Palgrave Studies in European Union Politics

Series Editors
Michelle Egan
American University
Washington, USA

Neill Nugent
Manchester Metropolitan University
Manchester, UK

William E. Paterson
Aston University
Birmingham, UK

Following on the sustained success of the acclaimed European Union Series, which essentially publishes research-based textbooks, Palgrave Studies in European Union Politics publishes cutting edge research-driven monographs. The remit of the series is broadly defined, both in terms of subject and academic discipline. All topics of significance concerning the nature and operation of the European Union potentially fall within the scope of the series. The series is multidisciplinary to reflect the growing importance of the EU as a political, economic and social phenomenon. To submit a proposal, please contact Senior Editor Ambra Finotello ambra.finotello@palgrave.com. This series is indexed by Scopus.

Editorial Board
Laurie Buonanno (SUNY Buffalo State, USA)
Kenneth Dyson (Cardiff University, UK)
Brigid Laffan (European University Institute, Italy)
Claudio Radaelli (University College London, UK)
Mark Rhinard (Stockholm University, Sweden)
Ariadna Ripoll Servent (University of Bamberg, Germany)
Frank Schimmelfennig (ETH Zurich, Switzerland)
Claudia Sternberg (University College London, UK)
Nathalie Tocci (Istituto Affari Internazionali, Italy)

More information about this series at
http://www.palgrave.com/gp/series/14629

Marianne Riddervold · Jarle Trondal ·
Akasemi Newsome
Editors

The Palgrave Handbook of EU Crises

Editors
Marianne Riddervold
Inland School of Business and Social Sciences
Inland University
Rena and Lillehammer, Norway

The Norwegian Institute of International Affairs (NUPI)
Oslo, Norway

Institute of European Studies
University of California
Berkeley, CA, USA

Akasemi Newsome
Inland School of Business and Social Sciences
Inland University
Rena and Lillehammer, Norway

Institute of European Studies
University of California
Berkeley, CA, USA

Jarle Trondal
Department of Political Science and Management
University of Agder
Kristiansand, Norway

ARENA - Centre for European Studies
University of Oslo
Oslo, Norway

ISSN 2662-5873   ISSN 2662-5881 (electronic)
Palgrave Studies in European Union Politics
ISBN 978-3-030-51790-8   ISBN 978-3-030-51791-5 (eBook)
https://doi.org/10.1007/978-3-030-51791-5

© The Editor(s) (if applicable) and The Author(s), under exclusive license to Springer Nature Switzerland AG 2021, corrected publication 2021
This work is subject to copyright. All rights are solely and exclusively licensed by the Publisher, whether the whole or part of the material is concerned, specifically the rights of translation, reprinting, reuse of illustrations, recitation, broadcasting, reproduction on microfilms or in any other physical way, and transmission or information storage and retrieval, electronic adaptation, computer software, or by similar or dissimilar methodology now known or hereafter developed. The use of general descriptive names, registered names, trademarks, service marks, etc. in this publication does not imply, even in the absence of a specific statement, that such names are exempt from the relevant protective laws and regulations and therefore free for general use.
The publisher, the authors and the editors are safe to assume that the advice and information in this book are believed to be true and accurate at the date of publication. Neither the publisher nor the authors or the editors give a warranty, expressed or implied, with respect to the material contained herein or for any errors or omissions that may have been made. The publisher remains neutral with regard to jurisdictional claims in published maps and institutional affiliations.

Cover credit: Magic Lens/Shutterstock

This Palgrave Macmillan imprint is published by the registered company Springer Nature Switzerland AG
The registered company address is: Gewerbestrasse 11, 6330 Cham, Switzerland

Preface

This Handbook is a primer on the European Union (EU) crisis. Europe has faced a decade of profound crises and this volume takes stock of their consequences for the EU. Despite having emerged from the devastation of WWII, the EU faces an unprecedented situation given the multiplicity, magnitude and cross-domain nature of recent crises. Times of profound crisis pave the way for analyzing what remains the same and what is changing as a result of these shocks. We also want to know why we have continuity in some areas and change in others and to do that we identify factors that might determine causation. Our work has been to generate competing scenarios for the EU in the short, medium and long term—from *breaking down* to *heading forward*. As politicians search for new and diverse forms of political association in Europe, scholars seek analytical categories and explanatory mechanisms. They have attempted to explain how and why 'Brexit' happened, as well as the most likely consequences for the future of the EU. This Handbook *comprehensively* explores the EU's institutional and policy responses to crisis across policy domains and institutions, what this tells us about the EU's ability to cope with unforeseen events, and what one should subsequently expect for the future of the EU. This volume addresses a variety of research questions on institutional change and continuity, decision-making behavior and processes, and public policy-making. We offer a systematic discussion of how the existing repertoire of theories understand crisis and how well they have been able to capture periods of unrest and events of disintegration such as «Brexit».

More generally, the Handbook aims to understand how public organizations cope with crisis, and thus probes how sustainable and resilient public organizations are in times of crisis and unrest. Periods of political and economic turbulence call for studying conditions for political order and sustainable public service delivery. Political science harbors competing ideas on the robustness of governments and public organizations. Yet, where a vast body of scholarly literature suggests that public sector organizations are profoundly unstable and unsustainable in the long run, few comprehensive studies exist. Our ambition is to provide a sweeping bird's eye view of EU crisis, and to make a significant research contribution on how the EU handles crisis. The book thus zooms into different crisis-ridden policy-areas and institutions, and also allows some distance to analyzes polity implications at the aggregate level.

At the same time, our Handbook presents state-of-the-art research in an easily accessible way for teaching purposes as well as for practitioners. In this way, the Handbook should be seen both a contribution to research on European crisis as well as a state-of-the-art primer. The editors are very happy—and proud—to have assembled such high quality research from a select group of specialists at the top of their respective fields, as well as promising younger academics. We strove to build bridges across the Atlantic between established scholars and a new generation of students of European integration. One need to look no further for proof of our success to a lively and packed reception in a downtown Denver restaurant where the editors organized a reception for the Handbook to coincide with the biennial European Union Studies Association (EUSA) conference in May 2019.

The editors would like to thank several people who have contributed in different capacities to the Handbook. First of all, we would like to acknowledge the contributors to this book. All top experts in their field, they did not hesitate to add yet another commitment to their already busy schedules. Almost all the authors that were invited were able to take part. A special thank you to Christian Kaunert, Bev Crawford, Mike Smith, Jolyon Howorth, and Martin Shapiro who provided critical guidance to this project in its very early stages. We are also very grateful to the anonymous reviewers for helpful questions and suggestions and to the series editors, who have provided invaluable feedback throughout the entire process. These inputs substantially increased the quality of the book. The editors would also like to thank Amund Botillen, Hans Peter Riise Tranøy, and Haakon Sandvold for fantastic research assistance when preparing the book, and Anne Birchley-Brun, Ambra Finotello and Preetha Kuttiappan at Palgrave Macmillan for all their help shepherding this volume through the publication process. The editors gratefully acknowledge financial support from the Jean Monnet Centre of Excellence Grant 2018–2021 at the Institute of European Studies, University of California, Berkeley.

With this book we also want to honor the memory of John Peterson, Professor of International Politics at the University of Edinburgh. John passed away suddenly in May 2019 and was an enthusiastic supporter of this book from the outset. Somehow he managed to be both a brilliant and kind colleague. We will miss him. John's intellectual legacy is inescapably present, of course, in this book as we have grappled with many of his sharp insights on crisis and the EU.

Oslo/Rena, Norway　　　　　　　　　　　　　　　　Marianne Riddervold
Kristiansand, Norway　　　　　　　　　　　　　　　　　　　Jarle Trondal
Berkeley, USA　　　　　　　　　　　　　　　　　　　Akasemi Newsome

The original version of the book was revised: In the list of contributors, the affiliation for "Hubert Zimmermann" has been corrected. The correction to the book is available at https://doi.org/10.1007/978-3-030-51791-5_46

Contents

Part I Introducing the Study of European Union Crisis

1 **European Union Crisis: An Introduction** 3
   Marianne Riddervold, Jarle Trondal, and Akasemi Newsome

Part II Theoretical Approaches to Crisis

2 **Theoretical Approaches to Crisis: An Introduction** 51
   Marianne Riddervold, Jarle Trondal, and Akasemi Newsome

3 **Liberal Intergovernmentalism** 61
   Frank Schimmelfennig

4 **Classical Realism** 79
   Alexander Reichwein

5 **Neorealism** 99
   Hubert Zimmermann

6 **Neofunctionalism** 115
   Arne Niemann

7 **Institutionalism** 135
   Christopher Ansell

8 **Organizational Theory** 153
   Jarle Trondal

9	**Cleavage Theory** Gary Marks, David Attewell, Jan Rovny, and Liesbet Hooghe	173
10	**Social Constructivism** Mai'a K. Davis Cross	195
11	**Deliberative Theory** Claudia Landwehr	213

Part III Crisis, Continuity, and Change in European Union Institutions

12	**Crisis, Continuity, and Change in European Union Institutions: An Introduction** Jarle Trondal, Marianne Riddervold, and Akasemi Newsome	231
13	**The Council** Jeffrey Lewis	239
14	**The European Parliament** Akasemi Newsome and Matthew Stenberg	259
15	**The Court of Justice of the European Union** Lisa Conant	277
16	**The European Commission** Hussein Kassim and Luc Tholoniat	297
17	**European Union Agencies** Michelle Everson and Ellen Vos	315
18	**The European Central Bank** Ingrid Hjertaker and Bent Sofus Tranøy	339
19	**The European External Action Service** Heidi Maurer	357

Part IV Policy Areas: Crisis, Continuity, and Change

20	**The Financial Crisis: An Introduction** Akasemi Newsome, Marianne Riddervold, and Jarle Trondal	375

21	**The EU's Response to the Financial Crisis** Espen D. H. Olsen and Guri Rosén	381
22	**Failing Forward in Financial Stability Regulation** Eirik Tegle Stenstad and Bent Sofus Tranøy	401
23	**The Euro in a Triple Crisis Context and Its Impact on the European Union** James A. Caporaso	421
24	**The Migration Crisis: An Introduction** Akasemi Newsome, Marianne Riddervold, and Jarle Trondal	443
25	**The EU's Response to the Migration Crisis: Institutional Turbulence and Policy Disjuncture** Kaija Schilde and Sara Wallace Goodman	449
26	**The Refugee Crisis and the EU Border Security Policies** Ruxandra-Laura Bosilca	469
27	**Moral Leadership or Moral Hazard? Germany's Response to the Refugee Crisis and Its Impact on European Solidarity** Beverly Crawford	489
28	**Brexit: An Introduction** Jarle Trondal, Marianne Riddervold, and Akasemi Newsome	507
29	**The EU's Response to Brexit** Benjamin Martill and Tim Oliver	511
30	**The Security and Defense Aspect of Brexit: Altering the Third Country Balance?** Øyvind Svendsen	525
31	**Crisis and EU Foreign and Security Policy: An Introduction** Marianne Riddervold, Jarle Trondal, and Akasemi Newsome	545
32	**The EU's Response to the Ukraine Crisis** Ana E. Juncos and Karolina Pomorska	553

33 *Heading Forward* in Response to Crisis: How the Ukraine Crisis Affected EU Maritime Foreign and Security Policy Integration 569
Marianne Riddervold

34 The EU's Comprehensive Response to Out of Area Crises: Plugging the Capability-Expectations Gap 585
Pernille Rieker and Steven Blockmans

35 EU–US Relations in Times of Crises 603
Marianne Riddervold and Akasemi Newsome

36 The Legitimacy Crisis: An Introduction 619
Akasemi Newsome, Marianne Riddervold, and Jarle Trondal

37 The EU's Crisis Response Regarding the Democratic and Rule of Law Crisis 627
Kolja Raube and Francisca Costa Reis

38 Responding to Crises—Worries About Expertization 647
Cathrine Holst and Anders Molander

39 Rebound? The Short- and Long-Term Effects of Crises on Public Support and Trust in European Governance 667
Pieter de Wilde

Part V Commentaries

40 A Differentiated European Union 687
Stefan Gänzle, Benjamin Leruth, and Jarle Trondal

41 The European Union, Crisis Management, and International Order 707
Michael Smith

42 Crises and the EU's Response: Increasing the Democratic Deficit? 725
Anne Elizabeth Stie

43 The Perfect Storm 739
Martin Shapiro

44	**The COVID-19 Pandemic: Failing Forward in Public Health** Scott L. Greer, Anniek de Ruijter, and Eleanor Brooks	747
45	**A Series of Unfortunate Events: Crisis Response and the European Union After 2008** Jeffrey J. Anderson	765

Correction to: The Palgrave Handbook of EU Crises   C1
Marianne Riddervold, Jarle Trondal, and Akasemi Newsome

Index   791

Notes on Contributors

Jeffrey J. Anderson is Professor at Georgetown University.

Christopher Ansell is Professor and Department Chair at the University of California Berkeley.

David Attewell is Professor at the University of North Carolina at Chapel Hill.

Steven Blockmans is Head of EU foreign policy and Head of Institutional Affairs at CEPS and a Professor of EU External Relations Law and Governance at the University of Amsterdam.

Ruxandra-Laura Bosilca is Research Fellow at the Inland Norway University of Applied Sciences.

Eleanor Brooks is Lecturer at the University of Edinburgh.

James A. Caporaso is Professor of Political Science at the University of Washington.

Lisa Conant is Professor and Chair at the University of Denver.

Francisca Costa Reis is Ph.D. Candidate at the University of Leuven.

Beverly Crawford is Professor Emerita University of California, Berkeley.

Mai'a K. Davis Cross is the Edward W. Brooke Professor of Political Science and Professor of political science and international affairs at Northeastern University.

Anniek de Ruijter is Associate Professor at the University of Amsterdam.

Pieter de Wilde is Professor at the Norwegian University of Science and Technology.

Michelle Everson is Professor of Law, University of London, Birkbeck.

Stefan Gänzle is Jean Monnet Chair and Professor of Political Science at University of Agder.

Sara Wallace Goodman is Associate Professor of Political Science at the University of California, Irvine.

Scott L. Greer is Professor at the University of Michigan, School of Public Health.

Ingrid Hjertaker is Ph.D. Fellow, Inland Norway University of Applied Sciences, Norway.

Cathrine Holst is Professor at the University of Oslo.

Liesbet Hooghe is the W.R Kenan Distinguished Professor of Political Science at the University of North Carolina at Chapel Hill and recurring Robert Schuman Fellow at the EUI, Florence.

Ana E. Juncos is Professor of European Politics at the University of Bristol.

Hussein Kassim is Professor of Politics, University of East Anglia.

Claudia Landwehr is Professor of Public Policy (Politics and Economy) at Johannes-Gutenberg-University, Mainz.

Benjamin Leruth is Assistant Professor in Politics and Public Administration at the Institute for Governance and Policy Analysis, University of Canberra.

Jeffrey Lewis is Professor in Political Science at Cleveland State University, College of Liberal Arts and Social Sciences.

Gary Marks is Burton Craige Professor of Political Science at UNC-Chapel Hill.

Benjamin Martill is Dahrendorf Post-Doctoral Fellow at London School of Economics and Political Science.

Heidi Maurer is Lecturer in European Politics at University of Oxford, Department of Politics and International Relations.

Anders Molander is Professor at the Oslo Metropolitan University.

Akasemi Newsome is Associate Director at the Institute of European Studies and Executive Director at the Peder Sather Center for Advanced Study, University of California Berkeley.

Arne Niemann is Professor at Johannes Gutenberg-Universität Mainz.

Tim Oliver is Senior Lecturer for the Institute for Diplomacy and International Governance, Loughborough University London.

Espen D. H. Olsen is Associate Professor at Oslo Metropolitan University and Senior Researcher at the ARENA Centre for European Studies, University of Oslo.

Karolina Pomorska is Associte Professor at the University of Leiden.

Kolja Raube is Assistant Professor at the University of Leuven.

Alexander Reichwein is Postdoctoral research associate at Justus-Liebig-Universität Gießen, department of political science.

Marianne Riddervold is Professor of Political Science at the Inland Norway University of Applied Sciences and the Norwegian Institute of International Affairs (NUPI), and a Senior Fellow at UC Berkeley Institute of European Studies.

Pernille Rieker is Senior Researcher at the Norwegian Institute of International Affairs (NUPI).

Guri Rosén is Associate Professor of Political Science at Oslo Metropolitan University.

Jan Rovny is Associate Professor in Political Science, Sciences Po, Paris.

Kaija Schilde is Associate Professor of International Relations at the Pardee School of Global Studies, Boston University.

Frank Schimmelfennig is Professor in European Politics and member of the Center for Comparative and International Studies. He is also a Schuman Fellow at the Robert Schuman Centre for Advanced Studies of the European University Institute in Florence.

Martin Shapiro is Professor emeritus in law at the University of California, Berkeley, School of Law.

Michael Smith is Professor in European Politics at the University of Warwick.

Matthew Stenberg is Ph.D. fellow at University of California Berkeley, Department of Political Science.

Eirik Tegle Stenstad is research assistant, Kristiania University College.

Anne Elizabeth Stie is Associate Professor at the University of Agder.

Øyvind Svendsen is Ph.D. Fellow at the Department of Political Science, University of Copenhagen and a Research Fellow at the Norwegian Institute of International Affairs, NUPI.

Luc Tholoniat was an economic advisor to President Jean-Claude Juncker's team.

Bent Sofus Tranøy is Professor of Political Science, Kristiania University College and Inland Norway University of Applied Sciences (INN University). He is also affiliated to ARENA Centre for European Studies, University of Oslo.

Jarle Trondal is Professor of Political Science University of Agder and at the ARENA Centre for European Studies, University of Oslo.

Ellen Vos is Professor of European Union law, Maastricht University, Faculty of Law.

Hubert Zimmermann is Professor at Philipps-University of Marburg, Marburg, Germany.

List of Figures

Fig. 9.1   Socio-structural differences between party families (*Note* Data from 2002 to 2016 ESS. The thickness and color of the lines reflects the extent to which the electorate of two party families is distinctive on a social characteristic. Black = >30% difference; Red = 20–30% difference; Yellow = 10–20% difference; Green = <10% difference)   183

Fig. 9.2   Social distinctiveness among younger and older voters: the GALTAN vs. left-right divide (*Note* 2002–2016 ESS voting data aggregated to the party family. Structural distinctiveness is estimated as the average difference in a social characteristic between GAL (left) and TAN (right) parties divided by two   184

Fig. 9.3   Party ideology and party structuration (*Note* 169 individual political parties by their GALTAN position (CHES) and their score on party structuration (ESS), whereby low scores indicate an overrepresentation of voters with social characteristics associated with anti-transnationalism and high scores indicate an overrepresentation of voters with social characteristics associated with transnationalism)   188

Fig. 15.1   Percent who tend to trust the European Court of Justice, 1993–2018 (*Source* European Commission. [1993–2018]. *Eurobarometer.* Survey question 'Trust in European Institutions: European Court of Justice.' http://ec.europa.eu/commfrontoffice/publicopinion/index.cfm/Chart/getChart/themeKy/9/groupKy/28. Accessed 28 Feb 2019)   282

Fig. 21.1   Overview of publications on the Eurozone crisis (This overview is based on a search for "euro crisis" and "Eurozone crisis" between 2008 and 2018. There is bound to be some overlap between the articles in each search, but the distribution nevertheless demonstrates the change over time)   387

Fig. 22.1   Three dimensions of a comprehensive financial stability framework (*Source* Stenstad 2017: 31)   405

Fig. 23.1	Greece and Germany in the eurozone crisis	431
Fig. 23.2	Refugee crisis	433
Fig. 23.3	EU and UK (Brexit)	437
Fig. 39.1	Public Mood about the EU, 2007–2018 (Net Image and Net Optimism have been calculated where "very positive" and "very optimistic" are recoded as 2; fairly optimistic and fairly positive as 1; neutral as 0; fairly pessimistic and fairly negative as −1; and very pessimistic and very negative as −2. Both indicators thus run from a maximum of +2 to a minimum of −2.)	673
Fig. 39.2	Indifference about the EU (Y-axis reports fraction of the population answering «Don't Know»)	674
Fig. 39.3	Trust in the European Commission	675
Fig. 39.4	Trust in the European Parliament	676
Fig. 39.5	Trust in the European Central Bank	676

List of Tables

Table 9.1	Socio-structural biases by party family (all countries)	181
Table 9.2	Party structuration and party ideology	186
Table 19.1	A decade of European External Action Service and European crisis	361
Table 22.1	Comparison of the two main belief systems of finance	404
Table 39.1	Comparative trends in trust in institutions	677
Table 45.1	The time horizons of different causal accounts	771

PART I

Introducing the Study of European Union Crisis

CHAPTER 1

European Union Crisis: An Introduction

Marianne Riddervold, Jarle Trondal, and Akasemi Newsome

Europe will be forged in crises and will be the sum of the solutions adopted for those crises. (Jean Monnet 1978)

INTRODUCTION

What is the impact of crisis on European Union (EU) integration? Exploring continuity and change in EU policies and institutions, this Handbook takes stock of how and in what way crisis influences the EU. Since its inception, the EU integration project has been characterized by a mix of incremental change

---

M. Riddervold (✉) · A. Newsome
Inland School of Business and Social Sciences, Inland University, Rena and Lillehammer, Norway
e-mail: marianne.riddervold@inn.no

Institute of European Studies, University of California, Berkeley, CA, USA

A. Newsome
e-mail: akasemi@berkeley.edu

M. Riddervold
The Norwegian Institute of International Affairs (NUPI), Oslo, Norway

J. Trondal
Department of Political Science and Management, University of Agder, Kristiansand, Norway
e-mail: jarle.trondal@uia.no

ARENA - Centre for European Studies, University of Oslo, Oslo, Norway

© The Author(s) 2021
M. Riddervold et al. (eds.), *The Palgrave Handbook of EU Crises*,
Palgrave Studies in European Union Politics,
https://doi.org/10.1007/978-3-030-51791-5_1

and integration spurts that usually have followed major crises. Understanding EU crisis and the EU response is thus key also to our understanding of the EU more generally, and the empirical findings and theoretical arguments will have relevance for the EU integration literature beyond the EU's immediate responses to crises.

The numerous crises confronting the EU today combine to form the 'perfect storm' of conditions that make this particular historical moment in European integration so crucial to understand, theoretically, conceptually, and empirically (Riddervold and Newsome 2018). Over the last decade, the EU has faced an unprecedented number of challenges on multiple fronts. At the time of writing, the EU is embroiled in what has been referred to as its gravest crisis 'since the integration project began' (Fabbrini 2020). Summing up the EU's initial lack of a common response to the Corona crisis, Greer (2020) writes: 'A union that speaks often of solidarity between peoples initially saw little solidarity. A union often reproached for technocracy showed none of it. A union built on the freedom of movement of people and goods has become a chaotic continent of closed borders and export bans.' The Corona crisis came on top of the many other crises the EU has faced in recent years. With the Brexit vote, one of the EU's biggest and most influential member-states decided to leave the Union, posing existential challenges to the EU after sixty years of integration. Internally, populist parties and anti-EU sentiments have mobilized people across the continent, and member-states such as Poland and Hungary are facing new political threats as they drift further away from democratic governance. Culminating with the annexation of Crimea in March 2014, the EU has to contend with a more aggressive Russia making territorial claims or interfering militarily in the EU's near abroad. Other areas of concern include Russia's territorial claims in the Arctic and its intervention in the Syrian conflict from 2015. As a result of conflicts in Syria and other developing world hotspots, the EU has also witnessed an explosion of migrants coming to Europe in search for a better life—more than one million in 2015 alone. The EU must also confront a number of more long-term challenges with potentially far-reaching implications, not least the global financial crisis and challenges facing the Economic and Monetary Union (EMU) and a changing and more volatile international environment (cf. Caporaso and Rhodes 2016; Cross and Karolewski 2017; Hall 2014; Hume and Pawle 2015; MacFarlane and Menon 2014; Mearsheimer 2014; Pop 2015; M. Smith 2018; M. E. Smith 2018).

The case of Brexit illustrates that Europe might be in a stage of accelerating turbulence and crises (Ansell et al. 2017) that has triggered 'institutional soul-searching' among most EU member-states and within the EU institutions themselves. Similarly, the Corona crisis, with its very wide direct and indirect consequences for all sectors of society, has triggered a discussion on European solidarity, EU competences, and the future of the European project (Fabbrini 2020; Greer 2020). The European Commission's White Paper on the future of the EU also illustrates how crises trigger debates that go to the core of how the

EU should respond and how it should develop in the future. The White Paper established five scenarios for the EU by 2025, ranging from disintegration (what this volume refers to as a *breaking down* scenario) to more EU collective action. In short, these scenarios have been captured under the following titles: '1: Carrying on,' i.e., following the current path of *muddling through* without any major changes and reforms; '2: Nothing but the Single Market' excluding areas such as migration, security, and defence; '3: Those who want more do more' based on coalitions of the willing; '4: Doing less more efficiently' with a strong focus on further market integration leaving nonmarket-related affairs aside, and, eventually; '5: Doing much more together' across a wide range of areas (European Commission 2017: 15–25).

By developing and exploring the relevance of a set of theoretically derived scenarios of the EU's resilience in the face of crises, this Handbook aims to provide a comprehensive understanding of how crisis affects the EU and the drivers of EU integration. We start from the observation that scholars tend to expect that the cascade of crises facing the EU is likely to influence EU integration and governance. Often, these parallel crises are expected to *undermine* and threaten the EU project, not least due to what is seen by observers and scholars as the EU's lack of appropriate policy responses (see for example Macfarlane and Menon 2014; Mearsheimer 2014; Posen 2014; Walt 2014). Others have argued that further EU integration has often followed in response to crisis, and that although of a different magnitude, today's crises are also likely to lead to more and not less integration (Cross and Karolewski 2017; Cross and Ma 2015; McNamara 2015; Mény 2014; Genschel and Jachtenfuchs 2014; Schmitter 1970).

Against this background, this Handbook comprehensively explores the EU's institutional and policy responses to crisis. Our analysis, moreover, aims to generalize empirical and conceptual knowledge on how the EU responds to crisis and what resulting predictions can be made about the EU's future developments. This Handbook also offers a systematic discussion of how different EU integration theories understand and explain crisis. Our analytical apparatus thus serves as a toolbox for other studies and as a basis for discussions on the relevance of theoretical perspectives in capturing not only EU integration but also EU crisis and potential disintegration. Although there are numerous studies of various EU crises and crisis responses, the literature lacks a comprehensive overview like the one offered by this Handbook (see 'State of the art' below). At the same time, most of the chapters in this Handbook are stand-alone chapters on particular crises, institutions, policy areas, and theories. Whereas some chapters discuss a particular theory's relevance for understanding and explaining crisis (Part II), others zoom in on various institutional responses (Part III) or examine specific policy crises and the EU's response to each of them (Part IV). A final set of chapters offer commentaries on the broader relevance of this analysis (Part V).

We organize the remainder of this introductory chapter as follows. We first unpack the concept of crisis and describe how it is applied in this volume. Next, we develop three theoretically deduced scenarios on the EU's putative response to crisis. The three scenarios build on different theoretical approaches in EU integration scholarship and are discussed in the chapters that follow. We also briefly discuss some methodological challenges involved when seeking to tease out the extent to which different mechanisms influence EU policies and institutions. The chapter then sums up novel empirical findings from different parts of the Handbook on the impact of crisis on EU policies and institutions, as well as the applicability of various theories to understanding these observations. The summary of findings also systematically addresses the Handbook's main questions, focusing on what the case studies tell us about continuity and change in the EU, and hence the future of the Union. Overall, we use the structuring of the chapter sections to synthesize empirical findings across chapters, before discussing the overall impact of crises on the EU as such.

Although empirical insights vary across chapters, and so far with the exception of the EU's (limited) response to the severe democratic challenges in Hungary and Poland, the volume finds that the EU has been surprisingly resilient in the face of crises owing to its ability to adapt and absorb, and if necessary, change, in response to crisis. This in turn suggests that the EU has reached a stage in its development where it has sufficiently consolidated to adapt to and cope with multiple and simultaneous crisis situations. Thus, although clearly demanding, crises arguably no longer challenge the fundamental core of the EU. There are, however, democratic challenges attached to the responses applied, and the EU's responses also have implications for our wider understanding of the EU polity. There are for example implications related to a potential further differentiation of the Union, and the EU's aspiring role on the global scene. The EU's silent and very slow response to the undermining of democracy in Poland and Hungary—a situation exacerbated by increased executive powers in response to the Corona crisis—has led observers to question whether the EU is *breaking down* when it comes to the protection of core democratic values. We also see challenges for the EU project originating from polarization and voter mobilization not only linked to European integration but also globalization more broadly. These issues are discussed in great detail in the Handbook's four commentary chapters (Part V of this book) and at the end of this chapter. This chapter finally closes with some suggestive avenues for future research.

Before proceeding, however, a common understanding of 'integration' is needed, as it has not often been provided in the literature. The meaning of the term 'integration' varies across theoretical perspectives in literature and will subsequently vary across the chapters in this volume (Wiener et al. 2019). Overall, we choose a less attended and general definition of integration suggested by James G. March (1999: 134) who sees integration as the imagination of 'a world consisting of a set of parts. At the least, integration is gauged by some measure of the density, intensity, and character of relations among the elements of that set.' Subsequently, he suggests three parameters for integration: consistency among the parts, interdependence among the parts, and structural connectedness among the parts. On this basis, disintegration would imply a lower degree of density and intensity of the consistency, interdependence, and structural connectedness among these parts.

INTRODUCING CRISIS

Our understanding of crisis departs from Ikenberry's definition of crisis as 'an extraordinary moment when the existence and viability of the political order are called into question' (Ikenberry 2008: 3; Cross and Ma 2015). A crisis represents 'a serious threat to the basic structures or the fundamental values and norms of a system, which under time pressure and highly uncertain circumstances necessitates making vital decisions' (Rosenthal et al. 1989: 10). According to Boin et al. (2005: 3–4), key properties of crisis are *threat*, *urgency*, and *uncertainty*. A crisis occurs where an urgent response is required in an uncertain situation that threatens fundamental values or life-sustaining systems. Crisis, however, is not the same as turbulence. Ansell et al. (2017) define turbulence as interactions of events or demands that are highly variable, inconsistent, unexpected, or unpredictable. Although turbulence itself may 'threaten' basic structures or values, it is also possible that organizations regard turbulence as the 'normal' state of affairs (Ansell et al. 2017). As an analytical concept, turbulence complements, but is not identical to, the concept of crisis. This has been noted for organizations operating in 'high velocity environments' (Eisenhardt and Bourgeois 1988), for 'garbage can' decision-making (Cohen et al. 1972), for high reliability organizations (Casler 2014), and for 'reforming organizations' where reform has become routine (Brunsson and Olsen 1993). Turbulence may be seen as an endogenous, constitutive, and systemic part of the fabric of organizations. To say these organizations are in crisis stretches the concept beyond its useful limits. Turbulence and crisis, however, may also be related in important but poorly understood ways. The Eurozone faced turbulence long before the sudden financial crisis hit Greece. But this latent turbulence remained unnoticed until the crisis revealed it. Turbulence may also continue long after the immediate response to a crisis and may reverberate beyond the specific domain of the crisis. The George W. Bush administration created the US Department of Homeland Security in response to 9/11 as an amalgamation of 22 separate agencies; this unprecedented reorganization produced ongoing turbulence for these agencies that lasted well beyond the immediate crisis.

Most accounts of crisis and turbulence regard the phenomena as exogenous environmental properties that trigger responses inside organizations. A few scholars, however, have noted that crisis and turbulence are not just a property of the environment but also endogenous properties of organizations. This point is particularly relevant for public organizations which are led by political leadership and ultimately accountable to legislatures. The empirical focus on private firms rather than on political organizations may be one reason why this point has been less appreciated in literature. Yet, this Handbook focuses on how crises as an *exogenous* property of the environment hit institutions, politics, and policies. All crises examined in this volume are characterized precisely by exogenous chains of events, varying between periods of turbulence and more immediate situations of crises.

Three Scenarios of the EU's Functional Response to Crisis

In order to fully grasp the EU's institutional and policy response to polycrisis, the contributors to this volume incorporate three models of the EU's crisis response. The first challenge that public organizations confront in the face of crisis is whether to stabilize *or* change, or even combining stability *and* change. Limits to organizational design, however, often prevent public organizations from rational responses to crises. Organizational designers are likely to face limitations to their own instrumental reasoning, notably short-sightedness coupled with short time horizons (Lodge and Wegrich 2016; Pierson 2000). The limits to design might moreover be greater in complex organizational orders with 'nested rules' (Goodin 1996a: 23) such as supranational institutions such as the EU than in single organizations such as government ministries or agencies (e.g., Gilardi 2005).

Crisis often creates pressures to reinforce well-known organizational solutions and governing arrangements because governance systems and governance practices under stress may revert to or reinforce preexisting organizational traditions, practices, and formats, reinforcing institutional path dependencies. Although crisis is likely to create an impetus for public organizations to stabilize their operations, it might simultaneously produce pressure for rapid change. To avoid mismatches with their environment, organizations sometimes quickly adapt the organization to these changing conditions. Public organizations are therefore often pulled between the impulse to stabilize and the impulse to transform themselves in response to turbulence. From the outset, the literature harbor contending theoretical perspectives on the extent to which, and how, crisis affects public organizations' institutional framework and policy responses.

This Handbook has developed three analytically distinct scenarios on how the EU may cope with crises. Scenario 1 suggests that the EU is unable to cope with crisis (*breaking down*), whereas Scenarios 2 and 3 hold that the EU adapts, in different ways, to crises—either through incremental processes (*muddling through*) or pathbreaking processes (*heading forward*).

Scenario 1. Change: Breaking Down

A first scenario suggests that the EU as we know it is likely to break apart or disintegrate in one or more policy areas when facing crisis, largely owing to member-states' unwillingness to deal collectively with major risks or to popular anti-EU sentiments. This *breaking down* scenario has already been suggested by a number of neorealist scholars. Following the neorealist assumptions of strategic states operating in an anarchical state order where they always aim at increasing their relative power, it is difficult to see why states would cooperate or delegate sovereignty to supranational authorities in the first place (Macfarlane and Menon 2014; Mearsheimer 2014; Posen 2014; Walt 2014. Also see Zimmerman, this volume). The EU's limited ability to deal with the migration crisis, or the actions of a revisionist Russia, is hence not very surprising. Simply put, following a realist perspective, the EU is fragile in the face of crisis: Only to the extent that the member-states perceive integration or cooperation to be necessary owing to their foremost strategic interests will they agree to common policies. In times of crisis, one would expect member-states to be more concerned with securing their own interests, borders, and citizens' instant security, which could thus limit their ability to reach agreement on common policies or to delegate authority and capacity to EU institutions. Member-states are also less likely to share sovereignty or contribute to redistribution in times of austerity, or when faced with an EU sceptic population and would ultimately strive to preserve their autonomy as sovereign nation-states.

Also, post-functionalism theorizes the possibility that the EU might breakdown in times of crisis. Focusing instead on how conflicts between European integration and local identities may come to the forefront in times of crisis, an increase in anti-EU sentiments may limit the EU's ability to collectively respond to crisis or even breakdown in affected areas. According to Hooghe and Marks (2018; Marks et al. 2020), functional pressures created by transnationalism create a clash with local identities, over time leading to the development of a new and increasingly salient transnational party cleavage. At its core, this new party divide is linked to a conflict over the role of the nation-state and hence also linked to voters' perceptions and parties' positions on the EU. While GAL (green, alternative, libertarian) parties embrace open societies and international governance, parties on the other side (TAN: traditionalist, authoritarian, nationalist parties) favor a strengthening of national control over external forces such as the EU. The political implications of this divide become particularly visible when the EU faces crisis, with the transnational cleavage narrowing the EU's response options due to TAN mobilization (ibid.).

Scenario 2. Continuity: Muddling Through
A second scenario suggests that the EU is likely to muddle through crisis through path-dependent incremental responses building on pre-existing institutional architectures, functional spillover, or by 'failing forward.' Rather than breaking up, crisis may reinforce well-known organizational solutions and governing arrangements and thus either have few profound effects on EU integration and governance, or crisis may engender changes that develop gradually over longer periods of time. Institutional and organizational approaches suggest that governance systems and practices under stress may revert to or reinforce pre-existing organizational traditions, practices,

and formats, buttressing institutional path dependencies (Olsen 2010; Pierson 2004; Skowronek 1982). This may occur because organizations are thrown into a reactive mode of response. The lack of time for creating new institutions, for example, may render decision-makers' 'pursuit of intelligence' bounded and their search for solutions local (March 2010: 19). Decision-makers may hence have a tendency to replicate structures or procedures that are perceived as successes in the past. More precisely, building on a historical-institutional approach, the EU is likely to muddle through crises via processes of path dependency: It basically assumes that institutional change is contingent on and locked in by pre-existing institutional formats, and thus profoundly stable, sustainable, and robust. Organizations are seen as experiential learners that base future choices on past experiences. Institutions create elements of robustness, and concepts such as 'historical inefficiency' and 'path dependence' suggest that the match between environments—e.g., crises—and institutional solutions is not automatic and precise (March and Olsen 1998; Olsen 2009, 2010; Trondal, this volume). Faced with crises, new governing arrangements are thus likely to be extrapolated from and mediated by pre-established institutional frameworks (Skowronek 1982). However, there might also be less reactive reasons for institutional path dependence in the face of crisis. Pre-existing institutions may serve as an important source of stability in the face of crisis, enabling organizations to ride out stressful times. This argument thus assumes that organizations facing crises might improvise, called institutional syncretism, responding in a syncretic fashion that is neither path-dependent nor punctuated. Institutional change is thus described as a process of recombination, refashioning, or repurposing of existing institutions in an adaptive fashion. This view of institutional change emphasizes the ability of actors to combine existing institutions and new institutional innovation in a creative or improvisational way (Ansell et al. 2017; Ansell, this volume).

The EU may also muddle through crisis as a result of the EU 'failing forward' through unsuccessful bargaining processes where the member-states try, but ultimately fail, to find a lasting solution to a looming crisis due to their inability to provide crisis responses above the lowest common denominator (Jones 2018; Hjertaker and Tranøy, this volume). This mechanism is a theoretical synthesis of liberal intergovernmentalism and neo-functionalism, in which 'intergovernmentalism captures the dynamic at work in critical junctures and neo-functionalism describes the mechanism linking one critical juncture to the next' (Jones et al. 2016: 1013). In a dynamic process of 'failing forward,' intergovernmental lowest common denominator bargaining produces incomplete integration arrangements, which spark crises, in which intergovernmental bargaining produces more but again incomplete integration.

Third, the EU might muddle through as a result of functional spillover processes driven by supranational institutions. Neo-functionalists assume that decisions are taken by rational and self-interested actors with imperfect knowledge of their consequences (Haas 1970: 627). Implicit is the assumption that integration processes evolve over time and take on their own dynamic. Some political decisions may fail to anticipate likely consequences, which increases the likelihood of later problems and potentially crisis (Schmitter 1970). Consequently, neo-functionalists assume that the integration process is driven slowly forward by unintended consequences. Haas (1958) thus stressed incremental decision-making over grand designs. Moreover, seemingly marginal adjustments that in sum may lead to more integration are driven by the unintended consequences of previous decisions. This effect arises from the incapacity of most political actors to engage in long-term purposive behavior. Following the idea of functional spillover, the EU's lack of competences and thus inability to provide a common response would create a functional pressure to integrate further, driven not least by supranational institutions, such as the European Commission (Niemann, this volume; Webber 2019).

Scenario 3: Change: Heading Forward
A last scenario suggests that crisis is likely to trigger more integration to address common challenges, leading to policy innovations and delegation of new capacities to EU institutions in new policy fields (Cross and Karolewski 2017; McNamara 2015; Mény 2014; Genschel and Jachtenfuchs 2014; Schmitter 1970). There are several ways in which crisis may lead to such institutional and policy innovations. First, following an institutionalist approach (see Ansell, this volume), crisis may entail a fundamental questioning of pre-existing governance arrangements and 'long-cherished beliefs' in existing solutions, and cause institutional soul-seeking and the raising of fundamental questions about the nature of the *res publica* (Emery and Giauque 2014: 24; Lodge and Wegrich 2012: 11). Crisis may produce critical junctures that generate 'windows of opportunity' for significant policy change (Kingdon 1984) and novel organizational solutions (Jones and Baumgartner 2005: 5). Or, crisis may trigger organizational meltdown and create opportunity structures for the creation of new organizations (Padgett and Powell 2012). This is so as organizations facing crisis may experience a disruption of equilibrium conditions—for example, a disruption of the balance between political leadership and independent expertise, between transparency and secrecy, between electoral representation in parliament and interest group involvement, and so on. Crisis may thus also spur the emergence of entirely new policies or institutional arrangements. Recent examples include the rise of EU financial surveillance agencies and the structuring of an EU banking union in the aftermath of the financial crisis, and the emergent European energy union in the aftermath of energy and climate crises (Trondal and Bauer 2017).

This scenario builds on the idea that crisis may function as a 'window of opportunity' in unsettled situations and for under-institutionalized organizations. The garbage can model was originally presented as a characterization of how choices in organizations sometimes happen when faced with problematic preferences, unclear technology, and fluid participation (Cohen et al. 1972). Organizational processes were pictured as non-standardized, fluid, discontinuous, and loosely organized where sudden windows of opportunity or external shocks activate problems, initiatives, solutions, and participants that are packed more or less randomly together (Heimer and Stinchcombe 1999: 28). In open societies such as in Europe, events exogenous to the government, for example crises, might call for its attention. Anything from an earthquake to the miscarriage of justice may call for immediate governmental reaction (Olsen 2009, 2010). According to a garbage can approach, external shocks sometimes offer the opportunity to shift agendas within policy areas that are perceived to be gridlocked. In garbage-can situations choice is ambiguous and open to creative decision-making, leadership, policy innovations, and sudden unforeseen turns.

Second, following a liberal intergovernmentalist approach, big steps toward more EU integration may follow from intergovernmental treaty bargaining processes. According to this perspective, EU integration is the sum of the member-states' preferences and relative strengths. Member-states may agree to share sovereignty if they are likely to see that negative effects from a crisis are better solved by common solutions. Particularly in intergovernmentally organized policy domains—such as foreign and security policy, health, and social policies, and external immigration, or when negotiating treaty changes to the Union—policy-making outcomes may follow processes of member-state bargaining, where strategically motivated actors strive to maximize predetermined and fixed preferences (Moravcsik and Schimmelfennig 2009). Interdependence and the cost of non-integration are mechanisms that may explain member-states' willingness to take steps to reduce negative impacts of crisis. The member-states least affected by a crisis are moreover most likely to influence the outcomes (Schimmelfennig this volume). In such cases, they may find that it serves their interests better to integrate further, which is how this approach explains leaps forward in EU integration through treaty changes (Moravscik 1998; Schimmelfennig, this volume). National interest groups—such as organized businesses—play a key role in defining these interests and could strongly influence states in pushing for common responses to protect particular interests.

Lastly, while neo-realists expect the EU to breakdown, classical realism instead allows for the possibility that the EU may head forward under the leadership of the most powerful EU states, France and Germany, or what Pedersen refers to as the EU's 'dual cooperative hegemony' (Pedersen 1998; Reichwein, this volume). *Heading forward* might be in the national interest of both Germany and France since both have strong economic but relatively limited military power capabilities and both (for different reasons) seek integration to (re)shape their regional environment, i.e., EU institutions and regulations.

STATE OF THE ART

Much of the existing literature on EU crisis is empirically oriented and has engaged with already prevalent theoretical approaches and methodological tools. This section reviews several significant contributions to this empirical and theoretical work and suggests how this Handbook intervenes in new ways.

Owing to the number of studies that have emerged in recent years, this section focuses mainly on recent and systematic studies of crisis, several of which have been published in journal Special Issues.

Prevalent theories in EU studies have been mainly focused on explaining the integration process—that is the ups and downs of the process of integration of European states. Among the diverse set of factors applied in the study of integrative moves toward what often—both empirically and theoretically—is perceived as 'an ever closer Union' include interdependence, functional and political spillover, bargaining, arguing, institutional processes of socialization and path dependency, shared norms, and actors' perceptions. Recent years' crises have therefore witnessed an increasing number of scholarly discussions on the relevance of various theoretical approaches for understanding EU crisis and potential disintegration, both in individual articles and in special issues with more comparative aims. The most comprehensive discussions of crisis and EU integration theory prior to this Handbook have been conducted by Schimmelfennig (2017, 2018a, b); Börzel and Risse (2018), and in two *Journal of European Public Policy* (JEPP) special issues edited by Hooghe et al. (2018) and Hooghe and Marks (2019). With contributions from Hall (2018), Pontusson and Weisstanner (2018), Kriesi (2018), Börzel and Risse (2018), and Hooghe and Marks (2018), guest editors Hooghe, Laffan and Marks (2018: 1) asked 'leading scholars of varieties of capitalism, democracy, re-distributional politics, European integration and political parties to engage the theoretical implications of Europe's multiplex crisis,' focusing both on applicability and the need for theoretical revisions. Moving on from this, the second JEPP special issue edited by Hooghe and Marks in 2019 set out to systematically reengage the three grand theories of European integration—neo-functionalism, intergovernmentalism, and post-functionalism—by exploring their ability not only to explain integration but also crisis and potential disintegration. Evaluating these theories, Hooghe and Marks (2019: 1) ask in their introductory article whether they 'explain the genesis, the course, and the outcome of four episodes of European (dis)integration that we have witnessed since 2008: the Eurocrisis, the migration crisis, Brexit, and illiberalism.' Rather than treating the three perspectives as competing accounts of EU crises, Hooghe and Marks find that they—on the basis of their different focus and assumptions—allow us to understand different aspects of crises, together providing a more comprehensive account than if simply applying one perspective: 'At one and the same time, the Eurocrisis, the migration crisis, Brexit, and illiberalism can be viewed as episodes of intergovernmental bargaining, path-dependent spillovers, and ideological conflict' (ibid.: 16).

Further in this vein, Kuhn (2019) assesses the three theories' applicability in understanding the increasing importance of collective *identity* politics for European integration. Concluding that 'neo-functionalism and both classical and liberal intergovernmentalism have underestimated the disruptive potential of identity politics in European integration' (ibid.: 1226), Kuhn calls for future research 'to investigate under which conditions politicization turns in favour or against further European integration, and under which conditions public opinion succeeds in influencing policy making' (ibid.: 1227). The argument that identity is a key factor in EU integration echoes Börzel and Risse's conclusion from 2018. According to Börzel and Risse, none of the grand theories can by themselves sufficiently account for the impact and response to EU crises and should therefore 'take insights from social constructivism with regard to identity politics' (Börzel and Risse 2018: 102). In their contribution to the 2019 JEPP special issue on grand theories and crisis, Börzel and Risse (2019) move on to discuss the applicability of grand theories from a comparative regional perspective, asking whether these theories can travel beyond the EU. Contrary to the neo-functional and liberal intergovernmental assumption that economic interdependence drives integration, Börzel and Risse show that there is weak correlation between the two. Building on post-functionalist theory, they therefore develop a new comparative regionalist account which is not only able to explain regional cooperation more generally but also 'fits better the European experience than standard theories of integration' (ibid.: 1231).

Schimmelfennig and Winzen (2019) further explore the relevance of grand theories in understanding differentiated integration, focusing on Treaty making from 1992 to 2016. Deriving hypotheses from all three theories—liberal intergovernmentalism, neo-functionalism, and post-functionalism—they conclude that although a combination of the three approaches maximizes overall explained variance, more detailed variations remain unexplained by the three grand theories. Applying a new intergovernmentalist approach and a utility maximization ontology, Hodson and Puetter (2019) explore the role of key member-states in moving forward with integration in response to crisis by circumventing Eurosceptic party politics. Echoing Stie's warnings in this Handbook, these short-term solutions to crisis, however, risk adding to Europe's disequilibrium, with the EU now being 'at risk not only from Eurosceptic challengers but [also] from member state governments' determination to circumvent them' (ibid.: 1167). Focusing, *inter alia*, on the so-called 'migration crisis,' Webber (2019) further expanded on post-functionalism, arguing that Hooghe and Marks' (2009) post-functionalist approach is best equipped to understand the consequences of the crisis on European integration, in that '[m]ass politicization and the growth of identity politics are likely to create "downward pressure on the level and scope of integration"' (Webber 2019: 8, citing Hooghe and Marks 2009: 21). Lastly, turning instead to the question of how media coverage of EU affairs affects the European integration process, Peter de Wilde (2019) confronts media theory with key aspects of the three grand theories to identify a set of mechanisms and corresponding hypotheses of media impact: public interest spillover, democratic spillover, new supranational entrepreneurship, populist preference formation, and discursive intergovernmentalism. In a first exploration of their applicability, de Wilde finds that media coverage in particular 'favors member state governments, reconstructing European politics decidedly toward a form of discursive intergovernmentalism' (ibid.: 1208). Media also creates opportunities for a new supranational entrepreneurship that 'is executive in nature, where charismatic EU officials with significant competencies engage with powerful adversaries in moments of crisis' (ibid.: 1209). Adding to this theoretical discussion from a constructivist perspective, Mai'a K. Davis Cross (2017) has conducted one of the most comprehensive, theoretically informed comparative studies of crisis to date. Rather than seeing crisis as a given, Cross' argument is that crisis, with all its potential institutional and policy implications, is socially constructed, in particular by the media. In fact, the media can generate a crisis where none exists, if coverage of an event underscores said event's ability to splinter and fragment Europe and 'emphasizes a kind of "us vs. them" conflict' (Davis Cross 2017: 35). Also moving beyond EU integration theory, Maher (2020) reminds us of the relevance of international relations theories for understanding European integration and the future of the European project. Although not studying their relevance across empirical cases, Maher shows how the basic assumptions of each of the three big IR theories—liberalism, realism, and constructivism—can 'generate both optimistic and pessimistic variants on the future of European integration' (Maher 2020: 3), hence suggesting a wide range of theoretically deduced expectations of future EU integration that can be applied to empirical studies. As such, 'a reengagement between general IR theory and European integration holds promise for generating new insights in both domains' (ibid.: 20). Quoting Mark Pollack: 'EU studies… are in many ways the vanguard of international relations theory, insofar as the EU serves as a laboratory for broader processes such as globalization, institutionalization, and socialization' (Pollack 2005: 368 in Maher 2020: 21).

Despite facing conceptual and explanatory challenges, much of the literature discussing theoretical applicability and rehabilitation has focused on the grand theories, leaving the mid-range accounts less discussed. One reason may be that 'existing theoretical arguments … are ill-equipped to go in reverse' (Jones 2018: 440); another may be that big theoretical ideas are comparably better equipped to explain general trends than the particularities of cases, such as crisis management, institutional resilience, etc. (e.g., Boin and Lodge 2016). One comprehensive attempt to explain crisis and European *dis*integration is conducted by Vollaard (2014), written in the context of the Eurocrisis. Vollaard suggests that studies of differentiated (dis)integration, such as Leuffen et al. (2012), 'only explain why some member-states do not join all integrative steps, and not whether the EU could become less integrated' (Vollaard 2014: 1143). Following Vollaard (2018), integration is seen as multifaceted processes that coexist with disintegrative ones. Rather than discussing theoretical applicability and development per se, there has thus been an increase in studies applying mid-range theories to describe or explain various crises and the EU's response, and studies which seek to understand the mechanisms the EU uses to tackle crisis, for example through disintegration (Vollaard 2018), or by pushing the EU toward differentiation (Leruth et al. 2019) or segmentation (e.g., Bátora and Fossum 2020).

Douglas Webber's paper in the *European Journal of International Relations* (2014) was one of the first academic articles to discuss the possibility of European disintegration as well as bringing states back into the study of European (dis)integration. In so doing, his work also makes a broader plea for mid-range theories which explain how exogenous shocks are absorbed in ways that reflect the endogenous bias of already existing rules and routines. When applied to how the EU adapts to crisis, institutional perspectives have focused on how institutional segmentation of the EU fosters differentiated crisis sensitivity and crisis management within different policy domains. Consequently, crisis in one policy area does not necessarily spillover to neighboring policy areas, thus not reverberating across entire systems. Put generally, 'bad' solutions may therefore be implemented in parts of organizations without ruining it all (Ansell and Trondal 2018). Similar ideas from Genschel and Jachtenfuchs (2018) suggest that processes of (dis)integration may unfold differently in policy domains of core state powers (through institutional capacity-building) and noncore state market integration (through regulatory measures). Exploring the financial crisis from a historical institutionalist perspective, Verdun (2015) argues that although the crisis also encouraged unilateral member-state behavior, over time the crisis has led to the development of new institutions on the basis of already existing structures and institutions. Also drawing on institutionalist reasoning, Falkner argues in a Special Issue of the *Journal of European Integration* (2016b) that crisis pressure was unequally distributed between nine policy areas and that the effects were mediated by the EU's decision-making 'modes' and layered on top of existing elements. In line with this Handbook's findings, Falkner (2016b: 229) shows that no policy area experienced integration 'failures' and a renationalization of competences and capacities. In short, polycrisis contributed to 'an even greater role to the EU,' partly due to spillover by stealth (Mèny 2014). The latter observation led Mèny (2014) to argue that crisis has contributed to a possible 'federalism of executives,' with a shift of power toward executive institutions, albeit segmented across different policy sub-systems (Bátora and Fossum 2020). This finding is buttressed by our Handbook, suggesting that executive dominance has spiraled in the wake of polycrisis.

Some of the recent literature on crisis, disintegration, and differentiation in Europe also combines explanations based on collective actors' cost–benefit calculations—such as the promotion of equality of opportunity among EU members (Jones 2018) and institutionalist explanations focusing on how crises are channeled through and mediated by pre-existing institutional frameworks and resources (e.g., Bátora and Fossum 2020). Consistent with the conclusions of this Handbook, both Vollaard (2018) and Bátora and Fossum (2020) suggest that the EU mainly *muddles through* crisis, either by means–end calculating member-states balancing different strategies of exit, voice, and loyalty (Vollaard 2018), or through institutional lock-in mechanisms influenced by pre-existing segmented institutional orders (Bátora and Fossum 2020).

Similarly, by combining insights from studies of European disintegration, post-functionalism, and differentiated integration, attempts have recently also been made to draw on the Brexit crisis as a groundbreaking case of differentiated disintegration to explore the mechanisms underlying these processes (Leruth et al. 2019). Brexit has reinvigorated differentiated integration as a nascent focus of research in EU studies. Common to this literature is the idea of crisis as a catalyst of increased European differentiation. According to Bátora and Fossum (2020), Schimmelfennig (2017); Schimmelfennig and Winzen (2019) and a Symposium in the *Journal of Common Market Studies* by Leruth et al. (2019), differentiation is a persistent and embedded phenomenon in the EU—a *systemic feature* and not a mere episode in the history of integration. The process of European integration is abundant with examples of fundamental crises, such as the ones triggered by the failure of the European Defence Community in 1954, the empty chair crisis of 1965–1966 or the 'euro-sclerosis' of 1970, to name but a few. Yet, the full *dis*integration of the Union has never happened and is in line with the findings of this volume not likely to happen according to Vollaard (2018: 259). Theorizing this phenomenon, scholars have argued that differentiation is driven by the need to find functional or constitutional compromises (Leuffen et al. 2012; Schimmelfennig 2017; Schimmelfennig and Winzen 2019), and linked mechanisms of supply and demand: those on the demand side mostly consist of the national governments of one country or a group of countries that do not wish to follow the integrationist path taken by the inner core of the EU, while the supply side consists of pro-integrationist governments from member-states that accept the demands to move away from uniformity (Leruth et al. 2019). Differentiation, arguably, not only covers processes where groups of member-states proceed with more integration but also processes under which a member-state withdraws from participation in the process of European integration (full exit) (Leruth et al. 2019), or component parts of member-states withdraw (partial exit), leading to processes of differentiated disintegration (Vollaard 2018: 233).

Recent studies also provide rich, theoretically informed, empirical probes of how the EU has responded to crisis across different policy fields. Exploring the financial crisis, Copelovitch, Friedan, and Walter's 2016 Special Issue in *Comparative Political Studies* argues that whereas economists have neglected the political causes of the Eurozone crisis, political scientists have similarly mischaracterized economically feasible reform paths. A paper in this Special Issue, by Jones et al. (2016), coined the term 'failing forward,' with reference to the financial crisis and its impact on future EU integration. This has later been applied and developed in other studies, including in Stenstad and Tranøy's chapter in this Handbook. Other scholars have proposed solutions to the Eurozone crisis, such as Begg (2009) who recommended a 'quasi federal system' for financial regulation. The Caporaso and Rhodes volume (2016) on the Eurozone crisis is a particularly incisive and broad investigation of the causes and implications of the crisis as stemming from several causes and enabling the empowerment of individual member-states and not of supranational institutions. Caporaso (2018) has also extensively explored the ways in which Eurozone crisis shaped Brexit and the migration crisis in ways that engendered their own dynamic for future integration. In our Handbook, Caporaso extends his analysis of interactions among crises further in order examine how these interactions impact the prospects of further integration in the EU. In a *West European Politics* special issue on the financial crisis, Hall (2014) argues that the divide between creditor and debtor nations reflected in the resulting austerity policies grows out of different regional approaches to capitalism in the north where most firms are export to international markets in contrast with southern and eastern economies powered by internal consumption. Rather than explaining crisis, studies have also focused on the question of governance, as investigated by Graziano and Halpern's 2016 Special Issue in *Comparative European Politics* and particularly as concerns the leading role of the European Commission in handling the Euro crisis (see also Graziano and Hartlapp 2019). Contributors to Graziano and Halpern's project explored different tools available to the European Commission in addition to fines such as withdrawal of funding as well as 'shaming' (Falkner 2016a: 36, 48). However, specific implementation of the methods of soft governance by the European Commission, EU agencies (Saurugger and Turpan 2016), and the European Central Bank (Kudrna 2016) after crisis were not explored. Our Handbook thus picks up where Graziano and Halpern left off and considers several instances of governance reforms across the EU institutions, including several of minor interest to Graziano et al. such as the European Parliament and the European Court of Justice.

Published before the migration crisis hit, Guiraudon (2014) looks at the impact of the austerity in response to the Eurozone crisis on migrant integration policy, addresses questions of legitimacy of the European social model under duress, and considers whether it can cushion all residents, including migrants and their descendants, in an economic crisis by asking what the effects of financial crisis are in this area. Several studies examine the migration crisis in comparison mainly to the financial crisis. A key example is Schimmelfennig's 2018 study, in which he finds that member-states were more willing to delegate to supranational institutions as a result of the financial crisis but held onto sovereignty in response to migration crisis (Schimmelfennig 2018a: 982). Even if member-states in both cases have become reliant on supranational governance, Schimmelfennig argues that although a regulatory regime existed at supranational level in both policy areas, the supranational institutions were weaker in migration policy than for finance (ibid.: 985). The special issue by Roos and Zaun (2016) in *Journal of Ethnic and Migration Studies* considers the Eurozone crisis and its impact on migration, noting that migration policy has changed, but not as a result of the financial crisis. Roos and Zaun (2016) point out that crisis in and of itself does not lead to policy developments. Political actors have to perceive a crisis as a moment for reform (ibid.: 1585), a perception which may be variable across member-states. A key set of papers authored by Niemann and Zaun (2018) looks specifically at the migration crisis. They posit that European integration theories are useful for generating explanations for why member-states resist the supranationalization of migration policy. Their special issue's main finding is that 'European co-operation, particularly in the area of core state powers, does not always equal European integration,' and the EU–Turkey statement is the main evidence for this finding (Niemann and Zaun 2018: 5).

The EU's Common foreign and security policy (CFSP) has also been explored systematically in special issues through the lens of crisis. Although with some variation, much of the literature in this domain suggests that the Ukraine crisis has served to unite EU member-states in the CFSP, leading to a strengthening of integration in the domain—a finding further supported in this Handbook by Juncos and Pomorska, Riddervold and Newsome, Blockmans, and Rieker and Riddervold. Systematically exploring EU policies in response to the Ukraine crisis, in an edited volume of *Journal of Common Market Studies*, Cross and Karolewski (2017) asked how this crisis has affected the EU's foreign policy power. Applying a common framework on crisis and EU power in exploring various dimensions of EU foreign policy in reaction to the crisis, most of the contributions to that special issue found that the EU was affected by the crisis; however, they also observed variation. Two articles argued that rather than *heading forward* or *muddling through*, the EU has become more constrained as a consequence of the Ukraine crisis. According to Howorth (2017), although the EU did agree on common responses, for example through sanctions, the EU has remained incoherent vis-à-vis Russia and Ukraine following the Russian annexation of Crimea. Similarly, Kuzio (2017) argued that member-states' relations with Russia trumped EU foreign policy values, resulting in a weak coordinated EU response compared to other crisis responses. In sharp contrast to this, Sjursen and Rosén (2017) observed that the EU did respond strongly to Russian aggression owing to an already institutionalized norm of cooperation in response to external crisis. Focusing on member-states' reactions to the Ukraine crisis, Orenstein and Kelemen (2017) found that responses were two-sided. On the one hand, core member-states took strong positions vis-à-vis Russia, and as a consequence, the EU came out as a stronger actor. On the other hand, the EU's powers were constrained by certain member-states referred to as 'Trojan Horses' that continued helping Russia. Several contributions argued that the crisis caused increased EU powers by increasing the level of *de facto* supranationalism in the domain. Although still a 'secondary track,' Nitoiu and Sus (2017) found that the Ukraine crisis led to an increased use of transnational diplomacy as a foreign policy tool, due to increased coordination of diplomatic action between the European External Action Service, the European Commission, the European Parliament, and member-states' diplomacy. According to Natorski and Pomorska (2017), the crisis increased member-states' trust in EU institutions, such as the European Commission and the Councils Coreper. By exploring defence spending and strategic focus, Schilde (2017) revealed that the crisis has led to an increased focus on developing European defence. Focusing instead on how EU crisis, combined with a changing US foreign policy orientation or what Anderson (this volume) refers to as the 'Trump crisis,' affected the EU's relationship with its traditional ally the US, a Special Issue in the *Journal of European Integration* (Riddervold and Newsome 2018) also came to similar conclusions, suggesting that the EU is *moving forward*, or at least *muddling through* in the CFSP (M. E. Smith 2018; Howorth 2018; Riddervold and Rosén 2018). Studies of the EU's role in international governance came to a more nuanced conclusion, arguing that the EU in certain multilateral arenas is becoming more united (Cross 2018) but in others, it struggles to agree internally (Newsome 2018), and that member-states seek special relationships with the US (M. Smith 2018). Studies of other recent external challenges and conflicts such as the Syrian conflict, where the EU has played a limited role, also reveal that EU unity in the CFSP sometimes can be a cumbersome process (see Jørgensen et al. 2015; Novotna 2017).

Notwithstanding these valuable studies of EU crises, there are no accounts of EU crisis comparable to this Handbook. Two of the most comprehensive books so far are the anthology *The European Union in Crisis* edited by Dinan et al. (2017) and Webber's book *European Disintegration? The Politics of Crisis in the European Union* (2018). Discussing the financial crisis, the migration crisis, the Ukraine crisis, and Brexit, and in sharp contrast to one of the main findings in this Handbook, Webber (2018) argues that European disintegration, or what this volume refers to as a *breaking down* scenario, is a tangible prospect. According to Webber, existing integration theories fall short of explaining the EU's response to these crises. Instead, EU integration and hence EU stability depends on a 'stabilizing force'—a role that so far has been taken on by Germany. With Germany according to Webber not being able to play this dominant role in the integration process, the future of the EU will depend on whether or not other forms of 'stabilizing leadership' is found. The anthology *The European Union in Crisis* edited by Dinan et al. (2017) is a comprehensive study of EU crises that combines both theoretical discussions and empirical studies of various crises and EU institutions. The book's editors and other leading experts examine not only the set of problems the EU has faced during polycrisis but also the crisis of European integration more broadly. In addition to the introduction by the three editors, the book covers theoretical discussions of EU integration theories (Schimmelfennig 2017) and one general chapter on EU's institutions and policy processes (Nugent 2017). Empirically, chapters explore the historical contexts (Dinan 2017) and political economy of crisis (Rosamond 2017) before going into depth on the eurozone crisis (de la Porte and Heins 2017; Dyson 2017; Laffan 2017), Brexit (McGowan and Phinnemore 2017), the migration crisis (Buonanno 2017), and the legitimacy challenge (Schweiger 2017). The book also covers country and policy chapters, including on Germany (Bulmer and Paterson 2017), Greece (Featherstone and Papadimitriou 2017), Central and Eastern Europe (Haughton 2017), and a separate chapter on Ukraine (Seibel 2017). Two chapters, by Webber (2017) and the concluding chapter by the editors (Dinan et al. 2017), reflect on the EU's future. This anthology is, however, foremost written as a first (and before this Handbook, most comprehensive) textbook in the field, and does not provide systematic theoretically informed studies of the EU's institutional and political crisis responses and their broader consequences to the comprehensive extent done in this volume. Similarly, as discussed here and in other parts of the Handbook, there are many studies both on particular crises, theories' applicability, the role and reform of the various EU institutions, and the long-term consequences of the measures adopted. Yet, no attempts have previously been made to take the bird's-eye perspective on the EU as a whole. Even if looking at the different parts of the book, they are unique compared to existing literature due to the systematic comparative discussions of the grand theories of European integration, all the main institutions and all the main cases. Issues of governance also concern us, but rather than exploring key institutions or key crises in isolation, the contribution of this Handbook is also to comprehensively contextualize the efforts made by each institution in light of other prominent EU institutions, for example exploring the European Commission's interactions with the European Parliament, the European Central Bank, and the Council. We also examine each individual crisis on its own as well as consider interactive dynamics across crises. In so doing, while we also 'emphasize the primacy of domestic politics' (Copelovitch et al. 2016), and thus also relate to our earlier studies of crisis and transatlantic relations (Riddervold and Newsome 2018), this Handbook focuses on the combined role of EU institutions and is thus not limited to the role played by only certain institutions such as the European Central Bank or the European Commission. Some studies have also proposed solutions to the crises, something this Handbook does not do. Rather than identifying ideal reform policies or trajectories, the Handbook assesses the policies and institutional changes which have been implemented, and subsequently considers what this implies for European integration.

In addition to this being a comprehensive account on EU crisis, what is unique about this Handbook is also that all chapters relate to a common analytical framework as outlined above. Moreover, by contextualizing the analytical approach, this Handbook engages in a broader debate on the extent to which, and under what conditions, crisis poses a threat, or not, to the European integration project. Our framework is cognizant both of increased prospects for future integration and the co-existence of unintended disintegrative consequences. With this Handbook, we thus not only aim to provide a comprehensive, systematic, and comparative account of the EU's institutional and policy responses to crisis; we also hope to provide a comprehensive, systematic, and comparative account of European (dis)integration as such.

STRUCTURE OF THE VOLUME

To do this, the Handbook consists of five parts: Part I contains this introductory chapter. Next, Part II includes chapters discussing how important theoretical approaches to EU integration understand and explain crisis, focusing in particular on the theories' ability to explain continuity and change in the face of crisis. Part III addresses the impact of crises on the EU institutions, exploring putative changes in their competences and roles as well as their influence and role in crisis response. Chapters in Part III of the volume also illuminate the variety of EU responses that evolve over longer courses of time, allowing us to examine how multiple crises influence individual institutions as well as the EU polity as a whole. Part III also examines how institutional continuity or change can be accounted for. In sum, this broad institutional analysis allows to comprehensively map institutional continuity and change in the face of crisis. Next, Part IV studies how crisis has influenced different policy domains, with chapters on the financial crisis, the migration crisis, Brexit, foreign and security policy crises, as well as crises attached to EU legitimacy. The volume concludes with Part V, which provides commentaries that draw broader implications on how crisis influences the EU and what this tells about the nature, functioning, and legitimacy of the EU polity. Relating to the Handbook's overall findings, it closes with a chapter discussing the EU's responses to the Corona crisis.

In order to more easily synthesize knowledge, each part of the Handbook opens with an introduction that sums up key arguments and findings in each chapter that follows, and discusses the broader implications of the empirical observations presented. The Handbook contains seven introductions for each thematic area: one for the theory chapters, one for the institutional chapters, and one for each of the five policy crises discussed.

When studying the impact of crisis on the EU's policies and institutions, a methodological challenge facing most contributions relates to casual identification. Without having a positivist understanding of causality, the Handbook builds on the general assumption that crisis somehow triggers effects on (some) EU policies and/or institutions and that observers are able to draw inferences about the extent to which, how, and why this unfolds. A methodological challenge is thus to control for intervening causal factors—i.e., to isolate whether putative effects indeed are influenced by crisis and not mainly by other causal drivers. In the end, this is a challenge that is carefully dealt within each chapter. Chapter authors were invited to measure the impact of crisis through various methodological techniques and data sources, such as process tracing, counterfactual arguing, larger data sets, and/or triangulation. These are ways of examining EU responses, the extent to which and how these fit the different scenarios outlined above, the applicability of the theories as well as the broader implications of these findings.

KEY FINDINGS

Part II: Theoretical Approaches to Crisis

Part II covers a set of the most important theoretical approaches to EU studies: intergovernmentalism (Frank Schimmelfennig), classical realism (Alexander Reichwein), neo-realism (Hubert Zimmerman), neo-functionalism (Arne Niemann), institutionalism (Christopher Ansell), organizational theory (Jarle Trondal), cleavage theory (Gary Marks, David Attewell, Jan Rovny and Liesbet Hooghe), social constructivism (Mai'a K. Davis Cross), and deliberative theory (Claudia Landwehr). These chapters discuss how each theory studies, understands, and explains crisis' putative impact on the EU. To do this, all authors were invited to discuss a set of joint questions: How does the suggested theoretical perspective envision how crises are likely to influence EU institutions and policies? What are the causal mechanisms accounting for continuity or change in public policy and governing institutions? And to what extent have these perspectives been able to explain continuity and change in the EU in the face of crisis?

This Handbook is not the first to address these questions (see 'State of the art' above and the introduction to Part II for a selection of key scholarly work). However, no volume has thus far made a comprehensive theoretical study of crisis to the extent offered by this volume. The chapters in Part II suggest first, that European integration theories have relevance also for explaining EU crisis. Due to their different focus and different ontological assumptions, their applicability varies across cases, and particular crises can be understood through different theoretical lenses. Future research should hence systematically test alternative theories across different cases (see Hooghe and Marks 2019). Second, no one theory provides a full picture or explanation of the EU's many crisis-responses, suggesting that there might be a need also to revisit existing theoretical frameworks to more adequately encompass *dis*integration and crisis (Webber 2014). Third, overall, we find that the EU's crisis response to a large extent has been to (incrementally) integrate further. Whether a different outcome—if the EU was breaking up in the face of crisis—could have been equally explained by the existing integration theory toolkit, however, remains an open question also after this endeavor. In some cases, where outcomes do not fit various integration logics, existing theories have struggled to provide robust explanations, for example in the case of Brexit. As argued by Frank Schimmelfennig, there is thus room for theoretical innovation, for example by combining insights from existing theories or by further developing prevailing theories to better understand both continuity and change, as discussed in Ansell's chapter. Lastly, theorizing on the impact of crisis on EU institutions, policies and the processes of integration should move on to establish more systematic knowledge on the *scope conditions* under which the three conceptual scenarios—breaking up, *muddling through*, and *heading forward*—are more or less likely to play out in response to crisis.

Our ambition is that this Handbook will provide a constructive contribution to all these research challenges.

Part III: Crisis, Continuity and Change in European Union Institutions

This section examines the (European Union) Council (Jeffrey Lewis), the European Parliament (Akasemi Newsome and Matthew Stenberg), the Court of Justice of the European Union (Lisa Conant), The European Commission (Hussein Kassim and Luc Tholoniat), EU agencies (Michelle Everson and Ellen Vos), the European Central Bank (Ingrid Hjertaker and Bent Sofus Tranøy), and the European External Action Service (Heidi Maurer). As an overarching observation, the section shows that EU institutions have responded to the multiple set of crises mainly by *muddling through* based on familiar ways of governing and by introducing incremental changes, and yet in some cases also by *heading forward* with new institutional arrangements or structures. Contrary to what one would expect if the EU was *breaking down* under the weight of crises, we hardly find evidence of institutional breakdown or even of minor reductions in the role of EU institutions—either vis-à-vis other EU institutions or vis-à-vis member-state institutions. To the contrary— the EU institutions have proved to be fairly resilient and able to deal with crisis by drawing on their already established tools and structures, or by developing new ones. If anything, crisis has strengthened what was already a strong element of expert governance and 'rule by the knowers' in the EU: All executive institutions—the European Commission, EU agencies, and the European Central Bank—have gained more influence as a consequence of the crises explored. The case of EU agencies further illustrates this by their increased but highly contested role. The chapter on EU agencies discusses how crises have heightened underlying concerns about the appropriate place of autonomous governance institutions within the broader scheme of democratic politics and government. A similar tension is observed in the case of the European Central Bank. Experts and executive institutions' increased roles have not been fully compensated by an equally strengthened role for the European Parliament. Member-states have also wanted a stronger role for themselves in response to crises, with for example the European Council meeting more often. Finally, the observations in sum also suggest that multiple institutions can potentially be strengthened in tandem as a consequence of multiple crises, and that winners do not take all as in 'zero-sum' games.

Part IV: Policy Areas: Crisis, Continuity and Change

To systematically and comprehensively explore the impact of crises on continuity and change across policy fields, this core part of the Handbook consists of five sections, each exploring the impact of a particular crisis. These are (i) the financial crisis, (ii) the migration crisis, (iii) Brexit, (iv) crisis and EU foreign and security policy, and finally (v) the legitimacy crisis. Each section opens with an editorial introduction, followed by a set of chapters containing detailed empirical studies of each crisis. The chapters map the chronology of each crisis and offer state-of-the-art empirical observations. Moreover, each chapter systematically addresses the question of what, if any, impact the crisis had in each policy domain. Finally, each chapter relates to the three scenarios outlined above and thus draw general conclusion on how crisis hits the processes of European integration.

The Financial Crisis
A first section explores the Eurozone crisis, describing how it unfolded, before shifting to analyzes of how the EU addressed the crisis, its effect on integration, and what the nature of the crisis suggests for the future of the EU. Espen D.H. Olsen and Guri Rosén, Eirik Tegle Stenstad and Bent Sofus Tranøy, as well as James Caporaso arrive at the same conclusion, characterizing the EU's response to the financial crisis primarily as *muddling through*. At the same time, the chapters disagree on what the implications the financial crisis are likely to have for the future of the EU integration. Espen D.H. Olsen and Guri Rosén point out that the reforms in European Monetary Union after the crisis provoked protest across Europe against national leaders and Brussels-based institutions. Their study highlights the absence of a role for citizen participation in the expansion of powers for the ECB in response to crisis. Olsen and Rosén thus reject characterizing finance policy postcrisis as *heading forward*. On the other hand, Eirik Tegle Stenstad and Bent Sofus Tranøy argue that the finance sector reforms undertaken by the EU did not go far enough as they did not call into question the normative role of finance and banking as a public good. James Caporaso analyzes the Eurozone crisis and considers how it was interconnected with the migration crisis and Brexit. Caporaso offers the insight that the EU's a la carte approach to integration, initially useful for keeping the UK engaged, contributed to Brexit as the sheer number of policy fields other member-states opted into left Britain increasingly isolated.

The Migration Crisis
The chapters in the second section analyze the migration crisis. Whereas the migration crisis polarizes domestic political debates within member-states about whether migration is compatible with the nation, it also has a similar effect at the supranational level. Contributors Kaija Schilde and Sara Wallace Goodman, Ruxandra-Laura Bosilca, and Beverly Crawford engage with questions of national and European identity, interests, and previous decisions to trace the EU's policy responses to migration historically and in the context of the 2015 crisis. Schilde and Wallace Goodman conclude that the EU struggles to adequately solve the migration crisis in part because it has struggled to do so in the past. While member-states have been willing to work with EU institutions to develop common border security policies, they have resisted and disagreed repeatedly on asylum management. Schilde and Wallace Goodman show that while border security contains examples of deeper integration,

asylum management policy has followed the scenarios of *breaking down* and *muddling through*. Bosilca concurs with Schilde and Wallace Goodman's finding that member-states have rejected common asylum policy over the years and in the recent 2015 case. At the same time, when member-states found common ground for cooperation in migration policy in response to crisis, member-states still took the step of avoiding the supranational institutions as they hammered a joint policy. Lastly, Crawford's chapter highlights Germany as a pivotal actor in the EU's response to the migration crisis. Where the other authors are pessimistic about the possibilities for deeper integration in migration policy in the future, Crawford contends that Germany has been able to push for deeper integration in this policy area as befitting *muddling through* and *heading forward*.

Brexit
This section focuses on the consequences of the United Kingdom (UK)'s decision to leave the EU. Although much of the new relationship between the UK and the EU will depend on the UK–EU negotiations, Brexit will be a groundbreaking and thus unpredictable case of differentiated *dis*integration. It is still unclear what kind of relationship the UK will achieve with the EU, and what the consequences Brexit will have for the future of European integration. It is likely to take years before scholars and practitioners are able to grasp the consequences of Brexit for all those involved and determine whether it will trigger integration slowdown (Scenario 1), accelerated integration (Scenario 3), or merely path-dependent processes of *muddling through* (Scenario 2). So far, however, EU member-states have kept a united front in the Brexit negotiations. Perhaps more than anything, the Brexit process has revealed how interwoven the EU member-states have become, with the EU influencing all aspects of society and national legislation now largely originating from EU legislative processes. Rather than leading to more member-states discussing a possible departure from the EU, the challenges involved in a Brexit also seems to have increased public support for the EU. The Brexit part of the Handbook covers two chapters. The chapter by Tim Oliver and Benjamin Martill provides an overview of the criticisms levelled against the EU's approach to Brexit. Brexit is examined as a series of overlapping processes and debates involving multiple actors in Britain, in the EU, in the rest of Europe, as well as globally. These processes are also analyzed across various time frames. The chapter breaks down the EU's mistakes on Brexit into three broad groups: misguiding Britain over its place in the EU; misreading what Brexit means; and mishandling how Brexit has been negotiated. Secondly, the chapter by Øyvind Svendsen examines security and defence aspects of Brexit. The chapter answers two questions: What room is there for the inclusion of third countries in EU security and defence initiatives, and how does Brexit alter the politics of such inclusion? The chapter argues that whereas the EU internally heads forward on security and defence, how it deals with like-minded third country partners is likely to be characterized by *muddling through*.

Crisis and the EU Foreign and Security Policy
While the other chapters in this part of the Handbook discuss how each crisis has played out in the EU and how each has affected EU integration in a specific field, the four chapters in this section examine the impact of externally induced crises on EU integration in the EU Common Foreign and Security policy (CFSP) only. The four chapters by Ana E. Juncos and Karolina Pomorska, Marianne Riddervold, Pernille Rieker and Steven Blockmans, and Marianne Riddervold and Akasemi Newsome focus in particular on the impact of three external crises with EU foreign and security policy implications taking place within, and contributing to a more uncertain international context: The Ukraine Crisis, 'the Trump Crisis,' and the 'instability crisis' in the EU's neighborhood. All chapters suggest empirically that the EU seems able to cope with crisis and that crisis has led to a strengthening of the CFSP mainly by *muddling through* but in some instances also *heading forward*. This is a surprising result given the CFSP's intergovernmental character in which several member-states have been reluctant to push for more EU policy integration. Indeed, all chapters discuss how this reluctance combined with the formal CFSP procedures pose challenges to the EU's ability to efficiently act with one voice, something also seen in other international conflicts, for example in Syria and Libya. As such, the cases explored in the CFSP section of the volume may not give the whole picture of this policy domain. However, what we can say on the basis of our findings and in contrast to what some observers have maintained, the CFSP does *not* seem to be *breaking down* in the face of crisis. Instead, when looking at some of the main external crisis the EU has faced in recent years, not least in Ukraine and linked to the US' turn in foreign policy, as well as the EU's ability to launch crisis-management operations, the EU and its member-states seem to have reacted by joining forces to become more resilient. Overall, this suggests that the EU is likely to *muddle through* and *head forward* with more and stronger cooperation also in the future of CFSP.

The Legitimacy Crisis
The chapters in this final section conceptualize the crisis of democratic legitimacy in the EU and examine how the question of legitimacy shapes the prospects for further integration in the crisis context. Most recently in response to the coronavirus outbreak, democracy in Hungary and Poland, but also the Czech Republic and Romania, has been endangered for the past decade by right-wing populist governments that seek to undermine the rule of law, judicial independence, the free press, and human rights conventions to which many EU member-states are signatories. At the same time, populist parties have mobilized voters in opposition to the technocratic responses to this crisis made by the EU and have cast the EU as distant, untrustworthy, and fundamentally undemocratic, while also using EU funds to expand party mobilization capacity. However, this Handbook does not limit the legitimacy crisis

solely to the growth of illiberal parties and movements.[1] Chapters in this section additionally analyze the broader phenomenon of expertization and examine Eurobarometer measures of trust in the EU across member-states. Given these complex dimensions of the EU legitimacy crisis, this section assemble evidence that the EU is *muddling through* in response to its democratic legitimacy crisis, suggesting that the EU continues to take limited steps toward greater integration in response to the legitimacy crisis. These limited steps in the short-term, of course, cannot wholly rule out unintended disintegrative effects in the medium and long-term. Kolja Raube and Francisca Costa Reis' chapter examines the legitimacy crisis as a threat to the EU's identity, as a threat to the EU's ability to reap compliance from member-states, and as a threat to how outsiders perceive the EU. Undoubtedly, the EU's lack of response to Polish juridical reforms and increased executive powers in Hungary—most recently in response to the Corona crisis—suggests that the EU is *breaking down* in its defence of democratic values. At the same time, however, Raube and Coast Reis show that there are several ongoing processes in the EU with regards to these countries' breach of the EU's core and treaty-based principles, suggesting that there is not a complete EU-wide breakdown in these areas. These are slow and not always efficient processes but might over time suggest that the EU overall is *muddling through* also in this domain. Although Rauba and Costa Reis demonstrate mainly incremental steps taken by the EU in response to the legitimacy crisis, they also find support for *heading forward* in the CJEU's innovative use of Article 19 TEU on judicial independence in case rulings. Catherine Holst and Anders Molander's chapter looks closely at how expert advice in policy-making has contributed to the contemporary crisis in EU legitimacy. The authors recommend reforms to EU institutions that would change experts' behavior and allow civil society and citizens to play a more active role in both the selection of experts to develop policy solutions and in the policy-making process itself. For these authors, the plausibility of the different scenario's hinges on the likelihood of reforms. As they deem gradual reforms most likely, they conclude that *muddling through* best describes the EU's response to the technocracy dimension of the legitimacy crisis. Pieter de Wilde's chapter addresses the short- and long-term effects of crises on public support for and trust in European governance. As EU citizens remain evenly divided on the issue of trust in the EU, de Wilde also suggests that *muddling through* is the most likely scenario.

---

[1] For an important dimension to the legitimacy crisis and a discussion of how various EU crises impacted trans-European networks of social movement building, see Philip Ayoub (2019) for a study of successful social movement building around LGTBI rights across EU member states including in Poland and Hungary.

Main Conclusions—Polycrisis and EU Policy Developments

Taking a step back from the in-depth discussions of these five crises, one central conclusion is that in every policy domain the EU has made some response to address the crisis at hand and that it has often reached for trusted practices that have served it well in the past. Across the policy areas of finance, migration, and foreign and security policy, the Union has foremost made incremental steps in order to address the challenges it faced. Notwithstanding challenges the EU has faced in dealing with severe democratic challenges in some member-states, for Brexit, and for the legitimacy crisis, our contributors found evidence of *muddling through*. This assessment of *muddling through* is also coupled with instances of *heading forward* across policy cases, in which the EU's response to crises also included windows of opportunity through which innovative organizational structures or new policies could be created with the goal of solving the crisis through deepening integration. A few examples of *heading forward* bear repeating: Post financial crisis, the ECB is newly now the lender of last resort for the Eurozone. As democracy is in decline in some parts of Central Europe, national courts and the European Commission sought and received guidance from the CJEU on judicial independence in member-states, as subject to EU enforcement. The EU has strengthened its own foreign and security policy in response to aggressive steps taken by Russia in Ukraine, a unity that is strengthened also by Brexit and a changing US foreign policy orientation. And not least—faced with its newest and perhaps most severe crisis to date—the Corona crisis—the EU is both *muddling through* and *heading forward*, with the mutualization of debt by some observers even being referred to as a 'revolutionary step,' 'remarkably integrative,' and the EU's 'Hamiltonian moment' (see Greer, Ruijter and Brooks, this volume). When it comes to our first *breaking down* scenario, our authors also suggest that the migration and legitimacy crises and the EU's response to them can be partly characterized as instances of *breaking down*. At least for now, the EU seems to be *breaking down* in its guarding of EU democratic values but is at the same time *muddling through* institutionally and legally to deal with some of the democratic challenges in Hungary and Poland. Chapters on the migration crisis provide a long view of repeated failed attempts by the European Commission and the European Parliament to develop common asylum policy followed by refusals from member-states to cede sovereignty in this area. Member-states have been able to agree to invest in border security and yet Bosilca highlights a lack of commitment by member-states in the immediate aftermath of the 2015 migration crisis to preserve the Schengen system, choosing instead to resurrect national borders within the EU. Although proving remarkably unified in the negotiations, Brexit in one sense also involves a *breaking down* scenario with one of the most important members of the EU leaving the Union. It is also noteworthy that there was not a response from the EU to the UK with the aim of dissuading the UK from leaving. And internally, the EU has been surprisingly unified.

A final conclusion from the policy section of the Handbook and that we will return to at the end of this chapter also concerns the issue of the EU responses' unintended consequences over time and across policy areas. For example, for the financial crisis and Brexit, the Handbook suggests that the disintegrative implications of deeper integration in one area in response to crisis are not yet known for other areas. *Heading forward* by empowering the ECB unleashed civil unrest in both Greece and Germany about the democratic legitimacy of the ECB's postcrisis financial policy. All in all, however, the EU seems to incrementally and functionally integrate further in its responses to crisis. Future studies of the EU's response to the Corona crisis will be a key test of the generalizability of our findings. So far, studies of this crisis proves us right. Conducting the first systematic study of the impact of the Corona crisis to date, Greer, Ruijter, and Brooks (this volume) finds that the EU indeed is *heading forward* in response to the crisis, arguing that the EU in terms of response 'has actually had a good crisis.' While the first phase characterized by egoism and national protection lasted a month, in May and June 2020 the EU 'created a substantial new first-face health policy agenda, reasserted its second-face market-preserving powers, and shifted its fiscal stance in a much more supportive direction' (Greer et al., this volume). Predicting the future is always risky. However, on the basis of the findings in this Handbook, we thus expect the EU to prove resilient in the face of the Corona crisis also in the longer run, *muddling through* and *heading forward* with new policies both in the public health domain and neighboring and affected policy domains. As summed up by Greer, Ruijter, and Brooks in this volume, the crisis 'exposed European Union member-states' interdependence. It has, so far, also led to integration.'

Part V: Commentaries

The final part of the Handbook brings together empirical findings of the Handbook and offers commentaries on the EU as a differentiated polity, the EU's external crisis response and broader role in a multilateral changing global order, EU crises and their implications for democracy and popular support, the EU's first responses to the Corona, crisis as well as the longer term challenges facing the EU.

In a first commentary chapter, Gänzle, Leruth, and Trondal discuss the relationship between crisis and differentiated European integration, understood as a holistic term encompassing both (differentiated) integration and *dis*integration. Differentiation is seen as a likely outcome of crisis integration and disintegration. The EU has to a large degree developed in response to crisis, as a functional way to solve disagreements has often been to find differentiated solutions, either in the short-term or through constitutional, longer-term solutions (also see Leuffen et al. 2012). As a consequence, rather than being an exception, differentiation is increasingly the natural state of affairs in the EU, and it is likely to increase in the future as the EU continues to face various crises. Having discussed the development of a growing literature on differentiated integration and its increased relevance for understanding the EU, Gänzle, Leruth, and Trondal move on to discuss avenues of further research in the field. With prospects for more differentiated disintegration, new questions and scenarios arise for the Union and the field of inquiry, and old ones have reappeared. Given the wide range of publications related to differentiation and following the Brexit vote, the authors consider differentiated disintegration to be the next key topic in EU studies. In relation to the three scenarios outlined in the Handbook, the authors argue that future EU studies should treat the dependent variable as a continuum rather than as alternative models and should further develop this in the study of differentiation. As discussed in Part II in this Handbook, we should also expect the study of European (dis)integration to largely follow existing theoretical threads within EU studies. Moreover, another avenue for future theorizing of differentiation thus lies in determining the conditions under which each of the three scenarios outlined in this Handbook plays out in the case of differentiated (dis)integration.

A second overall theme discussed in Part V of this volume is the link between crisis and the EU's role in the world. Mike Smith argues that the future of the EU as an international actor and crisis manager will reflect both the hybrid nature of the EU and the complexity of the challenges it faces, both internally and externally. Mike Smith starts from the observation that not only the EU but also the global arena is currently characterized by a number of intersecting crises and increased volatility that serve to undermine the post-WWII international, rule-based order. Since the EU's international credibility and legitimacy to a large extent is linked to this order, the EU will be profoundly challenged by these global crises, while at the same time facing challenges to internal unity. In terms of this volume's three scenarios, Mike Smith on the one hand argues in line with a *breaking down* scenario that the EU has proved incapable of dealing with several key international crises, for example in the Middle East. There is, however, on the other hand also evidence of a *muddling through* scenario, as crises have been met with incremental adjustments of the EU's policies and institutional structures, for example in terms of environmental and commercial policies, in the Common security and defence policy, and in relation to Brexit. Internal and external polycrisis, combined with the EU's hybrid institutional structures, have in other words led to a number of differentiated EU responses. Lastly, in terms of the *heading forward* scenario, the above examples also show that the EU indeed may be moving forward on various external topics. A complicating factor is that that the EU is not operating in a vacuum but instead is strongly influenced not least by the ongoing changing power structures and the potential undermining of the post WWII international order—factors the EU cannot control. Eventually, Mike Smith argues, the EU's future role on the world stage will depend on its answer to the question of who or what its external crisis management is for—whether it will reflect the internal needs of the Union, the external opportunities available to it, or the EU's capacity to establish a stable identity and role for itself in relation to the emerging European and world order.

A third commentary chapter by Anne Elizabeth Stie discusses the Handbook's findings in relation to the question of the EU's democratic legitimacy, asking if the EU's response to polycrisis has served to further increase the EU's democratic deficit. In answering that it has, the chapter makes two interrelated arguments. Firstly, Stie argues that democratic decision-making requires both citizen participation (input legitimacy) and expertise (output legitimacy). This implies that the EU's output legitimacy can only to some extent compensate for the lack of democratic input legitimacy. In the EU, the reliance on output legitimacy has been written into the structural architecture from the start but has now developed too far, making populists and Eurosceptics big winners. Secondly, not only does Stie find that democracy is hollowed out—at both the national and the European levels—the credibility of expertise is increasingly also at risk in the EU. In a polity where insulated and relatively independent technocratic institutions dominate and when decisions taken by these institutions are (no longer) neither perceived as desirable nor as contributing in solving, but rather exacerbating, citizens' problems (as many found in the euro and migration crises), people start questioning the credibility of these institutions and consequently also the quality of the expertise they claim to hold. In other words, Stie argues that EU's handling of crises mainly through technocratic solutions could end up being a self-defeating strategy for the EU—that prior to the crises also suffered from legitimacy deficits. Hence, the EU's strategy is (seemingly) counterproductive as clogging the citizens' possibility to influence decision-making through democratic contestation rather seems to promote more populism, polarization, and fragmentation. The only way out of such a democratic quagmire, Stie argues, is to stay away from 'expertocratic shortcuts' and rather acknowledge that there is no quick fix for democratic self-government but to opt for the 'long road' and increase democracy at the EU level.

Next, Martin Shapiro comments on what he calls the 'perfect storm' for the EU, and which according to Shapiro now hovers over both sides of the Atlantic. Going back to the end of the Cold War and the victory of Liberalism, Shapiro argues that the problems of the EU today are many, complex, and constantly changing. Discussing the various challenges facing not only the EU but also national, transnational, and international governance on both sides of the Atlantic, Shapiro argues that the EU's main problem (and hence potential solution) is associated with dynamics of distrust and anti-establishment feelings: Driven by factors such as economic globalization and rapid technological change, large population displacements, evident income gaps between different groups of the population, and the divide between winners and losers of globalization, we have witnessed a popular movement that does not trust government, bureaucrats, experts, professional politicians, and the 'chattering classes.' This challenge may according to Shapiro thus also be the main reason why this volume observes that the EU is largely *muddling through* in response to crises rather than taking dynamic action by *moving forward* in an attempt to radically deal with them. Although there are many underlying factors of this distrust, at its core Shapiro argues that this phenomenon seems to be linked more to psychological processes than to typical political science explanatory factors such as economic self-interest, party identification, or the like. While the solution to this challenge indeed might be difficult to find, Shapiro thus reminds us that it is important not to shy away from trying to understand this phenomenon and to combine analytical insights from other academic disciplines when studying the EU and its member-states.

Scott L. Greer, Anniek de Ruijter, and Eleanor Brooks relate the analytical framework to the latest and perhaps most severe crisis facing the EU, namely, the Corona crisis. In their discussion of the impact of Covid-19 on the EU integration, they find that although EU member-states initially did not display a common purpose in fighting the pandemic, overall this crisis provides evidence of *heading forward*. While the issue area of public health remained firmly within the bounds of member-state sovereignty preceding the Corona crisis, several developments rendered this issue area new territory for expanded integration. Greer, Ruijter, and Brook point out that funding of public health for supranational institutions has increased from EUR 445 million to more than EUR 10 billion in response to the crisis. Additional mechanisms for coordination among member-states now exist and, most importantly for Greer et al., stand a likely chance for becoming deeply entrenched as success in stemming the Coronavirus will require increasing coordination and harmonization of public health standards and procurement over several years. Most importantly, the ensuing economic crisis resulting from Covid-19 delivered what the authors refer to as 'a remarkably integrative step' and by others as Europe's 'Hamiltonian moment,' in which the ECB issued European debt without conditions in response to the contraction of the economy during the pandemic. The authors also expect a long-lasting crisis to have a longer term integrative impact on the EU, both through *muddling through* and *heading forward* processes across different domains, in particular in health and finance. As noted elsewhere in this introductory chapter and the volume at large, EU policy-making can be a slow process, and the longer the crisis, the authors argue, the more likely it is that there will be calls for more integration through hard law and increased budgets.

Lastly, in the final chapter of the Handbook Jeffrey Anderson compares some of the contemporary crises with previous EU crises and considers how various EU crises are interlinked. Jeff Anderson revisits the dominant theories of European integration in order to clarify the conditions of polycrisis afflicting the EU. Building on the insight that scholars have underspecified crisis not only in terms of explaining the origins of the EU but also that when crisis appears it is limited conceptually to crises emanating from external sources, Anderson's chapter underscores the iterative, interactive, and overlapping nature of contemporary crises in the EU. Using environmental metaphors, he also explores the forces internal to the EU generating crisis. The most critical event is, in his view, the Eurozone crisis, owing in no small part to the way it deepened multiple cleavages such as those between actors favoring austerity over greater public investment; between the largest and smallest economies; as well as within member-states between national and local governments. For Anderson, given the tensions resulting from the Eurozone crisis, the emergence of the Russia/Ukraine crisis offered an opening for Russia to divide Europe further in its own pursuit of regional hegemonic status. Discussions of the refugee crisis reveal the ways in which populist movements exploited the cleavages widened by the financial crisis, including the populists who engineered Brexit. Lastly, Anderson examines the Trump crisis and characterizes the presence of US President Trump at the helm of power as thus far unsuccessful in doing much more than dispensing rhetoric derisive and dismissive of the transatlantic relationship. Anderson concludes that while the polycrisis context will increase the need for deeper integration in order to problem-solve more effectively, while at the same time polycrisis narrows the possibilities for more integrative reforms.

Crisis and the Future of the EU

Overall and as already mentioned in the introduction, the studies presented in this Handbook suggest that the EU is *functionally* skilled to handle crisis. It has the requisite capacity to cope with crisis, and most often to solve them. Despite some variation across cases, not least as regards the migration crisis and the legitimacy crisis, the empirical observations in the volume suggest that the EU has proved resilient in the face of crises. Rather than *breaking down*, the EU has to a large extent incrementally adapted to and in some cases developed new policies in response to challenges that arrive, which is largely in line with the two scenarios of *muddling through* and *heading forward*. Moreover, this ability suggests that the EU has reached a stage in its development where it is sufficiently consolidated and settled to adapt to and cope with multiple and simultaneous crises. In functional terms, crises arguably no longer challenge the fundamental nature and core of the EU.

Earlier studies suggest that increased integration to deal with crisis is also the EU population's preferred response. According to a large-N study conducted by the Council on European Relations on how the Corona crisis has affected the European public's worldview, a majority of the surveyed replied that the EU had not lived up to their expectations during the crisis (Krastev and Leonard 2020). However, contrary to the often-heard claim that the EU's initial lack of a common response to the crisis will result in the resurge of anti-European sentiments, 'large majorities of people in all surveyed countries say that they are now more firmly convinced of the need for further EU cooperation than they were before the crisis' (Krastev and Leonard 2020:

14). The long-term effect on public opinion remains to be seen, but at least so far, and corresponding to the expectation that the EU would integrate further in response to crisis, citizens' support for EU-level solutions to crises seems to be rising.

Yet, functional capabilities for risk prevention and crisis handling might have consequences beyond what might have been intended. Arguably, successful crisis governance in the short-term or within particular institutions or policy domains can cause new problems in the longer term or across institutions and policy fields. One question thus becomes apparent: If the EU seems to be capable of dealing functionally and successfully with crisis of different kinds and magnitudes—what new challenges might appear as a consequence? We see at least three long-term implications from the politics of crisis that warrant attention and further studies: unintended consequences across policy fields and over time, differentiated European integration, and the EU's democratic legitimacy. These questions are indeed discussed throughout this Handbook but might also open future research agendas since these challenges are both fairly general as well as moving targets.

Crisis Response and Unintended Consequences

As already noticed, crisis management might have consequences that reach beyond what was intended or expected. Crisis that emerges in one policy domain or one institution might for example cause unintended consequences in other policy areas or institutions, or potentially also reverberating across entire systems. In cases where crisis or crisis governance is not contained, we are likely to observe polity level consequences as an unintended consequence of accumulated crisis in separate policy and institutional domains. To illustrate the argument, the potential for integration in one policy or institutional domain might positively or negatively affect the likelihood of integration in others. *Heading forward* in certain areas as well as in the short-term at EU level—such as in EU's economic integration—might for example, have unintended consequences toward the *breaking down* of democratic modes of governance in the longer run.

Policy solutions to certain crisis might also have polity implications on a broader scale. Technocratic and functional EU-level solutions to crisis—such as creating EU agencies—might for example lead to popular dissent and contestation at national or sub-national levels (see Marks, Attewell, Rovny and Hooghe in this volume). Solutions to crisis can thus lead both to the popular mobilization toward *heading forward or breaking down*. Situations of unintended consequences have also been observed in what has been coined 'turbulence of scale' (Ansell et al. 2017). This appears when what happens at one level of governance (e.g., within the EU) affects what happens at another level (e.g., national level of governance). In effect, a perceived 'good solution' at one level of governance might be conceived of as a 'bad' solution and thus a problem at another level. Unintended consequences that cause turbulence of scale typically characterizes federal or multilevel systems such as the EU. Each scenario might in other words be conceived of as casually connected in complex ways. How they are connected and by what mechanisms are puzzles that deserve further scholarly attention.

Crisis and Differentiation

Analytically, the above scenarios offer distinct predictions as to the extent to which and how crisis might affect the EU and how the EU may handle crisis. In empirical terms and given the complexity of the EU, we expect that crisis in the longer term may spur a variety of responses and that a blend of the above scenarios may thus materialize across policy fields and institutions. At the outset, we distinguish between what is often referred to as *differentiated integration* (see Gänzle, Leruth, and Trondal in this volume; Leuffen et al. 2012), where only some member-states decide to continue with deeper integration in certain or all policy fields, or when certain member-states decide to exit in certain policy domains (partial exit) or from the EU as a whole (full exit), and *undifferentiated integration* in which all member-states commit to common policies and/or institutional changes in response to crises. As suggested by the idea of differentiated integration, it might be that in the longer run, the EU may be conducive to varied crisis responses where parts of the EU face more profound transformation than other parts. While the EU for example might *muddle through* in some policy fields, new policy and institutional solutions might be found (or integration breakdown) in others, such as in the field of migration. The Eurozone is already per definition differentiated, and even though the Euro group has found new common crisis solutions, not all the member-states are involved. At the same time, as the EU is a highly sectorally differentiated system, this may be a contributing factor for why we find that the EU overall has been able to functionally cope with crises. After all, differentiation is often conceptualized as a functional response to divergent member-states preferences or other challenges to EU unity (Leuffen et al. 2012). Due to sectoral specialization of organizations, a *breaking down* scenario in one policy field does not necessarily spillover to other policy areas (but might have unintended consequences for other sectors, as discussed above) (Egeberg and Trondal 2018). The migration crisis is a telling example. Even though the EU, at least so far, has not been able to sufficiently respond to and deal with this crisis, the EU has muddled through or headed forward in most other policy areas. In spite of their different positions on migration, member-states have stood united for example in Brexit negotiations. Both the impact of differentiation on the EU's ability to cope with crisis and the future (un)differentiation of the EU clearly warrant further studies. In particular, although the different scenarios developed in this chapter build on a variety of expectations as to how the EU copes with crises, they do not specify what this implies in terms of policy content or particular institutional designs, for example as regards differentiation. These are empirical questions and are examined in the individual case studies throughout the volume. They are however also important questions that merit further scholarly attention beyond this Handbook.

Crisis and the EU's Democratic Legitimacy

The main focus of this Handbook is on how crisis affects EU institutions and policy-making, and EU's subsequent ability to cope with and respond to crisis. However, a focus on EU crisis resilience explored through the lens of theories of European integration risks overlooking important implications of crisis on the broader legitimacy of the EU's institutional and policy developments. Functional responses to crises might cause challenges to legitimate governance both at EU and member-state level. Indeed, when the EU functionally *muddles through* in what seem sufficient and relevant responses to particular challenges, the EU might at the polity level and in the long run become less democratic, more expert ridden, and over time less popular among EU citizens. Or, alternatively, crisis response may in the long run offer opportunities for democratic reform and more pro-European integration forces. To deal with these challenges, several chapters in this volume also engage with questions of EU legitimacy and democracy. Kolja Raube and Francisca Costa Reis discuss the crisis of democracy and the rule of law in Poland and Hungary. Cathrine Holst and Anders Molander discuss the democratic implications of the EU's often overly technocratic ways of dealing with crises. According to Holst and Molander, some view the use of knowledge-based policy as necessary to address the EU's polycrisis. A competing view is however that experts themselves are to blame for polycrisis and the crisis of democratic legitimacy. Other chapters discuss populism, Euroscepticism, trust, and voter mobilization. The chapter by Gary Marks, David Attewell, Jan Rovny, and Liesbet Hooghe discusses how EU voters mobilize across a new transatlantic divide. After all, voters must be engaged and participate for democracy to work, and the authors conclude that we see voter mobilization and party organization on issues specifically linked to transnationalization—and thus to the EU as such. Moreover, Pieter de Wilde observes a pro- and anti-EU divide among EU voters. The financial and migration crises have had a substantive negative effect on citizens' trust in EU institutions, yet most of this decline is temporary, suggesting that the effect of crisis on public support toward EU institutions is merely short-term. However, de Wilde also documents a steady reduction in the percentage of citizens who do not know whether to trust EU institutions or not. These 'undecided' voters are moving instead to pro-EU or Eurosceptic points of view. The EU's handling of the ongoing Corona crisis might even serve to strengthen this trend further.

Although not a main emphasis of this Handbook, some broader implications of the empirical findings might also be derived as regards the EU's legitimacy. Overall, findings across chapters suggest that there are broader democratic implications of the EU's polycrisis response that warrant further studies. One such aspect is linked to the institutional implications of the EU's crisis response: As discussed above and in the introduction to Part III of the volume, the chapters indicate a (further) strengthening of EU executive governance, through the actions and influence of the EU agencies, the European Central Bank, the European Commission, and member-states' executive branch of government—without this being met with a parallel reinforcement of the European Parliament or national parliaments. Executive dominance has long been a main reason for the EU's well-known democratic deficit. But the EU's tendency to *muddle through* crisis by ways of technocratic and functional modes of governance serves to strengthen this imbalance even further. Some studies suggest that member-states have gained more influence, (see for example Bickerton, Hodson, and Puetter's (2015) work on 'New Intergovernmentalism'). However, as the EU with some exceptions continues to integrate further in response to crisis, this type of indirect legitimacy—via member-states' elected governments—faces difficulties in compensating for increased executive dominance at the EU level (Eriksen and Fossum 2012). Two chapters in this volume directly address the democratic implications of EU polycrisis. Underlining the EU's large democratic deficit, Claudia Landwehr argues that polycrisis may, if feeding into a deliberative and institutionalized process, prove to be an opportunity for reducing the EU's democratic deficit. As only the 'long road' of inclusive large-scale deliberation can ensure legitimate decision-making in the EU, crisis may serve to re-politicize the integration process and thus bring the questions of national control and the future of EU integration back to the center of the political agenda. We have already seen that the financial crisis and the migration crisis brought these debates to a wider public. Although 'inclusive meta-deliberative re-constitutionalization is required to ensure a broader procedural consensus,' Landwehr argues that a Europe-wide meta-deliberation 'is thus not entirely unrealistic and may still come to be realized and succeed.' Anne Elizabeth Stie (this volume) is more sceptical of the prospect of reducing the EU's democratic deficit. Similar to Landwehr, Stie argues that the EU's traditional reliance on output legitimacy cannot compensate for the lack of democratic participating and procedures. Democratic decision-making requires both citizens' participation and a role for experts. However, supported by the EU's mode of *muddling through* crises, democracy is undermined both at the national and European level. Stie moreover argues that polycrisis puts the credibility of expertise at risk in the EU, with citizens starting to question EU institutions and consequently also the quality of the expertise they claim to hold.

WHERE DO WE GO FROM HERE?

Crises, such as the Corona crisis, financial instabilities, the migration crisis, the ups and downs of civic unrest, together with other long-term challenges such as the emergent climate crisis and artificial intelligence, continuously produce surprises and challenges for public governments and organizations. Times of societal ruptures and political crisis call upon public organizations to adapt, anticipate, reform, and innovate—ruinously and at greater speeds. They are increasingly called upon to manage the unexpected, and in democratic states public entities are expected to do so in a democratically legitimate way. Turbulent times and crises also challenge the scholarly community to modify existing theories and frameworks, and to invent new ones. This Handbook aims to fill a lacuna in contemporary studies, not only in European Union studies but also in public governance more generally, by examining how the EU is affected by crisis, how it governs uncertainty, and what mechanisms and factors drive decisions and responses. The questions in focus are many, such as what tools public organization favor when handling situations of crisis and uncertainty? How does the EU manage dilemmas, such as stability and change, innovation and resilience, integration and differentiation, and so on? What are the long-term institutional and democratic implications of the decisions made, and how does this impact citizens' mobilization? Moreover, what theoretical lenses are helpful in mapping and explaining how the EU manages crisis, how the EU approaches complex and unfamiliar problems and solutions, and how the EU potentially tries to establish order out of disorder?

The theory section provides this Handbook with a conceptual and causal apparatus for understanding European integration and the consequences of crisis. For example, 'thin' and 'thick' conceptions of institutions and integration derive different readings of the consequences of crisis, and thus also lead them to different conclusions (Ansell and Trondal, this volume). Yet, theoretical disagreements and the unintended consequences of crisis also make conclusions on what 'good' crisis governance is ambiguous and open to debate. Brexit suggests that how member-states should behave as 'good citizens' becomes unclear but also that future studies should engage with how member-states maneuver in a crisis-ridden Union. This also relates to the unintended consequences of EU integration for member-states. Solutions at one level might cause problems at the next level. Future studies should thus also add a multilevel approach to understanding crisis in the EU, in addition to the numbers of areas that warrant further studies.

As a general conclusion of this volume, the EU tends to adapt fairly effectively to crisis and as a consequence makes EU policies and institutions relatively sustainable over the longer courses of time. The Handbook suggests that the EU is sustainable as a polity and that EU-level sustainable public governance to a large extent rests on its institutionalized organizational fabric. Yet, crisis governance comes with unintended consequences. To advance our understanding of public governance sustainability, future studies should invest in (collaborative) longitudinal studies both within national governments and international organizations. Understanding the nuts and bolts of sustainable public governance at national and international levels is vital in safeguarding sustainable public service delivery and understanding the various causes of stabile political order (e.g., Hooghe and Marks 2019). Indeed, as Martin Shapiro concludes in his essay (this volume), the many different aspects and implications of crisis discussed in this book mean that 'there are many volumes to come' in the study of EU crisis.

References

Ansell, C., & Trondal, J. (2018). Governing Turbulence: An Organizational-Institutional Agenda. *Perspectives on Public Management and Governance, 1,* 43–57. https://doi.org/10.1093/ppmgov/gvx013.

Ansell, C. K., Trondal, J., & Øgård, M. (Eds.). (2017). *Governance in Turbulent Times*. Oxford and New York, NY: Oxford University Press.

Ayoub, P. (2019). Intersectional and Transnational Coalitions During Times of Crisis: The European LGBTI Movement. *Social Politics, 26*(1), 1–29.

Bátora, J., & Fossum, J. E. (Eds.). (2020). *Towards a Segmented European Political Order: The European Union's Post-Crises Conundrum* (Routledge Studies on Democratising Europe). Abingdon, Oxon, and New York, NY: Routledge.

Begg, I. (2009). Regulation and Supervision of Financial Intermediaries in the EU: The Aftermath of the Financial Crisis. *JCMS: Journal of Common Market Studies, 47,* 1107–1128. https://doi.org/10.1111/j.1468-5965.2009.02037.x.

Bickerton, C. J., Hodson, D., & Puetter, U. (Eds.). (2015). *The New Intergovernmentalism: States and Supranational Actors in the Post-Maastricht Era*. Oxford: Oxford University Press.

Boin, A., Hart, P. 't, Stern, E., & Sundelius, B. (2005). *The Politics of Crisis Management: Public Leadership Under Pressure* (1st ed.). Cambridge: Cambridge University Press.

Boin, A., & Lodge, M. (2016). Designing Resilient Institutions for Transboundary Crisis Management: A Time for Public Administration. *Public Administration, 94,* 289–298. https://doi.org/10.1111/padm.12264.

Börzel, T. A., & Risse, T. (2018). From the Euro to the Schengen Crises: European Integration Theories, Politicization, and Identity Politics. *Journal of European Public Policy, 25,* 83–108. https://doi.org/10.1080/13501763.2017.1310281.

Börzel, T. A., & Risse, T. (2019). Grand Theories of Integration and the Challenges of Comparative Regionalism. *Journal of European Public Policy, 26*(8), 1231–1252. https://doi.org/10.1080/13501763.2019.1622589.

Brunsson, N., & Olsen, J. P. (1993). *The Reforming Organization*. Bergen: Fagbokforlaget.

Bulmer, S., & Paterson, W. E. (2017). Germany and the Crisis: Asset or Liability? In D. Dinan, N. Nugent, & W. E. Paterson (Eds.), *The European Union in Crisis* (pp. 212–232). London: Palgrave.

Buonanno, L. (2017). The European Migration Crisis. In D. Dinan, N. Nugent, & W. E. Paterson (Eds.), *The European Union in Crisis* (pp. 100–130). London: Palgrave.

Caporaso, J. A. (2018). Europe's triple crisis and the uneven role of institutions: The euro, refugees and brexit. *Journal of Common Market Studies, 56*(6), 1345–1361.

Caporaso, J. A., & Rhodes, M. (Eds.). (2016). *The Political and Economic Dynamics of the Eurozone Crisis*. Oxford: Oxford University Press.

Casler, J. G. (2014). Revisiting NASA as a High Reliability Organization. *Public Organization Review, 14,* 229–244. https://doi.org/10.1007/s11115-012-0216-5.

Cohen, M. D., March, J. G., & Olsen, J. P. (1972). A Garbage Can Model of Organizational Choice. *Administrative Science Quarterly*, 17, 1. https://doi.org/10.2307/2392088.

Copelovitch, M., Frieden, J., & Walter, S. (2016). The Political Economy of the Euro Crisis. *Comparative Political Studies*, 49, 811–840. https://doi.org/10.1177/0010414016633227.

Cross, M'.a. K. D. (2018). Partners at Paris? Climate Negotiations and Transatlantic Relations. *Journal of European Integration*, 40, 571–586. https://doi.org/10.1080/07036337.2018.1487962.

Cross, M.'a. K. D., & Karolewski, I. P. (2017). What Type of Power Has the EU Exercised in the Ukraine-Russia Crisis? A Framework of Analysis. *JCMS: Journal of Common Market Studies*, 55, 3–19. https://doi.org/10.1111/jcms.12442.

Cross, M.'a. K. D., & Ma, X. (2015). EU Crises and Integrational Panic: The Role of the Media. *Journal of European Public Policy*, 22, 1053–1070.

Davis Cross, M'.a. K. (2017). *The Politics of Crisis in Europe*. Cambridge: Cambridge University Press.

De La Porte, C., & Heins, E. (2017). The Aftermath of the Eurozone Crisis: Towards Fiscal Federalism? In D. Dinan, N. Nugent, & W. E. Paterson (Eds.), *The European Union in Crisis* (pp. 149–166). London: Palgrave.

de Wilde, P. (2019). Media Logic and Grand Theories of European Integration. *Journal of European Public Policy*, 26, 1193–1212. https://doi.org/10.1080/13501763.2019.1622590.

Dinan, D. (2017). Crises in EU History. In D. Dinan, N. Nugent, & W. E. Paterson (Eds.), *The European Union in Crisis* (pp. 16–32). London: Palgrave.

Dinan, D., Nugent, N., & Paterson, W. E. (Eds.). (2017). *The European Union in Crisis*. London: Palgrave.

Dyson, K. (2017). Playing for High Stakes: The Eurozone Crisis. In D. Dinan, N. Nugent, & W. E. Paterson (Eds.), *The European Union in Crisis* (pp. 54–76). London: Palgrave.

Egeberg, M., & Trondal, J. (2018). *An Organizational Approach to Public Governance*. Oxford: Oxford University Press.

Eisenhardt, K. M., & Bourgeois, L. J. (1988). Politics of Strategic Decision Making in High-Velocity Environments: Towards a Midrange Theory. *Academy of Management Journal*, 31, 737–770. https://doi.org/10.2307/256337.

Emery, Y., & Giauque, D. (2014). The Hybrid Universe of Public Administration in the 21st Century. *International Review of Administrative Sciences*, 80, 23–32. https://doi.org/10.1177/0020852313513378.

Eriksen, E. O., & Fossum, J. E. (Eds.). (2012). *Rethinking Democracy and the European Union* (Routledge Studies on Democratising Europe, Vol. 7). London: Routledge.

European Commission. (2017). *White Paper on the Future of Europe: Reflections and Scenarios for the EU27 by 2025*. https://ec.europa.eu/commission/future-europe/white-paper-future-europe_en.

Fabbrini, S. (2020). The Future of Europe Is Being Decided Now. *Social Europe*, 3/4-2020 athttps://www.socialeurope.eu/the-future-of-europe-is-being-decided-now

Falkner, G. (2016a). Fines Against Member States: An Effective New Tool in EU Infringement Proceedings? *Comparative European Politics*, 14, 36–52. https://doi.org/10.1057/cep.2015.8.

Falkner, G. (2016b). The EU's Current Crisis and Its Policy Effects: Research Design and Comparative Findings. *Journal of European Integration, 38,* 219–235. https://doi.org/10.1080/07036337.2016.1140154.

Featherstone, K., & Papadimitriou, D. (2017). Greece: A Crisis in Two Level Governance. In D. Dinan, N. Nugent, & W. E. Paterson (Eds.), *The European Union in Crisis* (pp. 233–252). London: Palgrave.

Genschel, P., & Jachtenfuchs, M. (Eds.). (2014). *Beyond the Regulatory Polity? The European Integration of Core State Powers* (1st ed.). Oxford: Oxford University Press.

Genschel, P., & Jachtenfuchs, M. (2018). From Market Integration to Core State Powers: The Eurozone Crisis, the Refugee Crisis and Integration Theory. *JCMS: Journal of Common Market Studies, 56,* 178–196. https://doi.org/10.1111/jcms.12654.

Gilardi, F. (2005). The Institutional Foundations of Regulatory Capitalism: The Diffusion of Independent Regulatory Agencies in Western Europe. *The ANNALS of the American Academy of Political and Social Science, 598,* 84–101. https://doi.org/10.1177/0002716204271833.

Goodin, R. E. (1996a). Institutions and Their Design. In R. E. Goodin (Ed.), *The Theory of Institutional Design* (pp. 1–53). Cambridge: Cambridge University Press.

Goodin, R. E. (Ed.). (1996b). *The Theory of Institutional Design.* Cambridge: Cambridge University Press.

Graziano, P., & Hartlapp, M. (2019). The End of Social Europe? Understanding EU Social Policy Change. *Journal of European Public Policy, 26,* 1484–1501. https://doi.org/10.1080/13501763.2018.1531911.

Graziano, P. R., & Halpern, C. (2016). EU Governance in Times of Crisis: Inclusiveness and Effectiveness Beyond the 'Hard' and 'Soft' Law Divide. *Comparative European Politics, 14,* 1–19. https://doi.org/10.1057/cep.2015.6.

Greer, S. L. (2020, April 6). How Did the E.U. Get the Coronavirus So Wrong? And What Can It Do Right Next Time? *The New York Times.* Morning Briefing. https://www.nytimes.com/2020/04/06/opinion/europe-coronavirus.html.

Guiraudon, V. (2014). Economic Crisis and Institutional Resilience: The Political Economy of Migrant Incorporation. *West European Politics, 37,* 1297–1313. https://doi.org/10.1080/01402382.2014.929335.

Hall, P. A. (2014). Varieties of Capitalism and the Euro Crisis. *West European Politics, 37,* 1223–1243. https://doi.org/10.1080/01402382.2014.929352.

Hall, P. A. (2018). Varieties of Capitalism in Light of the Euro Crisis. *Journal of European Public Policy, 25,* 7–30. https://doi.org/10.1080/13501763.2017.1310278.

Haas, E. B. (1958). *The Uniting of Europe: Political, Social, and Economic Forces, 1950–1957.* Stanford: Stanford University Press.

Haas, E. B. (1970). The Study of Regional Integration: Reflections on the Joy and Anguish of Pretheorizing. *International Organization, 24*(4), 606–646.

Haughton, T. (2017). Central and Eastern Europe: The Sacrifices of Solidarity, the Discomforts of Diversity and the Vexations of Vulnerabilities. In D. Dinan, N. Nugent, & W. E. Paterson (Eds.), *The European Union in Crisis.* London: Palgrave Macmillan Education.

Heimer, C. A., & Stinchcombe, A. L. (1999). Remodeling the Garbage Can: Implications of the Origins of Items in Decision Streams. In M. Egeberg, & P. Laegreid

(Eds.), *Organizing Political Institutions: Essays for Johan P. Olsen*, (pp. 25–57). Scandinavian University Press.

Hodson, D., & Puetter, U. (2019). The European Union in Disequilibrium: New Intergovernmentalism, Postfunctionalism and Integration Theory in the Post-Maastricht Period. *Journal of European Public Policy, 26,* 1153–1171. https://doi.org/10.1080/13501763.2019.1569712.

Hooghe, L., Laffan, B., & Marks, G. (2018). Introduction to Theory Meets Crisis Collection. *Journal of European Public Policy, 25,* 1–6. https://doi.org/10.1080/13501763.2017.1310282.

Hooghe, L., & Marks, G. (2009). A Postfunctionalist Theory of European Integration: From Permissive Consensus to Constraining Dissensus. *British Journal of Political Science, 39,* 1–23. https://doi.org/10.1017/S0007123408000409.

Hooghe, L., & Marks, G. (2018). Cleavage Theory Meets Europe's Crises: Lipset, Rokkan, and the Transnational Cleavage. *Journal of European Public Policy, 25,* 109–135. https://doi.org/10.1080/13501763.2017.1310279.

Hooghe, L., & Marks, G. (2019). Grand Theories of European Integration in the Twenty-First Century. *Journal of European Public Policy, 26,* 1113–1133. https://doi.org/10.1080/13501763.2019.1569711.

Howorth, J. (2017). 'Stability on the Borders': The Ukraine Crisis and the EU's Constrained Policy Towards the Eastern Neighbourhood. *JCMS: Journal of Common Market Studies, 55,* 121–136. https://doi.org/10.1111/jcms.12448.

Howorth, J. (2018). Strategic Autonomy and EU-NATO Cooperation: Threat or Opportunity for Transatlantic Defence Relations? *Journal of European Integration, 40,* 523–537. https://doi.org/10.1080/07036337.2018.1512268.

Hume, T., & Pawle, L. (2015, December, 22). Number of Migrants Reaching Europe This Year Passes 1 Million. *CNN.* https://www.cnn.com/2015/12/22/europe/million-refugees-enter-europe/index.html.

Ikenberry, G. J. (2008). Explaining Crisis and Change in Transatlantic Relations: An Introduction. In G. J. Ikenberry, J. J. Anderson, & T. Risse-Kappen (Eds.), *The End of the West? Crisis and Change in the Atlantic Order* (Cornell paperbacks). Ithaca: Cornell University Press.

Jones, B. D., & Baumgartner, F. R. (2005). *The Politics of Attention: How Government Prioritizes Problems.* Chicago, Il.: University of Chicago Press.

Jones, E. (2018). Towards a Theory of Disintegration. *Journal of European Public Policy, 25,* 440–451. https://doi.org/10.1080/13501763.2017.1411381.

Jones, E., Kelemen, R. D., & Meunier, S. (2016). Failing Forward? The Euro Crisis and the Incomplete Nature of European Integration. *Comparative Political Studies, 49,* 1010–1034. https://doi.org/10.1177/0010414015617966.

Jørgensen, K. E., Aarstad, Å. K., Drieskens, E., Laatikainen, K., & Tonra, B. (Eds.). (2015). *The SAGE Handbook of European Foreign Policy* (pp. 99–120). London: SAGE.

Kingdon, J. W. (1984). *Agendas, Alternatives, and Public Policies.* Boston: Little, Brown.

Krastev, I. & Leonard, M. (2020). Europe's Pandemic Politics: How The Virus Has Changed The Public's Worldview Policy Brief June 2020, *European Council of Foreign Relations.* Available at https://www.ecfr.eu/page/-/europes_pandemic_politics_how_the_virus_has_changed_the_publics_worldview.pdf.

Kriesi, H. (2018). The Implications of the Euro Crisis for Democracy. *Journal of European Public Policy, 25*, 59–82. https://doi.org/10.1080/13501763.2017.131 0277.

Kudrna, Z. (2016). Governing the EU Financial Markets. *Comparative European Politics, 14*, 71–88. https://doi.org/10.1057/cep.2015.10.

Kuhn, T. (2019). Grand Theories of European Integration Revisited: Does Identity Politics Shape the Course of European Integration? *Journal of European Public Policy, 26*, 1213–1230. https://doi.org/10.1080/13501763.2019.1622588.

Kuzio, T. (2017). Ukraine Between a Constrained EU and Assertive Russia. *JCMS: Journal of Common Market Studies, 55*, 103–120. https://doi.org/10.1111/jcms.12447.

Laffan, B. (2017). The Eurozone in Crisis: Core-Periphery Dynamics. In D. Dinan, N. Nugent, & W. E. Paterson (Eds.), *The European Union in Crisis* (pp. 131–148). London: Palgrave.

Leruth, B., Gänzle, S., & Trondal, J. (2019). Differentiated Integration and Disintegration in the EU After Brexit: Risks Versus Opportunities. *JCMS: Journal of Common Market Studies, 57*, 1383–1394. https://doi.org/10.1111/jcms.12957.

Leuffen, D., Rittberger, B., & Schimmelfennig, F. (2012). *Differentiated Integration: Explaining Variation in the European Union* (The European Union Series). Basingstoke: Palgrave Macmillan.

Lodge, M., & Wegrich, K. (Eds.). (2012). *Executive Politics in Times of Crisis* (Executive Politics and Governance). Basingstoke: Palgrave Macmillan.

Lodge, M., & Wegrich, K. (2016). The Rationality Paradox of Nudge: Rational Tools of Government in a World of Bounded Rationality. *Law & Policy, 38*, 250–267. https://doi.org/10.1111/lapo.12056.

MacFarlane, N., & Menon, A. (2014). The EU and Ukraine. *Survival, 56*, 95–101. https://doi.org/10.1080/00396338.2014.920139.

Maher, R. (2020). International Relations Theory and the Future of European Integration. *International Studies Review*. https://doi.org/10.1093/isr/viaa010

March, J. G. (1999). A Learning Perspective on the Network Dynamics of Institutional Integration. In M. Egeberg & P. Lægreid (Eds.), *Organizing Political Institutions*. Oslo: Scandinavian University Press.

March, J. G. (2010). *The Ambiguities of Experience*. Ithaca: Cornell University Press.

March, J. G., & Olsen, J. P. (1998). The Institutional Dynamics of International Political Orders. *International Organization, 52*, 943–969. https://doi.org/10.1162/002081898550699.

Marks, G., Attewell, D., Rovny, J., & Hooghe, L. (2020). The Changing Political Landscape in Europe. In M. Cotta & P. Isernia (Eds.), *The EU Through Multiple Crises* (pp. 20–44). London: Routledge.

McGowan, L., & Phinnemore, D. (2017). The UK: Membership in Crisis. In D. Dinan, N. Nugent, & W. E. Paterson (Eds.), *The European Union in Crisis* (pp. 77–99). London: Palgrave.

McNamara, K. R. (2015). *The Politics of Everyday Europe: Constructing Authority in the European Union* (1st ed.). Oxford: Oxford University Press.

Mearsheimer, J. J. (2014, September). Why the Ukraine Crisis Is the West's Fault. Foreign Affairs. https://www.foreignaffairs.com/articles/russia-fsu/2014-08-18/why-ukraine-crisis-west-s-fault. Accessed 10 Feb 2020.

Mény, Y. (2014). Managing the EU Crises: Another Way of Integration by Stealth? *West European Politics, 37,* 1336–1353. https://doi.org/10.1080/01402382.2014.929338.
Monnet, J. (1978). *Memoirs.* London: Collins.
Moravscik, A. (1998). *The Choice for Europe: Social Purpose and State Power from Messina to Maastricht.* Ithaca: Cornell University Press.
Moravcsik, A., & Schimmelfennig, F. (2009). Neoliberal Intergovernmentalism. In A. Wiener, T. A. Börzel, & T. Risse (Eds.), *European Integration Theory.* Oxford: Oxford University Press.
Natorski, M., & Pomorska, K. (2017). Trust and Decision-Making in Times of Crisis: The EU's Response to the Events in Ukraine. *JCMS: Journal of Common Market Studies, 55,* 54–70. https://doi.org/10.1111/jcms.12445.
Newsome, A. (2018). Credible Champions? Transatlantic Relations and Human Rights in Refugee Crises. *Journal of European Integration, 40,* 587–604. https://doi.org/10.1080/07036337.2018.1487964.
Niemann, A., & Zaun, N. (2018). EU Refugee Policies and Politics in Times of Crisis: Theoretical and Empirical Perspectives. *JCMS: Journal of Common Market Studies, 56,* 3–22. https://doi.org/10.1111/jcms.12650.
Nitoiu, C., & Sus, M. (2017). The European Parliament's Diplomacy—A Tool for Projecting EU Power in Times of Crisis? The Case of the Cox-Kwasniewski Mission. *JCMS: Journal of Common Market Studies, 55,* 71–86. https://doi.org/10.1111/jcms.12440.
Novotna, T. (2017). The EU as a Global Actor: United We Stand, Divided We Fall. *Journal of Common Market Studies, 55,* 177–191. https://doi.org/10.1111/jcms.12601.
Nugent, N. (2017). The Crisis and the EU's Institutions, Political Actors, and Processes. In D. Dinan, N. Nugent, & W. E. Paterson (Eds.), *The European Union in Crisis* (pp. 167–187). London: Palgrave.
Olsen, J. P. (2009). Change and Continuity: An Institutional Approach to Institutions of Democratic Government. *European Political Science Review, 1,* 3–32. https://doi.org/10.1017/S1755773909000022.
Olsen, J. P. (2010). *Governing Through Institution Building: Institutional Theory and Recent European Experiments in Democratic Organization.* Oxford: Oxford University Press.
Orenstein, M. A., & Kelemen, R. D. (2017). Trojan Horses in EU Foreign Policy. *JCMS: Journal of Common Market Studies, 55,* 87–102. https://doi.org/10.1111/jcms.12441
Padgett, J. F., & Powell, W. W. (Eds.). (2012). *The Emergence of Organizations and Markets.* Princeton: Princeton University Press.
Pierson, P. (2000). The Limits of Design: Explaining Institutional Origins and Change. *Governance, 13,* 475–499. https://doi.org/10.1111/0952-1895.00142.
Pierson, P. (2004). *Politics in Time: History, Institutions, and Social Analysis.* Princeton: Princeton University Press.
Pollack, M. A. (2005). Theorizing the European Union: International Organization, Domestic Polity, or Experiment in New Governance? *Annual Review of Political Science, 8,* 357–98.
Pontusson, J., & Weisstanner, D. (2018). Macroeconomic Conditions, Inequality Shocks and the Politics of Redistribution, 1990–2013. *Journal of European Public Policy, 25,* 31–58. https://doi.org/10.1080/13501763.2017.1310280.

Pop, V. (2015, October). Europe's Migrant Crisis Puts Open Borders at Risk. *Wall Street Journal*. https://www.wsj.com/articles/europes-migrant-crisis-puts-open-bor ders-at-risk-1446140263. Accessed 10 Feb 2020.

Posen, Barry, R. (2014, May). Ukraine: Part of America's "Vital Interests"? *The National Interest*.

Riddervold, M., & Newsome, A. (2018). Transatlantic Relations in Times of Uncertainty: Crises and EU–US Relations. *Journal of European Integration, 40*, 505–521. https://doi.org/10.1080/07036337.2018.1488839.

Riddervold, M., & Rosén, G. (2018). Unified in Response to Rising Powers? China, Russia and EU–US Relations. *Journal of European Integration, 40*, 555–570. https://doi.org/10.1080/07036337.2018.1488838.

Roos, C., & Zaun, N. (2016). The Global Economic Crisis as a critical Juncture? The Crisis's Impact on Migration Movements and Policies in Europe and the U.S. *Journal of Ethnic and Migration Studies, 42*, 1579–1589.

Rosamond, B. (2017). The Political Economy Context of EU Crises. In D. Dinan, N. Nugent, & W. E. Paterson (Eds.), *The European Union in Crisis* (pp. 33–52). London: Palgrave.

Rosenthal, U., Charles, M. T., & Hart, P't (Eds.). (1989). *Coping with Crises: The Management of Disasters, Riots and Terrorism*. Springfield, IL: Charles C Thomas Publisher.

Saurugger, S., & Terpan, F. (2016). Resisting 'New Modes of Governance': An Agency-Centred Approach. *Comparative European Politics, 14*, 53–70. https://doi.org/10.1057/cep.2015.9.

Schilde, K. (2017). European Military Capabilities: Enablers and Constraints on EU Power? *JCMS: Journal of Common Market Studies, 55*, 37–53. https://doi.org/10.1111/jcms.12444.

Schimmelfennig, F. (2017). Theorising Crisis in European Integration. In D. Dinan, N. Nugent, & W. E. Paterson (Eds.), *The European Union in Crisis* (pp. 316–336). London: Palgrave.

Schimmelfennig, F. (2018a). European Integration (Theory) in Times of Crisis: A Comparison of the Euro and Schengen Crises. *Journal of European Public Policy, 25*, 969–989. https://doi.org/10.1080/13501763.2017.1421252.

Schimmelfennig, F. (2018b). Liberal Intergovernmentalism and the Crises of the European Union. *JCMS: Journal of Common Market Studies, 56*, 1578–1594. https://doi.org/10.1111/jcms.12789.

Schimmelfennig, F., & Winzen, T. (2019). Grand Theories, Differentiated Integration. *Journal of European Public Policy, 26*, 1172–1192. https://doi.org/10.1080/135 01763.2019.1576761.

Schmitter, P. C. (1970). A Revised Theory of Regional Integration. *International Organization, 24*(4), 836–868.

Schweiger, C. (2017). The Legitimacy Challenge. In D. Dinan, N. Nugent, & W. E. Paterson (Eds.), *The European Union in Crisis* (pp. 188–211). London: Palgrave.

Seibel, W. (2017). The European Union, Ukraine, and the Unstable East. In D. Dinan, N. Nugent, & W. E. Paterson (Eds.), *The European Union in Crisis* (pp. 269–293). London: Palgrave.

Shapiro, M. M., & Stone Sweet, A. (2002). *On Law, Politics, and Judicialization*. Oxford: Oxford University Press.

Sjursen, H., & Rosén, G. (2017). Arguing Sanctions: On the EU's Response to the Crisis in Ukraine. *JCMS: Journal of Common Market Studies, 55*, 20–36. https://doi.org/10.1111/jcms.12443.

Skowronek, S. (1982). *Building a New American State: The Expansion of National Administrative Capacities, 1877–1920*. Cambridge: Cambridge University Press.

Smith, M. (2018). The EU, the US and the Crisis of Contemporary Multilateralism. *Journal of European Integration, 40*, 539–553. https://doi.org/10.1080/07036337.2018.1488836.

Smith, M. E. (2018). Transatlantic Security Relations Since the European Security Strategy: What Role for the EU in Its Pursuit of Strategic Autonomy? *Journal of European Integration, 40*, 605–620. https://doi.org/10.1080/07036337.2018.1488840.

Trondal, J., & Bauer, M. W. (2017). Conceptualizing the European Multilevel Administrative Order: Capturing Variation in the European Administrative System. *European Political Science Review, 9*, 73–94. https://doi.org/10.1017/S1755773915000223.

Vollaard, H. (2014). Explaining European Disintegration. *JCMS: Journal of Common Market Studies, 52*, 1142–1159. https://doi.org/10.1111/jcms.12132.

Vollaard, H. (2018). *European Disintegration: A Search for Explanations* (Palgrave Studies in European Union Politics). London: Palgrave Macmillan.

Verdun, A. (2015). A Historical Institutionalist Explanation of the EU's Responses to the Euro Area Financial Crisis. *Journal of European Public Policy, 22*(2), 219–237.

Walt, S. M. *Would You Die for That Country? Foreign Policy*. https://foreignpolicy.com/2014/03/24/would-you-die-for-that-country/. Accessed 10 Feb 2020.

Webber, D. (2014). How Likely Is It That the European Union Will Disintegrate? A Critical Analysis of Competing Theoretical Perspectives. *European Journal of International Relations, 20*(2), 341–365.

Webber, D. (2017). Can the EU Survive? In D. Dinan, N. Nugent, & W. E. Paterson (Eds.), *The European Union in Crisis* (pp. 336–359). London: Palgrave MacMillan.

Webber, D. (2018). *European Disintegration? The Politics of Crisis in the European Union*. London: Palgrave Macmillan.

Webber, D. (2019). Trends in European Political (Dis)Integration. An Analysis of Postfunctionalist and Other Explanations. *Journal of European Public Policy, 26*, 1134–1152. https://doi.org/10.1080/13501763.2019.1576760.

Wiener, A., Boerzel, T.A., & Risse, T. (Eds.). (2019) *European Integration Theory* (3rd Edition). Oxford: Oxford University Press.

PART II

Theoretical Approaches to Crisis

CHAPTER 2

Theoretical Approaches to Crisis: An Introduction

Marianne Riddervold, Jarle Trondal, and Akasemi Newsome

Each of the nine chapters in this section of the Handbook discusses essential EU integration and International Relations approaches and how they study, understand, and explain crisis' putative impact on the EU. For this purpose, each chapter sets out the theory's basic assumptions before addressing the following questions: (1) How does each theoretical perspective expect crisis to influence EU institutions and policies? What are the causal mechanisms to account for continuity or change in public policy and governing institutions? (2) To what extent has the perspective so far been able to explain change or continuity in the EU in the face of crisis? Has it been applied in crisis studies?

M. Riddervold (✉) · A. Newsome
Inland School of Business and Social Sciences, Inland University, Rena and Lillehammer, Norway
e-mail: marianne.riddervold@inn.no

Institute of European Studies, University of California, Berkeley, CA, USA

A. Newsome
e-mail: akasemi@berkeley.edu

M. Riddervold
The Norwegian Institute of International Affairs (NUPI), Oslo, Norway

J. Trondal
Department of Political Science and Management, University of Agder, Kristiansand, Norway
e-mail: jarle.trondal@uia.no

ARENA - Centre for European Studies, University of Oslo, Oslo, Norway

© The Author(s) 2021
M. Riddervold et al. (eds.), *The Palgrave Handbook of EU Crises*, Palgrave Studies in European Union Politics,
https://doi.org/10.1007/978-3-030-51791-5_2

Has it proved relevant? Has crisis led to revisions of the theory? Moreover, rather than discussing mid-range theories, this section focuses on the main EU integration perspectives that are commonly used in the scholarly literature and in teaching material: Liberal Intergovernmentalism, Classical Realism, Neo-realism, Neofunctionalism, Institutionalism, Organizational Theory, Cleavage Theory, Social constructivism, and Deliberative Theory.

Below is a summary of the main arguments made in the theory chapters. The main implications are discussed at the end of this chapter.

The first chapter by *Frank Schimmelfennig* discusses *Liberal Intergovernmentalism*'s relevance and applicability in studies of EU crisis. At the outset, Liberal Intergovernmentalism theorizes the conditions of integration—not crisis or disintegration. When Andrew Moravcsik published his seminal work in the 90s, European integration was on a path of *heading forward*. Focusing on interest groups' role in defining national preferences, asymmetrically interdependent member states' bargaining processes, and the facilitating effect of EU institutions, Liberal Intergovernmentalism has mainly been concerned with theorizing and explaining the big steps of EU the integration project. Nonetheless, Schimmelfennig argues, this traditional focus on explaining integration is no reason to disregard the relevance of Liberal Intergovernmentalism in studies of if and how crisis influences change and continuity in the EU: The general drivers and conditions of European integration stipulated by Liberal Intergovernmentalism can be applied both in regular negotiations and crisis negotiations. Having developed three hypotheses of crisis integration, Schimmelfennig goes on to discuss how three of the crises discussed in other chapters of this book—the Euro/Financial Crisis, the Schengen/Migration crisis, and the Brexit crisis—would be explained from a liberal intergovernmentalism. Schimmelfennig concludes that the member states' preferences to a large degree were in accordance with Liberal Integovernmentalism key assumptions in the Euro and Schengen cases, but that the theory is less able to explain May's—and other UK governments—preference for a hard Brexit. Schimmelfennig concludes that although providing helpful tools in explaining crisis negotiation, Liberal Intergovernmentalism suffers from a major explanatory gap: Since crisis is treated as exogenous to member states' bargaining, the theory neglects any feedback effects of already existing integration on these bargaining processes. Crisis can thus not be explained as a consequence of (deficient) integration. Schimmelfennig refers to Erik Jones, Dan Kelemen, and Sophie Meunier synthesis of liberal intergovernmentalism and neofunctionalism in their concept of "failing forward" as a possible way of dealing with these challenges through theoretical innovation.

Two chapters discuss *realist accounts* of crisis and EU integration. As *Zimmermann* discusses in his chapter, neither classical nor neo-realist accounts have been much applied in EU studies, despite their prominence in international relations studies more broadly. After all, realist perspectives are grand theories that seek to explain and predict broader historical trends. The parsimonious focus on power politics and structural power relations among states leave little room for explaining, let alone expecting, supranational cooperation such as in the EU. As such, realist scholars are not surprised when the EU faces crisis and potential disintegration—to the contrary, this is precisely what one would expect in an international environment characterized by anarchy and self-interested states keen to maintain their sovereignty, and is why many prominent realist scholars have predicted a development toward the "breaking up" scenario discussed in the Introduction to this volume. In a changing and more volatile international environment, realist perspectives may thus provide a relevant tool in understanding the potential *disintegrative* effects of crises. Such perspectives may also be valuable in explaining (short term) common foreign and security policies in response to changing power constellations and external threats.

In his chapter on *Classical Realism, Alexander Reichwein* discusses whether realism, often presumed to be a theory of non-integration, can contribute to the debate on EU in times of crisis. Reichwein argues that classical realism, applied from an historical perspective, indeed is of added value by reminding us of a key factor in the European integration process, namely the *German-French axis*. Empirically, Reichwein explores the two countries' role by exploring two questions: How did both powers achieve integration in the past? And how can and should they go about to deal with the challenges the EU is facing today? Analytically, to shed light on this, the chapter draws on the realist concept of *dual hegemony*. The main argument in the paper is presented in three steps: First, Reicwein argues that current EU crises can only be understood by exploring the history of the European integration project. Secondly, an historical analysis reveals that German–French cooperation was a precondition of the EU's birth in the 1950s. And third, that this *dual leadership* has been key to understand integrative steps up until today. On this basis, Reichwein argues that it is likely to assume that the France and Germany's shared leadership will be crucial for whether the EU is able to handle crises, and to move on with European integration, or not. Empirically reminding us of France and Germany's historical role in EU integration, theoretically, Reichwein also makes the theoretical argument that there is more variation in the realist international relation tradition than so far has been reflected in the EU literature. Neo realist studies tend to treat (EU)rope as a secondary phenomenon in international politics. However, realist insights about states, national interests, hegemony, and the logic of diversity may provide helpful tools for explaining EU crisis and disintegration.

In his chapter on *Neo-Realism, Hubert Zimmermann* discusses the neo-realism's relevance in explaining EU politics and EU crisis, using the Ukraine crisis, the Eurozone/financial crisis, and Brexit as empirical cases. Zimmermann finds that neo-realist assumptions may provide convincing explanations of the EU's response to recent crises, as the member states come together in the face of common external threats or uncertainties. There is however an inherent challenge in the application of neo-realism linked to the geographical scope of the study. If focusing on the EU level and thus member states' interests and intra-EU power relations, the internal challenges resulting in crisis and disintegration may be explained. However, if focusing on global level variables, on global power asymmetries and the EU's place in this structure, one would instead expect the member states to unify in their response to changing global power patterns: The UK would stay in the EU to be collectively stronger in a more uncertain world, the member states would remain united vis a vis Russia. Regarding the relevance of neo-realism for understanding and explaining crisis, Zimmermann therefore concludes that neo-realism provides a valuable source of and inspiration for theories of disintegration, but that it is likely to remain rather peripheral in EU studies. Regarding the three scenarios set out in the introduction, a neo-realist perspective would focus on the first, i.e., that of *breaking down*. Although external challenges and global crises might offer windows of opportunity and change the member states' interests in favor of integration in certain policy fields, such cooperation comes with a limited time horizon and will face breakdown or deadlock as soon as the erstwhile impetus wears off and diverging interests come to the fore. Given that these options are often ambiguous or indeterminate, a strategy of *muddling through* (scenario 2) might also be compatible with a neo-realist account.

Neofunctionalism, discussed by *Arne Niemann*, was developed as a theory of EU integration, focusing on how factors like functional spillover create pressure for further integration. Neofunctionalism may however also provide important insights for theorizing crisis. According to Niemann, there is in principle no reasons why "transformations have to be positive, i.e., in terms of moving the process forward or avoiding (public) contestation." First, as most political actors tend to "stumble" from one decision into the next, integration processes tend to be driven by unintended consequences rather than long-term planning. Actors may moreover fail to anticipate a policy's likely consequences, which increases the likelihood of later problems. Crisis may also be the result of the integration process itself due to unresolved functional spillover pressures. And slow or inadequate crisis management may amplify unresolved dysfunctionalities. Learning is another concept that is key to understand crisis and crisis response: Since policy-making involves contestation and choice, learning processes may not necessarily result in further integration, but potentially also in integration crises. According to Niemann, and drawing on insights from "soft" constructivism, functional logics only have effect if actors *perceive* them as plausible or compelling. Learning and socialization are moreover contingent on certain conditions including a commonly shared "lifeworld," insufficient knowledge, and low levels of politicization. Niemann illustrates neofunctionalism's relevance in a study of the financial crisis. Niemann shows that the EU's response can be explained by the dysfunctionalities created by the incomplete Maastricht EMU architecture. These functional rationales were moreover reinforced by integrative pressures exerted by supranational institutions, transnational interests, and markets. Spillover mechanisms—functional, political, and cultivated—in other words provide important insights for understanding the integrative steps taken during the crisis. So far, there is little evidence to support the theory's relevance for explaining the response to other recent crises, such as the migration crisis. Rather than dismissing the theory, Niemann however argues that neofunctionalism should be further revised by specifying the scope conditions of crises' impact on EU integration.

Various types of *Institutionalism* and how they have been applied in studies of institutional change and stability are discussed in *Chris Ansell's* chapter. Rather than being a specific theory of EU integration, institutionalism is a broad umbrella term used in the social sciences to describe the study of institutions and their importance in social, economic, and political life, including historical, rational choice, sociological, and discursive institutionalism. Critiques of institutionalism have argued that it is better at explaining stability than change due to its traditional emphasis on how institutions persist over time due to processes of path dependency, feedback effects, and "taken for granted" cognitive scripts. Although also discussing variables of incremental change, in general, the concept of "critical juncture" has been the central concept used to describe relatively short periods where (radical) institutional change is more likely, in the EU context hence allowing for a *"heading forward* scenario." Critical juncture has also largely been linked to crisis. Although this chapter has uncovered several meanings of crisis (e.g., conjunctural, structural). Ansell however underlines how institutional scholars have begun to problematize this analytical linkage between crisis, critical junctures, and institutional change. Illustrating his argument in a discussion of the EU's response to the financial/Eurozone crisis, Ansell argues that institutional changes in response to crisis are not necessarily radical. Rather than leading mainly to a *heading forward* institutional response, institutional responses to crisis are likely to be a combination of new institutional arrangements and the continuation and consolidation of old ones—of both path dependencies, radical change, and incremental adjustments, more in line with the *muddling through* perspective. Critical junctures may moreover not lead to change, even in the case of crisis.

Jarle Trondal moves on from this broader discussion of institutional theory to discuss one particular version, namely an *organizational theory* approach and in particular how this theory emphasizes institutional crisis response through meta-governance and institutional organizing. Rather than explaining or describing crisis and its effects on EU policies and governance as discussed in the other theory chapters, Trondal links the relevance of organizational theory in relation to crisis to how theoretical insights may be used in response to crisis to (re)design public policy through (re)designing organizational structures. An organizational approach accounts for the *politics of organizing* crises and it provides organizational tools that institutions and governments might use to handle, or in effect, muddle through crisis. As institutional approaches more generally, organizational theory tends to focus more on stability than change, and is thus better at explaining *muddling through* (Scenario 2) than *breaking down* (Scenario 1) or *heading forward* (Scenario 3). In addition to providing tools for *muddling through* a crisis, crisis can however also be seen as an opportunity for EU governments and institutions to head forward—as an enabling environment where governments and organizations find innovative solutions and thereby ways out also through more radical organizational change.

In their chapter *A Cleavage Perspective* on European Party Competition, *Gary Marks, David Attewell, Jan Rovny, and Liesbet Hooghe* address the issue of how political parties have responded to Europe's crises and how, in turn, these crises have affected the structure of political conflict by exploring a new and increasingly salient transnational cleavage linked to the meaning and implications of transnational community. Applying neo-cleavage theory on a large data set on European voters, the authors find that the conventional left-right divide has faded. However, rather than suggesting a process of dealignment where voters are more oriented toward individual preferences on a case to case basis, the analysis suggests that parties in Europe have become more polarized around a new socioeconomic transnational divide and that this cleavage is both structured and durable. Voters' behavior can be distinguished on a number of variables, including gender, education, occupation, and where they live, and these differences are clearer among younger voters. Neo-cleavage theory shares classic cleavage theory's that broader structural changes in the division of voters are caused by major exogenous shocks. Based on their findings, Marks, Attewell, Rovny, and Hooghe suggest that it is the gradual perforation of national states that is producing the transnational cleavage. At its core, this new party divide is linked to a conflict over the role of the national state and national community in an era of transnationalism and hence also linked to voters' perceptions and parties' positions on the EU. While parties on one side of this new divide embrace open societies and international governance (GAL; green, alternative, libertarian parties), parties on the other (TAN; traditionalist, authoritarian, nationalist parties) favor a strengthening of national control over external forces, including the EU. With the EU's crises, the political implications of this divide have become very visible, with the transnational cleavage narrowing the EU's response options not least due to TAN mobilization. This is particularly evident with regard to the migration crisis, where issues such as national border control and national identity, not only in the Visegrad countries but also in traditionally open and liberal countries such as Sweden and Germany, influenced the member states and EU's response. Questions on the new divide linked to national control also affected the EU's response to the Euro crisis. By bringing these issues to the forefront, EU crises have also contributed to accelerating the ongoing restructuring of party competition in Europe. Although TAN mobilization so far has been more pronounced than GAL mobilization the 2019 European Parliamentary elections may suggest that this is changing

Mai'a K. Davis Cross studies and explains crisis from the perspective of *Social Constructivism*. While other perspectives discussed in the book focus either on systemic and structural or statist behavioral factors when explaining crisis and crisis responses, Cross argues that crisis itself is a social construction that needs to be understood if wanting to explain and analyze EU crisis. From a constructivist or sociological perspective, a crisis is a subjective interpretation of events that is socially constructed through interaction. By offering insight into these processes, the added value of this approach in crisis studies is thus that it can help us understand why some events evolve into crises, while others do not. The approach also provides insights into how the perception of a crisis can feed back into the unfolding of the crisis itself and thus have self-fulfilling effects. Sociological and constructivist scholars have argued that political elites, interest groups including the media and the general public are the key actors in creating and spreading perceptions of crisis, with varied focus put on the three groups. In her chapter, Cross argues that all three groups should be analyzed in crisis studies but that the media has had a particularly strong role in constructing EU crises: In most cases, an event is first defined as a crisis in news coverage. More precisely, Cross draws on her own concept of integrational panic to explain the emergence of EU crisis through media construction, illustrating its relevance in a study of the Eurozone crises and the Constitutional treaty crises. Examining the causes of crisis also helps explain why the EU tends to respond to crises by *muddling through* or by *heading forward*. If a crisis takes on a self-fulfilling prophecy dynamic, *breaking down* becomes more of a possibility.

The final chapter in this section of the book is written by *Claudia Landwehr on Deliberative theory*. Landwehr's chapter is concerned with the normative implications of poly-crisis and in particular its implications for EU democracy. Two issues are addressed. First, deliberative theory's potential for understanding today's EU crises, and second, whether deliberative theory can offer a normatively attractive perspective on further EU integration and the possibility of European democracy. Regarding the first, Landwehr concludes that deliberative theories have been (mis)used to justify expert-oriented, technocratic, and elitist decision-making processes in the EU. However, rather than dismissing deliberative theory, Landwehr argues that a systemic, institutionalist account of deliberative democracy that takes its participatory promises seriously would provide a better understanding of the deliberative and democratic deficits that remain inimical to the European project. What is more—from this perspective, EU crises may actually have a positive impact on EU democracy by re-politicizing the integration process and thus bring the future of EU integration back to the center of the political agenda. While typically being discussed mainly by political and academic elites, not least the Euro crisis and the populist backlash have brought deliberation and debate about national control and the future of EU to a much wider public. The British Brexit decision has moreover illustrated the risks of disintegration and enabled what many would refer to as an unpredicted unity among European leaders. As a consequence, although (or precisely because) decision-making in response to crises is still difficult in many areas, deliberation has in other words moved one level up to address constitutional matters and institutional design, as well as the very foundations of supranational cooperation, which if translating into EU reform may serve to reduce the EU's democratic deficit. Landwehr refers to this as meta-deliberation, which occurs where rules and norms of interaction and collective decision-making have not yet been established or where existing rules and norms are challenged.

Takeaways from Part II

Existing theories in EU studies have focused primarily on explaining the integration process (exceptions include, among others, Hodson and Puetter 2019; Jones 2018; Vollard 2018). Factors like the need to cope with common economic challenges linked to interdependence, functional and political spillover, supranational dynamics, institutional processes of socialization and path dependency, common norms, and actors' perceptions are among the diverse set of factors applied in studies of integrative moves towards what often—both historically and theoretically—is perceived as an ever closer union. Although crises implicitly or explicitly are conceptualized differently in several integration theories, crises have often been "considered unavoidable moments to move forward the integration process" (Lequesne 2018: 289 in Svendsen, this volume). As such, EU integration theories face a potential challenge when the EU confronts poly-crisis: How do theories developed and applied to study EU integration deal with crisis and potential disintegration? Can existing theories adequately account for integration in reverse gear? After all, all crises examined in this Handbook "meet the definition of integration crises: situations that acutely threaten the EU with disintegration, i.e., the reduction of its membership or the renationalization of its policies" (Schimmelfennig 2018a, 2018b). The Handbook is indeed not the first attempt to address this question. Recently, in a Special Issue of *Journal of European Public Policy* (*JEPP*, Volume 26:8) Hooghe and Marks (2019: 1113) asked how three main theories designed to understand integration—neofunctionalism, intergovernmentalism, and postfunctionalism—"explain the genesis, the course, and the outcome of four episodes of European (dis)integration that we have witnessed since 2008: the Eurocrisis, the migration crisis, Brexit, and illiberalism." In addition to the arguments put forward by the various authors in this *JEPP* Special Issue (Börzel and Risse 2019; de Wilde 2019; Hodson and Puetter 2019; Kuhn 2019; Schimmelfennig and Winzen 2019; Webber 2019), other discussions on the applicability of EU integration theories in crisis studies include, but are not limited to, Börzel and Risse (2018), Cross and Karolewski (2017), Dinan et al. (2016), Genschel and Jachtenfuchs (2018), Rosamond (2019), and Schimmelfennig (2017, 2018a, 2018b). However, no studies have thus far made a comprehensive theoretical study of crisis to the extent done in this volume.

The chapters in Part II suggest that the existing menu of theoretical approaches to European integration have relevance also for the purpose of explaining the EU's responses to crisis. They have their strengths and weaknesses when faced with the task of explaining EU crisis response, and are sometimes more able to explain certain aspects of crisis and its affect than others. The observation that these theories' applicability varies across crisis is perhaps not surprising: Most of the theories discussed in this volume are mid-range theories rather than grand theories, or in the case of realism, in its basic assumption already prone to expect EU crisis and disintegration. Not least, the variation in the theories' applicability is not surprising given their somewhat different focus and different ontological assumptions. After all, as underlined by Hooghe and Marks (2019), different theories start from different standpoints, they pose different questions and apply different mechanisms both when studying integration and when seeking to understand crisis. As such, their contribution and applicability also vary, and the same phenomenon can be understood from different theoretical lenses. In this sense, we can echo Hooghe and Marks' conclusion that future research should focus on applying alternative theories to develop "conflicting hypotheses that can be systematically tested against each other. However, prior to this, it can be illuminating to engage a theory in its own terms, and to probe its use value in explaining phenomena for which it was not designed, but which are in its field of vision" (Hooghe and Marks 2019: 1128–1129). This volume has contributed in this regard. Importantly, no one theory provides a full picture or explanation of the EU's many crises-responses, suggesting that there indeed might be a need also to revisit existing theoretical frameworks to more adequately encompass disintegration and crisis. What is more: The Handbook finds that the EU has muddled through and in some cases headed forward in response to crises across policy sectors and institutions. In other words, the response has largely been to (incrementally) integrate further. Whether a different outcome than the one we find in this volume—if the EU indeed was *breaking down* in response to crises—could have been equally well explained by the existing integration theory toolkit thus remains an open question also after this endeavor. In some cases, where outcomes do not fit various integration logics, existing theories have struggled more to provide robust explanations. In particular, as several authors discuss in their chapters, Brexit has proved difficult to explain on the basis of existing integration theories. We can thus also echo Frank Schimmelfennig's conclusion both in this chapter and elsewhere that there is room for theoretical innovation, for example by combining insights from different theories. Or, alternatively, by further developing existing theories to better understand continuity and change, as discussed in Ansell's chapter. Future theorizing on the impact of crisis on EU integration should moreover also move on from this by seeking to establish more systematic knowledge on the scope conditions under which the three scenarios set out in Chapter 1 are more or less likely to play out.

References

Börzel, T., & Risse, T. (2018). From the Euro to the Schengen Crises: European Integration Theories, Politicization, and Identity Politics. *Journal of European Public Policy, 25*(1), 83–108.

Börzel, T. A., & Risse, T. (2019). Grand Theories of Integration and the Challenges of Comparative Regionalism. *Journal of European Public Policy, 26*(8), 1231–1252.

Cross, M., & Karolewski, P. (2017). What Type of Power Has the EU Exercised in the Ukraine-Russia Crisis? A Framework of Analysis. *Journal of Common Market Studies, 55*(1), 3–19.

de Wilde, P. (2019). Media Logic and Grand Theories of European Integration. *Journal of European Public Policy, 26*(8), 1193–1212.

Dinan, D., Nugent, N., & Paterson, W. (2016). *The European Union in Crisis* (pp. 316–336). Basingstoke: Palgrave Macmillan.

Genschel, P., & Jachtenfuchs, M. (2018). From Market Integration to Core State Powers: The Eurozone Crisis, the Refugee Crisis and Integration Theory. *Journal of Common Market Studies, 56*(1), 178–196. https://doi.org/10.1111/jcms.12654.

Hodson, D., & Puetter, O. (2019). The European Union in Disequilibrium: New Intergovernmentalism, Postfunctionalism and Integration Theory in the Post-Maastricht Period. *Journal of European Public Policy, 26*(8), 1153–1171.

Hooghe, L., & Marks, G. (2019). Grand Theories of European Integration in the Twenty-First Century. *Journal of European Public Policy, 26*(8), 1113–1133.

Jones, E. (2018). Towards a Theory of Disintegration. *Journal of European Public Policy, 25*(3), 440–451.

Kuhn, T. (2019). Grand Theories of European Integration Revisited: Does Identity Politics Shape the Course of European Integration? *Journal of European Public Policy, 26*(8), 1213–1230.

Rosamond, B. (2019). Theorising the EU in Crisis: De-Europeanisation as Disintegration. *Global Discourse: An Interdisciplinary Journal of Current Affairs, 9*(1), 31–44.

Schimmelfennig, F. (2017). Theorising Crisis in European Integration. In D. Dinan, N. Nugent, & W. Paterson (Eds.), *The European Union in Crisis* (pp. 316–336). Basingstoke: Palgrave Macmillan.

Schimmelfennig, F. (2018a). Liberal Intergovernmentalism and the Crises of the European Union. *Journal of Common Market Studies, 56*(7), 1578–1594.

Schimmelfennig, F. (2018b). European Integration (Theory) in Times of Crisis. *Journal of European Public Policy, 25*(7), 969–989.

Schimmelfennig, F., & Winzen, T. (2019). Grand Theories, Differentiated Integration. *Journal of European Public Policy, 26*(8), 1172–1192.

Vollaard, H. (2018). *European Disintegration: A Search for Explanations*. Basingstoke: Palgrave Macmillan.

Webber, D. (2019). Trends in European Political (Dis)integration: An Analysis of Postfunctionalist and Other Explanations. *Journal of European Public Policy, 26*(8), 1134–1152.

CHAPTER 3

Liberal Intergovernmentalism

Frank Schimmelfennig

INTRODUCTION

Liberal intergovernmentalism (LI) is a theory of integration progress rather than integration crisis. Andrew Moravcsik published his seminal article (Moravcsik 1993) and his book on the 'Choice for Europe' (Moravcsik 1998) in the 1990s, arguably the decade of the most dynamic progress in European integration. The EU had just completed its Single Market Program, agreed on Economic and Monetary Union, introduced the Schengen free-travel area, and embarked on the EFTA and Eastern enlargements that would more than double the EU's membership. Correspondingly, LI focused on explaining 'major steps toward European integration' (Moravcsik 1998: 4).

Whereas the LI account of European integration from 'Messina to Maastricht' (Moravcsik 1998) covers several episodes of negotiation and integration failure such as French President de Gaulle vetoes of the British accession to the EU or the 'empty-chair crisis' in the 1960s, these were episodes of stagnation rather than crisis. LI theorizes the factors of integration, not the conditions of crisis, let alone disintegration.

This is no reason to disregard LI. LI is formulated in sufficiently abstract terms, and it stipulates general drivers and conditions of European integration, which operate in principle in regular as well as crisis negotiations and decisions. This chapter first recapitulates the basic assumptions and propositions of LI on European integration and applies them to the special context of integration

---

F. Schimmelfennig (✉)
ETH Zurich, Center for Comparative and International Studies, Zürich, Switzerland
e-mail: frank.schimmelfennig@eup.gess.ethz.ch

© The Author(s) 2021
M. Riddervold et al. (eds.), *The Palgrave Handbook of EU Crises*,
Palgrave Studies in European Union Politics,
https://doi.org/10.1007/978-3-030-51791-5_3

crises. In a second step, it reviews how LI explains three recent crises of the EU—the Euro, Schengen, and Brexit crises.

On the one hand, I claim that LI offers only a partial account of state preferences in the EU's recent crises. Whereas LI accounts convincingly for preferences in the Euro and Schengen crises, this is not the case in the Brexit crisis. On the other hand, LI captures the negotiation dynamics and outcomes of all three crises well. The biggest deficit of LI is its failure to specify a feedback mechanism that could account for integration crises and crisis outcomes as consequences of earlier integration decisions.

Liberal Intergovernmentalism: An Overview

Andrew Moravcsik's liberal intergovernmentalism builds on traditional or realist intergovernmentalism (Hoffmann 1966), with which it shares the focus on the centrality of governments, their interests, and their power for the process and outcomes of European integration. Yet it complements this intergovernmentalist core in two ways. First, it draws on a liberal theory of preference formation, which attributes the 'national interest' to a domestic politics process: governmental preferences reflect the interests and power of societal groups, mediated by domestic political institutions (Moravcsik 1993: 481). Second, it incorporates a neoliberal, functional theory of international institutions (Keohane 1984), which explains the EU's supranational institutions as instruments to facilitate international cooperation in an interdependent international system and to strengthen governments' commitment to and compliance with the integrated policies.

LI proposes a three-stage explanation for European integration. The first stage is the domestic formation of state or governmental preferences. At the second or negotiation stage, the intergovernmental constellation of preferences and power explains the substantive integration outcomes. The final stage concerns the establishment of EU-level institutions.[1]

While general demand for regional integration results from international policy externalities, concrete integration preferences come primarily from 'the commercial interests of powerful economic producers' (Moravcsik 1998: 3). Governments pursue integration as 'a means to secure commercial advantages for producer groups, subject to regulatory and budgetary constraints' (Moravcsik 1998: 38). Depending on how competitive these powerful producers are on the regional market, states demand either market liberalization or protectionist policies. Moreover, they seek agreement on regulatory policies that benefit the competitiveness of domestic producers.

Domestic economic interests most clearly shape state preferences, the 'more intense, certain, and institutionally represented and organized' they

---

[1] This overview of LI draws mainly on Moravcsik's original writings from the 1990s. For recent reappraisals of LI, see Kleine and Pollack (2018), Moravcsik (2018) and Moravcsik and Schimmelfennig (2019).

are (Moravcsik 1998: 36) and the less 'uncertainty there is about cause-effect relations' (Moravcsik 1999: 171). Conversely, 'the weaker and more diffuse the domestic constituency behind a policy' (ibid.) and the more uncertain and modest 'the substantive implications of a choice', the less predictable are national preferences (Moravcsik 1998: 486–489; Moravcsik and Nicolaïdis 1999: 61). Typically, domestic producers most clearly determine national preferences in commercial policies. General public policies, including macroeconomic, environmental, or social policies, usually involve broader and more diverse constituencies including mass publics.

Governmental autonomy depends on how unified and organized societal interests are. It is highest with regard to issues that do not affect citizens or domestic social groups directly, such as the design of institutions or general foreign policy. Moreover, the less member states are capable of calculating the effects of regional integration on themselves, the more ideological or geopolitical preferences are likely to shape state preferences (Moravcsik 1993: 487–496).

At the negotiation stage, governments are the relevant actors. They negotiate both on the establishment or further development of integration and on the substantive rules of the integrated policies. Finally, they need to decide on the institutional design of regional integration. Even though Moravcsik categorizes institutional design as a separate—third—stage of the explanatory model, these negotiations are only analytically distinct: they go on in parallel and need to be concluded together successfully to produce integration.

First, successful integration requires mutually beneficial arrangements for all participating states. For regional integration to produce mutual benefits, states need to have both mutual interdependence and compatible preferences. Without mutual policy externalities, governments do not see value in integration; without compatible policy preferences, governments are unable to agree on a common policy.

Second, in addition to producing mutual benefits, intergovernmental negotiations consist in hard bargaining about their distribution among the participating governments, including 'credible threats to veto proposals, to withhold financial side-payments, and to form alternative alliances excluding recalcitrant governments' (Moravcsik 1998: 3). The distribution of integration benefits is mainly conditioned by state bargaining power, which is a function of asymmetric interdependence and outside options between states. Those states that are less dependent on integration because they are less affected by negative externalities, or have credible alternative options to deal with them, are in a position to influence the distribution of gains in their favor and extract concessions and side-payments by the more dependent states.

Third, governments negotiate on the institutions designed to secure their agreements. Institutional choice is again driven by governments—and by their concern about each other's commitment to and future compliance with the substantive deals reached. Supranational institutions are instruments of the states. Delegation and pooling serve to remove agreements from the influence of domestic actors who might build up pressure for non-compliance if their integration costs or losses increase. They also remove them from decentralized intergovernmental control, which may be too weak to secure compliance, in particular if powerful member states violate the rules and domestic opposition is strong (Moravcsik 1998: 9, 73). The degree to which governments pool and delegate their decision-making competences depends on the value they place on the issues and substantive outcomes in question and on their uncertainty about the future behavior of other governments. The more a government benefits from a cooperative agreement, and the higher the risks of non-compliance are, the higher is its readiness to cede competences to the EU to prevent potential losers from revising the policy (Moravcsik 1998: 9, 486–487).

LI explains European integration as a sequence of intergovernmental negotiation episodes, each of which ends with a substantive and an institutional integration outcome. LI does not theorize any systematic feedback processes of regional integration. LI assumes that European integration remains under the control of national governments; its working reflects and reproduces the intergovernmental constellation of preferences and power that produced it. The institutions that governments establish lock in these intergovernmental bargains; they do not enable autonomous supranational agency leading to endogenous change. If change occurs, it is exogenous to the integration process. It could either originate in the international environment outside the EU or bottom-up in the domestic environment of the member states. If interdependence spreads to policies or countries outside the existing framework of integration, the deepening or widening of European integration is likely. Moreover, the convergence of policy preferences among governments creates opportunities for more integration.

Liberal Intergovernmentalism and Integration Crisis

Liberal intergovernmentalism is not a theory of integration crisis. Its focus is on explaining why and how the member states of EU agree to move integration forward and which member state(s) have been able to shape the substantive integration outcomes (most). The most important cases of European integration that Moravcsik has focused on in developing the theory are the 'big decisions' of European integration: the agreements on the European Economic Community, the Common Agricultural Policy, the Single Market, and Economic and Monetary Union. Nor does LI offer explicit expectations regarding the origins and causes of integration crises. Its explanation starts with the interdependencies and preferences of major European states and ends with the treaties that establish integrated policy regimes. LI's functional theory of institutions explains how international institutions stabilize international cooperation, but it does not offer an account of unintended institutional effects—such as crises. In sum, LI theorizes the conditions of integration but not the conditions of integration crises.

Moreover, the recent crises of the EU have featured actors, processes, and policies that do not play a significant role in the LI account of European integration. In contrast to the LI focus on commercial policies and their characteristic actor constellations (producers, consumers, and their interest groups) and material cost-benefit calculations, the crises have developed around core state powers in macroeconomic, border, and migration policies. In contrast to the low electoral salience that Moravcsik attributed to EU politics (Moravcsik 2002: 615), issues of European integration topped the list of citizens' concerns across the EU and became the dominant issues in domestic politics and national elections. LI thus faces serious challenges in explaining crises of European integration.

On the other hand, LI has all the theoretical building blocks to analyze and explain the international politics of integration crises. First, the fact that integration crises occur does not contradict LI. Given its assumption of minimal state rationality (Moravcsik 1993: 481), LI does not claim that governments are able to foresee or prevent crises that may affect, or emanate from, their integrated policy regimes.

Second, regardless of their causes and origins, integration crises constitute international negotiating and decision-making situations—the focus of the intergovernmentalist explanatory program. In some ways, integration crises may even privilege an intergovernmentalist approach over alternative approaches. For one, integration crises are situations of heightened interdependence, i.e. pronounced (negative) international policy externalities that create particularly strong demand for policy coordination (Moravcsik 1993: 485). In addition, crisis decision-making tends to be centralized and limited to the core decision-makers. This corresponds with the LI assumption that governments—and the governments of the largest member states in particular—are the relevant actors in European integration.

Moreover, crises commonly have significant distributional implications. The crisis burdens are likely to be unequally distributed (Moravcsik 1993: 486–487). The asymmetrical way in which member states are affected by the crises give rise to unequal bargaining power. Those states that are hardest hit by the crisis and stand to gain most from (more) integration or lose most from disintegration, find themselves in a weak bargaining position and most willing to compromise. Conversely, states that are least affected by the crisis are best able to achieve their preferred policy and extract concessions (Moravcsik 1993: 497–507). Finally, it seems plausible that crisis negotiations are highly likely to feature particularly hard intergovernmental bargaining—in line with another LI proposition.

To explain the politics of integration crises and the variation in preferences, power, and outcomes, we can thus draw on standard assumptions of LI. The following LI hypotheses on integration crises are based on LI's three-stage explanatory model and concern national preferences, intergovernmental bargaining outcomes, and institutional choice (Schimmelfennig 2015). In an integration crisis, in which an EU policy regime—or the EU as a whole—is acutely threatened by disintegration, the status quo is not viable. Member states thus have a basic choice between integration and disintegration, i.e. trying to overcome the crisis by investing more authority and resources in the EU or by coping with the crisis outside the EU framework, by national or unilateral means. The LI crisis hypotheses thus concern the conditions under which governments chose and attain integration as a crisis response.

National preferences are shaped both by the overall extent of international interdependence in the crisis and by how strongly the crisis affects individual member states (or powerful interest groups within the member state societies). It is assumed that states generally seek to protect both their national autonomy and their national resources in integration crises, but agree to supranational delegation and the commitment of resources if they expect net benefits. This is the case in particular if their national capacity to manage the crisis is weak and the costs of disintegration are high.

(H1a) The more interdependence the integration crisis creates among the member states, the more likely they prefer integration.

(H1b) The more negatively a member state is affected by the integration crisis, the more likely it prefers integration.

Taking, H1a and H1b together, if all member states (or their dominant societal groups) are equally vulnerable to the crisis, i.e. expect similarly high losses from disintegration and do not have the capacity to overcome them by national means, they are similarly willing to strengthen the powers and resources of the EU. If interdependence is asymmetrical, member state preferences on the integrated policies diverge. The less affected states are less willing to transfer national authority and resources and to engage in burden-sharing than the more affected states (who can expect to reap net benefits from integration). Finally, if interdependence is low and member states are capable of dealing with the crisis alone, they reject further integration and are willing to accept disintegration.

At the second stage, negotiations on the crisis response reflect the intergovernmental constellation of national preferences and bargaining power. Bargaining power results from asymmetrical interdependence: states that are less vulnerable to interdependence gain less from integration. In turn, they can successfully bargain for side-payments or terms of integration that work in their favor.

(H2) The less a member state is negatively affected by the integration crisis, the more likely it can shape the integration outcome according to its preferences.

Finally, the member states negotiate on the establishment and reform of EU institutions during integration crises. For one, H2 holds for intergovernmental bargaining on the institutional design, too: Those states that are least negatively affected by the crisis and most satisfied with the institutional status quo, possess the strongest bargaining power and have the largest influence on the design of common institutions.

In addition, the design follows the cooperation problem and the integration stakes at hand. In integration crises, governments are the more willing to delegate and pool sovereignty, the more the crisis exhibits failure of formerly decentralized institutions and the higher the costs of disintegration and the likelihood of defection by other governments or domestic actors are.

> (H3) *The higher the risks of disintegration are in the integration crisis, the more likely the member states are to establish or strengthen supranational institutions.*

In the remainder of the chapter, I apply LI and these hypotheses to the three major recent crises of the EU.[2]

The Euro Crisis[3]

The Euro crisis resulted from a balance-of-payment crisis of several Euro area countries, which put in question their ability to retain the Euro as their currency. During the Euro crisis, national preferences combined a common interest in preserving the Euro and conflicting distributional preferences on the rescue between north and south. The Eurozone states engaged in hard bargaining, in which they tried to avoid and shift the costs of preserving the Euro until bankruptcy and breakdown appeared imminent. Owing to asymmetrical interdependence, the rescue terms reflected the preferences of the surplus countries predominantly. Finally, institutional reform was designed to strengthen the credibility of member state commitments to the single currency.

Preference Constellation

Because the Euro crisis was in essence a financial market crisis turned into a fiscal crisis, the preferences of the member states reflected their financial market and fiscal positions as surplus/creditor and deficit/debtor countries (Armingeon and Cranmer 2018; Schimmelfennig 2015: 182–183). In Moravcsik's original formulation, macroeconomic policies are generally less likely to have strong or clear substantive implications for specific interest groups than market-making or market-regulating rules. Therefore, he expected integration preferences in this area to reflect 'the macro-economic preferences of ruling governmental coalitions' (Moravcsik 1998: 3). In the Euro crisis, however, the short-term welfare implications of the major policy alternatives were clear and strong. For this reason, LI would assume material interests to prevail over ideological preferences. Accordingly, the Euro crisis

---

[2]The following sections build on Schimmelfennig (2018a) and further published work.
[3]For more on the Euro/financial crisis, see Tranøy and Stenstad this volume and Olsen and Rosén this volume.

pitted a predominantly 'northern' coalition of surplus countries against a mainly 'southern' coalition of deficit countries.[4]

According to the mainstream scenarios, a breakdown of the Eurozone would have produced prohibitive economic costs for *all* euro area countries.[5] For the deficit countries, abandoning the euro would have meant sovereign default, a likely breakdown of the monetary and financial system, and hyperinflation. Moreover, contagion effects were widely expected. Whereas the other Euro countries would probably have been able to cope with a default and exit of Greece, there was reason to fear that financial markets would lose trust in the Euro more generally, withdraw from further debt countries, and force the Eurozone to back countries (such as Spain and Italy) that were too big to rescue. For the surplus countries, a breakdown of the euro would have resulted in a steep appreciation of their currencies, a concurrent slump in exports, and deep and long-lasting recession. The high negative interdependence in the case of disintegration generated a common interest in preserving the Eurozone (H1a).

This common interest was accompanied, however, by distributional conflict between north and south. Simply put, the costs of adjustment in the crisis could be mutualized, e.g. in the form of Euro bonds or fiscal equalization schemes, in which case the creditor countries would pay for the debtors. Alternatively, adjustment could be nationalized through fiscal austerity, wage, and price depression, thus putting the burden of adjustment on the debtor countries. Accordingly, the north rejected the mutualization of debt and demanded that deficit countries adjust internally. By contrast, the southern countries pushed for the 'Europeanization' of sovereign debt and soft adjustment policies. Thus, all member states sought to shift the costs of preventing disintegration away from themselves. Yet whereas the most negatively affected southern states sought stronger fiscal integration, the northern countries were interested in limiting their financial commitment to the Eurozone (H1b). The intergovernmental preference constellation developed early in the crisis and remained stable. All issues from the first bailouts via the establishment of the rescue funds and the reforms of budget monitoring policies to the development of banking union were structured by the same basic conflict and coalitions.

---

[4] It is, however, not possible to explain the leading role of France in the southern coalition without taking into account long-standing ideological differences with Germany about macroeconomic policy and Eurozone governance. Although the French fiscal position was weaker than that of the northern coalition, it was more similar to the north than to the south. See the discussion in Schimmelfennig (2015: 183).

[5] 'The choice', *The Economist*, 26 May 2012; Petersen and Böhmer (2012).

Intergovernmental Bargaining

The mixed motives of an overarching common interest in preserving the Eurozone and conflicting burden-shifting incentives constituted an iterated 'chicken game' with hard bargaining and brinkmanship (Schimmelfennig 2015: 184–185). The solvent countries repeatedly rejected and delayed (additional) support to the crisis countries and pushed them to make fiscal cuts up to the point at which sovereign default was imminent. The indebted countries, in turn, sought to postpone painful adjustment measures and demonstrate their incapacity to counter financial market pressure until the solvent countries came to their rescue.

Interdependence in the Euro crisis was strong but asymmetrical. Whereas the stakes were high for all Eurozone countries, the immediate consequences of the crisis and potential disintegration were significantly more painful for the debtor countries. As a result, the creditors were in a better position to realize their preferences (H2). At each stage of crisis decision-making, Germany and its allies shaped the terms of integration in return for ending its opposition to bailouts. Germany prevented the introduction of Euro bonds or any other formally mutualized sovereign debt. In addition, Germany was able to link financial assistance to strict austerity conditionality, the strengthening of the EU's monitoring and sanctioning of national budgets, and the adoption of the Fiscal Compact and its balanced budget rules. Whereas the citizens of the debtor countries have suffered huge losses in wages, subsidies, social security benefits, and increases in taxation, the creditor states have successfully opposed the write-off of their rescue money.

The major crisis management and reform deals were reached in intergovernmental negotiations. This is especially true for the bailout packages, the rescue funds, and the Fiscal Compact, all based on intergovernmental agreements. The guidelines for the reforms of the procedures to monitor EU budgets and banking union were also hammered out in intergovernmental negotiations before they entered the legislative process.

Institutional Choice

The Euro crisis revealed several enforcement problems in EMU. First, the Stability and Growth Pact (SGP), established to commit countries to fiscal discipline, had already proven malleable ahead of the financial crisis. Second, the crisis demonstrated that exogenous shocks and sudden stops could even hit countries without excessive budget deficits (such as Ireland or Spain). In this case, the enforcement problem was to commit other member states to coming to their rescue. Finally, the Euro crisis highlighted the inadequacies of national banking supervision and resolution: lax supervision due to cozy relations between bankers and politicians, regulatory arbitrage across member states, and burden- as well as blame-shifting among national regulators when transnationally operating banks ran into trouble.

The three major blocks of institutional reform are clearly linked to these problems. The Fiscal Compact and the legislation on the surveillance of member states' fiscal and economic policies are intended to overcome the enforcement problems of the SGP. The legislation on banking union tackles the sovereign-bank nexus and the enforcement problems of national regulation in an integrated financial market; and the European Stability Mechanism commits surplus countries to the rescue of deficit countries.

In addition, however, the design of the common institutions largely follows the preferences of the northern countries. Their institutional preferences were linked strongly and consistently to their material preferences: whereas they sought to strengthen the credibility of the debtors' commitment to fiscal discipline, they tried to limit their own financial commitment and exposure. Therefore, the new and reformed institutions feature intergovernmental financial assistance with a fixed limit on lending capacity, supranational fiscal and economic surveillance, and a banking union that combines supranational banking supervision with more intergovernmental banking resolution (which may involve international transfers).

The Schengen Crisis[6]

Whereas the number of migrants across the Mediterranean Sea had been increasing for several years, in 2015 migration flows shifted from the Central to the Eastern Mediterranean, and the number of asylum-seekers in the EU doubled in comparison with the previous year. As in the Euro crisis, the member states engaged in burden-shifting behavior. In the end, however, they failed to develop a common interest in consolidating the Schengen regime. Moderate disintegration costs and sufficient national capacity allowed member states to pursue unilateral policies, avoid costly mutual commitments, and resist significant further integration (Schimmelfennig 2018b).

Preference Constellation

The Schengen crisis developed in the EU's Area of Freedom, Security and Justice (AFSJ), which includes home policies such as border security, asylum, and immigration. This policy area is even more distant from LI's focus on commercial policies and economic interest group politics than EMU. It is a policy area that is sensitive to state sovereignty and national identity and therefore likely to be driven by ideological public policy preferences. The short-term policy issue of the crisis was, however, the management of migration pressure: how the EU should limit and distribute the burden of sustaining the refugees and processing their asylum requests. Just as in the Euro crisis, the distributive implications of policy alternatives were certain and substantial. National policy

---

[6]For more on the migration crisis, see Bosilca this volume, Crawford this volume and Schilde this volume.

preferences mainly resulted from how strongly the migration flow affected the member states; their affectedness depended on their position toward the main migration routes; and this position was a function of geography and economic as well as regulatory asylum conditions.

Because of their geography, frontline member states like Greece and Italy are most immediately affected by the migrant flows but do not offer attractive asylum conditions. Destination states like Germany and Sweden are remote from the origins of the migration flow, but strongly affected by secondary migrant movement, owing to attractive conditions as prosperous countries with a comparatively liberal asylum regime. Transit countries such as Hungary and Slovenia are positioned on the migration routes from the frontline to the destination states. Bystander countries are located off-route and therefore not directly affected. As in the Euro crisis, each member state engaged in burden-minimizing behavior. The heavily affected frontline and destination states pushed for the redistribution of refugees across the EU, whereas transit and bystander countries opposed relocation (Biermann et al. 2019).

The preference constellation in the Euro and Schengen crises was structurally similar in that all member states preferred to minimize their own adjustment costs and to shift the burden of crisis management to other member states. Moreover, the most affected countries supported integrated European solutions (H1b). Yet the Schengen crisis produced less interdependence than the Euro crisis (H1a). First, many Schengen member states (the bystander countries) were not directly affected at all by the surge in the number of asylum-seekers. Second, even weaker and smaller member states were capable of reducing their affectedness by national means. They could reestablish border controls, build fences, and wave through migrants to their neighbors. By contrast, states threatened by sovereign default in the Euro crisis could not have coped without an international bailout. Third, whereas the Schengen free-travel area is a popular policy of European integration, the costs of disintegration were manageable. Even according to the most pessimistic scenario of several studies that have appeared during the migrant crisis, the annual 'cost of non-Schengen' would not have amounted to more than 0.2% of GDP annually (European Parliament 2017).

Intergovernmental Bargaining

In the absence of a strong common interest in cooperation, intergovernmentalist studies describe the bargaining structure of the migrant crisis as a 'suasion game', in which one side has the dominant strategy to defect, leaving the other side dissatisfied (Biermann et al. 2019; Zaun 2018: 48). In the Schengen crisis, bystander countries had no interest in cooperation because migration passed them by. Frontline countries were heavily affected but could simply stop registering asylum-seekers and let them move on. Transit countries helped migrant groups to cross their countries. Consequently, destination countries ended up with the weakest bargaining power (H2).

Correspondingly, common solutions to the burden-sharing problem have largely failed. The EU only agreed to a *one-time* reallocation of up to 160'000 refugees in 2015, but even this ad hoc measure met with opposition and legal challenges by several Eastern member states. It was also poorly implemented: less than 20% of the envisaged relocations had taken place by the end of the agreed period in 2017. A Commission proposal for a permanent quota system for the allocation of asylum seekers was rejected not only by the Eastern member states but also by Western member states such as France and Spain—all of them countries at the margins of the 2015 migration routes (Biermann et al. 2019; Zaun 2018: 54).

Because they were not in a position to induce the other member states to integrate, the destination countries were left with three options: they could reduce their attractiveness to migrants, close and fortify their borders, and offer the countries of origin side-payments for cooperation. Accordingly, Sweden and Germany tightened their asylum rules considerably and reintroduced border controls. In addition, Germany was the main driver behind the March 2016 agreement between the EU and Turkey, at the origin of the Eastern Mediterranean migration route. Austria—half destination country, half transit country—orchestrated an agreement of the countries along the Balkan migration route to close their borders to migrants. Both measures led to a significant reduction in migrant arrivals and asylum requests after March 2016.

Institutional Choice

Given weak interdependence and incompatible preferences, intergovernmental bargaining during the Schengen crisis did not result in substantial further integration. Rather, we observe a mix of unilateral measures producing temporary disintegration and additional support to EU agencies without authority transfer.

Because of the unilateral actions taken by the member states, the Schengen/Dublin regime has been up in the air since the summer of 2015. Starting with Germany in September 2015, several Schengen states (Austria, Denmark, France, Norway, and Sweden) reintroduced controls at some of their internal Schengen borders. Whereas these measures were legal under the Schengen Borders Code and authorized by the EU, they were prolonged several times even though migrant flows quickly returned to pre-crisis levels.

The two EU agencies active in the border and asylum regime of the EU—the European Asylum Support Organization (EASO) and Frontex—have seen a major expansion of their budget and personnel but have not acquired supranational competencies (Carrera et al. 2017). The competences of EASO continue to be limited to supporting and coordinating member state authorities in the implementation of EU asylum rules. It can help to promote but not enforce uniform asylum decisions across Europe. In the case of Frontex, the Commission proposed supranational competences: the right to return rejected migrants and to deploy guards to the borders of EU states without the consent of the government. These proposals did not pass, however.

THE BREXIT CRISIS[7]

The Brexit crisis resulted from the June 2016 UK referendum on EU membership, which produced a narrow majority for Leave. For the first time in the history of the EU, a member state decided to withdraw from the Union. In November 2018, the EU and the UK finished negotiations on a withdrawal agreement. Because the British Parliament failed to ratify the agreement, however, the EU and the UK agreed on an extension of the March 2019 deadline. Whereas LI cannot convincingly account for national preference formation, the EU's superior bargaining power has led the UK to make major concessions in the withdrawal negotiations.[8]

Preference Constellation

Brexit is not a single-issue crisis but affects the membership of the UK in the EU as a whole. Essentially, however, the British participation in the internal market is at stake—a policy area, in which intense and concrete material interests and domestic economic (producer) interest groups should carry the day and determine state preferences. Indeed, the Remain campaign focused on the negative economic consequences of Brexit. Economists from international organizations such as the OECD and the IMF, the British Treasury, think tanks, and private consultancies were in almost full agreement about the harm that Brexit would do to the UK economy. In addition, the UK business community and its major interest groups have been overwhelmingly in favor of remaining in the EU and its market (Jensen and Snaith 2016: 1304–1305). By contrast, the victorious Leave campaign focused on self-determination and identity issues, above all immigration, which resonated strongly with the major concerns of the Leave voters (Clarke et al. 2017: 161–165).

The Leave vote did not prescribe the specific form of non-membership arrangement. The two essential options were 'soft Brexit', which would keep the UK in the customs union and/or single market, and 'hard Brexit'. After months of vagueness ('Brexit means Brexit'), Prime Minister May came out in favor of a 'hard Brexit' in her Lancaster House speech in January 2017. May excluded membership in the internal market because it would mean accepting EU legislation, the jurisdiction of the Court of Justice, the freedom of movement for labor, and 'vast contributions' to the EU budget. Whereas the UK government was simultaneously seeking full market access for financial services

---

[7] For more on the Brexit crisis, see Oliver this volume and Whitman this volume.
[8] I exclude the negotiations on the new settlement for the UK between November 2015 and February 2016, which took place before the crisis erupted.

and selective industries to minimize the economic harm of Brexit, it consistently stuck to these 'red lines'. In prioritizing self-determination, 'hard Brexit' followed the Leave campaign, the Eurosceptic camp in the Conservative Party, and the majority of Tory voters. Thus, the Tory government followed the concerns of its voters rather than the business community. In sum, the British government position is inconsistent with LI expectations.

For the remaining EU member states, LI expects that national preferences vary with the intensity of their economic relations with the UK. Clearly, Ireland is most heavily exposed, followed by regions in Germany, the Netherlands, Belgium, and France (Chen et al. 2018). In addition, Ireland has a special interest in avoiding a hard border across the island that could undermine the Good Friday peace agreement. According to LI reasoning, these member states should be most in favor of a 'soft Brexit' and most ready to make concessions to the UK on selective market access should it opt for a 'hard Brexit'. Yet in spite of their diverse economic preferences, the EU-27 have made a strong show of unity on Brexit, and many of the more exposed member states have taken a particularly tough position. The Irish government threatened to reject any agreement that would introduce a hard customs border between Northern Ireland and the Republic. The German government, on whose interest in keeping access to the British export market the proponents of Brexit had placed high hopes, made clear on several occasions that a common EU position and the rejection of 'cherry picking' were its preponderant preference (Schimmelfennig 2018c).

In the European Council's negotiation guidelines, the EU set out several core principles: preserving the integrity of the single market, making sure that non-members cannot enjoy the same rights and benefits as members, and conducting negotiations as a single package and exclusively through Union channels. In other words, no cherry picking, no separate negotiations, and no separate agreements (European Council 2017). As in the case of the Euro crisis, this overarching common interest of the member states in preserving the integrity of the single market results from high interdependence: the EU-27's benefits from the single market strongly exceed their benefits from the bilateral relationship with the UK.

Intergovernmental Bargaining and Institutional Choice

The EU enjoyed superior bargaining power in the negotiations on the withdrawal agreement—both materially and institutionally. Materially, the EU and the UK are likely to lose from Brexit, but interdependence favors the EU. According to Chen et al. (2018: 38), the UK's economic exposure to Brexit is almost five times higher than that of the rest of the EU.

Institutionally, the Article 50 negotiations favor the EU, too. First, the exiting state negotiates with the EU as a whole, represented by the European Commission. This procedure strengthens the unity and bargaining power of the EU. Second, the withdrawal agreement requires the consent of the European Parliament. Third, Article 50 negotiations are limited to two years. If the exiting state rejects a withdrawal settlement and a future relationship that is acceptable to the remaining member states, it leaves the EU without any agreement at all—the most materially detrimental outcome. Only unanimous agreement of the remaining member states can extend the negotiating period.

The withdrawal negotiations between the UK and the EU have produced an agreement in November 2018. In line with the expectations of LI (H2 and H3), the material and institutional provisions of the agreement predominantly reflect the negotiating positions of the EU-27 (Schimmelfennig 2018c). First, the UK accepted the EU position that negotiations on a follow-up agreement would only start after sufficient progress on the terms of withdrawal. Second, the UK pledged to honor all of its financial obligations under the current financial framework (running out in 2020), after initially refusing to pay beyond the exit date. Third, the UK government accepted the need for a transitional phase after exit, during which it would remain bound by the legal obligations, but without the decision-making rights, of a member state. Third, the UK guaranteed avoiding a hard border in Ireland and consented to the so-called 'Irish backstop' securing a customs union and regulatory alignment of Northern Ireland with the EU should other solutions fail. Finally, in an area of more genuine compromise, the UK agreed to guarantee the rights of EU citizens residing in the UK but obtained limits in the EU Court's jurisdiction after withdrawal.

In the first three months of 2019, Prime Minister May failed three times to obtain a majority for the withdrawal agreement. Yet the EU refused to reopen negotiations and accommodate the hard-liners in Parliament. To avoid a high-risk no-deal Brexit, May requested two extensions of the original March 29 deadline. In spite of his earlier rejection of the agreement, May's successor Boris Johnson accepted the Irish backstop and secured ratification in Parliament in January 2020. On 31 January 2020, the UK left the EU.

Conclusions

Even though LI was not developed as a theory of crisis and has no specific propositions on national preferences, intergovernmental negotiations, and integration outcomes in the context of integration crises, its general assumptions and hypotheses can be reformulated and applied easily for the purpose. Moreover, they hold up generally well against the evidence on the three major recent crises of the EU: the Euro, Schengen, and Brexit crises.

It is true that LI fails to explain the UK vote to leave the EU and the May and Johnson governments' preference for a hard Brexit. As Brexit is about commercial policy, affects intense and well-organized interests, and is predicted to produce negative effects with high certainty, British preferences contradict LI on its home turf. This is, however, the only clear explanatory failure of LI.

In all other cases, preferences match LI expectations overall. Generally, member state preferences reflect the position of the state in international interdependence and distributional conflicts. More precisely, common preferences for preserving and deepening integration result from common expected losses of disintegration and lack of national, unilateral capacity to master the crises, whereas conflicting preferences mirror conflicting costs and benefits from sharing the burdens of crisis adjustment. Even in the cases of non-commercial public policies such as macroeconomic and migration policy, which leave room for ideological preferences according to LI, high and clear short-term material effects have structured member state preferences and coalitions.

Most importantly, LI provides a convincing account of the crisis bargaining processes. Intergovernmental negotiations featuring hard bargaining constitute the most important process linking preferences and outcomes in the crises. In the crises, established European rules and procedures of policy-making typically fail, and intergovernmental negotiations fill the void. Asymmetric interdependence accounts for the bargaining power of governments and the material and institutional integration outcomes. Interdependence explains why the Euro crisis produced more integration, whereas the Schengen crisis did not. Asymmetry tells us how the costs of crisis adjustment were distributed, and whose preferences gained the upper hand.

Yet, LI suffers from a major explanatory gap. Whereas its three-stage explanatory model covers the process from national preference formation to integration agreement, it neglects the consequences of integration agreements and the endogenous or feedback effects of integration on interdependence, preferences, and bargaining power. Crises cannot be explained as consequences of (deficient) integration but remain exogenous to the LI mode. This is not a novel observation. Already in the 1990s, Paul Pierson criticized the distortions resulting from LI's '"snapshot" view' on European integration as a series of independent intergovernmental bargains (1996: 127).

To bridge this gap, Erik Jones, Dan Kelemen, and Sophie Meunier propose a theoretical synthesis of LI and neofunctionalism in their analysis of the euro crisis, in which 'intergovernmentalism captures the dynamic at work in critical junctures, whereas neofunctionalism describes the mechanism linking one critical juncture to the next' (Jones et al. 2016: 1013). In a dynamic process of 'failing forward', intergovernmental lowest common denominator bargaining produces incomplete integration arrangements, which spark crises, in which intergovernmental bargaining produces more but again incomplete integration. Both Marco Scipioni (2018) and Sandra Lavenex (2018) applied the 'failing forward' argument to the Schengen crisis. The EU's integration crises have thus not only broadly corroborated the LI analysis of European integration but also produced attempts to develop the theory further.

REFERENCES

Armingeon, K., & Cranmer, S. (2018). Position-Taking in the Euro Crisis. *Journal of European Public Policy, 25*(4), 544–564.

Biermann, F., Guérin, N., Jagdhuber, S., Rittberger, B., & Weiss, M. (2019). Political (non-) Reform in the Refugee Crisis: A Liberal-Intergovernmentalist Explanation. *Journal of European Public Policy, 26*(2), 246–266.

Carrera, S., Blockmans, S., Cassarino, J., Gros, D., & Guild, E. (2017). *The European Border and Coast Guard. Addressing Migration and Asylum Challenges in the Mediterranean?* Brussels: Center for European Policy Studies.

Chen, W., Los, B., McCann, P., Ortega-Argilés, R., Thissen, M., & Van Oort, F. (2018). The Continental Divide? Economic Exposure to Brexit in Regions and Countries on Both Sides of the Channel. *Papers in Regional Science, 97,* 25–54.

Clarke, H., Goodwin, M., & Whiteley, P. (2017). *Brexit: Why Britain Voted to Leave the European Union.* Cambridge: Cambridge University Press.

European Council. (2017). Special Meeting of the European Council (Art. 50) (29 April 2017)—Guidelines (EUCO XT 20004/17).

European Parliament. (2017). The Cost of Non-Schengen: Impact of Border Controls Within Schengen on the Single Market, PE 581.383 (April 2016). Available at http://www.europarl.europa.eu/RegData/etudes/STUD/2016/581383/EPRS_STU(2016)581383_EN.pdf.

Hoffmann, S. (1966). Obstinate or Obsolete? The Fate of the Nation-State and the Case of Western Europe. *Daedalus, 95*(3), 862–915.

Jensen, M., & Snaith, H. (2016). When Politics Prevails: The Political Economy of a Brexit. *Journal of European Public Policy, 23*(9), 1302–1310.

Jones, E., Kelemen, R. D., & Meunier, S. (2016). Failing Forward? The Euro Crisis and the Incomplete Nature of Integration. *Comparative Political Studies, 49*(7), 1010–1034.

Keohane, R. (1984). *After Hegemony: Cooperation and Discord in World Political Economy.* Princeton: Princeton University Press.

Kleine, M., & Pollack, M. (2018). Liberal Intergovernmentalism and Its Critics. *Journal of Common Market Studies, 56*(7), 1493–1509.

Lavenex, S. (2018). 'Failing Forward' Towards Which Europe? Organized Hypocrisy in the Common European Asylum System. *Journal of Common Market Studies, 56*(5), 1195–1212.

Moravcsik, A. (1993). Preferences and Power in the European Community: A Liberal Intergovernmentalist Approach. *Journal of Common Market Studies, 31*(4), 473–524.

Moravcsik, A. (1998). *The Choice for Europe. Social Purpose and State pPower from Messina to Maastricht.* Ithaca: Cornell University Press.

Moravcsik, A. (1999). The Choice for Europe: Current Commentary and Future Research: A Response to James Caporaso, Fritz Scharpf, and Helen Wallace. *Journal of European Public Policy, 6,* 168–179.

Moravcsik, A. (2002). In Defence of the "Democratic Deficit": Reassessing Legitimacy in the European Union. *Journal of Common Market Studies, 40*(4), 603–624.

Moravcsik, A. (2018). Preferences, Power and Institutions in 21st-century Europe. *Journal of Common Market Studies, 56*(7), 1648–1674.

Moravcsik, A., & Nicolaïdis, K. (1999). Explaining the Treaty of Amsterdam: Interests, Influence, Institutions. *Journal of Common Market Studies, 37,* 59–85.

Moravcsik, A., & Schimmelfennig, F. (2019). Liberal Intergovernmentalism. In A. Wiener, T. Börzel, & T. Risse (Eds.), *European Integration Theory* (pp. 64–84). Oxford: Oxford University Press, 3rd ed.

Petersen, T., & Böhmer, M. (2012). *Economic Impact of Southern European Member States Exiting the Eurozone (Future Social Market Economy Policy Brief 2012/06).* Gütersloh: Bertelsmann Stiftung.

Pierson, P. (1996). The Path to European Integration: A Historical Institutionalist Analysis. *Comparative Political Studies, 29*(2), 123–163.

Schimmelfennig, F. (2015). Liberal Intergovernmentalism and the Euro Area Crisis. *Journal of European Public Policy, 22*(2), 177–195.

Schimmelfennig, F. (2018a). Liberal Intergovernmentalism and the Crises of the European Union. *Journal of Common Market Studies.*

Schimmelfennig, F. (2018b). European Integration (Theory) in Times of Crisis. *Journal of European Public Policy, 25*(7), 969–989.

Schimmelfennig, F. (2018c). Brexit: Differentiated Disintegration in the European Union. *Journal of European Public Policy, 25*(8), 1154–1173.

Scipioni, M. (2018). Failing Forward in EU Migration Policy? EU Integration After the 2015 Asylum and Migration Crisis. *Journal of European Public Policy, 25*(9), 1357–1375.

Zaun, N. (2018). States as Gatekeepers in EU Asylum Politics: Explaining the Non-Adoption of a Refugee Quota System. *Journal of Common Market Studies, 56*(1), 44–62.

CHAPTER 4

Classical Realism

Alexander Reichwein

INTRODUCTION

The European Union (EU) is in a deep crisis (Waever and Wivel 2018: 2). How far can realism help to understand and explain this crisis and its impact on the EU? How far can it help to discuss how to respond to challenges the EU is faced with? And how far can realists offer practical solutions to practitioners how to go on with the European integration process? Realism is presumed by most IR and EU scholars to be an under-theorized theory of non-integration (Collard-Wexler 2006), or a "theory of dis-integration" (Rosamond 2016). Consequently, many observers of EU affairs discard realism in the belief that this theory of power politics cannot grasp politics of dialogue, compromise, and cooperation. However, this rejection is based more on a false stereotypical view of realism without any differentiation than on the insights on the EU generated by various realist approaches (Rynning 2005). *Neo-* and *structural* realists are indeed sceptical about institutions, cooperation, and delegating sovereignty to supranational authorities. And they are not really surprised about a revisionist Russia and the Ukraine war (Mearsheimer 2010, 2014; see Waever and Wivel 2018: 4–5), the Brexit or a failed EU migration policy. Quite the contrary, neo-realists explain these crises and disintegration dynamics within the EU as a predictable self-fulfilling prophecy (see Zimmermann in this volume). *Classical* realism which traditionally focuses on history, the state, and state strategies, and which assumes maximizing *influence* as the

---

A. Reichwein (✉)
Department of Political Science, Justus-Liebig-University, Giessen, Germany
e-mail: alexander.reichwein@sowi.uni-giessen.de

© The Author(s) 2021
M. Riddervold et al. (eds.), *The Palgrave Handbook of EU Crises*, Palgrave Studies in European Union Politics,
https://doi.org/10.1007/978-3-030-51791-5_4

most important goal of states trying to shape international institutions and rules and the regional environment they are embedded in, is quite different.

This chapter presents a variety of classical realism represented by three generations of European realists which deals with a key factor of the European integration process that is not dealt with in the other chapters. The role of Germany and France, and with how both great powers can and should go on to achieve an integrated Europe. The chapter sheds light on a unique category in classical realism, namely *German–French axis*, from a historical perspective. The argument which makes the historical lens an added value is threepart: First of all, you need to look back and know the history of the European integration process in order to understand and deal with current crises. Classical realism helps in this regard. Secondly, German–French cooperation was a precondition of the birth of the European Community (EC) in the 1950s. Finally, this *dual leadership* is a requirement of the ongoing integration process until today. This shared leadership will also be key to whether or not the EU member states are able to handle today's crises, and to move on with deepening and widening (EU)rope, or not. In line with this argument, I explore the history of European integration by focusing on Germany and France, and Pedersen's realist model of *dual hegemony* (Pedersen 1998, 2002). In the first part, I work out some limitations of structural neo-realism and some promises of classical realism when dealing with German–French relations embedded in the European integration process. In the second part, I argue in a historical vein that classical realism with its categories and assumptions about states and national interests, power politics and its limitations such as the balance of power, and about what Stanley Hoffmann introduces as *national situations* and the *logic of diversity* is well prepared to expect and to explain the EU in trouble, and to identify the implications on fragmented EU institutions and inconsistent policies. Finally, I present how today's realists take history seriously and deal with EU in crisis. Which solutions do they offer to scholars and practitioners on how to respond to challenges and go on with the integration process.

REALISM(S), HISTORY, AND EUROPEAN INTEGRATION

Realism is not well known as a dominant European integration theory "[…] because the EU is commonly perceived as capable of transcending power politics as we used to know it" (Rynning 2011: 23). Rather, realism is presumed by most integration scholars to be a marginalised theory in the field. And realists, it is asserted in the institutional-liberal-constructivist camp, cannot explain the ongoing European integration process. Because during and after the Cold War, history treats the EU rather nicely.

Realists' Predictions on Post-Cold War Europe

The realist dilemma seems to be obvious: it is the belief in determined and law-like history. The—unexpected—demise of the Soviet Union in 1991, the resulting gradual withdrawal of Europe's American pacifier (Joffe 1984) and the rise of unified Germany did *unbalance* Europe again (Zimmer 1997; see Waever and Wivel 2018: 4). The end of bipolarity caused uncertainty and fear again about Germany's future role in Europe.[1] Most realists those days did expect the renaissance of the *German Question* (Hoffmann 1990). And they did expect the return to nineteenth-century-like power politics in Europe, and an old imperial Germany pursuing its national interests unilaterally. Given a more powerful Germany in terms of material capabilities and economic resources, landmass and population (Baumann et al. 2001) and an improved geographical position (Waltz 1993), multipolarity and the traditional struggle for power, and disorder and instability coming along with this was the expected old new nightmare scenario (Mearsheimer 1990; Zelikov 1992). As a best case scenario in offensive realism, Mearsheimer did suggest Germany to become the nuclear-armed European hegemon. Germany would first of all exploit and in the medium term leave the EU. And in the long run, it would dominate the new European Concert of powers including Russia. Mearsheimer's hope was that the German hegemon would provide order, stability, and a cold peace (see also Mearsheimer 2010, 2014). As a rational response, defensive realists (Waltz 2000) did expect power balancing by France, Great Britain, and Russia *against* rising Germany.[2] Against the background of the deepening and widening of the EU since the Maastricht Treaty, Germany's rather benign leading role (Otero-Iglesias and Zimmermann 2016) and the German–French axis, it is obvious that Waltz and Mearsheimer did predict future developments in Europe wrong.

Balancing Against Germany? Limitations of Neo-Realism

Structural and neo-realists are sceptical about institutionalized and durable forms of state cooperation, shared power and leadership, or dual hegemony. They treat the European integration process as a secondary phenomenon

---

[1] Anderson/Goodman (1993); Bulmer/Paterson (1996); Kaelberer (1997); Markovits/Reich/Westermann (1996); Reichwein (2019: 85–97); Wessels (2001).

[2] Whereas Mearsheimer feared a Hobbesian state of anarchy within Europe, Waltz was quite optimistic. To him, European anarchy was rather benign. Consequently, he did expect unified Germany to try to control its surroundings by pursuing defensive strategies of power balancing—if necessary—in order to preserve the post-Cold War status quo of the power distribution among states. According to Waltz, satisfied Germany just aimed preserving its own new beneficial position by means of increased conventional military resources and/or bi- and multilateral alliance-building against any revisionist state. For a summary of the—different—realist predictions in the early 1990s concerning Europe see Hoffmann (1995b: 281–285), Reichwein (2012: 39/40; 2019: 86/87), Rynning (2005, 2011: 25–28).

in international politics (Waltz 1993, 2000; Grieco 1988, 1995; Simón 2017). Given the current crises in Europe, these realists are validated in their pessimistic stance towards integration. To them, Europe is internally characterized by power asymmetries and egoistic, opportunistic, and self-interested actors. Actors with divergent security and economic interests and cost-benefit calculations, seeking for sovereignty and autonomy vis-à-vis other states. This is in particular the case for the Eastern European member states. According to neo-realists, the EU is externally confronted by revisionist powers such as Russia, Turkey, Iran, or China. This leads to a continuous and inescapable security dilemma. And there is little other to be expected than individual security policies in line with individual and mostly different *national* security interests (Mearsheimer 2001: 29–54). Nevertheless, some neo-realists did revise theory in the face of the 1990s and 2000s ongoing European integration process. According to these revisionists, EU member states may act together as an alliance or common actor in external affairs. They do so towards other main powers and in the face of challenges and threats. This is in line with Waltz's balance of power and Walt's balance of threat propositions (Waltz 1979: 102–128; Walt 1987: 17–50). Accordingly, the insight of these revisionist realists about a dual balancing behaviour of European states can be a fruitful theoretical alternative (Waever and Wivel 2018: 3–4). The internal dimension means balancing of EU member states against Germany trying to define the EU agenda, or acting unilaterally at the expense of the EU or other states. Balancing is not against Germany *as such*. The migration issue and Germany's demand for a European solution is an exemplary case. The external dimension is balancing together with Germany against competing powers outside the EU such as Russia. Or soft diplomatic balancing against the U.S. in order to get more autonomy within NATO.[3] The neo-realist dual balancing hypothesis helps to explain the origins of the EC/EU a balance of power configuration and rationality. It helps to make sense of the current transatlantic divide when it comes to burden-sharing within NATO. It helps to discuss opportunities as well as the limitations of the integration project in the so-called high politics issues security and defence. It enables to formulate expectable but rather pessimistic future scenarios in (EU)rope (see Zimmermann in this volume). But, neo-realism is too parsimonious and not adequate to understand the political dimension of the peace project (EU)rope, and German–French axis.

---

[3]For a revised neo-realist explanation of European integration in the realm of security and defence and the dual power balancing argument, see Hyde-Price (2012); Jones (2007: 18–56); Posen (2006); Rosato (2011); Rynning (2011); Wivel (1998, 2008); for a summary see Reichwein (2015).

German–French Relationship: The Promises of Classical Realism

Classical realism is quite different. The concept of history is not deterministic but dynamic. States' internal structure, interests, strategies, and behaviour can change over time. The changeful German–French relationship, a puzzle for most neo-realist thinking in terms of inescapable and perpetual security dilemmas (see Loriaux 1999: 355), is a case in point. It is to be distinguished from Mearsheimer's "[...] gloomy view of a Europe of states returning to its troublesome past [...]", namely an endless contest for power in order to guarantee survival under the conditions of anarchy, "[...] resulting not from any empirical evaluation of present-day Europe, but from a theory [...]" (Hoffmann 1995b: 281). First of all, classical realism differentiates between different states that are not functional alike, as Waltz (1979) argues. States are more or less satisfied, cooperative, or revisionist depending on structural modifiers such as history and political culture, geographical position, vulnerability because of economic interdependence, or domestic affairs. Secondly, neo-realists do not open the black box state in order to evaluate the internal characteristic of a state. Analyzing domestic politics and other (cognitive) factors driving and shaping a state's external behaviour (Reichwein 2012) is not on the neo-realist agenda. Germany is maybe the best example that the domestic level matters. Germany remains a *Mittelmacht*. But, is it still the same Germany over centuries? Mearsheimer does not differentiate between the empire (*Kaiserreich*), the Third Reich, and the Federal Republic in German history. Reading *Back to the Future*, you ask: "[...], is there really no difference between the revisionist imperial Germany in clumsy search of a world role, the rabid revolutionary Germany of Hitler, and the satisfied, cooperative and world-shy new united republic?" (Hoffmann 1995b: 284). Economic interdependence among industrial societies in welfare states, attractive economic and security institutions as magnets for member states (Hoffmann 1995b: 284–285) and the German–French center of gravity are sources of peace within (EU)rope. And given the historically proven inadequacy of military power and force in particular in Europe, you can state: "In real life, it makes a difference whether one is in, say, the Europe of rival alliances of 1914 and 1939, or the Europe of today" (Hoffmann 1995b: 283). Also in Paris, decision-makers did learn during the twentieth-century decades that "[...] today's Europe, and, in particular, Germany differ from the Europe and Germany of 1913 or 1938 [...]" (Hoffmann 1995b: 282). This was the precondition for German–French reconciliation and rapprochement after World War II and later cooperation and integration. Finally, classical realism focusses on the state, state interests, and state strategies (Mastanduno and Kapstein 1999). Statesmen and stateswomen, and domestic institutions and politics constitute the foreign policy decision-making process. The core classical realist insight is that foreign policy *is made* by individuals and governments who "[...] sit at the intersection of domestic and international political systems" (Lobell 2009: 56). Interests are a matter and subject of external pressure *and* domestic bargains, but not externally given. Classical realists do not assume that systemic constraints condition or even determine the behaviour of rational units fixed once for all. Classical realists assume that maximizing *influence* is the most important goal of states trying to shape international institutions and rules, and the regional environment they are embedded in and cannot escape (Brooks 1997). Accordingly, there are various options of rational responses to given challenges or opportunities *beyond* power balancing or regional hegemony-seeking. Accordingly, states are assumed by classical realists as innovative actors being able to learn, adjust, and modify and change interests and strategies (Pedersen 1998: 13–21). As the third part of the chapter illustrates, Germany and France throughout the history of the European integration process, and the way both deal with crises and go on with integration is a case in point through realist lens. To begin with, classical realism can explain crises. Realists classify disintegration dynamics, spill-backs, and fragmentation as integral parts of EU integration.

Looking Back, Moving Ahead: Explaining the EU in Motion and Crisis

The Interwar Idea: German–French Reconciliation and Europe

The first generation of European inter- and postwar classical realists such as Hans J. Morgenthau dealt—affirmatively—with the European Integration project. The key question was *how* rational and prudent governments can and should act and go on achieving a united and peaceful Europe. Go on in line with the "[…] objective and insuperable laws with inescapable consequences that governs politics […]" (Morgenthau 1954: 4). Morgenthau's original idea was a peaceful revision of Versailles, and close German–French relations and partnership. This dual leadership was based on a legal order provided by the League of Nations as the arena, international law as a functional tool serving the national interests of states and negotiations between former opponents of war. The result was the Treaty of Locarno (1925) and Rapallo (1922) about territories, the nonuse of force, and a system of war prevention. These means should serve a twofold end: peace and Germany's comeback in Europe. To most classical realists in the interwar period, peace between France and Germany was not only a bilateral but a European concern (Morgenthau 1929). The precondition was German–French reconciliation and rapprochement, Germany's reintegration into the international community and a shared political will to cooperation based on common interests (ibid.; see Andréani 1998; Loriaux 1999: 358). Unpacked, European institutions and the dual leadership should have been the robe of German rehabilitation and resocialization as a European power. A peaceful one pursuing national interests and influencing institutions. This failed in the 1930s because of a weak League without sanction mechanisms, reckless revisionism in imperial

Nazi Germany and fascist Italy, and the failed Western policy of Appeasement towards revisionist states.

The Postwar Roots of Diplomatic Europe: A "Collaborative" **Balance of Power**

After WWII, the Western states treated Germany different than in 1919. Realists did learn that international law cannot work and operate in the context of explosive power competition and rivalry among nations. But they did not give up a vision of a peaceful and integrated Europe. They just changed their opinion concerning *how* to achieve this. To most realists those days it was clear: Given the new distribution of power among European states in a divided Europe after 1945, it took something different in order to establish a postwar settlement. The task was twofold: Given Soviet military presence in Berlin, *containment* towards the Soviet Union (Kennan 1946/1947) was the strategy to respond to the new rising threat (Morgenthau 1951: 81–82). Given Germany's position in the midst of Europe, its population and industrial potential and natural superiority, and the unwillingness of France to accept this superiority (Morgenthau 1951: 76), there was another challenge to respond to.

The solution was threefold, and in line with classical realist suggestions to practitioners: to divide Germany and to deny West-German resources and allegiance to the Soviet Union; to restore West Germany to political and economic health through the Marshall Plan; and to restrain and *control* West Germany. The control worked by means of West Germany's integration into the West, and close German–French cooperation. And by restoring the double balance of power system: internally within Western Europe against West Germany, and externally as united and invigorated West vis-à-vis the Warsaw Pact (Morgenthau 1951: 77, 81, 84, 85). In other words: Realists argue in favour of a balance of power leading to an equilibrium in Europe (Morgenthau 1951: 77, 78, 83). *But*, this balance of power is not understood as a solely economic or military order. Or as a temporary and fragile stabilization of smoldering conflicts between states bringing actors into a power equilibrium by a permanent process of generating, evaluating and adjusting power capabilities in order to minimize the security dilemma. This balance of power was not understood as just a regulative regularity preventing one power gaining coercive hegemonic status over the other smaller powers. In this rather functional and narrow understanding, power is made to check power, a logic which did fail in the interwar period towards Nazi Germany. In fact, the balance of power is understood by classical realists as an effective *political* structure producing a status quo stability, but also providing a policy advice for governments leading to a *social* alive and *just* relationship among nations. A relationship based on the shared principles of sovereignty, coexistence, equality, self-determination leading to the preservation of stable peace. And the means to this aim is prudent diplomacy. The European diplomatic system (Calleo 2001, cited according to Rynning 2011: 29) of the eighteenth and nineteenth century is the realist archetype of a "collaborative balance of power" in the postwar period in Europe (Calleo 2009: 137, cited according to Rynning 2011: 31). The driving force behind is the common European history or "Europe's shared heritage" (ibid.), namely the "political collapse of Europe" (Hoffmann 1995a: 78). For Morgenthau, Calleo, and other classical realists, the balance of power is both: a functional regularity and institutionalized system of checks and balances. And a normative guidepost for governments (Morgenthau 1954: 184–201). From this perspective "the balance of power is the only available alternative to the domination of one state or group of states over the other" (Wolfers 1940, cited according to Scheuerman 2011: 30). And according to Wolfers, the balance of power in Europe "was the one and only way to limit the growth of German power" (ibid.).

West Germany became a member of the NATO in 1949 and of the EC founded in 1951. The argument was a very strategic one, and beneficial to all: *Kontrolle durch Einbindung* (control through integration). The aim was to "strengthen the West against the Soviet Union through closer partnership with West Germany" including a remilitarization of Germany and a rearmed Western Europe (Morgenthau 1951: 81–82). Through classical realist lens, this was the best way to ensure that the U.S. could intervene into European affairs. France was promised security guarantees. And West Germany was getting back its sovereignty step by step (Morgenthau 1951: 84–87, 1954: 497–498). It took the U.S. some time to convince France of the rearmament of West Germany. Hoffmann argues that it was "wily France's invention" (1995b: 283). In the long run, there was a win-win-win situation (Hyde-Price 2009: 1–24; Loriaux 1999: 357–358). Morgenthau cited a Speaker in the House of Commons, saying in 1946: "What we want to do is to make Germany so strong as to be able to frighten the Russians but not so strong as to make the French afraid" (Morgenthau 1951: 86). The aim was peace in Europe, and the solution of the German question after WWII was bringing West Germany back into shared power. The means, or price to pay from the French perspective, was "to use German power for the purposes of the over-all defense of Western Europe" (ibid.). In Hoffmann's words: "After the failure of a 'traditional' hostile approach to the solution of the 'German problem' [...]", there was a new shrewd European strategy: "[...] to 'balance' German power not by building a coalition *against* Germany but by bandwagoning (and cooperating) *with* Germany" (Hoffmann 1995b: 283). Morgenthau highlighted the end of a so often in history failed balance of power against Germany. Instead, a French-lead strategy "to draw Germany into its arms in order to disarm it and to make the superior strength of Germany innocuous" by means of the EC (Morgenthau 1954: 498) was the news strategy to handle Germany. He honoured Churchill for making a difficult endeavour and double task real: "to make Western Europe, and first of all the U.S., strong enough to be able to negotiate with the Russians successfully, but not so strong as to frighten the Russians into a war" (Morgenthau 1951: 87). The response to crises and conflicts in a divided Europe after WWII was the U.S. as pacifier (Joffe 1984). And a *balance of power* system directed by Washington. This strategy kept the Americans in, the Soviets out, and the Germans down. It did enable the U.S. to assist France and Great Britain to control West Germany and thereby to preserve the *Status Quo* of peaceful coexistence in a bipolar Cold War Europe. The question realists today are debating is whether to integrate and collaboratively balance Russia within a Pan-European order, or not. A Russia whose motives are rather unclear (see Götz 2015, 2018; Rynning 2015).

European Integration in Crisis: Diverging National Interests

U.S. security protection was the precondition which enables Germany, France, and the West-European states to cooperate from the 1950s on. And to integrate from a bureaucratic, economic, and technological Coal and Steal Community in the so-called low politics-fields such as agriculture, transport, or electricity into a political EU serving political purposes in the so-called high politics such as security and defence, currency or migration (Loriaux 1999: 355–359; Morgenthau 1954: 497–499). Nevertheless, since the 1950s the European integration process is characterized by spill-overs and spill-backs. Classical realists are not really surprised about this. They expect disintegration resulting from different national interests and a lack of political will to integrate. Common European institutions and interests in high politics issues are rather an exceptional case (Morgenthau 1964). In a realist world, the *national interest defined in terms of power* is assumed to guide political decision-making and action. The national interest is, and should be, the yardstick and compass for rational foreign policy makers (Morgenthau 1954: 5–8). But *what* is in the national interest of a state is not defined and fixed once for all. It is *rather* a matter of a particular period of history, and the political and cultural context in which a state is embedded: "The goals that might be pursued by nations in their foreign policy can run the whole gamut of objectives any nation has ever pursued or might possibly pursue" (Morgenthau 1954: 8–10).

The integration process is in no way a fast-selling item, working and going on just on the level of bureaucracy, technical cooperation, and economic trade. Out of a series of functional units, political unity will *not* grow organically (Morgenthau 1954: 498). According to classical realism, there are three preconditions for the success of the European peace project: a clearly defined distribution of power among EC/EU member states; the degree of unity among the member states in the high politics-fields, and the degree of divergency because of the different national interests; and the relations between member states and nonmembers, and with the U.S. (Morgenthau 1954: 498–499). The former becomes important because of the Brexit, the latter in a Trumpian age of protectionism. The realist message is: If the Europeans wanted to exploit the fruits of unification and institutionalization, "[…] the jump from national to European sovereignty must be made by an act of will" by political decisions in order to coordinate the divergent interests, and "[…]

to keep recalcitrant members in check" (Morgenthau 1964, cited according to Scheuerman 2010: 268). According to classical realists, European unification is desirable and necessary. But it is insufficient and it cannot flourish as long as there are no common institutions helping to generate collective policies. And as long as there is no political will of the governments and nations. And as long as nation-states oppose supranational and/or common decision-making procedures in the name of national interests. Italy, Hungary, or Poland and the lack of willingness to contribute to Germany's suggested migration policy is a case in point here. The second-generation realist key figure Stanley Hoffmann did deal with this realist concerns during the Cold War. He was influenced by the so-called *Eurosklerose* in the 1960s. French President Charles de Gaulle and his administration did oppose the decision-making process in the European Council of Ministers because of French national interests of serving the French agricultural sector (Hoffmann 1995a: 89). Hoffmann's categories and basic assumptions about the fate of the nation-state (Hoffmann 1966, 1995a) and the diversity among European states making European integration that difficult helps us to expect the worst and to explain the EU in times of crisis.

Migration, Russia, Brexit: Diverging National Situations

According to Hoffmann, the key actor in the European integration process is the sovereign nation-state. The states share, pool and/or delegate, but do not give away sovereignty to Brussels institutions (Hoffmann 1995a: 72, 102; see also Rynning 2011: 28–29). The nation-state is constituted by *nationalism* in a sense of the amalgamation of historical tradition and legacy, territory, culture and language, and the idea of the defence of the nation. The drama with nationalism is its destructive part in a sense of a nationalist policies leading to conflicts at the expense of integration and peace (Hoffmann 1995a: 71, 76–77). Russia's Crimea annexation motivated by geopolitics, irredentism, and status aspirations are cases in point (Götz and Merlen 2019: 135–137; Piontkovsky 2015). Hoffmann also introduced the realist concept of the *national situation* of a state. The *diversity* of the national situations of states is the insuperable condition of all policy decisions and choices in the EC/EU (Hoffmann 1995a: 76, 79, 80, 97). The national situation is constituted by the following factors: power capabilities in terms of territory, population, economic resources compared to other competing states; domestic politics and institutions (Hoffmann 1995a: 72, 92); a state's geographical position and relations and formal commitments to neighbor states and security claims coming along with this (Hoffmann 1995a: 73, 93); a state's *national consciousness* in a sense of having vital interests and a kind of assessment of losses and gains when cooperating with other states (Hoffmann 1995a: 75, 84); social and political culture (Hoffmann 1995a: 75); history and historical legacy (Hoffmann 1995a: 93). And there is *national sensitivity*. According to Hoffmann, the national situations make European states different.

The German attitude towards the EC/EU after WWII was and still is positive. German EU policies is a mixture of supranational and intergovernmental approaches, and a balancing act between Washington and Paris. U.S. hegemony in Europe during the Cold War was assessed and accepted by the West-German governments as the only way to get back what Grieco (1995) calls *voice opportunity* within Euro-Atlantic structures, and welfare (Hoffmann 1995a: 77, 80, 82, 83, 90, 93). "For West-Germany, integration meant a leap from opprobrium and impotence to respectability and equal rights" (Hoffmann 1995a: 93). There is continuity after 1990 (see Reichwein 2019). But even Germany steps out of line. During the Balkan Wars, the EU was suffering German unilateralism in the issue of recognition of Croatia and Slovenia (Crawford 1996; see Reichwein 2019). British conceptions of Europe after joining the EC in 1973 was rather defensive and pessimistic. It is a former world and nuclear great power's strategy of persistently downplaying or opposing common policies emanating from either the supranational Brussels authorities or proposed by other member states. London was rather interested in widening the EU because of the free trade zone, but not deepening. And it resisted any supranational decision-making and the extension of majority vote in high politics (Hoffmann 1995a: 90). The British and the Eastern European member states' core aim is to maintain close ties with the U.S. within NATO (Hoffmann 1995a: 97). A consequence of this was the division of the EU in the Iraq War in 2003 (Crowe 2003; Hill 2004; Mouritzen 2006). The Brexit is therefore not surprising at all. It can be classified as a reaction to the EU's labour market policy and migration crisis. It is also a response to Germany's claimed leadership role, coercive diplomacy and pressure to ensure compliance from other member states in the field of the Euro and Greek crisis, sanctioning Russia, and migration policy aiming for a common European burden-sharing. This burden-sharing is against British interests and will. And it simply overburdens states such as Czech Republic, Hungary, Poland, or Croatia (Bulmer and Paterson 2017: 213; Hellmann 2016: 7–9; see Zimmermann in this volume). And France, *La Grande Nation* with interests in Europe and overseas? Paris did bemoan and struggle with U.S. hegemony over Europe during the Cold War. It did oppose U.S. unilateralism in the Iraq War. And it tries to prevent German domination of the common decision-making process in Europe. Actually, France's aim after WW II was to play the single leadership role in Europe, and to shape European affairs. But, Paris did fear a close German-British leadership which was to be prevented by the strategy of close cooperation and dual leadership with West- and later unified Germany. A leadership based on both supranational and intergovernmental methods (Hoffmann 1995a: 78, 79, 82, 85–87, 93, 94) and balancing the U.S. and Great Britain. Given the German–French catalyst of European Integration (Calleo 1998; van Ham 1999), the French governments did succeed at the expense of exclusive leadership, but in line with and in terms of French security concerns and claims (Hoffmann 1995a: 93).

The Logic of Diversity

What are the implications for EU institutions and EU policies? It is the logic of diversity, and the effects of national differences (Hoffmann 1995a: 94) that characterize the integration process. This leads to a "permanent confrontation of national interests of the units engaged in an attempt to integrate" (Hoffmann 1995a: 98), and to a "logic of competition" (Hoffmann 1995a: 101). According to Hoffmann, there is a "dialectic of fragmentation and unity" (ibid.), of spill-overs and spill-backs, of disintegration and integration. In contrast to a *logic of integration*, the diversity within Europe sets limits for spill over-dynamics. It limits and curtails the state governments' freedom of action in particular in the high politics-fields (Hoffmann 1995a: 84):

> The logic of diversity [...] suggests that, in areas of key importance to the national interest, nations prefer the self-controlled uncertainty of national self-reliance, to the uncontrolled uncertainty of the blending process [...] The logic of diversity implies that losses on one vital issue are not compensated for by gains on other issues (especially not on other less vital issues): nobody wants to be fooled. (ibid.)

HOW TO KEEP (EU)ROPE TOGETHER: THE GERMAN–FRENCH AXIS

How can the EU deal with diversity? How can it respond to challenges and crises? And how can the EU go on with the integration process? Classical realism helps again. Third-generation European realists suggest a solution which is in line with a realist analysis of the history of the European integration: German–French *cooperative hegemony* (Loriaux 1999; Pedersen 1998: 34–67, 2002; Waever and Wivel 2018: 3). Germany and France are the most powerful states in Europe. They share the same security concerns such as terrorism. And both are faced by military threats such as formerly Soviet Union and today's Russia (Calleo 1998: 5). Both are immigration countries interested in coordinating migration and refugee policies. There are some more motives making Germany and France defenders of a crisis-ridden (EU)rope. According to Loriaux (1999: 375–379), French and German leaders have what classical realists define as leadership qualities of rational, moral, and prudent statesmen. They support the integration process because it is built on institutions serving their individual interests in the realm of money, trade, and security. And they support integration because it is built on norms of "common life" becoming customary commitment in both nations. The cultivation of common institutions and norms is a circular thing: "The Europeans - above all the French and Germans - embrace integration because they fear that the prudential norms they have developed in the postwar period will become inoperative if the pan-European ideal loses strength" (Loriaux 1999: 378). In Loriaux's understanding, Germany and France are bound to cooperate, lead, and integrate. Integration is a one-way road and another realist self-fulfilling prophecy. German–French peculiar relationship is a matter of historical experiences, legacy, and learning (Calleo 1998: 10). Both build a common destiny (*Schicksalsgemeinschaft*). Even though German–French history is characterized by such violent animosity (Loriaux 1999: 355–358), the trauma of 1871, 1914, and 1940 and the fear of another mutual suicidal competition are the foundation of the "*integrationist enterprise*" (Loriaux 1999: 379). France's belief that "only full participation of Germany in the European construction makes it possible to look with serenity on the inevitable reunification of the two Germanies"[4] is part of the French political culture. And it is in the national interest of Germany to deepen and widen the EU. This is a win-win-scenario on the part of both states that explains integration and makes it the German–French political project (Calleo 1998: 1, 4–5).

The German–French Engine of Integration

Germany and France build the so-called "engine of European integration" (Calleo 1998: 1; Loriaux 1999: 360), and the center of gravity (van Ham 1999). The German–French partnership becomes more and more important in times of crisis: "Since the end of the Cold War, the EU's capacity to meet its new challenges depends heavily on whether the partnership remains vital and durable" (Calleo 1998: 1). This dual leadership succeeded to solve the German Question in postwar Europe and in the early 1990s. Germany and France found a compromise on how to end the Balkan Wars (Loriaux 1999: 368–369). Since the late 1990s, there is a Franco-German political vision and an ambitious program of deepening and widening the EU (Tewes 2002: 81–139): Realists make sense of this: "[...] integration should serve as the essential anchor of stability for the continent as a whole. This process should lead to an ever growing EU, accepting transfers of sovereignty but continuing to build on the existing nation-states and falling short of turning into a new statehood entity. The Union should be opened up to new members [...]. Russia should take part, recognizing her dual nature as a European and global power" (Andréani 1998, cited according to Calleo 1998: 5). Germany and France responded U.S. attempts to divide the EU during Iraq War. One may ask: Will Russia manage to divide the EU? Despite challenges and crises, it seems that Germany and France will go on, even though it is an "ambitious integrationist enterprise" (Loriaux 1999: 379). And they can go on because dual leadership is accepted by third states: "[...] the Franco-German relationship [...] has become so central and so obvious, [...]. Third countries [...] recognize it as a key element to the stability of Europe and the conduct of European Union's policies [...]" (Andréani 1998, cited according to Calleo 1998: 3).

---

[4]French former President Francois Mitterand in an interview with the Le Nouvel Observateuer, January 1996 (cited according to Loriaux 1999: 372/373).

German–French Cooperative Hegemony

Germany and France build what Pedersen calls an EU institutional embedded "*dual cooperative hegemony*", or directional hegemony (Pedersen 1998: 195–208, 2002; see Waever and Wivel 2018: 3). Both reflect their political and economic but military limited power capabilities. Therefore, both have the political will to share power with the privileged partner. And both agree upon the prudent strategy to embed the dual leadership within European institutions, and to act multilaterally. Both seek for *influence* to (re)shape the regional environment, concretely EU institutions and rules instead of maximizing autonomy. Given these conditions, the European integration process was, is and will be *in* the national interest of both for very different reasons and calculations outlined in this chapter. Both define the EU agenda, and thereby increase influence and power. This is what Pedersen calls *tactical gradualism* (Pedersen 1998: 34–67). This German–French magnetic center of gravity is attractive for smaller states to join. These states follow voluntarily for different reason such as economic or security claims. It is a kind of bandwagoning for profit. Neither Poland nor Hungary or Croatia oppose German–French leadership as such. These states just oppose German dictated migration policy because they lack economic resources or the political will and culture to contribute. In general, Germany and France are successful in convincing the other EU member states about the benefits of European integration. What makes the states following is that they do not feel marginalized because they have voice opportunity within the institutions. By doing concessions by strategies of cooptation and institutionalization of power, Germany and France prevent uncertainty and fear among EU member states, and a balance of power coalition against the center. Instead, the tandem gains trust, loyalty, and following (see Pedersen 1998: 1–12, 195–208). The best case scenario is that all member states are, for very different reasons, satisfied with the given power distribution and the individual position within the setting (Pedersen 1998: 34–67). Great Britain is the first exception. It will lose voice opportunity and influence, and becoming isolated. The German–French tandem makes the EU what the EU is (Hyde-Price 2009: 25–50; Loriaux 1999: 360–374; Pedersen 1998: 195–208). Not only realists ask: Who else could do this job?

German–French Future Agenda

To cope with the current crisis requires that Germany together with France will go on leading the EU in the future (Waever and Wivel 2018: 3). An institutionalized and economic strong German–French leadership is the bulwark against economic chaos within the EU. Through classical realist lens, it is up to Germany and France to define the rules of economic games. And to launch a new Marshall Plan in order to intensify economic cooperation and interdependence within Europe. This is in particular necessary in South and Eastern Europe to enable these member states to solve the problems of labor *e*migration and to contribute to the common European migration policy. And it is up to both dealing with Russia in the economic and security realm. The core aim and objective must be to revive the old 1990s idea of a *Pan*-European security architecture (Haslam 1998; Joetze 2006) including Russia and the Ukraine.

A regional system in which diplomatic rules and bargains resting on a balance of power are formalized and guaranteed. A community which binds its members and rules and guides the behavior of the member states (Waever and Wivel 2018: 1–2). This would make the EU again the unique realist archetype of a cooperative and *integrative balance of power system* (Wivel 1998; Waever and Wivel 2018: 3–4). This would equip and provide the EU with "[…] a capacity for power-sharing vis-à-vis smaller states in a region, for power aggregation on the part of the predominant regional state(s) and for commitment to a long-term regionalist policy strategy" (Pedersen 2002: 684). This would lead to a *rebalanced* order and stability, welfare, security, and peace in Europe. And this would make German–French dual hegemony even stronger.

Conclusions

The core argument of this chapter was twofold: First of all, that looking back and knowing about the history of the European integration process helps to understand, explain, and deal with current crises. Neo-realists are wrong expecting crisis generally to undermine and threaten the EU. Classical realism teaches us that crises have been part of successful integration. Secondly, that German–French cooperation and dual leadership is the condition and requirement of the ongoing integration process. This shared leadership will be key to whether or not the EU member states are able to handle future crises, and to move on, or not. The European integration process was launched in order to check and control the former pariah state Germany by means of a rational strategy of integration (Loriaux 1999: 371–372). Throughout the decades, the geopolitical setting, challenges, and threats and in particular Germany's role (Bulmer and Paterson 2017; Hellmann 2016; Reichwein 2019) have changed. Germany has become a power combining political stability, economic strength, and other power capabilities with historical legacy, moral responsibility, and coercive diplomacy in order to deal with new challenges and crises in EUrope. Germany has become more assertive, but: "Germany does shape the future of Europe without waking old demons because the policy remains EU-centered" (Waever and Wivel 2018: 6). Germany has underpinned not undermined European integration process since the 1990s by using its growing power. From a classical realist perspective focusing on the state, strategy, and influence, this is a rational strategy: "European integration has allowed Germany to rise peacefully without provoking a counter-balance, but, by allowing this development, the process of integration has become the most important outcome for Germany" (Waever and Wivel 2018: 7). It seems to be clear and widely shared: Germany is the power center in Europe. It will use the power vacuum left by the self-marginalization of a more isolationist U.S., and by Great Britain after the Brexit to maximize its influence. Leadership is in line with German economic and security interests, but also with responsibility. Germany is an interest-driven (Bulmer and Paterson 2017), "grown-up" and "self-confident" (Hellmann 2011) but also normative power. A power playing the decisive role as a "shaping power" within a crisis-ridden EUrope (Hellmann 2016; see also Reichwein 2019). A power fulfilling a 'chief facilitator' in the Ukraine crisis (Waever and Wivel 2018: 6) aiming for restoring a balance of power order (Waever and Wivel 2018) and to keep EUrope together. An imperial Germany in the Bismarckian or Wilhelminian tradition trying to dominate the continent is out of any imagination. A DExit, leaving France alone, would be a worst case scenario for the future of the EU. But not EUrope lead by Germany abreast with France. This is what European history teaches us so far.

References

Anderson, J. J., & Goodman, J. (1993). Mars or Minerva? A United Germany in a Post-Cold War Europe. In R. Keohane, J. S. Nye, & S. Hoffman (Eds.), *International Institutions and State Strategies in Europe, 1989–1991* (pp. 23–62). Cambridge, MA: Harvard University Press.

Andréani, G. (1998). The Franco-German Relationship in a New Europe. In D. P. Calleo & E. R. Staal (Eds.), *Europe's Franco-German Engine* (pp. 21–35). Washington D.C.: Brookings Institution Press.

Baumann, R., Rittberger, V., & Wagner, W. (2001). Neorealist Foreign Policy Theory. In V. Rittberger (Ed.), *German Foreign Policy Since Unification. An Analysis of Foreign Policy* Continuity *and Change* (pp. 37–67). Manchester: Manchester University Press.

Brooks, S. G. (1997). Dueling Realisms. *International Organization, 51*(3), 445–477.

Bulmer, S., & Paterson, W. (1996). Germany in the European Union: Gentle Giant or Emergent Leader? *International Affairs, 72*(1), 9–32.

Bulmer, S., & Paterson, W. (2017). Germany and the Crisis: Asset or Liability? In D. Dinan, N. Nurgent, & W. E. Paterson (Eds.), *The European Union in Crisis* (pp. 212–232). London: Palgrave.

Calleo, D. (1998). Introduction. In D. P. Calleo & E. R. Staal (Eds.), *Europe's Franco-German Engine* (pp. 1–19). Washington, DC: Brookings Institution Press.

Calleo, D. (2001). *Rethinking Europe's Future*. Princeton: Princeton University Press.

Calleo, D. (2009). *Follies of Power: America's Unipolar Fantasy*. Cambridge: Cambridge University Press.

Collard-Wexler, S. (2006). Integration Under Anarchy: Neorealism and the European Union. *The European Journal of International Relations, 12*(3), 398–432.

Crawford, B. (1996). Explaining Defection from International Cooperation: Germany's Unilateral Recognition of Croatia. *World Politics, 48*(4), 482–521.

Crowe, B. (2003). A Common European Foreign Policy After Iraq? *International Affairs, 79*(3), 533–546.

Götz, E. (2015). It's Geopolitics, Stupid: Explaining Russia's Ukraine Policy. *Global Affairs, 1*(1), 3–10.

Götz, E. (2018). Strategic Imperatives, Status Aspirations, or Domestic Interests? Explaining Russia's Nuclear Weapons Policy. *International Politics, 56*(6), 810–827.
Götz, E., & Merlen, C. R. (2019). Russia and the Question of World Order. *European Politics and Society, 20*(2), 133–153.
Grieco, J. M. (1988). Anarchy and the Limits of Cooperation: A Realist Critique of the Newest Liberal Institutionalism. *International Organization, 42*(3), 485–507.
Grieco, J. M. (1995). The Maastricht Treaty, Economic and Monetary Union and the Neo-Realist Research Programme. *Review of International Studies, 21*(1), 21–40.
Haslam, J. (1998). Russia's Seat at the Table: A Place Denied or a Place Delayed? *International Affairs, 74*(1), 119–130.
Hellmann, G. (2011). Normatively Disarmed, But Self-Confident. German Foreign Policy 20 Years After Reunification. *Internationale Politik Global Edition, 3*, 45–51.
Hellmann, G. (2016). Germany's World: Power and Followership in a Crisis-Ridden Europe. *Global Affairs, 2*(1), 3–20.
Hill, C. (2004). Renationalizing or Regrouping? EU Foreign Policy Since 11 September 2001. *Journal of Common Market Studies, 42*(1), 143–163.
Hoffmann, S. (1966). Obstinate or Obsolete? The Fate of the Nation State and the Case of Western Europe. *Daedalus, 95*(3), 862–915.
Hoffmann, S. (1990). Reflections on the "German Question". *Survival, 32*(4), 291–298.
Hoffmann, S. (1995a). Obstinate or Obsolete? France, European Integration, and the Fate of the Nation State. In S. Hoffmann (Ed.), *The European Sisyphus: Essays on Europe, 1964–1994* (pp. 71–106). Boulder: Westview Press.
Hoffmann, S. (1995b). Balance, Concert, Anarchy, or None of the Above. In S. Hoffmann (Ed.), *The European Sisyphus: Essays on Europe, 1964–1994* (pp. 281–300). Boulder: Westview Press.
Hyde-Price, A. (2009). *Germany and European Order. Enlarging NATO and the EU*. Manchester: Manchester University Press.
Hyde-Price, A. (2012). Neorealism: A Structural Approach to CSDP. In X. Kurowska & F. Breuer (Eds.), *Explaining the EU's Common Security and Defence Policy. Theory in Action* (pp. 16–40). London: Palgrave.
Joetze, G. (2006). Pan-European Stability: Still a Key Task? In: H.-W. Maull (Ed.), *Germany's Uncertain Power. Foreign Policy of the Berlin Republic* (pp. 152–165). Basingstoke: Palgrave Macmillan.
Joffe, J. (1984). Europe's American Pacifier. *Foreign Policy, 54*, 64–82.
Jones, S. (2007). *The Rise of European Security Cooperation*. Cambridge: Cambridge University Press.
Kaelberer, M. (1997). Hegemony, Dominance or Leadership? Explaining Germany's Role in European Monetary Cooperation. *European Journal of International Relations, 3*(1), 35–60.
Kennan, G. F. (alias X) (1946/1947). The Sources of Soviet Conduct. *Foreign Affairs, 25*(4), 566–582.
Lobell, S. (2009). Threat Assessment, the State, and Foreign Policy: A Neoclassical Realist Model. In S. E. Lobell, N. M. Ripsman, & J. W. Taliaferro (Eds.), *Neoclassical Realism, The State, and Foreign Policy.* (pp. 42–74). Cambridge: Cambridge University Press.
Loriaux, M. (1999). Realism and Reconciliation: France, Germany, and the European Union. In E. B. Kapstein & M. Mastanduno (Eds.), *Unipolar Politics. Realism and*

State Strategies After the Cold War (pp. 354–384). New York: Columbia University Press.
Markovits, A., Reich, S., & Westermann, X. (1996). Germany: Hegemonic Power and Economic Giant? *Review of International Political Economy, 3*(4), 698–727.
Mastanduno, M. & Kapstein, E. B. (1999). Realism and State Strategies After the Cold War. In E. B. Kapstein & M. Mastanduno (Eds.), *Unipolar Politics: Realism and State Strategies After the Cold War* (pp. 1–27). New York: Columbia University Press.
Mearsheimer, J. (1990). Back to the Future: Instability in Europe After the Cold War. *International Security, 15*(4), 5–56.
Mearsheimer, J. (2001). *The Tragedy of Great Power Politics*. New York: Norton.
Mearsheimer, J. (2010). Why Is Europe Peaceful Today? *European Political Science, 9*, 387–397.
Mearsheimer, J. (2014). Why the Ukraine Crisis Is the West's Fault: The Liberal Delusions That Provoked Putin. Foreign *Affairs, 93*(5), 77–89.
Morgenthau, H. J. (1929). Stresemann als Schöpfer der deutschen Völkerrechtspolitik. *Die Justiz, 3*, 169–176.
Morgenthau, H. J. (1951). Germany: The Political Problem. In H. J. Morgenthau (Ed.), *Germany and the Future of Europe* (pp. 76–88). Chicago: Chicago University Press.
Morgenthau, H. J. (1954). *Politics Among Nations: The Struggle for Power and Peace* (2nd ed.). New York: Knopf.
Morgenthau, H. J. (1964). The Future of Europe. *New York Times Magazine*.
Mouritzen, H. (2006). Choosing Side in the European Iraq Conflict: A Test for New Geo-Political Theory. *European Security, 15*(2), 137–163.
Otero-Iglesias, M. & Zimmermann, H. (2016). A Benign Hegemon: Germany's European Vocation. In H. Zimmermann & A. Dür (Eds.), *Key Controversies in European Integration* (2nd ed.) (pp. 243–250). London: Palgrave.
Pedersen, T. (1998). *Germany, France and the Integration of Europe: A Realist Interpretation*. London: Pinter.
Pedersen, T. (2002). Cooperative Hegemony: Power, Ideas and Institutions in Regional Integration. *Review of International Studies, 28*(4), 677–696.
Piontkovsky, A. (2015). Putin's Russia as a Revisionist Power. *Journal on Baltic Security, 1*, 6–13.
Posen, B. R. (2006). European Union Security and Defense Policy: Response to Unipolarity? *Security Studies, 15*(2), 149–186.
Reichwein, A. (2012). The Tradition of Neoclassical Realism. In A. Toje & B. Kunz (Eds.), *Neoclassical Realism in European Politics: Bringing Power Back In* (pp. 30–60). Manchester: Manchester University Press.
Reichwein, A. (2015). Realism and European Foreign Policy: Promises and Shortcomings. In K. E. Jørgensen, et al. (Eds.), *The SAGE Handbook of European Foreign Policy* (pp. 99–120). London u.a.: Sage.
Reichwein, A. (2019). Germany's Growing Power in Europe: From Multilateral Collectivism Towards Re-Nationalization and Destabilization? In R. Belloni, P. Viotti, & V. Della Sala (Eds.), *Fear and Uncertainty in Europe: The Return to Realism?* (pp. 85–108). London: Palgrave Macmillan.
Rosamond, B. (2016). Brexit and the Problem of European Disintegration. *Journal of Contemporary European Research, 12*(4), 864–871.

Rosato, S. (2011). Europe's Troubles. Power Politics and the State of the European Project. *International Security, 35*(4), 45–86.
Rynning, S. (2005). Return of the Jedi: Realism and the Study of the European Union. *Politique Européenne, 3*(17), 10–33.
Rynning, S. (2011). Realism and the Common Security and Defence Policy. *Journal of Common Market Studies, 49*(1), 23–42.
Rynning, S. (2015). The False Promise of Continental Concert: Russia, the West and the Necessary Balance of Power. *International Affairs, 91*(3), 539–552.
Scheuerman, W. (2010). The (Classical) Realist Vision of Global Reform. *International Theory, 2*(2), 246–282.
Scheuerman, W. (2011). *The Realist Case for Global Reform*. Cambridge, UK: Polity Press.
Simón, L. (2017). Neorealism, Security Cooperation, and Europe's Relative Gains Dilemma. *Security Studies, 26*(2), 185–212.
Tewes, H. (2002). *Germany, Civilian Power and the New Europe. Enlarging NATO and the EU*. Basingstoke and Houndmills: Palgrave Macmillan.
Van Ham, P. (1999). Europe's Precarious Centre: Franco-German Co-operation and the CFSP. *European Security, 8*(4), 1–26.
Waever, O., & Wivel, A. (2018). The Power of Peaceful Change: The Crisis of the European Union and the Rebalancing of Europe's Regional Order. *International Studies Review, 20*(2), 317–325.
Walt, S. (1987). *The Origins of Alliances*. Ithaca, NY: Cornell University Press.
Waltz, K. N. (1979). *Theory of International Politics*. New York: McGraw-Hill.
Waltz, K. N. (1993). The Emerging Structure of International Politics. *International Security, 18*(2), 44–79.
Waltz, K. N. (2000). Structural Realism After the Cold War. *International Security, 25*(1), 5–41.
Wessels, W. (2001). Germany in Europe: Return of the Nightmare or Towards an Engaged Germany in a New Europe? In D. Webber (Ed.), *New Europe, new Germany, Old Foreign Policy? German Foreign Policy Since Unification* (pp. 107–116). London: Cass.
Wivel, A. (1998). New Threats and Old Dilemmas: European Integration in the International System. In A. Wivel (Ed.), *Explaining European Integration* (pp. 166–189). Copenhagen: University Press.
Wivel, A. (2008). Balancing Against Threats or Bandwagoning with Power? Europe and the Transatlantic Relationship after the Cold War. *Cambridge Review of International Affairs, 21*(3), 289–305.
Wolfers, A. (1940). Armistice Day Address. *Yale Alumni Review, 4*(8), 5.
Zelikov, P. (1992). The New Concert of Europe. *Survival, 34*(2), 12–30.
Zimmer, M. (1997). Return of the Mittellage? The Discourse of the Centre in German Foreign Policy. *German Politics, 6*(1), 23–38.

CHAPTER 5

Neorealism

Hubert Zimmermann

INTRODUCTION

Since at least a decade, the EU seems to stumble from one crisis into the next. This sorry state of affairs does not really come as a surprise to neorealist theorists. In fact, it appears to validate their skeptical stance with regard to the durability of institutionalized cooperation among states. As consequence of this skepticism, neorealism traditionally has given short shrift to the phenomenon of the postwar European integration project. The neglect was mutual since EU scholars regarded their object of study as major argument for the obsolescence of theories based on the materiality of power. Antje Wiener et al. (2018) hardly mentioned the word "neorealism" in their widely used textbook on theories of European Integration. The neorealist emphasis on the structural constraints imposed by anarchy on the actors in the international system, on the dominant role of states in this system, and on the all-important consequences of power asymmetries did not sit well with the multifaceted emergence and the complicated workings of the Union. Nor did it fit with its pervasively legalized polity, its emphasis on consensus-building and trust, and its denunciation of pure power politics. This incompatibility marginalized neorealism's contribution to EU studies. Despite its enormous and rising prominence as IR theory since the mid-1970s, it played a small role in early interpretations of European integration.

H. Zimmermann (✉)
Philipps-University of Marburg, Marburg, Germany
e-mail: hubert.zimmermann@uni-marburg.de

© The Author(s) 2021
M. Riddervold et al. (eds.), *The Palgrave Handbook of EU Crises*, Palgrave Studies in European Union Politics,
https://doi.org/10.1007/978-3-030-51791-5_5

When the end of the Cold War dissolved the geopolitical constellation that had forced the EU's current member states under the protective and paternalistic umbrella of competing superpowers, prominent neorealists expected a progressive withering away of European integration. They had explained the advance of European integration in the postwar decades as a reaction to the more or less benevolent prodding of the hegemons and as search for security in an alliance with a dominant power (bandwagoning). Simultaneously, in the Western alliance, the deepening of European integration could also be seen as an attempt to preserve the autonomy of European states in this alliance. However, after the end of bipolarity these conditions did not apply anymore. Not only was the common enemy, the Soviet empire, disintegrating, with many of the shattered pieces actually seeking admission to the EU. Furthermore, the American hegemon slowly loosened its grip, reducing its military presence and pivoting openly towards Asia. In a series of widely quoted articles, neorealists claimed that the time-bound rationalities that had underpinned the European project would give way to a dissolution of the ties that united hegemons and followers, as well as the followers among themselves (Waltz 1993; Mearsheimer 1990, 1994; Layne 1993). European integration had lost its rationale.

None of these predictions held much water in the 1990s and 2000s. When the EU undertook a quantum leap with the ratification of the Maastricht Treaty, the theory was unable to explain this phenomenon. The supposed new hegemon, Germany, gave away the core instrument of its power, the Deutsche Mark. Germany also continued to accept strict limits on its military potential while at the same time placing its weight firmly behind the idea of pooling European defense capabilities. The EU, on the other hand, despite its economic potential, showed few signs of equipping itself with the attributes of a superpower. These developments directly contradicted the core claims of eminent neorealists who had expected a return to power politics in Europe with the end of the constraints caused by the dependence of EU member states on protection by the United States. Despite the spectacular deepening and the no less spectacular widening of the Union, most neorealist scholars, after this brief flurry of interest, continued to mention the EU only in passing. As Collard-Wexler wrote, the EU remained "dreadfully undertheorized" (2006: 398) in neorealist thought about international politics (see also Pollack 2001).

However, the claims of the obsolescence of the nation state uttered by enthusiastic supporters of supranational governance at the turn of the millennium had to endure a massive challenge emanating from the rising nationalism of the 2010s. National interests and power politics, core concepts of realist thought (see Reichwein in this volume) dominate the discourse of global politics. The EU, somewhat reluctantly, has acknowledged these global dynamics and tries to adapt to them, although its strategic autonomy is still in its infancy. In addition to the permanent state of crisis within the Union since almost two decades, neorealists are not surprised by such shortcomings and the crises from which they result. This is what the theory predicted after all, and it is quite likely that the state-centered concepts of neorealism might experience a revival. As the future direction of European integration appears to switch from widening and deepening to shrinking and unravelling, neorealism might indeed become one of the most prominent theories of disintegration, as Ben Rosamond (2016: 865) speculated. The theory offers a very straightforward account of disintegration dynamics, especially compared to traditional theories of European integration which, to varying degrees, are rather optimistic about the prospects of the EU (Webber 2019a). Neorealism also seems less ambiguous than the most prominent current theory of disintegration, post-functionalism, which argues that politicized identity dynamics create a constraining dissensus which ultimately may lead to less integration (Hooghe and Marks 2009). Such identity dynamics, however, can be quite unstable and unevenly distributed across countries, as Eurobarometer polls and the European Parliamentary elections of May 2019 show. Neorealism offers a far more radical account, claiming sustained pressure toward disintegration.

This contribution will deal with this claim. It will first briefly sketch the core concepts of neorealism with respect to crisis, change and continuity in the EU. I will then look at how these concepts were used to explain some of the most important recent instances of crises in the EU, i.e., the Ukraine conflict, the euro crisis, and Brexit/migration crisis. Finally, the explanatory potential of neorealism in the face of crises in the EU will be evaluated.

Neorealism and Crisis in the EU

The central tenets of neorealism are so well-known that they need not be repeated at length in this article. Put briefly, in the neorealist world the international system is structured by the logic of anarchy which forces rationally acting states to secure their survival through the pursuit of power politics relative to other states (Waltz 1979). The core variable explaining the behavior of states, the central actors in the system, is the "distribution of relative power capabilities" (Hyde-Price 2012: 18). Therefore, it seems to constitute an instance of anomalous and sub-optimal behavior by states to give up power resources as well as to surrender their autonomy to the imperatives of an intrusive international organization such as the EU. In the long run, such behavior will be self-destructive. Predictions of this kind are stressed particularly by the offensive variant of neorealism which expects states to continue their pursuit of power even after they reach a secure position (Mearsheimer 2003). Defensive realists, on the other hand, argue that at such a point states will seek to maintain their position in the system since the cost of expansionary policies will be getting progressively higher, ending in a self-destructive spiral (Waltz 2000). Nonetheless, states still will strive to preserve their capacity of autonomous action vis-à-vis other states. Thus, both offensive and defensive neorealism do not expect international institutions to have sustained independent effects and to be stable in a longer term perspective.

In the case of the EU, it is important to stress that these neorealist predictions have an external, global, and an internal, regional dimension. In the external dimension, the EU as a collective reacts to macro-developments in the international system. European states will cooperate in the face of an external, superior threat and try to balance it (Rosato 2011), for example during the Cold War, but not in the absence of such a threat. This balancing behavior could be either "soft" via non-military, diplomatic or economic measures, or "hard," involving the creation of rival military capabilities (Walt 2011: 115–123). In the internal, regional dimension, power politics structures political conflict within the EU. The focus is on the dynamics of relations between big and small EU member states. These two dimensions are not clearly separated in most analyzes inspired by or critical of neorealism; they privilege either the global or the regional systemic level (but see: Simón 2017). Actually, as will be shown later in the empirical examples, often the neorealist logic works in opposing directions, depending on whether the referent object is the EU as unified actor in the global arena, or its internal dynamics. Thus, an external crisis with a rising and aggressive power might suggest balancing behavior by the EU as a whole, and enhanced cooperation among the member states, while at the same time a neorealist perspective focused on internal consequences would stress the different interests of these states and therefore expect more conflict. As test for neorealist hypotheses derived from an external crisis, the Ukraine conflict will be used. This conflict revitalized the perception of a fundamentally threatening Russia and thus might have triggered a balancing strategy by the EU focused on enhanced defense cooperation.

The most existential EU crises of recent times, however, undoubtedly have their origins in internal developments. To neorealists this reflects the return of intra-European power politics, made possible by the progressive retrenchment of the United States as external moderator (Mearsheimer 2010). They furthermore claim that as soon as European integration reached a certain threshold, threatening the autonomy and ultimately the very substance of European states, disintegrating dynamics were likely. Neorealists such as Seth Jones (2003) predicted that the late nineteenth-century inner-European security dilemma would reemerge as a consequence of American retrenchment and the rise of Germany. This would cause balancing and bandwagoning behavior, i.e., either smaller states band together to forge an alliance against potential hegemons or they align with stronger powers to protect their existence (Schweller 1994). Such a situation would underline the importance of relative gains among competing European powers. Given the economic preponderance of Germany, states such as France and Italy would probably try to forge a balancing coalition, whereas smaller countries might ally (bandwagon) with Germany. Particularly in such a scenario, the neorealist concept of relative gains becomes relevant. Scholars such as Robert Gilpin (1981) and Joseph Grieco (1988) stressed that states are more interested in gains relative to potential rivals than in the realization of absolute gains. Relative gains led to asymmetric benefits which make the breakdown of cooperation likely. From this the hypothesis follows that a sustained situation of asymmetric benefits accruing to specific countries at the expense of others will sooner or later influence the dynamics of EU policy-making negatively, as, for example, the euro crisis might show. Brexit might also constitute an example, as large parts of the British political establishment and the population felt that the country lost power relative to other nations in the EU.

The disintegrating potential of relative gains can be mitigated though. For one, most scholars tend to agree that the relative gains dilemma is less acute in the economic realm than in security issues (Simón 2017: 193). Issue linkages might create the potential to set off relative gains in one area with relative losses in another, and thus change the cost–benefit calculations of the states involved in the transaction (Werner 1997). Defensive neorealists also have stressed that states act power-maximizing only if they feel threatened (Walt 1985). This feeling can be averted in case a benevolent hegemon exists, providing the collective goods that are necessary to overcome collective action problems. This concept was first formulated by Charles Kindleberger (Kindleberger 1973) and later popularized by neorealist scholars such as Robert Gilpin (1987). Some scholars have argued that Germany might assume such a role as benevolent hegemon (Otero-Iglesias and Zimmermann 2016; Reichwein 2018). Recent neorealist scholarship has attributed the recurrent crises of the EU to the failure of Germany to accept this role and act accordingly (Matthijs 2016; Webber 2019b: 17). Absent the role of hegemons, internal or external, the traditional great power rivalries in Europe might reemerge.

Overall, thus, neorealism provides a profoundly skeptical account of the EU. Crises are natural consequences of an anarchic state system that continues to exert pressure towards the self-interested pursuit of power and therefore disintegration. How well do these predictions hold when confronted with recent crises in the EU?

UKRAINE AND A COMMON EUROPEAN SECURITY POLICY[1]

Already since its earliest days, international crises originating abroad had ambiguous repercussions on cooperation in the EU. The then European Community experienced deep divisions in the 1970s dealing with issues such as the Israeli–Palestine conflict or the breakdown of the Bretton Woods system. It reacted with timid or insufficient steps toward more integration, in the form of European Political Cooperation (EPC) and the European Monetary System (EMS). Far from offering a coherent and effective answer to the civil wars that erupted on its own doorsteps in the 1990s after the disintegration of former Yugoslavia, the EU had to rely on the reluctant United States to provide an effective response. This gave rise to a renewed attempt at integration in security and defense policies, most famously with the British–French initiative of

---

[1] for more on the Ukraine crisis, see Juncos and Pomorska, this volume and Riddervold, this volume.

St. Malo in 1998 (Posen 2006, 2014). Yet, harmony and impetus were of limited duration. The disunited response to American unilateralism after 9/11, in particular with respect to the Iraq war of 2003, but also the Libya intervention in 2011 which saw Germany on the sidelines, provided ample evidence for European divisions in the area of defense and security policies.

Thus, while the global configuration of power after the Cold War exerted pressure to unite and pursue (soft) balancing behavior by creating effective military capabilities, as for example Posen (2004) and Hyde-Price (2012: 34) maintained, the dynamics of regional power rivalries and diverging interests have undermined these efforts time and again (Reichwein 2015). Neorealist theory can provide an explanation for this inconsistent pattern, with cooperation happening in fits and starts. Intense global or regional crises affecting the EU provide an impetus to forge ahead with common security, defense, monetary, or energy policies. However, such initiatives peter out, particularly in the high politics area of security and defense policy, as soon as mutual rivalries and incompatible interests kick in.

The Ukraine crisis of 2013/14 was such a geopolitical event. It revived the specter of the Russian threat, and posed a direct challenge to EU policies and many of its fundamental values. To neorealists, Russia's reaction to EU neighborhood policies, in particular the prospective EU–Ukraine association agreement, came as no surprise. Already in 2010, Mearsheimer predicted that conflict between Russia and the Ukraine was very likely, and that it would entail a geopolitical dimension. He argued that only the continued presence of the United States would impede a resulting security competition between Russia and Germany (Mearsheimer 2010: 396). When the "Orange Revolution" in Ukraine turned into a major crisis, culminating in the annexation of the Crimea and an undeclared war between Russia and the Ukraine in the Eastern part of that country, neorealists urged caution. The West should not meddle in a region in which it had no essential national interests, contrary to Russia (Walt 2015; Mearsheimer 2014). By doing so and thus neglecting essential Russian interests, it would take on its share of responsibility for the resulting bloodshed (Mearsheimer 2014; MacFarlane and Menon 2014).

Whatever the shortcomings of EU actions prior to the events, the consequences were a profound shock to those speculating about the possibility of an EU-dominated zone of prosperity, including Russia. The Ukraine crisis posed a unique test to the EU, as a neighboring power fundamentally challenged not only specific EU policies but also core values and norms promoted by the EU (Howorth 2017). Quite outspokenly, Russia pushed back vigorously against EU ambitions. At the same time, the former hegemon, the United States, made clear that it did not see the Ukraine as essential national interest. After the election of Donald Trump, it even seemed to prefer Putin's authoritarian regime to its traditional allies. Neorealist theory would expect that the Russian threat and the unreliability of the United States would force the Europeans towards a balancing behavior, the expression of which would be first and foremost the creation of capable European military force. In fact, the

EU presented a quite united front, imposing repeatedly sanctions on Russia as the crisis escalated. It supported Ukraine economically and took the lead in brokering ceasefire talks between Russia and the Ukraine (the Minsk I and II talks). Countries, such as Hungary or Slovakia, which had hesitated to support the sanctions, toed the EU line. This was facilitated by the fact that Germany, after some hesitation, prioritized a strong response to its traditional close economic relations with Russia, acting as a benevolent hegemon (Karolewski and Cross 2017: 141). At the same time, however, the Russian government successfully courted "Trojan Horses" in the EU (Orenstein and Kelemen 2017), that is, governments that were willing to extend economic and political benefits to Russia during or soon after the crisis. This squares with the neorealist prediction that member states would continue to pursue their national interests. In fact while the Ukraine crisis for some time became a "catalyst for a more diverse and specialized European defence policy" (Karolewski and Cross 2017: 139), this effect soon wore off. The shock of Brexit and the election of Donald Trump were necessary to breathe new life into European defense cooperation in the form of PESCO (Permanent Structured Cooperation), inaugurated in November 2017. How long this renewed drive will last, is open to speculation, since, in the neorealist imagination, it depends on the durability of major external threats.

The Euro Crisis and Neorealism[2]

The crisis in the Eurozone began in autumn 2009 when the extent of Greece's budget deficits became known. It soon mushroomed into a full-scale financial crisis that almost destroyed the common currency. The crisis has been explained in very diverse ways, for example as a result of the dynamics of global financial markets, the deficiencies of domestic politics and institutions in debtor countries, the institutional setup of the Eurozone, the incompatibility of varieties of capitalism in the Eurozone, and the influence of neoliberal ideas with their emphasis on permanent austerity. Associated with this last argument was the debate about Germany's role in the crisis and its pursuit of austerity policies (Bulmer 2014). It was obvious from the outset of the turmoil that the German government would play the pivotal role in the decision-making processes that shaped the outcome of the crisis, just as it had done during the creation of the European Monetary Union. Research that focused on the role of Germany tended to be more open towards explanations that borrowed from the concepts of the neorealist tradition than neo-functionalist, intergovernmental, or constructivist accounts of the rise and near-fall of the common currency. Thus, realist-inspired accounts have stressed the increasing constraints on German autonomy in the aftermath of the breakdown of Bretton Woods when the United States abused its hegemonic privileges.

[2] For more on the Euro crisis, see Trondal and Stenstad, this volume and Olsen and Rosén, this volume.

They interpreted the subsequent attempt at monetary integration as (soft) counterbalancing against a dominant dollar (Zimmermann 2008). Another prominent argument is that EMU represents a strategy by other European states to constrain German hegemony, particularly after reunification, and that Germany as benign hegemon chose to be entangled in a currency union in order to deal with renewed concerns about its preponderance (Grieco 1995, 1996; Pederson 1998). However, to argue the voluntary acceptance of permanent institutional constraints tends to run into many logical problems and forces these interpretations to rely on ad hoc assumptions, such as quite fundamental misperceptions by many Eurozone members about the costs and constraints of monetary union (Legro and Moravcsik 1999: 41–43). Thus, neorealist explanations of monetary union remain problematic.

Has this changed with the onset of the euro crisis? A neorealist account of this crisis would stress above all the power asymmetries built into the construction of the Eurozone which became glaringly obvious during the conflicts about the various rescue packages which became necessary. It would see the no-bailout clause of the Maastricht treaty as an expression to preserve the autonomy of creditor states. Germany and France's flagrant bending of the rules of the Stability and Growth Pact in 2004 are, in this view, an example of great power politics within the insufficient constraints of EMU. In addition, creditor states imposed their monetary philosophy on the rest, causing highly asymmetric relative gains (Matthijs 2016). A relatively low exchange rate of the euro, for example, boosted Germany's export competitiveness. During the crisis, Germany resisted all steps toward a mutualisation of debt which would have institutionalized mutual solidarity and greatly strengthened the confidence of markets in the sustainability of the common currency (Schieder and Guarneri 2018).

Still, an interpretation focusing solely on the national interests of Germany and other creditor states have difficulties to account for the survival of the Eurozone and the apparent deepening which occurred after the crisis, for example through the creation of the European Stability Mechanism or the project of Banking Union (Niemann and Ioannou 2015; Schimmelfennig 2018). In a recent book, Shawn Donnelly employed Realist Institutionalism to explain these integrationist steps (Donnelly 2018). He argues that the dominant powers in the Eurozone, particularly Germany, will create institutions outside the legal framework of the EU to allow them to pursue their specific interests, for example the European Stability Mechanism (ESM) or the Single Resolution Mechanism (SRM). No common deposit insurance system was setup which would have linked the national banking systems and effectively installed a strong mutual solidarity mechanism. Germany's "reluctant leadership" (Newman 2015) was therefore motivated by the pursuit of national interests which prevented the necessary completion of the institutional architecture of the Eurozone (Schoeller 2018).

A (still to be written) neorealist account of the Eurozone and its crisis would therefore remain deeply skeptical about the longevity of the euro. The current

Italian government's blatant repudiation of the deficit rules of monetary union and its open flirtation with an exit from the euro is an obvious case strongly suggesting that the travails of monetary union are not over (Jones 2018).

BREXIT AND THE MIGRATION CRISIS[3]

Brexit is the result of a rational act by the leaders and the population of a country that realized that it derived more disadvantages than benefits from its membership. Hence, by leaving the Union, Britain attempted to preserve its autonomy, confronted as it was with the progressive withering away of core state competencies. Essential British interests, such as control over immigration, the negotiation of commercial treaties, and the regulation of the domestic economy seemed to have moved into the hands of a domineering bureaucracy armed with a massive, irremovable and inscrutable body of treaties, laws and regulations. In addition, given its many global connections and its close relations with major powers such as the United States ("the special relationship"), Britain can expect to wield much more influence without the constraints of EU membership.

This is how neorealists would explain Brexit, and their view is echoed in the leavers' slogan "Take Back Control." As the UK's former Secretary of State for International Trade, Liam Fox, stated: "I fundamentally, constitutionally, believed that the whole concept of 'ever closer union' was dated and that in an era of globalisation, it would not be in Britain's national interest to be tied too closely politically and economically to a model that was designed for the world of the second half of the 20th century" (Fox 2018). Instead, the United Kingdom would forge new alliances, constructing (or reconstructing) a new role as "Global Britain" (Daddow 2019). To neorealists, the only surprising thing in all this would be that the exit from the EU happened so late, and that (apart from Greenland and Algeria) other states have not yet come to the realization that they might be better off outside the EU. Given neorealism's distrust of the effectiveness and longevity of international institutions, instances of disintegration should not be exceptional, but rather regular occurrences. A neorealist perspective stresses the importance of the often-stated perception of Eurosceptic politicians and media that the United Kingdom gained consistently less from its membership in the EU than other European powers, in particular Germany and France. Brexit is thus less a consequence of the populist surge in the United Kingdom, or a jingoistic and xenophobic media-scape, or the effects of globalization in regions suffering from industrial decline which paved the way for referendum. These are dependent variables, reflecting reactions to Britain's declining position in the EU and the wider world. When it became clear during the renegotiation of Britain's terms of

---

[3] For more on Brexit, see Oliver, this volume and Whitman, this volume. For more on the migration crisis, see Bosilca, this volume, Crawford, this volume and Schilde, this volume.

membership by the government of David Cameron, that the United Kingdom would not be able to realize what it perceived to be fundamental national interests, in particular the control of migration, Brexit became a rational strategy. The migration crisis of 2015 signaled that Britain might not be the only country on this track. Countries such as Hungary and Poland were adamant in refusing to take on even a small number of migrants despite intense pressure. Germany, too, stuck to its interests and did not provide the kind of leadership hoped for by the Cameron government during the renegotiation of the terms of British membership. It refused to compromise European principles and to risk upsetting the Eastern Europeans by granting concessions on the free movement of persons (Parker 2016). In addition, the opening of the German borders in autumn 2015 to more than a million of refugees was interpreted by many European countries as a blatant unilateral act and its aftershocks provided an important context to the Brexit referendum (Outhwaite 2019).

Overall, neorealism provides a consistent account of intra-European power rivalries that might have been a decisive structural factor behind Brexit. Much more research on the international dimension of the run-up to the Brexit referendum would be necessary to thoroughly back up this account. However, it will not remain without ambiguities, particularly when the level of analysis is broadened beyond an exclusively intra-European perspective. The dynamics of global power shifts in the years leading up to the referendum would rather lead to the prediction that Britain as medium power would try to balance against the potential and the actual threats represented by China, Russia, and the United States. It would therefore move closer to Europe, particularly in the field of defense cooperation. And of course, the crucial domestic dynamics are not captured by neorealist concepts, as Ben Rosamond noted: "Realism's insistence that exit decisions would be driven by *raison d'état* in light of external security calculus does rather make it a hard sell as a theory capable of explaining the nuances of Brexit" (Rosamond 2016: 867). It also has problems to account for the attitude of EU member states which have very strong security and economic rationales to keep Britain in. Though the extent of the impact of Brexit on the relative power position of the EU in the international system is debated, it certainly is not inconsequential. With the United Kingdom, the EU loses about 25% of its combined defense spending and a high percentage of its most advanced weapons systems (Giegerich and Mölling 2018). Of course, from the point of view of rival powers to the EU such as Russia and more recently the United States their involvement on the side of the Brexiteers would make clear sense in a neorealist world.

Neorealism as a Theory of Disintegration

Neorealism is a grand theory that tries to explain broad historical trends, not specific instances of crisis. Its general pessimism regarding constraining and entangling forms of state cooperation that imply a loss of sovereignty has rendered it unable to advance a strong and convincing explanation of the progress of European integration. However, as this article has shown, with respect to disintegration dynamics neorealism appears much more promising. Its concepts suggest convincing and evocative explanations for recent EU crises. As stressed in the theoretical discussion and substantiated in the case studies, it is necessary to specify the geographic scope of the application of the theory, i.e. whether it is global or intra-European. Otherwise, ambiguities and contradictions undermine the neorealist cause. These ambiguities can be removed if the neorealist argument is reduced to its most parsimonious form, a search for survival in an anarchic world. In that case, the global level would take precedence. As the case studies have demonstrated, however, such theoretical parsimony would make neorealism unable to explain recent crises of the EU, since the member states could be expected to be able to forget their petty squabbles given the geopolitical realities and relative European decline. Manifestly, this is not the case.

One instance that demonstrated this pattern is the case of the Ukraine crisis. It temporarily united EU member states, helped by the active leadership of Germany, and it caused evidence of balancing behavior vis-à-vis Russia. However, the case study also suggests that, like in earlier crises, the unity was soon undermined by divergent interests and opportunistic behavior. Countries such as Italy and Hungary recently made advances toward Russia which are difficult to explain from a geopolitical point of view. A similar pattern emerged during the Eurozone crisis. While the creation of the euro might be explained as a strong example of soft-balancing, restoring monetary autonomy, the crisis showed the persistence of power asymmetries and the pursuit of national interests by the member states of the Eurozone. Still, as long as the current deep institutionalization of the common currency survives, neorealism will have a problem to explain why member states continue to forgo the advantages of an autonomous monetary policy. Brexit is interpreted by neorealists as a strategy to pursue essential British interests in the global arena. Britain regains the option to bandwagon with the United States or join the remainder of the EU in its efforts to balance against rival great powers. Again, however, this account is somewhat indeterminate since it presupposes a degree of rational calculation by British leaders which is hard to reconcile empirically with the political process leading to Brexit.

All in all, the neorealist vision would privilege the first of the three scenarios outlined in the introduction to this volume, i.e., change and *breaking down*. While external challenges and global crises might offer windows of opportunity and move the material interests of member states towards integrating steps in selected policy fields, such cooperation comes with a limited time horizon and will face breakdown or deadlock as soon as the erstwhile impetus wears off and diverging interests come to the fore. The EU's relations with the United States and China will most likely be characterized by such a pattern as member states evaluate their options in security and economic policies. Given that these options are often ambiguous or indeterminate, a strategy of *muddling through* (scenario 2) might also be compatible with a neorealist account.

The configuration of global power asymmetries and the EU's place in this configuration is the principal causal mechanism the theory employs to explain change and continuity in the Union's reaction to crisis. Modified variants of neorealism, operating with variables such as threat perception or institutions can help explain the emergence of crisis in the EU, but they are inadequate to explain the specific dynamics of crisis management in the EU. Neorealism therefore provides a valuable source of and inspiration for theories of disintegration, but in the field of EU studies per se it will remain rather peripheral.

References

Bulmer, S. (2014). Germany and the Eurozone Crisis: Between Hegemony and Domestic Politics. *West European Politics, 37*(6), 1244–1263.

Collard-Wexler, S. (2006). Integration Under Anarchy: Neorealism and the European Union. *The European Journal of International Relations, 12*(3), 398–432.

Daddow, O. (2019). *The Real Meaning of Global Britain: A Great Escape from the EU*. LSE Blog. https://blogs.lse.ac.uk/brexit/2019/04/04/the-real-meaning-of-global-britain-a-great-escape-from-the-eu/. Accessed 28 May 2019.

Donnelly, S. (2018). *Power Politics, Banking Union and EMU: Adjusting Europe to Germany*. Milton Park: Routledge.

Fox, L. (2018). *Brexit and Beyond: Britain's Place in the World in the 2020s*. The Brexit Lectures. https://www.gov.uk/government/speeches/brexit-and-beyond-britains-place-in-the-world-in-the-2020s. Accessed 7 May 2019.

Giegerich B., & Mölling C. (2018). *The United Kingdom's Contribution to European Security and Defence: Military Balance Blog: Posts from the IISS Defence and Military Analysis Programme Paper*. https://dgap.org/en/think-tank/publications/further-publications/united-kingdoms-contribution-european-security-and. Accessed 24 June 2019.

Gilpin, R. (1981). *War and Change in World Politics*. Cambridge: Cambridge University Press.

Gilpin, R. (1987). *The Political Economy of International Relations*. Princeton: Princeton University Press.

Grieco, J. M. (1988). Anarchy and the Limits of Cooperation: A Realist Critique of the Newest Liberal Institutionalism. *International Organization, 42*(3), 485–507.

Grieco, J. M. (1995). The Maastricht Treaty, Economic and Monetary Union and the Neo-Realist Research Programme. *Review of International Studies, 21*, 21–40.

Grieco, J. M. (1996). State Interests and Institutional Rule Trajectories: A Neorealist Reinterpretation of the Maastricht Treaty and European Economic and Monetary Union. In B. Frankel (Ed.), *Realism: Restatements and Renewal* (pp. 262–305). London: Frank Cass.

Hooghe, L., & Marks, G. (2009). A Postfunctionalist Theory of European Integration: From Permissive Consensus to Constraining Dissensus. *British Journal of Political Science, 39*(1), 1–23. https://doi.org/10.1017/S0007123408000409.

Howorth, J. (2017). 'Stability on the Borders': The Ukraine Crisis and the EU's Constrained Policy Towards the Eastern Neighbourhood. *Journal of Common Market Studies, 55*(1), 121–136.

Hyde-Price, A. (2012). Neorealism: A Structural Approach to CSDP. In X. Kurowska & F. Breuer (Eds.), *Explaining the EU's Common Security and Defence Policy. Theory in Action* (pp. 16–40). London: Palgrave.

Jones, E. (2018, November 2). Italy's Dangerous Budget Showdown with Europe. *Foreign Affairs*. https://www.foreignaffairs.com/articles/italy/2018-11-02/italys-dangerous-budget-showdown-europe.

Jones, S. (2003). The European Union and the Security Dilemma. *Security Studies, 12*(3), 114–156.

Karolewski, I. P., & Cross, M. D. (2017). The EU's Power in the Russia-Ukraine Crisis: Enabled or Constrained? *Journal of Common Market Studies, 55*(1), 137–152.

Kindleberger, C. (1973). *The World in Depression 1929–1939*. London: The Penguin Press.

Layne, C. (1993). The Unipolar Illusion: Why New Great Powers Will Rise. *International Security, 17*(4), 5–51.

Legro, J. W., & Moravcsik, A. (1999). Is Anybody Still a Realist? *International Security, 24*(2), 5–55.

MacFarlane, N., & Menon, A. (2014). The EU and Ukraine. *Survival, 56*(3), 95–101.

Matthijs, M. (2016). The Failure of German Leadership. In H. Zimmermann & A. Dür (Eds.), *Key Controversies in European Integration* (2nd ed., pp. 236–242). London: Palgrave.

Mearsheimer, J. J. (1990). Back to the Future: Instability in Europe After the Cold War. *International Security, 15*(4), 5–56.

Mearsheimer, J. (1994). The False Promise of International Institutions. *International Security, 19*(3), 5–49.

Mearsheimer, J. J. (2003). *The Tragedy of Great Power Politics*. New York: Norton.

Mearsheimer, J. J. (2010). Why Is Europe Peaceful Today? *European Political Science, 9*, 387–397.

Mearsheimer, J. J. (2014, August 18). Why the Ukraine Crisis Is the West's Fault. *Foreign Affairs*. https://www.foreignaffairs.com/articles/russia-fsu/2014-08-18/why-ukraine-crisis-west-s-fault. Accessed 24 June 2019.

Newman, A. (2015). The Reluctant Leader: Germany's Euro Experience and the Long Shadow of Reunification. In M. Matthijs & M. Blyth (Eds.), *The Future of the Euro* (pp. 117–135). Oxford: Oxford University Press.

Niemann, A., & Ioannou, D. (2015). European Economic Integration in Times of Crisis: A Case of Neofunctionalism? *Journal of European Public Policy, 22*, 196–218.

Orenstein, M. A., & Kelemen, R. (2017). Trojan Horses in EU Foreign Policy. *Journal of Common Market Studies, 55*(1), 87–102.

Otero-Iglesias, M., & Zimmermann, H. (2016). A Benign Hegemon: Germany's European Vocation. In H. Zimmermann & A. Dür (Eds.), *Key Controversies in European Integration* (2nd ed., pp. 243–250). London: Palgrave.

Outhwaite, W. (2019). Migration Crisis and "Brexit". In C. Menjivar, M. Ruiz, & I. Ness (Eds.), *The Oxford Handbook of Migration Crises* (pp. 93–110). Oxford: Oxford UP.

Parker G. (2016, December 18). How David Cameron Lost His Battle for Britain. *Financial Times*. https://www.ft.com/content/3482b434-c37d-11e6-81c2-f57d90f6741a. Accessed 20 June 2019.

Pederson, T. (1998). *Germany, France, and the Integration of Europe: A Realist Interpretation*. Washington, DC: Pinter.

Pollack, M. A. (2001). International Relations Theory and European Integration. *Journal of Common Market Studies, 39*(2), 221–244.

Posen, B. R. (2004). ESDP and Structure of World Politics. *International Spectator, 39*(1), 5–17.

Posen, B. R. (2006). European Union Security and Defense Policy: Response to Unipolarity? *Security Studies, 15*(2), 149–186.

Posen, B. R. (2014). *Restraint: A New Foundation for US Grand Strategy*. Ithaca, NY: Cornell University Press.

Reichwein, A. (2015). Realism and European Foreign Policy: Promises and Shortcomings. In K. E. Jørgensen et.al. (Eds.), *The Sage Handbook of European Foreign Policy* (pp. 99–120). London: Sage.

Reichwein, A. (2018). Germany's Growing Power in EUrope: From Multilateral Collectivism Towards Re-Nationalization and Destabilization? In R. Belloni, V. della Sala, & P. Viotti, (Eds.), *Fear and Uncertainty in Europe. The Return to Realism* (pp. 85–108). London: Palgrave.

Rosamond, B. (2016). Brexit and the Problem of European Disintegration. *Journal of Contemporary European Research, 12*(4), 864–871.

Rosato, S. (2011). Europe's Troubles: Power Politics and the State of the European Project. *International Security, 35*(4), 45–86.

Schieder S., & Guarneri C. (2018). Germany's Leadership Role in the Eurozone Crisis Revisited. *REScEU! Reconciling Economic and Social Europe: The Role of Ideas, Values and Politics*, Available at: www.euvisions.eu. Accessed 20 June 2019.

Schimmelfennig, F. (2018). Liberal Intergovernmentalism and the Crises of the European Union. *Journal of Common Market Studies, 56*(7), 1578–1594.

Schoeller, M. (2018). Germany, the Problem of Leadership and Institution-Building in EMU Reform. *Journal of Economic Policy Reform*. https://doi.org/10.1080/17487870.2018.1541410.

Schweller, R. (1994). Bandwagoning for Profit: Bringing the Revisionist State Back in. *International Security, 19*(1), 72–107.

Simón, L. (2017). Neorealism, Security Cooperation, and Europe's Relative Gains Dilemma. *Security Studies, 26*(2), 185–212.

Walt, S. M. (1985). Alliance Formation and the Balance of World Power. *International Security, 9*(5), 3–43.

Walt, S. M. (2011). Alliances in a Unipolar World. In G. J. Ikenberry, M. Mastanduno, & W. C. Wohlforth (Eds.), *International Relations Theory and the Consequences of Unipolarity* (pp. 99–140). Cambridge: Cambridge University Press.

Walt, S. M. (2015, February 9). Why Arming Kiev Is a Really, Really Bad Idea. *Foreign Policy*. https://foreignpolicy.com/2015/02/09/how-not-to-save-ukraine-arming-kiev-is-a-bad-idea/?wp_login_redirect=0. Accessed 20 June 2019.

Waltz, K. (1979). *Theory of International Politics*. Reading, MA: Addison-Wesley.

Waltz, K. (1993). The Emerging Structure of International Politics. *International Security, 18*(2), 44–79.

Waltz, K. (2000). Structural Realism After the Cold War. *International Security, 25*(1), 5–41.

Webber, D. (2019a). Trends in European political (Dis)Integration: An Analysis of Postfunctionalist and Other Explanations. *Journal of European Public Policy.* https://doi.org/10.1080/13501763.2019.1576760.

Webber, D. (2019b). *European Disintegration? The Politics of Crisis in the European Union.* London: Macmillan/Red Globe Press.

Werner, S. (1997). In Search of Security: Relative Gains and Losses in Dyadic Relations. *Journal of Peace Research, 34*(3), 289–302.

Wiener, A., Börzel, T. A., & Risse, T. (2018) (Eds.), *European Integration Theory* (3rd ed.). Oxford: Oxford University Press.

Zimmermann, H. (2008). West German Monetary Policy and the Transition to Flexible Exchange Rates, 1969–1973. In D. M. Andrews (Ed.), *Orderly Change: International Monetary Relations Since Bretton Woods* (pp. 155–176). Ithaca: Cornell University Press.

CHAPTER 6

Neofunctionalism

Arne Niemann

INTRODUCTION

Neofunctionalism stands out among early theories of European integration in its sophistication and in the amount of criticism that it has attracted. The theory was first formulated in the late 1950s and early 1960s by Ernst Haas in response to the establishment of the European Coal and Steel Community (ECSC) and later the European Economic Community (EEC). The theory was in its prime until the mid-1960s, during which time the evolution of European integration seemed to vindicate its assumptions. Shortly before the publication of Haas' seminal book, *The Uniting of Europe*, in 1958, cooperation on coal and steel under the ECSC had "spilled over" into the EEC and the European Atomic Energy Community (Euratom). In addition, the formation of the customs union ahead of schedule and the progress made on the Common Agricultural Policy supported the neofunctionalist claims.

From the mid-1960s, however, several adverse developments culminating in the "empty chair" crisis of 1965–1966 when French President Charles de Gaulle effectively paralyzed the Community, cast doubt on the theory's apparent assumption that integration would essentially progress automatically. Despite some attempts to revise certain hypotheses and claims in the late 1960s and early 1970s, Haas eventually declared the theory to be "obsolescent" (Haas 1976). With the resurgence of the European integration process in the

---

A. Niemann (✉)
Department of Political Science, Johannes Gutenberg University Mainz, Mainz, Germany
e-mail: arne.niemann@uni-mainz.de

© The Author(s) 2021
M. Riddervold et al. (eds.), *The Palgrave Handbook of EU Crises*, Palgrave Studies in European Union Politics,
https://doi.org/10.1007/978-3-030-51791-5_6

mid-1980s, neofunctionalism made a comeback in academia. Since the 1990s, several efforts have been made to revise and extend the original approach.

Crises as critical junctures and hard cases should particularly lend themselves for theory development (cf. Rosamond 2000: 9), specifying the boundaries within which, and conditions under which, a theory may have explanatory value. It is therefore probably no coincidence that the first substantial wave of neofunctionalist revision occurred after the Community's first considerable crisis (the "empty chair" crisis).

This chapter argues that while neofunctionalism is not as such a theory of crisis, it still provides important insights for theorizing crisis. In addition, since it has been developed in precrisis times and as it has proven to be a dynamic/evolving theory, it may be further developed into such direction, not least by working on the specification of scope conditions for analyzing and explaining integration crises.

I proceed as follows: the first part of this chapter will provide an overview of neofunctionalism, including its intellectual roots, its main initial assumptions and hypotheses, including the central notion of spillover, as well as its later revisions. In Part 2, I specify the neofunctionalist take on the phenomenon of crisis. The following section will probe and exemplify neofunctionalism, focusing on the Eurozone crisis. Finally, I will draw some conclusions.

Neofunctionalism: An Overview

Neofunctionalism has its intellectual roots at the juncture between functionalist, federalist, and communications theories. Haas and Lindberg, the two most influential and prolific neofunctionalist writers, combined functionalist mechanisms with federalist goals. Like functionalism, neofunctionalism emphasizes the mechanisms of technocratic decision-making, incremental change, and learning processes. However, although the theory has been dubbed neofunctionalism, this is in some respects a case of "mistaken identity" (Groom 1978), since it departed significantly from Mitrany's functionalism (Mitrany 1966). Whereas functionalists held that form, scope, and purpose of an organization was determined by the task that it was designed to fulfill, neofunctionalists attached considerable importance to the autonomous influence of supranational institutions and the emerging role of organized interests. While the former did not limit integration to any territorial area, the latter gave it a specifically regional focus. Moreover, where Mitrany attached importance to changes in popular support, neofunctionalists privilege changes in elite attitudes. Another important figure in neofunctionalism's intellectual inheritance was Jean Monnet, who indicated to the importance of functional dynamics in political practices.

Both Haas and Lindberg held integration to be a process and agreed that the latter involved the creation and role-expansion of regional institutions. Moreover, they both stressed change in expectations and activities on the part of participating actors. Haas (1958: 16) defined integration as:

the process whereby political actors in several distinct national settings are persuaded to shift their loyalties, expectations and political activities toward a new center, whose institutions possess or demand jurisdiction over the preexisting national states. The end result of a process of political integration is a new political community, superimposed over the preexisting ones.

Lindberg (1963: 6) offers a somewhat different definition:

(1) The process whereby nations forego the desire and ability to conduct foreign and domestic policies independently of each other, seeking instead to make joint decisions or to delegate the decision-making process to new central organs: and (2) the process whereby political actors in several distinct settings are persuaded to shift their expectations and political activities to a new centre.

It should be noted that, unlike Haas, Lindberg, in not suggesting any end point for the integration process, implicitly acknowledged that the breadth and depth of integration could be in constant flux. Lindberg also suggested that political actors merely shift their expectations and not their loyalties to a new center. Thus, Lindberg's conception and definition of integration can be seen as more cautious.

Basic Tenets

The essence of the theory can be derived from a set of fundamental maxims: Firstly, in line with the mainstream of US political science of the time, the early neofunctionalists aimed at general theory-building. In its initial conception, neofunctionalism understood itself as a "grand" or general theory of integration—claiming applicability regardless of when and where it occurred (Haas 1961). Second, integration is understood as a process. Neofunctionalists fundamentally differ from intergovernmentalists who tend to look at isolated events and assume them to be repetitions of the same power politics. Implicit in the notion of process is the contrary assumption that integration processes evolve over time and take on their own dynamic. Third, neofunctionalism is "pluralist" in nature. In contrast to realist theories, it contests both that states are unified actors and that they are the only relevant actors. Instead, neofunctionalists assume that regional integration is characterized by multiple, diverse, and changing actors who are not restricted to the domestic political realm but also interact and build coalitions across national frontiers and bureaucracies (Haas 1964: 68ff). Fourth, neofunctionalists see the Community primarily as "a creature of elites." While Haas (1958: chs. 5 and 6) devoted much of his attention to the role of nongovernmental elites, Lindberg (1963: ch. 4) largely focused on governmental elites. Neither ascribed much importance to the role of public opinion. The conclusion was that there was a "permissive consensus" in favor of European integration (Lindberg and Scheingold 1970: 41) and that this would suffice to sustain it.

Fifth, neofunctionalists assume rational and self-interested actors (Haas 1970: 627), who (nevertheless) have the capacity to learn and change their preferences. Interest-driven national and supranational elites, recognizing the limitations of national solutions, learn from the benefits of regional policies and from their experiences in cooperative decision-making (Haas 1958: 291). Sixth, early reformulations of the theory stressed the primacy of incremental decision-making over grand designs. Moreover, seemingly marginal adjustments are often driven by the unintended consequences of previous decisions. This effect arises from the incapacity of most political actors to engage in long-term purposive behavior (Haas 1970: 627). Seventh, neofunctionalists reject the conventional realist axiom that all games played between actors are necessarily zero-sum in nature. In the Community setting exchanges are often better characterized as positive sum-games and a "supranational" style of decision-making, which Haas defined as "a cumulative pattern of accommodation in which the participants refrain from unconditionally vetoing proposals and instead seek to attain agreement by means of compromises upgrading common interests" (Haas 1964: 66).

The Concept of Spillover

The neofunctionalist conception of change is succinctly encapsulated in the notion of "spillover." Haas (1958: 383) described an "expansive logic of sector integration" whereby the integration of one sector leads to "technical" pressures pushing states to integrate other sectors. The idea is that some sectors are so interdependent that it is impossible to isolate them from the rest. Thus, the integration of one sector at the regional level is only practicable in combination with the integration of other sectors, as problems arising from the functional integration of one task can only be solved by integrating yet more tasks. Haas (1958: 297) held that sector integration "begets its own impetus toward extension of the entire economy...". For example, the viability of integration in the coal and steel sectors would be undermined unless other related sectors such as transport policy followed suit, in order to ensure a smooth movement of necessary raw materials. In the literature the term *functional spillover* later came to denote the functional-economic rationale for further integration (Lindberg and Scheingold 1970).

Haas and Lindberg also considered support for the integration process among economic and political elites to be of great significance. National elites had to come to perceive that problems of substantial interest could not be effectively addressed at the domestic level, not least because of the above-mentioned functional-economic logic. This should lead to a gradual learning process whereby elites shift their expectations, political activities, and—according to Haas—even loyalties to a new European center. Consequently, national elites would come to promote further integration, thus adding a political stimulus to the process. Hence, the integrative pressures exerted by (national) elites were later termed *political spillover* in the literature (Tranholm-Mikkelsen 1991: 5). Two stands of political spillover can be distinguished.

First, Haas (1958: 312–313) in particular focused on the pressures exerted by nongovernmental elites. Those pressures include the altered perceptions of political parties, business and professional associations, trade unions or other interest groups. This implies that integration in a particular sector leads the relevant interest groups to move part of their activity to a higher level of aggregation and therefore gradually shift their focus and expectations to European institutions. Presuming that they would perceive positive benefits from their regional experiences, these private organizations should support further integration (Haas 1958: chs. 8 and 9). Second, Lindberg attributed greater significance to the role of governmental elites and socialization processes. He drew attention to the proliferation of EU working groups and subcommittees which, by bringing thousands of national officials into frequent contact with each other and Commission officials, had given rise to a complex system of bureaucratic interpenetration. These interaction patterns, Lindberg argued (1963: ch. 4), increase the likelihood of socialization processes occurring among national civil servants within the Council framework. Given the effect of these mechanisms, neofunctionalists challenged the classic intergovernmental vision of Community decision-making as based only on national strategic bargaining and postulated the existence of a "supranational" problem-solving process, "a cumulative pattern of accommodation in which the participants refrain from unconditionally vetoing proposals and instead seek to attain agreement by means of compromises upgrading common interests" (Haas 1958: 66). It was further implied that these socialization processes, by fostering consensus formation among agents of member governments, would eventually lead to more integrative outcomes (Lindberg 1963: chs. 1 and 4).

A further impetus for regional integration would be provided by the role of supranational institutions. Haas emphasized how the High Authority of the ECSC and, later, the European Commission facilitated agreement on integrative outcomes. As opposed to lowest common denominator bargaining, which he saw as inherent in strictly intergovernmental decision-making, supranational systems were characterized by "splitting the difference" and more significantly a bargaining process of "upgrading common interests." Parties agree that they should have a common stand in order not to jeopardize those areas in which consensus prevails. The participants in such negotiations tend to swap concessions in related fields under the auspices of an institutionalized mediator such as the Commission. Governments do not feel as if they have been bullied. Common interests are upgraded to the extent that each participant feels that, by conceding something, it has gained something else. In addition, Haas saw the Commission as the main actor cultivating the underlying logic of functional-economic interdependence. Haas foresaw the gradual expansion of its mandate as commensurate with the increasing breadth and depth of integration, thus providing the process with yet more impetus (Haas 1961: 369ff). Lindberg (1963) emphasized the Commission's cultivation of ties with national elites. He pointed out that it occupies a privileged position of centrality and authority, enabling it not only to direct the dynamics of relations among states but also the relations of interest groups within each state. The integrative role attributed to the Commission (or supranational institutions more generally) was later termed *cultivated spillover* (Tranholm-Mikkelsen 1991: 6).

Modifications and Revisions

Neofunctionalist theory was in its prime until the mid-1960s, during which time the evolution of European integration seemed to vindicate its assumptions. From the mid-1960s, the theory was increasingly criticized, particularly in the face of several adverse empirical developments (Niemann 2006: 20–23). In response, neofunctionalists undertook to reformulate their theory in the 1960s and early 1970s. Some of their modifications provide useful insights, while others have proved of limited utility. Critics would say that the theory became increasingly reactive to ad hoc occurrences and, therefore, so undetermined as to provide no clear direction for research (Moravcsik 1993: 476). By the mid-1970s, most academic observers had dismissed neofunctionalism as either out-of-date or out-of-touch and Haas himself (1976) declared the theory to be "obsolete." However, with the resurgence of the European integration process in the mid-1980s, neofunctionalism made a substantial comeback. Some authors suggested that the approach still contains some useful building blocks for contemporary theorizing (Keohane and Hoffmann 1991; Marks et al. 1996; Pierson 1996). Others even argued that it may be worth resurrecting the theory in light of the Community's revival (Taylor 1989; Tranholm-Mikkelsen 1991).

Although it is noticeable that some of the later approaches bear considerable resemblance to neofunctionalism, such as multilevel governance and institutionalist scholarship on the EU (Niemann 2006: ch. 5), few authors have given explicit credit to the theory. Most plainly drawing on neofunctionalist thought (without however seeming to intend to revise the theory), Stone Sweet and Sandholtz (1997) put forward their "supranational governance" approach, which emphasizes the role of transnational exchange, EU rules, and supranational institutions. They argue that cross-border transactions generate a demand for Community rules, which EC institutions seek to supply. Once Community legislation develops, supranational society emerges as (business) actors realize that one set of rules is preferable to numerous sets of (national) rules. As a result of actors testing the limits of EC rules and clarifications from Community adjudicators, rules develop ever further away from member governments' original intentions. Stone Sweet and Sandholtz argue that the transfer of competence to the Community is uneven and depends on the intensity of demands for EC regulation in a given issue area. They most significantly depart from (early) neofunctionalism by leaving open whether actors' loyalties and identities eventually shift to the European level and by laying greater emphasis on the relevance of intergovernmental bargaining in EC politics.

Only few scholars have overtly deliberately sought to revise the original theory. Philippe Schmitter first turned to the task of revision in the early 1970s and then again thirty years later. Schmitter (1970, 2004) illustrates the dynamic of his revised approach through a model of decision cycles. "Initiating cycles," which the present EU has passed through long ago, are followed by "priming cycles" that account for the changing dynamics of Member States in between decision cycles. (Schmitter 2004: 61). As regional processes begin to have greater effect, national actors may become more receptive to changing the competencies and authority of regional institutions. However, in his revised theory Schmitter rejects the "automaticity of spillover" assumption. Strategic responses other than spillover are conceptualized, such as (a) "spill-around," the proliferation of functionally specialized independent, but strictly intergovernmental, institutions; (b) "build-up," the concession by Member States of greater authority to the supranational organization without expanding the scope of its mandate; (c) and (d) "spill-back," which denotes withdrawal from previous commitments by member states. He points out that so far each of the EC/EU decision cycles has generated further imbalances and contradictions thus avoiding "encapsulation," a state of stable self-maintenance. He also implies that the EU has not yet reached the "transforming cycle," where the potentialities for functionally integrating their economies (would) have been exhausted and the emphasis would be placed on the integration of polities.

Another revised neofunctionalist framework was developed by Arne Niemann (1998, 2000, 2004, 2006). He departs from the original approach in several ways. First, the ontological scope is slightly broadened—beyond what Haas (2001) post hoc described as "soft rational choice" for the original neofunctionalist account—toward a more inclusive ontology by encroaching upon "soft" constructivism. Second, integration is no longer viewed as an automatic and exclusively dynamic process, but rather occurs under certain conditions and is better characterized as a dialectic process, i.e. the product of both dynamics (driving forces) and countervailing forces (Tranholm-Mikkelsen 1991). Two concrete countervailing forces are accommodated in his revised neofunctionalist framework: "sovereignty-consciousness" and "domestic constraints and diversities." Third, Niemann expands the scope of functional spillover, freeing the concept from its deterministic ontology. He argues that the degree of interdependence between policy areas is not the sole determinant of the strength of functional spillover and that functional structures do not determine actors' behavior in a mechanical or predictable manner. Rather, for functional logics to gain traction they must be *perceived* as plausible or compelling (Niemann 2006: 30f). Fourth, Niemann refined the concept of political spillover. He argues that not only the quantity but also the *quality* of interaction impacts on cooperative norm socialization and learning processes.

Learning and socialization are no longer regarded as constant (as implied by early neofunctionalists), but contingent on certain conditions including a commonly shared "lifeworld," insufficient knowledge, and low levels of politicization. Under such conditions, actors are predisposed to deliberate, reason, argue, and persuade, rather than bargain, and may consequently undergo more deeply rooted (reflexive) learning.[1]

In his final contribution Haas (2004) suggested that neofunctionalism may be considered a forerunner, and part of, constructivism. He also argued that revised neofunctionalist approaches would benefit from institutionalist thinking, as a result of which the neofunctionalist tradition, in his view, "has a new lease on life" and should be considered "no longer obsolescent" (Haas 2004: liii).

Neofunctionalism and (Integration) Crisis

Neofunctionalism is not as such a theory of crisis (of integration). Instead, its main focus is on accounting for the dynamics of integration, i.e. on explaining why and how the integration process moves forward. However, neofunctionalism still provides important insights for theorizing crisis, and may be developed further into such direction.

Crisis Through the Lens of General Neofunctionalist Assumptions

Crises are by no means epiphenomenal from a neofunctionalist perspective (and may be seen as in keeping with some of its core assumptions): Neofunctionalists assume that the integration process tends to be driven by unintended consequences, as most political actors are incapable of long-range purposive behavior but rather "stumble" from one decision into the next as a result of earlier decisions. Decisions are normally taken with imperfect knowledge of their consequences and frequently under deadline pressure (Haas 1970: 627). Some (over-)ambitious political decisions may fail to anticipate likely consequences, which increases the likelihood of later problems and potentially crisis (Schmitter 1970).

In addition, neofunctionalism is "transformative": it has repeatedly demonstrated its capacity to retain its core concepts, mechanisms, and hypotheses while incorporating changes in the conditions that affect them (Niemann et al. 2019). There is no reason, in principle, that these transformations have to be positive, i.e. in terms of moving the process forward or avoiding (public) contestation. Part of neofunctionalism's transformative nature is that actors are capable of learning. Insofar as politics involves choice and contestation, learning processes may lead to different directions being recommended or taken, not necessarily resulting in further integration—but potentially also

---

[1] Cf. Niemann (2004; 2006) who builds on Habermas (1981), Risse (2000), and Checkel (2001).

in crises of integration—as the result of learning processes (Niemann 2006: 271). Also worth mentioning in this context is that neofunctionalists had already avoided talking about a political Community as possible end-state of integration from the early 1960s (cf. Haas 1960; Lindberg 1963: 6). Thus, setbacks and stagnation constitute processes within neofunctionalism's explanatory range.

Crises as the Result of Existing, and Amplifier of Subsequent, Functional Pressures

For some neofunctionalists crises have been an integral part of the process of regional integration. Schmitter (1970) incorporated the notion of intrinsic crisis into his revised neofunctionalist framework five decades ago. Building on this notion, from a neofunctionalist understanding, crises are (above all) endogenous in nature, i.e. result from the integration process itself.[2]

It may even be said that crises, to some/a large extent, emerge due to the success, progressiveness, or "the very functioning of the integration process" (Lefkofridi and Schmitter 2015: 8; Schmitter 1970). For example, despite the neofunctionalist assumption of the "permissive consensus," one could argue that politicization is the logical outcome of the dynamics of integration. With progressing functional integration, European/EU politics was bound to become politicized at some stage because national sovereignty would be increasingly "engaged." Hence, what we have now is the logical development of successful functional integration, for which neofunctionalists had hypothesized the relevant (spillover) processes. Put somewhat differently, functional spillover pressure may (also) explain the emergence of crises. The latter can, at least in part, be seen as the result of existing functional pressures. If functional pressures are not to be resolved through further integrative steps, this can promote crises (Niemann and Ioannou 2015; cf. following section).

However, crises may not just be seen as the result of existing, but also as an amplifier of subsequent, functional pressures: if crisis management is slow and/or inadequate the unresolved dysfunctionalities will remain and enhance the perception of strong functional necessities for change. This eventually tends to trigger the necessary steps of integration, especially if conditions are favorable. Existing path dependencies may prevent dysfunctionalities to be resolved by spill-back (Niemann and Ioannou 2015).

Schmitter translates this into a more general trend by suggesting that "with each successive crisis resolved [...] regional-level rules [...] gain in significance to the point that they begin to overshadow the opinions and actions of national governments, associations and individuals" (Schmitter 2004: 61). As regional processes begin to have greater effect, national actors may become

---

[2] However, an exogenous shock or event, i.e. one that is not related to the European integration processes itself, may have an effect on, and co-function with, existing (functional) interdependencies and other spillover logics Bergmann and Niemann (2018).

more receptive to changing the competencies and authority of regional institutions. While it was assumed that such crises exposed tensions, problems, or dysfunctionalities in the integration process, it was usually argued that these would be resolved by additional integrational steps, but may under certain conditions also result in disintegration—this again being dependent on scope conditions (Schmitter 1970; Niemann and Ioannou 2015).

Overall, in terms of the three scenarios of coping with crises developed in the introduction to this volume, scenario 2 (*muddling through*) and especially scenario 3 (*heading forward*) are the most likely from a neofunctionalist perspective, given a certain propensity for incrementalism and path dependencies on the one hand (pointing toward scenario 2), and the (progressive) questioning of current/preceding governance arrangements due to functional discrepancies and pressures on the other (pointing toward scenario 3).

The Eurozone Crisis

The sovereign debt crisis arguably constitutes a crucial case for the neofunctionalist approach, since it has manifestly penetrated to the arena of "high politics," i.e. issues close to the heart of national sovereignty, and therefore has become substantially politicized (Hobolt and Wratil 2015). Neofunctionalism was previously confined to the analysis of "low politics," i.e. conflicts that did not (yet) threaten the core features of national identity and sovereignty, and attracted little attention from political parties or the public (Hoffmann 1966).

As regards the degree of European economic integration, the precrisis institutional framework considerably advanced in all main policy areas of EMU. Particularly worth mentioning is, in terms of fiscal and macroeconomic surveillance, the so-called "six-pack" of legislative measures, adopted to strengthen the fiscal rules of the Stability and Growth Pact (SGP) and the national fiscal frameworks and to set up a framework to tackle macroeconomic imbalances. These were supplemented by the so-called "two-pack" and the Fiscal Compact, increasing the coordination of fiscal and budgetary policy (Begg 2013). In the financial sphere, the creation of the banking union, i.e. a centralized banking supervision at the European Central Bank (ECB) and its resolution counterpart, the Single Resolution Mechanism at the Commission, deepened to a remarkable degree European economic integration (Merler 2014). The impact of, and response to, the crisis ranges somewhere between scenario 2 (*muddling through*) and scenario 3 (*heading forward*), probably closer to the latter (cf. introduction, this volume).

Subsequently, the relevance of the various neofunctionalist spillover dynamics for explaining the management of the crisis and the drive toward a more complete Economic and Monetary Union (EMU) will be assessed. In a nutshell, integrative outcomes that emerged can be explained by significant dysfunctionalities that arose from the incomplete EMU architecture created in Maastricht. These functional rationales were reinforced by integrative pressures exerted by supranational institutions, transnational-organized interests, and markets. Spillover mechanisms thus provide important insights for understanding the integrative steps taken during the crisis.[3]

Functional Spillover

The progress toward deeper economic integration that came about during the process of managing the crisis can be explained as steps taken to alleviate functional pressures arising from an incomplete architecture created in Maastricht. Policy that would normally take place at the same level of governance has been allocated to different levels under the Maastricht EMU design. While monetary and exchange rate policy is an exclusive EU competence, fiscal policies are largely determined at the national level. Financial sector regulation is determined at the European and national level, while financial sector supervision and structural policies (beyond the single market) are loosely coordinated at the EU level, but legislated at the national level.

Three dysfunctionalities brought about substantial integrative pressures during the crisis. First, the creation of crisis management tools such as the ESM and a tighter fiscal and economic framework sought to alleviate the functional dissonances between a stable single currency and the "no-bailout" clause and decentralized national policies leading to public over-indebtedness. Second, the establishment of the banking union reflects steps taken to reduce the functional dissonances emanating from European financial stability and integration on the one hand, and a banking system that was functioning under essentially national policy allowing private over-indebtedness on the other. The third dysfunctionality arose from the interaction of the first two in what became known as the bank-sovereign nexus (European Council 2012). Fragile public and private debt developments became intertwined at the national level, either because domestic banks were overexposed to failing domestic sovereign debt, or because the sovereign had to rescue the systemically important credit institutions. A close correlation thus arose between sovereign and bank debt with European-wide financial instability implications, simultaneously interrupting the smooth transmission of monetary policy by the banking system. The nexus thus endangered the EU- and Euro area-wide public goods such as financial stability and the single currency. A combination of fiscal backstops like the ESM (and the possibility of bank recapitalization) together with a centralized supervisory and resolution framework sought to alleviate the bank-sovereign nexus.[4]

---

[3]This section draws on Niemann and Ioannou (2015).

[4]As pointed out by Niemann and Ioannou (2015), the functional spillover logic was strong also because alternative solutions to reach the original goal (the stability of EMU and safeguarding the Euro) were considered politically and economically far too costly and/or risky.

The crisis can, at least in part, be seen as the result of existing, and amplifier of subsequent, functional pressures. If functional pressures are not resolved through further integrative steps, this can promote crises, which in turn cause further functional pressures during the process of crisis management, thereby eventually triggering the necessary steps of integration. At least some elements of the crisis can be attributed to the first two dysfunctionalities described above (Schmidt 2012: 76). Moreover, the lack of crisis management tools led to the third dissonance, whereby the support of illiquid banks to ensure financial stability became difficult for over-indebted national governments (Dyson 2013: 216).

Political Spillover

Next, we examine the integrative role played by nongovernmental elites by discussing the role of interest associations and financial markets.

The role of interest associations: Many Europe-wide organized interest groups—especially those representing large-scale businesses—have a strong preference for further integration. Survey data suggest that 78% of Eurozone business leaders are positive about the overall impact of joining the Euro, 94% support the survival of the Euro, and 89% favor further economic integration (Grant Thornton International Business Report 2013). Their position papers, reports, and statements further corroborate their interest in supranational solutions (BusinessEurope 2011; European Roundtable of Industrialists 2011, 2012). Also, in line with neofunctionalist assumptions, much of the corporate interest representation and articulation during the crisis took place through Brussels-based umbrella organizations and/or in a transnationally coordinated fashion. More importantly, specific associations have been able to influence outcomes. For example, in the negotiations for the "six-pack," BusinessEurope acted as a policy entrepreneur, arguing for stricter binding sanctions—both in terms of greater automatism and transfer of fines to a crisis resolution fund—even before this was taken up by the Commission or Task Force (Knedelhans 2014).[5]

The role of the financial markets: Although financial markets may be treated simply as arenas in which actors play out their individual strategies and respond to each other (Overbeek 2012: 40), a majority of authors have viewed them (mostly implicitly) as actors during the crisis (Schimmelfennig 2012: 396; Yiangou et al. 2013: 16ff). They acted, largely autonomously, both directly and indirectly to promote integration during the crisis (Schmidt 2012: 24). They may not have been organized as a unitary actor, but due to the high uncertainty and herd-like behavior observed during the crisis (Dyson 2013: 220), their actions appeared unitary vis-à-vis EU policy-makers and exerted significant pressure toward the adoption of integrative measures

---

[5] Compare BusinessEurope (2010) with European Commission (2010a, b) and European Council (2010). Also cf. Knedelhans (2014).

(Schimmelfennig 2012: 396). In particular, they bluntly revealed the dysfunctionalities of the original EMU design and became a serious threat to the Euro area through the radical reassessment of a variety of economic and credit risks. During numerous "historic" summits, where decision-makers attempted to persuade the markets of their ability to solve the problems, original positions gradually subsided to the pressure of financial markets, leading to more sustainable measures such as the six-pack, Fiscal Compact, and Banking Union (Vilpišauskas 2013: 372). From a neofunctionalist perspective, financial markets became a "revealer" of, and barometer for, the degree to which functional dissonances were addressed: when significant crisis management and integrative measures were taken, markets generally reacted positively, reducing pressure on sovereign bonds. By contrast, investors withdrew rapidly from these markets when they saw policy-making inactivity and hesitation.

Cultivated Spillover

The Commission, the European Parliament, and especially the European Central Bank shared a clear preference for substantial action toward further integration. The Commission sought to exploit the opportunity through proposals that would reinforce its authority in fiscal, budgetary, and banking arenas—and even raised the prospect of a "quantum leap" toward political union (Lefkofridi and Schmitter 2015: 6). The resulting regime of economic and financial governance provided the Commission with new opportunities for influence—primarily through new implementation powers (Bauer and Becker 2014). Though somewhat marginalized during the crisis, the EP exerted a lot of pressure so that the ESM and the Fiscal Compact were subjected to revisions (Fabbrini 2013: 1022f). In the end, the EP's mobilization resulted in its stronger involvement in the new regulatory framework—its role was strengthened compared to the previous version of the Stability and Growth Pact and to national parliaments (Fasone 2014).

The ECB reacted with standard and nonstandard monetary policy measures, including the rapid reduction of its key interest rates; changes to its collateral policy and Long Term Refinancing Operations (LTROs); the adoption of three Covered Bond Purchases Programmes (in 2009, 2011, and 2014); the Securities Markets Programme (SMP) in 2010 and the announcement of Outright Monetary Transactions (OMT) in 2012, both with the aim of enhancing the transmission of monetary policy through purchases of securities in secondary markets under different conditions. Beyond monetary measures, the ECB was an early advocate of integrative deepening to buttress EMU (Van Rompuy et al. 2012) and played an advisory role in assisting the authorities to shape and monitor EU-financed economic adjustment programs. The ECB's role in advancing integration was most evident in the development of the banking union. In neofunctionalist terminology, the ECB's advocacy to adjust and deepen the EMU framework is understood as resolving functional dissonances between the different policy domains under EMU that jeopardized the ECB's independence and its ability to shield the Euro and deliver price stability. Menz and Smith (2013: 203) even suggest that the ECB was a "decisive, at times even shrewd actor in pursuing its favoured strategy. In fact, much of the empirical story reads like one of quiet, yet powerful, mission creep". They further claim that ECB "officials [were] dedicated to not only salvaging the Euro at any cost, but also pushing for fiscal union."

Favorable Conditions for Spillover

It can be argued that the conditions for neofunctionalist spillover have been rather favorable in this case. We could witness a considerable presence of all main neofunctionalist pressures—something that under a non-deterministic neofunctionalist account cannot be taken for granted (Niemann 2006): compelling functional interdependencies and discrepancies, supportive market actors, and strong supranational agency. As a result, a fertile structural context could be exploited by effective agency. In addition, two (other) conditions have been conducive to the spillover process.

First, high levels of politicization[6] can be assumed to potentially obstruct neofunctionalist spillover because functional logics, socialization processes, reasoned debate tend be overshadowed by domestic/national constraints and supranational agents are likely to be kept under tighter control of national principals (Niemann 2006). The Eurozone crisis led to a certain/substantial politicization of EU politics. The public began to pay attention to the process and to mobilize their respective interest representations and party (representatives) to an unprecedented extent (Kriesi and Grande 2016), often not advocating further integration. Having said that, it has been argued that—despite the augmented overall level of politicization—policy-makers "successfully managed to depoliticise and shield decision-making against public scrutiny and silence public debates by avoiding treaty reforms, using secondary legislation (for example, Six Pack, Two Pack), establishing treaties outside the EU framework (for example, the Fiscal Compact)" (Börzel 2016: 17; Börzel and Risse 2018).

[6]Interestingly, politicization was first taken seriously by neofunctionalist scholar. They did so by the late 1969 and early 1970s. Schmitter (1969) thought that politicization would lead to "*a manifest redefinition of mutual objectives* that will probably occur [...] along with "*a shift in actor expectations and loyalty* toward the new regional center" Schmitter (1969: 166: emphasis in original). However, Schmitter's account of the potential impact of politicization became more cautious soon afterwards, when he suggested such a prediction only applied to exceptionally dynamic (integration) processes, while the more normal result of politicization would be "encapsulation," a state of rest or stagnation Schmitter (1970). Lindberg and Scheingold (1970) suggested that the relatively benign climate in which the EC was able to grow during its early years could be transformed into a politicized, conflictual one. Such developments, however, were "not likely to be felt in the years immediately ahead" Lindberg and Scheingold (1970: 278). For an approach that focuses specifically on the emergent process of politicization, see the "post-functionalist" work of Hooghe and Marks (2009).

A related condition is the relative technical complexity of the issues negotiated in the process of reforming the EMU regime and the strong possibility for experts in the process. The assumption here is that technically complex issues require expertise, and that experts are more prone to pursue functionally sound solutions, while keeping the negotiations away from the political limelight. That the issues negotiated during the crisis were technically complex has been recognised by observers (e.g. Wyplosz 2015; 201). Schmitter and Lefkofridi (2016: 21) thus consider the crisis management process as substantially influenced by a (neoliberal) epistemic community that largely internalized its conflicts. As suggested by Rosenhek (2013: 23; quoted from Schmitter and Lefkofridi 2016: 21) the "interpretative plots of the crisis were not offered by outsiders, but rather by established and powerful actors, such as the Fed and the ECB, with recognized expertise and high epistemic authority."

Conclusion

The above analysis suggests that neofunctionalism provides substantial utility in explaining the Eurozone crisis. As for the theory's usefulness in shedding light on other recent EU crises, there is limited evidence so far. While Niemann and Speyer (2018) have been able to make a similarly convincing case for the 2016 reform of Frontex, accounts dealing with the Schengen/refugee crisis more general (including the redistribution of refugees issue), seem somewhat problematic in terms of neofunctionalist spillover logics. It is interesting to note that the latter seems to be accompanied by less favorable conditions. The refugee crisis has been substantially more politicized and seemingly less technically complex (requiring less epistemic authority). At the same time, attempts at depoliticization, for example by masking redistributive issues behind regulatory policy, have failed because core issues of (national) sovereignty and identity were touched upon and because nationalist positions had been strengthened domestically, partly due to discontent over the isolation of controversial issues from political and electoral accountability during the preceding Euro crisis (Börzel 2016: 17–18). In addition, Schimmelfennig (2018) points out that the Schengen crisis, compared to the Eurozone crisis, has been characterized by less supranational capacity and transnational interdependence, thus adversely affecting important neofuctionalist pressures for integration.

Although neofunctionalism is not as such a theory of crisis, it still provides important insights for theorizing crisis, and may be developed further into such direction. There are several reasons for that: first, as the case illustration has indicated, neofunctionalism (still) has a very useful toolkit for analyzing salient issues, explaining EU decision processes and policy outcomes. Second, rather than confining its relevance to the specific conditions prevailing at the time of its formulation, neofunctionalism should be regarded as an evolving theory that has proven capable of reformulation, partly owing to the nature of its core assumptions, concepts, and hypotheses, and partly to its authors' propensity for self-reflection and self-criticism. Its scope of application has been usefully delimited through the above analysis, suggesting that moderate levels of politicization (or possibilities of depoliticization), and technical complexity (enabling epistemic authority), which directly affect supranational capacity, are important scope conditions for the neofunctionalist spillover logic, particularly relevant to the context of crisis.

This chapter also suggests one important shortcoming of neofunctionalism to the analysis of crisis: the way the theory developed until the 1970s mainly concentrates on the dynamics of integration, and, thus, struggles to explain its limits since it lacks an account of pressures that may counter the integration process (yet see Niemann, 2006).

There is continued potential for developing the theory, not least in further specifying the conditions under which the pressure of different types of spillover is likely to emerge (in terms of crises but also more generally) and affect the subsequent strategic responses for further integration or eventual disintegration. Hence, neofunctionalism is open-ended and inconclusive, which should be taken as a challenge for further developing it rather than as an excuse for dismissing it as an approach for analyzing and explaining integration crises.

REFERENCES

Bauer, M. W., & Becker, S. (2014). The Unexpected Winner of the Crisis. *Journal of European Integration, 36*(3), 213–229.

Begg, I. (2013). Are Better Defined Rules Enough? *Transfer: European Review of Labour and Research, 19*(1), 49–62.

Bergmann, J., & Niemann, A. (2018). From Neo-Functional Peace to a Logic of Spillover in EU External Policy. *Journal of Common Market Studies, 56*(2), 420–438.

Börzel, T. (2016). From EU Governance of Crisis to Crisis in EU Governance. *Journal of Common Market Studies, 54*(1), 8–23.

Börzel, T., & Risse, T. (2018). From the Euro to the Schengen Crises. *Journal of European Public Policy, 25*(1), 83–108.

BusinessEurope. (2010).*Combining Fiscal Sustainability and Growth: A European Action Plan*. https://www.businesseurope.eu/content/default.asp?PageID=568&DocID=25979.

BusinessEurope. (2011). *Letter to Council President Van Rompuy*. https://www.businesseurope.eu/Content/Default.asp?PageID=568&DocID=28181.

Checkel, J. T. (2001). Why Comply? *International Organization, 55*, 553–588.

Dyson, K. (2013). Sworn to Grim Necessity? *Journal of European Integration, 35*(2), 207–222.

European Commission. (2010a). *Reinforcing Economic Policy Coordination* (COM (2010) 250 Final). Brussels: European Commission. https://eurlex.europa.eu/LexUriServ/LexUriServ.do?uri=COM:2010:0250:FIN:EN:PDF.

European Commission. (2010b). *Enhancing Economic Policy Coordination for Stability, Growth and Jobs*. Brussels: European Commission.https://ec.europa.eu/economy_finance/articles/euro/documents/com_2010_367_en.pdf.

European Council. (2010). *Strengthening Economic Governance in the EU* (Report of the Task Force to the European Council). Brussels: European Council. https://www.consilium.europa.eu/uedocs/cms_data/docs/pressdata/en/ec/117236.pdf.
European Council. (2012). *Euro Area summit Statement of 29 June 2012.* https://www.consilium.europa.eu/uedocs/cms_data/docs/pressdata/en/ec/131359.pdf.
European Roundtable of Industrialists. (2011). *'Euro crisis: European industry leaders call for coordinated actions to reinforce EMU*. https://www.ert.eu/sites/default/files/Euro%20-%20ERT%20Press%20Release%20FINAL%20121011.pdf.
European Roundtable of Industrialists. (2012). *'Creating growth in Europe'*. https://www.ert.eu/sites/default/files/2012%20January%20-%20ERT%20Statement%20on%20Creating%20Growth%20in%20Europe.pdf.
Fabbrini, S. (2013). Intergovernmentalism and Its Limits: Assessing the European Union's Answer to the Euro Crisis 1. *Comparative Political Studies, 46*(9), 1003–1029.
Fasone, C. (2014). European Economic Governance and Parliamentary Representation. *European Law Journal, 20*(2), 164–185.
Grant Thornton International Business Report. (2013). *The future of Europe.* http://www.internationalbusinessreport.com/files/IBR2013_Future_Europe_FINAL.pdf.
Groom, A. J. R. (1978). A Case of Mistaken Identity. *Political Science, 30,* 15–28.
Haas, E. (1958). *The Uniting of Europe, 1950–7*. London: Stevens.
Haas, E. (1960). *Consensus Formation in the Council of Europe.* Berkeley, CA: University of California Press.
Haas, E. (1961). International Integration. *International Organization, 15,* 366–392.
Haas, E. (1964). Technocracy, Pluralism and the New Europe. In S. Graubard (Ed.), *A New Europe?* (pp. 62–88). Boston, MA: Houghton Mifflin.
Haas, E. (1968). *The Uniting of Europe, 1950–7*. Stanford, CA: Stanford University Press.
Haas, E. (1970). The Study of Regional Integration. *International Organization, 24,* 607–644.
Haas, E. (1976). Turbulent Fields and the Theory of Regional Integration. *International Organization, 30,* 173–212.
Haas, E. B. (2001). Does Constructivism Subsume Neo-functionalism? In T. Christiansen, K.E. Jørgensen, & A. Wiener (Eds.), *The Social Construction of Europe* (pp. 22–31). London: Sage.
Haas, Ernst, & Schmitter, P. (1964). Economics and Differential Patterns of Political Integration. *International Organisation, 18*(4), 705–737.
Haas, & Ernst, B. (Ed.). (2004). Introduction: Institutionalism or Constructivism? In *The Uniting of Europe: Politics, Social and Economic Forces, 1950–1957* (pp. 13–56). Notre Dame: University of Notre Dame Press.
Habermas, J. (1981). *Theorie des kommunikativen Handelns, 2 volumes.* Frankfurt/Main: Suhrkamp.
Hobolt, S. B., & Wratil, C. (2015). Public Opinion and the Crisis. *Journal of European Public Policy, 22*(2), 238–256.
Hoffmann, S. (1966). Obstinate or Obsolete. *Daedalus, 95*(3), 862–915.
Hooghe, L., & Marks, G. (2009). A Postfunctionalist Theory of European Integration. *British Journal of Political Science, 39*(1), 1–23.

Keohane, R., & Hoffmann, S. (1991). Institutional Change in Europe in the 1980s'. In T. N. E. Community (Ed.), *Keohane, Robert and Hoffmann* (pp. 1–40). Boulder, CO: Westview Press.

Knedelhans, M. (2014). The Influence of Non-Governmental Interest Groups on the European Sovereign Debt Crisis Management. Master Thesis, University of Mainz, Mainz, Germany.

Kriesi, H., & Grande, E. (2016). The Euro Crisis. In Hütter et al. (Eds.), *Politicising Europe*. Cambridge: Cambridge University Press.

Lefkofridi, Z., & Schmitter, P. C. (2015). Transcending or Descending? *European Political Science Review, 7*(1), 3–22.

Lindberg, L. (1963). *The Political Dynamics of European Integration*. Princeton, NJ: Princeton University Press.

Lindberg, L., & Scheingold, S. (1970). *Europe's Would-Be Polity*. Englewood Cliffs, NJ: Prentice Hall.

Marks, G., Hooghe, L., & Blank, K. (1996). European Integration from the 1980s. *Journal of Common Market Studies, 34*, 341–378.

Menz, G., & Smith, M. (2013). Kicking the Can Down the Road to More Europe? *Journal of European Integration, 35*(3), 195–206.

Merler, S. (2014). *Banking Union and Beyond*. Brussels Think Tank Dialogue. Brussels: Think Tank Dialogue. https://www.bruegel.org/publications/public ation-detail/publication/808-banking-union-and-beyond-discussion-papers-for-bru ssels-think-tank-dialogue/.

Mitrany, David (1966). *A Working Peace System*. Chicago, IL: University of Michigan.

Moravcsik, A. (1993). Preferences and Power in the European Community. *Journal of Common Market Studies, 31*, 473–524.

Niemann, A. (1998). The PHARE Programme and the Concept of Spillover. *Journal of European Public Policy, 5*, 428–446.

Niemann, A. (2000). The Internal and External Dimensions of European Union Decision-Making: Developing and Testing a Revised Neofunctionalist Framework. Ph.D. Thesis, University of Cambridge, Cambridge.

Niemann, A. (2004). From Pre-Theory to Theory? (p. 11). Dresdner Arbeitspapiere Internationale Beziehungen, No: Developing a Revised Neofunctionalist Framework.

Niemann, A. (2006). *Explaining Decisions in the European Union*. Cambridge: Cambridge University Press.

Niemann, A., & Ioannou, D. (2015). European Economic Integration in Times of Crisis: A case of Neofunctionalism? *Journal of European Public Policy, 22*(2), 196–218.

Niemann, A., Lefkofridi, Z. and Schmitter, P. (2019). Neo-functionalism. In A. Wiener, T. Börzel, & T. Risse (Eds.), *Theories of European Integration* (3rd ed.). Oxford: Oxford University Press.

Niemann, A., and Speyer, J. (2018). A Neofunctionalist Perspective on the 'European Refugee Crisis': The Case of the European Border and Coast Guard. *JCMS: Journal of Common Market Studies, 56*(1), 23–43.

Overbeek, H. (2012). Sovereign Debt Crisis in Euroland. *The International Spectator, 47*(1), 30–48.

Pierson, P. (1996). The Path to European Integration. *Comparative Political Studies, 29*, 123–163.

Risse, T. (2000). Let's Argue! *International Organization, 54*, 1–39.

Rosamond, B. (2000). *Theories of European Integration*. London: Macmillan.
Rosenhek, Z. (2013). Diagnosing and Explaining the Global Financial Crisis: Central Banks, Epistemic Authority, and Sense Making. *International Journal of Politics, Culture, and Society, 26*(3), 255–272.
Sandholtz, W., & Stone Sweet, A. (1998). *European Integration and Supranational Governance*. Oxford: Oxford University Press.
Schimmelfennig, F. (2012). Zwischen Neo—und Postfunktionalismus: Die Integrationstheorien und die Eurokrise. *Politische Vierteljahresschrift, 53*(4), 394–413.
Schimmelfennig, F. (2018). European Integration (Theory) in Times of Crisis. *Journal of European Public Policy, 25*(7), 969–989.
Schmidt, S. (2012). *Das Gesetz der Krise*. Munich: Droemer Verlag.
Schmitter, P. (1969). Three Neo-functional Hypotheses About International Integration. *International Organization, 23*(2), 161–166.
Schmitter, P. (1970). A Revised Theory of Regional Integration. *International Organization, 24*, 836–868.
Schmitter, P. C. (2004). Neo-Neofunctionalism. In A. Wiener & T. Diez (Eds.), *European Integration Theory* (pp. 46–74). Oxford: Oxford University Press.
Schmitter, P. C., & Lefkofridi, Z. (2016). Neo-functionalism as a Theory of Disintegration. *Chinese political science review, 1*(1), 1–29.
Sweet, S., & Alec and Sandholtz, Wayne. (1997). European Integration and Supranational Governance. *Journal of European Public Policy, 4*, 297–317.
Taylor, P. (1989). The New Dynamics of EC in the 1980s'. In J. Lodge (Ed.), *The European Community and the Challenge of the Future*. New York, NY: St. Martin's Press.
Tranholm-Mikkelsen, J. (1991). Neo-Functionalism: Obstinate or Obsolete? *Millenium, 20*, 1–22.
Van Rompuy, H., Barroso, J. M., Juncker, C., & Draghi, M. (2012). *Auf dem Weg zu einer echten Wirtschafts—und Wa¨hrungsunion'*. https://www.consiliumeuropa.eu/uedocs/cms_data/docs/pressdata/de/ec/134206.pdf.
Vilpišauskas, R. (2013). Eurozone Crisis and European Integration? *Journal of European Integration, 35*(3), 361–373.
Wyplosz, C. (2015). The Eurozone Crisis: Too Few lessons Learned. In R. Balwin & F. Giavazzi (Eds.), *The Eurozone Crisis*. London: CEPR Press.
Yiangou, J., O'Keeffe, M., & Glöckler, G. (2013). 'Tough Love': How the ECB's Monetary Financing Prohibition Pushes Deeper Euro Area Integration. *Journal of European Integration, 35*(3), 223–237.

CHAPTER 7

Institutionalism

Christopher Ansell

What Is Institutionalism?

Institutionalism is a broad umbrella term used in the social sciences to describe the study of institutions and their importance in social, economic, and political life. The intellectual sources of this tradition are eclectic, ranging from the classical sociology and political economy of authors such as Emile Durkheim, Karl Marx, Thorstein Veblen, and Max Weber (Stinchcombe 1997), to the formal-legal study of politics (Rhodes 2011), to the analysis of organizations (Selznick 1996). In the 1970s and 1980s, a "new institutionalism" began to take shape, becoming codified in the early 1990s (Williamson 1975; March and Olsen 1983, 1989; Shepsle 1989; Powell and DiMaggio 1991; Steinmo et al. 1992; Hall and Taylor 1996; Immergut 1998; Thelen 1999; Pierson and Skocpol 2002). As it developed, new institutionalism became differentiated around different assumptions about what institutions are and how they matter.

In an influential article, Hall and Taylor (1996) identified three variants of "new institutionalism"—historical, rational choice, and sociological institutionalism. Historical institutionalism grew out of an examination of how institutions structure the interaction between states and markets and also between market actors (Steinmo et al. 1992). Rational choice institutionalism developed out of studies of how rules governing U.S. Congressional behavior affected the creation of majorities and also out of the "new economics of organization" (Moe 1984; Shepsle 1989). Sociological institutionalism grew

C. Ansell (✉)
University of California, Berkeley, CA, USA
e-mail: cansell@berkeley.edu

out of a critique of organizational rationality and reflected a "cognitive turn" in sociology (Powell and DiMaggio 1991). As Thelen (1999) subsequently pointed out, the boundaries between these different versions of new institutionalism are not clear cut, and many authors draw on more than one. Others have proposed additional variants. Schmidt (2008) proposed a fourth version of institutionalism she called "discursive institutionalism" and a number of authors have suggested a version influenced by Pragmatist philosophy (Berk and Galvan 2009; Ansell 2011).

Although the boundaries between these variants of institutionalism are fuzzy, it is possible to point to some important starting points for understanding their view of crisis and institutional change. In rational choice institutionalism, institutions can be understood as either "exogenous constraints" or as an "exogenously given *game form*" (Shepsle 2006: 24). As exogeneous constraints, they can be thought of as "the rules of the game" that affect what actors can and cannot do. As a game form, such rules shape how actors interact strategically, producing a "structure-induced equilibrium." However, institutions may also be more endogenous and are thus conceived as simply "equilibrium ways of doing things" (Shepsle 2006: 26). Institutions may be formal or informal (North 1990; in Shepsle's terms "structured" or "unstructured").

Key elements of historical institutionalism were first codified by an edited volume by Steinmo et al. (1992) and have developed rapidly since. Two critical concepts in historical institutionalism are *critical juncture* and *path dependence*. Summarizing this body of ideas, Fioretos writes that:

> [t]he most distinguishing mark of historical institutionalism is the primacy it accords to temporality—the notion that the timing and sequence of events shape political processes. In more specific terms, historical institutionalism suggests that timing and sequence contribute to unpredictability (outcomes may vary greatly), inflexibility (the more time passes, the more difficult it is to reverse course), nonergodicity (chance events may have lasting effects), and inefficiencies (forgone alternatives may have been more efficient). (2011: 371)

However, in contrast with rational choice institutionalism historical institutionalism "tend[s] to emphasize historical process over equilibrium order" (Thelen 1999: 384).

Sociological institutionalism has deep roots that can be traced back to the work of Durkheim and Weber, among other classical theorists, and it has been particularly prominent in the field of organization studies. In the 1960s, a "new" sociological institutionalism began to differentiate itself from Talcott Parson's functional sociology (Powell and DiMaggio 1991). Berger and Luckmann's (1991) *Social Construction of Reality* was a landmark work emphasizing that social interactions lead to the development of taken-for-granted role structures. As the title of their book suggested, this version of institutionalism stressed the "socially constructed" nature of institutions. This constructivist perspective leads to the view that institutions are "constitutive," as explained by Jeffrey Checkel:

> Sociological institutionalists are unabashedly thick institutionalists. Not only in the distant future, but in the near-term, institutions constitute actors and their interests. What exactly does it mean for institutions to constitute? It is to suggest that they can provide agents with understandings of their interests and identities. (1999: 547)

Socialization and social learning mechanisms are therefore important aspects of sociological institutionalism. A key implication here is that "institutions constrain and shape politics through the construction and elaboration of meaning" (From 2002: 226). Institutions are thus sometimes interpreted as cultural norms that establish a rule-like "logic of appropriateness" (March and Olsen 1996).

A fourth version of institutionalism is discursive institutionalism (Schmidt 2008). Discursive institutionalism focuses on the role of ideas and discourse in producing both institutional change and continuity. There is now an extensive literature on the role of ideas that explores why some ideas stick, while others do not. Discursive institutionalism builds on this literature, but suggests that ideas are embedded in wider "coordinative discourses" ("the individuals and groups at the center of policy construction who are involved in the creation, elaboration, and justification of policy and programmatic ideas") and "communicative discourses ("the individuals and groups involved in the presentation, deliberation, and legitimation of political ideas to the general public") (Schmidt 2008: 310). Analyzing the process of discursive interaction is a way of understanding why some ideas succeed while others fail. With its focus on meaning, discursive institutionalism shares much with sociological institutionalism, but emphasizes that actors exercise agency through discourse. In making this point, they distinguish their position from the mere compliance with norms that they associate with sociological institutionalism (Schmidt 2008: 320).

A final variant of institutionalism is pragmatist institutionalism. Although pragmatist institutionalism can trace its roots back to Chicago school sociology, institutional economics, and organizational sociology, it has recently been reinvigorated (Sabel and Zeitlin 2008; Berk and Galvan 2009; Herrigel 2010; Ansell 2011; Farjoun et al. 2015; Jabko and Sheingate 2018). A distinctive feature of the philosophy of pragmatism is that it emphasizes both the power of habit *and* the possibilities for creative action (Jabko 2019). Thus, Berk and Galvan argue that institutions can be understood in terms of pragmatism's distinctive understanding of habit as skillful action rooted in experience:

> …[I]nstitutions are composed of rules that are not enacted schemas, but lived skills. Institutions are social because they're temporal. Institutions are not

> constraints on action, they're made through action. Order is not a prior or necessary condition of institutions, but a possible result of particular forms of experiencing rules in action. (2009: 552)

From this perspective, pragmatism suggests that institutions can be recombined and reinterpreted through action in a manner similar to what the French anthropologist Claude Lévi-Strauss (1966) called "bricolage."

Based on this very brief introduction to these different variants of institutionalism, we can now examine more closely how each of them approaches the issue of explaining institutional change and stability.

Mechanisms of Institutional Continuity or Change

The traditional emphasis in institutionalism is on how institutions persist through time. There is an initial assumption that institutions are "sticky" or inertial, as expressed in the idea that institutions are path dependent and reinforced through feedback effects, that they are in a self-reinforcing equilibrium, or that they are "taken for granted" cognitive scripts. This emphasis on the stability of institutions through time creates a challenge for explaining institutional change (Mahoney and Thelen 2010). While the assumption of institutional stability remains dominant, institutional theorists now clearly appreciate the need to have a complementary concept of change.

Historical institutionalism has been particularly focused on developing a complementary theory of stability and change. To explain stability, they have drawn on the concept of path dependence as initially developed by economists studying technological development (Pierson 2000). However, Kathleen Thelen has argued that this model of lock-in via positive feedbacks was both too contingent and too deterministic to capture the path dependence of political institutions. As she writes:

> It is too contingent in that the initial choice (call it a "critical juncture") is seen as rather open and capable of being "tipped" by small events or chance circumstances, whereas in politics this kind of blank slate is a rarity, to say the least... [It] is also too deterministic in that once the initial choice is made, then the argument becomes mechanical. There is one fork in the road, and after that, the path only narrows... However, [in politics] the losers do not necessarily disappear, and their adaptation can mean something very different from embracing and reproducing the institution, as in the technology model. (1999: 385)

At the time she wrote her review article in 1999, Thelen argued that historical institutionalists had not given sufficient attention to how particular national trajectories or institutional legacies are reinforced over time. She argued that a "cognitive" conception of path dependence, advanced by sociological institutionalism, was not a good match for highly contested political processes.

However, she noted that the literature on "feedback effects" was notable for providing a clearer understanding of these mechanisms (Pierson 1993).

Historical institutionalists see institutions as the product of political contestation, but where outcomes can have long-lasting legacies. Thelen notes two such mechanisms. One mechanism is that institutions create incentives for behaviors that reinforce existing institutional pathways. A second mechanism is that institutions reinforce the distribution of power in such a way that they may support certain pathways while undermining the possibility of others. Discussing historical institutionalism, Fioretos (2011) summarizes four causal feature of institutional lock-in: (1) the creation of vested interests; (2) the production of positive feedbacks; (3) the role of increasing returns; and (4) self-reinforcing qualities created by interdependence with other institutions.

Once path dependent processes are in place, historical institutionalists must then explain change. The concept of "critical juncture" has been the central idea in this tradition for describing the period in which it is possible to shift paths (Collier and Collier 2002; Capoccia and Kelemen 2007). Capoccia and Keleman define critical junctures as "relatively short periods of time during which there is a substantially heightened probability that agents' choices will affect the outcome of interest" (2007: 348). The duration of a critical juncture is short relative to the longer "path" of development that follows from it. They observe that although the outcomes of critical junctures are contingent, it is also possible that the result of such a period may be a "re-equilibration" of an existing institutional path. Furthermore, junctures become more critical to the extent that the period of the juncture is short relative to its long-term effects ("temporal leverage") and to the extent that the probability of a particular path increases ("probability jump") (Capoccia and Kelemen 2007: 361).[1]

In an analysis of the causal dynamics of critical junctures, Soifer (2012) distinguishes between permissive and productive conditions. Permissive conditions relax structural constraints on action, whereas productive conditions foster particular outcomes. A permissive condition creates a "window of opportunity" for change but does not explain the change that occurs. Understood as a point of time where the path of institutional development diverges from the status quo, Soifer argues that *both* permissive and productive conditions are necessary and causally relevant for producing a critical juncture. He distinguishes these two different types of conditions from a "critical antecedent." Unlike permissive conditions, antecedent conditions are present before the critical juncture, but they do influence the importance of productive conditions during the juncture.

The critical juncture model tends to see change as driven by exogenous factors that disrupt existing paths or equilibrium. This image of "punctuated

---

[1] Soifer says it somewhat differently, saying that a juncture becomes more critical to the extent that "the outcomes generated in one historical moment persist over time" (2012: 1577).

equilibrium" driven by external shocks has been a prominent feature of institutionalist perspectives, but it has also led theorists to consider different patterns of change. A number of scholars, for instance, have sought to break down the dualism between punctuated equilibrium and gradual incremental change. Stark (2018) tries to do this by reconceptualizing critical junctures. He argues that critical junctures should be understood as periods where radical, incremental, and no change coincide. He observes that "[w]e also need to consider those 'near misses' where change has not occurred and re-equilibrium is the order of the day. In these instances, we must conceptualise a smaller critical juncture in which a window for change opens quickly, permissive conditions allow for the possibility of change but the status quo reasserts itself and no change occurs" (2018: 36). Studlar and Cairney (2014) describe the idea of "phased transitions" that occur gradually over time without being precipitated by major crises or events.

Other scholars have explored patterns of endogenous change. Mahoney and Thelen (2010) argue that one mechanism of institutional change is produced by shifts in the distributional balance of power that underpin institutional stability. Another source of change is associated with the ambiguity of rules, which can be interpreted in different ways. Institutional change can therefore occur through shifts in interpretation. Change can also occur due to gaps between institutions and their enforcement. Coalitional shifts, ambiguity, and enforcement gaps provide the basis for endogenous change in institutions. Building on these ideas, they identify four types of gradual institutional change: *displacement* is "the removal of existing rules and the introduction of new ones"; *layering* is "the introduction of new rules on top of or alongside existing ones"; *drift* is "the changed impact of existing rules due to shifts in the environment"; and *conversion* is "the changed enactment of existing rules due to their strategic redeployment" (2010: 15–16).

Mahoney and Thelen (2010) then develop an analytical framework to predict the type of institutional change that one might expect. This framework depends on two broad factors. First, are there political actors who are in a good position to veto change? Second, to what extent are actors able to exercise discretion in the interpretation and enforcement of institutions? Where veto power is strong and discretion is limited, they predict that institutional change will take the form of layering. Where veto power is strong, but discretion is more extensive, they predict drift. Where discretion is more extensive, but veto power is weaker, they expect institutional change to be characterized by conversion. Finally, where discretion is limited and veto power is weak, institutional displacement is likely to occur.

Recent work in the tradition of historical institutionalism argues that "institutional plasticity" also matters for understanding institutional change. Ikani (2019) argues that historical institutionalism adopts a "contextual causality" that places explanations of change in a temporal context. A critical juncture can be understood as making temporal context more salient. Ikani argues that it is the interaction of institutional plasticity and temporal context that explains the pattern of institutional change during the Ukraine Crisis.

In rational choice institutionalism, institutional stability and change are understood in terms of equilibria outcomes. In an early paper, Shepsle (1989) spelled out a useful general framework. On the one hand, he wrote, institutions can be understood as structures that constrain and channel individual choices. They produce what he called a "structure-induced equilibrium." On the other hand, he wrote, to explain why the structure itself is stable, we need to study "equilibrium institutions." He posited that institutions could be understood to be an *ex ante* selection of rules that will apply to a particular situation. They are like contracts. However, as with contracts, there is a good deal of uncertainty involved and the ex ante selection may not be robust in the face of changing conditions. An institution is robust (stable) over time if no coalition wishes to change it.

Adopting a rational choice-historical institutionalist view of institutions, Lindner defines institutional change as "as the introduction of new rules or rule interpretations that supplement or replace existing rules and interpretations" (2003: 913). This description builds on the important work of the economic historian Douglass North, who argues that institutions tend to change gradually and incrementally. North argues that this is because "the economies of scope, the complementarities and the network externalities that arise from an existing institutional matrix" will often bias actors to stick with the existing rules of the game (1993: 64). Change will therefore occur at the margins of existing institutions. More radical change occurs when the actors are unable to reach compromises under existing institutional constraints.

Greif and Laitin (2004) discuss the challenges of explaining endogenous institutional change from a game-theoretic perspective that regards institutions as equilibrium outcomes. Their solution to this challenge is to develop two concepts—quasi-parameters and institutional reinforcement. A quasi-parameter is treated as exogenous in the short run, but endogenous in the long run. While a quasi-parameter can reinforce institutions, they can also undermine them. In other words, for endogenous change to occur, quasi-parameters have to shift from reinforcing to undermining. Thus, Greif and Laitin suggest that "institutional change should have a quality of punctuated equilibria…where change is in actuality evolutionary but apparently abrupt, typically associated with a 'crisis' revealing that the previous behavior is no longer an equilibrium" (2004: 639).

Sociological institutionalism's understanding of institutional change has, in part, focused on how institutions diffuse and on why there is convergence on similar institutional forms over time—that is, institutional isomorphism. In a now classic article, DiMaggio and Powell (1983) identified three different mechanisms—coercive, normative, and mimetic influences—that explain the convergence of institutions on a particular form (e.g., institutional isomorphism). Beckert (2010) has emphasized that this model of institutional isomorphism can also be used to explain institutional change and divergence.

Coercive influences imply that power is exercised to force institutional change. Normative influences, Beckert argues, work by a mechanism of attraction, whereby institutional entrepreneurs are attracted to particular institutional models. Mimetic influences work by emulation and tend to occur where uncertainty and the need for legitimation is high. To these three mechanisms, Beckert adds competition, which he suggests explains institutional change through evolutionary selection pressures. Finally, he stresses that while sociological institutionalism tends to stress the homogenizing impact of these influences, these mechanisms can also explain institutional diversification.

Discursive institutionalism investigates the role of ideas and the nature of discursive interaction in order to explain institutional change. Schmidt writes that "historical institutionalist approaches do very well in describing how the rules and institutions continue or change incrementally over time but not so well in explaining why. This is because they do little to elucidate how and why agents engage in layering, let alone inventing or reinterpreting the rules – other than to categorise them as change agents" (2016: 1036). Rational choice institutionalism, she argues, does capture the role of agency in institutional change, but does not adequately capture "the complexity of real agents' changing ideas about their interests in incrementally developing institutions, as member state agents engage in a constant process of dialogue, deliberation, and contestation in their 'coordinative' discourses of policy construction and 'communicative' discourses of political legitimation" (2016: 1036).

What these approaches miss, Schmidt argues, is the role of ideas and discourse in producing institutional change. To illustrate her argument, she discusses a now classic paper by Peter Hall (1993), which argued that policy change could be understood in terms of the transformation of "policy paradigms." Drawing an analogy with Thomas Kuhn's well-known conception of scientific paradigms (Kuhn 1962), Hall distinguished three different "orders" of change. A first order change occurs when overall policy goals and instruments remain stable, but policy practices (e.g., the "settings" of policy instruments) are adapted in order to better meet these goals and deploy these instruments. A second order of policy change occurs when policy goals remain stable, but when the policy instruments for achieving these goals change. A third order of change occurs when not only policy instruments and their settings, but also the hierarchy of goals behind the policy, change. Hall suggests that a policy paradigm refers to the ideas behind a particular constellation of goals and instruments—ideas through which policy actors understand and make sense of a particular policy area. He suggests that "normal policymaking" refers to first and second order change—that is, where policy instruments or their settings change. Third order change is more radical and refers to a "paradigm shift." Policy paradigm shifts are likely to be political rather than scientific and are likely to be driven by the accumulation policy failures or experiments that are viewed as anomalous from the perspective of the reigning paradigm.

Schmidt (2011) argues that Hall's account does not help us understand when a paradigm shift has occurred (which she equates to a "critical juncture"). She also argues that the paradigm shift may come about through relatively abrupt and radical change or through incremental change over a longer period. She also suggests that the concept of paradigm may be overly monolithic, since typically there are many competing policy ideas in a particular domain. Elsewhere, she argues that ideas must be understood in terms of discursive interaction and that institutional change occurs through a discursive battle over ideas (Schmidt 2010).

Writing from a pragmatist institutionalist perspective, Berk and Galvan (2009) articulate a model of institutional change that they call "creative syncretism." They suggest that to appreciate institutional change we must first envision institutional "structures" as mutable rather than fixed constraints. Institutions are not simply objective conditions that exist like rocks in social space. Part of their mutability comes from the fact that they are typically more loosely coupled than typically envisioned by rational choice or historical institutionalist perspectives. In building on Berk and Galvan, Jabko (2019) puts this nicely, arguing that institutions are "[l]oosely articulated and evolving repertoires, rather than systematic templates of action…" (2019: 14). Moreover, it takes work to maintain them, a point that Jabko and Sheingate (2018) have recently elaborated. Thus, for Berk and Galvan, syncretism is a "label and metaphor [that] highlights the openness and mutability of seemingly coherent structures" (2009: 544). Actors engage with institutions not as objective constraints, but instead they skillfully deploy and appropriate them. Thus, syncretism is creative because actors engage with institutional rules in improvisational ways.

Both discursive and pragmatism institutionalism seek to introduce more agency into explanations of institutional change. But their efforts point to a wider rethinking of the nature of stability and change itself. A number of authors have begun to challenge the usefulness of thinking of stability and change as a dualism. According to Marsh (2010), this dualism misleadingly demarcates time into periods of stasis and periods of rapid change. Marsh points to the possibility, for instance, that one paradigm may create the context for and mediate the development of an alternative paradigm, an argument he makes in defense of an historical institutionalist view of path dependence— noting that "path dependency is not synonymous with path determinacy" (2010: 99). Marsh points to how this dualism rests on a particular view of agency and structure: "If one argues that successful crisis narratives, that is ideas, drive change, then one almost inevitably focuses on the agents who proselytize the ideas" (Marsh 2010: 92). By contrast, Marsh argues for a more dialectical view of the relationship between structure and agency. Institutional structures place constraints on ideational change, but agents of change may (or rather must) exploit the contradictions or tensions in existing structures and attack the bases of institutional reproduction.

In a defense of historical institutionalism, Stephen Bell poses the wider issue of understanding institutional change: "[m]ore broadly, the challenge is how to describe and explain contingent degrees of agent-centred discretion (arguably the ultimate propellant of institutional change) within a context of constraint, conditioning and empowerment associated with institutionally embedded agents" (2011: 884). He also arrives at a "dialectical" view of the relationship between structure and agency. To put this idea into practice, Bell formulates several key points: (1) "agents interpret and construct the experience of their institutional situation using subjective and inter-subjective cognitive and normative frameworks and discursive processes" (2011: 893); (2) "despite the role of institutional shaping, agents still have contingently variable degrees of agential space or 'bounded discretion' within institutional settings and can change institutions over time" (2011: 894); and (3) "a further innovation is to see institutions not just as sources of constraint but also as having important empowering and enabling effects which interpretive agents may be able to exploit" (2011: 895). This move, he argues, enables historical institutionalism to transcend the dualism between "exogenous" and "endogenous" change and between "change" and "stasis."

Institutionalist Perspectives on Crisis

The term "crisis" has a long history, with many layered meanings (Kosolleck 2006). In contemporary discourse, crisis is often understood to be a delimited period of time in which communities and institutions must confront exceptional threats or challenges, such as a major flood, a humanitarian emergency, or a terrorist attack. These challenges and threats are understood to require effective "crisis management" to prevent or survive them. A somewhat different interpretation of crisis comes from the political economy tradition, which stresses the "crisis of capitalism" or the "crisis of the state." Building on the work of Claus Offe, Colin Hay captures the different meanings at stake here by distinguishing between a "conjunctural" and a "structural" intervention in response to crisis. Where a conjunctural intervention seeks solutions "within the pre-existing and largely unmodified structures of the state regime," a structural intervention restructures the system itself (1999: 329).

Institutionalism has not been particularly attuned to the use of the concept of crisis. However, from the political economy perspective just described, Hay understands a crisis "as a moment of decisive intervention in the process of institutional change" produced by "perceptions of systemic failure" (1999: 320, 324). Other scholars, however, note that crisis can reinforce existing institutions (Peters 2011). Existing institutions may be a "safe harbor" in a crisis. (Bell 2017). Building on behavioral psychology, Bell argues "…that agents often use fast thinking, cognitive short-cuts, heuristics, emotions, social narratives and social emulation, and they rely on rules and institutions to operate in an uncertain world, to secure greater predictability and to feel as safe and right as possible" (2017: 730–731). Similarly, Hooren et al. (2014) find that economic shocks produced primarily incremental change in welfare institutions in Australia, Belgium, the Netherlands, and Sweden and conclude that there is "only a very loose association between the depth of the crisis and policy change" (2014: 616). They suggest that a "threat-rigidity" dynamic may be at work—an old argument that threat makes decision-makers conservative (rigid).

Perhaps the central concept in institutionalism with respect to crisis is "critical juncture." Ikani, for example, argues that the Ukraine Crisis was a critical juncture for the European Neighborhood Policy (ENP), creating "…a moment of heightened contingency as calls for reform mounted and the EU launched a formal reform round of the ENP" (2019: 27). As such, all the issues discussed in the previous section with respect to critical junctures are relevant for explaining institutional change processes during crises. Notably, Soifer (2012) argues that the relationship between crisis and institutional change can be understood in terms of his distinction between permissive and productive conditions. A crisis may produce permissive conditions for change, but the productive conditions pushing for particular changes may or may not be present.

Historical institutionalism also associates a crisis with the concept of "punctuated equilibrium," which implies an exogenous shock that disrupts an existing institutional equilibrium (Peters 2011). However, scholars have criticized this perspective. Colin Hay has argued that social constructivist versions of institutionalism (e.g., sociological institutionalism, discursive institutionalism) do not assume that institutions are "self-equilibrating" and he notes that "constructivism is perhaps particularly sensitive and attuned to such disequilibrating dynamics, to moments of crisis and, above all, to their political constitution (and the politics of their constitution)" (Hay 2016: 530). In his earlier work, Hay (1999) proposed the idea of "punctuated *evolution*" to call attention to ways that new ideas often outrun the structural transformation of state institutions (1999: 327; my emphasis).

From a discursive or sociological perspective, a crisis is itself a social construction—that is, an interpretation of events. Hay (2016) argues that a social constructivist perspective provides insight into how a crisis can feed back into the unfolding of the crisis itself. In essence, a crisis is a crisis because it "challenge[s] conventional conceptions of normality – violating codified norms which govern our expectations" (Hay 2016: 531). A discursive construction of a crisis—that is, a crisis narrative—recruits specific instances of failure as symptoms of deeper and more systemic problems. Ultimately, Hay argues, crisis is the process in which narratives about the need for intervention are contested and constituted. For example, through acts of solidarity, Hassan (2010) argues that Europe narrated the crisis precipitated by the September 2001 terrorist attacks in the U.S. as its own.

An important implication of a discursive institutionalist perspective is that crisis narratives themselves require explanation (Kern et al. 2014). Schmidt (2011) argues that although discursive institutionalism tends to share with historical institutionalism a demarcation of institutional change into periods of crisis-driven and incremental change, discursive institutionalism treats crises as "objects of explanation, in which agents' constructive ideational and discursive engagement with events become the basis for future ideational (re)constructions and actions" (2011: 108). Although she notes that historical institutionalism is interested in endogenous change, it tends to focus on "how" this occurs, whereas discursive institutionalism emphasizes the "why and the wherefore of incremental change by reference to agents' own ideas and discourse about how they go about layering, reinterpreting, or converting those institutions" (2011: 108).

Thus, discursive institutionalism focuses attention on the framing of the crisis itself, and the rival narratives that provide interpretations of the crisis (Schmidt 2013, 2014). Although discursive institutionalism finds the idea of "paradigm" important (see Hall 1993), it is less useful during a crisis where ideas appear to be in flux. Schmidt suggests that during a crisis, we must understand the interplay of two aspects of communication: *coordinative discourse* among policy actors and *communicative discourse* with the public about the legitimacy of certain measures.

From a pragmatist institutionalist perspective, Jabko and Sheingate (2018) argue that crises are more pervasive than institutionalism typically appreciates and they define crises as "…moments of disorder when problems outrun the institutional capacity of the political system to contain conflict" (2018: 313). Crises are expressions of multiple tensions, but according to Jabko and Sheingate they do not always produce critical junctures. Political elites may produce responses to crisis in ways that strengthen the existing order rather than producing radical change.

Ansell et al. (2016) suggest that the outcomes of institutional crises depend upon the degree of institutionalization of a policy sector (weak or strong) and the degree of agency of those institutions that must respond to the crisis (weak or strong). A strongly institutionalized sector with weak capacity (agency) to adapt to crises is likely to be highly path dependent and resistant to change until a powerful external shock ("punctuated equilibrium") forces significant change. However, a weakly institutionalized policy sector with strong agency to adapt is likely to lead to "agenda reinvention" through "recombination, realignment and active improvisation" (2016: 429). This logic follows the creative syncretist model of Berk and Galvan (2009, 2013), which argues that loosely coupled institutions and creative agency will produce a pattern of improvised bricolage.

EU Institutions in the Face of Crisis[2]

What does institutionalism suggest about how EU institutions will respond in the face of crises? As suggested in the previous sections, expectations differ depending on which of the variants of institutionalism you adopt. Analyzing Europe's financial crisis from an historical institutionalist perspective, Verdun (2015) points to the inadequate nature of EU institutions prior to the financial crisis. She also supports the view that the crisis itself encouraged member-states to act unilaterally. However, gradually, new institutions were constructed and she argues that "they were built on previous institutions or were inspired by structures that had been created before" (2015: 231). Building on Fritz Scharpf's rational choice analysis of European Union politics, which stresses what Scharpf calls "joint decision traps" leading to lowest common denominator negotiating outcomes, Falkner's analysis of the impact of the financial crisis on nine policy sectors found that "[t]he most relevant finding is that the crisis-induced pressures frequently made earlier preferences change and new compromise solutions possible, including exits from joint-decision traps" (2016: 231).

Jones et al. (2016) combine rational choice and historical institutionalism to explain the EU's response to the Eurozone crisis. They ask why the EU only adopted incomplete and piecemeal reforms in the face of the financial crisis. They argue that the character of reforms is explained by intergovernmental bargaining and minimum winning coalitions. But they also ask why these reforms have deepened integration over time rather than eroding it. To explain this puzzle of "failing forward," they adopt an historical institutionalist argument on temporal sequencing, arguing that intergovernmentalism characterizes critical junctures, while neofunctionalism characterizes periods between critical junctures. They summarize the implications of this argument as follows:

> Our "failing forward" argument—based on a fusion of liberal intergovernmentalism and neofunctionalism—has a number of observable implications. If this dynamic is at work, we should observe the following: (a) member governments should introduce incomplete governance structures as a result of lowest common denominator bargains, (b) at least some national leaders involved in these bargains should indicate that they believe the incomplete governance structures are likely to prove inadequate, (c) the incomplete governance structures should generate functional spillovers that help spark future crises, and (d) the cycle should repeat itself. (Jones et al. 2016: 1017)

An interesting feature of their argument is that crises become nearly continuous because incomplete governance structures create their own subsequent crises.

---

[2] See Tranøy and Stenstad, this volume, and Olsen and Rosén, this volume, for in depth analyses of various aspects of the EU financial crisis.

From a discursive institutionalist analysis of the Euro crisis, Schmidt (2016) argues that the focus must be on how EU actors develop ideas that reinterpret existing rules. In managing the financial crisis, she observes that the "coordinative discourse" was highly restricted due to the intergovernmental nature of the bargaining. During a crisis, leaders have a tendency to become trapped by their own rhetoric. However, she notes that the European Central Bank and the European Commission utilized a "communicative discourse" to provide cover for a more flexible reinterpretation of the rules. Papadimitriou et al. (2019) draw discursive and historical institutionalism together to demonstrate that the Greek financial crisis produced significant narrative shifts in elite discourse.

Finally, from a pragmatist institutionalist perspective, Jabko and Sheingate (2018) argue that European leaders responded to the Eurocrisis by combining significant elements of both continuity and change—and notably, "Leaders generally coped with crisis by adopting drastic new measures designed to buttress the existing order" (2018: 317). The discourse of leaders aimed to both defend the existing order and to transform it through experimentation.

Conclusion

Institutionalism is a venerable perspective in the social sciences, one that has generated a rich literature on the importance and impact of institutions. With the rise of "new institutionalism" in the 1970s and 1980s, institutionalism underwent a differentiation that has led to the articulation of several different versions of institutionalism, including rational choice, historical, sociological, discursive, and pragmatist institutionalism. This chapter has explored these different versions of institutionalism, focusing on how they explain both institutional stability and institutional change. Broadly, the differences relate to expectations about (1) the extent to which institutions constrain human agency, (2) the degree to which institutional change arises exogenously versus endogenously, (3) the extent to which institutions are themselves malleable in the face of human agency, and (4) how to conceptualize the nature of institutional change (radical, incremental, syncretist).

This volume as a whole explores how crises are likely to influence EU institutions and policies, with a focus on explaining the patterns of change and continuity of EU institutions. In addressing this issue from the perspective of institutional theory, perhaps the central concept is the idea of "critical juncture," which is understood to be a relatively delimited period of time in which radical or at least significant institutional change becomes more likely or possible (Capoccia and Keleman 2007). Although this chapter has uncovered several meanings of crisis (e.g., conjunctural, structural) that might be significant for understanding the nature of institutional change, the institutionalist literature tends, in general, to view a crisis as a critical juncture where significant institutional change is likely.

Institutionalist scholarship, however, has begun to problematize this association of critical junctures with radical change and intervening periods with gradual incremental change. More recent perspectives tend to view institutional change during a crisis as far more uneven, with some forces working to defend and consolidate existing institutions and others working to experiment with new institutions. As our brief investigation of the EU's response to the Eurozone crisis suggests, patterns of institutional change during a crisis are likely to blend old and new. Some change will be used to shore up the existing order, while some existing institutions will provide the raw materials for experimenting with new institutional forms.

REFERENCES

Ansell, C. K. (2011). *Pragmatist Democracy: Evolutionary Learning as Public Philosophy*. Oxford: Oxford University Press.

Ansell, C., Boin, A., & Kuipers, S. (2016). Institutional Crisis and the Policy Agenda. In N. Zahariadis (Ed.), *Handbook of Public Policy Agenda Setting*. Cheltenham, UK: Edward Elgar Publishing.

Beckert, J. (2010). Institutional Isomorphism Revisited: Convergence and Divergence in Institutional Change. *Sociological Theory, 28*(2), 150–166.

Bell, S. (2011). Do We Really Need a New 'Constructivist Institutionalism' to Explain Institutional Change? *British Journal of Political Science, 41*(4), 883–906.

Bell, S. (2017). Historical Institutionalism and New Dimensions of Agency: Bankers, Institutions and the 2008 Financial Crisis. *Political Studies, 65*(3), 724–739.

Berger, P. L., & Luckmann, T. (1991). *The Social Construction of Reality: A Treatise in the Sociology of Knowledge*. Garden City, NY: Anchor Books

Berk, G., & Galvan, D. (2009). How People Experience and Change Institutions: A Field Guide to Creative Syncretism. *Theory & Society, 38*, 543–580.

Berk, G., & Galvan, D. (2013). Processes of Creative Syncretism: Experiential Origins of Institutional Order and Change. In G. Berk, D. C. Galvan, & V. Hattam (Eds.), *Political Creativity: Reconfiguring Institutional Order and Change* (pp. 29–54). Philadelphia: University of Pennsylvania Press.

Capoccia, G., & Kelemen, R. D. (2007). The Study of Critical Junctures: Theory, Narrative, and Counterfactuals in Historical Institutionalism. *World Politics, 59*(3), 341–369.

Checkel, J. T. (1999). Social Construction and Integration. *Journal of European Public Policy, 6*(4), 545–560.

Collier, R. B., & Collier, D. (2002). *Shaping the Political Arena: Critical Junctures, the Labor Movement, and Regime Dynamics in Latin America*. Notre Dame: University of Notre Dame Press.

DiMaggio, P. J., & Powell, W. W. (1983). The Iron Cage Revisited: Institutional Isomorphism and Collective Rationality in Organizational Fields. *American Sociological Review*, 147–160.

Falkner, G. (2016). The EU's Current Crisis and Its Policy Effects: Research Design and Comparative Findings. *Journal of European Integration, 38*(3), 219–235.

Farjoun, M., Ansell, C., & Boin, A. (2015). Pragmatism in Organization Studies: Meeting the Challenges of a Dynamic and Complex World. *Organization Science, 26*(6), 1787–1804.

Fioretos, O. (2011). Historical Institutionalism in International Relations. *International Organization, 65*(2), 367–399.
From, J. (2002). Decision-Making in a Complex Environment: A Sociological Institutionalist Analysis of Competition Policy Decision-Making in the European Commission. *Journal of European Public Policy, 9*(2), 219–237.
Greif, A., & Laitin, D. D. (2004). A Theory of Endogenous Institutional Change. *American Political Science Review, 98*(4), 633–652.
Hall, P. A. (1993). Policy Paradigms, Social Learning, and the State: The Case of Economic Policymaking in Britain. *Comparative Politics, 25*, 275–296.
Hall, P. A., & Taylor, R. C. (1996). Political Science and the Three New Institutionalism. *Political Studies, 44*(5), 936–957.
Hassan, O. (2010). Constructing Crises, (In) Securitising Terror: The Punctuated Evolution of EU Counter-Terror Strategy. *European Security, 19*(3), 445–466.
Hay, C. (1999). Crisis and the Structural Transformation of the State: Interrogating the Process of Change. *British Journal of Politics and International Relations, 3*(1), 317–344.
Hay, C. (2016). Good in a Crisis: The Ontological Institutionalism of Social Constructivism. *New Political Economy, 21*(6), 520–535.
Herrigel, G. (2010). *Manufacturing Possibilities: Creative Action and Industrial Recomposition in the United States, Germany, and Japan*. New York: Oxford.
Hooren, F. V., Kaasch, A., & Starke, P. (2014). The Shock Routine: Economic Crisis and the Nature of Social Policy Responses. *Journal of European Public Policy, 21*(4), 605–623.
Ikani, N. (2019). Change and Continuity in the European Neighbourhood Policy: The Ukraine Crisis as a Critical Juncture. *Geopolitics, 24*(1), 20–50.
Immergut, E. M. (1998). The Theoretical Core of the New Institutionalism. *Politics & Society, 26*(1), 5–34.
Jabko, N. (2019). Contested Governance: The New Repertoire of the Eurozone Crisis. *Governance, 32*(3), 493–509.
Jabko, N., & Sheingate, A. (2018). The Practices of Dynamic Order. *Perspectives in Politics, 16*(2), 312–327.
Jones, E., Kelemen, R. D., & Meunier, S. (2016). Failing Forward? The Euro Crisis and the Incomplete Nature of European Integration. *Comparative Political Studies, 49*(7), 1010–1034.
Kern, F., Kuzemko, C., & Mitchell, C. (2014). Measuring and Explaining Policy Paradigm Change: The Case of UK Energy Policy. *Policy & Politics, 42*(4), 513–530.
Koselleck, R. (2006). Crisis. *Journal of the History of Ideas, 67*(2), 357–400.
Kuhn, T. S. (1962). *The Structure of Scientific Revolutions*. Chicago: University of Chicago Press.
Lévi-Strauss, C. (1966). *The Savage Mind*. Chicago: University of Chicago Press.
Lindner, J. (2003). Institutional Stability and Change: Two Sides of the Same Coin. *Journal of European Public Policy, 10*(6), 912–935.
Mahoney, J., & Thelen, K. (2010). A Theory of Gradual Institutional Change. In J., Mahoney & K. Thelen (Eds.), *Explaining Institutional Change: Ambiguity, Agency, and Power* (pp 1–37). Cambridge: Cambridge University Press.
March, J. G., & Olsen, J. P. (1996). Institutional Perspectives on Political Institutions. *Governance, 9*(3), 247–264.
March, J. G., & Olsen, J. P. (1983). The New Institutionalism: Organizational Factors in Political Life. *American Political Science Review, 78*(3), 734–749.

March, J. G., & Olsen, J. P. (1989). *Rediscovering Institutions*. Simon and Schuster.
Marsh, D. (2010). Stability and Change: The Last Dualism? *Critical Policy Studies*, 4(1), 86–101.
Moe, T. M. (1984). The New Economics of Organization. *American Journal of Political Science*, 28(4), 739–777.
North, D. C. (1990). *Institutions, Institutional Change, and Economic Performances*. Cambridge: Cambridge University Press.
North, D. C. (1993). Toward a Theory of Institutional Change. *Political Economy: Institutions, Competition, and Representation*, 31(4), 61–69.
Papadimitriou, D., Pegasiou, A., & Zartaloudis, S. (2019). European Elites and the Narrative of the Greek Crisis: A Discursive Institutionalist Analysis. *European Journal of Political Research*, 58(2), 435–464.
Peters, B. G. (2011). Governance Responses to the Fiscal Crisis—Comparative Perspectives. *Public Money & Management*, 31(1), 75–80.
Pierson, P. (1993). When Effect Becomes Cause: Policy Feedback and Political Change. *World Politics*, 45(4), 595–628.
Pierson, P. (2000). Increasing Returns, Path Dependence, and the Study of Politics. *American Political Science Review*, 94(2), 251–267.
Pierson, P., & Skocpol, T. (2002). Historical Institutionalism in Contemporary Political Science. In I. Katznelson & H. Milner (Eds.), *Political Science: The State of the Discipline* (pp. 693–721). Washington, DC: American Political Science Association.
Powell, W. W., & DiMaggio, P. J. (Eds.). (1991). *The New Institutionalism in Organizational Analysis*. Chicago: University of Chicago press.
Rhodes, R. A. (2011). Old Institutionalisms: An Overview. In In R.A. W. Rhodes, S. Binder, & B. Rockman (Eds.), *The Oxford Handbook of Political Institutions*. Oxford: Oxford University Press.
Sabel, C. F., & Zeitlin, J. (2008). Learning from Difference: The New Architecture of Experimentalist Governance in the EU. *European Law Journal*, 14(3), 271–327.
Schmidt, V. A. (2008). Discursive Institutionalism: The Explanatory Power of Ideas and Discourse. *Annual Review of Political Science*, 11, 303–326.
Schmidt, V. A. (2010). Taking Ideas and Discourse Seriously: Explaining Change Through Discursive Institutionalism as the Fourth 'New Institutionalism'. *European Political Science Review*, 2(1), 1–25.
Schmidt, V. A. (2011). Speaking of Change: Why Discourse Is Key to the Dynamics of Policy Transformation. *Critical Policy Studies*, 5(2), 106–126.
Schmidt, V. A. (2013). Arguing About the Eurozone Crisis: A Discursive Institutionalist Analysis. *Critical Policy Studies*, 7(4), 455–462.
Schmidt, V. A. (2014). Speaking to the Markets or to the People? A Discursive Institutionalist Analysis of the EU's Sovereign Debt Crisis. *The British Journal of Politics and International Relations*, 16(1), 188–209.
Schmidt, V. A. (2016). Reinterpreting the Rules 'By Stealth' in Times of Crisis: A Discursive Institutionalist Analysis of the European Central Bank and the European Commission. *West European Politics*, 39(5), 1032–1052.
Selznick, P. (1996). Institutionalism 'Old' and 'New'. *Administrative Science Quarterly*, 41, 270–277.
Shepsle, K. A. (1989). Studying Institutions: Some Lessons from the Rational Choice Approach. *Journal of Theoretical Politics*, 1(2), 131–147.

Shepsle, K. A. (2006). Rational Choice Institutionalism. In R. A. W. Rhodes, S. Binder, & B. Rockman (Eds.), *The Oxford Handbook of Political Institutions* (pp. 23–38). Oxford: Oxford University Press.

Soifer, H. D. (2012). The Causal Logic of Critical Junctures. *Comparative Political Studies, 45*(12), 1572–1597.

Stark, A. (2018). New Institutionalism, Critical Junctures and Post-Crisis Policy Reform. *Australian Journal of Political Science, 53*(1), 24–39.

Steinmo, S., Thelen, K., and Longstreth, F. (Eds.). (1992). *Structuring Politics: Historical Institutionalism in Comparative Analysis*. Cambridge: Cambridge University Press.

Stinchcombe, A. L. (1997). On the Virtues of the Old Institutionalism. *Annual Review of Sociology, 23*(1), 1–18.

Studlar, D. T., & Cairney, P. (2014). Conceptualizing Punctuated and Non-Punctuated Policy Change: Tobacco Control in Comparative Perspective. *International Review of Administrative Sciences, 80*(3), 513–531.

Thelen, K. (1999). Historical Institutionalism in Comparative Politics. *Annual Review of Political Science, 2*(1), 369–404.

Verdun, A. (2015). A Historical Institutionalist Explanation of the EU's Responses to the Euro Area Financial Crisis. *Journal of European Public Policy, 22*(2), 219–237.

Williamson, O. E. (1975). *Markets and Hierarchies*. New York: The Free Press.

CHAPTER 8

Organizational Theory

Jarle Trondal

INTRODUCTION

This chapter outlines an organizational approach to crisis governance. An organizational approach accounts for the *politics of organizing* crises. The relevance of organization theory to the study of crisis relates particularly to how crises might be organizationally handled and tamed, and thus how organizations and governments thus might use organizational tools to muddle through crisis (see Chapter 1 in this volume). This chapter first outlines the organizational approach, and then shows how the approach is relevant in understanding how crisis may be tackled through meta-governance (see below). In doing so, the relevance of organization theory thus relates to how it might be practically used to (re)design public policy through (re)designing organizational structures.

Times of crisis call upon organizations to adapt, anticipate, reform and innovate. The EU has faced multiple existential crises for more than one decade. This chapter argues that political systems facing continuous crisis tend to respond with ambitions for innovation in order to muddle through and cope with ongoing challenges through organizational means (see Chapter 1 in this volume). As a consequence, the organization of crisis management and innovation "has climbed to the top of government agendas,

J. Trondal (✉)
Department of Political Science and Management, University of Agder, Kristiansand, Norway
e-mail: jarle.trondal@uia.no; jarle.trondal@arena.uio.no

ARENA - Centre for European Studies, University of Oslo, Oslo, Norway

© The Author(s) 2021
M. Riddervold et al. (eds.), *The Palgrave Handbook of EU Crises*, Palgrave Studies in European Union Politics,
https://doi.org/10.1007/978-3-030-51791-5_8

perhaps earlier in the US than in Europe" (Ansell and Torfing 2014: 3). This chapter makes two key arguments: First, organizations and governments facing crises might use meta-governance innovate, and secondly that such endeavors are subject to organizational design. In sum, therefore, this chapter argues how organizations can manage the unexpected such as crisis through meta-governance—that is forward-looking problem-solving in situations marked by uncertainty and imperfect information (Simon 1983: 83; Weick and Suttcliffe 2001). Following scenario 1 from Chapter 1, crises is thus seen as an opportunity to organizations and governments—as an enabling environment for organizational change.

A decade of European crises has called upon member-state governments and EU institutions to become organizational designers. This is characterized by a search for new solutions to muddle through or head forward, and thus escape the break-down scenario (see Chapter 1 in this volume). This chapter offers an organization theory approach to meta-governance, and thereby also a theory of how organizations and governments might cope with crisis by (re-)designing organizational architectures. Ideally, the knowledge basis for organizational design (meta-governance) consists of evidence-based insights into how organization's structure might shape or at least make a difference in governance processes. Thus, our scholarship is closely linked to the realities of practice, concerned not just with how things are, but *how things might be* (Gulick 1937; Meier 2010: 284). Given certain goals, such as innovation and change as discussed in this chapter, organization designers should be capable of recommending particular structural solutions that would work.

Moreover, this discussion illuminates an old academic debate between pure "science" and applied "craft." Whereas science and craft are typically orthogonal and mutually disregarded (Galbraith 1980), our approach advocates that organization theory as "craft" *requires* organization theory as "science." Political systems are created and arguably open to design thinking (Hood 1983; Stoker 2013). However, a design approach, we argue, needs to take broader organizational contexts into account (Clarke and Craft 2019; Egeberg and Trondal 2018). Put together, knowledge about how organizational factors affect public governance, as well as knowledge about conditions for organizational change, are necessary preconditions for using organization theory to meta-govern. As advocated already by Luther Gulick (1937), "craft" and "science" are complementary joint ventures, not opposing endeavors. The challenge is thus for political science, as any social science, to implement stacks of knowledge for practical use. An organizational approach to meta-governance, we argue, should serve as an action program for political science, making it practically relevant for solving societal challenges (Bennis 1966: 97; Clarke and Craft 2019; Egeberg and Trondal 2018; Stoker 2013).

The chapter is organized as follows: The next section outlines two organization theory ideas on crisis governance: The idea of dyadic public administration, and the idea of compound public administration. Next, this section also briefly outlines the organizational approach to meta-governance and briefly discusses its relevance with regard to the contemporary crises discussed in this book. It closes by discussing organizational theories' contribution to crisis studies by summing up the discussion on how public innovation might be engineered through (i) routinization of reform, (ii) loose coupling, (iii) organized complexity, and (iv) temporal sorting.

Two Organization Theory Ideas on Crisis Governance

How do public organizations innovate in times of crisis? The organizational theory literature discerns two broad strategies. One strategy is to *stabilize*; the other is to *adapt* (Kupers 2014). Arguably, these two strategies are not mutually exclusive and may be complementary. Meta-governance entails balancing continuity and stability on the one hand with adaptability and experimentation on the other (Ansell and Trondal 2017; March 1991). Yet, these strategies also suggest different patterns of institutional change and modes of organizational and governance response: First, if public organizations and governance systems opt to stabilize in the face crisis, they will produce a pattern of path dependence and *muddling through* (Pierson 2004). They may do this by reactively coping with crisis, erecting various kinds of buffers or decoupling to protect themselves from future environmental shocks, creating centralized capacity, and formalizing network agreements. We call this strategy "static resilience" because it tries to maintain the status quo (Ansell and Trondal 2017). Should this strategy fail, more sweeping change—a punctuated equilibrium—may be the solution and thus meta-governance toward innovation. If public organizations and governance systems opt to adapt to crisis, they may produce a pattern of institutional change, leading to more continuous but less dramatic meta-governance. They do this by adopting a wider variety of strategies often of a hybrid nature, acting in an improvisational and experimental fashion, favoring flexible structures and decentralized initiatives, and developing informal networks and other interstitial arrangements to achieve coordination in rapidly evolving situations (see below). This is often seen in the aftermath of several of the EU crises, for example with the creation of ever-more EU agencies as institutional compromises between supranationalism and intergovernmentalism (see Hussein this volume). We call this strategy "dynamic resilience," building on ideas of adaptive bureaucracies in which public organization adapts continuously in the face of crisis. Yet, the extent to which systems are resilient remains empirical (Meier et al. 2018). It is the behavior of the system that demonstrates, after a crisis, if the organization was resilient.

Although crisis creates an impetus for public organizations to stabilize their operations, it often simultaneously produces pressure for rapid change. Environments change quickly and unexpectedly and may exhibit high volatility. To avoid mismatches with their environment, organizations are pressed to quickly adapt the organization to these changing conditions (Bourgeois and Eisenhardt 1988; McCann et al. 2009). Public organizations are therefore often pulled between the impulse to stabilize and the impulse to transform themselves in response to crisis. Studies show that crisis push public organizations to balance both stability and flexibility (Volberda et al. 2012). This perspective is reinforced by recent research that shows that as organizational environments become more unpredictable, "[t]he tension between too much and too little structure is challenging and crucial to manage" (Davis et al. 2009: 438). In the logic of dynamic resilience, stability and change are not such sharply drawn distinctions (Easton 1965; Farjoun 2010). Governing organizations use stability to help them change and use change to help them to stabilize. No clear "equilibrium" between the organization and its environment is easily discerned and the organization appears to be continually changing as a "reforming organization" (Brunsson and Olsen 1993). Dynamic resilience emphasizes the importance of building flexibility into organizational and institutional arrangements by absorbing complexity and incorporating requisite variety. It emphasizes the importance of maintaining multiple repertoires that can be flexibly redeployed to meet changing circumstances. This will be discussed below when illuminating innovation as an organizational response to crisis.

The Dyadic Public Administration

This approach rests on ideas of "static resilience." The idea builds on the simple conjecture that public administration runs in a world of dyadic and opposing governing dynamics: normal vs. abnormal, change vs. stability, and so on. This idea builds on an image of bureaucracies as fundamentally rigid. Crisis is thus understood to be fundamentally *dysfunctional*—that is, as exceptional, dangerous, or contradictory. Seen in this light, crisis may push organizations and institutions to their limits and threaten surprising cascading dynamics that test the sustainability of existing governance arrangements. Or it might produce maladaptive behaviors that trap governance into suboptimal outcomes. From this perspective, the emphasis is not how governing institutions manage crisis, but how they withstand it.

The Compound Public Administration

This approach contends that public administration is complex and involves multiple actors, resources, governing logics, and dynamics (Fabbrini 2007; Olsen 2017; Trondal et al. 2010). The idea builds on the notion of "dynamic resilience" and sees crisis as a *condition* for public governance, not as a dysfunction (Ansell and Trondal 2017; also see Ansell this volume). If an intensification of speed, complexity, and conflict is understood to be a condition of contemporary crisis governance, then the implication is that efficient and effective governing institutions must manage crisis as a critical condition of the governing process. Public governance, consequently, should be analyzed on the basis of continuous variables that might be dynamically interactive

(Ansell et al. 2017). In this light, public administration has been pictured as hybrid and compound (Emery and Giauque 2014), partly reflecting how public administration relates to a larger political orders and partly how this order is under profound change and deep stress (Olsen 2018). The idea of the compound institutional order goes beyond "the tyranny of dichotomies" and study "mixed political orders blending different forms of governance and organization" (Olsen 2008: 5–6). The ensuing discussion of this chapter follows this idea. Consequently, meta-governance needs to take crisis as *condition*, not dysfunction, for its endeavor (Ansell et al. 2017; Easton 1965). The following discussion should thus be read with this caveat in mind (Weick and Suttcliffe 2001: 157).

An Organizational Approach to Meta-Governance

Knowledge about the conditions for meta-governance is pertinent when recurrent crises in Europe call for major reforms (Lodge and Wegrich 2012; Emery and Giauque 2014; Torfing et al. 2012). This section argues that organizational factors may influence meta-governance in two ways: first, the *existing* organization structure may affect reform processes, and second, reform processes themselves may be deliberately *organized* on a temporary basis in order to achieve particular goals. This section privileges the latter since this has greatest design implications. Our focus is thus on how to organize the meta-governing process, such as in response to crisis. Concerning the enabling and constraining role of the *existing* organization structure, whether a reform process is anchored within a ministry or within an agency may, for example, affect the kind of actors which are deemed legitimate participants, in which arguments are seen as appropriate, and thus on the overall governability of the reform process. Particularly affected parties like external interest groups and internal trade unions tend to have greater influence at the agency level than at the ministry level where a political (hierarchical) control is more acceptable (Egeberg and Trondal 2018). Moreover, reform processes that encompass not one but several ministries are likely to become more complicated since they usually rely on horizontal coordination mechanisms. Finally, since the ordinary governing apparatus has to run everyday business while engaging in reorganization, the question is how much requisite capacity is left for handling crisis (March and Olsen 1983).

Organization theory may thus be helpful in understanding how different ways of *organizing* reform processes may give different reform trajectories and thus different crisis outcomes. The idea sees reform processes as *decision-making processes* that allocate attention, resources, capabilities, roles, and identities. Reform organizations have structures, demographics, and locations that distribute rights and obligations, power and resources, and normally do so unevenly. The question is how the (reform) decision-making processes are (or should be) organized. The organizational structure of a reform limits the set of actors, the number of sequences involved, the access of affected external groups, the role of political leaders, the degree of leeway for major change, and so on. Therefore, effects of reform organizations on the governing of reform processes are, in principle, parallel to effects of organizational structure on substantial decision-making processes. Insight into the effects of the organization of reforms thus has implications for knowledge of its impact on public sector governance on a broader scale (Lægreid and Roness 1999: 302).

The following section discusses four dimensions on the organization of reforms and their design implications: specialization of reforms, reforms as routine, the ecology of reforms, and the temporal dimension of reforms. These dimensions are relevant in relation to crisis, as such situations often accompany demands for crisis management.

Specialization of Meta-Governance

Crisis governance requires attention of decision-makers. One tool thereof is organization of attention. Even though political organizations tend to engage in continuous reforms (Brunsson and Olsen 1993), such organizations have also been described as not very "changeful" (Brunsson 2000: 163) since they involve multiple actors with adjacent agendas that in turn may jam decision-making processes. One way to mobilize change is to organizationally specialize meta-governance by separating "thinking" and "acting" into separate reform sub-units. At a more general level, reform processes may be organized into specialized or non-specialized structures—both vertically and horizontally. Organizational specialization is a way of decomposing and isolating problems and solutions into autonomous parts, "to reduce large problems into their component parts" (March 1994: 12). While specialized reform structures limit the access to actors and concerns, non-specialized structures open reform processes to a broader spectrum of actors and concern (Simon 1983: 88).

First, vertical specialization expresses the intended division of labor across hierarchical levels within or between organizations. A vertically specialized reform organization limits the access of actors from lower levels of the hierarchical chain and favors the access of leaders. This organizational solution establishes communication barriers between organizational levels and reduces information flows across the chains. Vertical specialization is a mechanism for opening reform organizations to change through increasing sub-unit autonomy (Leavitt 1965: 1147). Yet, sub-unit autonomy might hinder reform implementation. This general argument has been illustrated in how governments have organized innovation labs and digital transformation units across a spectrum of countries (Clarke and Craft 2019). Timeus and Gasco (2018) show that the city of Barcelona established innovation labs organizationally isolated from their parent organizations, which hindered innovation in the labs from being transported to the organization at large. One "takeaway" implication for crisis governance is that vertical specialization of reform organizations reduces actor constellations and conflicts over problems and solutions.

In short, vertical specialization reduces reform resistance and increases reform speed that might be critical in crisis situations.

Second, horizontal specialization expresses how different issues and policy areas, for example, energy and climate change, are supposed to be linked together or decoupled from one another. Those areas that are encompassed by the same organizational unit are supposed to be more coordinated than those that belong to different units (Gulick 1937). One implication of horizontal specialization is increasing exploitation and thus the use of well-known solutions in crisis governance. "Exploitation includes such things as refinement, choice, production, efficiency, selection, implementation, execution" (March 1994: 127). Horizontal specialization mobilizes decision-making myopia, in which problems and solutions outside own "turfs" are neglected or seen as illegitimate, fuzzy, and distant. One consequence might also be inconsistencies in crisis governance where the "global" outlook across organizational borders is sacrificed for "local attention" and siloization. A similar argument goes for the specialization of expertise in crisis governance: if dominated by one profession—for example economists as in the case of the Six Pack (see Hussein this volume), reforms are likely to search locally and narrowly—for example by focusing on marked-conforming efficiency policies to a larger extent than if reforming organizations are staffed with a blend of different expertise (Christensen 2017). More generally, demographically de-specialized crisis governance will mobilize multiple problems and solutions to a larger extent than crisis governance that are demographically specialized—and thus mobilize exploration and innovation.

The "takeaway" design implication for crisis governance is that exploration and innovation thrives on horizontal de-specialization. Increasing exploitation, and thus the likelihood of getting reform ideas through and thus to solve crises, requires specializing the reform structure.

Meta-governance and capacity: Since crisis governance requires capacities to launch and implement solutions, one important variable in meta-governance is organizational capacity. Even ad hoc reforms need capacity to be launched and implemented. Yet, launching reforms might be easier than implementing them (Pressman and Wildavsky 1984). Nonetheless, literature harbors competing ideas on the effects of capacity in meta-governance. One idea sees meta-governance as ad hoc events. Organizations are pictured as stable equilibrium-seeking bodies, only interrupted by sudden occasional changes. Organizational-institutionalist literature advocates that institutions are "settled, stable, and integrated" (Selznick 2015: 15) making them robust vis-à-vis their task environments. Change happens incrementally and gradually, and less as a reflex of deliberate reforms (e.g., Mahoney and Thelen 2010; March and Olsen 1989; Streek and Thelen 2005). A competing idea sees meta-governance as routine activity and subject to deliberate intervention (Brunsson and Olsen 1993). A pragmatist literature has offered a middle ground in which organizations both defend core values at the same time as they adapt to ongoing problems (Ansell 2011; Ansell et al. 2015).

Following the pragmatist argument, stability and change might coexist in crisis processes (March 1981: 563). For example, crisis and reform in certain parts of an organization might happen parallel to stability in other parts. This might happen if reform organizations are horizontally specialized, enabling solid borders between those parts of organizations that are subject to reform and those focusing on business-as-usual. The late Selznick (1992: 321) suggested that mindful institutional leadership implied that the designing of organizational change combines elements of change and continuity. Essential was for leaders to draw on what he calls the "institutional character" as a source of direction. Meta-governance will thus not challenge the deeper personality of the organization, while at the same time adjusting to environmental demands of the day (Krygier 2012: 77). One way of crafting this is by routinizing meta-governance by allocating continuous attention to it through permanent organizational capacity (Brunsson and Olsen 1993). This may safeguard the institutional character in the long term, while routinely updating the organization in the face of crisis at the same time (Ansell et al. 2015). Meta-governance becomes "the new normal" and would represent some kind of organized and structured "stability" (Brunsson and Olsen 1993: 33).

One way of routinizing attention to meta-governance is to form permanent organizational attention and recruit permanent staff earmarked to reform. Less routinization would be the result if embedded in temporary organizations with contracted short-term staff (Bakker et al. 2016). The routinization of administrative reform in states is typically done by the creation of ministries and agencies for government reform (Brunsson and Olsen 1993). In the EU, independent implementation structures have been installed notably by establishing EU agencies (Egeberg and Trondal 2017), which has fortified EU-level control on exploitation processes. Essential to this book, EU agencies have typically been created and strengthened as responses to crises. The migration crisis, for example, has fostered ideas to strengthen Frontex and make it even more independent of member-states (regarding the migration crisis, see Bosilca this volume, Crawford this volume, and Schilde this volume).

More generally, democracies can be seen as an organizational (and institutional) arrangement that routinizes reforms by embedding opposition and disagreement into governments, parliaments, and courts. Democracies have embedded competing claims for how the state should be structured and governed, and thereby increase states' capacity for routinized and continuous calls for reforms and thus meta-governance (Ansell 2011; Dahl 2000). As such, democracies are indeed "changeful" due to its organizational capacity to mobilize exploration from within and thus structures suited for crisis governance. The "takeaway" design implication for crisis governance is that meta-governance as routine requires requisite stand-by organizational capacity.

Ecology and Meta-Governance

Since crises typically hit across policy domains and institutions, meta-governance processes often do not live alone. They may intersect and feed on one another (Brunsson and Olsen 1993: 33). As a consequence of major crises, responses are sometimes surprisingly small and incremental. Yet, if such small responses are seen as elements in the ecology of large-scale reforms, they might aggregate into profound change (Ansell 2011: 44). Moreover, reform processes at one place, and in the future, tend to be affected by reform processes elsewhere, and in the past. Meta-governance should thus be analyzed as parts of ecologies of nested and coevolving reforms (Olsen 2010).

If seen in an ecological organizational perspective, reforms might be designed in ways that make them mutually interdependent. Two such factors are important: First, isolated reforms might be tied into larger reforms through organizational linkages or bridges. We may think of small reforms as parts of larger ones and thus as "co-evolving processes" creating interactive effects (March 1994: 97; Olsen 2010: 14). We may also think of large-scale reforms as not typically "designed" per se, but as the product of smaller reforms converging into transformative change. Incremental change often has the advantage of being politically feasible to launch. Linking small reforms into a wider "meta-reform" makes it more likely that decisions made in smaller reform processes feed into one another, generating aggregated transformation. One organizational solution is through secondary structures that are temporary in nature—notably collegial structures such as committees and project organizations (Bakker et al. 2016: 1705), as well as contracted personnel. In sum, organizational reform programs serve as a design factor that balances multiple concerns—such as order and change, long- and short-term horizons, exploitation and exploration, and change at different scales (Bolman and Deal 1997: 60; Olsen 2010: 10).

Secondly, if crisis governance processes are organized through non-specialized and open structures, it is more likely that available time and energy among reformers might be used elsewhere—i.e., in adjacent reform processes. This suggests that anarchic design of crisis governance might increase mutual learning and information exchange across different parts of the process. Perceptions of legitimate and efficient solutions to problems might thus be transferred between reform processes. The flip-side of organized exploration might be less control over the overall reform trajectories and outcomes. Reforms in one organization might kick into neighboring reforms to the surprise of reform leaders.

Time and Meta-Governance

Since crisis is characterized by short time horizons, the time variable is important in crisis governance. Time concerns factors such as speed, the number and types of tempi, and the sequencing of reforms (e.g., Ansell and Trondal

2017; Goetz 2014). Moreover, the temporal logic of meta-governance may be organizationally designed. First, organizational design might affect the speed of reform, for example, by setting tight deadlines. With increased speed comes a tendency for repetition. During reforms when tempo increases, established ideas and practices are likely to be subject to test, yet pre-existing solutions are likely to be selected due to the sheer lack of time for search. High-speed meta-governance processes are thus likely to experience a tendency of repeating past successes, or what are perceived as past successes (March 2010: 16). By repeating in this way, organizations may be victims of trained incapacity to improvise—merely due to high speed of conduct.

Perhaps even more critical, reforms may come too late. This speaks to the need to organize requisite proactive capacities in organization to anticipate the unforeseen. Yet, this strategy is probably most helpful when organizational challenges are in the distant horizon. Following the above discussion on capacity, organizing for future surprises requires establishing organizational capacities for meta-governance that may do foresight activities that preempt crises. Put together, these arguments speak to the need for organizing capacity for temporal diversity in reform programs. If several speeds are organized into reform programs, this may buffer the need for combining exploitation and exploration (March 2010), combining continuity and change (Ansell et al. 2017), or combining both conservative and dynamic elements in the face of crisis (Selznick 1958).

Organizing for Public Sector Innovation in Times of Crisis

Crisis calls for innovative solutions. Big problems sometimes request big solutions. If so, how can innovation be more than the result of diffusion and imitation, or mere luck? This section challenges ideas that public sector innovation can solely be facilitated by *certain* organizational architectures and that some kind of *optimal* design exists for innovation, notably in crisis situations. Optimal design literature suggests that innovation follows from certain types of structures, such as the institutionalization of single-purpose organizations, collaborative structures, semi-autonomous agencies and state-owned enterprises, and competition-based incentive structures (e.g., Christensen and Lægreid 2006; Friedman 2008; Torfing and Sorensen 2016). This chapter argues that *a variety of* organizational characteristics may spur public sector innovation, and thus that crisis may have multiple organizational responses. Moreover, crisis governance involves both exploration and exploitation (March 1994). This section privileges the role of *exploration or innovation* in crisis governance since this has the largest problem-solving capacity (March 1994: 237), which entails "improving the variety of the novelty in the process" (Dong et al. 2017: 8). By innovation we do not think of ideas that the establishment would easily accepts and supports. Quite opposite. Truly innovative ideas would be seen as "an alien intruder that organizations and societies will react to ... in a negative way" (Dong et al. 2017: 9). Thus, innovation goes opposite to assumptions in much organizational reform rhetoric geared toward maximizing expected value and finding optimal solutions.

Yet, an organizational theory approach does not assume that organizational structures are subject to free "choice." Organizational designers face constraints of resources, institutional histories, and limitations to their attention and imagination (Margetts and Dunleavy 2013). Their "relative autonomy" and their "power to command" is circumscribed (Goodin 1996: 13). However, 'insofar as the social world is accident-prone, we might want to design around the risk of accidents, seeking robust institutions that can withstand the various shocks that will inevitably befall them' (Goodin 1996: 29). Despite there are often no single design or designer, we assume that public innovation might be crafted through organizational engineering. This section examines how crisis governance might be organizationally engineered through (i) routinization of reform in crisis, (ii) loose coupling in crisis governance, (iii) organized complexity in crisis governance, and (iv) temporal sorting of crisis governance.

Routinization of Reform in Crisis

First, innovation is often seen as the ability of organizations to reform. Routinizing reform in organizations is a way of allocating continuous attention to innovation and thus create a permanent stand-by capacity to tackle, anticipate, or even preempt future crises. Innovation and crisis management can become routine if permanent attention is allocated to organizational change, possibly preempting crisis to unfold. Innovation does not thrive only on actors´ motivations; it requires the supply of organizational resources around it. The case of Brexit and the ensuing negotiations illustrates how lack of stand-by organizational capacities made the event a surprise (for more on Brexit, see Oliver this volume and Whitman this volume). It more importantly made the ensuing negotiations subject to improvization due to lacking routinization. In EU´s external relations, by contrast, stand-by organizational capacities existed before the Ukraine crisis, making the crisis governance relatively more subject to rules and routines (for more on the Ukraine crisis, see Juncos and Pomorska this volume and Riddervold this volume). In this case, organizational capacities translated to slack resources in which the crisis response represented some kind of organized and structured organizational "stability" for the EU (Brunsson and Olsen 1993: 33). One way of routinizing attention toward organizational reform is to establish permanent organization and staff earmarked to reform. Permanent organizational attention to reform would thus be safeguarded to a larger extent than if embedded in temporary organizations with contracted short-term staff. One often-used measure of routinizing administrative reform is to install separate ministries or agencies responsible for government reform. Yet, the flip-side of this might be lack of flexibility of participants and ideas (Agranoff 2014). Moreover, innovation through reforms might be achieved by organizing reforms as ecologies of reforms as outlined above. If so, innovative ideas developed in one reform might spill over to adjacent governance processes and increase the sum of innovation accomplished. One way of routinizing this is by organizing networks among units to achieve what is commonly coined collaborative governance (Ansell and Torfing 2014). This is an often-used tool in the EU multilevel administrative networks and much used in EUs migration governance in which Frontex typically cooperate with member-state agencies through administrative networks.

It is typically argued in innovation literature that the traditional characteristics of public organizations favor stability and predictability over innovation capacity. Studies suggest that governments see the establishment of separate administrative units as ways to introduce innovation capacity without disrupting the traditional bureaucratic structure (Bason and Carstensen 2002; Karo and Kattel 2015). A recent study by Tõnurist et al. (2017), for example, shows that temporary "labs" within the government apparatus have become a preferred organizational tool to introduce innovation because their structure and mandate allow them to circumvent certain characteristics of the traditional public administration that are often seen as barriers to public innovation. Yet, Tõnurist et al. (2017) also show that such labs often isolate them from the rest of the organization. Similarly, the creation of semi-autonomous EU agencies as a response to crisis makes them sometimes independent from other EU bodies, despite they are more strongly connected to Commission DGs than the Council and the European Parliament (Egeberg and Trondal 2017. Also see Hussein this volume).

One organizational device to build bridges between reforms is through secondary structures such as reform committees and project organizations (Bakker et al. 2016: 1705) or through actor-oriented solutions such as the recruitment of contracted personnel that are involved across several reform process. In a recent study, Agger and Sorensen (2014) showed how the establishment of committees, politicians, and citizens resulted in a learning process in which politicians, administrators, and citizens came to share similar views on city innovation. Similar to Timeus and Gasco (2018), Agger and Sorensen (2014) showed that the challenge for such committee processes is to organize a feedback-loop to the primary structure, and thereby to implement innovation ideas. If not, great expectations may easily be dashed (Pressman and Wildavsky 1984). In times of crisis, secondary structures are often established temporarily to handle the first stage of a crisis. At later stages after the first chock, such temporary structures—such as administrative networks—might be permanently established as for example in the case of EU agencies.

Loose Coupling in Crisis Governance

Secondly, innovation and crisis governance may be paired with ideas from garbage can theory, which emphasizes fluidity and randomness (Hood 1999). Garbage can processes may be organizationally designed so that decision situations become deliberately ambiguous through loose coupling. A tightly coupled organized system is likely to increase actors´ risk averse behavior. Loose coupling of organizations opens opportunities for discretionary behavior and leeway for actors to choose new policy solutions. Loose coupling reduces coherences inside organizations and "provide agents with greater leeway for choosing between competing goals and/or instruments" (Koreh et al. 2019: 8). Loosely coupled structures thus open crisis governance to a logic of exploration (March 1991). In this way, organizational structures might be designed to "encourage disharmony and hence dynamics, to force us to reconsider and perhaps to change the way we are doing things from time to time" (Goodin 1996: 38–39). As argued by Hood (1999: 62), "elements of the garbage can model might be deliberately introduced into organizational design." The abovementioned secondary structures are one way to deliberately increase garbage-can elements in meta-governance processes—basically by increasing fluid participation and unclear objectives into governing processes. According to Hood (1999: 64), "such structures can be considered discovery systems ...". 0). In governments´ responses to crises, loosely coupled structures might thus be more effective organizational forms than tightly coupled structures—such as bureaucratic organizations. Since the EU multilevel system is a fairly loosely coupled system writ large—both internally at EU level and externally vis-à-vis member-state governments—, it is thus rigged for crisis responses. One major challenge, however, is that loosely coupled systems such as the EU are likely to suffer from lower levels of implementation—and thus exploitation–during crisis than tightly coupled systems such as unitary states.

Organized Complexity in Crisis Governance

Third, innovation during crisis may be facilitated by deliberately designing complex organizational structures. Innovation can be facilitated in crisis governance processes by installing conflicting organizational principles, and thereby the number of conflicting concerns that actors mobilize. Typical examples are hybrid and interstitial organizational forms that are recurrent in the administrative structures of EU's external relations governing system (Bátora 2017; Trondal 2017). They characteristically combine components from various organizational forms and induce "chaos" in the meta-governing process where different parts of the meta-organization mobilize rival means-ends relationships. Hybrid organizations as wholes are thus rigged for innovation and crisis response to a larger extent than non-hybrid structures (Ansell and Trondal 2017). Organizational complexity is likely to mobilize a variety of skills, ideas, and visions for public innovation (Agranoff 2014). In the same vein, a mix of professional skills might trigger creative thinking as well. A recent study of innovation in Danish municipalities suggests that hybrid organizational structures boost intra-organizational conflicts, leaving the hybrid municipal organization with more innovation capacity than other non-hybrid municipal organizations (Thorup 2017). Similarly, the multilevel complexity in EU´s economic governance system, made the EU creative in its exploration, yet less than effective in its implementation.

Temporal Sorting of Crisis Governance

Crisis are marked by being temporally brief. Innovation in crisis governance might be facilitated by designing the temporality of the processes (Ansell and Trondal 2017). Organizing multiple speeds into crisis governance might be one organizational solution. Multiple speeds increase the likelihood of ambiguity as to *when* actors are legitimate participants and what concerns are appropriate to mobilize at *what point in time*. Multi-speed or poly-rhythmic governance processes are thus arguably more likely to boost innovation and discovery than mono-temporal processes. In addition, innovation might be facilitated by organizing crisis governance processes in slow tempo. It has been argued that with increased speed in governance processes come a tendency for repetition (March 2010). By contrast, slow tempo meta-governing processes increase the likelihood that several actors have time to mobilize and that potential critics are activated throughout the process. Slow tempo leaves more time for each actor to attend to multiple problems and solutions and thus to question pre-existing solutions. Innovation thus takes time. The challenge during crisis is that time is a scarce resource. Solutions might come too late. In sum, this argument suggests that innovation as crisis management may be crafted through carefully structuring the temporality of public meta-governance.

CONCLUSIONS

To establish dynamic resilience and permanent capacity of organizations and governments to meet crises, organizational structures such as bureaucracies facilitates innovation given their long time horizons, their relative permanence, as well their ability to breakdown problems into their component parts. Permanent organization with permanent staff recruited for life are more explorative than temporary organizations staffed with temporary agents. Elected executives with short time frames due to their electoral cycles, thus have limited capacities for exploration than non-elected executive heads (Meier et al. 2018). Taken together, multi-speed, slow tempo, and permanent organizational capacities increase the mobilization of contrasting ideas and thus the overall likelihood of innovation in the public domain.

An organizational theory approach illuminates how organizations and governments facing crisis may organize meta-governance in order to find innovative solutions, and thereby ways out. The chapter has discussed an organization theory approach to meta-governance, and thereby also offered a theory of how organizations and governments might cope with crisis through (re-)organizing. In sum, therefore, organization theory cannot predict crises, yet it might understand how to manage them through careful and knowledgeable organizational craft. Moreover, organization theory is, as institutional approaches more generally (see Ansell this volume) perhaps better equipped to explain continuity than change in crisis governance, and thus better at explaining *muddling through* (Scenario 2) than *breaking down* (Scenario 1) and *heading forward* (Scenario 3). Finally, the chapter has outlined the contours of a design approach in political science (see Egeberg and Trondal 2018; Haberstroh 1965). This ambition illuminates an old academic debate between pure "science" and applied "craft" Whereas science and craft are often mutually disregarded, our approach suggests that organization theory as "craft" *requires* organization theory as "science." Put together, knowledge about how organizational factors affect public governance, as well as knowledge about conditions for organizational change, are necessary preconditions for using organization theory to meta-govern. "Craft" and "science" are complementary joint ventures, not opposing endeavors. The challenge is thus for political scientists to suggest ways to make for practical use of accumulated knowledge. An organizational approach to meta-governance, it is argued here, should serve as an action program for political science, making it practically relevant for solving societal problems.

Emphasizing organizational factors, moreover, does not exhaust the causal identification of crisis governance (Timeus and Gasco 2018). Giving analytical priority to organizational factors, many well-known mechanisms are left out on meta-governance, notably financial resourcing and individual agency (Goetz and Patz 2017). We thus argue that innovation and crisis governance is more than the result of entrepreneurial leadership and clear policy goals (Meier et al. 2018). The chapter thereby argues against one-size-fits-all recipes for crisis governance and innovation—such as requiring cross-boundary collaborative and interactive processes (Torfing et al. 2012; Ansell and Torfing 2014), contracting out, getting the incentives right, and as a consequence commercialization of the public sector (Osborne and Gaebler 1993), as well as the development of certain entrepreneurial leadership styles or attributes among executive heads (Bason 2014; Knill et al. 2016). Since organizational responses to crisis range from mundane reforms to large-scale organizational transformations, the number of explanatory factors needed exceeds organization theory. The set of explanatory mechanism needed to fully explain the latter is likely to exceed the set needed to explain the former. Organizational designers should be aware of the many things that tend to make processes of organizational change complex and difficult; such as ambiguous and composite goals, shortage of attention and capacity to monitor the process, previous conflicts that could be reopened, the stickiness of existing organizational arrangements, and the influence of organizational fad and fashion (see Egeberg and Trondal 2018 for an overview). Therefore, in the practical pursuit of meta-governance in crisis situations, organizational designers might also benefit from being aware of factors influencing organizational change (Egeberg and Trondal 2018). We suggest how organizational factors mediate meta-governing processes generally and public sector innovation particularly, and thus how organizational factors are essential tools for organizations and governments to muddle through crises.

References

Agger, A., & Sorensen, E. (2014). Designing Collaborative Policy Innovation: Lessons from a Danish Municipality. In C. Ansell & J. Torfing (Eds.), *Public Innovation Through Collaboration and Design*. London: Routledge.

Agranoff, R. (2014). *Managing Within Networks*. Georgetown: Georgetown University Press.

Ansell, C. (2011). *Pragmatist Democracy*. Oxford: Oxford University Press.

Ansell, C., Boin, A., & Farjoun, M. (2015). Dynamic Conservatism: How Institutions Change to Remain the Same. In M. S. Kraatz (Ed.), *Institutions and Ideals*. Emerald: Bingeley.

Ansell, C., & Torfing, J. (Eds.). (2014). *Public Innovation Through Collaboration and Design*. London: Routledge.

Ansell, C., & Trondal, J. (2017). Governing Turbulence: An Organizational-Institutional Agenda. *Perspectives on Public Management and Governance, 1*(1), 43–57.

Ansell, C., Trondal, J., & Ogard, M. (Eds.). (2017). *Governance in Turbulent Times*. Oxford: Oxford University Press.

Bakker, R. M., DeFillippi, R. J., Schwab, A., & Sydow, J. (2016). Temporary Organizing: Promises, Processes, Problems. *Organization Studies, 37*(2), 1703–1719.

Bason, C. (2014). Design Attitude as an Innovation Catalyst. In C. Ansell & J. Torfing (Eds.), *Public Innovation Through Collaboration and Design*. London: Routledge.

Bason, C., & Carstensen, H. V. (2002). Powering Collaborative Policy Innovation: Can Innovation Labs Help? *The Public Sector Innovation Journal, 17*, 2–26.

Bátora, J. (2017). Turbulence and War: Private Military Cooperations and the Reinstitutionalizing of War-Making. In C. Ansell, J. Trondal, & M. Ogard (Eds.), *Governance in Turbulent Times*. Oxford: Oxford University Press.

Bennis, W. G. (1966). *Changing Organizations*. New York: McGraw-Hill Book Company.

Bolman, L. G., & Deal, T. E. (1997). *Reframing Organizations*. San Francisco: Jossey-Bass.

Bourgeois, L. J., III, & Eisenhardt, K. M. (1988). Strategic Decision Processes in High Velocity Environments: Four Cases in the Microcomputer Industry. *Management Science, 34*(7), 816–835.

Brunsson, N. (2000). *The Irrational Organization*. Bergen: Fagbokforlaget.

Brunsson, N., & Olsen, J. P. (1993). *The Reforming Organization*. Bergen: Fagbokforlaget.

Christensen, J. (2017). *The Power of Economists Within the State*. Stanford: Stanford University Press.

Christensen, T., & Lægreid, P. (2006). Agencification and Regulatory Reform. In T. Christensen & P. Lægreid (Eds.), *Autonomy and Regulation*. Cheltenham: Edward Elgar.

Clarke, A., & Craft, J. (2019). The Twin Faces of Public Sector Design. *Governance, 32*, 5–21.

Dahl, R. (2000). *On Democracy*. New Haven: Yale University Press.
Davis, J. P., Eisenhardt, K. M., & Bingham, C. B. (2009). Optimal Structure, Market Dynamism, and the Strategy of Simple Rules. *Administrative Science Quarterly*, 54(3), 413–452.
Dong, J., March, J.G., & Workiewicz, M. (2017). On Organizing: An Interview with March, J. G. *Journal of Organization Design*, 6(14), 1–19.
Easton, D. (1965). *A Systems Analysis of Political Life*. New York: Wiley.
Egeberg, M., & Trondal, J. (2017). Researching European Union Agencies: What Have We Learnt (and Where Do We Go from Here). *Journal of Common Market Studies*, 55(4), 675–690.
Egeberg, M., & Trondal, J. (2018). *An Organizational Approach to Public Governance*. Oxford: Oxford University Press.
Emery, Y., & Giauque, D. (2014). The Hybrid Universe of Public Administration in the 21st Century. *International Review of Administrative Sciences*, 80(1), 23–32.
Fabbrini, S. (2007). *Compound Democracies*. Oxford: Oxford University Press.
Farjoun, M. (2010). Beyond dualism: Stability and Change as a Duality. *Academy of Management Review*, 35(2), 202–225.
Friedman, B. L. (2008). Policy Analysis as Organizational Analysis. In M. Moran, M. Rein, & R. E. Goodin (Eds.), *The Oxford Handbook of Public Policy*. Oxford: Oxford University Press.
Galbraith, J. R. (1980). Applying Theory to the Management of Organizations. In W. M. Evan (Ed.), *Frontiers in Organization and Management*. New York: Praeger Publishers.
Goetz, K. H. (2014). Time and Power in the European Commission. *International Review of Administrative Sciences*, 80(3), 577–596.
Goetz, K. H., & Patz, R. (2017). Resourcing International Organizations: Resource Diversification, Organizational Differentiation, and Administrative Governance. *Global Policy*, 8, 1–10.
Goodin, R. E. (1996). Institutions and Their Design. In R. E. Goodin (Ed.), *The Theory of Institutional Design*. Cambridge: Cambridge University Press.
Gulick, L. (1937). Notes on the Theory of Organizations: With Special References to Government in the United States. In L. Gulick & L. Urwick (Eds.), *Papers on the Science of Administration*. New York: Institute of Public Administration, Columbia University.
Haberstroh, C. J. (1965). Organization Design and Systems Analysis. In J. G. March (Ed.), *Handbook of Organizations*. Chicago: Rand McNally.
Hood, C. (1983). *The Tools of Government*. Chatham: Chatham House.
Hood, C. (1999). The Garbage can Model of Organization: Describing a Condition or a Prescriptive Design Principle? In M. Egeberg & P. Lægreid (Eds.), *Organizing Political Institutions*. Oslo: Scandinavian Political Press.
Karo, E., & Kattel, R. (2015). *Innovation Bureaucracy: Does the Organization of Government Matter When Promoting Innovation?* Unpublished paper, Lund University, Sweden.
Knill, C., Eckhard, S., & Grohs, S. (2016). Administrative Styles in the European Commission and the OSCE Secretariat: Striking Similarities Despite Different Organizational Settings. *Journal of European Public Policy*, 23(7), 1057–1076.
Koreh, M., Mandelkern, R., & Shpaizman, I. (2019). *A Dynamic Theoretical Framework of Gradual Institutional Changes*. Unpublished paper, University of Haifa, Israel.

Krygier, M. (2012). *Philip Selznick: Ideals in the World*. Stanford: Stanford Law Books.
Kupers, R. (2014). *Turbulence*. Amsterdam: Amsterdam University Press.
Leavitt, H. J. (1965). Applied Organizational Change in Industry: Structural, Technological, and Humanistic Approaches. In J. G. March (Ed.), *Handbook of Organizations*. Chicago: Rand McNally.
Lægreid, P., & Roness, P. G. (1999). Administrative Reform as Organized Attention. In M. Egeberg & P. Lægreid (Eds.), *Organizing Political Institutions*. Oslo: Scandinavian University Press.
Lodge, M., & Wegrich, K. (Eds.). (2012). *Executive Politics in Times of Crisis*. Houndmills: Palgrave Macmillan.
Mahoney, J., & Thelen, K. (Eds.). (2010). *Explaining Institutional Change*. Cambridge: Cambridge University Press.
March, J. G. (1981). Foodnotes to Organizational Change. *Administrative Science Quarterly, 26*(4), 563–577.
March, J. G. (1991). Exploration and Exploitation in Organizational Learning. *Organization Science, 2*(1), 71–87.
March, J. G. (1994). *A Primer on Decision Making*. New York: The Free Press.
March, J. G. (2010). *The Ambiguities of Experience*. Ithaca: Cornell University Press.
March, J. G., & Olsen, J. P. (1983). Organizing Political Life: What Administrative Reorganization Tells Us About Government. *American Political Science Review, 77*(2), 281–297.
March, J. G., & Olsen, J. P. (1989). *Rediscovering Institutions*. New York: The Free Press.
Margetts, H. and Duneavy, P. (2013). *The Second Wave of Digital-Era Governance: A Quasi-Paradigm for Government on the Web*. Royal Society Publishing. http://rsta.royalsocietypublishing.org/.
McCann, J., Selsky, J., & Lee, J. (2009). Building Agility, Resilience and Performance in Turbulent Environments. *People & Strategy, 32*(3), 44–52.
Meier, K. J. (2010). Governance, Structure, and Democracy: Luther Gulick and the Future of Public Administration. *Public Administration Review, 70*(1), 284–291.
Meier, K. J., Compton, M., Polga-Hecimovich, J., Song, M., & Wimpy, C. (2018). *Politics, Bureaucracy, and Successful Governance: The Problem of Political Failure*. Paper presented at the 2018 Annual Meeting of the American Political Science Association, Boston MA.
Olsen, J. P. (2008). The Ups and Downs of Bureaucratic Organization. *Annual Review of Political Science*, 11, 13–37.
Olsen, J. P. (2010). *Governing Through Institutional Building*. Oxford: Oxford University Press.
Olsen, J. P. (2017). *Democratic Accountability, Political Order, and Change*. Oxford: Oxford University Press.
Olsen, J. P. (2018). Democratic Accountability and the Changing European Political Order. *European Law Journal, 24*(1), 77–98.
Osborn, D., & Gaebler, T. (1993). *Reinventing Government*. Harmonthsworth: Middlesex.
Pierson, P. (2004). *Politics in Time*. Princeton: Princeton University Press.
Pressman, J. L., & Wildavsky, A. (1984). *Implementation*. Berkeley, CA: University of California Press.
Selznick, P. (1958). *Leadership in Administration*. Berkeley, CA: University of California Press.

Selznick, P. (1992). *The Moral Commonwealth*. Berkeley, CA: The University of California Press.
Selznick, P. (2015). On Sustaining Research Agendas: Their Moral and Scientific Basis. In M. S. Kraatz (Ed.), *Institutions and Ideals: Philip Selznick's Legacy for Organizational Studies*. Emerald: Bingley.
Simon, H. A. (1983). *Reason in Human Affairs*. Stanford: Stanford University Press.
Stoker, G. (2013). Designing Politics: A Neglected Justification for Political Science. *Political Studies Review, 11,* 174–181.
Streek, W., & Thelen, K. (Eds.). (2005). *Beyond Continuity*. Oxford: Oxford University Press.
Thorup, M. L. K. (2017). *Hybride organiseringer i danske kommuner*. PhD thesis. Roskilde: University of Roskilde.
Timeus, K., & Gasco, M. (2018). Increasing Innovation Capacity in City Governments: Do Innovation Labs Make a Difference. *Journal of Urban Affairs, 40*(7), 992–1008.
Tõnurist, P., Kattel, R., & Lember, V. (2017). Innovation Labs in the Public Sector: What They are and What They Do? *Public Management Review, 19,* 1455–1479.
Torfing, J., Peters, B. G., Pierre, J., & Sorensen, E. (2012). *Interactive Governance*. Oxford: Oxford University Press.
Torfing, J., & Sorensen, E. (2016). Metagoverning Collaborative Innovation in Governance Networks. *American Review of Public Administration, 47*(7), 826–839.
Trondal, J. (2017). Organized Turbulence. In C. Ansell, J. Trondal, & M. Ogard (Eds.), *Governance in Turbulent Times*. Oxford: Oxford University Press.
Trondal, J., Marcussen, M., Larsson, T., & Veggeland, T. (2010). *Unpacking International Organisations*. Manchester: Manchester University Press.
Volberda, H. W., van der Weerdt, N., Verwaal, E., Stienstra, M., & Verdu, A. J. (2012). Contingency Fit, Institutional Fit, and Firm Performance: A Metafit Approach to Organization–Environment Relationships. *Organization Science, 23*(4), 1040–1054.
Weick, K. E., & Suttcliffe, K. M. (2001). *Managing the Unexpected*. San Francisco: Jossey Bass.

CHAPTER 9

Cleavage Theory

Gary Marks, David Attewell, Jan Rovny, and Liesbet Hooghe

INTRODUCTION

Europe's politics and policy have been swept up in a deep divide about the meaning and implications of transnational community. This divide has its roots in institutional reforms beginning in the 1990s that opened up states to trade, immigration, and international authority. One side embraces open societies and international governance; the other favors strengthening national control over external forces. This conflict about transnationalism is cultural as well as economic.

The Eurocrisis, migration, and Brexit have made the political implications of the divide starkly transparent, but the conflict predates these crises. So we

---

G. Marks (✉) · L. Hooghe
Department of Political Science, University of North Carolina at Chapel Hill and Robert Schuman Fellow, EUI, Chapel Hill, NC, USA
e-mail: marks@unc.edu

L. Hooghe
e-mail: hooghe@unc.edu

D. Attewell
University of North Carolina at Chapel Hill, Chapel Hill, NC, USA
e-mail: dattew@live.unc.edu

J. Rovny
Sciences Po, Paris, France
e-mail: jan.rovny@sciencespo.fr

© The Author(s) 2021
M. Riddervold et al. (eds.), *The Palgrave Handbook of EU Crises*, Palgrave Studies in European Union Politics,
https://doi.org/10.1007/978-3-030-51791-5_9

need to ask how the political conflict over transnationalism has come into being and whether it takes the form of a social as well as a political divide.

If conflict over transnationalism is a new dimension of conflict, is it more than just a series of issues on which individuals and political parties have transient preferences? Is the conflict evidence of dealignment, of diminishing association between party competition and social structure? Or is this a new cleavage that juxtaposes socially distinctive groups? The answer bears directly on our understanding of how political parties have responded to Europe's crises and how, in turn, these crises have affected the structure of political conflict.

Our point of departure is the classic cleavage model, and in the next section, we discuss alternative ways of explaining its decline. In the following sections, we argue that transnationalism has generated social conflict that escapes the old left-right divide, and we set out expectations for why and when political parties have socially distinct constituencies on the new divide. We then put our cleavage argument to the test: we compare the extent to which voters and parties are structured by higher education, occupation, rural/urban location, religion, and gender across the old and new divides, pooling cross-national data from eight waves of the European Social Survey. We find that conventional parties on the left-right have become much less socially structured. However, parties on the socio-cultural transnational divide—GAL (green, alternative, libertarian) and TAN (traditionalist, authoritarian, nationalist)—have sharply divergent social bases. In the conclusion, we discuss how this transnational divide has narrowed the parameters for tackling Europe's crises, and how Europe's crises have accelerated the restructuring of party competition in Europe.

Dealignment or a New Divide?

The point of departure for theorizing party competition is the decline of the historical cleavages described by Lipset and Rokkan in their 1967 paper. The decline appears to be over-determined (Dalton et al. 1984; Franklin et al. 1992; Knutsen 2006; van der Brug 2010). The closed social milieus that bonded voters to parties have fragmented. The decline of religion, the diversification of working life, and greater occupational and spatial mobility have weakened the social ties that bind individuals to traditional social strata. Individuals lead lives that are only tenuously encased by durable and homogenous social groupings. Trade unions have declined. Fewer people go to church. Economic transformation has muddied the class divide. Social change points in the same direction. Mass education has increased political sophistication, and this arguably loosens the effect of social background while enhancing individual choice. Because these trends are time-bound, their effect appears to increase with each new generation of voters (van der Brug 2010; Walzcak et al. 2012).

There are two ways of making sense of this. One is to conceive the decline of traditional cleavages as part of an ongoing process of dealignment in which political choice becomes short-term and oriented to particular issues or personalities. Political preferences become a matter of *individual* choice (Franklin et al. 1992; Dalton 2007). Political parties compete to attract voters by strategically framing manifestos, making populist overtures, and having appealing candidates. In short, dealignment produces destructuration in which political parties are no longer defined by the stable support of specific social groups, but instead fish for voters in a fluid political environment. Destructuration should be particularly strong among educated voters and voters who have the cognitive resources to judge issue positions and leaders for themselves. It should also be strongest among younger generations who have come of age in an era of loosening social moorings.

Another view is to conceive the weakening of traditional cleavages as a phase in the re-articulation of political conflict (Dalton 2018; Inglehart 1977; Kriesi 1998; Kriesi et al. 2006; Bornschier 2010; Hooghe and Marks 2018). This literature emphasizes the growing salience of value conflict. Cultural issues—postmaterialism, individual lifestyle choice, multiculturalism, immigration—have produced a dimension of political conflict that is only loosely associated with traditional left-right competition. Inglehart (1971: 991) diagnoses a "transformation ... in the political cultures of advanced industrial societies, [which] seems to be altering the basic value priorities of given generations, as a result of changing conditions influencing their basic socialization." Kitschelt (1988, 1995) relates these patterns of value change to the rise of green and radical right parties. Kriesi (1998: 180) highlights "the emergence of yet another new cleavage – the cleavage opposing the new middle-class winners of the transformation of Western European societies to the group of losers of the very same process." Inglehart and Norris (2016: 4) observe that "the silent revolution launched in the 1970s seems to have spawned a resentful counter-revolutionary backlash today."

To say that a divide is cultural does not settle whether it has a basis in social structure. Values and social structure can be complementary explanations for political conflict. Cleavage theory theorizes an intimate connection between values and social structure. It conceives value conflict as structured by social divides that have a lasting impact on the formation of social movements and political parties (Bartolini and Mair 1990). These divides arise from large-scale processes that shape the lives and the livelihoods of those in a society. Lipset and Rokkan (1967) identify three: the building of national states across Europe from the sixteenth century, the emergence of Protestantism in Northern Europe from the seventeenth century, and the industrial revolution from the nineteenth century.

Old divides may lose the power to shape human relations as the socializing effect of prior institutions attenuates from generation to generation. As prior divides exhaust their shaping force, there is the ever-present possibility that a new cleavage arises to overlay the old. The organizations that reinforced the religious and class cleavage have declined, but there is reason to suspect that political parties competing on the new cultural divide have distinct constituencies with recognizable social characteristics.

This is the basis for neo-cleavage theory (Hooghe and Marks 2018). The chief propositions of neo-cleavage theory are that the dynamism in party systems arises from exogenous social change; that the party-political response comes chiefly in the form of new political parties that rise on a new cleavage; and that processes of alignment and dealignment coexist as new divides become solidified among voters while old divides lose causal power. Neo-cleavage theory does not anticipate a wholesale restructuring of the electorate. A significant degree of volatility is likely to persist alongside structuration. This is because transnationalism concerns certain social categories more than others, and it is those individuals most directly affected who are most likely to form intense, durable political allegiances.

A Transnational Cleavage

At the core of the contemporary cultural divide is a sharp rise in transnationalism with profound social and economic consequences. Transnationalism advanced in a series of reforms following the Reagan-Thatcher years that opened up Western societies to immigration and trade. In the process, and particularly in Europe, the architecture of political life was transformed. The Single European Act and the Maastricht Treaty reconceived Europe as a political union with common citizenship and a single currency. Ten Eastern European countries joined the EU in the mid-2000s. The end of the Cold War released in Europe alone the westward migration of one hundred million people, and many more from the African continent. From the 1990s to the present, major indices of transnationalism, including foreign investment, trade, and immigration have grown at historically high rates. National borders have been perforated by immigration, international trade, and by the melding of states in a multilevel EU polity (Hooghe et al. 2019).

Transnationalism is combustible because immigration, trade, and European integration are *political* choices that profoundly affect people's lives (Hooghe et al. 2018; Zürn 2018). The intermixing of peoples with diverse beliefs, norms, and behavior holds the potential for intense conflict. To this one may add the economic consequences, because transnationalism tends to benefit those with human and financial capital, while those who lack capital face greater competition for jobs and housing. From the perspective of cultural and economic losers, transnationalism has devalued national citizenship.

The divide pits those who defend national ways of life from external influence against those who conceive their identities as consistent with international governance and who welcome, rather than oppose, the dense interpenetration of societies (Hooghe and Marks 2018). Public opinion is sharply divided on immigration, European integration, and transnationalism (De Vries 2018; van Elsas et al. 2016; Hooghe and Marks 2009; Rooduijn et al. 2017).

There are signs that this divide is producing new political parties with distinctive social constituencies (Aichholzer et al. 2014; Bornschier 2010; Hobolt and Tilley 2016; Häusermann and Kriesi 2015; Hutter et al. 2016; Lubbers and Coenders 2017; Rohrschneider and Whitefield 2016). Radical nationalist parties, or TAN parties, mobilize stark opposition to immigration and European integration and drive one side of this divide. Green parties, or GAL parties, take the most pronounced transnationalist positions.[1]

Occupation and class were the chief social markers that sorted individuals on the left-right divide. What kind of social characteristics structure political choice on the transnational divide?

Education appears key on the new divide. Higher education is associated with attitudes sympathetic to transnationalism, including tolerance for ethno-cultural diversity and positive views on European integration (Ceobanu and Escandell 2010; Hakhverdian et al. 2013; Hainmueller and Hiscox 2006). Education is also a path to economic security in a transnational world. It is worth noting that education seems to be more a marker than a cause. Panel studies suggest that acquiring education has little effect on a person's political affinities over time (Kuhn et al. 2017; Lancee and Sarrasin 2015). Instead, education tells one about a person's parents, how a person was raised, and a person's station in life—in short, it tells us something important about a person's social and material background.

The role of education in the neo-cleavage model contrasts sharply with the expectation, central to dealignment theory, that education erodes social structuration. With the expansion of mass education, dealignment theorists suggest an increasing proportion of voters have gained the cognitive capacity to make their own choices, to act on their political preferences as individuals rather than as members of a group. In short, dealignment theory suggests that education releases a person from the chains of inherited social structure.

---

[1] The GALTAN concept was introduced by Hooghe et al. (2002) to characterize a second, non-economic or cultural, new politics dimension, which had been gaining strength since the 1970s. The concept was further developed by Marks et al. (2006: 157 and note 3): "This dimension summarizes several noneconomic issues—ecological, lifestyle, and communal—and is correspondingly more diverse than the Left/Right dimension. In some countries, it is oriented around environmental protection and sustainable growth; in others, it captures conflict about traditional values rooted in a secular-religious divide; and in yet others, it is pitched around immigration and defense of the national community. Therefore, we describe the poles of this dimension with composite terms: green/alternative/libertarian (GAL) and traditionalism/authority/nationalism (TAN) … Gender and color connotations intended." The CHES surveys on party positioning have been estimating political parties' position on this dimension since 1999 with a question that is biased toward the libertarian element in green/alternative/libertarian and the authoritarian element in traditionalism/authority/nationalism (Steenbergen and Marks 2007; see also https://chesdata.eu). This imposes a useful conservatism because these elements are distant from the sovereignty aspects of European integration and immigration, which motivate the transnational cleavage.

The two sides on the transnational divide appear also to be occupationally distinctive (Häusermann and Kriesi 2015). Professionals—e.g., managers, teachers, nurses, doctors, social workers—exercise discretion at work and are engaged in face to face relations with diverse others. Such people tend to have GAL values, whereas manual workers, low-grade service workers, and those whose work is chiefly technical tend to be more TAN.

This is reinforced by an economic logic. Production workers are precariously placed in the international division of labor where they produce traded goods in competition with former peasants from developing countries. While mobile capital threatens to outsource jobs abroad, the presence of recent immigrants increases domestic competition for blue-collar jobs. This puts TAN parties, which demand national closure, in direct competition with social democratic parties, which have been the home base for production workers (Oesch and Rennwald 2018). For professionals who have financial or social capital, an internationalized market multiplies economic opportunities and immigration is a source of cheap labor.

Hence, our expectation is that the transnational cleavage cuts across the class divide. Lipset once noted that a signal attribute of socialist parties was to turn those towards the bottom of society in an internationalist cosmopolitan direction. Radical nationalist parties have arisen on the new divide that do just the opposite.

Rural or urban location also sorts individuals on either side of the transnational cleavage (Maxwell 2019). Cities have always been known for trade, the flow of ideas, and cultural openness, and they tend to attract those who are comfortable with transnationalism. A nine-country comparative study concludes that "identical social groups living in metropolitan places with distinct interests and lifestyles behave in starkly different ways" (Sellers et al. 2013: 419, 448–449). TAN parties do well in small towns and suburbs that are ethnically less diverse and economically peripheral, while green parties do best in cities.

Gender and age, inert characteristics on the conventional left-right, are clear markers on the transnational cleavage (Dolezal 2010). Positive views on transnationalism tend to go together with positive views on gender and transgender equality, and younger people, on the whole, have been socialized under conditions of social diversity and multilevel politics that characterize the transnational world. The role of religiosity in the new divide is less clearcut. On the one hand, secularism has been associated with the postmaterialist value change that underpins transnationalism (Inglehart 2008). On the other hand, church attendance still appears capable of nurturing loyalty to Christian parties, even while many religious voters support TAN positions on immigration or multiculturalism (Immerzeel et al. 2013; Minkenberg 2017).

Education, occupation, location, gender, religion are not transitory choices that a person makes. They shape a person's life, who they work with, who their friends are, and in an increasing proportion of cases, who they marry. While the incidence of organizational membership has declined, the impact of social networks of friends, family, or co-workers on political preferences may have grown (Fitzgerald 2011; Zuckerman et al. 2007).

Conflict between mainstream political parties has softened with the decline of the class cleavage, but conflict between green and TAN parties is acute and has become sharper over time. The model we posit is not one of realignment in which new conflicts replace old ones. It is, instead, akin to a geological process in which cleavages are formed in succession and overlay each other so that the resulting structure of conflict reflects both emerging and eroding tensions. So neo-cleavage theory builds on classic cleavage theory but relaxes the assumption that cleavages are frozen. Instead, we expect destructuration and restructuration to coexist. This produces a diversified party landscape in which parties with socially distinctive electorates compete with socially generic parties.

Data and Measurement

Neo-cleavage theory has different expectations from dealignment on three basic questions: (1) Are political parties competing on the transnational cleavage more or less socially distinctive than those competing on left/right? (2) To what extent does education sort voters on the transnational cleavage? (3) How does this play out over time with younger generations of voters?

To answer these questions, we pair individual-level data from the European Social Survey (ESS) (eight rounds, every two years between 2002 and 2016) with estimates on party positioning from the Chapel Expert Survey (five waves: 2002, 2006, 2010, 2014, 2017). We select those individuals who say that they voted in the last national election for a political party, provided that the party has at least 25 voters in one ESS round or a total of 75 across all ESS rounds.[2] This produces a dataset with 147,671 respondents who have voted for 169 parties in 24 European countries. We aggregate individual-level information on vote and social characteristics to the party family or, for the multivariate analysis, to the individual party.

The dependent variables are five structural characteristics hypothesized to predispose an individual to transnationalism: higher education, professional occupation, urban location, female, and secularism. *Higher education* encompasses individuals with postsecondary or tertiary education. *Professional*, derived from Oesch's ISCO categorization, consists of managers and socio-cultural professionals. *Urban* describes people in cities or suburban communities. *Secular* refers to those who never attend religious services or only on special occasions.

---

[2] We restrict the sample to voters who were at least 21 years old at the time of the survey to avoid the confounding effect of people with incomplete education. We impose a minimum number of respondents to reduce the odds on drawing a biased sample of voters. The same concern for reducing sampling bias motivates us to pool party respondents across ESS rounds. The time span in the ESS—just fourteen years—is too short to pick up meaningful shifts in the social composition of parties' voters.

Party ideology is operationalized in two ways. Party family—TAN, conservative, liberal, Christian democratic, social democratic, radical left, and green—is a standard classification to "summarize the accumulated historical experience of cleavages" (Marks and Wilson 2000: 439). Our baseline is the categorization in the CHES dataset (Polk et al. 2017; Bakker et al. 2015; Hooghe and Marks 2018), which is highly correlated with Parlgov's classification (Döring and Manow 2016). We can then compare the distinctiveness of voters across party families and contrast twenty-one binary party family pairs.

Second, we estimate parties' ideological positions in a two-dimensional political space, consisting of a left-right dimension tapping the role of government and equality versus economic freedom, and a cultural GALTAN dimension, using the Chapel Hill Expert Survey (Hooghe et al. 2002; Marks et al. 2006).[3]

We control for party size on the intuition that smaller parties may find it easier to sustain a distinctive social base. *Vote share* is a party's average vote share in the national election of the survey year or the nearest prior year. Country-fixed effects account for the fact that respondents and parties are nested within countries.

Results

We begin by comparing party families. The expectations are that social characteristics are more powerful in differentiating political parties on the transnational cleavage than on the class cleavage, and that social structuration on the transnational cleavage is more pronounced for younger generations while it is the opposite on the left-right.

Table 9.1 reports the overrepresentation or underrepresentation of a social group by party family.[4] The first column does this for the 34.1% of the ESS sample of respondents who have completed postsecondary or tertiary education. Each row shows the percentage difference in highly educated people relative to the mean for the sample. Hence, higher educated voters are 21.2% overrepresented in green political parties. In absolute terms, more than half (55.3%) of their voters are highly educated. The probability that this distribution would arise randomly is less than one in one hundred million. This contrasts with an underrepresentation of 12.4% for TAN parties. On average, just one in five (21.7%) of TAN voters are highly educated. The educational gap between green and TAN voters is 33.6% (the absolute difference between 21.2 and 12.4). Education produces the largest difference among all social characteristics.

[3] CHES data are available for five time points between 2002 and 2017. We interpolate between rounds.

[4] Results are robust when using more narrowly focused categorizations for education (tertiary educated vs. all others) or occupation (socio-cultural professionals vs. others; production workers vs. others). We prefer more encompassing categories because they divide the population into more equivalently sized groups.

Table 9.1 Socio-structural biases by party family (all countries)

	Education *Higher*	*Occupation* *Socio-professional or manager*	*Urban-rural* *Urban*	*Gender* *Female*	*Religion* *Secular*
Greens	+21.20	+12.86	+11.56	+7.18	+13.99
Liberals	+9.24	+5.91	+1.43	−0.17	+8.55
Radical left	2.69	−0.33	+7.36	−1.72	+13.15
Social democrats	−5.17	−2.43	+1.38	+1.15	+5.68
Christian democrats	+0.80	+1.96	−6.49	0.02	−23.38
Conservatives	−0.48	−1.20	0.98	0.09	−6.07
Radical Tan	−12.38	−8.91	−4.49	−9.55	−1.61
Overall electorate	*34.12%*	*26.26%*	*31.32%*	*52.69%*	*73.20%*

Note Each cell shows the overrepresentation (+) or underrepresentation (−) of a group having this characteristic in a party family compared to the overall population (21 years or older).
Source ESS (2002–2016) for 18 countries

These data are consistent with neo-cleavage theory. First, political parties that anchor the GALTAN dimension—green and TAN—are at the extremes in sorting highly educated persons, professionals and managers, females, and urban people.[5] The social distinctiveness of party families on the left-right cleavage is much weaker. The major party families on the left-right—social democrats, Christian democrats, liberals, conservatives—are much alike on education, occupation, gender, and (except for Christian democrats) on urbanization. This similarity extends even to the radical left. These party families reflect the social structure of the overall electorate, and deviations from the overall mean are, with one exception, smaller than eight percentage points. Hence, the old cleavage structure built on class and occupation is now only dimly evident in the party families that motivate Lipset and Rokkan's analysis. Remarkably, green and TAN parties are more occupationally distinctive than parties that compete on the class cleavage. The gap between green (12.9) and TAN (−8.9) parties in professionals and managers is 21.8%, compared to 8.3% between the next two most dissimilar parties, liberals (5.9), and social democrats (−2.4). Conversely, TAN parties draw heavily from the traditional core constituency of left political parties. Production and service workers are overrepresented by 6.6% in TAN parties, compared to 5.5% for social democratic parties and 2.5% for radical left parties.

Religion has some bite on the transnational divide. Secular voters are strongly overrepresented in green parties (14.0%) and radical left parties (13.1%) and underrepresented in TAN parties (−1.6%). However, religiosity's greatest power lies in differentiating Christian democrats from other party

---

[5] TAN and green voters have the lowest and highest concentrations of the first three of these characteristics, and almost for the fourth: while green voters are the most urbanized party, TAN voters are the second-most rural group just behind Christian democratic voters.

families. In a predominantly secular Europe, religiosity remains a distinctive marker for partisan choice (van der Brug et al. 2009; Rovny and Polk 2017).

The sharp contrast between green and TAN parties goes hand in hand with relatively moderate stances on classic left-right issues. TAN parties tend to blur positions on the left/right (Rovny 2012, 2013).[6] Greens and TAN parties conceive their mission in relation to the transnational cleavage, taking polar positions on immigration and Europe. This is what sorts their voters in socio-structural camps. These findings are robust across subregions (northwest, south, and east), older and younger electorates, and when controlling for party size.

Figure 9.1 visualizes the difference between every paired combination of party families for four social characteristics. Black lines represent a difference of at least 30%, red lines a difference between 20 and 30%, yellow lines a difference between 10 and 20%, and green lines a difference of less than 10%. In every case, the largest contrast between party family dyads involves green or TAN parties, and for education, occupation, and gender the green & TAN dyad exhibits the greatest gap. While it is valid to say that a value divide has emerged alongside the conventional left-right cleavage, this does not imply a decline in the role of social structure in differentiating political parties. Education most sharply distinguishes green and TAN voters, and while class location is almost imperceptible in differentiating parties on the class cleavage, the gap is wide and significant across green and TAN parties.

Hence, the evidence presented here is consistent with the neo-cleavage expectations that (1) political parties competing on the transnational cleavage are more socially distinctive than those competing on left-right, and (2) that education is the strongest sorter of voters on the transnational cleavage.

Does the social structuration of political parties increase or decrease from generation to generation? We split the sample in the ESS dataset into three roughly equally sized generational groups of voters: those born before 1950, those born between 1950 and 1970, and those born after 1970. Figure 9.2 aggregates these comparisons for parties that compete on GALTAN (green and radical right) and for parties that compete on left-right (conservative, Christian democrat, liberal, social democrat, and radical left). The social distinctiveness of party families for the pre-1950 generation of voters is indicated by the light bar in each frame, and that for the post-1970 generation is dark. Each bar averages the extent (in percent) to which voters deviate from the population mean. Hence, the higher the bar, the more a generation of voters sorts itself on a social characteristic into different parties.

Neo-cleavage theory shares with dealignment theory the expectation that social distinctiveness has declined for left-right political parties. We see mixed evidence for this. For these parties, the post-1970 generation of voters is less sharply sorted than the pre-1950 generation on higher education, gender, and religion, but more sharply on occupation and rural–urban location. However,

---

[6]This is why we describe these parties as *TAN* rather than radical right.

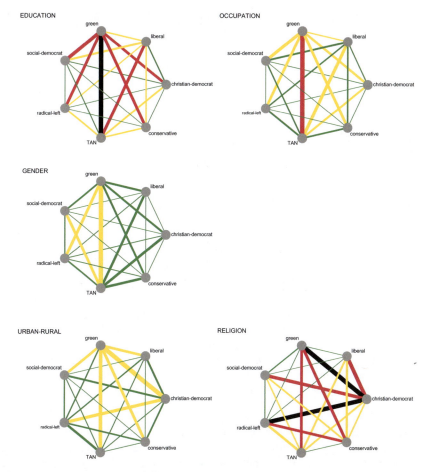

Fig. 9.1 Socio-structural differences between party families (*Note* Data from 2002 to 2016 ESS. The thickness and color of the lines reflects the extent to which the electorate of two party families is distinctive on a social characteristic. Black = >30% difference; Red = 20–30% difference; Yellow = 10–20% difference; Green = <10% difference)

in all but religion, the difference across generations is 2% or less. Hence, we see quite stable rates of social sorting for left-right parties across generations, with the exception of religion.

Other expectations are more clearly confirmed. One is that social differentiation is considerably greater among parties competing on GALTAN than among those competing on left-right. This is the case for education, occupation, rural–urban location, and gender. Left-right parties are more differentiated on religion than GALTAN parties, though the difference with GALTAN parties has almost disappeared for voters born after 1970.

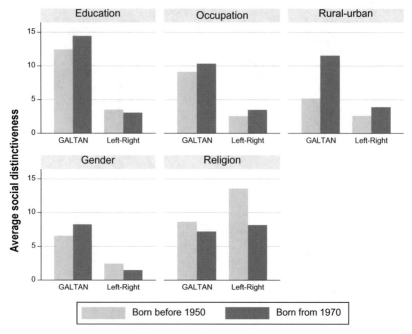

Fig. 9.2 Social distinctiveness among younger and older voters: the GALTAN vs. left-right divide (*Note* 2002–2016 ESS voting data aggregated to the party family. Structural distinctiveness is estimated as the average difference in a social characteristic between GAL (left) and TAN (right) parties divided by two

Finally, and perhaps most decisively, neo-cleavage and dealignment theory have contrasting expectations regarding generational change. Dealignment theory expects the social distinctiveness of political parties to decline with successive generations, whereas neo-cleavage theory expects that a new cleavage will retain, or even increase, its distinctiveness. We find that social distinctiveness on the GALTAN divide is sharper for the post-1970 generation than for the pre-1950 generation on education, occupation, rural–urban location, and gender. Overall, these comparisons are in line with neo-cleavage theory and fit poorly with dealignment theory. The social distinctiveness of party families is much greater on the GALTAN side than on left-right, and while, in general, left-right distinctiveness has diminished across generations of voters, that on the GALTAN side has increased.

The analysis so far has taken the party family as the building bloc. The final step in our analysis is examine individual political parties. The dependent variable in our analysis is party structuration, which is a factor of the five social characteristics (education, occupation, rural/urban, gender, religion) obtained through principal components analysis. The factor, *party structuration*, has an eigenvalue of 2.25 and explains 44.9% of the variance. Higher values reflect structuration on social characteristics associated with transnationalism, lower values reflect structuration on characteristics opposed to transnationalism, while middle values (0) reflect lack of structuration.[7]

We can now estimate the effect of the positioning of a political party on GAL vs. TAN and left vs. right for its social structuration. Neo-cleavage theory expects significant structure whereby positioning on the GALTAN dimension has a much greater effect than positioning on the left-right dimension. All model specifications include a variable tapping the percentage vote of a political party on the ground that smaller parties may be more structured.

The first model in Table 9.2 reveals the power of party family in accounting for variation in structuration at the individual party level. TAN parties are the reference category, and all other party families have a more transnational social profile, that is, their electorate tends to be more educated, urban, professional, female, and secular than that of a typical TAN party. Green parties as a family are most strongly different from TAN parties, and Christian democrats are least different. This model explains around two-thirds of the variance in party structuration.

Party families are telling shortcuts for the worldview that a political party claims to defend. However, we can tap this more directly through party ideology or an individual party's stance on dimensional issues, and by relating this to its structural distinctiveness.

We expect party ideology to explain a party's structural distinctiveness, and the remaining models in Table 9.2 test this. Across each of the models, the social structure of a party is strongly predicted by its GALTAN position. In Model 2 and Model 6, the left-right position of a party has a significant effect, but its causal power is about one third of that of GALTAN. This is what one would expect if the traditional class divide had lost structural coherence and a new cultural divide came into force. When we consider party social structure for the entire electorate, the model explains around 74% of the variance.

If transnationalism is driving structuration, a party's stances on immigration and European integration should have a strong effect on its social structure. Model 3 replaces GALTAN and left-right position with party stances on immigration and European integration as estimated by Chapel Hill experts. The model is strongly predictive of the social character of the party. Political parties that are less restrictive on immigration and more supportive of European integration tend to have a distinctly more structured electorate. Model 4 repeats the exercise for redistribution, which is arguably the central issue on the classical left-right divide. Party stances on redistribution do not appear to be a systematic predictor of a party's social-structural make up. Model 5 then juxtaposes the transnationalism and left-right dimensions. This suggests that positioning on transnational issues (immigration, in particular) is a much more powerful predictor of a party's social distinctiveness than redistribution. At the same time, once we control for immigration and European integration

---

[7]The results are similar when the dependent variables are centered around the country mean or when using nonlinear modeling.

Table 9.2 Party structuration and party ideology

	Model 1 Party family model	Model 2 Ideology model	Model 3 Trans-nationalism model	Model 4 Classic left-right model	Model 5 Trans-nationalism vs. left-right	Model 6 Ideology model for parties with 5–15% vote
Party family (ref = Radical Tan)						
Conservatives	1.608*** (.297)					
Liberals	1.843*** (.255)					
Christian democrats	0.782* (.313)					
Social democrats	1.584*** (.299)					
Radical left	1.302*** (.301)					
Greens	2.720*** (.304)					
GALTAN		− 0.371*** (.030)				− 0.397*** (.046)
Left-right		0.138*** (.033)				0.155** (.053)
Immigration			0.239*** (.036)		0.377 (.046)***	

| | Model 1
Party family model | Model 2
Ideology model | Model 3
Trans-nationalism model | Model 4
Classic left-right model | Model 5
Trans-nationalism vs. left-right | Model 6
Ideology model for parties with 5–15% vote |
|---|---|---|---|---|---|---|
| European integration | | | 0.190** (.055) | | 0.071 (.061) | |
| Redistribution | | | | 0.034 (.049) | −0.183 (.046)*** | |
| Vote | −0.032*** (.009) | −0.026*** (.006) | −0.035*** (.008) | −0.034*** (.009) | −0.030 (.007)*** | −0.138** (.047) |
| Country dummies | YES | YES | YES | YES | YES | YES |
| R^2 | 0.681 | 0.735 | 0.689 | 0.394 | 0.729 | 0.827 |
| Number of parties | 169 | 162 | 157 | 152 | 152 | 72 |

Note OLS unstandardized coefficients with standard errors in brackets; ***sign < .001 **sign < .01 *sign < .05. *Source* 2002–2016 ESS voting aggregated to the party for the dependent variable; CHES data for the independent variables positions, a party's position on redistribution appears significantly related to structural distinctiveness. This is consistent with neo-cleavage theory, which anticipates that new cleavages overlay older ones rather than replace them. Party system formation is akin to a geological process whereby the structure of conflict reflects both emerging and eroding tensions.

Party size is significantly related to structuration, but the substantive effect is small, which gives us confidence that the results are not driven by the smaller size of green and radical-TAN parties relative to many mainstream parties. Model 6, which limits the sample of parties to those with a vote share greater than 5% and less than 15%, allows a direct test of the party size effect. Seventy-two parties are in this band of vote share, and their structuration is powerfully explained by their GALTAN position. Left-right position is much weaker.

Figure 9.3 illustrates how GALTAN and social structuring go hand in hand, and it reveals that party families are rather coherent with respect to their structuration. TAN and green parties are bunched at opposite ends of the regression line. Liberal parties, as in other respects, are the most diverse party family, with the other party families falling in-between.

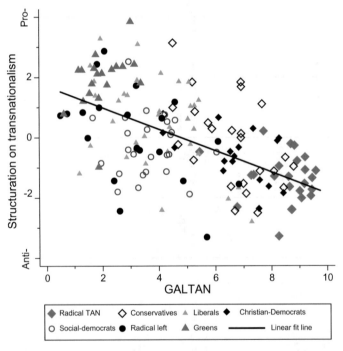

Fig. 9.3 Party ideology and party structuration (*Note* 169 individual political parties by their GALTAN position (CHES) and their score on party structuration (ESS), whereby low scores indicate an overrepresentation of voters with social characteristics associated with anti-transnationalism and high scores indicate an overrepresentation of voters with social characteristics associated with transnationalism)

Conclusion

The evidence presented here throws into doubt both the continued preeminence of the classic cleavages theorized by Lipset and Rokkan's frozen landscape thesis and the chief counter-claim, that individual party preferences are increasingly unstructured. We find plenty of support for the contention that the structural distinctiveness of the left-right divide has faded; that class location and education only weakly distinguish mainstream left versus right parties; and that these phenomena are particularly marked among younger generations of voters. However, we also find that voters for political parties on the transnational divide—green and TAN parties—are distinguished by their level of education, their occupation, where they live, and whether they are female or male. These differences do not appear to be diminishing over time. They are *more* pronounced among younger generations of voters than older generations.

Consequently, we are drawn to reassess the idea that socially structured political cleavages are a thing of the past. Among the implications of neo-cleavage theory are that the dynamism in party systems arises from exogenous social change; that the party-political response comes chiefly in the form of new political parties that rise on a new cleavage; that processes of alignment and dealignment coexist as new divides become solidified among voters while old divides lose causal power; and that the decline of social structure among parties on a prior cleavage can go hand in hand with considerable social structuration on a new cleavage.

The rise of a transnational cleavage suggests that, far from being frozen, party systems are subject to exogenous shocks that can produce durable divides. As Lipset and Rokkan stressed, cleavages overlay and interact with each another—and so prior cleavages constitute a prism that affects the incidence of a more recent cleavage. The chief intermediary institutions of Lipset and Rokkan's era—churches and unions—have lost much of their socializing force, but this does not mean that voters behave as atomized individuals. Research on social networks—family, friends, neighborhood, and work, alongside the digital sources of information into which people self-select—is vital in probing how sociality shapes political preferences and behavior.

A premise that neo-cleavage theory shares with classic cleavage theory is that change comes in response to major exogenous shocks. The shocks that Lipset and Rokkan observe are the rise of the national state which produced a centre-periphery cleavage and a religious cleavage; and the industrial revolution which produced an urban–rural and a class cleavage. We suspect that the perforation of national states is producing a transnational cleavage. The first cleavage arose with the breakdown of a supranational order and the establishment of strong territorial bureaucracies imposing national religions and languages. The most recent cleavage is, at its core, a conflict over the role of the national state and national community in an era of transnationalism.

The rise of the transnational cleavage narrowed options for responses to Europe's crises. This is most transparent with respect to the migration crisis which "touched a nerve of national identity because it asked Europe's populations to harbor culturally dissimilar people" (Hooghe and Marks 2019: 8–9). Börzel and Risse (2018) argue that the mobilization of these identities by TAN parties explains to a large extent why elites failed to coordinate when the Dublin system collapsed under the weight of the refugee flows. TAN parties, using tabloid and social media as willing mediums, compelled governments to introduce restrictions, not only in the Visegrad countries but also in Germany, Austria, and Sweden where the public response was initially positive. Countermobilization—on the part of the GAL side—was meek. Exclusive nationalism also delayed and limited the response to the Eurocrisis. TAN parties took the initiative by framing the crisis as a contest among nations and a fight against Brussels. Northern governments were acting as party coalitions acutely sensitive to public opinion, and largely ignored the advice of the World Bank and the IMF to increase domestic consumption in order to rebalance the Eurozone. European-wide solidarity in the shape of bailouts, a stimulus package, or even Eurobonds was not on the cards. The Euro came close to collapse, but—contrary to the migration crisis—coordination failure was averted. A cocktail of partial and technical fixes was agreed mostly outside the limelight of party politics. A long-term solution, including fiscal union, seems off the table.

GAL mobilization has been much less pronounced than TAN mobilization. But this is not written in stone. The 2019 European Parliamentary elections have seen the green vote rise sharply in several European countries. Partisanship in Europe has become decidedly more polarized around the transnational cleavage. Our analysis of voters and political parties suggests that the new cleavage is structured and durable.

References

Aichholzer, J., Kritzinger, S., Wagner, M., & Zeglovits, E. (2014). How Has Radical Right Support Transformed Established Political Conflicts? The Case of Austria. *West European Politics, 37*(1), 113–137.

Bakker, R., Edwards, E., Hooghe, L., Jolly, S., Marks, G., Polk, J., et al. (2015). Measuring Party Positions in Europe: The Chapel Hill Expert Survey Trend File, 1999–2010. *Party Politics, 21*(1), 143–153.

Bartolini, S., & Mair, P. (1990). *Identity, Competition, and Electoral Availability: The Stabilisation of European Electorates, 1885–1985*. Cambridge: Cambridge University Press.

Bornschier, S. (2010). *Cleavage Politics and the Populist Right: The New Cultural Conflict in Western Europe*. Philadelphia: Temple University Press.

Börzel, T. A., & Risse, T. (2018). From the Euro to the Schengen Crises: European Integration Theories, Politicization, and Identity Politics. *Journal of European Public Policy, 25*(1), 83–108.

Ceobanu, A. M., & Escandell, X. (2010). Comparative Analyses of Public Attitudes Toward Immigrants and Immigration Using Multinational Survey Data: A Review of Theories and Research. *Annual Review of Sociology, 36,* 309–328.

Dalton, R. J. (2007). Partisan Mobilization, Cognitive Mobilization, and the Changing American Electorate. *Electoral Studies, 26*(2), 274–286.

Dalton, R. J. (2018). *Political Realignment: Economics, Culture, and Electoral Change.* Oxford: Oxford University Press.

Dalton, R. J., Flanagan, S. C., & Beck, P. A. (Eds.). (1984). *Electoral Change in Advanced Industrial Democracies: Realignment or Dealignment?.* Princeton, NJ: Princeton University Press.

De Vries, C. (2018). *Euroscepticism and the Future of European Integration.* Oxford: Oxford University Press.

Dolezal, M. (2010). Exploring the Stabilization of a Political Force: The Social and Attitudinal Basis of Green Parties in the Age of Globalization. *West European Politics, 33*(3), 534–552.

Döring, H., & Manow, P. (2016). *Parliaments and Governments Database (ParlGov): Information on Parties, Elections and Cabinets in Modern Democracies.* Development Version. http://www.parlgov.org.

Fitzgerald, J. (2011). Family Dynamics and Swiss Parties on the Rise: Exploring Party Support in a Changing Electoral Context. *Journal of Politics, 73*(3), 783–796.

Franklin, M., Mackie, T. T., & Valen, H. (Eds.). (1992). *Electoral Change: Responses to Evolving Social and Attitudinal Structures in Western Countries.* Cambridge: Cambridge University Press.

Hainmueller, J., & Hiscox, M. J. (2006). Learning to Love Globalization: Education and Individual Attitudes Toward International Trade. *International Organization, 60*(2), 469–498.

Hakhverdian, A., van Elsas, E., van der Brug, W., & Kuhn, T. (2013). Euroscepticism and Education: A Longitudinal Study of Twelve EU Member States, 1973–2010. *European Union Politics, 14*(4), 522–541.

Häusermann, S., & Kriesi, H. (2015). What Do Voters Want? Dimensions and Configurations in Individual-Level Preferences and Party Choice. In P. Beramendi, S. Häusermann, H. Kitschelt, & H. Kriesi (Eds.), *The Politics of Advanced Capitalism* (pp. 202–230). Cambridge: Cambridge University Press.

Hobolt, S. B., & Tilley, J. (2016). Fleeing the Centre: The Rise of Challenger Parties in the Aftermath of the Euro Crisis. *West European Politics, 39*(5), 971–991.

Hooghe, L., Lenz, T., & Marks, G. (2018). Contested World Order: Delegitimation of International Governance. *Review of International Organizations.* https://doi.org/10.1007/s11558-0189334-3.

Hooghe, L., Lenz, T., & Marks, G. (2019). *A Theory of International Organization.* Oxford: Oxford University Press.

Hooghe, L., & Marks, G. (2009). A Postfunctionalist Theory of European Integration: From Permissive Consensus to Constraining Dissensus. *British Journal of Political Science, 39*(1), 1–23.

Hooghe, L., & Marks, G. (2018). Cleavage Theory Meets Europe's Crises: Lipset, Rokkan, and the Transnational Cleavage. *Journal of European Public Policy, 25*(1), 109–135.

Hooghe, L., & Marks, G. (2019). Grand Theories on European Integration in the 21st Century. *Journal of European Public Policy.* https://doi.org/10.1080/13501763.2019.1569711.

Hooghe, L., Marks, G., & Wilson, C. (2002). Does Left/Right Structure Party Positions on European Integration? *Comparative Political Studies, 35*(8), 965–989.
Hutter, S., Grande, E., & Kriesi, H. (Eds.). (2016). *Politicising Europe: Integration and Mass Politics*. Cambridge: Cambridge University Press.
Immerzeel, T., Jaspers, E., & Lubbers, M. (2013). Religion as Catalyst or Restraint of Radical Right Voting? *West European Politics, 36*(4), 946–968.
Inglehart, R. (1971). The Silent Revolution in Europe: Intergenerational Change in Postindustrial Societies. *American Political Science Review, 65*(4), 991–1017.
Inglehart, R. (1977). *The Silent Revolution: Changing Values and Political Styles Among Western Publics*. Princeton, NJ: Princeton University.
Inglehart, R. (2008). Changing Values Among Western Publics from 1970 to 2006. *West European Politics, 31*(1–2), 130–146.
Inglehart, R., & Norris, P. (2016). *Trump, Brexit, and the Rise of Populism: Economic Have-Nots and Cultural Backlash*, presented at the American Political Science Association Annual Meeting, Philadelphia, 1–4, September.
Kitschelt, H. (1988). Left-Libertarian Parties: Explaining Innovation in Competitive Party Systems. *World Politics, 40*(2), 194–234.
Kitschelt, H. (1995). *The Radical Right in Western Europe: A Comparative Analysis*. Ann Arbor: University of Michigan Press.
Knutsen, O. (2006). *Class Voting in Western Europe: A Comparative Longitudinal Study*. Lanham, MD: Lexington Books.
Kriesi, H. (1998). The Transformation of Cleavage Politics: The 1997 Stein Rokkan Lecture. *European Journal of Political Research, 33*(2), 165–185.
Kriesi, H., Grande, E., Lachat, R., Dolezal, M., Bornschier, S., & Frey, T. (2006). Globalization and the Transformation of the National Political Space: Six European Countries. *European Journal of Political Research, 45*(6), 921–956.
Kuhn, T., Lancee, B., & Sarrasin, O. (2017). *Educational Differences in Euroskepticism: Utilitarianism, Values Acquired at School, or Parental Socialization?* (Unpublished Paper).
Lancee, B., & Sarrasin, O. (2015). Educated Preferences or Selection Effects? A Longitudinal Analysis of the Impact of Educational Attainment on Attitudes Towards Immigrants. *European Sociological Review, 31*(4), 490–501.
Lipset, S. M., & Rokkan, S. (1967). Cleavage Structures, Party Systems, and Voter Alignments: An Introduction. In S. M. Lipset & S. Rokkan (Eds.), *Party Systems and Voter Alignments: Cross-National Perspectives* (pp. 1–64). Toronto: The Free Press.
Lubbers, M., & Coenders, M. (2017). Nationalistic Attitudes and Voting for the Radical Right in Europe. *European Union Politics, 18*(1), 98–118.
Marks, G., Hooghe, L., Nelson, M., & Edwards, E. (2006). Party Competition and European Integration in East and West: Different Structure, Same Causality. *Comparative Political Studies, 39*(2), 155–175.
Marks, G., & Wilson, C. (2000). The Past in the Present: A Theory of Party Response to European Integration. *British Journal of Political Science, 30*(3), 433–459.
Maxwell, R. (2019). Cosmopolitan Immigration Attitudes in Large European Cities: Contextual or compositional effects? *American Political Science Review*. https://doi.org/10.1017/S0003055418000898.
Minkenberg, M. (2017). Between Christian and Multicultural Democracy: Religious Legacies and Minority Politics. *West European Politics, 41*(1), 53–79.

Oesch, D., & Rennwald, L. (2018). Electoral Competition in Europe's New Tripolar Political Space: Class Voting for the Left, Centre-Right and Radical Right. *European Journal of Political Research, 57*(4), 783–807.

Polk, J., Rovny, J., Bakker, R., Hooghe, L., Koedam, J., Kostelka, F., et al. (2017). Explaining the Salience of Anti-Elitism and Reducing Political Corruption for Political Parties in Europe with the 2014 Chapel Hill Expert Survey Data. *Research & Politics*, January–March, 1–9.

Rohrschneider, R., & Whitefield, S. (2016). Responding to Growing European Union-Skepticism? The Stances of Political Parties Toward European Integration in Western and Eastern Europe Following the Financial Crisis. *European Union Politics, 17*(1), 138–161.

Rooduijn, M., Burgoon, B., van Elsas, E. J., & van de Werfhorst, H. G. (2017). Radical Distinction: Support for Radical Left and Radical Right Parties in Europe. *European Union Politics, 18*(4), 511–535.

Rovny, J. (2012). Who Emphasizes and Who Blurs? Party Strategies in Multidimensional Competition. *European Union Politics, 13*(1), 269–292.

Rovny, J. (2013). Where Do Radical Right Parties Stand? Position Blurring in Multidimensional Competition. *European Political Science Review, 5*(1), 1–26.

Rovny, J., & Polk, J. (2017). New Wine in Old Bottles: Explaining the Dimensional Structure of European Party Systems. *Party Politics, 25*(1), 12–24.

Sellers, J. M., Kübler, D., Walks, R. A., Rochat, P., & Walter-Rogg, M. (2013). Conclusion—Metropolitan Sources of Political Behaviour. In J. M. Sellers, D. Kübler, M. Walter-Rogg, & R. A Walks (Eds.), *The Political Ecology of the Metropolis* (pp. 419–478). Colchester, UK: ECPR Press.

Steenbergen, M., & Marks, G. (2007). Evaluating Expert Judgments. *European Journal of Political Research, 46*(3), 347–366.

van der Brug, W. (2010). Structural and Ideological Voting in Age Cohorts. *West European Politics, 33*(3), 586–607.

van der Brug, W., Hobolt, S., & de Vreese, C. (2009). Religion and Party Choice in Europe. *West European Politics, 32*(6), 1266–1283.

van Elsas, E. J., Hakhverdian, A., & van der Brug, W. (2016). United Against a Common Foe? The Nature and Origins of Euroscepticism Among Left-Wing and Right-Wing Citizens. *West European Politics, 39*(6), 1181–1204.

Walzcak, A., van der Brug, W., & de Vries, C. (2012). Long- and Short-Term Determinants of Party Preferences: Inter-Generational Differences in Western and East Central Europe. *Electoral Studies, 31*(2), 273–284.

Zuckerman, A. S., Dasovic, J., & Fitzgerald, J. (2007). *Partisan Families: The Social Logic of Bounded Partisanship in Germany and Britain.* Cambridge: Cambridge University Press.

Zürn, M. (2018). *A Theory of Global Governance: Authority, Legitimacy, and Contestation.* Oxford: Oxford University Press.

CHAPTER 10

Social Constructivism

Mai'a K. Davis Cross

INTRODUCTION

The dominant accounts that explain change in international relations (IR) tend to rely on statist structural frameworks of explanation. To offer an alternative viewpoint, the aim of this chapter is to explain how the construction of crises is often the product of societal perceptions and beliefs about events. In general, constructivism assumes that identity, ideas, norms, and perceptions matter and material resources and interests take on meaning only through social interaction (Wendt 1999). Social interaction can come in the form of persuasion, learning, norm diffusion, deliberation, and argument, among other processes. Common to all crises, especially existential crises, is a *perception* of threat, and a *belief* in the need to find new ways to deal with these critical junctures. That is, crises must be *seen* to threaten whatever defines the current order of things (Boin et al. 2005: 2). It takes opinion-makers (defined as those who have a high-level of influence in shaping what others think because of their status or expertise), the mass media, political leaders, and various other *social* actors to construe an event as a crisis in order for it to be recognized as such. So far, however, the mechanisms behind the socially constructed dynamic of crises

---

The theory and research in this chapter draw upon Cross (2017).

Mai'a K. Davis Cross (✉)
Northeastern University, Boston, MA, USA
e-mail: m.cross@northeastern.edu

© The Author(s) 2021
M. Riddervold et al. (eds.), *The Palgrave Handbook of EU Crises*, Palgrave Studies in European Union Politics,
https://doi.org/10.1007/978-3-030-51791-5_10

remain underexplored. I build upon the sociological theory of *moral panic* to put forward a *societal panic* approach to understanding international crises.

In this chapter, I first provide an overview of some existing perspectives on the origins of international crises. Second, I explain my adaptation of moral or societal panic—what I call *integrational panic* in the context of the EU—as an approach for understanding the social construction of crisis. Indicative of societal panic are exaggerated narratives about crises, and subsequently, self-fulfilling prophecies. In the third section, I briefly describe two illustrative case studies of EU crises to show how integrational panic and the social construction of crisis plays out. I argue that we must explore the role of societal perception and reaction in explaining the origins of crises. In each EU crisis, certain segments of society are essential not only in defining crises as such, but also in constructing them. This chapter is more focused on the origin of crises than their resolution, but the concluding section explains how the construction of EU existential crises has a bearing on the three scenarios discussed in the introduction to this book.

Perspectives on the Origins of Crises

Across the social sciences, there are at least three broad perspectives—systemic, behavioral, and sociological—that grapple with crises, and seek to explain how and why they happen (Geva et al. 2000: 447–471; see also Schmitt 2004; Gamble 2006; Neal 2010).

Systemic/Structural Perspectives

One major approach to the explanation of the origins of crises includes systemic and structural perspectives. These sorts of arguments see crises as resulting from "unfolding events" that enable "destabilizing forces" in the international system to disturb routine patterns, undermine institutions, and ultimately threaten the nature of the existing structure (Young 1968: 6–15). The assumption is that crisis events simply occur, and then decision makers must find a way to reinstate stability, which may require fundamentally changing the system in place. This approach takes as given that crises are objective, structural phenomena, and that human perceptions do not matter (Young 1968; Verba 1971; Gourevitch 1984; Jo 2007).

Organizational theory is one example of this structural approach (Seeger et al. 2003; Rochlin 1996). As Boin et al. argue, "the cause of the crisis lies in the inability of a system to deal with the disturbance" (2005: 5). It assumes that crises originate from factors built into the system "that come to represent an undeniable threat to the system" (Boin et al. 2005: 5). Along these lines, closely related to organizational theory is the crisis management approach. By taking the "crisis state" as given, a crisis management argument is that we can recognize a crisis when institutions and social structure reach a "breaking point" and there is a sharp decline in the legitimacy of the system in place (Boin 2004: 167–168). While legitimacy and societal trust are not necessarily easily measurable, certain variables like media reporting, political initiatives, and social mobilization provide evidence of declining trust in the existing system (Alink et al. 2001).

While crisis management theories can explain specific kinds of structural crises, it is not really generalizable beyond this. Moreover, approaches that prioritize discontinuities in the system or disturbances in social or institutional structure encounter potentially serious difficulties in explaining instances in which potential triggering events and even systemic change are neither seen as crises nor treated that way. Not all crisis ingredients are simply waiting in the wings, so to speak. The systemic approach cannot account for cases in which the "dog didn't bark."

Behavioral Perspectives

The second major type of approach to explaining the origins of crisis is the *behavioral perspective*. Rather than assuming that the ingredients for crises are somehow embedded in the international system, it prioritizes the behavior of individuals as they relate to the system around them. From this perspective, one explanation is that crises emerge when an event:

> (1) threatens one or more important goals of a state, that is, the group of authoritative policy makers who constitute the state, (2) allows only a short time for decision before the situation is significantly transformed, and (3) occurs as a surprise to the policy makers. (Hermann 1972: 187)

This definition seems relatively unproblematic in terms of recognizing a crisis, but beyond this, behavioralists see the study of crises as objective in that these are measurable events with certain thresholds that can be determined through analysis of the observable "facts" involved. According to this approach, ascertaining these facts and thresholds can even enable prediction of future crisis patterns.

Along these lines, some behavioralists have actually emphasized *perception of threat* as defining the threshold for the onset of crisis in the wake of a triggering event, but as Billings et al. argue, it generally depends on "the perceived value of possible loss, probability of loss, and time pressure" (Billings et al. 1980: 303–304). They define "loss" as the difference in one's state of being before and after the triggering event. So, from this perspective, there is still a *measurable* threshold that is determined through calculation of the costs involved. Billings et al. go on to argue that after the triggering event, there must be a sense of time pressure and stress, otherwise the actors involved will not seek to deal with the perceived threat immediately.

Thus, the emphasis on individual cost calculation as well as scientific measures of crisis triggers and thresholds still denies the importance of social processes that are so fundamental to the origins of crises. Rational cost calculation, in particular, does not fit well in explaining many types of crisis. For example, during the Eurozone crisis, investors and speculators took advantage of market fluctuations, which in turn aggravated the crisis, but this was not the same as rational behavior. Rather, they acted based on perceptions about the viability of the euro and the media-driven belief that the European Union (EU) might fall apart. Moreover, Europeans often willingly take on *more* cost during and after crises to keep integration moving forward, as they did with the repeated bailouts during the Eurozone crisis. To understand cost or loss calculation, it is necessary to investigate what people value, which in the case of the EU may also include the *idea* of a supranational entity (Cross 2012: 229–246).

Sociological Perspectives

The third major perspective on crises draws upon sociology, and fully delves into the socially constructed and "subjectively perceived" nature of crises (Hay 1999: 317–344). Colin Hay, for example, argues that shared narratives about crises are what bring them into existence. Similarly, Carroll L. Estes argues that social construction "does not deny or ignore the existence of objective phenomena....Social action, however, is inseparable from the socially constructed ideas that define and interpret these phenomena" (1983: 446). These arguments support Alexander Wendt's classic work on the social construction of IR, which argues that there is a material reality, but that ideas play a strong role in constituting material causes in the first place (1999).

One of the key debates within the sociological perspective is the question of which constituent of society is most central to the social construction of crises. Classic Marxist theories tend to emphasize the power of elites in engineering crises out of minor issues to serve their own selfish purposes, such as to divert public attention away from real issues of concern (Chambliss and Mankoff 1976; Reinarman and Levine 1997; Hall et al. 1978, as cited in Goode and Ben-Yehuda 2009: 62–66). On the opposite end of the spectrum, scholars who subscribe to a more grassroots model emphasize the importance of the general public in constructing crises (Morin 1971; Victor 1993; Brunvard 2001 as cited in Goode and Ben-Yehanel: 55–57). The argument is that instead of elites engineering the terms of the crisis narrative, they are simply feeding off of the sentiments that already exist in the regular public. In between these two extremes is the argument that "interest groups" in the middle of the social hierarchy matter most in constructing crises. Interest groups, in this sense, are defined as groups of opinion-makers, such as the media, epistemic communities, NGOs, businesses, lobbying groups, professional organizations, and so on. They may construct crises either for material or normative reasons. For example, the media may choose to frame events as crises because "bad news sells," while a professional organization of human rights experts may craft a crisis narrative about the need to stop trafficking in humans because of an overwhelming belief that it is the right thing to do.

These three arguments within the sociological approach—emphasizing the role of elites, the regular public, or interest groups like the media—differ as a matter of emphasis. In every case study and context, one or another societal actor may be most important in originating crises, but all three should be examined in studies of these events. As will be argued below, contemporary EU crises in particular seem to have a heavy media-driven component, and it may be true that in most cases, an event is first defined as a crisis in news coverage. It then takes on a crisis narrative that can turn into a self-fulfilling prophecy. Overall, the added value of this sociological perspective is that it takes human interpretation into account, and this has valuable explanatory power because it can tell us why various events evolve into crises, while others do not.

An Integrational Panic Approach

How and why are some EU crises socially constructed and subjectively perceived? To grapple with this core question, I describe in this section, the concept of societal panic—or more specifically to the EU, *integrational panic* (Cross 2017). Societal or integrational panic draws upon the widely researched concept of *moral panic* from the field of sociology. Integrational panic occurs when there is some form of overreaction to events, as well as the consolidation of narratives about these events, defining them as crises of EU integration. This disproportional reaction often brings pre-existing societal tensions to the surface that are not even directly related to the crisis event itself, further demonstrating its socially constructed nature.

To recognize cases of societal/integrational panic in IR, there should be (1) evidence of disproportionate rhetoric about events—primarily in the international media—that exaggerate the implications or severity of a potential crisis event; (2) an emphasis on social tensions and the presence of sharp divisions (us vs. them); and (3) growth in the perception that societal or political breakdown of some kind is imminent. Besides the actual terms of the potential crisis event, research on crises could focus on public speech acts, such as media interviews or protests, statements from leaders or opinion-makers within society, and public opinion. The severity of these factors in shaping crises can vary, but the more distressing they become, the more likely they result in a self-fulfilling prophecy. Above all, in this increasingly fast-paced, information-centric international environment, the recognition of the media's role in the social construction of crises is an important dimension to consider in investigating the origins of crises.

The vast literature on moral panic, combined with other research from sociology, media studies, communications, psychology, and leadership, is valuable in explaining why societal panic incites crises, as well as understanding the actors involved. The theory of moral panic, first developed in the 1960s, seeks to explain specific instances of societal overreaction to what is perceived to be a growing problem within that society (Rohloff and Wright 2010: 404). As Charles Krinsky writes,

> A moral panic may be defined as an episode, often triggered by alarming media stories and reinforced by reactive laws and public policy, of exaggerated or misdirected public concern, anxiety, fear, or anger over a perceived threat to social order. (Krinsky 2013: 1)

Thus, the purpose of the theory is to show how and why societal actors, especially the mass media, construct concern or anxiety over a social issue that constitutes an out-of-proportion reaction (Cohen 1972). This public concern builds up to such an extent that it can change the rules and laws within society, and result in a perceived threat to the existing social order. In other words, moral panics are crises, according to the standard definition—they are seen as "a serious threat to the basic structures or the fundamental values and norms of a social system" (Rosenthal et al. 1989: 10).

The notion of moral panic was first used to describe anything that threatened social order and led to disagreements over how to confront these threats. These episodes have typically centered on a wide range of taboo issues that have triggered moral indignation, such as witch-hunts, pornography, the Red Scare, anti-Semitism, and human trafficking. Even though the theory of moral panic was developed to explain how some actors within society come to be defined as threats to dominant social values, an adaptation of the framework is valuable in understanding other kinds of crisis that do not involve issues of morality. This is the purpose of the societal panic approach advanced here, which is closely related to moral panic, but also distinctive as it encompasses many more types of socially driven instances of crisis construction, including those that occur at the international level, and those with particular relevance to the EU (i.e., integrational panic).

Who Panics?

Sociologists who have researched moral panics have tried to operationalize the various components of it (Goode and Ben-Yehuda 2009: 2). Key questions that arise are: Who is panicking? In other words, must *all* of society panic to qualify as societal panic, or can this be confined to just one constituent of society? What type of behavior is characteristic of this type of panic? And what types of events might trigger societal panic?

Stanley Cohen's approach to moral panics is useful in *breaking down* the dynamics in societal panic. He sees segments of society as actors in a drama. These actors may be different depending on the nature of the crisis, but consistent players in these dramas are the media, the public, and the agents of social control (Goode and Ben Yehuda 2009: 22; Cohen 1972). Societal panic follows similar lines, but since these panics may not be moral in nature, any type of leader at the national or international levels can be thought of as the "agents of social control" in Cohen's conceptualization. Thus, the various constituents involved in societal panic are typically the regular public, the media (and other interest groups), and political leaders. These actors may make claims about whether an event constitutes a crisis and the meaning behind this (Critcher 2003). And while many societal actors interact to contribute to the perception of crises, it is not necessary for all to be involved.

In particular, I suggest that it is unlikely that the public *on its own* would be able to craft a coherent crisis narrative, but they must either contribute to or buy into the perception that there is a crisis for it to build momentum. Thus, public participation in the social construction of crises is necessary, but not sufficient. Along with moral panic scholars, I contend that no societal actor is as powerful as the media in enabling public perceptions of crisis to build around specific narratives. The media has the unique ability to pick up and amplify the perceptions of other societal actors, especially other opinion-makers and leaders.

The Media, Leaders, and the Public

On a practical level, the media has the power to disseminate information, and to reach a large audience in ways that no other actor does. Beyond the media's power to reach many, however, manipulation, exaggeration, or misinterpretation of events is common, particularly in light of the intense pressure to provide news first and to update that information more quickly than the competition. In the process, communications scholars have shown that the media tends to spin events in a negative direction (Critcher 2003). As Seeger et al., write, "Media coverage of crisis has become more aggressive and frequent, with the proliferation of news magazines and 24-hour news programs" (2003: 8).

The media typically serves as the "primary definer" of a crisis (Critcher 2003: 15). In the early stages of a potential crisis, the media can play a particularly strong role (Cohen 1972: 30). In these situations, it tends to over-report, exaggerate, and distort events as well as predict that the worst is still to come (Goode and Ben-Yehuda 2009: 23). It also uses the power of language to create ready symbols of each crisis (Critcher 2003: 12). Since the public needs information about each crisis in order to react, the media is at the heart of whether publics understand an event to be a crisis or not (Cohen 1972). As Critcher argues, "[Media discourses] define, describe and delimit what it is possible to say and not possible to say" (2003: 170; also see Fairclough 1995; Bell and Garrett 1998; Fowler 1991). Discourses or narratives are at the heart of how publics construct their perceptions of a problem. Numerous studies also show a clear causal link between the way journalists frame news and how people think about issues (Price et al. 1997 as cited in Valkenburg et al. 1999).

Of course, there is an interaction effect that ensues between media framing and public or elite narratives about an event. In the first place, journalists have to feel that if they report a story that emphasizes conflict it will gain traction among elites and the public. To report with disproportionality, as happens during times of societal panic, they must be even *more* confident that this will attract an audience. Naturally, journalists do not craft such stories out of thin air. Perhaps a leader makes a statement, or an interest group—like rating agencies or lobbyists—speaks a little louder about an issue of concern. There is no predicting how a media frenzy will evolve each time. Nonetheless, the media can either make or break a potential crisis depending on its collective choices about framing and volume of coverage.

The public itself also matters in defining crises.[1] In the field of sociology, social reaction theory recognizes that important events like crises result in multiple reactions. Some of these reactions may be related to the real problem or tension that has occurred, and others may be wholly unrelated (Garland 2008: 23). As Cohen (1972) points out, in the very disproportionality of moral panics is the symbolic indication that there exists some deeper source of tension within or across societies. In effect, the crisis event that the media talks up often becomes an excuse for the public to air pre-existing tensions. The European case, discussed in the next section, suggests that this is indeed true. There are wide-scale themes that form a dominant narrative about each recent crisis in Europe, for example, East vs. West, public vs. elite, and North vs. South.

Leaders certainly play their part in this dynamic as well, especially as they exist at both the elite, political level, and at the activist or grassroots level. They may be experts on the issue involved in a particular crisis, or official bureaucrats charged with addressing the matter. Like the media, what leaders share in common is the ability to shape public opinion. During the build-up of crises, elite opinion-makers are instrumental in persuading others of the nature of the problem and oftentimes assigning blame. Leaders, of course, are still subject to the overwhelming power of the media, which continually selects and interprets their statements. What leaders say to the public is nearly always filtered through the media. The end result is that sometimes leaders can be ignored, and at other times, certain statements they make can be disproportionately amplified.

Crises are complex phenomena, but they are fundamentally *social* phenomena. They have multiple social causes, and these factors interact with each other, leading to the origination of crises that may often be unanticipated.

European Crises and Integrational Panic

Every few years, the international media announces that the "end of Europe" is at hand. The instances are many and are typically described as such, with notable examples stretching from the 1965 Empty Chair crisis to the 1999

---

[1] Some scholars discount the public role almost entirely, and argue that elites basically orchestrate public opinion (Hall et al. 1978).

Commission resignation crisis right up through the Schengen and refugee crisis of 2011 (Thies 2012). Yet, none of these predictions have actually played out, and doomsday scenarios continually prove to be overblown, which begs the question: why are these errors in perception repeated over and over again?

These repeated instances of existential crisis in Europe make sense when examined through the lens of societal or integrational panic. Numerous events such as disagreement over foreign policy, questions over whether a new treaty will be approved, or a debt problem in a small member state occur frequently and are relatively routine events, but only some grow into seeming existential crises for the EU.

As the societal panic approach anticipates, social processes, especially the disproportional reaction of the media, determine whether an event is defined as a crisis. Elite and public actors are also involved to varying degrees, solidifying narratives about crises, and bringing certain tensions to the surface, enabling the media to further amplify the crisis build-up. These narratives then become self-fulfilling prophecies, as certain events are perceived to threaten the very existence of the EU.

2005 Constitutional Treaty Crisis

In the lead-up to the constitutional crisis, there began to surface tensions between European elites and the general European public. At some point in the 1990s, the so-called permissive consensus, defined as tacit public consent for the European project, came to an end. With the implementation of the 1992 Maastricht Treaty—which created a clear political dimension to the EU, significant areas of social and internal security policy, and the eventual advent of monetary union—the effects of EU integration began to be felt by regular European citizens. They became politicized in their thinking about European integration, and became increasingly involved in transnational debates about key European issues (Risse 2010).

Around the same time that this occurred, Brussels officials engaged in significant efforts to democratize EU processes, making their institutions more transparent, legitimate, open, and with due respect to subsidiarity. However, despite having an electorate that was increasingly aware and affected by EU issues, various national elites continued to use the EU as a scapegoat for their own failures and to campaign on exclusively national issues. The media also seriously downplayed any coverage of EU issues that might work as a positive counterbalance to such national scapegoating (Sutton 2005: 9).

In this climate, European leaders agreed to a new treaty, formally known as the Treaty Establishing a Constitution for Europe, which was actually intended to help simplify, streamline, and democratize the EU, among other things. On October 29, 2004, all 25 heads of state signed this constitutional treaty. The next stage was for each member state to follow its own ratification procedures. Agreement on EU treaties must be unanimous, but this is naturally easier to achieve through parliamentary votes rather than through referenda. However, a few months before, on April 20, 2004, British Prime Minister Tony Blair had unexpectedly promised a referendum on the constitutional treaty, a procedure he had previously rejected. Subsequently, seven other member states—Denmark, France, Ireland, Luxembourg, the Netherlands, Spain, and Portugal—also announced that they would hold referenda on the constitution.

This ratification process provided the grounds for the development of this crisis, but in no way should this event has threatened the very existence of the EU. Indeed, at this early stage in October 2004, the possibility of a failed Treaty was viewed as a setback in the minds of many, but not necessarily something that could escalate into a full-blown existential crisis for the EU. Nearly every major EU/EC treaty that had come before, except for the founding Treaties of Rome, had resulted in initial negative referenda, including the 1986 Single European Act, 1992 Maastricht Treaty, and 2001 Nice Treaty. As a result, leaders were relatively unconcerned as they looked toward the upcoming ratification process. They either assumed that ratification would be unproblematic or that failed referenda could be resolved in the same way as in the past—with adjustments to the treaty and another round of voting.

Nonetheless, well before the referenda had taken place, a crisis narrative solidified around the perception that the EU had reached the end of the road in terms of integration (Gamble 2006). Journalists and other opinion-makers led the charge. Representative of the media rhetoric during this period is a September 25, 2004 *Economist* article stating, "Gentlemen, you are trying to negotiate something you will never be able to negotiate. But if negotiated, it will not be ratified. And if ratified, it will not work." Similarly, Wolfgang Munchau, a regular *Financial Times* columnist, wrote on October 3, 2004, "The bandwagon against the European constitutional treaty is rolling...it is worth asking whether there is such a thing as a Plan B. The answer is no, at least not officially" (Munchau 2004). Media coverage like this not only shows oft-repeated negative predictions about the prospects for the treaty, but also a strong belief that the EU would not be able to find a way forward after its predicted failure. Anticipating that the votes would fail, commentators suggested that this could lead to departures of some member states, or alternatively, a two-speed Europe with a more-integrated core and a less-integrated periphery (for example, see *The Economist*, June 2, 2005). Some even talked about the need to cede sovereignty away from Brussels and back to the member states (ibid.).

Why did a relatively typical treaty ratification process become an existential crisis for the EU? I suggest that integrational panic offers a strong explanation. The media clearly played a role in construing this as a crisis for Europe through its negative and exaggerated coverage of the ratification process before it had even taken place. Indeed, major international presses had a high percentage of predictions of failure before the French referendum had even occurred: 89% for *Time Magazine*, 79% for *The Economist*, 100% for the *International Herald*

Tribune, and 68% for the *Financial Times*.[2] With this outcome then assumed, media content focused almost exclusively on what would happen if the treaty failed.

The regular public also played a significant role in bringing pre-existing public-elite tensions to the surface. As the crisis gained momentum from the barrage of negative media coverage, narratives about the crisis emphasized various aspects of public-elite tensions, whether the focus was on EU or national leaders, such as: fear of losing national identity and sovereignty; citizens' unhappiness with the current government, unemployment, and the role of migrant workers; a feeling that the EU was remote, that the Eurozone and single market would take precedence over citizens' rights; and the fear of what future enlargements would bring. Moreover, during the period of October 29, 2004 to May 28, 2005, stories about the constitutional treaty emphasized public-elite tensions 89% of the time in *Time Magazine*, 60% in the *Economist*, 100% in the *International Herald Tribune*, and 84% in the *Financial Times* (Cross and Ma 2015; Cross 2017).

The constitution did not fail because of anything inherent about its terms nor did it fail because of widespread agreement that more Europe was a bad thing. The negative referenda in France and the Netherlands were not wholly based on the actual substance of the treaty. For example, many French voters saw this as a referendum on French President Jacques Chirac's government. A *Time Magazine* article captured it well in March 2005: "There's growing desire to punish leaders, and blame Paris and Brussels alike for everything going wrong…Most people are basing how they'll vote on anything but the constitution itself" (Crumley 2005). As indicative of this, and despite this explicit recognition of what was going on, only 2% of the news coverage in major international papers—the very outlets that would be expected to cover the issue, and all widely read across Europe—actually dealt with the substantive terms of the constitutional treaty itself (Cross and Ma 2015; Cross 2017).

In short, the media construed even the *possibility* of a negative referendum as the end of the road for integration, although nearly every treaty before had at first experienced negative referenda. Public-elite tensions did not cause the constitutional treaty crisis, but they characterized its central narratives, highlighting the socially constructed nature of the crisis. While the systemic approach to understanding crises would assume that the negative referenda sparked this crisis, the "end of Europe" rhetoric actually emerged well before the ratification process even began. Thus, the timing of the crisis also reveals the role of integrational panic in the origin of this crisis. The negative referenda in May and June 2005 may even have occurred as a result of a self-fulfilling prophecy. While a possible negative result was anticipated in the UK, this was

---

[2]This data reflects the crisis build-up period from October 29, 2004 to May 28, 2005. The remaining percentage of articles for *Time Magazine* and *The Economist* were not positive predictions, but simply offered no predictions. For the *Financial Times*, 10% of the articles had positive predictions, while 22% offered no predictions.

unexpected in France and the Netherlands, two founding member states of the EU. But the media frenzy and negative predictions were hard to escape.

2010–2012 Eurozone Crisis

Another instructive case is the 2010–2012 Eurozone crisis. In the years leading up to this, North–South tensions had indeed emerged as an increasing source of concern.[3] These tensions were present for some time as a result of the apparent differences in economic cultures across Europe. After 2008, however, North–South tensions became far more noticeable for a variety of reasons: (1) the global economic crisis put the entire European economy on shakier ground, (2) there was increasing evidence that the South was not being as fiscally conservative as the North, (3) new member states, like Poland, made it their explicit aim to emulate the member states of the North rather than those of the South, (4) there was a growing sense of divide between those EU countries that had adopted the euro and those that had not (Miliband 2011), (5) the rise of German economic power alongside growing German economic leadership raised concerns and insecurity in other member states, and finally (6) with the tightening of domestic budgets and enlargement of EU membership, the division between net contributors and net detractors to the EU budget became more contentious.

However, the first and perhaps most significant of these events, the subprime mortgage and financial deregulation crisis that brought down Wall Street in 2008, was obviously not a result of these tensions in Europe. Indeed, the US-triggered global financial crisis did not really reach European shores, in the way it eventually would, until at least two years later. Certainly, Greece—a country that represented only 2% of the Eurozone economy—was in trouble. But why did a debt crisis in a tiny country turn into a full-blown existential crisis for the EU itself? May 2011 likely marks the point at which integrational panic began fully to take hold. The event that made this possible was the realization that Greece would require a second bailout, and Portugal was also in trouble. Even still, these two countries only represented 3–4% of the whole Eurozone economy.

In this crisis, like in the others, the media played a large role in constructing a crisis narrative. The covers of *The Economist* were particularly striking:

> February 28, 2009, *The Bill that could Break up Europe*
> May 1, 2010, *Acropolis Now: Europe's Debt Crisis Spins out of Control*
> January 15, 2011, *The Euro Crisis: Time for Plan B*
> July 16, 2011, *On the edge: Why the euro crisis has just got a lot worse*
> November 26, 2011, *Is this Really the End?* (with an image of a euro coin going down in flames).

---

[3] Some in the media and academia have referred to this as center-periphery tensions, with Greece, Spain, Portugal, and Italy as the periphery. See, for example, Jabko (2012).

At the time, very few elites recognized this largely disproportional ratcheting up of crisis narratives, but there were a few notable exceptions coming from former political leaders who must have felt more freedom to voice their concerns. Former British foreign secretary MP David Miliband wrote in an op-ed, "I don't know whether to weep or laugh. Eurozone leaders have turned a €50bn Greek solvency problem into a €1,000bn existential crisis for the European Union" (2011). Similarly, former French President Valery Giscard d'Estaing said in a speech:

> Greece is a great culture but a small country in our financial sphere and there is no basis for it rocking the euro at this point, had it not been constantly prodded by speculators and by banks from outside the euro area. (Rettman 2011)

And former German chancellor Helmut Schmidt added to this, stating, "This talk of a crisis of the euro is merely hot air emanated by journalists and politicians" (ibid.). He described the atmosphere of the time as psychopathic, and emphasized that it was really the Anglo-Saxon media that was to blame.

But these appeals to reason fell on deaf ears. Many media reports and op-eds argued that either Greece would have to leave the EU, or it would bring the rest of Europe down with it. Others predicted that the only way Greece could repair its own economy and save itself was to leave the EU. News stories like, "It's Time to Admit the Euro has Failed" (Sivy 2011), and "10 Reasons the Euro was a Dumb Idea" (Gersemann 2011), became commonplace. News coverage of the Eurozone crisis in the international press spiked from September 2011 to January 2012, and these stories depicted a negative outlook for the euro 77% of the time in *Time Magazine*, 78% in the *Economist*, 66% in the *International Herald Tribune*, and 57% in the *Financial Times* (Cross and Ma 2015; Cross 2017). Despite this media frenzy, at no point did the European Commission or any EU head of state suggest that Greece (or any other country) might have to leave the EU. This, among other things, indicates that the perception of crisis had gone far beyond the actual circumstances.

There are a variety of ways in which European member states could have responded to the Greek debt crisis. As with all crises, there are multiple narratives at work, but the one that stood out most often in this case was hostility between the North and the South (ibid.: 31). While this certainly reflected some pre-existing tensions, other tensions about the crisis that arguably would have made much more sense in this context were: blame for US neglect in upholding financial regulation, criticism of Wall Street, criticism of the global banking sector for greed and corruption, questioning of capitalism in general, or complaining of growing inequality between the rich and the poor. However, these were either far less prominent or non-existent in media coverage, again demonstrating the socially constructed origins of this crisis. Europeans (except for those in the South) often talked about these tensions through the language of stereotypes. Northern European were assumed to be "hard-working, law-abiding people who live within their means," while Southern Europeans were "work-shy, rule-bending, and profligate" (Mahony 2012). These stereotypes sharpened and became widespread as the dominant narrative during 2011 and 2012.

The origins of the Eurozone crisis essentially boil down to a crisis of confidence caused by widespread integrational panic at the international level. Speculators, investors, rating agencies, and others cast doubt on the viability of the euro. As this integrational panic grew, the Eurozone crisis became a self-fulfilling prophecy complete with a contagion effect, spreading to other countries within Europe—France, Italy, Spain, and Cyprus to name a few—and exploiting their economic weaknesses. Certainly, all economies have vulnerabilities, even during strong periods of growth. But no economy can weather the storm of severe and unexpected crises of confidence that drive up borrowing costs and undermine the very engines of growth that make spending and investment possible. I argue that without the widespread integrational panic that ensued, this crisis, like the others before it, might also have played out in far milder terms. Human perceptions influence financial crises with particular strength because of the ability of markets to adjust in real time. Forecasts about the direction of markets are regularly covered in the media, making reactions and overreactions in the actual economy virtually instantaneous.

The EU is naturally still a work-in-progress, and is not without its challenges. There are often visible disagreements among member states' governments, and there is sometimes a lingering sense of disillusionment at the societal level when things go wrong. However, it is worth noting that such internal discord is common in every democracy. The question is not why this discord exists, but rather why some of these episodes are seen as existential crises for the EU. Indeed, the EU continues on today, and is arguably stronger and more-integrated than ever.

Conclusion

We call many things crises, but only events that are perceived to be relatively unique, urgent, and unexpected should be understood as such. And while certain crises are undeniable because they stem from systemic or structural properties, most events are subject to societal interpretation. They can either be perceived to constitute a crisis or not, and the nature of this perception has important ramifications for how crises develop, and how they are ultimately resolved. To some extent, all events are subject to a degree of human interpretation, but beyond "acts of nature," there is value in recognizing the socially constructed quality of many crises.

While this chapter has been more focused on the causes of crises rather than their resolution, examining the causes helps to explain why the EU typically responds to crises either with continuity (Scenario 2) or deepening integration (Scenario 3). Crises that are largely based on perceptions, panic, and reaction, can also be significantly diminished when leaders recognize that panic is not necessary or the media shifts its attention elsewhere. If the crisis narrative goes away and perceptions of crisis dissipate, it becomes much easier to continue or find a path toward more integration. At the same time, if a crisis takes on a self-fulfilling prophecy dynamic, it takes on tangible qualities—as in the case of the Eurozone crisis—and this make crisis resolution more difficult. Ultimately, breakdown (Scenario 1) becomes a possibility.

Thus, it is important to look for solutions to manage the impact of crises as enhancing our understanding of the origins of crisis can also help with their resolution. Some crises do not have to be as severe as society perceives them to be—the self-fulfilling prophecy dynamic of recent European crises is a case in point. The recognition of other crises can be desirable and might enable change to occur, such as the overthrow of dictatorships or finding solutions to systemic problems like climate change. Future research on the origins of crises can shed light on the role of societal processes, especially the power of the media, in the construction of crises. A better understanding of crisis patterns in IR can help channel human energy into more productive directions, whether it is to solve problems or avoid pitfalls.

References

Alink, F., Boin, A., & 'T Hart, P. (2001). Institutional Crises and Reforms in Policy Sectors: The Case of Asylum Policy in Europe. *Journal of European Public Policy*, *8*(2), 286–306.

Bell, A., & Garrett, P. (Eds.). (1998). *Approaches to Media Discourse*. Oxford: Blackwell.

Billings, R., Milburn, T., & Schaalman, M. L. (1980). A Model of Crisis Perception: A Theoretical and Empirical Analysis. *Administrative Science Quarterly*, *25*(2), 300–316.

Boin, A. (2004). Lessons from Crisis Research. *International Studies Review*, *6*(1), 165–194.

Boin, A., 'T Hart, P., Stern, E., & Sundelius, B. (2005). *The Politics of Crisis Management: Public Leadership Under Pressure*. New York: Cambridge University Press.

Brunvard, J. H. (2001). *Encyclopedia of Urban Legends*. New York: W. W. Norton.

Chambliss, W., & Mankoff, M. (Eds.). (1976). *Whose Law? What Order?* Chichester, UK: John Wiley.

Cohen, S. (1972/2002). *Folk Devils and Moral Panics: The Creation of the Mods and Rocker*, third edition. London: Routledge.

Critcher, C. (2003). *Moral Panics and the Media*. Philadelphia: Open University Press.

Cross, Mai'a K. D. (2012). Identity Politics and European Integration. *Comparative Politics*, *44*(2), 229–246.

Cross, Mai'a K. D. (2017). *The Politics of Crisis in Europe*. New York: Cambridge University Press.

Cross, Mai'a K. D., & Ma, X. (2015). EU Crises & Integrational Panic: The Role of the Media. *Journal of European Public Policy*, *22*(8), 1053–1070.

Crumley, B. (2005, March 20). Switching Sides? *Time Magazine.* Available at: http://www.time.com/time/magazine/article/0,9171,1039679,00.html. Accessed 3 July 2012.
Estes, C. L. (1983). Social Security: The Social Construction of a Crisis. *The Millbank Memorial Fund Quarterly, 61*(3), 445–461.
Fairclough, N. (1995). *Media Discourse.* London: Edward Arnold.
Fowler, R. (1991). *Language in the News: Discourse and Ideology in the Press.* London: Routledge.
"The Future of Europe: The Europe That Died." *The Economist.* (2005, June 2). Available at: http://www.economist.com/node/4033308. Accessed 3 July 2012.
Gamble, A. (2006). European Disunion. *British Journal of Politics & International Relations, 8*(1), 34–49.
Garland, D. (2008). On the Concept of Moral Panic. *Crime, Media, Culture, 4*(1), 9–30.
Gersemann, O. (2011, November 25). 10 Reasons the Euro Was a Dumb Idea. *TIME Magazine.* Available at: http://www.time.com/time/world/article/0,8599,2100059,00.html. Accessed 13 July 2012.
Geva, N., Mayhar, J., & Skorick, M. (2000). The Cognitive Calculus of Foreign Policy Decision Making: An Experimental Assessment. *Journal of Conflict Resolution, 44*(4), 447–471.
Goode, E., & Ben-Yehuda, N. (2009). *Moral Panics: The Social Construction of Deviance* (2nd ed.). Chichester, UK: Wiley-Blackwell.
Gourevitch, P. (1984). *Politics in Hard Times: Comparative Responses to International Economic Crises.* Ithaca: Cornell University Press.
Hall, S., Critcher, C., Jefferson, T., Clarke, J., & Roberts, B. (1978). *Policing the Crisis: Mugging, the State, and Law and Order.* London: Macmillan.
Hay, C. (1999). Crisis and the Structural Transformation of the State: Interrogating the Process of Change. *British Journal of Politics and International Relations, 1*(3), 317–344.
Hermann, C. (1972). Threat, Time, and Surprise: A Simulation of International Crises. In C. Hermann (Ed.), *International Crises: Insights from Behavioral Research.* New York: Free Press.
Jabko, N. (Ed.). (2012). The Eurozone Seen from the Periphery. *European Union Studies Association Review.*
Jo, S.-S. (2007). *European Myths: Resolving the Crises in the European Community/European Union.* Lanham, MD: University Press of America.
Krinsky, C. (Ed.). (2013). *The Ashgate Research Companion to Moral Panics.* Burlington, VT: Ashgate.
Mahony, H. (2012, February 22). National Stereotyping—The Eurozone's Other Story. Euboserver.com. Available at: http://euobserver.com/political/115340. Accessed 30 Apr 2013.
Miliband, D. (2011, November 14). Don't Split Europe; Make It Stronger. *Financial Times.* Available at: http://blogs.ft.com/the-a-list/2011/11/14/dont-split-europe-make-it-stronger/. Accessed 5 July 2012.
Morin, E. (1971). *Rumor in Orléans* (P. Green, Trans.). New York: Pantheon Books.
Munchau, W. (2004, October 3). Europe Is Likely to Split. *Financial Times.* Available at: http://www.ft.com/intl/cms/s/1/3eacd454-1565-11d9-8997-00000e2511c8.html#axzz2Ry8Fa6lt. Accessed 4 Dec 2013.

Neal, A. (2010). *Exceptionalism and the Politics of Counter-Terrorism: Liberty, Security and the War on Terror*. New York: Routledge.

Price, V., Tweksbury, D., & Powers, E. (1997). Switching Trains of Thought: The Impact of News Frames on Readers' Cognitive Responses. *Communication Research, 24*, 481–506.

Reinarman, C., & Levine, H. G. (Eds.). (1997). *Crack in America: Demon Drugs and Social Justice*. Berkeley, CA: University of California Press.

Rettman, A. (2011, October 20). *EU Institutions Hit Back at Markets, Rating Agencies*. EUObserver.com. Available at: http://euobserver.com/economic/113999. Accessed 30 Apr 2013.

Risse, T. (2010). *A Community of Europeans? Transnational Identities and Public Spheres*. Ithaca, NY: Cornell University Press.

Rochlin, G. I. (1996). Reliable Organizations: Present Research and Future Directions. *Journal of Contingencies and Crisis Management, 42*(2), 55–59.

Rohloff, A., & Wright, S. (2010). Moral Panic and Social Theory: Beyond the Heuristic. *Current Sociology, 58*(3), 403–419.

Rosenthal, U., Charles, M. T., & 'T Hart, P. (1989). The World of Crises and Crisis Management. In U. Rosenthal, M. T. Charles, & P. 'T Hart (Eds.), *Coping with Crises: The Management of Disasters, Riots, and Terrroism*. Springfield, IL: Charles C. Thomas.

Schmitt, C. (1922/2004). *Political Theology: Four Chapters on the Concept of Sovereignty* (G. D. Schwab, Trans.). Chicago: University of Chicago Press.

Seeger, M. W., Sellnow, T. L., & Ulmer, R. R. (2003). *Communication and Organizational Crisis*. Westport, CT: Praeger.

Sivy, M. (2011, September 11). It's Time to Admit the Euro Has Failed. *TIME Magazine*. Available at: http://business.time.com/2011/09/12/its-time-to-admit-the-euro-has-failed/. Accessed 12 July 2012.

Sutton, A. (2005, June 3). *Treaty Establishing a Constitution for Europe: Impact of negative votes in the French and Dutch referenda* (White Paper). White & Case.

Thies, W. J. (2012). Is the EU Collapsing? *International Studies Review, 14*(2), 225–239.

Valkenburg, P., Semetko, H. A., & Vreese, C. H. (1999). The Effects of News Frames on Readers' Thoughts and Recall. *Communication Research, 26*(5), 550–569.

Verba, S. (1971). Sequences and Development. In L. Binder et al., (Eds.), *Crises and Sequences in Political Development* (pp. 283–316). Princeton: Princeton University Press.

Victor, J. S. (1993). *Satanic Panic: The Creation of a Contemporary Legend*. Chicago: Open Court Press.

Wendt, A. (1999). *Social Theory of International Politics*. Cambridge: Cambridge University Press.

Young, O. (1968). *The Politics of Force: Bargaining During International Crises*. Princeton, NJ: Princeton University Press.

CHAPTER 11

Deliberative Theory

Claudia Landwehr

INTRODUCTION

Over the 1980ies and 1990ies, a kind of co-evolution could be witnessed in European integration and in democratic theory. With the single European Act and the Maastricht treaty, European integration took a major leap forward, leading to the establishment of the European Union with its single market and joint currency and to its enlargement to post-communist countries in central Europe. In the mid-1990ies, it seemed as if the dream of an "ever wider and closer union" had become true (Dinan 2010). At the same time, democratic theory took a "deliberative turn" away from radical pluralist theories that regarded democratic decision-making merely as a process of aggregating inalterably materialistic and stable preferences (Goodin 2008). Instead, the exchange of arguments in deliberative processes of opinion- and will-formation became the new focus of analysis and the normative starting point in the justification of democratic institutions. In the study of international relations, the observation that not only self-interested bargaining, but also the collaborative construction of norms and institutions by way of arguing and justification drive relationships between states represented a new and fertile perspective (Risse 2000). Scholars of European integration thus quickly embraced deliberative theory, seeing that it offered both an attractive normative re-description of a political process they were largely supportive of and a plausible explanation for

C. Landwehr (✉)
Johannes-Gutenberg-University, Mainz, Germany
e-mail: landwehr@politik.uni-mainz.de

processes and developments they were observing empirically (e.g. Eriksen and Fossum 2002; Neyer 2006, 2010).

More recent events such as the Euro-crisis, the EU's failure to find an adequate joint response to Russian aggression in Ukraine and war in Syria as well as persistent national egoism in the face of mass immigration and the threats of climate change have cast significant doubts on the Union's capacity to address some of the most pressing political problems. At the same time, its "democratic deficit" that consists in the gap between citizens' expectations and their actual opportunities for effective political participation further undermines the EU's legitimacy, leading to an erosion of support and increasing protest. The resulting lack of both "input" and "output" legitimacy (Scharpf 2009) seems to culminate in a rise of populist parties and the British Brexit vote, apparently moving the EU toward the brink of disintegration and break-down. These developments have not only curbed the enthusiasm for deliberative perspectives on integration, but have also turned deliberative democracy into the culprit of an interesting theoretical trial. In the eyes of EU-critics on the political left, such as Peter Mair, deliberative theory bears responsibility for providing the normative justification for the erection of an executive-centred, expert-dominated technocratic order in Europe, which leaves no room for political parties and citizen participation (Mair 2013).[1]

In order to assess the potential deliberative theory has for providing a better understanding of the present crisis of the EU and to explore whether it can still offer a normatively attractive perspective on further integration and the possibility of a European democracy beyond the nation-state, this chapter will proceed in three steps. First, I will try to identify a core of normative assumptions that unites the numerous distinct conceptions of democracy offered by authors subsumed under the heading of "deliberative democracy". Moreover, I will point out that while the theory of deliberative democracy is in its essence a normative account of democracy, it also implies a set of empirical assumptions about the preconditions for successful deliberation and its effects on preferences and decisions. These assumptions have since inspired an "empirical turn" within deliberative democracy that produced a large body of quantitative and qualitative research. Secondly, I will ask whether deliberative democracy has any specific explanations or predictions to offer when it comes to the present crisis. Drawing on Cristina Lafont's recent account of the theory, I point out that decision-making in the EU is subject to a number of "shortcuts" that undermine its efficacy and legitimacy. At the same time, I reject the interpretation of deliberative democracy as a justification for a technocratic European polity and argue that instead, the theory offers a normative defence of the processes of argument-based interest mediation that are essential to representative party democracy. Finally, I conclude by pointing out that a revival

---

[1] For a similar argument, although not made in the specific context of European integration, see Buchstein and Jörke (2007).

of the European integration process will depend on the possibility of establishing large-scale and inclusive deliberative processes beyond national publics and of moving deliberation one level up: meta-deliberation about the merits and shortcomings of existing institutions and about possible innovations is required to enable a re-constitutionalization of the European Union and to win back support from its citizens.

Deliberative Democracy as a Normative and Empirical Theory

In the 1980s, economic theories had gained dominance in political science, especially in the United States. While these approaches were primarily empirical ones, aiming to formally model and explain electoral and legislative behaviour, their premises also featured in normative accounts of democracy: the assumption that collective decision-making essentially consists in the aggregation of pre-defined preferences derived from material interests, which, as shown by Arrow (1963), is ridden with the severe difficulties, if not impossibility, leads to liberal or even libertarian conceptions of democracy. Riker, for example, turned the impossibility theorem into an argument for a minimal state, claiming that if the results of aggregation are not meaningful anyway, we should minimise the number and reach of democratic decisions (Riker 1982). Early proponents of a deliberative understanding of democracy formulated their theories in explicit demarcation from these economic or rational choice approaches (e.g. Dryzek 1990; Elster 1986, 1997; Habermas 1999). They redirected the focus to the processes of argumentative opinion—and will-formation that precede majoritarian political decisions, coining the term "deliberation" to describe both an empirical mode of interaction and a normative ideal. As a normative ideal, deliberation requires participants to engage in communication under conditions of equality where only the "forceless force of the better argument" (Habermas) should drive decisions and where individual differences in resources and power should not play a role. Moreover, deliberators may not allow own material interests to influence argumentation, but instead aim at decisions that maximize a common good. The input to deliberation, and eventually, to democratic decisions thus consists in judgments rather than interests, thereby enabling not only meaningful aggregation, but also resolving the notorious conflict between individual and collective rationality (Estlund 1990; Dryzek and List 2003). The reasons that are named in deliberation to justify respective judgments accordingly have to be at least potentially transferable ones, i.e. they should constitute reasons not only for oneself, but also for others to support a specific decision. If reasons are transferable and if the better argument commands support, consensus appears a cogent outcome of deliberation.

In democratic theory, however, the place and role of deliberation remains controversial. Whereas researchers writing the US context locate deliberation in congress (Bessette 1980) and importantly, in courts (Gutmann and

Thompson 1996), Habermas regarded it as a non-institutionalizable process between legislators and the public sphere (Habermas 1996). Others want to institutionalize deliberation in participatory citizen forums (Fishkin 1991; Ackerman and Fishkin 2003; Bächtiger et al. 2014) or, in the EU context, view it as realized in the Open Method of Coordination or the comitology system (Joerges and Neyer 1997; Borrás and Conzelmann 2007).[2] Two central and related normative questions remain here. The first is the question of how not only equality within the deliberative forum itself, but also inclusiveness with regard to all those to be bound and affected by the decision taken can be achieved. As Gutman and Thompson argue, deliberation only qualifies as democratic in so far as it is inclusive (Gutmann and Thompson 2004, ch. 1). At the same time, "scaling up" deliberation (Niemeyer 2014) to the level of modern mass democracies is difficult, as it seems impossible that each and every group's or even individual's reasons are given adequate consideration in a deliberative forum. One possible response here is to redefine the concept of democracy itself in a way that replaces democratic authorisation on the basis of the one-person-one-vote principle with merely discursive representation (Bohman 2007), especially in the international and global sphere, where majoritarian democratic decisions are not (yet) possible. The second possibility consists in a return to the more systemic perspective originally offered by Habermas, which directs legitimacy claims to the political system as a whole rather than single deliberative forums within it (Parkinson and Mansbridge 2012). The second major question that arises from the latter approach is to specify the adequate role of deliberative forums in relation to majority decisions. Aggregation clearly remains necessary not only empirically (because consensus is rarely, if ever, achieved) but also in light of any defensible normative conception of democracy in order to guarantee authorization and to provide decisions with transparent legitimation. How can and should pre-aggregation deliberation be organized and rendered maximally inclusive? How can recommendations developed in deliberative forums be subjected to majoritarian democratic decisions? And how can we deal with cases where results of deliberative decision-making and majority votes clearly diverge? These normative issues remain pressing in deliberative democratic theory.

Since the turn of the century, however, the theory has attracted attention from empirical researchers in a variety of disciplines and research areas, among them, European integration scholars (e.g. Joerges and Neyer 1997; Eriksen and Fossum 2002; Pollack 2003; Borrás and Conzelmann 2007). At the same time, deliberative democrats were keen on proving the benefits of deliberation and started to organize and evaluate more and more deliberative polls, mini-publics and experiments (Fishkin and Luskin 2005; Bächtiger et al. 2010; Bächtiger, Grönlund et al. 2014). This line of research thus addresses

---

[2] For a more nuanced and critical perspective, see Pollack (2003).

the empirical assumptions that are implicitly or explicitly entailed in normative accounts of deliberative democracy and treats its promises as falsifiable hypotheses (see Mutz 2008; Thompson 2008). The most important assumption deliberative democracy makes on the level of individuals concerns the way in which political opinions and preferences over alternative policy options are formed and transformed. Where economic approaches treated these as stable and exogenous to the decision-making process, deliberative democrats regard them as endogenous to and the result of the communicative processes that have to precede aggregation. Opinions, or preferences, thus have to be formed in interaction with other citizens and they are assumed to be transformable rather than stable. While evidence for this micro-level assumption can easily be found (and rational choice scholars are quick to point out that they exogenize preferences only for purposes of formal modelling), the effects of deliberation on the macro, or collective, level are more difficult to track.

One hypothesis that suggests itself for empirical testing can be derived from the promise that deliberation will eventually enable a consensual decision, which all decision-makers support for the same reasons. While the obvious sparseness of consensual decisions in politics seems to prove the opposite, deliberation might also lead to a convergence of preferences that garners more support for decisions and improves compliance. Dryzek and List have argued that deliberation enables at least a consensus on the dimensions according to which options can be assessed, thus leading to single-peaked preferences that make aggregation meaningful (Dryzek and List 2003). Some degree of convergence between participants' beliefs and opinions can also be found in most deliberative mini-publics and experiments (Luskin et al. 2002).

Even if we have reasons to believe that deliberation produces preference convergence, it is a different matter whether the direction of convergence is the "right" one. In other words: Does deliberation lead to better decisions because of the "laundering" or filtering effect it has on individual preferences (Goodin 1986)? The difficulty with this question is that while deliberative democrats typically have progressive policy preferences that might serve as a touchstone for evaluation, the identification of "rational" preferences or "reasonable" decisions is, according to their own theory, not possible from the position of a researcher. Michael Neblo has described this problem as "progressive vanguardism", meaning that deliberative democrats regard deliberation as successful in so far as it leads to more progressive preferences (Neblo 2005). Among European integration scholars, there seems to be a similar tendency to regard deliberation as successful in so far as it produces more pro-European attitudes and enables further integration.

Although participants in many deliberative experiments do indeed tend to move toward more progressive positions, there are also counter-examples in which group-think phenomena seem to lead to more radical positions, for example on immigration, and to increased polarization (see Sunstein 2003; Lindell et al. 2017). Despite these problems, deliberative democracy can go some way in explaining how and why deliberation sometimes produces support for decisions even in collectives characterized by fundamental disagreements and deep divisions (O'Flynn 2006). What is more, it can identify ways in which deliberative deficiencies undermine support for decisions and institutions. These potentials enable the theory to provide a fertile perspective on European integration and the European Union—which is without doubt characterized by both deep divisions and deliberative deficiencies.

Deliberation and EU Crisis

As noted before, European integration scholars have described decision-making within European institutions, and in particular, within its comitology system as deliberative (see, for example, Joerges and Neyer 1997). The normative ideal deliberation seemed to resemble the type of interaction they were witnessing empirically: a respectful, well-informed, rational exchange of arguments, leading to reasonable decisions that were acceptable and largely complied with by all those involved in the decision-making process. At the same time, they were deeply aware of the democratic deficit that continued to exist in the European Union (Featherstone 1994; Majone 1998; Follesdal and Hix 2006). Under these conditions, deliberative democracy as a normative theory also seemed to offer a justification for viewing the integration process as a "transnational experiment" (Eriksen and Fossum 2018; with reference to Cohen and Sabel 1997; Bohman 2007). In this experiment, an uninterrupted legitimation chain that provides decisions with majoritarian authorisation seemed dispensable. Instead, representation was conceived of as functional and discursive: if experts and civil society actors, despite the fact that they do not have an explicit democratic mandate, can represent all discourses and arguments relevant to a decision, a decision based on high-quality deliberation could be justified to all those affected by it, even if they did not have an explicit say in it (Dryzek and Niemeyer 2008; Neyer 2010).

These pragmatist or experimental approaches, however, failed to see that deliberation cannot in itself bear the burden of democratic legitimation, but depends upon institutional requirements to lend legitimacy to decisions (Eriksen and Fossum 2018: 847). Moreover, the forums and interactions they described as deliberative were instances of technocratic, de-politicizing deliberation rather than democratic deliberation (Landwehr 2010; 2017). Putting the presumed benefits of deliberation for rational problem-solving before democratic authorisation means subscribing to an epistemic conception of democracy that is ridden with numerous problems. Most importantly, locating deliberation solely or primarily in expert communities constitutes what Cristina Lafont calls an "expertocratic shortcut" to political decisions (Lafont 2019, ch. 3.1).

What happens where the "shortcut" rather than "the long road" is taken is that presumably passive and ignorant citizens are asked to "blindly defer" to decisions taken by a more knowledgeable elite. However, the apparent shortcut in fact becomes a dead end, because citizens eventually cannot be bypassed as decision-takers (ibid.):

> It is one thing to contend – against deep pluralists – that political disagreements can be overcome. It is quite another to stipulate political disagreement away in assuming that, once decision-makers hit on the right political answers, agreement by decision-takers will simply follow. [...] It is one thing to assume – as deliberative democrats do – that over time political struggles may lead to agreement on the best answers to some political questions. It is quite another to ignore or stipulate away *the need for such political struggles to actually take place and succeed* – as epistocrats do. (Lafont 2019: 98)

In other words, citizens will be unlikely and unwilling to blindly defer to decisions in which they could not participate. Moreover, the implementation and effectiveness of decisions are significantly reduced where citizens are unable to understand and share the reasons they are based on. For example, decisions intended to improve equal rights and non-discrimination are unlikely to change the circumstances of life in a society that remains racist, misogynistic and homophobic. Accordingly, there is no alternative to the inclusion and participation of ordinary citizens in the decision process.

Not only scholars of integration, but also actors within European institutions have acknowledged the need for more citizen participation on the European level. The European Citizen Initiative introduced with the Lisbon treaty is perhaps the most notable instrument to enhance opportunities for participation. However, deliberative citizen participation has also been attempted. In 2006 and 2007, over 1800 European citizens took part in a deliberative consultation process on the future of the European Union (Goldschmidt et al. 2008). While these consultations took place in 27 separate national forums, the EuroPolis deliberative poll organized before the 2009 European elections gathered a representative group of citizens from all member states in Brussels for three days of deliberation (Isernia and Fishkin 2014). More recently, the French president Emmanuel Macron suggested a series of participatory deliberative events to strengthen European identity and move integration forward—an initiative that failed to gain traction.

If opportunities for participation have been considerably improved, why does the support for European integration and institutions remain so reluctant in many countries? While deliberative citizen participation has enhanced pro-European attitudes in participants, it has failed to resonate with a wider public. Moreover and more importantly, even if the European mini-publics had been empowered to take decisions on European policies, these decisions would have demanded the same blind deference from all non-included citizens as technocratic decisions, as Lafont points out: "Empowering the few is hardly ever a way of empowering the many" (Lafont 2019: 109). Whereas in the case of technocratic institutions, citizens defer to the superior knowledge of experts, they are expected to defer to a better version of themselves in the case of mini-publics (ibid.). This is because they are effectively asked to accept that they, too, would have arrived at the same results if only they had the opportunity to deliberate sufficiently on the issue in question. In the end, empowering deliberative forums, whether on the national or European level, simply constitutes just another problematic shortcut, this one labelled "lottocratic" by Lafont.[3]

Recognizing the numerous expertocratic shortcuts, but also the inevitable failure of lottocratic ones can explain how and where democratic deliberation remains insufficiently realized at the European level. The technocratic nature of EU decision-making and the lack of democratic control in it have long been discussed as a major cause for political alienation (Mair 2013). Colin Crouch described the resulting political order as a "post-democratic" regime in which seemingly democratic institutions only serve as a façade, behind which elites and business interests rule the continent (Crouch 2002). The surge of populist parties over the last ten years has been interpreted as a response to the "unpolitical disfigurement" (Urbinati 2014) democracy has suffered in Europe, and to democracy's promise of effective political participation being incessantly broken (Jörke 2019). Populism has also been described as a kind of corrective to de-politicized, overly rationalistic modes of policy-making, placing technocracy and radical pluralism at one end of the spectrum and morally and emotionally charged populism at the other end (Canovan 1999; Plattner 2010).

Although the putative will of the "ordinary people" as opposed to "corrupt elites" takes centre stage in populism (Mudde 2004), the juxtaposition between populism and technocracy (or elitism) is problematic. Both are effectively based upon an instrumental justification of democracy, in which the legitimacy of decisions depends on their substance, not on the procedures by which they have been taken. Bickerton and Accetti argue that this apparent confrontation masks a deeper opposition between representative party democracy and its critics, where both technocracy and populism are to be found on the same side (Bickerton and Accetti 2017). In line with a similar argument made by Caramani (Caramani 2017), they show that both lines of political thinking reject the ideas of representation, interest reconciliation and mediation.

While neither Bickerton and Accetti nor Caramani explicitly refers to deliberation, the democratic proceduralism they contrast with both populism and technocracy is also inherent in the participatory conception of deliberative democracy defended by Lafont. According to such a conception, only democratic procedures, if properly designed and applied, can produce decisions that are legitimate and that promise to be reasonable and effective because they

---

[3] Deliberative polls and mini-publics are typically based on a stratified random sample from the population. If every citizen has the same chance be selected and empowered, pure procedural justice is realized through the lottery principle. The idea that decision-makers should be chosen randomly from the population is termed "lottocratic."

are based on considered public opinion (Lafont 2019: 101). Importantly, however, democratic procedures must not be reduced to elections or even plebiscites. Instead, the deliberative processes that take place within political parties, in legislatures and in the broader public sphere constitute *the* central foundation for democratic procedures.

While it is obvious that a European public sphere is at best beginning to emerge and that European integration is of only inferior importance in intra-party deliberations and national parliaments, majoritarian procedures without deliberation can neither resolve the EU's legitimacy problems nor fill the democratic deficit. The referenda on the draft European constitution in France and the Netherlands in 2005, which pushed the EU into its first major crisis since the 1980ies, as well as the British Brexit vote in 2016, which is symptom and cause of its present crisis, illustrate how attempts to achieve a majoritarian mandate for integration failed. Seeking to overcome divisions and to end a bothersome debate by way of a plebiscite is just another type of apparent shortcut that leads to a dead end. In the UK, a seemingly democratic decision that followed campaigns characterized by outright lies, manipulation and horror scenarios has left the country in a deep constitutional crisis. In hindsight, David Cameron's decision to take the question of whether the UK should remain in the European Union to the people can easily be recognized as the "proceduralist shortcut" it was, making it clear that there is simply no alternative to taking the "long road" of inclusive mass deliberation (Lafont 2019).

What can we thus learn from deliberative theory about the causes of the EU's present crisis? And what predictions can we derive from deliberative theory with regard to the EU's resilience in times of crisis and with regard to perspectives for further integration? First, a systemic perspective on deliberation that recognizes the importance of large-scale and inclusive mass deliberation as well as the institutional requirements for democratic legitimacy allows us to recognize the numerous *expertocratic shortcuts* built into the EU's decision-making processes, as well as their detrimental effects on legitimacy and political support (Lafont 2019). At the same time, it dampens expectations where democratic innovations such as deliberative mini-publics or referenda are concerned. While deliberative mini-publics do have potential to enrich public debates, this potential can only be realized where they are embedded into these debates, not where they are regarded as a substitute for them. Empowering mini-publics that remain detached from the wider public sphere and from representative institutions constitutes a *lottocratic shortcut* that will not produce legitimate and accepted decisions (see Lafont 2019). Referenda, too, can have potential for effective citizen participation. The Irish case, where intensive and inclusive deliberation within and beyond citizen assemblies and a constitutional convention prepared the way for a series of referenda seems to be model case here (Farrell et al. 2013; Farrell 2014). Unless referenda are preceded by high-quality large-scale deliberation, however, they constitute a *proceduralist shortcut* that will deepen divides and that risks undermining representative democratic institutions.

However, if despite its gaping democratic deficit and limited success in responding to challenges such as climate change, mass migration and rising inequality, the EU has faced the Euro crisis, the surge of populism and the Brexit turmoil with surprising resilience, it must also possess deliberative resources to draw on. Although major leaps forward in the integration process are only conceivable if they are based on large-scale deliberation, the EU's stability in a state imperfect democratization and in the face of intense struggles over its future can be given a deliberative reading. In the following section, I want to argue that the persistent debates about the destination of European integration, the design of EU institutions and the values shared by European societies constitute a meta-deliberative process which, while it cannot in itself move integration forward, reinforces at least a minimal procedural and constitutional consensus that stabilizes the EU.

META-DELIBERATIVE RE-CONSTITUTIONALIZATION: A WAY FORWARD?

In modern, secular and pluralist societies, or under "post-metaphysical conditions", only procedures can lend legitimacy to political decisions (Eriksen 2005).[4] This insight leads to an institutionalist rather than pragmatist perspective on democracy and deliberation in the European Union (Eriksen and Fossum 2018), which, as a systemic account of deliberative democracy, recognizes egalitarian electoral procedures as indispensable for democracy within and beyond the nation-state (Schmalz-Bruns 2007). The design of European institutions and the degree to which they enable democratic control has been a much-contested issue over the last decades. While discussions of the EU's democratic deficit have been largely limited to academic and political elites, the destination of the integration process and the definition of national and European competencies are of concern to a much wider public. The Euro crisis and the populist backlash against the EU triggered by it may be much deplored by pro-Europeans, but they have had the positive side-effect of re-politicizing the integration process and challenging the merely permissive consensus on European integration, thus bringing its future back to the centre of the political agenda (Kriesi 2020). The British Brexit decision, leading the country into chaos and deep uncertainty, and threatening severe economic and financial upheavals, has illustrated the risks of disintegration and enabled an unpredicted unity among European leaders. In the European public sphere(s), these impressions seem to have induced a positive reappraisal of the benefits of integration and enhanced support for the EU (European Commission 2019).

---

[4]For an earlier and similar argument made outside the context of deliberative democracy, see Luhmann (1983).

What we are witnessing here is that while, and in part because, substantial policy-making is stalling, deliberation is moved one level up to address constitutional matters and institutional design, as well as the very foundations of supra-national cooperation. I have elsewhere labelled this type of deliberation "meta-deliberation" (Landwehr 2015).[5] Meta-deliberation occurs where rules and norms of interaction and collective decision-making have not yet been established or where existing rules and norms are challenged. It can address individual rights and duties, the design of decision-making procedures and institutions as well as more informal norms and conventions of interaction and cooperation. We can consider meta-deliberation, like deliberation, both as a mode of interaction and as a normative ideal. As a mode of interaction, meta-deliberation should not significantly differ from deliberation. However, it can be hampered where fundamental norms of communicative interaction (such as a ban on verbal and physical violence) are not (yet) consensual. Moreover, decision-making procedures that are contested in meta-deliberative processes cannot be successfully used to resolve conflicts. As a normative ideal, meta-deliberation requires broad, inclusive and egalitarian participation and promises to enable a consensus on a set of fundamental norms and decision-making procedures. Such a procedural consensus is a prerequisite for dealing with deep substantial conflicts peacefully, productively and deliberatively.

Although the focus is consistently moved to a meta-level and back to the substantial level wherever deliberation takes place, more systematic reassessments of basic rules, norms and decision-rules that involve the wider public are much rarer in democracies. After the German reunification, civil rights activists in the former GDR had hoped to give the re-unified country a new constitution to be drafted in an inclusive participatory process. While this option was possible according to the constitution, the window of opportunity for re-constitutionalization was quickly closed with the decision to extend the area of application of the Basic Law (the German constitution) to the East German states (Kaiser 1990). It also seems surprising that in countries like the United States, where a high degree of disproportionality is caused by a majoritarian electoral system and enhanced by gerrymandering tactics, challenges to decision-making structures remain comparatively rare, probably because changes to the constitution seem unrealistic. This could be different in the United Kingdom, where many rules and institutions may become up for grabs in the Brexit crisis. The above-mentioned case of the Irish Constitutional Convention, also called in a time of economic crisis (that followed the Lehman Brothers collapse), may be seen as an example of successful meta-deliberation and could constitute a model for the UK.[6]

---

[5] See also Dryzek (2010: p. 12) and Dryzek and Stevenson (2011).

[6] Other cases of institutionalized meta-deliberation include British Columbia, where a citizen assembly prepared a recommendation for a new electoral system that was later defeated in a referendum (Warren and Pearse 2008) and New Zealand, where the majoritarian electoral system ended up being replaced with proportional representation in 1993.

At the European level, however, meta-deliberation has accompanied the integration process from its very beginnings. While the Charter of Fundamental Rights and the common market (although not of all its implications) have, after initial struggles, garnered relatively strong support, the goals of the integration process have always been controversial and the institutional set-up, decision-rules and competencies of the Union contested. This contested nature of the European polity's evolving "constitution" (de facto, if not by name) continues to prevent important decisions, in particular in the areas of positive integration and global and security politics. At the same time, however, the ongoing and public debates about the European project and about the institutions that are to serve it show that the EU remains subject to a permanent re-constitutionalization that could, where it is successful, be described as meta-deliberative. This kind of meta-deliberation may often prevent decision-making, but it also enables those engaged in it to reappreciate the European project itself, thus lending the EU and its institutions a surprising degree of stability. If the EU is to move beyond stability and toward deeper integration, however, much more far-reaching and inclusive Europe-wide meta-deliberation is required. Such meta-deliberation cannot be limited to civil society organizations and an unorganized public sphere, but will have to be initiated and accompanied by representative institutions on the national level, first and foremost the parliament and political parties.

Regarding the possible scenarios for the European Union's future development from its present situation of crisis—break-down, *muddling through* or *heading forward*—deliberative theory can only offer conditional predictions. Given the well-established, if deficient and insufficiently inclusive deliberative structures and the meta-deliberative reappraisal of the European project under conditions of crisis, a break-down of the integration process seems rather unlikely. Further *muddling through* by way of incremental, temporary solutions and compromises is a far more realistic scenario. Given the permanent contestation of decision-rules, institutions and the EU's goals and destination, major leaps forward seem unlikely as long as a procedural consensus remains out of reach.

Conclusion

Deliberative theories have often been (mis-)used as a justification for expert-centred, technocratic and essentially elitist decision-making processes in the European Union. Adopting a systemic, institutionalist account of deliberative democracy that takes its participatory promises seriously, however, allows for a better understanding of the deliberative and democratic deficits that remain inimical to the European project. Cristina Lafont's call for a "democracy without shortcuts" (Lafont 2019), in particular, enables a perceptive understanding of the ways in which expertocratic shortcuts have undermined support for the EU, which neither lottocratic nor proceduralist shortcuts could correct. Only the "long road" of inclusive large-scale deliberation can ensure legitimate and accepted decisions. Before such decisions become conceivable on the most pressing, but also most divisive and conflict-ridden issues we are presently confronting, however, inclusive meta-deliberative reconstitutionalization is required to ensure a broader procedural consensus. While Europe-wide meta-deliberation remains an ambitious project, it is not entirely unrealistic and may still come to be realized and succeed.

REFERENCES

Ackerman, B., & Fishkin, J. (2003). Deliberation Day. In J. Fishin & P. Laslett (Eds.), *Debating Deliberative Democracy* (pp. 7–30). Malden, MA: Blackwell.

Arrow, K. (1963). *Social Choice and Individual Values*. New York: Wiley

Bächtiger, A., Grönlund, K., & Setälä, M. (2014). *Deliberative Mini-Publics: Involving Citizens in the Democratic Process*. Colchester, UK: ECPR Press.

Bächtiger, A., Niemeyer, S., Neblo, M. A., Steenbergen, M. R., & Steiner, J. (2010). Disentangling Diversity in Deliberative Democracy. *Journal of Political Philosophy*, 18(1), 32–63.

Bächtiger, A., Setälä, M., & Grönlund, K. (2014). Towards a New Era of Deliberative Mini-Publics. *Deliberative Mini-publics: Involving Citizens in the Democratic Process*, 203–224.

Bessette, J. M. (1980). Deliberative Democracy: The Majority Principle in Republican Government. In R. A. Goldwin & W. A. Schambra (Eds.), *How Democratic Is the Constitution?* (pp. 102–116). Washington, DC: American Enterprise Institute for Public Policy Research.

Bickerton, C., & Accetti, C. I. (2017). Populism and Technocracy: Opposites or Complements? *Critical Review of International Social and Political Philosophy*, 20(2), 186–206.

Bohman, J. (2007). *Democracy Across Borders: From Demos to Demoi*. Cambridge: MA, MIT Press.

Borrás, S., & Conzelmann, T. (2007). Democracy, Legitimacy and Soft Modes of Governance in the EU: The Empirical Turn. *European Integration*, 29(5), 531–548.

Buchstein, H., & Jörke, D. (2007). Redescribing Democracy. *Redescriptions: Yearbook of Political Thought and Conceptual History*, 11, 178–202.

Canovan, M. (1999). Trust the People! Populism and the Two Faces of Democracy. *Political Studies*, 47(1), 2–16.

Caramani, D. (2017). Will vs. Reason: The Populist and Technocratic Forms of Political Representation and Their Critique to Party Government. *American Political Science Review*, 111(1), 54–67.

Cohen, J. and Sabel, C. (1997). Directly-Deliberative Polyarchy. *European law journal*, 3(4), 313–342.

Crouch, C. (2002). *Post-Democracy*. Cambridge, MA: Polity Press.

Dinan, D. (2010). *Ever Closer Union: An Introduction to European Integration*. Basingstoke & London: Palgrave Macmillan.

Dryzek, J., & Niemeyer, S. (2008). Discursive Representation. *American Political Science Review*, 102(4), 481–493.

Dryzek, J. S. (1990). *Discursive Democracy: Politics, Policy, and Political Science*. New York: Cambridge University Press.

Dryzek, J. S. (2010). *Foundations and Frontiers of Deliberative Governance*. Oxford: Oxford University Press.
Dryzek, J. S., & List, C. (2003). Social Choice and Deliberative Democracy: A Reconciliation. *British Journal of Political Science, 33*(1), 1–28.
Dryzek, J. S., & Stevenson, H. (2011). Global Democracy and Earth System Governance. *Ecological Economics, 70*(11), 1865–1874.
Elster, J. (1997 [1986]). The Market and the Forum: Three Varieties of Political Theory. In J. Bohman & W. Rehg (Eds.), *Deliberative Democracy* (pp. 3–34). Cambridge, MA: MIT Press.
Eriksen, E. (Ed.). (2005). *Making the European Polity: Reflexive Integration in the EU*. London: Routledge.
Eriksen, E. O., & Fossum, J. E. (2002). *Democracy in the European Union: Integration Through Deliberation?* London: Routledge.
Eriksen, E. O., & Fossum, J. E. (2018). Deliberation and the European Union. In A. Bächtiger, J. S. Dryzek, J. Mansbridge, & M. E. Warren (Eds.), *The Oxford Handbook of Deliberative Democracy* (pp. 842–855). Oxford: Oxford University Press.
Estlund, D. (1990). Democracy Without Preference. *The Philosophical Review, XCIX*(3), 376–442
European Commission. (2019). *Eurobarometer Series, No 91*. Brussels.
Farrell, D. M. (2014). The 2013 Irish Constitutional Convention: A Bold Step or a Damp Squib? *Comparative Reflections On, 75*, 191–200.
Farrell, D. M., O'Malley, E., & Suiter, J. (2013). Deliberative Democracy in Action Irish-Style: The 2011 We the Citizens Pilot Citizens' Assembly. *Irish Political Studies, 28*(1), 99–113.
Featherstone, K. (1994). Jean Monnet and the 'Democratic Deficit' in the European Union. *JCMS: Journal of Common Market Studies, 32*(2), 149–170.
Fishkin, J. (1991). *The Voice of the People: Public Opinion and Democracy*. New Haven: Yale University Press.
Fishkin, J., & Luskin, R. (2005). Experimenting with a Democratic Ideal: Deliberative Polling and Public Opinion. *Acta Politica, 40*(3), 284–298.
Follesdal, A., & Hix, S. (2006). Why There Is a Democratic Deficit in the EU: A Response to Majone and Moravcsik. *JCMS: Journal of Common Market Studies, 44*(3), 533–562.
Goldschmidt, R., Renn, O., & Köppel, S. (2008). *European Citizens' Consultations Project: Final Evaluation Report*.
Goodin, R. E. (1986). Laundering Preferences. In J. Elster (Ed.), *Foundations of Social Choice Theory* (pp. 75–102). Cambridge: Cambridge University Press.
Goodin, R. E. (2008). *Innovating Democracy: Democratic Theory and Practice After the Deliberative Turn*. Oxford: Oxford University Press.
Gutmann, A., & Thompson, D. (1996). *Democracy and Disagreement*. Cambridge, MA: Belknap Press.
Gutmann, A., & Thompson, D. (2004). *Why Deliberative Democracy?*. Princeton University Press: Princeton.
Habermas, J. (1996). *Between Facts and Norms*. Cambridge, MA: Blackwell.
Habermas, J. (1999). Drei normative Modelle der Demokratie. In J. Habermas (Ed.), *Die Einbeziehung des Anderen. Studien zur politischen Theorie* (pp. 277–292). Frankfurt am Main: Suhrkamp.

Isernia, P., & Fishkin, J. S. (2014). The EuroPolis Deliberative Poll. *European Union Politics, 15*(3), 311–327.
Joerges, C., & Neyer, J. (1997). From Intergovernmental Bargaining to Deliberative Political Processes: The Constitutionalisation of Comitology. *European Law Journal, 3*(3), 273–299.
Jörke, D. (2019). *Die Größe der Demokratie*. Berlin: Suhrkamp.
Kaiser, K. (1990). Germany's Unification. *Foreign Aff., 70,* 179.
Kriesi, H. (2020). Backlash Against European Integration. *British Journal of Politics and International Relations*. https://doi.org/10.1177/1369148120947356.
Lafont, C. (2019). *Democracy Without Shortcuts: A Participatory Conception of Deliberative Democracy*. Oxford: Oxford University Press.
Landwehr, C. (2010). Democratic and Technocratic Policy Deliberation. *Critical Policy Studies, 3*(3–4), 434–439.
Landwehr, C. (2015). Democratic Meta-Deliberation: Towards Reflective Institutional Design. *Political Studies, 63,* 38–54.
Landwehr, C. (2017). Depoliticization, Repoliticization, and Deliberative Systems. In P. Fawcett, M. Flinders, C. Hay, & M. Wood (Eds.), *Anti-Politics, Depoliticization and Governance* (pp. 49–67). Oxford: Oxford University Press.
Lindell, M., Bächtiger, A., Grönlund, K., Herne, K., Setälä, M., & Wyss, D. (2017). What Drives the Polarisation and Moderation of Opinions? Evidence from a Finnish Citizen Deliberation Experiment on Immigration. *European Journal of Political Research, 56*(1), 23–45.
Luhmann, N. (1983). *Legitimation durch Verfahren*. Frankfurt am Main: Suhrkamp.
Luskin, R. C., Fishkin, J. S., & Jowell, R. (2002). Considered Opinions: Deliberative Polling in Britain. *British Journal of Political Science, 32,* 455–487.
Mair, P. (2013). *Ruling the Void: The Hollowing of Western Democracy*. London: Verso Trade.
Majone, G. (1998). Europe's 'Democratic Deficit': The Question of Standards. *European Law Journal, 4*(1), 5–28.
Mudde, C. (2004). The Populist Zeitgeist. *Government and Opposition, 39*(4), 541–563.
Mutz, D. C. (2008). Is Deliberative Democracy a Falsifiable Theory? *Annual Review of Political Science, 11,* 521–538.
Neblo, M. A. (2005). Thinking Through Democracy: Between the Theory and Practice of Deliberative Politics. *Acta Politica, 40,* 169–181.
Neyer, J. (2006). The Deliberative Turn in Integration Theory. *Journal of European Public Policy, 13*(5), 779–791.
Neyer, J. (2010). Justice, Not Democracy. *Journal of Common Market Studies, 48*(4), 903–921.
Niemeyer, S. (2014). Scaling up Deliberation to Mass Publics: Harnessing Mini-publics in a Deliberative System. In A. Bächtiger, K. Grönlund, & M. Setälä (Eds.), *Deliberative Mini-Publics: Involving Citizens in the Democratic Process* (pp. 177–202). Colchester, UK: ECPR Press.
O'Flynn, I. (2006). *Deliberative Democracy in Divided Societies*. Edinburgh: Edinburgh University Press.
Parkinson, J., & Mansbridge, J. (2012). *Deliberative Systems: Deliberative Democracy at the Large Scale*. Cambridge: Cambridge University Press.
Plattner, M. F. (2010). Democracy's Past and Future: Populism, Pluralism, and Liberal Democracy. *Journal of Democracy, 21*(1), 81–92.

Pollack, M. A. (2003). Control Mechanism or Deliberative Democracy? Two Images of Comitology. *Comparative Political Studies, 36*(1–2), 125–155.

Riker, W. H. (1982). *Liberalism Against Populism: A Confrontation Between the Theory of Democracy and the Theory of Social Choice*. San Francisco: Freeman.

Risse, T. (2000). "Let's Argue!" Communicative Action in World Politics. *International Organization, 54*, 1–39.

Scharpf, F. W. (2009). Legitimacy in the Multilevel European Polity. *European Political Science Review, 1*(2), 173–204.

Schmalz-Bruns, R. (2007). On the Political Theory of the Euro-Polity. In E. O. Eriksen (Ed.), *Making The European Polity* (pp. 71–95). London: Routledge.

Sunstein, C. R. (2003). The Law of Group Polarization. In J. S. Fishkin & P. Laslett. Malden (Eds.), *Debating Deliberative Democracy* (pp. 80–101). Cambridge, MA: Blackwell.

Thompson, D. F. (2008). Deliberative Democratic Theory and Empirical Political Science. *Annual Review of Political Science, 11*, 497–520.

Urbinati, N. (2014). *Democracy Disfigured*. Cambridge, UK: Harvard University Press.

Warren, M. E., & Pearse, H. (2008). *Designing Deliberative Democracy: The British Columbia Citizens' Assembly*. Cambridge: Cambridge University Press.

PART III

Crisis, Continuity, and Change in European Union Institutions

CHAPTER 12

Crisis, Continuity, and Change in European Union Institutions: An Introduction

Jarle Trondal, Marianne Riddervold, and Akasemi Newsome

As set out in Chapter 1, each of the chapters of this section offers an overview of the respective institutions before discussing how each of them has been affected by crises and how they have coped with them. Three questions guide all chapters: First, what, if any, has been the impact of crises within each of these institutions? Second, to what extent and how have they changed? Finally, how can institutional continuity and change be accounted for? To determine causality, each chapter draws selectively on the theoretical apparatus as outlined in Part II of this volume. One crucial focus of this section is hence to determine institutional change in EU institutions as a consequence of polycrisis

J. Trondal (✉)
Department of Political Science and Management, University of Agder, Kristiansand, Norway
e-mail: jarle.trondal@uia.no

ARENA - Centre for European Studies, University of Oslo, Oslo, Norway

M. Riddervold · A. Newsome
Inland School of Business and Social Sciences, Inland University, Rena and Lillehammer, Norway
e-mail: marianne.riddervold@inn.no

Institute of European Studies, University of California, Berkeley, CA, USA

A. Newsome
e-mail: akasemi@berkeley.edu

M. Riddervold
The Norwegian Institute of International Affairs (NUPI), Oslo, Norway

© The Author(s) 2021
M. Riddervold et al. (eds.), *The Palgrave Handbook of EU Crises*, Palgrave Studies in European Union Politics,
https://doi.org/10.1007/978-3-030-51791-5_12

(Zeitlin et al. 2019). In doing so, this section aims to determine the extent to which each EU institution, and thus the EU system as a whole, has been subject to what Chapter 1 outline as transformative change through breakdown (Scenario 1) or *heading forward* (Scenario 3). The alternative Scenario (Scenario 2) is incremental change through processes of *muddling through*.

The Council

The first chapter by *Jeffrey Lewis* is on the Council, which has been no stranger to dealing with crises. The Council's institutional architecture itself is forged and reforged in crisis. This chapter examines patterns of continuity and change in Council politics during an era of what is called "turbulent" integration crises (Ansell and Trondal 2017). The chapter applies an organizational culture perspective to help reveal the durable system attitude found in the Council's social fabric, and political sociology offers insight into the outsize durability of consensus-seeking as part of a *habitus* of cooperation and *sens practique* of what works and what does not inside the Brussels bubble. The chapter shows evidence of path dependence and institutional syncretism in these patterns, with an accent on bricolage and the crafty agency of informal rulebooks as a source of innovative, improvisational change. The pooling of national sovereignty and its collective rearticulation at the EU level makes the Council system a central interlocutor in developing a "community of practice" to manage the political-administrative implications of such power. But the chapter also stresses that the EU's system attitude and "doxa" of integration is not immutable. A deeply internalized style of cooperative negotiation should not be treated as taken for granted, since norm-erosion, contestation, and delegitimation are possible. Tangled complexities of flexible integration have created both external and internal differentiation patterns of insider–outsider status, making the invisible hierarchies of power more even more difficult to map out. The risk of different "classes" of membership is that a "system attitude" may become thinner or patchier among different Council networks, or even encourage some members to become more self-isolated rather than make the extra efforts. Despite widespread changes in procedural and substantive processes of decision-making, the counterintuitive finding is that the Council's *habitus* of integration has obtained an outsize durability over time.

The European Parliament

Here, *Akasemi Newsome and Matthew Stenberg* examine the degree to which polycrisis has undermined the Parliament as an institution or triggered the expansion of its powers. Their central finding is one of an EP *muddling through* crises and repeating modes of engagement with other supranational institutions and the member states that it has relied upon in the past. One challenge unique to the EP is that posed by the polarization of domestic member state politics by Euroscepticism. Whereas similar to other EU institutions, the EP must consistently make the case for increased competencies for itself, the presence of parliamentarians from Eurosceptic parties renders the task of building shared consensus particularly onerous. Interestingly, with the case of Brexit, the Parliament energetically addressed its own polarization by Eurosceptic parties by naming an EP Brexit coordinator to offer a single EP view on Brexit when participating in the Parliament's hard-won spot in the Brexit negotiations process. The EP's gained its priorities, particularly for EU and British citizens' rights, yet these were also shared by the Commission and the Council. During the migration crisis, the EP sounded the alarm early for the need for a common functioning asylum policy in the union that involved shared burdens across member states hosting asylum seekers. Not only did member states refuse to implement the EP's preferred policy, member states circumvented the EP's formal role in assenting to treaties by concluding a non-treaty—the EU-Turkey statement—in response to the refugee crisis. Even when the EP has a larger portfolio of formal roles, the EP's ability to articulate and implement positions on polycrisis distinctive from the member states and the Commission remains elusive.

THE COURT OF JUSTICE OF THE EUROPEAN UNION

This chapter by *Lisa Conant* introduces the Court of Justice of the European Union (CJEU) and discusses how it has influenced recent crises afflicting the EU. The European Commission, national judges, and private parties sent disputes to the Court concerning the Eurozone, democratic backsliding, migration, Russian aggression in Ukraine, and British exit (Brexit). The chapter suggests that litigation has not generated a crisis for the Court itself, but the withdrawal of the United Kingdom (UK) from the EU risks the first "breakdown" of the EU's institutional order according to Scenario 3 as set out in Chapter 1. If the UK leaves the EU, the chapter argues, ending free movement of persons and CJEU jurisdiction over most legal domains, Brexit will entail the first-ever case of "spillback." The chapter explains the origins of resentments fueling Brexit and warns that these resentments challenge the Court's legitimacy even in member states committed to remain in the EU.

THE EUROPEAN COMMISSION

Hussein Kassim and Luc Tholoniat introduce the European Commission role in EU crisis management, but also makes a comparative assessment with the European Council. It does so since a growing literature on EU crises highlights the role played by the European Council. Emphasizing the role of heads of government, scholarly consensus has emerged that only the European Council has the authority and the capacity to address the severe challenges that have confronted the EU. Much of the literature has focused exclusively on the European Council and disregarded or overlooked the contribution made by other institutions. This chapter contests this view. While not disputing that the European Council has often played an important part in crisis management, it highlights the key role played by the Commission. Taking examples since 2014, it examines the contribution made by the Commission, underlining how it has approached a series of crises and assessing its input to the EU response. It argues that there are actions of which only the Commission is capable, which have been neglected by the scholarly literature, including by studies that focus on the consequences of crises. It also sheds further light on the "political" role which the Commission has claimed under the Juncker Commission. Drawing on instances of crisis response on the part of the EU between 2014 and 2019, the chapter illustrates the importance of looking beyond the European Council when considering how the EU responds to crises. It considers four "hard cases": Ukraine, the refugee influx, the second Greek bailout, and the wave of terrorist attacks in Europe. All four cases—external action, emergency eurozone measures, migration, as well as security and foreign policy—represent both sensitive policy areas and relatively new areas of EU competence where the literature would anticipate a primarily intergovernmental response and a limited degree of Commission involvement. In all cases, the chapter documents how the Commission has been able to muddle through crisis (Scenario 2) and in fact increased its own role (Scenario 3). Thus, the chapter argues against the picture of a "withering" Commission, and rather suggests that the Commission has used crisis to expand its role.

EUROPEAN UNION AGENCIES

This chapter by *Michelle Everson and Ellen Vos* investigates the particular difficulties which EU agencies face within a crisis-ridden Union. In accordance with Scenario 3, the chapter suggests that polycrisis have slightly strengthened the role of EU agencies, both by creating ever-more EU agencies in ever-more crucial policy areas, but also that they have got stronger *de jure* powers. Yet, this change has not come easily. At one level, the institutional position of autonomous European regulators has been challenged both in European law and by the coordination demands of a broader European crisis regime. Within the European System of Financial Supervision (ESFS) alone, for example, the European Securities and Market Authority (ESMA) has found its 'regulatory' powers challenged before the Court of Justice (CJEU); meanwhile, the European Banking Authority (EBA) has lost various of its functions to the European Central Bank (ECB) within the crisis busting institution of Banking Union, comprising the Single Supervisory Mechanism (SSM) and Single Resolution Board (SRB). At a far deeper level, however, crisis has also heightened underlying concerns about the appropriate place of autonomous governance institutions within the broader scheme of democratic politics and government, as political indecision or political failure have created a problem of "mandate overload" for the ESFS, as well as individual agencies. Similarly, mandate overload finds its counterpart in renewed calls for the enhanced legitimation of agency operation, a phenomenon which itself is claimed to undermine agency functionality. Autonomous administration thus finds itself the subject of problems of accountability overload and of reputational risk. Finally, EU agencies are also implicated within a modern epistemological crisis which pitches a technocratic arm of administration against a rising tide of politics, or 'populism', that sometimes doubts the "truths" of scientific method or refuses to view it as a basis for democratic decision-making. As such, when crises have strengthened the role of EU agencies in EU governance (Scenario 2), this has triggered challenges to the appropriate role of such nonelected body in democratic EU governance.

THE EUROPEAN CENTRAL BANK

This chapter by Ben Sofus Tranøy *and Ingrid Hjertaker* suggests that the European Central Bank's (ECB's) changed role over the last 10 years can be conceptualized by distinguishing between three different modes of crisis handling: *Denial, Mission Creep* and *Mission Leap*. The chapter argues that the ECB was never intended to be a lender of last resort, but with the financial crisis, this was precisely what eurozone financial institutions needed. As the crisis evolved, member states needed a sovereign lender of last resort, something the ECB was explicitly designed *not* to be. The great contrast between the narrow, technocratic institution the ECB was designed to be, and the powerful, political institution it has become, opened up an integration dilemma but also a window of opportunity. The chapter offers a review of the ECBs action in the crisis and attempts to explain how the ECB came to take the powerful position it did over the past decade and discuss where the ECB might go from here. The chapter introduces the history of the ECB and the design of its mandate. It is argued that the ECB has "muddled forward" to a position of considerable strength. In terms of *outcomes*, the monetary union is moving forward (Scenario 3) toward giving the ECB a position of considerable strength. As a response to crises, it has become a sovereign lender of last resort, something the ECB was explicitly designed *not* to be. Thus, *muddling through* (Scenario 2) almost seems too weak a description of the constitutionally messy *process* that led the ECB through the crisis. In combining the two scenarios, the chapter argues that the ECB has "muddled forward" to a position of considerable strength.

THE EUROPEAN EXTERNAL ACTION SERVICE

The final chapter by *Heidi Maurer* examines the European External Action Service (EEAS) and how it has been affected by EU crises. The EEAS evolved from 2010 onward amidst various crises that shaped its identity construction and policy thinking. The chapter argues that the dominant austerity discourse of the financial crisis embedded the notions of budget-neutrality and providing added value firmly in the EEAS identity. The chapter also suggests that the inability and inadequacy of the EEAS to manage the rising insecurity after the Arab spring or the Syria conflict triggered a reconsideration of EU foreign policy objectives. Security for the EU and its citizens was anchored prominently as the main priority in the revised European Neighborhood Policy strategy in 2015 and the EU global strategy in 2016. Crises did not make or break the EEAS, but in their interplay with other dynamics they left a considerable mark on the formative first decade of the EEAS. As such, the chapter suggests that the EEAS mainly muddled through crises processes (Scenario 2).

Key Findings

Summing up key empirical findings from this section, we find that overall, the EU institutions have responded to polycrisis mainly by *muddling through* based on familiar ways of governing and by introducing incremental changes, and in some cases, also *heading forward* with new institutional arrangements or structures. Contrary to what one would expect if the EU was *breaking down* under the weight of crises, we hardly find evidence of institutional breakdown or even of minor reductions in the role of EU institutions—either vis-à-vis other EU institutions or vis-à-vis memberstate institutions. To the contrary—the EU institutions have proved to be resilient and able to deal with crises by drawing on their already established tools and structures or by developing new tools building on the already established institutional patterns. If anything, crises have strengthened what was already a strong element of expert governance in the EU, as all the expert institutions—the Commission, the agencies and the Central Bank—have gained more influence during the polycrisis. The member states have also wanted a stronger role for the EU in response to crises, with for example the European Council meeting more often. Experts and executive institutions' increased role have not been compensated by an increased role for the European Parliament (democratic implications are discussed by Stie, this volume).

The analysis of the Council of the European Union (Council) shows evidence of path-dependent behavior and what is termed institutional syncretism, suggesting that polycrisis has not changed the workings of the Council substantially. As such, overall, the workings of the Council during crises mostly reflect Scenario 2, suggesting that is has muddled through, resorting to its traditional procedures and ways of doing things also when seeking to deal with various crises. Findings, however, also suggest that the "system attitude" or norm of consensus-seeking may have become thinner or patchier among different Council networks as a result of crisis, which may have consequences in the long run, if divisions within the Council become more explicit. In the case of the European Parliament (EP), we see a fairly consistent picture of *muddling through* behavior in the face of polycrisis, without observing any major changes. Certainly, there have been some procedural gains for the EP, but this is combined with a lack of articulated or implemented distinctive policy goals from this institution. If anything, the

European Parliament has not been able to increase its influence in response to crisis. In the case of the European Court of Justice (ECJ), polycrisis has not generated a crisis for the Court itself. The withdrawal of the UK from the EU, however, arguably risks becoming the first breakdown of the EU's institutional order, with possible longer-term implications for the court (Scenario 1). The chapter on the European Commission highlights the key role played by the Commission in managing polycrisis, and thus also continuity in the incrementally strengthened role of the Commission in EU governance.

More generally, the EU's crises responses seem to have strengthened expert governance and "rule by the knowers" in the EU. The case of EU agencies illustrates this by their increased but highly contested role. The chapter on EU agencies discusses how crises have heightened underlying concerns about the appropriate place of autonomous governance institutions within the broader scheme of democratic politics and government. A similar tension is observed in the case of the ECB. In terms of *outcomes*, the monetary union is moving forward (Scenario 3) toward giving the ECB a position of considerable strength. As a response to crises, it has become a much stronger institution—as a sovereign lender of last resort. Thus, *muddling through* (Scenario 2) almost seems too weak a description of the constitutionally messy *process* that led the ECB through the crisis. In combining the two scenarios, the ECB has, similar to most EU institutions, "muddled forward" toward a more prominent position in EU governance. These observations thus also suggest that multiple institutions can potentially be strengthened in tandem, and that winners do not take all.

References

Ansell, C., & Trondal, J. (2017). Governing Turbulence: An Organizational-Institutional Agenda. *Perspectives on Public Management and Governance, 1*(1), 43–57.

Zeitlin, J., Nicoli, F., & Laffan, B. (2019). Introduction: The European Union Beyond the Polycrisis? Integration and Politicization in an Age of Shifting Cleavages. *Journal of European Public Policy, 26*(7), 963–976.

CHAPTER 13

The Council

Jeffrey Lewis

INTRODUCTION

The Council of the European Union (EU) and the European Council are institutionally designed to represent national interests in the European integration process and, taken together, amount to a "meta-network" of negotiation and bargaining at the heart of the EU legislative process.[1] With more than 4200 official meetings per year and an annual operating budget in excess of 540 million euros, the "Council," at all levels of political seniority and expertise involves some 62,000 national officials in EU governance (Lewis 2019a). However, the Council system is not only an institutional bargaining space at the EU level, it is a social order with its own rules of the game and a distinct organizational culture. Across the many layers that compose it, from heads of government and ministers to preparatory specialists and technical experts, the Council deliberately institutionalizes "club-like" networks of like-minded national agents to meet in repeat, face-to-face interactions and make collective decisions in mostly non-transparent (*in camera*) settings of insulation from domestic audiences. Rather than simply provide a redoubt

---

[1] This analysis treats the Council of the EU (née "Council of Ministers") and the European Council as part of a singular "Council system" of decision-making. While strictly speaking, since the 2009 Lisbon Treaty, the European Council is a freestanding EU institution it still relies heavily on Council preparatory (and follow-up) work and is still logistically serviced by the General Secretariat of the Council (GSC).

J. Lewis (✉)
Cleveland State University, Cleveland, OH, USA
e-mail: J.LEWIS07@csuohio.edu

© The Author(s) 2021
M. Riddervold et al. (eds.), *The Palgrave Handbook of EU Crises*, Palgrave Studies in European Union Politics,
https://doi.org/10.1007/978-3-030-51791-5_13

for national sovereignty and autonomy, Council networks exchange "classical" Westphalian sovereignty for "pooled" sovereignty and joint decision-making in what Adler-Nissen (2009) calls "late sovereign diplomacy."[2]

The Council system has changed considerably over the years, although the genealogy proves older than the current era of crises. Start with the accretion of executive-like authority to the European Council as a "history-making" institution. The crises have added to the high profile of "emergency" summitry. This applies to external relations (e.g.,—Russia's annexation of Crimea) and differentiated formats for Euro Summits and Art. 50 (EU27) meetings over Brexit. Add to this the ascent of eurozone finance ministers as the Eurogroup, a pattern predating but enhanced by the crisis, and economic policy coordination bodies such as the EFC and EGWG that act as a highly autonomous network of financial/economic governance (Puetter 2006). Or consider the normalization of "co-decision" rights for the EP in the legislative process as the now "ordinary legislative procedure" (OLP) between the eras of Maastricht and Lisbon. Looking back on the firewalled "pillar" design of the Maastricht Treaty in the 1990s, which left wide swaths of EU competence subject to national vetoes, one would be surprised to see today's extent of qualified majority voting (QMV). And the autonomous profile of "permanent" or internally selected leadership positions such as the President of the European Council, the Chairs of the Eurogroup and EGWG, and the High Representative of the Foreign Affairs Council now make distinctions of who counts as a "supranational entrepreneur" in the EU something of a trick question.

At the same time, continuities in the basic reality of life inside the "Brussels bubble" stand out as well. The Council system is not a public vote machine. The penchant for consensus-seeking practices to avoid formal voting still holds. All layers of Council business still treat formal voting as a kind of last resort, despite the widespread application of majority voting rules. The closed "policy community" segmentation of the Council's work is as true as ever,[3] as is the deliberate discretion afforded by shuttling dossiers up-and-down the informal hierarchies of expert, preparatory, and ministerial levels to help avoid politicization and "keep a lid" on nationally sensitive topics (this can range from glyphosate regulation to strategic Chinese investment). There is still a basic individual expectation of explaining and justifying problems to the group and a shared expectation for mutual responsiveness. Even a member hopelessly isolated on an issue can receive group legitimation for exemption, derogation, or special circumstances. New leadership jobs have not hollowed out the Council's tradition of "rotating presidency" which still serves as a parity

---

[2] For more on this point, see Keohane (2002), Waever (1995), Bickerton (2012), Sbragia (1994).

[3] The "policy community" concept comes from the anthropological tradition of network research. See for example, Marsh and Rhodes (1992), Marsh and Smith (2000), Bevir (2013: 91).

mechanism between big-small, new-old members and, crucially, acts to create a stakeholder role in seeing the EU legislative process succeed. Elemental norms of reciprocity, trust, and trustworthiness have been tested but not effaced (such as *pacta sunt servanda*). The in-group dynamics of Council networks still instill a sense of joint enterprise, hard to quantify and perhaps easy to overstate, based on a shared responsibility to find EU solutions and deliver results with a palpable sense of failure should the legislative process logjam.

The remainder of the chapter contrasts such continuity and change in Council politics during an era of "turbulent" integration crises. The aim is to assess how EU crises impact the Council as an institutional environment, and, in turn, how a mature organizational culture responds to turbulence. The next section offers an overview of how EU crises impact the Council and how the Council's organizational culture has obtained resilience over time. A key metric is the ethos of a "system attitude" that now appears as if hardwired into Council politics and hardly touched at all by today's integration crises. This is followed by a section that focuses on key patterns of "turbulence," comparing trends of institutional path dependence and more improvisational forms of institutional syncretism. The implication is that the Council is now a transnational governance space of both durable *habitus* and ever-changing institutional hybridity.

How EU Crises Impact Council Institutions

Crises expose fault lines and unintended consequences, follow path dependencies, but are also moments of institutional plasticity where improvisation and creative agency come to the fore. The "turbulence" found in European integration affects the Council in particular ways. For one thing, the Council's component parts have differential relationships to patterns of "turbulence of scale" between the EU and domestic levels. Whereas the European Council is the EU's *ne plus ultra* political shock absorber often living with "turbulence of scale" from the eye of the storm, much of the politico-administrative machinery is deliberately insulated and buffered from such effects.[4]

Overall, the Council has experienced a string of EU crises that, on the one hand, place strain on the Council's tried-and-true working methods. In recent years, the complex ins and outs of differentiation and principled objections to EU migration policy have made *in camera* deliberation and consensus-seeking a more contestable and politicized set of practices. The image of elitist insider politics within the "Brussels bubble" has added fuel to Europe's angry populism and euroskeptic public opinion views (Schweiger 2017; Bruter 2012). The current rhetoric of "Brussels' made us do it" found in Rome,

---

[4]The concept of "turbulence of scale" comes from Ansell and Trondal (2017). The Council's hybridity to insulate certain policy networks from such effects is analogous to their idea of "decoupling" techniques as a "device for coping with the turbulence of scale by buffering parts of organizations" (ibid.: 293).

Budapest, Warsaw, and elsewhere shows signs of a more openly confrontational and uncompromising style of negotiation (De Gruyter 2018).

On the other hand, the Council's institutional architecture and the practices that sustain it are forged and reforged *during* crises, a trend established as early as the 1960s (Ludlow 2006). In many ways, the Council system fits the general observation made by Ansell et al. (2017: 8) that "turbulence" can be "almost a constitutive part of the institutional fabric" in an organizational culture. Indeed, if by crisis we mean "a serious threat to the basic structures or the fundamental values and norms of a system" (Rosenthal et al. 1989, cited in Ansell et al. 2017: 7) then the Council has experienced more institutional continuity than change over the last decade.

The serial crises of the EU *have* resulted in significant changes in Council institutions. Start with the eurozone crisis. The European Council has enhanced "executive federalism," institutionalized regular Euro Summits, and elevated the status of the Eurogroup network of eurozone finance ministers. Thirty or so European Council summits with an emergency reform theme during the heat of the eurozone crisis earned the impression of *muddling through*, yet the EU now has new euro crisis mechanisms, a conditional bailout regime, and real banking union (Jabko 2019). The migration crisis contested the legitimacy of QMV practices in forcing mandatory asylum relocation quotas onto reluctant member-states and principled opposition produced a rarely seen "voting bloc" in Council politics (i.e.,—the so-called Visegrad Four (V4) of Poland, Hungary, Slovakia, and the Czech Republic).[5] The concept of durable voting coalitions or blocking minorities has remained largely hypothetical until now; however, the possibilities for the "political effects" of crises to generate new cleavages—between East-West, new-old, debtor-creditor, liberal-illiberal and so on—are now more likely than in the past.[6] Brexit, whatever its eventual outcome, adds a radically new dynamic of "exit, voice, and loyalty" options and cements patterns of differentiated integration in ways that the Maastricht-era "opt-outs" merely foreshadowed. The crises of external relations have gradually upgraded EU administrative capacities with the Lisbon Treaty roles for the High Representative and EEAS as well as growing member-state support for an extension of QMV-based foreign policy actions under the "shadow of the vote." Last, though not least, the ongoing legitimacy crisis has produced a series of transparency reforms (including a public Transparency Register of lobbyists and interest groups) and attempts to ring-fence EU fundamental values with formal sanctioning procedures (such as the excessive deficit procedure or the Article 7 process).

---

[5] Actually, the V4 was not a cohesive voting bloc in the mandatory asylum case: Poland publicly opposed the quotas but sided with the majority and did not contest the outcome. The "noes" included the Czech Republic, Slovakia, Hungary, and Romania (with Finland abstaining) (Council Decision (EU) 2015/1523, OJ L 239, 15/9/2015).

[6] For example, in EU migration policy the V4 has "found a new ally in an Austrian government containing the far-right Freedom Party" (Geddes 2018: 128–129).

And yet, the organizational culture of the Council has an enduring quality that such change patterns do not seem to erode. If the Council system were equated to a "corporate culture" (Kreps' term), then the process of consensus-seeking would be the most patently observable feature over time. There is now broad but not universal agreement that the Council as a social order rests on a distinctive "culture of consensus" (Smeets 2015: 1) albeit one that varies internally by specialized configuration (Wallace and Reh 2015: 80) or as "sub-societies" with distinct normative and behavioral expectations (Lewis 2019b). The roots of this culture are in the foundational era of European integration, originally what neofunctionalists observed as a "system attitude" or a "willingness to behave according to an accepted bargaining code keyed primarily to a determination to succeed" (Lindberg and Scheingold 1970: 242, 119). Weiler's concept of EU "infranationalism" is helpful to understand a consensus-seeking culture as an "underlying ethos" that is "managerial and technocratic" and dilutes a purely "national element" in the joint decision-making process (Weiler 1999: 272,283).[7] The infranational dimension of the Council's consensus culture is comparable in institutional durability and soft law functions as that in other "cooperative" styles of federalism. In describing EU infranationalism, Weiler mentions intriguing parallels to the inclusiveness of viewpoints that is hardwired into consociational polities or the accommodation style found in neo-corporatist countries that avert a confrontational style of politics (Weiler 1999: 282–285). Consider the comparison to a "spirit of accommodation" found in Lijphart's (1968) seminal study of Dutch politics. If one replaces "Dutch" with "EU," you find a description of Council-style consensus-seeking that has a striking similarity. In Lijphart's (1968: 103–104) words:

> Dutch politics is a politics of accommodation. That is the secret of its success. The term accommodation is here used in the sense of settlement of divisive issues and conflicts where only a minimal consensus exists. Pragmatic solutions are forged for all problems, even those with clear religious-ideological overtones on which the opposing parties may appear irreconcilable, and which therefore may seem insoluble and likely to split the country apart. A key element of this conception is the lack of a comprehensive political consensus, but not the complete absence of consensus. Dutch national consensus is weak and narrow, but it does contain the crucial component of a widely shared attitude that the existing system ought to be maintained and not be allowed to disintegrate. The second key requirement is that the leaders of the self-contained blocs must be particularly convinced of the desirability of preserving the system. And they must be willing and capable of bridging the gaps between the mutually isolated blocs and of resolving serious disputes in a largely nonconsensual context.

From an organizational cultural perspective, the central concept here is that of a widely shared "system attitude," namely, that the system ought to be

---
[7]For more on this theme, see Lewis (2015), Heisenberg (2007).

maintained, that the norms and principles of consensus-seeking not erode into disuse, that the collective decision-making process itself has value, and the obligation of finding results is a shared responsibility.[8] The resort to nonconsensual outcomes can likewise compare to the Council's formal "shadow of the vote" under QMV. "Accommodation" does not mean the same as making "generous concessions" (see Naurin 2015 for a study that conflates the terms). The key aspect is the system attitude that the legislative process should succeed, that important national positions are not simply bigfooted or outvoted, that everyone finds themselves with instructions at times that are isolating or hopelessly unpersuasive, and so forth. A classic illustration is the bevy of Council preparatory structures such as Coreper, the EFC, and the PSC that all have unwritten mandates from the ministers to find solutions at their level and, wherever possible, reach consensus outcomes that everyone can live with (described by participants as "a global, permanent instruction"). The formal decision rule helps to hardwire this system attitude since the "shadow of the vote" compels a logic of explaining and justifying positions, listening and responding to each claimant's demands, and providing group deliberated collective legitimation of outcomes. The policy segmentation of the Council's work, into discreet networks of like-minded policy specialists, also helps in moments of crisis (or "turbulence of scale") to create an institutional "loose coupling" that "deter the failure of one component from reverberating across the entire system" (Ansell and Trondal's terms 2017: 293). This helps explain how the dramatic mandatory asylum quota vote in 2015 did not leech into broader QMV practices in the Council as well as the containment of the toxic mistrust generated by the frictions of the eurozone crisis within circles of finance and banking policymakers.

Institutional Patterns of Turbulence

The academic distinction between crisis and turbulence is instructive when taking stock of patterns of continuity and change in the Council. If one applies Ikenberry's (2008: 3) definition of a "crisis" as "an extraordinary moment when the existence and viability of the political order are called into question," then the Council has a remarkably stable organizational culture of decision-making over time. New and more heterogeneous members, majority voting as the "ordinary" decision rule, Treaty reforms and institutional reengineering, the normalization of the EP's legislative "co-decision" rights, and so forth—none of these trends have called into question the Council's prevailing *modus operandi* and least of all the "system attitude" that Adler-Nissen depicts as an unspoken "doxa" of integration that is taken for granted and undisputed as a self-evident truth (Adler-Nissen 2014). But simultaneously, the notion of "turbulence" as "interactions of events or demands that are highly

---

[8]The primordial foundations of such a system attitude shares much in common with what Levitsky and Ziblatt (2018: 106–111) describe as norms of "institutional forebearance."

variable, inconsistent, unexpected or unpredictable" (Ansell et al. 2017: 2) appears as a near permanent feature of the Council's operating environment. The Council's institutional environment offers empirical validity to the possibility that "turbulence" can be an "endogeneous, constitutive, and systematic part of the fabric of organizations" (Riddervold et al. 2019: 3). In a recent volume on "turbulent governance," the editors identify three generic change responses: profound change characterized by punctuated equilibria, path-dependent change, and institutional syncretism (Ansell et al. 2017: 10–12). Council "turbulence" does not fit the pattern of profound change but excels at generating the latter two types as this section will further detail.

First, turbulence exhibits a pattern of *institutional path-dependence* in the Council's evolving organizational culture. In this view, "governance systems and governance practices under stress revert to or reinforce pre-existing organizational traditions, practices, and formats" (Ansell et al. 2017: 11). The path dependence of informal norms and the stability of governing practices is a venerable characteristic of Council politics. At the macro-historical level, the tendency to work by process of consensus-seeking and eschew formal voting is now a robust empirical finding.[9] While the hard paper trail only dates to 1993 and Maastricht transparency reforms to make voting records public, the overall trend from 1994 to 2004 sees consensus outcomes in nearly 85% of all legislative acts (Hayes-Renshaw and Wallace 2006: 259). Even more, we know from the pioneering study of Hayes-Renshaw et al. (2006) that "contested voting" (that is, all public votes where at least one "no" or "abstention" is recorded) tends to cluster in a slender bandwidth of cases involving agriculture, trade, and the internal market. These sectors account for more than 60% of all contested votes between 1995 and 2010 (Van Aken 2012: 34). More recently, the evidence shows an uptick in contested votes under QMV to 35% of cases between 2009 and 2012, again with a clustering around a few areas: economic and monetary affairs, the environment, and public health (VoteWatch Europe 2012: 8). Still, over the same reference period of 2009–2012, the overall trend is nearly 98% of all votes were cast in favor as a percentage of all possible votes in favor (covering 343 proposals that had public votes) (ibid.: 9, Fig. 4).

The path dependence of consensus-seeking practices does not necessarily imply outcomes to make everyone happy, rather they evolve under the so-called "shadow of the vote" and the calculation of hypothetical blocking minorities under QMV. Qualitative evidence reveals a continual alertness

---

[9]There is a big difference between consensus as process and outcome. The former reflect shared practices to find collective solutions in a cooperative style of decision-making (Lewis 2010; Heisenberg 2012; Aus 2008; Niemann 2006). This includes informal expectations of mutual responsiveness in a deliberative environment of explaining and justifying individual demands or positions. Consensus outcomes are no more than an "absence of explicit opposition" (Novak 2013: 1094) and may reflect "procedural acquiescence" (Smeets 2016: 35) rather than unanimous support in favor. For more on the distinction see Novak (2013), Smeets (2015), Urfalino (2007), Lindell (1988), Lewis (2017).

by the Council presidency, the Commission, and the GSC of hypothetical blocking coalitions during all stages of the negotiation process (Novak 2013; Piris 2000: 19). The implication is that the Chair is more willing to state a sufficient majority exists or move towards a formal vote in circumstances where a clear blocking minority is no longer a valid threat. The formal option of "indicative voting" is to supply a signaling device in the coalition-building process for emerging majorities or potential blocking minorities (Häge 2012). The meaning of how indicative voting is used in practice clearly shows us that Council consensus-seeking is not really about trying to make everyone equally happy with the outcome.

Indicative voting reflects a permanent "counting practice" to efficiently identify majority win sets (Deloche-Gaudez and Beaudonnet 2010: 4). But the formal use is interpreted within the context of informal rules for mutual accommodation and responsiveness expectations. Diana Panke (2010) reveals this in her case analysis of the EU "spirit drinks" negotiations over vodka labeling. Britain developed a credible blocking coalition through subtle club methods to broaden a narrow definition whereas Poland applied "hard ball tactics" with an unwillingness to make concessions over a purist-conception of vodka (only from cereals and potatoes) that led to isolation and blocking minority threats that lacked credibility (Panke 2010: 144–164). By using the indicative vote, group leverage on a single isolated delegation can be especially intense, and some delegations openly mention having a standing instruction to "avoid isolation." Overall, counting and indicative voting practices have given a procedural sophistication to consensus-seeking under QMV that shows path-dependent change patterns over time.

There does appear to be a safety-in-numbers aspect to public contestation under QMV. Comparing data from 2002–2004 and 2004–2006, Dehousse and Deloche-Gaudez (2009: 26, Fig. 4) find a considerable decline in "one-State minorities" (from 56 to 35% of all cases) and an attendant rise in multimember minorities of three or more states (from 5 to 27% of all cases). This has been interpreted as a sign that EU enlargement and the heterogeneity of members create a functional necessity for higher reliance on voting rather than mutual accommodation. But informal rules counterbalance this trend in path-dependent directions. For example, there are newly invigorated procedural methods designed as outlets for dissent *without* publically contested votes. A good illustration is the surge in reading "formal statements" into the minutes (Hagemann and De Clerck-Sachsse 2007; Hagemann 2008). Statements in the minutes can be considered a close cousin to the practice of abstention under unanimity (what Jensen describes as a "mild form of dissent").[10] If 1999–2006 data are representative, the outlet of formal statements lowers the incidence of publically contested votes by something like

---

[10]See Jensen (2009). William Nicoll (1993) notes statements hold no legal value. But as an outlet of contestation, they serve to put "gloss" on what may have been a lost battle without a publically contested vote (Nicoll 1993: 564–565).

10–20 percent per year or more (Hagemann 2008). The appeal of statements is "governments are able to enact a sense of "willingness to cooperate" without at the same time sending a political signal of having deviated from their initial policy preferences" (Hagemann 2008: 47). This inference is important in helping us understand the prevalence of consensus-seeking trends in Council decision-making even during turbulent times and in response to crises. The use of statements shows the fiction of consensus as "outcome" (i.e.,—that everyone is equally pleased with the result) compared to consensus as "process" which represents a social environment of collective standards for assessing individual preferences and (de)legitimating them in an atmosphere of cooperative bargaining. In addition, there are also signaling and accommodation standards that informally operate at the group level that determine the extent to which the Council will "spend extra time" to find agreements everyone can live with.

As a path-dependent social order, the Council system is an integral element of the so-called "Brussels bubble," akin to a world of its own, with its own diplomatic capital in a "social field" where tacit understandings and shared meanings constitute a *sens practique*, or "feel for the game" that "define agency and make action intelligible" (Adler-Nissen 2014; Smeets 2015; Rasmussen 2016). The EU's Council system has evolved a set of governing practices that create *habitus*, or stable dispositions of 'how things are done' inside the Brussels bubble. The reinforcing quality of social practices becomes an "inherited tradition" over time which acts to demarcate "what does and does not work around here" and are "embodied in rituals and routines" (Bevir 2013: 44, 68). Consensus-seeking practices are a largely taken for granted "inherited tradition" but since they rest entirely on an informal normative rulebook they are thus *always* subject to interpretation and potential contestation. The organizational culture of the Council is passed on and reinforced over time through processes of socialization and mimetic emulation, which hews to both a logic of appropriateness and a complex institutional memory of social influence. The returns to scale that such "inherited traditions" produce in everyday negotiations in the Council are what instantiate a distinct consensus-seeking *habitus* and deepen the *sens practique* of what works (Adler-Nissen 2014; Cornut 2018; Kleine 2013). On a more pathological note, EU policy can also become entrapped in a "muddle through" approach of path dependence where turbulence leads to a reinforcement of the status quo (witnessed in euro crisis reforms, the migration crisis and the Dublin asylum system, or the window dressing transparency reforms to hold select public ministerial debates post-Maastricht). Even hidebound national safeguards like the infamous Luxembourg Compromise (LC) are path-dependent—despite a deprecated practice of making legitimate "very important interest" claims (discussed below), member-states have never formally revoked the LC principle.[11]

Turbulence also generates a pattern of *institutional "syncretism"* which is a change process neither profound nor path-dependent but "a process of recombination, refashioning, or repurposing of existing institutions in an adaptive fashion" (Ansell et al. 2017: 11). Syncretic change tends to rely on improvisation and produces institutional hybridity over time, especially in complex organizations like the Council where there is a "dynamic resilience" or "continuous change that adapts to the [institutional] environment without seeking to maintain or restore an equilibrium" (Ansell 2017: 95). A structural illustration of this is how the relative authority of different ministerial Councils is neither fixed nor formalized. The odd-bin formal status of the Eurogroup (technically not a formation of the Council at all) and elevation of finance ministers' networks is one post-Maastricht trend, as is the attendant decline in status for the foreign ministers and General Affairs. The institutional reengineering capacity of the European Council (promoting the Eurogroup, or disinviting foreign ministers from summits) and the "special oversight powers" over the individual ministerial Councils (Puetter 2014) enhances "dynamic resilience" and allows for improvisation.

At the level of practices, syncretic improvisational change abounds. A central insight of the IR "practice turn" is how a "competent performance" (Adler and Pouliot 2011) is not only tied to knowing what the informal rules are or how to use them, but how to apply them creatively. As Cornut (2018: 717) tells us, "practices are not only ways of doing, but also ways of improvising." QMV practices display this type of significant, but gradual change, also known as "institutional bricolage." Bricolage is a change process where actors can "reinterpret the meaning of rules and redeploy them under significantly altered circumstances" (Carstensen 2017: 140). This can entail novel interpretations of existing rules or redeploying them to solve new problems (ibid.: 143). During the "relaunch" era of European integration the 1980s and the legislative agenda of the "1992 Project," Council QMV practices underwent significant repurposing. Perhaps little noticed at the time, but votes infrequently began from the late 1970s on, clustering around certain issues where formal QMV was an option, including the budget, CAP implementation, and technical trade issues (Hayes-Renshaw and Wallace 2006: 268). By the time of the SEA in 1986, the issue of Single Market liberalization and decision-making reform had become tightly coupled (Dooge Report 1985). In his insider ethnography, de Bassompierre recounts a "turning point" moment in 1982 when the Belgian presidency rejected a British veto threat over setting annual agricultural prices and "decided to go ahead and call for a vote anyway" (de Bassompierre 1988: 27). By his account, "a modest, but significant,

---

[11] See Lewis (2017) for a more detailed analysis. See Cruz (2006) for an insightful overview of the Luxembourg Compromise as a "legal and political myth."

psychological breakthrough was achieved, which led all succeeding presidencies, including the French and British, to call more and more often for a vote" (ibid.: 28). In any event, this was a clear instance where the British invoked an LC claim (that "very important interests" were at stake) but were rebuffed by the group. Swinbank (1989: 309) notes "it was partly a matter of chance" that the Belgians held the rotating presidency during the first half of 1982 when the CAP price review came up, noting "Belgium has always been particularly dubious about the Luxembourg Compromise." He goes on to describe the event as a "watershed" since this was the first time the annual CAP price review was settled by majority vote (ibid.: 310).

As Council voting practices were refashioned, formal recourse to QMV gradually became a more effective deterrent to those with uncompromising positions. During the 1980s, "the vote was used in an abrupt way in the early years, without any real diplomatic niceties, like a 'procedural guillotine', to use the words of one representative" (Novak 2011: 15). One advisor in the Council's legal service estimates there were perhaps 20 votes per year by 1982, 40 or so in 1984 and 1985, and 80 in 1986 (Dewost 1987, cited in Novak 2011: 15, fn. 18). But over time, QMV practices evolved to become more "sophisticated" especially through the leadership capacities of the presidency to build compromise and allow those in the minority to "join the majority without losing face" (Novak 2011: 15). Thus, over the decade of the 1980s, formal voting, implicit vote counting, and consensus practices evolved considerably, to the point where "the language of negotiations is now the language of voting. Officials and even occasionally ministers are prepared to use the vocabulary of majorities and minorities" (Wallace 1989, cited in Sbragia 1993: 102). What one scholar calls "one of the most hard-fought battles in the political history of the EU" (Dinan 2015: 209) was effectively improvised by repurposing the "shadow of the vote" in a bricolage fashion over time.

Another improvised voting practice is the selective use of the so-called "silent procedure" where the group spotlights an intransigent position that prevents a collective agreement under unanimity. Jonathan Aus depicts its use as an informal variant of the formal "written procedure" that was innovated in common action domains for foreign policy and JHA. The practice shifts the onus onto the delegation that has a special problem (typically in the form of an unwavering "reserve") and requires them to speak up by a certain date and time or else live with the "consensus" agreement in place. The case documented by Aus involves the Danish presidency (who chaired the JHA Council despite Denmark's "opt-out") creating a silent procedure deadline in 2002 to overcome intransigent Italian and Greek reservations over the Dublin II asylum agreement (Aus 2008: 112–113). Likewise, the British presidency used the silent procedure in a similar fashion to overcome endgame reserves on the EU's 1996 blocking measure to U.S. "extraterritoriality" embedded in the Helms-Burton Cuba embargo. In that instance, the British went out on a limb to overcome several hold outs, including the French. Basically, the UK Permanent Representative Stephen Wall told his colleagues at 8:00 p.m. on a

Sunday, "if anyone has trouble with this agreement, have your head of government call Blair by tomorrow morning." In general, the rare but surprisingly effective improvisation of the silent procedure tells us the meaning of "being isolated" is contextually specific even under different formal voting rules. As Smeets (2016: 24) finds, even with unanimity voting (and formal veto player options) "isolation can become untenable." The silent procedure, in effect, is a mechanism that raises the "degree of exposure of the loners" in Smeets' formulation and shows how the Council's club-like rules can involve collective legitimation of individual claimants' demands and positions (ibid.: 35).

An even newer improvised practice is reverse qualified majority voting (RQMV) to restructure the meaning of how abstentions count and raise the bar for blocking coalitions by flipping the "blocking minority" logic around. Abstaining under QMV counts as a "no" since it does not add to the minimum majority threshold requirement to successfully adopt a proposal.[12] But under RQMV abstentions count as votes in favor, to enhance the enforcement power of Commission recommendations and make a blocking coalition harder to achieve. RQMV has been introduced in a few select areas such as EU anti-dumping decisions (since 2004), economic surveillance under the revised stability and growth pact (SGP) regarding the "excessive deficit procedure" (since 2011), and the fiscal compact (since 2012) (Van Aken and Artige 2013). Under the old rules, a simple blocking minority could reject Commission recommendations (i.e.,—at least four member-states representing at least 35% of the EU's population), but RQMV "significantly lowers the majority threshold to pass legislation" since a blocking vote now requires a qualified majority to do so (ibid.: 153). In effect, RQMV is a procedural adaptation of formal rules designed to influence informal voting behavior (especially "counting" practices). While RQMV has untested legitimacy in the case of Commission "excessive deficit" (EDP) recommendations (Scharpf 2013), the procedural ingenuity is to create a formal shadowing device that makes transgressive behavior policed by group standards under a significantly foreshortened shadow of the vote. The novelty of the device in policing national budgets as part of the eurozone reforms is to build on the informal procedural sophistication of QMV practices that were already durably institutionalized.

Institutional syncretism is a key "turbulence" dynamic in how the collective meanings of Council rules can change over time. Consider again the mythical notoriety of the LC as an ultimate emergency brake for "very important interests." The LC was a procedural improvisation to end the French boycott during the 1965 empty chair crisis, still considered by many as "the greatest constitutional crisis in the history of European integration" (Dinan 2015: 209). Boiled down to its procedural essence, the LC is a "set of non-binding conclusions" with "a difference of opinion on what precisely would happen when a complete resolution of a dispute within the Council was not achieved"

---

[12] Post-Lisbon, this requires a "double majority" of at least (1) 55% of member-states, and (2) 65% of the total EU population.

(Teasdale 1993: 569). It was, in short, a politically (but not legally) binding agreement to disagree on the need for unanimity in cases involving very important interests. In a fundamental sense, the LC is an informal social convention, not a formal rule at all. This distinction is confirmed time and again by official Council replies to written questions regarding the status of the LC. The Council even goes to lengths to avoid using the terminology as such. Instead, the Council refers to the LC as "the conclusions of the extraordinary Council meeting in Luxembourg on 17, 18, 27 and 28 January 1966."[13]

Nor has the LC ever formally been invalidated. During the Dooge Committee deliberations on institutional reform (that contributed to the 1986 Single European Act), the final report contains a footnote reference insisting the LC was not a negotiable point of reform (Wallace and Winand 2006: 40–41).[14] But the social context of invoking LC claims has evolved considerably over time, and its invocation has severely deprecated in practice. To operate, the LC requires an informal rulebook: who can invoke it, under what circumstances, and when and how the group will affirm what constitutes "very important interests" depends on the exact circumstances and the social environment in which these rules operate.

The patchy unevenness of when the LC has been invoked and whether it was successful attests to the social order in which it operates. By Teasdale's calculations, the LC was formally invoked maybe 10 times in the 15 years after 1966 and became essentially unusable by the latter 1980s (Teasdale 1993: 570, 578). One key reason its use deprecated in practice is that it was highly uncertain to work, and could result in a "vital interest" claim being rejected by the group. This happened on several occasions to agricultural ministers who attempted to wield it during the 1980s (including Greece and Germany) (Teasdale 1993). Teasdale states the British government *contemplated* the LC during 1992–1993 social policy negotiations for both parental leave and working time, "but rejected it on the grounds that the exercise might backfire" (ibid.: 578). More recently, Poland invoked the LC discourse during the February 2006 reform of the sugar sector, but this was explicitly rebuffed by the AGFISH Council (Jakubek 2008: 97). Teasdale's risk of "backfire" seems to attach in this case to harm Poland's reputation. In her detailed interview evidence, Novak singles out the "case of a non-conforming Polish delegation" which was repeatedly cited by Council participants for not behaving "in accordance with the Council's norms" (Novak 2013: 1098; Heisenberg 2012: 387).

Over time, the procedural sophistication of QMV practices seems to have hollowed out the validity of successfully invoking an LC-grade infringement of national interests. The history of the LC's legacy status offers a great

---

[13] For example, see the Council reply to a written question, OJ C 217, 26/07/1996, pg. 22.

[14] For more on the Dooge Committee and the SEA, see Cameron (1992). For a full text of the Dooge Report, see: http://aei.pitt.edu/997/.

application of Adler-Nissen's (2014: 61) concept of "diplomatic capital" as a group-legitimated form of social power. Who might have the diplomatic capital to invoke an LC claim as "valid currency" (Adler-Nissen's term) cannot be determined apart from the social field in which it operates (Kuus 2015). The legacy status of the LC shows us the meaning of "what counts" as a legitimate national safeguard claim is something that has evolved over time through improvised QMV practices, a dynamic of syncretic change at the heart of Council politics that contributes to the unspoken *doxa* of integration over time.

Conclusion

The Council is no stranger to dealing with crises. It would not be much of an exaggeration to say that the Council's institutional architecture itself is crisis forged and re-forged over time. Take the landmark "empty chair crisis" of 1965 and resultant Luxembourg Compromise (LC). Did the crisis resolution of protecting very important interests with an ambiguous "veto player" right represent a profound intergovernmental control mechanism as conventional wisdom holds? Or did the crisis enhance consensus-seeking practices and a group deliberative environment of joint decision-making? Did the LC narrow the pipeline of politically acceptable win sets and grind the legislative process to a slow halt? Or did the LC lead to syncretic adaptation with the 1980s "new approach" and re-introduction of majority voting practices? The organizational culture perspective helps reveal the durable system attitude found in the Council's social fabric and political sociology offers insight into the outsize durability of consensus-seeking as part of a *habitus* of cooperation and *sens practique* of what works (and what does not) inside the Brussels bubble. The "new intergovernmentalism" theory's emphasis on the need for "permanent consensus generation" (Bickerton et al. 2015) presupposes such a *habitus* but is largely silent on the genealogy of where it comes from and what sustains it. The procedural sophistication of QMV practices, discussed above, offer an important illustration of why this genealogy matters. Treating the Council system as a "corporate culture" helps reveal both the timeworn "inherited traditions" and the constant bricolage adaptability that is possible in such an organizational ecosystem. The evidence of path dependence and syncretism in the Council's evolution and the reinforcing processes for consensus-seeking practices share much in common with Greif and Laitan's (2004) innovative concept of a "quasi-parameter" that again spotlights an important, if underexamined, system attitude which Council politics hardwires into the *doxa* of integration in ways that today's crises do not seem to affect much at all.

But it should also be stressed that the EU's consociational-like system attitude and *doxa* are hardly immutable. A deeply internalized style of cooperative negotiation should not literally be treated as taken for granted, since norm erosion, contestation, and delegitimation are always possible. Equating the

Council's consensus culture to a "quasi-parameter" keeps us alert to the possibility that today's self-enforcing behaviors could gradually change or become less applicable in more situations, and institutional environments within the Council ecosystem might develop new reinforcing or undermining dynamics, including the "intentional selection of alternative behaviors" (Greif and Laitan 2004: 639). Today's tangled complexities of flexible integration have created both external and internal differentiation patterns of insider–outsider status, making the invisible hierarchies of power even more difficult to map out (Rittberger et al. 2014). The implication of different "classes" of membership is that a "system attitude" may become thinner or patchier among different Council networks, or even encourage some members to become more self-isolated rather than make the extra efforts and psychological compensatory behavior reported by Adler-Nissen in the opt-out cases of Denmark and the UK. And who knows at this point what "competent practices" *could* emerge from the traumas of Brexit? The Art. 50 (EU27) meeting format is perhaps unknowingly a bricolage incubator for future areas of enhanced cooperation such as PESCO as well as sharpening the edges of group sanctioning skills that could apply to future Article 7 proceedings concerning "fundamental values." As a mature organizational culture, what is most distinctive overall is how the Council combines a durable *habitus* with ever-changing institutional hybridity. In effect, the pooling of national sovereignty and its collective rearticulation at the EU level makes the Council system a central interlocutor in developing a transnational "community of practice" to manage the political-administrative implications of such power.

References

Adler, E., & Pouliot, V. (2011). International Practices: Introduction and Framework. In E. Adler & V. Pouliot (Eds.), *International Practices* (pp. 3–35). Cambridge: Cambridge University Press.

Adler-Nissen, R. (2009). Late Sovereign Diplomacy. *The Hague Journal of Diplomacy, 4,* 121–141.

Adler-Nissen, R. (2014). *Opting Out of the European Union: Diplomacy, Sovereignty and European Integration.* Cambridge: Cambridge University Press.

Ansell, C. (2017). Turbulence, Adaptation, and Change. In C. Ansell, J. Trondal, & M. Ogard (Eds.), *Governance in Turbulent Times* (pp. 77–104). Oxford: Oxford University Press.

Ansell, C., & Trondal, J. (2017). Coping with Turbulence. In C. Ansell, J. Trondal, & M. Ogard (Eds.), *Governance in Turbulent Times* (pp. 285–302). Oxford: Oxford University Press.

Ansell, C., Trondal, J., & Ogard, M. (2017). Turbulent Governance. In C. Ansell, J. Trondal, & M. Ogard (Eds.), *Governance in Turbulent Times* (pp. 1–23). Oxford: Oxford University Press.

Aus, J. (2008). The Mechanisms of Consensus: Coming to Agreement on Community Asylum Policy. In D. Naurin & H. Wallace (Eds.), *Unveiling the Council of the European Union: Games Governments Play in Brussels* (pp. 99–118). Basingstoke: Palgrave Macmillan.

Bevir, M. (2013). *A Theory of Governance*. Berkeley, CA: University of California Press.
Bickerton, C. (2012). *European Integration: From Nation-States to Member States*. Oxford: Oxford University Press.
Bickerton, C., Hodson, C., & Puetter, U. (2015). The New Intergovernmentalism and the Study of European Integration. In C. Bickerton, C. Hodson, & U. Puetter (Eds.), *The New Intergovernmentalism: States and Supranational Actors in the Post-Maastricht Era* (pp. 1–48). Oxford: Oxford University Press.
Bruter, M. (2012). The Difficult Emergence of a European People. In J. Hayward & R. Wurzel (Eds.), *European Disunion: Between Sovereignty and Solidarity* (pp. 17–31). Basingstoke: Palgrave Macmillan.
Cameron, D. R. (1992). The 1992 Initiative: Causes and Consequences. In A. Sbragia (Ed.), *Euro-Politics: Institutions and Policymaking in the "New" European Community* (pp. 23–74). Washington, DC: The Brookings Institution.
Carstensen, M. (2017). Institutional Bricolage in Times of Crisis. *European Political Science Review*, 9(1), 139–160.
Cornut, J. (2018). Diplomacy, Agency, and the Logic of Improvisation and Virtuosity in Practice. *European Journal of International Relations*, 24(3), 712–736.
Cruz, J.B. (2006). The Luxembourg Compromise from a Legal Perspective: Constitutional Convention, Legal History or Myth? In J-M. Palayret, H. Wallace, & P. Winand (Eds.), *Visions, Votes and Vetoes: The Empty Chair Crisis and the Luxembourg Compromise Forty Years on*. (pp. 251–77). Brussels: P.I.E. Peter Lang.
de Bassompierre, G. (1988). *Changing the Guard in Brussels: An Insider's View of the EC Presidency*. New York: Praeger.
De Gruyter, C. (2018, October 19). *The Brussels "Kicking Post": Polarised Debate on the EU*. European Council on Foreign Relations.
Dehousse, R., & Deloche-Gaudez, F. (2009). Voting in the Council of Ministers: The Impact of Enlargement. In A. Ott & E. Vos (Eds.), *Fifty Years of European Integration: Foundations and Perspectives* (pp. 21–30). Hague: T.M.C. Asser Press.
Deloche-Gaudez, F., & Beaudonnet, L. (2010, June). *Decision-Making in the Enlarged EU Council of Ministers: A Softer Consensus Norm as an Explanation for Its Apparent Adaptability?* Paper prepared for the Fifth Pan-European Conference on EU Politics, Porto, Portugal, 23–26.
Dewost, J.-L. (1987). "Le vote majoritaire: simple modalite de gestion ou enjeu politique essential?" [The majority vote: simple management tool or essential political tool] In Baden-Baden and Nomos Verlagsgesellschaft (Eds.,). *Du droit international au droit de l'integration, Liber amicorum Pierre Pescatore*. (pp. 167–175).
Dinan, D. (2015). The Political System of the European Union. In J. Magone (Ed.), *Routledge Handbook of European Politics* (pp. 202–218). London: Routledge.
Dooge Report. (1985). *Ad Hoc Committee for Institutional Affairs: Report to the European Council*. Brussels, 29–30 March.
Geddes, A. (2018). The Politics of European Union Migration Governance. *Journal of Common Market Studies*, 56, Annual Review, 120–130.
Greif, A., & Laitin, D. (2004). A Theory of Endogenous Institutional Change. *American Political Science Review*, 98(4), 633–652.
Häge, F. (2012). Coalition Building and Consensus in the Council of the European Union. *British Journal of Political Science*, 43, 481–504.
Hagemann, S. (2008). Voting, Statements and Coalition-Building in the Council from 1999 to 2006. In D. Naurin & H. Wallace (Eds.), *Unveiling the Council of the*

European Union: Games Governments Play in Brussels (pp. 36–63). Basingstoke: Palgrave Macmillan.

Hagemann, S., & De Clerck-Sachsse, J. (2007, March). *Old Rules, New Game: Decision-Making in the Council of Ministers After the 2004 Enlargement*. Centre for European Policy Studies, Special Report.

Hayes-Renshaw, F., & Wallace, H. (2006). *The Council of Ministers* (2nd ed.). New York: St. Martin's Press.

Hayes-Renshaw, F., Van Aken, W., & Wallace, H. (2006). When and Why the EU Council of Ministers Votes Explicitly. *Journal of Common Market Studies, 44*(1), 161–194.

Heisenberg, D. (2007). Informal Decision-Making in the Council: The Secret of the EU's Success? In S. Meunier & K. McNamara (Eds.), *The State of the European Union: Making History: European Integration and Institutional Change at Fifty* (pp. 67–87). Oxford: Oxford University Press.

Heisenberg, D. (2012). Informal Governance and the Decision-Making of the Council of Ministers. In T. Christiansen & C. Neuhold (Eds.), *International Handbook on Informal Governance* (pp. 374–394). Cheltenham: Edward Elgar.

Ikenberry, J. (2008). Introduction. In J. Andersen, J. Ikenberry, & T. Risse (Eds.), *The End of the West? Crisis and Change in the Atlantic Order* (pp. 1–27). Ithaca: Cornell University Press.

Jabko, N. (2019). A Genealogy of Eurozone Governance. In M. Bevir & R. Phillips (Eds.), *Decentring European Governance* (pp. 121–141). Abingdon and New York: Routledge.

Jakubek, J. (2008). Polish Experiences with European Policy Coordination. In M. Myant & T. Cox (Eds.), *Reinventing Poland: Economic and Political Transformation and Evolving National Identity* (pp. 91–106). New York: Routledge.

Jensen, T. (2009). *Time and the Consensus Norm: Examining the Dynamics of Voting in the Council*. ETH Zurich.

Keohane, R. (2002). Ironies of Sovereignty: The European Union and the United States. *Journal of Common Market Studies, 40*(4), 743–765.

Kleine, M. (2013). *Informal Governance in the European Union: How Governments Make International Organizations Work*. Ithaca: Cornell University Press.

Kreps, D. (1990). Corporate Culture and Economic Theory. In J. Alt & K. Shepsle (Eds.), *Perspectives on Positive Political Economy* (pp. 90–143). Cambridge: Cambridge University Press.

Kuus, M. (2015). Symbolic Power in Diplomatic Practice: Matters of Style in Brussels. *Cooperation and Conflict, 50*(3), 368–384.

Levitsky, S., & Ziblatt, D. (2018). *How Democracies Die*. New York: Crown.

Lewis, J. (2010). How Institutional Environments Facilitate Cooperative Negotiation Styles in EU Decision Making. *Journal of European Public Policy, 17*(5), 650–666.

Lewis, J. (2015). The Council of the European Union and the European Council. In J. Magone (Ed.), *Routledge Handbook of European Politics* (pp. 219–234). Abingdon and New York: Routledge.

Lewis, J. (2017). The Council of Ministers of the European Union. *Oxford Research Encyclopedia of Politics*. Online publication date: May 2017. https://doi.org/10.1093/acrefore/9780190228637.013.253. Available at: politics.oxfordre.com.

Lewis, J. (2019a). The European Council and the Council of the European Union. In M. Cini & N. Perez-Solorzano Borragan (Eds.), *Politics in the European Union*. Sixth edition (pp. 157–175). Oxford: Oxford University Press.

Lewis, J. (2019b). EU Council Networks and the "Tradition" of Consensus. In M. Bevir & R. Phillips (Eds.), *Decentring European Governance* (pp. 142–170). Abingdon and New York: Routledge.

Lijphart, A. (1968). *The Politics of Accommodation: Pluralism and Democracy in the Netherlands*. Berkeley, CA: University of California Press.

Lindberg, L., & Scheingold, S. (1970). *Europe's Would-Be Polity*. Englewood Cliffs, NJ: Prentice-Hall.

Lindell, U. (1988). *Modern Multilateral Negotiation: The Consensus Rule and Its Implications in International Conferences*. Lund: Lund Political Studies, Studentlitteratur.

Ludlow, N. P. (2006). *The European Community and the Crises of the 1960s: Negotiating the Gaullist Challenge*. London and New York: Routledge.

Marsh, D., & Rhodes, R. A. W. (1992). Policy Communities and Issue Networks: Beyond Typology. In D. Marsh & R. A. W. Rhodes (Eds.), *Policy Networks in British Government* (pp. 249–268). Oxford: Clarendon Press.

Marsh, D., & Smith, M. (2000). Understanding Policy Networks: Towards a Dialectical Approach. *Political Studies, 48*, 4–21.

Naurin, D. (2015). Generosity in Intergovernmental Negotiations: The Impact of State Power, Pooling and Socialisation in the Council of the European Union. *European Journal of Political Research, 54*, 726–744.

Nicoll, W. (1993). Note the Hour—And File the Minute. *Journal of Common Market Studies, 31*(4), 559–566.

Niemann, A. (2006). *Explaining Decisions in the European Union*. Cambridge: Cambridge University Press.

Novak, S. (2011, November). *Qualified Majority Voting from the Single European Act to Present Day: An Unexpected Performance*. Notre Europe.

Novak, S. (2013). The Silence of Ministers: Consensus and Blame Avoidance in the Council of Ministers. *Journal of Common Market Studies, 51*(6), 1091–1107.

Panke, D. (2010). *Small States in the European Union: Coping with Structural Disadvantages*. Surrey: Ashgate.

Piris, J.-C. (2000). The Mackenzie Stuart Lecture 2001, The Treaty of Nice: An Imperfect Treaty But a Decisive Step Towards Enlargement. *Cambridge Yearbook of European Legal Studies, 3*, 15–36.

Puetter, U. (2006). *The Eurogroup: How a Secretive Group of Finance Ministers Shape European Economic Governance*. Manchester: Manchester University Press.

Puetter, U. (2014). *The European Council and the Council: New Intergovernmentalism and Institutional Change*. Oxford: Oxford University Press.

Rasmussen, M.K. (2016). "Heavy Fog in the Channel. Continent Cut Off?" British Diplomatic Relations in Brussels After 2010. *Journal of Common Market Studies, 54*(3), 709–724.

Riddervold, M., Trondal, J., & Newsome, A. (2019). *"Background and Question" for Handbook on EU Crisis*. Palgrave Macmillan (forthcoming).

Rittberger, B., Leuffen, D., & Schimmelfennig, F. (2014). Differentiated Integration of Core State Powers. In P. Genschel & M. Jachtenfuchs (Eds.), *Beyond Regulatory Polity? The European Integration of Core State Powers* (pp. 189–210). Oxford: Oxford University Press.

Rosenthal, U., Charles, M., & t'Hart, P. (1989). *Coping with Crises: The Management of Disasters, Riots and Terrorism*. Springfield: Charles C. Thomas.

Sbragia, A. (1993). Asymmetrical Integration in the European Community: The Single European Act and Institutional Development. In D. Smith & J. L. Ray (Eds.), *The 1992 Project and the Future of Integration in Europe* (pp. 92–109). New York: M.E. Sharpe.

Sbragia, A. (1994). From 'Nation-State' to 'Member-State': The Evolution of the European Community. In P. Lützeler (Ed.), *Europe After Maastricht: American and European Perspectives* (pp. 69–87). Providence: Berghahn Books.

Scharpf, F. (2013). Monetary Union, Fiscal Crisis and the Disabling of Democratic Accountability. In A.Schäfer & W. Streeck (Eds.), *Politics in the Age of Austerity* (pp. 108–142). Cambridge: Polity Press.

Schweiger, C. (2017). The Legitimacy Challenge. In D. Dinan, N. Nugent, & W. Paterson (Eds.), *The European Union in Crisis* (pp. 188–211). Basingstoke: Palgrave Macmillan.

Smeets, S. (2015). *Negotiations in the EU Council of Ministers: 'And All Must Have Prizes'*. Colchester: ECPR Press.

Smeets, S. (2016). Consensus and Isolation in the EU Council of Ministers. *Journal of European Integration, 38*(1), 23–39.

Swinbank, A. (1989). The Common Agricultural Policy and the Politics of European Decision Making. *Journal of Common Market Studies, 27*(4), 303–322.

Teasdale, A. (1993). The Life and Death of the Luxembourg Compromise. *Journal of Common Market Studies, 31*(4), 567–579.

Urfalino, P. (2007). La décision par consensus apparent. Nature et propriétés. *Revue Européenne de Science Sociales, XLV*(136), 47–70.

Van Aken, W. (2012, 2 September). Voting in the Council of the European Union: Contested Decision-Making in the EU Council of Ministers, 1995–2010. *Swedish Institute for European Policy Studies*. Fiesole, Italy: European University Institute.

Van Aken, W., & Artige, L. (2013). Reverse Majority Voting in Comparative Perspective: Implications for Fiscal Governance in the EU. In B. de Witte, B, A. Héritier, & A. Trechsel (Eds.), *The Euro Crisis and the State of European Democracy* (EUI ebook) (pp. 129–161). Fiesole, Italy: European University Institute.

VoteWatch Europe (2012). *Agreeing to Disagree: The Voting Records of the EU Member States in the Council Since 2009*. Annual Report, July.

Waever, O. (1995). Identity, Integration and Security: Solving the Sovereignty Puzzle in EU Studies. *Journal of International Affairs, 48*(2), 389–431.

Wallace, H. (1989). *Dealing in Multiple Currencies: Negotiations in the European Community*. Unpublished paper.

Wallace, H., & Reh, C. (2015). An Institutional Anatomy and Five Policy Modes. In H. Wallace, M. Pollack, & A. Young (Eds.), *Policy-Making in the European Union* (7th ed., pp. 72–112). Oxford: Oxford University Press.

Wallace, H., & Winand, P. (2006). The Empty Chair Crisis and the Luxembourg Compromise Revisited. In J-M. Palayret, H. Wallace, & P. Winand, P. (Eds.), *Visions, Votes and Vetoes: The Empty Chair Crisis and the Luxembourg Compromise Forty Years on* (pp. 21–42). Brussels: P.I.E. Peter Lang.

Weiler, J. H. H. (1999). *The Constitution of Europe: "Do the New Clothes Have an Emperor?" and Other Essays on European Integration*. Cambridge: Cambridge University Press.

CHAPTER 14

The European Parliament

Akasemi Newsome and Matthew Stenberg

INTRODUCTION

Multiple crises have buffeted the EU in recent years, and this chapter explores continuity and change in how the European Parliament (EP) has fared as an institution in response to the crisis environment. We address the degree to which crises have undermined the Parliament and triggered further integration. This chapter then discusses whether, on balance, crisis has resulted in institutional changes to and different competences for the Parliament. Our discussion points to a scenario in which the EP is *muddling through* the crisis context, reproducing familiar practices in which it asserts itself in order to defend and enlarge its procedural position in an incremental way.

Existing theories of European integration and their implications for how crisis affects the EU are not only unable to account for the full scope of crises but also tend to ignore the role of the European Parliament in particular. Part of the challenge posed in the application of theories of EU integration to the EP's response to crisis is that these theories are heavily informed by a

A. Newsome (✉)
Institute of European Studies, University of California, Berkeley, CA, USA
e-mail: akasemi@berkeley.edu

Inland School of Business and Social Sciences, Inland University, Rena and Lillehammer, Norway

M. Stenberg
Department of Political Science, University of California, Berkeley, CA, USA
e-mail: stenberg@berkeley.edu

© The Author(s) 2021
M. Riddervold et al. (eds.), *The Palgrave Handbook of EU Crises*, Palgrave Studies in European Union Politics,
https://doi.org/10.1007/978-3-030-51791-5_14

focus on member states as central to European integration and do not account for divergent interests among supranational actors. Other studies conceptualize the EP as though it were a national bicameral parliament and thus fail to provide specific understandings for how crisis could impact the EP. Crisis could generate more obstacles for an EP seeking to smooth inter-party differences within its body if parties become more polarized in response to the polarization of member state electorates. This development would then result in less interest on the part of parties to form consensus policies, which historically have allowed the EP to provide a unified policy perspective. Parties in the EP would then be likely to renationalize and discard their European approach to EU politics (Ripoll Servent 2019: 295). On the other hand, when the EP is able to overcome party polarization, the question remains of how distinct the consensus interests expressed by the EP are in comparison to those of the Commission and the Council of the European Union? The EP also shares the challenge of framing, faced by other supranational actors, in that it is not clear that the EP is able to shape the understanding of a crisis as an issue best addressed by supranationalism and that would not be a threat to the "core state powers" of member states (Biermann et al. 2019). Can the EP pitch the solution to a common crisis in a way to influence member state perspectives and increase the inclination to cooperate through supranational institutions?

Our chapter reveals that the record of the EP in maintaining its institutional position and pushing for further integration in a crisis context has been mixed. While the EP has informally expanded its role in responding to the multiple crises beyond its formal powers, it is unclear whether its growth in informal powers has resulted in increased capacity of the EP to secure objectives that are either different from or in opposition to other supranational actors, the member states, or both. Similarly, the EP's efforts at framing recent crises in a way to be favorable to further integration have been inconsistent. On the one hand, where the EP has succeeded in overcoming internal divisions, as in its response to Brexit, the EP's priorities were virtually identical to those of the Commission and member states. On the other hand, when the EP has distinct interests from the Commission, as in the Eurozone crisis, this may weaken the EP further. The capacity for the EP to convince member states that common solutions are worth pooling sovereignty has been mixed in the crises. For example, in the Eurozone crisis, the EP was able to show that forging a common solution would not threaten core state powers. However, during the migration crisis, the EP was not successful in framing the crisis and a common solution as a boon rather than a threat to core state powers (Biermann et al. 2019).

This chapter is organized as follows: first, we provide an overview of the origins and function of the EP, describing the parliamentary electoral process and recent formal expansions of the EP's powers under the 2009 Treaty of Lisbon. We also discuss party dynamics within the EP, the results of the 2019 elections, and the EP's relative position vis-à-vis the other key supranational actors in the EU. Then, we turn to the Parliament's response to crises, with subsequent sections examining in turn: the migration crisis, Brexit, the Eurozone crisis, the democratic legitimacy crisis, and the Ukraine crisis in external relations.

Parliament Overview

The European Parliament (EP) is one of the two primary legislative bodies of the European Union and, unique among the core institutions of the European Union, is made up of democratically elected members (MEPs). Direct election of MEPs began in 1979, and European elections are held across all member states every five years, with the most recent elections held from May 23–26, 2019. Candidates are nominated by national political parties, though the exact procedures differ across member states. In some member states, regional lists are used, so as to maintain some degree of geographical proportionality of the elected representation. In other states, national party lists are used.

With the implementation of the Lisbon Treaty on December 1, 2009, the policy domains in which the European Parliament is institutionally coequal to the Council of the European Union were expanded.[1] The ordinary legislative procedure, previously called co-decision, is the primary form of legislative decision-making in the European Union, and the Council of the EU and Parliament both have powers of amendment and approval. While Lisbon expanded the policy domains subject to the ordinary legislative procedure, the Parliament still has only consultative capacity in some areas.[2] In addition to its legislative responsibilities, the European Parliament has several other capacities in which MEPs can influence and oversee policymaking in the European Union, including reports, committee hearings (Neuhold 2001; Whitaker 2011), and written questions (Proksch and Slapin 2011; Stenberg 2019), all of which can be used to both hold to account but also steer the European agenda (Poptcheva 2019). Perhaps its most important non-legislative function is budgetary approval. The EP may not have an explicit veto on budgets, but it does have the power of amendment, can participate in the joint conciliation committee for budgetary matters, and can delay implementation, all of which allow it significant influence on the final budget itself (Crombez and Høyland 2015). While the Council has won in various explicit budgetary standoffs, the Parliament's budgetary authority has been a key mechanism in recent years to extend the purview and authority of the EP in various policy domains.

The European Parliament has steadily had its relative power increased vis-à-vis the other major institutions of the European Union, generally gaining some capacities or authority with each major treaty revision (Follesdal and Hix 2006; Hix and Høyland 2013). By empowering the European Parliament, the

---

[1] The ordinary legislative procedure was extended to matters of agriculture, services, migration, structural and cohesion funds, and some judicial courts (Craig 2008: 110–111).

[2] Since the Lisbon Treaty, the Ordinary Legislative Procedure has been used in 77% of directives and 30% of regulations (Chalmers and Chaves 2014: 165–166).

European Union has sought to respond to charges of its democratic deficit (Featherstone 1994; Sánchez-Cuenca 2017). The Lisbon Treaty's extension of the ordinary legislative procedure for the Parliament was one clear attempt to increase responsiveness in European policymaking. At the same time, empowering the European Parliament has been argued to be an insufficient response to the democratic deficit. Although survey data showed that 76% of EU citizens considered the Parliament to be "totally important," a far smaller number (32%) considered that the EP had gained authority (Schweiger 2017: 193), in spite of the structural gains built-in by the Lisbon Treaty. Voter involvement in European elections has declined over time (Bhatti and Hansen 2012; Hobolt 2015; Fiorino et al. 2017), though this trend was bucked in many member states in the 2019 elections.

The European Parliament has also been an active institutional entrepreneur, seeking to expand its power relative to the other major European institutions (Lord 2011; Rosén 2015; Wiesner 2018). Some of these gains were substantively codified with the implementation of the Lisbon Treaty; however, the EP has continued to seek to extend its powers since 2009. Foreign and security policy has been one major domain in which the Parliament has been a clear policy entrepreneur (Riddervold and Newsome 2019). The EP actively leveraged its budgetary authority in the creation of the European External Action Service, the new European diplomatic corps, in order to ensure it had greater influence over EU diplomatic efforts (Raube 2012; Wisniewski 2013). The Parliament was able to use more community-based framing of defense issues to have influence in the implementation phase, even when they lack decision-making authority (Riddervold and Rosén 2016). And it has taken an important informal role in trade and other transnational policy domains in order to exert its preferences on final agreements (Meissner 2016). Broadly, this entrepreneurship has allowed the Parliament greater influence in policy domains where the ordinary legislative procedure is not in effect and the EP should structurally have less input on European policymaking (Farrell and Héritier 2003).

Political contestation in the European Parliament is organized primarily on a left-right political spectrum, with competition between ten European Political Parties (Europarties). In practice, there is not much coordination within Europarties as each is a federation, and national parties organizing candidate selection. While the left-right spectrum is organizationally dominant, there is increasingly a pro-/anti-Europe cleavage present in voting (Roger et al. 2017). Elected MEPs of these parties are then organized into political groups, which manage political activities of the parliamentary agenda. Europarties do not have a one-to-one relationship with party groups and may incorporate other like-minded MEPs; in the 8th Parliament (2014–2019), there were eight party groups, in addition to several non-attached MEPs. The largest party groups are the center-right European People's Party (EPP) (affiliated with the similarly-named European People's Party) and the Progressive Alliance of Socialists & Democrats (S&D), which is largely composed of members affiliated with the Party of European Socialists (PES). In recent parliaments, these two party groups have functionally governed in a grand coalition and agreed to alternate control of the President of the Parliament, with each group getting a 2.5 year term in charge (Ripoll Servent 2018: 45–47), although this arrangement fell apart in 2017. Generally speaking, national party preferences are the strongest prediction of voting behavior for individual MEPs (Hix 2002). National party membership in Europarties is sometimes politically contested itself, most clearly demonstrated by controversy regarding the ongoing membership of Hungary's Fidesz party in the European People's Party amidst domestic democratic backsliding under its rule (Alemanno et al. 2018; Bokros 2018; Rankin and Walker 2018). This controversy ultimately resulted in a February 2019 Fidesz ad campaign against European Commission President Jean-Claude Juncker—a fellow representative of the EPP—which brought about criticism from EPP party president Joseph Daul and led Juncker to call for Fidesz's expulsion from the EPP (EurActiv 2019). In other cases, the desire for far right parties to signal respectability to domestic audiences impacts which party groups they seek to affiliate with at the European level (McDonnell and Werner 2019).

The increasing membership in Euroskeptic party groups in the European Parliament has knock-on effects beyond a mere expression of voter discontent. Nathalie Brack's (2018) recent examination of Euroskeptic MEPs points out many ways in which they have opportunities to reduce the functionality of the institution: rhetorically attacking the chamber from within, refusing to compromise in deliberations. Euroskeptic parties are able to parlay success in a European election in several ways. First, and most fundamentally, the success of Euroskeptic parties encourages mainstream parties to become more Euroskeptic themselves. This has happened perhaps most notably and directly in the United Kingdom, where the success of the UK Independence Party pushed the Conservative Party in more Euroskeptic directions, ultimately leading to Prime Minister David Cameron's decision to hold the Brexit referendum (Bale 2018). Dinas and Riera (2018) find that the socialization effects of European Parliament elections lead younger voters to be less likely to support major parties in other elections. Even if Euroskeptic actors do not impact the positions of other parties, they are able to use the resources gained by being in the Parliament to have both more credibility and resources (Reungoat 2015) or higher turnout (Franklin 2017) in future elections. And the European Parliament can serve as an important venue for transnational cooperation among radical right groups, allowing them to build a network of cooperation and share best practices across national borders (Dolan 2018).

After several election cycles with declining citizen interest, EU citizens turned out in record numbers to vote as 51.0% of the eligible electorate voted in the 2019 EP elections thus constituting the greatest number of citizens voting in 25 years. The 2019 Eurobarometer survey also provided evidence that, on average, more citizens trust the EU, in fact citizens are more likely to express trust in the EU than in their own countries and institutions

(Bolin et al. 2019: 13; De Wilde, this volume). However, the two largest party groups, the center-right European People's Party and the center-left Socialists & Democrats, both lost a large number of seats and, importantly, a parliamentary majority between them. The new, explicitly pro-Europe Renew EU group, created as a result of a merger of the liberal ALDE group with MEPs from French President's Emmanuel Macron's La République en Marche party, was brought into the leadership of the European institutions for the first time. While far right parties made electoral gains, ultimately they gained fewer seats than many had predicted. The 2019 EP elections suggested that there are limits to the ability of Euroskeptic parties to exert influence in that the political goal of leaving the EU remains a "highly marginal position in EU politics"—especially considering the challenges of implementing Brexit—with only one hard Euroskeptic party expressly listing "exit" as the goal of political engagement, in contrast with soft Euroskeptic parties preferring less integration (Bolin et al. 2019: 26).

THE PARLIAMENT IN TIMES OF CRISIS

As the European institution is most directly accountable to voters, we might expect the European Parliament to be especially affected by crises. If voters perceive a crisis, they may expect politicians to come up with radical responses. In turn, this might lead for voters to support more radical politicians. The Parliament has consequently increasingly been a battleground for voters responding to crisis. Dissatisfaction with the European Union's handling of the financial crisis led voters to support more Euroskeptic parties (Hobolt and de Vries 2016), whose representatives were more willing to challenge the European Union's belief in the necessity of austerity measures by offering Keynesian alternatives, for example. Although in the run up to the 2019 European Parliament elections, scholars and commentators predicted that these elections would be seen as a referendum on Europe's handling of the migration crisis, as far right parties sought to use the influx of Syrian refugees since the 2014 election to galvanize electoral support (Lehne and Grabbe 2018; Newsome 2018), election returns reflected a waning in importance of the migration crisis as a mobilizing concern, and far right party groups gained fewer seats than their most optimistic projections. Together, the recent crises have impacted and continue to shape transnational politics in the European Union, as all the parties react to the new electoral cleavages created by the financial and migration crises: a pro-Europe majority in opposition to a Euroskeptic minority (Otjes and van der Veer 2016; Hooghe and Marks 2018).

The Migration Crisis

Over the past decade, the EP has become more active in migration policy and issued statements identifying shortcomings in member state-driven migration policies, including the Common European Asylum System (CEAS), and called for a unified approach across member states to international migration. In 2009, the EP drew attention to the problems generated by fragmented approaches to processing asylum claims across EU countries (European Parliament 2009: 11). Here the EP noted that member states were practically unable to deter asylum seekers from lodging claims across multiple EU member states owing to gaps in data sharing by member states to the Eurodac database. The EP also developed a common position on the European Asylum Support Office (EASO) and highlighted the need for increased member state funding of the EASO so that it could more effectively ease the burden of migrant processing in Mediterranean border states. Despite polarization among constituent parties on how far to pursue policy integration, the EP also urged member states to pool asylum policy in a new European Union Asylum Agency (EUAA). The EUAA would verify and assess asylum cases and thus replace the "responsibility principle" animating asylum policy under the Dublin Convention with a "capacity principle" that considered each member state's available resources to host asylum seekers (Newsome 2018: 596; Ripoll Servent 2019: 301).

Although the EP has been able to overcome internal party differences and articulate majority positions on migration and asylum policies, this has not been enough to push the EP's views forward in the context of the migration crisis. Rather, the migration crisis itself has rendered the prospect of deeper EU integration more controversial to EU member states, since they view common action as a choice to relinquish or retain sovereignty over core state powers in justice and home affairs (Ripoll Servent 2019: 294). The migration crisis has resulted in the EP's challenging member states more willing to invest their resources in the European Council for the purpose of blocking expanded supranationalism, including efforts by the European Parliament to push for common solutions (Schilde and Wallace Goodman; Bosilca, this volume).

The EU–Turkey deal provides an example of the weakness of the EP in pushing supranational solutions to the migration crisis. Member states, led by German Chancellor Angela Merkel, negotiated with Turkey so that it could be designated as a safe country of refuge for asylum seekers coming to the EU in exchange for financial aid and liberalized visa requirements, easing access for Turkish citizens to the EU. If the EU–Turkey deal had been an international agreement officially between the EU and Turkey, the deal could not enter into force without the EP's review and assent of the agreement. The European Parliament was in fact critical of the agreement and suggested it amounted to the EU ignoring fundamental rights violations in Turkey (Saatçioğlu 2020). However, member states released the settlement reached by the national governments of EU member states and Turkey as a "statement" which rendered it not legally binding and it was not "adopted as part of the EU architecture" (Niemann and Zaun 2018: 9; for an alternative view, see Crawford this volume). The EU–Turkey statement is thus significant as an instance of coordination among EU member state leaders for a common policy solution while rejecting EU supranational institutions, including the EP, as the means for reaching a common solution (Slominski and Trauner 2018: 109).

Brexit

In the negotiations around the United Kingdom's exit from the European Union, it is clear that notwithstanding the divisions among parties, that the EP was able to develop a unified position and set of interests—both internally and with the other major European institutions. The EP sought to bolster its own standing and support the survival of the EU as an entity (Bressanelli et al. 2019: 348) and successfully created a streamlined procedural process to facilitate its ability to speak with one voice. The European Parliament's Conference of Presidents appointed Guy Verhofstadt, the Chair of the ALDE (liberal) party group, as the EP's Brexit Coordinator. Verhofstadt was backed by a Steering Committee, with prominent members of the left-wing and centrist party groups. This consolidation of high-level leadership from a range of political parties allowed the EP to play a more assertive role in Brexit negotiations in spite of its limited formal role, which was limited to approval of the agreement (McGowan 2017: 82). At the same time, the Parliament broadly shared the same institutional goals as the Commission and the Council—especially EU (and British) citizens' rights—so while the Parliament asserted its position in Brexit negotiations (Brusenbauch Meislova 2019), the other major institutions likely provided less resistance than they might in the case of differences of opinion.

The Parliament itself will be tangibly affected in response to Brexit. Brexit has had a clear institutional impact: the overall number of MEPs has been reduced from 751 to 705; the remainder of the 73 MEPs previously allocated to the United Kingdom was distributed among the remaining member states in response to population changes on the continent. Spain and France each gained five seats as the biggest winners, but 14 of the 27 members gained seats (European Parliament 2018). However, as the Brexit deadline was extended to January 31, 2020, UK voters selected 73 new British MEPs, including 29 from the newly launched Brexit Party. The Brexit Party played a fairly limited role in the ninth EP as the only party with the single issue platform of exit from the EU.

The Eurozone Crisis

While the European Parliament has most clearly been affected by the EU in crisis through its tangible effects on party contestation, crises have affected the inter-institutional balance of power in the European Union as well. Crises have had both direct and indirect effects on both the structure and the capacities of the European Parliament. In some spheres, the response to crises has been to create new institutional avenues for oversight and MEP participation, as the European Union seeks to expand the supranational capacity to respond to major disruptions. This was especially true in the case of the European financial crisis. The European Parliament was given increased *de jure* supervisory authority over financial issues and the European Central Bank in the series of legislative efforts that followed the crisis. Most concretely, this consisted of a series of supervisory dialogues allowing for increased oversight as part of the Single Supervisory Mechanism, with additional oversight for the Parliament incorporated into the two-pack and six-pack legislative provisions designed to make the European Central Bank (ECB) more accountable (Fromage 2018). However, while the EP's authority to hold hearings and conduct oversight increased, it lacks the capacity to enforce significant consequences on the ECB (Amtenbrink and Markakis 2017).

Did the EP act to further supranational integration in the context of the Eurozone crisis? In order to answer this question, new intergovernmentalism (Schimmelfennig 2015, this volume) is particularly useful in that it specifies how supranational institutions can simultaneously seek to enhance their voice in decision-making processes dominated by member states yet do so in a way that advances both the substantive policy preferences of member states as well as their desire to maintain dominance of the policy area more broadly. While a supranational body such as the EP may act in its own interest to gain a seat at the table, once among the decision-makers that same body may be motivated *strategically* to support member state positions, including those that limit the impact of supranational actors. In the case of the Eurozone crisis, the EP was initially barred from participation in the Taskforce led by European Council President Van Rompuy (Warren 2018: 639). Once the deliberations of the Taskforce advanced and the Commission decided to preempt the Taskforce's proposed reforms of the Eurozone with its own six-pack of legislative proposals, the EP utilized issue linkage in order to increase its influence on the content and the direction of the reform proposal. In this case of the Eurozone crisis, while the European Council and the Commission nominally accepted the EP's interpretation of co-decision to extend to this reform package via issue linkage, neither the ECON committee of the EP nor the EP as a whole advanced a perspective on EMU reform that differed significantly from that of the European Council or the Commission. This was owing to the left-right party division present in the EP, in which center-right parties supported a reform package aligned with austerity and fiscal discipline espoused by the member states (particularly Germany) and the Commission, and center-left parties favored a neo-Keynesian approach that sought to preserve jobs in the impacted indebted countries such as Greece (Warren 2018: 640). Members of both the European's People's Party (EPP) and the Alliance of Liberals and

Democrats (ALDE) on the ECON committee underscored the need for a "sound and sustainable fiscal governance framework." In contrast, the MEPs from the center-left Progressive Alliance of Socialists and Democrats (S&D) stated "austerity alone won't resolve the eurozone crisis" and proposed "a strong system of Eurobonds, a real European budget…and a Growth and jobs pact" (Warren 2018: 641). Not only was the EP unable to bridge the divide among parties on pro-austerity and anti-austerity approaches, but the Council and the Commission sought to exploit this divide to advance the pro-austerity consensus these bodies had reached without the EP: "The Council sought to 'divide and rule' the Alliance of Liberals and Democrats for Europe (ALDE) to ensure that the EP's plenary did not support the suggestions by the Committee on Economic and Monetary Affairs (ECON) to introduce a Redemption Fund in the Two Pack" (Dionigi and Koop 2019: 781). In fact, as Warren points out, all the Parliament could agree upon was an enlarged role for the EP; however, MEPs could not agree on the content of the reform or successfully push for increased decision-making on economic reform to be moved out of the intergovernmental arena into supranational purview.

Although the EP could neither spearhead the EMU reform package nor steer its execution, the EP took advantage of the Eurozone crisis and increased its oversight capacity (Dionigi and Koop 2019: 776). The EP succeeded in formalizing regular updates from the ECB to the ECON committee to address Banking Union, and the EP also formalized information sharing from the Commission with ECON on "countries under enhanced and post-programme surveillance" as well as updates on the implementation of fiscal reform in these countries (Dionigi and Koop 2019: 781). One of the weaknesses of EMU was the limited ability of citizens to access channels to shape policy, which was seen to signify the lack of a leading role for the EP. Indeed, the EP argued that enhancing its own role was key to safeguarding democratic integrity of the EU (Dionigi and Koop 2019: 784).

The limited effectiveness of the EP's oversight capacity gained over the ECB is representative of many of the EU's institutional changes made in response to crises: the actual authority gained by the European Parliament with these new powers has been somewhat blunted. The politics of crisis response, which often require quick, decisive action, do not necessarily lend themselves to the legislative policymaking cycles of the European Parliament (White 2014). Instead, the emphasis on executive policymaking minimizes the role of the EP, helping to contribute to the European Union's legitimacy crisis, as the elected representatives are functionally denied the opportunity to shape reforms and exercise substantive oversight (Dawson and de Witte 2013; Hobolt 2018). While the European Parliament has attempted to remain involved in the policymaking through hearings, resolutions, and oversight, it has not been able to drive crisis response (Nugent 2017: 175–176).

Democratic Legitimacy Crisis

One of the prime positions taken by the EP as justification for expanding policy areas under its purview has been its role as the only directly elected supranational institution and therefore the substantive guarantor of democratic legitimacy within the EU. However, one of the crises afflicting the EU has been the threat to democratic legitimacy, embodied by the slide into illiberalism experienced in Eastern European member states. In these specific situations, the EP has struggled to enforce democratic norms within its own body. Illiberal parties won electoral contests for EP seats and many play major roles within the European Parliament, even if ultimately a majority of MEPs have moved to sanction illiberal parties for their violations of democratic norms.

The European Union has two primary means of sanctioning member states for violations: infringement procedures and Article 7 of the Treaty on European Union. While infringement procedures are best suited for specific violations, the invocation of Article 7 is the strongest means of sanctioning a member state for persistent undemocratic and/or illiberal behavior (Kochenov and Pech 2015). While the EP has no formal role in infringement procedures, it plays a concrete role in Article 7 procedures. Article 7 has two variants: preventative and sanctioning. Both require EP approval to enact; however, the Parliament only has the power to initiate a preventative instance, the weaker of the two procedures.[3] The European Council or European Commission can initiate the sanctioning procedure, which results in stronger penalties. Either procedure requires a simple majority of total MEPs, as well as a 2/3 majority of votes cast, in order to pass the Parliament.

Article 7 has been preliminarily invoked by the European Union twice: initiated by the Commission against Poland in 2017 and by the Parliament against Hungary in 2018. However, party politics at the European level, including in the European Parliament, plays an important role in the sanctioning of member states. Because Europarties often want to defend national members, it can be difficult to mobilize action (Sedelmeier 2014; Kelemen 2017, 2020; Raube and Costa Reis, this volume). The case of backsliding in Hungary provides a clear example of this. For example, when faced with Fidesz's curtailment of the independent judiciary and of free speech by the media in Hungary, MEPs were initially unable to secure the votes necessary to sanction Fidesz and Hungary in 2015. One of the main obstacles to sanctioning Fidesz was its caucusing with the European People's Party, the center-right party group in the EP, which was unwilling to support sanctions that would weaken its own position in the Parliament (Kelemen 2017). However, by 2018, the mood in the EP shifted. After receiving a report from MEP Judith Sargentini, the rapporteur responsible for the European Parliament's report on violations of fundamental values in Hungary, enough center-right political parties in the EP

---

[3] Passing the sanctioning procedure would suspend a member state's voting rights in the Council.

supported triggering Article 7 and sanctioning Fidesz for violating democratic norms to reach the necessary parliamentary majority. When confronted with a similar challenge to democratic norms from the Law and Justice Party (PiS) in Poland, the center-right political party grouping in the EP took a stance in favor of publicly reprimanding PiS, joining MEPs in the center-left and leftist party groupings (Laffan 2019: 9–10). PiS, as a member of the much smaller ECR party group, lacked the political protections to delay action (Kelemen 2017: 229–230), so Article 7 procedures were opened against Poland before Hungary, in spite of Hungary's several-year head start on backsliding.

While these preventative Article 7 procedures against both Hungary and Poland have been opened and passed by the European Parliament, sanctions have not been invoked on either country because they remain blocked in the European Council. Full implementation of Article 7 procedures is a high bar to clear politically (Sedelmeier 2017). Even where the European Parliament has been able to overcome the self-interest of party groups to move against backsliding member states, it has ultimately been unable to push sanctions through the more intergovernmental European institutions.

Ukraine and the Crisis in External Relations

With the Ukraine crisis, the EP consolidated some gains it had made in attaining new informal powers in common foreign and security policy (CFSP), including powers it has executed in opposition to member state interests, despite the lack of specific guidelines in the Lisbon Treaty increasing the role of the EP in EU external relations. This was not without precedent. Previously, the EP shaped the Atalanta mission on the high seas beyond the expressed interests of member states by extending its purview from long-haul boats containing industrial and commercial goods to also include fishing fleets (Riddervold and Rosén 2016: 694). In response to the Ukraine crisis, the EP inserted itself into the opportunity created by disagreement among member states on a common response and suggested a parliamentary envoy get involved (Nitoiu and Sus 2017: 79; Riddervold, this volume).

When member state governments balked in 2011 at identifying a common response to illiberal developments in Ukraine such as the jailing of members of parliament, the EP moved quickly to nominate and dispatch its own observers to the region—former Polish President Aleksander Kwaśniewski and former EP President Pat Cox (Fonck 2018; Nitoiu and Sus 2017: 79). One of the main goals of the EP observers was to interact with the imprisoned former head of government, Yulia Tymoshenko, and use their presence as a safeguard against procedural irregularities during her trial. In this way, the EP gained new competences as a supranational diplomatic actor (Nitoiu and Sus 2017: 78–79). As a result of their efforts, the EP envoy convinced the Azarov government to relax punitive measures for dissent and emancipate some detainees from state detention. Cox and Kwaśniewski argued that such steps taken by the Azarov government would only cement the likelihood of future cooperation between the EU and Ukraine. At the close of the EP mission, Ukraine had not fulfilled the criteria required to conclude formal association status. At the same time, this case shows the competitive nature of the European Parliament in foreign policy, as it seeks to expand its institutional role and overtake some of the traditional roles of diplomats (Nitoiu and Sus 2017: 73; Riddervold and Newsome 2019).

Conclusion

The European Parliament has offered solutions to the crises afflicting EU that have not always been welcomed by the Commission and the member states. The migration crisis undermined the EP, in that the member states not only have not been receptive to the Parliament's arguments for common asylum reform, but member states circumvented the supranational institutions in the EU–Turkey statement. On the other hand, with Brexit, the EP bolstered its institutional position by expanding its role from mere assent to the terms of negotiation and succeeded in securing a seat at the table for the EP Brexit coordinator Verhofstadt at the beginning of the process. When it comes to the substance of the Brexit agreement, we evaluate this as beneficial for further integration in that the EP and the Commission were able to reach agreement on the three key issues of EU citizens' rights, the financial settlement, and the Irish border (Bressanelli et al. 2019: 358). At the same time, owing to the fact that the EP did not have different views from the Commission on any of the three issues, we do not view this as directly improving the EP's influence as a supranational actor.

The series of crises affecting the European Union has also reduced some of the avenues for political entrepreneurship that might have otherwise been open to the European Parliament after the Lisbon Treaty. Müller Gómez et al. (2019) find that the response to the European financial crisis was dominated by the member states through the European Council, minimizing the enhanced formal powers gained by the European Parliament in the post-Lisbon era. Civil society has seemingly responded to the disempowerment of the EP on financial issues by reducing its emphasis on the Parliament as a means of furthering its goals on issues of financial oversight and instead pursuing other channels (Crespy and Parks 2019), potentially weakening long-standing ties with civil society. While the European Parliament has made incremental *de facto* and *de jure* gains in response to the crises facing the European Union in several areas, it has been overruled by other European institutions when their goals come into conflict and has not found a clear path to future institutional enhancement.

REFERENCES

Alemanno, A., Kelemen, R. D., & Pech, L. (2018). Europe's Shameful Silence—An Open Letter to EU Leaders from Jean Monnet Chairs. *Verfassungsblog* (blog). Available at: https://verfassungsblog.de/europes-shameful-silence-an-open-letter-to-eu-leaders-from-jean-monnet-chairs/. Accessed 10 Dec 2018.

Amtenbrink, F., & Markakis, M. (2017). *Towards a Meaningful Prudential Supervision Dialogue in the Euro Area? A Study of the Interaction Between the European Parliament and the European Central Bank in the Single Supervisory Mechanism* (Working Paper 2017/081). ADEMU Working Paper Series. A Dynamic Economic and Monetary Union. Available at: https://www.ssrn.com/abstract=3218861.

Bale, T. (2018). Who Leads and Who Follows? The Symbiotic Relationship Between UKIP and the Conservatives—And Populism and Euroscepticism. *Politics, 38*(3), 263–277. Available at: https://doi.org/10.1177/0263395718754718.

Bhatti, Y., & Hansen, K. M. (2012). The Effect of Generation and Age on Turnout to the European Parliament—How Turnout Will Continue to Decline in the Future. *Electoral Studies, 31*(2), 262–272. Available at: https://doi.org/10.1016/j.electstud.2011.11.004.

Biermann, F., Guérin, N., Jagdhuber, S., Rittberger, B., & Weiss, M. (2019). Political (Non-)Reform in the Euro Crisis and the Refugee Crisis: A Liberal Intergovernmentalist Explanation. *Journal of European Public Policy, 26*(2), 246–266. Available at: https://doi.org/10.1080/13501763.2017.1408670.

Bokros, L. (2018). Populist Threats to Democracy in Europe: The Responsibility of Mainstream Parties in the West. In C. Y. Robertson-von Trotha (Ed.), *NationEUrope: The Polarised Solidarity Community* (pp. 87–94). Baden-Baden: Nomos.

Bolin, N., Falasca, K., Grusell, M., & Nord, L. (Eds.). (2019). *Euroflections: Leading Academics on the European Elections 2019*. Sundsvall: Mittuniversitetet. Available at: https://www.euroflections.se.

Brack, N. (2018). *Opposing Europe in the European Parliament: Rebels and Radicals in the Chamber*. London: Palgrave Macmillan.

Bressanelli, E., Chelotti, N., & Lehmann, W. (2019). Negotiating Brexit: The European Parliament Between Participation and Influence. *Journal of European Integration, 41*(3), 347–368.

Brusenbauch Meislova, M. (2019). The European Parliament in the Brexit Process: Leading Role, Supporting Role or Just a Small Cameo? In T. Christensen & D. Fromage (Eds.), *Brexit and Democracy* (pp. 235–261). London: Palgrave Macmillan.

Chalmers, D., & Chaves, M. (2014). EU Law-Making and the State of European Democratic Agency. In O. Cramme & S. B. Hobolt (Eds.), *Democratic Politics in a European Union Under Stress* (pp. 155–179). Oxford: Oxford University Press. Available at: https://doi.org/10.1093/acprof:oso/9780198724483.003.0009.

Craig, P. (2008). The Role of the European Parliament Under the Lisbon Treaty. In S. Griller & J. Ziller (Eds.), *The Lisbon Treaty: EU Constitutionalism Without a Constitutional Treaty?* (pp. 109–134). Vienna: Springer. Available at: https://doi.org/10.1007/978-3-211-09429-7_5.

Crespy, A., & Parks, L. (2019). The European Parliament and Civil Society. In O. Costa (Ed.), *The European Parliament in Times of EU Crisis* (pp. 203–223). Cham:

Springer International Publishing. Available at: https://doi.org/10.1007/978-3-319-97391-3_10.

Crombez, C., & Høyland, B. (2015). The Budgetary Procedure in the European Union and the Implications of the Treaty of Lisbon. *European Union Politics, 16*(1), 67–89. Available at: https://doi.org/10.1177/1465116514552202.

Dawson, M., & de Witte, F. (2013). Constitutional Balance in the EU After the Euro-Crisis. *The Modern Law Review, 76*(5), 817–844. Available at: https://doi.org/10.1111/1468-2230.12037.

Dinas, E., & Riera, P. (2018). Do European Parliament Elections Impact National Party System Fragmentation? *Comparative Political Studies, 51*(4), 447–476. Available at: https://doi.org/10.1177/0010414017710259.

Dionigi, M., & Koop, C. (2019). Losing Out on Substance But Winning Procedurally? The European Parliament and Accountability in Crisis Legislation. *West European Politics, 42*(4), 776–802.

Dolan, L. (2018). *Radical Right-Wing Populism as a Transnational Movement*. Paper presented at the 59th International Studies Association Convention, San Francisco.

EurActiv. (2019, February 19). Hungary's Ruling Party Doesn't Belong in EPP, Says Juncker. *EurActiv*. Available at: https://www.euractiv.com/section/eu-elections-2019/news/hungarys-ruling-party-doesnt-belong-in-epp-says-juncker/.

European Parliament. (2009). *Multi-Annual Programme 2010–2014 Regarding the Area of Freedom, Security and Justice (Stockholm Programme): European Parliament Resolution of 25 November 2009 on the Communication from the Commission to the European Parliament and the Council—An Area of Freedom, Security and Justice Serving the Citizen—Stockholm Programme*. Available at: http://www.europarl.europa.eu/sides/getDoc.do?type=TA&reference=P7-TA-2009-0090&format=XML&language=EN.

European Parliament. (2018, February 1). *EU Elections: How Many MEPs Will Each Country Get in 2019?* Available at: http://www.europarl.europa.eu/news/en/headlines/eu-affairs/20180126STO94114/eu-elections-how-many-meps-will-each-country-get-in-2019.

Farrell, H., & Héritier, A. (2003). Formal and Informal Institutions Under Codecision: Continuous Constitution-Building in Europe. *Governance, 16*(4), 577–600.

Featherstone, K. (1994). Jean Monnet and the 'Democratic Deficit' in the European Union. *JCMS: Journal of Common Market Studies, 32*(2), 149–170.

Fiorino, N., Pontarollo, N., & Ricciuti, R. (2017). *Supra National, National and Regional Dimensions of Voter Turnout in European Parliament Elections* (JCR Technical Reports EUR 28856 EN). Brussels: European Commission.

Follesdal, A., & Hix, S. (2006). Why There Is a Democratic Deficit in the EU: A Response to Majone and Moravcsik. *JCMS: Journal of Common Market Studies, 44*(3), 533–562. Available at: https://doi.org/10.1111/j.1468-5965.2006.00650.x.

Fonck, D. (2018). Servants or Rivals? Uncovering the Drivers and Logics of the European Parliament's Diplomacy During the Ukrainian Crisis. In K. Raube, M. Müftüler-Baç, & J. Wouters (Eds.), *Parliamentary Cooperation and Diplomacy in the EU* (pp. 306–323). Cheltenham: Edward Elgar.

Franklin, M. N. (2017). EP Elections as Stepping-Stones to Eurosceptic Party Success. In J. H. Nielsen & M. N. Franklin (Eds.), *The Eurosceptic 2014 European Parliament Elections* (pp. 223–238). London: Palgrave Macmillan UK. Available at: https://doi.org/10.1057/978-1-137-58696-4_11.

Fromage, D. (2018). The European Parliament in the Post-Crisis Era: An Institution Empowered on Paper Only? *Journal of European Integration, 40*(3), 281–294. Available at: https://doi.org/10.1080/07036337.2018.1450405.

Hix, S. (2002). Parliamentary Behavior with Two Principals: Preferences, Parties, and Voting in the European Parliament. *American Journal of Political Science, 46*(3), 688. Available at: https://doi.org/10.2307/3088408.

Hix, S., & Høyland, B. (2013). Empowerment of the European Parliament. *Annual Review of Political* Science, *16*(1), 171–189. Available at: https://doi.org/10.1146/annurev-polisci-032311-110735.

Hobolt, S. B. (2015). The 2014 European Parliament Elections: Divided in Unity?: European Parliament Elections. *JCMS: Journal of Common Market Studies 53*(September), 6–21. Available at: https://doi.org/10.1111/jcms.12264.

Hobolt, S. B. (2018). The Crisis of Legitimacy of European Institutions. In O. Bouin, J. Caraça, G. Cardoso, J. B. Thompson, & M. Wievorka (Eds.), *Europe's Crises* (pp. 243–268). Cambridge: Polity.

Hobolt, S. B., & de Vries, C. (2016). Turning Against the Union? The Impact of the Crisis on the Eurosceptic Vote in the 2014 European Parliament Elections. *Electoral Studies, 44*(December), 504–514. Available at: https://doi.org/10.1016/j.electstud.2016.05.006.

Hooghe, L., & Marks, G. (2018). Cleavage Theory Meets Europe's Crises: Lipset, Rokkan, and the Transnational Cleavage. *Journal of European Public Policy, 25*(1), 109–135. Available at: https://doi.org/10.1080/13501763.2017.1310279.

Kelemen, R. D. (2017). Europe's Other Democratic Deficit: National Authoritarianism in Europe's Democratic Union. *Government and Opposition, 52*(2), 211–238.

Kelemen, R. D. (2020). The European Union's Authoritarian Equilibrium. *Journal of European Public Policy, 27*(3), 481–499. Available at: https://doi.org/10.1080/13501763.2020.1712455.

Kochenov, D., & Pech, L. (2015). *Upholding the Rule of Law in the EU: On the Commission's 'Pre-Article 7 Procedure' as a Timid Step in the Right Direction* (EUI Working Paper RSCAS 2015/24).

Laffan, B. (2019). The European Parliament in Turbulent Political Times: Concluding Reflections. *Journal of European Integration, 41*(3), 347–363.

Lehne, S., & Grabbe, H. (2018, December 11). *2019 European Parliament Elections Will Change the EU's Political Dynamics*. Brussels: Carnegie Europe. Available at: https://carnegieeurope.eu/2018/12/11/2019-european-parliament-electi ons-will-change-eu-s-political-dynamics-pub-77922.

Lord, C. (2011). The European Parliament and the Legitimation of Agencification. *Journal of European Public Policy, 18*(6), 909–925. Available at: https://doi.org/10.1080/13501763.2011.593317.

McDonnell, D., & Werner, A. (2019). *International Populism: The Radical Right in the European Parliament*. London: Hurst.

McGowan, L. (2017). *Preparing for Brexit: Actors, Negotiations and Consequences*. London: Palgrave Macmillan.

Meissner, K. (2016). Democratizing EU External Relations: The European Parliament's Informal Role in SWIFT, ACTA, and TTIP. *European Foreign Affairs Review, 21*(2), 269–288.

Müller Gómez, J., Wessels, W., & Wolters, J. (2019). The European Parliament and the European Council: A Shift in the Balance of Power? In O. Costa (Ed.),

The European Parliament in Times of EU Crisis (pp. 53–76). Cham: Springer International Publishing. Available at: https://doi.org/10.1007/978-3-319-97391-3_3.

Neuhold, C. (2001). The 'Legislative Backbone' Keeping the Institution Upright? The Role of European Parliament Committees in the EU Policy-Making Process. *European Integration Online Papers, 5*(10). Available at: https://doi.org/10.2139/ssrn.302785.

Newsome, A. (2018). Credible Champions: Transatlantic Relations and Human Rights in Refugee Crises. *Journal of European Integration, 40*(5), 587–604.

Niemann, A., & Zaun, N. (2018). EU Refugee Policies and Politics in Times of Crisis: Theoretical and Empirical Perspectives. *JCMS: Journal of Common Market Studies, 56*(1), 3–22.

Nitoiu, C., & Sus, M. (2017). The European Parliament's Diplomacy—A Tool for Projecting EU Power in Times of Crisis? The Case of the Cox-Kwasniewski Mission. *JCMS: Journal of Common Market Studies, 55*(1), 71–86.

Nugent, N. (2017). The Crisis and the EU's Institutions, Political Actors, and Processes. In D. Dinan, N. Nugent, & W. E. Paterson (Eds.), *The European Union in Crisis* (pp. 167–187). New York: Palgrave Macmillan.

Otjes, S., & van der Veer, H. (2016). The Eurozone Crisis and the European Parliament's Changing Lines of Conflict. *European Union Politics, 17*(2), 242–261. Available at: https://doi.org/10.1177/1465116515622567.

Poptcheva, E. (2019). Parliamentary Oversight: Challenges Facing Classic Scrutiny Instruments and the Emergence of New Forms of 'Steering' Scrutiny. In O. Costa (Ed.), *The European Parliament in Times of EU Crisis* (pp. 25–52). Cham: Springer International Publishing. Available at: https://doi.org/10.1007/978-3-319-97391-3_2.

Proksch, S., & Slapin, J. B. (2011). Parliamentary Questions and Oversight in the European Union. *European Journal of Political Research, 50*(1), 53–79. Available at: https://doi.org/10.1111/j.1475-6765.2010.01919.x.

Rankin, J., & Walker, S. (2018, April 5). EU Centre-Right Bloc Accused of Sheltering Hungary's Orbán. *The Guardian*, sec. World News. Available at: https://www.theguardian.com/world/2018/apr/05/eu-centre-right-bloc-accused-of-sheltering-hungarys-orban.

Raube, K. (2012). The European External Action Service and the European Parliament. *The Hague Journal of Diplomacy, 7*(1), 65–80. Available at: https://doi.org/10.1163/187119112X614657.

Reungoat, E. (2015). Mobilizing Europe in National Competition: The Case of the French Front National. *International Political Science Review, 36*(3), 296–310.

Riddervold, M., & Newsome, A. (2019). Chapter 3: The Role of EU Institutions in the Design of the EU Foreign and Security Policies. In E. C. Perez (Ed.), *The Routledge Handbook of EU Security Law and Policy*. London: Routledge.

Riddervold, M., & Rosén, G. (2016). Trick and Treat: How the Commission and the European Parliament Exert Influence in EU Foreign and Security Policies. *Journal of European Integration, 38*(6), 687–702. Available at: https://doi.org/10.1080/07036337.2016.1178737.

Ripoll Servent, A. (2018). *The European Parliament*. London: Palgrave Macmillan.

Ripoll Servent, A. (2019). Failing Under the 'Shadow of Hierarchy:' Explaining the Role of the European Parliament in the EU's 'Asylum Crisis.' *Journal of European*

Integration, 41(3), 293–310. Available at: https://doi.org/10.1080/07036337.2019.1599368.

Roger, L., Otjes, S., & van der Veer, H. (2017). The Financial Crisis and the European Parliament: An Analysis of the Two-Pack Legislation. *European Union Politics, 18*(4), 560–580. Available at: https://doi.org/10.1177/1465116517716311.

Rosén, G. (2015). EU Confidential: The European Parliament's Involvement in EU Security and Defence Policy. *Journal of Common Market Studies, 53*(2), 383–398.

Saatçioğlu, B. (2020). The European Union's Refugee Crisis and Rising Functionalism in EU-Turkey Relations. *Turkish Studies, 21*(2), 169-187. Available at: https://doi.org/10.1080/14683849.2019.1586542.

Sánchez-Cuenca, I. (2017). From a Deficit of Democracy to a Technocratic Order: The Postcrisis Debate on Europe. *Annual Review of Political Science, 20*(1), 351–369. Available at: https://doi.org/10.1146/annurev-polisci-061915-110623.

Schimmelfennig, F. (2015). Liberal Intergovernmentalism and the Euro Area Crisis. *Journal of European Public Policy, 22*(2), 177–195.

Schweiger, C. (2017). The Legitimacy Challenge. In D. Dinan, N. Nugent, & W. E. Paterson (Eds.), *The European Union in Crisis* (pp. 188–211). New York: Palgrave Macmillan.

Sedelmeier, U. (2014). Anchoring Democracy from Above? The European Union and Democratic Backsliding in Hungary and Romania After Accession. *JCMS: Journal of Common Market Studies, 52*(1), 105–121.

Sedelmeier, U. (2017). Political Safeguards Against Democratic Backsliding in the EU: The Limits of Material Sanctions and the Scope of Social Pressure. *Journal of European Public Policy, 24*(3), 337–351.

Slominski, P., & Trauner, F. (2018). How Do Member States Return Unwanted Migrants? The Strategic (Non-)Use of 'Europe' During the Migration Crisis. *JCMS: Journal of Common Market Studies, 56*(1), 101–118.

Stenberg, M. (2019). *Regional Variation in the European Parliament: Differences in Parliamentary Questions Between MEPs Representing Post-Socialist and Western Member States*. Paper presented at the 115th American Political Science Association Conference, Washington, DC.

Warren, T. (2018). The European Parliament and the Eurozone Crisis: An Exceptional Actor. *The British Journal of Politics and International Relations, 20*(3), 632–651.

Whitaker, R. (2011). *The European Parliament's Committees: National Party Influence and Legislative Empowerment*. London: Routledge.

White, J. (2014). Politicizing Europe: The Challenge of Executive Discretion. In O. Cramme & S. B. Hobolt (Eds.), *Democratic Politics in a European Union Under Stress* (pp. 87–102). Oxford: Oxford University Press. Available at: https://doi.org/10.1093/acprof:oso/9780198724483.003.0005.

Wiesner, C. (2018). The Micro-Politics of Parliamentary Powers: European Parliament Strategies for Expanding Its Influence in the EU Institutional System. *Journal of European Integration, 40*(4), 375–391. Available at: https://doi.org/10.1080/07036337.2018.1462351.

Wisniewski, E. (2013). The Influence of the European Parliament on the European External Action Service. *European Foreign Affairs Review, 18*(1), 81–101.

CHAPTER 15

The Court of Justice of the European Union

Lisa Conant

INTRODUCTION

The Court of Justice of the European Union (CJEU) exercises authority over European Union (EU) institutions, member states, and private actors. Comprised of the Court of Justice (ECJ) and General Court, the CJEU interprets EU law to promote uniform enforcement. Consisting of two judges from each EU country as of 2019, the General Court sits in a variety of panel formations and primarily resolves disputes concerning competition law, State aid, trade, agriculture, and trademarks for individuals and companies that are directly addressed by (or concerned with) an EU act. These rulings may be appealed on points of law to the ECJ, which also (1) issues preliminary rulings that interpret EU law in response to references from national courts, (2) decides whether member states have violated EU law in infringement proceedings initiated by the European Commission (Commission), and (3) hears claims from EU institutions and member states that EU institutions failed to take required action or violated EU treaties or fundamental rights. With one judge from each member state, the ECJ hears cases on three-to-five-judge panels, a Grand Chamber of fifteen judges, or the full Court, and it receives opinions in important cases from one of eleven advocates general. Fines for ongoing infringements and financial liability for failures to apply EU law give the CJEU more bite than most international courts. ECJ preliminary rulings "constitutionalized" the EU treaties, establishing the supremacy and direct

L. Conant (✉)
Department of Political Science, University of Denver, Denver, CO, USA
e-mail: conant@du.edu

effect of EU law, where EU law is given primacy over competing national laws and can be applied by national courts in the absence of domestic implementing measures. Substantively, preliminary rulings expanded free movement, equal treatment, fundamental rights, and EU citizenship. The ECJ's activism in developing these rights contributed to the most serious threat to EU judicial authority in the form of British exit (Brexit).

This chapter discusses how all EU crises generated disputes whose adjudication risked damaging political confrontations for the CJEU. It demonstrates that only the withdrawal of the United Kingdom (UK) from the EU constitutes a disintegrative "breakdown" for the EU and its Court of Justice. This chapter explains the origins of resentments that fueled Brexit and warns that these resentments challenge the legitimacy of the Court even in member states with no intention to leave the EU.

EU Crises and the Court of Justice: Why Brexit Eclipses Other Challenges

All five EU crises—Eurozone, democratic backsliding, migration, Ukraine, and Brexit—inspired CJEU litigation, and Brexit rejects ECJ jurisdiction. During the Eurozone crisis, the ECJ dodged a showdown when it fielded the German Federal Constitutional Court's first-ever reference, which questioned the EU legality and German constitutionality of the European Central Bank's (ECB) Outright Monetary Transactions (OMT) program that restored confidence in the Euro (Hinarejos 2015). The German court's acceptance of the preliminary ruling upholding the OMT (ECJ 16 June 2015) deferred to the ECJ, allowing the ECB to deploy a tool that relied on Germany (Payandeh 2017).

With respect to democratic backsliding, Hungary and Poland have come under fire for actions that defy fundamental values concerning the rule of law and democracy under Article 2 of the Treaty on European Union (TEU) (Kelemen and Orenstein 2016; Blauberger and Kelemen 2017). Commission discretion, however, has blunted infringement proceedings against Hungary. Deploying narrow legal bases rather than fundamental civil and political rights, the Commission also settled cases in the wake of symbolic compliance (Batory 2016). As a result, efforts to challenge Viktor Orban's authoritarianism have proceeded through a censure vote in the European Parliament under Article 7 TEU (Staudenmaier 2018)[1] and at the European Court of Human Rights (ECtHR), which is institutionally separate from the EU and controls its own docket rather than relying on any Commission or national judges to refer disputes. The rise in (1) applications alleging human rights violations and (2) pending ECtHR cases against Hungary between 2010 and 2016 (Bozóki and

---

[1] Hungary's vulnerability to any sanctions now rests with the Council of the EU, where four-fifths of national governments must agree to penalties for violations of the EU's fundamental values (BBC 12 September 2018).

Hegedus 2018) suggests that national courts in Hungary are gatekeepers insulating the regime from ECJ scrutiny. By contrast, the Commission invoked Article 7 TEU against Polish reforms forcing the retirement of Supreme Court judges over age 65, which enabled the Law and Justice party to appoint new judges and threaten judicial independence. In these infringement proceedings, the ECJ issued an interim order to suspend the Polish law, on grounds it infringed Article 19 TEU prohibiting age discrimination and Article 47 of the EU Charter of Fundamental Rights guaranteeing a fair and public hearing by an independent and impartial tribunal (ECJ 19 October 2018). Once the Polish government complied and reinstated judges forced into retirement (BBC 17 December 2018), the ECJ escaped another challenge to its authority.

Meanwhile, disputes concerning the migration crisis raise provocative choices. Responding to a Belgian reference, the ECJ ruled that EU law did not require an embassy abroad to grant visas to Syrians hoping to apply for asylum, deferring to the national immigration office and thereby skirting obligations to those displaced in Lebanon, Jordan, and Turkey (ECJ 7 March 2017). The opposite decision risked increasing refugee arrivals when the EU was acting to limit them.[2] Yet infringement proceedings against Poland, Hungary, and the Czech Republic for their refusal to admit refugees in an EU relocation scheme (ECJ pending) have no easy solution. These states led the opposition to EU redistribution of refugees, and are expected to resist enforcement. Relieving countries of responsibility to help front-line states receiving the most refugees, however, will infuriate Italy's nationalist government. The Commission may spare the ECJ from this lose-lose proposition by stalling its prosecution while the EU tries to secure its external borders (Deutsche Welle 29 June 2018).

In the crisis of Russian aggression against Ukraine, several Russian entities lost challenges against EU sanctions before the General Court. Interpreting the EU–Russia Partnership Agreement, the General Court upheld sanctions as proportionate to penalize Russian violations of Ukraine's territorial integrity, sovereignty, and independence (General Court 13 September 2018). Although EU sanctions failed to moderate Russian interference in Ukraine, and the losing parties may appeal to the ECJ on points of law, these challenges from foreign enterprises are unlikely to threaten the CJEU.

By contrast, Brexit poses a fundamental crisis for the ECJ. Both post-Referendum Conservative governments seek to end the Court's jurisdiction over the UK (Department for Exiting the European Union 2018; Commission 2019a). This situation fits John Ikenberry's definition of crisis as "an extraordinary moment when the existence and viability of the political order are called into question" (2008: 3). The ECJ sits atop the institutional structure that has resolved EU-related disputes concerning the UK for nearly half a century. If the UK negotiates new dispute resolution mechanisms with the EU, or if it

---

[2] The Syrians lodged applications for humanitarian visas over six months after the EU negotiated its March 2016 deal with Turkey to reduce irregular migration.

"crashes out" of EU transitional arrangments without any new trade agreement, the institutional order between the EU and UK "breaks down." Even if the UK softens Brexit by opting for a variant of the "Norway model" within the European Economic Area (EEA), institutional transformation ensues. The European Free Trade Area (EFTA) Court exercises jurisdiction over three non-EU EEA members (Iceland, Liechtenstein, Norway) and interprets EU law on the single market, but it does not cover common policies in the fields of agriculture, fisheries, taxation, foreign policy, and currency. Moreover, although the EFTA Court usually follows ECJ case law to promote uniform application of single market provisions across the entire EEA (including the EU-28), it has also "gone its own way" on "essential questions of European single market law" (Baudenbacher 2017). Institutionally, the EFTA Court is independent of and different from the ECJ: the EFTA Court has not recognized ECJ doctrines of direct effect and supremacy, national courts of last instance have no formal obligation to make references to it, and its "advisory opinions" in response to references are not formally binding on referring courts (EFTA Court 2018; Baudenbacher 2017). These institutional differences make becoming a party to EEA institutions without full EEA membership—"docking into" the EFTA Court—potentially appealing to the UK (Wright 2018).

Avoiding the "Brexit break down" required that the UK remain in the EU. The ECJ offered the British government a chance to reverse course when it enabled the UK's unilateral revocation of Article 50 and maintenance of its membership terms in a preliminary ruling responding to a Scottish court's reference (ECJ 10 December 2018). Governments led by Theresa May and Boris Johnson rejected that olive branch as violating the referendum outcome, and Johnson's government presided over the UK's withdrawal from the EU on January 31, 2020. Appeals from a case before the General Court offered the ECJ an opportunity to limit the damage that Brexit poses for EU citizens. A group of UK expats—prohibited from voting in the referendum because they had resided in other EU member states for 15 years or longer—challenged the Council's decision to begin withdrawal negotiations on the grounds that their exclusion from an election that eliminates their EU citizenship rights constituted discrimination on the basis of residence. Dismissing the action because negotiations take away no rights and an agreement could preserve rights (26 November 2018), the General Court dodged the controversy. Ruling before withdrawal negotiations were finalized, the ECJ rejected appeals (19 March 2019 and 11 July 2019) even though prevailing withdrawal terms reduced EU citizenship rights for all British nationals and non-British EU citizens already resident in the UK—terms which have now come into force (Council 12 November 2019).

The only way to avoid the "Brexit break down" would be for the UK to remain in the EU. The ECJ enabled the UK's unilateral revocation of Article 50 and maintenance of all existing membership terms in a preliminary ruling responding to a Scottish court's reference (ECJ 10 December

2018). Governments led by Theresa May and Boris Johnson reject this olive branch as violating the referendum outcome, but another government could hold a second referendum that legitimizes remaining. If Johnson's government tries to leave the EU without a deal, however, an appeal from a dispute in the General Court could offer the ECJ another opportunity to intervene. A group of UK expats—prohibited from voting in the referendum because they had resided in other EU member states for 15 years or longer—challenged the Council's decision to begin withdrawal negotiations on the grounds that their exclusion from an election that eliminates their EU citizenship rights constituted discrimination on the basis of residence. Dismissing the action because negotiations take away no rights and an agreement could preserve rights (26 November 2018), the General Court dodged the controversy. Ongoing disagreements over negotiated withdrawal arrangements risk the UK's "no-deal crash out" of the EU, abruptly ending EU citizenship rights for all British nationals and non-British EU citizens currently living in the UK. If the ECJ accepted the appeal, it could restore EU citizenship rights indefinitely for the British expats. An alternative intervention to invalidate (or rerun) the Brexit referendum on those grounds would be incendiary, eclipsing controversial judgments that inflamed Euroscepticism for decades. The fact that ECJ jurisdiction became a "red line" in the UK's Brexit negotiations should give rise to some institutional soul searching. Even if no other "exits" from the EU seem plausible, this does not mean that the ECJ's role in the Brexit crisis has no broader implications. Resentments that fueled the vote to leave exist across the EU, and British grievances about the role of the ECJ and its rulings are shared by governments and citizens in several other member states. As a result, this chapter focuses on the relationship of the Brexit crisis to the ECJ.

Brexit and the ECJ: Theorizing British Aversion to EU Judicial Jurisdiction

Neofunctionalist and liberal intergovernmentalist theories cannot explain why ending ECJ jurisdiction is among the "red lines" of UK governments. Predicting ongoing spillovers to the ever-closer union, neofunctionalism and related approaches such as transactionalism and historical institutionalism, with their one-way ratchets intensifying integration and sticky path-dependency, preclude any end to ECJ jurisdiction. Neofunctionalist accounts describe a lost past, where the ECJ insulates itself from politics through the "mask and shield" of legal reasoning and the relationships it cultivates with legal professionals serving the beneficiaries of integration (Burley and Mattli 1993). Liberal intergovernmentalism (Moravcsik 1998) and related rationalist institutionalist accounts do no better at predicting why the British are so frustrated that they insist on ending ECJ jurisdiction. Conceptualizing the ECJ as an agent that enforces bargains member states agreed, interstitially specifies legislation, and remains vulnerable to legislative overrule or noncompliance, the principals should not need to terminate their agent.

By contrast, the actor-centered institutionalism of Fritz Scharpf theorizes grounds for backlash against the ECJ. Because the intergovernmental consensus necessary for agreements impedes the correction of unwelcome decisions imposed by supranational institutions, the democratic legitimacy of EU institutions suffers (Scharpf 2006). The ECJ's enforcement of liberal treaties that privilege negative integration and strain national social systems exacerbates this problem (Scharpf 2010). Observing the left's critique of market bias, Liesbet Hooghe and Gary Marks develop a postfunctionalist theory to explain how the extension of European integration into areas associated with state sovereignty and national identity—including EU citizenship—mobilized opposition from the right and resulted in mass politicization of integration (2008) (see Marks et al., in Chapter 9). Surveys demonstrate that popular trust in the ECJ plummeted from 1993 to 1999, and remained low through March 2018 in all of the largest states except Germany (Fig. 15.1). The clash between nationalism and neoliberalism in the British Conservative party since the Maastricht era, and the popularity of the UK Independence Party (UKIP) (Hooghe and Marks 2008) coincide with popular trust falling most steeply among the British over the 1990s and remaining lower than other large member states until the Eurozone austerity era, when Italians, and ultimately the French, became similarly distrusting.

Protracted conflict over Brexit among elected politicians includes no champions of the ECJ, even while governments tolerate its temporary jurisdiction over the UK as a necessary evil of the transitional period and a more long-standing role in Northern Ireland (Commission 2019b). The next section

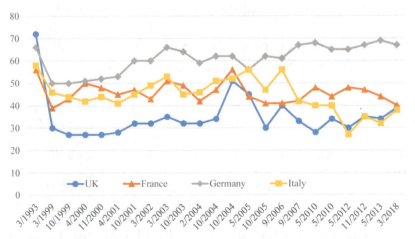

Fig. 15.1 Percent who tend to trust the European Court of Justice, 1993–2018 (*Source* European Commission. [1993–2018]. *Eurobarometer.* Survey question 'Trust in European Institutions: European Court of Justice.' http://ec.europa.eu/commfrontoffice/publicopinion/index.cfm/Chart/getChart/themeKy/9/groupKy/28. Accessed 28 Feb 2019)

draws on ECJ scholarship to explain why the UK wants out from under that Court, but may nonetheless agree to a limited degree of future ECJ influence.

Breach of Contract? Why the ECJ Generates Resistance

After decades of scholarship lauding the ECJ as the engine of European integration, critical voices multiplied. That the ECJ offers an escape from the dysfunctional EU legislative process (Falkner 2011) is no cause for celebration to its critics. In these accounts, (over)constitutionalized case law removes choices from elected representatives, threatening democratic legitimacy (Bellamy 2007; Grimm 2015; Scharpf 2016; Schmidt 2018). The ECJ created mandates to which national governments never agreed in EU primary (treaties) or secondary law (regulations and directives) when it pioneered solutions to promote the free movement of goods. Resentments emerged when the ECJ applied these principles to workers, but it took further extensions to "persons" and EU citizenship rights to fuel radical resistance to the EU (Schmidt 2018) and the ECJ (Kelemen 2016). Far from engaging in interstitial interpretation to "complete the contract" of general legislation, the ECJ breached the contracts member states made in EU law.

Constitutionalizing rulings declaring the direct effect and supremacy of EU law are ECJ inventions long contested by national supreme courts, whose challenges resurface (Komárek 2013; Dyevre 2016: 107–108; Madsen et al. 2017) and inspire justification from constitutional pluralists (Krisch 2010; Avbelj and Komárek 2012; Berman 2012). National judges in Nordic and Central/East European states refer disproportionately few cases to the ECJ for preliminary rulings that interpret EU law, shielding their governments from de-centralized EU enforcement (Bobek 2008; Wind 2010). British judges remain reluctant to engage the ECJ, making only 63% as many references for preliminary rulings as French judges and only 27% as many as German judges (Rabkin 2016: 95). Marlene Wind (2010) attributes such reticence to majoritarian political culture in countries such as Denmark, Sweden, and the UK, where constitutional review to overturn legislation does not exist. It was so alien to the British that Parliamentary debates about the UK's adoption of the European Communities Act 1972—years after the ECJ declared the direct effect and supremacy of EU law—show no realization that parliamentary sovereignty was at stake (Nicol 2001).[3]

The functional logic for the direct effect and supremacy of EU law is compelling since member states could otherwise free themselves from rules through new national legislation. However, deploying these doctrines to expand rights and obligations beyond the letter of the law in substantive areas

---

[3] Nicol shows that the government understood the implications of ECJ doctrines but did not enlighten MPs. The French Conseil d'État's rejection of supremacy until 1989 and other national courts' resistance to direct effect may have led the 1972 UK government to expect that constitutionalization was unenforceable.

is not necessary. Scholars disagree about the extent to which the ECJ responds to member state preferences, but several argue it is a strategic actor that avoids unacceptable rulings that would provoke (1) override through treaty revision or legislative correction or (2) pervasive noncompliance (e.g., Carruba et al. 2008, 2012). Historical accounts of the early period demonstrate that the ECJ was aware of strong preferences and tried to make rulings tolerable (Pollack 2013). A study of social policy jurisprudence on health care found that the Court narrows unwelcome legal principles to limit negative impacts of controversial decisions, simplifying implementation, and increasing compliance (Obermaier 2008).

Yet Olof Larsson and Daniel Naurin (2016: 398) reveal that the ECJ is more responsive to national governments who confirm the judicial bias of advancing integration, finding that observations supporting "more Europe" before the ECJ were four times more influential than those hoping to maintain "more domestic control". While this proclivity was uncontroversial for trade in goods (Larsson and Naurin 2016: 396), it helped precipitate the Brexit backlash because rulings were much less likely to respect state views concerning free movement of workers. The Court was also more attuned to national preferences in areas with qualified majority voting (QMV), acting in its strategic interest to avoid override since QMV makes it easier to overturn judgments with new EU legislation (Larsson and Naurin 2016: 401). Paradoxically, this renders the ECJ obtuse in the most sensitive areas: those where member states maintained vetoes. Taxation and social security/social protection are among the five policy domains requiring unanimity after the Lisbon Treaty (EU 2018). Disputes about free movement of workers/persons often concern benefits drawing on general taxation in states most annoyed by the ECJ's citizenship jurisprudence. Compounding these frustrations, Larsson and Naurin (2016: 392) found that the UK intervened more often than any other state. Although the British often argue for "more Europe" regarding competition policy and free movement of goods, services, and capital, they joined several states demanding "more autonomy" for free movement of persons.

Widespread acknowledgment of judicial retrenchment over the past several years exposes the neofunctionalist mask as a myth. Growing ranks of legal scholars see the Court shifting toward a more restrictive interpretation of EU citizen rights (Shuibhne 2015; Thym 2015; Verschueren 2015; O'Brien 2016; Sadl and Madsen 2016), which a team of political scientists attributes to its responsiveness to mass politicization (Blauberger et al. 2018). A blatant instance includes the ECJ upholding nationality discrimination in an infringement proceeding only days before the Brexit referendum (ECJ 14 June 2016). Assailing the judgment as part of the trend to dismantle EU citizenship rights, Charlotte O'Brien (2017, 209) argues that the "ECJ has played politics and lost," thereby sacrificing "the last vestige of EU citizenship on the altar of the UK's nativist tendencies." Quantitative analysis reveals that this propensity to "play politics" peaks in years coinciding with treaty revisions and shortly prior to signature, theorized to be a strategic effort to avoid irritating governments when they are best positioned to rollback the Court's jurisdiction or rulings (Castro-Montero et al. 2017).

Others have contested these arguments on grounds that treaty revision is too difficult to pose credible threats (Pollack 1997; Alter 1998; Höpner and Schäfer 2012; Davies 2016). This difficulty renders override through legislative correction futile, given that (over)constitutionalization enables the ECJ to reassert its preferences by declaring "politically corrective" secondary legislation incompatible with the treaty (Davies 2014; Schmidt 2018). Exhibiting faith in the law, Gareth Davies claims that the restrictive turn in EU citizenship rights results from less deserving litigants (2018).[4]

Meanwhile, evidence of overrides and noncompliance reflect a more nuanced picture of judicial politics. Scholarship identifies that the ECJ has been defied in ways that deprive its rulings of impact. Treaty change deserves attention in three respects. First, treaty revisions that contest past ECJ rulings exist. The Barber and Grogan Protocols to the Maastricht Treaty did not overturn judgments, but they circumscribed their impact, communicating the limits of toleration (Curtin 1992; Garrett et al. 1998). In the Amsterdam Treaty, Article 141 (4) overrode the ECJ's 1995 *Kalanke* ruling that rejected a German affirmative action measure (Conant 2002: 235). The rarity of these events could result from either a politically strategic court or the difficulty of attaining unanimous consent. Denying their significance, however, is folly, as they addressed pensions, abortion, and gender discrimination, all of which are salient, and the first had dire fiscal consequences.

Second, while member states never removed a competence that the ECJ possessed, they repeatedly excluded or limited ECJ jurisdiction for new areas from the Maastricht to Lisbon treaties. The exclusion of Justice and Home Affairs from ECJ jurisdiction in Maastricht has only partially eroded, as states negotiated opt-ins and opt-outs in subsequent treaties. The mechanism of decentralized EU law enforcement through national courts is truncated since only courts of last instance refer disputes to the ECJ for preliminary rulings concerning asylum and immigration, and states decide to allow or forbid references from lower courts in areas related to policing and judicial cooperation (Due 1998; Conant 2002). Reserving references for courts of last instance constrains access to justice since it forces parties to appeal through the national judicial hierarchy and then requires cooperation from the judges who are least likely to make references in most states, regardless of formal obligations. Despite net gains overtime, the ECJ had its authority over Article 7 TEU[5]

---

[4] Portraying Trojani or Brey as more deserving than Alimanovic, and casting Sala as more deserving than Dano requires a thick lens of white, male, and/or Christian privilege. The only unambiguously more deserving litigant is Baumbast, who was economically active abroad and possessed sufficient resources to support a family (2018). The ECJ's demographic composition makes these biases unsurprising (Gill and Jensen 2018).

[5] The provision under which the Council may suspend a member state's voting rights for violations of democratic values and fundamental rights.

limited to reviewing procedural requirements, and it remains largely excluded from the Common Foreign and Security Policy (Barents 2010).

Third, discussions about curbing the Court reflect the politicized context prevailing since the 1990s. The informal British proposal to overturn ECJ rulings through QMV in the Council of Ministers (Garrett et al. 1998) foreshadowed Scharpf's arguments that states be able to subject rulings to support from a majority of governments in the European Council (2009, 2010). European Parliament debates repeatedly addressed eliminating the right of lower courts to make references to the ECJ in the early 1990s (European Union 14 September 1993). In official proposals to the 1996 Intergovernmental Conference, the UK called for an appeals procedure within the ECJ, an expedited procedure for important references, and Council competence to initiate proceedings to correct judicial interpretations of legislation (UK 1996: 2–16). These proposals sought more voice for national governments, and Schmidt (2018) now emphasizes how the exclusive right of the Commission to propose all new EU legislation ratchets up integration because it privileges the Court's expansive interpretations of the treaties over explicit wording in secondary legislation. Parallel ideas for legislative overrides from a Conservative British government in the mid-1990s and progressive German academics today suggest that Luxembourg has a problem. The ECJ has unified not only the mainstream right and left in ire, but also those from majoritarian and constitutional democracies.

Meanwhile, legislative overrides in EU secondary law happen. Explicit regulatory reversals of rulings are rare, but as with treaty revision, they concern disputes over salient social policies affecting individual rights. The Council adopted an amending regulation in 1980 in order to overrule an ECJ judgment and reassert national control over access to cross-border health care, a restrictive approach later affirmed by both the Council and European Parliament in the patient rights directive (Martinsen 2015: 227). In response to a series of judgments expanding access to noncontributory social benefits, member states acted unanimously in the Council to overturn the Court's more generous approach with another amending regulation in 1992 (Conant 2002: 193; Martinsen 2015: 227).

More commonly, both EU and national legislative resistance to unwelcome ECJ rulings takes the form of "restrictive application as policy," "preemption" (Conant 2002: 32–33), "modification" (Martinsen 2015: 36), or "compensatory measures" (Schmidt 2018: 209–211) all of which entail legislation to limit jurisprudence. Examples encompass policy areas including the balance between mutual recognition and regulatory harmonization, liberalization of electricity and transportation, posting workers, collective bargaining, EU citizenship, and cross-border health care. Usually successful at the EU level, this strategy enjoys variable success when deployed unilaterally by national governments in domestic law (Conant 2002: 194–195; Blauberger 2012; Schmidt 2018: 209–210). Despite resistance, the ECJ long failed to take the hint, chipping away at restrictions in EU legislation until opposition became loud and widespread (Blauberger et al. 2018). Expansive interpretations of rights associated with the free movement of workers and their extension to "persons" in the advent of EU citizenship have been particularly controversial (Schmidt 2014; Blauberger and Schmidt 2017).

Given the difficulty in passing EU legislation, innovative case law often generates legislative gridlock and legal uncertainty about how principles developed for specific disputes apply more generally (Martinsen 2015; Schmidt 2018). Obedience to this creative case law is possible (Blauberger 2014; Schmidt 2018: 211), but confusion about implementation and "pushback" prevails. Schmidt observes that "the sheer complexity of the regulatory framework, which is driven by case law, is actually resulting in 'dis-unity', as national administrations and EU citizens ... make sense of ... the complicated legal regime in very different ways" (2018: 243). Lack of uniformity offers opportunities for national governments to avoid unacceptable policies, which reduces the risk of backlash against the ECJ (Conant 2002; Martinsen 2015; Werner 2016), but also results in unequal treatment (Schmidt 2018). Commission prosecution of questionable choices by national administrations can result in infringement proceedings. Yet in adjudicated disputes, compliance with ECJ judgments is delayed in half of all cases and resisted in another 10% (Hofmann 2018: 12). Even more cases are closed after symbolic compliance or payment of fines despite ongoing defiance, to protect constituencies or avoid costly implementation (Kilbey 2010; Batory 2016; Falkner 2015).

Decentralized enforcement through national courts directly applying EU law is unlikely to yield different outcomes. References constitute a minute fraction of EU law cases before national courts (Mayoral 2013; Hübner 2017; Pollack 2017). National judges in France, Germany, and the UK (Conant 2002: 190) and Denmark, Norway, and Sweden (Wind 2018: 336) prefer their own interpretations: they all cite treaties, conventions, and EU legislation more frequently than ECJ rulings that interpret these texts. Existing studies of national judicial interpretation indicate that outcomes vary across courts and often diverge from existing ECJ case law. Early studies found that British judges refused to overturn national provisions that were incompatible with EU law (Chalmers 2000), German and French judges independently interpreted EU law in ways that contradicted ECJ rulings (Conant 2002: 173, 209–210), and Spanish judges gave precedence to national case law when it conflicted with ECJ jurisprudence (Romeu 2006). Such resistance continues, with more recent studies finding that national courts enjoy discretion in their application of EU law (Davies 2012; Schmidt 2018: 219–224); national high courts across twenty-five EU member states failed to enforce EU law in a majority of cases (Mayoral 2015); and French, German, and Italian courts did not enforce the EU Race Equality Directive a decade after its adoption (Hermanin 2012).

To the extent that ambiguities persist and national administrations do not anticipate enforcement, governments may evade obligations. National administrators routinely "contain compliance" with unwelcome ECJ obligations by obeying the judgment with respect to the parties to the case and ignoring the broader ramifications for similar situations unless legal or political mobilization generates pressures for general application (Conant 2002). A growing literature confirms that such narrow compliance (Helfer 2013) and other evasions characterize many areas of attempted ECJ intervention, with several studies reinforcing the finding that domestic responses to ECJ principles determine practical impact. Judicial efforts to subjugate national labor relations to the free movement of services in the single market from the mid-2000s achieved their intended effects in Sweden and the UK but fell flat in Denmark, Germany, and Italy, owing to different constellations of interests and structures (literature reviewed in Hofmann 2018) or intransigent national courts (Perinetto 2012). Member states contested ECJ expansions of eligibility for social benefits and residence rights to migrating EU and third-country nationals long before these issues attracted mass attention, and national administrations consistently demonstrated their ability to limit access in practice (Conant 2002).

Equal Treatment, Migration, and the Absence of European Solidarity

Resistance is striking considering that few workers exploited free movement rights historically, with the exception of mass Italian migration in the early period of integration (Straubhaar 1988). Eastern enlargement transformed migration after 2004 as Ireland, Sweden, and the UK immediately accepted workers from newer member states, and opportunities for firms to post workers led to elevated migration in countries imposing the seven-year delay in free movement (Schmidt 2018: 210, 216). Mass migration ensued (Drew and Sriskandarajah 2007), and the social rights of EU citizenship captured the popular imagination (Blauberger and Schmidt 2017). Often portrayed as a reaction against eastern "others," frustration develops even when obligations extend equal treatment to wealthier westerners: Austria and Belgium oppose the free movement of German and French students in medicine and veterinary sciences (de Witte 2012).

Yet despite all the acrimony over "welfare migration," Austria and Germany succeed in denying EU citizens minimum subsistence benefits (Heindlmaier and Blauberger 2017), the UK deploys mass administrative procedures (rather than individual assessments) to exclude claimants from eligibility (Blauberger and Schmidt 2017), and Denmark and the Netherlands creatively "quarantine" mobile EU citizens from benefits coverage (Kramer et al. 2018). In cross-border health care, Danish courts insulated the national system from ECJ principles until prolonged pressure from the Ombudsman resulted in legislative reform while the Spanish legislature ignored its national courts' efforts to apply EU law (Martinsen and Mayoral 2017). Poland adopted EU requirements on cross-border care in legislation, but administrative practices remain restrictive and national courts look the other way (Vasev et al. 2017), displaying a pattern of legal change with no implementation that is common in post-communist democracies (Falkner and Treib 2008; Conant 2014). A case study of Danish welfare utilization reveals that local administrators follow the more restrictive provisions of EU legislation rather than the more expansive eligibility declared by the ECJ, enabling Denmark to limit residence rights to EU citizens who provide for themselves and grant full benefits only after a substantial work history (Martinsen et al. 2019).

Evasion and controversy concerning EU citizenship indicate that the ECJ exceeded the boundaries of solidarity. All "political corrections" of judgments relate to social policy (three treaty revisions and two legislative overrides), and reference rights to the ECJ remain restricted to courts of last instance in areas concerning asylum and immigration. Despite this history, judges displayed a slow learning curve when they overrode restrictions in the Citizenship Directive of 2004/38 for a decade before reversing course with the *Dano* judgment of 2014 (Blauberger et al. 2018).

BREXIT AND THE ECJ: BRITISH EXCEPTIONALISM OR WARNING BELL?

Blauberger et al. (2018) attribute the timing of ECJ retrenchment to judicial accommodation of the public mood rather than government preferences. If true, this was a blunder. Elected governments are more attuned to public sentiments than judges, and heeding government warnings would have been wiser than waiting until entitlements inflamed hostile attitudes about immigration. Often dismissed as exceptional, British Euroscepticism can be a harbinger of trouble. As leaders of two political corrections (Barber and exportability of noncontributory benefits), the British secured unanimous agreement. David Cameron's demands to reduce incoming EU citizens' access to benefits during negotiations for a better membership deal (Glencross 2016: 26–33) reflected common frustrations. British calls to curb the Court[6] and anti-immigrant Brexit grievances are wake-up calls. Even while campaigning to "Remain" as Home Secretary, May advocated working "to limit the role of the Court of Justice" (2016). She and her then shadow counterpart, Yvette Cooper, responded to animosity toward unlimited EU migration by claiming that talks about migrant quotas could follow a Remain victory (Glencross 2016: 33). As Prime Ministers, May and Johnson held fast to ending free movement of persons, and their negotiated withdrawals have UK courts merely taking "due regard" of CJEU decisions after the end of the transitional period (Council 19 February and 12 November 2019). Due regard requires fair consideration of all the facts, but it is not direct effect, which requires enforcement. Even if migration serves economic interests, national competence can limit rights to the economically active and/or self-sufficient. Granting equality to migrants who contribute for qualifying periods is all that governments agreed to in EU law; it is not a uniquely British preference.

---

[6]The UK also spearheaded the 2012 Brighton Declaration's agenda to reign in the ECtHR (Madsen 2016).

EU institutions heeding the limits of agreement may be the only hope to "head forward" even if this does not produce "more integration" (see Chapter 1 in this volume). Respecting the limits of legislation may even entail "spillback" relative to ECJ rulings, but tolerating a greater degree of national differentiation may be the only means to preserve most benefits of integration. By contrast, with Brexit and an end to free movement of people and ECJ jurisdiction, the disintegrative scenario of "break down" occurs.[7] Extending rights to resident EU citizens after the transitional period and a close trade and customs regime constitute *muddling through*, where path-dependent and incremental responses build on preexisting institutional structures.

As EU–UK negotiations continue while this goes to press, the EU has persistently insisted on "all freedoms or no freedoms" within the single market. Pragmatic compromises might serve the EU better in the long run. Europhiles and progressives may detest these trade-offs, but pretending that judges can impose unwelcome solutions is folly. Courts do not operate in vacuums, and judges become fickle friends in the wake of sustained pressure. Persistently defying democratically elected governments provokes backlash against judges and the beneficiaries of their generosity. Advocates seeking a more progressive, cosmopolitan Europe need to mobilize for this goal politically in democratic venues and socially in communities where national identity remains salient, rather than relying on legal rationality in the court house.

References

Alter, K. (1998). Who Are the Masters of the Treaty? *International Organization*, 52(1), 121–147.
Avbelj, M., & Komárek, J. (2012). *Constitutional Pluralism in the European Union and Beyond*. Oxford: Hart Publishing.
Barents, R. (2010). The Court of Justice After the Treaty of Lisbon. *Common Market Law Review*, 47, 709–728.
Batory, A. (2016). Defying the Commission. *Public Administration*, 94(3), 685–699.
Baudenbacher, C. (2017, August 25). *How the EFTA Court Works*. London School of Economics, Brexit. http://blogs.lse.ac.uk/brexit/2017/08/25/how-the-efta-court-works-and-why-it-is-an-option-for-post-brexit-britain/. Accessed 10 May 2019.
Bellamy, R. (2007). *Political Constitutionalism*. Cambridge: Cambridge University Press.
Berman, P. (2012). *Global Legal Pluralism*. New York: Cambridge University Press.
Blauberger, M. (2012). With Luxembourg in Mind. *Journal of European Public Policy*, 19(1), 109–126.
Blauberger, M. (2014). National Responses to European Court Jurisprudence. *West European Politics*, 37(3), 321–336.

---

[7] However, several years of domestic Brexit conflict, including two prime ministerial resignations and no foreseeable end to internal divisions over EU membership, suggest that the UK could face more disintegration than the EU.

Blauberger, M., Heindlmaier, A., Kramer, D., Martinsen, D., Thierry, J., Schenk, A., et al. (2018). ECJ Judges Read the Morning Papers. *Journal of European Public Policy*. https://doi.org/10.1080/13501763.2018.1488880.

Blauberger, M., & Kelemen, R. D. (2017). Can Courts Rescue National Democracy? *Journal of European Public Policy*, 24(3), 321–336.

Blauberger, M., & Schmidt, S. (2017). Free Movement, the Welfare State, and the European Union's Over-Constitutionalization. *Public Administration*, 95(2), 437–449.

Bobek, M. (2008). Learning to Talk. *Common Market Law Review*, 45(6), 1611–1643.

Bozóki, A., & Hegedus, D. (2018). An Externally Constrained Hybrid Regime. *Democratization*. https://doi.org/10.1080/13510347.2018.1455664.

British Broadcasting Corporation (BBC). (2018, September 12). *What Sanctions can the EU Impose on Hungary?* https://www.bbc.com/news/world-45485994.

British Broadcasting Corporation (BBC). (2018, December 17). *Poland Reinstates Supreme Court Judges Following EU Ruling*. https://www.bbc.com/news/world-europe-46600425.

Burley, A. M., & Mattli, W. (1993). Europe Before the Court. *International Organization*, 47, 41–76.

Carruba, C., Gabel, M., & Hankla, C. (2008). Judicial Behavior Under Political Constraints. *American Political Science Review*, 102(4), 435–452.

Carruba, C., Gabel, M., & Hankla, C. (2012). Understanding the Role of the European Court of Justice in European Integration. *American Political Science Review*, 106(1), 214–223.

Castro-Montero, J., Albas, E., Dyevre, A., & Lampach, N. (2017). *The Court of Justice and Treaty Revision*. Social Science Research Network (SSRN). https://papers.ssrn.com/sol3/papers.cfm?abstract_id=2978615. Accessed 30 June 2018.

Chalmers, D. (2000). *The Much Ado About Judicial Politics in the United Kingdom* (Jean Monnet Working Paper No. 1/100). Cambridge, MA: Harvard University.

Commission. (2019a, October 17). *Revised Text of the Political Declaration*. https://ec.europa.eu/commission/publications/revised-political-declaration_en. Accessed 18 Oct 2019.

Commission. (2019b, October 17). *Revised Protocol on Ireland and Northern Ireland included in the Withdrawal Agreement*. https://ec.europa.eu/commission/publications/revised-protocol-ireland-and-northern-ireland-included-withdrawal-agreement_en. Accessed 18 Oct 2019.

Conant, L. (2002). *Justice Contained*. Ithaca, NY: Cornell University Press.

Conant, L. (2014). Compelling Criteria? *Journal of European Public Policy*, 21(5), 713–729.

Council. (2019, February 19). Agreement on the Withdrawal of the United Kingdom of Great Britain and Northern Ireland from the European Union and European Atomic Energy Community. *Official Journal of the European Union*, C-66 I/1.

Council. (2019, November 12). Agreement on the withdrawal of the United Kingdom of Great Britain and Northern Ireland from the European Union and the European Atomic Energy Community. *Official Journal of the European Union*, C-384 I,1.

Curtin, D. (1992). Case C-159/90, The Society for the Protection of Unborn Children Ireland Ltd. v Grogan, Judgment of 4 October 1991. *Common Market Law Review*, 29(3), 585–603.

Davies, G. (2012). Activism Relocated. *Journal of European Public Policy, 19*(1), 76–91.
Davies, G. (2014). Legislative Control of the European Court of Justice. *Common Market Law Review, 51,* 1579–1608.
Davies, G. (2016). The European Union Legislature as an Agent of the European Court of Justice. *Journal of Common Market Studies, 54*(4), 846–861.
Davies, G. (2018). Has the Court Changed or Have the Cases? *Journal of European Public Policy,* https://doi.org/10.1080/13501763.2018.1488881. Accessed 30 June 2019.
De Witte, F. (2012). Transnational Solidarity and the Mediation of Conflicts of Justice in Europe. *European Law Journal, 18*(5), 694–710.
Department for Exiting the European Union. (2018, July 12). *The Future Relationship Between the United Kingdom and the European Union.* https://www.gov.uk/government/publications/the-future-relationship-between-the-united-kingdom-and-the-european-union. Accessed 20 July 2018.
Deutsche Welle. (2018, June 29). *EU Leaders Reach Migration Deal After Marathon Talks in Brussels.* https://www.dw.com/en/eu-leaders-reach-migration-deal-after-marathon-talks-in-brussels/a-44451703. Accessed 5 July 2018.
Drew, C., & Sriskandarajah, D. (2007). *EU Enlargement in 2007.* Washington, DC: Migration Policy Institute.
Due, O. (1998). Impact of the Amsterdam Treaty Upon the Court of Justice. *Fordham International Law Journal, 22,* 48.
Dyevre, A. (2016). Domestic Judicial Defiance in the European Union. *Yearbook of European Law, 35*(1), 106–144.
European Court of Justice (ECJ). (2015, June 16). *Gauweiler and Others v Deutscher Bundestag,* C-62/14.
European Court of Justice (ECJ). (2016, June 14). *Commission v United Kingdom,* C-308/14.
European Court of Justice (ECJ). (2017, March 7). *X and X v État belge,* C-638/16.
European Court of Justice (ECJ). (2018, October 19). *Commission v Poland,* C-619/18 R.
European Court of Justice (ECJ). (2018, December 10). *Wightman and Others v Secretary of State for Exiting the European Union,* C-621/18.
European Court of Justice (ECJ). (2019, March 19). *Shinder v Council,* C-755/18 P.
European Court of Justice (ECJ). (2019, July 11). *Shinder v Council,* C-755/18 OST.
European Court of Justice (ECJ). (Pending). *Commission v Poland,* C-715/17.
European Court of Justice (ECJ). (Pending). *Commission v Hungary,* C-718/17.
European Court of Justice (ECJ). (Pending). *Commission v Czech Republic,* C-719/17.
European Free Trade Area (EFTA) Court. (2018). *EFTA Court: Questions and Answers.* http://www.eftacourt.int/the-court/jurisdiction-organisation/questions-and-answers/. Accessed 3 Aug 2018.
European Union (EU). (1993, September 14). Debates of the European Parliament. *Official Journal of the European Communities,* Annex No. 3–434, 50.
European Union (EU). (2018). *Unanimity.* EUR-Lex. https://eur-lex.europa.eu/summary/glossary/unanimity/html. Accessed 18 Aug 2018.

Falkner, G. (2011). In and Out of EU Decision Traps. In G. Falkner (Ed.), *The EU's Decision Traps* (pp. 237–258). New York: Oxford University Press.
Falkner, G. (2015). Fines Against Member States. *Comparative European Politics, 14*(1), 36–52.
Falkner, G., & Treib, O. (2008). Three Worlds of Compliance or Four? *Journal of Common Market Studies, 46*(2), 293–313.
Garrett, G., Kelemen, R. D., & Schulz, H. (1998). The European Court of Justice, National Governments, and Legal Integration in the European Union. *International Organization, 52*(1), 149–176.
General Court. (2018, September 13). *Rosneft and Others v Council...*, T-715, 732, 734, 735, 737, 739, 798, 799/14.
General Court. (2018, November 26). *Shindler and Others v Council*, T-458/17.
Gill, R., & Jensen, C. (2018). Where Are the Women? *Politics, Groups, and Identities..* https://doi.org/10.1080/21565503.2018.1442726.
Glencross, A. (2016). *Why the UK Voted for Brexit*. London: Palgrave.
Grimm, D. (2015). The Democratic Costs of Constitutionalism. *European Law Journal, 21*(4), 460–473.
Heindlmaier, A., & Blauberger, M. (2017). Enter at Your Own Risk. *West European Politics, 40*(6), 1198–1217.
Helfer, L. (2013). The Effectiveness of International Adjudicators. In C. P. R. Romano, K. Alter, & C. Avgerou (Eds.), *The Oxford Handbook of International Adjudication* (pp. 464–483). Oxford: Oxford University Press.
Hermanin, C. (2012). *Europeanization Through Judicial Enforcement?* Ph.D. Thesis, European University Institute, Florence, Italy.
Hinarejos, A. (2015). Gauweiler and the Outright Monetary Transactions Programme. *European Constitutional Law Review, 11*, 563–576.
Hofmann, A. (2018). Resistance Against the Court of Justice of the European Union. *International Journal of Law in Context, 14*(2).
Hooghe, L., & Marks, G. (2008). A Postfunctionalist Theory of European Integration. *British Journal of Political Science, 39*, 1–23.
Höpner, M., & Schäfer, A. (2012). Embeddedness and Regional Integration. *International Organization, 66*(3), 429–455.
Hübner, D. (2017). The Decentralized Enforcement of European Law. *Journal of European Public Policy.* https://doi.org/10.1080/13501763.2017.1376701.
Ikenberry, G. J. (2008). Introduction. In J. Anderson, G. J. Ikenberry, & T. Risse (Eds.), *The End of the West?* (pp. 1–27). Ithaca, NY: Cornell University Press.
Kelemen, R. D. (2016). The Court of Justice of the European Union in the Twenty-First Century. *Law and Contemporary Problems, 79*, 117–140.
Kelemen, R. D., & Orenstein, M. (2016, January 7). Europe's Autocracy Problem. *Foreign Affairs.* https://www.foreignaffairs.com/print/1116396. Accessed 1 Mar 2016.
Kilbey, I. C. (2010). The Interpretation of Article 260 TFEU (ex 228 EEC). *European Law Review, 35*(3), 370–386.
Komárek, J. (2013). The Place of Constitutional Courts in the EU. *European Constitutional Law Review, 9*(3), 420–450.
Kramer, D., Thierry, J., & van Hooren, F. (2018). Responding to Free Movement. *Journal of European Public Policy, 25*(10), 1501–1521. https://doi.org/10.1080/13501763.2018.1488882.
Krisch, N. (2010). *Beyond Constitutionalism*. Oxford: Oxford University Press.

Larsson, O., & Naurin, D. (2016). Judicial Independence and Political Uncertainty. *International Organization, 70*(2), 377–408.

Madsen, M. (2016). The Challenging Authority of the European Court of Human Rights. *Law and Contemporary Problems, 79*, 141–178.

Madsen, M., Olsen, H. P., & Sadl, U. (2017). Competing Supremacies and Clashing Institutional Rationalities. *European Law Journal, 23*(102), 140–150.

Martinsen, D. (2015). *An Ever More Powerful Court?*. Oxford: Oxford University Press.

Martinsen, D., & Mayoral, J. (2017). A Judicialisation of Healthcare Policies in Denmark and Spain? *Comparative European Politics, 15*(3), 414–434.

Martinsen, D., Rotger, G., & Thierry, J. (2019). Free Movement of People and Cross-Border Welfare in the European Union. *Journal of European Social Policy, 29*(1), 84–99. https://doi.org/10.1177/0958928718767300.

May, T. (2016, April 25). *Remain Speech During Brexit Campaign*. https://www.conservativehome.com/parliament/2016/04/theresa-mays-speech-on-brexit-full-text.html. Accessed 30 June 2019.

Mayoral, J. (2013). *The Politics of Judging EU Law*. PhD dissertation, Department of Political and Social Sciences, European University Institute.

Mayoral, J. (2015). *The Politics of Judging EU Law*. Madrid: Instituto Juan March de Estudios e Inv.

Moravcsik, A. (1998). *The Choice for Europe*. Ithaca, NY: Cornell University Press.

Nicol, D. (2001). *EC Membership and the Judicialization of British Politics*. Oxford: Oxford University Press.

O'Brien, C. (2016). Civis Capitalist Sum. *Common Market Law Review, 53*, 937–978.

O'Brien, C. (2017). The ECJ Sacrifices EU Citizenship in Vain. *Common Market Law Review, 54*, 209–244.

Obermaier, A. (2008). *Fine-Tuning the Jurisprudence* (Working Papers of the Vienna Institute for European Integration Research). https://ideas.repec.org/p/erp/eifxxx/p0002.html. Accessed 20 June 2018.

Payandeh, M. (2017). The OMT Judgment of the German Federal Constitutional Court. *European Constitutional Law Review, 13*(2), 400–416.

Perinetto, P. (2012). Viking and Laval. *European Labour Law Journal, 3*(4), 270–299.

Pollack, M. (1997). Delegation, Agency, and Agenda Setting in the European Community. *International Organization, 52*(1), 177–209.

Pollack, M. (2013). The New EU Legal History. *American University International Law Review, 28*(5), 1257–1310.

Pollack, M. (2017). Learning from EU Law Stories. In B. Davies & F. Nicola (Eds.), *EU Law Stories* (pp. 557–602). New York: Cambridge University Press.

Rabkin, J. (2016). A Strange Institution. In H. Zimmerman & A. Dür (Eds.), *Key Controversies in European Integration* (pp. 91–96). London: Palgrave.

Romeu, F. (2006). Law and Politics in the Application of EC Law. *Common Market Law Review, 43*, 395–421.

Sadl, U., & Madsen, M. (2016). Did the Financial Crisis Change European Citizenship Law? *European Law Journal, 22*(1), 20–40.

Scharpf, F. (2006). The Joint Decision Trap Revisited. *Journal of Common Market Studies, 44*(4), 845–864.

Scharpf, F. (2009). Legitimacy in the Multilevel European Polity. *European Political Science Review, 1*(2), 173–204.

Scharpf, F. (2010). The Asymmetry of European Integration. *Socio-Economic Review, 8*(2), 211–250.
Scharpf, F. (2016). *De-constitutionalization and Majority Rule* (Max-Planck-Institut für Gesellschaftsforschung Discussion Paper 14). Cologne: MPIfG.
Schmidt, S. (2014). Judicial Europeanisation. *West European Politics, 37*(4), 769–785.
Schmidt, S. (2018). *The European Court of Justice & the Policy Process*. Oxford: Oxford University Press.
Shuibhne, N. (2015). Limits Rising, Duties Ascending. *Common Market Law Review, 52*, 889–938.
Staudenmaier, R. (2018, September 12). *EU Parliament Votes to Trigger Article 7 Sanctions Procedure Against Hungary*. Deutsche Welle. https://www.dw.com/cda/en/eu-parliament-votes-to-trigger-article-7-sanctions-procedure-against-hungary/a-45459720. Accessed 15 Sept 2018.
Straubhaar, T. (1988). International Labour Migration Within a Common Market. *Journal of Common Market Studies, 27*(1), 45–62.
Thym, D. (2015). The Elusive Limits of Solidarity. *Common Market Law Review, 52*, 17–50.
United Kingdom (UK). (1996). *Memorandum by the United Kingdom on the European Court of Justice*. London.
Vasev, N., Vrangebaek, K., & Kreplka, F. (2017). The End of Eastern Territoriality? *Comparative European Politics, 15*(3), 459–477.
Verschueren, H. (2015). Preventing "Benefits Tourism" in the EU. *Common Market Law Review, 52*, 363–390.
Werner, B. (2016). Why Is the Court of Justice of the European Union Not More Contested? *Journal of Common Market Studies, 54*(6), 1449–1464.
Wind, M. (2010). The Nordics, the EU, and the Reluctance Towards Supranational Judicial Review. *Journal of Common Market Studies, 48*(4), 1039–1063.
Wind, M. (2018). Laggards or Pioneers? In M. Wind (Ed.), *International Courts and Domestic Politics* (pp. 319–342). Cambridge: Cambridge University Press.
Wright, G. (2018, January 31). *EFTA Court Could Answer Post-Brexit Judicial Quandry*. Chatham House. https://www.chathamhouse.org/expert/comment/efta-court-could-answer-post-brexit-judicial-quandary#. Accessed 30 Mar 2018.

CHAPTER 16

The European Commission

Crisis and Crisis Management in the European Union: The European Council and European Commission Revisited

Hussein Kassim and Luc Tholoniat

INTRODUCTION

In the now voluminous scholarly literature on the crises that have consumed the European Union (EU) since the failed ratification of the draft Constitutional Treaty, the European Council has generally been presented as the European Union's 'crisis manager.' Most accounts have taken the view that the European Council alone among EU institutions possesses the necessary authority to take decisions, mobilize and commit resources, and put in place protective measures and the appropriate institutional arrangements. The story of the EU's response to numerous crises has subsequently been told largely in terms of action taken by heads of state and government at summits or

---

Luc Tholoniat is writing in a personal capacity and his views should not be seen to represent those of his employer or any EU institution.

The original version of this chapter was revised: The duplication of author name H. Kassim has been corrected and the disclaimer for Luc Tholoniat has been added. The correction to this chapter is available at https://doi.org/10.1007/978-3-030-51791-5_46

H. Kassim (✉)
University of East Anglia, Norwich, UK
e-mail: H.Kassim@uea.ac.uk

L. Tholoniat
European Commission, Brussels, Belgium
e-mail: luc.tholoniat@ec.europa.eu

in other intergovernmental forms (van Middelaar 2019). Since decisions are held to have been taken in one or many intergovernmental arenas, explanations for how the EU has reacted has been largely sought with reference to national preferences and the positions adopted by member states (Krotz and Maher 2016; Frieden and Walter 2017; Armingeon and Cranmer 2018; Schimmelfennig 2018; Moravcsik 2019; see Csehi and Puetter 2017 for an overview). With the exception of the ECB (see Hjertaker and Trangy, this volume) and the financial and economic crisis, the assumption has been—exaggerating only slightly—that the input of other EU institutions, notably, the European Commission (Commission) has been nugatory, and that the only meaningful interactions at the EU level have been those involving the member states (though see Backman and Rhinard 2018; Beach and Smeets 2020a, 2020b; Dehousse 2016; Rhinard 2019 for alternative perspectives).

This chapter contends that the view that the EU's response to crises can be told only in terms of the action taken by the European Council and the positions adopted by the member states is misleading. Although the European Council has unique authority and can play a key role where it chooses to intervene, the time that it can devote to any one issue is limited its capacity for action is sometimes limited by a lack of agreement among heads of government, and it depends on other institutions for its decisions to be enacted. Nor is the European Council always uniquely competent to take action. Other institutions, notably the Commission, have responsibilities, resources in the form of staff, expertise, funding and other instruments, as well as a permanence, that may allow them to be more immediately responsive. There is also always a question of agency; namely, whether incumbents in leadership positions decide to frame a particular issue as a 'crisis,' what actions they believe should follow, and how other actors in the EU system respond. These intra-institutional processes and inter-institutional interaction need to be taken into account.

Drawing on instances of crisis response on the part of the EU between 2014 and 2019, this chapter illustrates the importance of looking beyond the European Council when considering how the EU responds to crises. It considers four 'hard cases': Ukraine, the refugee influx, the second Greek bailout, and the wave of terrorist attacks in Europe. All four cases—external action, emergency eurozone measures, migration, security, and foreign policy—represent both sensitive policy areas and relatively new areas of EU competence where the literature would anticipate a primarily intergovernmental response and a limited degree of Commission involvement.

The discussion below is divided into two parts. The first offers a brief critical review of the literature on the EU and crises. It argues that scholarly attention has been overly focused on the actions of the European Council and therefore the positions taken by member states, thereby overlooking the possibility that the Commission has played a key role. It then discusses the respective capacities of the European Council and Commission and highlights the importance of leadership. The second part considers how the EU has responded to four crises since 2014. Particular attention is paid to the role of the Commission.

The EU and Crisis Management

There is now a substantial literature on the difficulties, disruptions, and challenges confronted by the EU over more than a decade. By definition, crises are extraordinary events, and it is no surprise that they have commanded high levels of attention. Scholars have investigated both the experience of individual sectors, and the overall impact and effects. They have also addressed the multiple aspects and dimensions of each crisis. The Eurozone and the refugee crisis have attracted particular attention (Buonanno 2016; Niemann and Zaun 2018; Trauner 2016; Carrera et al. 2016). The literature considers the positions adopted by individual member states and the EU institutions, as well as processes of preference formation (Laffan 2016a; Târlea et al. 2019; Schmidt 2019; Degner and Leuffen 2019; Fontan and Saurugger 2019; Kassim et al. 2019; Morlino and Sottilotta 2019). The literature also examines the institutional consequences of the crisis and crisis measures, considering, for example, the extent to which particular institutions 'won' or 'lost' (see, e.g., Bauer and Becker 2014; Dehousse 2016).

According to a general consensus, the European Council has taken the lead or been the decisive actor in responding to moments of crisis (see Puetter 2014, 2015; Laffan 2016b; Dinan and Nugent 2017; van Middelaar 2019). Whether the Commission has failed to deliver on account on partisan considerations (Hodson 2013) or an inability to propose measures that are acceptable to the member states, or simply that heads of government have decided to intervene, the European Council has invariably assumed responsibility. In these instances, the Commission's role has typically been restricted to the production of reports or studies for consideration by the European Council, or to the implementation of decisions following meetings of heads of government, in keeping with the conceptualization of Eurozone issues and foreign policy as part of the 'intergovernmental union' (Puetter 2012, 2014; Fabbrini 2016) within the EU's dualist framework that has evolved since Maastricht (Fabbrini and Puetter 2016).

Since it follows from the focus on the European Council that the key to explaining EU action lies in the positions adopted by member governments, accounts have focused on processes of national preference formation on the part of national capitals. Some scholars have applied variants of liberal intergovernmentalism (Armingeon and Cranmer 2018; Schimmelfennig 2015, 2018). Others have used core concepts—'preferences' and 'preference formation'—that are traditionally associated with liberal intergovernmentalism, but have incorporated them within competing theoretical perspectives. The latter include the 'new intergovernmentalism' (Bickerton et al. 2015), 'deliberative institutionalism' (Puetter 2012), or 'discursive institutionalism' (Crespy and Schmidt 2014) (see also Section II, this volume).

Many of these accounts see no or little decision-making role for the Commission. They also appear to discount input from the Commission as a factor in decision-making by the European Council or otherwise shaping the EU's response, and pre-decisional interaction between the two institutions whether on the basis of cooperation, competition or rivalry as an important stage that influences the form taken by the final output, as well as how in practice they decide to divide labor. Yet, the Commission participates in the European Council. It also has important competencies under the treaty that are engaged by crisis, as well as a responsibility to act in the general interest of the European Union (Article TFEU). Indeed, the Commission is often best positioned to act first when a crisis emerges and often does, which has consequences for the EU's response.

Moreover, although the European Council was strongly empowered by changes introduced by the Treaty of Lisbon, its resources remain limited. Lisbon recognized the European Council as an EU institution for the first time, and entrusted the heads of government with responsibility for defining the general political guidelines for the EU. It also created the (semi-)permanent Presidency, which altered the operation of the European Council, separated the European Council from the Council of the European Union, and equipped the European Council with a leadership capacity that it had lacked hitherto. Importantly, Herman Van Rompuy, the first President of the European Council, worked organizationally on undergirding the Presidency with a strong cabinet that enjoyed close links with prime ministers' offices in the national capitals. He also strengthened the leadership role of the European Council by his creative use of convening power, establishing special summits devoted to a single topic and Eurozone summits alongside its normal meetings (Puetter 2015). As well as 'convening power', which enables him to bring heads of government together, the President can issue statements, which then guide the work of the other Institutions.

Despite significant strengthening since Lisbon and a broadening of its policy involvement (Puetter 2014; Fabbrini and Puetter 2016), however, the European Council's ability to deal with crises is not unlimited. Crises are dealt with by the European Council because the President of the European Council decides to table the issue at a normal summit or to call an extraordinary meeting (Puetter 2014). Thus, the incumbent of that office plays a crucial agenda-setting role in defining an issue as a crisis. The reasons can be various, ranging from the inability of the sectoral Council to reach the necessary agreement, or an unwillingness on the part of the latter to endorse decisions that are 'too big,' the fact that the crisis at hand is not easily covered by existing formations of the Council, to situations where the crisis as already been resolved by a sub-group of member states and the European Council is asked to rubber-stamp the results.

As well as lacking law-making power and its dependence on other institutions—including not only the Commission, but the Council of European Union—to carry out its decisions, the European Council has limited bureaucratic resources. It can call on the Council Secretariat, which is some 3000-people strong, but two-thirds of its staff are mainly concerned with logistics and only a small proportion provide direct support for the President. Furthermore, since as presidents or prime ministers its members are mainly preoccupied with domestic matters, they have limited time to devote to EU matters, and multiple issues compete for their attention. Although the creation of the Presidency has created a degree of permanence, the capacities of the office should not be exaggerated.

Several further points are important. First, the very fact of calling a meeting of EUCO has consequences. It may force the Council to agree something before the meeting of the European Council takes place or it could paralyze or disempower the Council. Moreover, since conclusions of the European Council have force, it is rare that a crisis is solved on the day of a meeting. A key question is whether the sectoral Council is able to follow this up—the task of the rotating Presidency. Furthermore, it is important to note that national governments, following years of crisis, have become increasingly fragile and are more often coalitions. As a result, the Minister of Finance or the Minister of the Interior may come from a different party to the prime minister, which can lead to problems in coordinating national positions.

The Commission, by contrast, has considerable resources. As well as a staff of around 33,000, it commands very substantial policy and legal expertise, financial resources under various budgetary headings, and important political linkages to the European Parliament. There are also a range of sectoral, sub-sectoral and transversal instruments at the Commission's disposal.

As with the European Council, leadership is a key variable. Processes of presidentialization following the Treaties of Amsterdam and especially of Nice have concentrated power in the hands of the Commission President (Kassim 2012; Kassim et al. 2013). The decision to respond to a crisis, to launch an initiative, or proactively to seek cooperation with the European Council, are largely in the power of a single individual. Different Presidents are likely to arrive at very judgments about whether, when or how to act. Their decisions reflect different values, different levels of experience and different evaluations of, for example, the importance of collaborating with the European Council (Bocquillon and Kassim 2019).

For these reasons, this chapter argues for a broader appreciation of the EU system in explaining the EU's response to crises and its management of them.

REVISITING THE EU AND CRISIS RESPONSES

The chapter draws on crises experienced during the Juncker Commission to illustrate the importance of these variables. The Juncker Commission, which took office on November 1, 2014, was the first to be headed by a winner of the *Spitzenkandidaten* process (Westlake 2015; Christiansen 2016; Kassim and Laffan 2019). As a result of the decision of most European parties to nominate a candidate for the Commission Presidency ahead of the elections to the European Parliament in 2014, and with the strong encouragement of the European Parliament itself, the electoral campaign took on an EU-wide dimension, with parties setting out detailed policy agendas for the coming five-year term.

These attempts to program EU action, however, were made at a time of considerable uncertainty. The EU was emerging from the worst economic, financial and social crisis it had experienced since the Second World War. The financial crisis which started in 2008 had led to a double-dip economic recession in the euro area, and unemployment peaked at 12% toward the end of 2012. Even if the economic situation had started to improve in the course of 2013–2014, protracted slow growth, if not deflation, was anticipated for the near future. More broadly, the crisis had had far-reaching political consequences. Populist and anti-establishment movements, old and new, were performing well across Europe, and Eurosceptic and anti-European sentiment were on the rise. National governments had become weakened. Many had narrow parliamentary majorities and were composed of fragile coalitions. Mistrust between member states, especially between 'north' and 'south' was fueled by tensions over unprecedented financial assistance programs.

The political manifestos published in the run-up to the 2014 European elections reflected these concerns, putting economic recovery and social fairness at their center. However, a series of new challenges arose. The EU was faced by what the then candidate for Commission President Jean-Claude Juncker termed a 'polycrisis,' illustrating the multiplicity of sudden and severe problems the EU now confronted on top of the difficult economic and social situation the incoming Commission had inherited. This chapter examines the respective roles of the European Council and the Commission played in responding to five of these crises: Ukraine, the second Greek economic collapse, the migration and refugee crisis, security and the fight against terrorism, and Brexit. It focuses principally on intra- and inter-institutional processes, and, underlining the scope for contingency, the role that is played by key actors at particular points. It notes that there are different routes by which an issue becomes a crisis, that crises assume different forms, and that there are different ways in which crises can be addressed.

Ukraine

In the EU context, external relations, especially those involving international conflict, are traditionally perceived as national and thus essentially intergovernmental matters, despite the existence of the High Representative of the Union for Foreign Affairs. However, such a reading neglects the significance of EU actors and instruments. The case of the Ukraine illustrates the importance of the latter.

In 2013, the government of the newly elected President decided to suspend the Association Agreement that was being negotiated by Ukraine and the EU as part of a broader policy to strengthen the Ukraine's ties with Russia. Several months of demonstrations and protests led to a rallying of pro-EU forces and a change of government. In response, Russia launched a military intervention in February 2014, leading to the illegal annexation of Crimea in March 2014 and war in the Donbass region in April 2014.

As a traditional reading of EU action in external relations would have predicted, Berlin and Paris largely shaped the initial response on the part of the Union. France and Germany moderated the talks that led to the Minsk Agreements, and a fragile ceasefire between Russia and Ukraine. However, the Minsk Agreements were not the final word. The President of the European Council and the High Representative both played a role in steering and coordinating a broader EU response, essentially Europeanizing policy toward the Ukraine. In addition to backing diplomatic efforts, the European Council agreed a set of restrictive measures against Russia, which were then later extended. The Commission also set up a dedicated Support Group for Ukraine, in April 2014, as a way to concentrate and coordinate the channelling of resources and supply of expertise in fields, including governance and the rule of law, justice and home affairs, economic governance, agriculture, energy, infrastructure, health, education, and communication.

Building on the Association Agreement that was eventually signed in March 2014, the EU provided support on several fronts. First, alongside the International Monetary Fund, the Commission activated a number of programs of macro-financial assistance to keep the country afloat. Since the outbreak of the crisis, the Commission has disbursed a total of EUR 2.8 billion in macro-financial assistance through three programs of low-interest loans—the highest amount ever made available by the EU to a third partner. These programs linked the disbursement of tranches to progress on reforms, for instance to fight corruption, which required close monitoring of developments on the ground, and interaction with the broader economic and policy dialogue.

Second, the EU stepped up its support for Ukraine's real economy. The biggest international donor to Ukraine, the EU was able to tap into an envelope of EUR 11 billion for direct support over the period 2014–2020. As Ukraine's largest trade partner, the EU also sought to provide new opportunities and strengthen trade ties. The EU and Ukraine signed a Deep and Comprehensive Free Trade Agreement, which entered force in January 2016, and will gradually reduce tariffs on goods and services. The EU also decided (in April 2014) to lift temporarily the customs duties on Ukrainian exports to the EU, a measure worth EUR 500 million per year. In parallel, the Commission—through its Support Group—rolled out technical assistance projects for capacity building in the public sector and for private sector development, and the European Investment Bank provided funding for dedicated projects.

Third, the EU was concerned to prevent energy black-outs in the Ukraine and to strengthen the country's energy security. The Commission—at the level of one of its Vice-Presidents—took the lead in moderating regular energy talks between Russia, Ukraine and the EU. In spite of a tense political context, this helped prevent major disruptions of gas delivery to both Ukraine and the EU.

Fourth, the EU sought to boost political ties and people-to-people exchange. The political and cooperation provisions of the Association Agreement were provisionally applied as of November 2014, in anticipation of its entry into force. A bilateral Visa Facilitation Agreement was finalized in

February 2014 and the EU approved visa-free travel for Ukrainian citizens in May 2017. Half a year later, more than half a million Ukrainians had made use of this new opportunity. Several cooperation projects in the field of education and research were also initiated.

This panoply of instruments, their rapid deployment following the 2014 crisis and further deepening over the years, illustrate the role that EU actors, including the Commission and the European External Action Service (EEAS) (see Maurer, this volume), play in international crisis situations. They show how EU action in response to a crisis situation, includes, but also goes beyond, purely diplomatic efforts.

Averting 'Grexit'

As noted above, the scholarly literature on the financial and economic crisis in Europe between 2008 and 2013 tends to stress the central role of the EU's member states, as well as intergovernmental settings, including the 'Eurogroup,' the regular gathering of euro area Finance Ministers, and 'Euro Summits' (see e.g., Puetter 2012). Such instances are not strictly speaking EU institutions, but they played a central steering role and had been responsible for the most sensitive decisions, which often resulted in further intergovernmental arrangements, such as the European Stability Mechanism (ESM), Europe's new financial firewall. The focus on 'last chance' summits, which was a notable feature of media coverage, overlook the role played by other EU actors, including the European Parliament and the Commission, in designing new initiatives and operating new instruments, alongside the European Central Bank.

From the first attempt at a coordinated response through a 'recovery plan' in November 2008 to the 'Youth Guarantee' of 2013, from the changes to the Stability and Growth Pact brought about by the 'six-pack' and 'two-pack' legislation to the launch of the European Semester of economic policy coordination, from the Four Presidents' Reports on the future of Europe's Economic and Monetary Union to the wave of EU legislation passed to reform Europe's financial and banking sectors, much of the substantial work of containing and overcoming the crisis was undertaken by EU Institutions. By the time of the European elections of spring 2014, the economic and political situation had improved: most countries that had recourse to financial assistance from the euro area had exited their adjustment programs, and only Greece was still due to complete its second program. Yet, Eurozone reform remained unfinished and President Juncker's political guidelines—the program he presented as candidate Commission President—made the deepening of Europe's Economic and Monetary Union a central priority for the following five years. The political guidelines also included important messages for countries in need of financial assistance: the end of the 'Troika'; the commitment to carry out a social impact assessment before any new program; and greater accountability and parliamentary control.

These commitments were not intended to be put into immediate effect. With Greece gradually able to tap the markets in the course of 2014, no new program was in sight. Yet, the election of a new government in Greece in January 2015 changed that prospect. After refusing such move at first, Greece requested an extension of the deadline of its program from February to June 2015. As negotiations started, uncertainty led opponents of the euro, as well as those opposed to Greece's participation in it, to become more vocal. The risk of 'Grexit'—the exit of Greece from the euro—became especially severe in the early summer as Greece defaulted on a payment to the International Monetary Fund and introduced capital controls. Following a radical turn of political events, including a referendum, Greece requested a new financial assistance program in July.

Detailed accounts of how this crisis unfolded have started to appear, which put a new light on the role played by actors including the staff of the Eurogroup and the Commission. While the Commission had been vilified by many in the new Greek government, it turned out to be an important channel of communication for Athens and a defender of Greek interests. With the direct intervention of President Juncker, the Commission provided constant behind-the-scenes assistance to convey the requests of the Greek government, often negotiating on its behalf, and moderating contacts between the Greek government with other member states and bodies including the European Central Bank, the International Monetary Fund, and the European Stability Mechanism. These efforts paved the way for a new Stability Support Programme which, for the first time, was submitted by the Commission to an ex-ante *social* impact assessment.

The Commission also designed a plan to support Greece's real economy. In July 2015, it proposed to scrap the co-financing requirements of EU funds and to frontload the EUR 35 billion planned for Greece under various funding programs for the period 2014–2020. With the creation of its new Structural Reform Support Service in October 2015, the Commission provided and coordinated far-reaching technical support to help Greece build the necessary administrative support for reforms and boost the absorption of EU funds, with Greece becoming the best EU performer as a result.

In parallel, the Commission President took the initiative to coordinate a report on the deepening of Europe's Economic and Monetary Union, together with the Presidents of the European Parliament, the European Council, the European Central Bank and the Eurogroup, the so-called 'Five Presidents' Report.' This report was released in June 2015, at the peak of the crisis, as way to stabilize expectations about the euro area, assert its integrity, and chart out a clear future.

The Euro Summit of 12–13 July 2015 is often mentioned as the moment when 'Grexit' was finally averted, with the decision of EU Leaders to move toward a new program. Yet, much of the substance of the reforms still needed to be fleshed out and there was still a risk of a further aggravating default of Greece on its debt later that month. It was only by activating a bridging loan of EUR 7 billion under the European Financial Stabilisation Mechanism, the precursor of the ESM, backed up by the EU budget, that the Commission was able to avert the risk of further financial accidents in Greece. The Memorandum of Understanding initiating a new Stability Support Programme was signed on 20 August 2015. Three years later, Greece emerged from its program, with fiscal targets met, economic growth averaging 2% and unemployment falling. A total of EUR 61.9 billion had been mobilized in loans. Capital controls were lifted in September 2019.

Tackling the Migration and Refugee Crisis

Migration featured as a priority for the European Council (2014) in its 2014–2019 Strategic Agenda and as one of the ten priorities of the incoming Juncker Commission. Migration was also made a designated Commission portfolio for the first time. The scale of the refugee crisis, however, was not anticipated. Toward the end of 2015, the United Nations High Commissioner for Refugees reported the largest number ever of displaced persons. With wars on the EU's borders and within the wider neighborhood, the number of refugees arriving rose dramatically in 2015 from around 40,000 in May to more than 200,000 in October. For Europe, this was arguably the largest crisis since the Second World War.

Ensuring a common EU response was an immediate challenge. In May 2015, the Commission announced a comprehensive 'European Agenda for Migration,' while the European Council discussed the crisis at meetings in June, October, and December. However, unilateral action, notably the re-imposition of internal borders along the so-called Western Balkans route, reflecting a rise in the salience of migration, domestic political pressures on governments, and an increase in anti-migrant sentiment, threatened the unity of the EU and the integrity of the Schengen area.

The Commission took the initiative of holding regular conference calls with the 'sherpas' of the member states concerned. It also appealed to international and European financial organizations to secure additional funding. The need for coordination at the highest level was such that the Commission eventually hosted in its premises a meeting on the Western Balkans route in October 2015, where the leaders of eleven countries endorsed a dedicated action plan. The decisive step came a few months later, with the EU-Turkey agreement of March 2016, which led to a radical reduction in the number of arrivals.

Several new initiatives were developed very rapidly at EU level, often backed up by EU staff and funding. Several European operations were organized to rescue lives at sea. 'Hotspots' gathering staff of the European Asylum Support Office (EASO), the European Border and Coast Guard Agency (HYPERLINK "https://ec.europa.eu/home-affairs/what-we-do/networks/european_migration_network/glossary_search/european-border-and-coast-guard-0_en"Frontex", HYPERLINK "https://ec.europa.eu/home-affairs/what-we-do/networks/european_migration_network/glossary_search/eur opean-border-and-coast-guard-0_en"), Europol and Eurojust were set up to assist frontline member states— Greece and Italy foremost—to facilitate the registration of asylum seekers (see Everson and Vos, this volume). New mechanisms for the resettlement of refugees from outside the EU were also put in place. The concept of a European Border and Coast Guard (EBCG) was rapidly agreed, with significant new powers transferred to the corresponding Agency. New ways to support and engage with countries of origin and transit were developed through the creation of dedicated Trust Funds and the launch of an External Investment Plan.

By contrast, divisions among member states, which were reflected in increasingly tense relations between the Commission and the European Council, prevented the reform of EU legislation, notably in asylum. The Commission tabled 30 legislative initiatives in the field of migration between 2014 and 2019, but 16 remain on the table of the EU legislator. While the European Parliament was able to reach a compromise on some files, the Justice and Home Affairs Council were very divided on others. The fact that member states were not always represented at the appropriate ministerial level is a symptom of the difficulties for the sectoral Council to follow up decisions of the European Council in this field.

For a number of member states, there was a case of 'too much, too fast, too far' in regard to the Commission's proposals. 'Too much,' when instead of directives—allowing for a gradual convergence of legislation—regulations were proposed to harmonize sensitive policy domains. 'Too fast,' when a second proposal for the EBCG Agency was presented before the first one was really finalized. 'Too far,' when the Commission, early on in the crisis, proposed a quota-like system of assessment of asylum applications based on principles of solidarity. Although a system informed by the latter was eventually adopted by the Council against opposition from a minority of member states, it has not yet been implemented. Moreover, a number of governments are now blocking attempts at a broader revision of the rules.

The need for lasting solutions remains particularly obvious in the Mediterranean Sea. When a rescue vessel arrives on European shores, it is the Commission that plays the—largely informal and unnoticed—role of ad hoc coordination, contacting EU member states to ask them to volunteer to welcome a number of the refugees concerned and organising relocation. Thus, the EU system, although responsive and forward-looking at the peak of the crisis, was able to devise and implement a number of instruments, but proved unable to renew EU legislation. The migration case underlines the importance of looking beyond the actions of the European Council and member state preferences when examining how the EU responds to crises.

Security and the Fight Against Terrorism

The shooting of the French cartoonists of 'Charlie Hebdo' in Paris in January 2015 was the first in a series of terrorist attacks on European soil—Paris again,

Brussels, Nice, Berlin, London, Stockholm, Manchester, Barcelona—between autumn 2015 to the summer of 2017. More than 300 people were killed and over 1100 injured. For many observers, these attacks laid bare the limitations of bilateral and EU-wide cooperation in security. Competences had only started to emerge at EU level for a decade. They also led to the questioning of how the EU's internal and external borders functioned, and the Schengen area, with France deciding to re-establish internal border controls on security grounds, while several other countries did so in response to the refugee crisis.

After only a few months in office, the Commission issued an action plan—a 'European Agenda on Security'—in April 2015. A year later, as the European Commissioner of British nationality decided to leave following the 'Brexit' referendum, the President appointed a Commissioner exclusively dedicated to security matters. A new 'security taskforce' was also set up within the Commission, which was able to cut across and draw on the expertise of several established Directorates-General. Since 2014, the Commission has proposed 22 legislative initiatives, of which 15 have been agreed by the EU legislator. These include: a law to criminalize and more heavily sanction related offenses, restricted access to firearms within the single market—legislation drafted by Commission services during the weekend following the 'Bataclan' attack in November 2015; improved interoperability of information systems; and revised rules on anti-money laundering and a Cybersecurity Act. Unfinished business includes the proposal to extend the mandate of the European Public Prosecutor's Office to fight cross-border terrorism and legislation removing terrorist content online.

Beyond legislative action, effort has been expended in efforts to (re)build trust among European actors, as well as to strengthen operational cooperation between law enforcement authorities and with EU agencies. Some of these initiatives gained international recognition and have the potential to set new standards. In the wake of the 'Christchurch' attack, in May 2019, the President of the French Republic and the Prime Minister of New Zealand invited the President of the Commission to an international meeting with other global leaders and CEOs of digital platforms to discuss the European approach to fighting on-line extremism.

Security concerns have also led to an increased focus on defense. Significant steps have been taken at EU level over recent years, ranging from pilot projects on industrial and research cooperation to the establishment of a fully fledged European Defence Fund. As a measure of the achievement in the historical context of the EU's development, the congratulations offered by the President of the French Republic to the Commission for its work on security and defense matters in his remarks following the June 2017 European Council are richly symbolic.

CONCLUSION

Although the existing literature focuses largely on the European Council, this chapter has argued for the importance of looking across the EU system when investigating how the EU responds to crisis. Since the European Council is widely considered to be the EU's 'crisis manager,' scholars have sought to explain the EU's response to crises in terms of the positions adopted by member states and ultimately in processes of national preference formation. However, this focus may be unduly narrow. The importance of other institutions has often been overshadowed by the 'summitry' associated with major crises. It may also lead to an underestimation of the EU's resilience.

The experience of the four crises shows that heads of government do not always take the lead or play the lead role when the EU is confronted by extraordinary difficulties. In three of the four cases—the Ukraine, averting 'Grexit,' and the refugee crisis—the European Council had significant involvement, while in the fourth—security and defense—it played a limited role. The attention of the European Council may be directed elsewhere, or member states may be divided on what course of action to take, thereby preventing the European Council (or the sectoral Council) from reaching a decision.

Moreover, the above discussion highlights the role played by the Commission and the range of instruments deployed by the EU in response to four crises experienced since 2014. Contrary to the image of public bureaucracies as slow and unresponsive, the Commission demonstrated its ability to react to sudden threats or challenges. The cases show the range of resources at its disposal. They include the breadth and depth of specialist expertise among its staff, access to varied policy instruments, permanence, and relations with international bodies, as well as a capacity to improvise in the absence of pre-existing routines. Initiative on the part of Commission President was also important, underlining the role of agency.

As well as underlining the importance of looking not only at, but beyond, the European Council, the discussion also suggests avenues for future enquiry. First, since it is often argued that crises lead to creative solutions, legislation, financing instruments and structures, one possibility would be to examine the longevity of measures that were introduced as emergency responses. The quality of the legislation passed, or measures adopted, could be compared with those enacted during 'normal' periods. The comparison, particularly given the limited scrutiny given to emergency measures under 'better regulation' procedures, could be instructive. Second, the responsiveness of the EU system departs from the more traditional gradualism of EU affairs, which raises questions about the ownership of EU decisions in the medium term. How do emergency measures adopted during the heat of a crisis fare when they are implemented at a later date by governments? Are they likely to be robust or are they the result of compromise under pressure and therefore difficult to put into practice? Third, what would detailed analysis reveal about issue attention during periods of crisis. The fact that crises overlap each other is of significance. For instance, it is clear that many EU Leaders were eager to close the 'Grexit' by the summer of 2015 to be able to refocus their attention and political capital on tackling the migration crisis—with Greece accidently at the heart of both. Is 'one crisis at a time' the best recipe?

References

Armingeon, K., & Cranmer, S. (2018). Position-Taking in the Euro Crisis. *Journal of European Public Policy*, 25(4), 546–566. https://doi.org/10.1080/13501763.2016.1268642.

Backman, S., & Rhinard, M. (2018). The European Union's Capacities for Managing Crises. *Journal of Contingencies and Crisis Management*, 26(2), 261–271. https://doi.org/10.1111/1468-5973.12190.

Bauer, M. W., & Becker, S. (2014). The Unexpected Winner of the Crisis: The European Commission's Strengthened Role in Economic Governance. *Journal of European Integration*, 36(3), 213–229. https://doi.org/10.1080/07036337.2014.885750.

Beach, D., & Smeets, S. (2020a). New Institutionalist Leadership–How the New European Council-dominated Crisis Governance Paradoxically Strengthened the Role of EU institutions. *Journal of European Integration*, 42(6), 837–854. https://doi.org/10.1111/1475-6765.12354.

Beach, D., & Smeets, S. (2020b). The Unseen Hands: Collaborative Instrumental Leadership in the British Renegotiation Case. *European Journal of Political Research*, 59(2), 444–464. https://doi.org/10.1111/1475-6765.12354.

Bickerton, C. J., Hodson, D., & Puetter, U. (2015). *The New Intergovernmentalism: States and Supranational Actors in the Post-Maastricht Era*. Oxford.

Bocquillon, P. & Kassim, H. (2019). *The European Commission and the European Council: Setting the EU's Agenda in the Post-Lisbon Era* (Unpublished Paper).

Buonanno, L. (2016). The European Migration Crisis. In D. Dinan, N. Nugent, & W. E. Paterson (Eds.), *The European Union in Crisis*. London: Palgrave.

Carrera, S., Blockmans, S., Gros, D., & Guild, E. (2016, December 2015). *The EU's Response to the Refugee Crisis: Taking Stock and Setting Policy Priorities* (CEPS Essay, No. 20/16). https://www.ceps.eu/wp-content/uploads/2015/12/EU%20Response%20to%20the%202015%20Refugee%20Crisis_0.pdf.

Christiansen, T. (2016). After the Spitzenkandidaten: Fundamental Change in the EU's Political System. *West European Politics*, 39(5), 992–1010. https://doi.org/10.1080/01402382.2016.1184414.

Crespy, A., & Schmidt, V. A. (2014). The Clash of Titans: France, Germany and the Discursive Double Game of EMU Reform. *Journal of European Public Policy*, 21(8), 1085–1101.

Csehi, R., & Puetter, U. (2017). *Problematizing the Notion of Preference Formation in Research About the Euro Crisis* (EMU Choices Working Paper Series). https://emuchoices.eu/2017/10/18/csehi-r-and-puetter-u-2017-problematizing-the-notion-of-preference-formation-in-research-about-the-euro-crisis-emu-choices-working-paper-2017/. Accessed 13 Sept 2019.

Degner, H., & Leuffen, D. (2019). Crises and Responsiveness: Analysing German Preference Formation During the Eurozone Crisis. *Political Studies Review*. https://doi.org/10.1177/1478929919864902.

Dehousse, R. (2016). Why Has EU Macroeconomic Governance Become More Supranational? *Journal of European Integration, 38*(5), 617–631. https://doi.org/10.1080/07036337.2016.1180826.

Dinan, D., & Nugent, N. (2017). *The European Union in Crisis*. Houndmills: Palgrave Macmillan.

Fabbrini, S. (2016). From Consensus to Domination: The Intergovernmental Union in a Crisis Situation. *Journal of European Integration, 38*(5), 587–599. https://doi.org/10.1080/07036337.2016.1178256.

Fabbrini, S., & Puetter, U. (2016). Integration Without Supranationalisation: Studying the Lead Roles of the European Council and the Council in Post-Lisbon EU Politics. *Journal of European Integration, 38*(5), 481–495. https://doi.org/10.1080/07036337.2016.1178254.

Fontan, C., & Saurugger, S. (2019). Between a Rock and a Hard Place: Preference Formation in France During the Eurozone Crisis. *Political Studies Review*. https://doi.org/10.1177/1478929919868600.

Frieden, J., & Walter, S. (2017). Understanding the Political Economy of the Eurozone Crisis. *Annual Review of Political Science, 20*(1), 371–390.

Hodson, D. (2013). The Little Engine that Wouldn't: Supranational Entrepreneurship and the Barroso Commission. *Journal of European Integration, 35*(3), 301–314. https://doi.org/10.1080/07036337.2013.774779.

Kassim, H. (2012). The Presidency and Presidents of the European Commission In J. Erik, M. Anand, & W. Stephen (Eds.), *The Oxford Handbook of the European Union* (pp. 219–232). Oxford: Oxford University Press.

Kassim, H., James, S., Warren, T., & Hargreaves Heap, S. (2020). Preferences, Preference Formation and Position Taking in a Eurozone Out: Lessons from the United Kingdom. *Political Studies Review*. https://doi.org/10.1177/1478929919864774.

Kassim, H. & Laffan, B. (2019). *The Juncker Commission: The Political Commission in Theory and Practice* (Unpublished Paper).

Kassim, H., Peterson, J., Bauer, M. W., Connolly, S., Dehousse, R., Hooghe, L., & Thompson. A. (2013). *The European Commission of the Twenty-First Century*. Oxford: Oxford University Press.

Kassim, H., Saurugger, S., & Puetter, U. (2019). The Study of National Preference Formation in Times of the Euro Crisis and Beyond. *Political Studies Review*. https://doi.org/10.1177/1478929919873262.

Krotz, U., & Maher, R. (2016). Europe's Crises and the EU's 'Big Three'. *West European Politics*, *39*(5), 1053–1072. https://doi.org/10.1080/01402382.2016.1181872.

Laffan, B. (2016a). Europe's Union in Crisis: Tested and Contested. *West European Politics*, *39*(5), 915–932. https://doi.org/10.1080/01402382.2016.1186387.

Laffan, B. (2016b). The Eurozone in Crisis: Core-Periphery Dynamics. In D. Dinan, N. Nugent, & W. E. Paterson (Eds.), *The European Union in Crisis*. Palgrave: Houndmills.

Moravcsik, A. (2019). Liberal Intergovernmentalism. In A. Wiener, T. Borzel, & T. Risse (Eds.), *European Integration Theory*. Oxford: Oxford University Press.

Morlino, L., & Sottilotta, C. E. (2019). Southern Europe and the Eurozone Crisis Negotiations: Preference Formation and Contested Issues. *South European Society and Politics*, *24*(1), 1–28. https://doi.org/10.1080/13608746.2019.1603697.

Niemann, A., & Zaun, N. (2018). EU Refugee Policies and Politics in Times of Crisis: Theoretical and Empirical Perspectives. *Journal of Common Market Studies*. https://doi.org/10.1111/jcms.12650.

Puetter, U. (2012). Europe's Deliberative Intergovernmentalism: The Role of the Council and European Council in EU Economic Governance. *Journal of European Public Policy*, *19*(2), 161–178. https://doi.org/10.1080/13501763.2011.609743.

Puetter, U. (2014). *The European Council and the Council: New Intergovernmentalism and Institutional Change*. Oxford: Oxford University Press.

Puetter, U. (2015). The European Council: The Centre of New Intergovernmentalism. In C. J. Bickerton, D. Hodson, & U. Puetter (Eds.), *The New Intergovernmentalism*. Oxford: Oxford University Press.

Rhinard, M. (2019). The Crisisification of Policy-making in the European Union. *JCMS: Journal of Common Market Studies*, *57*, 616–633. https://doi.org/10.1111/jcms.12838.

Schimmelfennig, F. (2015). Liberal Intergovernmentalism and the Euro Area Crisis. *Journal of European Public Policy*, *22*(2), 177–195.

Schimmelfennig, F. (2018). Liberal Intergovernmentalism and the Crises of the European Union. *Journal of Common Marked Studies*, *56*(7), 1578–1594.

Schmidt, V. A. (2019). Politicization in the EU: Between National Politics and EU Political Dynamics. *Journal of European Public Policy*, *26*(7), 1018–1036. https://doi.org/10.1080/13501763.2019.1619189.

Târlea, S., Bailer, S., Degner, H., Dellmuth, L. M., Leuffen, D., Lundgren, M., et al. (2019). Explaining Governmental Preferences on Economic and Monetary Union Reform. *European Union Politics*, *20*(1), 24–44. https://doi.org/10.1177/1465116518814336.

Trauner, F. (2016). Asylum Policy: The EU's 'Crises' and the Looming Policy Regime Failure. *Journal of European Integration*, *38*(3), 311–325. https://doi.org/10.1080/07036337.2016.1140756.

van Middelaar, L. (2019). *Alarums and Excursions: Improvising Politics on the European Stage*. Agenda publishing.

Westlake, M. (2015). *Spitzenkandidaten procedure and the. Election of Jean-Claude Juncker as European Commission President* (LSE Europe in Question Discussion Paper Series Paper No. 102/2016). https://www.lse.ac.uk/european-institute/Assets/Documents/LEQS-Discussion-Papers/LEQSPaper102.pdf.

CHAPTER 17

European Union Agencies

Michelle Everson and Ellen Vos

Introduction

It is a popular academic conceit, shared by the authors of this chapter, that European Union (EU) agencies have benefitted greatly from conditions of crisis (Everson and Vos 2014; Vos 2000). Just as the 1990s 'mad cow disease' (BSE) crisis appears to have given impetus to the EU agency vehicle, the 2008 financial crisis can be thanked for the institutionalization of the most powerful agencies yet seen at EU level, or the three European Supervisory Agencies (ESAs) established to oversee the financial services market. However, for all that autonomous agencies have proven themselves to be a useful tool in 'muddling through', or in the ad hoc mastering of crisis situations (see Chapter 1, this volume), recent European malaise can also be argued to have posed very significant challenges both to individual agencies, as well as to the concept of independent (technocratic) administration within the EU.

First sketching out the history of EU agencies in crisis, as well as their contested place within the scheme of EU governance (II), this chapter investigates the particular difficulties which EU agencies now face within a Union, which is still experiencing challenges, if no longer an existential crisis (III). At one level, such problems are easy to grasp, as the institutional position of

M. Everson (✉)
University of London, London, UK
e-mail: m.everson@bbk.ac.uk

E. Vos
Maastricht University, Maastricht, The Netherlands
e-mail: e.vos@maastrichtuniversity.nl

autonomous European regulators has been challenged both in European law and within the coordination demands of a broader European crisis regime. Within the European System of Financial Supervision (ESFS) alone, for example, the European Securities and Market Authority (ESMA) has found its 'regulatory' powers challenged before the Court of Justice (CJEU), and the European Banking Authority (EBA) has lost various of its functions to the European Central Bank (ECB) within the crisis busting institution of Banking Union. At a far deeper level, however, crisis has also heightened underlying concerns about the appropriate place of autonomous governance institutions within the broader scheme of democratic government, as political indecision or failure might be argued to have created a problem of 'mandate overload' for the ESFS, as well as individual agencies, such as the European borders agency (Frontex). Similarly, mandate overload finds its counterpart in renewed calls for the enhanced legitimation of agency operation, a phenomenon which is itself claimed to undermine agency functionality. Autonomous administration thus finds itself the subject of, for example, problems of 'accountability overload' (III), or of 'reputational risk' (Stansfield 2006). Finally, and perhaps the most intractable of all challenges, EU agencies are also implicated within a governing crisis which pitches a technocratic arm of administration against a rising 'populist' tide of politics that sometimes doubts the 'truths' of scientific method, or refuses to view it as a basis for democratic decision-making.

CRISIS, GOVERNANCE AND CHARACTERISATION

Crisis-Driven Agencification

The ESFS was established by a series of EU regulations in 2010,[1] and then comprised the European Systemic Risk Board (ESRB, chaired by the ECB President) dedicated to macro-prudential supervision, the three ESAs, who administer a complex series of common financial regulations for Banks, Insurers and Financial Markets, and National Supervisory Authorities, formally responsible for micro-prudential supervision at member state level. The ESFS was not the first endeavour to coordinate financial supervision at supranational level. It built instead upon the national regulatory networks and standard-setting committees for the financial services, established following the report of the 'Lamfalussy Committee' on the Regulation of European Securities Markets in early 2001.[2] However, lying between the Commission's establishment of its

---

[1] Regulation (EU) No 1092/2010 (ESRB Regulation); Regulation No 1096/2010 (ECB Regulation); Regulation (EU) No 1095/2010 (European Securities and Markets Authority); Regulation (EU) No 1093/2010 (European Banking Authority); Regulation (EU) No 1094/2010 (European Insurance and Occupational Pensions Authority).

[2] Known as the European Financial Services Action Plan, and comprising, in particular, Commission Decisions, 2001/527/EC and 2001/528/EC (EU Securities Committee and Committee of European Securities Regulators); Commission Decision 2004/10/EC (Committee of European Banking Supervisors; Commission Decision 2004/9/EC (Committee of European Insurance and Occupational Pensions Supervisors).

own comitology system and a far broader Union commitment to the ESFS, we find the collapse of Lehman Brothers, a significant change in the rhetorical justification for EU institutional reform, a host of new financial regulations, and a notable widening of supranational regulatory structures founded in independent expertise.

The Lamfalussy group was primarily concerned with the establishment of a globally competitive European market for financial services. Unwieldy EU regulation and discrepancies in national implementation were seen as regulatory failings because they led to differential treatment of financial instruments, both 'violating the pre-requisite of the neutrality of financial supervision' in the EU market, and delaying adaption of European financial services 'to the pace of global financial market change'.[3] By rhetorical contrast, the 'high-level' de Larosière group convened in response to financial melt-down appeared to have returned to a more traditional concept of market failure, concluding that the system of European regulation must be strengthened to improve an 'inadequate mix' of regulatory and supervisory skills and to create a coordinated early-warning system 'to identify macro-systemic risks of a contagion of correlated horizontal shocks'.[4] As a consequence, in addition to imposition of stricter capital requirements on financial institutions, the regulatory and supervisory structure was significantly enhanced with the creation of the new, semi-autonomous authorities for regulation and supervision of financial services. This final development was particularly significant. Facing financial meltdown, the European Parliament (EP) 'enthusiastically' welcomed the ESFS, discarding its long-standing opposition to further consolidation of EU technocratic governance,[5] in particular by means of supranational 'agencification' (Moloney 2011).

The vital point to note is one that agencies have not always been popular within EU institutional circles, and have instead been vigorously opposed by a EP concerned with limiting the growth of technocratic governance, and a Commission jealous of its own executive competences. Commission acceptance of, if not enthusiasm for EU agency governance, may be traced back to crisis or to the failings in comitology structures exposed by BSE. BSE still functions as a potent warning to proponents of technocratic governance, especially with regard to the problem of what to do when expertise can no longer provide answers, or of how to respond when diffuse hazard cannot be concretised as risk 'because the science has run out' (Van Asselt and Vos 2008: 359). In the 1990s, however, the failure of scientific expertise was primarily viewed

[3] http://ec.europa.eu/internal_market/securities/docs/lamfalussy/wisemen/final-report-wise-men_en.pdf.

[4] http://ec.europa.eu/internal_market/finances/docs/de_larosiere_report_en.pdf.

[5] EP had rejected a proposed Institutional Agreement on a common operating framework for EU agencies COM (2005) 59 final creating a factual moratorium on their establishment by demanding that the Commission undertake further review of the operations of such bodies already operating at EU level; see 'European Agencies—the Way Forward', COM (2008) 159 final.

within an institutional paradigm stressing the need to act to improve its quality and delivery. Lack of transparency within ad hoc scientific committees established to ensure food safety had exacerbated a lack of scientific expertise at EU level and foreclosed potential for epistemic scientific review. Highlighting the 'obscurantism' of the comitology model (Dehousse 2003: 798), the BSE saga also revealed a need for permanently funded EU expertise in order to facilitate long-term research upon the basis of which hazards could be transformed into manageable risks, as well as a demand for permanent oversight of implementation of EU standards at Member State level (Vos 2000). Transparency, independence, and permanence are characteristic of expert agency operation (Demortain 2010), and a radical expansion in their use naturally followed BSE. By the same token, financial crisis overcame long-standing national and parliamentary opposition to a further consolidation of EU regulatory function in the financial services sector: ESAs would lift the veil on riskily obscure financial operations, providing transparency in financial markets.

The Efficiency of New Public Management?

Crisis has undoubtedly played its part in the evolution of EU agencies. Nevertheless, 'agency fever' (Egeberg and Trondal 2016: 1), or an exponential increase in 'non-majoritarian' (Majone 1996; Majone 1997) EU governance structures also relates to factors other than crisis. Limiting our analysis to the so-called decentralised agencies, or public law bodies that are institutionally separate from EU institutions, have their own legal personality and a degree of administrative and financial autonomy, as well as legislatively specified tasks, 37 such agencies now exist and are accruing an increasingly broad range of powers. Unforeseen by the founding treaties, decentralised EU agencies have slowly become an integral part of the EU's institutional structure, and are 'an established part of the way the EU operates'.[6] In this, the EU is far from alone. Pragmatic resort to agencies by public authorities to assist them in the carrying out of executive tasks is a very old phenomenon within national executives (Egeberg and Trondal 2016), albeit that more recent 'agencification' processes, whereby new entities have been created in the public sector, or whereby existing agencies have been given greater autonomy to carry out specific tasks, also have their roots in the generalized retreat of centralized state administrations and modern theories of public management (Jacobsson and Sundström 2007: 5).

Seen in this light, the establishment of ESAs in particular might be argued not only to derive from the need for effective crisis management, but also to represent the renewed pursuit of pre-millennial tropes of efficient governance within a fourth branch of government. This point is significant, since,

---

[6] Joint Statement of the EP, the Council and the European Commission on decentralised agencies adopted on 19 July 2012; http://europa.eu/agencies/documents/joint_statement_and_common_approach_2012_en.pdf, Accessed on 29 April 2016.

within this model, the establishment of autonomous regulatory agencies operating at arms' length from government is justified not simply by the argument that areas requiring complex technical oversight are best governed by experts (Vibert 2007), but is also bolstered by the view that autonomous market governance is legitimated by alterations in the manner in which the relationship between exercise of political power and economic operation is viewed. The argument traditionally used to justify independent central banks—prevention of manipulation of exchange rates for short-term political gain (Majone 1996)—finds far more general application within the permissive consensus that market operation should take place within its own autonomous sphere. Efficiency is the leading criterion within a modern paradigm that seeks to refashion regulation in order to separate out the pursuit of general redistributive goals from sectoral regulatory aims. Assuming a higher normative commitment to autonomous markets, efficiency-based regulatory models argue that the distorting statist tendency to conflate micro-economic regulation with redistributive macro-economic goals can be combatted by establishing independent regulatory expertise (Everson 1995).

Autonomous regulatory models also gain in normative legitimacy as postulation of a concept of *pareto*-efficiency itself mediates against concerns that executive power should never be endowed with too broad a mandate. Discretionary powers may be delegated to independent agencies where they have no redistributive consequences, or the subject-matter of regulation is value-neutral in terms of general welfare losses (Majone 1994). Accordingly, and to the degree that pursuit of economic efficiency has become a self-limiting principle within the polity, the independence of EU regulatory agencies is transformed from a potential challenge to democratic government to a positive governing good that finds its *raison d'être* in the shielding of regulatory expertise from political contingency. Famously, legitimacy of autonomous agencies is also argued to be further secured by a scheme of control that ensures that independent expertise is both capable of fulfilling its regulatory functions and performs them well. 'Transparent' agencies must consequently be made accountable to traditional constitutional institutions (government, legislature, and courts), and to the general public, in a manner that does not endanger autonomy. This is generally achieved applying a scheme of multiple institutional oversight—drawn from US experience—which determines that 'no-one controls the agency, yet the agency is under control' (Moe 1990).

A Crisis of Categorisation and Incomplete Constitutionalism

The global ideological shifts which have seen state-based economic steering cede to notions of market-conform regulation claim their own self-contained legitimacy. As such, for all that EU agencies have blossomed, especially during crisis, their ideal-typical operation would not be considered challenging to the EU institutional architecture, European publics, or the democratic principle. Nevertheless, significant concerns do now arise for three distinct reasons: the first, a notable historical anxiety about the underlying impact of 'politicised administration' upon democratic government, even in its efficiency-based form; the second arises with regard to the growing conundrum of how to categorize agencies which have taken on a far broader set of functions within a distinctive and still evolving polity. The third problem relates to and is also a cause of these preceding issues: lacking a proper basis and purpose within the European treaties, EU agencies continue to pose fundamental constitutional questions.

Modelled on their US counterparts, EU agencies might nevertheless claim to be distinguished from them, at least to the degree that where the celebrated wave of agency creation during the economically interventionist US New Deal served largely to compensate for market failure, EU agencies are seemingly designed to support the internal market, ring-fencing its autonomous operation. However, although idealized agency governance is per se concerned solely with technical implementation tasks, wholesale delegation of executive function to autonomous governance bodies has always given rise to suspicions about the nature and the consequences of the political impetus for agency creation, the potential for unfair or politicized decision-making within agency operation (Shapiro 2005), as well as the nature of the relationship established between agencies and the citizenry (Stewart 2005). Profound and widespread throughout the history of agency creation, such concerns have met their countermovement in vigorous efforts to constrain agency operations through heightened accountability, most famously within the fiercely proceduralized ambit of the 1946 US Administrative Procedures Act.[7] It would be illusionary to expect them not to have arisen within the EU, especially to the degree that the creation of the single market can also be argued to be a substantive political goal; a reverse image of Roosevelt's program of renewal, but one to which considerable political resources have been committed since the 1980s.

Equally, within a European setting, where agencies have been assigned an ad hoc mixture of tasks, reaching from information collation to decision making, they have likewise played their part in a more general process of the functional decentralization of the EU executive, which compensates, on the one hand, for administrative *lacunae* within Commission administrative capacity, but similarly, acts to mediate the continuing tensions of multi-level governance. The intense interaction of EU agencies with national authorities, experts and/or stakeholders within governance networks (Vos 2014), also places them firmly within an integrated multi-level administration (Hofmann 2008). Seen in this light, the particular character of EU agencies might accordingly be argued to have little to do with efficiency, or with political goals such as completion of the internal market, nor yet even have much to do

---

[7] For the evolution of the US APA as a means to pluralize democracy, or allow for post-legislative challenge of agency acts, see Shapiro (1996).

with the regulatory function at all. In turn, this gives rise to a crisis of categorization. Academic literature struggles: EU agency operation may be part of the broader global trend to market-conform regulation, but also happens within the confines of an evolving EU polity, with its on-going negotiations between national and supranational competence. Egeberg and Trondal (2016) capture this difficulty, presenting not one, but three broad conceptual images of agencification as being intergovernmental, transnational, or supranational in character. The intergovernmental label reflects the view that EU agencies are set up to implement or monitor the implementation of policies agreed upon by member states. By contrast, transnationalism presupposes that EU agencies are 'loosely coupled' to national and EU institutions, consequently underlining the role of agencies as network regulators. Finally, the supranational classification considers agencies to be integral elements of the EU administration, more specifically, of the Commission. These three images highlight 'overlapping, supplementary, co-existing and enduring governance dynamics within and among EU agencies', which, according to Egeberg and Trondal (2016: 2–3), are likely to co-exist, but also to change over time and within each separate agency.

The EU polity is a polity on the move, and the institutional framing of agencies is necessarily contingent on patterns of Union evolution. What is clear from this analysis, however, is the fact that the agency phenomenon has induced a shift away from the Community Method of indirect administration, whereby EU policies were implemented by member states to a more direct form, whereby implementation is either carried out at the EU level or through the co-option of national agencies by EU institutions—mostly, the Commission (Egeberg and Trondal 2016: 8; Keading and Versluis 2014). For Egeberg and Trondal (2016: 9), this is indicative of an ongoing trend of the supranationalization of executive power within the EU. Importantly, however, agencies have not thus undermined Commission executive power, as they largely perform functions that the Commission cannot perform itself because its lack of expertise or by virtue of political resistance toward it. Busuioc and Groenleer (2014: 179) argue that agencies have been established within the Union, because it was felt that it would not be *politically* appropriate to entrust certain tasks to the Commission as the latter would be too bureaucratic, too politicized, and composed only of generalists.

A similar trend toward direct administration and supranationalization may also be identified within the operation of EU agencies within regulatory networks, whereby agencies such as the European Food Safety Agency, although not being placed at a hierarchical apex within the network, nonetheless manoeuvre as a form of *primus inter pares* between national counterparts and/or stakeholders (Vos and Wendler 2006). The fact that EU agencies contribute to a reinforcement of EU executive power and lead to a pluralization of the EU executive (Hofmann and Morini 2012), is not, however, in itself conclusive in determining the precise location of agencies within the political-administrative setting, although Egeberg and Trondal argue that these agencies lean more toward the Commission than any other potential principal (2016: 11).

By contrast, legal literature often connects the phenomenon of EU agencies with a depiction of the Union as a composite or shared administration. Agencies are, 'betwixt and between' (Curtin and Egeberg 2008) or 'hierarchy beaters' (Everson 1995). This makes EU agencies 'interesting hybrids' (Everson 2009). The hybridity of EU agencies is expressed, both institutionally, in their relationship with and their (in)dependence from the EU institutions and the member states, as well as substantively, in their multiple tasks (Rijpma 2012: 90). Representatives of both member states and the EU institutions sit in their steering boards, who, by virtue of their 'double-hats' serve both national and EU authorities (Egeberg and Trondal 2011). Thus, potential tension, competition, and/or conflicts between national and European interests seem to be inherent to the composite character of the EU executive.

Hybridity and complexity is only increased where account is taken of the fact that agencies not only assist EU institutions, but may also act for the member states (Chamon 2012; Ott et al. 2014). The European Aviation Safety Agency (EASA), for example, even acts as 'the authorised representative of EU member states', concluding arrangements at the global level (Interstate Aviation Committee) and with various third countries, such as Australia and Brazil.[8] Further, although the 'borrowing' of EU agencies by member states to implement EU law, as permitted by EU law, is not as such troublesome in practice,[9] it does raise more general concerns about their accountability: to whom are EU agencies accountable, for what purposes and when?

The latter is a general problem that is inherent to the hybrid character of EU agencies. 'Inbetweeners', beholden both to the EU institutions, particularly the Commission, and to the member states (Everson et al. 2014), EU agencies, in contrast to their US and national counterparts, present very specific accountability problems: whose agenda are they pursuing when and why? How easily can they be suborned by their respective masters, or how easily can they escape all supervision? The problems are myriad, and are only heightened within a context of the incomplete constitutionalization of the EU agency structure.

Unforeseen within the Treaties, the proliferation of agencies within the EU's institutional setting understandably gave rise to historic concerns about their place within the emergent EU polity. Their rise has accordingly also demanded many adjustments within EU constitutional principles, above all within the principle of the institutional balance, and the formal recognition

---

[8] See working arrangement on the airworthiness between EASA and the Interstate Aviation Committee, https://www.easa.europa.eu/system/files/dfu/intl_appro_IAC_EASA.pdf, Accessed on 29 April 2016.

[9] In view of the Court's liberal attitude towards the 'borrowing' of EU institutions by Member States when implementing an international agreement outside the EU legal framework. See De Witte and Beukers (2013).

of agencies within the Lisbon Treaty must now be welcomed,[10] above all with regard to the enhanced jurisdiction of the Court of Justice. Codifying longstanding practice,[11] the Court may now review the legality of agency acts 'intended to produce legal effects vis-à-vis third parties' and their failure to act, while it may also interpret agency acts in preliminary rulings,[12] ensuring greater legal certainty in the judicial review of agency acts.[13]

The belated constitutional recognition that agencies form a part of the EU executive and must accordingly be made subject to the constitutional values of transparency, openness, and participation is undoubtedly important. However, it is also very true that the strictures of the Lisbon Treaty do little to regularize comprehensively the status of agencies within the EU with regard to the clear stipulation of their purpose, their exact relations with the varied centres of political power within the EU, or indeed, fully address the issue of how agencies might be comprehensively controlled.

At legal level, an incomplete constitutionalization of EU agencies is immediately noticeable in the continuing failure to establish an EU Administrative Act (Curtin et al. 2013), which might augment the opportunities afforded to the public to challenge both the procedural character (*ultra vires*) and the substance of agency-led decision-making. Whether this is an indication of the failure of anti-agency forces in Europe to muster their 'constitutionalised' strength, or is a simple result of a still-traditional suspicion of modern, pluralist models of administrative law within European legal systems,[14] the Lisbon Treaty has similarly left three pressing legal concerns about EU agency operation unanswered: the legal basis for creation of EU agencies, delegation of powers to EU agencies, and the status of agency decision-making within the hierarchy of norms system that was also introduced by the Lisbon Treaty (Articles 291 and 292 TFEU) (Vos 2018).

---

[10] The Lisbon Treaty has also imposed EU standards upon agencies with regard to internal security, financial measures and ECB independence, the jurisdiction of the Ombudsman, audits, fraud, and citizenship. Agencies are also made subject to the principle of transparency (including access to documents), personal data protection requirements and the own-language rights of individual citizens. They are also required to establish an open, efficient and independent administration.

[11] Whilst having no constitutional basis for this, the founding regulation of the European trade mark regulation provided for the possibility to have decisions of OHIM's board of appeal reviewed by the Court, see Article 65 of Regulation 207/2009 on the Community trade mark, OJ 2009 L 78/1.

[12] Article 263 TFEU permits that the founding regulation of agencies lay down specific conditions and arrangements concerning actions brought by natural or legal persons against acts of these bodies, offices or agencies intended to produce legal effects in relation to them.

[13] See the Court's rulings in Case T-411/06, *supra* n. 72 and Case T-70/05 *Evropaiki Dynamiki* v. *EMSA*, ECLI:EU:T:2010:55. See Saurer (2010) and Alemanno and Mahieu (2008).

[14] As Stewart (2005) has famously demonstrated, the US Administrative Procedures Act has also become a mechanism whereby legislative programmes may be challenged during the course of their implementation.

Crisis, Constitutional Concern and Political Failure
Legal Lacunae and Political Tensions

'Short-Selling'

A headline happening within EU (financial and sovereign debt) crisis, the 2012 case of *ESMA* (Case C-270/12), better known as the *'short-selling'* case, proves highly illustrative to the analysis, acting as exemplar both for the incomplete constitutionalization of EU agencies, and for the heightened challenges of agency operation under conditions demanding immediate 'emergency' action. In seeking the annulment of Article 28 of Regulation 236/2012, the UK Government challenged the conferral of direct powers upon the ESMA to issue legally binding measures against financial institutions of the member states in the event of a threat to the orderly functioning and integrity of financial markets, or to the stability of the whole or part of the financial system in the EU.[15] Concomitantly, the UK questioned both the basis for agency action and the legality of the direct intervention powers conferred upon the Authority, as well as—most significantly—the status of 'discretion' within the burgeoning EU executive.

A first point of concern for the UK Government was the use of Article 114 TFEU, and the EU notion of 'approximation' of national market measures, in order to justify granting of direct powers to the agency to impose a measure of individual application. Reiterating earlier rulings that the EU legislature may deem it necessary to provide for the establishment of 'an EU body responsible for contributing to the implementation of a process of harmonisation',[16] the Court[17] dismissed this argument and approved the use of the Article 114 TFEU as a legal basis for the establishment of autonomous authorities as long as they contribute to the implementation of 'a process of [market] harmonisation'[18]—a fairly low barrier to agency creation reflecting a functionalism that facilitates competence creep to the European level. For the UK at least, political suspicion of the motivation behind agency creation within the internal market sphere, may explain recurring challenge: is deployment of the agency model less a matter of technical market regulation and more an issue of executive expansion at European level? The summary treatment of such suspicions by the CJEU, however, may be an indication of its simple desire to ensure the continuing functioning of the Single Market.[19]

---

[15] EP and Council Regulation 236/2012 on short selling and certain aspects of credit default swaps, OJ 2012 L86/1.

[16] Case C-270/12, para 104.

[17] But not AG Jääskinen, who argued that the correct legal basis of this regulation should have been Article 352 TFEU. See Opinion AG Jääskinen in Case C-270/12, para 54.

[18] Ibid.

[19] See Case C-66/04, *United Kingdom* v *European Parliament and Council* [2005] ECLI:EU:C:2005:743, para 44 and Case C-217/04, *United Kingdom* v *European Parliament and Council* [2006] ECLI:EU:C:2006:279.

The *short-selling* case is also notable for a further UK argument that the exercise of direct powers by the ESA contradicted or fell outside the hierarchy of norms laid down by the Lisbon Treaty. The Court was explicitly asked to judge whether Articles 290 and 291 TFEU were intended to establish a single framework under which certain delegated and executive powers may be attributed solely to the Commission, or whether other systems for the delegation of such powers to Union agencies may be contemplated by the EU legislature.[20] In its judgment, the Court affirmed the latter notion, and found no difficulty in circumventing the carefully crafted hierarchy of norms within the Treaty. The Court deduced from the inclusion of agencies in other Treaty provisions, more specifically, Article 263 (judicial review) that the possibility exists to confer powers upon such bodies.[21]

At the core of the hierarchy of norms debate lies the question of delegation: Articles 290 and 291 TFEU were meant to settle, once and for all, the terms upon which power would be delegated to a burgeoning EU executive. Given this fact, the neglect, or lack of mention of agencies in Articles 290 and 291 is extraordinary. Once again, however, political factors, external to the practical problems of delegation may explain the gap: in particular, the 2001 Commission White Paper on European Governance took care to present the Commission as 'as the lone hero of European policy-making and implementation' (Scharpf 2001: 8), and thus acted as counterweight to a degree of national support for an independent legal basis for agencies (Vos 2014) that might have diluted Commission competence within competing power centres.[22] Instead, the Commission preferred to refocus attention on the traditional Community Method (see below), whereby agencies would simply aid in traditional implementation of EU legislation.

The resultant logic of the hierarchy of norms established by Articles 290 and 291 TFEU is wholly inadequate to the reality of governance within the EU, especially under conditions of crisis. The inability to grasp the realities of European decision-making and regulation, however, extends far beyond this specific debate, leaving its indelible mark on the underlying principles of the EU legal and governance system as whole. In *Short-selling*, the CJEU struggled to reconcile the powers afforded to ESAs in crisis with the *Meroni* doctrine[23] and asserted a traditional, 'anti-delegation' or 'limited-delegation' approach to delegated powers within the EU.

---

[20] Case 270/12, *supra* n.XX, para 78.

[21] 'A number of provisions in the FEU Treaty none the less presuppose that such a possibility exists.' Case 270/12, paragraph 79.

[22] Speech by R. Prodi before the EP, 3 October 2002, SPEECH/00/352, see http://europa.eu/rapid/press-release_SPEECH-00-352_en.htm?locale=EN, Accessed on 29 April 2016.

[23] Cases 9/56 and 10/56 Meroni v. High Authority [1957–1958] ECLI:EU:C:1958: 7.

Boiling down in a final analysis to a mode of protection for the principle of the institutional balance, which safeguards the respective political competences of national and supranational instances, the *Meroni* limited-delegation doctrine nevertheless disguises tension between portions of the Commission which, in their policy-oriented character, have recognized the functional need to confer more powers on agencies to address the growing complexity of EU tasks, and the Commission's Legal Service which has sought to uphold the strict interpretation of the doctrine (Majone 2002). A European manifestation of the age-old clash between constitutional imperatives and the simple need to get things done, it is thus unsurprising that legislative reality is characterised by a far more indulgent attitude toward the delegation of powers (Vos 2014). This is especially so under conditions of crisis, as evidenced by the wide-ranging soft law powers conferred upon ESMA in the wake of financial collapse (Ottow 2014).

Objecting to exactly these powers, the UK Government's challenge in *Short-selling* was consequently rejected by the Court, which instead crafted a 'Meroni 2.0' approach to EU delegation (Vos 2018). *Meroni* was declared to still be good law (Lenaerts 2014). The Court was nevertheless visibly torn between its outdated strictures and a functional recognition that ESMA needs must be allowed to carry out the crisis busting tasks bestowed upon it. The CJEU does not therefore entirely rule out delegation of discretionary powers and limits rather than excludes ESMA's discretion.[24] Above all, the Court laid value on the fact that powers delegated to ESMA were 'circumscribed by various conditions and criteria which limited ESMA's discretion'.[25] The decision is elegant, but, in a final analysis, the Court's assertion that 'ESMA is not vested with "a very large measure of discretion"',[26] must be recognized for the very convenient fiction that it is.

Short-selling is a case decided at the very limits of the rule of law; it is a case within which, by virtue of continuing political conflicts within the evolving EU polity (Commission primacy within the EU executive) the Court is faced with the task of bridging a gap between normative provisions (the treaties) and functional reality (delegation to agencies under conditions of crisis). Seen in this light, the Court might be praised for its adaptation of the *Meroni* doctrine to the twenty-first century. Yet, in bridging the 'constitutional gap in EU executive rulemaking', (Marjosola 2014) the Court is also cavalier in its approach to ESMA's decision-making processes, or to the fact that they may encompass important political, economic, or social choices (Schammo 2011). Functional reality is simply ignored.[27]

---

[24] Case 270/12, *supra* n. 68, e.g. paras 45 and 50.

[25] Case 270/12, *supra*, para 45.

[26] Case 270/12, *supra*, para 54.

[27] See Case T-187/06, *Schräder* v *CPVO* [2008] ECLI:EU:T:2008: 511, para 59, and Case T-96/10, *Rütgers Germany GmbH* v. *ECHA* [2013], ECLI:EU:T:2013:109 for an alternative approach by the Court where necessary discretion is recognized.

Banking Union

The basic institutional refusal to acknowledge that crisis busting measures taken in the wake of financial and sovereign debt crises are more than technical in nature, also extends beyond the ESFS to encompass its potentially disruptive partner within the European Banking Union, established in 2014 by the Single Supervisory Mechanism (SSM) and Single Resolution Mechanism (SRM).[28] The ECB is the lead actor within Banking Union. It is charged with the direct micro-prudential supervision of 'significant' Eurozone banks, defined by their size, importance, and volume of cross-border activities,[29] and is required to act within a framework of macro-prudentially oriented oversight, in which it may apply contagion-busting mechanisms, such as heightened capital adequacy buffers.[30] Moreover, it is obliged by Article 3 of the SSM Regulation to pursue 'economic growth' in the 'integrated market'; a generalist obligation, which itself translates into a very specific Commission goal: Banking Union 'will put an end to the era of massive bailouts paid for by taxpayers and will help restore financial stability. This, in turn, creates the right conditions for the financial sector to lend to the real economy, spurring economic recovery and job creations'.[31]

Banking Union is designed to promote a market-driven exit from crisis. However, the paradigm of market-conform technical regulation may once again be doubted, above all with regard to the consequence-filled choices made within the function of macro-prudential supervision (see below). Equally, a political-institutional tension may be noted in the potential conflict between the ECB and the EBA, certain of whose competences the ECB has now assumed. The move away from the EBA to the ECB in the matter of supervision of systemically relevant Eurozone banks is a clear matter of political choice, swimming against the tide of 'technical' economic rationality: in many national settings, 1980s liberalization also found its corollary in re-allocation of banking supervision powers away from central bankers to autonomous agencies, not only as a demand for specialist oversight grew, but also as the newly apportioned competences of central banks to set interest rates were perceived as being in conflict with direct oversight of the Banking system, as interest rates play a central role in sectorial liability assessments (Heffernan 1996). Equally, where the Commission underlines its apparent belief in the

---

[28] Council Regulation (EU) No 1024/2013 of 15 October 2013 conferring specific tasks on the European Central Bank concerning policies relating to the prudential supervision of credit institutions and Regulation (EU) No 1022/2013 of the EP and of the Council of 22 October 2013 amending Regulation (EU) No 1093/2010 establishing a European Supervisory Authority (European Banking Authority) as regards the conferral of specific tasks on the European Central Bank pursuant to Council Regulation (EU) No 1024/2013.

[29] Article 6 SSM Regulation.

[30] Article 5 SSM Regulation.

[31] European Commission Memo (Brussels, 15 April 2014) Banking union: restoring financial stability in the Eurozone. Available at: http://ec.europa.eu/internal_market/finances/docs/banking-union/banking-union-memo_en.pdf.

pareto-efficient character of European regulation, asserting that '[Mo]netary policy tasks [of the ECB] will be strictly separated from [its] supervisory tasks to eliminate potential conflicts of interest between the objectives of monetary policy and prudential supervision',[32] technocratic isolationism is immediately undone within the highly discretionary character of ESFS-SSM governance structures. Within the broader EU setting, establishment of a discretionary Banking Union framework is prescribed by the additional tensions of heightened European differentiation, or by potential incompatibility between the interests of member states who are and who are not participating within the SSM. Certainly, the SSM makes a clear effort to preserve EBA functions and thus the interests of non-participating member states: '[T]he ECB should not replace the exercise of those tasks by the EBA' (Recital 32 SSM Regulation). Nevertheless, coordination between the two systems is necessarily a matter for greatly enhanced executive (ECB) discretion (Everson 2015).

Mandate Overload, Accountability Overload, and Reputational Risk

The political uncertainties which mark the still-to-be-fully-negotiated relationship between Banking Union and a Single Market, within which EU agencies reign supreme, give the lie to the efficiency-based argument for the legitimation of autonomous authorities, at least to the degree that regulatory outcomes can no longer be held to be a matter of neutral science. '[A] central bank is not an appropriate institution for macro-prudential supervision because central bankers are not legitimate politically to make decisions that involve important trade-offs between political and economic objectives [.] [S]uch decisions should be left with finance ministries and other elected officials' (Ferran and Alexander 2010: 771). What is true of central banks may also be argued to be true of EU agencies, and especially so, the ESAs who operate within the EFSF.

The problem is perhaps less a matter of a traditional concern that agencies might expand and break their mandates, regardless of the principle of limited-delegation, and more a feature of a contemporary abdication of political responsibility within a blind faith in market-driven welfare and the corrective powers of technocratic executive oversight. The fault is perhaps more in the master than the servant, in Government rather than the administration. Remaining within the ambit of the ESFS, we are reminded that crisis precipitated regulatory opportunity within European financial services. Most commentators agree that regulatory arbitrage under Lamfalussy weighed most heavily in favour of the unexpected hardening of the supranational supervisory competence in crisis (Snowdon and Lovegrove 2011; Andenas and Chui 2013). The preparedness of member states to manipulate residual national regulatory competence in order to assert their varying degree of tolerance

---

[32] COM (2012) 511.

for the risks posed by financial markets (Andenas and Chui 2013) undoubtedly played its part in crisis-inducing contagion. Nevertheless, at least to the degree that regulatory arbitrage created its own particularly obdurate competition barrier, crisis has also provided further opportunities for permissively integrative interventionism within European markets in line with global trends (See also Chapter 3 this volume). Hardened regulatory prescriptions apart, the ESFS is also a responsive creature of market utility: the three ESAs, led by specialist national regulators but shielded from national political influence, have been inserted into the existing supervisory paradigm, wherein they are charged with unavoidably conflicting roles of 'improving the functioning of the internal market', 'ensuring the integrity, efficiency and orderly functioning' of markets, combatting 'regulatory arbitrage', and securing 'consumer protection'.[33] ESAs, with their dual rulemaking and supervisory function now find themselves on the discretionary front-line of simultaneous promotion of innovation and security within financial markets. Given the key role of elaborating the new EU legislation which implements Basel III,[34] ESAs have also accrued unprecedented supervisory powers, including, controversially (Moloney 2010), emergency intervention powers in national financial instruments markets, where informational asymmetries threaten financial stability (MiFiD II[35]).

As *Short-selling* amply demonstrates, EU agencies have been called upon to address and master ever more complex situations with still-developing tools and indistinct consequences: the emergence of systemic risk within financial markets—for which 'there is no universally accepted definition, let alone an accepted measure of quantification' (Arnold et al. 2012: 3127)—is a new phenomenon, whose exact causes and ramifications are as yet only dimly perceived in economic literature (Skilos 2014; Born et al. 2012). Nevertheless, where, in the minds of policy-makers, systemic risk equates with financial instability 'so widespread that it impairs the functioning of a financial system to the point where economic growth and welfare suffer materially',[36] 'waiting is not an option', such that 'policies have moved ahead of academic research' (Arnold et al. 2012: 3127). Part and parcel of a new regime is discretion: where, for example, a new supervisory fulcrum of macro-supervision—exercised jointly by ESAs and the ECB within Banking Union/ESRB—remains as ill-defined as the systemic risk it is designed to combat, the discretionary rather than prescriptive character of supervision, just as surely allows for continual

---

[33] Article 1 of the ESMA, EBA and EIOPA Regulations, see n. XX above.

[34] In elaboration of framework Directives for European financial services markets. Mirroring old-style comitology procedures and in accordance with Article 290 TFEU, the EBA drafts BTS which are given legal force as Commission Implementing Acts.

[35] Directive on markets in financial instruments, Directive 2014/65/EU (MiFID 2) repealing Directive 2004/39/EC and the Regulation on markets in financial instruments (Regulation (EU) No 600/2014 on markets in financial instruments).

[36] Jean-Claude Trichet, then ECB Chair, 2010, 13th Conference of the ECB-CFC Research network; cited by Arnold et al. (2012: 3127).

corrective adjustment in the oversight function (Skilos 2014). Yet, and perhaps far more critically, where 'the ultimate goals of the policy are still the usual macro-economic ones of output and welfare', (Arnold et al. 2012: 3132) post-crisis oversight schemes are similarly implicated within socio-economic choices, within decisions about the amount of risk the financial system should carry and when. As historical arbitrage also demonstrates, variations in risk appetites do exist and are just as much demonstrative expression of the political nature of trade-off between lost opportunity gains and immediate, if utility-dampening, security as of a desire to protect national markets.

Caught in an incomplete constitutional framework, trapped within tensions between the Single Market and other areas of EU competence/policy (monetary policy), implicated within the continuing stresses and strains of shifting patterns of intergovernmentalism, transnationalism, and supranationalism (Egebert and Trondal 2016), it is little wonder that agency operation cannot but spring the confines of the traditional model of non-delegation which infuses European legal principles. The additional assertion that any traditional administrative model is confounded by 'mandate-overload', or abdication on the part of political process, at national and EU level, of responsibility for the difficult economic and social choices to be made in any regulatory setting might appear, initially at least, to be an assertion too far. However, writing in mid-2019, a pattern of evasive technocratisation, of avoidance of the need to establish clear, political lines of responsibility for EU policy-making can now only be argued to have been repeated within recent reforms to the EU borders agency, Frontex. With the European Parliament now having agreed to the re-establishment of Frontex with its own human and material resources, and an enhanced role with regard to the Integrated Border Management of the Schengen Zone,[37] it is very hard to resist the conclusion that continuing political disagreement about European asylum and immigrational policy has been masked within agencification; within a depoliticization and technocratisation of a *lacking political will*.[38] Years of uproar within the European polity, of continuing discord and distrust among member states translate simply into the technical task of Frontex directly to manage removals and returns from the Schengen area.

Subject now to increasing concerns that it will be implicated in fundamental rights violations (Ekelund 2017; Meissner 2017), Frontex joins the ranks of autonomous regulatory institutions increasingly concerned about the phenomenon of 'reputational risk'[39] (Griffin 2014). For private companies, and more especially financial companies, the 'intangible', or non-accountable

---

[37] http://www.europarl.europa.eu/news/en/press-room/20190410IPR37530/european-border-and-coast-guard-10-000-strong-standing-corps-by-2027.

[38] See for details, Mariana Gkliati, Ph.D. researcher at Leiden University, working on the accountability of Frontex for human rights violations during its operations, http://eulawanalysis.blogspot.com/2019/04/the-new-european-border-and-coast-guard.html.

[39] With specific reference to the role of Central Banks in managing macro-prudential supervision, Born et al. (2012: 180).

commodity of reputation is priceless: 'damage to an institution's reputation (and the resulting loss of consumer trust and confidence) can have very tangible consequences (Stansfield 2006). Within markets, a hit to reputation makes itself felt, however untraceably, in a bottom line of profit as stakeholders withdraw their support from the commercial enterprise. By contrast, reputational risk is a relative newcomer within the public sphere (Vardy 2015/2016). This should not come as a surprise given the existence of mandate overload, and an increasing concern that where autonomous authorities are required to make regulatory choices, with a political flavour, they might face reputational ruin since they are perceived to have made the wrong one. The bigger surprise should instead be one that the notion has ever attained currency within a public sphere at all, where authority was once predicated upon a mixture of coercion and accountability (Jackson and Gau 2015).

'Behind the façade of parliamentary democracy, both political conflict and the resolution of policy issues increasingly takes place within organisations which are unknown to democratic theory' (Offe 1980: 8): an observation made by Claus Offe three decades ago, little would appear to have changed, especially as regards a growing technocratic preference. And yet, a difference may still be noted, at least to the degree that the extension of the administrative function has brought about its own pragmatic efforts to bring an emergent, experimental, and 'politicised administration' within the confines of democratic practice. 'Governance' has become such a commonplace term at all levels of private and public organization that it is all too easy to forget its particular meaning and promise within the EU governing system. Long in vogue within international relations theory, governance was adopted by European political scientists to describe the decision-making processes formed within the EU system from the 1990s onwards (Jachtenfuchs 2002); above all, the institutions and procedures developed during and after the completion of the internal market in the awareness that the internal market program called for proactive initiatives across all sectors to acknowledge and master its unforeseen economic and social implications. As such, the term governance, as deployed within the European context, is characterized by its own analytical vagueness, or openness to the evolving institutions and modes of governing the expanding competences of the Union.

This is not to criticize the notion. Granted, the concept is vague, yet it also usefully designates 'a distinctive method/mechanism for resolving conflicts and solving problems that reflects some profound characteristics of the exercise of authority that are emerging in almost all contemporary societies and economies' (Schmitter 2001). It is a virtue of the concept that it captures actor configurations and problem-solving activities, which have emerged as responses to functional exigencies. Modern governance depends on, and similarly builds on, expert knowledge and the management capacities of enterprises and organizations. Seen in this light, the 'formalised' adoption by Romano Prodi of governance within the Commission White Paper of 2001 was an act full of promise and innovation, especially as regards the autonomous administrative function. For years the Union had played host to extra-legal developments and institutional innovations that had widened the discrepancies between the EU's activities and its formal legal structures. The governance debate admitted of this reality and sought to identify new forms of legitimation for the process of *muddling through*.

Yet, this debate has inevitably disappointed: 'governance' rather than 'government and administration' captures modern political action, its emphasis upon the social knowledge and the management capacities of enterprises and organizations, its eschewal of command and control policy-making and policy implementation, and its response to real social problems and to bottlenecks within the political system and its administrative machinery. This is the desired outcome, but it is also the problem, the point at which 'is' and 'ought' part company and the search for a sustaining legitimation is revealed as a simple chimera. The Commission underestimated the weight of the underlying legal-normative question, responding to the legitimacy question with principles of openness, participation, accountability, effectiveness, and coherence, which, while individually worthwhile, merely reproduced the individual mechanics of traditional administrative legitimacy. Mainstream European legal thought remained trapped within the functionalist outlook, returning to a traditional Community Method of centralized control as the failure to translate European governing *praxis* into a language of legitimacy found its counterpart in the return of the final version of the White Paper to the language of inherited legal categories. As noted above, 'Strengthening the Community Method!'—this is the illusionary *legal* leitmotiv of the Governance White Paper. This is the chimera which sees decentralized agencies complain of a crisis of 'accountability overload' (TARN, Debate and Dialogue),[40] as politicization of the agency function also precipitates calls for a further strengthening of an inadequate mode of administrative legal oversight.

An Agency of Political Wills?

'To grant a role to expert knowledge does not require us to accept the immaculate conception of expertise' (Turner 2006): Recent European crisis lends weight to this assertion, albeit also requiring us to clarify our categories further. In the experimentalism of prudential efforts to re-establish financial stability within European markets, or in the techniques of people management that substitute for good political will within a reinforced Frontex, we find the limits to expertise; but not simply because a science of money management has 'run out' in the face of systemic risk (endogenous limits), but also because political decision-making instances are unwilling or unable to make hard choices that might precipitate popular backlash (exogenous limits). At the

---

[40]TARN Dialogue, Brussels 13 April 2018, https://tarn.maastrichtuniversity.nl/publications/dialogue-2/.

same time, however, expertise has still proven its vital worth in the management of complex and uncertain processes across multiple and contested centres of political power and administration. For all that many dangers remain, European financial markets have yet to collapse. Meanwhile, populist backlash against asylum and immigration policies has been contained if not eliminated, albeit in a highly cynical manner: in crisis, as in mundane normality, 'we can safely say the EU can no longer function without its agencies' (Everson et al. 2014).

Executive competence, be it within the traditional and traditionally inadequate non-delegation model, or be it within indistinct and quite possibly chimeric governance discourses, has always been a necessary but always potentially subversive companion to a process of (democratic) political will formation, which is only ever complete if it disposes of the means to affect its will (Everson 1995, 2008). But herein—in the notion of 'will'—lies the particular problem that must be most urgently addressed within debate on the future of EU agencies. Giandomenico Majone, academic father of European agencies as a part of the fourth branch of government, has related processes of agencification within the EU to a need to differentiate memberships within a future integration *telos*, made up of distinct plural aims (Majone 2016). The thesis is electric, notable for Majone's implicit rejection of earlier *pareto* arguments, and his re-concretisation of his continuing support for technocratic governance around a classical language of will formation and effective actio

'A theory of clubs' stands for a rationalized, but all the more democratic European future, as member states agree among themselves who among them will pursue with political goals, in which combinations and using which executive/technocratic vehicles. It cannot ever hope to fully overcome traditional concerns about the potential subversions of executive acts, neither can it breathe rationalizing life into more modern governance notions, which seek to admit of contingency and muddle through in contemporary governing (see Chapter 1, this volume). However, where Majone seeks to answer the contemporary crisis within the European integration *telos*, to defend the EU from populist assault on supposed democratic deficit, he also releases technocratic governance, and EU agencies, from the deceptive dominations of a paradigm of immaculate expertise. He highlights and corrects the exogenous limitations of non-majoritarian governance: a political will must exist. Contemporaneously, he reveals and allows us to accept the internal limitations of agencies: expertise will always run out, this is its very nature.

References

Alemanno, A., & Mahieu, S. (2008). The European Food Safety Authority before European Courts: Some Reflections on the Judicial Review of EFSA Scientific Opinions and Administrative Acts. *European Food and Feed Law, 5*, 320–333.

Andenas, M., & Chui, H.-Y. (2013). Financial Stability and Legal Integration in Financial Regulation. *European Law Review, 38*(3), 335–359.

Arnold, B., Borio, C., Ellis, L., & Moshirian, F. (2012). Systemic Risk: Macroprudential Policy Frameworks, Monitoring Financial Systems and the Evolution of Capital Adequacy. *Journal of Banking & Finance, 36*(12), 125–139.

Born, B., Hermann, M., & Fratzscher, M. (2012). Communicating About Macro-Prudential Supervision—A New Challenge for Central Banks. *International Finance, 15*(29), 179–203.

Busuioc, M., & Groenleer, M. (2014). The Theory and Practice of EU Agency Autonomy and Accountability: Early Day Expectations, Today's Realities and Future Perspectives'. In M. Everson, C. Monda, & E. Vos (Eds.), *European Agencies in Between Institutions and Member States*. Alphen a/d Rijn: Wolters Kluwer.

Chamon, M. (2012). The Influence of "Regulatory Agencies" on Pluralisms in European Administrative Law. *Review of European Administrative Law, 59*, 61–91.

Curtin, D., & Egeberg, M. (2008). Tradition and Innovation: Europe's Accumulated Executive Order. *West European Politics, 31*(4), 639–61.

Curtin, D., Hofmann, H., & Mendes, J. (2013). Constitutionalising EU Executive Rule-making Procedures: A Research Agenda. *European Law Journal, 19*, 1–21.

Dąbrowska, P. (2010). EU Governance of GMOs: Political Struggles and Experimentalist Solutions? In C. F. Sabel & J. Zeitlin (Eds.), *Experimentalist Governance in the European Union*. Oxford: Oxford University Press.

De Witte, B., & Beukers, T. (2013). Case C-370/12, Thomas Pringle v. Government of Ireland, Ireland, The Attorney General, Judgment of the Court of Justice (Full Court) of 27 November 2012. *Common Market Law Review, 50*, 805–848.

Dehousse, R. (2003). Comitology: Who Watches the Watchmen? *Journal of European Public Policy, 10*, 798–813.

Demortain, D. (2010). *Scientists and the Regulation of Risk: Standardising Control*. London: Edward Elgar.

Ferran, E., & Alexander, K. (2010). Can Soft Law Bodies be Effective? The Case of the European Systemic Risk Board. *European Law Review, 35*(6), 751–776.

Egeberg, M., & Trondal, J. (2011). EU-Level Agencies: New Executive Centre Formation or Vehicles for National Control? *Journal of European Public Policy, 18*(6), 883–884.

Egeberg M., & Trondal, J. (2016). Agencification of the European Union Administration: Connecting the Dots (TARN Working Paper No 1). Oslo: University of Oslo.

Ekelund, H. (2017). Normative Power FRONTEX? Assessing Agency Cooperation with Third Countries (TARN Working Paper 15). Oslo: University of Oslo.

Everson, M., Monda, C., & Vos, E. (2014). What is the Future of European Agencies? In M. Everson, C. Monda, & E. Vos (Eds.), *European Agencies in Between Institutions and Member States*. Alphen a/d Rijn: Wolters Kluwer.

Everson, M. (1995). Independent Agencies: Hierarchy Beaters? *European Law Journal, 1*(2), 180–204.

Everson, M. (2008). Three Intimate Tales of Law and Science: Hope, Despair and Transcendence. In M. Everson & E. Vos (Eds.), *Uncertain Risks Regulated*. London: Routledge.

Everson, M. (2009). Agencies: The 'Dark Hour' of the Executive? In H. C. H. Hofmann & A. Türk (Eds.), *Legal Challenges in EU Administrative Law*. Cheltenham: Edward Elgar.

Everson, M., Monda, C., & Vos, E. (2014). European Agencies in between Institutions and Member States. In M. Everson, C. Monda, & E. Vos (Eds.), *European*

Agencies in between Institutions and Member States. Wolters Kluwer: Alphen a/d Rijn.
Everson, M. (2015). Banking on Union. In M. Dawson, H. Enderlein, & C. Joerges (Eds.), *The Governance of Europe's Economic, Political and Legal Transformation.* Oxford: Oxford University Press.
Griffin, A. (2014). *Crisis, Issues and Reputation Management.* London: Kogan.
Heffernan, S. (1996). *Modern Banking in Theory and Practice.* London: Wiley.
Hofmann, H. C. H., & Morini, A. (2012). Constitutional Aspects of the Pluralisation of the EU Executive through "Agencification". *European Law Review, 37*(4), 419–443.
Hofmann, H. C. H. (2008). Mapping the European Administrative Space. *West European Politics, 31*(4), 662–676.
Jachtenfuchs, M. (2002). The Governance Approach to European Integration. *Journal of Common Market Studies, 39,* 245–264.
Jackson, J., & Gau, J. M. (2015). Carving Up Concepts? Differentiating Between Trust and Legitimacy in Public Attitudes Towards Legal Authority. In E. Shockley, T. M. S. Neal, L. M. PytlikZillig, & B. H. Bornstein (Eds.), *Interdisciplinary Perspectives on Trust Towards Theoretical and Methodological Integration.* Berlin: Springer.
Jacobsson, B., & Sundström, G. (2007). *Governing State Agencies Transformations in the Swedish Administrative Model* (Scores Report Series 5). Stockholm: Scores rapportserie.
Keading, M., & Versluis, E. (2014). EU Agencies as a Solution to Pan-European Implementation Problems. In MEverson, C. Monda, & E. Vos (Eds.), *European Agencies in between Institutions and Member States.* Alphen a/d Rijn: Wolters Kluwer.
Lenaerts, K. (2014). EMU and the EU's Constitutional Framework. *European Law Review, 39*(6), 753–769.
Majone, G. (1994). Independence vs. Accountability: European Non-Majoritarian Institutions and Democratic Government in Europe (EUI Working Papers (SPS) 9). Florence: European University Institute.
Majone, G. (1996). *Regulating Europe.* London: Routledge.
Majone, G. (1997). The New European Agencies: Regulation by Information. *Journal of European Public Policy, 4*(2), 262–275.
Majone, G. (2002). Delegation of Regulatory Powers in a Mixed Polity. *European Law Journal, 3*(3), 319–239.
Majone, G. (2016). European Integration and its Modes: Function vs. Territory (TARN Working Paper 2). Oslo: TARN.
Marjosola, H. (2014). Bridging the Constitutional Gap in EU Executive Rulemaking: The Court of Justice Approves Legislative Conferral of Intervention Powers to the European Securities and Markets Authority. *European Constitutional Law Review, 10*(3), 500–527.
Meissner, V. (2017). *The European Border and Coast Guard Agency Frontex Beyond Borders: The Effect of the Agency's External Dimension* (TARN Working Paper Series 16). Oslo: TARN.
Moe, T. M. (1990). Political Institutions: The Neglected Side of the Story. *Journal of Law Economics and Organization, 6,* 213–253.
Moloney, N. (2010). EU Financial Market Regulation after the Global Financial Crisis: "More Europe" or more Risks? *Common Market Law Review, 47*(5), 1317–1383.

Moloney, N. (2011). The European Securities and Markets Authority and Institutional Design for the EU Financial Market—A Tale of Two Competences: Part 1: Rule-Making. *European Business Organization Law Review, 12,* 41–86.

Offe, C. (1980). The Separation of Form and Content in Liberal Democratic Politics. *Studies in Political Economy, 3,* 5–16.

Ott, A., Vos, E., & Kund, F. C. (2014). European Agencies on the Global Scene: EU and International Law Perspectives. In M. Everson, C. Monda, & E. Vos (Eds.), *European Agencies in between Institutions and Member States*. Alphen a/d Rijn: Wolters Kluwer.

Ottow, A. (2014). The New European Supervisory Architecture of the Financial Markets. In Everson, C. Monda, & E. Vos (Eds.), *European Agencies in between Institutions and Member States*. Alphen a/d Rijn: Wolters Kluwer.

Rijpma, J. J. (2012). Hybrid Agencification in the Area of Freedom, Security and Justice and its Inherent Tensions: The Case of Frontex'. In M. Busuioc, M. Groenleer, & J. Trondal (Eds.), *The Agency Phenomenon in the European Union*. Manchester: Manchester University Press.

Saurer, J. (2010). Transition to a New Regime of Judcial Review of EU Agencies. *European Journal of Risk Regulation, 1*(3), 325–327.

Schammo, P. (2011). The European Securities and Markets Authority: Lifting the Veil on the Allocation of Powers. *Common Market Law Review, 48*(6), 1879–1887.

Scharpf, F. W. (2001). *European Governance: Common Concerns vs. The Challenges of Diversity* (Jean Monnet Working Paper 6/01). New York, NY: New York University.

Schmitter, P. (2001). What is There to Legitimize in the European Union, and how Might this be Accomplished? In C. Joerges, Y. Mény, & J. H. H. Weiler (Eds.), *Symposium: Mountain or Molehill? A Critical Appraisal of the Commission White Paper on Governance* (Jean Monnet Working Paper 6/01). New York, NY: New York University School of Law.

Shapiro, M. (1996). A Golden Anniversary? The Administrative Procedures Act of 1946. *Regulation, 3,* 40–48.

Shapiro, M. (2005). "Deliberative", "Independent", Technocracy v Democratic Politics: Will the globe echo the EU? *Law and Contemporary Problems, 68,* 341.

Skilos, P. L. (2014). *Communication for Multi-Taskers: Perspectives on Dealing with Both Monetary Policy and Financial Stability. The Rimini Centre for Economic Analysis* (Working aper 11–04). Italy: Rimini.

Snowdon, P., & Lovegrove, S. (2011). The New European Supervisory STRUCTURE. *Compliance Officer Bulletin, 83*(1), 1–31.

Stansfield, G. (2006). Some Thoughts on Reputation and Challenges for Global Financial Institutions. *The Geneva Papers, 31,* 470–479.

Stewart, R. B. (2005). US Administrative Law: A Model for Global Administrative Law? *Law and Contemporary Problems, 68*(63), 63–108.

Turner, S. (2006). What is the Problem with Experts? In E. Selenger & C. Robert (Eds.), *The Philosophy of Expertise*. New York, NY: Columbia University Press.

Van Asselt, M., & Vos, E. (2008). Science, Knowledge and Uncertainty in EU Risk Regulation. In M. Everson & E. Vos (Eds.), *Uncertain Risks Regulated*. London: Routledge.

Vardy, J. (2015/16). *Reputational Risk Management in Central Banks* (Central Bank of Canada, Staff Discussion Paper/Document d'analyse du personnel). Ottawa, ON: Bank of Canada.

Vibert, F. (2007). Better Regulation and the Role of EU Agencies. In S. Weatherhill (Ed.), *Better regulation*. Oxford: Hart Publishing.

Vos, E., & Wendler, F. (2006). Food Safety Regulation at the EU Level. In E. Vos & F. Wendler (Eds.), *Food Safety Regulation in Europe*. Intersentia: Antwerp-Oxford.

Vos, E. (2000). EU Food Safety Regulation in the Aftermath of the BSE Crisis. *Journal of Consumer Policy, 23,* 227–255.

Vos, E. (2014). European Agencies and the Composite EU Executive. In M. Everson, C. Monda, & E. Vos (Eds.), *European Agencies in between Institutions and Member States*. Alphen a/d Rijn: Wolters Kluwer.

Vos, E. (2018). EU Agencies on the Move: Challenges ahead (SIEPS Working Paper 01). Stockholm: SIEPS.

CHAPTER 18

The European Central Bank

Ingrid Hjertaker and Bent Sofus Tranøy

INTRODUCTION

The past decade has seen the European Central Bank (ECB) move from being a powerful technocratic institution within a clearly delimited operational range, to emerge as a powerful political actor, with opinions on and influence over policies that have until now been viewed as the prerogative of democratic politics. This has been achieved through a series of unconventional monetary policies, a massively expanded balance sheet, increased power through its role in new regulatory agencies, and above all, as a member of the troika. Through the troika, the ECB sought to influence the structural reform and bail-out policies of member states, using access to funds as leverage to achieve its desired policy outcomes in non-monetary policy areas, in what has been termed "democratic blackmail" (Sandbu 2015: 101).

The ECB threatened Ireland with bankruptcy if it didn't structure its bank bailout in a way that made taxpayers foot the bill rather than private creditors. It threatened Greece and Spain along similar lines, requesting, for example, labor market liberalization in exchange for liquidity support to distressed banking systems. In Italy and Greece, the ECB was also controversially involved in the November 2011 events that resulted in two democratically elected prime ministers being replaced with unelected, Troika-friendly technocrats (Mody 2018: 330). The ECB has moved far beyond the scope of central banking without any formal changes to its intentionally narrow mandate or the already weak mechanisms under which it is held accountable (Braun 2017; Dawson et al. 2019).

At its inception, the ECB was given a very narrow mandate of price stability, with a second clause on its independence and a third clause prohibiting policies aimed at financing the budgetary policies of member states. The mandate that was given to the ECB reflected views both of what a central bank should do (managing price stability through managing aggregate demand through short-term interests rates) and what would be the greatest threat (the ECB used for member state debt financing). It was not designed to be a lender of last resort, i.e., to be the provider of funds to stabilize markets when everyone else panics. This is a function central banks are increasingly expected to play since it has gradually achieved a taken-for-granted status among the ECB's peers–since first being formulated in the late 1800s (Bagehot 1873/2008).

After ten years of crisis management, we ask where the ECB stands today. Is monetary policy and central banking an area where the EU is moving forward (Scenario 3), *muddling through* (Scenario 2) or facing a breakdown (Scenario 1)? Our short answer is that in terms of *outcomes* the monetary union is moving forward with a strengthened central bank. The ECB has a larger toolkit and has survived legal challenges against its interpretation of its own mandate. However, *muddling through* almost seems too weak a description of the constitutionally messy *process* that led us here, from an initial reluctance by the ECB to act at all, to subsequent radical policy innovation and unchecked transgressions into the realm of democratic politics.

The financial- and euro crises became the ECB's first real test as central bank. Prior to the crisis, the ECB had ten years of what on the surface appeared to be plain sailing. This inspired a slew of self-congratulatory reporting of the central bank's own achievements, primarily low inflation and economic convergence between the Eurozone's members (Trangy and Schwartz 2019). The crisis would force the ECB, de facto if not officially, to confront the limitations of both its understanding of financial markets and its mandate.

We suggest that the ECB's changed role over the last 10 years can be conceptualized by distinguishing between three different modes of crisis handling: *Denial, Mission Creep,* and *Mission Leap*. The ECB was hesitant about acting as lender of last resort. However, this was precisely what Eurozone financial institutions needed when the crisis hit. As the crisis got worse, the member states themselves needed a sovereign lender of last resort, something the ECB was explicitly designed *not* to be. It's perhaps not that surprising then, that the ECB's initial reaction was denial. Furthermore, it was slower than other central banks to lower interest rates, and in fact raised them in the middle of the crisis. It took half a decade for the ECB to join the other central banks in doing quantitative easing. The severity of the crisis gradually set in motion a series of processes in which the bank started to experiment with granting more long-term loans at favorable rates before diving in and engaging in the outright purchase of financial assets (QE).

Reflecting the *muddling through* scenario (Scenario 2), we label these innovations "mission creep," a term borrowed from security studies and defined by the Oxford dictionary of current English as: *a gradual shift in objectives during the course of a military campaign, often resulting in an unplanned long-term commitment.* These innovations are in some sense merely technical policy innovations falling under the "lender of last resort"-function which most central banks perform. Yet they are also policies that blur the boundaries between monetary policy (which the ECB should be doing), and fiscal and industrial policy (which the ECB should not be doing).

Reflecting the *heading forward* scenario (Scenario 3), we coin the term "mission leap" for the transgressions that the ECB made into the democratic politics of member states, to denote that the actions the ECB took in negotiations with member states over bail-outs could not be termed "monetary policy" by any stretch of the imagination. The ECB threatening to withhold monetary support unless member states enacted structural reforms.

The rest of the chapter is structured as follows: The three different modes of crisis handling we have identified—Denial, Mission Creep and Mission Leap—organize our narrative in subsequent sections. We argue that the ECB has "muddled forward" to a position of considerable strength. In Section "Muddling Through to a Powerful New Normal" we analyse the process that yielded such a puzzling range of crisis responses, looking at how both interests and ideas shaped the ECB's response. We also discuss what role the ECB now will take when European markets are less distressed, arguing that a return to the "old normal" is not possible. The extraordinary constitutional protection granted to the ECB was predicated on an old normal, on an understanding of how the economy works and what the appropriate role of a central bank should be, which no longer holds. In short, safeguards erected to defend an old normal will make it difficult to reform an emergent institutional form in dire need of a democratic rethink.

Denial

With the onset of the financial crisis, the ECB would be confronted with the severe limitations of its deliberately narrow mandate and with the inherently difficult territory of being a central bank for multiple countries with different economic needs. The challenges the ECB would face were not immediately obvious at the outset of the crisis. Nor was it clear at the beginning that the currency union itself would come to face an existential threat. The ECB was late in lowering interest rates and raised them again while the continent was still in deep crisis. It delayed in pursuing the kinds of unconventional monetary policies that other central banks were doing, and initially explicitly rejected them (ECB 2009). We term this early crisis response "denial",[1] and show that it fits both the ECB's initial response on interest rates and liquidity measures.

A central bank's primary tool is interest rates. So how did the ECB use its interest rate during the crisis? The ECB's approach diverged from other major central banks. The Federal Reserve started aggressively cutting rates when the markets showed signs of distress in 2007, lowering from 5.25 to 4.25% by the end of 2007, and in 2008 would cut further all the way down to 0.25%, the level at which the Federal funds rate would remain for almost a decade. The ECB kept their rate at 4% through the latter half of 2007 and into 2008, even after it had enacted early liquidity measures to combat the crisis. In July 2008, when global markets were highly distressed following the early bank bankruptcies, the ECB *raised* its interest rate to 4.25%. Only in October 2008, after Lehman's collapse and the ensuing financial calamity, did the ECB start cutting. The rate came down to 1% by July 2009, but the ECB was hesitant to follow the Fed and other central banks in cutting the rate further. The ECB would keep its rate at a 1% "floor" for several years, despite steady worsening economic conditions.

In 2011, while Europe was in deep recession, the ECB decided to swim again the tide and start *raising* interest rates again. On April 7th, the ECB raised rates to 1.25%, and Jean Claude Trichet defended the decision by citing signs of rising inflation (Stewart 2011). This was true for Germany, which experienced a doubling of demand for German cars and machinery from China between 2009 and 2012, thanks to the Chinese government stimulus. Yet, most of the rest of the eurozone was facing a far greater risk from deflation than inflation. At the press conference, Trichet was pressed by journalists whether he feared that the crisis-ridden periphery countries would suffer from the rate rise. Trichet's answer is worth quoting in full:

> Price stability is of extreme importance for growth and job creation in the euro area as a whole. Of course, all countries would benefit directly or indirectly from the fact that the euro area as a whole will have more growth and more job creation, in particular, because, with inflation-expectations being well-anchored, we will have a financial environment in which medium and long-term interest rates in the market will be lower than if inflation expectations were higher. This is pure arithmetic. I would also add that high inflation is a particular burden for the most vulnerable and the poorest of our fellow citizens. We call upon all countries, not only the countries you have mentioned, to be ahead of the curve in terms of their public finances, in terms of maintaining their costs at a competitive level; and last but not least in terms of embarking on the appropriate structural reforms. This is very important, particularly the structural reforms. (ECB 2011)

Here Trichet expressed clearly that the ECB remained narrowly focused on price stability, and saw inflation as the greatest threat, even in the midst of

---

[1] A term also used by Mody (2018) and Whelan (2012).

a deep recession. Trichet was not alone in his view. The decision to raise rates was unanimous in the ECB's governing council. Mario Draghi, then head of the Italian central bank but soon to succeed Trichet, told the Wall Street Journal that monetary policy "had been expansionary for a long time" (Draghi, quoted in Koeppen and Blackstone 2011). This was a remarkable statement given that the ECB's monetary policy had been far tighter than most other central banks'. A few months later, the ECB raised rates yet again, to 1.5%, inflicting what the IMF chief economist for Europe termed "a grievous wound" on the European economy (Mody 2018: 293).

Markets did not react well, and bond market panic spread from periphery countries to Italy and Spain, the Eurozone's third and fourth largest economies. The ECB then realized the error of its ways, and a majority of the governing council voted to abandon Trichet's 1% floor and lower rates. Ironically, once the ECB finally pursued a low interest rate policy, it went further than many other central banks, and by 2014 was experimenting with negative rates.

From denial to innovation is also the path the ECB took with its liquidity measures. Here the ECB started out conservatively and dragged its feet for half a decade before engaging in unconventional monetary policy. When the global financial crisis began on August 9 2007, the ECB, the Fed and a few other central banks responded with the first of what would become a series of liquidity measures. The ECB inserted a combined €94.8 billion to 49 banks that first day, and on the following day 62 banks took another €61.1 billion. Similar operations continued throughout the fall. These "Fine-Tuning Operations" were aimed at lowering short-term interbank rates and were part of the central bank's regular market operations, although the amounts in question were certainly irregular.

The ECB's initial liquidity measures in 2007 and early 2008 were similar in type and scope to the other central banks'. When these measures quickly proved ineffectual in the face of the largest financial crisis since the 1930s, other central banks, with the Fed leading the way in 2008, engaged in unconventional monetary policies, such as QE. These were aimed at lowering longer-term market rates, in the hope of resuscitating a lifeless economy. Trichet refused to follow, arguing that the ECB was to target short-term rates only (Jones 2010). Other governing council members agreed, seeing QE as inflationary or/and as a mandate-violating bail-out of crisis countries (Evans-Pritchard 2009).

Both in interest rate policy and early liquidity measures, the ECB showed it was in denial about the severity of the financial crisis and the eurozone's desperate need for its central bank to act as lender of last resort. It was therefore a radical change when an ECB governor would tell the world two years later that the ECB would do "whatever it takes."

Mission Creep

As the crisis grew worse and threatened to break the currency union itself, it became clear the ECB needed to do more. Over the course of just four years, from 2011 to 2015, the ECB would shift from a "no, never"-approach to unconventional monetary policy to leading the pack. The three policies that we label "mission creep" are the long-term refinancing operations beginning in 2011, the Outright Monetary Transaction policy presented in 2012, and the asset purchasing program (QE) that began in 2015. Our use of this label does not signal a normative stance on our part. We label these policies mission creep because they were far outside what the limited mandate of the ECB specifies, and far from the limits ECB officials set for themselves at the beginning of the crisis.

Long Term Refinancing Operations

As the crisis persisted and even worsened, the ECB realized it would also have to target longer-term interest rates. To begin with, the ECB started extending 3-month loans to financial institutions against collateral, under a new program called "Long-Term Refinancing operations." LTROs would be the first of the three policy measures the ECB would itself label "non-standard." In 2011 the ECB extended this program in the form of 3-year loans. This effectively gave the banks interest-free loans (the nominal rate was 1%). While Trichet had early on denied that the ECB would do QE, several observers saw this LTRO innovation as a form of "QE light" (Pisani-Ferry and Wolff 2012). 3-year LTROs certainly stretched the concept of a "crisis liquidity measure." Draghi defended the move, stating that LTROs were "obviously not at all equivalent to the ECB stepping up bond-buying" (Draghi, quoted in Tooze 2018: 421).

The ECB had finally established a lender of last resort system and was doing what any other modern central bank would do in a crisis. Instead of feeling justified, being a lender of last resort "made Frankfurt queasy to the extreme" (Sandbu 2015: 99). At the end of 2011, as the euro crisis was entering what would be its most dramatic year with a real threat of an EMU breakdown, rather than looking for ways to do more, the ECB was looking for exit strategies for its unconventional monetary policy (ibid.). Yet at the same time, it was using the opportunities the crisis created to pursue its preferred policies in non-monetary issue areas. The different "modes" of crisis handling are here at display at the same time, with both an extremely limited and an extremely expansive view of what central banks could do co-existing in the ECB's operating procedures.

Doing Whatever It Takes—Outright Monetary Transactions

Bond market panic spread to larger Eurozone countries in 2012. Spain and Italy faced market interest rates of 6 and 7%, a rate at which rolling over government debt becomes difficult. The potential for default or a Spanish or Italian "exit" from the euro posed a much larger threat to the EMU writ large than Greece or Portugal ever did. It became clear to the ECB that LTROs would not be enough and they would need to roll out a bigger gun. In a speech given in the summer of 2012, Mario Draghi assured journalists that the ECB would do "whatever it takes" to save the euro, "within their mandate." The markets heard the "whatever it takes"-part as a strong commitment to bail-out Italian and Spanish bonds. Market rates came down considerably in the days and weeks that followed (Randow and Speciale 2018), despite that it would take two months before the ECB formally announced the Outright Monetary Transactions-program to which Draghi was referring. The OMT enabled the ECB to buy almost unlimited amounts of sovereign bonds in the secondary markets, subject to certain conditionalities. The three words spoken by Draghi have been credited with "saving the euro" (Randow and Speciale 2018). The existential crisis of the eurozone was averted, and the OMT program did not need to be used (and has yet to be). The creation of OMT would however reveals cracks in the consensus that had characterized the ECB's policies in the early crisis years. Jens Weidmann, the Bundebank's representative on the ECB's governing board, voted against the OMT program. Chancellor Merkel, however, came out in support, and finance minister Schauble even publicly criticized Weidmann's opposition (Blackstone and Walker 2012).

Quantitative Easing

Quantitative easing is a technical term for the central bank creating money to purchase government and corporate bonds in the secondary market, and in some cases also buying corporate stocks. It is a departure from other liquidity measures in that the central bank is not simply holding these securities as collateral against loans to financial institutions, *but actually buying them*. The other major central banks, Bank of England, the Federal Reserve and the modern pioneer of this strategy, the Bank of Japan, all began QE programs from 2008 on, in an effort to combat the crisis. The ECB delayed for more than half a decade, realizing eventually that it would need to become "buyer of last resort" in certain bond markets.

When the ECB finally did embark on QE in August 2015, it was designed as open-ended from the very beginning—with a fixed monthly amount for asset purchases (beginning at €60bn/month then increased to €80bn in 2016) but no fixed total amount for the program. Here the ECB seemingly learned from the Fed. The Fed began in 2008 with a fixed total amount, but then had to create a second QE program when the first program expired, and finally created "QE3" that was designed to be open-ended. When the ECB announced it was winding down its QE program in December 2018, it had purchased assets for €2.6 trillion over less than four years, at a pace of €1.3 million per minute (Carvalho et al. 2018). At its peak, the ECB's balance sheet was equivalent to more than a third of Eurozone GDP, making it a much larger QE program than the Fed's (at its peak 25% of US GDP).

Because QE blurs the boundaries between monetary policy and fiscal and industrial policy, it was a controversial policy also in other countries. Yet, in the ECB's case it became especially controversial as the ECB decided that not all countries were to be included in the program. The program was designed in a way that disqualified Greek bonds. Paul de Grauwe's (2016) argues that the ECB's QE program meant debt relief for all euro members except for the one that needed it the most. The ECB defended its QE program as simply a program that was designed to improve the "transmission mechanism" for its conventional monetary policy (Andrare et al. 2016). Argued in these terms, purchasing up to a third of member countries' government debt was not monetary debt financing (and thus a violation of the ECB mandate), but simply a way for the ECB to ensure price stability.

And while the QE program was (and in 2019 is still being) challenged legally on the grounds that it violated the debt financing-prohibition of the ECB, it would not be stopped or actively opposed by the powerful member states after initiation. QE is now part of the permanent toolkit of the ECB.[2] As Germany and other parts of the Eurozone slipped back into recession over the summer of 2019, the ECB announced in August it was considered re-upping its QE program in September 2019.

Mission Leap

Extraordinary liquidity measures that challenged the boundaries between monetary and fiscal policy were being undertaken by many central banks. Yet, the ECB would also expand its power in a sense that was unprecedented. The Troika, an informal but extremely powerful alliance of the IMF, the European Commission and the ECB coordinated the financial assistance given to member states in crisis. Both as a part of, and alongside its role in the Troika, the ECB began actively pressing member states on non-monetary issues.

Creditor countries, or international creditor institutions such as the IMF, usually attach conditionalities to loans, conditions that include politically controversial structural reforms. The novelty of the troika, in this respect, was that this coalition of creditors included a non-creditor and supposedly politically independent central bank. During the crisis, the ECB attempted to influence structural reforms relating to fiscal and labour market policy, to decide the distribution of costs associated with bank bail-outs, and even who should be prime minister in some crisis countries. These are issue far beyond the purview of a central bank. While these interventions into the realm of democratic politics were widely criticized, by the governments themselves, by the media, and by economists, these transgressions were left unchecked; There

[2]https://www.ecb.europa.eu/explainers/show-me/html/app_infographic.en.html.

are few reasons to think the ECB will not take the same role in the next crisis, or even possibly seek to influence non-monetary policy in non-crisis periods.

With the bailouts (Ireland, Portugal, Greece, and Cyprus), the semi-bailout (Spain), and the almost bailout (Italy), the ECB engaged in direct efforts at political interference, some including threats of withholding monetary support if certain (non-monetary) policies were not enacted. In this section we briefly present some of the most controversial cases. The scope of this chapter means we cannot do justice to the full "litany of sins" committed by the ECB during the crisis, nor the criticism they garnered. They have, however, already been skillfully catalogued by journalists and academics (e.g., Sandbu 2015; Stiglitz 2016; Henning 2017; Mody 2018; Tooze 2018).

In the case of *Ireland*, the ECB pushed for the Irish government to seek a bailout from the EU when the Irish were trying to deal with their crisis alone. Trichet especially was adamant that the Irish should not structure their bailout in a way that would force a haircut on creditors. Ireland, while in a fiscally much stronger position than Greece and Portugal, was in trouble due to the massive banking crisis in the country. The government had issued an ill-advised blanket guarantee of bank liabilities, putting a great deal of pressure on the government's finances. Over the fall of 2011, interest rates on Irish government bonds were rising. In the latter half of 2011, the Irish government was looking to change its laws in order to make the bank guarantee less generous, seeking to "bail-in" senior bondholders and force creditors of Allied Irish Bank and Irish Countrywide to share in some of the losses. The ECB was not pleased. On November 12, Reuters ran a story quoting official sources that Ireland was in talks with the EU over seeking bailout (Strupczewski and Halpin 2012). The Taoiseach and finance minister denied this, at the time and afterwards. Ireland only had a debt level of 25%/GDP and had a sovereign wealth fund constituting 15%/GDP and felt confident they could weather the spike in interest rates. Three days later, the finance minister received a letter from Trichet, urging Ireland to seek assistance. Trichet threatened to withdraw the emergency liquidity assistance to the Bank of Ireland should Ireland not comply, an assistance the Irish banks were dependent on. Less than a week later, the governor of the Bank of Ireland announced while on a visit to Frankfurt, that Ireland was in bailout talks.

The ECB denied this story and what Ireland's finance minister claimed the letter contained, and Trichet instead said Ireland came to apply for assistance voluntarily (Hirst 2014). To the subsequent embarrassment of the ECB Trichet's letter was leaked to a newspaper three years later, supporting the Irish finance minister's version of events. In the letter, Trichet stressed the amount of liquidity the ECB had provided Irish banks over the preceding couple of weeks, and warned that the assessment of the ECB's exposure to Irish banks "…depends very much on progress in economic policy adjustment, enhancing financial sector capital and bank restructuring" (ECB 2014).

It is puzzling that the ECB should be so insistent that senior bondholders be spared any losses. Even after Ireland sought assistance, the structuring of the bank guarantee was not part of the Troika's memorandum of understanding (Whelan 2012). The IMF admitted later in its evaluation of its Irish program that it had supported bailing-in creditors, but had been overruled by the ECB, and that the IMF considered not sharing losses with creditors was a mistake (IMF 2015). Nor does it seem that Trichet here had the support of the Eurozone's most powerful member. Merkel publicly disagreed with Trichet:

> The president of the European Central Bank has the view that he wants to do everything to ensure that markets take a calm view of the euro zone. We are also interested in that, but we also have to keep in mind our people, who have a justified desire to see that it's not just taxpayers that are on the hook, but also private investors. (Merkel, quoted in Mody 2018: 279).

The politicians saw the need to share some of the bail-out costs with the financial sector for them to be palatable to their domestic constituents, described by commentators as "applying capitalism to banks" (Sandbu 2015: 98). The ECB was not having it. What the ECB and the Commission told Ireland was that they were worried about contagion to other European bank bonds, although market actors at the time saw little risk in this. Forcing these creditors to take a haircut would likely have caused little contagion to other bond markets (Stiglitz 2016: 157; Sandbu 2015: 104).

In the case of *Greece*, the ECB was also active in setting terms for the financial assistance received from the Troika, terms that included structural reforms to the economy, public sector wages, pensions, privatization, and even regulations of which type of milk could be labeled "fresh" in the Greek dairy market (Stiglitz 2016: 201). When Greek debt was to be restructured in 2012, following Sarkozy and Merkel's monumental Deauville agreement, the ECB also got involved. Trichet was active in the negotiations and advocated for a solution that would not trigger credit default swaps (a form of insurance) on Greek bonds, structuring the Greek "haircut" in such a way that it didn't trigger CDS' would punish the prudent investors—who had taken out insurance on their Greek investment. The only beneficiaries would be the European banks that had sold the credit default swaps and would thus have to pay out in the event that Greek bonds "defaulted" under the contract terms (Sandbu 2015: 141). While it was no secret that there were disagreements among the member states and among the Troika institutions on the best solutions for Greece, Trichet made his disapproval of the Deauville agreement public, stating that it would be contradictory to ask bond investors to accept haircuts on government bonds for Greece while at the same time expecting them to remain confident in the government bonds of other peripheral member states (Henning 2017: 108).

On August 5 2011 Draghi, together with his predecessor Trichet, sent a letter to the *Italian* government under Berlusconi, urging them to undertake certain economic reform measures "as soon as possible" in order to save the Italian economy and the euro. The Italian cabinet called a press conference the same day announcing new measures, and the Italian press described a "secret letter" sent from the ECB (Vaciago 2012). The ECB refused to publish the letter at first but published it after it had been leaked to an Italian newspaper two months later. The letter contained policy recommendations that were far outside the scope of monetary policy, including recommending that the regional administrative level in Italy be removed, in addition to privatization and labor market liberalization (Corriere della Sera 2011). While Italy was not under any formal assistance program with the Troika, the Bank of Italy was heavily dependent on emergency liquidity assistance from the ECB, and the entire Italian banking system would be vulnerable should those taps be turned off.

This would become only the beginning of tensions between Italy and the ECB, with Berlusconi publicly blaming the ECB and Commission for his resignation in November 2011, calling it a "plot" to remove him and insert the technocrat Mario Monti in his place (Mackenzie 2014). Dismissed at the time, Berlusconi would later receive support for his account when former US Treasury Secretary Tim Geithner published his financial crisis-memoir. Geithner wrote that several EU leaders approached Obama, asking him to join a plan to remove Berlusconi, a request Obama turned down (quoted in Evans-Pritchard 2014).

While this is not a full account of all the ECB interactions with member states in this period, they exemplify the ECB's highly political activities. We have called these "unchecked transgressions" as they are not only far outside the formal scope of the ECB's mandate, but also violate the existing norms of how central bankers should and shouldn't engage in political questions that are under the jurisdiction of elected politicians (Pisani-Ferry 2015; Buiter 2015). The ECB had become "Europe's sledgehammer" (Stiglitz 2016: 165), a tool to force member states in line and on board with structural reform.

MUDDLING THROUGH TO A POWERFUL NEW NORMAL

This chapter is centered on two ambitions. The first is a stock-taking exercise about gauging output and outcomes, while the second is to analyze the process of how the ECB got to where it is in 2019. Where can we place the EU's monetary policy, and by extension the ECB's position, on a continuum running from "moving forward" to "breakdown"? Our answer on this score is unequivocal. The currency union and in particular the ECB could be used to illustrate the old adage that "what doesn't kill you makes you stronger." Faced with the threat of collapse the ECB, if belatedly and sometimes reluctantly, pulled out all the stops, awarding itself new tools and tasks along the way. The ECB is more powerful in 2019 than it was in 2007. It is also difficult to envisage how this new power could be rolled back, as the ECB's already limited system of political accountability has not been expanded. The ECB now has "almost unrestrained" emergency powers and has not been placed under checks and balances to balance this power democratically (t'Klooster 2018). The legal challenge of the ECB's actions was resolved in the European Court of Justice in 2015, with a win for the ECB. Changing the ECB's mandate or accountability structure requires a treaty change and thus unanimity among member states, a high bar to clear even on far less controversial topics.

This gives rise to a deep constitutional irony. The irony is that the legitimacy of this arrangement partly hinged on the narrowness of the ECBs mandate. Giving the bank one task and one tool—controlling inflation through short-term interest rates—in principle makes it fairly straight forward to hold the bank accountable. It either delivers low inflation or it does not. The combination of a vastly enlarged operational range and an unchanged narrow mandate instead forces the ECB to engage in a convoluted form of policy-making that obscures the nature of its activities, thereby rendering political scrutiny more *difficult*. Simultaneously, narrow mandates limit the scope of issues that can be contested about ECB decisions, so that all questions become procedural. (Dawson et al. 2019).

We have illustrated some of the ECB's key decisions and policy innovations, showing three modes of crisis response; denial, mission creep, and mission leap. This curious mix of responses, and the justifications given for them, present a puzzle. One way of establishing analytically distinct (but often empirically overlapping) explanations is to look for ideas, interests, and institutional logics (Hall 1997). Our ambition is not to develop hypotheses in order to explain a clearly delimited phenomenon. Instead we will illustrate how interest-driven, institutional, and ideational approaches can help us make sense of some of the ECBs key actions.

In a technocratic field like central banking, where normative justifications and mandate formulation draws directly on economic theory, a natural starting point for an *ideational approach* is to examine the assumptions underlying the mix of ordoliberal and new macroeconomic theory upon which the banks mandate and modus operandi was founded (Tranøy and Schwartz 2019). That is, rational expectations and the neutrality of money. The problem with starting a sense-making exercise from this world view is that it has precious little to say about financial crises. To the rational expectations school, a financial crisis is an anomaly, which unless can be attached to a grave policy mistakes, or an external shock, is impossible to make sense of. It offers no blue print for how to deal with a crisis, apart from a deep skepticism towards the ability of governments and democratic politics to deliver fiscal and monetary discipline (se for instance Kydland and Prescott 1977), which in turn can be seen as an argument for the ECBs resistance to be the lender of last resort for governments.

An *interest driven approach,* of which the inter-govermentalist perspective in EU-studies is a fine example, places economic interests and power at the center of analysis. It directs attention to the relationship between the major powers of the EU and their domestic banks (see also Chapter 20 this volume).

Simply put, if the existence of big German, British, or French banks were threatened by a defaults or restructurings that would confer huge losses on these banks, this perspective would lead us to expect that the ECB would come to their rescue with cheap loans (lender of last resort) and policy stances that protect creditors at the expense of taxpayers when countries are bailed out. To a large degree these expectations are borne out by the data, but the way the ECB dragged its feet before starting to subsidize banks big time via the LTRO program in December 2011, indicates that even in a deep crisis material interests are not directly translated into policy by an independent central bank. This points us in the direction of a perspective which gives pride of place to institutional identity.

An *identity-centered approach* directs attention toward the ECB as a (by comparison to its peers the Bank of England and The Fed for example) new institution trying to arrange its adolescent feet in a complex world prone to throwing unpleasant surprises in its face. According to such a perspective, we need to ask: What would be appropriate actions for a self-conscious institution seeking to establish its credentials as the purveyor of monetary policy and financial stability for the Eurozone and the EU's internal market for capital? Firstly, this perspective helps us make sense of the bank's initial reluctance to act as a lender of last resort, even though this is considered an obligation for all of its peers. Instead it guarded this unique omission against its mandate for as long as it could. Secondly, this perspective can help us understand why the ECB took the stance it took in the Irish case. Even in the face of direct calls to the opposite in the shape of the Deauville declaration and Merkel's statement about bailing-in creditors, the bank was willing to lie and manipulate in order to save creditors from taking haircuts. One institutional interpretation is that the ECBs actions during the crisis were guided by a sense of pride in the Eurozone's as an attractive arena for investment and thus responsible for protecting the reputation of the internal market for capital. Haircuts and defaults to any European bonds, even the bonds of countries that had long been in crisis so that markets had priced that risk in, was not acceptable to the ECB under Trichet.

Conclusion

The financial and euro crises were crises for which the ECB was unprepared—intellectually as well as in terms of its toolkit. The limited view of central banking that underpinned the creation of the ECB would come to be confronted with the harsh realities of both modern financial markets and the inherent problems of the currency union. The mandate would end up being unchanged formally, but radically altered in practice, and the policy toolkit of the ECB would be massively expanded to include targeted long-term financing, negative interest rates, and large-scale asset purchases.

The ECB had multiple and contradictory modes of dealing with the crisis, interpreting its own mandate narrowly and expansively at the same time. On the one hand, it jealously defended its narrow price stability mandate, refusing for two crisis-ridden years to take on the lender of last resort function that central banks long have been expected to perform. It was selective in its rescue operations, giving preferential treatment to creditors over taxpayers, and with both its interest rate policy and its liquidity, serving the interests of core member countries over peripheral ones—all the while defending its action with referral back to the sole mandate of price stability. On the other hand, the ECB willingly and aggressively entered unchartered territory for a central bank in seeking to influence fiscal policy and using the threat of withdrawal of lender of last resort-help as leverage.

The ECB short history falls neatly into two time periods. First 10 years of apparent stability bearing out the wisdom of the founding fathers followed by 10 chaotic years of crisis and crisis management from which the ECB has emerged stronger, but also more unruly than ever. The current strength and position of the ECB would appear to leave both sides of the debate on central bank independence unhappy. If one thinks of the first 10 years as the true normal, where the central bank (on the face of things) could deliver price stability by managing aggregate demand through short-term interest rates, one will likely see the expanded lender of last resort functions and QE as threats. Not only to the mandate of price stability, but also an invitation to "politicize" central banking and in so doing threaten its independence over time. The alternative position is to take the policy innovations of the last 10 years as the new normal, as necessary but also more political, and with more far-ranging distributional consequences than anything the ECB had previously been up to. From this vantage point, the impossibility of making a clean cut between technocratic central banking and democratic policy-making comes clearly into view. This position makes it difficult to accept the pretense involved in pursuing with the old mandate, and the weak accountability mechanisms which the ECB's operational realities have long since outgrown.

REFERENCES

Andrade, P., et. al. (2016). *The ECB's Asset Purchase Program: An Early Assessment* (ECB working paper No. 1956.) Available at https://www.ecb.europa.eu/pub/pdf/scpwps/ecbwp1956.en.pdf.

Bagehot, W. (1873/2008). *Lombard Street: A Description of the Money Market*. Sioux Falls: NuVision Publications.

Blackstone, B., & Walker, M. (2012, October 2). How ECB Chief Outflanked German Foe in Fight for Euro. *Wall Street Journal*. Available at https://www.wsj.com/articles/SB10000872396390443507204578020323544183926. Accessed 4 July 2019.

Braun, B. (2017). *Two Sides of the Same Coin? Independence and Accountability at the European Central Bank*. Report for Transparency International EU. Available at https://transparency.eu/ecb-needs-democratic-oversight-if-the-euro-is-to-survive-the-next-crisis/.

Buiter, W. H. (2015, May 21–23). *"Unemployment and Inflation in the Euro Area. Why has Demand Management Failed to badly?"*, ECB Forum on Central Banking. Sintral. Available at https://www.ecb.europa.eu/pub/pdf/other/ecbforumoncentralbanking2015en.pdf.

Carvalho, R., Ranasinghe, D., & Wilkes, T. (2018, December 12). *The Life and Times of ECB Quantitative Easing*. Reuters. Available at https://www.reuters.com/article/us-eurozone-ecb-qe/the-life-and-times-of-ecb-quantitative-easing-2015-18-idUSKBN1OB1SM. Accessed 22 April 2019.

Corriere della Sera. (2011, September 29). La Lettera Original in Inglese: Trichet e Draghi: un'azione pressante per ristabilire la fiducua degli investitori. *Corriere della Serra*. Available at https://www.corriere.it/economia/11_settembre_29/trichet_draghi_inglese_304a5f1e-ea59-11e0-ae06-4da866778017.shtml. Accessed 10 June 2019.

Dawson, M., Akbik, A., & Bobić, A. (2019). Reconciling Independence and Accountability at the European Central Bank: The False Promise of Proceduralism. *European Law Journal, 25*, 75–93.

De Grauwe, P. (2016, May 19). The ECB Grants Debt Relief to All Except Greece. *Social Europe*. Available at https://www.socialeurope.eu/ecb-grants-debt-relief-eurozone-nations-except-greece.

ECB. (2009, May 7). *Introductory Statement with Q&A, Jean Claude Trichet and Lucas Papademos*. Available at https://www.ecb.europa.eu/press/pressconf/2009/html/is090507.en.html.

ECB. (2011, April 7). *Introductory Statement with Q&A, Jean Claude Trichet and Vítor Constâncio*. Frankfurt. Available at https://www.wsj.com/articles/SB10001424052748703858404576214500818460200.

ECB. (2014, November 14). *Irish Letters*. Press release. Available at https://www.ecb.europa.eu/press/html/irish-letters.en.html.

Evans-Pritchard, A. (2009, May 7). European Central Bank Falls into Line and Embraces Quantitative Easing. *The Telegraph*. Available at https://www.telegraph.co.uk/finance/financialcrisis/5292781/European-Central-Bank-falls-into-line-and-embraces-quantitative-easing.html. Accessed 13 June 2019.

Evans-Pritchard, A. (2014, November 12). Tim Geithner Reveals in His New Book How European Officials Tried to Commit Financial Suicide. *The Independent*. Available at https://www.telegraph.co.uk/finance/economics/11226828/Tim-Geithner-reveals-in-the-raw-how-Europes-leaders-tried-to-commit-financial-suicide.html. Accessed 10 June 2019.

Hall, P. A. (1997). The Role of Interests, Institutions, and Ideas in the Comparative Political Economy of the Industrialized Nations. In M. I. Lichbach & A. S. Zuckerman (Eds.), *Comparative Politics: Rationality, Culture and Structure* (pp. 174–207). Cambridge, MA: Cambridge University Press.

Henning, R. (2017). *Tangled Governance: International Regime Complexity, the Troika, and the Euro Crisis*. Cambridge, MA: Oxford University Press.

Hirst, T. (2014, November 6). Here's The Secret Letter That Shows The ECB Forced Ireland to Ask for a Bailout. *Bloomberg Insider*. Available at https://www.businessinsider.com/heres-the-secret-letter-that-shows-the-ecb-forced-ireland-to-ask-for-a-bailout-2014-11?r=US&IR=T. Accessed 10 June 2019.

IMF. (2015). *Ireland: Ex-post Evaluation of Exceptional Access Under the 2010 Extended Agreement* (IMF Country Report No. 15/20). Washington, DC: The

International Monetary Fund. Available at https://www.imf.org/en/Publications/CR/Issues/2016/12/31/Ireland-Ex-Post-Evaluation-of-Exceptional-Access-Under-the-2010-Extended-Arrangement-42656.

Jones, M. (2010, November 13). *Trichet: ECB Support Temporary Not QE, Backs Recovery*. Reuters. Available at https://www.reuters.com/article/us-ecb-trichet/trichet-ecb-support-temporary-not-qe-backs-recovery-idUSTRE6AC10P20101113. Accessed 13 June 2019.

Klooster, J. V. (2018). Democracy and the European Central Bank's Emergency Powers. *Midwest Studies in Philosophy*. https://doi.org/10.1111/misp.12094.

Koeppen, N., & Blackstone, B. (2011, March 22). Trichet Signals Rate Rise Still Likely *Wall Street Journal*. Available at https://www.wsj.com/articles/SB10001424052748703858404576214500818460200. Accessed 6 July 2019.

Kydland, F. E., & Prescott, E. C. (1977). Rules Rather Than Discretion: The Inconsistency of Optimal Plans. *Journal of Political Economy*, 85(3), 473–491.

Mackenzie, J. (2014, May 14). *Italy's Berlusconi Says He Was Forced Out by EU 'Plot'*. Reuters. Available at https://www.reuters.com/article/us-italy-berlusconi/italys-berlusconi-says-he-was-forced-out-by-eu-plot-idUSBREA4D0N720140514. Accessed 10 June 2019.

Mody, A. (2018). *Euro Tragedy: A Drama in Nine Acts*. New York: Oxford University Press.

Pisani-Ferry, J. (2015, May 21–23). *Central Bank Advocacy of Structural Reform: Why and How? Remarks at ECB Forum on Central Banking*. Sintra. Available at https://www.ecb.europa.eu/pub/pdf/other/ecbforumoncentralbanking2015en.pdf.

Pisani-Ferry, J., & Wolff, G. (2012, May 3). Is LTRO QE in Disguise? *VoxEU*. Available at https://voxeu.org/article/ltro-quantitative-easing-disguise. Accessed 10 June 2019.

Randow, J., & Speciale, A. (2018, November 28). 3 Words and $3 Trillion: The Inside Story of How Mario Draghi Saved the Euro. *Bloomberg*. Available at https://www.bloomberg.com/news/features/2018-11-27/3-words-and-3-trillion-the-inside-story-of-how-mario-draghi-saved-the-euro. Accessed 2 July 2019.

Sandbu, M. (2015). *Europe's Orphan: The Future of the Euro and the Politics of Debt*. Princeton, N.J.: Princeton University Press.

Stewart, H. (2011, April 7). European Central Bank Raises Interest Rates to 1.25%. *The Guardian*. Available at https://www.theguardian.com/business/2011/apr/07/interest-rates-held-again-at-record-low.

Stiglitz, J. E. (2016). *The Euro: How a Common Currency Threatens the Future of Europe*. New York: W.W. Norton & Co.

Strupczewski, J., & Halpin, P. (2012, November 12). *Ireland in Aid Talks with EU, Rescue Likely-Sources*. Reuters. Available at https://uk.reuters.com/article/uk-g20-ireland/ireland-in-aid-talks-with-eu-rescue-likely-sources-idUKTRE6AB0NV20101112. Accessed 13 June 2019.

Tooze, A. (2018). *Crashed: How a Decade of Financial Crisis Changed the World*. New York: Allen Lane.

Tranøy, B. S., & Schwartz, H. M. (2019). Illusions of Convergence: The Persistent Simplification of a Wicked Crisis. In J. Batora & J. E. Fossum (Eds.), *Crises, EU Trajectories and the Question of Resilience*. London: Routledge.

Vaciago, G. (2012, August 3). La lettera da Francoforte che ha cambiato l'Italia. *Il Sole 24 ore*. Available at https://www.ilsole24ore.com/art/commenti-e-idee/2012-08-03/lettera-francoforte-cambiato-italia-063800.shtml?uuid=AbZPWYIG.

Whelan, K. (2012). *The ECB's Role in Financial Assistance Program. Policy Paper for the European Parliament*, June. Available at https://www.karlwhelan.com/EU-Dialogue/Whelan_June2012.pdf.

CHAPTER 19

The European External Action Service

Heidi Maurer

INTRODUCTION

The European External Action Service (EEAS) has been formally created with the Lisbon Treaty in 2009 and started operating in December 2010. This was another step in the reform process to further institutionalize European foreign policy cooperation in Brussels and to support member states in coordinating the EU's international activity (Allen 2012). The underlying idea was to unite the various strands of European foreign policy expertise in Brussels from the European Commission (Commission) and the Council Secretariat into one service. It would serve as a quasi-foreign ministry for the European Union (EU), with the High Representative (HR/VP) as foreign minister at its helm. Originally an idea of the constitutional draft treaty, it survived the reform crisis that haunted the EU after 2007, when French and Dutch voters rejected the constitutional draft treaty in referenda. The state-like jargon of foreign minister was dropped, but overall the idea of one service, led by the HR/VP survived and made its way into the Lisbon Treaty. Nevertheless, the timing of setting up a foreign service on the EU level was paired with economic and internal security issues redirecting political attention away leading to fading enthusiasm for strengthening the foreign policy identity of the EU. Additionally, various crises in the following decade shaped the evolution of the EEAS and its head, the HR of the Union for Foreign Affairs.

H. Maurer (✉)
University of Oxford, Oxford, UK
e-mail: heidrun.maurer@politics.ox.ac.uk

© The Author(s) 2021
M. Riddervold et al. (eds.), *The Palgrave Handbook of EU Crises*,
Palgrave Studies in European Union Politics,
https://doi.org/10.1007/978-3-030-51791-5_19

This chapter discusses how subsequently various crises like the European financial debt crisis (2010–2012), the Arab spring (2010 onwards), the turmoil in Ukraine (2014/2015), the migration crisis (2015/2016), have not only driven EU institutional change, but how those crises fundamentally shaped the underlying idea of the EEAS and how its position within the EU institutional framework has been implemented. The various European crises did not necessarily cause the notion of efficiency and being of service to the member states (financial crisis impact), the increased focus on securitization and European interest representation (Arab spring, migration crisis), as well as the repeated plea for necessary ownership by member states (Ukraine and populism), but they were reinforced and mitigated. Those notions have evolved in parallel and also reinforce and complement each other throughout the first decade of the EEAS.

The contested nature of the EEAS and the timing of its evolution reinvigorated the impact of those crises on this new service in the making. For established EU actors those crises have been triggers for change and continuity, like many other moments of contestation before. But their impact on the EEAS was more fundamental due to the timing of those crises during the early formative years of the EEAS (Scenario 3). Nevertheless, the EEAS also showed continuity in its emphasis on security and crisis management, as well as its complementary set-up next to the foreign policies of the EU member states (Scenario 2).

The chapter shows how the various crises left their marks on the conception, set-up, and identity construction of the EEAS. It will first provide the necessary context about what the EEAS was meant to be when it was created with the Lisbon Treaty at the end of 2009, emphasizing the contested nature of the EEAS, which was a compromise between different visions for EU foreign policy action, as well as its unusual status of a service that fulfils foreign ministry tasks without being a foreign ministry in the traditional sense. In a next step, we will focus on two developments that have been reinforced by the ongoing internal and external crises that the EU had to deal with: first, the set-up of the EEAS and how the dictum of "cost-neutrality," "efficiency," and "being of use to member states" triggered by the European financial crisis has shaped the initial set-up but also identity construction of the EEAS from 2010 onwards. Secondly, how the political instability following the Arab spring, the Ukraine crisis, and the migration crisis reinforced the focus of EU foreign policy thinking on European (internal) security and on delivering for European citizens.

The EEAS: A Kind of Foreign Ministry for a Non-State Foreign Policy Actor

More coherence, more efficiency, and more unity were the three mantras that the Lisbon Treaty innovations aimed for in EU foreign affairs. In order to achieve this strengthening of the EU foreign policy identity without changing the underlying unanimous decision-making power of member states in EU foreign policy, EU member states agreed to strengthen the role of the HR/VP and to create an administrative body to support the work of this invigorated role. According to the treaties, the HR/VP is there to support the member states in foreign policy-making by setting the agenda and implementing the Common Foreign and Security Policy (CFSP). The HR/VP does so as chair of the Foreign Affairs Council, as head of the EEAS, as Vice-President of the Commission, and as head of the European Defence Agency (EDA).

Since the Lisbon Treaty, the EEAS and its 140 EU delegations support the HR/VP in the daily EU foreign policy work. It was formally established by Council decision of 26 July 2010 establishing the organization and functioning of the EEAS (Council of the European Union 2010) and started operating in December 2010. Next to assisting the HR/VP it shall work *"in collaboration with the diplomatic services of the Member States"* (Art. 27(3) Treaty on European Union). Staff for the EEAS has been drawn from three different sources, and the underlying idea was to merge the foreign policy expertise present in Brussels from the Commission, the Council Secretariat, and the member states. In addition, the former Commission delegations were upgraded to fully fledged EU delegations and made part of the EEAS. They took over the role of representing the EU politically to third countries from the rotating Council presidency, and now not only represent the community competences but the whole of the EU politically outside of the EU. They are to coordinate with the diplomatic missions of the member states, represent now also joint CFSP decisions to third countries and deliver diplomatic demarches, once those have been adopted by the Foreign Affairs Council in Brussels under the leadership of the HR/VP (Bicchi and Maurer 2018). It must be noted though that the EEAS has been devised as a "service" and not an EU "institution" (see also Van Vooren 2011). It, therefore, does not have the same institutional standing like e.g., the Commission or other EU institutions.

The size of the EEAS and its network of EU delegations is comparable to the diplomatic service of a mid-sized European country (Bicchi and Maurer 2018; see also Austermann 2014). 2805 people were transferred from the Commission (of which 1084 were local staff) and 674 staff came from the Council Secretariat. "Today the EEAS has 3611 staff, including 1551 working in Brussels and 2060 in delegations" (EEAS 2011). In the EU delegations, heads of delegation, deputy heads, staff from the political sections, press and public diplomacy, and administration staff were transferred to the EEAS, although most EU delegations on average only have one EEAS AD post (i.e., the ambassador) (EEAS Human resources report 2015). Next to the EEAS staff working in EU delegations, there are more than 3500 Commission staff posted to the EU delegations. Merging Commission and EEAS staff led to controversy in the first year, as officials continued to receive instructions from both the Commission and EEAS, respectively. An interinstitutional agreement from 2012 (European Commission and HR/VP 2012) tackled this issue and aimed at a smooth and effective cooperation among all EU actors involved by enforcing a double-hatted position of the EU ambassador who would now be the linchpin for both lines of communication and command.

Creating a new service from scratch is a time-consuming task. Forging a new service from different institutions, each-other often opposing parts that is based on a weak compromise by its masters about its (in)dependence and role (Morgenstern-Pomorski 2018; see also Dinan 2011: 112–114). It meant full attention by the upgraded HR/VP and its office holder from 2009 onwards, Catherine Ashton. Ashton was repeatedly criticized for neglecting her role as vice-president of the Commission and for not doing enough in pushing forward new initiatives, as for example, the following account illustrates:

> In its first year of operation the EEAS found itself fully occupied with just keeping the EU's diplomatic show on the road and with coming to terms with the new institutional arrangements which have given rise both to a new set of 'turf wars' and to an enhanced and more significant role for the EP in EU external relations. For this, and other reasons discussed above, the EU was limited almost exclusively to reacting to events and was not able to produce any significant external policy initiatives. (Allen and Smith 2012: 176)

Yet, it is also repeatedly acknowledged that the job description of the reinvigorated HR/VP is nearly impossible for one single person to achieve. In the foreword of the 2013 EEAS review, the HR reflects on those first few months in the following manner:

> There is much that could be written about those early days – and of the extraordinary events that took place as we started to build the service, turning a few words in the Lisbon Treaty into a global foreign policy service of 3400 staff and 139 delegations. I have linked it to trying to fly a plane while still bolting the wings on. The institutional challenges, and sometimes battles, were many. Different ideas on how the service should work and what impact it would have on existing institutions led to difficult decisions and sometimes lost opportunities. (Catherine Ashton in EEAS 2013)

The EEAS and its diplomatic network of EU delegations are neither meant nor equipped to replace the foreign ministries and diplomatic services of the EU member states. The EEAS is to support the HR/VP and complement the diplomatic activities of the member states. Its delegations and the EU ambassadors are now representing the EU politically to third countries, but there had been hardly any additional staff or resources made available. Also, the diplomatic networks of EU member states did not shrink or vanish because of this adaptation. Quite on the contrary, Bicchi and Maurer (2018) shows that despite the set-up of the EEAS and its diplomatic network, member states kept growing their diplomatic networks and reshuffling their diplomatic resources according to their national foreign policy priorities.

The EEAS has also not evolved into a traditional foreign ministry, but it remains an interstitial organization (Bátora 2013). It fulfils most tasks that also foreign ministries in member states take care of, but due to the EU competence division it sometimes can only do less, while on the other hand—when it comes to the coordination of member states—it does more than what traditional foreign policy actors would do (see Duquet 2018). It represents EU foreign policy *cooperation*, but not the foreign policy of a sovereign state. The EEAS, its ambassadors, and EU delegations can only represent the EU position internationally, if all EU member states agreed to this decision beforehand. Nothing changed in this regard with the Lisbon Treaty, and it leaves the EEAS a comparably unusual foreign policy actor.

The timing for getting the EEAS up and running shaped the evolution of this new service considerably. David O'Sullivan, the Chief Operating Officer responsible for establishing this new EU diplomatic service from 2010 onwards, remarked that

> 2011 was a challenging year in which to launch the EEAS. (Like fixing an engine while it's running). It was marked by the eruption of the Arab Spring and the eurozone crisis, which frankly used up most of the political bandwidth available at leaders' level. (O'Sullivan 2012)

This difficult start was exacerbated by the distinct nature of EU foreign policy cooperation and by the also still apparent disagreement between member states and other actors of what the EEAS should be. The Lisbon Treaty as well as the Council decision provided the legal basis but remained vague on details (Maurer and Morgenstern-Pomorski 2018: 307). They "provided the basic parameters of the new service, but gaps remained to be filled" (O'Sullivan 2012), and those gaps had to be filled in the context of several crises impacting the evolution and consolidation of the EEAS in different ways.

The first decade of the EEAS was accompanied by various crisis moments in Europe, as Table 19.1 illustrates. These crises, however, did not only impact the EEAS, but they fundamentally shaped its creation and its evolution during its first decade. In addition to the internal challenges of not being sure about its identity and place in the EU institutional framework, the European financial

Table 19.1 A decade of European External Action Service and European crisis

Year	European crises		EEAS Milestones
2009			**Catherine Ashton** appointed as HR/VP (December 2009)
2010	European debt crisis	From Arab spring to instability in Mediterranean (especially Syria)	Council Decision **establishing** the organisation and functioning of the **European External Action Service** (26 July 2010)
2011			
2012			
2013			**EEAS Review** (September 2013)
2014		Euromaidan, Russian annexation of Crimea	**Federica Mogherini** appointed as HR/VP (November 2014)
2015	Migration crisis		
2016			
2017	Populist rise		**EU global strategy** (June 2017)
2018			

crisis and its "efficiency" and "cost-neutrality" dictum left a considerable mark on the EEAS, as did the Arab spring, the following increase in insecurity in the Mediterranean and the Ukraine crisis. The chapter will in the following show how two distinct but interconnected trends left their mark on the EEAS that were shaped by various crises: Before we look at the impact of the security challenges (crisis after Arab spring, migration crisis) and the readjustment of EU foreign policy priorities to the EU's own security and stability, the next part is going to illustrate how the early years of the EEAS—in the spirit of the European financial crisis and the subsequent national budget cuts—were marked by the notion of "being of service," achieving added value without costing extra ("budget-neutrality") and using the available resources most efficiently.

The EEAS: A Budget-Neutral and Value Delivering Service Built During the Financial Crisis

The EU financial crisis was in full swing when the EEAS started operating in December 2010. Most EU member states had ordered national budget cuts that impacted also their national foreign services (see Balfour and Raik 2013). With economic recession and austerity across Europe, also the EU institutions had to reduce their spending and readjust their budgets. Discussions about the budget had for the EEAS, however, already started before the financial crisis brought cuts on the agenda of policy-makers. This is not specific to the EEAS but most foreign ministries had experienced cuts in financial and human resources during the past two decades, also because of the claimed loss in salience and importance within national political systems. Already during the negotiations of the convention for the constitutional draft treaty, member states had pushed the idea of budget-neutrality of the new service forward. It should provide added value, but not cost more than the foreign policy structures that had already been in place before the Lisbon Treaty reforms. It was the European Parliament (EP), who had insisted on EEAS budget increases over time to make the service fit for purpose (Morgenstern-Pomorski 2018: 157).

Already the 2010 Council decision on establishing the EEAS stipulated that the new service "should be guided by the principle of cost-efficiency aiming towards budget neutrality." For 2011, the EEAS had a total of EUR 464 million at its disposal with a slight increase over the years to EUR 633 million in 2016 (Morgenstern-Pomorski 2018: 137). The draft budget for 2019 allocates EUR 682 million to the EEAS.[1] While a direct comparison is difficult to draw, it still provides useful food for thought to consider that the annual administrative budget for the EEAS is similar to the one for the foreign ministry of the Netherlands,[2] while member states like Spain, Italy, Germany,

---

[1] See Eur-lex Online budget: https://eur-lex.europa.eu/budget/www/index-en.htm.
[2] Budget of the Dutch Foreign Ministry: https://www.government.nl/ministries/ministry-of-foreign-affairs/policy-and-budget/foreign-affairs-budget-2018.

France, or UK spend considerably more on their foreign ministries (for a comparison see Balfour and Raik 2013). The challenge of meagre resources was also acknowledged by O'Sullivan:

> A major challenge for the service will be to fulfil its numerous duties with the existing resources made available to it, since, in addition to carrying on the work previously done by the Commission and Council in the external relations field, we have taken on new functions: we have assumed the rotating presidency role, the chairing of Political and Security Committee and the different geographical and thematic Council Working Groups, while the HR/VP has been chairing the Foreign Affairs Council for a year already. This also includes the so called political dialogue meetings with third counties and international organisations. (Literally hundreds of meetings per year) (O'Sullivan 2011)

The HR also reiterated the difficult economic and henceforth political starting position that the EEAS had to face in her report to the EP the Council and the Commission in December 2011:

> More generally, it would seem that insufficient provision has been made for the needs of the EEAS as an autonomous body in financial and administrative terms. [...] The political and economic context for the launch of the EEAS has been particularly challenging. The global economic crisis and tensions within the euro zone, together with the Arab Spring, have dominated the international agenda. At the same time, public administrations across Europe are under acute budget pressure, with consequences for the diplomatic services of Member States. This is hardly the ideal backdrop for the launch of a new service for the external relations of the Union. (EEAS 2011: paragraph 3)

The limited resources and, more importantly, the amount that was considered justified to spend on the new service within the discourses of national budget cuts and austerity in light of the EU financial crisis shaped the first years of the EEAS. It is not far-fetched to assume that the EEAS would look and be quite different today, if it would have been set-up only ten years earlier and equipped with more substantial financial and human resources. The financial crisis, therefore, did not directly harm the EEAS but the political and economic environment considerably limited what member states considered opportune and justified to spend on the new service. Among informed policy-makers and experts it was no secret that the financial resourcing was insufficient to match the high expectations for an EU international role, as also the following report summary illustrates:

> The broad perception among interviewees is that the EEAS is too understaffed and underequipped to achieve the ambitious objectives of the Lisbon Treaty. Although Member States agreed to establish the EEAS, there is a broad perception that subsequently they did not wish to grant the necessary budget and resources to conduct an effective common foreign policy. (Wouters et al. 2013: 30)

The financial crisis embedded the already low starting point due to resistance of some member states to grant more resources to the new service into a discursive political environment that made it impossible for those who wanted a more fully fletched quasi-foreign ministry to justify higher spending.

For the emerging EEAS, identity was equally important, though, the justifications that EU policy-makers were emphasizing during those formative years were built upon a cost–benefit rationale. In speeches and public interventions, they repeatedly felt the need to justify the very existence of the EEAS by pointing to its usefulness and the added value that it provides for EU foreign policy and for EU member states. "The EEAS and its EU delegations developed the notion of 'being of service to EU member states' in EU foreign policy making as their unique selling point" (Maurer and Morgenstern-Pomorski 2018: 305). In EU terms, having a strong legal footing provides legitimacy, and the EEAS clearly felt like it was lacking this stronghold due to the vagueness of the Lisbon Treaty and the 2010 Council decision. This strong emphasis on justifying the existence of the EEAS left the impression that the EEAS and its leadership often were not too sure about its legitimate role in the first place, or at least that they felt the need to remind other actors about it. The long-term challenge for the EEAS though will be that pragmatic legitimacy construction based on self-interested calculation (i.e., other actors consider the EEAS legitimacy mostly due to the added value that the EEAS provides for them) is only able to provide for a weak form of legitimacy (Maurer and Morgenstern-Pomorski 2018: 308), while it contravenes the creation of cognitive or moral legitimacy based on common understanding (i.e., having the EEAS is the right policy choice). This self-inflicted overemphasis on being of added value is, for example, tellingly illustrated by this passage in the 2011 EEAS report:

> As national diplomatic services are scaling back their resources to concentrate on national priorities, the value added of the delegations is ensuring the EU is properly represented throughout the world. This is not about replacing national diplomatic services, but in making a more effective and cost-efficient use of resources. (EEAS 2011: paragraph 4)

The repeated justifications that the EEAS is providing value for (little) money instead of, for example, constructing an argument based on the need of the EU to have the EEAS due to changing international affairs has been shaped by the political context of the time in light of the financial crisis. This institutional insecurity had been partly home-made by the merger of different political and bureaucratic actors into one new service. Spence (2012: 6–7) had already noted that "the sorely needed formation of a 'we group' and an esprit de corps has not so far been achieved," and Juncos and Pomorska (2014: 316) suggest that "high esprit de corps is especially important for organizations in times of crisis and would therefore benefit the EEAS at a time when EU Member States are trying to deal with the effects of the eurozone crisis." The continued focusing of political energy and will on fixing the Eurozone instead of tackling challenges in the immediate neighborhood further fuelled this institutional insecurity (Whitman and Juncos 2013: 155). And it does not help that, according to Aggestam and Johansson (2017), European and national diplomats developed divergent views about leadership in EU foreign policy in the post-Lisbon system. National diplomats emphasize EU external representation as the main strength of the EEAS, while EEAS officials predominantly refer to their leadership role in agenda-setting and delivering proposals.

The first five EEAS years under the HR/VP leadership of Catherine Ashton focused on consolidation and were shaped by notions of budget-neutrality, efficiency, and being perceived as useful. The EEAS in this regard evolved very much as a child of its times, with the prevailing discourses and justifications not only determining the directions of its set-up but also its identity and legitimacy construction. The appointment of Federica Mogherini as HR/VP in 2014 marked a new stage of the EEAS and its vision for EU foreign policy. Mogherini, as former Italian foreign minister, encouraged on the one hand a more politicized presentation of the EEAS and on the other hand accelerated the politicization of European foreign policy agenda.

The EEAS Delivering (Security) for European Citizens in a Chaotic and Contesting World

Crises that had been in the making for quite some time also shaped the post-2014 EEAS development. EU external crises (Arab winter, Syria, Ukraine) picked up already looming EU-internal challenges (policy stagnation in neighborhood and increasing sense of irrelevance next to new big power game in international affairs) and were followed by institutional and policy adaptation leading to a politicization and securitization of EU foreign policy. Political pressures to show the ability to provide policy solutions after the evolving European migration crisis reinforced the prioritization of European security. EU foreign policy was not able to herald any success in shaping its environment and the ongoing conflicts (with the exception of the Kosovo-Serbia accord in 2013 and the Iran deal in 2015), and at the same time the "crisis in Ukraine brought security concerns close to home" (Natorski and Pomorska 2017: 54). While those different trends did not directly cause a certain EEAS institutional or policy development, they interacted and influenced each other and locked in particular problem identifications. This in turn shaped the policy thinking of the EEAS and the EU, leading to a politicization and securitization of the EU foreign policy agenda and the EU foreign policy strategy, also visibly consolidated in the EU global strategy of 2017.

By 2014, the EEAS had firmly been put in place and many of the internal shortcomings that had been identified in the 2013 review had been addressed. The new HR/VP appointed in 2014, Federica Mogherini brought as former Italian foreign minister a new political impetus to the EEAS. Two characteristics of the EEAS stood out in particular, as they interlinked with other ongoing internal and external trends: a stronger focus on communicating the added value of the EEAS for citizens and a firm situating of security and crisis management units within the EEAS. First, Mogherini put a stronger emphasis on her role as vice-president of the Commission and considerably strengthened the communication policy of the EEAS to the outside world and to EU citizens. This, in part, was in line with a more general trend in diplomacy, where more and more foreign ministries emphasized the direct added value of their work for citizens. "It is in the interest of the European citizens, both inside and outside of the European Union" (Mogherini 2018), and Mogherini ensured that the EEAS would also communicate its added value not only to policymakers in Brussels but in a more colorful and professional manner to the wider world. It fitted with the earlier notion of the EEAS communicating its relevance within the background of the financial crisis, but it placed the main argument on a slightly different and more self-confident footing. Secondly, Mogherini continued the notion of dealing with crisis as a strong asset of the EEAS, which had already developed under Ashton:

> There has been a significant upgrade in the crisis response capabilities of the EEAS […] In addition, the EEAS has recently created a new Situation Room to provide a 24/7 contact and information service […] these arrangements have already demonstrated their value added in the EU response to events in Ivory Coast, Libya and Yemen. The EEAS is working to consolidate the EU's position in other crisis regions, including in particular in meeting the evolving challenges in Afghanistan and Syria. (EEAS 2011: paragraph 5).

In the EEAS organigram, CSDP and crisis management units take up a comparably big space next to the traditional geographical and thematic desks. Foreign ministries normally do not have such units, as those would rather be in the ministry of defence, but in the EEAS these units had been institutionalized over time to deliver for EU crisis management. Mogherini also put political energy behind security and defence development as one concrete output of the EU global strategy, culminating in the signing of the treaty on Permanent Structured Cooperation on Security and Defence (PESCO) in November 2017.

Allen and Smith (2012: 163; for similar argument see also EEAS 2011: paragraph 5) argue that the Arab spring next to various challenges also provided opportunities for the EEAS and the HRVP, as it asked for the coordination of different policy tools and initiatives toward a coherent response, which should confirm the very rationale for creating the EEAS. And at first, those coordinated actions also worked and kept the EEAS busy in its crisis management mode. Yet, as already in the past the EU seemed better to deliver on small technocratic objectives than to provide the big political momentum that would have been needed to facilitate political stabilization in the region:

The overall feeling is one of continuity rather than change in the approach of the EU to the neighbourhood as it continues to deal with problems in a technocratic manner. There is a general lack of EU political imagination – and political will – to make a significant impact in the region through diplomatic and security initiatives. (...) Further, the substantive impact of the European External Action Service (EEAS) on policy formulation and implementation towards the challenges of the EU's neighbouring states remains limited. (Whitman and Juncos 2013: 155)

The stagnation of political progress in the neighborhood and the deteriorating political stability in the aftermath of the Arab spring resulted in a vast deterioration of the security situation in Libya and later in Syria. Ashton, for example, remained active and tried to engage in the Middle East Peace Process, but her role was handicapped due to different positions of member states (Whitman and Juncos 2013: 160–161). Due to the lack of necessary high politics or military tools the EU kept focusing on "on medium and long-term reconstruction and democratization" (Juncos and Whitman 2015: 201). Those reform agendas were, however, not sufficient to have an impact on the increasingly fragile political situation on the ground. In the Libyan as well as in Syrian conflict, the UK and France had been actively involved but often engaged outside of the EU framework with international partners. Once the conflict escalated, the EU had "not played any meaningful diplomatic role so far and no other (military) role is envisaged for the EU, beyond the provision of humanitarian assistance for the Syrian refugees" (Whitman and Juncos 2014: 7).

The Ukraine crisis left a similar mark on the EU foreign policy apparatus and the EEAS, next to the growing instability in the Mediterranean. During the early phase of the crisis in late 2013 and during Euromaidan in spring 2014, the HR/VP and the EU member states kept sending messages of support for the protesters, calling for political dialogue and putting in place targeted sanctions (Juncos and Whitman 2015: 203). The HR/VP went on a diplomatic visit, and the EU attempted to go back to business as usual in supporting the reform processes. Yet, the EU toolkit very quickly proved insufficient, when tensions rose after the Russian annexation of Crimea in March 2014. From then onwards, "the HR/VP and the EEAS were bystanders to this diplomacy as the Member States, via Germany, drove the EU's diplomatic response" (Juncos and Whitman 2015: 206). The EEAS is often criticized for not having picked up the Russian thinking and resistance toward the development of the Eastern Partnership, although it inherited most of the policy thinking from the European Neighbourhood Policy, which had been in place since 2004. The EEAS and the Commission worked closely together in providing a comprehensive policy toward Ukraine, but the often more technocratic policy responses were not able to equip the EU with a political authority that would be needed to engage with the Russian government in this highly politicized context.

The EEAS and its political leadership repeatedly emphasized that EU foreign policy is ready and willing to facilitate the management of crises and turmoil, and that the invigorated EU foreign policy set-up would provide improved and suitable tools. The many conflict situations kept the EEAS busy, and there was a strong will to deliver. But the deteriorating situation in the Southern neighborhood after the Arab spring, the increasing political tension toward the East, and the perceived irrelevance in international affairs as illustrated during the Syria conflict which soon developed into a reality check for the EU and showed the inability or even inadequacy of the EEAS and the HR/VP to be recognized as interlocutor once conflicts hit a certain high politics threshold. This inability to deliver on this more politicized level fuelled disappointment and frustration, and tellingly reminded the EEAS and the HR/VP that they are not a traditional foreign policy actor on par with the foreign policy authority of other international players.

The experiences of the HR/VP and the EEAS as well as the EU member states with those two crises in the South and the East reinforced the shift to a more security-focused and interested-driven formulation of EU foreign policy goals. From 2014 onwards, the actions of EU actors confirmed that they shared the frustrating assessment that

> the EU's milieu-shaping goals and instruments are not equipped for these challenges. An EU response equivalent to the magnitude of these challenges did not take shape during the course of the year. (Juncos and Whitman 2015: 212)

This frustration of not being able to influence or, even worse, of not even being considered a relevant stakeholder by other parties meddling in the crises lead the EU to refocus on its own interests, which matched the growing demand to manage the massive wave of refugees to Europe via the Balkans and the changing public demand in late 2015 to tackle the European migration crisis more proactively. Political attention shifted to strengthening the EU external border controls via a military naval operation to prevent human smuggling in the Mediterranean Sea and via a boost for the EU border management agency Frontex. A second policy shift was the increasing reliance on negotiations with third countries for readmission cooperation, culminating in the November 2015 deal with Turkey to take back illegal migrants in exchange for humanitarian and financial support (for details see Pomorska and Vanhoonacker 2016: 211).

The HR/VP and the EEAS suggested to shift the EU foreign policy objectives from shaping its environment (milieu goals) to putting its own security interests to the fore (possession goals), due to the perceived lack of tools and of ability to manage the security challenges by engaging in the crises directly on the highest political level. There is also an increased European feeling of irrelevance in shaping international events next to foreign policy leaders like Putin or Trump. Since 2016 the HR/VP has time and again emphasised the more chaotic and insecure global environment that EU foreign policy and therefore also the EEAS will need to handle. The EEAS and its diplomatic network "contribute to avoid that the world collapses completely" and the HR/VP warns EU diplomats that it needs to be clearly communicated that despite all the challenges "Europe is not withdrawing from the world stage" (Mogherini 2018). The first paragraph of the EU global strategy puts a similar emphasis on the new threat perception that had emerged among EU foreign policy actors in reaction to the various crises:

> The purpose, even existence, of our Union is being questioned. Yet, our citizens and the world need a strong European Union like never before. Our wider region has become more unstable and more insecure. The crises within and beyond our borders are affecting directly our citizens' lives. [...] We will indeed have to rethink the way our Union works, but we perfectly know what to work for. (Mogherini in foreword of EEAS 2016)

The European Neighbourhood Policy review documents from 2015 onwards as well as the EU global strategy published in 2016 illustrate this shift toward "pragmatic idealism" (EEAS 2016) and "a more interest driven agenda with an explicit focus on security" (Pomorska and Noutcheva 2017: 165). Stabilization of the neighborhood and thus ensuring security for the EU and its citizens was put forward as the main objective, with democratic reforms becoming a secondary concern (Pomorska and Noutcheva 2017: 168). The EU global strategy additionally introduced the concept of "resilience" (Juncos 2017), and overall shows "a less transformative framing of the EU's foreign policy" (Barbé and Morillas 2019: 1). This shift in policy thinking is also illustrated in the 2019 implementation report of the EU global strategy, which lists "EU security" as the main priority before "state and societal resilience to our East and South" (EEAS 2019). The prioritization of the EU's own security and the introduction of a more joined-up policy approach (Barbé and Morillas 2019) further increased the securitization and politicization of EU foreign policy and EU external relations (Costa 2019).

Conclusion

The EEAS created in 2009 evolved amidst various crises that shaped its conception, identity construction, and policy thinking. The dominating austerity discourse of the financial crisis embedded the notions of budget-neutrality and being of added value firmly into the set-up and identity construction of the EEAS. The EEAS right from the start felt the need to justify its existence by showing what it delivers for EU member states and EU citizens in complementing the foreign policy activities of its member states and in supporting the HR in setting the agenda and implementing EU foreign policy. The inability and inadequacy of the EEAS and the HR to manage the rising insecurity in the aftermath of the Arab spring and to find a role in the devastating Syria conflict also reflected the EU experience in the Ukraine crisis.

As proactive and effective interlocutor in the early stages of the crisis the EU (and therefore also the EEAS) were side-lined when the crisis escalated and big member states had to take over to engage in high politics negotiations with the Russian government and Ukraine. Those experiences left a considerable mark on the EU foreign policy identity and lead to a re-consideration of EU foreign policy prioritization. Security for the EU and its citizens was anchored prominently as main objective in the reviewed European Neighbourhood Policy strategy in 2015 and the EU global strategy in 2016.

The first decade of the EEAS was no easy ride (Scenario 2), and there is little hope to suggest that the next ten years of the EEAS will be less crises-driven. For the past two years there has been growing concern among EU foreign policy circles in Brussels that another EU-internal crisis is looming to challenge EU foreign policy: the increase of populist leaders in EU member states who threaten to block EU decisions (Politico 2019; EU Observer 2019) and an increasing disinterest of EU member states in taking ownership in EU foreign policy. EU policy-makers and diplomats keep emphasizing that it is of paramount importance for the EU, its member states, and its citizens to engage in managing crises proactively when and where they occur, despite all the challenges in the current international setting. It is too early to assess if this current trend in European politics remains a timely challenge or will grow into a more substantive crisis for EU foreign policy.

This chapter showed the impact of various crises from 2010 onwards on the EEAS and how those shaped both the institutional set-up and the policy thinking of this newly created EU foreign policy service. Crises did not make (Scenario 3) or break (Scenario 1) the EEAS, but they left a considerable mark, in conjunction with other trends, on the formative first decade of the EEAS (Scenario 2).

References

Aggestam, L., & Johansson, M. (2017). The Leadership Paradox in EU Foreign Policy. *Journal of Common Market Studies, 55*(6), 1203–1220.

Allen, D. (2012). The Common Foreign and Security Policy. In E. Jones, A. Menon, & S. Weatherwill (Eds.), *The Oxford Handbook of the European Union*. Oxford: Oxford University Press.

Allen, D., & Smith, M. (2012). Relations with the Rest of the World. *Journal of Common Market Studies, 50*(Annual Review), 162—177. https://doi.org/10.1111/j.1468-5965.2012.02277.x.

Austermann, F. (2014). *European Union Delegations in EU Foreign Policy: A Diplomatic Service of Different Speeds*. Basingstoke: Palgrave.

Balfour, R., & Raik, K. (2013). *The European External Action Service and National Diplomacies* (EPC Report). Available at: https://www.epc.eu/pub_details.php?cat_id=2&pub_id=3385. Accessed 29 Aug 2019.

Barbé, E., & Morillas, P. (2019). The EU Global Strategy: the Dynamics of a More Politicized and Politically Integrated Foreign Policy. *Cambridge Review of*

International Affairs (Early View). https://doi.org/10.1080/09557571.2019.158 8227.

Bátora, J. (2013). The "Mitrailleuse Effect": The EEAS as an Interstitial Organization and the Dynamics of Innovation in Diplomacy. *Journal of Common Market Studies, 51*(4), 598–613.

Bicchi, F., & Maurer, H. (2018). European Cooperation Abroad: European Diplomatic Cooperation Outside EU Borders. Introduction to the Special Issue. *The Hague Journal of Diplomacy, 13*(1), 1–19.

Costa, O. (2019). The Politicization of EU External Relations. *Journal of European Public Policy, 26*(5), 790–802.

Dinan, D. (2011). Governance and Institutions: Implementing the Lisbon Treaty in the Shadow of the Euro Crisis. *Journals of Common Market Studies, 49*(Annual Review), 103–121.

Duquet, S. (2018). Bound or Unbridled? A Legal Perspective on the Diplomatic Functions of European Union Delegations. *The Hague Journal of Diplomacy, 13*(1), 21–40.

EEAS. (2011, December 22). Report by the High Representative to the European Parliament, the Council and the Commission. Available at: http://www.eeas.europa.eu/images/top_stories/2011_eeas_report_cor.pdf. Accessed 29 Aug 2019.

EEAS. (2013). *EEAS Review.* Available at: http://eeas.europa.eu/library/publications/2013/3/2013_eeas_review_en.pdf. Accessed 05 Sept 2019.

EEAS. (2015). *Human Resources Report 2015.* Available at: https://eeas.europa.eu/sites/eeas/files/eeas_human_resources_report_2015.pdf.

EEAS. (2016). *Shared Vision, Common Action: A Stronger Europe.* A Global Strategy for the European Union's Foreign and Security Policy. Available at: https://eeas.europa.eu/sites/eeas/files/eugs_review_web_0.pdf. Accessed 29 Aug 2019.

EEAS. (2019). *The European Union's Global Strategy Three Years on, Looking Forward.* Available at: https://eeas.europa.eu/sites/eeas/files/eu_global_strategy_2019.pdf. Accessed 29 Aug 2019.

EU Observer. (2019, May 1). EU Ignores Hungary Veto on Israel, Posing Wider Questions. *EU Observer.* Available at: https://euobserver.com/foreign/144768. Accessed 29 Aug 2019.

European Commission & High Representative. (2012). Joint Decision of the Commission and the High Representative of the Union for Foreign Affairs and Security Policy of 28 March 2012 on Cooperation Mechanisms concerning the Management of Delegations of the European Union. JOIN (2012) 8 final.

Juncos, A. (2017). Resilience as the New EU Foreign Policy Paradigm: A Pragmatist Turn? *European Security, 26*(1), 1–18.

Juncos, A., & Pomorska, K. (2014). Manufacturing Esprit de Corps: The Case of the European External Action Service. *Journal of Common Market Studies, 52*(2), 301–319.

Juncos, A., & Whitman, R. (2015). The Arab Spring, the Eurozone Crisis and the Neighbourhood: A Region in Flux. *Journal of Common Market Studies, 52*(Annual Review), 147–161.

Maurer, H., & Morgenstern-Pomorski, J.-H. (2018). The Quest for Throughput Legitimacy: The EEAS, EU Delegations and the Contested Structures of European Diplomacy. *Global Affairs, 4*(2–3), 305–316.

Mogherini, F. (2018). *Speech by HR/VP Mogherini at the Opening Session of the 2018 EU Ambassadors Conference.* Brussels.

Morgenstern-Pomorski, J.-H. (2018). *The Contested Diplomacy of the European External Action Service: Inception, Establishment and Consolidation*. Abingdon: Routledge.

Natorski, M. & Pomorska, K. (2017). Trust and Decision-making in Times of Crisis: The EU's Response to the Events in Ukraine. *Journal of Common Market Studies, 55*(1), 54–70.

O'Sullivan, D. (2011, January 14). *Setting Up the EEAS: Notes from Podcast at IIEA Dublin*. Available at: http://www.eeas.europa.eu/archives/docs/speeches/2011_1201_dos_iiea_en.pdf. Accessed 29 Aug 2019.

O'Sullivan, D. (2012). *The European External Action Service One Year on: Note of Comments Made at European Policy Centre Breakfast Meeting on 25 January 2012*. Available at: http://eeas.europa.eu/images/top_stories/2012_dos_speech.pdf. Accessed 29 Aug 2019.

Politico. (2019, February 5). Black Monday. *Brussels Playbook*. Available at: https://www.politico.eu/newsletter/brussels-playbook/politico-brussels-playbook-black-monday-another-messy-day-in-brexit-trolling-romania/. Accessed 29 Aug 2019.

Pomorska, K., & Noutcheva, G. (2017). Europe as a Regional Actor: Waning Influence in an Unstable and Authoritarian Neighbourhood. *Journal of Common Market Studies, 55*(Annual Review), 166–176.

Pomorska, K., & Vanhoonacker, S. (2016). Europe as a Global Actor: Searching for a New Strategic Approach. *Journal of Common Market Studies, 54*(Annual Review), 204–2017.

Spence, D. (2012). The Early Days of the European External Action Service: A Practitioner's View. *The Hague Journal of Diplomacy, 7*(1), 115–134.

Van Vooren, B. (2011). A Legal-Institutional Perspective on the European External Action Service. *Common Market Law Review, 48*, 475–502.

Whitman, R., & Juncos, A. (2013). Stasis in Status: Relations with the Wider Europe. *Journal of Common Market Studies, 51*(Annual Review), 155–167.

Whitman, R., & Juncos, A. (2014). Challenging Events, Diminishing Influence? Relations with Wider Europe. *Journal of Common Market Studies, 52*(Annual Review), 157–169.

Wouters, J., De Baere, G., Van Vooren, B., & Raube, K. (2013). *Organisation and Functioning of the European External Action Service*. Study Requested by the European Parliament AFET Committee. Available at: http://www.europarl.europa.eu/RegData/etudes/etudes/join/2013/457111/EXPO-AFET_ET(2013)457111_EN.pdf. Accessed 29 Aug 2019.

PART IV

Policy Areas: Crisis, Continuity, and Change

CHAPTER 20

The Financial Crisis: An Introduction

Akasemi Newsome, Marianne Riddervold, and Jarle Trondal

The 2008 collapse of US investment bank Lehman Brothers, within days rapidly followed by the insolvency of US insurance firm AIG, had ripple effects throughout the world economy and a particularly devastating impact in Europe. Not only were the financial sectors of the Eurozone locked in a network of mutual interdependence; European banks were the largest holders of American subprime debt and, hand in hand with Wall Street banks, pushed for the extreme deregulation of global finance dually headquartered in both London and New York in the decades preceding the crisis (Tooze 2018; Cross 2017; Eichengreen 2012). Conventional accounts of the Eurozone crisis commence the timeline with the 2009 public release of information

A. Newsome (✉) · M. Riddervold
Institute of European Studies, University of California, Berkeley, CA, USA
e-mail: akasemi@berkeley.edu

Inland School of Business and Social Sciences, Inland University, Rena and Lillehammer, Norway

M. Riddervold
The Norwegian Institute of International Affairs (NUPI), Oslo, Norway
e-mail: marianne.riddervold@inn.no

J. Trondal
Department of Political Science and Management, University of Agder, Kristiansand, Norway
e-mail: jarle.trondal@uia.no

ARENA - Centre for European Studies, University of Oslo, Oslo, Norway

© The Author(s) 2021
M. Riddervold et al. (eds.), *The Palgrave Handbook of EU Crises*, Palgrave Studies in European Union Politics,
https://doi.org/10.1007/978-3-030-51791-5_20

by the Greek government admitting that it had significantly understated the size of its public debt. These chapters reach further back in time to uncover the roots of the crisis in European Monetary Union (Howarth and Quaglia 2015). Several important developments—the ensuing rollback of regulatory safeguards for finance, the onset of self-regulation by banks, the growth of non-bank financial institutions, the practice among European banks of borrowing sums larger than their capital holdings in order to lend—exacerbated sovereign debt burdens of European countries with the Euro currency (Ioannou et al. 2015). The chapters in this section provide an overview of the Eurozone crisis before discussing various dimensions of how the Eurozone coped, its impact on integration, and the crisis' implications for the future of the EU.

All the chapters converge on the scenario *muddling through* as characterizing the impact of the financial crisis on the integration prospects in finance policy for the EU. However, when it comes to the implications of integration in this area for other policy fields, the authors diverge. Guri Rosén and Espen D.H. Olsen note that reforms in European Monetary Union post crisis triggered citizen unrest in both debtor and creditor member-states directed at both member-state governments and the EU itself. Indeed, it is this assessment of the democratic deficit implicit in the empowerment of the ECB that causes them to refrain from categorizing finance policy post crisis as a case of *heading forward*. Bent Sofus Tranøy and Eirik Tegle Stenstad hint at the implications of the financial crisis for integration in other EU policy areas when they point out that post-crisis reforms did not interrogate how best the financial sector might serve society. James Caporaso directly examines the financial crisis in the polycrisis context and traces the ways in which the financial crisis crippled the EU's response to the migration crisis, which then in symbiotic fashion provided fodder for the Leave campaign in the UK. Caporaso echoes some of the concerns of Rosén and Olsen when he points out the way in which multi-speed Europe, deployed by the EU to keep the UK in, paradoxically helped to push it out, since Britain's desired exclusion from the Eurozone for example thinned its commitment and sense of efficacy in other EU areas where it was active. His chapter concludes that without the UK and its areas of differentiated integration, however, the prospects for future integration for the rest of the EU in areas beyond finance policy are favorable.

Rosén and Olsen's chapter on 'The EU's response to the financial crisis' underscores how the Eurozone crisis started as a problem of access to credit but then threatened to destabilize the Eurozone permanently. There was differential impact in that Spain and Italy had large public debt-to-GDP ratios, while Ireland and Greece's problems were so severe that the countries could no longer borrow money. They rely on a three-pronged approach assessing firstly, how political institutions responded, then turning to what the relevant divides were on how the EU should respond, before examining lastly the policies that the EU implemented. For Rosén and Olsen it is clear that the financial crisis spurred new and innovative actions by some EU actors during the crisis. For example, the European Central Bank (ECB) took the step of purchasing government bonds from the Eurozone countries such as Greece, which were locked out from credit markets in order to shore up their economies. As a result of the crisis, agencies such as the ECB gained new powers in the European Banking Union. The ECB would provide oversight for banks in Eurozone states; serve as a key regulator in executing the steps for bank failure via the 'single resolution mechanism;' and guarantee bank deposits with the introduction of an 'European Deposit Insurance Scheme' and the 'European Semester.' The latter provides Euro area governments with a binding framework for coordinating budgets and fiscal policy (see Tranøy and Hjertaker, this volume). Notwithstanding the new competences for the ECB, when Rosén and Olsen turn to the political process underpinning how these decisions were made, the authors surmise that the scenario that best describes the impact of financial crisis on integration is *muddling through*. This is owing to the fact that EU member-states were reluctant to use supranational institutions such as the Commission or the Parliament to reform the role of the ECB. Instead, they came together outside of the supranational structures in order to limit the loss of national sovereignty over banking.

Rosén and Olsen go as far as to identify the way in which the Commission and the Parliament were sidelined by member-states during the crisis and later brought back in order to execute and apply the reforms member-states were able to agree upon as policymaking under 'emergency Europe.' The authors broach the question of if in times of polycrisis, 'emergency Europe' has become the normal mode of business. Indeed, this question leads into a larger discussion by the authors about a mode of conducting politics in the EU that results from polycrisis and the ways in which this mode exacerbates the exclusion of citizen voices from the policymaking process. Along the same line, Rosén and Olsen are critical of the decisions by member-states to exclude politics from the financial crisis by empowering the ECB, an EU institution by design removed from citizen input and influence. They note that in this way, depoliticization, paradoxically, leads to increased politicization and polarization around the EU's role in finance, particularly when this role is experienced by citizens as harsh austerity measures and cuts to the public sector without accompanying visible declines in power and prestige for banks and financial elites. They note that 'redistributive conflicts became structured by the pro-/anti-EU dimension more strongly than before.' Although Rosén and Olsen pose the question of 'emergency Europe' as a way of getting things done in the polycrisis context, the other two chapters do not share this assessment. This is in part owing to the conclusion reached by Caporaso as well as Tranøy and Stenstad that the reforms did not go far enough.

In their chapter, 'Failing forward in financial stability regulation,' Tranøy and Stenstad expand the 'failing forward' thesis of Jones et al. to argue that although the Eurozone crisis resulted in innovative reforms and continued integration in the immediate aftermath of the crisis, the first reforms were not extensive enough to forestall another crisis and thus constituted, *muddling through.* Yet, in the current period the authors believe supranational interests have been more successful in gaining the upper hand vis-à-vis reluctant member-states and thus the longer-term response to the crisis shows evidence for *heading forward.* Their chapter identifies a mechanism key to explaining why the reforms fall short of what is needed—namely, 'social learning' in the context of Jones et al.'s earlier specified 'lowest common denominator bargaining' as well as 'functional spillover' dynamics among member-states. In other words, 'social learning' refers to the way in which policymakers view the menu of available policy choices while simultaneously taking into account the likely preferences of fellow policymakers and the possibilities of convincing others and being convinced by others of a specific policy choice. For the authors, a policymaker's grasp of the menu of policy choices in the case of the Eurozone crises depended in part on whether their diagnosis of the crisis was rooted in 'Chicago-style economics' or 'Keynesian thinking.' The former entails lightly regulating different sectors of finance separately as needed based on the assumption that markets are self-correcting. The latter involves comprehensive regulation of finance as a system based on the assumption that markets are regularly subject to erratic developments. Tranøy and Stenstad then consider how each diagnosis of the crisis, as needing either government regulation that is minimal and sectoral or alternatively new rules that are interventionist and systemic, fits with supranational governance.

In contrast to the other two chapters, Tranøy and Stenstad root their explanation of the post-crisis reform in disputes among member-states. Member-states had distinct opinions on how much sovereignty to cede to supranational interests—the French government was comfortable with ceding more oversight over its banks and the banking sector overall, whereas the Germans were split, favoring more oversight over large banks and wanting to keep smaller banks under national supervision. The UK favored less supranational regulation over the Eurozone banking system and also had the largest and most globalized finance sector. In the end, the UK was unable to block the desire of other member-states to create the Single Supervision Mechanism with oversight over '82 percent of the Eurozone banking assets.' Germany succeeded in exempting some of its smaller banks from supranational supervision and in carving a role for national bank officials in a supervisory board together with the ECB.

The authors identify a change in the dominant view of banking governance as a result of the crisis that qualifies the long-term impact of reforms as *heading forward.* Before the crisis, officials in the national Euro area banks and in the Commission subscribed to a perception of markets as trending toward greater efficiency and officials believed that the securitization reduced risk. Post crisis, Tranøy and Stenstad find evidence that 'thinking of markets as inefficient riddled with preferred habits…herding…and agents with less than idealized rationality' dominated and produced policy recommendations such as the de Laroisiére Report and the UN Stiglitz Commission, which underpinned post-crisis reforms. However, the authors signal that the reforms remain incomplete if new and innovative because officials' comprehension of market instability did not extend to the non-bank or shadow banking financial sector. Given that traditional banks are still very much interconnected with non-bank financial institutions, Tranøy and Stenstad see problems on the horizon with potential contagion across regulated and un-regulated nodes of the financial system.

In an approach marked by an acute awareness of the overlapping nature of crises afflicting the EU, Caporaso's chapter 'The Euro in a Triple Crisis Context and its Impact on the EU' analyzes how the Eurozone crisis was to and influenced by the simultaneous unfolding of Brexit and the refugee crisis. He argues that the financial crisis presents the greatest potential for *heading forward* while Brexit and the migration crisis offer conditions more suited to the *breaking down* of the EU. His chapter analyzes the role of institutions in enabling these crises and shows that there are limits to the ability of institutions to shape preferences in ways that further deeper integration. The case of the UK is unique in that the piecemeal use of differentiated integration via opt outs and exceptional clauses generated, in his words, a heightened sense within Britain that the nation-state had 'lost control' in the very areas of EMU and Schengen where the UK opted out in order to retain sovereignty in these domains. Caporaso also investigated political divisions within the EU on how best to tackle the Eurozone crisis by focusing either on austerity approaches designed to keep inflation low vs. Keynesian stimulus designed to jumpstart the economy. He then examined cleavages within and among member-states about whether either macroeconomic philosophy was appropriate to the EU or not. For Caporaso, these political divides made it especially difficult for member-states to embark on full fiscal union by giving the EU the ability to tax, although institutional reforms were implemented to create a 'lender of last resort' out of the ECB and the new regulatory agency, the European Stability Mechanism (ESM).

In terms of how the triple crisis context created challenges and opportunities for the deeper integration of EU member-states in finance, Caporaso points out that the refugee and financial crisis combined to generate an obstacle to further integration. In his view, 'Italy and Greece, the two primary first destinations, were ill equipped to respond [to the refugee crisis] since they both had sluggish economies as well as high levels of unemployment' and in this way served as 'the worst possible constellation of locations, interests and actors' needed to develop a common approach to the refugee crisis. This combination in Caporaso's estimate supported an environment in which *breaking down* of member-states' commitment to find supranational solutions to the refugee crisis, took place. On the other hand, Caporaso argued that the financial crisis and Brexit, and to a lesser extent, the refugee crisis interacted in ways that increased the potential for *heading forward* in financial integration. Public opinion polls indicated that the percentage of UK voters in favor of remaining in the EU declined with the unfolding of the refugee crisis in the run up to the vote in 2016. For Caporaso, once the UK has left the EU, reforms to the governance of the financial sector concluded by the Eurozone member-states, stand to take on more of the characteristics of fiscal union.

REFERENCES

Cross, M. K. D. (2017). *The Politics of Crisis in Europe*. New York: Cambridge University Press.

Eichengreen, B. (2012). European Monetary Integration with Benefit of Hindsight. *Journal of Common Market Studies, 50(1)*, 123–136.

Howarth, D., & Quaglia, L. (2015). The Political Economy of the Euro Area's Sovereign Debt Crisis. *Review of International Political Economy, 22(3)*, 457–484.

Ioannou, D., Leblond, P., & Niemann, A. (2015). European Integration and the Crisis: Practice and Theory. *Journal of European Public Policy, 22(2)*, 155–176.

Tooze, J. A. (2018). *Crashed: How a Decade of Financial Crises Changed the World*. New York: Penguin Random House.

CHAPTER 21

The EU's Response to the Financial Crisis

Espen D. H. Olsen and Guri Rosén

INTRODUCTION

This chapter addresses the EU's response to the financial crisis. In August 2007, credit difficulties of transnational investment banks and insurance companies upended the global economy, what is often referred to as the "subprime crisis" (Menéndez 2013: 463). This credit crisis developed into an institutional crisis that eventually put into question the very sustainability of the Euro as a common currency. As national and European institutions struggled to handle the effects of the crisis, the very rationale of a European system of integration was questioned. After the initial phase of the crisis, numerous countries in the Western world went into recession. Key member states of the Eurozone, showed more than a few signs of not being able to balance the books according to models of financial and economic stability. At the same time, smaller states suffered credit failures and the consequences of increased sovereign debt.

Most political and academic commentary has focused on the macroscopic consequences of crisis. The economy, financial systems, fiscal stability, budget deficits, and institutional breakdown have been widely discussed. We add a discussion on the *democratic* consequences of crisis reactions and institutional changes. In so doing, the chapter draws attention to the possibility that the

---

E. D. H. Olsen (✉) · G. Rosén
Oslo Metropolitan University, Oslo, Norway
e-mail: Espen.H.Olsen@oslomet.no

G. Rosén
e-mail: Guri.Rosen@oslomet.no

© The Author(s) 2021
M. Riddervold et al. (eds.), *The Palgrave Handbook of EU Crises*,
Palgrave Studies in European Union Politics,
https://doi.org/10.1007/978-3-030-51791-5_21

initial crisis measures have mutated into a form of "emergency Europe" where the "state of exception" becomes part of ordinary policymaking and institutional thinking. This normalization of emergency politics begs the question whether this can be theorized as a form of continuity of already existing patterns of EU decision-making or change either in the form of breakdown or institutional innovation. We do not conclude definitively on this issue but draw attention to different democratic problems with what some EU scholars see as institutional innovation and new budgetary politics in the Eurozone.

The EU reacted to the crisis through both short-term measures and longer-term institutional changes. In this chapter, we chart both these types of responses to the financial crisis. First by surveying the literature on the financial crisis, highlighting different understandings and conceptualizations of the financial crisis from subfields of the social sciences, such as EU studies, institutional theory, law, and political economy. We then utilize the main points from the literature survey as a starting point for a discussion of the EU's responses according to the framework of polity, politics, and policy. The financial crisis became more than a crisis of a few select financial institutions; it became a global, regional, and national crisis of economic and fiscal institutions due to the complex interdependence of states, national budgets, and flows of capital in our globalized world. As such, to chart the responses of a state or an international organization such as the EU, there is a need to analyze changes to *policy*, its effects on *politics* and patterns of conflict, as well as institutional ramifications of the *polity*. In utilizing this analytical scheme, this chapter will nuance the story of change and continuity in EU financial politics, which is an overarching aim of this handbook.

The chapter maps onto the three scenarios of possible crisis development this handbook centres around: (1) the *breaking down* of institutions; (2) *muddling through* in path-dependent and incremental responses; or (3) *heading forward* by policy changes and institutional innovation. The literature review and our discussion of policy, politics, and polity highlights that the EU has foremost resorted to some form of *muddling through* by relying on already existing concepts and policy repertoires, while at the same time also creating some new institutional frameworks. Yet, as we will show, EU scholars argue that this was no "revolution" in institutional terms, but rather followed some well-known logic of hybrid arrangements that are neither fully supranational nor intergovernmental. This varied approach to crisis resolution is moreover an indication of the debate on differentiated integration in the EU after the crises (see Leuffen et al. 2012; Batora and Fossum 2019).

This chapter is organized in the following manner: First, we give an account of the development of the financial crisis, focusing on short-term measures and longer-term policy and institutional changes, including banking union, the European Semester as well as other legislative and treaty changes. Secondly, we present an overview of the literature on the EU's *responses* to the crisis, which we subsequently draw on in our analysis. Thirdly, we examine the EU's response along the three dimensions of politics, policy, and polity before we sum up our analysis in our concluding remarks.

Development of the Crisis

Pollack et al. write (2010: 498): "The centrepiece of the EU is the creation of a single European market with common rules and rule-making, and, for the Eurozone members, with an experiment in common monetary and coordinated fiscal policy." It was precisely the latter experiment that was put to the test when the global financial crisis progressed into the Euro crisis and triggered a deep economic recession in several EU member states.

With the Maastricht Treaty, the EU member states resolved to "establish an economic and monetary union including, in accordance with the provisions of this Treaty, a single and stable currency." The ambition was that by 2002, the Euro would replace national currencies.[1] To join the common currency, the member states would have to ensure that the government deficit was kept within 3% of GDP and public debt levels to 60% of GDP. Prior to the introduction of the Euro, the member states agreed the Stability and Growth Pact,[2] which established a set of rules and regulations to secure budgetary discipline by reinforcing the monitoring and coordination of national fiscal and economic policies. According to Copelovitch et al. (2016: 814), the general perception of policymakers was that it had been a formidable success, even helping "Europe to weather the 2007–2008 global financial crisis." These optimistic assessments would soon be proven wrong.

One could say that the starting point of the Eurozone crisis was when Greece, in 2009, acknowledged that its debts were much higher than previously disclosed. When these news broke, the price of Greek bonds rose sharply, leaving the Greek government unable to pay off—or refinance—its debts. In the first instance, the EU, together with the International Monetary Fund (IMF), provided Greece with a bailout package in return for austerity policies and structural reforms. During the months and years that followed, also Cyprus, Ireland, Portugal, and Spain would turn to the EU for help. As will be further described below, while several of these countries eventually received bailout, the EU also devised a range of policies to stem the crisis. In the words of Howarth and Quaglia (2015: 458), the Eurozone crisis "prompted an unprecedented degree of policy intervention at the national, EU and international levels designed to prevent a potential domino effect of sovereign debt defaults."

The EU's main response can be described as twofold: First, a set of measures aimed at stabilizing the markets and preventing the crisis from

---

[1] At the time, the United Kingdom, Sweden, and Denmark, decided not to join the Euro.
[2] The original Stability and Growth Pact consisted of one European Council Resolution and two Council regulations.

spreading, and later also from emanating. Second, a set of reforms were developed to remedy the structural problems of the European Monetary Union (EMU), which many critics claim contributed to the severity of the crisis in the EU (e.g., Lane 2012; Copelovitch et al. 2016; Jones et al. 2016).

The measures aimed at crisis management centered on the provision of financial assistance. In May 2010, the European Financial Stability Facility (EFSF) was created as a mechanism. With a lending capacity of €440 billion, it was to provide financial help to countries in the Euro area in order to preserve financial stability. In addition, the European Commission could use the European Financial Stabilisation Mechanism (EFSM) to provide loans to countries that were experiencing, or were threatened by, "a severe economic or financial disturbance caused by exceptional occurrences beyond its control." From 2012, the tasks of the EFSF and EFSM were taken over by the European Stability Mechanism (ESM). ESM is an agency—hence a permanent rather than temporary mechanism—designed to fund future financial assistance, including direct loans and loans to recapitalize banks. Funding from the ESM is conditional on the recipient country enforcing policy measures, amending the treaty accordingly: "*The Member States whose currency is the euro may establish a stability mechanism to be activated if indispensable to safeguard the stability of the euro area as a whole. The granting of any required financial assistance under the mechanism will be made subject to strict conditionality*" (Article 136(3)). Between 2010 and 2016, the EFSF and ESM distributed more than 250 billion Euros.[3]

Facing massive pressure from the financial markets, the European Central Bank (ECB) also took measures to restore faith in the Eurozone through a series of bond-purchasing programs (Högenauer and Howarth 2019). As argued by Hjertaker and Tranøy (this volume), the crisis has meant that the ECB has ventured "far beyond the scope of central banking without any formal changes to its intentionally narrow mandate" (p. 340). These measures included the Security Markets Programme and the Outright Monetary Transactions Programme, which enabled the ECB to buy sovereign debt in the secondary market. Schmidt (2016) argues that the ECB's approach to the crisis initially was aimed at projecting credibility through keeping the inflationary target, while denying that the ECB had the role of "lender of last resort." With Mario Draghi at the helm, however, the narrative shifted to "stability," accompanying the bond-buying program, which was an instrument largely opposed by the German government (see Matthijs and McNamara 2015). The ECB wanted to make very clear that it would do whatever it took to stabilize the Euro (Högenauer 2019: 293). In 2012, Draghi gave a speech where he stated: "Within our mandate, the ECB is ready to do whatever it takes to preserve the euro. And believe me, it will be enough" (European Central Bank 2012).

---

[3] https://www.esm.europa.eu/about-us/history.

Among the larger structural reforms implemented in the wake of the Eurozone crisis were: (1) the Banking Union; (2) the European Semester; and (3) the reorganization of the Stability and Growth Pact through a collection of new laws and the Fiscal Compact, which is part of the Treaty on Stability, Coordination and Governance.

The financial crisis started ouSt with several banks experiencing liquidity problems, and the EU's Banking Union was set up to prevent new banking crises by enhancing the EU's capacity in regulation, supervision, and resolution (Weisman 2017: 1). Moreover, the Banking Union was argued to complete the EMU (Howarth and Quaglia 2013) and rests on three pillars: The Single Supervisory Mechanism, the Single Resolution Mechanism, and the European Deposit Insurance Scheme. The Single Supervisory Mechanism sets up a supervision system for the euro area and EU countries that have decided to join. The main supervisor of the banks is the ECB aided by national supervisory authorities as well as the European Banking Authority, an agency established in 2011, responsible for implementing the set of rules for EU banking. These rules are enshrined in the Single Rulebook, which constitutes the foundation for the Banking Union. The Single Resolution Mechanism aims to ensure orderly failure, so that member states will have a common approach to manage failing banks. In addition, it provides for resolution planning and early intervention measures (Howarth and Quaglia 2013). Finally, the European desposit ensurance scheme is meant to secure bank deposits, and essentially prevent a run on the banks, that is "panic withdrawals by customers of their bank deposits because of fear of collapse" (Howarth and Quaglia 2013: 107). However, this particular aspect of the Banking Union has proven hard won, and is yet to be realized (European Commission 2017).

The crisis also instigated reforms in the governance of EU economic policies, and especially in the area of budgeting and fiscal policy. The European Semester was a first effort to establish a framework for coordinating national policies, building on, and developing, existing procedures within the Stability and Growth Pact, the Broad Economic Policy Guidelines, and the Lisbon Strategy (Verdun and Zeitlin 2018: 138). The European Semester introduces a cycle of economic and budgetary reporting and monitoring, bringing together a range of other instruments established in the wake of the crisis. In 2011, a set of six legislative measures was decided aimed at strengthening the Stability and Growth Pact and introducing macroeconomic imbalance procedures. Known as the "Six Pack," it provides detailed rules for national budgeting, for example by strengthening the debt criterion of the Stability and Growth Pact, introducing limits to annual growth in expenditure, enhancing the surveillance of member states. In 2013, two new regulations (the "Two Pack") were decided, extending the existing legislation in the areas of surveillance and budgetary procedures. In the first half of January 2012, the EU agreed on the fiscal compact, aiming to create budgetary stability, foster budgetary discipline, and more generally to improve the governance of the Euro area. Based on the Treaty on Stability, Coordination and Governance, the fiscal compact sets limits for national expenses and debt, and—compared to the Stability and Growth Pact—correction mechanisms enter into force sooner, if countries break the rules.

Taken together, these measures testify to the comprehensive nature of the EU's response to the crisis, both in the immediate and long term. The reforms also encouraged a broad spectrum of academic research, which we address in the following section.

Research on the EU's Response to the Financial Crisis

The Eurozone crisis triggered a plethora of studies from various disciplines, aiming to chart, understand, and explain the consequences of the Eurozone crisis. In this chapter, we chart the literature based on political analysis of crisis responses in the *EU context*, coming mainly from political science, political economy, and law.[4] As Ioannou et al. (2015: 155) argue, there is a need to "(...) understand not only the economics but also the politics and institutions of the crisis." For instance, this is pivotal to understand why the crisis did not lead to the dissolution of the common currency or the breakdown of European institutions and the integration project. To exemplify the magnitude of work on the crisis, a search on Google Scholar shows how the Eurozone crisis spawned a large literature (Fig. 21.1).

In political science and law, research on crisis responses has mostly dealt with policy changes, institutional developments, and wider ramifications for the EU as a compound polity of supranational institutions and member states (for an overview, see Ioannou et al. 2015). Verdun (2015) for instance, traces the EU's responses to the financial crisis through a historical institutionalist lens. She shows how the EU followed the response favored by prominent political economists such as De Grauwe (2012), Eichengreen (2012), and Krugman (2011, 2012) which was to usher in new institutional innovations as a consequence of a failing system. Yet, despite "new" institutions such as the EFSF, the ESM, the European Semester, and the Fiscal Compact, the EU response followed, according to Verdun, well-known institutional structures. The new institutions followed a combined supranational and intergovernmental logic based on binding rules but with considerable room for member state involvement, especially from the creditor states.

Ioannou et al. (2015) underline the integrative steps taken by the EU in response to the crisis. They emphasize how the EU's response was incremental and stepwise, linking to a logic of supranational spill-over, while

---

[4] In this overview of existing research our aim is mainly to highlight different approaches and perspectives on the EU's response(s) to the financial crisis. It is not exhaustive in the sense that it covers the ground completely, as this would be too big a task for a short chapter. The main tendencies in the literature coming from EU research and political analysis are covered, focusing on policy decisions, institutional developments, and to some lesser degree the ramifications for EU integration writ large.

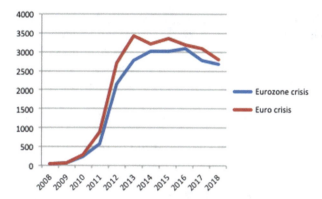

Fig. 21.1 Overview of publications on the Eurozone crisis (This overview is based on a search for "euro crisis" and "Eurozone crisis" between 2008 and 2018. There is bound to be some overlap between the articles in each search, but the distribution nevertheless demonstrates the change over time)

Schimmelfennig (2015, 2018) focuses on the relative importance of national preferences and interstate bargaining for the outcome of EU institutional reform. What unites most such institutional and EU studies-oriented accounts is that rather than "big bang" institutional developments changing the system radically or institutional breakdown, they show that these integrative steps were incremental and addressed specific problems that occurred as the crisis progressed. Moreover, it is claimed that "the resulting institutions contributed to overcoming the peak of the crisis… and will provide a better framework for preventing and managing future crises" (Ioannou et al. 2015: 164). A further argument is that the achievements of the EU in terms of institutional innovation and responses are "remarkable," visible for instance in the rapid institutionalization of a banking union only years after the fiscal coordination in the EU had been seen as "toothless" (ibid.: 164).

In their work on "the new intergovernmentalism," Bickerton et al. (2015) underline the "comeback" of the member states at the heart of EU affairs. They do this partly by arguing that the EU in responding to the onset of financial and institutional crisis from 2007 to 2008 did not increase powers of the Commission—its "executive branch"—but rather relied on intergovernmental solutions. This lack of institutional supranationalism in the wake of the crisis is augmented by an intensification of policy coordination between member states in the EU, both in responding to the financial crisis and in general. They go on to conceptualize such style of integration through so-called de novo bodies: Both the ECB and the ESM eschew traditional supranational mechanisms and rather "(…) considerable autonomy by way of executive or legislative power" (Bickerton et al. 2015: 705). The new intergovernmentalism approach argues that the EU responded to the financial crisis not only through a renewed focus on the member states but also on "depoliticized" bodies with considerable power that fall to the side of traditional channels of accountability and legitimacy.

The observation from Bickerton and his coauthors that the EU has chosen to eschew traditional democratic accountability for autonomous expert bodies represents a less sanguine take on the EU's handling of the financial crisis. Work coming from critical political economy, EU law, and democratic theory supports this impression. Tooze (2018) has written one of the most complete overviews of the financial crisis as an American, European, and global phenomenon. His conclusion of the EU and its response to the financial crisis is that it was "one of the worst self-inflicted economic disasters on record" (Tooze 2018: 10). Part of Tooze's argument is that the EU handled the crisis through a fragmented approach, where ultimately one country—Greece—was blamed for failure on the supranational and systemic level. Scharpf (2010) has taken a similar stance in his analyses of the socioeconomic, institutional, and domestic consequences of the European management of the financial crisis. Focusing less on the fact that EU institutions *did* something as immediate responses to instability and crisis in the financial sector, Scharpf (2011: 22) underlines that creation of the ESM and EFSF entailed that governments in need of assistance "had to accept extremely tough commitments to fiscal retrenchment and supply-side policy reforms." This, he argues, has become a model for a *general* system of fiscal supervision in the Eurozone over the budgets of independent and sovereign states. This stands in contrast to EU experts who laud the Union's achievements in institutional innovation.

Another example of a more critical account is the comprehensive overview of EU crisis management by Menéndez (2013), who claims that the EU faced an "existential crisis," which was governed in an inconsistent manner. Menéndez (2013: 508ff.) highlights how EU crisis responses both fostered and undid the market at the same time. One example is that the historical and contemporary rhetoric of the importance, if not, necessity of creating an unimpeded and "free" single market in Europe has met with considerable market-intruding measures in the role of the ECB in allocating financial resources in the EU. Moreover, the EU has taken on considerable new powers to perform macroeconomic coordination, yet not in a *European* sense, but rather through correcting *national* economies. This has led to a system of Eurozone management where a strengthened sanctions regime ultimately steered by the Commission may inflict strong demands on member states facing financial and fiscal distress (Menéndez 2013: 511).

The financial crisis was a systemic crisis and EU scholars with an interest in institutional theory and institutional change (or inertia) highlighted crisis-driven reforms. Their focus has been on the challenges that the financial crisis posed for the EU system of governance and they have sought to understand and explain the institutional outcomes of the EU's responses to this complex crisis. Yet, the EU is more than an international regime or international organization bent on decision-making within clearly delimited substantive fields. The EU is a political system of law-generating institutions, with considerable democratic implications, both on the European and domestic levels of decision-making. Discussions on the democratic aspects of crisis management have, however, been left largely to democratic theorists and, perhaps surprisingly, political economists. Scharpf (2015) provides a perceptive critique of the state of European democracy "after the crash." The new regime of Euro monetary and fiscal policy had demonstrable economic and distributional consequences, especially in the debtor states. The institutional responses from the EU continue to constrain domestic capacity to use national budgets to foster economic growth (Scharpf 2015: 390ff.). In terms of EU democracy, such developments have further constrained *democratically accountable* governments in the member states, while supervision from *technocratic* arrangements on the supranational level must be complied with for the sake of fiscal stability in the logic of the Euro Area.

Matthijs (2014) echoes this criticism, focusing especially on the effects of the crisis in Southern Europe. He argues that the crisis itself and the ensuing institutional responses by the EU highlighted the "tension between legitimate domestic democratic choices in the South and the demands from technocratic supranational institutions dominated by the North" (2014: 102). The subsequent question is whether national electorates have significant democratic agency post-crisis, again in stark contrast to the more positive angle taken by scholars who focus on institutional reform alone. Finally, a normative analysis of the Eurozone crisis claims that the EU has eschewed its traditional two-level or multilevel form of Euro Area governing in the pursuit of crisis resolution (Bellamy and Weale 2015). Bellamy and Weale (2015: 257) argue that for democratic quality to be reintroduced to the EMU, "member states must treat each other as equals and be representative of and accountable to their citizens on an equitable basis." The EU's response through, for instance, the Fiscal Compact as a form of supranational legal constitution was unjustifiable as it denies reasonable disagreement between citizens and among states on issues of economic policy (ibid.: 271).

These reflections on the *democratic* consequences highlight how the *muddling through* of initial crisis responses may lead to some form of *heading forward* in the scenario parlance of this book, albeit not necessarily change for the better from a democratic standpoint. As we have shown, the EU initially responded through relying on known institutional and policy frameworks, before innovating in some new institutional solutions. These solutions are, however, no panacea to the EU's democratic deficit or the more general legitimacy crisis of post-crisis Europe. Our survey of democratic theory on the EU in the financial crisis accentuates a differentiation not only in institutional terms, but also in the supranationalization of European democracy. The technocratic and extra-democratic procedures chosen to instill budgetary and fiscal *discipline* on some EU member states stand in danger of undermining basic principles of popular legitimacy and the democratic autonomy of national parliaments. The literature on the financial crisis has been dominated by the institutional and policymaking strands of EU studies, yet one could question whether this democratic downfall should receive more attention in future research.

A survey of the *Journal of Common Market Studies* shows that only five of 732 articles published between the launch of the Single Market and mid-2009 dealt with factors that led to the financial crisis of the EU (Ryner 2012). In following up this survey, Ryner (2015) takes a critical stance on the Eurozone crisis—from the vantage point of so-called critical political economy—its management by EU institutions, and the role of mainstream EU research. While research based on institutional theory, integration theory, market theory, social policy analysis, and democratic theory have much to teach us about the causes of and responses to the financial crisis in Europe, Ryner (2015: 275) argues that the scholarly response to "the anomalies that the EA crisis poses for European integration scholarship has been minimalist and complacent." Focusing on responses alone, simply charting these from some predetermined theoretical lens, may render results that do not highlight enduring structures and interests that condition the choices made (or not) by researchers. Highlighting possible alternative trajectories of EU institutions and dominant member states' crisis handling, Ryner (2015) concludes that the EU responded to the contradictions of an enduring monetary union based on a logic steeped in an "ordoliberal iron cage."

With this survey of different perspectives on the EU's response to the financial crisis, we have highlighted institutional and democratic issues of the Euro crisis. In the next sections of this chapter, we highlight some examples, issues, and putative consequences of the EU's crisis mode in terms of politics, policy, and polity.

Politics

The EU's bailout packages were hard-fought, and in the countries that received them, protests against their consequences broke out. Heads of the State and Government would quarrel over whether Greece should receive financial assistance, while the Greek people were taking to the streets, protesting the demands for austerity that they would have to bear (Dinas and Rori 2013). Thus, the Euro crisis had broad ramifications on the *politics* of the EU.

During the first years after the crisis hit, more or less permanent negotiations took place. There were multilateral talks within the EU, between the EU and the IMF and in the G20-format, but also extensive bilateral exchanges. Who were to finance the new financial instruments, and at what price? In this phase, the key arena was the European Council and the Council (Carstensen and Schmidt 2018), with member states from Northern Europe were at the demand side of the table (Biermann et al. 2019). The German government was particularly vocal in advocating against the creation of Eurobonds (Bulmer

2014). Germany was not only the largest potential contributor, but the Bundesbank was also highly skeptical about the ECB buying bonds "on principle." Once the ECB had decided to go further with its bond-buying, leader of the Bundesbank and representative on the ECB's governing board, Jens Weidmann, criticized the plan on several occasions (Bulmer 2014). However, Angela Merkel as well as the German finance minister, Wolfgang Schäuble, would express their support (Hjertaker and Tranøy, this volume).

As described above, the ECB was initially unwilling to act as a lender of last resort, but once it entered the scene in full capacity, it was resolute in shaping the EU's response. Hjertaker and Tranøy (this volume) argue that while the measures that enabled the ECB to buy sovereign debt were a form of competence-creep, albeit significant, the real leap forward was the conditionality accompanying monetary support to member states. They contend that the ECB, through its role in the Troika, put pressure on member states to initiate non-monetary reforms: "With the bailouts (Ireland, Portugal, Greece and Cyprus), the semi-bailout (Spain) and the almost bailout (Italy), the ECB engaged in direct efforts at political interference, some including threats of withholding monetary support if certain (non-monetary) policies were not enacted" (p. 347). Also in this respect, the ECB received ample backing from the German government. Bulmer (2014: 1254–1255) for example describes how the "discourse of austerity," fits into the German reliance on ordoliberal principles, both as an idea and concrete strategy (more on this below).

Although the problem was identified as one belonging to the structure of the Eurozone, solutions were decided outside the framework of the EU. The crisis made manifest a latent, geographical cleavage between member states from the North and South. Many of the net contributors to the EU's budget, and henceforth also to the bailout packages, the former group of member states demanded austerity policy in return for financial assistance. Matthijs and McNamara (2015: 230) make the argument that this narrative of urgently needed reforms was not a result of similar economic mismanagement in all the debtor countries: "Rather than correct the institutional flaws in the euro's design and build the necessary fiscal, financial, and political unions, leaders doubled down on a story of Northern Saints and Southern Sinners." They ascribe the resulting policy to a set of social structures where the ideas of academics, bankers, investors, and government officials dominated. Other authors emphasize the interplay between politics at the EU and national levels. Statham and Trenz (2013: 299) underline how national governments had to defend their position vis-à-vis their national electorate, and that justifying payments to fellow member states faced considerable domestic opposition, particularly in Germany. In a study of parliamentary debates about the European Financial Stability Fund (EFSF), however, Kinski (2018) shows a somewhat contradictory pattern where government parties defend the measures devised at the EU level with reference to the EU as a whole, rather than exclusive national interests.

Still, there is little doubt that the Euro crisis led to more contestation about the EU (e.g., Kriesi and Grande 2016; Leupold 2016; Statham and Trenz 2015; Wonka 2016). Examples from Germany show how the media would amplify the cleavages between member states. After Draghi had announced that the ECB would do "whatever it takes" to save the Euro, for example, the newspaper Bild declared that this was like a "blank cheque for debtor states" (quoted in Bulmer 2014: 1258). Not only did public confrontation of the European integration project increase, which we return to below, it also produced a heightened level of conflict within legislatures. Research has demonstrated how the cleavages in the European Parliament (EP) changed in the wake of the crisis, strengthening the pro-/anti-EU conflict in the chamber (Otjes and van der Veer 2016). Instead of amplifying economic voting patterns, i.e., the dominant left–right dimension, after the EU took control of national budgetary policies, redistributive conflicts became structured by the pro-/anti-EU dimension more strongly than before (ibid.: 257). Interesting in this regard is Rohrschneider and Whitefield's (2016) finding that European mainstream parties did not respond to the Eurozone crisis by questioning European integration, which left the field open to Eurosceptic parties.

Thus, increasing politicization of the EU's handling of the crisis did not mean, that the majority of MEPs opposed the EU's response. The majority of party groups in the EP put stability first (Roger et al. 2017), which meant that they tended to support the initiatives of the Commission and Council (see also Laffan and Schlosser 2016). As argued by Blumenau and Lauderdale (2018: 463), MEPs responded to the crisis by becoming "more tolerant towards policies that they might previously have opposed." This was because the crisis strengthened the agenda-setting powers of the European Commission, which contrasts with the argument made by others who claim that the Commission was "not very visible in early crisis management" (Puetter 2012: 172). While we return to the role of the Commission below, it is important to take note of the complexity of the EU's response to the crisis, which oscillates in focus between the institutions as well as overtime. As we describe further in the subsequent sections, this implies significant changes to the EU as a political order, but before we move to the discussion about the polity-side of the EU's response, we need to connect the politics to the policies.

Policy

As we saw from the overview of the research on EU crisis handling, responses by the EU were largely institutional and policy-oriented. Uniting these responses is their origins in some form of "rescue package." Such rescue packages were meant to first alleviate the short-term issues of crisis in financial systems and member states fiscal standing. Yet, they have also become mid- to long-term solutions that are becoming institutionalized as part of the Eurozone architecture. These rescue packages that originated from what White

(2015: 300) has called "the highest stakes – the necessity of bare survival" has to considerable extent become "normal" policymaking and policy-steering institutions on the supranational level. White (2015) argues that the EU's forging of an EU budgetary regime has the traits of what he calls "emergency Europe." This means that the crisis style of making rapid decision to avert the consequences of a crisis has become a way of doing policy also in the longer run. In other words, the responses of the EU have slowly developed into a policy style of its own, partly based on existing institutions as highlighted by scholars focusing on institutional issues, but *also* acts of "legal improvisation as much as suspension" (ibid.: 300). This may have consequences for the way policy is produced at the EU level, but also for its status as polity built on democratic ideals.

The obvious problem in terms of democracy is that crises understood as immediate emergencies may result in the arbitrary breach of legal norms and in the heightening of preexisting power imbalances, which are slowly being codified into specific emergency norms (White 2015) that endure way past the resolution of the immediate crisis. Moreover, the policy focus on emergencies may blur the understanding of the structural causes of the problems and foster a possible addiction to emergencies themselves with policy implications, not only for the response taken to handle the crisis but also in long-term policy processes. In the EU, this is clearly linked to the difficulty of tackling emergent societal challenges, visible for instance in the surprise among EU leaders and member states that structural issues of the Eurozone area could lead to a fiscal crisis of the magnitude seen in 2010. The EU tends to enter into a dynamic of procrastination and manifestly inadequate action, as argued by Tooze (2018) in the case of the financial crisis, which may paradoxically lead to emergency action. Not taking such emergency action is then often legitimized by the argument that inaction risk to damage vital public interests.

Analyzing the EU's response to the financial crisis as an instance of "emergency Europe" goes against the main thrust of the research we surveyed in the section on previous research. Yet, it may not be that simple. While highlighting that the institutional and policy solutions the EU made to counter the crisis were surprisingly effective, some EU scholars still would subscribe to the tenet that the EU is as White (2015: 312) highlights "an institutional arrangement produced incrementally and continually in a process of modification." Indeed, several of the researchers cited above would argue that the EU handled the crisis also through a form of incremental logic. No completely new institutions or policies were created, rather they did often build on existing solutions. Through such analysis, steeped in theories of European integration, we know much about the minute details of the EU's response to the financial crisis, yet this short discussion of its wider policy implications highlights the need for a broader scholarly debate on the consequences for how politics is done in the EU governance architecture. The perspective from critical political economy draws our attention to the possible existence of enduring frames and dominant ideas (an ordoliberal "iron cage") that conditions not only policy decisions but also the way most EU scholars understand and analyze the underlying problems as well as the chosen solutions of the financial crisis. We do not take sides as such between different perspectives on how the EU responded to the financial crisis and the consequences thereof, but would argue that looking at this solely from the perspective of the "classical" European integration theories only takes us so far. More critical perspectives are needed, as well as those that take a broader outlook on the effects of the crisis handling, not only for economies, member state budgets, or the financial system, but also for the democratic life of the EU and its member states. What further transpires from this is, then, that the policies created by the EU in the wake of the financial crisis also have implications for the Union as a political order, and it is to these responses that we now turn.

Polity

The Eurozone crisis led to a comprehensive debate not only about the future of the Union, but also about whether it had a future at all. So fundamental was the shock of the Eurozone crisis that the very existence of the polity was held to be at stake (Menéndez 2013; Eichengreen 2012). In this section, we focus on two dimensions of the EU's response to the financial crisis that had particular impact on the Union polity: The relationship between member states and supranational EU actors and the democratic implications of the crisis management.

The EU's response to the Eurozone crisis caused debate among researchers about whether and how it strengthened the member states and institutions such as the European Council and Council or rather supranational actors such as the Commission or the ECB (Bauer and Becker 2014; Bickerton et al. 2015; Niemann and Ioannou 2015; Puetter 2012; Schimmelfennig 2015). As described above, the conflict between the member states during the Euro crisis was pronounced. At the same time, massive policy reforms had to be undertaken, which could only be decided by the European Council, i.e., Heads of Government. Thus, a key argument of the new intergovernmentalists is that while the crisis entailed further integration in the realm of economic governance, it did not lead to the transfer of competence to supranational institutions (Bickerton et al. 2015). A key example is the Treaty on Stability, Coordination and Governance, which was negotiated and agreed outside the framework of the EU. Another illustration is the amendment of the Treaty of the European Union to accommodate for the establishment of the European Stability Mechanism, which was decided by-passing ordinary revision procedures, and hence intergovernmental conference. In the words of Puetter (2012: 162): "The European Council has emerged as the centre of political gravity in the field of economic governance" and "[t]he Council and the Eurogroup fulfil a crucial role as forums for policy debate." As described above, the German government used its leverage on several occasions to ensure that. Schoeller (2019: 3), however, underlines that German leadership very much depended on the issue at stake: "Especially in cases where Germany did not seek to provide leadership, supranational institutions such as the European Commission, the European Parliament, or the European Central Bank (ECB) had the chance – or were forced – to fill the leadership vacuum."

Thus, others argue that the pronounced role of the European Council only holds for the first phase of the crisis, and the first stages of the decision-making processes. Carstensen and Schmidt (2018: 610) suggest an interaction between the measures devised by the EU to stem the crisis and the balance between the institutions: "Increasing pressure to save the euro that followed from the adverse consequences of crisis management in the first part of the crisis opened up space for supranational actors to employ ideational and institutional power to leverage their expertise and implementation capacity in ways that challenged the coalition of Northern European member states, which themselves were no longer able to dominate the European Council." This ties in with the argument made by Bauer and Becker (2014): "During the crisis, the Commission may have kept a rather low profile, but its role in the reformed economic governance architecture appears not to be diminished but strengthened." In analyzing the European Semester, Verdun and Zeitlin come to a similar conclusion (2018: 138), describing how it is the EU institutions that are responsible for "monitoring, scrutinizing and guiding national economic, fiscal and social policies, specially within the euro area."

We will not attempt to settle the score on the debate on institutional balance here. Our point is rather to highlight the ramifications of the combination of formal leadership by the member states—obviously eager to signal that they are in charge—and the implementation stage where supranational actors reenter the fray. First, this risks reinforcing the image of technocracy and democracy, second, the Euro crisis has had some discernable effects on the institutional balance, if not at the executive level, then at least for the legislators. Although there is disagreement about the effect of the crisis on the European Council, ECB and Commission, there seems to be unison agreement that the European Parliament (EP) got the short end of the stick. Fasone (2015) for example, claims that the legislative acts meant to strengthen the Stability and Growth Pact only provided a small role for the EP, which risks undermining the principle of "no taxation without parliamentary representation" in the EU. In the establishment of the Banking Union, the EP complained that it was being side-lined (Howarth and Quaglia 2013) and throughout the European Semester it plays a similarly diminished role (Verdun and Zeitlin 2018). Although there is evidence of some variance across the different measures (Rittberger 2014), the Eurozone crisis clearly challenged the existing democratic order of the EU.

Furthermore, the lack of democratic influence and oversight also has implications beyond the EP as decision-maker. Högenauer (2019: 291) argues that while the efforts to depoliticize the management of economic policies and "reduced the opportunities for democratic contestation," this also "bred frustrations that led to politicization." Negotiated behind closed doors, citizens were left to wait while governments and technocrats hammered out the details. Intergovernmental decision-making processes, exemplified by the Treaty on Stability, Coordination and Governance, which was negotiated and agreed outside the framework of the EU, add to this tendency, inter alia by omitting involvement of the EP. This deliberate seclusion and exclusion of popular participation, contributed to the contestation of EU policies: "in so much as the governments' and EU institutions' attempts to depoliticize the crisis actually exacerbate popular perceptions about the EU's democratic deficit leading to public claims making" (Statham and Trenz 2015: 297, see also Hooghe and Marks 2019).

The EU's policies also had clear effects on public support. In the words of Matthijs and McNamara (2015: 231): "These effects were put on display during the Eurosceptic assault on Brussels in the May 2014 elections for a new European Parliament. Voters openly questioned the EU's democratic legitimacy and underscored their fundamental lack of trust in EU institutions." The geographical cleavage is also present in the patterns of public support, for example in attitudes toward policy and polity. Hobolt and de Vries (2016) underline how respondents from South and Eastern Europe back further integration, whereas respondent from the North is supportive of the EU regime, but express less support for further policy integration. While these diverging preferences present European politicians with a quandary about which direction to take the Union, it underlines how support for the EU is multidimensional (ibid.: 426). EU citizens do not only consider EU policies when expressing their level of support for the EU, they also take the polity dimension into account. This suggests that, to safeguard the legitimacy of the Union, politicians need to factor both dimensions when shaping their response, even during times of crisis.

Concluding Remarks

The financial crisis in the Eurozone struck the EU and its member states to the core of their political and economic systems, to the extent that some feared it would mean the end of the Euro project and ultimately European integration. Yet, despite this perception of the crisis, the EU's response was not to break down, but much closer to some form of *muddling through*. Initial crisis reactions were not highly coordinated and bore the sign of typical EU style of crisis management, which is some form of "wait and see." As the response of EU institutions and powerful member states became more concerted, the solutions chosen were still based on some structure of combining supranational and intergovernmental solutions, as shown by scholars with an institutional outlook. New institutions and arrangements such as the banking union or the EFSF were novel in that they surpassed the initial institutional structure of the EMU. Most EU scholars underline that this was no "revolution" in institutional terms, but rather followed some well-known logic of hybrid arrangements that are neither fully supranational nor intergovernmental. Moreover, as we have learnt from legal analysis and critical political economy, the institutional and policy solutions chosen have eschewed democratic channels of accountability and have perhaps led the EU even further into an "ordoliberal" iron cage.

In this sense, we would question whether the EU's response to the financial crisis really is a case of *heading forward* as one of the scenarios outlined in this book for overall assessment of EU crisis politics. The key tenets of the monetary union persist. The rules of the Stability and Growth Pact outlined thresholds for state debt and budget discipline. The new institutions and rules of the Eurozone Area post-crisis have added surveillance mechanisms, sanctions, and supranational oversight, which dig deeper into the fiscal and thereby democratic sovereignty of member states. In other words, the crisis response did not undermine the structure of Eurozone governance, but built on already existing mechanisms and added some features to increase supranational control over domestic budgets.

References

Batora, J., & Fossum, J. E. (Eds.). (2019). *Towards a Segmented European Political Order. The European Union's Post-Crises Conundrum*. London: Routledge.

Bauer, M., & Becker, S. (2014). The Unexpected Winner of the Crisis: The European Commission's Strengthened Role in Economic Governance. *Journal of European Integration, 36*(3), 213–229.

Bellamy, R., & Weale, A. (2015). Political Legitimacy and European Monetary Union: Contracts, Constitutionalism and the Normative Logic of Two-Level Games. *Journal of European Public Policy, 22*(2), 257–274.

Bickerton, C., Hodson, D., & Puetter, U. (2015). The New Intergovernmentalism: European Integration in the Post-Maastricht Era. *Journal of Common Market Studies, 53*(4), 703–722.

Biermann, F., Guérin, N., Jagdhuber, S., Rittberger, B., & Weiss, M. (2019). Political Non(reform) in the Euro Crisis and the Refugee Crisis: A Liberal Intergovernmentalist Explanation. *Journal of European Public Policy, 26*(2), 246–266.

Blumenau, J., & Lauderdale, B. E. (2018). Never Let a Good Crisis Go to Waste: Agenda-Setting and Legislative Voting in Response to the EU Crisis. *Journal of Politics, 80*(2), 462–478.

Bulmer, S. (2014). Germany and the Eurozone Crisis: Between Hegemony and Domestic Politics. *West European Politics, 37*(6), 1244–1263.

Carstensen, M. B., & Schmidt, V. (2018). Power and Changing Modes of Governance in the Euro Crisis. *Governance, 31*(4), 609–624.

Copelovitch, M., Frieden, J., & Walter, S. (2016). The Political Economy of the Euro Crisis. *Comparative Political Studies, 49*(7), 811–840.

De Grauwe, P. (2012). The Governance of a Fragile Eurozone. *Australian Economic Review, 45*(3), 255–268.

Dinas, E., & Rori, L. (2013). The 2012 Greek Parliamentary Elections: Fear and Loathing in the Polls. *West European Politics, 36*(1), 270–282.

Eichengreen, B. (2012). When Currencies Collapse. *Foreign Affairs, 91*(1), 117–134.

European Commission. (2017). Communication to the European Parliament, the Council, the European Central Bank, the European Economic and Social Committee and the Committee of the Regions on Completing the Banking Union, Brussels, 11.10.2017, COM (2017) 592 final.

European Central Bank. (2012, July 26). Speech by Mario Draghi, President of the European Central Bank at the Global Investment Conference in London. https://www.ecb.europa.eu/press/key/date/2012/html/sp120726.en.html.

Fasone, C. (2015). European Economic Governance and Parliamentary Representation: What Place for the European Parliament? *European Law Journal, 20*(2), 164–185.

Hobolt, S. B., & de Vries, C. (2016). Public Support for European Integration. *Annual Review of Political Science, 19,* 413–432.

Högenauer, A. L. (2019). 'The Politicisation of the European Central Bank and the Bundestag', *Politics and Governance, 7*(3), 291–302.

Högenauer, A.-L., & Howarth, D. (2019). The Democratic Deficit and European Central Bank Crisis Monetary Policies. *Maastricht Journal of European and Comparative Law, 26*(1), 81–93.

Hooghe, L., & Marks, G. (2019). Grand theories of European integration in the twenty-first century. *Journal of European Public Policy, 26*(8), 1113–1133.

Howarth, D., & Quaglia, L. (2013). Banking Union as Holy Grail: Rebuilding the Single Market in Financial Services, Stablizing Europe's Banks and 'Completing' Economic and Monetary Union. *Journal of Common Market Studies, 51,* 103–123.

Howarth, D., & Quaglia, L. (2015). The Political Economy of the Euro Area's Sovereign Debt Crisis: Introduction to the special issue of the *Review of International Political Economy*. *Review of International Political Economy, 22*(3), 457–484.

Ioannou, D., Niemann, A., & Leblond, P. (2015). European Integration and the Crisis: Practice and Theory. *Journal of European Public Policy, 22*(2), 155–176.

Jones, E., Kelemen, R. D., & Meunier, S. (2016). Failing Forward? The Euro Crisis and the Incomplete Nature of European Integration. *Comparative Political Studies, 49*(7), 1010–1034.

Kinski, L. (2018). 'Whom to represent? National parliamentary representation during the eurozone crisis', *Journal of European Public Policy, 25*(3), 346–368.

Kriesi, H., & Grande, E. (2016). The Euro Crisis: A Boost to the Politicisation of European Integration? In S. Hutter, E. Grande, & H. Kriesi (Eds.), *Politicising Europe: Integration and Mass Politics*. Cambridge: Cambridge University Press.

Krugman. P. (2011, November 11). This Is the Way the Euro Ends. *New York Times Blogs*. Available at: http://krugman.blogs.nytimes.com/2011/11/09/this-is-the-way-the-euro-ends-2/?_r=0.

Krugman, P. (2012, May 24). Greece and the Euro: Is the End Near? *Truthout*. Available at: http://truth-out.org/opinion/item/9358-greece-and-the-euro-is-the-end-near.

Laffan, B., & Schlosser, P. (2016). Public Finances in Europe: Fortifying EU Economic Governance in the Shadow of the Crisis. *Journal of European Integration, 38*(3), 237–249.

Lane, P. (2012). The European Sovereign Debt Crisis. *Journal of Economic Perspectives, 26*(3), 49–68.

Leuffen, D., Rittberger, B., & Schimmelfennig, F. (2012). *Differentiated Integration: Explaining Variation in the European Union*. Houndmills: Palgrave Macmillan.

Leupold, A. (2016). A Structural Approach to Politicisation in the Euro Crisis. *West European Politics, 39*(1), 84–103.

Matthijs, M. (2014). Mediterreanean Blues: The Crisis in Southern Europe. *Journal of Democracy, 25*(1), 101–115.

Matthijs, M., & McNamara, K. (2015). 'The Euro Crisis' Theory Effect: Northern Saints, Southern Sinners, and the Demise of the Eurobond. *Journal of European Integration, 37*(2), 229–245.

Menéndez, A. J. (2013). The Existential Crisis of the European Union. *German Law Journal, 14*(5), 453–526.

Niemann, A., & Ioannou, D. (2015). European Economic Integration in Times of Crisis: A Case of Neofunctionalism? *Journal of European Public Policy, 22*(2), 196–218.

Otjes, S., & van der Veer, H. (2016). The Eurozone Crisis and the European Parliament's Changing Lines of Conflict. *European Union Politics, 17*(2), 242–261.

Pollack, M., Wallace, H., & Young, A. R. (2010). EU Policy-Making in Challenging Times: Adversity, Adaptability, and Resilience. In H. Wallace, M. A. Pollack, & A. R. Young (Eds.), *Policy-Making in the European Union* (6th ed., pp. 481–502). Oxford: Oxford University Press.

Puetter, U. (2012). Europe's Deliberative Intergovernmentalism: The Role of the Council and European Council in EU Economic Governance. *Journal of European Public Policy, 19*(2), 161–178.

Rittberger, B. (2014). Integration without Representation? The European Parliament and the Reform of Economic Governance in the EU. *Journal of Common Market Studies, 52*(6), 1174–1183.

Roger, L., Otjes, S., & van der Veer, H. (2017). The Financial Crisis and the European Parliament: An Analysis of the Two-Pack Legislation. *European Union Politics, 18*(4), 560–580.

Rohrschneider, R., & Whitefield, S. (2016). Responding to Growing European Union-Skepticism? The Stances of Political Parties Toward European Integration in Western and Eastern Europe Following the Financial Crisis. *European Union Politics, 17*(1), 138–161.

Ryner, M. (2012). Financial Crisis, Orthodoxy, Heterodoxy and the Production of Knowledge About the EU. *Millennium: Journal of International Studies, 40*(3), 647–673.

Ryner, M. (2015). Europe's Ordoliberal Iron Cage: Critical Political Economy, the Euro Area Crisis and Its Management. *Journal of European Public Policy, 22*(2), 275–294.

Scharpf, F. W. (2010). The Asymmetry of European Integration, or Why the EU Cannot Be a 'Social Market Economy'. *Socio-Economic Review, 8*(2), 211–250.

Scharpf, F. W. (2011). *Monetary Union, Fiscal Crisis and the Preemption of Democracy* (LEQS Paper No. 36). Available at SSRN: https://ssrn.com/abstract=1852316 or http://dx.doi.org/10.2139/ssrn.1852316.

Scharpf, F. W. (2015). After the Crash: A Perspective on European Multilevel Democracy. *European Law Journal, 21*(3), 384–405.

Schimmelfennig, F. (2015). Liberal Intergovernmentalism and the Euro Area Crises. *Journal of European Public Policy, 22*(2), 177–195.

Schimmelfennig, F. (2018). Liberal Intergovernmentalism and the Crises of the European Union. *Journal of Common Market Studies, 56*(7), 1578–1594.

Schmidt, V. (2016). Reinterpreting the Rules 'by Stealth' in Times of Crisis: A Discursive Institutionalist Analysis of the European Central Bank and the European Commission. *West European Politics*, 39(5), 1032–1052.

Schoeller, M. (2019). *Leadership in the Eurozone: The Role of Germany and EU Institutions*. Basingstoke: Palgrave Macmillan.

Statham, P., & Trenz, H.-J. (2013). How European Union Politicization can Emerge through Contestation: The Constitution Case. *Journal of Common Market Studies*, 51(5), 965–980.

Statham, P., & Trenz, H.-J. (2015). Understanding the Mechanisms of EU Politicization: Lessons from the Eurozone Crisis. *Comparative European Politics*, 13(3), 287–306.

Tooze, A. (2018). *Crashed: How a Decade of Financial Crisis Changed the World*. London: Penguin.

Verdun, A. (2015). A Historical Institutionalist Explanation of the EU's Responses to the Euro Area Financial Crisis. *Journal of European Public Policy*, 22(2), 219–237.

Verdun, A., & Zeitlin, J. (2018). Introduction: The European Semester as a New Architecture of EU Socioeconomic Governance in Theory and Practice. *Journal of European Public Policy*, 25(2), 137–148.

Weisman, P. (2017, March 2017). *The European Central Bank (ECB) Under the Single Supervisory Mechanism (SSM): Its Functioning and Its Limits* (TARN Working Papers, Paper 1/2017). http://dx.doi.org/10.2139/ssrn.2925814.

White, J. (2015). Emergency Europe. *Political Studies*, 63(2), 300–318.

Wonka, A. (2016). The Party Politics of the Euro Crisis in the German *Bundestag*: Frames, Positions and Salience. *West European Politics*, 39(1), 125–144.

CHAPTER 22

Failing Forward in Financial Stability Regulation

Eirik Tegle Stenstad and Bent Sofus Tranøy

INTRODUCTION

The overarching issues of the book will be translated into three questions about outputs, processes, and outcomes. Firstly, to what degree has the European financial and debt crises spurred new policies and purposeful action toward improved financial stability regulation and thus more symmetry between market-making and market-correcting policies (output)? Secondly, given that Europe is still suffering in the aftermath of a systemic crisis that originated in the realm of finance, we ask if what has been achieved is likely to be sufficient (outcome)? And thirdly, how do we best theorize the processes that link crisis and policy?

Our answer to the third question draws on insights from liberal intergovermentalism, neofunctionalism and social constructivism (see Schimmelfennig; Niemann and Cross, this volume). We build on the "failing forward" argument of Jones et al. (2015), an approach that is particularly suited to understand policy-making in times of crisis, since it takes recurrent crises as a key premise. It does so by combining the integration pessimism of intergovernmentalism with the dynamism of functionalism. Intergovernmentalism predicts that the outcome of interstate negotiations will be the lowest common denominator, i.e., incremental, piecemeal, and incomplete reform. While it is the very incompleteness of lowest common denominator reforms, which stimulates "functionalist processes": Incompleteness gives rise to functional problems—often in the shape of crisis—that have to be dealt with. Thus, Jones et al. (2015) can move from the old functionalist adage of "falling forward" to "failing forward." To this, we add theories of social learning: Decision makers are not only constrained by diverging interests within a framework where every state holds veto power, but also by what we identify as epistemic deficits. We need to ask what ideas were available on the policy menu at any given point in time. The crude version of our answers to the first two questions about what has been achieved and if it is sufficient are "a lot", and "maybe not," respectively. In order to gauge the progress made toward further regulatory integration within finance, we have investigated policy change along three dimensions. These are level of aggregation, functional scope, and level of governance.

The aggregation dimension runs from a Chicago-school-inspired optimistic view of financial markets that considers micro-prudency as sufficient to ensure stability, to the more politically ambitious (and at heart Keynesian) concept of macro-prudential regulation. This dimension is fundamentally expert-driven and tends to evolve through a process of (re)learning. The functional scope dimension can also be seen in terms of Keynesianism versus Chicago-school economics. Keynesian thinking suggests that systemic risk needs to be addressed with a system-wide not sector-wise perspective. A system-wide approach means that banking, securities, and insurance markets should not be regulated separately. Finally, the governance dimension indicates to what degree the financial stability framework matches the current level of financial market integration. Level of integration is a fundamentally political question and tends to be decided by intergovernmental logic.

We proceed in three steps. The first step is to measure our answer to question number one (output), against the most optimistic scenario. We find that the crisis triggered more integration and clear new policy directions. In isolation, this strengthens the *heading forward* scenario. We do need, however, to modify this verdict in light of how we answer the two other questions. Firstly, we find the regulatory solutions chosen somewhat wanting, which pushes us toward the *muddling through* scenario. In turn this generates a forward-looking hypothesis of further failing forward-like decision-making activity, a process which clearly fits under the heading of *muddling through*.

The rest of the chapter is structured as follows. First, we flesh out the framework we use when conceptualizing the output variable. Then we revisit aspects of integration theory and present our expanded failing forward argument. The next section offers a descriptive analysis. It tracks changes to the regulatory regime along the three dimensions. After that we apply our version of the failing forward argument to the process behind the observed changes, while the concluding section returns to the "is it sufficient" question in the shape of closing reflections.

THEORETICAL DIMENSIONS OF FINANCIAL STABILITY REGULATION

We investigate policy change along three analytically distinct, but empirically overlapping dimensions: level of aggregation, functional scope, and level of governance. In order to clarify what we mean by level of aggregation and functional scope; we need to take a step back and introduce the mutually exclusive assumptions that differing positions on these two dimensions reflect. Thereafter we will provide a theoretical justification for the third dimension, level of governance. Finally, we operationalize the three dimensions.

The Economics of Level of Aggregation and Functional Scope

In the field of financial stability, we can distinguish between two main belief systems. According to the former chair of the UK Financial Services Authority (FSA) Lord Turner (2010: 1318), the rational expectations/Chicago-school perspective, with its micro-oriented efficient market hypothesis, was the "conventional wisdom" of financial regulation until the financial crisis. From this vantage point there is no role for discretionary stabilization, only clearly communicated rules of micro-prudential regulation. The alternative belief system is Keynesian. The core figure Minsky (2015 [1982]: xii) believed instability was inherent to the economic process, and "[o]nce instability is understood as a theoretical possibility, then we are well positioned to design appropriate interventions to constrain it." In the years leading up to 2008 Keynesianism had been banished to the margins of the discipline and out of the regulatory discourse, but it re-emerged in the guise of macro-prudential regulation after the crisis. Fundamentally, the two perspectives differ on how they perceive the market in general and the financial system in particular—as self-equilibrating or inherently unstable. Baker (2013b) summarizes the two belief systems succinctly (Table 22.1).

Thinking About the Level of Governance

The issue of macro-prudential regulation brings policy content into focus. But for financial stability policy to be effective it also needs sufficient geographical reach. Initially, European integration was symmetric (Menéndez 2016: 391). The scope of the economic ("market-making") and social protection ("market-correcting") communities was in constitutional parallel (Menéndez 2009: 39–40; Scharpf 2002: 549). Symmetric integration was slow and easily stuck, thus it hindered supranational solutions (Menéndez 2016: 392). The Single Market came as a response, and the four freedoms unleashed

Table 22.1 Comparison of the two main belief systems of finance

	Rational expectations tradition	*Keynesian tradition*
View on markets	• Largely efficient, prone to short-term disruptions, but should be left to their own devices as far as possible	• Inherently pro-cyclical and prone to herding • Financial innovation and increasing complexity can make the system prone to shocks and generally less stable
Instruments	• Market discipline • Enhanced transparency • Private risk management (VaR models)	• Leverage limits • Countercyclical capital buffers • Modularity/prohibition
Regulation in action	• Regulators ask banks and financial institutions what they do	• Regulators define limits for banks and financial institutions, what they must and must not do

Based on Baker (2013b: 117)

pro-integration forces. The Single Market was a clear case of "negative integration"; it ruled out national regulation that restricted the four freedoms or could be seen as discriminating against foreign business (Scharpf 1996: 142–143). The result was asymmetric integration. With the Single Market, the financial system became highly integrated; however, the infrastructure to support the system was not integrated at the same rate (De Haan et al. 2009: 323).

This state of affairs has led to what Schoenmaker (2008, 2013) labelled the financial trilemma. This holds that it is not possible for the EU to achieve the goals of a *stable* financial system which is *integrated* across borders, while financial stability policy is provided at the *national* level. One of the three must yield. The absence of legally binding mechanisms that address risk at the EU level poses a number of obstacles to the management of conflicts of national interest (De Haan et al. 2009: 322). The single market stimulated cross-border finance. Cross-border firms will sometimes generate negative externalities. National supervisors, however, will only address negative externalities to the degree that they appear in their jurisdiction, as they only had national mandates (Schoenmaker 2013: 24).[1]

---

[1] The American AIG had only about 40% domestic business in 2008 when they nearly failed (ibid.: 31). If the US government bailed out AIG, only 40% of the benefit would go to them. It was only saved because the Americans perceived the benefits for them to be large enough.

The Three Dimensions Operationalized

The *level of aggregation* (aggregation dimension) indicates that one needs a top-down approach to financial stability. To cope with systemic risk, one needs a macro approach. Financial stability instruments, spanning from crisis prevention to crisis management, can broadly be categorized as macro-prudential supervision, recapitalization, and resolution, respectively.

The *functional scope* dimension also builds on notions of network externalities and complex systems and indicates that one cannot supervise the financial system in a piecemeal fashion (Baker 2013a: 5; b: 116). The different parts are interconnected and sensitive to the same systemic risk. The financial crisis is a good example: The shadow banking system was the key provider of liquidity to the financial institutions, market makers, and the core funding markets (Moe 2014: 8–15). The American investment bank Lehman Brothers failed in 2008 and the American multinational *insurance* corporation AIG had to be rescued soon after. Therefore, it has become a tenant of macro-prudential thinking that financial stability frameworks need a system-wide approach.

The *governance* dimension can be deduced from the financial trilemma and the notion of asymmetric integration. What is beneficial for an individual country is not necessarily advantageous in an EU context. The choice along the continuum with national or supranational governance on either side, should be determined by the level of financial integration. Level of integration is a political question, and the EU has chosen deep financial integration through the Single Market. Thus, the appropriate level of governance is European.

Awareness of the three dimensions is a necessary, but not sufficient condition for coping with systemic risk. They provide the general framework, while the policy instruments and their calibration determine the efficiency. We can stylize the three dimensions, with their respective endpoints, graphically (Fig. 22.1).

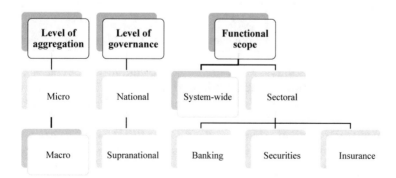

Fig. 22.1 Three dimensions of a comprehensive financial stability framework (*Source* Stenstad 2017: 31)

Theorizing Processes and Decisions

We build on liberal intergovernmentalism, neofunctionalism, and social learning when we theorize the processes that link crisis and policy. The fundamental insight from liberal intergovernmentalism's analysis of interstate bargaining is that governments only have a clear incentive to cooperate when national policy creates negative externalities for one another, and unilateral adjustment is ineffective (Moravcsik 1993: 486). Generally, during negotiations based on intensity of preferences, the need to compromise with the "least forthcoming government" drives the cooperation toward the "lowest common denominator" (Moravcsik 1993: 500–501). This means that governments with the position closest to the status quo can limit the reform, but it is generally in their interest to compromise rather than veto, thus the agreement will not precisely mirror their preferences. Comprehensive reforms demand convergence of national preferences.

Lowest common denominator bargaining and functional spillover are the two key mechanisms of the failing forward model. Our main gripe with this argument is that the existence of adequate policy options is taken for granted, and furthermore, that policy makers are aware of these options, a bold assumption that is explicit in Jones et al. (2015: 1018). This might be true in some cases, but it is unreasonable to hold it as a general assumption. Thus, we introduce the notions of *belief systems* that in turn delimit *policy menus*. This flows from an assumption that all policymaking materializes within a context of a specific set of ideas (Hall 1993: 289–292). Policy changes as a result of social learning. Hall (1993: 278) defines social learning as "a deliberate attempt to adjust the goals or techniques of policy in response to past experiences and new information". Hall distinguishes between three types of change in policy. When the levels or settings of the basic policy instruments are changed, while the overall goals and instruments are unaltered, we can call it a *first order change* in policy (Hall 1993: 278–280). *Second order change* is the result of a policy learning process where the policy instruments are changed, but the overall goals persist. When these overall goals are replaced, we can speak of a process of *third order change*.

We use the notion of a policy menu to explain how learning (or lack thereof) affects outcomes. The belief system mechanism establishes the content of the policy menu, while the lowest common denominator mechanism defines the limit for which "dishes on the menu" can be agreed upon. The relation is not a zero-sum game. Both mechanisms are always active. The belief system mechanism may reduce or expand the menu. When it reduces the policy menu—creating an epistemic deficit—the effect of the lowest common denominator mechanism can be trivial (Stenstad 2017).

From Lamfalussy to the Banking Union

Integration of financial supervision moved slowly until the end of the 1990s (Quaglia 2010: 24). The internal market for capital was institutionalized in 1992, but eight years passed before the EU made its first feeble attempts at positive integration. The Lamfalussy Framework institutionalized cooperation on regulatory micro-matters (aggregation dimension), and a sectoral approach (functional scope dimension) while it preserved supervision as a national competence (governance dimension). The Lamfalussy Framework thus deviated considerably from what our definition of comprehensive financial stability entails. The new committees did not execute prudential supervision, and macro issues were explicitly kept off the table. Crisis management was not part of the reform. It consolidated a framework where national autonomy and belief in the efficiency of financial markets were the main principles. The main goal was the creation of "a level playing field". The result was under provision of the collective good of financial stability.

The Financial Crisis—Financial Stability Back on the Agenda (The Larosière Framework)

The de Larosière Framework, or the European System of Financial Supervisors (ESFS), was a result of the financial crisis. This round of reforms introduced financial stability as an element of the institutional structures at the EU level through a new macro-prudential body. Financial stability policies remained a national competence, but EU conducted macro-prudential oversight on the systemic level. Despite the macro-prudential and systemic element, the framework underprovided the collective good of financial stability for two main reasons. Firstly, even though this period is marked by a burst of positive integration, market-correcting policies did not catch up with the negative integration/market-making that had gone on before. At the micro level this stage saw a piecemeal upgrading of the institutional framework (Quaglia 2013: 79; Spendzharova 2012: 318).

The ESFS framework consisted of two components: three micro-level European Supervisory Authorities (ESAs) and the European Systemic Risk Board (ESRB). The three ESAs are responsible for supervising banking (EBA), insurance and occupational pension schemes (EIOPA), and securities (ESMA). Functional scope remained sectoral. ESRB on the other hand, pushed the framework somewhat toward macro *level of aggregation*. It was set up as an independent body tasked with macro-prudential oversight over the entire financial system. The ESRB issued warnings and recommendations but were given no financial stability policy instruments apart from an "act or explain" mechanism: If the addressees did not act, they had to justify it. The *functional scope* of the ESRB is in and of itself system wide, but the ESRB has no financial stability instruments apart from its right to issue warnings and recommendations.

The *level of governance* of financial stability policy on the micro side took a step toward the supranational level by transforming what had previously been committees into agencies but regulation was still exercised at the national level, with a lot of room for discretion. Hence, the de Larosière reforms did not fully address the constitutional asymmetry between negative and positive integration. Regarding the macro side, the ESRB had no binding powers over Member States, it was a "reputational" body: Its most powerful measure was its moral authority (European Commission 2009: 5). The ECB and the central banks dominate the ESRB, but supervisors are also involved (OJ EU 2010). The ESRB relies on the goodwill of the different national micro-prudential bodies to get the information it needs.

The Banking Union Reforms of 2012–2013

The Banking Union reforms had many components, but the main developments were a move toward macro on the aggregation dimension, a consolidation of a banking-centered regime on the functional scope dimension and a move toward a much stronger supranational hue on the governance dimension. The move toward macro can be seen firstly from the introduction of macro-prudential instruments, the most obvious of which are countercyclical capital buffers and regulations that allow for restricting risk-taking by banks, particularly in the mortgage sector. The two most important of these regulations are loan-to-value ratios (LTVs) and debt-service-to-income (DSTI) (ESRB 2019). Furthermore, two new decision-making pillars were introduced. The Single Supervision Mechanism (SSM) and the Single Resolution Mechanism (SRM), both resting on the Single Rulebook for regulating, supervising, and governing the financial sector in all EU-countries. These pillars have mandates that cover both macro- and micro-level issues. At the micro level the SSM represents a further harmonization and standardization of practices, while the macro level responsibility of the SSM and the introduction of the SRM represent more radical innovations.

The most important concession to macro-thinking within the SSM is the notion that there are "systemically important institutions" (SIIs), that are now regulated by ECB in cooperation with national supervisors. Previously the implicit assumption had been that each bank could be supervised and regulated "on its own" by authorities in their respective home countries. This, the crises demonstrated, was highly problematic; it underestimated the complexity of the financial system the internal market had created. In particular, how network externalities arising from trouble in a single bank with cross-border activities could unbalance the whole system. The establishment of a SRM also reflects the post-crisis realization in regulatory circles that complex financial systems give rise to network externalities. Banks' fortunes are linked through various ties; from asset prices and confidence (one bank's losses can impact the value of another bank's assets) to their direct exposure to each other. This makes controlled troubleshooting, on a spectrum from recapitalization to orderly winding down procedures, crucial for systemic stability.

On the functional scope dimension, the system is still sectoral. The three separate ESAs (for banking, insurance, and securities) uphold their division of labor which, arguably, reflects the nature of micro-regulation. If one is concerned with one institution at the time, why not leave regulation to specialized agencies? Not so at the macro level where the ESRB's monitoring responsibility is toward the system as such. Furthermore, the ESRB's recommendations and warnings assumed increased significance with the new macro-prudential tools given to the ECB (which in turn is the dominant voice in the governance of the ESRB) as part of the Banking Union. On the other hand, if one goes through the ECB's (2018) list of systemically important institutions, only banks and holding companies owned by banks are to be found.

When it comes to the governance dimension, the system took important steps toward supranationality. Firstly, the Single Rulebook moved micro-level governance from intergovernmental harmonization toward supranational standardization, reducing the leeway for national discretion. Secondly, at the macro level, the granting of significant powers to the ECB, and thus indirectly also to the ESRB, marks a clear step toward supranational governance.

DISCUSSION

Output: **Heading Forward**

This book revolves around three scenarios, *change* in shape of *breaking down*, *continuity* via *muddling through*, and *change* as in *heading forward* toward further integration. We argue that the regulatory efforts of the EU in terms of *output* immediately after the global financial crisis qualifies as *muddling through*, that is path-dependent and incremental responses that built on preexisting institutional architectures. As the European debt crisis wore on however, new institutions were given new powers which altered the landscape of European financial regulation fundamentally. We are now in a situation that qualifies as *heading forward*. Confirming to the expectation that "crises may trigger more integration to address common challenges, leading to policy changes and the delegation of new powers to EU institutions" (see Chapter 1).

In terms of level of aggregation EU financial regulation is markedly different to what it was before the global financial and European debt crises. Macro-prudential regulation has in less than ten years gone from being nonexistent to a fundamental part of the EU's regulatory set-up. This is, however, mainly limited to banking. The ESRB is mandated to monitor systemic stability as such, which by definition includes insurance and securities (capital markets) as well as banking, but among the institutions defined as systemically important we find only banks. As regards level of governance, the supervision of these institutions who between them account for around 80% of the assets in the banking market in Europe, is performed by Joint Supervisory Teams heavily influenced, and probably dominated by, actors at the European level (the ECB and the ESRB). At the micro level the introduction of the Single Rulebook and the creation of three new agencies represent significant steps toward more integration. The standard-setting efforts of these micro-level agencies are more geared toward creating a level playing field when regulating and supervising individual institutions, than financial stability at the systemic level, and we therefore deem them less important for our analysis.

Process: Failing Forward

In general, the process toward a more ambitious and hopefully more adequate financial stability regulation, confirms to expectations generated by the failing forward plus social learning perspective. The belief system that surrounded regulators underwent a dramatic shift in the immediate aftermath of the financial crisis. The efficient market hypothesis was the pre-crises orthodoxy because it provided:

> [...] a set of ideas complex and internally consistent enough to have intellectual credibility, but simple enough to provide a workable basis for day to day decision-making. Complex human institutions—such as those which together form the policymaking and regulatory system—are difficult to manage without guiding philosophies—and guiding philosophies are most compelling when they provide clear answers. (Turner 2010: 1321–1322)

The financial crisis was an immense anomaly that the rational expectations tradition, in the guise of the efficient market hypothesis, could not explain. Thus, the hegemonic belief system was severely weakened. Before the crisis, the attitude was that securitization and "slicing and dicing [of] risk" made the system safer, but instead such a diversified system emboldened the financial institution to increase their risk-taking (Borio 2009: 34). The understanding in the European Commission that "all can be arranged by tailor-made regulation" disappeared (Caravelis 2010: 7). Deputy Governor for financial stability at the Bank of England Paul Tucker (2011: 2) encouraged a "Gestalt flip to thinking of markets as inefficient, riddled with preferred habitats, imperfect arbitrage, regulatory arbitrage, herding, and inhabited by agents with less than idealized rationality." The cognitive filter of policymakers "switched," and resulted in macro-prudential reports like the Turner Review, the de Larosière Report, the UN Stiglitz Commission, etc., that became the blueprints for reforms (Baker 2013a: 5–8).

For decision makers, the de Larosière Report translated this broader social learning into a policy menu. To fully understand the development of the policy menu, we need to assess change along the aggregation dimension.

The de Larosière Group found a lack of supervisory focus on "macrosystemic risk." As Baker (2013a) argues, it was not a paradigm shift that led to a change in all three orders, but rather a contingent ideational shift, paradoxically enough, without corresponding changes of a second and first order nature. De Larosière delivered a new view of how financial markets work and a clear focus on systemic risks, without recommending new tough instruments that corresponded to this ideational shift. Consequently, the financial crisis did not extend the policy menu beyond oversight and the "act or explain" mechanism. De Larosière et al. (2009: 58) explained the reasoning for rejecting a broader and more centralized option to a lack of "irrefutable arguments."

In the words of De Vries (2009):

> So what should be the role of a Systemic Risk Board if it has no clear goal, no instrument and may only give advice? This is like an ECB that cannot set the interest rate, but has to advise national central banks on the interest rate they should set. [...] As national interests prevail in a crisis, the advice is likely not heeded when it is most needed.

This damning judgement raises the question of why de Larosière did not go further. One reason is that the new "paradigm," at least not in the eyes of mainstream economists, had not been fleshed out yet. A joint report from the FSB, IMF, and BIS (2011: 3) put it this way: "the identification of systemic risk is a nascent field. No common paradigms yet exist. Further fundamental and applied research is needed, not least to better inform the collection and analysis of data underway." A second reason is related to the experts' judgment of what was politically feasible, an anticipation of what the intergovernmentalism literature speaks of as the lowest common denominator mechanism. In the words of de Larosière et al. (2009: 58), a further reason for limiting the policy menu was "doubts of it being implemented at this juncture."

The group's perception of political realities was most likely correct, because at this point in time the three core states, France, Germany, and the UK had diverging interests. France continued its longstanding support for more comprehensive solutions (Jabko 2012: 103–104). As France has a small, but consolidated financial sector, she preferred more integration as it could gain from a more ambitious, European solution (Buckley and Howarth 2010: 125–128).

Germany was more ambivalent as its financial sector was divided on the reform. Consequently, at least initially, Germany "dragged [its] feet" along with Britain (Jabko 2012: 103–104). As the proposed framework split the industry between the strong private banks who could see several advantages in a common European regulatory framework and the smaller saving banks, cooperatives, and semi-public banks that wanted to remain under the auspices of national agencies, the government did not voice strong opinions on the proposed framework of the de Larosière Report, but chose to back the French position during the negotiations (Buckley and Howarth 2010: 126–128; Hennessy 2014: 157).

Britain on the other hand, was a vocal supporter of preserving national autonomy. With a large financial sector, Britain has less to gain from centralization of supervision (Rixen 2013: 441). They wanted the systemic risk board to be an "informing agency" that reported to the Council, totally independent of the ECB, a less binding arrangement along the governance dimension (ibid.; House of Lords 2009: Q610–621). Despite the lack of EU level crisis management arrangement, Britain did not support EU supervisory powers that could overrule national governments. In the negotiations, Britain was the least forthcoming government and had national preferences closest to status quo and could threaten to block or veto proposals outside its bargaining space. This position gave her substantial bargaining power.

Britain underlined that the non-euro countries had to have equal representation at the board and for the participation of national supervisors, and won concessions there (Buckley and Howarth 2010: 127). In addition, the Council stated explicitly, to accommodate the British government, that the establishment of the ESRB was without legal personality, and that the new framework excluded any fiscal responsibilities for the Member States. Thus, we see that the lowest common denominator mechanism determined the choices made from the (already restricted) policy menu. The negotiations focused on the governance dimension, as this was the most controversial part of the policy menu for the Member States.

If de Larosière was a child of the financial crisis, the Euro crisis facilitated accelerated social learning, which in turn paved the way for Banking Union. The widespread sovereign debt crisis led to "successive waves of emergency policy action, both at the ECB and in the Council" (Jones 2015: 58). The urgency of the situation(s) sped up learning to such a degree that there was no time for blueprints. The most important lesson emerged from the ECBs support of the banks' investment in national debt (in disproportionate volumes), thereby strengthening the ties and the linked vulnerabilities between states and banks (Epstein and Rhodes 2016: 416). The result was a "doom loop"—a vicious circle—where declining state finances increased the vulnerability of the banks and vice versa (Gros 2013: 93). Thus, risk was increasingly concentrated in a set of individual debt-ridden Eurozone countries as the crisis progressed (Epstein and Rhodes 2016: 417). Financial stability became connected to the fate of the states themselves, and not only of the financial institutions.

Taken together, the blueprint-less actions of the EU leaders in this phase can be interpreted as a radical extension of the policy menu, and implicitly a radical evolution of the belief system thus fulfilling the *heading forward* scenario. The European debt crisis complemented the previously stand-alone third order change that followed the financial crisis, with macro-prudential instruments, i.e., second order policy. The Keynesian tradition with its macro-prudential thinking dominated, as the three orders of policy now coincided. The new policy menu contained instruments that addressed financial stability proactively (crisis prevention) and reactively (crisis management): macro-prudential supervision, recapitalization, and resolution. Supranational governance was available on the menu. It was now possible to address the constitutional asymmetry and systemic risk. However, the belief system mechanism did not extend the second order policy beyond banking.

The desire to combat the doom loop spawned three major initiatives; The SSM, the SRM, and the ESM. Since there are space-constraints and the European Stability Mechanism (ESM) is not formally a part of the banking union, nor the regulatory framework as such, we will not afford it further attention here.

The Single Supervision Mechanism—The Least Forthcoming Government Was Less Decisive

The negotiation over the SSM was not a matter of a micro or macro level of aggregation, but rather on the level of governance. The Member States accepted the need for single supervision as part of the new Banking Union. There were two points of disagreement: the scope of ECB powers—all banks or only cross-border banks, and definition of "significant" and "less significant" banks—and the relationship to non-Eurozone countries (Howarth and Quaglia 2015: 155).[2] The juxtaposition of divergent interests and therefore the dynamics of the negotiations resembled those over the ESRB, with one notable exception. The Banking Union was established within the Eurozone, which meant that the UK did not have formal role in the negotiations.

France had the most ambitious preferences—ECB supervision of all 6000 banks—while the German government had a position close to status quo— only ECB supervision of the few, major cross-border banks. Germany wanted a €50 billion threshold for direct ECB supervision to ensure that most of its domestic financial industry remained under German control (Epstein and Rhodes 2016: 422–424). The bargaining resulted in a compromise. The threshold ended up at €30 billion. National supervisors were to assume responsibility for the day-to-day supervision of those below this threshold, but ultimate power rested at the ECB. The ECB now directly supervises the 114 most significant banks, representing 82% of the Eurozone banking assets (ECB 2019). In addition, Germany won concessions through the creation of a supervisory board of ECB and national supervisory representatives to better secure separation of the monetary policy functions from the new micro-prudential banking tasks of the ECB, and in the shape of a mediation panel for conflicts between Supervisory Board and the ECB. The lowest common denominator mechanism was less influential in this round compared to the de Larosière

---

[2] The last conflict is not relevant for the three dimensions. However, non-Eurozone countries were allowed to opt in (Howarth and Quaglia 2013: 114–115).

negotiations. After all, the least forthcoming government could not stop what was a major transfer of sovereignty, but Germany did water down the ambition of France and the European Commission.

THE SINGLE RESOLUTION MECHANISM—A VERY COMPLEX COMPROMISE

Banking resolution can have great distributional consequences. Also, in times of a crisis, decisiveness will normally be essential to avoid self-fulfilling prophesies spinning out of control. In this case, level of governance was directly tied to fiscal risk, which only made matters more complicated. Echoing positions taken all the way back to Maastricht, Germany was concerned with the risk of moral hazard, that member states would be more permissive toward their banks when EU funds were available (Howarth and Quaglia 2014: 126–134). Therefore, Germany wanted "bail-in" rules (initial losses on private sector bonds and shareholders), and that EU funding could only be released after a complex intergovernmental process. France, Italy, and Spain were opposed to bail-in clauses and wanted simpler and faster decision-making. SRM bargaining circled around what Germany did and did not want. Germany had considerable bargaining power, and as it would become a net contributor, had little to gain and preferred a solution close to the status quo. It was the least forthcoming government, and largely defined the terms to integration for the new instrument. The original proposal was supranational, while the final agreement was highly intergovernmental. A minority of the Council has veto power on the use of Single Resolution Fund (SRF). To close a bank, there are considerable checks and balances. The decision-making authority, the Single Resolution Board (SRB), is intergovernmental, and the Member States control the mutualization of the SRF. The outcome tended toward the lowest common denominator. Thus, the lowest common denominator mechanism limited the selection from the policy menu along the governance dimension.

CLOSING REFLECTIONS ON POSSIBLE OUTCOMES: IS THIS SUFFICIENT?

In our introduction, we listed three levels at which we wanted to discuss the financial stability regulation regime of the EU: outputs, processes, and outcomes. In short, there has been at last a lot of output produced through the kind of failing forward-like processes that our theory predicted. This leaves us with our final questions. Is the outcome satisfactory, is this enough?

First a caveat: It is in the nature of the beast that it is difficult not only to predict, but also to prevent financial crises within systems that let credit and capital move freely. If it were not the case, crises would have been fewer and farther between. What we can do, however, is gauge the output produced against our model of a fully integrated regulatory regime. Europe's internal market for capital (or finance) has been highly integrated since the establishment of the internal market in 1992 and for practical purposes fully integrated since the inception of the euro around the turn of the millennium. Our story is therefore, basically, a story about stability regulation catching up: The EU gradually realize that it needed to overcome its Scharpfian joint-decision trap and re-establish symmetry between financial markets and their regulatory framework. The big picture that emerges is that the EU is getting there, but is not quite there. Substantial progress has been made along all three dimensions. Governance is now in the main located at the supranational level, macroprudential regulation has been institutionalized, and the functional scope of regulation is somewhat increased. Upon closer inspection, however, several chinks in the armor come into view.

The most obvious evidence for *heading forward* is to be found in the degree to which regulation now has a broad enough functional scope. The ESRB is tasked with monitoring the system as such, but when one looks at the institutions actually covered by the instruments of ECB, a bank-centric pattern is revealed. This is both interesting and problematic. It is theoretically interesting because it reflects the nature of what we termed the blueprint-less learning that took place during the European debt crisis. The doom loop that emerged between banks and their domestic governments became the major conundrum. Thus, banks were at the center of regulatory attention when the Eurozone sought to fix its broken system. The bank-centric pattern is problematic because "the next" financial crisis never crops up exactly the same place as where the last one broke out. Financial markets are dynamic and the borders between institutional spheres like credit, capital, insurance, and brokerage are constantly challenged by actors seeking to find new ways to make a profit, often in direct response to the last round of regulation. This means that innovative business models and the "new" risks associated with them are highly likely to surface outside of the sphere that is usually referred to, and regulated as, banking.

When it comes to the level of governance issue, we believe that the most important weakness is to be found in the cumbersome routine established for releasing funds from the SRM. Here German fiscal concerns clearly trumped the functional demand for speedy resolution, in effect threatening to undermine the logic behind establishing a resolution mechanism in the first place. One lesson (relearned) in the crisis of 2008 and the subsequent European debt crisis is that when crises hits there is never enough time. If resolution drags out, then panic spreads and the system as such, or large parts of it, gets dragged down. Therefore, regulatory efforts toward facilitating orderly resolution of banks in crisis through resolution funds and "living wills" have been on the agenda in all regulatory agencies since 2008, but with limited progress made on either (Hjertaker and Tranøy 2017).

Finally, the most important potential weakness with the new macroprudential regime is associated with the underlying worldviews and ontology upon which it rests. As we shall see political economists have criticized the macro-prudential efforts of both the Bank for International Settlements (BIS) and the EU for trying to add macro-prudential regulation to a regulatory structure that is based on ontological priors that are incompatible with the intellectual underpinnings of the Minsky-Keynes tradition. As a consequence, the regulation—or policy menu from which this is chosen—does not go far enough. The key issues are an insistence on continued quantification of risk (at the cost of thinking more in terms of fundamental uncertainty), the notion that risk resides in institutions rather than in the network and more fundamentally that macro-prudential regulation as it stands now does not to a sufficient degree problematize the relationship between finance and the societies which finance notionally serves (Kranke and Yarrow 2018). In short the predatory, value extracting, and socially useless aspects of modern finance are never addressed.

According to Baker (2018: 293), who has followed the macro-prudential process outside and inside the EU since the first macro-murmurs appeared in 2010, the macro-prudential regulation which has been produced so far falls short because "[…] a variety of epistemological, professional, institutional and political barriers have impeded relevant expert groups and political actors' willingness and ability to actively translate macro-prudential ontology into a systemic vision, or sense of social purpose […]." Taken together these three weaknesses along our three dimensions lead us to conclude that there is a good chance that further progress in financial stability regulation will follow the now established pattern of "failing forward." A more radical interpretation is that the EU is selling *muddling through* as *heading forward* thereby risking a more severe breakdown further down the line.

References

Baker, A. (2013a). The Gradual Transformation? The Incremental Dynamics of Macroprudential Regulation. *Regulation & Governance, 7*(4), 417–434.

Baker, A. (2013b). The New Political Economy of the Macroprudential Ideational Shift. *New Political Economy, 18*(1), 112–139.

Baker, A. (2018). Macroprudential Regimes and the Politics of Social Purpose. *Review of International Political Economy, 25*(3), 293–316.

Borio, C. (2009). Implementing the Macroprudential Approach to Financial Regulation and Supervision. *Financial Stability Review [Bank of France], 13,* 31–41.

Buckley, J., & Howarth, D. (2010). Internal Market: Gesture Politics? Explaining the EU's Response to the Financial Crisis. *JCMS: Journal of Common Market Studies, 48*(1), 119–141.

Caravelis, G. (2010). *The EU Financial Supervision in the Aftermath of the 2008 Crisis: An Appraisal* (EUI Working Papers No. 2010/11). Robert Schuman Centre for Advanced Studies. San domenico di Fiesole.

De Haan, J., Oosterloo, S., & Schoenmaker, D. (2009). *European Financial Markets and Institutions*. Cambridge: Cambridge University Press.

De Larosière, J., Balcerowicz, L., Issing, O., Masera, R., McCarthy, C., Nyberg, L., et al. (2009). *Report of the High-Level Group on Financial Supervision in the EU*. Brussels: DG Internal Market and and DG Economic and Financial Affairs.

De Vries, C. (2009). *The Systemic Risk Board*. Eurointelligence: A Return to the EMS.

ECB. (2018). *List of Supervised Entities*. https://www.bankingsupervision.europa.eu/ecb/pub/pdf/ssm.list_of_supervised_entities_201812.en.pdf. Accessed 22 June 2019.

ECB. (2019). *Single Supervisory Mechanism*. https://www.bankingsupervision.europa.eu/about/thessm/html/index.en.html. Accessed 10 Aug 2019.

Epstein, R. A., & Rhodes, M. (2016). The Political Dynamics Behind Europe's New Banking Union. *West European Politics, 39*(3), 415–437.

ESRB. (2019). *A Review of Macroprudential Policy in the EU in 2018*. Frankfurt am Main: ESRB.

European Commission. (2009). *Proposal for a Regulation of the European Parliament and of the Council on Community Macro Prudential Oversight of the Financial System and Establishing a European Systemic Risk Board* (COM(2009) 499 final). Brussels: EUR-Lex.

FSB, IMF, & BIS. (2011). *Macroprudential Policy Tools and Frameworks: Progress Report to G20*. Retrieved from https://www.imf.org/external/np/g20/pdf/102711.pdf.

Gros, D. (2013). Banking Union with a Sovereign Virus. *Intereconomics, 48*(2), 93–97.

Hall, P. A. (1993). Policy Paradigms, Social Learning, and the State: The Case of Economic Policymaking in Britain. *Comparative Politics, 25*(3), 275–296.

Hennessy, A. (2014). Redesigning Financial Supervision in the European Union (2009–2013). *Journal of European Public Policy, 21*(2), 151–168.

Hjertaker, I., & Tranøy, B. S. (2017). *Ustabilitetens politiske økonomi: Om fremveksten av finansialisert kapitalisme*. Oslo: Cappelen Damm akademisk.

House of Lords. (2009). *The Future of EU Financial Regulation and Supervision* (HL Paper 106-II). London: Authority of the House of Lords.

Howarth, D., & Quaglia, L. (2013). Banking Union as Holy Grail: Rebuilding the Single Market in Financial Services, Stabilizing Europe's Banks and 'Completing' Economic and Monetary Union. *JCMS: Journal of Common Market Studies, 51*(S1), 103–123.

Howarth, D., & Quaglia, L. (2014). The Steep Road to European Banking Union: Constructing the Single Resolution Mechanism. *JCMS: Journal of Common Market Studies, 52*(S1), 125–140.

Howarth, D., & Quaglia, L. (2015). The New Intergovernmentalism in Financial Regulation and Banking Union. In C. Bickerton, D. Hodson, & U. Puetter (Eds.), *The New Intergovernmentalism: States and Supranational Actors in the Post-Maastricht Era* (pp. 146–162). Oxford: Oxford University Press.

Jabko, N. (2012). International Radicalism, Domestic Conformism: France's Ambiguous Stance on Financial Reforms. In R. Mayntz (Ed.), *Crisis and Control: Institutional Change in Financial Market Regulation* (pp. 97–118). Frankfurt: Campus.

Jones, E. (2015). The Forgotten Financial Union: How You Can Have a Euro Crisis Without a Euro. In M. Matthijs & M. Blyth (Eds.), *The Future of the Euro* (pp. 44–69). New York: Oxford University Press.

Jones, E., Kelemen, R. D., & Meunier, S. (2015). Failing Forward? The Euro Crisis and the Incomplete Nature of European Integration. *Comparative Political Studies, 49*(7), 1010–1034.

Kranke, M., & Yarrow, D. (2018). The Global Governance of Systemic Risk: How Measurement Practices Tame Macroprudential Politics. *New Political Economy, 24*, 1–17.

Menéndez, A. J. (2009). When the Market Is Political: The Socio-Economic Constitution of the European Union Between Market-Making and Polity-Making. In R. Letelier & A. J. Menéndez (Eds.), *The Sinews of European Peace: Reconstituting the Democratic Legitimacy of the Socio-Economic Constitution of the European Union* (pp. 39–62). Oslo: ARENA.

Menéndez, A. J. (2016). The Refugee Crisis: Between Human Tragedy and Symptom of the Structural Crisis of European Integration. *European Law Journal, 22*(4), 388–416.

Minsky, H. P. (2015 [1982]). *Can "It" Happen Again? Essays on Instability and Finance*. New York: Routledge.

Moe, T. G. (2014). *Shadow Banking: Policy Challenges for Central Banks* (Levy Economics Institute Working Paper, 802), pp. 1–32.

Moravcsik, A. (1993). Preferences and Power in the European Community: A Liberal Intergovernmentalist Approach. *JCMS: Journal of Common Market Studies, 31*(4), 473–524.

OJ EU. (2010). *Regulation (EU) No 1092/2010 of the European Parliament and of the Council of 24 November 2010 on European Union Macro-Prudential Oversight of the Financial System and Establishing a European Systemic Risk Board*, L 331/1 C.F.R.

Quaglia, L. (2010). *Governing Financial Services in the European Union: Banking, Securities and Post-Trading* (Vol. 12). London: Routledge.

Quaglia, L. (2013). Is European Union Governance Ready to Deal with the Next Financial Crisis? In H. K. Anheier (Ed.), *Governance Challenges and Innovations: Financial and Fiscal Governance*. Oxford: Oxford Scholarship Online.

Rixen, T. (2013). Why Reregulation After the Crisis Is Feeble: Shadow Banking, Offshore Financial Centers, and Jurisdictional Competition. *Regulation & Governance, 7*(4), 435–459.

Scharpf, F. W. (1996). Democratic Policy in Europe. *European Law Journal, 2*(2), 136–155.

Scharpf, F. W. (2002). The European Social Model: Coping with the Challenges of Diversity. *JCMS: Journal of Common Market Studies, 40*(4), 645–670.

Schoenmaker, D. (2008). *The Trilemma of Financial Stability*. Paper Presented at the CFS-IMF Conference, A Financial Stability Framework for Europe: Managing Financial Soundness in an Integrating Market, Frankfurt am Main.

Schoenmaker, D. (2013). *Governance of International Banking: The Financial Trilemma*. New York: Oxford University Press.

Spendzharova, A. (2012). Is More 'Brussels' the Solution? New European Union Member States' Preferences About the European Financial Architecture. *JCMS: Journal of Common Market Studies, 50*(2), 315–334.

Stenstad, E. T. (2017). Failing Forward Towards Reduced Instability? Integration and Aggregation in EU Financial Regulation. *ARENA Report 4/17*. Oslo: ARENA.

Tucker, P. (2011, February 18). *Discussion of Lord Turner's Lecture, "Reforming Finance: Are We Being Radical Enough?"* [Keynote Speech]. Clare Distinguished Lecture in Economics. Cambridge.

Turner, A. (2010). The Crisis, Conventional Economic Wisdom, and Public Policy. *Industrial and Corporate Change, 19*(5), 1317–1329.

CHAPTER 23

The Euro in a Triple Crisis Context and Its Impact on the European Union

James A. Caporaso

INTRODUCTION

The eurozone crisis of the European Union (EU) occurred simultaneously with two other crises concerning refugees and Brexit. There are other crises facing Europe today but I choose to examine how these two interact with the financial crisis because it is instructive for our purposes. The arrangement of preferences among the key actors in these crises as well as the differential opportunities for improvement through institutional changes, provide us with opportunities for learning about the prospects and limits of institutions. In line with the three scenarios developed in the introduction of this book, I argue that the financial crisis presents the most capacity for *heading forward* among member states, whereas both the refugee crisis and Brexit constitute *breaking down* for the EU. In the discussion that follows, this chapter will show how the three crises intersect and feed on one another. Each crisis is best understood as part of a larger complex of challenges to the EU rather than in isolation. The chapter will also demonstrate that while institutions can often help, they are not panaceas. When preferences of member states diverge, institutions may prove to be of little help in moving integration forward. Existing scholarship on the EU often implies that the EU operates far from

---

Revised and reprinted version of an original article: Caporaso (2018).

J. A. Caporaso (✉)
University of Washington, Seattle, WA, USA
e-mail: caporaso@uw.edu

its institutional frontier and that substantial improvements in welfare are just around the corner if only we "get our institutions right." But institutional fixes do not exist for all problems. From the very beginning, the basic political structure of the Economic and Monetary Union (EMU) was sub-optimal (Heipertz and Verdun 2010; Sims 2012). Institutional improvements, in fiscal capacity, banking, and surveillance of macroeconomic imbalances, provided the prospect of collective gains. Institutional improvements are less available for the refugee crisis and Brexit though they are far from absent. In what follows, I will first describe the three crises, then move to the intersections between the financial crisis, the refugee crisis and Brexit, followed by a discussion of what institutions can and cannot do well, given the distribution of preferences among the member states.

THE EUROZONE CRISIS

The eurozone crisis had all the characteristic features of a financial crisis (Kindleberger and Aliber 2005): cheap undifferentiated credit priced almost identically for all countries, excessive lending and borrowing, and a psychological mania in that money appeared "free" (see Rosén and Olsen; Tranøy and Stenstad in this volume). Consumption was very high especially in the south of Europe (Greece, Italy, Spain, and Portugal) and Ireland. Kindleberger and Aliber would have seen this pattern as a bubble and of course bubbles always burst. A small event, one out of all proportion to the underlying economic fundamentals, can burst bubbles. There is no plateau regarding asset prices or economic growth. Once a bubble bursts, confidence plummets and credit dries up very quickly (Merler and Pisani-Ferry 2012).

The natural question to ask is "why?" The most popular explanation, not confined to the tabloids, is a cultural one. There are two Europes. First there is Northern Europe which is fiscally responsible, works hard, invests wisely, and lives within its means. Northern Europe includes Germany, Austria, the Netherlands, and Finland. Then there is Southern Europe (Greece, Italy, Portugal, and Spain) which is fiscally lax, doesn't work hard, engages in periodic consumption binges, and does not save, invest, and grow. It's a story of virtue vs. indulgence, saints and sinners, Calvinists and Catholics (Matthijs and McNamara 2015).

This version of the financial crisis finds expression in ordoliberalism, an economic doctrine in which ideas shape and rationalize interests at the same time. The eurozone crisis occurred because of the clash of ideas between the north (largely Germany, but also the Netherlands, Austria, Finland, and Belgium) and the south (Greece, Italy, Portugal, and Spain). Economics is not only about interest rates, money supply, credit and debts, and trade. It is of course about these "things" but also about the ways they are conceptualized. German leaders, particularly economic leaders, are guided by the economic philosophy of ordoliberalism. There may be few academic economists in Germany who identify as ordoliberals, but in the making of economic policy, this viewpoint is important (Brunnermeier et al. 2016; Matthijs and McNamara 2015; Jacoby 2017).

As described by Brunnermeier et al. (2016), there is a clash of economic philosophies between the north and the south of the eurozone. The northern vision is about rules, rigor, and consistency while the southern view (of which France is the champion) is more about the need for flexibility, adaptability, and innovation. Economic policymakers attempt to capture these differences in the simple rules vs. discretion dichotomy. It is Walter Eucken and the Freiburg School against Keynes.

Conceptual frameworks shape policy preferences. In terms of policy-relevant beliefs, ordoliberals worry about moral hazard while others (Keynesians) worry about collapse of demand and political fragmentation. Why, for example, does Germany not pursue the goal of helping the periphery of Europe to recover, as a way of assuring that German loans are repaid, rather than imposing austerity reforms and in the process shrinking their economies? Pure self-interest does not adjudicate between the two interpretations. If repayment were the only goal, it is plausible that aiding the periphery would be the appropriate strategy. After all, healthy economies are more likely to be productive and capable of servicing their debts.

Policy implications flow from different visions of the eurozone. The first concerns economic governance. The Germans (ordoliberals) favor a stability culture to control inflation. Growth is best dealt with by supply-side measures. For France and the South of Europe, "gouvernance economique" implies a certain way of thinking about the role of government intervention in the economy, stimulating demand when the economy is in recession, and slowing down the economy when it is overheated (Brunnermeier et al. 2016: 3). This implies a strong countercyclical role for the fiscal authorities, a role accepted in German domestic politics but rejected at the European level.

A second policy implication involves liquidity and solvency. The southern discretionary approach tends to see many economic problems (deficits, trade imbalances) as "temporary liquidity problems that can be easily solved by an injection of new lending" (Brunnermeier et al. 2016: 4). If the problem is liquidity, credit can be extended and loans can be paid back. However, if there is lack of trust that central institutions will correct temporary deficits, liquidity problems can easily become solvency problems. DeGrauwe (2011) has discussed this situation as one where multiple equilibria are possible and where outcomes (good and bad) depend on institutional factors. Countries that have institutionalized lender of last resort facilities do better at holding the line and preventing liquidity problems from becoming solvency problems (DeGrauwe and Li 2013).

Finally, the policy responses on the German side are austerity, fiscal tightening, and domestic reform. Reform of the tax system in Greece, cutbacks in government employees, and spending controls were put in place. Among debtors, there was support for bailouts and debt write-downs. Both approaches were presented as "saving EMU," the Germans through fiscal discipline and countering moral hazard and the southern view that sought to assure that liquidity problems did not become solvency problems.

Political institutions to ensure stability in the eurozone, particularly in the event of asymmetric shocks, were weak from the start. Out of numerous gaps in the institutional architecture, the lack of a lender of last resort was most crucial. Design of the eurozone "... seemed to require elimination of national lender of last resort functions for central banks, without creating as strong a replacement at the European level" (Sims 2012: 1). This gap created incentives to alter the institutional framework but provided no overall direction for institutional change, such as whether the central bank should be more or less autonomous or whether fiscal transfers should be part of the eurozone's governance system.

REFUGEE CRISIS

The European refugee crisis erupted in the summer of 2015 with hundreds of thousands of people from the Middle East and Africa attempting to cross the Mediterranean. Pressures for the dramatic movement of refugees were building with the civil war in Syria and the Arab Spring dating from December 2010 (See Schilde and Wallace Goodman in this volume). State failure and civil unrest in Sub-Saharan Africa and central Asia also contributed to the refugee crisis (Hollifield 2016).

The refugee crisis has opened up new cleavages among countries in the EU. One such cleavage is between frontline southern states (Italy and Greece) vs. rearguard states in Northern Europe (France, Austria, Finland). A bigger and more politically charged divide has opened up between member states in the north and west of Europe, and some refugee-rejecting states from eastern Europe chief of which are Hungary, the Czech Republic, Poland, and Slovakia. Victor Orban of Hungary calls Juncker's refugee plan "mad" and Angela Merkel's acceptance of refugees "moral imperialism" (See Crawford this volume). Reactions of governments in Poland and Hungary to acceptance of refugees have been strongly negative. In September of 2015, EU member states agreed to accept 160,000 refugees, but as of May 2017 fewer than 30,000 had been accepted and resettled. The intervening event was the election of the Law and Justice Party in Poland in October 2015. Before that, Poland had agreed to accept 10,000 refugees but after the elections, this decision was reversed. This prompted the EU to open sanction procedures—infringement procedures—against Hungary, Poland, and the Czech Republic on June 13, 2017. The outcomes of these legal actions are not yet known but the divisions between central and eastern Europe and many other older members of the EU, are now a reality. These divergent preferences thus serve as an obstacle to deeper integration and make *breaking down* as a scenario more likely in this policy field. The multiple cleavages among member states on the refugee crisis and refugee policy integration contrasts with the predominant creditor–debtor cleavage in the financial crisis. The financial crisis on its own offers more potential for *heading forward* in common fiscal and monetary policy. Institutional changes in the architecture of EMU held out the hope of overcoming collective action problems and systemic failure, potentially benefitting all, while Brexit and the refugee situation posed clearer costs and benefits for specific dissidents and cooperators (the UK for Brexit and the Visegrad countries for refugees).

One of the ironies of the triple crisis concerns the alliance of Germany and Greece regarding refugees. As representatives of their respective northern and southern coalitions regarding the financial crisis, they are antagonists locked in a bitter and prolonged creditor–debtor struggle. The refugee crisis brings Germany and Greece together with a new configuration of interests. As Offe puts it (2015: 140), Germany and Greece are now "playing major roles in the refugee crisis, with the important difference being that they antagonized each other in the debt crisis while they now are both severely and commonly affected victims of their fellow Europeans' refusal to share the burdens of the wave of refugee migration for which the EU was entirely unprepared" (2015: 140). Possibilities for a bargain focus on Germany and Greece with Germany holding the card of debt forgiveness and Greece capable of offering even greater acceptance of refugees and control of its northern borders.

BREXIT

On June 23, 2016 a referendum was held in the UK in which approximately 52% of the voters cast their ballots for leaving the EU. The vote to leave was in many ways a surprise, though not a big one. The pollsters got it wrong, but not by much (2–3%). While the polls were off in their predictions, the broad trends were captured by social media and patterns of tweeting. Of course, tweets are not held to the same standards as scientific polls. Tweets are seldom randomly sampled, their "predictions" are not stated with confidence intervals, and we do not have good models of "eligible tweeters" as with "eligible voters." We do not know if there is selection bias as to who tweets and who does not. The relevance of social media to macro political events such as referenda and elections is not well known and study of these relationships is in its infancy (Howard and Kollanyi 2016; Llewellyn and Cram 2016). Nevertheless, the patterns of tweeting dramatically increased in the summer of 2015, just as the refugees crossing the Mediterranean increased (Porcaro and Mueller 2016: Figure 1). It was impossible not to notice the correlation between refugee flows and pro-Brexit sentiment. In this way, differential integration which allowed the UK to opt out of Schengen and EMU also had the effect of increasing the perception among many in the UK that their nation state was less able to control policy in these areas.

Predictions about the results of Brexit range from economic catastrophe to little effect to actual improvement in performance of the UK economy.

In addition, there were several noneconomic reasons for Brexit, including restoring sovereignty and regaining control of one's borders (see Oliver et al. this volume). Many in the UK saw themselves as liberal with regard to trade in goods and services and capital flows, but much more interventionist on immigration. The desire to control borders holds for immigration from outside the EU as well as eastern Europe. As Matthijs points out, between 2004 and 2014 about 2 million people moved from Poland to Germany and the UK (2017: 93). These movements no doubt sensitized UK citizens to the subsequent waves of migrants from the Middle East and North Africa.

The stakes for Brexit, both for the UK and the EU, are high but asymmetric. British trade with the EU is over 46% on the export side while EU exports to the UK are around 8%. Gravity models of trade tell us that the UK's trade partners are not likely to dramatically shift, since trade patterns are dominated by geographic location and trade volumes of importing and exporting countries. It is not likely that there will be a large redirection of trade toward New Zealand, Australia, or Canada. Commonwealth effects are likely to be already "baked into" existing trade levels. When trade negotiations enter the hard-bargaining stage, asymmetric interdependence implies that bargaining leverage should lie with the EU.

Intersections

How does the financial crisis interrelate with the refugee crisis and Brexit? What prospects for deeper integration and differential integration does this crisis context offer? The causal sources of the crises appear separate at first: institutional flaws, a credit-induced boom and structural imbalances in trade and capital flow for the financial crisis, wars and instability in the Middle East and Africa for the surge in refugees, and a mixture of economic, demographic, and identity factors for Brexit. Even if the sources are different, they come together in distinct historical conjunctures. I see at least three intersections.

The first intersection is between the financial crisis and the refugee crisis. The financial crisis worsened the refugee situation, increasing the likelihood of *breaking down*. Refugees arrived in 2015 and 2016 when growth was sluggish and unemployment was high on Europe's periphery. Italy's unemployment rate was almost 13% while unemployment in Greece was over 26% overall, with youth unemployment higher. Both countries experienced other economic hardships, including pension cuts, a rise in temporary contracts, and an increase in the "working poor" (Giglioli 2016). While recovery had started, the GDP of the eurozone in the final quarter of 2015 was still below its pre-crisis peak in 2008 (*Economist* 2016). Italy and Greece, the two primary first destinations, were ill-equipped to respond. One sad fact about the geography of the financial and refugee crises is that it presented the worst possible constellation of locations, interests and actors. From the standpoint of geography what was needed was a southern Europe experiencing an economic boom with high employment close to refugees emigrating from adjacent areas. Though far from a uniform pattern, the most accepting countries were/are in the north and the least enthusiastic in the south and east. This simple fact, high unemployment and sluggish growth in Europe's southern periphery combined with the fact that the initial destination of many refugees included Italy and Greece, exacerbated an already toxic situation.

The second intersection relates to the effect of the refugee crisis and intra-EU migration on Brexit. In the UK, there was a small bias for "remain" in the first half of 2015 but this margin dissipated quickly in the summer of 2015 with dramatic increases in the flows of refugees across the Mediterranean, thus preparing the conditions for *breaking down*. Anti-refugee sentiment continued throughout the year, punctuated by significant moments in the campaign itself, for example, the announcement of the date for the vote (Porcaro and Mueller 2016). Internal EU migrations to the UK also added fuel to the Brexit fires (McBride 2017). The enlargements of 2004 and 2007 added 12 new members to the EU. Both of these expansions caused spikes in migrations from the new members to the UK. The number of Polish immigrants in the UK surpassed 800,000 by 2011. There were also considerable numbers of immigrants from Lithuania, Latvia, and Slovakia. By 2015 net migration to the UK surpassed 300,000 a year, a number which David Cameron called "unsustainable" (McBride 2017).

The third intersection took place between Brexit and the eurozone financial crisis. The way in which these two events interacted is more subtle than the others. The UK was never part of the eurozone and tried to stay as aloof as possible from developments inside the monetary union. Nevertheless, the interactions between Brexit and the financial crisis are multiple and important. First, at the purely economic level, the eurozone crisis created uncertainty and depressed economic growth. Shrinking markets within the eurozone countries were bound to adversely affect British trade and finance.

Second, the economic recession in the eurozone meant greater migration from eurozone and non-eurozone countries to the UK. Migrations increased from Poland, Czech Republic, Slovakia, Latvia, and Lithuania. While these were not refugee movements—they all came from within the EU and were economic migrants—they no doubt gave rise to resentment and primed the UK to be negatively disposed to the 2015 surge of refugees.

Thirdly, with few exceptions (see Fabbrini 2015; Henning 2017) very little attention has been paid to the ways in which the governance system of the eurozone alienated the UK from political and institutional developments inside the EU. Fabbrini (2015) has brought to our attention the emergence within the EU of two distinct systems of governance, one centered on the traditional "community method" involving the making of laws on the basis of Commission proposals and co-decision by the Council of Ministers and the European Parliament and the other centering on the intergovernmental method employed in the European Council. The second governance system regulates issues traditionally close to core state powers (security and foreign policies, large parts of justice and home affairs) and particularly the economic policy of the eurozone. The UK is not a member of the eurozone and is therefore not represented in the distinctive institutions of the eurozone, such as the Eurogroup and the Euro Summit. This is appropriate on the grounds that only members of the eurozone should participate in its governance. However, there are policy externalities. The UK is correct when it sees itself as excluded from having a voice in the overall democratic nature of the eurozone (see Oliver et al. this volume). The new intergovernmental treaties—Fiscal Compact, European Stability Mechanism, Single Resolution Fund—were taken outside the Lisbon Treaty so as to isolate those states who might want to veto actions relating to monetary policy (Fabbrini 2015: 263). On the one hand, the financial crisis allows for deeper integration and *heading forward* among those member states in EMU seeking to prevent the next crisis. Intergovernmental governance has deepened integration in the eurozone, giving rise in the UK to fears of exclusion and (in the eurozone's member state publics) to a perception of a general loss of legitimacy of the EU's institutions.

Lessons for Institutionalists

Institutions can be defined in general terms as "… the rules of the game in a society or … humanly devised constraints that shape human interaction" (North 1990: 3). Similarly, Keohane defines institutions as "persistent and connected sets of rules … that prescribe behavioral roles, constrain activity, and shape expectations" (1989: 3). Institutions defined as rules are related to, but distinct from, formal institutions which are also called organizations. They are similar in that organizations embody rules as defined above. Indeed, an organization may have been created precisely to carry out a set of rules. But "persistent and connected sets of rules" do not require an organizational vehicle. The institution of multilateralism (Ruggie 1993), a core set of rules about how to structure international economic relations, exists apart from any particular organization (such as the IMF or NATO) which adopts multilateral principles. One reason to distinguish between rules and organizations is that the latter have agency. Organizations such as the EU can "act" in the standard sense (sign treaties, consider applications for membership) while a rule (such as the Dublin Regulation) cannot.

Institutions are pervasive but their existence may signify different things. They may reflect the interests of the powerful (Knight 1992), may provide solutions to problems of cooperation (Keohane 1984), be purely ceremonial (Meyer and Rowan 1977), or be utterly pathological (Barnett and Finnemore 1999). The dominant approach within political science and economics sees institutions as solutions to problems of market failure. Institutions may solve problems of deficient equilibria if these problems are associated with low levels of trust, weak or asymmetric information, or the inability to monitor and enforce bargains. Thus, transparency, reporting, monitoring, and third-party adjudication are often part and parcel of the institutional toolkit.

This template carries over into regional integration studies. Many scholars see chronic institutional underperformance in the EU, implying that there are "big bills left on the sidewalk" (Olson 1996) in terms of unexploited cooperative gains. Some expect that all problems can be solved with the right mix of information and institutional engineering. Like the economist who is expected to create a market for every externality or failed exchange, the political scientist is to create the right set of rules to respond to any and all challenges. This view is flawed. We should be wary of institutional hubris every bit as much as market hubris. We can appreciate this point better if we see institutions in context next to their kindred analytic tools: preferences, resources and ideas (Moravcsik 2003, 2010). Preferences are what people want, their goals, how they trade-off different goals. Resources are the means people have at their disposal to pursue these goals. Ideas, including causal beliefs, link resources to actor goals. Institutions refer to the framework of rules within which actors pursue their goals.

Failure to achieve goals can be due to different causes. Sometimes actors aren't successful because of scarce (inadequate) resources; sometimes, they lack the basic knowledge to achieve goals; sometimes they fail due to inefficient institutions; and sometimes they fail due to the arrangement of preferences among the actors. In short, if the quartet of terms—preferences, resources, ideas, and institutions—is to have integrity, we must allow all four to vary independently. We must allow for failures due to scare resources, divergent preferences or inadequate information (ideas) and inadequate rules. Which brings us to the cases at hand: the eurozone crisis, the refugee crisis, and Brexit. My view is that the latter two crises, especially Brexit, are less about institutional failures, or inadequate resources, and more about the distribution of preferences.

It is often difficult to distinguish between an institutional failure and a failure due to the constellation of preferences. However, collapsing these two categories creates a muddle and intractable analytic difficulties. A necessary step to clarity is to distinguish between fundamental (basic) and situational preferences. Basic preferences refer to what individuals want in settings that are pre-strategic while the latter refers to preferences that depend on particular circumstances. Perhaps a better term for basic preferences is interests. As Moravcsik puts it, "State preferences … comprise a set of fundamental interests defined across 'states of the world'" (2003: 164). A country's basic preference may be survival and security from physical harm while its strategic preferences may be for alliances, divide and rule, or neutrality. The introduction of a new institution (as a rule) can change a preference for a strategy from defect to co-operate, by making the defect strategy more costly. This definition of preference accords with usage in economics. A firm in a duopoly may act on the basis of market share while one in a competitive setting pursues absolute gains. Basic preferences do not change. Rather, variation in economic structure accounts for differences in situational preferences.

Role of Institutions in the Eurozone Crisis

Of the three crises, the one most amenable to an institutional solution is the eurozone crisis, and the capacity of the EU for *heading forward* in this policy area is significant. From the very beginning, the institutional architecture of the eurozone was radically incomplete. Gaps were evident in banking regulations, the monitoring and control of structural imbalances, and fiscal deficits. The biggest institutional gaps were in the areas of fiscal imbalances and lender of last resort functions (LLR). As Sims (2012) points out, the EMU eliminated the LLR function at the national level without providing an equivalent mechanism at the European level. The Stability and Growth Pact set out criteria for debts and deficits, but there was a virtual absence of institutions at the center of EMU to deal with deficits should they occur. EMU lacked centralized fiscal resources to deal with country indebtedness and in any case, the EU was legally prohibited from bailouts and monetary financing. The problem was both inadequate resources and lack of centralized institutions, with resource scarcity largely endogenous to institutions.

The lack of a central LLR function leads to a situation where a manageable budget deficit might generate anxiety out of proportion to the underlying problem. Localized deficits might spread beyond their point of origin. Liquidity problems could easily become solvency problems. This has elements of a classic social dilemma in the sense that the structure of the situation could easily lead to a bad equilibrium (a situation that is stable even though it is no one's first preference): high interest rates, difficulty paying off debt, shrinkage of affected economies aggravating debt, and ability to repay. A "good" equilibrium is available with different institutions (DeGrauwe and Ji 2013: 17). DeGrauwe and Ji (2013) conducted an empirical test in which they compared bond markets in eurozone countries with bond markets outside the eurozone with respect to sensitivity of these markets to national debt. Eurozone bond markets were notably more fragile in the sense that they registered higher interest rate spreads with German ten-year bonds than bond markets in "stand-alone" countries.

We can model the incentives facing Germany and Greece in the eurozone crisis as an approximation to a prisoner's dilemma game as illustrated in Fig. 23.1. Germany's incentives are in favor of austerity and no bailout with accompanying reforms in Greece. Greece's incentives are to resist reforms and to advocate for bailouts. Each prefers to not cooperate and push for the other to give in. Both would be better off with cooperation and certainly both countries want to avoid a eurozone collapse. On the other hand, Germany mostly wants to avoid moral hazard by setting an example that the costs of domestic spending cannot be externalized. Greece wants to avoid domestic collapse on the part of the government in power. Institutions which clarify expectations about what happens in case of crisis could play a positive role and indeed one such example is the European Stability Mechanism set up by member states to provide liquidity to troubled Euro area economies during the crisis.

		Greece	
		C	D
Germany & Creditors	C	Cell 1 **Supports fiscal union** **Greece restraint** Greater stability Less tendency for small disturbances to become large	Cell 2 **Supports fiscal union** **Greece overspends** Moral hazard realized
	D	Cell 3 **No bailout funds;** **Germany insists on costly reforms** **Greece tries to control spending, but** Shrinking Greek GDP Greece unlikely to be able to pay off debt	Cell 4 **No fiscal union** **Greece chronic overspending** Fiscal deficits Growing gap between Germany and Greece

Fig. 23.1 Greece and Germany in the eurozone crisis

I do not think the eurozone crisis perfectly fits the prisoners' dilemma game but it is a useful approximation. While Germany would like Greece to undertake reforms, Germany may also think that it is unlikely for Greece to be able to carry out these reforms without wrecking their economy. Some politicians in Greece may also welcome the idea of externally imposed reforms.

The Role of Institutions in Refugee Crisis

The refugee crisis will not be easily solved by institutions. The interactions among the crises and the distribution of preferences among member states, along with demanding voting rules, work against easy resolution (see Bosilca, this volume).

Instabilities in North Africa, the Middle East, and Sub-Saharan Africa paint a bleak picture. As Miliband (2016) points out in a sobering article, modern warfare, particularly civil wars, are protracted affairs, often lasting over three decades (2016). Correlated with the length of wars we observe that refugees are displaced for an average of 17 years and for internally displaced people the figures are even higher. Many lament the dire situation posed by the refugee crisis. While institutional solutions are difficult, they are not impossible. EU institutions are strained but not overwhelmed. To be overwhelmed is to find oneself in the situation where one is seriously committed to helping but lacking in the wit or resources to do so. This is not the situation with regard to the EU in the refugee crisis. There is little in the EU's political constitution (the treaties and the institutions they have created) that prevents measured responses. Yet, talk of "institutional failure," "institutional weakness," or "the crisis of EU institutions" is widespread.

Similarly, resource limitations do not provide a compelling argument for inaction on refugees. As EU scholars know, budgetary restrictions are very tight, but budgets are endogenous to preferences. EU budgets are the products of collective choices. We know from the financial crisis that there are many ways these restrictions can be circumvented. That these restrictions were circumvented improves the prospects for deeper integration. Member states can contribute from their own budgets rather than requiring the EU to violate its budgetary ceiling. Special purpose institutions, along the lines of those created for the eurozone crisis, can be created which raise their own funds and operate outside the formal legal structure of the EU and the eurozone. There is much room for creativity when the will of member states is present but little when there is disagreement on objectives.

Many see a chronic institutional underperformance of the EU in addressing the refugee crisis. My view is that the crisis is less about the EU falling short of its institutional potential and more about divergent preferences among key member states, domestic political processes that reward anti-immigrant behavior, and demanding EU voting rules. In short, this is not institutional failure. It is a "failure" of preferences to align in such a way as to allow for cooperative solutions. Unless one argues that institutions can change fundamental (not just strategic) preferences, then one is brought to the inevitable conclusion that the preferences of the leaders of Hungary, Slovakia, the Czech Republic, and Poland cannot be brought into line with those of other more pro-refugee countries such as Germany and Sweden. The difficulty of designing institutions that could change the preferences of member states and member state publics on immigration creates the conditions for *breaking down* in the migration policy area. While Poland and Hungary violate the "liberal" part of liberal democracy, these countries enjoy a depressingly high level of electoral support. Unlike in Western Europe where anti-immigrant attitudes come from anti-system parties of the right and left, in the Visegrad countries 'anti-immigrant rhetoric comes from the very center of the political space' (Hunyadi and Molnar 2016: 1) which makes it difficult to delegitimize the mainstream political parties (see Raube et al. and Newsome and Stenberg in this volume).

To illustrate the array of preferences, see Fig. 23.2. If both Germany and Hungary prefer acceptance of refugees but prefer to free ride while others shoulder the burdens, one could think of this as a prisoners' dilemma game. The familiar preference orderings would conform to a prisoner's dilemma game: DC>CC>DD>CD and CD>CC>DD>DC (players 1 and 2, respectively). The problem is that preferences do not follow the standard prisoners' dilemma structure. Hungary prefers mutual non-cooperation (both Hungary and Germany do not accept refugees) to an outcome where Germany accepts and Hungary free rides on German generosity. This claim is supported by

		Hungary/Visegrad Countries	
		C	D
Germany	C	Cell 1 **Germany co-operates** **Hungary co-operates** (Not Likely)	Cell 2 **Germany co-operates** **Hungary does not co-operate**
	D	Cell 3 **German does not co-operate** **Hungary co-operates** (No)	Cell 4 **Germany does not co-operate** **Hungary does not co-operate** (Not Likely)

Fig. 23.2 Refugee crisis

the strenuous reactions of Orban to Merkel's generous "willkommenskultur," calling it "moral imperialism."[1]

As stated previously, we must theoretically allow for failures due to scarce resources, divergent preferences, scarce or faulty information, and weak or inefficient institutions. Voting rules are endogenous to institutions, which in turn are endogenous to preferences. Provided those rules are democratically created, it would be odd to blame the rules themselves. A different response to the refugee crisis, a better one according to many, was not forthcoming because of the preferences of the member states and their adopted rules. The old-time religion of integration theory would have called this "a failure of will" but whatever one calls it, it is not an institutional failure.

If institutions cannot fix a serious problem, maybe moral suasion can change hearts and minds. A good case can be made that the refugee crisis is a humanitarian crisis. As Betts (2015: 364) argues, moral philosophy starts with the idea of obligation and the notion that we have a special duty toward those in need. One can invoke Rawls and the veil of ignorance. What kind of world would we choose if we did not know which position we would occupy in it? Most of us would choose a world where others would be obligated to take us in. By forcing us to assume a disinterested position, Rawls's ethical experiment clarifies our values. Communitarians might be less likely to open the borders fully to refugees but would nevertheless be likely to accept some level of responsibility. True, the communitarian state takes care of its own first, but even if we see the state as a lifeboat with limited capacity, we have to be honest about how much room we have. Lebanon has 1.2 million refugees and a total population of 4 million. Germany, the most generous country in the EU, made commitments to accept 800,000 and has a population of over 80 million. The EU has a population of over 440 million. Yet, the 120,000–160,000 that Merkel suggested be taken in by the rest of the EU appears to be too much for some countries.

An obstacle to finding an institutional solution involves the current decision-making rules. These rules set a high bar for agreeing on what constitutes a breach to a member state's obligations insofar as refugees are concerned. Article 7 of the Lisbon Treaty allows for the use of material sanctions and suspension of voting rights for serious breaches. If a breach is decided, the vote on sanctions is by qualified majority in the European Council (Sedelmeier 2017: 239) but the existence of a breach presents a higher barrier, unanimity minus one in the European Council. Given that there are several members opposed to the mandatory refugee quotas, it appears impossible to garner the necessary votes.

---

[1] Admittedly, other interpretations are plausible, including one in which Orban sees German generosity as relieving pressure on Hungary to accept more refugees.

We should not exaggerate the obstacles flowing from the current rules (Art. 7). Rules can be very flexible. They can be stubbornly or flexibly applied, they can be bent, amended, and made subject to extensive exception-seeking. They can be circumvented, which is what the European Council did when it created the European Financial Stability Facility (EFSF) and Fiscal Compact outside of the legal architecture of the EU. They can be made more complex for special reasons, which is what the heads of state and governments did when they made the International Monetary Fund (IMF) part of the Troika (Henning 2017). The EU has employed coalitions of the willing, opportunistic opt-outs and opt-ins regarding Schengen and EMU, treaty rewrites, and heroic treaty interpretations related to monetary financing. Much could be done within the overall institutional structure of the EMU and EU to creatively use what is now available to facilitate further integration.

The Role of Institutions in Brexit

At first, the Brexit negotiations appear to offer little room for institutional improvement. The UK wants to leave, the EU prefers that they remain, and neither side plans to make it easy for the other. If this is the understanding of the situation, we have something close to a game of redistribution where trade-offs and compromises are grudgingly made. However, a more careful look reveals a number of areas where there are common as well as divergent interests. There is ample room to think about the efficient as well as distributive role of institutions.

In an interesting document prepared for the European Parliament, with the title "The United Kingdom's Exit from and New Partnership with the European Union" (2017) the authors identify a number of key interests motivating the UK. Among them are ensuring free trade of goods, services, and free movement of capital. These objectives are three out of four of the fundamental freedoms central to the EU. These are followed by "securing the rights of EU and UK nationals," a matter of mutual concern to EU and UK nationals.

Admittedly, there are also divergent interests. An important one has to do with control over borders, both to regulate movements within the EU and outside the EU. Migration and control over borders were important issues in the election. Many members of the EU would like to see free movement of peoples within the EU and for the UK to accept more refugees from outside the EU borders. This is an issue where disagreements run deep and are hard to resolve.

A second divergent interest has to do with ending the jurisdiction of the Court of Justice of the European Union (CJEU). The direct effect and supremacy doctrines run counter to the British concept of parliamentary sovereignty since supremacy implies that the EU treaties are themselves higher normative orders than national laws.[2] With exit from the EU it follows that the CJEU no longer has jurisdiction over the UK legal order. However, the CJEU is not only guardian of the Treaty, but is also the vehicle for resolving disputes within the single market. Since the UK and the EU seem to have convergent interests regarding the benefits of the single market (minus the free movement of labor), the future role of the CJEU is not so clear-cut. Also, getting rid of the CJEU's jurisdiction for new cases may be relatively easy, but what does one do about the ways that complex judicial reasoning and case law are already baked into "domestic law" (Jupille and Caporaso 2009). Both of these divergent interests constitute *breaking down* albeit in different ways. While the loss of the UK as a member state and the ensuing reduction in the scope of EU's legal regime signifies the literal breaking apart of the Union, more significant is the potential that unravelling expands to include the exit of other states, and the contention of differentiated integration measures designed to keep member states at their own desired depth and breadth of integration, leads in turn to a parallel alienation from the European project.

A third divergence is symbolic. The EU does not want to establish a precedent that it is easy to leave because each country may feel free to strike its own bargain. The EU wants to make clear that "Europe cafeteria style" is not acceptable. The strategy that flows from this premise is anything but straightforward. It may involve situations in which the EU threatens to pursue actions which are welfare-decreasing to the member states simply for reputational reasons, such as to discourage others from using the Brexit as a precedent. The opportunity cost to membership should be high and the way to do this is to threaten to use the structural power of the EU (27 members, large market, asymmetric reliance of the UK on the EU) to extract concessions.

With such a mix of interests, it is hard to represent Brexit–EU relations as a simple game, but we can approximate their respective situations if we simplify and focus only on the four fundamental freedoms. Looking at Fig. 23.3 (EU and UK–Brexit) below we see that Cell 1 is not really a possibility since the UK will not accept labour mobility and the EU will not unpack the four freedoms. Similarly, Cells 2 and 3 are not really attainable because both actors are not going to cave in on such a basic goal. It follows that the EU prefers Cell 2 to Cell 3 and the UK prefers Cell 3 to Cell 2. There is little room for institutions to coordinate expectations and preferences in this stark situation. Preferences are arranged in such a way that cooperation will not improve outcomes for either actor.

---

[2] This is hotly contested in several countries not least of which is Germany.

		EU	
		C	DC
UK	C	Cell 1 UK accepts EU accepts (Not Realistic)	Cell 2 EU maintains position Soft Brexit, accepts EU conditions
	DC	Cell 3 UK opposes EU accepts (UK wins)	Cell 4 Both hold firm Implies Brexit

Fig. 23.3 EU and UK (Brexit)

Conclusion

This paper advanced two themes: the interrelatedness of the eurozone crisis with the refugee and Brexit crises and the variable effectiveness of institutions. The relations among the crises are for the most part self-aggravating, each one making the other one worse. Refugees from Africa and the Middle East put additional administrative and financial stress on Greece and Italy, two countries least equipped to handle displaced people. Migrations from Greece, Italy, and central and eastern European countries to the UK sensitized the UK to refugees from the Middle East and Africa. Austerity policies hit not only citizens of the EU's periphery but also the migrants and refugees who fled to Greece and Italy. Austerity increased the chances of unemployment for refugees as well as citizens, unemployment increased the prospects for losing one's residency papers, and this in turn decreased the prospects of remaining inside a host country.

Solutions to Europe's triple crisis will take place partly outside the EU. The refugee crisis was sudden and involved the movement of millions of people in 2015 from poorer, war-torn, and dysfunctional states to richer democratic ones (Betts and Collier 2017). Ending the wars in Iraq, Afghanistan, and Syria, while not an immediate prospect, would certainly help to relieve the refugee situation but by itself this is not enough to solve the problem. Dysfunctional regimes in South Sudan, Nigeria and Somalia, where there are chronic food shortages, will continue to fuel the refugee situation. Over 90% of the world's displaced peoples are living in the less developed world. Poor countries such as Iran, Lebanon, Jordan, and Ethiopia have provided a haven of sorts to refugees. The EU may see itself at the center of the refugee question but most of the help, on the ground, comes from poorer countries outside the EU.

Waiting for wars to end is not a policy but pinning hopes on the generosity of EU countries does not seem a realistic alternative. Merkel has not been successful in convincing other EU members to accept even the small (120,000–160,000) numbers of refugees she has proposed. Macron in France has vowed not to allow the 'jungle' in Calais to continue. Central and Eastern European countries are firm in their determination to keep their borders closed. Italy and Greece are not equipped to deal with the problem on a long-term basis, even if their rescue efforts have been valuable. The EU has shown itself to be limited in the face of a crisis that revolves around identity concerns more than economic issues (Boerzel and Risse 2018). Indeed, the refugee crisis and the prospects for *heading forward* in monetary and fiscal union compounded the paradoxically desired exclusion of the UK from common migration and financial policy.

The EU has made a lot of reforms to alleviate the financial crisis. The banking system has been reformed. Regulations regarding finance have been harmonized. The Commission has been given added powers with regard to monitoring macro-economic imbalances, competitiveness, and budget deficits. The eurozone crisis has been stabilized. There will be long, drawn-out negotiations between Greece and the Troika, but Greece's problems are not likely to become problems for the whole eurozone. In addition, perhaps there is a hidden exchange lying in wait between Greece, geographically well-situated with respect to accepting refugees but badly in need of debt relief, and Germany which supports acceptance of more refugees by the EU, and also has the power to grant debt relief to Greece. So, a swap—a political bargain— is within reach whereby Greece continues to accept refugees, regulates its northern border, in return for a write-down of debt and increased funds to manage the refugees (*Financial Times* 2016). In this way, it could be possible that *breaking down* in refugee policy may partially be converted into reforms across policy areas through political bargaining.

This takes us to the second theme, the limits of institutional solutions. I have found liberal institutionalism helpful in addressing the three crises. Some variants of liberalism treat institutionalism as separate (Moravcsik 2003, 2010) with liberalism focusing on preferences and institutionalism on information. I prefer to join the two concerns and see the success of institutions as linked to both changes in incentives and changes in information. Many market failures are due to scarcities or asymmetries of information, as the "market for lemons" instructs us. Yet the supply of sanctions, as in punishment for not pursuing a cooperative strategy (such as overfishing, exploiting the commons), is also part and parcel of institutional solutions.

Liberal institutionalism provides a better explanatory account of the triple crisis than realism (relying on coercive abilities) and constructivism, relying on communication, socialization and malleability of preferences. The Brexit and refugee crises are not due to market failures, information shortages or asymmetries in the distribution of information. Knowing more about what Orban and Merkel want (both basic and strategic preferences) will not help. The environment of the eurozone is information-rich and symmetric rather than information-poor and asymmetric. Institutional changes will not make these preferences align. Basic differences cannot be made compatible as they can in instances of market failures. Of course, this does not mean there is no room for improvement (see Bordignon and Moriconi 2017). I am struck by the ingenuity of the member states concerning the eurozone crisis (Fiscal Compact, Troika) compared to the institutional inertia and paralysis concerning the refugee crisis. Perhaps the EU still has some cards to play regarding both refugees and impending UK exit. However, the UK is now outside the EU and many refugees will have suffered years of needless hardship (Bully 2017). The Brexit outcome can feature either a soft or hard landing and there is still time to make a difference regarding refugees, with or without the help of the least cooperative EU members.

References

Barnett, M. N., & Finnemore, M. (1999). The Politics, Power, and Pathologies of International Organizations. *International Organization, 53*(4), 699–732.

Betts, A. (2015). The Normative Terrain of the Global Refugee Regime. *Ethics and International Affairs, 29*(4), 363–375.

Betts, A., & Collier, P. (2017). *Refuge: Rethinking Refugee Policy in a Changing World*. Oxford, England: Oxford University Press.

Boerzel, T. A., & Risse, T. (2018). From the Euro to the Schengen Crises: European Integration Theories, Politicization, and Identity Politics. *Journal of European Public Policy, 25*(1), 83–108.

Bordignon, M., & Moriconi, S. (2017). The Case for a Common European Refugee Policy. Bruegel Policy Contribution Issue 8. Bruegel, Brussels, Belgium, 1–13.

Brunnermeier, M. K., James, H., & Landau, J. P. (2016). *The Euro and the Battle of Ideas*. Princeton, NJ: Princeton University Press.

Bully, D. (2017). Shame on EU? Europe, RtoP, and the Politics of Refugee Protection. *Ethics and International Affairs, 31*(1), 51–70.

Caporaso, J. A. (2018). Europe's Triple Crisis and the Uneven Role of Institutions: The Euro, Refugees and Brexit. *Journal of Common Market Studies, 56*(6), 1345–1361.

DeGrauwe, P. (2011). Only a More Active ECB Can Solve the Euro Crisis. No. 250, August. Brussels, Belgium. *Center for European Policy Studies*, 1–8.

DeGrauwe, P., & Ji, Y. (2013). Self-Fulfilling Crises in the Eurozone: An Empirical Test. *Journal of International Money and Finance, 34*, 15–36.

Economist. (2016, February 18). Taking Europe's Pulse. *Economist*.

Fabbrini, S. (2015). *Which European Union?*. Cambridge, England: Cambridge University Press.

Giglioli, I. (2016). Migration, Austerity, and Crisis at the Periphery of Europe. *Othering and Belonging, Issue One, Summer*. http://www.otheringandbelonging.org/wp-content/uploads/2016/07/OtheringAndBelonging_Issue1.pdf.

Heipertz, M., & Verdun, A. (2010). *Ruling Europe*. Cambridge: Cambridge University Press.

Henning, R. C. (2017). *Tangled Governance: International Regime Complexity, the Troika, and the Euro Crisis*. Oxford, England: Oxford University Press.

Hollifield, J. F. (2016). The Refugee 'Crisis' in Europe and the Policy Responses. *Policy Brief*, 1–3. Washington, DC: Woodrow Wilson Center.

Howard, P., & Kollanyi, B. (2016). Bots, #Strongerin, and #Brexit. *Comprop Research Note, 2016*, 1–6.

Hunyadi, B., & Molnar, C. (2016). *Central Europe's Faceless Strangers: The Rise of Xenophobia*. Washington, DC: Freedom House.

Jacoby, W. (2017). *Surplus Germany* (Paper Series No. 8, 1–32). Washington, DC. Transatlantic Academy.

Jupille, J., & Caporaso, J. A. (2009). Domesticating Discourses: European Law, English Judges, and Political Institutions. *European Political Science Review, 1*(2), 205–228.

Keohane, R. O. (1984). *After Hegemony*. Princeton, NJ: Princeton University Press.

Keohane, R. O. (1989). *International Institutions and State Power*. Boulder, CO: Westview Press.

Kindleberger, C., & Aliber, R. (2005). *Manias, Panics, and Crashes*. New York: Wiley.

Knight, J. (1992). *Institutions and Social Conflict*. Cambridge, England: Cambridge University Press.

Llewellyn, C., & Cram, L. (2016). Analyzing Opinion on UK-EU Referendum on Twitter. *Proceedings of the Tenth International AAAI Conference on Web and Social Media* (ICWSM 2016).

Matthijs, M. (2017, January/February). Europe After Brexit. *Foreign Affairs, 96*(1), 85–95.

Matthijs, M., & McNamara, K. (2015). The Euro Crisis' Theory Effects: Northern Saints, Southern Sinners, and the Demise of the Eurobond. *Journal of European Integration, 37*(2), 229–245.

McBride, J. (2017). What Brexit Means. *Council on Foreign Relations*. Available at: https://www.cfr.org/backgrounder/what-brexit-means. Accessed 21 August 2017.

Merler, S., & Pisani-Ferry, J. (2012). *Sudden Stops in the Euro Area* (pp. 1–16). Brussels, Belgium, Bruegel: Bruegel Policy Contribution.

Meyer, J. W., & Rowan, B. (1977). Institutionalized Organizations: Formal Structure as Myth and Ceremony. *American Journal of Sociology, 85*(2), 340–363.

Miliband, D. (2016, October 13). The Best Way to Deal with the Refugee Crisis. *New York Review of Books, 63*(15).

Moravcsik, A. (2003). Liberal International Relations Theory: A Scientific Assessment. In C. Elman & M. F. Elman (Eds.), *Progress in International Relations Theory* (pp. 159–204). Cambridge, MA: MIT Press.

Moravcsik, A. (2010). *Liberal Theories of International Relations: A Primer*, 1–15. Princeton, NJ: Princeton University, unpublished manuscript.

North, D. C. (1990). *Institutions, Institutional Change, and Economic Performance*. Cambridge, England: Cambridge University Press.

Offe, C. (2015, postscript 2016). *Europe Entrapped*. Cambridge, England: Polity Press.

Olson, M., Jr. (1996). Big Bills Left on the Sidewalk: Why Some Nations are Rich and Others Poor. *Journal of Economic Perspectives, 10*(2), 3–24.

Porcaro, G., & Mueller, H. (2016). *Tweeting Brexit: Narrative Building and Sentiment Analysis*. Bruegel, Brussels, Blog Post. http://bruegel.org/2016/11/tweeting-brexit-narrative-building-and-sentiment-analysis/.

Rachman, G. (2016, January 25). Greek Debt Is the Key to Refugee Crisis. *Financial Times*.

Ruggie, J. G. (1993). Multilateralism: The Anatomy of an Institution. In J. G. Ruggie (Ed.), *Multilateralism Matters: The Theory and Praxis of an Institutional Form* (pp. 3–47). New York: Columbia University Press.

Sedelmeier, U. (2017). Political Safeguards Against Democratic Backsliding in the EU: The Limits of Material Sanctions and the Scope of Social Pressure. *Journal of European Public Policy, 24*(3), 337–351.

Sims, C. A. (2012). Gaps in the Institutional Structure of the Euro Area. *Banque de France. Financial Stability Review, 16*(April), 1–7.

CHAPTER 24

The Migration Crisis: An Introduction

Akasemi Newsome, Marianne Riddervold, and Jarle Trondal

Migration is a perennial issue in European politics. Yet, the recent refugee crisis of 2015–2016 laid bare a new cleavage hitherto poorly understood. Not only are national parties divided about whether migration is a threat to national identities, but national governments and EU officials disagree about what implications migration has for European identity and the European project. In many ways, the chapters by Kaija Schilde, Sara Wallace Goodman, Ruxandra-Laura Bosilca and Beverly Crawford to follow map different sets of disagreements and debates about what kind of policy and institutional response

---

A. Newsome (✉) · M. Riddervold
Inland School of Business and Social Sciences, Inland University, Rena and Lillehammer, Norway
e-mail: akasemi@berkeley.edu

Institute of European Studies, University of California, Berkeley, CA, USA

M. Riddervold
e-mail: marianne.riddervold@inn.no

M. Riddervold
The Norwegian Institute of International Affairs (NUPI), Oslo, Norway

J. Trondal
Department of Political Science and Management, University of Agder, Kristiansand, Norway
e-mail: jarle.trondal@uia.no

ARENA - Centre for European Studies, University of Oslo, Oslo, Norway

© The Author(s) 2021
M. Riddervold et al. (eds.), *The Palgrave Handbook of EU Crises*,
Palgrave Studies in European Union Politics,
https://doi.org/10.1007/978-3-030-51791-5_24

challenges migration poses more broadly via the lens of the specific migration crisis. The 2015–2016 migration crisis captured the world's attention owing to three notable developments. Firstly, there was an increase in the number of people traveling to Europe over a matter of months, some crossing the Mediterranean from North Africa and others later making the maritime trip between Turkey and Greece. Secondly, there were growing numbers of people dying in the attempt to reach Europe. People fleeing to Europe originated overwhelmingly from areas riven by war (Ceccorulli 2019; Zaun 2016). For example, a Migration Policy Institute Europe report notes that 'during 2015 around 90 percent of those arriving in Greece by sea were from Syria, Afghanistan or Iraq' (Collett and Le Coz 2018: 9). Initially, the uncoordinated response offered by individual member-states in response to growing numbers of migrants taking the dangerous trip to Europe in order to escape inhospitable home countries was 'rescue,' as Italy did with Operation Mare Nostrum (Riddervold 2018; Sciopini 2017). A concern for rescue began to be superseded by the priority of limiting the numbers of people coming, which resulted in EUNAVOR Sophia and its pursuit of human traffickers coupled with the launch of 'hotspots' as a supranational effort 'to identify, register and fingerprint incoming migrants' (Collett and Le Coz 2018: 10). As the numbers of migrants reached their height in late summer 2015, the EU and member-states confronted repeated failures of coordination, communication, and resource sharing. These failures were symptoms of the more profound inability to define the objective of EU action and if indeed the EU was the right actor for the job (Collett and Le Coz 2018: 14; Newsome 2018). By the end of 2015, member-states and EU officials had coalesced around the goal of limiting the numbers of people entering Europe and in various Council, European Council, and Commission forums had decided to work with Turkey outside of supranational forums to relocate migrants already in Europe and prevent future flows (Collett and Le Coz 2018: 18).

Previous scholarly and media treatments have been quite detailed in terms of describing the impact of refugee flows on individual member-states at the height of the crisis. The authors featured here offer readers a longer time horizon on the migration crisis and foreground the decades of policy choices and their repercussions that landed the EU in the contemporary crisis.

Kaija Schilde and Sara Wallace Goodman's chapter, 'The EU's Response to the Migration Crisis: Institutional Turbulence and Policy Disjuncture,' argues that the EU has difficulty addressing the migration crisis owing at least in part to turbulence the EU itself has generated through contradictory policy decision making in border security in contrast to asylum management. Schilde and Wallace Goodman show that while border security contains examples of deeper integration, asylum management policy has followed the scenarios of *breaking down* and *muddling through*. The authors thus identify directions in which these policies are moving and also uncover the ways in which policies can create additional dynamics in related areas. Crisis is indeed a factor for policy development. However, one of the unintended consequences of deeper integration in one policy area is turbulence, followed by disintegration, in another policy area. To further show that deeper integration is not an unalloyed good, Schilde and Wallace Goodman also rely on historical institutional approaches to build their case, as does Bosilca in this section. To the contrary, they argue that closer cooperation of EU member-states through supranational institutions in border policy has 'accelerated the criminalization of unauthorized movement and the subsequent rise in the dangers associated with migration, including an increase in violence and death at border zones.'

External border security differs from other migration policy areas in that member-states have been more willing to provide more resources and autonomy to supranational institutions policing the border, namely Frontex. This is in contrast to asylum policy where member-states have balked repeatedly at the prospect of a 'central agency to pool resources or coordinate registration processing or resettlement.' For Schilde and Wallace Goodman, 'policy development sequencing' played a key role in pushing integration forward. Their chapter examines common asylum policy as an afterthought for member-states preoccupied with setting up the single market. Border policy on the other hand is an example of 'reactive sequencing' where member-states band together to roll back the Commission's attempts to liberalize and unify migration policy within the EU. Although Schilde and Wallace Goodman provide evidence for policy development sequencing in explaining the trajectories of different areas of migration policy, some other explanations remain unexplored. It is interesting to note from their chapter that while Germany in 1993 proposed common asylum laws, one year later Germany joined other member-states in rejecting rights for 'legal residents and asylum seekers' on par with citizens. In fact, Schilde and Wallace Goodman suggest that Germany had an interest in supranational devolution only if the common standard were to be more restrictive. Schilde and Wallace Goodman trace the shared origins of integrated border policy and fragmented asylum policy to the meetings in the 1970s of the Trevi Group, the 1989 Palma document, and the 1990 Dublin convention. Echoing later chapters by Bosilca and Crawford, Schilde and Wallace Goodman underscore the deficiencies of the Dublin convention in particular as paving the way for the contemporary refugee crisis.

Ruxandra-Laura Bosilca's chapter, 'The Refugee Crisis and the EU Border Security Policies' seeks to explain the lack of shared approaches at the EU level among member-states to address the migration crisis. Bosilca finds evidence for *breaking down* in addition to minimal reforms of border security policy that constitute *muddling through*. Even for the areas of agreement for common reform, member-states repeatedly chose to go outside of supranational institutions in order to stem the tide of refugees and find solutions maintaining the Schengen system of internal border free movement. What is novel about Bosilca's approach is her use of the theoretical perspectives of historical institutionalism and multiple streams models to infer firstly, the form that integration might take according to the three scenarios described in this book's introduction and secondly, the expectations observers should have about the kinds of developments in migration and border policy given her application of these theoretical parameters to our possible paths of EU integration in times of crisis. In this sense, Bosilca's analysis has much in common with Trangy and Stenstad's work on the financial crisis in this volume in that she is also interested in how policy makers understand available policy options and how they make choices. She considers the degree to which policy options mesh with existing norms and values among policy makers as particularly critical for the decision-making process.

For the purpose of interrogating how *breaking down* occurred in the migration crisis, Bosilca isolates indicators for this scenario from theories of liberal intergovernmentalism and compares the specific expectations suggested by this narrow theoretical lens with the empirical data. One of her findings is that regardless of if a member-state encountered high numbers of migrants as a 'front-line' or 'destination country' or very few migrants at all, member-states displayed a low degree of interest in protecting the border free movement success story of Schengen during the crisis. Instead, member-states moved independently to re-establish national borders largely in response to the anti-immigrant preferences of national voters. Bosilca acknowledges that member-states selectively and 'temporarily' did support Commission reforms of Frontex into an empowered European Border and Coast Guard agency (EBCG). However, given that funding for the EBCG's new duties depended on case-by-case decision making on the part of the member-states, this development constitutes *breaking down* in its rejection of supranationalization and *muddling through* at best since the EBCG is nominally strengthened.

When Bosilca turns to assess the evidence for *muddling through* in the migration crisis, she notes the problems in institutional design of the Dublin system of asylum: from the very beginning, countries of reception on the EU's border would be overtaxed by asylum requests. Although the Dublin system had rules stipulating asylum seekers could apply to only one member-state at a time for asylum, these rules did not functionally prevent simultaneous applications, streamline processing by border states, or improve the application procedure for asylum seekers owing to the lack of integration among member-states in implementing Dublin. Relying in this case on historical institutionalist theory to interpret Dublin plus reforms in response to the migration crisis, Boslica finds evidence of incremental changes constituting *muddling through* in this policy area. Member-states refused repeatedly to accept refugees languishing in the southeastern coastal EU member-states, and reforms including resettlement quotas had to be abandoned in favor of those providing resources for these coastal states to get through the legal backlog of asylum claims. Another example of an incremental change in response to the migration crisis can be seen in the EU campaign to intercept maritime human trafficking routes from North Africa to the EU. Bosilca points out that EUNAVOR MED 'Sophia' reproduces previous patterns of 'militarization' of migration policy. The EU also revised earlier attempts to manage migratory flows by concluding diplomatic agreements with non-EU member-states. Bosilca shows that the EU-Turkey agreement, while pursued outside of the supranational procedures for a treaty, reinvigorated the 'Rabat and Khartoum Processes' set up with significant Commission and European Parliament participation, to curtail the numbers of people coming to the EU closer to their countries of origin.

This chapter also considers the degree to which there is evidence for further integration as a result of the migration crisis. Bosilca defines further integration as both 'an expanded Community portfolio' as well as the 'increasing empowerment of supranational agents' in this policy field and considers how EU actors delineated the policy challenge, ascertained possible paths forward to address the policy challenge, and took advantage of political coalitions and appetites in support of a given policy path. Bosilca details the way in which the Commission, also at times in partnership with the Parliament, sought to transform Frontex into the EBCG with new resources and powers and increased transfer of migration policy from member-states to the EU. Although the Commission took advantage of the policy opening posed by the high incidence of migrant deaths near Lampedusa in Spring 2015 and the growing agreement among different political actors including the European Council and the Parliament on strengthening Schengen and reforming Frontex into the EBCG, this did not result in deeper integration in migration policy. Rather, the attempt by the Commission to remove politics from EBCG expansion by framing it as a technical and efficient solution to the migration crisis did not work. Member-states refused to accept an EBCG that would assess problems with migration and border policy, formulate and suggest policies for member-states to implement, and then, if the member-state did not act, act on its own (including on member-state territory) without member-state permission. Memberstates also opposed a 'mandatory and automatic distribution mechanism' for refugees and circumscribed the EBCG's ability to act by reserving for themselves the ability to consider and veto EBCG activities and resource allocations as a matter of course.

Beverly Crawford's chapter, 'Moral leadership or moral hazard? Germany's response to the refugee crisis and its impact on European solidarity,' takes on the broader question of Germany's role in the EU by analyzing its behavior across the refugee crisis and the financial crisis. While acknowledging the challenge posed by extreme right populism, Crawford expresses the view that the migration crisis provides evidence both of *muddling through* and *heading forward* and is thus more optimistic than either Schilde and Wallace Goodman or Bosilca about the overall prospects for EU integration in this policy area. A key factor for Crawford in this study is the role of leadership, as she argues that crisis is not enough on its own to initiate change in integration. Crawford builds on theories of collective action to show that leadership is a necessary condition for integration, if it is accompanied by the leader's resources and willingness to offer incentives and sanctions needed to push for further integration or disintegration. She states that Germany offers a model of 'soft leadership' and engages in process tracing to show how across different crises German leaders would model the behavior they desired from other member-states by 'making domestic sacrifices for new areas of cooperation within the EU's institutional structure.' Then Germany would 'ask… for burden sharing,' and lastly, to motivate others further, it would distribute 'side payments' that in Crawford's view 'ensured the stability of existing institutions and expanding the EU's institutional competences.' Crawford contrasts Germany's behavior in the refugee crisis with the financial crisis, where it was seen as a 'coercive hegemon' in the latter but as a 'moral leader' in the former.

Crawford also engages directly with the idea that European integration has become more contentious in German politics, and this is clearly illustrated by the rise of the Alternative für Deutschland. EU institutions are not perfect—and even when Germany overcomes internal polarization, Crawford argues that EU institutions hamper Germany's ability to push for further integration. As seen in the chapters by Bosilca and Schilde and Wallace Goodman, Crawford also singles out the Dublin convention as an EU institution unsuited for unified asylum policy. Where Crawford parts ways with other contributors in this section is in her assessment of the EU-Turkey statement as a symbol of EU solidarity and thus integration. As the EU-Turkey Statement circumvented the traditional EU treaty procedure, and Schilde and Wallace Goodman list the empowerment of supranational institutions as fundamental to *heading forward*, they count the Statement as indicating *muddling through* at best rather than further integration.

REFERENCES

Ceccorulli, M. (2019). Back to Schengen: The Collective Securitization of the EU Free-Border Area. *West European Politics, 42*(2), 302–322.

Collett, E., & Le Coz, C. (2018). *Report: After the Storm: Learning from the EU Response to the Migration Crisis*. Brussels: Migration Policy Institute Europe.

Newsome, A. (2018). Credible Champions? Transatlantic Relations and Human Rights in Refugee Crises. *Journal of European Integration, 40*(5), 587–604.

Riddervold, M. (2018). A Humanitarian Mission in Line with Human Rights? Assessing Sophia, the EU's Naval Response to the Migration Crisis. *European Security, 27*(2), 158–174.

Sciopini, M. (2017). Failing Forward in EU Migration Policy? EU Integration After the 2015 Asylum and Migration Crisis. *Journal of European Public Policy, 22*(1), 1–19.

Zaun, N. (2016). Why EU Asylum Standards Exceed the Lowest Common Denominator: The Role of Regulatory Expertise in EU Decision-Making. *Journal of European Public Policy, 23*(1), 136–154.

CHAPTER 25

The EU's Response to the Migration Crisis: Institutional Turbulence and Policy Disjuncture

Kaija Schilde and Sara Wallace Goodman

INTRODUCTION

The European Union faces ongoing and multidimensional turbulence when it comes to migration. On the one hand, EU migration policy has proven incapable of responding to turbulence and crisis. The deadly civil war in Syria created an unprecedented flow of asylum seekers to European borders—almost 2 million detections of illegal crossing along the external border (Frontex 2016: 6).[1] As border states along Eastern Europe began to close off land routes, Syrians joined with asylum seekers and migrants from other developing world hotspots in attempting an often-deadly Mediterranean crossing—earning the description of "world's deadliest border" (Jones 2016: 12). If migrants made it to European shores, border states proved largely unable (and some uninterested) to comply with some of the directives from the Common European Asylum System. The refugee crisis eventually de-escalated owing to member state behavior (Germany) and declining violence in Syria (See Crawford, this volume).

[1] This 2015 figure—the highest recorded within one year—was "more than six times the number of detections reported in 2014, which was itself an unprecedented year."

K. Schilde (✉)
Boston University, Boston, MA, USA
e-mail: kschilde@bu.edu

S. W. Goodman
University of California, Irvine, CA, USA
e-mail: swgood@uci.edu

At the same time EU migration policy struggles to *respond* to turbulence, it also does a fair job in *producing* turbulence. Early path differentiation within migration policy—where border security and asylum management institutionally diverged—created non-complementary policy trajectories. Exhibiting stasis in some aspects of policy integration, a political crisis the size of the refugee crisis also makes unified and coordinated solutions more difficult. Political crisis and institutional turbulence exacerbate and reduce the likelihood of any durable political solutions to the humanitarian crisis at the EU's borders or internally when it comes to migration-adjacent issues, like security. So, while crisis catalyzes some aspects of migration policy integration, e.g., border security, it stunts others, like asylum management, coordination, and treatment. Migration policy, then, has different integration paths: path-dependent dynamics within asylum policy make more likely that the EU will continue to "muddle through" in this area of integration, while integration of member state external border policy appears to be *heading forward*, with accelerating integration in this area fueled by crisis dynamics.

This chapter evaluates the complex relationship between migration, policy integration turbulence, and EU governance. This chapter primarily documents *turbulence*—following Ansell et al.'s (2017) definition as interactions of events or demands that are highly variable, inconsistent, unexpected, or unpredictable—rather than *crisis*, using Ikenberry's meaning of an "extraordinary moment when the existence and viability of the political order are called into question" (Ikenberry 2008: 3), in the domain of EU migration policy. Indeed, the EU has not so much experienced crisis in migration as its turbulence has produced it.

We argue through evolving institutional asymmetries, where migration policy diverged and developed at different speeds, intensities, and sequences, EU policy today is—as a result—highly differentiated, often uncoordinated, and ultimately weak to crisis. Our analyses of EU migration policy are centered within institutionalist or organizational theories of political development and European integration, focusing on timing and sequencing of migration policymaking. In short, we trace EU migration policy integration from a common origin (same committees and projects) to today's policy landscape, in which different temporal sequences have made different types of migration policy. In asylum, relative sequencing and lock-in has produced a "stuck" or stalled integration area, while reactive sequencing accelerated integration to produce external border security and internal free movement. Integration in these latter, coordinated policy areas reflect and reify strong EU political authority, experiencing sustained political development toward an entity with "core state powers" (Genschel and Jachtenfuchs 2014). However, the differentiation between policy areas leaves EU migration policy imbalanced, uncoordinated in crisis, and ultimately contributing its own turbulence. Future EU integration in migration heads forward, but with a focus on security over humanitarian concerns, making the next migration crisis potentially more catastrophic.

Multiple, Overlapping, and Complex Migration Turbulence and Crises

There is no one migration crisis in the EU; there are multiple migration crises. These crises are both a cause and a consequence of EU policymaking, preserving a negative feedback loop of policy craft and evidenced in the problematic gaps in EU authority and cleavages among member state preferences. Some may claim the diverging preferences over asylum policy and refugee redistribution—between member states as well as the vertical disagreements between EU institutions and member states—constitutes Ikenberry's level of a crisis, as it is alleged to have shaken the very foundation of the European integration project. EU states are also drifting further apart on their ability to negotiate treaties or reforms to a Common European Asylum System (CEAS), with Dublin IV negotiations at a standstill. However, it is at the domestic political level that we observe the actual Ikenberry-level of crisis. A political crisis over asylum has disrupted domestic political parties, catalyzing populist campaigns from Sweden to Italy and nearly bringing down Chancellor Angela Merkel twice (in the federal election of 2017 and a June 2018 coalition leadership challenge).[2] In fact, these challenges have effectively moved Germany from a "*Willkommenskultur*" (welcome culture) and "*Wir schaffen das*" (We can do it) spirit to an increasingly restrictive approach (see Crawford this volume). Moreover, domestic laws and policy are highly variable cross-nationally, deeply institutionalized, checked by courts, and less fluid than intergovernmental bargaining positions among EU states at the council level.

Exacerbating the domestic political crises is the unclear, unsettled, or partially developed nature of EU integration in the area of migration. Domestic political crisis exposes and potentially worsens the institutional turbulence of migration governance at the EU level, as the direction of domestic politics is drifting further from parties interested in streamlined solutions, at least over asylum and refugee resettlement. EU migration policy has variously been described as a "puzzlingly flawed" (Kelemen and McNamara 2018: 16) case of "no integration," (Schimmelfennig 2018) "disintegration," (Heldt 2018) or the "failure of integration" (Börzel and Risse 2017). These outcomes have also been variously diagnosed as a result of institutional design gaps between "preferences for closure and control" (Goodman 2014), intentions and outcomes (Cornelius et al. 2004), or between institutional design and implementation, where, for example, Sandra Lavenex describes EU asylum policy as a form of "organized hypocrisy," reflecting an "unconscious organizational strategy to cope with irreconcilable demands" (Lavenex 2018). In addition to the intergovernmental and inter-institutional turbulence in EU migration governance, EU migration policy itself has differentiated integration, where EU asylum policy is *muddling through* a status

---

[2] https://www.npr.org/2018/07/02/625406632/germanys-merkel-faces-leadership-challenge-sparked-by-migrant-issue.

quo of dysfunction, while other aspects of EU migration policy are *heading forward* with rapid institutional development. In sum, the EU has increasingly integrated via directives and other policy in politically "hard" and sovereignty-sensitive migration areas of visa, internal movement, and borders and security, while EU asylum and refugee policy has been frozen in place in a state of non-functionality since inception (Goodman 2018).

The tangible consequences of institutional turbulence and domestic political crisis dynamics are the direct worsening of the humanitarian components of migration. In addition to the deadly EU external border, states such as Hungary have implemented extreme control measures in multiple dimensions, most recently in a punitive 25% tax on NGOs working to support migrants,[3] and Italy now turns away migrant boats and is cracking down on charity NGOs.[4] While domestic political crises and EU institutional turbulence have worsened the ability, capacity, or willingness of policymakers to find solutions to asylum or refugee redistribution problems, accelerated integration in the areas of freedom of movement and increased border security have exacerbated human security crises, particularly around internal domestic security and refugee response. In this light, the EU *heading forward* toward more integration in migration has accelerated the criminalization of unauthorized movement and the subsequent rise in the dangers associated with migration, including an increase in violence and death at border zones (Lori and Schilde 2020). States may increasingly associate migrants with "security threats," but as Jones (2016: 5) explains, "the hardening of the border through new security practices is the source of the violence, not a response to it."

EU Integration Literature and Migration Policy

Theories of European integration have evolved swiftly to keep up with evidence of turbulent institutional dynamics, moving from how integration progresses (Moravcsik 1998; Sandholtz and Stone Sweet 1997; Schimmelfennig, this volume; 2003) toward explaining crisis (Cross 2017), disintegration (Jones 2018; Vollaard 2014), or differentiated integration outcomes (Hooghe and Marks 2009; De Vries and McNamara 2018; Schimmelfennig et al. 2015). The explanations, too, are distinct—from original theories predicting dynamic change and integration (neofunctionalism) or status quo effects (intergovernmentalism), current accounts characterize outcomes as a result of "failing forward" (Jones et al. 2016), an incomplete process of state-formation (Kelemen and McNamara 2018), or a political process requiring an "amendment to postfunctionalism" (Hooghe et al., this volume; Börzel and Risse 2017). In contrast, in alignment with the introduction to this handbook, we view integration turbulence as a "normal" state of affairs that may

[3] https://www.ft.com/content/1be350e0-8c3b-11e8-bf9e-8771d5404543.
[4] https://www.nytimes.com/2018/06/11/world/europe/italy-migrant-boat-aquarius.html.

"threaten" basic structures or values but generally does not rise to the level of crisis. Indeed, the EU suffers from turbulence and crisis in its migration policy and within its migration institutions, but this may be more "normal" than not, and when studying the EU, "sometimes normal may be a little weird" (Newman 2018). This is especially the case when explaining policy and political turbulence.

Institutionalist theories are particularly useful to analyzing turbulence (Ansell this volume; Farrell and Newman 2010, 2015; Fioretos 2011, 2017; Newman and Posner 2016), where timing, sequencing, and cumulation can bear a direct effect on institutional outcomes (Farrell and Newman 2015). Given common origin but a divergence of spatial and temporal variation, we look specifically at dynamics of sequencing, which are less dependent on early events but driven by a configuration of choices or patterns over time (Howlett 2009; Howlett and Goetz 2014). Sequential turbulence can result from variation in governmental attention, or addressing one political problem at a time (Baumgartner and Jones 2009; Baumgartner et al. 2009). Sequences connect "events in different time periods" as processes of "reiterated problem solving," and they are differentiated not by crises as critical junctures but by contingent political solutions for recurring and turbulent problems (Haydu 1998: 354).

In the next section, we describe the sequencing patterns that have characterized European integration of migration policy and, we argue, will determine the future paths of integration in migration policy. However, there are different kinds of sequencing patterns at work that ground our analysis. Asylum and internal movement policies have been characterized by *relative sequencing*, where the order of policy decisions drove policy outcomes, whereas border security policy has been driven by a *reactive sequencing*, where "each event in the sequence is both a reaction to antecedent events and a cause of subsequent events" (Mahoney 2000: 509). These sequences are not only determined by policy choices within their respective domains but also parallel decisions in adjacent domains wherein, for example, border security policy accelerated in reaction to initial sequencing choices of internal movement asylum policies. In a relative sequence, shifting governmental priorities drive political phases. In a reactive sequence, phases are marked by a discontinuity in actors or preferences, as political actors have agency and use it to react to past outcomes in an attempt to change or reverse them. Distinct from path-dependent or self-reinforcing sequences, early events trigger subsequent development not by reproducing a given pattern but by setting in motion a chain of tightly linked reactions and counter reactions.

Crisis and Turbulence in the EU Migration Domain

Before the 1970s, Europe was largely a place people left to seek opportunity and employment elsewhere. By the twenty-first century, the EU became a top destination.[5] In just a few decades, European states had to quickly adapt to these changes while simultaneously establishing a borderless and liberalizing European economic community. Both free movement and asylum are located within the broader policy field of Justice and Home Affairs (JHA). Free movement concerns date to the original 1957 Treaty of Rome, though it did not provide language nor specify authority. It presented the goal of achieving the common (internal) market by eliminating barriers and simplifying laws across the EU's four freedoms—the free movement of goods, services, capital, and people. "People" here refers to labor.[6] JHA was formally launched as an intergovernmental domain in the 1992 Maastricht treaty, out of a series of ad hoc, intergovernmental committees assembled in the late 1970s and 1980s, and transferred to EU authority with in 1997. Under the 1997 Amsterdam Treaty, part of JHA was subsumed under the Community (supranational) method of decision making and governance (Uçarer 2013). These competencies include areas such as border security, immigration and visa policy, asylum procedures, and rules for judicial cooperation in civil matters.[7] The 2003 Treaty of Nice further Europeanized JHA with additional majoritarian decision voting rules, and the 2009 Lisbon Treaty substantially supranationalized JHA governance.

Parts of EU migration policy have been Europeanized, while other parts have remained intergovernmental. In the case of *within-Europe* migration ("second country nationals," i.e., from one EU member state to another), free internal movement has grown to encompass nearly the entire EU, far from the small group of five Schengen countries that initially established a borderless zone in 1985. Meanwhile de facto authority over migration and the legal status of people and workers *from outside of the EU* ("third country nationals")—including asylum seekers—remains firmly under the control of member states (Bosilca this volume; Uçarer 2013).

Migration policies are controversial and high-profile public policy issues. Although fears that EU enlargement would prompt a massive influx of internal immigration from the East to West—concerns echoing Portugal's ascension in 1995—this did not materialize to the degree feared by policymakers. Instead, there was a massive influx of economic and humanitarian migrants from the Middle East and Africa, as hundreds of thousands fled Afghanistan, Iraq, Sri Lanka, Eritrea, and other war-torn regions (Uçarer 2013). Migrants have settled disproportionately in a few states, such as Italy or Germany, and have

---

[5] https://www.pewforum.org/2012/03/08/religious-migration-destination-spotlights/#spotlight-on-europe.

[6] https://eur-lex.europa.eu/LexUriServ/LexUriServ.do?uri=CELEX:12008E045:en:HTML.

[7] Afterwards, the intergovernmental third pillar of JHA covered only police and judicial cooperation in criminal matters.

led those countries to call for greater burden sharing in the EU over migrant policy. High-profile refugee crises in Mediterranean states such Spain, Malta, and Greece have also raised the profile of irregular immigration across the EU and calls for common solutions. Millions of third-country nationals reside across Europe, and the issue of external immigration and border control is an explosive domestic issue within member states (Geddes and Scholten 2016).

This unchecked flow of people within Europe effectively externalized the problem of migration to the boundary of the EU. Despite these pressures, and consistent prioritization by the European Commission, there has been little harmonization in EU immigration policy (Newsome 2018). The Commission has generated numerous policy proposals, although most have died in the intergovernmental European Council. Of the adopted policies, few have survived legal interpretation, implementation, and compliance.

Indeed, it is external border security that proves exceptional as a migration policy, where a supranational agency (Frontex) was created to coordinate monitoring external EU borders and extraditing refugees. Since its 2005 inception, Frontex has developed a "securitized" border policy for criminalizing immigration. Increases in border security resources and authority have been overwhelmingly supported by member states. Recent examples include increased Frontex budgets and authority, and treaty agreements to "deepen EU defense cooperation through treaty-based, 'binding commitments' to jointly develop defence capabilities and make them available for EU military operations," including the Operation Sophia CSDP military mission deployed to the Mediterranean to address (and stem) migration (See also Riddervold 2018).[8]

This development and support are in stark contrast to asylum. With no central agency to pool resources or coordinate registration, processing, or resettlement, member states retain significant control and discretion in asylum policy and, as a result of distinct domestic administrative processes—from asylum bureaus to courts—and political preferences, produce a patchwork of unharmonized practices across the EU. Despite the eventual adoption and labeling of a "Common European Asylum Policy," the design remains faithful to the origin intent of EU asylum policy: that they place minimal burden on states, where interests and regulatory expertise of powerful, core members states exert uneven power in shaping policy (Zaun 2016). What the Commission was able to coordinate was a series of directives on procedures, reception conditions, and qualifications, as well as regulations on EURODAC (EU-wide asylum fingerprinting database) and the Dublin Convention, which chiefly aims to "determine rapidly the member state responsible [for an asylum claim]," typically being the state through which the asylum seeker first entered

---

[8]Council Decision (CFSP) 2015/778 of 18 May 2015 on a European Union military operation in the Southern Central Mediterranean (EUNAVFOR MED). Available at http://eurlex.europa.eu/legalcontent/EN/TXT/PDF/?uri=CELEX:32015D 0778&qid=1435825940768&from=EN.

the EU.[9] This arrangement has been characterized by its "restrictive and weakly integrated core" (Ripoll Servent and Trauner 2014) as well as a "critical lack of solidarity" (Scipioni 2017).

This presents a puzzle: the humanitarian crisis of increasing migration and the institutional turbulence of divided authority over migration policy have accelerated the development of EU border control policy but not asylum policy. The 2015 refugee crisis exposed institutional design flaws in both Schengen (internal free movement) and Dublin (which governs state responsibility for registering asylum seekers upon entering the EU). They are, of course, mutually dependent. Strong procedures (from registration to removal) buttress wider internal movement freedoms. The Schengen area also "made it possible for asylum-seekers to move across borders and thus introduced grounds for Member States to dispute responsibility regarding asylum claims" (Fratzke 2015). Under Schengen and Dublin, states retained the right to unilaterally reintroduce border controls and to return asylum seekers to the first country of entry, but in practice Dublin rules exacerbated distributional conflicts among member states, eventually provoking a collapse of the Greek asylum system, as well as political crises in other border states such as Hungary and Italy (see Lavenex 2018, Newsome and Stenberg this volume). Thus, while external border policy coheres around common goals and is materially supported through sufficient contributions by both the EU and private interest groups, asylum policy cooperation—from renegotiating Dublin procedures to considering "fair" burden and refugee resettlement—remain as distant as ever. In the language of the introductory framework, asylum policy is *muddling through* without *breaking down*, but external border policy is *heading forward* toward more integration. In the following case studies, we account for this as a function of policy development sequencing.

Asylum

Asylum had every opportunity to become a coherent, harmonized, even coordinated policy, like internal movement or security. But because it was shaped from *relative sequencing*, where the order of policy decisions drove policy outcomes, it remains the most marked by institutional turbulence. Specifically, institutional arrangements kept asylum as a secondary concern to achieving the Single European Act's goal of obtaining the free internal market by January 1, 1993 (including movement) and grounded asylum firmly in intergovernmental hands. The substantive consequence of this was asylum explicitly developed as an ancillary, compensatory policy. In other words, harmonizing achievements were to make other policies work better (e.g., expulsion rules make free movement more possible), not particularly to reach asylum policy goals in their own

---

[9]http://eur-lex.europa.eu/legal-content/EN/TXT/PDF/?uri=CELEX:32003R0343&from=EN.

right. The institutional consequence of this sequence is that early intergovernmental power dynamics became locked-in and continued to exert a force long after authority transferred to supranational governance. In the near-total absence of interest mobilization and transnational actors to provide external leverage to speed up harmonization (Schilde 2017) or define shared political will later on, there is little that is "common" or "European" about today's Common European Asylum System.

We necessarily begin by describing asylum and border security's common origin in the same ad hoc group, in order to show the consequences of sequencing, policy prioritization, and lock-in. Transnational immigration was first mentioned in the 1975 Tindemans Report, and formally addressed 1976 Trevi Group, which formed to coordinate state responses to terrorism, migration, and security (Mitsilegas et al. 2003: 25). The first institutional outcome of these EU level groups was the 1985 Schengen Agreement, famous for abolishing internal border controls but also significant as the origin of what is now the Common European Asylum System by establishing the system of responsibility for examining asylum claims (Uçarer 2013). In 1986, under the UK Presidency, the Interior Ministers set up the Ad Hoc Group on Immigration (heretofore, AHI) to do work distinct from that of Trevi (which focused on security, terrorism, drug trafficking, etc.). But while their remits were different, they both pointed toward the same goal: completion of the internal market.

This objective necessarily prioritized certain issues over others. As stated in the Declaration of the Belgian Presidency, "realization of free movement within the Community, as the Single European Act provides for" required member states to "intensify cooperation in the fight against terrorism, illegal immigration and drug trafficking" (Bunyan 1997: 9–11). These prioritized areas were under the remit of the Trevi Ministers, whose objective was to "pool resources in order to strengthen their capacity" in areas like combating terrorism and drug trafficking (Bunyan 1997). Moreover, for both the Commission and the Council, "that there was a strong link between the removal of controls at internal frontiers and the strengthening of controls at external frontiers. These two objectives clearly need to be pursued simultaneously since only in this way can adequate standards of security be preserved, while at the same time the best possible use be made of the human technical resources available to the Member States."[10] As external movement was essential to realizing internal free movement and asylum was not, AHI prioritized visa policy as it pertained to the external border. Remaining preoccupations regarding asylum consisted of system abuse (e.g., procedures for combating pre-arrival, examining requests, false documents, etc.).

---

[10]"Communication of the Commission report on the abolition of controls on persons at intra-Community borders," Com (88) 640.

Thus, as early as the 1990 Dublin Convention (the very first, major step in cooperation on asylum policy between member states), asylum policy-making was tied to serving free movement goals. This objective was explicit; its Preamble emphasizes the "joint objective of an area without internal frontiers" and suggests a number of "implementing measures" to determine host state responsibility. It is worth pausing to reflect on this point: the purpose of establishing basic principles on host state responsibility was not to improve the asylum process, address the sources of asylum, or identify a joint European goal. Rather, member states sought to establish accountability and were tied to regulation of the external border, whereby "crossing of the external border of the Member States … is closely linked to other instruments necessary for the realization of Article 8a … and, in particular, to the Convention determine the state responsible for examining applications for asylum." [11] Objections to the former were unsurprisingly intergovernmental in nature: the Netherlands did not want to implement Dublin until Denmark got on board; Spain argued the UK should extend its responsibilities to Gibraltar.

But it was not merely realizing the internal market was a priority that impeded progress on asylum policy; assigning member state responsibility for examining an asylum request was no easy task. Intergovernmental preferences played a dominant role and "good will" in procedural discipline between states was low. This sequence of policies—both realized and abandoned—was a direct product of intergovernmental preferences but also of the institutions themselves. Given Community priorities, free movement interests were supervised by a "Coordinators group on the free movement of persons," established in 1988 to ensure cooperation between the many migrant-related policies being discussed at the time (e.g., customs, drugs, asylum, etc.) but, as the group title states, with realization of the internal market a central goal. In 1989, this group produced the Palma Document, serving as a further cornerstone in a series of institutional transformations that took internal free movement from an ad hoc intergovernmental group to a new European position under the K4 Coordinating Committee after the Maastricht Treaty. Palma was nominally interested in asylum, suggesting a "common policy will be based on member states' obligations," but said little else on the matter.[12] The consequences of prioritization were clear: after Dublin was adopted, the

---

[11] "Declarations in the minutes of the Conference of Immigration Ministers of the Member States of the European Communities", SN 2836/93 (WGI 1505), Dublin, 15 June 1990.

[12] When asylum was moved to the Third Pillar under Maastricht and, even later under the Community pillar under Amsterdam, it retained its ancillary role to servicing border goals. As Lavenex (2018) notes retrospectively, "the CEAS was framed in view of protecting the EU's internal 'Area of Freedom, Security and Justice' and not as a genuine European policy of refugee protection."

Coordinators group concluded "no further work is required on the substantive provisions of the External Frontiers convention that are not related to the last remaining problem," referencing explicitly the Dublin Convention.[13]

Only once the internal market had been realized could AHI—and member states more generally—begin to think about harmonization of asylum policy and rules. This belated thinking about the "idea" of harmonization and what it would and could achieve necessarily limited the scope of possibilities. And there was no paucity of limitations. The first was political will. The idea for harmonization originated at the request of German delegation to the Luxembourg European Council meeting, asking Ministers responsible for immigration to submit proposals on the harmonization of immigration and asylum policies at its meeting in Maastricht.[14] The Council, in response to this "rather unanticipated German proposal" (Papagianni 2006), drew an arbitrary line for dialogue, achieving "more thorough harmonization post-Dublin without dealing with the vexed issue of the institutional framework."[15]

Beyond authority, a degree of institutional turbulence also inhibited forward movement. Whereas visa policy moved to the first pillar of European Community competence, asylum was nominally incorporated into the third pillar as an intergovernmental issue. The Commission, in their Communication on the Right of Asylum (1991), identified the "complex nature of the issues involved, the many and varied aspects of the problems involved have been discussed in a number of different fora."[16] They continue by offering a number of policy priorities, to "clarify the rather confused picture and to refocus the strategy so as to keep the overall programme, and each individual part of it, on target,"[17] including abuse, concern with the ratification of Dublin, regulating travel by asylum seekers to member states, coordinate practice of granting asylum, and fast-tracking removal for "manifestly unfounded" applications. But, in general terms, the Commission was also sounding a clarion call for vision: "a need for acceleration and a new political impulse which only the Council can provide ... there is a need to pull together the work being done in the various fora identified in this paper to ensure that there is a coherent approach to the very similar problems which arise in each area."[18] When asylum was finally moved to the first pillar to become a Community

[13]"Report to the European council in Edinburgh from the Coordinators' Group on Free Movement of Persons". CIRC 3687/1/92. 3 Dec 1992.

[14]Compilation of texts on European practice with respect to asylum (no. prev. doc. WGI 1343 REV 1). "Report from the Ministers responsible for immigration to the European Council meeting in Maastricht on immigration and asylum policy" SN *2836/93* (WGI 1505). Brussels 14 May 1993.

[15]Report from the Ministers Responsible for Immigration to the European Council meeting in Maastricht on immigration and asylum policy. SN 4038/91 (WGI 930) 3 December 1991.

[16]SEMDOC, p. 3.

[17]Ibid.

[18]Ibid.

competence with the Treaty of Amsterdam, there was little the Commission could change by this point, evidenced by record non-compliance and minimal policy change.

To summarize, harmonizing asylum policy was preoccupied with determining responsibility, and never became a project of coordination for the EU, nor a rallying point for interest mobilization, nor could they be partners together in this enterprise. This was due to several factors: first, institutional arrangements and ideational; assignment also is a clear case of pneumonia through commitment to the internal market relegated asylum to a secondary, ancillary policy to buttress this goal. The downstream effects of the sequence of policy prioritization and adoption, as well as the reserving asylum to intergovernmental purview, was such that post-Dublin ambition was modest, opportunities were circumscribed, and momentum lackluster, despite period calls for harmonized immigration policy.

External Borders

EU Asylum policy illustrates the consequences of policy prioritization, where asylum was demoted to favor free movement and border policy, but what explains the rapid integration, or *heading forward* of EU border security? Many observers point to the role of crisis, claiming that the 2015 migration crisis at the EU borders resulted from a lack of EU border management resources and reluctant member states with sovereignty concerns over further cooperation (European Commission 2015). However, EU integration over external border policy both preceded crisis and was accelerated by earlier phases of institutional turbulence over integral movement and asylum policy. Indeed, both the sequencing of EU policies over time and political domestic crisis have served to accelerate European integration in this area. Member states have reliably endorsed increases in EU border security funding and institutional authority in response to the migration crisis (European Council 2015). In sum, border security has been driven by crisis and turbulence, rather than suffered from it, and has been heading forwards toward more integration to "strengthen Frontex significantly and develop it into a fully operational European border and coast guard system" (Juncker 2015), resulting in the 2016 European Border and Coast Guard Agency (EBCGA), with a doubled budget and staff (from €143 million in 2015 to €322 million in 2020, and from 402 staff in 2015 to 1000 by 2020).[19]

Like asylum, the institutional roots of border policy are in the internal market. Following the European Council meeting in Fontainebleau in June 1984 (d'Appollonia 2012), five countries (West Germany, France, Belgium, Luxembourg, and the Netherlands) signed the Schengen Agreement to allow for free movement within internal borders, create common external borders,

---

[19] https://europa.eu/rapid/press-release_MEMO-15-6332_en.htm.

coordinate immigration issues, harmonize visa policies, and control immigration within a borderless area. Schengen management focused on reducing barriers to migration within Europe, while at the same time managing or restricting immigration from outside Europe (Uçarer 2013). The 1999 Amsterdam Treaty incorporated the non-EU Schengen system into EU law, eliminating internal EU borders and creating a common external border. The Tampere Agreement (1999–2004), the Hague Programme (2005–2009), and the Stockholm Programme (2010–2015) all advanced internal freedom of movement and EU external border policy. In December 2003, the EU adopted a security strategy—intended to address defense strategy—with a number of implications for border policy. It advanced "a comprehensive approach that included: closer police cooperation at European level, centralized collection of data [...] and integrated management of EU external borders..." (Council of The European Union 2005: 28).

EU border policy is marked by reactive sequences, in which the Commission's progressive ambition was continuously checked by reactive member states, leading to accelerated border closure and least-common-denominator policy outcomes. The Commission first attempted a progressive migration policy in 1985, in parallel to the intergovernmental Schengen agreement, issuing a guideline and official decision on liberalizing immigration and access for non-EU migrants (Commission of the European Communities 1985). The five member states brought their opposition to the case before the ECJ, and it annulled the decision in 1987. This subsequently constrained the Commission's competence to the free movement of EU citizens within EU borders. The Single European Act of 1986 then mandated the creation of an internal market without internal frontiers and included a political declaration of intent on the immigration of third-country nationals (Nanz 1994).

Member states initially reacted to early Commission attempts by setting a more securitized migration agenda via informal channels such as the Trevi Group. They convened in a 1991 emergency meeting to discuss "terrorist threats caused recently by Iraqi leader Saddam Hussein, of terrorist actions in the Western Europe in coming days," ordering tightened security at "airports, seaports, border check points, especially on foreigners from non-EC countries. Nations are reinforcing their security control on their common borders against increasing threats of terrorism, radicalism, extremism and international violence."[20] Two days after the Maastricht Treaty took effect, the informal K4 Committee met to "inaugurate an era of unprecedented inter-governmental co-operation on security matters in the new EU," with an agenda including preventing additional refugee migration from Bosnia, coordinating migrant expulsions, an automated European Data Archive Collection (EURODAC) for fingerprinting refugees, and creating an immigration database (European

---

[20] "EC Nations Strengthening Border Security Control," *Central News Agency—Taiwan*, January 24, 1991, accessed May 6, 2010.

Information Service (Doyle 1993). Policies such as EURODAC,[21] as well as a computerized identity system to prevent immigration fraud,[22] were eventually adopted in 1998.

In the early 1990s, migration policy was still firmly within the Pillar III area of intergovernmental politics and national control—but that did not stop the Commission liberalization attempts. A 1994 Commission report proposed that legal residents and asylum seekers should enjoy the same rights, freedoms, and benefits as EU citizens (Evans 1994). Transnational NGOs predicted member state opposition due to "public opinion and re-election concerns ... but without a clear European immigration policy we won't be able to fight xenophobia, which is rooted in ignorance, fear and the impression that the government doesn't control the phenomena" (Evans 1994). The Commission proposal was eventually blocked by Germany, after two German commissioners delayed the report and their interior ministers voted against it in the Council due to German citizenship laws.

The 1997 Treaty of Amsterdam and the 1999 Tampere Council conclusions were turning points in the migration policy integration within an area of freedom, security, and justice (AFSJ).[23] In 1999, there was a double movement in the reactive sequencing process already underway: the Commission renewed its effort to liberalize migration policy, and member states sharpened their reactive opposition to these policies. Commission policies included illegal immigration and illegal residence, rights and conditions under which nationals of third countries may reside in other member states, standards on procedures for issuing long-term visas and residence permits, and conditions of entry and residence within the EU (Palomar 2004). While EU migration regulation was binding after Amsterdam, member states had unanimous voting procedures in the European Council (Geddes 2008). Some observers attribute the radical treaty changes in the Treaty to Commission negotiators confusing member state negotiators with three-thousand pages of regulations over the incorporation of the Schengen Convention, with other dramatic changes to JHA policy embedded within the technicalities (Guiraudon 2003). After this point, member states tipped in further opposition to any Commission migration policymaking.

The Commission immediately interpreted its first pillar right of initiative under Amsterdam and began proposing progressive asylum policy initiatives. In 1998, it created proposals for joint actions on the temporary protection of displaced persons, the integration of refugees into the EU, and burden

---

[21] Bulletin of the European Communities, January–February 1998.

[22] Bulletin of the European Communities, December 1998, 1.4.8.

[23] Bulletin of the European Communities, October 1999, I.4; Bulletin of the European Communities, October 1999, I.1.

sharing of refugee costs between member states.[24] In 1999, the Commission adopted a European refugee fund from its own budget to support and encourage member states to receive refugees. The fund covers reception, integration, and voluntary repatriation measures, divided across member states by the number of refugees accommodated.[25] Between 1999 and 2004, it pushed for a comprehensive migration policy agenda, including directives over the status and rights of long-term resident migrants, reunification of family members inside and outside the EU, and visa and asylum application centralization. After 2000, the EU initiatives on migration pursued three main directions: broadening the rights provided for third-country nationals, urging on the adoption of integration policies for migrants, and undertaking long-term measures on migration.

EU summits in Seville (in 2002) and Thessaloniki (in 2003) accelerated a security and control agenda.[26] Member states at Seville "invoked populist electoral breakthroughs in various European elections to step up the fight against illegal migration."[27] The UK and Spain proposed EU legislation linking punitive measures such as trade sanctions or aid reductions to foreign refusal to accept rejected asylum seekers.[28] At Thessaloniki, the Commission proposed and states accepted a plan to locate asylum detention centers outside the EU's borders and to create a border agency.[29]

The 2004 Hague Treaty proposed a five-year timeline to strengthen the external borders and migration management of the EU by giving the European Commission the exclusive right of legislative initiative in matters of JHA under the community pillar. It introduced qualified majority voting in the intergovernmental European Council, effectively eliminating any member state vetoes over illegal immigration and border control policy. It also gave the European Parliament co-decision power with the Commission, meaning Parliament could propose policy amendments and veto Commission legislation (Uçarer 2013).

---

[24] European Council on Refugees and Exiles, 1 September 1998; Bulletin of the European Communities, December 1998, 1.4.4; Bulletin of the European Communities, December 1998, 1.2.25.

[25] Bulletin of the European Communities, December 1999, 1.5.8.

[26] Communication from the Commission to the Council and the European Parliament, Biannual Update of the Scoreboard to review progress on the creation of an area of "Freedom, Security and Justice" in the European Union, first half of 2003, Brussels, May 22, 2003, COM (2003) 291 final.

[27] Guiraudon, "The Constitution of a European Immigration Policy Domain," 264.

[28] "EU Plans to Sanction Countries over Immigration," *EU Observer*, Accessed May 5, 2010. http://EU Observer/?aid = 6623.

[29] Commission of the European Communities, Third annual report on the development of a common policy on illegal immigration, smuggling and trafficking of human beings, external borders, and the return of illegal residents, Brussels, March 9, 2009 Sec (2009) 320 final. p. 4.

As the EU bureaucracy most directly connected to border security funding, Frontex has experienced a remarkable growth and development in terms of its mandate, activities, and financial and human resources (Frontex Final Report 2016). The legal personality of Frontex is governed by specific rules, dictated by risk and forecasting analysis (Frontex Management Board Decision No 1/2014). Since the establishment of the agency, there have been three significant developments in Frontex authority (Schilde 2017). Regulation (EC) No. 863/2007 of the EP and of the Council established a mechanism to create Rapid Border Intervention Teams (RABITs) and implemented regulation of the responsibilities and power of guest officers. The amendment allowed organized officers to bear arms and use force without the consent of Member States and stipulated emergency funding for the agency depending on the urgency of the circumstances (Regulation (EC) No. 863/2007). Further regulations streamlined Frontex budgetary and deployment authority, enabling it to co-lead border patrol operations with EU member states, deploy liaison officers in third countries, coordinate joint return operations, and launch and finance pilot projects. A 2011 regulation increased Frontex's authority over preparing, coordinating, and implementing border operations, allowing it to co-lead border patrol operations with states, deploy liaison officers in third countries, coordinate joint return operations, and launch and finance pilot projects (Schilde 2017). A 2013 Regulation established the European Border Surveillance System (Eurosur) to detect, prevent, and combat illegal immigration and cross-border crime (Schilde 2017).

In summary, integration patterns in EU border policy are marked by turbulence in the form of reactive sequences, in which the Commission's progressive ambition was continuously checked by reactive member states, leading to increased border closure and least-common-denominator policy outcomes. Frontex authority has been accelerating over the last decade, but with a focus on security and surveillance over humanitarian resources such as search and rescue operations.

Conclusion

The various strands that make up EU migration policy all stem from the same integration projects of internal freedom of movement within Europe, but their various policies have different integration dynamics and types of turbulence, where different types of migration policy experience different kinds of turbulence. In asylum, relative sequencing and lock-in has produced a "stuck" or stalled integration area, where EU institutions will continue to muddle through at an extremely low level of functionality or capacity. On the other hand, early attempts by the European Commission to create more progressive integration in EU asylum policy led migration policy down a path of reactive sequencing, where member states moved more toward closure and control, while moving forward on an accelerated EU integration of external border security and internal free movement. The differentiated integration within migration policy makes the EU imbalanced, uncoordinated in crisis, and ultimately, contributing to its own turbulence. While the EU will continue to move forward on migration integration, the turbulence produced by tensions within its differentiated migration policies have potentially disastrous crisis implications for democracy in European states, for the human security of migrants seeking safety in Europe, and perhaps, for the health of the EU project in the long run.

References

Ansell, C. K., Trondal, J., & Øgård, M. (Eds.). (2017). *Governance in Turbulent Times*. Oxford University Press.

Baumgartner, F., Berry, J. M., Hojnacki, M., Leech, B. L., & Kimball, D. C. (2009). *Lobbying and Policy Change: Who Wins, Who Loses, and Why*. Chicago, IL: University of Chicago Press.

Baumgartner, F., & Jones, B. (2009). *Agendas and Instability in American Politics*. Chicago, IL: University of Chicago Press.

Börzel, T. A., & Risse, T. (2017). From the Euro to the Schengen Crises: European Integration Theories, Politicization, and Identity Politics. *Journal of European Public Policy, 25*(1), 83–108.

Bunyan, T. (Ed.). (1997). *Key Texts on Justice and Home Affairs, From Trevi to Maastricht* (Vol. 1 (1976–1993), p. 1997). Statewatch: London.

Commission of the European Communities. (1985). *Guidelines for a Community Policy on Migration*. Luxembourg: Office for Official Publications of the European Communities, 1986.

Cornelius, W., Tsuda, T., Martin, P., & Hollifield, J. (Eds.). (2004). *Controlling Immigration: A Global Perspective* (2nd ed.). Palo Alto, CA: Stanford University Press.

Council of the European Union. (2005, January 1). "*Living in an Area of Freedom, Security and Justice*,", 28.

Cross, M. (2017). *The Politics of Crisis in Europe*. New York, NY: Cambridge University Press.

d'Appollonia, A. C. (2012). *Frontiers of Fear: Immigration and Insecurity in the United States and Europe*. Ithaca, NY: Cornell University Press.

De Vries, C., & McNamara, K. R. (2018, May 14). How Choice Can Save Europe: The EU Needs Less Technocracy and More Democracy. *Foreign Affairs*. https://www.foreignaffairs.com/articles/europe/2018-05-14/how-choice-can-save-europe.

Doyle, L. (1993, November 12). Secret Plans for Brave New World of EU Security; New intelligence Networks will be Well Beyond the Reach of Elected Officials. *The Independent*.

European Commission. (2015). *Refugee Crisis: European Commission Reports on Progress in Implementation of Priority Actions*. IP/15/5839.

Evans, M. (1994, February 24). EU offers Immigrants Glimmer of Hope Report Urges Granting Legal Residents Same Rights and Freedoms as Citizens. *The Globe and Mail*.

Farrell, H., & Newman, A. (2010). Introduction: Making Global Markets: Historical Institutionalism in International Political Economy. *Review of International Political Economy, 17*, 609–638.

Farrell, H., & Newman, A. (2015). The New Politics of Interdependence: Cross-National Layering in Trans-Atlantic Regulatory Disputes. *Comparative Political Studies, 48*(4), 497–526.

Fioretos, O. (2011). Historical Institutionalism in International Relations. *International Organization, 65,* 367–399.

Fioretos, O. (2017). *International Politics and Institutions in Time.* Oxford: Oxford University Press.

Fratzke, S. (2015). *Not Adding Up: The Fading Promise of Europe's Dublin System.* Florence, Italy: Migration Policy Institute Europe.

Frontex, (2016). *Risk Analysis for 2016.* Warsaw, Poland: Frontex.

Geddes, A. (2008). *Immigration and European Integration: Beyond Fortress Europe?* Manchester, UK: Manchester University Press.

Geddes, A., & Scholten, P. (2016). The Politics of Migration and Immigration in Europe. London: Sage.

Genschel, P., & Jachtenfuchs, M. (2014). *Beyond the Regulatory Polity?: The European Integration of Core State Powers.* Oxford: Oxford University Press.

Goodman, S. W. (2014). Immigration policy-making in Europe. In J. M. Magnon (Ed.), *Handbook of European Politics.* London: Routledge.

Goodman, S. W. (2018). *Institutional Origins of Europe's Refugee Crisis.* Irvine, CA: University of California, Irvine.

Guiraudon, V. (2003). The Constitution of a European Immigration Policy Domain: A Political Sociology Approach. *Journal of European Public Policity, 10*(2), 270.

Haydu, J. (1998). Making Use of the Past: Time Periods as Cases to Compare and as Sequences of Problem Solving. *American Journal of Sociology, 104,* 339–371.

Heldt, E. (2018). *European Policy Failure During the Refugee Crisis: Partial Empowerment, Reluctant Agents, a Cacophony of Voices, and Unilateral Action* (Robert Schuman Centre for Advanced Studies, Research Paper No. RSCAS, 2018/36). Available at SSRN: https://ssrn.com/abstract=3293864.

Hooghe, L., & Marks, G. (2009). A Postfunctionalist Theory of European Integration: From Permissive Consensus to Constraining Dissensus. *British Journal of Political Science, 39*(1), 1–23.

Howlett, M. (2009). Process Sequencing Policy Dynamics: Beyond Homeostasis and Path Dependency. *Journal of Public Policy, 29,* 241–262. https://doi.org/10.1017/S0143814X09990158.

Howlett, M., & Goetz, K. H. (2014). Introduction: Time, Temporality and Timescapes in Administration and Policy. *International Review of Administrative Sciences, 80,* 477–492. https://doi.org/10.1177/0020852314543210.

Ikenberry, G. J. (2008). Explaining crisis and change in Transatlantic relations: An introduction. *The end of the West,* 1–27.

Jones, E. (2018). Towards a Theory of Disintegration. *Journal of European Public Policy, 25*(3), 440–451.

Jones, E., Kelemen, R. D., & Meunier, S. (2016). Failing Forward? The Euro Crisis and the Incomplete Nature of European Integration. *Comparative Political Studies, 49*(7), 1010–1034.

Jones, R. (2016). *Violent borders: Refugees and the Right to Move.* London: Verso Books.

Juncker, J. C. (2015). State of the Union 2015: Time for Honesty, Unity and Solidarity. *European Commission,* 9.

Kelemen, R. D., & Mcnamara, K. R. (2018). *How Theories of State-Building Explain the EU*. Working Paper Presented at the Council of Europeanists, with R. Daniel Kelemen, Chicago, IL, March 28–30.

Lavenex, S. (2018). "Failing Forward" Towards Which Europe? Organized Hypocrisy in the Common European Asylum System. *JCMS: Journal of Common Market Studies, 56*(5), 1195–1212.

Lori, N., & Schilde, K. (2020, forthcoming). A Political Economy of Global Security Approach to Migration and Border Control. *Journal of Global Security Studies*.

Mahoney, J. (2000). Path Dependence in Historical Sociology. *Theory and Society, 29*, 507–548.

Mitsilegas, V., Monar, J., & Rees, W. (2003). *The European Union and Internal Security: Guardian of the People?*. Basingstoke: Palgrave Macmillan.

Moravcsik, A. (1998). *The Choice for Europe*. New York, NY: Cornell University Press.

Nanz, K. (1994). The Harmonisation of Asylum and Immigration Legislation Within the Third Pillar of the Union Treaty—A Stocktaking. In J. Monar & R. Morgan (Eds.), *The Third Pillar of the European Union: Co-Operation in the Field of Justice and Home Affairs* (pp. 123–133). Bruges: European Interuniversity Press and College of Europe.

Newman, A. L. (2018). Global European Union Studies: Sometimes Normal is a Little Weird. *Journal of European Public Policy, 25*(7), 959–968.

Newman, A., & Posner, E. (2016). Structuring Transnational Interests: The Second-Order Effects of Soft Law in the Politics of Global Finance. *Review of International Political Economy, 23*, 768–798.

Newsome, A. (2018). Credible Champions? Transatlantic Relations and Human Rights in Refugee Crises. *Journal of European Integration, 40*(5), 587–604.

Palomar, T. (2004). Migration Policies of the European Union. In J. Blaschke, (Ed.), *The Politics of Immigration in the EU* (pp. 88–92). Berlin: Parabolis, 2004.

Papagianni, G. (2006). *Institutional and Policy Dynamics of EU Migration Law*. Leiden: Martinus Nijhoff Leiden.

Riddervold, M. 2018. A Humanitarian Mission in Line with Human Rights? Assessing Sophia, the EU's Naval Response to the Migration Crisis. *European Security, 27*(2), 158–174.

Ripoll Servent, A., & Trauner, F. (2014). Do Supranational EU Institutions Make a Difference? EU Asylum Law Before and After "Communitarization.". *Journal of European Public Policy, 21*(8), 1142–1162.

Sandholtz, W., & Stone Sweet, A. (1997). European Integration and Supranational Governance. *Journal of European Public Policy, 4*(3), 297–317.

Schilde, K. (2017). *The Political Economy of European Security*. New York, NY: Cambridge University Press.

Schimmelfennig, F. (2003). *The EU, NATO and the Integration of Europe: Rules and Rhetoric*. New York, NY: Cambridge University Press.

Schimmelfennig, F. (2018). European Integration (Theory) in Times of Crisis. A Comparison of the Euro and Schengen Crises. *Journal of European Public Policy, 25*(7), 969–989.

Schimmelfennig, F., Leuffen, D., & Rittberger, B. (2015). The European Union as a System of Differentiated Integration: Interdependence, Politicization and Differentiation. *Journal of European Public Policy, 22*(6), 764–782.

Scipioni, M. (2017). Failing Forward in EU Migration Policy? EU Integration after the 2015 Asylum and Migration Crisis. *Journal of European Public Policy, 53*, 1–19.

Uçarer, E. (2013). The Area of Freedom, Security, and justice. In *European Union Politics* (pp. 281–295). New York, NY: Oxford University Press.

Vollaard, H. (2014). Explaining European Disintegration. *JCMS: Journal of Common Market Studies, 52*(5), 1142–1159.

Zaun, N. (2016). Why EU Asylum Standards Exceed the Lowest Common Denominator: The Role of Regulatory Expertise in EU Decision-Making. *Journal of European Public Policy, 23*(1), 136–154.

CHAPTER 26

The Refugee Crisis and the EU Border Security Policies

Ruxandra-Laura Bosilca

INTRODUCTION

When more than one million asylum seekers arrived in Europe and hundreds of thousands lost their lives at sea in 2015, a new crisis hit the European Union (EU). The EU responded through a comprehensive set of immediate and medium-term measures in the areas of border control, asylum, and migration intended to develop a "common European migration policy" to manage migration flows more effectively (European Commission 2015a: 2). More importantly, the unprecedented scale and depth of the crisis posed a direct threat to core EU values, and jeopardized the existence of flagship integration projects such as Schengen (Ceccorulli 2019; Fink 2018). Faced with these challenges, member states would be expected to formulate common solutions to safeguard the mutual gains of integration. Furthermore, past episodes of migratory pressures had often opened up 'windows of opportunity' for the EU to revamp border control agents (Carrera and den Hertog 2016), upgrade border management tools and technologies (Pawlak and Kurowska 2012), or expand the scope of migration policies (Moreno-Lax 2019). Then, such crises would normally create impulses for major policy reforms, driving integration forward (Jones et al. 2016).

Yet, the jumble of disparate and unilateral responses which followed offered a very different picture. The massive influx of refugee arrivals and the faulty management of the crisis put immense strain on the EU's asylum system and jeopardized the very existence of Schengen. Then the question arises,

R.-L. Bosilca (✉)
Inland Norway University of Applied Sciences, Rena, Norway

why has the EU been unable to generate new common solutions to these shared problems? The chapter suggests that the crisis has led to a mixture of provisional and limited disintegration, on the one hand, and incremental and unsubstantial reforms, on the other hand. Member states starkly opposed distributional policies such as the refugee quotas proposed by the Commission, as well as any significant transfer of authority to EU bodies. In sharp contrast, national governments reached rapid agreement on incremental, modest policy reforms intended to reduce asylum pressures and prevent the collapse of the Schengen system.

The analysis aims to contribute to the growing literature on the politics of crisis, migration, and borders in the EU context (Moreno-Lax 2018; Fink 2018; Schimmelfennig 2018; Ryan 2019). A large part of these studies has frequently drawn on one particular conceptual framework, or has focused on single empirical cases and outcomes (but see Niemann and Zaun 2018; Genschel and Jachtenfuchs 2018; Hooghe and Marks 2019). This body of work is important, yet leaves ample room for further empirical and conceptual explanations.

The chapter adheres to the conceptual framework developed in this Handbook to (re)appraise the usefulness and limitations of key theoretical perspectives on European integration. It thus builds on conceptual approaches rooted in international relations, such as liberal intergovernmentalism (LI), as well as in comparative politics and public policy, including historical institutionalism (HI), and the 'garbage can'/multiple-streams models (MSM). Whereas LI has been widely applied to studies on the EU response to crises (Zaun 2018; Schimmelfennig 2018; this volume; Biermann et al. 2017), HI and MSM have attracted much less empirical testing. By bringing together the two theoretical clusters, this chapter seeks to capture a broader picture of European (dis)integration, through complementary perceptions of the EU as an international organization and a 'state-like' political system (Saurugger 2014: 1–3).

The analysis assumes that the empirical complexity of EU crisis politics transcends the boundaries of any one theoretical perspective. Each approach casts a different light on EU crisis response and border governance, in a complementary rather than competing perspective (Ferguson 2015). The chapter adopts a 'problem-solving' approach which focuses on a central analytical issue instead of testing the robustness of a particular theory (Lynggaards et al. 2015: 9). For this purpose, it draws on EU official documents, reports issued by various bodies in the field of asylum and migration, news articles, as well as the scholarly literature on the refugee crisis.

The chapter unfolds as follows. I first develop three sets of theoretical expectations about the impact of the crisis on EU border policies, based on the tripartite scenario laid out in the introduction to this Handbook. According to the first scenario (*breaking down*), the refugee crisis would trigger intense distributional conflicts between member states with asymmetrical preferences and bargaining power. Tensions would prevent member governments from banding together to respond to the crisis, and would thus render the EU vulnerable to disunity and disintegration. Such manifestations would be found, for instance, in the empowerment of national governments at the expense of supranational regimes, the prioritization of unilateral solutions over a common response, or the member states' blatant non-compliance with their obligations under EU and international law. In a second scenario (*muddling through*), the EU would react to the escalating crisis by making incremental adjustments to previous policies rather than completely overhauling them. Due to institutional 'stickiness' and path-dependent processes, established structures and policies would be hard to change despite their ineffectiveness. Finally, the third scenario (*heading forward*) suggests that the refugee crisis would act as a 'window of opportunity' for further integration, prompting major policy revisions and the creation of new governance structures.

I then examine each of these lines of inquiry empirically by concentrating on key developments during 2015 and 2016 at the height of the crisis. Space precludes an in-depth analysis of each scenario and the theoretical propositions are presented in a condensed form. Notwithstanding these limitations, the chapter draws attention to the value of theoretically informed analyses of the refugee crisis and paves the way for future studies. The concluding section summarizes the main points.

MIGRATION, CRISIS, AND EU BORDER SECURITY: THREE LOGICS OF RESPONSE CHOICES

Crises occur when exceptional phenomena threaten the fundamental structures or core values of a system, warranting urgent decision-making under conditions of uncertainty (Boin et al. 2005). For their part, border and migration policies involve multiple risks and uncertainties concerning their impact on individuals, communities, societies, and states (Williams and Baláž 2012). Building on the conceptual framework outlined in the introductory chapter, the scenarios below distinguish three potential effects of the refugee crisis on the EU border policies: disintegration, *muddling through*, and deepened integration.

The *first scenario* predicts a 'vertical' disintegration of the EU in the area of border security and asylum, whereby particular 'EU policies are transferred back to member states' (Leruth et al. 2019). The renationalization of competences and a scaling back of policies at the supranational level are explained through the three-stage rationalist model of LI involving domestic preference formation, intergovernmental bargaining, and institutional choice.

First, LI assumes that state preferences are articulated by national governments in response to competing pressures from domestic constituencies and societal groups. In the refugee crisis, domestic actors are expected to be mainly interested in curbing migration fluxes rather than protecting asylum seekers or restoring the normal functioning of the Schengen space (Moravcsik and Schimmelfennig 2019). As the main goal of national decision-makers is to remain in office, member states would 'share a primarily and stable national interest in managing issue-specific social interdependence by reducing migration to levels tolerable to the prevailing domestic political consensuses in their countries' (ibid.: 75).

Second, governments enter interstate negotiations in order to manage interdependence more favorably through collective action rather than through 'go-it-alone' or loosely coordinated policies. The decisive factor in the outcome of the negotiation process is the actors' relative bargaining power, which is determined by the intensity of national preferences, the availability of unilateral or multilateral alternatives, and the opportunities for compromise and linkage (Moravcsik 1998: 63). In this case, the uneven effects of the refugee crisis are expected to result in asymmetrical preferences and bargaining power across member states with different geographies, economic conditions, and asylum policies (Schimmelfennig 2018). Intergovernmental bargaining would thus focus on the distributional consequences of the crisis: states most adversely affected by the crisis and expecting to gain most from deeper integration would have scant bargaining power, and would be more likely to make concessions. Conversely, states that were least affected by the crisis would be the most likely to resist cooperation or to impose firm conditions to pursue their preferred course of action (ibid.).

Third, national governments might decide to pool and delegate sovereignty to EU supranational structures to increase the credibility of their mutual commitments (Moravcsik 1998). In practice, however, national governments often opt for policy coordination mechanisms, and only rarely delegate extensive regulatory powers to supranational institutions (Moravcsik and Schimmelfennig 2019). Member states are thus expected to institutionalize their border cooperation (see also Schilde and Wallace Goodman in this volume) as a means to enforce agreements and prevent defections. These institutions, however, would act in the member states' national interest, and would ultimately remain under intergovernmental control.

The *second* scenario elaborates on HI to explain institutional continuity and change. Within this framework, established preferences and patterns of political action are hard to change—even if they result in sub-optimal outcomes—due to self-reinforcing processes of 'positive feedback' and 'increasing returns' (Pierson 2004). This results in long-lasting path-dependent processes, in which early decisions shape and constrain subsequent institutional and policy choices (ibid.).

Despite their stability and resilience, institutions are not immutable. Institutional transformation may occur as a result of exogenous shocks during 'critical junctures', which are defined as *'relatively* short periods of time during which there is a *substantially* heightened probability that agents' choices will affect the outcome of interest' (Capoccia and Kelemen 2007: 348, emphasis in original). Change is expected to take place when agents respond to a 'window of opportunity', which opens following a relaxation of structural constraints on action (Mahoney 2002).

Critical junctures, however, do not always cause abrupt and sweeping transformations in institutional configurations and policies. Instead, due to the high unpredictability and uncertainty surrounding decision-making, the outcome may be a return to the pre-critical juncture status quo (Capoccia and Kelemen 2007). When change nonetheless occurs, it takes gradual and incremental forms rather than being the result of an isolated break point (Mahoney and Thelen 2010). Based on these premises, the refugee crisis would open a window of opportunity and lead to new policies, yet these would largely reproduce patterns of the past.

Finally, the third *scenario* posits that the refugee crisis propels integration forward, resulting in an expanded EU portfolio and an empowerment of supranational agents. It assumes that 'policy outputs are neither exclusively rational nor solely a function of the institutional design' (Zahariadis 2008: 515). Instead, the EU policy processes may be more akin to an unpredictable 'garbage can' decision-making model characterized by problematic preferences, unclear technologies, and fluid participation (Cohen et al. 1972). Policy makers act under conditions of high ambiguity, imperfect information, and shifting coalitions, which are further exacerbated during crises. Problems, solutions, and decision-makers are therefore interconnected in a way which depends on their temporal order and access to choice opportunities, and much less on a particular consequential sequence (March and Olsen 1989: 12).

The MSM explains EU policy choice as the result of three relatively independent 'streams'—problems, policies, and politics—which are 'coupled' by 'policy entrepreneurs' at an opportune time (Kingdon 1984). The *problem stream* includes the totality of conditions that policy makers and/or citizens wish to alter. Different issues can attract the decision-makers' limited attention through policy-relevant indicators, feedback mechanisms, and 'focusing events', which 'are relatively conducive to agenda setting campaigns' (Cairney and Zahariadis 2016: 98). The *policies stream* encompasses competing solutions that seek to respond to perceived problems and challenges. Initiatives which are technically feasible and congruent with the main norms and values of a policy community are likely to prevail (Zahariadis 2003: 28). The *politics stream* highlights the importance of 'the time of politics' (Borrás and Radaelli 2011: 475). Salient factors include the 'European Parliament elections, Council summits and the renewal of the European Commission at regular intervals of time' (ibid.). Finally, policy entrepreneurs need to bring together problems and solutions during policy windows. These may briefly open in the problem stream and/or in the political stream, due to predictable events such as elections or budget negotiations, or due to unforeseen occurrences such as crises (Kingdon 1984). Entrepreneurs, acting as power brokers, exploit these opportune moments to 'bias choice towards some options and away from others' (Zahariadis 2008: 520).

Based on this model, change in the EU border policies is likely to occur when a problem is acknowledged (the unmanageable influx of asylum seekers), for which at least one viable solution exists (e.g., reinforcing external borders control), in a political context conducive to supranational initiatives (e.g., the favorable position of national governments and/or EU actors). Windows of opportunity would provide the context and catalyst for policy choice, whereas supranational entrepreneurs would seize the opportunity to promote their policy preferences.

Empirical Analysis

First Scenario: 'Breaking Down'

During the first stage of the LI model, governments articulate domestic political interests into a consistent set of national preferences. At the height of the refugee crisis, migration was seen as the chief concern at the EU level, with large parts of the European electorates opposing more arrivals (European Commission 2015b). The spike in asylum seekers resulted in a broad support for more restrictive policies, which was further fueled by right-wing populist parties (Zaun 2018). Most national governments aligned their preferences with their voters' views to avoid electoral punishment, and hence focused on managing the refugee inflows advantageously, or preventing their arrival altogether (ibid.). Consequently, the distributional consequences of different policy options were 'clear and substantial' (Schimmelfennig 2018: 8).

As LI would predict, the crisis generated negative policy externalities, which triggered demand for international cooperation; interdependence, however, was asymmetrical as not all member states were equally affected (ibid.: 3). Frontline coastal states, in particular Italy and Greece, were hit the hardest by the crisis, while lacking adequate capacities to handle the mass arrivals. In turn, destination states such as Germany or Sweden were affected by massive secondary movements from the first countries of arrival. Transit countries experienced variable migratory pressures; finally, other states remained outside the main migratory routes (ibid.).

In the second stage, member states took the domestically constituted national preferences to the EU arena, where they engaged in hard bargaining to minimize their crisis costs and maximize cooperation gains. Frontline states pushed hard for a fairer redistribution mechanism, yet exerted little bargaining leverage: they could neither 'wave through' asylum seekers with transit and destination countries threatening to close their borders, nor 'push back' those in need of international protection, as they would bluntly violate human rights law (Moravcsik and Schimmelfennig 2019). In April 2015, following the deadliest single shipwreck in the Mediterranean in decades, Prime Minister Tsipras (2015) called for 'an immediate increase in the emergency financial and logistical support to Member States in the front line' and an 'equitable distribution of the financial burdens and the hospitality responsibility'. Similarly, Italy deplored the lack of solidarity 'which Europe has shown in other instances', while Malta accused member states of 'turning a blind eye' to the tragedies in the Mediterranean (BBC 2015).

By contrast, transit and destination countries supported more restrictive border controls, and enjoyed higher bargaining power due to the availability of unilateral options. States could decide to seal their borders and deflect asylum seekers from their territories, or force them to remain in the first state of arrival (Moravcsik and Schimmelfennig 2019). Transit countries feared large numbers of refugees being stranded throughout their territories, and thus tolerated or facilitated the transit of asylum seekers to their destination countries. In turn, long-term recipient countries tempered their open policies as migration flows steadily increased by imposing tighter asylum conditions or returning applicants to their countries of origin (Daley 2015). A number of transit countries along the Balkan route, including Hungary, Macedonia, Austria, and Slovenia, as well as receiving countries such as Norway, installed barbed wire fences and fortified walls to control movement. Finally, non-affected states had no interest in cooperation whatsoever, as both common action to reinforce borders and refugee redistribution arrangements left them worse off (Moravcsik and Schimmelfennig 2019). In other words, the distribution of asylum seekers eventually came down to a 'zero-sum' game in which any outcome favorable to one group of states was inescapably unfavorable to the other group (ibid.). Consequently, negotiations focused on the more politically feasible options of preventing irregular entries into Europe and facilitating return to third countries, as evidenced by the EU-Turkey resettlement agreement, and the EU partnerships with key third countries (Moravcsik and Schimmelfennig 2019: 78; also Crawford in this volume).

Then, during the third stage, it is hardly surprising that member states opposed the Commission's reform agenda and sought to retain firm control over border and asylum policies. In mid-September 2015, Germany temporarily suspended the Schengen Agreement and reintroduced internal border checks at its southern border, triggering a domino effect along the Balkan corridor. Austria, Slovenia, Hungary, Sweden, Denmark, and Norway soon followed suit. This chain of uncoordinated responses not only entailed high costs for both member states and the EU but also risked jeopardizing the Schengen regime (Ceccorulli 2019).

The member states' inability to reach common ground was also revealed by their failure to reform the Dublin regime or to supplement it with functional mechanisms of shared responsibility. In September 2015, the Council set up a temporary and exceptional relocation mechanism for 160,000 asylum seekers from Greece and Italy to alleviate the disproportionate burden of frontline states. This decision, however, was taken *despite* the vehement opposition of various Eastern member states—and thus by breaking the informal rule of consensus in the Council (European Commission 2016a). Furthermore, implementation was fraught with problems and inefficiencies, not least due to the national governments' faltering pledges, prolonged response time to relocation requests, and unjustified rejections of applicants (ibid.). As expected, the Commission encountered even more fervent opposition when it proposed a permanent relocation mechanism. This 'would have been a strong and binding solidarity mechanism [...], and a significant step towards deeper European integration' (Zaun 2018: 57). The idea was pushed through by host countries—in particular Germany, Austria, and Sweden—and supported by border and transit countries, as well as by recipient states such as the Benelux countries. However, a broad coalition of 'up to 15 member states', including the Visegrád states and the Baltic countries along with France and Spain, vetoed the initiative to avoid receiving more asylum claims (ibid.). The Commission's plans for a voluntary and ad hoc resettlement scheme were hindered by similar obstacles. In July 2015, member states agreed to resettle 22,500 refugees from the Middle East, the Horn of Africa, and Northern Africa over a two-year period. Nonetheless, the wavering political commitments, discretionary selection of asylum seekers, lengthy procedures, and inadequate capacity and logistics of some of the destination states resulted in a patchy and slow response (Grün 2018).

Member states also opposed the Commission's proposals for increasing the supranational competencies of two pivotal agencies in the EU 'area of freedom, security, and justice' (AFSJ): Frontex, relabeled as the 'European Border and Coast Guard Agency' (EBCG), and the European Asylum Support Office (EASO), which was meant to become a fully fledged 'European Union Agency for Asylum' (EUAA). Similarly, the European Parliament signaled the deficiencies of Dublin and supported a substantial reform of the EBCG and EASO (Newsome 2018). However, these institutional innovations were rapidly dismissed as 'unwelcome incursions into national sovereignty' by national governments and were significantly watered down during negotiations (ibid.: 598). As a result, EASO continued to assist member states in the implementation of EU asylum rules, yet without having decision-making powers regarding asylum applications, or enforcement competencies on the ground. Likewise, the EBCG has neither been conferred executive tasks, nor its own border personnel and resources. As expected by LI, member states pursued unilateral policies which triggered 'temporary disintegration and additional support to EU agencies without authority transfer' (Schimmelfennig 2018: 10).

Second Scenario: 'Muddling Through'

A useful starting point for understanding the refugee crisis from a HI perspective goes back to the adoption of the Schengen Agreement (1985) and the Schengen Convention (1990) aimed at gradually removing controls on persons at the internal frontiers of signatory states. The creation of an area of free movement was accompanied by a set of 'compensatory measures' to secure the external frontiers of the Union through tougher border controls and more restrictive immigration and asylum policies (Lavenex 1999). The growing need for cooperation in asylum opened parallel negotiations on the Dublin Convention of 1990, which subsequently led to the Dublin II (2003) and Dublin III (2013) Regulations. The Schengen and Dublin systems developed in close tandem, sharing the common goal of 'preventing the uncontrolled movement of asylum seekers in the EU and limiting their access to member states territories and asylum procedures' (ibid.: 41). As a result, '[t]he decision not to undertake a more profound harmonization but to settle for minimum standards has locked several policy areas, such as asylum and legal migration, into a path of incremental changes' (Scipioni 2018: 1361).

The Dublin regime has been long criticized for its dysfunctional design which placed a disproportionate burden on the EU's southern member states. These systemic flaws, however, passed unnoticed as long as immigration remained at tolerable levels. The situation changed drastically with the arrival of an unprecedented number of asylum seekers into Europe in 2015. More than 1300 people died at sea during the month of April, sparking an international outcry and throwing the EU into emergency mode (UNHCR 2015). The events constituted a critical juncture in the EU border policies in at least two respects. First, the massive arrivals and the member states' uncoordinated responses triggered an internal crisis which led to the suspension of Dublin and menaced the very existence of Schengen. Second, the crisis exposed the shortcomings of the EU's border and asylum systems, thus forcing a rethinking of existing policies. The need for institutional reform accelerated the adoption of pre-existing plans, as in the case of the EU-Turkey agreement or the establishment of the EBCG (Ceccorulli 2019). Additionally, the crisis facilitated agreement on new solutions that would otherwise have been unacceptable, such as the EU-led naval operation *Sophia* (Riddervold 2018).

While this critical juncture opened the *possibility* of significant change (Capoccia and Kelemen 2007), no drastic transformation occurred in the EU policies. On the one hand, member states strived to retain discretion over the decision-making process to avoid 'being outvoted by other governments in the Council and overruled by supranational institutions' (Beach 2016: 53). One the other hand, there was no centralized body at the EU level that could help member states cope with the crisis. National governments thus turned to unilateral decisions dictated by the urgency of the moment; in the longer run, however, the severity and complexity of the crisis required common management, not least to prevent further refugee arrivals and a complete breakdown of Schengen/Dublin. As a compromise solution, member states agreed on a series of incremental strategies, either by enhancing existing institutions or by setting up new structures inspired by previous policies.

In the first case, the EU has reformed its policies by adding new rules and structures on top of existing ones, through what Mahoney and Thelen (2010) called 'layering'. In the area of asylum, for instance, the Commission settled for a more modest proposal for a 'Dublin plus' regulation after member states rejected burden-sharing quotas (Niemann and Zaun 2018). This preserved existing rules but introduced a 'corrective allocation mechanism' or 'fairness mechanism' enabling the relocation of asylum seekers in times of intense migratory pressures (ibid.). Another example is the EU 'hotspot approach', which created a system to identify, filter, and channel protection seekers into asylum or return. Despite some elements of novelty, the approach reflected limited change as the new rules were simply 'layered' over the existent Dublin system without replacing it (Trauner 2016: 320).

The EU took a similar approach to cooperation with third countries for preventing unauthorized entry and facilitating returns. A good example is the EU-Turkey 'deal' whereby Turkey accepted the return of irregular migrants from Greece in exchange for increased financial aid for the refugee burden, visa liberalization, and a reanimation of accession talks (Council 2016a). The deal was described by the Commission as 'unprecedented' as it 'established new ways to bring order into migration flows and save lives' (European Commission 2016b: 2–3). Yet, notwithstanding its broader scope and ambition, the EU-Turkish deal continued along the same lines as previous negotiations on readmission. The agreement also formed part of a long tradition of border externalization policies whereby European states have intercepted, deterred, or 'pushed-back' protection seekers (Basilien-Gainche 2017). This model was rapidly mainstreamed into broader EU initiatives on migration such as the Migration Partnership Framework (MPF), which aimed to coordinate the full range of 'instruments, tools and leverage' of the EU and member states 'to reach comprehensive partnerships (compacts) with third countries to better manage migration' (European Commission 2016b: 6). The MPF was heralded as a key innovation for the EU's success in 'stemming the flows of irregular migrants' (ibid.: 2). Compared to past policies, the framework had a broader geographical and policy reach, placed heavier emphasis on return and readmission, and relied more on positive and negative incentives. Its underlying intentions and effects remained, however, unchanged, which indicated 'merely an upgrade, albeit a powerful one' (Collett and Ahad 2017: 2). For instance, the EU drew on previous cooperation within regional forums—such as the Rabat and Khartoum Processes, or the EU-Africa summits—to strengthen ties with third countries that could tackle migration 'upstream' (ibid.). Similarly, the financial instruments underpinning the MPF, such as the Facility for Refugees in Turkey or the Emergency Trust Fund for Africa, reflected a 'reorganization or re-labeling of existing EU funds' rather than a novel addition (den Hertog 2016: 5).

With regard to operational responses, member states reinforced Frontex operations *Triton* and *Poseidon*, which displayed striking continuities with EU past practices of border securitization (Moreno-Lax 2018). Another telling example of layering is the creation of the EBCG. This was presented as a major institutional breakthrough meant to address the limitations in Frontex's resources, mandate, and autonomy vis-à-vis member states. The initiative failed, nevertheless, to establish a genuinely integrated management of external borders, and perpetuated the agency's institutional and functional dependency on member states (Carrera and den Hertog 2016). As a result, the newly created structure amounted to little more than an 'emergency-driven Frontex-Plus' (ibid.: 2).

In the second case, political actors created new tools inspired by the logic and mode of operation of previous policies. This fits Verdun's (2015: 232) ideal-type of 'copying' in the sense that 'new institutions are created by borrowing in some way from earlier institutions'. The EU-led naval operation *Sophia* exemplifies this practice. Launched under the Common Security and Defence Policy (CSDP), the operation's aim was to 'disrupt the business model of human smuggling and trafficking networks in the Southern Central Mediterranean', by 'undertaking systematic efforts to identify, capture and dispose of vessels and assets used or suspected of being used by smugglers and traffickers' (Council 2015a). Operation *Sophia* included several new elements, including an openly coercive mandate under UN Chapter VII which set it apart from the bulk of EU civilian and low-intensity missions, as well as the use of an instrument of external security governance to address an internal security issue (Tardy 2015). Its underpinning logic, however, further reproduced and reinforced old patterns of securitization and militarization in EU border management (Moreno-Lax 2018). As such, the operation primarily focused on countering migrant smuggling, seen as a criminal activity and a pull factor, rather than saving lives at sea. This is made evident in the operation's strategic review which quotes as main results 'the apprehension of 148 suspects' and the 'neutralization of some 550 assets' (EEAS 2018: 5). Moreover, destroying suspected vessels failed to reduce the number of arrivals, while also resulting in more dangerous crossings at sea and threatening the lives of passengers onboard (House of Lords 2017).

Overall, these examples illustrate well the incremental response of the EU to the refugee crisis in line with the HI view. As radical departures from the status quo were politically unfeasible, gradual and limited amendments facilitated common solutions without challenging the existing institutional context.

Third Scenario: 'Heading Forward'

In Kingdon's (1984) model, policy outputs emerge from the coupling of problems, solutions, and politics. In the problem stream, the surge in irregular sea crossings and spiraling fatalities sparked public outcry and fervent political debates. The year of 2015 marked a decisive quantitative shift from previous statistics (IOM 2015). This sudden deterioration in indicators immediately grabbed the policy makers' attention by signaling the magnitude of the crisis and revealing the limitations of the EU border regime. Concurrently, a haphazard mix of solutions competed for political influence in the policy stream. As distributional policies of resettlement and relocation proved technically complicated and politically undesirable, the Commission focused on more acceptable proposals geared towards 'noticeable centralization and harmonization' in border management (Niemann and Zaun 2018: 12).

Its flagship initiative was the creation of the EBCG, regarded as the first move towards a centralized governance of European borders. The idea first emerged in the early 2000s, when growing concerns about terrorism and the eastward enlargement prompted the need for a more robust control of Schengen's external frontiers (Monar 2006). Frontex was thus set up in 2004 to coordinate the operational cooperation between member states in the area of external border security. The agency, however, enjoyed limited powers vis-à-vis member states and remained chronically under-resourced. As a result, the Commission has strongly supported the establishment of the EBCG, which 'reserved an important position for itself and [...] added to the EU's remit of action' (Scipioni 2017: 6).

Two policy windows enabled the Commission to move forward with its plans. The first opened in the problem stream in April 2015, after hundreds of migrants lost their lives in two major shipwrecks near Lampedusa. The main focusing event, however, was not the worsening humanitarian crisis but rather the exposed weaknesses in the external border systems which threatened to unravel Schengen (Fink 2018; Ceccorulli 2019). After this episode, a wide consensus emerged in favor of reinforcing external borders and upgrading Frontex (European Commission 2015c). As European Commission First Vice-President Timmermans put it, external border governance was 'a shared responsibility' which required 'a truly integrated system of border management' (European Commission 2015d). The Commissioner for Migration, Home Affairs and Citizenship, Dimitris Avramopoulos, echoed these views and called for 'a truly European approach' (ibid.).

A second policy window opened in the political stream towards the end of 2015 and early 2016. Two institutional developments were particularly relevant. First, the European Council conclusions on migration in December 2015 stressed the need to safeguard Schengen and demanded a swifter political agreement on the EBCG (Council 2015b). Second, the Dutch Presidency endorsed the Commission's proposal, making EBCG its first priority (Niemann and Speyer 2018). The Presidency facilitated consensus among coalitions with divergent preferences, cooperated with other delegations, crafted compromise solutions, and used different bargaining strategies (ibid.).

Once these new policy windows opened, policy entrepreneurs within the Commission seized the opportunity to advance their proposal on the EBCG. President Juncker (2015) announced that turning Frontex into 'a fully operational European border and coast guard system' was one of the core priorities of his mandate. Moreover, the General Secretariat, DG Migration and Home Affairs, and the Legal Service in the Commission maintained close cooperation and exchanged information frequently during EBCG negotiations (Niemann and Speyer 2018). The Commission hence managed to manipulate preferences towards its preferred outcome by gaining access to the agenda-setting and negotiation process, and by brokering agreement during trilogues (ibid.).

The Commission used two main strategies to reach agreement on the ECBG. First, it selected a policy option that met both the criteria of value acceptability (a wide consensus already existed on a need for a European solution) and technical feasibility (the initiative built on the existent structures of Frontex rather than setting up a body *ex novo*). Second, the proposal was framed as an indispensable part of the EU's exit strategy from the refugee crisis. Specifically, the EBCG was introduced as a remedy for the weak and ineffective control of external borders, faltering Schengen cooperation, and rising concerns about terrorism (European Commission 2015e).

The Commission also sought to depoliticize negotiations by recasting sensitive issues as 'technical or functional requirements' (Niemann and Speyer 2018: 33). The EBCG was justified as a technocratic solution to the limitations of Frontex such as the 'inadequate resources in terms of staff and equipment, an inability to initiate and carry out return or border management operations, and the absence of an explicit role to conduct search and rescue operations' (European Commission 2015c: 2). By doing so, it managed to fend off potential opposition from member states fearing a dramatic shift in power from national to supranational institutions. Conversely, the Commission's efforts to depoliticize redistributional policies by framing them as technical measures utterly failed. For instance, the idea of a mandatory and automatic distribution mechanism based on 'objective' and 'quantifiable' criteria such as the member states' size, wealth, or capacity was met with staunch opposition from national governments, and was abandoned in favor of more flexible arrangements (Börzel 2016).

The Commission tabled its proposal on 15 December 2015 as part of its 'Borders Package'. The text was ambitious and granted the EBCG substantial new powers and resources. For example, the agency was tasked to conduct mandatory 'vulnerability assessments' to determine the member states' capacity to manage their external borders, including by dispatching liaison officers on the ground and by setting out corrective actions (European Commission 2015e). Furthermore, if a member state failed to implement these measures, or if the migratory pressures at its borders threatened Schengen, the EBCG could invoke a right to intervene—even without the consent of that state. The agency also acquired more important roles in return operations and interventions, coordination with third countries, and the protection of fundamental rights. Border policing was further reinforced by incorporating national coast guards performing border control tasks into the EBCG. Finally, the agency's capacity was increased through the establishment of a rapid reserve pool of 1500 border guards and a technical equipment pool, drawn from the member states' contributions. The EBCG could also acquire and deploy its own equipment. In sum, the Commission's proposal involved 'both an increased breadth (more tasks for the agency) and depth of integration (such as shifting competencies to EU institutions)' (Niemann and Speyer 2018: 28).

The proposal was adopted in a 'record' time of only nine months and entered into force on 6 October 2016 (European Commission 2016c). On this occasion, Commissioner Avramopoulos rushed to announce the birth of 'a fully-fledged European Border and Coast Guard system' while the Executive Director of the agency declared 'a historic moment' (European Commission

2016d). In reality, however, the bold provisions originally envisaged by the Commission were substantially diluted in the final form of the legislation. For example, the proposal for the agency's 'right to intervene' based on a decision issued by the Commission was seen as encroaching on national sovereignty and was thus rejected outright (Scipioni 2017). Instead, the Commission's role was limited to proposing measures to be implemented by the EBCG, which then had to be submitted to the Council for consideration (Council 2016b). Member states thus managed to maintain their primacy over border policies and block further communitarization. Contrary to the expectations under this scenario, the EBCG was granted limited decision-making powers and resources, which marked only slight and symbolic changes from the status quo.

Conclusion

This chapter set out to examine the impact of the refugee crisis on the border policy developments in the EU. Following the conceptual framework outlined in this Handbook, three theory-driven scenarios were considered: *breaking down*, *muddling through*, and *heading forward*. Given the severity of the crisis and the threat to major European integration projects such as Schengen, member states would normally be expected to work towards common policies rather than take unilateral action. Yet, contrary to this assumption, the crisis has not resulted in a supranationalisation of the EU border security regime, but in a mixture of temporary and limited disintegration on the one hand, and incremental and marginal reforms of existing policies, on the other hand. These outcomes best correspond to the first (*breaking down*) and second (*muddling through*) scenarios.

Building on insights from LI, the first scenario has shown that all national governments shared a common interest in minimizing the number of asylum seekers in their respective territories to appease domestic constituencies. However, member states were not equally vulnerable to migratory pressures and thus held different policy preferences. Frontline states and traditional recipients of refugees bore the brunt of the crisis and called for fairer responsibility-sharing arrangements; by contrast, countries receiving a smaller number of applicants favored unilateral solutions and opposed a quota system that would have left them worse off. The outcome of this 'zero-sum' game was a vehement rejection of distributional mechanisms. Accordingly, negotiations at the EU level shifted towards measures aimed at reducing the refugee influxes altogether, as in the case of the EU-Turkey agreement, as well as the partnerships with third countries. As member states sought to retain firm control over their border and asylum policies, they opposed a transfer of substantial national competencies to centralized bodies such as Frontex and EASO.

The second scenario, which builds on HI, can help explain the coexistence of partial disintegration and incremental change. The massive refugee arrivals in 2015 marked a critical juncture in the EU border policies, unmasking the structural deficiencies in its Dublin/Schengen regimes and triggering institutional change. While this critical juncture set out the context for reform, no major shifts in the EU's policies took place, not least because member states attempted to retain firm control over their border and asylum regimes. Member states thus initially opted for unilateral decisions at the expense of common strategies. Yet, when faced with the escalating crisis, EU member states eventually agreed on a set of incremental reforms. These changes have taken two main forms: first, introducing new rules and structures on top of existing ones, as in the cases of the 'Dublin Plus' and 'hotspot approach', the EBCG, and the cooperation with third states; and second, developing new tools inspired by previous practices or policies, as illustrated by the EU naval operation *Sophia*.

Conversely, the third scenario has not been supported by sufficient empirical evidence. As the refugee crisis topped the EU policy-making agenda and various solutions competed for political attention, two main windows of opportunity opened up possibilities for policy change. The first window, located in the problem stream, emerged after the boat disasters of April 2015; the second one opened in the political stream following the European Council's meeting in December 2015 and the Dutch Presidency of the Council. The Commission and the European Parliament acted as reform-oriented entrepreneurs and exploited these openings to advance proposals aimed at greater centralization, notably including the creation of the EBCG. While member states agreed on the proposal in a record time, they were not willing to transfer important powers to the supranational level. Overall, these findings are consistent with a number of analyses which explain the EU response to the refugee crisis as *muddling through*—notwithstanding a slight yet unsystematic centralization in border policies (see Hooghe and Marks 2019; Webber 2017).

From a theoretical standpoint, this chapter has demonstrated the relevance of different analytical lenses for examining the effects of the refugee crisis on the EU policies. By focusing on divergent national preferences, intergovernmental bargaining under conditions of asymmetry and weak institutional centralization, LI has provided a compelling account of why member states favored national solutions over supranational policy-making. Meanwhile, HI—particularly through its key concepts of critical junctures and path dependence—has captured the ways in which the member states' past institutional choices have restricted substantial change. Whereas the refugee crisis threatened the weak Dublin/Schengen regime and created possibilities for change, the outcomes remained contingent upon past policies. By contrast, the MSM has failed to predict the crisis outcome, as the modest refurbishment of existing institutions such as Frontex has not translated into a genuine supranationalisation of border governance in the EU. The model, nevertheless, has the merit of drawing attention to the important role of windows of opportunity and supranational entrepreneurship in devising common solutions.

References

Basilien-Gainche, M. (2017). Leave and Let Die: The EU Banopticon Approach to Migrants at Sea. In V. Moreno-Lax & E. Papastavridis (Eds.), *'Boat Refugees' and Migrants at Sea: A Comprehensive Approach. Integrating Maritime Security with Human Rights* (pp. 327–350). Leiden: Brill.

BBC. (2015, April 20). Mediterranean Migrant Deaths: EU Faces Renewed Pressure.

Beach, D. (2016). A Stronger, More Supranational Union. In H. Zimmermann & A. Dür (Eds.), *Key Controversies in European Integration* (pp. 48–54). 2nd edition, London, New York: Palgrave.

Biermann, F., Guérin, N., Jagdhuber, S., Rittberger, B., & Weiss, M. (2017). Political (Non)-Reform in the Euro Crisis And The Refugee Crisis: A Liberal Intergovernmentalist Explanation. *Journal of European Public Policy, 26*(2), 246–266.

Boin, A., Hart, P., Stern, E., & Sundelius, B. (2005). *The Politics of Crisis Management: Public Leadership Under Pressure.* Cambridge: Cambridge University Press.

Borrás, S., & Radaelli, C. M. (2011). The Politics of Governance Architectures: Creation, Change and Effects of the EU Lisbon Strategy. *Journal of European Public Policy, 18*(4), 463–484.

Börzel, T. (2016). From EU Governance of Crisis to Crisis of EU Governance: Regulatory Failure, Redistributive Conflict and Eurosceptic Publics. *Journal of Common Market Studies, 54*(S1), 8–31.

Cairney, P., & Zahariadis, N. (2016). Multiple Streams Approach: A Flexible Metaphor Presents an Opportunity to Operationalize Agenda Setting Processes. In N. Zahariadis (Ed.), *Handbook of Public Policy Agenda Setting* (pp. 87–106). Cheltenham, Northampton: Edward Elgar Publishing.

Capoccia, G., & Kelemen, R. (2007). The Study of Critical Junctures: Theory, Narrative, and Counterfactuals in Historical Institutionalism. *World Politics, 59*(3), 341–369.

Carrera, S., & den Hertog, L. (2016, March). *A European Border and Coast Guard: What's in a Name?* CEPS Paper in Liberty and Security in Europe No. 88. Brussels: CEPS.

Ceccorulli, M. (2019). Back to Schengen: The Collective Securitization of the EU Free-Border Area. *West European Politics, 42*(2), 302–322.

Cohen, M. D., March, J. G., & Olsen, J. P. (1972). A Garbage can Model of Organizational Choice. *Administrative Science Quarterly, 17*(1), 1–25.

Collett, E., & Ahad, A. (2017). *EU Migration Partnerships: A Work in Progress.* Transatlantic Council on Migration and Migration Policy Institute. Available at https://www.migrationpolicy.org/research/eu-migration-partnerships-work-progress. Accessed 14 May 2019.

Council of the EU (2015a). *Council Decision (CFSP) 2015/972 of 22 June 2015 Launching the European Union Military Operation in the Southern Central Mediterranean (EUNAVFOR MED)*, OJ 157/51.

Council. (2015b). *European Council Meeting (17 and 18 December 2015): Conclusions.* EUCO 28/15, 18 December, Brussels.

Council. (2016a). *EU-Turkey Statement.* Press release 144/16, 18 March. Available at https://www.consilium.europa.eu/en/press/press-releases/2016/03/18/eu-turkey-statement/. Accessed 14 May 2019.

Council. (2016b). *Proposal for a Regulation of the European Parliament and of the Council on the European Border and Coast Guard and Repealing Regulation (EC)*

No 2007/2004, *Regulation (EC) No 863/2007 and Council Decision 2005/267/EC-Mandate for negotiations with the European Parliament*. 7649/16, Brussels.
Daley, S. (2015, November 15). Nordic Countries, Overwhelmed by Migrants, Retreat from Generous Traditions. *The New York Times*.
den Hertog, L. (2016, May). *EU Budgetary Responses to the 'Refugee Crisis': Reconfiguring the Funding Landscape* (CEPS Paper No. 93). Brussels: CEPS.
EEAS. (2018). *Strategic Review on EUNAVFOR MED Op Sophia, EUBAM Libya & EU Liaison and Planning Cell*. Working document of the EEAS, EEAS(2018) 835.
European Commission. (2015a). *Communication: A European Agenda on Migration*. COM(2015)240 final, 13 May, Brussels.
European Commission. (2015b). *Standard Eurobarometer 83 Spring 2015: European Citizenship*. 31 July 2015, Brussels. Available at https://europa.eu/rapid/press-release_IP-15-5451_en.htm. Accessed 14 May 2019.
European Commission. (2015c). *Communication on a European Border and Coast Guard and Effective Management of Europe's External Borders*. COM(2015) 673 final, 15 December, Strasbourg.
European Commission. (2015d). *A European Border and Coast Guard to protect Europe's External Borders*. Press release IP/15/6327, 15 December, Strasbourg.
European Commission. (2015e). *Proposal for a Regulation of the European Parliament and of the Council on the European Border and Coast Guard*. COM(2015)671 final, 15 December, Strasbourg.
European Commission. (2016a). *Communication: Final Report on Relocation and Resettlement*. COM(2016)165 final, 16 March, Brussels.
European Commission. (2016b). *Communication on Establishing a New Partnership Framework with Third Countries Under the European Agenda on Migration*. COM(2016)385, 7 June, Strasbourg.
European Commission. (2016c, October 20). *European Council 20–21 October 2016: European Border and Coast Guard—from Policy Decision to Operational Implementation*. Available at https://ec.europa.eu/commission/publications/european-council-20-21-october-2016-european-border-and-coast-guard-policy-decision_ro. Accessed 14 May 2019.
European Commission. (2016d). *Securing Europe's External Borders: Launch of the European Border and Coast Guard Agency*. Press release IP/16/3281, 6 October. Available at https://europa.eu/rapid/press-release_IP-16-3281_en.htm. Accessed 14 May 2019.
Ferguson, Y. H. (2015). Diversity in IR Theory: Pluralism as an Opportunity for Understanding Global Politics. *International Studies Perspectives, 16*(1), 3–12.
Fink, M. (2018). *Frontex and Human Rights: Responsibility in 'Multi-Actor Situations' Under the ECHR and EU Public Liability Law*. Oxford: Oxford University Press.
Genschel, P., & Jachtenfuchs, M. (2018). From Market Integration to Core State Powers: The Eurozone Crisis, the Refugee Crisis and Integration Theory. *Journal of Common Market Studies, 56*(1), 178–196.
Grün, G. C. (2018, November 28). *How The EU's Resettlement Plan is Failing to Meet Its Goal*. DW.
Hooghe, L., & Marks, G. (2019). Grand Theories of European Integration in the Twenty-First Century. *Journal of European Public Policy, 26*(8), 1113–1133.
House of Lords. (2017). *Operation Sophia: A Failed Mission*. 2nd Report, Session 2017–19, HL Paper 5.

IOM. (2015, December 22). *Irregular Migrant, Refugee Arrivals in Europe Top One Million in 2015: IOM..* Available at https://www.iom.int/news/irregular-migrant-refugee-arrivals-europe-top-one-million-2015-iom. Accessed 14 May 2019.

Jones, E., Kelemen, D., & Meunier, S. (2016, July 5). Is Europe failing, or Is it "failing forward"? *The Washington Post.*

Juncker, J. C. (2015). *State of the Union 2015: Time for Honesty, Unity and Solidarity.* Strasbourg, 9 September. Available at: https://europa.eu/rapid/press-release_SPEECH-15-5614_en.htm. Accessed 14 May 2019.

Kingdon, J. W. (1984). *Agendas, Alternatives, and Public Policies.* Boston: Little Brown.

Lavenex, S. (1999). *Safe Third Countries: Extending the EU Asylum and Immigration Policies to Central and Eastern Europe.* Budapest: CEU Press.

Leruth, B., Gänzle, S., & Trondal, J. (2019). Exploring Differentiated Disintegration in a Post-Brexit European Union. *Journal of Common Market Studies, 57*(5), 1013–1030.

Lynggaards, K., Manners, I., & Lofgren, K. (2015). *Research Methods in European Union Studies.* Basingstoke: Palgrave Macmillan.

Mahoney, J. (2002). *Legacies of Liberalism.* Baltimore, MD: Johns Hopkins University Press.

Mahoney, J., & Thelen, K. (2010). A Theory of Gradual Institutional Change. In J. Mahoney & K. Thelen (Eds.), *Explaining Institutional Change: Ambiguity, Agency and Power* (pp. 1–27). New York: Cambridge University Press.

March, J. G., & Olsen, J. P. (1989). *Rediscovering Institutions: The Organizational Basis of Politics.* New York: Free Press.

Monar, J. (2006). The Project of a European Border Guard: Origins, Models and Prospects in the Context of the EU's Integrated External Border Management. In M. Caparini & O. Marenin (Eds.), *Borders and Security Governance: Managing Borders in a Globalised World* (pp. 193–208). Geneva: DCAF.

Moravcsik, A. (1998). *The Choice for Europe: Social Purpose and State Power from Messina to Maastricht.* Ithaca: Cornell University Press.

Moravcsik, A., & Schimmelfennig, F. (2019). Liberal Intergovernmentalism. In A. Wiener, T. Börzel, & T. Risse (Eds.), *European Integration Theory* (pp. 64–84). 3rd edn. Oxford: Oxford University Press.

Moreno-Lax, V. (2018). The EU Humanitarian Border and the Securitization of Human Rights: The "Rescue-Through-Interdiction/Rescue-Without-Protection" Paradigm. *Journal of Common Market Studies, 56*(1), 119–140.

Newsome, A. (2018). Credible Champions? Transatlantic Relations and Human Rights in Refugee Crises. *Journal of European Integration, 40*(5), 587–604.

Niemann, A., & Speyer, J. (2018). A Neofunctionalist Perspective on the European Refugee Crisis: the Case of the European Border and Coast Guard. *Journal of Common Market Studies, 56*(1), 23–43.

Niemann, A., & Zaun, N. (2018). EU Refugee Policies and Politics in Times of Crisis: Theoretical and Empirical Perspectives. *Journal of Common Market Studies, 56*(1), 3–22.

Pawlak, P., & Kurowska, X. (2012). The Fog on the Border: The Fragmentation of the European Union's Border Policies. In C. Kaunert, S., S. Léonard, & P. Pawlak (Eds.), *European Homeland Security. A European strategy in the making?* (pp. 126–144). Abingdon: Routledge.

Pierson, P. (2004). *Politics in Time: History, Institutions and Social Analysis*. Princeton, NJ: Princeton University Press.

Riddervold, M. (2018). A Humanitarian Mission in Line with Human Rights? Assessing Sophia, the EU's Naval Response to the Migration Crisis. *European Security, 27*(2), 158–174.

Ryan, B. (2019). The Migration Crisis and the European Union Border Regime. In M. Cremona & J. Scott (Eds.), *EU Law Beyond EU Borders: The Extraterritorial Reach of EU Law* (pp. 197–228). Oxford: Oxford University Press.

Saurugger, S. (2014). *Theoretical Approaches to European Integration*. London: Palgrave Macmillan.

Schimmelfennig, F. (2018). Liberal Intergovernmentalism and the Crises of the European Union. *Journal of Common Market Studies, 56*(7), 1–17.

Scipioni, M. (2017). *De Novo* Bodies and EU Integration: What is the Story Behind EU Agencies' Expansion? *Journal of Common Market Studies, 56*(4), 768–784.

Scipioni, M. (2018). Failing Forward in EU Migration Policy? EU Integration After the 2015 Asylum and Migration Crisis. *Journal of European Public Policy, 25*(9), 1357–1375.

Tardy, T. (2015, September). *Operation Sophia: Tackling the Refugee Crisis with Military Means, EUISS Brief Issue No. 30*. Available at https://www.iss.europa.eu/content/operation-sophia-tackling-refugee-crisis-military-means. Accessed 4 October 2020.

Trauner, F. (2016). Asylum Policy: The EU's 'Crises' and the Looming Policy Regime Failure. *Journal of European Integration, 38*(3), 311–325.

Tsipras, A. (2015, April 23). *Main Points of the Prime Minister's, Alexis Tsipras. Intervention at the EU Special Summit on Migration*. Available at http://primeminister.gr/english/2015/04/24/main-points-of-the-prime-ministers-alexis-tsipras-intervention-at-the-eu-special-summit-on-migration/. Accessed 14 May 2019.

UNHCR. (2015, July 3). The Sea Route to Europe: The Mediterranean Passage in the Age of Refugees. Available at http://www.unhcr.org/5592bd059.html. Accessed 14 May 2019.

Verdun, A. (2015). A Historical Institutionalist Explanation of the EU's Responses to the Euro Area Financial Crisis. *Journal of European Public Policy, 22*(2), 219–237.

Webber, D. (2017). Can the EU survive? In D. Dinan, N. Nugent, & W. E. Paterson (Eds.), *The European Union in Crisis* (pp. 336–359). London: Palgrave Macmillan.

Williams, A. M., & Baláž, V. (2012). Migration, Risk, and Uncertainty: Theoretical Perspectives. *Population, Space and Place, 18*(2), 167–180.

Zahariadis, N. (2003). *Ambiguity and Choice in Public Policy: Political Decision Making in Modern Democracies*. Washington, DC: Georgetown University Press.

Zahariadis, N. (2008). Ambiguity and Choice in European Public Policy. *Journal of European Public Policy, 15*(4), 514–553.

Zaun, N. (2018). States as Gatekeepers in EU Asylum Politics: Explaining the Non-Adoption of a Refugee Quota System. *Journal of Common Market Studies, 56*(1), 44–62.

CHAPTER 27

Moral Leadership or Moral Hazard? Germany's Response to the Refugee Crisis and Its Impact on European Solidarity

Beverly Crawford

INTRODUCTION

The UK's vote to leave the European Union cast grave doubt on future of the European project. Furthermore, President Trump's assertion that the EU was simply a "vehicle for Germany" underscored a fundamental question that had been brewing for years about Germany's role in Europe and the world. Is the EU simply a "vehicle" to achieve Germany's national interests to the detriment of EU solidarity or has Germany become Europe's benign "leader,"

Although the Schuman Declaration of May 9, 1950 is considered by most scholars to be the founding document of European integration, Robert Schuman did not use the word "integration," but rather the word "solidarity" in his Declaration. I use the word "solidarity" here in the sense that he used it: "Europe will not be made all at once, or according to a single plan. It will be built through concrete achievements... which create a de facto solidarity." Solidarity—or a strong sense of unity—was at the center of the European project, and for Schuman it meant that collective achievements would create European unity and a sense among the members of a common European destiny, which, in turn, would help them to overcome their national rivalries. For Schuman, the new Community would need strong institutions that could create those achievements and overcome collective action problems. My argument is closest to the "liberal institutionalist" school of thought on European integration as indicated by the creation, strength,

B. Crawford (✉)
University of California, Berkeley, Berkeley, CA, USA
e-mail: bev@berkeley.edu

© The Author(s) 2021
M. Riddervold et al. (eds.), *The Palgrave Handbook of EU Crises*, Palgrave Studies in European Union Politics,
https://doi.org/10.1007/978-3-030-51791-5_27

strengthening European integration? I address these questions by examining the case of the European refugee crisis of 2015–2016 and its impact on EU solidarity and strength. At first glance, the refugee crisis and its political aftermath appear to confirm doubts about the EU's future and point to the first scenario put forth by the editors of this volume: a weakening and potential breakup of the European Union. Certainly—thanks, in part, to the refugee influx of 2015–2016—ethnic nationalism has reared its head in most European states, including Germany. The rise of right-wing nationalist parties suggests that many EU member states no longer wish to engage in collective action to solve emergent problems. I would argue, however, that there are signs that recent challenges, including the refugee crisis, can trigger new and innovative solutions to the collective action problem, suggesting at the very least a successful effort to "muddle through" or even movement toward *heading forward*. The refugee crisis did not "break" the EU, but did point to institutional deficiencies that must be addressed in order to ensure that future crises will not weaken the European project.

The essential ingredient determining the direction the EU will take in the future is leadership. In their Introduction, Newsome, Riddervold, and Trondal argue that crisis need not lead to a breakdown but can more deeply entrench existing institutions or even cause deeper integration. My argument here is that crisis itself will do neither. Two additional conditions are necessary for the realization of both scenarios: First, drawing on theories of collective action in large groups,[1] my chapter suggests that both institutional stability in the face of crisis and deeper integration require the leadership of a powerful liberal hegemon to provide public goods that will underwrite institutional legitimacy (Crawford 2007; Newsome 2018).[2] The leader must be strong enough to

---

and scope of EU institutions and governing structures (Gilpin 2001; Eichengreen 2006; Sadeh and Verdun 2009), rather than in the broader sense of political and cultural integration. I use the term "solidarity" to signal a departure from the transactional feature of intergovernmentalism and to critique the liberal institutionalist approach by suggesting that institutions in and of themselves can only lead to deeper integration if "solidarity" is achieved.

[1] In large groups, coordination problems arise because communication among potential participants is difficult and "free riding" is easy. Furthermore, cross-cutting cleavages in large groups cloud an understanding of the "common good" to be pursued, and costs and benefits are diffuse and uncertain. Under these conditions, the incentive to engage in collective action is low. Olson argues these obstacles can be overcome through selective incentives (side payments for cooperation), which increase the benefits of collective action and lower the cost of participation, Strong institutions can provide those incentives. I argue that in the EU, those institutions must be backed by a powerful leader who can pay the lion's share of the costs of the EU's public goods.

[2] Newsome makes an interesting argument about the important role of an *external* hegemon, or leader in fostering transatlantic unity. She argues that the umbrella of U.S. leadership helped to achieve unity in the Kosovo refugee crisis, and it was the absence of U.S. leadership that undermined that unity in the Syrian refugee crisis. It can be argued that the United States as an external hegemon was an important facilitator of European cooperation in the early post-World War II period.

deliver side payments for cooperation (carrots) to both maintain and expand multilateral institutions in a liberal regime like the EU and must avoid the use of coercion (sticks). If the hegemon coerces its partners to adhere to its preferences, particularly if institutions in the targeted policy area are weak, cooperation is endangered. Indeed, a hegemon in Europe who uses its power unwisely can destabilize the European project. Second, European institutions must be constructed at the outset to weather crisis. Weak institutions, with or without a hegemonic leader, can be easily destroyed by crisis.

Germany's commitment to the task of helping to forge European solidarity, both on everyday levels and in the face of crisis, has been crucial to the success of the European Union, both in *muddling through* and moving forward. Long Europe's economic powerhouse, but afraid to utter the words "European hegemon" or even "leader" and the connotations of unwanted European dominance it conjured, Germany played the role of Europe's "patron" of integration behind the scenes, using its greater weight and influence in Europe to provide public goods in the service of forging European solidarity while strongly influencing the terms but avoiding unilateral moves to do so (Crawford 2007). Germany creates conditions necessary for moving forward in achieving cooperation and solidarity across a number of issue areas.

In supporting European cooperation, Germany seemed to look beyond its own parochial interests to exercise "soft" leadership in the EU: first setting examples by making domestic sacrifices for new areas of cooperation within the EU's institutional structure, then asking for burden sharing, and finally, providing carrots, or "side payments" to sweeten the pot, ensuring the stability of existing institutions and expanding the EU's institutional competences. Germany's intent was always to move Europe forward within the EU's institutional constraints.

This "soft leadership" is threatened by two obstacles that have emerged in recent times of crisis. The first is the threat that domestic politics will change Germany's pro-European stance and constrain its benevolent leadership role in Europe. Beginning with the Iraq war in 2003, the rise of mass politics and public awareness of the domestic consequences of foreign policy decisions have begun to directly impact voter preferences (Newman 2015). Euroscepticism in mass protest and in new political parties disrupted but has not erased the entrenched elite consensus on Germany's European role. An anti-European and anti-American agenda began to shape electoral incentives in issue areas such as transatlantic trade (TTIP) (Chan and Crawford 2017), European and global climate policy, European regulations on net neutrality and digital privacy, and Germany's role in the European sovereign debt and refugee crises. A previously insulated pro-European stance of political leaders and Germany's leadership of the EU evidenced a new vulnerability to domestic opposition, threatening the leadership necessary for the EU's stability.

A second factor influencing the success of German leadership is the flawed nature of key EU institutions, created in an era of harmony among member states, but rendered weak and ineffective in times of crisis. Germany is embedded in those institutions. Its "soft" leadership is viable when institutions are strong, but it is constrained when they are weak. In recent years, attempts to expand areas of EU competence have exposed defects in institutional design that exacerbated and even *caused* crises or, at best, left EU policies meaningless in addressing them. Without the backing by an authoritative EU structure, Germany's efforts to create EU policy was ineffective—as sanctions regime in the Ukraine crisis demonstrated. And acting within weak EU institutions, Germany made highly unpopular demands on its partners—as in the Greek and refugee crises—which were perceived as unilateral and coercive, triggering a backlash that threatened EU solidarity.

I illustrate this argument with the case of the European refugee crisis of 2015. Beginning in 2013, refugees from Syria, Iraq, and Afghanistan poured into Europe, seeking asylum. The EU had very limited institutional capacity to adequately respond. Germany's response raises important questions about its influence and role in Europe and about the conditions for European unity. Was German leadership in this crisis effective? Or did its response, coming on the heels of the Greek debt crisis, suggest the reemergence of a powerful and increasingly nationalist Germany on the European continent destined to pull Europe apart in the face of an EU that is not fully equipped to deal with crisis? (Kundnani 2014) Alternatively, did Germany try but fail to strengthen the EU asylum regime?

In addressing these questions, I begin by recalling brief examples in which Germany influenced European solidarity (both strengthening it and undermining it) through the use of example, domestic sacrifice, burden sharing requests, carrots, sticks, agenda setting, and unilateralism. Applying this framework and using the method of process-tracing, I then turn to an analysis of the European refugee crisis of 2015. I conclude that Germany's search for a resolution through both resettlement and restriction critically influenced the strength and scope of European solidarity in both positive and negative ways, but ultimately preventing further EU integration in asylum and migration policy and implementing institutions.

Examples of German Leadership: Successes and Failures in Strengthening EU Solidarity

German leadership in Europe has not *always* been necessary to the European project, and when it was exercised it was usually exercised quietly. The process of European integration through the growth of institutions, expansion of rules ("directives"), and acquisition of new members was most often that of *muddling through* described in Newsome and Riddervold's second scenario. Germany has encouraged this process of European integration by making cooperation easier for its partners *at its own expense*. When it became the largest net contributor to the EU budget in the 1980s, Germany eased the burden of European integration for weaker states. And it remains in this position to this day, consistently paying in almost twice as much as it has received, providing weaker European countries and regions with the lion's share of funding for economic development[3] in order to forge "cohesion" between richer and poorer EU members.

In numerous issue areas, Germany led by domestic example and then asked its EU partners to share the burden and provided incentives to do so. For example, in order to stem the tide of WMD proliferation, it successfully founded a European export control regime by being the first to withhold its own dual-use high technology exports from the market, then asking its European partners to follow suit and share the burden of high technology restrictions (Crawford 2007). Again, in helping to forge a common EU environmental policy, Germany first imposed environmental standards in its own industries and then successfully asked its European partners to impose the same restrictions on their polluting industries. Similarly, Germany, with its leadership in climate-friendly innovations, set a domestic example that served as a basis for the EU's renewable energy directive. In the European Monetary System (EMS) of the 1980s, Germany's Bundesbank provided a model for achieving and maintaining exchange rate stability within a Europe of multiple currencies. Germany encouraged cooperation by spending its reserves to buy falling currencies in order to maintain their value. And the Bundesbank lowered the discount rate to provide counter-cyclical lending to European debtors. Under German leadership, the EMS proved remarkably successful in stabilizing exchange rates and strengthening the single market. When EMU replaced the EMS, Germany insisted that the ECB be created on the model of the Bundesbank and that EMU members adopt the German model of price stability. The rules of monetary union were set according to German preferences. Perhaps it is telling that Germany made few domestic sacrifices to underwrite cooperation in monetary policy, did not contribute to burden sharing, and EMU almost crumbled under the Greek debt burden.

Germany famously undermined European solidarity once in the early years after unification (Crawford 1996). In 1991 a newly united and sovereign Germany extended unilateral diplomatic recognition to Croatia and Slovenia in their attempt to break away from Yugoslavia. The decision was in direct contravention of the preferences of its European partners in their nascent effort not to offer recognition without the promise of securing minority rights. Germany's *unilateral* recognition of Croatia in the absence of that promise was possible because the diplomatic institutional structure of the EU was still weak, and its flaws stymied European unity. Domestic politics shaped Berlin's unilateral decision: the Greens/Bundnis 90 had become an outsized moral force in German politics despite their minimal political power, because they argued vociferously for *self-determination* that had been a long-standing principle in West German foreign policy. Despite the fact that the principle had historically referred to the importance of self-determination *for*

---

[3]In contrast, France and the UK have managed to maintain relative parity between payments and receipts.

those Germans living in the GDR, Green politicians and their supporters used the concept in the wake of German unification to argue persuasively for the self-determination of the Croatian people. Minority rights of Serbs living in Croatia were ignored in that argument. And the ruling CDU/CSU coalition moved toward the Green/Bundnis 90 position to pave the way for unilateral recognition to the detriment of European diplomatic cooperation (Crawford 1996).

The second decade of the twenty-first century presented a series of crises that revealed weaknesses in EU institutions and unmasked Germany's quiet dominance in Europe. The Greek debt crisis exposed this institutional weakness. Beginning with the 2008 financial crisis, the euro's stability was shaken by the absence of Eurozone banking and fiscal regulations to control the accumulation of sovereign debt. In 2010, Greek debt soared, and with the goal of preserving the euro's value, Germany initially paid more than any other member state in financing the costs (Crawford and Rezai 2017). But Germany insisted on in the creation of a weak EMU—without the creation of a transfer and banking union that would assist debtors in shoring up their solidarity with creditors. As a result, Greece needed a "bailout" to prevent bankruptcy. Domestic German opposition to the bailout was so strong that a new political party, Alternative for Germany (AfD) was created in 2013 to oppose both Germany's participation in the common European currency. In order to assuage this domestic political pressure and still maintain the stability of the euro without the institutional support of a transfer or fiscal union, the German government demanded Greek austerity policies in exchange for loans. As the biggest lender and author of austerity demands, Germany unilaterally set the terms of European cooperation and refused to use its resources to provide the stimulus that was necessary to ease the burden of Greek debt. Although Germany was able to gather a coalition of creditors in the ECB to support austerity demands, Eurozone cooperation began to unravel when all debtor countries rebelled. Many observers seized upon the German role in the Greek crisis to raise questions about Germany's more general commitment to solidarity with its European partners. In both the Yugoslav and Greek cases, EU institutions were weak and had difficulty withstanding the crisis. Germany did nothing to strengthen them and was under domestic pressure to take action that undermined EU solidarity.

When the EU imposed sanctions on Russia in 2014 as a response to Russian invasion of Ukraine, Germany shifted its approach and led its European partners in creating a sanctions regime by putting up the highest stakes. At first, Merkel defied powerful domestic exporters by putting them on notice that if EU sanctions were imposed their business with Russia might end. Because Germany's trade with Russia was the largest in the EU, German business had the most to lose if Russia retaliated. Ultimately, though, pressure from the powerful business lobby weakened Merkel's resolve on tough sanctions, and she agreed that existing contracts with Russia would be honored in any sanctions regime. And as a concession to her EU partners, she backed the inclusion of important exceptions to the sanctions: gas imports were exempted (some EU members depend on Russia for 100% of their natural gas needs. France was in the process of completing delivery of two warships commissioned by Russia, and ExxonMobil saw no interruption in its business). These pressures insured that the sanctions would be quite modest—even just symbolic and largely ineffective in actually halting the war—but EU cooperation on imposing them was achieved through consensus under German leadership.

The Refugee Crisis of 2015: Strengthening EU Border Control Within a Weak Common Integration Regime

The world is currently experiencing an unprecedented refugee crisis, with an unparalleled number of people worldwide seeking asylum from persecution and violence. In 2014, 630,000 asylum requests were registered in EU member countries, a number last reached during the 1992 Bosnian war. By November 2015, Germany alone had registered 964,574 asylum seekers (EU Observer 2016). By 2016, 1.3 million asylum seekers would enter Europe. The central objective of EU migration policy has always been to prevent migrants from entering Europe. To that end, the Frontex program was created to coordinate cooperation in border control between member states. In 2005, the EU entered into agreements with Moammar Gadhafi's government to intercept and turn back migrants attempting to make their way through Libya to Europe. The arrangement was partly successful; by 2009, there was a drastic reduction in the flow of migrants to Italy and Malta. But after Gadhafi's 2011 death and the subsequent collapse of the government, migrants again began to surge across the Mediterranean Sea, and Frontex, least of all, proved incapable of stemming the tide. By 2015, migration had become a specific component of the EU's Common Security and Defense Policy with the aim of deploying a military mission that would strengthen EU border protection. Strong borders keeping migrants out remove the refugee problem for those who have promised to not turn them back. Because there is no "refugee visa" that would permit normal air travel, asylum seekers are forced to take the death-defying journey by sea, then enter the EU on the shores of Greece and Italy, or by land, outwitting border control to enter on foot through the barbed wire fences of Bulgaria, Hungary, and Estonia. Between 1994 and 2018, over 34,000 migrants died trying to cross the Mediterranean, attempting to exercise their legal right to asylum.[4] Others died inside refrigerator trucks, and in winter, many died from the cold. If they survive however, once within the EU, the authorities are forbidden by law to send them back to their country of origin if they fear persecution and death. Only then are they entitled to apply for asylum. It is for this reason that the authorities try to keep them out.

[4]https://missingmigrants.iom.int/region/mediterranean?migrant_route%5B%5D=1376.

Aside from asserting the fundamental right to asylum, a common EU asylum policy does not exist. Once within the EU, asylum seekers are dependent on the asylum policies of member states. The EU Dublin Regulation ensures that they must request asylum in the first state they enter, placing the burden of asylum application processing on border states. To assist them in this task, EURODAC was created, which allowed national law enforcement access to the EU database of the fingerprints of asylum seekers. And to further assist them in processing and housing asylum seekers, a small and ineffective European Refugee Fund,[5] a Temporary Protection Directive, and a European Asylum Support Office was created. Other Directives aimed to help family reunification and create more humane refugee reception centers. But as Akasemi Newsome argues, "European institutions and decision-making processes were too weak and fragmented to respond to the human rights crises set in motion by the Syrian civil war" (Newsome 2018).

GERMANY'S INITIAL RESPONSE

The EU's efforts to keep refugees out of Europe had worked in the past, but in the summer of 2015, the sheer number of asylum seekers proved the barriers too weak. As they poured over Europe's borders, Germany's initial response was to welcome them in Germany and to take steps to create and strengthen EU asylum policy, focusing on resettlement. That response followed a familiar pattern: First lead by domestic example, then ask for resettlement burden sharing within the EU, offering carrots and, if necessary, sticks to bring EU partners on board. Angela Merkel openly acknowledged this strategy of leadership: In a speech to the German parliament on September 9, 2015, she stated: "If we show courage and lead the way, a common European approach is more likely." "If Europe fails on the refugee issue, we would lose one of the key reasons for founding a united Europe, namely universal human rights." Germany's strength and power in cooperation with its partners, she stated, would be the key to solving the crisis (Goebel 2015).

Setting an Example: Public Enthusiasm and Industry Support

Three unilateral decisions taken in August and September of 2015 formed Merkel's effort to set a domestic example. First, she unilaterally announced that Germany would keep its borders open to Syrian refugees and pave the way for refugee integration into the labor force. "Those who come to us as asylum seekers or as war refugees need our help so they can integrate quickly," Merkel told the parliament, adding that it would be necessary to help them learn German quickly and find a job. Second, she stopped enforcing the EU's Dublin Agreement which stipulated that refugees must register in the first EU

---

[5] https://ec.europa.eu/home-affairs/financing/fundings/migration-asylum-borders/refugee-fund.

country they entered. Because Hungary, a "frontline state," had refused to process refugee applications, Merkel's suspension of Dublin meant that they could now come directly to Germany and register there. She thus lowered the hurdle for refugees from Syria to enter the EU, going even beyond what was required by the Geneva Convention.

Both UNHCR and Germany's European partners saw this suspension as helpful: UNHCR claimed that the regulation abused the rights and welfare of refugees because they were not always permitted to access an asylum procedure in the "frontline" countries (Fratzke 2015). By June 2015, Hungary was so overburdened with applications that it would not allow applicants back in if they left Hungary. Germany's unilateral suspension of the agreement eased that burden considerably; the European Commission hailed it as an act of European solidarity. Where Germany had been reviled as a *coercive hegemon* with its austerity demands of Greece, it was now praised as a *moral leader*, again seeming to set a strong example for Europe and again, making a domestic sacrifice to demonstrate its resolve. A third decision expanded an interpretation of the German constitution to provide refuge to those fleeing war rather than simply those fleeing persecution, required by the 1951 Refugee Convention. The decision was significant, because German refugee policy had been tightening since the 1980s (Crage 2016).

In tandem with this expansive reinterpretation of the German constitution, Merkel refused to set an upper limit on the number of refugees Germany would accept. In 2015 over 90% of Syrian applicants received three-year residence permits, an important milestone in the asylum application process (Bundesamt für Migration und Flüchtlinge 2016). The majority of the German public was solidly behind Merkel's decisions. With the tragic sight of three-year-old Aylan Kurdi lying face down on a Turkish beach, Germans opened their arms to Syrian refugees. Auguring well for the embrace of refugees was Germany's labor shortage and desperate need for immigrants to contribute to the growing bill for pensions and health care. With its aging population and low birth rate, the German population growth rate is declining, and the number of job vacancies continues to grow (Trading Economics 2019). Chancellor Merkel met with industry leaders to discuss a reform of labor regulations to bring refugees quickly into the labor force. Siemens put together an internship program for refugees, and several other firms followed suit.

Germany and the EU: Seeking Burden Sharing with Sticks and Carrots and Expanding Institutional Competency

Merkel did not stop by setting an example, however. She wanted to take the first step in creating a common asylum policy by requiring her fellow EU member states to share the burden of refugee resettlement. A plan for a common EU asylum policy which she had long encouraged, had been lying dormant for months, and Merkel intended to resurrect it. Her goal was to spread the growing refugee burden by resettling refugees in all EU member states. If successful, this would be the first time that the EU has exercised authority over the relocation and resettlement of refugees, removing that decision-making power from its members.

Angela Merkel fully intended for Germany to lead this burden-sharing effort, stating that "without clear guidance, Europe will probably fail to find a way through this historic crisis." She alluded to the central problem of collective action in the EU by stating further that the mandatory quota system for all was necessary because it would not be possible to simply set a limit and then leave it up to just a few to take in all of the refugees. "This must be a European responsibility, and only then will all member states care about the causes of migration" (*Frankfurter Allgemeine Zeitung* 2015). While recognizing that any relocation plan would not resolve the European refugee crisis, she argued that a distribution of asylum seekers across all member states would galvanize them to find a way to address the conflicts driving people to flee to Europe.

Merkel's first step was to use persuasion and incentives or "side payments" in order to convince EU partners to expand EU competence in migration management. Propelled by the discovery of 71 dead migrants in a refrigeration truck in Austria, and a dead baby on a Turkish beach, the EU Council met in early September 2015, to consider a proposal to redistribute 160,000 refugees throughout member states through a *mandatory* quota system over two years. In order to sweeten the deal, The European Commission proposed to allocate 780 million euros to fund resettlement. Each receiving country would get €6000 per relocated person. In addition, Italy, Greece, and Hungary would get €500 per relocated person, to cover transport costs. Greece—the country most burdened by the influx of migrants—would receive another 5.9 million euros. And finally, the EU commission agreed to reinforce the EU's external borders to reduce the refugee flow.

With opposition among member state to relocation rapidly developing, the EU Commission, moved the debate from the European Council (heads of government), where a unanimous decision was required, to a meeting of the Council of interior ministers, in which qualified majority voting was the rule (European Commission 2015b). There, only a majority approval was needed to implement the plan. To gain that majority, German officials, including Merkel herself, had been lobbying the bigger, more populous states behind the scenes. Merkel would need to have France, Spain, and Italy on board. With Italy already in agreement, she first convinced French President Francois Hollande to relocate some of the refugees there, and to present the mandatory quotas as a joint French-German plan. She then persuaded the Spanish Prime Minister, who had been one of the most hostile opponents of the resettlement plan, to accept quotas (Kellner 2015). Germany would bear the bulk of the refugee burden: Merkel continued to refuse to accept an upper limit on the number of refugees it would take in, although others could set limits. Through her lobbying efforts, a majority voted to accept the resettlement plan.

Phase 2: Germany's Shaky Leadership in the Face of Opposition

But the use of qualified majority voting in this issue would have a negative impact on European solidarity—which, as the Russian sanctions case had demonstrated, is best achieved through consensus. It was clear that the plan could be forced through with the agreement of the large countries; nonetheless, when some members of the Visegrad group balked at mandatory quotas, Merkel's insistence grew harsher and she issued an implicit threat: "What isn't acceptable in my view is that some people are saying this has nothing to do with them. This won't work in the long run. There will be consequences." Thomas de Maiziere, Germany's Minister of the Interior, floated the idea that countries who rejected refugee quotas could receive less EU funding (Goebel 2015). As the largest contributor to the EU budget, would Germany use its EU contribution as a stick to punish those who did not cooperate? Merkel stopped short of this coercive step: the final agreement did not include de Maiziere's proposal.

Dissenters were defiant but for the most part compliant. Poland voted for the plan, and Viktor Orban voted against the plan but announced that his government would abide by the majority vote. Prime Minister Bohuslav Sobotka of the Czech Republic also voted against it, using the moral hazard argument. Nonetheless he agreed to abide by the majority opinion. Romania voted against and declared that it would refuse its allotment. But after the vote, President Klaus Iohannis accepted the majority decision saying: "I think Romania must show solidarity" (Chiriac 2015). Slovakia, declaring that it too would not respect the quotas at all, began legal proceedings at the ECJ protesting the plan. Threatening to leave the EU if his country was forced to take its quota of refugees, Prime Minister Robert Fico told his parliament's EU affairs committee that "As long as I am prime minister, mandatory quotas will not be implemented on Slovak territory." An emboldened Hungary then followed suit, planning to file its own court challenge to the compulsory plan (Robinson and Spiegel 2015).

With only one refusal, then, cooperation was barely achieved on refugee quotas and, implicitly, on the EU's bid to expand its competence into asylum policy. But an EU plan, spearheaded by Chancellor Merkel, for "compulsory and permanent" EU quotas was opposed by more than half of all EU members and landed dead in the water. And after the terror attacks on Paris on November 13, 2015, even opposition to the 2-year plan was bolder and more widespread. Although the plan was implemented and thousands of refugees were resettled, its quotas would not be met.

Before the September vote, Germany had taken another step—placing controls on its border with Austria, allowing in only those seeking asylum—which would strike an additional blow to Merkel's EU-wide effort to assist refugees. The speed and scale of the refugee influx had begun to strain Germany's ability to process applications and care for the asylum seekers. To slow down the flow, the federal government reintroduced temporary border checks on Germany's border with Austria, triggering similar moves in the Netherlands, Slovakia, and Austria. France had been operating police checks on its border with Italy for some time, citing security as a motive. EU interior ministers moved to temporarily suspend the Schengen agreement so that member governments could introduce border controls for up to two years. Germany reinstated the Dublin agreement.

Domestic politics had fueled opposition to the EU's nascent refugee policy in almost all member states. Right-wing populists across Europe used the refugees as scapegoats to stoke fear of Muslims and thereby bolster their political agenda of white supremacy and ethnic nationalism. Hungarian Prime Minister Viktor Orban boasts that he is building an "illiberal state" and has promoted a policy of "preserving ethnic homogeneity," denouncing the EU's migration policy as an effort to destroy Europe. Slovakia's Robert Fico followed suit, and Poland's Jaroslaw Kaczynski, the country's most powerful politician warned that immigrants could bring "parasites...and diseases" to Poland (Wasik and Foy 2017; Buckley and Foy 2016).

Bypassing Dissenters: The "Coalition of the Willing"

Merkel, however, did not give up. Responding to member state opposition to insistence on a mandatory EU resettlement policy, her next step was to bypass the EU dissenters and create what the press called a "coalition of the willing" (of EU member states) to voluntarily resettle Syrian refugees in Europe. Frustrated by the lack of support and the floundering relocation plan,[6] Merkel brought together the leaders of Sweden, Finland, Austria, the Netherlands, Luxembourg, Belgium, *and* Greece to support a voluntary plan for the resettlement of refugees from Turkey to Europe. The plan, presented by the EU Commission as a "recommendation," would create "legal migration" from Turkey to the EU and be accompanied by EU funding in exchange for Turkey's promise to secure its borders to the maximum extent (European Commission 2015a).

The plan would admit and resettle some Syrian refugees in EU countries, but the more crucial outcome was the strengthening of Europe's borders. Merkel persuaded Turkey's Recep Erdogan to seal Turkey's borders and accept the return of refugees who had made it to Greece. Her aim was to ensure that as few refugees as possible embark on the long journey to Europe and that

---

[6] By December, only 159 of the 160,000 refugees landing in Greece and Turkey had been relocated.

those denied asylum—e.g., Afghans, Libyans, and Somalis—could be repatriated to "safe" third countries. Her talks with Erdogan had paved the way for an agreement that emerged from the EU-Turkey summit at the end of November 2015. The EU agreed to provide Turkey with financial aid to improve conditions for Syrian refugees in Turkey, hasten the resettlement of some in Europe, tighten Turkey's borders by increasing coast guard and navy patrols in the Aegean Sea, and tighten border controls between Turkey and Bulgaria. In turn, the EU would loosen visa restrictions on Turks traveling to Europe and would speed up negotiations on Turkey's bid to join the EU. The final agreement—termed a "Statement," was signed on March 18, 2016. It held to these initial conditions and also permitted Greece to return to Turkey "all new irregular migrants" arriving after March 20. In exchange, EU Member States promised to provide Turkey with €6 billion to carry out its part of the bargain. By 2018, the agreement appeared to be holding, according to regular reports from the Commission to the Council and to the Parliament. Deutsche Welle (2018) reported that between 2016, when the agreement was signed and 2018, on its second anniversary, 12,489 Syrians from Turkey were resettled in EU countries. Germany took in the lion's share of 4313, the Netherlands 2608, France 1401 and Finland 1002 (Deutsche Welle 2018) Border controls were tightened. By 2017, the number of refugees who came to Greece via Turkey fell by 97% compared to the period before the agreement (European Commission 2017a).

Domestic Response to Refugees in Germany: A Constraint on German Leadership?

As the Summer of 2015 turned into Autumn, 10,000 asylum seekers a day arrived in Germany, and political opposition to Merkel's open door policy began to brew. It was always lurking in the background: extremists had been setting fire to refugee housing; the anti-euro party, Alternative fuer Deutschland (AFD), which had been losing in the polls once the euro crisis became less acute, quickly became an anti-immigrant party, and it rapidly gained adherents.

Germany would soon lose its status as a country safe from terror attacks, and refugees became the scapegoats. On December 31, 2015, hundreds of men "with an immigration background" gathered in the Cologne train station, harassing and robbing women as they passed by. In the summer of 2016, there were four terror attacks in multiple German cities, killing a total of 10 people; three were committed by asylum seekers. The Christmas market attack on December 19, 2016 left 12 people dead and 56 people wounded. The attacker was a deported immigrant who had slipped back into Germany. Right-wing and euro-skeptic politicians placed the blame on Merkel's refugee policy and the lack of border security.

These attacks brought new restrictions on immigration and asylum in Germany. Although Merkel continued to refuse to set limits on the number of asylum seekers Germany would accept, the government began to restrict the list of countries whose nationals can apply for asylum.[7] Subsequent decisions and laws were constructed to discourage asylum seekers at every stage of the asylum process. Refugees were required to stay longer in initial reception centers and lost their right to work, restricting their freedom of movement; Deportations were expedited and family reunions delayed. In January, 2016 Merkel promised a "national effort" to ensure that people who are not entitled to stay in Germany will be deported, and Germany began to give "financial incentives" to the embassies of some African countries to not only readmit rejected asylum seekers from their own countries but also to readmit—without the refugees' consent—those from third states who had traveled through those countries.

Despite this concerted effort to control migration flows and place new restrictions on asylum seekers in Germany, the populist right continued to gain ground in public protest and in German state and local elections. By 2019, the AfD had won seats in the Bundestag, having surged into third place behind the weakened CDU and the SPD. For the first time since the end of World War II, a far right party had gained enough votes to participate in governing Germany. Its presence in the Bundestag can be directly attributed to its cunning ability to engender fear and turn an underlying discomfort with Merkel's immigration policies into populist hatred of immigrants. In October 2018, Merkel announced that she would resign as the head of her party and would not seek re-election in 2021.

The EU Muddled Through

By July 2017, the EU Commission reported that 24,676 refugees had been relocated from Greece and Italy to other member countries under the mandatory 2-year resettlement plan (EU Commission 2017b). By 2018, no state except Malta had reached its relocation commitment. The EU relocation program was formally ended in 2017, but 20 member states had answered European Commission call to resettle at least "50,000 persons in need of international protection" by October 2019. By May, 2018, 34,689 had been resettled (European Migration Law.eu 2018). The EU continues to muddle through on resettlement, but as of mid-2019 there is no common asylum policy in sight. What these numbers suggest, however, is that although institutions making up a potential common asylum policy may be far from complete, the EU may nonetheless be "failing forward" toward integration in this issue area. Indeed, member states failed in the initial effort to resettle 160,000 refugees from Greece and Italy. But they settled on the lowest common

---

[7] In October 2015, Kosovo, Montenegro, and Albania were placed on a list of "safe countries of origin," and in February 2016, the list was expanded to include Algeria, Morocco and Tunisia. This meant that refugees from those countries would have little chance of winning asylum.

denominator—taking in as few refugees as possible, suggesting piecemeal steps toward a common asylum policy.

Taking an organizational-institutional approach to EU integration—defined above as the strengthening of EU institutions and governing structures—I have shown that one of Germany's attempted solutions to the EU refugee crisis of 2015–2016 creating a mandatory resettlement policy strained EU solidarity. In 1950 Schuman predicted that without solidarity among EU member states, institutional integration could not advance. True to his prediction, EU integration in migration and asylum policy and its implementation structures beyond the strengthening of external border structures was stymied. Resettlement did continue under the EU-Turkey Statement, but the process was not institutionalized. Therefore, the EU muddled through the crisis, reinforcing "well-known organizational solutions (border controls) and governing arrangements" (Newsome and Rittervold forthcoming) without a profound effect on governance institutions.

Conclusion

This chapter traced the impact of Europe's "refugee crisis" on European solidarity in achieving collective action in European Union and Germany's role in attempting to expand EU institutions to resettle refugees and strengthen efforts to block them from entering Europe. Following a familiar pattern of leading by example, asking for burden sharing, offering side payments for cooperation, and unilateral action, Germany took the lead in attempting to create an EU refugee resettlement regime. But this time Merkel went further, coercing acceptance of a *compulsory* program of resettlement to be imposed on its European partners. This "stick," of mandatory resettlement drove a wedge between the Eastern and Western members of the EU, weakening solidarity. The refugee crisis itself strained the bonds holding the European partners together. But compulsory quotas strained those bonds even further. While Germany demanded *too much* solidarity, its partners offered *too little*. The refugee crisis did not "break" the EU, but did point to institutional deficiencies that must be addressed in order to ensure that future crises will not weaken the European project.

German leadership in Europe floundered in the refugee crisis. Domestic politics both in Germany and across Europe certainly played a role in the EU decision to strengthen its external borders and prevent the expansion of EU asylum policy. But German leadership in Europe is less constrained by domestic politics than it is by its institutional *embeddedness* in European Union. The refugee crisis, like the euro crisis before it, exposes the weakness or "incompleteness" of EU institutions as it tried to expand its competence without strengthening the structures required to do so. And because Germany is embedded in those weak institutions, its ability to lead is limited. Its use of coercive power in Europe will only serve to undermine Europe's solidarity.

References

Buckley, N., & Foy, H. (2016, August 29). The Visegrad Four: Brussels' Eastern Critics. *Financial Times*. https://www.ft.com/content/e99d3b12-6b96-11e6-a0b1-d87a9fea034f. Accessed 15 March 2017.

Bundesamt für Migration und Flüchtlinge. (2016, December). *Asylgeschäftsstatistik*. https://www.bamf.de/SharedDocs/Anlagen/DE/Downloads/Infothek/Statistik/Asyl/201612-statistik-anlage-asyl-geschaeftsbericht.pdf?__blob=publicationFile. Accessed 20 March 2017.

Chan, A., & Crawford, B. (2017). The Puzzle of Public Opposition to TTIP in Germany. *Business and Politics, 19*(4), 683–708. https://doi.org/10.1017/bap.2017.32.

Chiriac, M. (2015, September 24). Romania Changes Heart on Refugee Quota. *Balkan Insight*. http://www.balkaninsight.com/en/article/romania-supports-now-eu-refugee-decision-09-23-2015. Accessed 4 February 2017.

Crage, S. (2016). The More Things Change ... Developments in German Practices Towards Asylum Seekers and Recognized Refugees. *German Politics, 25*(3), 344–365.

Crawford, B. (1996). Explaining Defection from International Cooperation: Germany's Unilateral Recognition of Croatia. *World Politics, 48*, 482–521.

Crawford, B. (2007). *Power and German Foreign Policy: Embedded Hegemony in Europe*. London: Palgrave Macmillan.

Crawford, B., & Rezai, A. (2017). The Euro, the Gold Standard, and German Power: A Cautionary Tale. *German Politics and Society, 35*(4), 77–104.

Deutsche Welle. (2018, March 18). *The EU-Turkey Refugee Agreement: A Review*. https://www.dw.com/en/the-eu-turkey-refugee-agreement-a-review/a-43028295. Accessed 19 August 2019.

Eichengreen, B. (2006). European Integration. In B. Weingast & D. Wittman (Eds.), *Oxford Handbook of Political Economy* (pp. 799–813). Oxford: Oxford University Press.

EU Observer. (2016, January 19). *EU Expects 3mn Migrants by 2017*. https://euobserver.com/migration/130979. Accessed 15 March 2017.

European Commission. (2015a, September 22). *Statement Following the Decision at the Extraordinary Justice and Home Affairs Council to Relocate 120,000 Refugees*. http://europa.eu/rapid/press-release_STATEMENT-15-5697_en.htm. Accessed 3 February 2017.

European Commission. (2015b, December 15). *Commission Presents Recommendation for a Voluntary Humanitarian Admission Scheme with Turkey for Refugees from Syria*. http://europa.eu/rapid/press-release_IP-15-6330_en.htm. Accessed 4 February 2017.

European Commission. (2017a). Report from the Commission to the European Parliament, the European Council and the Council. *Sixth Report on the Progress Made in the Implementation of the EU-Turkey Statement COM/2017/0323 Final*. https://eur-lex.europa.eu/legal-content/EN/TXT/?qid=1565826596342&uri=CELEX:52017DC0323. Accessed 10 August 2019.

European Commission. (2017b). Report from the Commission to the European Parliament, the European Council, and the Council. *Fourteenth Report on Relocations and Resettlement COM/2017/405 Final*. http://www.europeanmigrati onlaw.eu/documents/COM(2017)405-14th%20Report%20on%20Relocation.PDF. Accessed 12 August 2019.

European Migration Law.eu. (2018, April 3). *Relocation of Asylum Seekers from Italy and Greece*. http://www.europeanmigrationlaw.eu/en/articles/datas/reloca tion-from-italy-and-greece.html. Accessed 14 August 2019.

Frankfurter Allgemeine Zeitung. (2015, September 11). *Merkel: Grundrecht auf Asyl kennt keine Obergrenze*. http://www.faz.net/aktuell/politik/fluechtlingskrise/ merkel-grundrecht-auf-asyl-kennt-keine-obergrenze-13797029.html. Accessed 15 March 2017.

Fratzke, S. (2015, March). Not Adding Up: The Fading Promise of Europe's Dublin System. *Migration Policy Institute Working Paper*. https://www.migrationpolicy. org/research/not-adding-fading-promise-europes-dublin-system. Accessed 17 May 2017.

Gilpin, R. (2001). *Global Political Economy: Understanding the International Economic Order*. Princeton: Princeton University Press.

Goebel, N. (2015, September 9). Germany Must 'Lead the Way' in Refugee Crisis. *Deutsche Welle*. http://www.dw.com/en/germany-must-lead-the-way-in-refugee-cri sis/a-18702937. Accessed 5 March 2017.

Kellner, H. (2015, September 6). Druck von der Straße wächst. *Deutschlandfunk*. http://www.deutschlandfunk.de/spanien-und-die-fluechtlinge-druck-von-der-str asse-waechst.795.de.html?dram:article_id=330366. Accessed 1 April 2017.

Kundnani, H. (2014). *The Paradox of German Power*. London: Oxford University Press.

Newman, A. (2015). The New German Problem: Mass Politics and the Transatlantic Partnership. *Georgetown Center for German and European Studies* (Working Paper).

Newsome, A. (2018). Credible Champions? Transatlantic Relations and Human Rights in Refugee Crises. *Journal of European Integration, 40*(5), 587–604. https://doi.org/10.1080/07036337.2018.1487964.

Newsome, A., Riddervold, M., & Trondal, J. (forthcoming). *Introduction: Handbook on EU Crisis*. London: Palgrave Macmillan.

Robinson, D., & Spiegel, P. (2015, September 22). EU Ministers Force Through Refugee Quota Plan. *Financial Times*.

Sadeh, T., & Verdun, A. (2009). Explaining Europe's Monetary Union: A Survey of the Literature. *International Studies Review, 11*, 277–301.

Trading Economics. (2019). https://tradingeconomics.com/germany/job-vacancies. Accessed 22 August 2019.

Wasik, Z., & Foy, H. (2017, September 14). Immigrants Pay for Poland's Fiery Rhetoric. *Financial Times*. https://www.ft.com/content/9c59ba54-6ad5-11e6-a0b1-d87a9fea034f. Accessed 16 March 2017.

CHAPTER 28

Brexit: An Introduction

Jarle Trondal, Marianne Riddervold, and Akasemi Newsome

This section focuses on the consequences of the United Kingdom (UK)'s decision to leave the EU. One ambition of the chapters is to probe why Brexit took place, and what impact—integrative or disintegrative—it is likely to have on the post-Brexit EU. Chapters acknowledge that most will depend on the outcome of the UK–EU negotiations as Brexit will be a ground-breaking and thus unpredictable case of differentiated disintegration in the years to come (Leruth et al. 2019). Years have already passed since the referendum and it is unclear what kind of future relationship the UK will get with the EU as a whole as well as in specific policy areas. An equally unclear question is what

---

J. Trondal (✉)
Department of Political Science and Management, University of Agder, Kristiansand, Norway
e-mail: jarle.trondal@uia.no

ARENA - Centre for European Studies, University of Oslo, Oslo, Norway

M. Riddervold · A. Newsome
Inland School of Business and Social Sciences, Inland University, Rena and Lillehammer, Norway
e-mail: marianne.riddervold@inn.no

Institute of European Studies, University of California, Berkeley, CA, USA

A. Newsome
e-mail: akasemi@berkeley.edu

M. Riddervold
The Norwegian Institute of International Affairs (NUPI), Oslo, Norway

© The Author(s) 2021
M. Riddervold et al. (eds.), *The Palgrave Handbook of EU Crises*, Palgrave Studies in European Union Politics, https://doi.org/10.1007/978-3-030-51791-5_28

consequences Brexit will have for the EU and European integration. Brexit represents the first time a member state has sought to withdraw from the Union by triggering Article 50 of the Treaty on EU. The lack of precedent creates a series of challenges for both parties, as discussed in this section. It is thus likely to take years before scholars and practitioners can grasp the impact of Brexit for all actors involved and determine whether it will trigger an integration slow-down (Scenario 1), accelerated integration (Scenario 3), or merely path-dependent processes of *muddling through* (Scenario 2) (see Chapter 1 this volume).

Situations like Brexit pave the way for analyzing continuity and change as well as mechanisms that might determine causation. As politicians are in search of new and diverse forms of political association in Europe, analysts are in search of categories and mechanisms (Olsen 2007). Scholars have already attempted to explain how and why "Brexit" happened, as well as its most likely consequences for the future of the EU (e.g., Gänzle et al. 2020). Gänzle et al. (2020) categorize Brexit as a ground-breaking case of *differentiated disintegration*. This section offers contributions that aim to stimulate debate on how Brexit might be understood and analyzed. The Brexit case is interesting for understanding how strongly integrated member states are into EU institutions and processes. Will Brexit cause breakdown, *heading forward* or merely continuous *muddling through*? If conceived of as a deeply integrated politico-administrative order that spans levels of governance, one could imagine that administrative units such as agencies withdraw from cooperation within a member state, or that a member state withdraws from formal membership in the EU whilesome domestic agencies keep their membership in EU administrative networks. This idea is captured by the public administration approach to European integration that sees the Union as consisting of interconnected sets of agencies, ministries and regulatory networks (e.g., Bauer and Trondal 2015; Egeberg 2006; Heidbreder 2015; Knill and Bauer 2016). This account might consider Brexit to be a much less radical breakdown since patterns of administrative integration might coexist with processes of political disintegration. This account would parallel the idea of integration by *muddling through*, as outlined in Chapter 1 of this volume. By contrast, theoretical accounts that see the Union as less deeply integrated, such as intergovernmentalist approaches, are more likely to view Brexit as a radical—and member state driven—process geared toward integration breakdown (Scenario 1). Consequently, the case of Brexit serves as a living research laboratory in which we can examine theories of European (dis)integration. Are they equally able to explain patterns of disintegration and integration, or do we need new theoretical and conceptual tools in order to explain European integration in reverse gear (Radaelli and Salter 2020)?

THE EU'S RESPONSE TO BREXIT

This chapter by *Tim Oliver and Benjamin Martill* provides an overview of the criticisms levelled against the EU's approach more than a coherent case against it. As made clear in the introduction to this handbook, the overall aim is to raise questions about the EU's approach rather than to assess the effectiveness and legitimacy of the EU's response. The focus of the chapter is neither on any one part of the EU, such as the European Commission or specific member states. The chapter also defines Brexit carefully, since the (common) failure to do so can lead to significant conceptual errors. Brexit is thus not merely seen as a single event such as the referendum on June 23, 2016, or as a process such as those undertaken through the two-year timeframe of article 50, or any one deal such as the 2018 Withdrawal Agreement negotiated between the UK and EU. Nor is it only about the UK. Brexit is examined as a *series of overlapping processes* and debates involving multiple actors in Britain, in the EU, in the rest of Europe, as well as globally. These processes are also analyzed across various timeframes. This chapter breaks down the EU's mistakes on Brexit into three broad groups: misguiding Britain over its place in the EU; misreading what Brexit means; and mishandling how Brexit has been negotiated.

THE SECURITY AND DEFENSE ASPECT OF BREXIT: ALTERING THE THIRD COUNTRY BALANCE?

Øyvind Syvendsen discusses how Brexit changes the institutional and political dynamics in European security and defense cooperation. At the same time, security and defense cooperation in Europe more broadly is differentiated and therefore the potential outcome of the Brexit process for the future EU–UK relationship has generated massive scholarly interest as to what form future cooperation between the two parties is likely to take, and the potential consequences that Brexit will produce. The problem refers to *external differentiation* of the Union, and the chapter answers two questions in this regard: What room is there for the inclusion of third countries in EU security and defense initiatives, and how might Brexit alter the politics of such inclusion? The chapter turns to the practical power politics of third country participation in EU security and defense and makes a comparison between past EU practices toward Norway and the emerging question of the UK's future status as a third country. The chapter argues that whereas the EU internally heads forward on security and defence (Scenario 3), how it deals with like-minded third country partners is likely to be characterized by a continuation of the existing *modus operandi*, or *muddling through* as outlined in Chapter 1 to this volume (Scenario 2). The chapter concludes by arguing that the literature should continue to ask questions about the role of third countries in EU security and defense and their potential decision-shaping and making, beyond the EU as a closed system of governance.

REFERENCES

Bauer, M. W., & Trondal, J. (Eds.). (2015). *The Palgrave Handbook of the European Administrative System*. Houndmills: Palgrave Macmillan.

Egeberg, M. (Ed.). (2006). *Multilevel Union Administration*. Houndmills: Palgrave Macmillan.

Gänzle, S., Leruth, B., & Trondal, J. (Eds.). (2020). *Differentiated Integration and Disintegration in a Post-Brexit Era*. London: Routledge.

Heidbreder, E. G. (2015). Horizontal Capacity Pooling: Direct, Decentralized, Joint Policy Execution. In M. W. Bauer & J. Trondal (Eds.), *The Palgrave Handbook of the European Administrative System*. Houndmills: Palgrave Macmillan.

Knill, C., & Bauer, M. W. (2016). Policy-Making by International Public Administrations: Concepts, Causes and Consequences. *Journal of European Public Policy, 23*(7), 949–959.

Leruth, B., Gänzle, S., & Trondal, J. (2019). Exploring Differentiated Disintegration in a Post-Brexit European Union. *Journal of Common Market Studies, 57*(5), 1013–1030.

Olsen, J. P. (2007). *Europe in Search of Political Order*. Oxford: Oxford University Press.

Radaelli, C. M., & Salter, J.-P. (2020). Europeanization in Reverse Gear? In S. Gänzle, B. Leruth, & J. Trondal (Eds.), *Differentiated Integration and Disintegration in a Post-Brexit Era*. London: Routledge.

CHAPTER 29

The EU's Response to Brexit

Benjamin Martill and Tim Oliver

INTRODUCTION

For an organization so often the subject of criticism, the EU has been largely applauded for its response to Brexit. Compared to how it has handled many of the other crises covered in this book, on Brexit the EU has appeared united, focused, and well prepared. Of course, the British Government and British Eurosceptics would be the first to disagree. But if the EU's approach has received little by way of criticism, it is largely because the focus has been on Britain's dire handling of Brexit. David Cameron's decision to call a referendum, and the way he went about handling the preparation for it, have been the subject of an array of criticisms that connects to longer-running critiques of UK approaches to the EU (Glencross 2018). Britain's strategy for handling Brexit, or often the lack of, has also been regularly highlighted. Resignations, unsustainable and ill-thought through red-lines, and reactionary rather than careful approaches have tended to dominate. It consumed Theresa May's premiership, leaving her and many in her government and beyond confounded and humiliated. It has turned Britain into a country of 'lions misled by donkeys' (Oliver 2017b). This is not to say there have not been times when the UK has performed well with Brexit. However, overall things

---

B. Martill (✉)
London School of Economics and Political Science, London, UK
e-mail: benjamin.martill@ucl.ac.uk

T. Oliver
Loughborough University, Loughborough, UK
e-mail: t.l.oliver@lse.ac.uk

© The Author(s) 2021
M. Riddervold et al. (eds.), *The Palgrave Handbook of EU Crises*,
Palgrave Studies in European Union Politics,
https://doi.org/10.1007/978-3-030-51791-5_29

have been so bad that some UK officials are reported to have outlined in writing their concerns to ministers so as to ensure they have a defense in any post-Brexit inquiry (Johnstone and Schofield 2017).

That does not mean, however, that the EU's own approach should be spared from critical analysis, which is the approach this chapter takes. This is an important objective, for a number of reasons. The first is practical. The EU, like any other organization, has the capacity to learn from its mistakes. And if the Union's propensity to muddle through complex political and economic crises is anything to go by, there have been plenty of them (see Chapter 1, this volume). Understanding what went wrong in its approach to Brexit will allow the EU to learn important lessons and to adapt its approach to future events. The EU's approach has, like the UK's, been defined by its negotiators and institutions navigating their way through an unprecedented development. Their mistakes and the lessons to be learnt can provide an important learning experience for the future of Union. This is especially relevant in the current context where, whatever the fate of the withdrawal negotiations, the UK and the EU are likely to be locked into recurrent negotiations for many years to come. The second concerns politics. Brexit has injected an unhealthy dose of partisanship into the analysis and assessment of EU policies and priorities, such that Brussels can do no wrong in the eyes of "Remainers" (and vice versa for Leavers). Long-time critics of EU policies are forced onto the defensive, given the ease with which critical perspectives can be co-opted into arguments in favor of leaving the EU. (One may reasonably argue the same can be said for Leavers who continue to express value in some of the EU's achievements). This is problematic, at any rate, since it closes down avenues of legitimate criticism and risks politicising scholarship on European politics. The third reason to subject the EU's Brexit approach to critical examination is the contribution it can make to emerging topics in the study of European integration and EU politics. The study of Brexit from a European perspective, for instance, has often lagged behind domestic-focused accounts, at least in British academia. While a number of recent works have examined the consequences of Brexit for the EU (Martill and Staiger 2018b; Oliver 2018a), far less has been written on the EU's handling of the Brexit process. This book, with its three scenarios, offers a way of locating Brexit in broader questions about the future of European integration, something we return to briefly in the conclusion.

Many of the criticisms outlined here are, it must be said, subjective, with some clearly contradicting others. They are also time-sensitive, with a fuller analysis of the EU's—and UK's—approaches to Brexit being only possible at some distant future date. And they are relative, in the sense that—however strong the criticism levelled at the EU—other actors, including the UK, may well be subject to similar criticisms or stronger. This chapter therefore provides an overview of the criticisms leveled against the EU's approach more than a coherent case against it. As made clear in the introduction to this handbook, the overall aim is to raise questions about the EU's approach rather than to assess the effectiveness and legitimacy of the EU's response. Nor is the focus here on any one part of the EU, such as the European Commission or specific member states. We must also take care to define Brexit carefully, since the (common) failure to do so can lead to significant conceptual errors. Brexit is not a single event such as the referendum on June 23, 2016, a formal set of processes such as those undertaken through the two-year timeframe of article 50, or any one deal such as the 2018 Withdrawal Agreement negotiated between the UK and EU. Nor is it only about the UK. Brexit is a series of overlapping processes and debates taking place at and involving multiple actors in Britain, the remaining EU, the rest of Europe, and around the world. These processes are unfolding over various timeframes.

This chapter breaks down the EU's mistakes on Brexit into three broad groups: misguiding Britain over its place in the EU; misreading what Brexit means; and mishandling how Brexit has been negotiated.

Misguiding Britain

One way in which the EU can be viewed as somewhat less than perfect is in the messages it has sent the UK both before and after the referendum. Confusion at the EU level over the requirements (and nature) of membership, and where it sees the post-Brexit relationship going, has led to the EU misguiding the UK in a number of respects.

First, the EU has arguably misguided the UK over the requirements of EU membership and the extent to which these have changed over the years. As is well known, the basis of the UK's membership has differed in key respects from those of other member states. The UK has opt-outs from Schengen and the Euro, a distinct(ly lower) balance of financial returns from a number of EU policy areas (Felbermayr et al. 2018), a distinct national economic model (Hall and Soskice 2001), and—of course—a distinct view of integration as a principally economic venture (De Búrca 2018: 49). Within these strictures the UK has been more of a team player than has often been acknowledged. In some areas the UK was above the EU average, for example in its enviable record in enforcing EU law (Mastenbroek 2005: 1109). And, while Britain might have been "*an* awkward partner" (George 1998), it was not "*the* awkward partner" (a frequent misquote of the title of Stephen George's 1998 book), with lots of EU member states being difficult. Arguably it has become more challenging over the years to be a member of the EU while retaining this profile, since it fits awkwardly with European initiatives for the Eurozone and security and defence (e.g., Thompson 2017). Yet the EU has never taken sufficient measures to address the problems of varying levels of commitment, nor made clear to the UK how viable its membership would continue to be on the terms it had always set out. Ideas of a multispeed Europe have been much spoken about, but they have not lead to meaningful reforms, and case-by-case opt-outs and *muddling through* continue to inform the EU's *modus operandi*. Moreover, the failure of the renegotiation—indeed its very need—tells of how the EU has struggled to accept that some member states such as Britain would probably never join projects such as the Euro. In a sense, the failure to adapt to retain the participation of a large and important Member State may be seen as a reflection of the EU's inability to decide what to with those players not committed to further centralization and harmonization.

Second, the EU has misguided the UK in the post-Brexit era over where it sees the future relationship going. The EU, like the UK, has struggled to interpret what Brexit should mean in terms of some form of final destination. Brexit forms part of wider and difficult questions about where the EU is headed in terms of its own development and place in Europe. Within EU studies, it has reinvigorated discussion of "differentiated integration" (Chopin and Lequesne 2016; Hodson and Puetter 2018: 466; Martill and Sus 2018; Schimmelfennig 2018), and of the value of different forms of association, which will likely continue to proliferate post-Brexit. Proposals such as the "Continental Partnership" (Pisani-Ferry et al. 2017), which have tried to identify alternatives to exiting models of pan-European collaboration, have been accused of arguing for the EU to change to fit a departing UK's needs. Refusing to dance to a Brexit tune is understandable. Dismissing such proposals while offering no alternatives, however, does little to move the EU forward in facing a problem that won't go away. Something bespoke will inevitably be created to fit the UK, even if this evolves over a medium to longer-term timeframe. There is also, in this respect, a discernible hypocrisy in the EU's approach to agenda setting. Where it has benefited Brussels the reins have been tightly held, but in other respects—for example, over the Irish border—responsibility for devising workable solutions has been delegated to the UK. In other areas, intra-EU disagreement has caused further confusion. Asked to propose guidelines on the future security and defence relationship, for example, and reliably informed by member states that the EU27 wanted to keep the UK close in this respect, Britain's proposals were shot down by the Commission on the grounds they undermined the EU's decision-making autonomy and risked moral hazard (European Parliament 2018). This has not helped British politicians and civil servants to discern what the EU position is, and what may or may not be on the cards, ironically the very same concern Brussels has made of the British position. Ultimately, Brussels has been forceful where it knows specifically what it wants, but in other respects has been content either to kick the can down the road, or to hand the agency to the Brits, which does not help in the search for long-term solutions.

Misreading Brexit

Interpreting Brexit has been challenging for all involved because Britain's vote to Leave came as a shock to many, not least to many in the UK itself. It has provoked a mix of anger and regrets across the rest of the EU, but also hopes for both pro-Europeans and Eurosceptics. A number of mistaken assumptions can be identified in the EU's perceptions of the Brexit vote and its implications for the Union, all of which lead to a more optimistic—skeptics may say naïve—interpretation of the vote's consequences.

First, the EU has tended to downplay the potential disintegrative effects of Brexit by focusing on the immediate aftermath of the vote rather than thinking about the Brexit moment itself. Since the 2016 referendum, opinion polling across the EU has shown an increase in support for the EU after Britain's vote (Stokes et al. 2017). EU officials speak of unprecedented unity among the member states. This can be taken as a sign the EU need not worry about Brexit triggering some form of domino effect that would lead to the unravelling of the EU. And yet, as noted in the introduction, a common failure when thinking about Brexit is to see it as an event as opposed to a series of processes, some of which are potentially open-ended. In other words, some in the EU have forgotten that Brexit is for life, not just for the two-year timeframe provided in article 50. Britain's position vis-à-vis the EU in a decade or more may be more interconnected to the EU, complex and weaker than will appear on the surface. To publics elsewhere in the EU, however, that may appear a technicality if yet another crisis such as in the Eurozone engulfs the EU. The effect of Brexit on the EU will therefore be shaped by two effects. First, the success or failure of the UK outside the EU and how this is perceived by the publics and elites of the remaining member states. The empirical basis for this has not yet occurred, since the UK remains (at the time of writing) a member of the Union. Second, the EU's own ability to manage the systemic challenges it faces and so demonstrate its utility to EU citizens (Oliver 2018b). The EU should be careful not to assume the UK's problems will act as a long-standing deterrent to the publics of other member states. Moreover, many of the ostensibly positive effects unleashed by the vote are temporary, and this includes both the sense of existential crisis engendered among European citizens, as well as the easy agreement between the member states on the terms of British withdrawal, a question with limited scope for the kind of distributional bickering which often characterizes EU politics.

Second, Brexit has seemingly reinforced two long-standing myths regarding the nature of integration: first, that crises are what drives European integration; and second, that the greatest inhibitor of further integration has been the veto (or the threat of one) by the British. The idea of crisis as a driver of integration is deeply woven into the narrative of the EU, and there is some evidence that integration has indeed resulted from specific times of crisis (Börzel 2018: 475; Lefkofridi and Schmitter 2015: 4; Mény 2014: 1350). But as Dinan et al. (2017) has shown, closer inspection raises questions about the link between crises and European integration. Integration has been the result of a variety of factors, with crises sometimes playing a part, but by no means being the key factor and sometimes playing little or no part at all. Giving credit to crises distracts from longer-running developments and work that integration has depended on. Moreover, arguably only certain kinds of crises—those that highlight policy failures from incomplete contracts—facilitate further integration. Other crises, like Brexit, which call into question the basis on which the

Union is constructed, are less likely to spur greater integration. The idea of the British veto as a brake on integration also has a long lineage, and many continue to view the UK in these somewhat Gaullist terms. Yet here again the record bears close scrutiny. British efforts were integral to a number of initiatives which ultimately fostered greater integration, including both enlargement and the effort to complete the single market in the mid-1980s (Oliver 2017a: 522). Moreover, it is the worst kept secret in Brussels that other skeptical member states hid behind automatic British vetoes of initiatives they opposed, and these disagreements will become increasingly stark after Brexit.

Third, the EU downplayed the likelihood of Brexit occurring, and continues to do so to this day. Prior to the referendum, with the exception of the Irish Government (Oliver 2016: 1322), large parts of the EU's leadership and those who debate and discuss it, failed to take the idea of Brexit as seriously as they could have. To some extent, the vote shattered illusions in Brussels that the EU was on a firm and unstoppable path to "ever closer Union." However, something of a taboo surrounding the idea of a member leaving has persisted, helping to underpin the assumption that the UK is ultimately going to stay. Or, if not, that it would quickly seek to rejoin once it learned the error of its ways. This is a view frequently voiced in Brussels and it does not tally well with the stark reality of British politics. Both Theresa May and Boris Johnson committed to respecting the result of the referendum, the proportion of Leave supporters has not reduced significantly in the post-referendum period, the new Brexit party polled extraordinarily well on a "no deal" platform, and the government's credibility seems tied to implementing the Brexit mandate. Moreover, rejoining would be difficult. It would require a further referendum, a tortuous accession process, and much loss of face. Any pro-EU campaign would face an uphill struggle given that the underlying forces that drove the Leave vote have not disappeared. It would require the UK to rejoin a very different Union, in a worse position than it had occupied before (Begg 2018) but would likely require a political narrative stressing that the EU had changed to fit Britain's needs, and not the other way around. The persistent belief in some quarters of Europe that Britain will not leave, cannot leave, or would in any case swiftly rejoin is hubristic, and ignores important aspects of UK politics. It also reflects long-standing beliefs about the inexorable progress of European integration which may no longer hold true in an era of increasing Euroscepticism. Indeed, it may well be that disintegration is the order of the day; a difficult reality for the EU to get its head around (e.g., Jones 2018; Webber 2013).

Fourth, Brexit has been viewed as an anomaly, temporally and geographically, and with causes located in the specificities of British politics and society, when in reality Brexit highlights a number of broader failings in European politics. While the decision taken in the vote rested on a number of contingent and local factors, perceived European policy failings also loomed large. Frequent mention of the EU's response to the Eurozone crisis, or its "bullying" of the Greeks, can be found in the literature of the Leave campaign, as can mention of well-known distortions in the EU budget alongside familiar concerns about the lack of democratic oversight in the Commission (which the recent failed Spitzenkandidaten process has recently highlighted). Survey data, interestingly, shows that even Remain supporters held less than positive views of the EU (Clarke et al. 2017), suggesting that selling Europe is a difficult task in the present circumstances. Moreover, if EU policy failures featured in—and influenced—the campaign in the UK, they may also be seen as contributing to a broader malaise in European politics which is treated separately from Brexit discussions in Brussels yet which bears some striking similarities. Discontent with migration is rising across the Union, populist parties are capitalizing on distrust of mainstream politicians and the decline of social democratic parties, and in many countries the fallout from the great recession has resulted in austerity, wage stagnation and economic underperformance. In this environment, discontent with the EU (deserved or not) has been rising. Dismissing the Brexit vote as an anomaly reflective of Britain's history of awkwardness does little to help find a way to go about reform in the face of a continuing "constraining dissensus" that confronts European integration across the Union (Hooghe and Marks 2009; Hooghe and Marks, this volume).

Mishandling Brexit

As the previous two sections covered, the EU can be accused of two sets of mistakes: misguiding Britain in ways that contributed to causing Brexit; and misreading Brexit, whether by dismissing it as a British anomaly or thinking that it can only be a positive development for the EU. In this final section, we turn to the third set of criticisms that focus on how the EU has faced the practical challenges of Brexit.

First, there has been somewhat disingenuous in its strict adherence to the terms of the Article 50 procedure which was never likely to be used but which affords the EU significant bargaining leverage against departing states. Of course, the history of the Article 50 provision and the precise intentions behind it are a matter of contemporary dispute, and these reflect in large part the unclear history of its drafting during the 2001–2003 Convention on the Future of Europe (Eeckhout and Frantziou 2017). According to one history, it was drafted by British diplomat and the Convention's Secretary-General, Lord Kerr, so the EU would be prepared for an unprecedented development (Spinant 2003). Another history tells of it being inserted specifically to assist with the possible consequences of EU enlargement, which would lead to the entry of a number of small central and eastern European states who might be overwhelmed by membership or be liable, as Lord Kerr himself described it, to a "dictatorial regime" (Gray 2017; Mair 2019). During the European Convention those opposed to the inclusion of a withdrawal clause argued it was superfluous because under international law member states had the right to withdraw anyhow (Oliver 2013: 12). Whatever its history, it was clear before the UK triggered article 50 on 29 March 2017 that the article would lead to problems for all involved. Since it was triggered, the negotiations have been dogged by the Article's lack of clarity when it comes to the sequencing of negotiations, by uncertainty over whether (or how) Article 50 could be suspended or reversed, by the opaque role of British MEPs in any European Parliament votes on Brexit, and by the sheer inadequacy of the two-year timeframe. That some clarity on this matter, thanks to a ruling of the Court of Justice of the European Union (Court of Justice 2018), was only provided in the final few months of the article 50 process, pointing to how unclear and flawed the process of withdrawal is in practice.

Second, underlying this specific problem is the EU's legalistic and bureaucratic approach to what is an inherently political problem. This is noticeable in a number of respects, from the EU's rigid adherence to the Article 50 process to its intensely bureaucratic management of the negotiating process, and from its defense of its "four freedoms" and "decision-making autonomy" to the insistence that the British deal only with the Commission's Taskforce 50. Though this is perhaps not surprising for an organization with its own distinct legal architecture and bureaucratic modes of operation, it stands in marked contrast to the Union's propensity for *muddling through* (Scenario 2) and for negotiating political compromises, as well as opt-outs and deviations from established positions. Seemingly this rigidity has stood the EU well, since it arguably enhances its bargaining position in the negotiations. It has, if anything, put pressure on a series of negotiations that even a united and clear-minded UK government would have found difficult to manage. But it is not without its detractors. Some fear that it leads the EU down an inflexible path which will preclude the possibility of a deal that could be mutually beneficial. Others point to the need to view Brexit in terms of the full geopolitical significance of the UK's departure, and to weigh up the desire to see Britain lose out from Brexit against the benefits of keeping the UK on-side, which would boost capabilities in key areas and raise the EU's credibility insofar as the Brits would be seen to need it. The EU's negotiators would point out in their defence that the Union is by its nature based on law. As a result, it has to be overly legalistic because this is the best way to ensure the smooth and peaceful functioning of a Union of so many different states. But negotiating procedure and process before negotiating substance would have saved time in the two-year period and provided more transparency and clearer expectations for all involved. This would also have allowed the EU and UK to better come to terms with the reality of trying to negotiate several deals rather than one. As the Brexit negotiations have shown most obviously over the issue of the Northern Ireland backstop, negotiations over a withdrawal agreement and new relationship cannot be undertaken entirely in isolation from one another.

Third, the EU has been remarkably intransigent in its conduct of the Brexit negotiations, and at times even outright uncooperative. This may appear surprising, given the extent to which the UK has indulged in so-called "hard bargaining" in the first phase of the Brexit talks (James and Quaglia 2018; Martill and Staiger 2018a), framing the talks in zero-sum terms and frequently threatening either to quit the talks entirely, leave with no deal, or engage in competitive deregulation. But when one looks at how the talks have played out, it is clear that the UK has in most cases been ultimately forced into accepting the EU's terms, perhaps most evident in acquiescence to Brussels' proposed sequencing. The EU has dealt with the UK as it has any other third country, waiting until the other party comes around to the EU position. Moreover, the criteria on which British hard bargaining rests are predominantly rhetorical, whereas the EU appears to combine discursive reasonableness with practical rigidity. This has led at least one analyst to argue that, while the UK sounds like the hard bargainer, it is actually the EU that rather fits this description in practice (Figueira 2018). In some instances, moreover, the EU has been downright uncooperative. The leaking of documents on the negotiations, for example, especially those covering a dinner between Theresa May and Jean-Claude Juncker, cast an adverse light on the way some in Brussels operate and viewed the Brexit negotiations. The way the Commission and EU have communicated over Brexit—whether by talk of EU defense cooperation or talking about exact numbers when it came to the UK's budget contribution— have also left a lot to be desired. If anyone in Brussels held out any real hopes of the UK reversing its decision or moving to a second referendum, then the EU's communication strategy can sometimes have been taken as a sign they wanted to prevent that.

Fourth, the institutional process for managing Brexit on the EU side is convoluted and presents a number of opportunities for vetoes representing specific and marginal interests. Where the terms of withdrawal are concerned, consent is required from the Council and the Parliament; approving any agreement requires a super-majority in the Council, but extending Article 50 requires unanimity. The EU has streamlined this process by delegating much of the work to the Commission, and Barnier has worked hard to keep the Parliament and the member states on board. Nevertheless, the EU's de facto emphasis on unanimity, and the processes for extending Article 50, means member states have the ability to force their own concerns onto the table. Spain, for instance, threatened on a number of occasions to withhold its consent on key Brexit decisions if they did not deal specifically with the question of Gibraltar, on which it holds a territorial claim. Whether one regards this as reasonable depends on whether it is seen as a necessary safeguard or a political manoeuvre. But the EU process has been opened to capture on both grounds. Thus far the unity of the EU27 has prevented more examples like this, but as the talks move onto the future relationship, greater divergence between member state preferences is expected to emerge. Moreover, the process for agreeing the future relationship will be more complex, since approval of any agreement—which will likely take the form of a mixed agreement—will rest also with national (and in some cases regional) parliaments. Doubts still exist as to how many deals—agreements or treaties—will need to be reached between the UK and the EU. Beyond agreements over the withdrawal lie deals over the new relationships in trade, security and, potentially, a host of smaller areas. These will all have to be negotiated and agreed by all 27 remaining member states.

Conclusion

This chapter has laid out a number of errors (strategic or otherwise) made by the EU in dealing with Brexit. We have argued that the EU is guilty of misleading the UK in the years prior to Brexit, misreading the significance of the British decision, and mishandling the subsequent withdrawal process. Specifically, we have highlighted three failings in particular in the EU's handling of Brexit. First, the EU misled the UK over the viability of its membership of a Union which was increasingly heading down a path which diverged strongly with long-held British preferences, failing to devise suitable frameworks for more skeptical members. It has also misguided the UK over the direction in which it wishes to see the future relationship evolve, either reserving judgment or placing the onus on the UK to spell out options. Second, the EU has misread a number of fundamental aspects of the Brexit vote, in most cases endorsing the most optimistic or self-serving narrative. For instance, it has downplayed the potential disintegrative effects of British withdrawal, and it has clung to long-standing myths about integration regarding the positive role of crises and the negative role of the British veto. It also continues to downplay the likelihood of Brexit occurring in a permanent manner, and tends to view the vote as a consequence of British specificity rather than more general problems afflicting Europe. Third, the EU has mishandled the Brexit process itself, opting for a bureaucratic and legalistic approach to an inherently political problem and dogmatically adhering to the Article 50 procedure, which was never appropriate for the task at hand, but which bolstered the Union's bargaining power. Moreover, the EU has been intransigent and at times uncooperative in the negotiations—in spite of its rhetoric—and on a number of occasions member states have threatened to derail the process to support particular interests.

This is not intended as an exercise in character assassination or as a contribution to the anti-European literature in vogue in the UK at present. The EU's internal politics and maneuverings can look tame compared to the shenanigans of the UK where Her Majesty's Government has been in a perpetual state of infighting, with Ministers of the Crown, egos ablaze, leaking information, challenging prime ministerial leadership (often in a disorganized way that itself has been the subject of sustained criticism) and resigned when they cannot agree to deals they have been heavily involved in drafting. It's a reminder, again, that the above criticisms should not be seen in isolation. Nor do they provide a single, unified case for EU incompetence when it comes to Brexit. Some readers will inevitably disagree with some of the criticisms, while having sympathy with others. Furthermore, this chapter could be balanced by one looking at what the EU or UK have got right about Brexit. As this chapter began by pointing out, the way the EU has handled Brexit has been seen as a success story for a Union that has so often struggled to face crises. The UK's approach has also been the subject of sustained critical analysis, with little attempt to look for where the UK may have performed well. As noted earlier, critical analysis of the way the EU has handled Brexit is an important part of ensuring that any lessons learnt from Brexit can be applied to how the EU faces other very different crises now and in future.

Our attempt here has been motivated by a twin desire to balance the equation and to contribute to the healthy criticism of Brussels which animates critical European studies scholarship. Subjecting the EU's Brexit approach to a critical examination can tell us a lot about how the EU views itself, how it responds to crises, how it likes to negotiate, where its comfort zones do—and do not—lie, and how it views its own future. Applying a more cynical lens therefore shows how the EU fits all three of the scenarios outlined at the start of this book. In the face of an unprecedented development, the EU has made mistakes but muddled through, albeit so far in a much better way than the UK has. The shock of the referendum result, the uncertainty that has overhung the UK, and the need for EU unity in negotiations with the UK has created opportunities to accelerate, or at least strengthen, existing integration as outlined in scenario 3. The Union has therefore not succumbed to the first scenario of *breaking down*. However, as this critical review warns, the EU should not overlook the longer-term timeframe of Brexit and the pertinent question of where the UK fits into the European geopolitical order. In short, there is a lot of detail bound up in Brexit which is liable to be missed if undue attention is placed on British side of the equation, such as over what scenarios the UK faces. Most importantly, a critical lens helps us to understand the politics of Brexit on the EU side, and where the interests of the Union lie. While some of our above criticisms may be construed as errors or misunderstandings, others are more deliberate, the product of efforts in Brussels to manage the fallout from Brexit and ensure the continued viability of the European project. Painting the EU in a generous light, and contrasting it with the "unreasonable" UK, misses the most interesting aspect of the whole Brexit process—the politics.

What the future holds for Brexit is understandably uncertain and is likely to remain so for the foreseeable future. But the stakes are high enough that lessons need to be learnt fast, on both sides, in order that mutual understanding improves, and the worst scenarios do not come to pass. Both the UK and the EU have been guilty of mishandling Brexit at times, and we hope in this chapter to have spurred recognition that this is a two-way street.

REFERENCES

Begg, I. (2018, September 26). What If Britain Rejoined the EU? Breaking Up May Be Less Hard Than Making Up. *Dahrendorf Forum Blog*. Available at: https://www.dahrendorf-forum.eu/what-if-britain-rejoined-the-eu-breaking-up-may-be-less-hard-than-making-up/.

Börzel, T. A. (2018). Researching the EU (Studies) into Demise? *Journal of European Public Policy, 25*(3), 475–485.

Chopin, T., & Lequesne, C. (2016). Differentiation as a Double-Edged Sword: Member States' Practices and Brexit. *International Affairs, 92*(3), 531–545.

Clarke, H., Goodwin, M., & Whiteley, P. (2017). *Brexit: Why Britain Voted to Leave the European Union*. Cambridge: Cambridge University Press.

Court of Justice of the European Union. (2018, December 10). *Judgment in Case C-621/18: The United Kingdom Is Free to Revoke Unilaterally the Notification of Its Intention to Withdraw from the EU*. Press Release No. 191/18. Available at: https://curia.europa.eu/jcms/upload/docs/application/pdf/2018-12/cp180191en.pdf.

de Búrca, G. (2018). How British was the Brexit Vote? In B. Martill & U. Staiger (Eds.), *Brexit and Beyond: Rethinking the Futures of Europe*. London: UCL Press.

Dinan, D., Nugent, N., & Paterson, W. E. (2017). *The European Union in Crisis*. London: Palgrave.

Eeckhout, P., & Frantziou, E. (2017). Brexit and Article 50 TEU: A Constitutionalist Reading. *Common Market Law Review, 54*(3), 695–733.

European Parliament. (2018, May). CSDP After Brexit: The Way Forward. *Study Prepared by the DG for External Policies of the European Parliament's Policy Department*. Available at: http://www.europarl.europa.eu/RegData/etudes/STUD/2018/603852/EXPO_STU(2018)603852_EN.pdf.

Felbermayr, G., Gröschl, J., & Steiningerm, M. (2018, November 7). *Quantifying Brexit: From Ex Post to Ex Ante Using Structural Gravity* (CESifo Working Paper).

Figueira, F. (2018, September 5). *Brexit Negotiations: A Hard Bargain or Soft Consensus Ahead?* Paper Presented at the UACES Annual Conference, University of Bath.

George, S. (1998). *An Awkward Partner: Britain in the European Community* (3rd ed.). Oxford: Oxford University Press.

Glencross, A. (2018). Cameron's European Legacy: How Brexit Demonstrates the Flawed Politics of Simple Solutions. In B. Martill & U. Staiger (Eds.), *Brexit and Beyond: Rethinking the Futures of Europe*. London: UCL Press.

Gray, A. (2017, March 29). Article 50 Author Lord Kerr: I Didn't Have UK in Mind. *Politico*. Available at: https://www.politico.eu/article/brexit-article-50-lord-kerr-john-kerr/.

Hall, P. A., & Soskice, D. W. (2001). *Varieties of Capitalism: The Institutional Foundations of Comparative Advantage*. Oxford: Oxford University Press.

Hodson, D., & Puetter, U. (2018). Studying Europe After the Fall: Four Thoughts on Post-EU Studies. *Journal of European Public Policy, 25*(3), 465–474.

Hooghe, L., & Marks, G. (2009). A Postfunctionalist Theory of European Integration: From Permissive Consensus to Constraining Dissensus. *British Journal of Political Science, 39*(1), 1–23.

James, S., & Quaglia, L. (2018). The Brexit Negotiations and Financial Services: A Two-Level Game Analysis. *The Political Quarterly, 89*(4), 560–567.

Johnstone, R., & Schofield, K. (2017, September 22). Civil Servants Fear Chilcot-Style Inquiry into Brexit—Report. *Civil Service World*. Available at: https://www.civilserviceworld.com/articles/news/civil-servants-fear-chilcot-style-inquiry-brexit-%E2%80%93-report.

Jones, E. (2018). Towards a Theory of Disintegration. *Journal of European Public Policy, 25*(3), 440–451.

Lefkofridi, Z., & Schmitter, P. C. (2015). Transcending or Descending? European Integration in Times of Crisis. *European Political Science Review, 7*(1), 3–22.

Mair, E. (2019, March 20). Brexit: Man Who Wrote Article 50 Says It Was Drafted for Dictators. *LBC*. Available at: https://www.lbc.co.uk/radio/presenters/eddie-mair/man-article-50-eastern-european-dictatorships/.

Martill, B., & Staiger, U. (2018a). *Cultures of Negotiation: Explaining Britain's Hard Bargaining in the Brexit Negotiations* (Dahrendorf Forum Working Paper, No. 4). Available at: https://www.dahrendorf-forum.eu/publications/cultures-of-negotiation-explaining-britains-hard-bargaining-in-the-brexit-negotiations/.

Martill, B., & Staiger, U. (2018b). *Brexit and Beyond: Rethinking the Futures of Europe*. London: UCL Press.

Martill, B., & Sus, M. (2018). Post-Brexit EU/UK Security Cooperation: NATO, CSDP+, or 'French Connection'? *British Journal of Politics and International Relations, 20*(4), 846–863.

Mastenbroek, E. (2005). EU Compliance: Still a Black Hole? *Journal of European Public Policy, 12*(6), 1103–1120.

Mény, Y. (2014). Managing the EU Crises: Another Way of Integration by Stealth? *West European Politics, 37*(6), 1336–1353.

Oliver, T. (2013). Europe Without Britain: Assessing the Impact on the European Union of a British Withdrawal. *Stiftung Wissenschaft und Politik, Berlin*. Available at: https://www.swp-berlin.org/fileadmin/contents/products/research_papers/2013_RP07_olv.pdf.

Oliver, T. (2016). European and International Views of Brexit. *Journal of European Public Policy, 23*(9), 1321–1328.

Oliver, T. (2017a). Never Mind the Brexit? Britain, Europe, the World and Brexit. *International Politics, 54*(4), 519–532.

Oliver, T. (2017b, September 28). *Britain's Brexit Strategy: Lions Misled by Donkeys*. London: Dahrendorf Forum. Available at: http://www.dahrendorf-forum.eu/britains-brexit-strategy-lions-misled-by-donkeys/.

Oliver, T. (2018a). *The Impact of the UK's Withdrawal on EU Integration*. Brussels: European Parliament's Committee on Constitutional Affairs.

Oliver, T. (2018b). *Europe's Brexit: EU Perspectives on Britain's Vote to Leave*. London: Agenda.

Pisani-Ferry, J., Rottgen, N., Sapir, A., Tucker, P., & Wolff, G. B. (2017). *Europe After Brexit: A Proposal for a Continental Partnership*. Brussels: Brugel.

Schimmelfennig, F. (2018). Brexit: Differentiated Disintegration in the European Union. *Journal of European Public Policy, 25*(8), 1154–1173.

Spinant, D. (2003, April 3). Giscard Forum to Unveil Controversial EU "Exit Clause". *European Voice*. Available at: https://www.politico.eu/article/giscard-forum-set-to-unveil-controversial-eu-exit-clause/.

Stokes, B., Wikes, R., & Mamevich, D. (2017, June 15). Post-Brexit Europeans More Favourable Toward EU. *Pew Research Centre*. Available at: https://www.pewresearch.org/global/2017/06/15/post-brexit-europeans-more-favorable-toward-eu/.

Thompson, H. (2017). Inevitability and Contingency: The Political Economy of Brexit. *British Journal of Politics and International Relations, 19*(3), 434–449.

Webber, D. (2013). How Likely Is It That the European Union Will Disintegrate? A Critical Analysis of Competing Theoretical Perspectives. *European Journal of International Relations, 20*(2), 341–365.

CHAPTER 30

The Security and Defense Aspect of Brexit: Altering the Third Country Balance?

Øyvind Svendsen

INTRODUCTION

Brexit changes the institutional and political dynamics in European security and defense cooperation. Expert-practitioner Nathalie Tocci (2018) labelled 2017 a remarkable year because of the progress made on security and defense cooperation in the EU. Yet, security and defense cooperation in Europe more broadly is differentiated and therefore the potential outcome of the Brexit process for the future EU–UK relationship has generated massive scholarly interest as to what form future cooperation between the two parties will take and the potential consequences that Brexit will produce (e.g., Black et al. 2017; Blagden 2017; Dijkstra 2016; Dunn and Webber 2017; Howorth 2017; Keohane 2017; Martill and Sus 2018; Menon 2016; Svendsen 2019; Whitman 2016; Wyn 2017). As a more general phenomenon in EU security and defense cooperation, this question pertains to the role of so-called third countries in EU security and defense. This 'problem' has been there ever since the EU established its Common Security and Defence Policy (ESDP, now CSDP) in 1999 (Webber et al. 2002). The problem refers to so-called external differentiation (see Leuffen et al. 2013)[1] and it concerns the way in which the EU

[1] Because non-members are not formal members of CSDP, Schimmelfennig et al. (2015) argues that there is no external differentiation, yet I treat opt-ins as political processes towards a differentiated relationship with the EU for third countries.

Ø. Svendsen (✉)
Norwegian Institute of International Affairs (NUPI), Oslo, Norway
e-mail: OyvindS@nupi.no

© The Author(s) 2021
M. Riddervold et al. (eds.), *The Palgrave Handbook of EU Crises*,
Palgrave Studies in European Union Politics,
https://doi.org/10.1007/978-3-030-51791-5_30

has been build upon notions of inclusivity and how a credible EU depends on good cooperation with partner countries. On this backdrop, the chapter answers two questions: What room is there for inclusion of third countries in EU security and defense initiatives and how does Brexit alter the politics of such inclusion?

Using common conceptual frameworks Brexit constitutes an instance of disintegration, while in practice the security and defense aspect of the Brexit debate has to a large extent concerned the need for cooperation and partnership to emerge from Brexit (see European Council 2017, 2018; May 2017, 2018; UK Government 2017). Therefore, Ben Rosamond (2016) was right in arguing that European disintegration needs to be understood in its actual, processual nature and not through dichotomous concepts limiting our conclusions to merely integration *or* disintegration. Making Brexit, and indeed the future security and defense involvement of third countries in EU security and defense was and remain a struggle between integration and autonomy with an open-ended outcome.

The prospects for any future relationship between the EU and the UK in security and defense did not emerge in a vacuum. It could only be innovative in relation to existing third country arrangements, and if it were to exceed such agreements also those relationships would need to be reconsidered or even renegotiated in order to sustain a coherent and credible framework for how the EU relates to third countries. I am here thinking especially of countries with close cooperative ties to the EU. The EU's European partner and outlier to the north, Norway is particularly interesting in this context. The country is closely aligned with the EU in defense and as such its relationship to the EU in this area resembles the one that has been envisioned by the UK (Haugevik 2017; Martill and Sus 2018: 856; Tocci 2018: 138). The ways in which Norway is attached to the EU in defense and the affordances offered to it from the EU can shed light on the future of the third country role in EU security and defense.

In the chapter I draw on the different scenarios envisioned in the framework of this handbook in order to make my argument. The overall argument is that the emergent third country role needs to be conceptualized as an essentially power-political process, and that when it comes to EU security and defense cooperation at 27 Brexit is one of several variables that has contributed to the EU heading (if only slightly) forward as an actor in security and defense. Yet, as is the focus in this chapter, when it comes to how the EU relates to third countries in this area, power politics contributes to a continuation of the existing *modus operandi*, or *muddling through*. It is not so much institutional path-dependence in EU governance that is reinforcing status quo, but EU reluctance to differentiate security and defense cooperation beyond the exclusive 'EU club.' Thus, shared interests and threat assessments are structural factors contributing to cooperation, but power politics between the polities—endogenous to the European security community—determine the extent to which the third countries can be associated with EU security and defense and how Brexit contributes to alter the balance.

The chapter is structured as follows. First, I present the methodological framework of the chapter, setting out how I enable any form of speculation about the potential consequences of what is an essentially open-ended process. I theorize the power politics of the third country role as an endogenously generated power in practice (see Adler-Nissen and Pouliot 2014) and present the comparative mode of inquiry that structures the analysis. Second, I go to Oslo and Brussels, taking into account the Norwegian experience and the EU's views and past practices concerning third country status in EU security and defense. Third, I discuss the Norwegian and Brexit-UK cases with regard to (1) the domestic level of politicization and (2) EU affordances. Finally, on the basis of the discussion, I conclude on the potential consequences that Brexit might produce in terms of third country participation in EU security and defense, highlighting the fundamentally power-political basis from which it will emerge.

Approaching 'Third Country' Security and Defense Cooperation Beyond Brexit

For all academic fields interested in it, Brexit has presented itself as something new. Whether it pertains to the economic, social, cultural, or political aspects of the instance of formal disintegration in the EU, we have seen the emergence of refined and new approaches to understand the process. In traditional approaches to European integration the issue has been that despite crises being endogenous to the understanding of integration, they have been "considered unavoidable moments to move forward the integration process" (Lequesne 2018: 289). Ideas about interdependence and the Kantian peace that the EU has been considered to be built upon, has made the field of EU studies normatively laden to the extent that the opposite—disintegration—was inconceivable, also theoretically. Now, the *exit* option has become reality (Hirschman 1970). Brexit has thus already proven existing theories and concepts to be flawed. From now on, scholars must produce pathologies of European integration.

Approaches to differentiated disintegration (Leuffen et al. 2013; Leruth et al. 2019) and disintegration (Scheller 2015; Schmitter and Lefkofridi 2016) attempts to open up the 'integration' box and provide for more detailed understandings of how the flip-side European integration works and what its problem areas are. Yet, disintegration, differentiated or not, is often treated with too much of a focus on institutions, a priori theoretical assumptions and lack of empirical data (see Svendsen and Adler-Nissen 2019). As such, states can either integrate—á la carte—through institutional arrangements or one can choose not to integrate (see Leruth et al. 2017). The consequence is that our understanding of differentiation—of which EU security and defense cooperation with third countries is an example (Biscop 2017)—is limited to the outcomes that processes produce and not the processes themselves (Rosamond 2016).

In this analysis I mobilize the concept of power to inquire into what room there potentially will be for inclusion of third countries in EU security and defense initiatives and how Brexit alters the politics of such inclusion. I do not define power in realist terms, i.e., as material capabilities determining how one state has power to change the behavior of other states (see both Reichwein and Zimmermann in this volume). Rather, I draw on social conceptions of power as diffuse relations that work through social relations of constitution (Barnett and Duvall 2005). Herein, the theorization of power is drawn from the practice turn in IR (see Adler and Pouliot 2011; Adler-Nissen 2016; Neumann 2002a) Specifically, I draw on Adler-Nissen and Pouliot's (2014) notion of emergent power; Players seek to establish their mastery of the game, other players acknowledge or challenge claims for competence, and players 'cash out' on their skills by wielding non-coercive influence. Third country 'power games' play out in a field of socially (more or less) meaningful patterns of action (Pouliot 2016), and even though it often seems non-coercive, it is always based on struggles for competence in given practices (Adler-Nissen and Pouliot 2014). Thus, the making of the third country role in EU security and defense will be the product of emergent power in the social field of European security. The power politics of third country is structured by interacting domestic and cross-border dynamics in Europe. The role of third countries in EU security and defense is therefore assumed to be a product of both domestic levels of politicization and EU affordances. Both of these are elements of emergent power politics and the analysis illustrates how they contribute to our knowledge of potential futures for the third country role in EU security and defense cooperation.

First to the level of politicization. The defining and altering of the third country balance in EU security and defense in relation to Brexit is embedded in relations between polities, but also the degree of politicization in connection to domestic political preferences and the struggle between autonomy and integration (see Lequesne 2018: 295). On the surface, de-politicization is common when it comes to European cooperation on security and defense issues because of shared identities and interests, but the comparison between Norway and the UK will show the tension and variance in the level of politicization of security and defense cooperation with the EU, i.e., the power politics that makes certain possibilities and limitations emerge.

Schimmelfennig et al. (2015: 778–779) have argued that there is no external differentiation in the area of defense and that "politicization would increase [...] if defence policy competences were actually pooled in the EU and delegated to its supranational institutions." For them politicization, drawing on de Wilde (2011: 560), refers to "an increase in polarization of opinions, interests or values and the extent to which they are publicly advanced towards the process of policy formulation within the EU." Herein, politicization is not an outcome of formal pooling of defense competences, but a product of the process of Brexit and how it alters the third country balance. As such, the emergent nature of the power politics of the third country problem in EU security and defense can be assessed on the basis of processes of politicization.

Furthermore, the EU is also a power-political actor, both at the level of its internal dynamics but also as a polity that struggles for relevance as a security and defense actor, balancing between exclusivity and inclusivity toward its partners. Thus, emergent power politics in relation to Brexit will be dependent on EU affordances. These are not limited to formal inclusion and agreements, but to the social process of claiming competence. Engaging with the Brexit process and comparing Norway and the UK's relationship with the EU, this chapter attends to the problems outlined above, by looking beyond institutional factors and static state interests, instead focusing on the emergent power politics that structure third country participation in EU security and defense. The data material that is used in the analysis comprise of previous studies of EU–Norway security relations, some original interview material, as well as official documents and statements relating to Brexit.

Finally, a brief note on temporality and looking into the crystal ball. As authors in this handbook we were asked to tease out our grounds for predicting. In my case, how can I predict that the third country problem in EU security and defense will be characterized by *muddling through*? For one, I analyze past practices and Brexit related developments which have already unfolded. Furthermore, both past practices and the making of new lines of cooperation or non-cooperation matter in the power politics structuring the development of the third country role in EU defense. By looking at the emergence and enactment of power politics, I unravel political practices that are part of a "temporally embedded process of social engagement, informed by the past (in its habitual aspect), but also oriented toward the future (as a capacity to imagine alternative possibilities) and toward the present (as a capacity to contextualize past habits and future projects within the contingencies of the moment)" (Emirbayer and Mische 1998: 963). I do not claim to know the future as such but studying practices of making the future on the basis of past practices gets us somewhere toward informed prediction (see Berenskoetter 2011).

EU and Past 'Third Country' Practices: Lessons from Norway

Several countries are or could be considered third country partners in EU security and defense, but in relation to Brexit the Norwegian experience seems particularly apt when discussing how Brexit will alter the third country balance. Norway is closely associated in EU security and defense, just like the UK has expressed a desire for, in addition to being a NATO member sharing a similar identity with the UK as well as like-mindedness with the EU. As such, Norway and the UK in this context appear, at the outset, as most similar cases. The first step in the analysis that follows is to draw on the Norwegian experience as a third country and consider past EU practices and power politics when it comes to third country participation in EU security and defense. By so doing we can assess how a similar country has been attached to the EU in this domain prior to Brexit. Having been in staunch opposition to EU membership and rejected it in two referendums (1972 and 1994), Norway has been voluntarily confined to third country relations with the EU in security and defense.

The provisions of the EEA agreement that bind Norway to the single market do not pertain to security defense cooperation, yet an interesting puzzle has characterized the Norwegian approach to EU security and defense: despite not having to follow any EU provisions or policies, an apparently servile role has evolved in which "the various governments in Oslo have been eager to contribute significantly to this European policy" (Rieker 2006: 282). As such, Norway's political position with regard to EU security and defense cooperation has been based on consensus across the political spectrum.[2] A comprehensive government-commissioned report on Norway's relationship with the EU published in 2012 concluded that Norway had been seeking as close as possible relations with the EU in the area of security and defense. In line with the argument from Sjursen above, the report found that Norway's involvement in EU security and defense structures and initiatives has developed without political debate (NOU 2012: 724).[3] In concrete numbers, Norway had contributed with 181 personnel and 240 million NOK in civilian EU operations and approximately 220 personnel and 224 million NOK in military operations at the time of writing.

These contributions have been initiated within the framework of several agreements that Norway has with the EU on foreign, security, and defense policies. Norway is in fact the third country with the most agreements with the EU in security and defense. Adopting the EU's positions on security is more or less routine and the country normally contributes when invited to join crisis operations, there are Norwegian representatives in the Union's civil and military forces, notably Norway contributes to the EU's Battle Groups, and Norway is part of projects led by the European Defence Agency (EDA) as an associated member (Sjursen 2015: 222).

As we can see from the above the headline on Norway's involvement in EU security and defense cooperation is that access is possible and that contributions have been welcome. Why, however, has Norway sought the close relationship with the EU in this area, despite not being member of the union?[4] Explanations for Norway's integrationist attitude toward the EU in security

---

[2] Or as Sjursen (2015) describes the Norwegian foreign policy consensus: A consensus in name only due to the lack of real (Habermasian) deliberation on these issues. Whatever nature of the consensus, Norway has been a close partner to the EU in the area of defence and has shown an eagerness to take part both in defence institutions and defence policies.

[3] Helene Sjursen was also part of the group that wrote the report for the government.

[4] The scholarship on why Norwegians are reluctant to join the EU at all is interesting yet not widely discussed in English writing (for accounts see Archer 2005; Ingebritsen 1998; Neumann 2002b).

and defense have been forwarded. Some follow the more rationalist form of inquiry, presenting arguments such as the one that "the Norwegian approach to the ESDP may be described as a 'troops-for-influence' strategy, where Norwegian political influence in the ESDP structures is sought through the contribution of forces to the EU Headline Goals" (Græger 2002: 35). Græger (2008) has also argued that Norway unsuccessfully has tried to obtain political influence in ESDP structures, and that Nordic cooperation has been central in that process (Græger 2018: 3–4). The argument has also been made that the Norwegian practices of seeking to contribute to and have a voice in EU security and defense are conditioned by specific strategies that emerge from being a 'small state' in international relations (Carvalho and Neumann 2015).

Other explanations of the Norwegian position are rooted broadly within a more sociological frame. Pernille Rieker (2006) combines rationalist and non-rationalist explanations and argues that the Norwegian willingness to cooperate and even integrate with the EU on security and defense is a function of three mechanisms. First, she argues that aligning with the EU may be seen as Norway's best way of pursuing its national interest and/or path dependency given that a lot seemed to be happening in EU defense cooperation in the context that were considered 'post-Cold War' and one where no country could effectively secure itself (see EU 2003). Second, she considered the 'corporative' interest of the *corps diplomatique* which was an argument similar to the one above yet not with an emphasis on stigmatization but on norm convergence. Third, Rieker suggested that Norway's willingness to participate in EU's security policies stemmed from 'learning' in the sense that Norway was part of a process of Europeanization where security identities were converging.

Finally, one might argue that the willingness to cooperate with the EU on security defense concerns how EU leaders impose a stigma on Norway as an outsider (Svendsen 2016). This is not desirable for the people that 'run' Norwegian security and defense policy, because their own proclivities lean in the direction of EU membership also for the northern outpost, or the "little piggy that stayed at home" (Neumann 2002b). The stigma imposition on Norway then, has arguably led to Norwegian officials seeking to align closely with the EU not because of pure national interest, but through a process of stigma recognition (Adler-Nissen 2014; Goffman 1963) where to be perceived as a 'normal' player in European security, Norway has effectively acted as a member of the European Union and gone along with EU policies in this area. This latter argument highlights the seemingly non-coercive nature of the fundamentally power-political nature of making third country arrangements in EU security and defense. On the one hand Norway is partially welcomed into the club, but on the other the EU finds Norwegian outsider position 'incompetent' as a point of departure. One should not need to look far to find similar thinking with regard to the paradox of the UK wanting close cooperation post-Brexit, but still moving on with the process of exiting the union. Also, the Norwegian case illustrates that in the Norway-EU relationship in security and defense, the EU's claim to competence has been recognized by Norwegian policy makers, civil servants, and thus the state. When it comes to asking for Norwegian support for EU initiatives then, the EU has been successful in 'cashing out' on its competence with Norwegian support.

Norway-EU Cooperation in Light of Brexit

Norway has been active also with regard to Brexit, arguing that it would be essential for all parties that Brexit did not end up with a weakening of the EU's Common Security and Defence Policy (CSDP).[5] Rather, Brexit was seen as a moment of opportunity also for Norway because it would see a major player enter into the role as third country. Also, it illustrates how Brexit, if only partially, contributed to a politicization of the third country role in EU security and defense. State secretary Tone Skogen made this clear in her address to the European Parliament's Subcommittee on Security and Defence in early 2018:

> In particular, a closer involvement in discussions, "decision-shaping" and information sharing would make participation in, and contributions to, future CSDP operations and missions more attractive to partners like Norway. We believe such involvement could best be achieved through differentiation between various partner countries, taking into consideration their individual characteristics. In other words, - a more tailored approach. (Skogen 2018)

In addition to the existing institutional and political affiliations between Norway and the EU, the Norwegian government has had to adjust to and follow both the Brexit negotiations and the new developments in EU security and defense cooperation. After the Brexit vote made the exiting of the UK from the EU a realistic probability, Norway sought to align itself with the EU and position itself. Recent Norwegian efforts to get in on developments in the EU such as PESCO and the EDF illustrate this point. As noted by the Norwegian anti-EU membership organization 'Nei til EU,' "Norway is marching in line with the EU's defence pact" (Steinholt 2018).

Whereas the above shed light on what and why a third country like Norway might seek cooperation with the EU both before and as a consequence of Brexit, they do not take into account what the EU has been willing to give. These affordances are also embedded in the emergent power dynamics of claiming competence in this area. The EU language in terms of third country status is inclusive and positive, yet on the ground Norwegian officials have experienced frustrations as to how inclusive the EU has actually been. Interviewing a senior Norwegian military official in Brussels, I was told that the some of the fora in which Norway and the EU were at times considered frustrating. An example of this is the consultation meetings with the EU's military committee (EUMC), where the Norwegians usually leave feeling only that

---

[5]The Norwegian government also did all it could to have the British not vote for Brexit in the first place (see Haugevik 2017; Helm 2015; Politico 2016).

they have been told what has been going on in the EU since last time, that the conversations are hampered by EU secrecy ("we could tell you but it is unfortunately classified") and where no real invitations to cooperate deeper are brought up, even though Norway desires to do more. This might be related to a problem integral to the EU when searching to speak with one voice as a security and defense actor: On the one hand the EU engages in competence struggles with third countries such as Norway, yet the EU also has to consolidate the positions of all member states internally. Thus, the sometimes frustrating exclusion that emerges in Norway-EU relations might stem from the power struggles to define what is the appropriate role for the EU as a security and defense actor internally.

A similar dynamic which might contribute to nuance the image of the EU as an all-inclusive security and defense partner for like-minded third countries is the will to include Norway in recent initiatives such as the European defence fund (EDF) and Permanent Structured Cooperation (PESCO). Norway has indicated a clear will to be part of both of these initiatives, especially the former (see Søreide 2019). Yet, Norway has only been invited to participate in the research part of EDF, and third country access to PESCO projects remains to be squared, largely because of Brexit. These issues are sensitive also among the EU members, and therefore a third country like Norway—accepting EU competence in this field and wanting to be part of the initiatives—are partly excluded due to the process of squaring these issues internally in the EU. In summary thus far, as a third country Norway has been seeking close relations with the EU in security and defense, but the Norwegian experience has been tied to a sense that the EU, despite talking of inclusivity, practices some degree of exclusivity. Despite the EU *muddling through* in this area and Norway pushing for even more influence, such as Tone Skogen's plea for Norwegian involvement in decision-shaping, the processes remain largely under the radar in the Norwegian public discourse and its political character remains technical rather than politicized in broader society.

Enter Brexit: Moving Ahead or '*Muddling Through*' for Third Countries?

Brexit did not immediately change much in terms of the security and defense issues of both the EU and the UK. The EU (including the UK!) realized its shared security interests in its first strategy document on the issue already in 2003 (EU 2003), it underlined the presence of common values and shared threats in its updated strategy (EU 2016), and it has started to deliver on that strategy through such notable developments as establishing a Military Planning and Conduct Capability (MPCC), Coordinated Annual Review on Defence (CARD), A European Defence Fund (EDF), and Permanent Structured Cooperation (PESCO) (see Biscop 2017; Svendsen 2018). Because of the similarities in threat assessments with regard to the external environment, it was not really the security and defense infrastructures of the EU that the UK sought to leave with Brexit. Former UK prime minister Theresa May made it clear early on that the UK wanted a close relationship with the EU also in security and defense after the country had left the EU:

> With the threats to our common security becoming more serious, our response cannot be to cooperate less, but to work together more. [...] We will continue to work closely with our European allies in foreign and defence policy even as we leave the EU itself. (May 2017)

Speaking at the Munich Security Conference in 2018, Theresa May expanded her governments' view on the future partnership with the EU. On internal security, May asked for the EU and the UK to work together in countering the crime and the terrorist threat by continuing to work together through the European Arrest Warrant, Europol and the Schengen Information System II (May 2018: 5). On external security, the prime minster argued that the EU–UK should put in place diplomatic consultation mechanisms, coordinate operations together and cooperate on capacity development through the EDA and the EDF (May 2018: 8–9). Importantly, the government's vision was to create a partnership that no existing third country has with the EU, yet at the same time it should "respect both the decision-making autonomy of the European Union and the sovereignty of the United Kingdom" (HM Government 2018: 7).

The EU's position on the future relationship on security and defense was much like the UK's: because of shared values and common threats it was considered important to continue to work together and establish a partnership (European Council 2017: 8; European Council 2018: 2). The EU's negotiating team presented plans for a consultation mechanism on foreign and sanction policies, a Framework Participation Agreement (FPA) on CSDP operations and missions, an administrative agreement with EDA, and a Security of Information Agreement on exchange and protection of classified information (TF50 2018: 5). On PESCO, EDF, the Galileo satellite system and development, the Task Force referred to council decisions and EU regulations on third country participation. This summary illustrates a certain overarching discursive convergence on both sides of the channel. At the same time, there is some distance in practice between 'relationship beyond any existing third country arrangement' and the EU notion of 'UK becoming a third country like any other.' Thus, we should analyze the power politics of the third country problem in light of Brexit not only in the context of a cooperative discourse, but in how agents with stakes in this area struggle for competence by trying to establish their mastery of the security and defense 'game' with regard to (1) the level of politicization and (2) EU affordances.

(De)Politicization of Third Country Participation

Politicization refers to a situation where opinions on security and defense cooperation are polarized and take hold in the public debate about policies in the given area. As we saw in the Norwegian case, security and defense cooperation in the EU has not been politicized in the public, nor between political parties. Despite the question of EU/EEA membership being politically salient, security and defense cooperation goes under the radar. As such, Norwegian policy makers can seek cooperation with the EU without too much public scrutiny. This picture is quite different in the UK. EU defense integration is highly politicized in the UK and the prospects of an 'EU Army' held a significant place in the debate leading up to the Brexit referendum (Vote Leave n.d.). Thus, the potential ability for the EU to successfully claim competence in security and defense vis-à-vis the UK might be limited. There is also an ongoing debate in the UK about what the consequences of current government policies in the Brexit debate will be for the UK's autonomy in security and defense (see Edginton 2018; Riley 2019). Thus, the variation in level of politicization in the two countries might encounter quite different domestic pressures and opposition if and when closer cooperation with the EU in security and defense is on the table.

In terms of the 'people-elite' divide, the Norwegian and British cases also share some elements. The way in which there has been a discrepancy between the attitude that citizens have toward the EU (Norwegian membership referendums and Brexit referendum) and the visions of the respective countries' leadership (alignment and special partnership) clearly can be discussed in relation to each other. Perhaps there is also some theoretical and methodical take-away from this, namely that our gaze should in fact be, and are indeed, most often toward the powerful when we try to understand security and defense cooperation in Europe, and when we talk about 'Norway' or 'the UK' as doing, meaning or saying this or that, we are in fact speaking about a very specific group of people that belong to specific social fields, normally referred to as 'high politics.' In the case of third country relations with the EU in security defense in light of Brexit, those involved in the issue area seek cooperation wherever possible. This can of course change with domestic power-shifts. Existing arrangements and visions for the future were not only technical matters but embedded in power-political processes where domestic levels of politicization met international politics, and where power is continually negotiated. The third country role in EU security and defense is subject to domestic levels of politicization and any political or diplomatic attempts at claiming certain competence toward affiliation or non-affiliation will be structured by the level of domestic politicization of security and defense cooperation.

EU Affordances

(De)politicization refers primarily to the domestic level of opposition in the third countries wanting to be part of EU security and defense cooperation. However, the emergent power politics of redefining the third country role through competence claims is also a question of what the EU is willing to accept in terms of external differentiation. We have already seen that the EU has stuck to some degree of exclusivity, i.e., lack of will to include, Norway in all areas of security and defense, especially with regard to decision-making. A notable use of exclusivity that emerged in the Brexit process pertained to Galileo, the EU-led project to develop an alternative satellite system to the US's GPS (see Inkster 2018). The UK had invested large sums in the system, but the EU excluded the UK from the security component of the project. Furthermore, in a May (2018) speech, Michel Barnier (2018) made it clear that the future relationship between the EU and the UK would be with the UK as a third country and that he would "of course, consider the close relationship we already have with partners, such as Norway" (Barnier 2018: 2). Yet, as a third country, in Barnier's account of the post-Brexit European security architecture, there would be no room for UK decision-making, decision-shaping, or leadership in EU defense. Yet, within legal arrangements and mechanisms, he argued that there needed to be a close partnership between the parties. This can all be read as formalistic statements, but they indeed feed into the EU claiming exclusive competence (and coherence) in this area in during a process in which the union is working to make itself relevant as a player in security and defense.

Based on my own interviews in and around EU's Political and Security Committee, the notion that the UK would become a third country like any other seemed to be a shared understanding, confirming Barnier's position. All of the informants (N10) stressed the fact that the UK would need to leave behind its EU privileges as a member and become a third country with formal agreements that would limit UK privileges.

> Over time, once we enter into negotiations over the official relationship, I think there will be a manoeuvre space to find solutions which will be beneficial for both sides. But again, it will be close relations, but, you know, once you are out you are out. You cannot expect to have the same relations or rights as the member states. That's reality.[6]

This was of course a question of defending the values and benefits of staying inside of the EU. In security and defense, however, which already is intergovernmental and with PESCO also differentiated, there could be space to manoeuvre for the UK. As an Ambassador to the PSC said when I asked about the possibility for the UK to have a say on EU defense from outside of the EU, "also after April next year I am pretty sure that they will have a

---

[6] Interview with Head of CSDP Section, 21 September 2018.

strong say, as we are in fact quite attentive also toward what our American friends are conveying".[7] This illustrates the emergent and constant negotiation of competence that defines the politics of third country participation. The discourse about formal red lines in the EU might produce certain institutional limitations, but in practice the politics of cooperation does not stop at the institutions. For the EU, exclusivity is one way of attempting to cash out on its competences, yet its coherence and ultimate success in security and defense is also perceived to be linked with practicing inclusivity. It is at this nexus where the emergent power politics of the third country problem will evolve in the future.

Commenting on the third country issue in EU defense in relation to Brexit, prominent scholar-practitioner Thierry Tardy (2018: 3) has pointed out that

> An issue at the forefront of any debate on this topic is the precedent that would be created if the UK were given any preferential treatment: others – Norway and Turkey in particular – are likely to ask for the same conditions, provided they offer similar profiles. Either the EU accepts that the UK can be given such treatment and is prepared to explain this to other third countries with all the diplomatic risks that it entails, or the same treatment is somehow given to a selection of third countries, based on well-defined criteria.

This sounds orderly and neat. Yet at the same time Norway is a small state with considerably less influence than the UK in terms of diplomatic capital, material capability, financial resources, and experience in the area of defense. As such, the ability of third countries to cash out on its claims to security and defense competence is not to be underplayed as a contributing factor in how Brexit changes third country relationships in relation to the EU. As both Norway and the UK historically, as well as presently, considers NATO to be the main pillar of their security infrastructure, the share material capabilities they possess might not sufficiently account for how each party would react to varying third country agreements. While Norway is a status seeker that accepts its place in the international hierarchy as something like a small or middle power, the UK will have a different repertoire to deploy in its engagements regarding EU defense considering its military and diplomatic weight. Yet, as quite a speculative point, the degree of self-harm that the UK has inflicted on itself in and through the Brexit process might shape its standing as a competent player in security and defense. Despite its military weight and the impossibility for now to measure the 'losses,' EU affordances and willingness to include the UK in the future might be limited. Also, the competence claims that define third country affordances from the EU might be in Norway's favor given the loyalty (or subservience) that Norway has exercised toward the EU.

The enactment of power in practice means that the UK could possibly come to enjoy the pleasure of informal policy shaping to a larger extent than the

---

[7]Interview with PSC Ambassador, 21 September 2018.

'taker' Norway both because it would seek such influence, but also because its power is recognized in the EU, which in turn increases its possibilities for cashing out on both its ideational and material capabilities. The EU's way of listening to and aligning with the US (and as such NATO) on security and defense issues is testament to how particular states in practice can enjoy informal privilege's that others can't. Yet, the EU documents and the interview data from the PSC shows a consistency in the EU's approach to the future relationship that emphasize how as much as possible needs to be agreed to formally. Any preferential agreement with the UK would be cause for concern because of what Tardy was quoted on above: other third countries, perhaps especially Norway, would voice strong opinions in favor of getting the same deal. State secretary Tone Skogen's appeal to the European Parliament provides an early indication of that, but this does not null the fact that the struggle for competence in the third country issue possibly would have an altered balance when the UK becomes a third country.

Finally, The EU of course has to play a 'double power game' in the sense that the union needs to stake out its internal path in struggles and claims for competence in which different national cultures and strategic priorities clash. A recent report from the European Court of Auditors (2019) pointed out that very problem. Only on the basis of internal agreement may the EU as a polity engage coherently in power struggles with like-minded third countries such as Norway and the UK. However, such consistency is not as neat as one might think. Concerning Brexit, there have been deep disagreements internally as to how the EU should relate to the UK, as Eastern European and some notable NATO members close to the UK have pressed for close UK cooperation whereas others approach the UK with a higher degree of indifference in this area. Add to that the loss of good-will that the Brexit process has produced in the EU–UK relationship and the future becomes genuinely uncertain.

Conclusion

What room then, is there for inclusion of third countries in EU security and defense initiatives and how does Brexit alter the politics of such inclusion? In this chapter, I have argued that an answer to this question can be found by comparing the Norwegian experience with the Brexit process focusing on the emergent power politics, or claims for security and defense competence and its potential recognition, between the different polities. By discussing the third country problem at the level of past practices, the level of domestic politicization and EU affordances, I forwarded the argument that the EU most likely will continue to muddle through when it comes to third country participation as it moves forward on security and defense internally. Furthermore, the domestic levels of politicization in Norway and the UK will determine the extent to which, especially the UK, will seek to 'cash out' on EU security and defense cooperation in the future, and vice versa.

For the EU, it matters which external partners they cooperate with on security and defense, both practically and normatively. In this sense, Norway and the UK are both potential close partners because they are like-minded, western liberal states. In the publicly available Brexit debate, the nature of such cooperation has revolved around notions of institutional formality. There is ample reason to believe that the more self-serving principled pragmatism laid out in the EU's (2016) Global Strategy will pertain also to the union's dealings with third country partnerships also in the future. The EU also deals with internal struggles for competence in this area and thus has to play a 'double power game' that continues to keep the future open-ended. Thus, we should continue to ask questions about the role of third countries in EU security and defense and their potential decision-shaping and making, beyond the EU as a closed off system and toward the power politics of competence claims that construct the meaning of this form of cooperation, both within the EU and in its dealings with current and emerging third country partners.

REFERENCES

Adler, E., & Pouliot, V. (2011). International Practices. *International Theory, 3*(1), 1–36.

Adler-Nissen, R. (2014). *Opting Out of the European Union.* Cambridge: Cambridge University Press.

Adler-Nissen, R. (2016). Toward a Practice Turn in EU Studies: The Everyday of European Integration. *Journal of Common Market Studies, 54*(1), 87–103.

Adler-Nissen, R., & Pouliot, V. (2014). Power in Practice: Negotiating the International Intervention in Libya. *European Journal of International Relations, 20*(4), 889–911.

Archer, C. (2005). *Norway Outside the European Union.* London: Routledge.

Barnett, M., & Duvall, R. (2005). Power in International Politics. *International Organization, 59*(1), 39–75.

Barnier, M. (2018). *Speech by Michel Barnier at the EU Institute for Security Studies Conference.* Available at: https://ec.europa.eu/commission/presscorner/detail/en/SPEECH_18_3785. Accessed 30 April 2020.

Berenskoetter, F. (2011). Reclaiming the Vision Thing: Constructivists as Students of the Future. *International Studies Quarterly, 55*(3), 647–668.

Biscop, S. (2017). European Defence: What's in the CARDs for PESCO? *Egmont Security Policy Brief, 91,* 1–6.

Black, J., Hall, A., Cox, K., Kepe, M., & Silfversten, E. (2017). *Defence and Security After Brexit.* Available at: https://www.rand.org/pubs/research_reports/RR1786z1.html. Accessed 14 June 2017.

Blagden, D. (2017). Britain and the World After Brexit. *International Politics, 54*(1), 1–25.

Carvalho, B. D., & Neumann, I. B. (2015). *Small State Status Seeking.* Abingdon, Oxon: Routledge.

de Wilde, P. (2011). No Polity for Old Politics? A Framework for Analyzing the Politicization of European Integration. *Journal of European Integration, 33*(5), 559–575.

Dijkstra, H. (2016). UK and EU Foreign Policy Cooperation After Brexit. *RUSI Newsbrief, 36*(5), 1–3.

Dunn, D. H., & Webber, M. (2017). The UK, the European Union and NATO: Brexit's Unintended Consequences. *Global Affairs, 2*(5), 471–480.

Edginton, S. (2018). *Despite Brexit, the Government Has Covertly Signed Us Up to the EU's Defence Agenda*. Available at: https://brexitcentral.com/despite-brexit-government-covertly-signed-us-eus-defence-agenda/. Accessed 20 September 2019.

Emirbayer, M., & Mische, A. (1998). What Is Agency? *American Journal of Sociology, 103*(4), 962–1023.

EU. (2003). *A Secure Europe in a Better World*. Available at: http://www.consilium.europa.eu/uedocs/cmsUpload/78367.pdf. Accessed 5 May 2016.

EU. (2016). Shared Vision, Common Action: A Stronger Europe. *A Global Strategy for the European Union's Foreign and Security Policy*. Available at: http://europa.eu/globalstrategy/en/global-strategy-foreign-and-security-policy-european-union. Accessed 14 June 2017.

European Council. (2017). *Special Meeting of the European Council (Art. 50) (29 April 2017)—Guidelines*. Brussels: European Council.

European Council. (2018). *European Council (Art. 50) (23 March 2018)—Guidelines*. Brussels: European Council.

Goffman, E. (1963). *Stigma: Notes on the Management of Spoiled Identity*. Englewood Cliffs, NJ: Prentice Hall.

Græger, N. (2002). Norway and the EU Security and Defence Dimension: A "Troops-for-Influence" Strategy. In N. Græger, H. Larsen, & H. Ojanen (Eds.), *The ESDP and the Nordic Countries: Four Variations on a Theme* (pp. 33–89). Helsinki: The Finnish Institute of International Affairs.

Græger, N. (2008). Norway Between Europe and the US. In C. Archer (Ed.), *New Security Issues in Northern Europe* (pp. 94–114). Oxon: Routledge.

Græger, N. (2018). Need to Have or Nice to Have? Nordic Cooperation, NATO and the EU in Norway's Foreign and Security Policy. *Global Affairs, 4*(1), 1–14.

Haugevik, K. (2017). Hva betyr brexit for utenforlandet Norge? *Internasjonal Politikk, 75*(2), 152–166.

Helm, T. (2015). *Britain Will Lose Influence in the World If It Quits the EU, Says Norway*. Available at: http://www.theguardian.com/politics/2015/feb/22/norway-urges-uk-dont-leave-eu. Accessed 6 July 2015.

Hirschman, A. O. (1970). *Exit, Voice, and Loyalty: Responses to Decline in Firms, Organizations, and States*. Cambridge, MA: Harvard University Press.

HM Government. (2018). *Framework for the UK-EU Security Partnership*. Available at: https://assets.publishing.service.gov.uk/government/uploads/system/uploads/attachment_data/file/705687/2018-05-0_security_partnership_slides__SI__FINAL.pdf. Accessed 1 October 2018.

Howorth, J. (2017). EU Defence Cooperation After Brexit: What Role for the UK in the Future EU Defence Arrangements? *European View, 16*, 191–200.

Ingebritsen, C. (1998). *The Nordic States and European Unity*. Ithaca: Cornell University Press.

Inkster, N. (2018). Brexit and Security. *Survival, 60*(6), 27–34.

Keohane, D. (2017). *Three's Company? France, Germany, the UK and European Defence Post-Brexit*. Available at: http://www.realinstitutoelcano.org/wps/portal/rielcano_en/contenido?WCM_GLOBAL_CONTEXT=/elcano/elcano_in/zonas_in/ari1-2017-keohane-threes-company-france-germany-uk-european-defence-post-brexit. Accessed 17 October 2017.

Lequesne, C. (2018). Brexit and the Future of EU Theory. In P. Diamond, P. Nedergaard, & P. Rosamond (Eds.), *The Routledge Handbook of the Politics of Brexit* (pp. 289–296). London: Routledge.

Leruth, B., Gänzle, S., & Trondal, J. (2017). *Differentiated Integration and Disintegration in the European Union: State-of-the-Art and Ways for Future Research* (ISL Working Paper 1, 1–23).

Leruth, B., Gänzle, S., & Trondal, J. (2019). Exploring Differentiated Disintegration in a Post-Brexit European Union. *Journal of Common Market Studies*, Early View, 1–18.

Leuffen, D., Rittberger, B., & Schimmelfennig, F. (2013). *Differentiated Integration: Explaining Variation in the European Union*. Basingstoke: Palgrave Macmillan.

Martill, B., & Sus, M. (2018). Post-Brexit EU/UK Security Cooperation: NATO, CSDP+, or 'French Connection'? *The British Journal of Politics and International Relations*, 20(4), 846–863.

May, T. (2017). *Read Theresa May's Speech Laying Out the UK's Plan for Brexit*. Available at: http://time.com/4636141/theresa-may-brexit-speech-transcript/. Accessed 14 February 2017.

May, T. (2018, February 17). *PM Speech at Munich Security Conference*. Available at: https://www.gov.uk/government/speeches/pm-speech-at-munich-security-conference-17-february-2018. Accessed 1 October 2018.

Menon, A. (2016). *Don't Assume CSDP Will Flourish Without the UK*. Available at: https://www.europeanleadershipnetwork.org/commentary/dont-assume-csdp-will-flourish-without-the-uk/. Accessed 8 May 2018.

Neumann, I. B. (2002a). Returning Practice to the Linguistic Turn: The Case of Diplomacy. *Millennium, 31*(3), 627–651.

Neumann, I. B. (2002b). This Little Piggy Stayed at Home: Why Norway Is Not a Member of the EU. In L. Hansen & O. Wæver (Eds.), *European Integration and National Identity: The Challenge of the Nordic States* (pp. 88–129). London: Routledge.

NOU. (2012). *Utenfor og innenfor: Norges avtaler med EU*, 2. Oslo: Departementenes servicesenter.

Politico. (2016). *Norway to Britain: Don't Leave, You'll Hate It*. Available at: https://www.politico.eu/article/eu-referendum-look-before-you-leap-norways-pm-tells-brexiteers/. Accessed 1 October 2018.

Pouliot, V. (2016). *International Pecking Orders: The Politics and Practice of Multilateral Diplomacy*. Cambridge: Cambridge University Press.

Rieker, P. (2006). Norway and the ESDP: Explaining Norwegian Participation in the EU's Security Policy. *European Security, 15*(3), 281–298.

Riley, J. (2019). *Beware of the Threat to Our Defence Autonomy Coming from the EU (and Not Just in the Draft Brexit Deal)*. Available at: https://brexitcentral.com/beware-the-threat-to-our-defence-autonomy-coming-from-the-eu-and-not-just-in-the-draft-brexit-deal/. Accessed 20 September 2019.

Rosamond, B. (2016). Brexit and the Problem of European Disintegration. *Journal of Contemporary European Research*, 12(4), 864–871.

Scheller, H. (2015). *We've Studied European Integration: It's Time to Examine Its Flipside—Disintegration*. Available at: http://blogs.lse.ac.uk/brexit/2016/01/12/weve-studied-european-integration-its-time-to-examine-its-flipside-disintegration/. Accessed 24 October 2016.

Schmitter, P. C., & Lefkofridi, Z. (2016). Neo-Functionalism as a Theory of Disintegration. *Chinese Political Science Review*, 1, 1–29.

Schimmelfennig, F., Leuffen, D., & Rittberger, B. (2015). The European Union as a System of Differentiated Integration: Interdependence, Politicization and Differentiation. *Journal of European Public Policy*, 22(6), 764–782.

Sjursen, H. (2015). Enighet for enhver pris? Om legitimitetsgrunnlaget for norsk utenrikspolitikk. *Nytt Norsk Tidsskrift*, 32(3), 219–232.

Skogen, T. (2018). *Norwegian Security Policy—Including Participation in the CSDP*. Available at: https://www.regjeringen.no/en/aktuelt/norwegian-security-policy–including-participation-in-the-csdp/id2592184/. Accessed 1 October 2018.

Søreide, I. E. (2019). *Defending the Security Architecture in Europe*. Available at: https://www.regjeringen.no/no/aktuelt/forsvar_sikkerhet/id2628501/. Accessed 27 August 2019.

Steinholt, J. R. (2018). *Marsjerer i takt med EUs forsvarspakt*. Available at: https://neitileu.no/aktuelt/marsjerer-i-takt-med-eus-forsvarspakt. Accessed 1 October 2018.

Svendsen, Ø. (2016). Stigma i internasjonal politikk: Norge, EU og søken etter 'det normale' i en post-sovjetisk sikkerhetskontekst. *Internasjonal Politikk*, 74(1), 1–20.

Svendsen, Ø. (2018). European Defence and Third Countries After Brexit. *NUPI Policy Brief*, 3(2018), 1–4.

Svendsen, Ø. (2019). Brexit and the Future of EU Defence: A Practice Approach to Differentiated Defence Integration. *Journal of European Integration* [Online First], 1–15.

Svendsen, Ø., & Adler-Nissen, R. (2019). Differentiated (Dis)integration in Practice: The Diplomacy of Brexit and the "Low" Politics of "High" Politics. *Journal of Common Market Studies* [Forthcoming], 1–12.

Tardy, T. (2018). *What Third-Country Role Is Open to the UK in Defence?* Available at: https://www.ceps.eu/publications/what-third-country-role-open-uk-defence. Accessed 1 October 2018.

TF50. (2018). *Slides on Foreign, Security and Defence Policy*. Available at: https://ec.europa.eu/commission/publications/slides-foreign-security-and-defence-policy_en. Accessed 1 October 2018.

Tocci, N. (2018). Towards a European Security and Defence Union: Was 2017 a Watershed? *Journal of Common Market Studies*, 56, 131–141. https://doi.org/10.1111/jcms.12752.

UK Government. (2017). *Foreign Policy, Defence and Development: A Future Partnership Paper*. Available at: https://www.gov.uk/government/uploads/system/uploads/attachment_data/file/643924/Foreign_policy__defence_and_development_paper.pdf. Accessed 15 November 2017.

Vote Leave. (n.d.). *Being in the EU Undermines Our Defence*. Available at: http://www.voteleavetakecontrol.org/briefing_defence.html. Accessed 20 September 2019.

Webber, M., Terriff, T., Howorth, J., & Croft, S. (2002). The Common European Security and Defence Policy and the 'Third-Country' Issue. *European Security*, 11(2), 75–100.

Whitman, R. G. (2016). The UK and EU Foreign, Security and Defence Policy After Brexit: Integrated, Associated or Dethatched? *National Institute Economic Review, 238*(1), 43–50.

Wyn, R. (2017). America, Brexit and the Security of Europe. *The British Journal of Politics and International Relations, 19*(3), 558–572.

CHAPTER 31

Crisis and EU Foreign and Security Policy: An Introduction

Marianne Riddervold, Jarle Trondal, and Akasemi Newsome

This section discusses the impact of various external crises on the development of the EU's Common Foreign and Security Policy, the CFSP. Many of the crises discussed in other sections of this book are also linked to various external factors. The *financial crisis* was fueled by global economic patterns and financial crises outside of Europe, not least in the US (see Caporaso, this volume; Olsen and Rosén, this volume and Trangy and Stenstad, this volume). The *migration crisis* was also largely caused by factors originating outside of the EU, triggered by the internal EU challenges and disagreements that followed the sharp increase in migrants coming to the EU from 2015

M. Riddervold (✉) · A. Newsome
Inland School of Business and Social Sciences, Inland University,
Rena and Lillehammer, Norway
e-mail: marianne.riddervold@inn.no

Institute of European Studies, University of California, Berkeley, CA, USA

A. Newsome
e-mail: akasemi@berkeley.edu

M. Riddervold
The Norwegian Institute of International Affairs (NUPI), Oslo, Norway

J. Trondal
Department of Political Science and Management, University of Agder,
Kristiansand, Norway
e-mail: jarle.trondal@uia.no

ARENA - Centre for European Studies, University of Oslo, Oslo, Norway

© The Author(s) 2021
M. Riddervold et al. (eds.), *The Palgrave Handbook of EU Crises*,
Palgrave Studies in European Union Politics,
https://doi.org/10.1007/978-3-030-51791-5_31

(see Crawford, this volume; Schilde and Goodman, this volume). Much of the EU member states discussions on how to deal with this crisis have thus been linked to the external aspects of migration, including in areas falling under the CFSP (Bosilca, this volume). Similarly, as Svendsen and Whitman discuss in their chapters, the implications of *Brexit* will probably be very visible in the EU foreign and security domain, as one of the EU's strongest foreign policy powers leaves the Union. *Populism and nationalism* are not simply European phenomenon either. As discussed in various chapters, including by Hooghe et al. and by Anderson, there is a new and politically very salient cleavage between supporters and opponents of globalization also in the US, where a populist President Trump explicitly has presented himself as a nationalist, putting "America first." Indeed, in a globalized world, the distinction between domestic and international policies are increasingly blurred, and the strong link we observe between internal and external crises affecting the EU's responses are thus not particularly surprising (see Anderson, this volume for a discussion of the links between several of the crises discussed throughout the Handbook).

However, while the other chapters in this part of the Handbook—on the Financial Crisis, the Migration crisis, Brexit, and the Legitimacy crisis—discuss how each of these crises has played out in the EU and how they have affected EU integration in these fields, the four chapters in this section explicitly explore the impact of externally induced crises and challenges on EU integration in the CFSP only. The main reason for this is that the CFSP is different. Contrary to all other policy areas, the CFSP remains intergovernmentally organized. Rather than following the rules of the "ordinary legislative procedure," decision-making in the CFSP runs by special procedures, based on unitary decisions made by the member states. Consequently, the member states all have the power to veto any policy they might object, and the EU institutions' influence is formally limited. The Commission cannot take cases of noncompliance to the European Court of Justice, and it does not enjoy an agenda-setting monopoly. Neither does the (Union) Council share decision-making powers with the European Parliament. The various factors and intervening variables determining the EU's response to crisis are thus likely to be different from other policy areas. (There are a number of studies exploring the functioning of the CFSP and the various factors influencing developments in the domain. See among others the Handbook on EU Foreign Policy edited by Jørgensen et al. 2015; Sjursen 2011). EU member states have moreover explicitly resisted further foreign and security policy integration, not least in defence, because of the national sensitivity of the policy area. In this sense, the CFSP can be seen as a least likely case of further integration in the EU. If we see the CFSP moving forward in response to crisis, it might thus be indicative of more profound effects of polycrisis on the EU integration project.

Several factors lead us to expect that external crises influence EU foreign and security policy integration. First, the EU foreign and security policy takes place in an increasingly volatile and uncertain international environment. China and Russia have different perspectives on international rules and governance than those who have traditionally formed the basis of the transatlantic relationship. Wars and conflicts are raging in the EU's near abroad both in the wider Middle East and in Ukraine. Second, the uncertainty caused by the Ukraine crisis, escalating with the Russian annexation of Crimea in March 2014 and at the time of writing war is still ongoing on in Ukraine which has particular importance to European security. Indeed, as discussed by Juncos and Pomorska in this volume, both scholars and the EU itself have referred to this crisis as existential to the EU. Moreover, this is happening in parallel to a changing US foreign policy, not least under the Trump Administration. Trump has already challenged some of the core principles underlying transatlantic relations since the Second World War, including the US defense guarantee, open trade relations and the support for multilateral institutions and agreements such as the Paris accord on climate change and the Iran nuclear accord. Some observers have even claimed that Trump's policies serve to undermine the multilateral order itself (see Andersen, this volume; Riddervold and Newsome, this volume).

Chapters in this section explore how this increasingly more uncertain and crisis-ridden environment have affected developments in the CFSP. In particular, chapters focus on three external crises with EU foreign and security policy implications: The Ukraine Crisis, "the Trump Crisis" and the "instability crisis" in the EU's neighborhood caused not least by wars and conflicts in the wider Middle East. Two chapters discuss the EU's foreign and security policy responses to the Russian annexation of Crimea and the ongoing war in Ukraine, arguing that this crisis has strengthened EU foreign and security cooperation, through the scenarios of *muddling through* and *heading forward*.

Juncos and Pomorska explore the puzzle of why the EU was able to form a common policy in response to Russia's actions in Ukraine, in spite of this being a most likely of the first scenario developed in the Introduction, that of *breaking down*. Before the Ukraine crisis, member states had diverging policies vis-à-vis Russia, often reflecting strong economic or strategic interests. Given the fact that the CFSP formally remains in the hands of the member states, following the underlying assumptions of the *breaking down* scenario, one would thus not expect them to agree to any substantial common policies toward Russia. Yet, EU member states were able to exercise coherence by agreeing to impose sanctions against Russia. To explain this puzzle, Juncos and Pomorska draw on two key insights from institutional theory (see Ansell, this volume) linked to the concepts of critical junctures and path dependencies. Applying these in a study of the sanctioning regime, they find that although particular events in 2014 indeed functioned as a critical juncture, the path dependency from previous EU practices of cooperation is key to understand the EU's particular response. Juncos and Pomorska explain the development of the sanctioning regime in two steps. In a first step, they show how two events turned what was previously perceived as a turbulent EU–Russia relationship into a crisis that functioned as critical juncture or tipping point, namely the annexation of Crimea and the downing of the MH17 plane.

These events brought the member states closer together by changing the positions of key member states regarding Russia and the overall EU Russia policy in a way that that was unthinkable prior to the crisis, also reducing the gap between the pro-Russian and more "Russophobe" member states. However, although this was a critical turning point in the EU's Russia policies and led to a stronger focus on the European rather than the national interest, it did not change the already established patterns of cooperation in the EU Council. To the contrary, Juncos and Pomorska find that path-dependent behavior is key to understanding the agreement: It was the fall back to already established practices of consensus-seeking and information-sharing in the Council that enabled the member states to overcome their disagreements and agree on a joint response. Hence, rather than *breaking down* or *heading forward*, the EU's policies with regard to the Ukraine crisis suggest that there has been a lot of continuity and *muddling through*.

Also, *Riddervold* finds that the Ukraine crisis had a strong impact on EU Foreign and Security Policies. Similar to Juncos and Pomorska, Riddervold explores the puzzle of why the member states in recent year have agreed on new CFSP policies in spite of member states' diverging preferences. Discussing two cases of EU maritime foreign and security policies where there initially was much opposition to common EU policies—the EU Maritime Security Strategy and the EU's Arctic policies—Riddervold argues that the Ukraine crisis is key to understanding the adoption of both of these policies. The analysis thus suggests that the EU has responded to Russia's aggression toward Ukraine by deepening cooperation, but also in various other foreign policy areas not directly linked to the Ukraine crisis. In line with the historical institutional concept discussed by Ansell in this volume, this crisis functioned as a *critical juncture*, generating a "window of opportunity" for policy change by allowing member states and EU institutions with an interest in further EU maritime and or/foreign policy integration to place EU security policies on the top of the EU agenda and get support for policies that might otherwise not have been agreed to. None of the alternative theoretically derived hypotheses outlined in the chapter are sufficiently able to account for the adoption of EU policies. Riddervold finds no evidence to suggest that EU policies were part of a bigger balancing game vis-à-vis Russia in cooperation with the US, as a neorealist perspective might suggest, nor that certain norms were the key mobilizing concerns behind new EU policies, as constructivist approaches to EU foreign policy often highlight. Economic interests, often underlined by liberal intergovernmentalist accounts, facilitated EU agreement. Also supporting an institutional approach, the actions of the EU institutions—notably the European Commission and the European External Action Service—were a necessary condition for the adoption of both of these policies. However, it took member state agreement to actually adopt common policies within these domains, and the Ukraine crisis became the tipping point by which the EU member states saw the need for new EU foreign and security policies. Overall, the EU responded to external crises by reactively *heading forward* with new common foreign and security policies more broadly.

In the third chapter on crisis and the EU foreign and security policies, *Rieker and Blockmans* examine the EU's ability to deal with external crises more broadly on the EU's crisis management capacities. Although not traceable back to one particular event or change, the EU's neighborhood has been hit by severe crises in recent years, from the Ukraine to the many civil and interstate wars and conflicts in the Sahel region and the wider Middle East. Against this background, Rieker and Blockmans ask how the EU is managing external crisis. In an increasingly crisis-ridden and volatile external environment, effective and integrated crisis-management has become a top priority. But to what extent has the EU actually become more efficient in its out-of-area crisis management? To contribute with an answer, Rieker and Blockmans develop a theoretical framework that gives a more comprehensive approach to what Christopher Hill in 1993 called the EU foreign policy "capability–expectations gap," describing the EU member states' (insufficient) ability to agree on common policies, allocate resources and commonly deploy foreign policy instruments. To get a full picture of the EU's capacity for external crisis response, they show the importance of exploring two additional potential gaps—"the intentions–implementation gap" and "the implementation– reception/perceptions gap"—linked to the extent to which policy aims are implemented on the ground and to how the EU is perceived in the countries in which it employs its crisis management tools. Exploring EU crisis management in depth across four variables—decision-making capacity, resources, knowledge, and organizational skills—Rieker and Blockmans find that the EU has come a long way in strengthening its capacity as an actor in the realm of crisis response. Even when faced with a volatile external environment, the EU has identified clear crisis management goals and objectives, and developed a stronger institutional foreign policy framework and a crisis-management legal framework. Still, the EU's capacity to respond effectively to certain crises remains seriously hampered by several factors. In purely intergovernmental crisis response, slow decision-making capacity is still a concern. In other areas, the EU's capacity to respond to crises remains hampered by a lack of resources and the inability to effectively learn from experience to ensure a more conflict-sensitive approach to each crisis. In this sense, the authors conclude that recent years' developments of the EU's external crisis management capacity can best be characterized as *muddling through* processes. Faced with challenges linked to the unique intergovernmental character of the CFSP and the member states' willingness to change decision-making and resource allocation in this domain, EU crisis management has moved steadily forward.

Lastly, the fourth chapter in this section explores how the EU relationship with its traditionally strongest ally and friend, the US, has been affected by a background of EU crises and a parallel change in US foreign policies—the latter taking crisis proportions for the Europeans following the election of

Donald Trump, who according to some observers challenges the very foundation of the liberal international order on which the transatlantic relationship was built (also see Andersen, this volume). According to *Riddervold and Newsome* and similar to the two chapters on Ukraine, this crisis contributed to strengthening EU foreign and security policy. Riddervold and Newsome address two questions: How, if at all, have crises affected EU–US relations? And what, if any, has been the impact of potentially changing transatlantic relations on EU foreign policy integration? Drawing on their own empirical data and other studies of transatlantic relations, Riddervold and Newsome find strong evidence to suggest that the EU–US relationship indeed has been weakening against a background of EU crises and a changing US foreign policy under Trump, to the extent that it is even reasonable to speak of a crisis in transatlantic relations. As regards the impact of the Trump crisis, studies moreover suggest that this is not necessarily a temporary phenomenon. Instead one would expect EU–US relations to remain weakened also after Trump owing to the increasingly strong polarization of US policies. Studies show a somewhat mixed picture regarding the impact of a weakening of EU–US relations on EU foreign and security policy integration. According to some studies, the change in US policies has led to a fragmentation of a common EU stance, as the member states all seek "special relations" with their main security provider, the US. A majority of studies, however, suggest that the observed weakening of EU–US relations has mobilized more EU foreign policy cooperation. The EU has accordingly become more unified and autonomous of the US in its policies, seeking other solutions to international challenges than preferred by the US. Faced with a weakening transatlantic relationship, the EU seems to be on the path of *muddling through* or even *heading forward* in its relations with the US.

What broader implications and lessons learned can be drawn from this section? Do we see broader patterns that support any of the three scenarios set out in the introduction to this volume? All four chapters suggest that the EU seems able to cope with crises and that overall, crises and increased uncertainty have led to a strengthening of EU Common Foreign and Security policies. This is surprising, given the intergovernmental character of the domain and several of the member states' traditional reluctance to move EU policy integration further in the domain. Indeed, all chapters discuss how this reluctance combined with the formal CFSP procedures poses challenges to the EU's ability to efficiently act with one voice, whether by resisting new policies, seeking special relations to other states or struggling to implement efficient crisis responses. Agreement on common EU foreign policies, missions and crisis responses can be a cumbersome process, and we also know from other international conflicts that the EU member states often struggle to find a common approach, for example, in Syria and Libya (Schumaker et al. 2017; Novotna 2017; Jørgensen et al. 2015). The cases explored in this Handbook may hence not cover the whole picture of the CFSP. However, what we can say on the basis of our findings and opposite to what some observers have maintained, the CFSP does not seem to be *breaking down* in the face of crisis. Instead, when looking at some of the main external crisis the EU has faced during recent years, not least in Ukraine and linked to the US' turn in policies, the EU and its member states seem to react to by joining forces to become more resilient (also see M.E Smith 2018; Riddervold and Newsome 2018). Still facing challenges not least due to the intergovernmental character of CFSP, the EU has also become better at crisis management and crisis missions than one might expect due to its limited resources. And other studies have shown that Brexit has further served to "foster a sense of unity among the EU-27" (Novotna 2017: 6), driving cooperation in the CFSP forward, including the Commons Security and Defence Policy (Howorth 2018).

Thus, based on the studies conducted in this section, overall, the EU and its member states react to external crises by joining forces to become resilient. Notwithstanding mentioned challenges, and although the EU's foreign and security policy responses to crises indeed might be differentiated on the *external* dimension in the sense that various CFSP agreements and relationships will be formed with non-EU members such as the UK or Norway, these findings also suggest that the EU over time might become *internally* less differentiated in the face of crises in the foreign and security policy domain (see Gänzle et al., this volume). Rather than undermining EU and contrary to what one would expect if we are witnessing a more internally fragmented or differentiated EU foreign and security policy, crises seem over time to drive EU foreign policy integration forward.[1]

References

Jørgensen, K. E., Aarstad, Å. K., Drieskens, E., Laatikainen, K. V., & Tonra, B. (Eds.). (2015). *The SAGE Handbook of European Foreign Policy*. Los Angeles: Sage.

Howorth, J. (2018). Strategic Autonomy and EU-NATO Cooperation: Threat or Opportunity for Transatlantic Defence Relations? *Journal of European Integration, 40*, 523–537. https://doi.org/10.1080/07036337.2018.1512268.

Novotna, T. (2017). The EU as a Global Actor: United We Stand, Divided We Fall. *JCMS: Journal of Common Market Studies, 55*, 177–191. https://doi.org/10.1111/jcms.12601.

Riddervold, M., & Newsome, A. (2018). Transatlantic Relations in Times of Uncertainty: Crises and EU-US Relations. *Journal of European Integration, 40*, 505–521. https://doi.org/10.1080/07036337.2018.1488839.

Schumaker, T., Marchetti, A., & Demmelhuber, T. (2017). *The Routledge Handbook on the European Neighbourhood Policy*. London: Routledge.

---

[1] Denmark still has legally binding opt outs of the CSDP aspects of new CFSP actions and policies.

Sjursen, H. (2011). Not so Intergovernmental After All? On Democracy and Integration in European Foreign and Security Policy. *Journal of European Public Policy*, *18*(8), 1078–1095.

Smith, M. E. (2018). Transatlantic Security Relations since the European Security Strategy: What Role for the EU in Its Pursuit of Strategic Autonomy? *Journal of European Integration*, *40*, 605–620. https://doi.org/10.1080/07036337.2018.1488840.

CHAPTER 32

The EU's Response to the Ukraine Crisis

Ana E. Juncos and Karolina Pomorska

INTRODUCTION

This chapter seeks to explore how crises influence EU foreign policy, what this tells us about the nature and functioning of the policy, as well as what one might expect regarding how the EU might deal with future crises in its neighborhood. In order to examine the impact of crises on change and continuity, this chapter presents a case study of the Ukrainian crisis and the EU's response, in particular, the agreement among the member states to impose sanctions against Russia. Like in other policy areas, we argue that crises have had enduring effects on the EU's foreign policy—in line with Jean Monnet's warning that 'Europe will be forged in crises and will be the sum of the solutions adopted for those crises' (Monnet 1978).

The historical episode examined by this chapter has many characteristics that makes it the most likely case for scenario 1 (Change: *Breaking down*) described by the editors in their introduction to this edited volume (see Introduction). This is because it concerns the intergovernmental EU foreign and security policy. Within this policy, relations with Russia are firmly in the hands of the member states, while supranational institutions have more difficulties in exercising some influence. As we show in the chapter, in this case, the

---

A. E. Juncos (✉)
University of Bristol, Bristol, UK
e-mail: a.e.juncos@bristol.ac.uk

K. Pomorska
Leiden University, Leiden, Netherlands
e-mail: k.m.pomorska@fsw.leidenuniv.nl

© The Author(s) 2021
M. Riddervold et al. (eds.), *The Palgrave Handbook of EU Crises*,
Palgrave Studies in European Union Politics,
https://doi.org/10.1007/978-3-030-51791-5_32

key security and economic interests of the member states were also divergent. Given this model's assumption that member states pursue their own national interest, previous EU–Russia policy record, and existing divergences among the member states regarding EU–Russia policy, explaining EU-level agreement on imposing sanctions on Russia constitutes a challenge for this model. Why did member states come to an agreement? Against earlier assessments of policy failure (Macfarlane and Menon 2014; Mearsheimer 2014), we argue that the Ukraine crisis did not undermine the EU project, resulting instead in an unexpected degree of unity among the member states regarding the sanctions regime on Russia. The question is therefore, why has the EU not broken down in the face of such acute crisis at its borders? We show in this chapter that, in fact, it is scenario 2 (*muddling through*) that most resembles what happened.

In order to explain the EU's response to the Ukrainian crisis, we resort to historical institutionalism and two key insights from this approach. The first concept that guides our explanation is that of *critical juncture* and the associated *uncertainty* and *urgency* related to the crisis.[1] In particular, we argue that while first reactions to the crisis exhibited similar features than previous EU responses to the Georgian crisis, the Orange Revolution or the gas crises, the downing of the MH17 constituted a critical juncture (or tipping point) that changed the positions of key member states (Germany) and constrained those of other countries (e.g. The Netherlands). Secondly, and more importantly, we contend that *previous practices* mattered through *path dependency*, in particular, those of consensus building and information-sharing. Through 'falling back' on the established ways-of-doing-things, i.e. consensus-oriented practices in the Council, member states were able to overcome the traditional divides and agree on a joint response.[2]

A Historical Institutionalist Approach

A historical institutionalist (HI) approach is particularly helpful in explaining the EU's response to the crisis in Ukraine (on Institutionalism, see Chapter 7 of this volume) as it allows us to better understand policy continuity and change. As understood by Pollack, HI focuses on 'the effects of institutions over time, in particular, the way in which a given set of institutions, once established, can influence or constrain the behaviour of the actors who established them' (2004: 139). Hence, preferences are endogenously formed within a given institutional setting. One can only understand the current political context (organizations, rules, and practices) by understanding and analyzing their historical development. This understanding, however, does

---

[1] One can also argue that uncertainty and urgency also explain why actors resort to well-established practices (this is also a key insight in HI analyses).

[2] In this chapter we draw evidence from the official (EU) documents, secondary literature and 6 in-depth, semi-structured interviews conducted by the authors with EU officials and diplomats from the member states between 2014 and 2017.

not neglect the role of agency; instead, agency needs to be understood as strategic action within a particular institutional context. According to Hay and Wincott (1998: 954),

> Actors are strategic, seeking to realize complex, contingent and often changing goals. They do so in a context which favours certain strategies over others and must rely upon perceptions of that context which are at best incomplete and which may very often reveal themselves inaccurate after the event.

A HI approach is based on the premise that prior institutional structures limit available future options and lead one to expect resistance to change owing to institutional legacies. This is particularly true in the case of Common Foreign and Security Policy (CFSP) where prior institutional legacies and practices structure actors' responses. From this perspective, path dependency appears as an important explanatory factor (Bulmer 1998; Pierson 1996; Stacey and Rittberger 2003). According to this literature, earlier decisions constrain the range of options that actors can consider in later moments (Mahoney et al. 2016: 82). This means that not only does history matter, but what also matters is the particular sequence of events. External forces will not have the same result in every period; previous political outcomes will determine the impact of current external forces and then a specific historical development or 'path' (Pierson 2000: 251). According to Pierson, 'actors do not inherit a blank slate [...] instead [they] find that the dead weight of previous institutional choices seriously limits their room for manoeuvre' (in Reynolds 2007: 55). This will favor some decisions and exclude others, eventually, shaping the political outcome.

Yet, a HI approach should not be conceived as static. It does not exclude the possibility of change that might occur as a result of critical junctures, which are defined as '*relatively* short periods of time during which there is a *substantially* heightened probability that agents' choices will affect the outcome of interest' (Capoccia and Kelemen 2007: 348, emphasis in the original). Contingency and uncertainty are key features during critical junctures (and generally political crises). Drawing on the notion of 'punctuated equilibrium' (Krasner 1984; Thelen 1999), critical junctures can be understood as episodes during which: '(a) the range of possible outcomes that might take place in the future briefly but dramatically expands; (b) events occur that quickly close off future possibilities and set into motion processes that track specific future outcomes' (Mahoney et al. 2016: 77). In EU external action, these often occur as a consequence of external events (economic crises or military conflicts) or internal ones (for example, a new Intergovernmental Conference). Actors may exploit these 'windows of opportunity' to introduce innovative policy changes, producing a clear departure from previous policies. In this way, critical juncture also helps reconcile the notions of agency and structure. As explained by Mahoney 'critical junctures are moments of relative structural indeterminism when willful actors shape outcomes in a more voluntaristic fashion than normal circumstances permit ... these choices demonstrate the power of agency by revealing how long-term development patterns can hinge on distant actor decisions of the past' (quoted in Capoccia and Kelemen 2007: 347).

Path dependency and critical junctures have been linked in the literature by considering critical junctures as moments that launch the path dependency process. Nevertheless, one should not assume that critical junctures always lead to sudden or radical change (Capoccia and Kelemen 2007: 348); instead, it might be possible to observe no change or gradual change, turning into a 'slow-moving process of incremental shifts' (Mahoney et al. 2016: 83). In other words, '[i]f change was possible and plausible, considered, and ultimately rejected in a situation of high uncertainty, then there is no reason to discard these cases as "non–critical" junctures"' (Capoccia and Kelemen 2007: 352). This is particularly relevant when critical junctures are related to external crisis and shocks given that there is also an academic bias that sees crises as triggering change. However, crises do not always result in change (e.g. during the financial crisis) and might actually obstruct change (Natorski 2015).

When it comes to conceptualizing change, drawing on Wolfgang Streeck and Kathleen Thelen modes of institutional change—displacement, layering, drift, and conversion (Streeck and Thelen 2005), this chapter thus eschews more transformative forms of change (such as displacement and conversion) for the notion of drift, which refers to 'the changed impact of existing rules due to shifts in the environment' (Mahoney and Thelen 2010: 16). From this perspective, the Ukraine crisis created a window of opportunity and resulted in a new sanctions policy toward Russia, but the way actors coordinated their foreign policies still followed the foreign policy practices of the past.

In this chapter, we consider specifically how past CFSP practices shaped the response to the critical juncture represented by the Ukrainian crisis. These CFSP practices consist of collective rules that guide the behavior of actors. Most of these practices were already identified in the early years of the EPC/CFSP. Otto von der Gablentz, for instance, noted that diplomats involved in the EPC developed a special 'code of conduct' for undertaking common foreign policy in the absence of formal rules and distinguished several features in these interactions, notably 'a commitment to informal decision-making and a consistently communitarian tone of negotiation where, as a general rule, fait accomplis are rarely launched by single diplomacies, even if national interest is felt to be salient' (in Glarbo 1999: 646–647). The practices that will be examined in this chapter are those of coordination reflex and consensus-building. Other practices documented in the literature include the existence of domains reserves, the obligation to justify national positions, confidentiality, or the prohibition of hard-bargaining; ensuring vertical and horizontal consistency and respect for 'agreed' language (Manners and Whitman 2000; Nuttall 1992; Tonra 2001; Smith 2004; Juncos and Pomorska 2006, 2011). However, due to constraints of space, the latter are left out of the analysis.

The existence of a 'co-ordination reflex' dates back to the early years of the European Political Cooperation, with the Copenhagen Report (1973), which noted that the habit of working together had become 'a reflex of co-ordination [...] which has profoundly affected the relations of the member states between each other and with third countries' (as quoted in Allen and Wallace 1982: 26). As Nuttall (1992: 312) observed: 'an automatic reflex of consultation brought by frequent personal contacts with opposite members from other member states'. The coordination reflex refers to a process of sharing information with the rest of member states before a decision has been taken. Informal consultations prior to the meeting are part of everyday work of the representatives. Communicative practices take place through formal channels, such as the COREU network or official mailing lists (Bicchi 2011). Nonetheless, a large bulk of information-sharing is informal. National diplomats remain in close contact through e-mails, mobile phones and frequent meetings that often occur in the corridors and over lunch. Consultations might take place bilaterally, in a group formation (e.g. of 'like-minded' countries) or with the chair of the group (EEAS representative). During these informal negotiations, national representatives inform other colleagues about their positions, in particular 'red lines', or exchange other types of information that may help the decision-making process. These consultations help develop a common understanding among national representatives and, in turn, foster consensus-building.

Consensus-building has also been identified in the literature as a key CFSP practice when it comes to the adoption of decisions, by contrast to hard-bargaining or confrontational methods (Tonra 2001; Smith 2004). As noted before, CFSP is subject to intergovernmental bargaining with states, apart from a few exceptions, retaining their veto powers. Interestingly enough, member states do not generally make use of their veto power during negotiations; on the contrary, there is a general practice to 'keep everyone on-board' and to achieve consensus. Member states' diplomats try to generate a broad agreement regarding the decision, so no member state feels isolated. This is a two-way process because not only will the majority try to integrate the minority, but also the potentially isolated will try to find supporters, instead of behaving unilaterally. That is why CFSP policies are not the exclusive result of lowest common denominator decisions.

Socialization processes facilitate the adoption of these practices by actors participating in CFSP institutions (Juncos and Pomorska 2006, 2011). It is also worth mentioning that some of these practices such as consensus-building are not exclusive of CFSP policymaking, but can be found in other EU policy areas (see for example, Lewis 2005). The fact that there are no enforceable mechanisms in this field and that unanimity is the rule, however, makes their existence even more significant in CFSP.

The EU's Response to the Ukrainian Crisis

As mentioned above, the policies of the member states toward Russia had been a subject of ongoing disagreements in the European Union. Divergent historical experiences as well as economic and security interests challenged the Union's ability to deliver a unified response to Russia's actions, let alone a coherent policy. In fact, policy toward Russia is usually considered as a case which 'reveals internal differences and the incoherence of EU policy most sharply' (Schmidt-Felzmann 2013: 193). As put forward by Bechev, in the case of relations with Russia, we can observe a 'Europeanization deficit' (Bechev 2013; see also Pomorska 2017; David et al. 2013; Schmidt-Felzmann 2014), as they are mainly conducted bilaterally and not through the EU. Previous crises in Georgia and Ukraine, have brought member states' attention to the Union's relationship with Russia and, arguably, fostered the way into agreement over the so-called Eastern Partnership (EaP). Even when the crisis in Ukraine intensified and the 'little green man' appeared in Crimea, some member states were in disbelief that these were Russian troops on the ground (Ikani et al. 2020).

In the particular case of sanctions against Russia, the initial positions of the member states seemed difficult to reconcile. Austria, Hungary, Czech Republic, Slovakia, Cyprus, Finland, Greece, Luxembourg, the Netherlands, and Spain started off from rather reluctant positions on sanctions to avoid economic harm resulting from Russian reactions (Schult et al. 2014). Therefore, it is not surprising that the expectations were modest on whether the EU would produce a common, strong response to the events in Ukraine. Hence, the first scenario, linked by the editors to rationalist perspectives and intergovernmental policies, seems particularly relevant in this area of foreign and security policy. Here, policymaking is supposed to follow interstate bargaining and in a security crisis such as the one in Ukraine, the EU's decision-making is expected to stall or break down. One would expect the member states to focus on their own security interests, such as securing the borders.

Theoretically, the Ukrainian crisis could be considered as the most likely case for the first scenario, in line with realist and rationalist expectations. As shown in the literature, in situations of crisis, the European Council and the Council is in general strengthened as compared to other institutional actors on the EU (Rhinard 2019). In our case, the divergent security and economic interests of the member states in the Council were clear and their salience was high. For example, Germany had to consider its high dependence on Russia in economic and energy fields, while France had pending contracts on Mistral helicopter carriers (for more on this see: Natorski and Pomorska 2017: 59). In addition, as argued by Sjursen and Rosen (2017), supranational actors like the European Commission or the European External Action Service (EEAS) have more difficulty exerting any significant influence in intergovernmental policy fields, such as foreign and security policy (but see Morillas 2019). Moreover, the institutional features of the CFSP also explain the existence of Trojan horses within the EU in the form of pro-Russian member states and political parties (Orenstein and Kelemen 2017).[3]

Yet, the empirical evidence shows that the first scenario did not take place. On the contrary, the EU was able to deliver a collective response and national interests did not prevail in discussions within the Council. In fact, as one of the interviewed diplomats stated, the crisis brought people together. Consensus was easier to reach and it was only the 'return to normal' (out of crisis) situation that could open up the discussions over the necessity of sanctions. As one of our interviewees told us: 'During the Ukrainian crisis the EU overcame the traditional division into two blocks. France and Germany moved to the proactive block' (Interview 21). Two insights from HI—critical juncture and path dependence (the prevalence previous practices)—can help explain this (unexpected) outcome. In what follows, we discuss each of them in turn.

The Ukraine Crisis as a Critical Juncture

Following the understanding of critical juncture posited above, the crisis in Ukraine in 2014 can be understood as a critical juncture for the EU policies vis-à-vis Russia. As will be shown, the crisis opened up a period of heightened contingency, where changes to EU policies that were once unthinkable were made possible, even if ultimately, it did not lead to a drastic rethinking of EU policies toward Russia and, more broadly, the Eastern neighborhood. Several scholars agree that the nature of the events in Ukraine needs to be understood as a crisis, rather than just a continuation of previous turbulences in EU–Russia policies. Turbulence had characterized EU relations with Russia over the previous decade. The energy crises of 2006 and 2009, as well as the Russian–Georgian war in August 2008 had already created much distrust among the parties. In fact, turbulence was very much the 'normal' state of affairs in EU–Russia relations during this period, which culminated with the crisis that ensued after the Vilnius Summit and the Maidan Square protests at the end of 2013 (Cadier 2014; Haukkala 2015).

The difference in this case was that the 2014 events, in particular, the invasion of the Crimea and the downing of the MH17, led to a full-scale crisis, threatening the core values of the EU project and even the viability of the EU's integration project. For instance, Howorth (2017: 33) has argued that the Ukraine crisis 'is arguably the most severe crisis of the 21st century in Europe's neighborhood'. This is the case because it challenged 'the fundamental values, interests and even, potentially, the existence of the EU'. Ikani (2019: 20) also agrees with this assessment and argues that the crisis posed a 'severe geopolitical challenge' for the EU, and that the conflict in Ukraine 'significantly undermined the EU's economic and political integration initiatives in the region'. This sense of crisis is well reflected in EU strategic policy

---

[3] Orenstein and Kelemen (2017) mention Hungary, Italy, Greece, and Cyprus as Russian Trojan horses although they argue that this list is not definitive.

documents. The EU Global Strategy, drafted after the events in Ukraine, for instance, declares: 'We live in times of existential crisis, within and beyond the European Union. Our Union is under threat. Our European project, which has brought unprecedented peace, prosperity and democracy, is being questioned' (EUGS 2016: 13). The crisis in Ukraine is specifically mentioned in this passage: 'To the east, the European security order has been violated' (EUGS 2016: 13) and later on in the EU Global Strategy:

> peace and stability in Europe are no longer a given. Russia's violation of international law and the destabilisation of Ukraine, on top of protracted conflicts in the wider Black Sea region, have challenged the European security order at its core. (EUGS 2016: 33)

This statement also reflects a significant alteration of key member state positions (e.g. France and Germany) regarding Russia and of the overall EU–Russia policy, which was unthinkable prior to the crisis. As a result of the crisis, the gap between the Russophobe and pro-Russian member states was narrowed (Sjursen and Rosen 2017). Orenstein and Kelemen also agree that 'the severity of the crisis caused a convergence of perceptions and interests about the Russian threat among the most powerful Member States in the foreign policy arena – the UK, France and Germany' (2017: 89; also 95). Drawing on a historical institutionalist approach, Ikani (2019) also argues that the crisis can be understood as a critical juncture for the European Neighbourhood Policy (ENP) as it led to 'a profound rethink' of this policy. When presenting their consultation paper on the ENP review, the HR Federica Mogherini and the European Commissioner for Neighbourhood and Enlargement Negotiations, Johannes Hahn, stated that 'We need to review our policy, our way of working, our partnership with the countries of our region […]. In particular because as our region is in flames, both to the East and South, we have to use all the potential of our bilateral relations with partners in the region to have an effective impact on our region' (European Commission 2015).

Despite this rhetoric, Ikani distinguishes between *change* at the level of policy ambitions (with the 2015 ENP review aimed at responding to the 'return of geopolitics' in the East) and *continuity* in relation to policy objectives and tools. Other authors have highlighted the degree of continuity in EU neighborhood policies due to the legacies of previous rounds of enlargement (Phinnemore 2003), but also the way that the institutional governance of the ENP and the need to achieve agreement among the member states has favored continuity over change (Ikani 2019: 40; Natorski 2015, 2016; Noutcheva 2015).[4] In the case of the EU's policy toward Russia, Howorth (2017: 122)

---

[4]This argument is also in line with explanations of institutional inertia such as Scharpf's 'joint-decision trap' (1988). According to Scharpf, institutional change will be less likely in institutions characterized by intergovernmentalism, unanimity, and a default condition in which the status quo remains if there is a lack of agreement. According to Stacey and Rittberger (2003), a high number of institutional veto points (i.e. the number of actors

argues that despite agreement among the member states on a sanction policy, the EU still lacks 'a coherent or viable strategy towards Ukraine – or indeed towards its two neighborhoods (South and East) in general'. Hence, and despite the heighten sense of insecurity and uncertainty caused by the crisis, there remain a lot of continuity in the EU's approach to the East.

In line with Capoccia and Kelemen (2007), we argue that the understanding of the crisis as a critical juncture has less to do with the degree of change (the outcome) resulting from a crisis than with the fact that the nature of the crisis increased *substantially* the probability of a change in EU Eastern policies compared to prior to the crisis, regardless of whether the change happened in practice or not or the type of policy change (policy aims, objectives, tools). In fact, the unity that was shown by EU member states around the issue of sanctions was *unexpected*, especially considering previous assessments of EU relations vis-à-vis Russia (see Natorski and Pomorska 2017). For example, with the imposition of a sanctions regime on Russia, Orenstein and Kelemen noted that the EU 'exceeded expectations of many observers' and that 'the crisis *enabled* the EU to mount a concerted response to Russian aggression' (2017: 87, emphasis added).[5] As put forward by one of the interviewees, '[t]he crisis has shown that, contrary to some popular opinions, the EU is able to act, taking into account what is possible according to the Treaties' (Interview 21). The crisis was generally seen as a test case for the EU: 'on Russia sanctions, everyone realized that if the EU had not been able to come together and adopt sanctions then when would it be able to bring people together?' (Interview 26).

Two events, particularly, created the conditions for change that turned the crisis into a critical juncture: the annexation of Crimea and the downing of the MH17 plane. Most of the responses preceding these events followed the previous well-known script in EU–Russia relations that had been rehearsed in the past (e.g. during the gas crises or the Georgia-Russia war): rhetorical condemnation of Russian policies in the East, mediation by EU member states and institutions, a divide and rule strategy by Russia, and a conciliatory stance from EU friendly member states such as Germany and France. The first responses to the crisis followed this template and provided evidence of a cacophony of voices among EU member states and EU institutions vis-à-vis Russia (Howorth 2017: 129–130; Natorski and Pomorska 2017: 59; Pridham 2014: 56–57). After the annexation of the Crimea by Russia, the first signals questioning this script started to emerge, with some discussion of potential sanctions. Ikani (2019: 38) also argues that two weeks after the referendum in Crimea held in March 2014 was 'the first time since the eruption of the crisis

---

that can veto a decision on institutional change), divergences among actors about the desirability of institutional reform or uncertainties as to its potential pay-offs are factors explaining institutional inertia.

[5] Despite this remarkable show of unity, it has also been noted that some member states (or Russian Trojan horses) continued pursuing their bilateral pro-Russia policies, such as in the area of energy policy or military cooperation (Orenstein and Kelemen 2017).

that the possibility of ENP reform is proposed' at a meeting of the Weimar Triangle between the foreign ministers of Germany, France and Poland. A former Ambassador summarized the change that resulted from the Crimea annexation: 'The Russian aggression was a clear challenge to the architecture of the system; for three and a half years I was in a minority in COREPER and I had been trying to get out of such a scheme. The Russian aggression put an end to thinking that if I am left in peace then that's fine. This gap between the South and the East started to narrow' (Interview 22).

The downing of the MH17 can be seen even more as a turning point in EU policies toward Russia. The shooting down of a commercial plane over Eastern Ukraine on July 17, 2014, killing all 298 passengers on board not only shocked the European publics, but also EU policymakers. Several observers agree that this event led to a change in position of a number of key member states, namely, the Netherlands, but also Germany and France, resulting in the decision to trigger sectoral sanctions on Russia in the summer of 2014 (Howorth 2017; Ikani 2019). For Natorski and Pomorska (2017: 63), '[t]he downing of the plane increased uncertainty and escalated the crisis'. Orenstein and Kelemen (2017: 94) argue that '[t]he shooting down of MH17 and the Russian response to it caused the trust of EU leaders with Russia to break down completely, most importantly the relations between German Chancellor Angela Merkel and Russian President Vladimir Putin'. Hence, Merkel declared that the MH17 tragedy showed that 'the Ukraine crisis is by no means solely a regional issue. No, this example shows us: it affects all of us' (quoted in Ikani 2019: 39). One of our interviewees agreed that 'The first batch of sanctions was very small, symbolic, but the MH17 was a tipping point, it was very hard for countries to oppose [sectorial sanctions] after that' (Interview 26). Ikani (2019) also argues that this event provided 'fresh impetus to reform the ENP' in the months to come. Meyer et al. (2019) quote their interview with former Polish Foreign Minister Radek Sikorski, who explained that '[i]t was when the Russians shot down that Malaysian plane and when the Dutch, the sensible, commercially minded, predictable Dutch, when they described how they [the Russian-backed separatists] were treating the victims, what the evidence was and how unacceptable [this was], they carried the room. Some of the sanctions were extended out of sympathy with the Dutch position'. While the critical juncture opened up the possibility of change, preexisting CFSP practices shaped the way negotiations between the member states took place.

CONSENSUS-BUILDING AND COORDINATION IN RESPONSE TO THE CRISIS

The crisis in Ukraine, according to our evidence, did not result in the erosion of established practices within the Council. This would be expected if the first scenario (*breaking down*) was to take place. In such case, different national interests would prevail and result in a fragmented response to Russia. On the contrary, the practices of consensus-building and information-sharing became key in the process of agreeing on a common approach. As put by one of the interviewed diplomats, the crisis did bring about change in the form of an even stronger emphasis on the European common interest, rather than national preferences:

> The crisis has shown that, contrary to some popular opinions, the EU is able to act, taking into account what is possible according to the Treaties. The pressure of external events was so high that we hid our own national interests; this pressure concerns the values; the public opinion expected the EU to do something. Normally some member states push for their interests but in this case they felt "stupid" and it was easier to convince them to follow the EU-line, based on values. (Interview 21)

The consensus-building practice during the crisis was also noted in the literature. Orenstein and Kelemen (2017) argued that the EU had quickly engaged in the 'usual EU techniques of consensus-building through logrolling and side-payments'. We would emphasize another dimension of consensus-building, which manifested itself through keeping everyone on-board, respecting member states' vulnerabilities, and through solidarity. As discussed by Natorski and Pomorska (2017), the Commission and the EEAS played an active part in the consensus-building practice, especially by disseminating information among the member states. In the words of one of our interviewees, the crisis 'soothe[d] the edges; most delegates focused on big issues; on the case of sanctions, the key issue was whether the proposals were balanced, all due care was taken that the potential impact on the EU would not fall to few selected member states' (Interview 86; Natorski and Pomorska 2017). Attention was paid so that the sanctions that were discussed would 'be based on the principle of equal pain', as put by a British diplomat (quoted in MacFarlane and Menon 2014: 100).

As reported by one of the interviewees, France and Germany quickly begun a very close coordination, especially between the capitals, 'almost to the level of instructions' (Interview 21). This cooperation continued in the broader format of the so-called Weimar Triangle, which consists of Poland, France, and Germany. Here, it was Poland that linked with the member states in Eastern Europe and kept them 'in the loop'. Its presence in the Weimar format guaranteed that the voice of other Eastern EU member states would be included in narrower consultations. It is important to emphasize that even though consensus is often firstly built through smaller groups ('like-minded' groups or regional grouping; sometimes also called minilateralism), in this case, there was a concentrated effort to keep all member states informed, especially in advance of the preparation of Foreign Affairs Council conclusions. A case in point was the initiatives that were negotiated within the Weimar Triangle forum. As one interviewee put it: 'The Weimar Triangle was (…) a trust-building process with France. Then the others from the South were looking and thought, OK, if France is fine with it, so are we. This group was a laboratory of consensus-building between the South, the East and Germany. Our Eastern region learnt that the Weimar Triangle was a way for us to have any influence' (Interview 22).

Another important element of the consensus-building process is that member states must wait until a single position is agreed upon by the Union and must not speak out on their own prematurely. In the case of the Ukrainian crisis, this norm was followed, even by the big member states and those with key interests at stake. Sjursen and Rosen (2017: 25) show in their article evidence in support of this argument. The British Foreign Secretary and German government officials refused to outline the British position before the European Council met. A similar need for consultation was expressed by the Swedish foreign minister. Sjursen and Rosen also demonstrate in their study that member states altered their positions during the consensus-building process after they learnt the positions of their partners (Sjursen and Rosen 2017).

Yet, due to the nature of the crisis, the amount of information available to member states was unequal. Some were well-informed on the situation on the ground, while others needed to rely on their partners. The norm of information-sharing, therefore, became ever more important. Negotiations within the so-called Normandy format were a potential challenge to the information-sharing norm because the EU was represented by only two of its member states (Germany and France), while the High Representative was not taking part. But even in this situation, it was reported that both France and Germany, but in particular German Chancellor Merkel, made sure to keep the Council fully informed of the situation in Minsk and to reassure the other member states that Germany and France were acting in 'good faith' and in accordance with what was agreed in the Council. For example, Chancellor Merkel took care to keep Warsaw closely in the information-loop before and after the meetings (Interview 13). National diplomats in general considered the information shared as solid and reliable (Natorski and Pomorska 2017: 64).

CONCLUSION

This chapter has considered a case of a security crisis in the EU's closest neighborhood. At first sight, one would expect it to show the prevalence of the first (*breaking down*) scenario. Nonetheless, the way in which the EU handled the Ukrainian crisis fits the second scenario, of *muddling through*. The everyday code of conduct in the Council was observed by the member states. The strong norms of consensus-building and information-sharing prevailed over particular national interests, even in the context of an acute crisis, within an intergovernmental policy area (security), and in the case of policy toward Russia, which has historically divided the Union. We had argued that it was the adherence to these norms, in addition to the critical juncture caused by the downing of MH17 plane, that allowed for sanctions to be discussed and agreed upon.

Despite the agreement on sanctions, we still find that the overall EU foreign policy toward Ukraine and Eastern Europe shows a lot of continuity and 'muddling through'. As such, there is less evidence of the third scenario (*heading forward*). In policy terms, the hardening of the policy toward Russia may be perceived as a (limited) change in the EU's policy toward Russia. Similar to the case of the Georgia conflict, the Ukraine crisis brought the South and the East closer together. However, in terms of policy innovation and strategic outlook, there were (once again) no major changes. According to Howorth (2017: 132), '[b]eyond the sanctions, whose effects are debatable, there was no attempt to devise a common strategic approach to Russia via diplomacy or commerce, and no sign of any increase in European military preparedness via the Common Security and Defence Policy'.

In sum, this chapter has discarded the first scenario as the system did not break down in face of the Russian challenge in Ukraine and there was a common response on the part of the EU when it came to the imposition of sanctions on Russia. The rhetoric surrounding these actions was also more united and stronger than in the past. Similarly, when it came to the ENP and its reform, there was a consensus on the need to revise and reform this policy as a consequence of the crisis. The fact that there is still a lack of strategic consensus on what the medium- and long-term relations with Ukraine and Russia should look like suggests that we are still faced with a case of *muddling through* (see Howorth 2017; Natorski 2016).

Theoretically, the chapter showed the relevance of institutionalist approaches and in particular, the two historical institutionalist insights of critical juncture and path dependence. While the critical juncture resulting from the crisis brought the positions of the member states closer together, previous norms such as consensus-building or information continued to provide scripts for behavior in the Council during the response to a crisis of such magnitude as the annexation of Crimea and the shooting down of the MH17.

In more general terms, this chapter has shown how the strong procedural norms can hold the Union together, even in the face of a large security crisis at its borders. The chapter also confirms previous studies that have suggested that critical junctures might not necessarily lead to change in European foreign and security policy, but instead result in continuity. The findings also point to a possible future research agenda looking at the links between these procedural norms and the changes to the substance of EU's external policies.

REFERENCES

Allen, D., & Wallace, W. (1982). European Political Cooperation: The Historical and Contemporary Background. In D. Allen, R. Rummel, & W. Wessels (Eds.), *European Political Cooperation: Towards a Foreign Policy for Western Europe*. London: Butterworths.

Bechev, D. (2013). Bulgaria: The Travails of Europeanization. In M. Baun & D. Marek (Eds.), *The New Member States and the European Union: Foreign Policy and Europeanization*. London: Routledge.

Bicchi, F. (2011). The EU as a Community of Practice: Foreign Policy Communications in the COREU Network. *Journal of European Public Policy*, 18(8), 1115–1132.

Bulmer, S. (1998). New Institutionalism and the Governance of the Single European Market. *Journal of European Public Policy*, 5, 365–386.

Cadier, D. (2014). Eastern Partnership vs Eurasian Union? The EU-Russia Competition in the Shared Neighbourhood and the Ukraine Crisis. *Global Policy*, 5(October), 76–85. https://doi.org/10.1111/gpol.2014.5.issue-s1.

Capoccia, G., & Kelemen, R. D. (2007). The Study of Critical Junctures: Theory, Narrative, and Counterfactuals in Historical Institutionalism. *World Politics*, 59(3), 341–369.

David, M., Gower, J., & Haukkala, H. (2013). *National Perspectives on Russia: European Foreign Policy in the Making?* London: Routledge.

European Commission. (2015). Joint Press Conference by High Representative/Vice-President Federica MOGHERINI and Commissioner Johannes HAHN on European Neighbourhood Policy Review (Brussels). http://europa.eu/rapid/press-release_SPEECH-15-4553_en.htm.

Glarbo, K. (1999). Wide-Awake Diplomacy: Reconstructing the Common Foreign and Security Policy of the European Union. *Journal of European Public Policy*, 6(4), 634–651.

Haukkala, H. (2015). From Cooperative to Contested Europe? The Conflict in Ukraine as a Culmination of a Long-Term Crisis in EU–Russia Relations. *Journal of Contemporary European Studies*, 23(1), 25–40. https://doi.org/10.1080/14782804.2014.1001822.

Hay, C., & Wincott, D. (1998). Structure, Agency and Historical Institutionalism. *Political Studies*, 46(5), 951–957.

High Representative. (2016). Shared Vision, Common Action: A stronger Europe. *A Global Strategy for the EU's Foreign and Security Policy*. https://europa.eu/globalstrategy/sites/globalstrategy/files/eugs_review_web.pdf.

Howorth, J. (2017). 'Stability on the Borders': The Ukraine Crisis and the EU's Constrained Policy Towards the Eastern Neighbourhood. *Journal of Common Market Studies*, 55(1), 121–136.

Ikani, N. (2019). Change and Continuity in the European Neighbourhood Policy: The Ukraine Crisis as a Critical Juncture. *Geopolitics*, 24(1), 20–50. https://doi.org/10.1080/14650045.2017.1422122.

Ikani, N., Guttmann, A., & Meyer C. O. (2020). An Analytical Framework for Postmortems of European Foreign Policy: Should Decision-makers Have Been Surprised? *Intelligence and National Security*, 35(2), 197–215. https://doi.org/10.1080/02684527.2019.1704384.

Juncos, A., & Pomorska, K. (2006). Playing the Brussels Game: Strategic Socialization in the CFSP Council Working Groups. *European Integration Online Papers*, *10*(11), 1–17.

Juncos, A., & Pomorska, K. (2011). Invisible and Unaccountable? National Representatives and Council Officials in EU Foreign Policy. *Journal of European Public Policy*, *18*(8), 1096–1114.

Krasner, S. D. (1984). Approaches to the State: Alternative Conceptions and Historical Dynamics. *Comparative Politics*, *16*(2), 243–266.

Lewis, J. (2005). The Janus Face of Brussels: Socialisation and Everyday Decision Making in the European Union. *International Organization*, *59*(Fall 2005), 937–971.

MacFarlane, N., & Menon, A. (2014). The EU and Ukraine. *Survival*, *56*(6), 95–101.

Mahoney, J., & Thelen, K. (2010). *Explaining Institutional Change: Ambiguity, Agency, and Power*. New York: Cambridge University Press.

Mahoney, J., Mohamedali, K., & Nguyen, C. (2016). Causality and Time in Historical Institutionalism. In O. Fioretos, T. G. Falleti, & A. Sheingate (Eds.), *The Oxford Handbook of Historical Institutionalism* (pp. 71–89). New York: Oxford University Press.

Manners, I., & Whitman, R. (2000). *The Foreign Policies of European Union Member States*. Manchester: Manchester University Press.

Mearsheimer, J. J. (2014). Why the Ukraine Crisis is the West's Fault. *Foreign Affairs*, *93*(5), 1–12.

Monnet, J. (1978). *Memoirs*. UK: Third Millennium Publishing (republished 2015).

Morillas, P. (2019). Autonomy in Intergovernmentalism: The Role of de Novo Bodies in External Action During the Making of the EU Global Strategy. *Journal of European Integration*. https://doi.org/10.1080/07036337.2019.1666116.

Meyer, C., De Franco, C., & Otto, F. (2019). *Warning about War: Conflict, Persuasion and Foreign Policy* (pp. 250–251). Cambridge: Cambridge University Press.

Natorski, M. (2015). Epistemic (Un)Certainty in Times of Crisis: The Role of Coherence as a Social Convention in the European Neighbourhood Policy After the Arab Spring. *European Journal of International Relations*, *22*(3), 646–670.

Natorski, M. (2016). The EU and Crisis in Ukraine: Policy Continuity in Times of Disorder? In D. Bouris & T. Schumacher (Eds.), *The Revised European Neighbourhood Policy: Continuity and Change in EU Foreign Policy* (pp. 177–196). Basingstoke: Palgrave Macmillan.

Natorski, M., & Pomorska, K. (2017). Trust and Decision-Making in Times of Crisis: The EU's Response to the Events in Ukraine. *Journal of Common Market Studies*, *55*(1), 54–70.

Noutcheva, G. (2015). Institutional Governance of European Neighbourhood Policy in the Wake of the Arab Spring. *Journal of European Integration*, *37*(1), 19–36. https://doi.org/10.1080/07036337.2014.975987.

Nuttall, S. (1992). *European Political Co-operation*. Oxford: Clarendon Press.

Orenstein, M., & Kelemen, R. D. (2017). Trojan Horses in EU Foreign Policy. *Journal of Common Market Studies*, *55*(1), 87–102.

Phinnemore, D. (2003). Stabilisation and Association Agreements: Europe Agreements for the Western Balkans? *European Foreign Affairs Review*, *8*, 77–103.

Pierson, P. (1996). The Path to European Integration: A Historical Institutionalist Analysis. *Comparative Political Studies*, *29*(2), 123–163.

Pierson, P. (2000). Increasing Returns, Path Dependence, and the Study of Politics. *American Political Science Review,* 94(2), 251–267.

Pollack, M. (2004). The New Institutionalisms and European Integration. In A. Wiener & T. Diez (Eds.), *European Integration Theory* (pp. 137–156). Oxford: Oxford University Press.

Pomorska, K. (2017). Foreign Policies of Eastern EU States. In R. Whitman, I. Manners, & A. Hadfield (Eds.), *Foreign Policies of EU Member States.* London: Routledge.

Pridham, G. (2014). EU/Ukraine Relations and the Crisis with Russia, 2013–14: A Turning Point. *International Spectator: Italian Journal of International Affairs,* 49(4), 53061.

Rhinard, M. (2019). The Crisisification of Policy-Making in the European Union. *Journal of Common Market Studies,* 57(3), 616–633.

Reynolds, C. (2007). Governing Security in the European Union: Institutions as Dynamics and Obstacles. In D. de Bievre & C. Neuhold (Eds.), D*ynamics and Obstacles of European Governance* (pp. 51–76). Chelthenham: Edward Elgar.

Scharpf, F. (1988). The Joint-Decision Trap: Lessons from German Federalism and European Integration. *Public Administration,* 66(autumn 1988), 239–78.

Schmidt-Felzmann, A. (2013). Conducting Relations with a Difficult Neighbor: The EU's Struggle to Influence Russian Domestic Politics. In G. Noutcheva, K. Pomorska & G. Bosse (Eds.), *The EU and Its Neighbours: Values Versus Security in European Foreign Policy.* Manchester: Manchester University Press.

Schmidt-Felzmann, A. (2014). Is the EU's Failed Relationship with Russia the Member States' Fault? *L'Europe En Formation,* 374, 40–60.

Schult, C., Schindler, J., & Neukirch, R. (2014). *Why EU Sanctions are a Bluff.* Spiegel International.

Sjursen, H., & Rosen, G. (2017). Arguing Sanctions: On the EU's Response to the Crisis in Ukraine. *Journal of Common Market Studies,* 55(1), 20–36.

Smith, M. E. (2004). *Europe's Foreign and Security Policy: The Institutionalization of Cooperation.* Cambridge: Cambridge University Press.

Stacey, J., & Rittberger, B. (2003). Dynamics of Formal and Informal Institutional Change in the EU. *Journal of European Public Policy,* 10(6), 858–883.

Streeck, W., & Thelen, K. (2005). Introduction: Institutional Change in Advanced Political Economies. In W. Streeck & K. Thelen (Eds.), *Beyond Continuity: Institutional Change in Advanced Political Economies.* Oxford: Oxford University Press.

Thelen, K. (1999). Historical Institutionalism in Comparative Politics. *Annual Review of Political Science,* 2(1), 369–404. https://doi.org/10.1146/annurev.polisci.2.1.369.

Tonra, B. (2001). *The Europeanisation of National Foreign Policy: Dutch, Danish and Irish Foreign Policy in the European Union.* Aldershot: Ashgate.

CHAPTER 33

Heading Forward in Response to Crisis: How the Ukraine Crisis Affected EU Maritime Foreign and Security Policy Integration

Marianne Riddervold

INTRODUCTION

This chapter illustrates how crisis influences EU foreign and security policy integration by exploring the impact of the Ukraine crisis on EU maritime foreign and security policy integration across two least likely cases not directly linked to the crisis as such: The EU's Maritime Security Strategy (EUMSS) and the EU's Arctic policies. From the outset, it is puzzling that EU member states agreed to adopt these policies.[1] Many EU member states have strong economic and strategic maritime interests, and have preferred not to limit their ability to move freely in defense of these interests by committing to a common policy (Germond 2015; Riddervold and Rosén 2015). When first suggested by the Spanish Presidency in 2010, the idea of developing an EU Maritime Security Strategy was therefore met with mixed reactions, including resistance by several member states (Frontini 2014). Much opposition was initially also expressed toward a common EU Arctic policy: Member states either viewed

[1] Interviews (2010), (2013),(2014)— see below. Also see A. Frontini, 'The European Union Maritime Security Strategy: sailing uncharted waters?', 26 June (2014), http://www.epc.eu/pub_details.php?pub_id=4569; Germond (2015).

M. Riddervold (✉)
Inland School of Business and Social Sciences, Inland University, Rena and Lillehammer, Norway
e-mail: marianne.riddervold@inn.no

The Norwegian Institute of International Affairs (NUPI), Oslo, Norway

Institute of European Studies, University of California, Berkeley, CA, USA

Arctic issues as too sensitive given Russia's interests in the area, feared too much Commission involvement or simply regarded this as an area with no relevance for the EU (Germond 2015; Offerdal 2011; Riddervold and Cross 2019; Weber and Romanyshyn 2011). So, why did the member states agree to adopt an extensive maritime strategy and to develop a distinct EU Arctic policy within the CFSP framework in 2014?

This chapter argues that the answer to this question is linked to the Ukraine crisis. Agreement among the EU member states to adopt common EU policies in these domains was largely driven by the crisis caused by increased Russian aggression and in particular its annexation of Crimea in 2014. In line with the historical institutional concept discussed by Ansell in this volume, this crisis functioned as a *critical juncture*, generating a 'window of opportunity' for policy change by allowing member states and EU institutions with an interest in further EU maritime and or/foreign policy integration to place EU security policies at the top of the EU agenda and get support for policies that otherwise could have been rejected. In this sense, the EU is also a *reactive foreign policy power*, reacting to external, geopolitical events by developing common policies, also in areas not directly linked to crisis as such (Riddervold and Cross 2019).

To explain the EUMSS and EU Arctic policies and substantiate this argument, the chapter proceeds as follows. First, I briefly present the two cases explored. Thereafter follows the analysis, which is conducted in two steps. The first part explores the impact of the Ukraine crisis on the EUMSS and the development of an EU Arctic policy. To control for the influence of other theoretically deduced explanations of EU policies, in a second part I go on to discuss the relevance of four alternative explanations of EU policies, each building on various integration theories set out in the theory section of this volume. One, t the EUMSS and EU Arctic policies can be explained by a neorealist approach, suggesting that the member states developed these policies to defensively balance an increasingly aggressive Russia by bandwagoning with its traditional hegemon, the US, (see Reichwein and Zimmermann's chapters in this volume; Waltz 1979). Two, the EUMSS and the EU's Arctic policies reflect an attempt to promote certain foreign policy norms on the international stage, as a constructivist perspective might suggest (see Cross this volume). In particular, the EU is often referred to as a normative or humanitarian power, due to its focus on promoting democracy and human rights, its multilateral focus, and its reputation as being a leader in climate negotiations (Elgström and Smith 2008; Falkner 2007: Manners 2002). Third, member states adopted the EUMSS and EU Arctic policies to defend their own economic interests and concerns, in line with a liberal intergovernmentalist approach (on this approach see Schimmelfennig this volume; Meunier and Nicolaïdis 2006; Moravcsik 1998; Moravcsik and Schimmelfennig 2009). Finally, EU institutional actors—the Commission and the External Action Service (EEAS) drove the EUMSS and EU Arctic policy processes as these actors had—a vested interest in further EU integration in the domain, in line with a rational institutional approach (see Ansell this volume; Cram 1994; Dijkstra 2014; Pollack 1997: Tallberg 2003). I conclude by summing up the findings and discussing their broader relevance with regards to the debate on differentiated integration as well as the three scenarios of crisis and EU integration set out in the introduction to this volume.

Cases

Several EU member states have developed their own maritime security strategies and/or policies toward the Arctic. However, this chapter limits its treatment of the EU's Arctic and maritime security policies to the common EU policies decided within the framework of the EU's Common Foreign and Security Policy (CFSP). As discussed earlier in this section of this volume, CFSP is the only EU policy-area that is still intergovernmentally organized. In CFSP, decision-making powers lie exclusively with member states in the Council and its preparatory bodies, most importantly the member states' ambassadors in the Political and Security Committee (PSC), who decide on common policies and actions on the basis of unanimity among the member states. Consequently, formally, the supranational EU institutions have only limited or no competence in the field (Merket 2012). As opposed to other policy-domains, the Council does not share its decision-making powers with the European Parliament and the Commission does not have the right to initiate new legislation or to take cases of noncompliance to the Court of Justice of the European Union, the Commission and the EU foreign service, the EEAS, can suggest policies and actions on the basis of (European) Council priorities and conclusions, in the form of so-called Joint Communications. However, the EU's "foreign minister," the High Representative of the Union for Foreign Affairs and Security Policy (HR) in charge of the EEAS, "receives her instructions from the Council in CFSP," and is also tasked with *implementing* the decisions that are taken by the member states (Thym 2011: 14).

The member states adopted their first legal conclusions on an EU Maritime Security Strategy (EUMSS) in April 2010. In this conclusion, the HR (i.e., the EEAS) was tasked to work together with the Commission and the Member States in "preparing options for the possible elaboration of a Security Strategy for the global maritime domain." The member states underlined that "work will take place in the context of CFSP/CSDP" and thus remain strictly intergovernmental (Council 2010). The European Council meeting in December 2013 then called for "an EU Maritime Security Strategy by June 2014 on the basis of a joint Communication from the Commission and the High Representative, taking into account the opinions of the member states, and the subsequent elaboration of action plans to respond to maritime challenges" (European Council 2013: 4). The Joint Communication was published in March 2014. The final EUMSS was adopted at the General Affairs Council in June 2014, following the conventional CFSP procedures, i.e., discussions among the member states' Permanent Representatives (ambassadors) in the special foreign policy committee, the PSC (Council 2014a). As the content of the final EUMSS is multi-sectorial, the then Greek Presidency also activated the ad hoc expert "Friends of the Presidency group" (FoP) to prepare the Council discussions. To ensure implementation, an action plan was adopted in December 2014 under the Italian presidency (Council 2014b).

EU Arctic policies are still less developed than many other policy areas under the CFSP. However, big steps have been taken since 2014. Initially, EU policies toward the Arctic region go back to the adoption of a Northern Dimension policy in 2000, revised in 2006. In October 2008, the EU institutions took a first step in seeking to move forward with a distinct EU Arctic policy, first with a European Parliament a resolution on Arctic governance in October, and then a first Commission communication on the EU and the Arctic region in November. Given this background, in December 2009, the EU foreign ministers adopted their first Council Arctic Conclusions (Council 2009). New steps were taken following the establishment of the EEAS and in parallel to the work conducted by the EEAS and the Commission on the EUMSS from 2010, when the two started working on a Joint Communication that was presented in June 2012: "Developing a European Union Policy towards the Arctic Region: progress since 2008 and next steps" (Commission and EEAS 2012). Still, it was not until 2014 that things really started to happen with regard to a specific common EU Arctic policy. First, the new European Parliament passed a resolution in March 2014 and then the new Foreign Affairs Council issued a conclusion on developing an EU policy for the Arctic region (Council 2014c). In its conclusions, the Council asked "the Commission and the High Representative to present proposals for the further development of an integrated and coherent Arctic Policy by December 2015" (Council 2014c: 3). A Joint Communication entitled "An integrated European Union Policy for the Arctic" was presented by the Commission and the High Representative in April 2016 (Commission and EEAS 2016). Since 2008, the EU (Commission) has also applied for observer status in the Arctic Council. This has not yet been granted due to opposition from permanent members.

Although, as mentioned above, the initial reluctance among several EU member states toward adopting an EU maritime security strategy and an EU Arctic policy makes these cases particularly relevant to explore in order to study the impact of crisis on EU foreign policy integration. Being least likely cases of EU integration, if crisis had an impact on EU agreement in these cases, it is likely that crisis will impact EU decision-making and outcomes also in areas where there is less disagreement among the member states on the preferred outcome of EU negotiations. After all, as discussed above, the CFSP in itself a least likely policy area of further integration, as testified by member state insistence on keeping this an intergovernmental policy domain. So it is surprising that member states decided to integrate further in the maritime and Arctic policy domains.

How Crisis Influences the CFSP[2]
The Impact of the Ukraine Crisis on EU Maritime Foreign and Security Policies

Data across different sources clearly suggest that the Ukraine crisis was important for the discussions, context, and eventual adoption of the EU Maritime Security Strategy and the EU's Arctic policies. The steps taken so far toward developing a distinct EU Arctic policy have clearly been informed by the Ukraine crisis. This crisis functioned as a critical juncture, changing reluctant member states' positions to one in favor of developing a common policy that might otherwise not exist. This is so even if the Arctic is an area where cooperation between the EU and Russia, and with other Arctic states, is well developed and remains relatively well functioning, in spite of the tensions between Russia and the EU over Ukraine and other security related issues such as the Syria conflict. According to an 2015 EUISS report, following the Ukraine crisis, the only area where EU–Russia cooperation "has remained relatively calm and stable to date is the Far North or, seen from the EU, northeast – in and around the Arctic" (Missiroli 2015: 3). The frameworks that exist for cooperation in the Arctic can "potentially also maintain dialogue and build up trust during times of heightened tensions" (Jokela 2015: 42).

Before 2014, there was not much of a common EU Arctic policy. A few first steps were taken in response to the Russian planting of its flag on the North Pole in 2007, with an European Parliament resolution, a first Commission communication and a first Council conclusion on the topic in 2008 and 2009 (Riddervold and Cross 2019). This episode put Arctic policies on the EU agenda (Offerdal 2011). Prior to this, and with Sweden and Finland and later the Baltic States as the main exceptions, the EU member states considered the Arctic policies to be outside the scope of the EU's policies or had little interest in the area due to other strategic interests, for example in the EU's southern neighborhood (Offerdal 2011; interviews 2013, 2014). Member states however remained reluctant to move forward with an EU Arctic policy after this first step and did not follow up on the Commission and Parliament's call for an EU Arctic policy. The 2009 Council Conclusions were vague, in particular as regards policies linked to the CFPS. Rather than setting out a distinct EU policy, the member states concluded that any EU policies toward the Arctic should "address EU interests and responsibilities, while recognising member states' legitimate interests and rights in the Arctic" (Council 2009). As mentioned in the introduction, several member states, including big countries Italy, Germany, and the UK, either continued to oppose cooperation in

---

[2]The analysis combines findings from Riddervold (2018) Chapters 1, 4, 5, 8 and 11; Riddervold and Cross (2019); Riddervold and Trondal (2020). Quotes from individual interviews are referred to in the same way as in these studies. Each interviewee is given a code referring to the institution by which he or she comes from as well as a number. Interviewees from member states are referred to as NatDel#1, NatDel#2 etc., from the EEAS as EEAS#1 etc.

the area of (maritime) EU foreign and security policy, did not want to upset Russia, or had other interests in the region that they feared could be jeopardized by a common EU approach (interviews 2010, 2013, 2014). Denmark, who is the only EU member state bordering the Arctic, was concerned that EU would meddle with its sovereign rights as an Arctic state. In fact, there are several still ongoing territorial disputes in the Arctic, and several EU states did not want to compromise their good relations with Russia by developing a common EU policy that might contradict Russian interests in the area (interviews 2013, 2014; Haftendorn 2011; Offerdal 2011).

From 2014 on this picture changed significantly, with member states and EU institutions changing their rhetoric and substantially increasing their attention to the Arctic area. Member states and EU institutions started referring to the Arctic as an area of strategic importance and previously reluctant member states changed positions from opposition to support for developing an EU Arctic policy within the CFSP framework. Data across documents, interviews, and other studies suggest that the Ukraine crisis is key to understand this change and the eventual adoption of a common EU policy. Following the crisis and in sharp contrast to their 2009 conclusions, the member states in 2014 agreed to move forward with "further development of an integrated and coherent Arctic Policy" with reference to the Arctic as "a region of growing strategic importance" (Council 2014a, b, c). A similar shift in policy toward the Arctic is also clear in the 2016 Council Conclusions. Here, the member states justified such an EU policy by arguing that "an ambitious cross-spectrum and well-coordinated Arctic policy will contribute to the EU's engagement in an increasingly strategically important region. The Arctic is an area of active cooperation between major regional and global actors; reinforcing the EU's engagement in the Arctic is also important from a foreign and security policy point of view" (Council 2016: 2).

Our interviewees also referred to the impact of the Ukraine crisis for understanding that member states agreed to take these big steps forward in the development of an EU Arctic policy, finally following up on the calls made by the EU institutions several years earlier. One of our key EEAS informants who was directly involved both in the negotiations and in the development of the 2016 Joint communication, stated that EU maritime security policies became "all about security and strategic interests in this region" as a result of the crisis in Ukraine (EEAS#6/Natdel#14). After Ukraine, "it is security first" (ibid). Actively promoting a Northern dimension to EU foreign policies since becoming EU members in 1996 due to their closeness not only to the Arctic but also Russia, Sweden, and Finland have in particular "pointed to a potential future role for the EU in this area [Sweden explicitly so], signalling (a) broader interest in seeing (the) further development of the EU's Common Security and Defence Policy" (Depledge 2015a, b: 63). Following the Ukraine crisis, these countries have actively used Russian aggression as a justification for a stronger common policy in the Arctic. The Finish foreign minister, for example, argued that "we are treading in a delicate environment in our relations with Russia…This is a threat that must be collectively managed. No EU country can deal with these issues alone. To a large degree, balancing the military threat belongs to the remit of NATO, but the EU, too, has a lot to contribute" (Soini 2016). XX linked this explicitly to the need to also develop a stronger Arctic voice and stated "the Arctic has gained strategic importance and thus needs to become one of our foreign and security policy priorities" (ibid.).

More importantly, also previously reluctant member states changed positions in favor of a more coordinated and stronger EU policy toward the region, including in the CFSP domain. Germany is an illustrative example. Before the Ukraine crisis, Germany was reluctant to develop an EU Arctic policy, among other things due to its economic interests in keeping a good relationship with Russia. After Ukraine, we however see a change where it now "supports an active EU Arctic policy and the strategic and consistent integration of the Arctic interests into EU foreign and security policy as well as into policies in other fields such as the environment, research, industry and technology, energy and raw materials, transport and fishery" (German Federal Ministry for the Enviroment, Nature Conversation and Nucelar Safety 2017).

The same change toward a focus on the Arctic as an area of strategic importance is evident across the EU institutions. The 2016 Joint Communication issued by the Commission and the EEAS, for example, starts by arguing that: "A safe, stable, sustainable and prosperous Arctic is important not just for the region itself, but for the European Union [EU] and for the world. The EU has a strategic interest in playing a key role in the Arctic region" (Commission and EEAS 2016: 1). Similarly, while the High Representative of the Union for Foreign Affairs and Security Policy (HR) Mogherini initially "was not very keen on maritime security," including in the Arctic (CSekr#1), this clearly changed following Russia's annexation of Crimea. Following the Ukraine events Mogherini argued that: "A safe, sustainable and prosperous Arctic not only serves the 4 million people living there, our European Union and the rest of the world (…) The steps taken today underline our commitment to the region, its States and its peoples, and to ensuring that the region remains an example of constructive inter-national cooperation. Because the Arctic is also crucial in terms of regional and global security, and a strategic component of our foreign policy" (Commission 2016). The European Parliament has changed its focus when discussing the Arctic to become more strategically oriented. While early on arguing that the Arctic should be compared to Antarctica, the 2017 European Parliament Resolution "specifically highlights hard security risks, drawing particular attention to the expansion of military capabilities in the Russian North" (in Raspotnik and Stępień 2017: 3–4). Several other studies support the claim that the Ukraine crisis and the continuing Russian aggression is key to understanding the development of an EU Arctic policy. Depledge (2015a, b: 65), for example, argues that "the general deterioration of Russia-Western relations after the Ukraine crisis may negatively affect the security situation in the Arctic and possibly lead to a heightened level of tension at the interstate level. In a situation marked by a mutual lack of trust and transparency, the 'security dilemma' dynamics in the Arctic may become more prominent" (Depledge 2015b; Baev 2015). In line with the argument made in this paper, Jokela (2015: 6) finds that "the ongoing crisis in Ukraine and the deteriorating relations between Russia and the West provide the most topical example of how conflicts elsewhere might spill over into the Far North."

The impact of the Ukraine crisis on EU foreign policy integration is also very clear in the EU Maritime Security Strategy case. The Russian intervention in Crimea in March 2014 put security at the top of the EU agenda 12 days after the Joint EUMSS Communication was launched—just when the member states were to start their negotiations on its adoption. The uncertainty created by the Ukraine crisis directly affected member states' positions in favor of more EU security cooperation, of which the EUMSS is one facet. Due to the EUMSS process, member states were already sitting down and debating security issues in an informal, preparatory forum when this crisis escalated. And due to the crisis, negotiations were taken up a level of discussing EU security and defence cooperation more generally, eventually leading to agreement on the adoption of the security strategy that was on the table (NatDel#8–13. See Riddervold 2018 for an in-depth study of the EUMSS negotiations).

There is much data to support the impact of the Ukraine crisis on the EUMSS. First, all the interviewed member state representatives present at the EUMSS negotiations who were interviewed in between the meetings underlined the strong impact of the Russia/Ukraine crisis on their negotiations, arguing that it changed the content of the strategy and that it influenced their ability to agree (NatDel#8–13). One PSC ambassador, for example, argued that because of Russia's actions, "this is called a maritime strategy but the discussions have become about all of the CSDP" (the Common Security and Defence Policy) (NatDel#9). Other member state representatives underlined how the Ukraine crisis changed the member states' discussions to focus more on security and the need to come to an agreement on common EU policies in a profoundly different security environment than what was initially planned on the basis of the Joint Communication. To illustrate the crisis' impact, another PSC ambassador argued that new issues were taken into directly deal with this new threat: "For example, there was nothing about the Black Sea in the Communication, now we have Ukraine and everyone wants the Black Sea in... For the Baltic states the vital concern is sovereignty vis a vis Russia—they are really scared" (NatDel#11). An interviewee from the Council Secretariat present at all the member state negotiation meetings, noted that the maritime strategy "has turned very much to defence, because the real problems are defence related" due to Ukraine situation (CouncilSekr#1).

As we also saw in the Arctic case, there is evidence to suggest that previously reluctant member states changed their positions to support an EUMSS due to the Ukraine crisis. According to all the interviewees, including from big countries such as the UK and Poland, the crisis made it clear to them that the EU needed a distinct and coordinated maritime security policy in addition to those conducted by NATO. This was necessary not least because of the EU's much wider range of foreign policy tools including tools needed to deal with crises such as the one in Ukraine, which member states perceived to be a severe threat., without the constraints of NATO's specific mandate. According to member state representatives from countries in both NATO and the EU, Ukraine convinced them that a stronger foreign and security policy was necessary because "NATO is crucial but not enough because the EU is much broader" (NatDel#10). Furthermore, EU foreign policy "is not traditional security policies. This is very clear in Ukraine. The EU conducts a different type of policy than NATO" and has more tools to draw on when faced with crisis (NatDel#9). And when the crisis hit, it was the EUMSS that was the topic of discussion.

Second, the impact of Russian aggression and the new security situation in Europe is clearly visible in the different working drafts and in the final text that was discussed at the member states' negotiation meetings in 2014 (unpublished documents; Council 2014a, b, c). As a direct consequence of Ukraine, the Greek Presidency decided that it "wanted its own paper" instead of discussing the Joint Communication that the EEAS and the Commission had just published (Comm#4, NatDel#8–9). Given the crisis, the document it presented was much more security and defense oriented than the Joint Communication. For example, the Joint Communication that was written before the crisis only mentions the EU's neighborhood once, focusing on cooperation and the need to improve "information-sharing arrangements with international partners" (Council 2014a). In stark contrast, interviewees pointed out that the EUMSS makes a clear reference to Russia: "The Union stresses the importance of its assuming increased responsibilities as a global security provider, at the international level and in particular in its neighbourhood, thereby also enhancing its own security and its role as a strategic global actor"—including by the use of military tools (Council 2014a, b, c: 2; interviews with participants 2014).

Following the Russian annexation of Crimea, energy security also immediately emerged as a topic of discussions. There are no references to energy security in the 2014 Joint Communication from the Commission and the EEAS (Commission and EEAS 2014). However, after the crisis emerged, this came up as a main concern both in informal and formal documents and by the participants themselves. The first informal Greek draft discussed at the FoP meetings in early April 2014 is a telling example, where the second paragraph read: "Maritime transport is key to Europe's energy security…. 90% of oil is transported by sea" (author's copy). Following discussions, this was amended to "Europe's energy security largely depends on maritime transport and infrastructures" but clearly shows how the crisis directly affected the member states' discussions (Council 2014a). Similarly, due member states discussed adding "the protection of the EU against maritime security threats, the safeguarding of the supply of energy by the sea..." as an important EU security interest that needed a common EU response (second draft, unpublished document). This was amended back to the initial Joint Communication text, which mentioned "the protection of critical maritime infrastructure, such as specific areas in ports and port facilities, off-shore installations, energy supply by the sea, underwater pipelines..." (Council 2014a) but again clearly underlines the strong impact that the crisis had on member states' preferences and discussions. Controlling for other factors: Alternative explanations of the EUMSS and EU Arctic policies.

These findings are in line with Riddervold and Cross' (2019) argument that the EU in the CFSP is a "Reactive Power," where new policies often are developed reactively in response to external events: The EU responds to crisis and external geopolitical developments in one area by developing new policies not only in directly linked areas but also in other issues that previously divided them. Crisis brings member states closer together on issues that may have previously divided them (ibid.). As we have seen, Russian aggression in Ukraine and beyond put the Arctic higher on the EU agenda and it helped form agreement among the member states on the need to develop a distinct EU Arctic policy. Similarly, data suggests that reluctant member states changed positions on the EUMSS when Russia annexed Crimea, literally while they were sitting down and discussing the strategy. These findings are also in line with the historical institutional idea that crisis may trigger new policies by functioning as a "critical juncture." As discussed by Ansell, critical junctures are "relatively short periods of time during which there is a substantially heightened probability that agents' choices will affect the outcome of interest" (Capoccia and Keleman 2007: 348 in Ansell, this volume). Such critical junctures can cause policy change in response to crisis by generating a "window of opportunity" for policy change, in particular as it allows actors to put new issues on the agenda and get support for policies that might otherwise not have been agreed to. As we saw in the above analysis, this is very much what happened in the cases discussed in this chapter.

Neither of the alternative explanations set out in the introduction to this chapter can fully explain this development. True, also a neorealist perspective would suggest that foreign policy events are driven by external events, in particular geopolitical events that are linked to core state interests such as territorial defence. After all, Russian aggression represents one of the greatest threats to EU members' territorial security, and one would expect member states to "join forces" (Zimmermann this volume). In line with this expectation, the analysis suggests that the main developments of EU Arctic policies and the adoption of the EUMSS were related to geopolitical events, in line with what one would expect following a neorealist, traditional great power model of foreign policy: As external powers become more threatening, the EU member states' have come together to become collectively stronger too (also see Riddervold and Cross 2019). However, there is not much evidence suggesting that EU policies were part of a broader balancing game in the cases discussed here. The EU does not foremost seek increased territorial control and powers over the Arctic area for itself or some or all of the member states, as one would expect following a traditional, neorealist great power model, or to balance Russia directly in the Arctic. In fact, except for Denmark, which with Greenland is one of five countries with a coastline bordering the Arctic, none of the EU member states have a strong claim to the Arctic region. Neither is there any evidence to suggest that the EU is joining forces with the US as a junior partner in the Arctic (also see Riddervold 2018). Instead, several interviewees including from traditionally "Atlantist" member states argued as discussed above that the EU should develop maritime policies independently of the US. For example, a PSC ambassador argued that "we need NATO, that is, the US. But the US has its own interests that are not necessarily in line with the EU's. So we also need the EU, with military capabilities (…) NATO is a military organization. EU is a political and military organization, where like a country, defence is only a small part of it (…) So even if NATO is extremely important it is not enough with NATO. We also need the EU" (NatDel#11). Lastly, other studies suggest that the EU's Arctic policy tools and aims do not fit with what one would expect following a realist perspective. Rather than seeking territorial control, the EU's position is that the Arctic should be regulated and governed by international law to ensure its sustainable development (Riddervold 2018). In other words, although the EU reacts to external crises and events by developing new policies, it does not do so in a (neo-) realist defensive, strategic way. Instead, external geopolitical crises, such as that in Ukraine, have as we have seen an impact through the mechanism of critical junctures, allowing actors to push through policies that might otherwise not have been agreed to.

What then about the three other alternative hypotheses of the EUMSS and EU Arctic policies? As already mentioned, other studies suggest that EU Arctic policies and EU maritime policies in some cases have a normative underpinning one would expect following a constructivist perspective. The EU in particular, is focused on securing sustainable development of the marine environment and the high seas, including in the Arctic, through developing binding, institutionalized regulation, in line with the claim that the EU is a green, environmental power (Riddervold 2018). With this focus, according to Weber and Romanyshyn (2011: 860), the EU can moreover "play a vital role and contribute to the sustainable development of the region." However, while a constructivist perspective may help us understand what type of influence the EU wants to exert in the Arctic and in the maritime domain more broadly, it cannot explain the rather sudden change in reluctant member states' positions toward the EUMSS and EU Arctic policies we observe in 2014, nor the increased security focus of EU policies. On the contrary, as discussed above, the EU, for example, started out with a relatively weak interest in the Arctic and only recently changed its tune in 2014 even though the environmental challenges were known well before 2014.

The same is true for a liberal intergovernmentalist hypothesis linking EU policies to the member states' economic interests. If economic considerations were the main drivers of EU Arctic policies, one would expect EU policies to develop in line with increased knowledge of economic opportunities in the area. The economic opportunities opening in the Arctic were however well known before 2014. The US Geological Survey (Gautier et al. 2009) suggested the Arctic had great potential for large oil and gas finds in 2009. Undoubtedly, the EU and its member states are interested in securing access to natural resources and open waterways, are doing so (also see Wegge 2011), given that economic interests are a contributing factor for understanding EU Arctic policies. Yet, economic considerations cannot explain the leap and change we observe in EU policies from 2014. Similarly, the financial crisis hit the EU in 2009/2010, again suggesting that common EU maritime security policies should have come earlier if driven mainly by concerns for economic gain.

The most important factor for understanding EU Arctic policies and the EUMSS in addition to the Ukraine crisis is the influence of institutional actors, the Commission and the EEAS, in line with what one would expect following a rational institutional perspective. Importantly, the argument that member states' agreement on new EU foreign and security policies often are reactive and driven by crisis does not mean crisis in itself can explain all EU foreign and security policies by external events only. As we have also seen in other studies, EU institutions, often in alliance with certain member states, are key to understanding why certain topics and suggestions reach and remain on the EU foreign policy agenda, as well as the long-term EU foreign and security policies agreed to and conducted (see Riddervold and Cross 2019; Riddervold and Trondal 2020). After all, there is, for example, a lot in the EUMSS and in the EU's Arctic policies that have not been discussed by the member states but instead were developed by the EEAS and the Commission. And as we have seen above, their actions were a necessary condition for putting and keeping the EUMSS and the EU Arctic policies on the agenda, as well as for driving them forward so that there was something substantial to discuss when crisis hit. However, the Ukraine crisis was the turning point that led to EU agreement on these policies. As illustrated by one of the informants when interviewed about the EU's Arctic policy, "with the ice melting and with maritime issues becoming more and more popular… member states" attention toward the Arctic gradually increased from 2007/2008 onward. But the Ukraine crisis was the "catalyst to get this issue mainstreamed, to get member state support" for an EU policy (EEAS#6/NatDel#14).

Conclusions

This chapter set out to illustrate how the Ukraine crisis has influenced EU foreign and security policy integration by exploring its impact on a distinct policy field within this domain, namely maritime security policies. The analysis suggests that the EU has responded to Russia's aggression by deepening cooperation not only vis a vis Russia in regard to Ukraine (see Juncos and Pomorsko this volume) but also in various other foreign policy areas not directly linked to the Ukraine crisis as such. In both of the cases explored the Ukraine crisis functioned as a critical juncture, moving them to the top of the EU agenda and affecting member states' positions in favor of developing new EU policies. As noted by Ansell and Juncos and Pomorska, similar findings regarding the Ukraine crisis' impact have been suggested in studies of other areas of EU foreign policy. According to Ikani (2019: 27 in Ansell this volume) for example, the Ukraine Crisis functioned as a critical juncture that is key to understand recent changes in the European Neighborhood Policy (ENP), as the crisis created "…a moment of heightened contingency as calls for reform mounted and the EU launched a formal reform round of the ENP.' Findings in this chapter are also in line with Riddervold and Cross' concept of "Reactive Power Europe" (2019), suggesting that the EU responds to external crises and events by reactively forming new common foreign and security policies more broadly.

Instead of seeking differentiated solutions, EU maritime foreign and security policies have moreover been uniform on the internal dimension of integration, with the exception of Denmark's opt-outs to the CSDP aspects of the EUMSS. Thus, contrary to the expectation that many of the EU's crisis-responses will "include some form of differentiation by which one or several member state deviate in terms of functionality of integration temporarily or even permanently" (Gänzle et al., this volume), internally, the EU is becoming less differentiated in the face of crises in the maritime foreign and security policy domain. Rather than undermining EU unity and contrary to what one would expect if we are witnessing a more internally fragmented or differentiated EU foreign and security policy, this chapter suggests that crises drive EU foreign policy integration forward in a more uniform fashion.

None of the alternative theoretically derived hypotheses discussed in this chapter could sufficiently account for the adoption of the EUMSS and the key steps taken in the development of an EU Arctic policy since 2014. While economic considerations may have served as a facilitating factor, economic interests cannot in themselves explain the observed change in member states' positions and the EU policies adopted. Neither can norms such as environmental concerns explain the adoption of new EU policies. Both the environmental consequences and the economic opportunities in the Arctic were, for example, well known before 2014. Similarly, there is no evidence to suggest that EU policies are part of a bigger balancing game vis a vis Russia in cooperation with the US. The actions of the EU institutions the Commission and the EEAS were, on the other hand, a necessary condition for the adoption of both of these policies. It was after all these institutions who put and kept the issues on the EU agenda (Riddervold and Trondal 2020). However, it took member state agreement to actually adopt common policies within these domains, and before the Ukraine crisis there was less interest, among the member states to do so. The Ukraine crisis hence became the tipping point by which the EU member states saw the need for new EU security policies. These policies were on the table, and with the crisis, reached the top of the agenda and led to consensus by affecting reluctant member states' positions in favor of forming common policies. As such, the findings in this chapters are in line with the third scenario set out in the introduction to this volume, namely that the EU is *heading forward* in the foreign policy domain in response to crisis. Building on this and other studies presented in this book, other external crises, including the migration crisis and what Anderson in this volume calls "the Trump crisis" are likely to further strengthen this development toward more foreign and security policy integration (also see Riddervold and Newsome this volume).

References

Baev, P. K. (2015). Russia's Arctic aspirations. In J. Jokela (Ed.), *Arctic Security Matters ISS Report Arctic Matters* (pp. 24, 35–42). Paris: The European Union Institute for Security Studies (EUISS).

Capoccia, G., & Kelemen, R. D. (2007). The Study of Critical Junctures: Theory, Narrative, and Counterfactuals in Historical Institutionalism. *World Politics, 59*, 341–369. https://doi.org/10.1017/S0043887100020852.

Commission. (2016, April 27). *A New Integrated EU Policy for the Arctic Adopted*. Press release. Brussels. Available at: https://ec.europa.eu/commission/presscorner/detail/en/IP_16_1539.

Commission and EEAS. (2012, June 26). *Joint communication to the european parliament and the Council Developing a European Union Policy Towards the Arctic Region: Progress Since 2008 and Next Steps*, (JOIN/2012/19 final). Brussels.

Commission and EEAS. (2014). *Joint Communication to the European Parliament and the Council*. For an Open and Secure Global Maritime Domain: Elements for a European Union Maritime Security Strategy (JOIN/2014/09 final). Brussels.

Commission and the EEAS. (2016, April). *Joint Communication to the European Parliament and the Council: An integrated European Union policy for the Arctic*. Brussels. Accessed 25 October 2019.

Council. (2009). *Council Conclusions on Arctic issues*. 2985th Foreign Affairs Council. Brussels.

Council. (2014a, May 12). *Council conclusions on developing a European Union Policy towards the Arctic Region*. Brussels.

Council. (2014b, December 16). *European Union Maritime Security Strategy (EUMSS)*. Action plan, (OR. en), 17002/14. Brussels.

Council. (2014c). *European Union Maritime Security Strategy* (11205/14). Brussels.

Council. (2016). *Conclusions on the Arctic as Adopted by the Council on 20 June 2016* (10400/16 COEST 166). Brussels.

Council. (2010, April 26). *Council Conclusions on a Maritime security strategy*. 309th Foreign Affairs Council Meeting, Luxembourg.

Cram, L. (1994). The European Commission as a Multi-Organization: Social Policy and IT Policy in the EU. *Journal of European Public Policy, 1*, 195–217.

Depledge, D. (2015a). Hard Security Developments. In J. Jokela (Ed.), *Arctic Security Matters Iss Report Arctic Matters* (pp. 24, 59–68). Paris: The European Union Institute for Security Studies (EUISS).

Depledge, D. (2015b, April 25). *The EU and the Arctic Council: Commentary*. European Council on Foreign Relations.

Dijkstra, H. (2014). Approaches to Delegation in EU Foreign Policy: The Case of the Commission. In M. Wilga & I. P. Karolewski (Eds.), *New Approaches to EU Foreign Policy* (pp. 38–56, Routledge Advances in European Politics). London: Routledge.

Elgström, O., & Smith, M. (2008). *The European Union's Roles in International Politics: Concepts and Analysis* (Routledge ECPR studies in European Political Science, vol. 45). London: Routledge.

European Council. (2013). *European Council Conclusions*. EUCO 217/13, 19/20 December 2013. Brussels.

Falkner, R. (2007). The Political Economy of 'Normative Power' Europe: EU Environmental Leadership in International Biotechnology Regulation. *Journal of European Public Policy, 14*, 507–526.

Frontini, A. (2014). *The European Union Maritime Security Strategy: Sailing Uncharted Waters? EPC Commentary*, 26 June 2014.

Gautier, D. L. et al. (2009). Assessment of Undiscovered Oil and Gas in the Arctic. *Science, 324*, 1175–1179. https://doi.org/10.1126/science.1169467.

German Federal Ministry for the Enviroment, Nature Conversation and Nucelar Safety. (2017). *German Arctic Policy Guidelines*. Berlin: Federal Ministry for the Environment, Nature Conservation, Building and Nuclear Safety (BMUB).

Germond, B. (2015). *The Maritime Dimension of European Security: Seapower and the European Union* (Palgrave Studies in European Union Politics). Basingstoke: Palgrave Macmillan.

Haftendorn, H. (2011). NATO and the Arctic: Is the Atlantic Alliance a Cold War Relic in a Peaceful Region Now Faced with Non-Military challenges? *European Security, 20*, 337–361. https://doi.org/10.1080/09662839.2011.608352.

Jokela, J. (Ed.). (2015). *Arctic Security Matters* (ISS Report Arctic Matters (24)). Paris: The European Union Institute for Security Studies (EUISS).

Manners, I. (2002). Normative Power Europe: A Contradiction in Terms? *JCMS: Journal of Common Market Studies, 40*, 235–258.

Merket, H. (2012). The European External Action Service and the Nexus between CFSP/CSDP and Development Cooperation. *European Foreign Affairs Review, 17*(4), 625–651.

Meunier, S., & Nicolaïdis, K. (2006). The European Union as a Conflicted Trade Power. *Journal of European Public Policy, 13*, 906–925.

Missiroli, A. (2015). Forword. In J. Jokela (Ed.), *Arctic Security Matters ISS Report Arctic Matters* (24). Paris: The European Union Institute for Security Studies (EUISS).

Moravcsik, A. (1998). *The choice for Europe: Social Purpose and State Power from Messina to Maastricht* (Cornell Studies in Political Economy). Ithaca, NY: Cornell University Press.

Moravcsik, A., & Schimmelfennig, F. (2009). Liberal lntergovernmentalism. In A. Wiener & T. Diez (Eds.), *European Integration Theory* (2nd ed.). Oxford: Oxford University Press.

Offerdal, K. (2011). The EU in the Arctic: In Pursuit of Legitimacy and Influence. The Arctic is Hot, Part II. *International Journal, 66*, 861–877.

Pollack, M. A. (1997). Delegation, Agency, and Agenda Setting in the European Community. *International Organization, 51*, 99–134.

Raspotnik, A., & Stępień, A. (2017). *The European Parliament Heading Towards Icy Waters—Again*. ArCticles, Arctic Centre, University of Lapland, Finland.

Riddervold, M. (2018). *The Maritime Turn in EU Foreign and Security Policies*. Cham: Springer International Publishing.

Riddervold, M., & Cross, M. K. (2019). Reactive Power EU: Russian Aggression and the Development of an EU Arctic Policy. *European Foreign Affairs Review, 24*(1), 43–60.

Riddervold, M., & Rosén, G. (2015). Beyond Intergovernmental Cooperation: The Influence of the European Parliament and the Commission on EU Foreign and Security Policies. *European Foreign Affairs Review, 20*(3), 399–417.

Riddervold, M., & Trondal, J. (2020). The Commission's Informal Agenda-setting in the CFSP. Agenda Leadership, Coalition-building, and Community Framing. *Comparative European Politics*. https://doi.org/10.1057/s41295-020-00218-1.

Soini, T. (2016, January 28). Minister Soini's Opening Speech. *The EU's Strategic Vision for Relations with Russia and the Eastern Neighbourhood*. Finland: The Finnish Institute of International Affairs.

Tallberg, J. (2003). *European Governance and Supranational Institutions*. Abingdon, UK: Taylor & Francis.

Thym, D. (2011). Holding Europe's CFSP-CSDP Executive to Account in the Age of the Lisbon Treaty. *Serie Union Europea, 53*, 1–40.

Waltz, K. N. (1979). *Theory of International Politics*. Boston, London: McGraw-Hill.

Wegge, N. (2011). The EU and the Arctic: European Foreign Policy in the Making Arctic. *Review on Law and Politics, 3*(1), 6–29.

Weber, S., & Romanyshyn, I. (2011). Breaking the Ice: The European Unionand the Arctic. *International Journal: Canada's Journal of Global Policy Analysis, 66*, 849–860.

CHAPTER 34

The EU's Comprehensive Response to Out of Area Crises: Plugging the Capability-Expectations Gap

Pernille Rieker and Steven Blockmans

INTRODUCTION

Since adopting a "comprehensive approach" to crisis management in 2013, the EU has spent considerable time and energy on streamlining its approach and improving internal coordination. New and protracted crises, from the conflict in Ukraine to the rise of ISIS and the refugee situation in the South, have also had an impact and made the improvement of external crisis-response capacities a top priority (see Riddervold; Junkos and Pomorska, this volume for discussions of Ukraine). This explains why the EU has revised its Security Strategy from 2003. The EU's Global Strategy, presented to the European Council in June 2016, offers a practical and principled route to conflict prevention, crisis response and peacebuilding, fostering human security through an "integrated approach."

The analysis in this chapter is based on an article published in European Security (see Rieker & Blockmans 2019). It has been written within the framework of the Horizon 2020 project, EUNPACK (project ID:693337, homepage: http://www.Eunpack.Eu/)

P. Rieker (✉)
Norwegian Institute of International Affairs (NUPI), Oslo, Norway
e-mail: pernille.rieker@nupi.no

S. Blockmans
University of Amsterdam, Amsterdam, Netherlands
e-mail: steven.blockmans@ceps.eu

This terminological change indicates an expansion of the comprehensive approach beyond the development–security nexus to encompass the commitment to the synergistic use of all tools available at all stages of the conflict cycle, while paying attention to all levels of EU action, from local, to national, regional and even the global (EU Global Strategy 2016: 9; Council of the European Union 2016). It also recognises the need to overcome the EU's own legal, institutional, and budgetary internal/external dichotomies that have troubled a truly joined-up approach in the past. The question that remains, however, is whether this change has led to an actual improvement of the Union's capacity to act? In other words, has the Union's infamous "capability–expectations gap" identified in the early 1990s been plugged? Or should the EU's new integrated approach to external conflict and crisis be characterised as just another iteration in a long process of *muddling through* rather than *heading forward*?

According to Christopher Hill, the gap between the expectations of the EU's role in international affairs and its capacity to act had three primary components: the (in)ability to agree, to allocate sufficient resources and to make use of all the instruments the EU has at its disposal (Hill 1993: 315). While the gap has narrowed considerably over the past decades and that this progress must be seen as a direct consequence of the various crises and wars in the Union's immediate (Balkans), near (Georgia, Ukraine) and wider neighbourhoods (Afghanistan, Iraq, Libya…), it still exists. In order to capture where the remaining challenges are, we need to undertake a fine-grained analysis. While it is commonly argued that the (in)ability to agree or the lack of decision-making procedures capable of overcoming dissent is the core of the matter (Toje 2008a), it is not the full story as this argument tends to focus exclusively on the traditional foreign policy areas (CFSP and CSDP) that remain mainly intergovernmental, and ignore the many dimensions of EU crisis response that have become parallel or exclusive competences and are implemented by the Commission and/or its agencies on a daily basis. Thus, in order to assess how the EU is doing with regards to plugging the capability-expectations gap in the Union's integrated approach to external conflict and crisis, whether it is *muddling through* or fundamentally changing, a more holistic and granular stock-taking exercise is needed.

The aim of this chapter is therefore to contribute with a comprehensive and systematic analysis of how and to what extent the EU has managed to plug the aforementioned gap and thus become a more important actor in external crisis response. To do this we have adjusted a framework developed by James G. March and Johan P. Olsen for studying the efficiency of democratic governance, where they noted several conditions that must be met in order to achieve effective democratic governance (March and Olsen 1995). As we see it, the same five basic conditions must be met in the area of EU crisis response. First, the capacity to formulate clear objectives and make decisions accordingly. Second, the existence of administrative key capacities such as a well-developed legal framework specifying when and how the EU should act.

Third, the resources necessary to be able to respond to a given crisis (financial means, staff, suitable instruments and equipment). Fourth, the knowledge and competence about the crises and a capacity for learning, to ensure conflict sensitivity. And, finally, a well-developed set of organizational skills that can prepare the ground for effective coordination and a comprehensive/integrated approach.

EU Crisis Response and Capacity to Act

Much of the scholarly literature on the EU as an external crisis responder has been narrowly conceived, focusing on the EU actorness, coherence and effectiveness, often giving priority to the institutional framework and instruments in the area of CSDP over the quality and impact of its various crisis response activities. It is repeatedly argued that the EU is something special, *sui generis*, and that new concepts are required to capture the essence of its agency as an actor. The EU has been referred to as a "normative actor" (Manners 2002) and a "cosmopolitan actor" (Sjursen 2006), but also as a "small power" (Toje 2008b) or rather a "super power" (Moravcsik 2010; Mc Cormick 2007). In their introduction to a special issue on EU external policy, Niemann and Bretherton (2013) call for a shift in focus from notions of actorness to effectiveness. In this article, this is what we aim to do in the area of crisis response.

Key Objective—an Integrated Approach to Crisis Response

After the end of the Cold War, the concept of security had to be reassessed, given the new threats and risks too complex to be tackled by single actors, instruments and budgets. EU involvement in Bosnia, Iraq, and Afghanistan revealed the need for better coordination when engaging in crisis management. In response, the EU introduced the European Security Strategy (ESS), recognizing the link between internal and external aspects as well as between security and development (Council of the European Union 2003a). The EU discourse on the pre-Lisbon "comprehensive approach" shows how the EU did more than merely adopt NATO terminology: it also sought to promote coordination and cooperation among key actors (political, civilian, and military) in theater.

In the post-Lisbon period, the EU's comprehensive approach has been put into a much broader framework, encompassing all policy areas relevant to forging effective external action. This was the logical consequence of the amalgamation of foreign policy objectives in Article 21 of the Treaty of European Union (TEU) and the decision to assign greater responsibilities to the HRVP regarding policy initiation, coordination, and conduct (Blockmans and Koutrakos 2018). These developments have spurred academic reflection on the most appropriate instruments for providing added value in EU crisis management (Pirozzi 2013: 5–7; Post 2015: 79–80).

The EU's "comprehensive approach" not only implied the coordination of various compartmentalized tools such as diplomacy, defence and development, or between civil and military components and structures: it also aims at developing a coherent way of thinking as well as a "culture of coordination" (Drent 2011: 4; Weston and Mérand 2015: 337–338). This formed the basis for the ongoing organizational build-up of the EEAS into an integrated foreign affairs service (Blockmans and Hillion 2013; Bátora 2013; Cooper 2016; EU Global Strategy 2016). As such, the comprehensive approach was about defining a common strategic vision of the EU and the operational premises, permeating all areas of EU external action (European Commission and HRVP 2015), not just along the security–development nexus. Thus, the comprehensive approach had to be understood as a horizontal organizing principle, aimed at ensuring a holistic, coherent, and integrated response from the various EU institutions and instruments (European Commission and HRVP 2013: 2). Indeed, the EU's latest effort to develop its approach further, the European Union Global Strategy on Foreign and Security Policy, refers to an *integrated approach* to conflicts (EU Global Strategy 2016: 28).

To adopt an integrated approach to conflicts, not as an end in itself but as a way to respond to external crises and achieve sustainable peace, the roles and formal division of labor among the institutions and their relevant policy-making, decision-making, and implementation responsibilities must be clearly defined (Kempin and Scheler 2016a: 26). We ask: to what extent has the EU has managed to adapt its crisis response apparatus to enable implementation of this objective of delivering an integrated approach?

Institutions and Decision-Making Capacity

Emerging and acute crises require swift responses—to alleviate human suffering, prevent further escalation, promote dialogue, reconciliation and reconstruction, and protect populations. The capacity of the EU to meet the needs and challenges that arise, often unexpectedly, in natural and man-made emergencies depends crucially on its ability to take ad hoc decisions and actions in real time. Crises seldom follow a predictable pattern—but when they erupt, immediate attention and coordination are required. Responses to acute situations are thus complementary to medium- to long-term measures; they are an integral element in a comprehensive approach that includes conflict prevention and peace-building, CSDP missions and/or development programmes.

The EU commonly distinguishes between three phases in a crisis cycle—the pre-crisis phase, the actual crisis phase and the post-crisis phase. While many institutions will be involved in more than one of these three phases, individual EU bodies normally have their main responsibilities in one of the three. The pre-crisis response is largely taken care of by the EEAS and the

Commission, in line with their focus on early warning and conflict prevention. In the crisis response phase, the Council (see Lewis, this volume) and the intergovernmental decision-making structures with the European Council and the Council of the EU are involved to a greater extent (with diplomacy and CSDP missions), as well as the Commission (see Kassim, this volume), via its Humanitarian Aid and Civil Protection department (ECHO). Finally, in the post-crisis phase, the Commission's services (like the Directorate-General for International Cooperation and Development, DG DEVCO) are particularly important, as are the EEAS and the various CSDP stabilization missions.

The capacities at the EU-level in the *pre-crisis phase* are fairly extensive. While both the EEAS and the Commission are involved in this phase, it is primarily the former's newly established Directorate Integrated Approach for Security and Peace (ISP) which is in the lead. Established on 1 March 2019, Directorate ISP follows on from the ongoing institutional change process that seeks to smooth the way for the implementation of an integrated approach to external conflict and crisis. Already in January 2017, the EEAS unit for "Peacebuilding, Conflict Prevention, and Mediation" was upgraded into a division that directly reported to the Deputy Secretary General for the Common Security and Defence Policy (CSDP) as well as crisis response. This division became the focal point for EU responses to the conflict cycle, including the unit for "Prevention of Conflicts, Rule of Law/Security Sector Reform, Integrated Approach, Stabilisation and Mediation" (PRISM). Among other things, PRISM coordinated a working group—the so-called "Guardians of the Integrated Approach"—of like-minded souls within the EEAS and the Commission, whose ultimate aim was to enhance operational capacity in conducting an integrated approach to external conflict and crisis.

As a pillar responsible for crisis response and planning, Directorate ISP operates in parallel with a "policy pillar" and a "conduct pillar." While the policy pillar (Security and Defence Policy—SECDEFPOL) brings together all policies relating to security and defence (e.g., PESCO, the Coordinated Annual Review on Defence (CARD), cyber security), the conduct pillar combines the operational headquarters of both civilian ("Civilian Planning and Conduct Capability"—CPCC) and military ("Military Planning and Conduct Capability"—MPCC) CSDP missions. Thanks to this improved in-house logic and increased staff capacity (an upgrade from some 30 to 90 staff members), Directorate ISP hopes to forge a better division of labor among its four branches, as indeed between the EU institutions (Debuysere and Blockmans 2019). EU actions also benefit from the support of programmes implemented by the member states.

Concerning *the actual crisis phase* the EU has been accorded fewer competences by the member states, thereby limiting its decision-making capacity. The EU shifts into the crisis response mode when a situation is jointly identified as a crisis by the member states (whether through regular or emergency meetings of the PSC, Foreign Affairs Council or the European Council) or by the High Representative and the Crisis Response System (see below). A response must then be decided unanimously by the member states. The Commission and the European Parliament have a very limited role, except in areas like humanitarian aid and civil protection, defined outside the realm of Common Foreign and Security Policy (CFSP). However, through its Foreign Policy Instruments Service, the Commission maintains control of the disbursement of CFSP funds from the EU's general budget.

When decisions are to be made on crisis response, tensions may arise (Boin et al. 2013: 64). First, it must be determined whether the crisis requires a military, civilian, and/or humanitarian response (or a combination), as well as what methods and instruments should be deployed, and which institution(s) should be in charge. Second, for the response to be legitimate, consensus must be achieved among all EU member states. The HR plays an important role in negotiating such consensus, but this is often a difficult and time-consuming process, which limits the Union's capacity to be the swift crisis responder it aspires to be. While crisis response "implies the immediate mobilisation of EU resources to deal with the consequences of external crises caused by man-made and natural disasters",[1] such steps are taken only *after* the member states have reached a decision.

Directorate ISP, which performs an overall operational coordination function in support of the Deputy SG for "CSDP and crisis response", is responsible for activating the *EEAS Crisis Response System*, which includes the *Crisis Platform, the EU Situation Room and the Crisis Management Board*. The Crisis Platform—which includes services across the EU system and is chaired by the High Representative, the EEAS Secretary General or one of her deputies—can be convened on an ad hoc basis. This is a crucial mechanism that is activated to guarantee EU responsiveness during external crises. The Platform provides the EEAS (SECDEFPOL, CPCC, EUMS, EUMC, INTCEN, etc.) and the Commission (ECHO, DEVCO, FPI, etc.) with a clear political and/or strategic guidance for the management of a given crisis. Secretariat support is ensured by Directorate ISP on the basis of conclusions agreed at the Crisis Platform meetings. Here too, INTCEN and the EUMS provide a first assessment of an emerging crisis and coordinate with other parts of the EEAS (e.g., either of the five regional directorates). Still, the main challenge in this phase is to reach a decision that allows the EU to act. This requires the alertness to trigger the inter-service crisis response system at the EU's disposal. It also demands political urgency, which can be drummed up by the HR.

As effective crisis response has proven difficult, it is the post-crisis response with peace- and state-building as the main instruments that is the phase in which the EU often becomes deeply engaged. The EU's role in the peace and reconciliation processes in Aceh, Belgrade-Pristina, Mindanao, and South Sudan are cases in point (Blockmans 2014). Many of the same instruments identified as pre-crisis response can also be considered as post-crisis measures, as it is sometimes difficult to separate the two phases in the crisis cycle.

---

[1] https://eeas.europa.eu/topics/crisis-response/412/crisis-management-and-response_en.

The reconstruction of state institutions and the economy lies at the heart of the EU's post-conflict engagement, and reform and capacity-building of the judiciary and security sector have been part of its response. At the strategic level, there has been a shift from a focus on the concept of so-called "deep democracy"—political reform, elections, institution-building, anti-corruption, independent judiciary, and support to civil society as promoted by HR Ashton—toward a more pragmatic approach to security and stability of state institutions, with less emphasis on the democratic elements of governance, as set out in the EU's Global Strategy promoted by HR Mogherini. Disarmament, demobilization, and reintegration (DDR), as well as security sector reform (SSR) are key objectives here, and have been included in recent CSDP missions and operations.

Beyond the Council's role in the CSDP, the bodies tasked with post-crisis response are the EU Special Representatives (EUSRs), EU Delegations and the Commission's DG DEVCO. The EUSRs handle the EU's role in negotiating peace agreements/ceasefires and general regional stabilization. EU Delegations in the field provide political reporting, monitoring, and follow-up in negotiations with local stakeholders in third countries. They also provide a logistical base for teams of EU officials on field visits to post-crisis areas. Further, they serve as coordination hubs for the EU's diplomatic presence on the ground, including efforts to streamline the work of member state missions (Austermann 2014; Spence and Bátora 2015). The EU level (Commission and the EEAS) has extensive powers in the post-crisis phase, and stronger capacity to act. Also in areas where the main competence lies with the member states (e.g., CSDP stabilization missions) joint action is often less controversial and less urgent.

LEGAL FRAMEWORK

In line with the functions and tasks provided for in Title V of the TEU ("General Provisions on the Union's External Action and Specific Provisions on the Common Foreign and Security Policy"), in particular Article 21 TEU (objectives), Article 27(2) TEU (external representation and political dialogue by the HR) and Article 43(1) TEU ("Petersberg tasks," the EU has acted as a crisis manager in many guises (Rieker and Blockmans 2019: 7). The only task in which the EU has not yet engaged is what the Treaty erroneously calls "peace-making"—to be understood not in the UN sense of the word (i.e., peaceful settlement of disputes through diplomatic means) but as peace enforcement through military intervention (as with NATO's Operation Allied Force, the 1999 bombing campaign against the former Yugoslavia over the war in Kosovo) (Blockmans 2014).

Most of the tasks have involved various phases of the conflict cycle. A clear legal separation among the EU's crisis response tasks is difficult to make, as the legal basis may be found in the various provisions grouped together under Title V of the TEU, or indeed Part V of the Treaty on the Functioning of the

European Union (TFEU, "The Union's External Action"). Identifying EU crisis response in the strict sense may be somewhat easier, but here too the legal geography of the action may pertain to Articles under the TEU or the TFEU, especially if the EU responds to crises with both internal (homeland) and external (expeditionary) measures.

Since the Lisbon Treaty, the constituent treaties of the EU have included a "solidarity clause" and a "mutual defence clause" in connection with crisis response. Article 222 TFEU imposes the explicit obligation upon the EU and its member states to act jointly, "in a spirit of solidarity," if a member state is the object of a terrorist attack or the victim of a natural or man-made disaster. Although the two are closely related, this strand of the principle should not be confused with the "mutual defence clause" enshrined in Article 42(7) TEU.

Although the word "solidarity" appears 16 times in the treaties, its precise meaning remains unclear. Arguably, "solidarity" is in the eye of the beholder (Myrdal and Rhinard 2012). Unlike the "solidarity clause," the "mutual defence clause" is purely intergovernmental in nature: it binds member states without transferring any competence to EU institutions; nor does it require coordination at the EU level in situations when the mutual defence obligation is invoked (see Crawford, this volume for further discussion on solidarity and EU integration). Article 42(7) TEU reminds member states of their unequivocal obligation to provide aid and assistance "by all the means in their power" if a member state is the victim of "armed aggression" on its territory. In principle, this formulation allows for many forms of assistance, but in practice the explicit reference to "armed aggression" points to military means. Whereas large-scale aggression against a member state appears unlikely in the foreseeable future, the Treaty constitutionalises both traditional territorial defence and defence against new threats (e.g., cyber-attacks), while stipulating that, for the EU countries that are members of NATO, the latter remains the foundation of their collective defence and the forum for its implementation, and that commitments and cooperation in the area of mutual defense must be consistent with commitments under NATO (Hillion and Blockmans 2015; Riddervold and Newsome, this volume).

Organizational Skills

While the skills discussed above (clear objectives, legal framework, resources, conflict sensitivity, and the capacity of learning) are necessary in order to have the capacity to act, it will not be sufficient without organizational skills, "without organizational talents, experience, and understanding, the other capabilities are likely to be lost in problems of coordination and control [...]" (March and Olsen 1995: 95).

Many institutions at various levels have roles to play in EU crisis response: the EEAS, the Commission, the Council, independent agencies, and of course the member states (Maurer, this volume). They all contribute to the development and implementation of EU crisis response in different ways. Although there exists a legal framework for cooperation (see above), this is so general that uncertainties remain as to the distribution of specific responsibilities.

The Commission's DG ECHO, for instance, has a special role to play in the EU's integrated approach to external conflicts and crises, given the need to follow as closely as possible the principle of neutrality and independence that underlies humanitarian cooperation. This implies that its agents act autonomously from other EU and Commission bodies—to avoid misperceptions on the ground in operations—while also maintaining cooperation at the decision-making level. For this reason, DG ECHO's level of engagement in the integrated approach could be defined as "in, but out". Responses are to be directed where the needs lie, beyond other strategic, military, or economic concerns.

The need for improved coordination in the sphere of external relations and CFSP is nothing new, and various reform measures have sought to remedy these problems. The establishment of the EEAS and the strengthening of the role of the High Representative in the Lisbon Treaty have been the most visible measures for improving coordination between the Council and the Commission. This has solved several problems, but also created new coordination challenges. A well-documented problem is the relationship between the EEAS and the Commission, complicated by the fact that the EEAS sets the strategic objectives whereas the Commission executes the budget and manages the programmes. Procedures and managerial guidelines have been put in place to facilitate interservice cooperation, and measures have been initiated to promote intraservice coordination. A case in point is the Commissioners' Group on External Action (CGEA). The members of this group with an external dimension to their portfolio are expected to exercise their functions "in close cooperation with the HR in accordance with the Treaties." Under President Barroso, the group had a rather formalistic character and did not contribute to the Commission's strands of EU external action. In 2014, Commission President Juncker reactivated the CGEA, with greater emphasis on coordination and streamlining under the leadership of the HR and Vice-President and four core Commissioners (ECHO, NEAR, DEVCO, and Trade). With its monthly schedule, it is now better suited for working on structural issues and long-term trends (Blockmans and Russack 2015: 9). Also, from an organizational viewpoint, the fact that Mogherini shifted the HR office from the EEAS building to the Commission building has helped to provide better conditions for improving day-to-day cooperation and coordination with the relevant DGs in CGEA.

However, there are also coordination issues within the Council, with political as well as institutional dimensions. The political dimension concerns the traditional coordination problems between member states within a policy area where most formal decisions are taken by consensus, whereas the institutional dimension is about coordination problems between civilian and military personnel. The problems in the political dimension have no short-term solution and will continue to place restrictions on the EU's ability to (re)act, but those in the institutional dimension have led to the creation of structures designed to strengthen civil–military cooperation. The establishment of a civilian–military unit within the military staff in 2005 should be recognised as an attempt to do precisely that. Also, following the entry into force of the Lisbon Treaty, some of the association and cooperation councils with countries in the EU's neighborhood have been chaired by the foreign ministers of countries holding the rotating presidency of the Council. This is done in coordination with the HR and helps in generating consensus among member states and EU institutions (e.g., in the framework of CGEA) on specific aspects related to the ENP. While the lack of interinstitutional coordination is often cited as the main challenge to EU crisis response (see Kempin and Scheler 2016b; Pirozzi 2015; Rieker 2009, 2013), others view the innovative dimension of the EU's institutional complexity as a strength. For instance, Bátora (2013) sees the "interstitial" nature of the EEAS as a source of innovation in the institutionalised fields of diplomacy, defense, and development as the EEAS combines practices, norms and rules from these fields. Similarly, Weston and Mérand (2015) note that the EEAS' mixture of competences might make it a source of organizational innovation, so that drivers of conflict could be addressed across a broader spectrum, taking into account regional as well as local perspectives.

Despite the flow of new initiatives for improving coordination between EU institutions, the absence of rapid decision-making capacity (and thus a well-developed capacity for crisis response) is due mainly to the strongly intergovernmental nature of much of this policy area and the fact that unanimity is required to launch a common security and defence initiative. This strictly limits the HR and his/her role as Chair of the Foreign Affairs Council. A recurrent problem is the low political will among member states (Barry 2012: 5). From the cases of South Sudan, Mali and the Central African Republic, Furness and Olsen (2016: 116) observe how national interests of prominent EU member states can hamper the capacity for effective crisis response. There may also be ambiguity and uncertainty as to the roles of EEAS HQ and the EU Delegations on the ground (Spence and Bátora 2015) and struggle for influence and symbolic power with the diplomatic services of member states (Adler-Nissen 2014). Perhaps this vertical coordination challenge (and not the horizontal challenge between EU institutions) remains the main reason why the EU's potential as a security-political actor has not been fully exploited. This is the void that will have to plug under the authority of the EEAS' Directorate ISP (see above).

In addition to the vertical/internal coordination challenge, the EU also struggles to live up to its objective of effective multilateralism as a guiding principle. Basically, this included the EU's declared goal of strengthening its cooperation with the UN and NATO (European Council 2003, 2016) in particular. Nearly a decade ago, Joachim Koops published a book evaluating EU multilateralism through several case studies, focusing on crisis management. His main conclusion was that the EU had not achieved its objective of strengthening interorganizational cooperation; further, that the EU had failed to match EU-internal with EU-external interinstitutional integration, and that case studies showed that "the EU [had] – at its various levels – been more strongly concerned about focusing on the short-term goal of promoting its own visibility, capability, coherence and presence as a new international security actor" (Koops 2011: 439).

Since 2011, the EU has experienced various crises, internal and external. While the focus of the 2016 Global Strategy has been on strengthening the EU's capacity to act, rather than on interinstitutional cooperation per se, the idea of "effective multilateralism" remains alive and stronger EU/UN and EU/NATO cooperation is emphasized as a tool for improving the EU's capacity to act (see Smith this volume).

RESOURCES AND CAPABILITIES

In addition to the capacities discussed above, the resources in terms of *budgets*, *staff* and *equipment* is of course also required. However, in a multidimensional actor as the EU, it is important to include all the relevant capacities at the EU level, but also at the level of the member states. The literature on EU crisis response has been generally focused on the capabilities linked to military and civilian CSDP (Galavan 2015; Tovornik 2015; van der Heijden 2015; Schilde 2016; Riddervold 2018). This is an area where EU action is needed, but also where action is dependent on member state commitments (through headline goals, etc.) and their relatively limited resources.

As shown above, the EU level also has its own capacities for crisis response. These are softer capacities, like humanitarian aid and civil protection, far less vulnerable to shifts in the political will and financial capabilities of member states. Moreover, they can, in principle, be deployed at shorter notice. Still, the lack of resources is a constraint also here.

As to the budget, common financial resources for crisis response are rather limited. The EU's external policies are implemented through the use of specific external and security-related thematic instruments and agencies. These "tools" are established within the priorities and limits of the Multiannual Financial Framework (MFF), a budgetary plan that translates EU priorities into financial terms and sets the maximum annual amounts which may be spent in various areas. Instruments relevant for external action were grouped in a single section (Global Europe) for the 2014–2020 budget, which was allocated only 6%. This is now likely to be increased quite substantially in the new proposed MFF for the 2021–2027 (potentially 2,1% for security and defence, 9,6% to "Neighbourhood and the World"). While the envisaged increase is an important signal, it is more important how the funding will eventually be spent.

What about staffing? DG DEVCO is the largest directorate in the Commission, with almost 10% of the overall Commission staff. In addition came the EEAS staff, recruited from the Commission, the Council Secretariat, and national diplomats. Apart from its staff at headquarters, DG DEVCO has a field presence through EUSRs and 140 EU delegations. The current EEAS staff totals approximately 4200, of which fewer than 1000 are career diplomats; and two-thirds of the senior management positions in Brussels are occupied by diplomats from member states. Compared to the diplomatic services of some of the larger member states and seen in relation to the Union's ambitions in crisis response, there seem to be many institutions and agencies responsible for implementing EU crisis response, but rather limited human resources.

We find a similar situation regarding "equipment." This is the case for the necessary equipment for CSDP missions, both civilian (Juncos 2018) and military capabilities (Duke 2018), which is dependent on member state contributions—but also for other types of crisis response where the EU has competence but where budget constraints put limitations on the capacity to act. While initiatives have been taken to improve the Union's "equipment" especially in the defence area, with new instruments such as PESCO and the European Defence Fund, these processes will take time to produce and procure new kit with EU value added (Blockmans 2018).

Thus, it can be said that even though the EU has an improved capacity for crisis response, it does not yet have sufficient resources—even if we include the resources at the member state level—to meet its own objectives and expectations.

Learning Capacity

A final capacity that is required to claim actorness is knowledge and competence as well as a certain capacity for learning from experiences. Evaluations of the EU's crisis response capacity have indicated that the EU needs to reduce the distance between Brussels and the field, to ensure proper information flows and learn from experience (Bossong 2013; European Parliament 2012). Increasingly, the EU has been recognizing the importance of knowledge-management and lessons-learnt processes in external crisis response, and these mechanisms have now become integral elements in its structures and policy. The Union's comprehensive approach to external conflicts and crisis stipulated that EU missions should aim to "take stock of lessons learned, including within the EU institutions, with Member States and external actors, and feed them back into the comprehensive approach cycle starting from early warning and including prevention efforts, training and exercises" (European Commission and HRVP 2013). The EU has developed its own policy cycle, with feedback mechanisms. In recent years, serious efforts have been made to improve lessons-learnt procedures, including studies of the efficiency of these initiatives (Arnaud et al. 2017).

Having procedures for institutional learning is relevant, but it is more important that these are used and feedback into the planning of new missions and operations. A recent study has surveyed practices of lessons learnt and best practices in various parts of EU crisis response activities, asking whether conflict sensitivity has been a special concern (Rieker et al. 2016). It found the mechanisms and procedures for learning particularly well developed, both within the EEAS in relation to the CSDP, and within the Commission's DG ECHO as regards humanitarian aid. There exist certain evaluation procedures also for the FPI, although these appear less institutionalized and streamlined. Closer examination of the mechanisms developed for CSDP and ECHO, however, revealed the lack of a clear method for undertaking evaluations. Three key observations can be noted from that study (Rieker et al. 2016):

First, although there are well-developed procedures for lessons learnt and internal and external evaluations of EU activities in both CSDP and ECHO, there is little to indicate whether the lessons are actually fed back into the planning phase of new missions or activities. Second, we must distinguish between immediate assessment of missions and operations of EU crisis response on the one hand; and, on the other hand, assessment of the lessons-learnt processes, mechanisms and methods meant to improve how lessons learnt are practised. Both are important: lessons will not be followed up unless procedures for doing so are in place, and there is the risk of paying more attention to procedures than to the actual impact. Finally, the main focus seems to be on *horizontal learning*, or learning from crisis response in different regions. While important, such a focus may overshadow relevant aspects of vertical learning and important aspects such as local experiences with EU engagement and thus what is often referred to as *conflict sensitivity*. Creating concepts and best practices that can readily be transferred from one crisis or conflict to another may make it difficult to recognize the particularities of each conflict.

This means that, although there is a certain level of understanding as well as procedures for lessons learnt and best practices, uncertainty remains as to whether and to what extent this new knowledge is actually put to use. A case in point is how the EU has been able to incorporate the objective of conflict sensitivity, given the core assumption that the EU needs a conflict-sensitive approach in order to break the crisis cycle and foster sustainable peace (Chandler 2010; Osland 2014: 20–22; Mac Ginty 2011; Richmond 2009; Richmond and Mitchell 2012).

As the "central organising principle of the EU's external action" (European Commission and HRVP 2013: 2) the EU comprehensive approach to conflicts and crises emphasized the reciprocal relationship between security and development. It stressed an inclusive understanding of crisis management for addressing all phases and dimensions of a conflict, noting the interlinkage of different policy areas: "a coordinated and shared analysis of each country and/or regional specific context, the conflict dynamics and the root causes of crisis situation." Further, this entails earlier and more coordinated planning for "a smooth transition" from one form of EU engagement to another (especially the transition from short- or medium-term activity to longer-term development cooperation). Here the importance of "local ownership and the need for sustainable results" is stressed (Council of the European Union 2014: 2–3).

In this respect, the creation of a "Concepts, Knowledge Management and Training" unit in Directorate ISP will help not just to revive and operationalise important concepts (e.g., disarmament, demobilization, and reintegration (DDR), security sector reform (SSR) and human security), but also to boost a process of lessons learnt from past deployments in EU crisis response.

Conclusions

This chapter has surveyed the current state of EU external crisis response and whether the EU has managed to plug the capability–expectations gap which is needed in order to be an effective actor in this area. It has investigated the EU's comprehensive/integrated approach to external conflicts and assessed the Union's capacities in this field. In structuring the analysis, we have drawn on the work of March and Olsen (1995) to identify what is needed for *actor capacity in the realm of crisis response*. This has enabled us to identify clear objectives, with an institutional framework and a decision-making capacity to follow up on these objectives, as well as a set of administrative capacities like a legal framework, organizational skills (including the ability to learn from past experience), resources (budget, staff and equipment), and learning capacity.

Our analysis indicates that the EU has managed to identify fairly clear goals and objectives; that it has over time developed an institutional framework and a legal framework that is complex but functional. However, the capacity to act remains hampered by limited resources and a less-developed capacity to make use of existing knowledge to ensure a conflict-sensitive approach. Given the low political willingness to provide the EU with increased capacities, especially for the actual crisis-phase, better coordination between the EU and its member states is needed to compensate for this weakness. While this is crucial, it is still not sufficient. Being an effective actor in the area of crisis response also requires a well-developed understanding of the various conflicts and their dynamics—aspects that seem to have been neglected by both the EU and its member states. Although the EU has managed (at least partly) to close what we may refer to as "the intentions–implementation gap" in crisis response, the "implementation–reception/perceptions gap" is still wide open. This will not only require more resources and better coordination between the EU institutions and an improved decision-making capacity. It will also require more attention to the need for implementing a conflict-sensitive approach based on greater local ownership and an in-depth understanding of the nature of the crises to which the EU seeks to respond. This is perhaps the gap that most urgently needs to be plugged if the EU wants to have more impact in tackling crises abroad.

Identifying this prevailing gap in EU crisis response does not mean that the EU has not become more integrated in this area since the establishment of the European Union. The question is if this integration can be characterised as a process of *muddling through* or *heading forward* (Chapter 1). While it is the *muddling through* perspective that best fits the sluggish development in this field, a more radical change (*heading forward*) is what is needed for the EU to be able to plug the remaining gaps that we have identified.

References

Adler-Nissen, R. (2014). Symbolic Power in EU Diplomacy: The Struggle Between National Foreign Services and the EU's External Action Service. *Review of International Studies, 40*(4), 657–681.

Arnaud, Y., Barbieri, C, Deneckere, M., De Zan, T., & Flessenkemper, T. (2017, March). *Analysis of CSDP Institutional and Policy Aspects and Lessons Learned*. CIVILEX Report D2.1. http://civilex.eu/sites/default/files/civilex/public/content-files/article/D2.1%20Analysis%20of%20CSDP%20institutional%20and%20policy%20aspects%20and%20lessons%20learned%20-%20public.pdf.

Austermann, F. (2014). *European Union Delegations in EU Foreign Policy: A Diplomatic Service at Different Speeds*. Basingstoke: Palgrave.

Barry, L. (2012). *European Security in the 21st Century: The EU's Comprehensive Approach*. IIEA European Security and Defence Series. Dublin: Institute of International and European Affairs.

Bátora, J. (2013). The 'Mitrailleuse Effect': The EEAS as an Interstitial Organization and the Dynamics of Innovation in Diplomacy. *Journal of Common Market Studies, 51*(4), 598–613.

Blockmans, S. (2014). *Peacemaking: Can the EU Meet Expectations?* (NUPI Working Paper No. 840). Oslo: Norwegian Institute of International Affairs.

Blockmans, S., & Hillion, C. (Eds.). (2013). *EEAS 2.0: A Legal Commentary on Council Decision 2010/427/EU Establishing the Organisation and Functioning of the European External Action Service*. Stockholm: SIEPS.

Blockmans, S., & Russack, S. (2015). *The Commissioners' Group on External Action—Key Political Facilitator* (CEPS Special Report No. 125).

Blockmans, S. (2018). The EU's Modular Approach to Defence Integration. *Common Market Law Review, 55*(6), 1785–1825.

Blockmans, S., & Koutrakos, P. s (Eds.). (2018). *Research Handbook on the EU's Common Foreign and Security Policy*. Cheltenham: Edward Elgar.

Boin, A., Ekengren, M., & Rhinard, M. (2013). *The European Union as Crisis Manager: Patterns and Prospects*. Cambridge: Cambridge University Press.

Bossong, R. (2013). EU Civilian Crisis Management and Organizational Learning. *European Security, 22*(1), 94–112.

Chandler, D. (2010). *International Statebuilding: The Rise of Post-liberal Governance*. London: Routledge.

Cooper, R. (2016). *The EU's Global Strategy: Three Quotations*. Policy Brief, Berlin: Dahrendorf Forum, May 2015.

Council of the European Union. (2003, December 12). *A Secure Europe in a Better World. European Security Strategy*. Brussels: Council of the European Union. https://europa.eu/globalstrategy/en/european-security-strategy-secure-europe-better-world.

Council of the European Union. (2014). *Council Conclusions on the EU's Comprehensive Approach*. Brussels: Press. http://www.consilium.europa.eu/en/council-eu/configurations/fac/.

Council of the European Union. (2016). *Taking Forward the EU's Comprehensive Approach to External Conflict and Crises—Action Plan 2016–17*. SWD(2016) 254 final, July 19. Brussels: Council of the European Union. http://data.consilium.europa.eu/doc/document/ST-11408-2016-INIT/en/pdf.

Debuysere, L., & Blockmans, S. (2019, June 5). *Directorate ISP: No Deus Ex Machina for the EU's Integrated Approach*. PeaceLab Blog.

Drent, M. (2011). The EU's Comprehensive Approach to Security: A Culture of Co-ordination? *Studia Diplomatica*, 64(2), 3–18.

Duke, S. (2018). Capabilities and CSDP: Resourcing Political will or Paper Armies. In S. Blockmans & P. Koutrakos (Eds.), *Research Handbook on the EU's Common Foreign and Security Policy*. Cheltenham: Edward Elgar.

EU Global Strategy. (2016). *Shared Vision, Common Action: A Stronger Europe*. Brussels: EEAS. https://eeas.europa.eu/sites/eeas/files/eugs_review_web_0.pdf.

European Commission and HRVP (2013, December 11). *Joint Communication to the European Parliament and the Council—The EU's Comprehensive Approach to External Conflicts and Crises*, JOIN (2013) 30 final.

European Commission and HRVP. (2015). *Taking Forward the EU's Comprehensive Approach to External Conflict and Crises—Action Plan 2015*. Joint Staff Working Document. (SWD (2015) 85 final).

European Parliament. (2012). *CSDP Missions and Operations: Lessons Learned Processes*. Study prepared by the Policy Department. Brussels: Directorate-General for External Policies of the Union.

Furness, M., & Olsen, G. R. (2016). Europeanisation and the EU's Comprehensive Approach to Crisis Management in Africa. *European Politics and Society*, 17(1), 105–119.

Galavan, R. (2015). *Understanding Resources, Competences, and Capabilities in EU Common Security and Defence Policy* (Working Paper). http://www.ieceu-project.com/wp-content/uploads/2016/02/Galavan%20-%20Understanding%20Capabilities%20(IECEU).pdf.

Hayes-Renshaw, F., van Aken, W., & Wallace, H. (2006). When and Why the EU Council of Ministers Votes Explicitly. *Journal of Common Market Studies*, 44(1), 161–194.

Hill, C. (1993). The Capability-Expectation Gap, or Conceptualizing Europe's International Role. *Journal of Common Market Studies*, 31(3), 305–328.

Hillion, C., & Blockmans, S. (2015). Europe's self-defence: Tous pour un et un pour tous? *CEPS Commentary*, 20 November.

Hillion, C., & Wessel, R. (2009). Competence Distribution in EU External Relations After ECOWAS: Clarification or Continued Fuzziness? *Common Market Law Review*, 46, 551–586.

Juncos, A. (2018). Civilian CSDP Missions: The Good, the Bad and the Ugly. In S. Blockmans & P. Koutrakos (Eds.), *Research Handbook on the EU's Common Foreign and Security Policy*. Cheltenham: Edward Elgar.

Kempin, R., & Scheler, R. (2016a). *Joining Forces: Necessary Steps for Developing the Comprehensive Approach*. SWP Comments 31. Berlin: SWP.

Kempin, R., & Scheler, R. (2016b). *"Vom 'umfassenden' zum 'integrierten Ansatz': Notwendige Schritte zur Weiterentwicklung der EU-Außenbeziehungen am Beispiel der Sahelzone und des Horns von Afrika"*, SWP-Studie 8. Berlin: SWP.

Koops, J. A. (2011). *The European Union as an Integrative Power? Assessing the EU's "Effective Multilateralism" Towards NATO and the United Nations*. Brussels: VUB University Press.

Mac Ginty, R. (2011). *International Peacebuilding and Local Resistance*. Houndmills: Palgrave Macmillan.

Manners, I. (2002). Normative Power Europe: A Contradiction in Terms? *Journal of Common Market Studies, 40*(2), 235–258.

March, J. J., & Olsen, J. P. (1995). *Democratic Governance*. New York: Free Press.

McCormick, J. (2007). *The European Superpower*. New York: Palgrave Macmillan.

Merlingen, M. (2012). *EU Security Policy: What It Is, How It Works, Why It Matters*. Boulder, CO: Lynne Rienner.

Moravcsik, A. (2010). 'Europe, the Second Superpower'. *Current History (2010), 109*(725), 91–98.

Myrdal, S., & Rhinard, M. (2012). *The European Union's Solidarity Clause: Empty Letter or Effective Tool? An Analysis of Article 222 of the Treaty on the Functioning of the European Union*. UI Occasional papers 2. Stockholm: Swedish Institute of International Affairs (UI).

Niemann, A., & Bretherton, C. (2013). EU External Policy at the Crossroads: The Challenge of Actorness and Effectiveness. *International Relations, 27*(3), 261–275.

Osland, K. (2014). *Much Ado About Nothing? The Impact of International Assistance to Police Reform in Afghanistan, Bosnia and Herzegovina, Kosovo, Serbia and South Sudan*. Oslo: Faculty of Social Sciences, University of Oslo/Akademika.

Pirozzi, N. (2013). *The EU's Comprehensive Approach to Crisis Management*. EU Crisis Management Papers Series (June). Brussels: Geneva Centre for the Control of Armed Forces (DCAF).

Pirozzi, N. (2015). *EU Crisis Management After Lisbon—A New Mode to Address Security Challenges in the 21st Century?* Cambridge: Intersentia.

Post, S. (2014). Towards a Whole-of-Europe Approach. *Organizing the European Union's and Member States' Comprehensive Crisis Management*. Berlin: Springer.

Richmond, O. P. (2009). The Romanticisation of the Local: Welfare, Culture and Peacebuilding. *International Spectator, 44*(1), 149–169.

Richmond, O. P., & Mitchell, A. (2012). *Hybrid Forms of Peace: From Everyday Agency to Post-Liberalism*. Houndmills: Palgrave Macmillan.

Riddervold, M. (2018). *The Maritime Turn in EU Foreign and Security Policies*. Cham:Springer International Publishing.

Rieker, P. (2009). The EU—A Capable Security Actor? Developing Administrative Capabilities. *Journal of European Integration, 31*(6), 703–719.

Rieker, P. (2013). The EU Foreign and Security Policy: High Expectations, Low Capabilities. In F. Bynander and S. Guzzini (Eds.), *Rethinking Foreign Policy*, (pp. 150–162). London: Routledge.

Rieker, P., Bátora, J., Blockmans, S., Ferhatovic, E., Peters, I., Stambøl, E. M., & Strand, S. (2016). *Best Practices in EU Crisis Response and Policy Implementation*. EUNPACK Deliverable D.4.02. Oslo: NUPI. http://www.eunpack.eu/sites/default/files/deliverables/Deliverable%204.02.pdf.

Rieker, P., & Blockmans, S. (2019). Plugging the Capabilityexpectations Gap: Towards Effective, Comprehensive and Conflict-sensitive EU Crisis Response? *European Security, 28*(1), 1–21.

Schilde, K. (2016). European Military Capabilities: Enablers and Constraints on EU Power? *Journal of Common Market Studies, 55*(1), 37–53.

Sjursen, H. (2006). What Kind of Power? *Journal of European Public Policy, 13*(2), 169–181.

Spence, D., & Bátora, J. (Eds.). (2015). *The European External Action Service: European Diplomacy Post-Westphalia*. Basingstoke: Palgrave.

Toje, A. (2008a). The Consensus-Expectations Gap: Explaining Europe's Ineffective Foreign Policy. *Security Dialogue, 39*(1), 121–141.

Toje, A. (2008b). The European Union as a Small Power, or Conceptualizing Europe's Strategic Actorness. *Journal of European Integration, 30*(2), 199–215.

Tovornik, N.A. (2015). Civilian Capability Development. In *CSDP Handbook: Missions and Operations*. Vienna: Federal Ministry of Defence and Sports.

van der Heijden, P. (2015). Military Capability Development. In *CSDP Handbook: Missions and Operations*. Vienna: Federal Ministry of Defence and Sports.

Weston, A., & Mérand, F. (2015). The EEAS and Crisis Management: The Organisational Challenges of a Comprehensive Approach. In D. Spence & J. Bátora (Eds.), *The European External Action Service: European Diplomacy Post-Westphalia* (pp. 306–340). Houndmills: Palgrave Macmillan.

CHAPTER 35

EU–US Relations in Times of Crises

Marianne Riddervold and Akasemi Newsome

INTRODUCTION

How, if in any way, have crises affected EU–US relations? And what, if any, has been the impact of potentially changing transatlantic relations on EU foreign policy integration? In 2008, Anderson, Ikenberry, and Risse asked if the US-led invasion of Iraq and the resulting split between the US and several of its European allies had led to the "End of the West?" Although concluding that it had not, the very title underlines the importance of the EU–US relationship not only for EU and US foreign policies but also for the post WWII international order as such. The liberal international order refers to the system of multilateral institutions, rules, and norms established by the US since 1945 with the UN at its center (Ikenberry 2008; 2018), today covering almost all areas of international relations. The transatlantic relationship, defined here as "the overall set of relations between the European Union and the United

M. Riddervold (✉) · A. Newsome
Inland School of Business and Social Sciences, Inland University, Rena and Lillehammer, Norway
e-mail: marianne.riddervold@inn.no

Institute of European Studies, University of California, Berkeley, CA, USA

A. Newsome
e-mail: akasemi@berkeley.edu

M. Riddervold
The Norwegian Institute of International Affairs (NUPI), Oslo, Norway

© The Author(s) 2021
M. Riddervold et al. (eds.), *The Palgrave Handbook of EU Crises*,
Palgrave Studies in European Union Politics,
https://doi.org/10.1007/978-3-030-51791-5_35

States, within the broader framework of the institutional and other connections maintained via NATO and other institutions" (Mike Smith 2018: 539), goes to the very heart of this system. Transatlantic relations have been at the core of "the establishment, expansion and maintenance of the multilateral system, and of multilateralism as a set of international practices" (ibid.). As a result of continuous cooperation and as the European states have moved closer together in the European Union, today, no other regions of the world are as closely connected in economics, security, and politics as Europe and the United States of America (US) (Oliver 2016: 2, see also Alcaro et al. 2016; Frölich 2012; Hill et al. 2017; Ilgen 2016; Peterson and Pollack 2003; Sola and Smith 2009). As such, relations with the US form an integral part of the EU's foreign policies, relating to all areas of the EU's external dealings as spelled out in the EU's Global Strategy. Similarly, the US relationship to its European partner has been a key component of US external relations.

In light of the many crises discussed in this volume, and as US foreign policy changes under and beyond Donald Trump, scholars and observers have started questioning the viability of the transatlantic relationship and the liberal order more broadly, including its implications for Europe. In a recent issue of Foreign Affairs, Kagan (2019: 108) discusses what a potential "decoupling" from the United States would mean for Europe, in particular for Germany's role on the continent. Drezner (2019: 10) argues that compared to previous crises in the transatlantic (and other US) relationships such as the Iraq war, "this time is different." For Drezner, a decreasing level of trust in the US will to uphold and honor international treaties and relationships, suggests that US foreign policies will never recover from the foreign policy actions of Donald Trump, with severe consequences both for the transatlantic relationship and the US role in the multilateral international system more broadly. Stephen M. Walt (2019: 32) argues that "it is time for the United States to gradually disengage from NATO and turn European security over to the Europeans." Others have also argued that Trump's actions undermine the viability of the multilateral order as such (Zakaria 2017), and that other contemporary global geopolitical changes, including the rise of China and a more aggressive Russia, add to this demise (Rose 2018; Mike Smith 2018).

Although this change in US policies started under previous presidents, it escalated with Trump. The potential implications for the liberal international system challenge the very foundation of the EU's foreign policy behavior and identity. As argued by Anderson in this volume: "the Trump challenge has been pervasive and durable, testament to the single-minded consistency of the U.S. president when it comes to Europe." Trump's presidency not only threatens European defense prospects—it also challenges the status of the EU as a liberal multilateral order where cooperation, free trade and democracy is in everyone's interest and a moral imperative. The promotion of this order lies at the core of all the EU's foreign policies and is an integral part of the EU's identity (see Smith, this volume). Most international trade is moreover tied to the dollar, and the Bretton Woods institutions, the WTO and the IMF, are the centerpieces of the international open trade system that the EU profits from and seeks to promote (see Hjertaker and Tranøy, this volume). The EU has also been the main global promoter of binding regulations to limit climate change (Falkner 2007) and played a key role in establishing the Iran accord, just to mention a few areas where the EU's multilateral foreign policy plays out. Trump, on the other hand—in spite of much EU opposition—has withdrawn the US from the Paris and Iran accords, the Transatlantic Trade and Investment Partnership (TTIP), imposed tariffs on trade, and has even questioned US willingness to support its NATO allies in the case of an attack. Adding to this uncertainty, EU–US relations are changing in a more volatile geopolitical environment, with the Ukraine crisis as one of the most severe external challenges the EU has ever faced (see Juncos and Pomorska, this volume).

Against this background, this chapter draws on existing studies to systematically explore if and if so in what way crises have influenced the transatlantic relationship and what a potentially changing EU–US relationship implies for EU foreign policy integration. Particular focus is given to the transatlantic partners' increasingly diverging foreign policy orientations following a changing US focus and a changing geopolitical environment. We also discuss how Brexit and increasing populism on both sides of the Atlantic linked to the new transnational cleavage discussed by Marks, Attewell, Rovny, and Hooghe in this volume seem to influence contemporary and future EU–US relations (also see Anderson, this volume, Shapiro, this volume). However, also the other various EU crises discussed in this volume also add to the picture, as they together form a "perfect storm" of conditions potentially affecting EU–US relations and hence EU foreign policies more than at any other time since the second World War (Riddervold and Newsome 2018. Also see Chapter 1, this volume).

The chapter proceeds as follows. We first briefly discuss what we mean by the transatlantic relationship and what characterized this relationship before contemporary crises, drawing on Ikenberry's (2008) concept of the Atlantic Order (also see Anderson 2018). We then move on to discuss evidence to suggest that EU–US relations are weakening in the face of crises, discussing the EU and the US' increasingly diverging foreign policy orientations as well as the impact of Brexit and populism and the new transnational cleavage, before turning to the way in which a weakening EU–US relationship has influenced EU foreign policy integration more broadly. We end by discussing what a changing transatlantic relationship implies for EU integration in relation to the three scenarios set out in the introduction to this volume.

The Postwar Transatlantic Relationship

Perhaps not very surprisingly given its importance for the post world war international order, much has been written about the transatlantic relationship (Alcaro et al. 2016; Hanhimäki et al. 2012; Hill et al. 2017; Ikenberry 2008,

2018; Peterson and Pollack 2003; Sola and Smith 2009). Although at its broadest transatlantic relations refers to the economic, cultural, strategic, and other state and non-state relations between North America and Europe, we today foremost think of relations between the EU and the US bilaterally and in various institutional settings, as defined above. In this chapter we use the two terms, EU–US relations and transatlantic relations, interchangeably. Ikenberry referred to the transatlantic relationship as a distinctive form of international order—the "Atlantic Political Order," emerging on the basis not least of the US' experience with the two world wars. According to Ikenberry, the transatlantic relationship is based on four key pillars: "U.S. hegemony, mutual interests, political bargains, and agreed-upon rules and norms" (Ikenberry 2008: 9). It is a security alliance under US hegemony developed in response to the cold war developments, but it is also a community based on shared liberal values linked to free trade, multilateral cooperation, and the spread of democracy. The liberal international system and the transatlantic relationship are according to Ikenberry to the advantage of all, as these systems increase stability, peace, and economic prosperity. In particular, Ikenberry argues that the transatlantic relationship has rested on two mutually advantageous bargains between the U.S. and Europe. For the "liberal bargain', Europe accepts US leadership and in exchange, "the US provides its European partners with security protection and access to U.S. markets, technology, and supplies within an open world economy." Then in regard to "the realist bargain," the US "makes its [military] power safe for the world, and in return Europe … agrees to live within the U.S.-led system" (Ikenberry 2008: 9–10 in Anderson 2018: 622). Lastly, the transatlantic relationship is not least visible in the vast number of formal and informal rules and institutions that have developed between the EU and the US since WWII, both bilaterally and within the broader institutional landscape referred to as the liberal international order. As discussed in the introduction and as will be further elaborated below, the transatlantic relationship is both a driver of and a result of the existing multilateral international order (Mike Smith 2018).

A Weakening EU–US Relationship?

So, in what way, if any is, this transatlantic relationship changing in the face of contemporary crises? Ikenberry has predicted that the transatlantic relationship will withstand today's crises, including the one caused by Trump's policies, due to everyone's interest in upholding these liberal and realist institutionalized bargains. Indeed, the transatlantic relationship has proven resilient before, surviving crises such as the US intervention in Iraq, or disagreements over the Suez-canal crisis in the 50s. However, as mentioned in the introduction, there is increasing evidence to suggest that it might be different this time: that the Trump crisis, combined with geopolitical changes, increased populism both in the EU and the US and various other EU crises such as Brexit, indeed have led to a weakening of the EU–US relationship. Below we first discuss evidence to suggest that there is a weakening in EU–US relations due to their increasingly different foreign policy orientations. We thereafter discuss how Brexit and the Legitimacy crisis and in particular the new transatlantic divide and growth of populism of both sides of the Atlantic have influenced the relationship.

Diverging Foreign Policy Orientations and the Crisis in Multilateralism

Although the changes in US policies under Trump have gained a lot of attention amongst policy makers, scholars, and observers, surprisingly few systematic comparative studies of a putatively changing EU–US relationship exist. There are two main exceptions: In a recent issue of Foreign Affairs (Rose 2018) with the telling title "Letting go. Trump, America and World Order," leading scholars discuss foreign policy under Trump with a focus on the present and future of its leadership role in the international liberal order, including its relations with Europe (Rose 2018). In addition, a special issue of the Journal of European Integration from 2018 examined EU–US relations in the context of contemporary crises. Contributors to both publications concluded that the transatlantic relationship indeed seems to be weakening, and that in particular the US is becoming increasingly less concerned with upholding its traditional bonds to its Atlantic partner (Riddervold and Newsome 2018).

The set of papers in *Foreign Affairs* addressed the current instability of US hegemony as the result of the disappearance of "a relatively unified public at home and a lack of any serious rivals abroad" (Rapp-Hooper and Friedman Lissner 2019: 18). The new instability of US hegemony means that the US has become a less reliable actor on the world stage and European allies question the US commitment liberal international order, thus putting the transatlantic relationship on shaky ground. Instead, new contenders such as China and Russia jockey for primacy with the US and internet-based innovations empower minor states and groups to outsized impact. Rapp-Hooper et al. make the argument that the US should shift its energies from defending a liberal multilateral order to an approach that takes account of these new challenges—through a "defense of openness." Part of their reasoning lies in the fact the liberal multilateral order, even if US hegemony was still uncontested, does not have governance structures for the new phenomenon "AI, biotech and cyberspace" increasingly shaping the international system. Both the plausibility and capability of the US taking on this changed mission depends on the commitment on the part of its leaders to openness, something that cannot be taken for granted given that the Trump administration has supported authoritarian regimes, and EU member states have been backsliding away from democracy and toward authoritarianism notably in Hungary and Poland, but also in the Czech Republic and Romania (Walt 2019: 28–29; see also Brechenmacher 2018; Vachudova 2019; Raube and Costa Reis, this volume). Several of the authors suggest a strategy of cooperating with rising powers with the goal of convincing them "to accept the principles of openness and independence" and then ideally build on that foundation to then convince rising powers to both work with US hegemony and shape the next regime (Rapp-Hooper and Friedman Lissner 2019: 25). Walt in particular highlights the failures of US interventionism among these: "the bungled Middle East peace process, the misguided expansion of NATO, the botched wars in Afghanistan and Iraq, the CIA's torture of detainees in the war on terrorism, the National Security Agency's warrantless surveillance of Americans, the disastrous NATO intervention in Libya and the American machinations in Ukraine that gave Russia pretext to seize Crimea" (Walt 2019: 35) For him, the problem is that the experts who developed these campaigns experienced no sanctions for their errors in judgement (see Holst and Molander, this volume for further discussion of expertisation as a threat to democratic legitimacy). He urges the US to seek to counterbalance rising powers by rededicating energies to addressing democratic backsliding within its own territory given social discontent rooted in growing inequality and lack of political voice, and thus "restore the foundations of US power at home" (Walt 2019: 34). Echoing Walt, Schake also offers a critique of US liberal interventionism and use of force in Afghanistan and Iraq. She argues that there is a need for the US to rely on other countries to enforce global rules and support Europe and other allies in becoming more independent and capable in military matters. Key here, is for the post-Trump government to reaffirm the links between democratic values espoused by the US and its foreign policy. Schake also views the internal problems faced by the US, and the discontentment of US voters as having important implications for US foreign policy. She iterates a concern for technocracy as well and states that experts making foreign policy should "work harder to engage the public and open its ranks to more itinerant participation" (Schake 2019: 40).

Our previous work in a Special Issue in the *Journal of European Integration* in particular noted that although the long-term effects remain to be seen, "the transatlantic relationship is under more pressure today than in any other period since its establishment after the Second World War, putting the strength of the transatlantic, institutional structure to a particularly hard test" (Riddervold and Newsome 2018: 518). Whereas in the past the partners could agree on mutual interests and the importance of cooperation, the EU and the US are increasingly at odds with one another when it comes to protecting democratic principles and norms and bolstering the organizational architecture underpinning these principles and norms (Mike Smith 2018: 539–553). The EU–US partnership shows signs of wear and tear as the EU becomes a bolder and more cohesive actor. The main explanation for the shaky transatlantic partnership is the opposing view on topics such as climate, Iran and Russia as well as on the desirability of the US to continue to play policeman on a global scale (Drezner 2019; Riddervold and Newsome 2018; Rose 2018).

Supporting the claim that EU–US relations are weakening, several studies suggest that the EU is developing a stronger and more independent role vis a vis its traditional hegemon, the US. As argued by other authors such as

M.E. Smith (2018), this autonomy is very much linked to the different means applied by the EU in its policies. While the US has traditionally relied more on its so far unrivaled military force, the EU has mainly relied on dialogue to settle foreign policy matters. A recent investigation of the ways in which the emergence of new rivals to US hegemony shaped the transatlantic partnership and intra-European cooperation revealed that the EU has not simply followed the US's lead in foreign and security policy, as neo-realist approaches would predict. Instead, Riddervold and Rosén's (2018) analysis of EU–US relations vis a vis China and Russia in territorial conflicts in Ukraine and the South China suggests that the EU demonstrated that the EU set a course in line with its priorities, as well as an aspiration to act independently of the US. This is not to discount a general willingness of the transatlantic partners to develop a common security agenda in response to Russian and Chinese global ambitions. However Riddervold and Rosén do find evidence that the EU seeks to define an approach without the input of the US on these issues, thus potentially putting the transatlantic partnership under stress as the EU is no longer content to be the "junior partner" to the US.

In additional support for the argument that the EU–US relationship is weakening, Mike Smith (2018) shows how weakening transatlantic relations are both a reflection of what he refers to as a contemporary crisis of multilateralism as well as a contributor to it. Informal rules, structures, and bargaining are three themes that allow scholars to orient themselves in analysis of the transatlantic partnership in the international order. Several factors put pressure on this partnership, not least the view among US foreign policy elite that unilateral military action as preferable for defending US interests (Walt 2019: 34), notwithstanding the considerable successes the US has achieved through cooperation over the last 75 years.

Mai'a Cross (2018) also finds evidence to suggest that the EU–US relationship is weakening, not as a result of fragmentation, but rather from EU unity and diverging interests across the Atlantic. For Cross, the topic worthy of investigation is how EU member states were able to agree to pool resources in the Commission with the goal of building the international coalition needed to make the Paris Climate Accords a success. She examines this in a context of missing US leadership in the transatlantic response to climate change more broadly, but in the run up to the Paris Climate Summit specifically. The context is all the more interesting since the US subsequently presented itself as the architect of the Paris Climate Agreement. Cross uncovers the more significant role played by a unified EU in investing the resources in nations so that they were empowered to implement the policies and practices to stem climate change. Rather than uniting the EU and the US over climate change issues under Obama, Cross in other words shows a competition between the two and a lack of EU–US coordination. With Trump, the EU–US division over climate change negotiations have of course grown much stronger, with the EU and the US taking the opposite positions to if and how the climate crisis should be solved.

Brexit and EU–US Relationship

While Brexit is best conceptualized as a "series of processes" continuing to unfold (Oliver and Martill, this volume), the pace and tenor of the Brexit negotiations point to greater difficulties for the UK in a leadership role in Europe from outside of the EU when it is no longer a member (Oliver and Williams 2016). Of course, the UK might still be valuable to the US, in terms of the strategic asset of the British islands, the extensive surveillance cooperation between security agencies, and a general shared approach to foreign policy. Outside of the EU, and contrary to what is often heard from the UK "Brexit camp," the UK is however likely to be a less attractive partner to the US, since it will no longer be "a country with significant influence over the policies of a market of 450 million people" (Wilson 2017: 551).

For the EU–US relationship, Brexit could potentially lead to a strengthening, if a stronger EU finds together in a renewed partnership with the US, for example, in response to Russia and China (Riddervold and Newsome 2018; Riddervold and Rosén 2018). Perhaps more likely, Brexit could however also contribute to a further weakening of the relationship not least due to the strong "special relationship" that has existed between the UK and the US since the Second World War. The UK has provided a distinctive voice inside EU institutions often close to US perspectives, always for example arguing that NATO and not the EU should be the number one security provider in Europe. In this capacity, it has also been the main voice of the "Atlantist" EU member states, often in opposition to the French-led group of member states supporting a stronger foreign and security policy that is independent of the US (Marsh and Rees 2012). With the UK exiting the EU, EU foreign and security policies may in other words become less Atlantist, over time weakening the relationship. The development of new defense initiatives inside and outside of the EU and the UK's role in these however remain to be seen (see Svendsen, this volume). Brexit also highlights and potentially deepens already existing fault-lines in the US–EU relationship (Boffey 2019). In terms of security and defense, the UK has for example been an important agent for preserving the US military presence in Europe as the US expands its security and defense engagements in Asia.

Much has been made of the impact Brexit is likely to have on business and trade between the US and Europe. US firms often choose the UK as a favored location for operations in the European single market owing to language and cultural ties. Once the UK is no longer an EU member state, Wilson argues that the UK loses that gateway role (Wilson 2017: 550). In the finance sector, for example, other EU cities such as Frankfurt, Dublin, and Amsterdam stand to benefit from company relocations in response to Brexit. However it is unclear if other cities can duplicate the networks of exchange and learning that exist between London and New York post-Brexit. Although the individual UK economy is a key trading partner, trade barely generates 30% of the economic activity in the US economy. The UK in contrast is more heavily dependent on trade in general as more than half of its economic activity stems from trade (Wilson 2017: 549).

One may also argue that EU–US relations are weakening because the UK–US special relationship has changed. Under the best circumstances, the UK–US relationship offered on the one hand a kind of policy surrogate for the US in EU institutions. On the other hand, the EU could also take advantage of the privileged access of one its member states to push commonly held interests of its member states. The UK's decision not to join the US-led coalition in Libya in 2016 made so. The Trump crisis has however meant that the US–UK relationship cannot be taken for granted. Rachman (2019) offered the example of a recent firing of the former top UK diplomat in the US, by whom President Trump felt personally insulted. Trump has broken with past precedent by questioning whether NATO is relevant; he has made many statements and gestures supportive of Vladimir Putin for example. Successive UK governments have tried to preserve ties to the US by accommodating President Trump but this has not delivered any gains to the UK. For Theresa May, accommodation brought her into conflict with a significant segment of the British public and with parliament, as many in both groups did not support May's decision to invite President Trump to visit the UK as president (Wilson 2017: 553). Similarly, President Trump made clear his unwillingness come to favorable trade terms with the UK with the current Brexit terms Boris Johnson delivered to the British parliament (Sloat 2019; Douglass 2019).

Populism and the Transatlantic Relationship

Another important concern for transatlantic relations that is exacerbated by Brexit is the gains made by nationalist parties on both sides of the Atlantic. Populist movements around Brexit in the UK and around Trump's then presidential candidacy in the US have mirrored each other. Not only has there been overlap in terms of the themes, politicians from each country have visited the other country to build momentum and support. For example, Nigel Farage, a prominent Brexiteer, identified several targets as the sources of Britain's problems much as Donald Trump has done including elites, immigrants, international treaties and agreements (Wilson 2017: 545).

John Peterson (2018) has studied the impact of populism and popular movements on the transatlantic relationship, concluding that this new transnational divide is an important factor for understanding its strength. After examining the popular movements behind Brexit and Donald Trump's election as president, Peterson concludes that voters in both countries are deeply dissatisfied with the postwar global system and that this consequently also contributes to a weakening of EU–US relations. He underscores the link between the transatlantic partnership and respective domestic politics as under attack and inseparable from foreign policy aims. Leaders like US President Trump have a mandate for actions believed to be inconceivable until now based on the assumption that the US and its allies—elites and citizens alike—shared common interests. Absence of this domestic harmony results in, "a US administration taking the lead in shredding transatlantic relations by casting doubt on the validity of Article 5 of NATO, demanding billions from European allies for security guarantees, attacking free trade and expressing affinity with authoritarian leaders" (Peterson 2018). In this way, Peterson corroborates similar arguments about the role of domestic discontent with globalization and democracy as key to the fraying of EU–US relations.

Findings from these and other studies also suggest that this weakening due to the "Trump crisis" may continue after Donald Trump, due to the polarization of US policies. According to Drezner, one consequence of populism is eroded trust in the foreign policy experts and diplomats traditionally upholding multilateralist US foreign policies, including the transatlantic relationship (also see Holst and Molander, this volume; Marks, Attewell, Rovny and Hooghe, this volume; Shapiro, this volume; Stie, this volume). Furthermore, populism and polarization have undermined that traditional bipartisan agreement on US foreign policies, creating a polarized system where US strategies change from one election to the next. With such instability, in stark contrast to the traditional post war US multilateralist foreign policy, "only the credulous will consider U.S. commitments credible" (Drezner 2019: 16). Continuing challenges both within the EU and the US as well as in the multilateral system as such will according to Mike Smith (2018) also further serve to undermine the strength of the transatlantic relationship. Mike Smith (2018: 544–545) has argued that the crisis in multilateralism, both fueling and resulting from weakening EU–US relations stems largely from the increased uncertainty about the EU and US roles and positions on multilateralism. It is difficult to determine what views these two actors have on international institutions and cooperation when domestic politics within each is splinters on isolationism vs. international engagement. One factor that carries significant weight in explaining internal divisions in the US is the fact that new contender nations are jockeying for influence and the US is no longer the only superpower. Current US president Trump played to domestic anxieties in some quarters about these changes in the global system, casting outward oriented elites as unpatriotic and advocating for isolationism for ordinary people and the nation. Across the Atlantic, Europe has its own divisions to contend with as populist movements also stoke suspicions of "cosmopolitan orientations among political elites" (Peterson 2018). At the same time, individual countries try to attain privileged access to the US. This competition among EU member states for the ear of the US thus undercuts the EU's effectiveness as a cohesive actor. With domestic divisions and ambitious new rival nations on the horizon, both the EU and the US cannot be sure "which EU [or US] will show up in transatlantic and other multilateral forums" (Riddervold and Newsome 2018). This was the case with the unsuccessful trade negotiations as well as the collapse of the Iran nuclear deal supported by Obama. Not least, Mike Smith shows that the existing norms, past practices and rules-based organizational structures have not been sufficient to maintain the health of the EU–US partnership. For these reasons, Mike Smith argues the partnership will continue to erode.

WHAT IMPACT ON EU INTEGRATION?

To sum up our discussions so far, there is indeed evidence to suggest that EU–US relations are weakening. As stated by Riddervold and Newsome (2018: 518): "Individual actions, a multitude of crises combined with increasingly diverging perspectives on the value and importance of multilateral cooperation and norms, less public support, and a decrease in trust between the two allies together serve to weaken the transatlantic relationship."

So what, if any has been the impact of this weakening on the EU's foreign policies? Is the EU becoming more fragmented in its relations with the US and in its foreign policies more broadly, as the EU member states seek to strengthen its relations to the US while one of the main promoters of a tight transatlantic bond is Brexiting the EU? Do the EU institutions deal with these challenges incrementally, seeking to handle new challenges as they arise, to muddle through a changing foreign policy context? Or has a changing US policy in a more uncertain world served to strengthen EU foreign policy integration by functioning as a pull factor for more foreign policy cooperation?

Evidence collected through empirical studies so far show a somewhat mixed picture. Both Mike Smith (2018) and Akasemi Newsome (2018) argue that the EU is becoming more fragmented in its relations with the US and hence key aspect of its foreign policy more broadly. Newsome explores the EU–US relationship from the perspective of their external human rights policies. How supportive are the US and EU when it comes to human rights and do the US and EU act in concert to uphold human rights? Newsome (2018) answers these questions with evidence that EU member states struggled to come to agreement on if and how to live up to their commitments to human rights when faced with concrete opportunities to put these values into practice following the 2015 Syrian refugee crisis. This is puzzling not only because human rights is one of the constitutive values of the EU, member states were unable to agree to defend them. When faced with a similar refugee crisis in its near abroad in Kosovo in the 90s, the EU was able to overcome divisions among members states and act to address the crisis. Newsome's analysis comparing the policy response to the Kosovo refugee crisis and the Syrian refugee crisis posits that the transatlantic partnership is no longer as strong as it once was on human rights concerns. The comparison of the two crises moreover suggests that the key explanatory factor in the EU's ability to act forcefully to defend human rights of refugees in Kosovo versus the lack of a defense in the Syrian case was US leadership. Her study documents a change in the US role whereby in Syria, "the US has been unwilling to provide leadership, both militarily and diplomatically" (Newsome 2018). Lacking a strong US voice in favor of intra EU cooperation, the EU retreated from human rights issues: "While the Kosovo crisis led to increased transatlantic cooperation as the EU was pushed into greater cooperation under US leadership, in the Syrian refugee crisis, both the EU member states and the US have acted unilaterally and have not lived up to their human rights obligations" (Newsome 2018). Mike Smith arrives at similar conclusions about the erosion of the transatlantic partnership. Particularly in international relations, Mike Smith (2018) notes that EU member states splinter easily in multilateral forums as they clamor for a favored position for their nation and the US. Smith attributes this lack of cohesion within the EU to the increasing instability given rising ambitious states on the world stage and the surge in rightwing nationalist movements, thus limiting the prospects for further integration.

Overall, however, so far, most existing studies seem to support the volume's second and third scenario: That a weakening EU–US relationship has served to pull the EU member states together in closer foreign policy cooperation in order to deal with the various external challenges it faces, through incremental changes or in some cases by developing new. According to Anderson (2018: 627–628), for example, "The two crises relating to security concerns – Russia/Ukraine and Trump – have provided motive and impetus for greater coordination on economic diplomacy (sanctions; tariffs) as well as the first inklings of a change in the European vision of security." Other chapters in this volume suggest the same impact of crisis on EU integration, in particular as regards the Ukraine crisis. Both Juncos and Pomorska (this volume) and Riddervold (this volume) present evidence to suggest that this crisis has led to more foreign and security policy integration, including changing member states positions from opposition to support of concrete policy initiatives such as the EU's Arctic Policies and the EU Maritime Security Strategy. The impact of the Ukraine crisis on EU foreign and security policy integration has also been discussed extensively in a JCMS special issue from 2017 edited by Karolewski and Cross (2017). Several studies suggest that a weakening EU–US relationship and in particular the Trump crisis further serves to strengthen this trend. In a broad study of contemporary EU foreign policies rather than attribute weakening transatlantic relations solely to developments internal to the US, M.E. Smith (2018) points out that the EU is becoming a more independent and assertive actor particularly in light of its increased activity in diplomacy and defense. This is not to say that political events in the US are not meaningful for weakening transatlantic relations, rather the Trump crisis and weakening relationship generate greater efforts within the EU to integrate further. For M.E. Smith, the substance of the EU's new assertiveness in international relations consists of a distinctive perspective on the kinds of actions best suited to address conflict abroad in that the EU is less quick to rely on military intervention. While this distinctive perspective stems in part from the sizeable and significant gap in military capability between the EU and the US, M.E. Smith (2018: 512–513) points out that even in cases of "conflict intervention and involvement [the EU] is often viewed as more acceptable by other states than those conducted by the US or NATO." For these reasons, the EU stands to become more prominent, active, and visible in diplomacy and defense situations outside of its territory. The growing confidence exerted by the EU in global affairs suggests that the transatlantic partnership may become even more difficult to sustain as signs point to continued support among member states and among supranational institutions for an EU with "strategic autonomy" with a preference for "multilateral security cooperation" in contrast to the isolationist approach many foreign policy elites advocate for in the US.

Conclusion

This chapter has explored the impact of crises on EU–US relations, discussing whether there is evidence to suggest that the transatlantic relationship is weakening in the face of internal and external EU crises, focusing in particular on the Trump crisis and the one caused by Russia in Ukraine. We also discussed what a weakening of EU–US relations has meant for EU foreign policy integration.

Regarding our first question, we find evidence across various studies to suggest that the EU–US relationship indeed is weakening. As far as we know, there are no studies that argue the opposite, namely that crises have served to strengthen EU–US relations in the face of often common challenges, such as climate change, migration, and growing and more assertive powers China and Russia. Should push come to show for example in the South China Sea it is likely that the EU would stand with its traditionally ally and hegemon the US. But even in the game of great power politics, the EU is acting increasingly independently of the US. Most importantly, the transatlantic relationship is weakening because the EU and the US have increasingly different perspectives on international relations, multilateral cooperation, and foreign policy, including the value of the transatlantic relationship as such. Although there have been tensions before and the relationship was already changing under previous US administrations, the EU–US relationship today indeed seems to be in an unprecedented crisis, due to a lack of trust among the European countries in its American partner and their increasingly different foreign policy perspectives. While the EU continues to be a main promoter of multilateral cooperation, the US is withdrawing from various international treaties and obligations, and has made the Europeans less certain about the US' commitment to the security alliance. As discussed above, factors such as populism, the increasing polarization of US politics, and the ongoing crisis of multilateralism make it likely to assume that this trend will continue. Either way, as several authors discussed above have pointed to, trust is something that is difficult to build and that might influence EU–US relations in years to come, also with another president.

A weaker EU–US relationship is also influencing EU foreign policy integration. Although the picture is somewhat mixed, with many EU member states seeking special or stronger bilateral relations with the US, our main conclusion is that the EU is becoming more unified—that it is integrating further—in the foreign policy domain in the face of a weakening transatlantic relationship. The EU has become more unified and more autonomous of the US in its policies, continuing to look for multilateral solutions to international challenges that are very different from those of the US under Trump, such as in climate policy negotiations or in relation to Iran. In this sense, the EU is *muddling through* also in its foreign policies in spite of a changing EU–US relationship. At the same time Trump and other crises seem to have functioned as critical junctures, putting new policies of increased EU foreign and security policy integration on the table, in the longer term indicating that the EU may also head forward in the CFSP. Many European and national leaders for example argue that it is time to take more responsibility for Europe's security. Questions such as how far the EU will be able to replace the US in terms of defense, the extent to which it will remain in opposition to the US on key foreign policy issues and the extent to which the EU will be able to uphold the liberal order without the US remain to be seen.

REFERENCES

Alcaro, R., Greco, E., & Peterson, J. (Eds.). (2016). *The West and the Global Power Shift: Transatlantic Relations and Global Governance*. London: Palgrave Macmillan.

Anderson, J. G. (2018). Rancor and Resilience in the Atlantic Political Order: The Obama ears in 'Crises and EU–US Relations', special issue. *Journal of European Integration, 40*(5), 621–636.

Anderson, J. G., Ikenberry, J., & Risse, T. (Eds.). (2008). *The End of the West? Crisis and Change in the Atlantic Order*. Ithaca: Cornell University Press.

Boffey, D. (2019, August 16). Boris Johnson to Head to Paris and Berlin in Bid to Break Brexit Deadlock. *The Guardian*.

Brechenmacher, S. (2018). *Comparing Democratic Distress in the United States and Europe*. New York: Carnegie Endowment for International Peace.

Cross, M. K. D. (2018). Partners at Paris? Climate Negotiations and Transatlantic Relations. *Journal of European Integration, 40*(5), 571–586.

Douglas, J. (2019, October 31). Trump Says Hard to Do Trade Deal with UK Under Boris Johnson Brexit Deal. *Wall Street Journal*.

Drezner, D. W. (2019). This Time Is Different: Why U.S. Foreign Policy Will Never Recover. *Foreign Affairs, 98*(3), 10–17.

Falkner, R. (2007). The Political Economy of 'Normative Power' Europe: EU Environmental Leadership in International Biotechnology Regulation. *Journal of European Public Policy, 14*(4), 507–526.

Frölich, S. (2012). *The New Geopolitics of Transatlantic Relations: Coordinated Responses to Common Dangers*. Washington, DC: Woodrow Wilson Center Press.

Hanhimäki, J., Zanchetta, B., & Schoenborn, B. (2012). *Transatlantic Relations Since 1945: An Introduction*. Abingdon, Oxon: Routledge.

Hill, C., Smith, M., & Vanhoonacker, S. (2017). *International Relations and the European Union* (3rd ed.). Oxford: Oxford University Press.

Kagan, R. (2019). The New German question: What Happens When Europe Comes Apart? *Foreign Affairs, 98*(3), 108–120.

Karolewski, I. P., & Cross, M. K. (2017). The EU's Power in the Russia–Ukraine Crisis: Enabled or Constrained? *JCMS: Journal of Common Market Studies, 55*(1), 137–152.

Ikenberry, G. J. (2008). Introduction. In J. Anderson, G. J. Ikenberry, & T. Risse (Eds.), *The End of the West? Crisis and Change in the Atlantic Order*. Ithaca, NY: Cornell University Press.

Ikenberry, G. J. (2018). The End of Liberal International Order? *International Affairs, 94*(1), 7–23.

Ilgen, T. L. (Ed.). (2016). *Hard Power, Soft Power and the Future of Transatlantic Relations*. London: Routledge.

Marsh, S., & Rees, W. (2012). *The European Union in the security of Europe: From Cold War to Terror War*. Abingdon: Routledge.

Newsome, A. (2018). Credible Champions: Transatlantic Relations and Human Rights in Refugee Crises. *Journal of European Integration, 40*(5), 587–604.

Oliver, T. (2016, May). New Challenges, New Voices: Next Generation Viewpoints on Transatlantic Relations. *LSE Ideas—Dahrendorf Forum Special Report*.

Oliver, T., & Williams, M. J. (2016). Special Relationships in Flux: Brexit and the Future of the US–EU and US–UK Relationships. *International Affairs, 92*(3), 547–567.

Peterson, J. (2018). Structure, Agency and Transatlantic Relations in the Trump Era. In *Crises and EU–US Relations*, special issue. *Journal of European Integration, 40*(5), 637–652.

Peterson, J., & Pollack, M. A. (Eds.). (2003). *Europe, America, Bush: Transatlantic Relations in the Twenty-First Century*. London and New York: Routledge.

Rachman, G. (2019, July 12). US–UK Relations: Strains in the 'Greatest Alliance'. *The Financial Times*.

Rapp-Hooper, M., & Friedman Lissner, R. (2019). The Open World: What America Can Achieve After Trump. *Foreign Affairs, 98*(3), 18–25.

Riddervold, M., & Rosén, G. (2018). Unified in Response to Rising Powers? China, Russia and EU–US Relations, special issue. *Journal of European Integration, 40*(5), 555–570.

Riddervold, M., & Newsome, A. (2018). Introduction: Uniting or Dividing? In *Crises and EU–US Relations*, special issue. *Journal of European Integration, 40*(5), 505–522.

Rose, G. (2018). Letting Go: Trump, America, and the World. *Foreign Affairs, 97*(2), 1–192.

Schake, K. (2019). Back to Basics: How to Make Right What Trump Gets Wrong. *Foreign Affairs, 98*(3), 36–43.

Sloat, A. (2019, July 31). What Boris Johnson Means for US–UK Relations. *Brookings*.

Smith, M. (2018). The EU, the US and the Crisis of Contemporary Multilateralism. In *Crises and EU–US Relations*, special issue. *Journal of European Integration, 40*(5), 539–554.

Smith, M. E. (2015). The EU and the US. In K. E. Jørgensen, A. K. Aarstad, E. Driesken, K. V. Laatikained, & B. Tonra (Eds.), *The Sage Handbook of European Foreign Policy* (pp. 570–583). Los Angeles: Sage.

Smith, M. E. (2018). Transatlantic Security Relations Since the European Security Strategy: What Role for the EU in Its Pursuit of Strategic Autonomy? Special issue. *Journal of European Integration, 40*(5), 605–620.

Sola, N. F., & Smith, M. (2009). *Perceptions and Policy in Transatlantic Relations: Prospective Visions from the US and Europe*. New York and London: Routledge.

Vachudova, M. A. (2019). From Competition to Polarization in Central Europe: How Populists Change Party Systems and the European Union. *Polity, 51*(4), 689–706.

Walt, S. M. (2019). The End of Hubris: And the End of American Restraint. *Foreign Affairs, 98*(3), 26–35.

Wilson, G. K. (2017). Brexit, Trump and the Special Relationship. *British Journal of Politics and International Relations, 19*(3), 543–557.

Zakaria, F. (2017). FDR Started the Long Peace: Under Trump, It May Be Coming to an End. *Washington Post*. Available at: https://www.washingtonpost.com/opinions/global-opinions/fdr-started-thelong-peace-under-trump-it-may-be-coming-to-an-end/2017/01/26/2f0835e2-e402-11e6-ba11-63c4b4fb5a63_story.html?utm_term=.6c3a972974cd. Accessed 16 Oct 2018.

CHAPTER 36

The Legitimacy Crisis: An Introduction

Akasemi Newsome, Marianne Riddervold, and Jarle Trondal

As illiberal leaders take advantage of the Coronavirus epidemic to cement their grip on power, the EU is confronted with threats to democracy and the rule of law among its own member-states. In Hungary, where Viktor Orbán attained 'sweeping emergency powers' including rule by decree (Kelemen 2020b), and in Poland, where the Law and Justice (PiS) party of Poland muffled its competition weeks before the 2020 presidential election, the EU has not been able to reverse the collapsing commitment of these member-states to democratic norms and legal regimes (Erlanger 2020). Nor has the EU moved to take decisive action to reinstate the rule of law in Hungary or Poland, for example by terminating structural adjustment funds (Kelemen and Soll 2020).

A. Newsome (✉) · M. Riddervold
Institute of European Studies, University of California, Berkeley, CA, USA
e-mail: akasemi@berkeley.edu

Inland School of Business and Social Sciences, Inland University, Rena and Lillehammer, Norway

M. Riddervold
The Norwegian Institute of International Affairs (NUPI), Oslo, Norway
e-mail: marianne.riddervold@inn.no

J. Trondal
Department of Political Science and Management, University of Agder, Kristiansand, Norway
e-mail: jarle.trondal@uia.no

ARENA - Centre for European Studies, University of Oslo, Oslo, Norway

© The Author(s) 2021
M. Riddervold et al. (eds.), *The Palgrave Handbook of EU Crises*, Palgrave Studies in European Union Politics,
https://doi.org/10.1007/978-3-030-51791-5_36

In addition to the rise of autocratic political movements, papers in this section also examine the growth in Euroscepticism in Western and Eastern Europe, both fueled at least in part by dissatisfaction among parties and citizens with policy responses to crisis, and how these risks are (further) undermining the legitimacy of the EU. We conceptualize this crisis in democratic legitimacy faced by the EU as one with disintegrative implications. On the one hand, the appearance of first 'defective democracies' that turned in 'autocracies' among the member-states calls into question the effectiveness of enlargement and the legitimacy of the EU as a space for democratic consolidation (Kelemen 2020a; Vachudova 2005, 2019). On the other hand, intertwined with the success of populist authoritarian mobilization in the EU has been the critique of policy and political responses to polycrisis as overly reliant on technocratic solutions and thus undemocratic, owing to both specialized knowledge inaccessible to average citizens as well as the bias among experts in favor of certain kinds of political and policy solutions. The problem of member-states in violation of the EU's rule of law regime began in 2010 (Hegedüs 2019) as Fidesz began to consolidate power. Some scholars have looked further in the past and view outmigration by high skilled youth most committed to liberal democracy as a 1990s occurrence that spurred legitimacy crises within post-Communist EU member-states (Krastev 2018: 50).

The purpose of illiberal democracy is ending liberal democracy. One avenue pursued by illiberal regimes has been to block the ability of the courts to rule impartially, while another has been implementing restrictions for nongovernmental organizations, media, voters, and civic groups (Levitsky and Ziblatt 2018). The problem with illiberal democracy in one or two or a handful of states is that it can infect the forums where those states are participants. Although initially, experts characterized Hungary under Fidesz as an illiberal democracy (Plattner 2019), Freedom House recently downgraded Hungary further to a 'transitional/hybrid regime' outside the democratic category (*Deutsche Welle* 2020). Freedom House also determined that in Poland the rule of law faced 'frontal assault' from PiS, given that the ruling party has politicized the judicial process such that only those judges with PiS support can be confirmed, and should those judges move to counter PiS political objectives, judges face sanctions and potential removal (*Deutsche Welle* 2020). In Hungary, Fidesz used legislative power to alter the constitutional protections existing for the free press, courts, and civic groups. Article 2 of the Lisbon Treaty specifies the values of the EU, including rule of law and democracy. Article 7 contains the 'nuclear option' whereby offending member-states experience a loss of voice within the EU as long as they are in violation (Polyakova et al. 2019).

In our discussion to follow examining how the question of legitimacy poses a serious challenge to further integration of the EU, we define the EU's legitimacy crisis beyond the autocratization of Hungary and Poland to also include the issue of expertization and questions of citizen trust in the EU vis-à-vis their national governments. Our broader conceptualization of the legitimacy crisis is captured in chapters by Kolja Raube and Francisca Costa Reis, Cathrine Holst and Anders Molander, and Pieter de Wilde; it suggests that of the three scenarios detailed in the Handbook introduction, the EU is so far *breaking down* in some respects while it 'muddles through' in others in response to its legitimacy crisis. Unable to forge a wholly new path, supranational actors have so far not overcome institutional barriers to define a common response and then act to enforce the rule of law in Hungary and Poland. Incurring resistance from nation states about perceived incursions into member-state sovereignty, supranational actors have largely remained silent and wary of taking drastic steps to sanction member-state transgressions. Although Raube and Reis also show that the EU in parallel is *muddling through* a formal response to the democratic challenges facing Hungary and Poland, at the time of writing, this apparent lack of clear and common response might be referred to as *breaking down* of the protection of EU democratic values. In part, the inability thus far of the EU to act results from the unintended consequences of integrative reform that released disintegrative forces in the medium and long term. Kelemen argues persuasively in his work that the 'partial politicization of EU politics' has involved the introduction of novel democratizing processes which illiberal Europarties have been most successful at exploiting (Kelemen 2020a; see also Jakli and Stenberg 2020).

Kolja Raube and Francisca Costa Reis' chapter, 'The EU's crisis response regarding the democratic and rule of law crisis,' looks at the steps taken by the European Commission, the European Parliament, the (Union) Council, and the CJEU in response to active efforts by elected populist governments to undermine democratic governance. Raube and Costa Reis conceptualize the crisis as consisting of three dimensions; an identity crisis in which the EU is not a democratic order; a compliance and implementation crisis in which the EU cannot get member-states to obey the law; and a perception crisis in which democratic backsliding suggests the EU is not what it seems. Raube and Costa Reis have three key findings. The first is that the CJEU's innovative use of Article 19 on judicial independence in case rulings brought against democratic backsliding constitutes *heading forward*. The European Commission and national courts sought legal support from the CJEU to 'enforce the rule of law' in member-states and the CJEU ruled that member-states have a legal obligation to preserve the rule of law, including by maintaining judicial independence. The authors find the most evidence for *muddling through* in the incremental steps taken by the European Commission and the European Parliament to address persistent erosion of a free press and an unbiased court system in Hungary and Poland. These incremental steps included starting infringement proceedings against both member-states, attempting to engage the member-states about repairing the damage to the democratic rule of law, and lastly through invoking Article 7 TEU. However, Raube and Costa Reis underscore that the efficacy of these otherwise important steps addressing the crisis of illiberal democracy in the EU was undermined by partisanship. Both the European Commission and the European Parliament moved much more slowly to sanction Hungary compared with Poland as both the European Commission and the European Parliament relied on the political support of Hungary's governing party Fidesz, but did not rely on PiS. This chapter also documented a simultaneous tendency for *breaking down* in that the weakest response to democratic backsliding came from the Council and member-states. The Council in particular was reluctant to pursue more than the Framework on the Rule of Law dialogue. Raube and Costa Reis acknowledge that while Orbán expanded the scope of his executive power under the cover of Coronavirus mitigation and the Law and Justice party in Poland made political loyalty the key qualification for filling judicial benches, the absence of strong counteraction by the EU to preserve the rule of law among errant member-states does seem to point to *breaking down* within the EU. At the same time, they point out that these signs of the EU's struggle to surmount divisions among member-states on how best to defend democratic values, do not constitute a total collapse among all member-states in their commitment to democracy. What Raube and Costa Reis witness instead are modest steps taken by supranational actors and slowly unfolding community processes drawing on treaty-based principles to address these specific illiberal turns. Given that actions by the European Parliament, CJEU, and Commission are still developing, often in inefficient ways, in their view suggests that *muddling through* more accurately describes how the EU has responded to the legitimacy crisis.

Catherine Holst and Anders Molander's chapter, 'Responding to crises—worries about expertization,' examines the role of experts in the EU's crisis of democratic legitimacy. They identify two challenges in this realm. While some view the use of knowledge-based policy as necessary to address the EU's current polycrisis, others believe that experts themselves are to blame for polycrisis and the specific crisis in democratic legitimacy. This chapter makes the argument that the challenge of 'expertise in EU policy-making and approaches to crisis' is well met through institutional reforms. Holst and Molander provide a list of ten *epistemic* problems of technocracy. They base their claims about governance after the Eurozone crisis by detailing such citizen concerns: Members of the public are unable to identify who the experts are independent of other experts; the public would like to know the most moral option to a policy problem, but morality is difficult for experts to ascertain; there is the problem of fallible expertise; the policy recommendations of experts reflect ideological biases; experts are aligned with elites and less likely to criticize elites; and experts struggle to translate their knowledge into layman's terms. The authors also describe ten *democratic* concerns related to expertise—firstly, that expertise poses a threat to democracy defined as 'self-governance of free and equal citizens;' experts lack the numbers to arrive at the best decisions—i.e., the problem of collective wisdom; at what point does expertise push out elected authority?; there is the problem of civic deliberation by ordinary citizens—can it occur when so many lack expertise?; the depoliticization of politics through the use of expertise can be harmful for democracy;

and experts and the elites who listen to them are disconnected from the public and its concerns.

Holst and Molander find that these debates about the democratic and epistemic pitfalls generated through growing technocratic decision-making in Europe have resulted in 'repeated appeals to the intrinsic value of democratic norms of inclusion and equal participation (1), and justifications on this basis for a vastly reformed EU, with a larger role for citizens, stakeholders and elected assemblies, and a more substantive curtailment of executives, courts and expert bodies.' The authors recommend reforms to EU institutions to get experts to behave differently, to reform the mode and content of expert recommendations. Holst and Molander also underscore the need for accountability structures for experts, in which experts could openly acknowledge which of their recommendations did not work and experts would be required to develop policies in pluralist environments and accountability structures that include roles for ordinary citizens. The authors engage with the scenarios of the Handbook introduction by considering the likelihood that these reforms could remedy the democratic and epistemic challenges of technocracy. In their view, *heading forward* most requires these reforms to occur, a lack of reform will make *breaking down* more likely.

Pieter de Wilde's chapter, 'Rebound? The short and long-term effects of crises on public support and trust in European governance,' investigates whether people trust the EU less after EU polycrisis and how crisis impacted trust in the EU. De Wilde examines the aggregate descriptive trends present in Eurobarometer public opinion polls after multiple overlapping recent crises afflicting the EU and considers the degree to which there are long- and short-term effects of crisis on public trust in EU institutions. The rationale for research on public opinion in this Handbook are the ramifications for swings in public opinion for the prospects of European integration. According to de Wilde, to the degree that polycrisis depresses public trust in the EU, the greater the likelihood of EU disintegration. Furthermore, the existence of a growing population with low trust in the EU suggests a growing potential voter base for populist anti-EU parties. De Wilde also identifies a possible feedback loop, whereby a decline in trust renders EU policy less effective, which in turn creates more distrust. On the other hand, if analysis of public opinion research shows a weak connection between crises and public trust, then the EU could continue incremental integration. This chapter finds *heading forward* to be the least likely scenario, owing in part to de Wilde's decision to set Treaty changes as the bar for radical innovation in integration. In terms of the relevant theory for the relationship between public opinion and trust in EU institutions, post-functionalist theory offers the most purchase in explaining changes in public opinion, in that the Hooghe and Marks theorize the shift from 'permissive consensus' to 'constraining dissensus' as one that occurs as 'political parties increase contestation over the EU and the integration project and as media provide more coverage of EU affairs, more citizens become aware of the EU's existence, impact on their lives and its functioning.' De Wilde's contribution pays attention to the 'don't know' answers to the Eurobarometer survey rather than only the affirmatives and the negatives. He is thus able to show that the group of undecided and low-information citizens who respond 'don't know' to the survey is falling over time and that these voters are moving instead to pro-EU or Eurosceptic points of view. Because voters remain evenly split between pro-EU and Eurosceptic viewpoints, de Wilde suggests that *muddling through* is the most likely scenario.

In sum, this section provides evidence for continued partisanship and politicization in the EU's future as a result of the legitimacy crisis. In this way, this section echoes other chapters on different crisis cases (see for example Rosén and Olsen on the financial crisis, this volume). Precisely in those areas where there has been greater integration, depoliticization fuels repoliticization, by both Eurosceptic and pro-EU forces. A point made early in the chapter by Raube and Costa Reis is that the rise of illiberal democracies has repoliticized rule of law at the supranational level, although it had been believed to be settled in a way that has been detrimental for the prospects of deeper integration. Holst and Molander address repoliticization and the breakdown of EU integration as well in their discussion of expertization and in terms of the kinds of institutional solutions that would increase citizen participation in policymaking, without necessarily guaranteeing the commitment of a more active citizenry in the EU project. De Wilde has shown that despite the polycrisis context, trust in the EU is resilient among EU citizens and the EU has become a legitimate object of political contestation among ordinary citizens, although political contestation has had unintended effects.

REFERENCES

Erlanger, S. (2020, April 22). Poland and Hungary Use Coronavirus to Punish Opposition. *New York Times*. https://www.nytimes.com/2020/04/22/world/europe/poland-hungary-coronavirus.html.

Hegedüs, D. (2019). *What Role for EU Institutions in Confronting Europe's Democracy and Rule of Law Crisis?* Washington, DC: The German Marshall Fund of the United States.

Jakli, L., & Stenberg, M. (2020). Everyday Illiberalism: How Hungarian Subnational Politics Propel Single Party Dominance. *Governance*, Early View, 1–20. https://doi.org/10.1111/gove.12497.

Janjevic, D. (2020, May 6). Hungary's Orban Dropped Any Pretense of Respecting Institutions, Freedom House Reports. *Deutsche Welle*.

Kelemen, R. D. (2020a). The European Union's Authoritarian Equilibrium. *Journal of European Public Policy*, 27(3), 481–499.

Kelemen, R. D. (2020b, April 2). Hungary Just Became a Corona Virus Autocracy: Will Europe Respond to Orban's Power Grab? *The Monkey Cage, The Washington Post*. https://www.washingtonpost.com/politics/2020/04/02/hungary-just-became-coronavirus-autocracy/.

Kelemen, R. D., & Soll, J. (2020, May 13). The EU Is Undermining Its Democracies While Funding Its Autocracies. *Politico*. https://www.politico.eu/article/the-eu-is-undermining-its-democracies-while-funding-its-autocracies-coronavirus-covid19-rule-of-law/.

Krastev, I. (2018). Eastern Europe's Illiberal Revolution: The Long Road to Democratic Decline. *Foreign Affairs, 97*(3), 49–56.

Levitsky, S., & Ziblatt, D. (2018). *How Democracies Die*. New York: Viking.

Plattner, M. F. (2019). Illiberal Democracy and the Struggle on the Right. *Journal of Democracy, 30*(1), 5–19.

Polyakova, A., Taussig, T., Reinert, T., Kirisci, K., Sloat, A., Kirchick, J., et al. (2019). *Report: The Anatomy of Illiberal States: Assessing and Responding to Democratic Decline in Turkey and Central Europe*. Washington, DC: Foreign Policy at Brookings.

Vachudova, M. A. (2005). *Europe Undivided: Democracy, Leverage and Integration After Communism*. Oxford: Oxford University Press.

Vachudova, M. A. (2019). From Competition to Polarization in Central Europe: How Populists Change Party Systems and the European Union. *Polity, 51*(4), 689–706.

CHAPTER 37

The EU's Crisis Response Regarding the Democratic and Rule of Law Crisis

Kolja Raube and Francisca Costa Reis

Introduction

In this following chapter the focus is on the EU's response and crisis management toward an emerging democracy and rule of law crisis in Europe. For a long time the consolidation and global successes of liberal democracy, including the European Union and its transformative enlargement processes, have been taken for granted. Enlargement processes were seen as a flagship policy of the EU, able to transform societies and economic policies in Central and Eastern Europe, however with limited success regarding 'liberal democratic principles' (Sedelmeier 2014a). Critical voices, seeing the transformation of Europe's Eastern countries after the end of the Cold War as one of multiple streams and challenges—including democracy, human and minority rights, rule of law, economy and society—that would interrelate and eventually undermine a full liberal democratic transformation, were often underrepresented (Offe 1994).

Indeed, current events raise doubts as to whether democratization can be regarded as a one-way street. Freedom House (2020) paints a dark picture of democracy in crisis and sees, globally, a period of democratic retrenchment. The emergence of so-called illiberal democracies seems to have established itself as a new normal, presenting fundamental challenges to those who seek

K. Raube (✉) · F. Costa Reis
University of Leuven, Leuven, Belgium
e-mail: kolja.raube@kuleuven.be

F. Costa Reis
e-mail: francisca.costareis@kuleuven.be

© The Author(s) 2021
M. Riddervold et al. (eds.), *The Palgrave Handbook of EU Crises*,
Palgrave Studies in European Union Politics,
https://doi.org/10.1007/978-3-030-51791-5_37

to uphold and protect the foundational principles and institutions of liberal democracies (Freedom House 2018; Polyakova et al. 2019). Separating what once had been seen as two complementary and synergetic notions, liberalism, and democracy, a new wave of regimes present themselves as illiberal democracies: although democratically elected, once in government they systematically "ignore constitutional limits on their power and depri[ve] their citizens of basic rights and freedoms" (Zakaria 1997: 22; see also Mounk 2018).

Strangely enough, the rise of illiberal tendencies and consolidation of "defective democracies" (Müller 2017: 58), such as Poland and Hungary, is often not regarded as part of the multidimensional "polycrisis" that the EU has faced since the beginning of the "age of crisis" in 2009–2010, often associated with the financial debt crisis, migration crisis, Brexit and challenges in the EU's neighborhood (Dinan et al. 2017). However, given the normative character of the EU as a polity based on democracy and the rule of law, systematic challenges to these principles can be understood as a crisis of fundamental values which the EU as an "order" is based on,[1] in other words "an extraordinary moment when the existence and viability of the political order are called into question" (Ikenberry 2008: 3; see also Riddervold et al. 2020). Understanding democracy beyond polyarchic conditions of free and fair elections and accountable government (Dahl 1971) includes checks and balances and the independence of the judiciary. With this in mind, a liberal notion of democracy based on the rule of law as one of its essential pillars comes to the fore: "What makes a rule of law democratic [...] is that the legal system defends the political rights and procedures of democracy, upholds everyone's civil rights, and reinforces the authority of other agencies of horizontal accountability that ensure the legality and propriety of official actions" (Diamond and Morlino 2004: 23; see also O'Donnell 2004).

Along these lines, we understand that the EU as "order" is put into question by a democracy and rule of law crisis in its Member States in three different ways. First, it faces an *identity crisis*, as the EU could be seen as being changed from within in the direction of values which are contrary to its identity. Second, the EU is challenged by a *compliance and implementation crisis*, as serious breaches of the rule of law could be understood as undermining the ability of the EU to guarantee the implementation of secondary EU law and uphold the supremacy and direct effect of EU law at the level of Member States. Third, this could also trigger a *perception crisis* which can undermine the way how the EU is perceived both internally and externally in its efforts to portray itself as a community of values. Overall, considering the fact that the European Union's integration process has resulted in an interconnectedness, based on mutual trust, in regulatory and judicial fields, the disrespect for fundamental values and principles such as democracy and the rule of law in

---

[1] See Case 294/83 Partie Ecologiste 'Les Verts' v. Parliament [1986] ECR 1339, § 23. Cf. Opinion 1/91 EEA Agreement [1991] ECR 6097.

one Member State has the potential of negatively impacting its legitimacy and credibility in the international arena (Pech and Platon 2017).

Following a deeper understanding of why illiberal tendencies pose a crisis for the EU, the overarching aim of this chapter is to understand and assess EU actors' responses with regard to emerging democracy and rule of law challenges. In explaining how and why EU actors have responded to the emergence and consolidation of illiberal tendencies in Member States within the territorial borders of the EU, this chapter seeks to look into the EU's ability to face the democracy and rule of law crisis and how this shapes the future development of its integration project: The chapter opens with a reflection on the essence of the EU as a community of values and how this has been challenged by the rise of defective democracies, followed by a brief overview of the theoretical framework used to systematically discuss, understand, and explain the EU's response to rule of law backsliding within its own borders. By integrating the three scenarios *breaking down, muddling through* and *heading forward* (Riddervold et al. 2020) into a theoretical discussion of how we would expect the EU to react to an unfolding democracy and rule of law crisis, we are able to hypothesize which crisis management direction the EU and its institutions would take. Against this conceptual background, our analysis proceeds with the assessment of EU actors' responses to the crisis by looking at their disposal of instruments and procedures (section "The EU's Institutional Responses and Crisis Management"). At the same time, we look into how the theoretical framework helps us understand and explain such responses against the conventional wisdom of integration and democracy theories. Last but not least, we attempt to situate this crisis by relating the findings of the previous section to three possible scenarios—*breaking down, muddling through* and *heading forward*—which offer different nuanced expectations about the extent to which, and how, crisis and the different actor responses affect the future of the European Union.

Toward an Understanding of the EU's Crisis Response and Management

The EU as a Community of Values and the Rise of Defective Democracies

Over years, European integration has been linked to sectoral policy integration, which according to supranational and liberal intergovernmental theories, was a functional necessity for both Member States and supranational institutions in view of rising European and global interdependence (Schimmelfennig et al. 2015: 771). At the same time, the Union has also emerged as a "community of values" (Closa and Kochenov 2016: 174). Since the Maastricht Treaty on European Union (1992) the EU was anchored on the idea of a political project, which had to respect "the identity of the Member States, whose systems of government are founded on the principles of democracy" (Article F 1 TEU) and which continued to develop a Common Foreign and Security

Policy (CFSP) to internationally "develop and consolidate democracy and the rule of law, and respect for human rights and fundamental freedoms" (Article J.1 TEU). The identity of the political Union was further clarified with regard to future acceding states in the so-called Copenhagen criteria (1993), specifying that entering the Union required new Member States to recognize and live up to the principles of democracy, the rule of law and human rights. Subsequently, the Treaty of Amsterdam (1997) recognized the triad of principles in an amendment of Article F 1 TEU, which read from then on: "The Union is founded on the principles of liberty, democracy, respect for human rights and fundamental freedoms, and the rule of law, principles which are common to the Member States." Rooted in these principles, now enshrined in Article 2 TEU (Treaty of Lisbon 2007), the European Union is seen as "a polity in its own right" (Eriksen 2009b: 13) and a "normative power" beyond its own territory, often (but not exclusively) inspired by its own constitutional principles when conducting its foreign policy (Manners 2002).

In a two-directional way, "the Union is founded" on values that become the parameter by which to judge Member States, both at the time of their admission into the Union (Article 49(1) TEU) and at the time of their possible sanction or suspension in view of a violation of those values. From early judgments of the European Court of Justice characterizing the then European Community as one based on the rule of law to subsequent references in the EU's founding treaties, the rule of law was thus progressively recognized as one of the European Union's constitutive pillars, both internally and externally (Pech 2012). Despite this ambitious promotion and sanctioning mechanisms to protect the values on which the EU order is based, the overall noncompliance of EU Member States with the basic principles and values set out in Article 2 of the Treaty on European Union (TEU) has shook the "very core of the constitutional system" of the EU, presenting it with new existential and acute challenges to its very foundation (Closa and Kochenov 2016: 1; Kochenov et al. 2016; Magen 2016; Pech and Scheppele 2017).

Although coined decades ago, the term "illiberal democracy" (Zakaria 1997) has gained traction in the past years and the EU presents no exception to the *malaise* of an emerging "illiberal consensus" (Krastev 2018; see also Mounk 2018), as several of its Member States arguably participate in a broader assault on democratic institutions, curtailing judicial independence, upsetting checks and balances, cracking down on civil society, and tampering with electoral systems in view of consolidating the power of ruling parties (Kelemen and Orenstein 2016; Magen 2016; Polyakova et al. 2019; Plattner 2019).

Often linked to the rise of populism at large, illiberal tendencies are however not about establishing alternative forms of democracy, they aim at overcoming liberal democracy itself (Müller 2017). In this regard, "illiberal democracy" has been denounced as a misleading term, pointing to the impossibility of a merger between illiberal values and democracy (Müller 2017: 55–57). In the same vein, "authoritative populism" has been recently suggested as an appropriate term to understand the underlying developments and movements that eventually aim to overcome liberal democracies (Norris and Inglehart 2019). Once hit by authoritative populism and its consequences, democracies are likely to turn into defective democracies, in which liberal dimensions of the democratic order are overcome and come to be "in need for serious repair" (Müller 2017: 58). More specifically, by means of rule of law backsliding, democratically elected governments and legislative majorities work toward a hollowing out of key mechanisms and instruments by which democratic leaders and governments could originally be held accountable in liberal democracies (Levitsky and Ziblatt 2018). By changing constitutions and legal acts through legislative majorities, the demise of democratic checks and balances regularly includes overcoming judicial oversight mechanisms and the impartiality of (constitutional) courts. These changes are deemed democratic, their consequences are clearly not. What emerges is a democratic and rule of law crisis in single European countries, which can spin a wider crisis of regional organizations, such as the EU, the Council of Europe or NATO.

In Hungary, since the Hungarian Civic Alliance (Fidesz) party came to power in 2010, what has become known as the blueprint of consolidation of illiberal democracies has unfolded in the country (Pech and Scheppele 2017). Enjoying a parliamentary majority since then, the Fidesz government has continuously committed sustained assaults against vital components and principles of liberal democracies, including the country's media, judiciary, civil society, and many others (Sedelmeier 2014b). While the government's systematic capture of the state has been achieved through legal and constitutional manipulation after a democratic election, Hungary has transformed into an illiberal constitutional order, proudly acknowledged by Prime Minister Viktor Orbán, which does in no way resemble the liberal democratic values and principles of the European Union (Pech and Scheppele 2017; Scheppele 2011).

Poland has also followed suit in this path of illiberalism, pursuing Hungary's already tested recipe of constitutional capture. Since the election of candidates from the Law and Justice Party (PiS) to the presidency and majority of parliamentary seats in Poland, "PiS has embarked on a course of change that places it solidly in the illiberal camp" (Puddington 2017: 38). As in Hungary, PiS has targeted the freedom and pluralism of the media, clamped down on civil society, and sought to increase its political control over key institutions of Poland's judiciary, ultimately undermining the functioning of liberal democracy and arguably turning Poland into a defective democracy (Freedom House 2018; Szuleka 2018). However, as opposed to Hungary's consolidation of an illiberal constitutional order through the manipulation of legal means, the developments in Poland have been essentially characterized as a coup d'état being in blatant violation of the country's existing constitution (Sadurski and Steinbeis 2016).

Illiberalism, however, is not a phenomenon confined to Hungary and Poland. Illiberal tendencies have also been observed in other European countries, including the Slovak Republic and Romania. Such illiberal tendencies and the actual appearance of defective democracies on the map pose a serious challenge for the EU, creating fragilities in various dimensions and fields of EU policies, threatening the stability of the European normative consensus and challenging the existence and viability of the political order. Such a crisis of democracy and rule of law that emerges in the EU Member States prompts the EU to respond collectively, using its own crisis "toolbox" (Closa and Kochenov 2016). To this end, the EU can compel Member States to respect its foundational values laid upon Article 2 TEU, most directly through Article 7 TEU, the so-called "nuclear option."

The mechanism of Article 7 TEU has both a preventive and a coercive arm and foresees the participation of three main EU actors, the European Commission, the European Parliament (EP), and the Council (Kochenov 2017). Under the preventive arm (Article 7(1) TEU), the Commission, the EP or 1/3 of the Member States, can trigger a process whereby the Council, acting with a majority of 4/5 and the EP's consent, may agree that there is "a clear risk of a serious breach by a Member State of the values referred to in Article 2" after hearing the Member State in question and possibly addressing recommendations to it. However, according to Article 7(2)-(4) TEU, only 1/3 of the Member States or the Commission can trigger the coercive arm of Article 7 TEU. After being triggered, the Council, acting by unanimity and with the EP's consent, can determine a serious and persistent breach of the rule of law after the Member State in question submits its observations. If such a breach is in fact identified, the Council, acting by qualified majority, can sanction the Member State by suspending some of its rights, such as the right to vote in the Council (Article 7(3) TEU). Overall, commentators have been rather pessimistic with regard to how effective Article 7 TEU really is, concluding that it forms a rather "insufficient legal basis for a successful intervention" (Closa and Kochenov 2016: 179).

Conceptualizing the European Union's Crisis Response and Management

How then and why does the EU respond to the emergence and consolidation of illiberal tendencies in Member States within the EU? The three scenarios *breaking down*, *muddling through*, and *heading forward* (Riddervold et al. 2020) provide us with an opportunity to think about how, alongside a wider theoretical discussion, we would expect the EU to react to an unfolding democracy and rule of law crisis. Paired with theoretical insights of various theories, such as neofunctionalist, liberal intergovernmental, new intergovernmental, post-functional theories as well as normative democratic theory, these scenarios help us conceptualize the EU's crisis response and management regarding the looming democracy and rule of law crisis in Europe.

According to Riddervold et al. (2020), *breaking down* is one of the scenarios that allow us to make sense of how the EU treats or—rather—is treated by crisis. Heavily informed by realist, intergovernmental and liberal intergovernmental theories, Member States come to the fore in this scenario as they are (a) not able to agree on common interests or instruments to tackle the crisis with, and (b) challenging the EU project due to a fragmentation of their interests (unless they see a common need to further proceed with integration) (Riddervold et al. 2020). More specifically, we would expect Member States to rethink and re-shift their devotion to the common project, openly starting to think about alternative options, including dissolving treaty obligations, or incurring in treaty-changes and differentiated forms of integration.

However, according to some observers, intergovernmental theories would not necessarily fall into the breakdown scenario and project an overall negative crisis outlook (Schimmelfennig 2017: 320; this volume). Accordingly, we would rather expect that the ultimate "crisis outcome depends on the intergovernmental constellation of integration preferences and bargaining power" (Schimmelfennig 2017: 317). In the case of a looming democracy and rule of law crisis, we would, for example, expect Member States to carefully weigh their interests in maintaining 'good relations' on the European level and the negative impact that an 'intervention' in domestic matters of drifting Member States could have. In terms of the EU actors involved and measures taken, we expect a preference for intergovernmental collective actors, such as the Council, and measures that represent the lowest common denominator rather than far-reaching sanctions.

In the case of a democracy and rule of law crisis, illiberal tendencies are situated in the European Union (Pech and Scheppele 2017) and are likely to unfold as '*burning down the house*' from within. Post-functionalist theories tend to share this pessimistic outlook and the negative expectations regarding European crises (Schimmelfennig 2017). Championed by Hooghe and Marks (2009; see also this volume), post-functionalist theory sees domestic Euroscepticism as an endogenous crisis origin. Rooted in the idea of an overall politicization of European integration (De Wilde 2011), Hooghe and Marks see a looming Euroscepticism within Member States which limits governments' room for maneuvre to take (necessary) integration steps. In other words, Hooghe and Marks expect a mismatch of functionally efficient and politically feasible solutions. In view of democracy and rule of law crises, we would accordingly expect the recognition of the need for appropriate responses, but may not see this materialize into practice due to the ongoing party competition at the national level (heavily affected by Euroscepticism) and an overall "constraining dissensus" in European integration (Webber 2019: 33). However, EU actors may prevent a "break down" and eventually fight the fire, if they prove to be autonomous and insulated enough from such downward spiral of integration (Hooghe and Marks 2019; Schimmelfennig 2017).

The latter argument is shared by neo-functionalists and supranationalists who arguably have their "feet" in two scenarios—*muddling through* and *heading forward*. By and large, neofunctionalist and supranationalists argue that every crisis of European integration can eventually be turned into an opportunity or will, at least, not necessarily have a negative effect (Webber 2019: 30). Their optimism is rooted in the institutionalization of supranational and autonomous actors, such as the European Commission or the Court of Justice of the European Union, the sheer endless stream of transnational interactions that recreates demands for supranational integration and, finally, path-dependency of institutional responses (Schimmelfennig 2017; Webber 2019). In other words, if the European Commission and the Court prove to be autonomous institutions, engines, and safeguards of integration, then democracy and rule of law crises can find effective responses at the European level, allowing the EU to *head forward* with integration. However, crisis response may rather follow a piecemeal approach, reactive rather than proactive in nature, with the consequence that the crisis is rather dealt with as a *muddling through* exercise: "Rather than breaking up, crisis may reinforce well-known organizational solutions and governing arrangements and thus have few profound effects on EU integration and governance. Institutional approaches suggest that governance systems and governance practices under stress may revert to or reinforce pre-existing organizational traditions, practices and formats, reinforcing institutional path-dependencies" (Riddervold et al. 2020). In the democracy and rule of law crisis context, such a path-dependency argument would be plausible if actors were to hit the beaten paths of previous examples and institutionalized responses. The case of Austria, for instance, would provide a useful example to which actors on the European level could revert to when activating the Article 7 mechanism.

According to Jones et al. (2017), however, *muddling through* may not occur due to path-dependencies but rather due to the incomplete bargaining solution of Member States following a crisis. "Failing forward" is described as the way how Member States try, but ultimately fail, to find lasting solutions to looming crises (ibid.). The reason is their inability to provide crisis responses above the lowest common denominator. Any response remains incomplete and necessarily leads to a range of new crises (Jones et al. 2017). In the context of the democracy and rule of law crisis such a "falling forward" may be recognizable in the Council's and Commission's attempt to look for alternative and incomplete measures next to the activation of Article 7 TEU, which would be rather deliberative in nature, aiming at persuading drifting governments of returning to the adherence of EU fundamental principles.

Such attempts, however, appear in a different light, if we take on board the ideas of new intergovernmentalism (Bickerton et al. 2015). Rather than *breaking down* and *muddling through*, they would see intergovernmentalism in the light of *heading forward*. For new intergovernmentalism, crisis is predominantly taken on by intergovernmental institutions, such as the European Council and the Council and so-called de novo agencies (Bickerton et al.

2015). Not the European Commission, but intergovernmental actors are able to find solutions to crisis due to their ability to seek consensus and deliberate among Member States (Bickerton et al. 2015: 704). Interestingly in the context of the democracy and rule of law crisis the Council has indeed tried to play a key role in dealing with rule of law backsliding in Poland and Hungary, especially through its newly established rule of law dialogue, which tries to engage drifting countries in a deliberation about how to revert their backsliding tendencies.

Last but not least, normative democratic theorizing of the European Union, will give us clues how EU actors react or ought to react in democracy and rule of law crises by *heading forward*. According to normative democratic theory (Eriksen 2009a, b), the European Union is seen as "a polity in its own right," based on the principles of democracy and the rule of law (Eriksen 2009b). Accordingly, any attempt to overcome this order calls for EU responses in order to avoid a deeper European identity and perception crisis. Deliberative democratic theory would argue that appropriate EU responses have to try to persuade governments and citizens by reasonable arguments and through an engaged public discourse. This could, for example, take place in a discursive, transparent, and free parliamentary environment like that of the EP or national parliaments. At the same time, given the matter at stake, responses may have to be less deliberative, but rather—following Loewenstein (1937)—militant in nature, sanctioning noncompliant actors, and reducing their rights in an effort to defend democracy overall. In other words, while normative democracy theorists may be divided over how to respond, their overall assessment is that the EU must go ahead and prevent the crisis from spreading and, ultimately, undermining the order of the EU.

The EU's Institutional Responses and Crisis Management

The following section will trace back and analyze the responses of four selected EU actors—Commission, Parliament, Council, and the Court of Justice of the European Union—to the establishment of defective democracies within the EU by referring to the theories introduced above. As demonstrated in the following, while some theories would place hope on EU actors' actions in the face of a crisis, more often than not it is the more skeptical intergovernmental and post-functional approaches that best describe their responses.

From Safeguarding Democracy to Politicization: Mixed Responses by the European Commission and European Parliament

As previously mentioned, according to both normative as well as neofunctionalist and supranationalist theorizing of the European Union and its integration processes, EU actors (supranational or not) would be expected to respond to crises in such a way that would defend the Union's democratic order, functioning as engines that safeguard its integration. While, overall, this might be an overly optimistic view, both the European Commission and the European Parliament exhibited, in their initial reactions, the potential to do so.

The Commission, undoubtedly one of the most engaged actors in relation to rule of law breaches and the establishment of defective democracies, launched infringement procedures with rule of law significance against Hungary and Poland, created and activated its "Framework to Strengthen the Rule of Law" and, finally, ultimately activated the preventive stage of Article 7 TEU against Poland (European Commission 2019). Confronted with the unfolding events threatening the rule of law in its Member States, the European Commission soon realized the shortcomings of the procedure laid out in Article 7 TEU: the provisions were seen as a last-resort option and subject to high decision-making thresholds which revealed to be challenging to achieve (Kochenov and Pech 2016). Faced with the necessity of an additional instrument to safeguard the integrity of the European Union, the Commission adopted the "Rule of Law Framework" in 2014, a tool meant to enable it to enter into dialogue with the concerned Member State so as to avoid the escalation of emerging systemic threats to the rule of law which could, eventually, result in the triggering of Article 7 TEU (European Commission, n.d.). Rather than sanctioning, the mechanism tries to solve emerging crises by engaging the respective Member States through the issuing of opinions and recommendations regarding possible measures to be taken to resolve the situation (Kochenov and Pech 2016). As neofunctionalism and supranationalism would have expected, the European Commission emerged as a forceful crisis manager handling the rise of defective democracies, as also visible in its ultimate decision to trigger Article 7(1) in December 2017.

In line with this behavior, the European Parliament, too, has often been characterized as the most active and vocal institution in terms of engaging with rule of law breaches in Member States and calling for action by other actors since the problem was first identified back in 2012 (European Parliament 2015; Pech and Scheppele 2017; Sargentini and Dimitrovs 2016; Wilms 2017). One of the first systematic analyses of the breakdown of the rule of law in Hungary, came from the Tavares Report adopted in the EP in July 2013. The report harshly criticized the state of fundamental rights in Hungary, recommending the setting up of an independent monitoring mechanism, a "Copenhagen Commission," to follow the development of fundamental rights in the country (Committee on Civil Liberties, Justice and Home Affairs 2013). Moreover, it called on the Council to assess the necessity, or not, of resorting to Article 7(1) TEU in case of Hungary's noncompliance with the requirements of Article 2 TEU. In a recent resolution on the ongoing Article 7 procedures (this time also including Poland), the European Parliament "expresses its regret that the hearings have not yet resulted in any significant progress [...]" (European Parliament 2020). Consequently, along the lines of supranational and normative democratic accounts, expectations that the European Parliament would take an active role in the crisis were confirmed, even if these actions by the EP did not see any concrete follow-up by the Commission or Council (Pech and Scheppele 2017).

Despite what might seem a promising and proactive reaction by both the European Parliament and the Commission, a closer look into further developments as the rise of defective democracies ensued reveals a less positive picture, rather in line with post-functionalist theorizing and insights from comparative politics. While Poland was subjected to the Commission's three tools for dealing with rule of law challenges, Hungary was only subjected to infringement procedures, a differentiated treatment not expected on democratic normative grounds. It has been suggested that, instead, a partisan explanation could help to understand this: whereas in the case of Hungary the Commission's top leadership enjoys a cosiness with Victor Orbán and also a certain dependence on the EPP-majority of the European Parliament, Poland's PiS belongs to the smaller Eurosceptic ECR group, which enjoys no backing by the EPP (Kelemen 2017). While part of the Commission's unsuccessful response could be attributed to the inherent structural problems of Article 7 (once triggered against two Member States with similar normative agendas it could lead to ironically empowering those targeted by it to veto its further mechanisms), approaches including post-functionalism and "failing forward" help us understand the limited room for action and capacity in times of politicization, polarization, and contestation. In addition to the seeming differential treatment between both countries, the Commission has also been continuously criticized for an overall lack of decisive action (Mycielski and Pech 2020; Pech et al. 2020), particularly since the election of its new president, Ursula von der Leyen. Having been elected as the result of the failure of the lead-candidate (Spitzenkandidaten) system, which clearly illustrated the divisiveness created by ongoing rule of law challenges (see below), Von der Leyen enjoys a narrow support by the European Parliament that was mustered with the support of backsliding Member States like Poland, among others (Crum 2020). The president's dependence on such fragile coalitional politics, the lack of a Commissioner specifically entrusted with rule of law issues and the Commission's at best tacit reaction to the further destruction of the rule of law during the COVID-19 pandemic in Hungary all raise serious questions about its commitment to responding to the establishment of defective democracies decisively.

In the case of the European Parliament, too, post-funtionalist theory helps us to understand the EU as embedded in contestation and Euroscepticism (Hooghe and Marks 2009). By 2015 the partisan dimension in the EP came fully to the fore and undermined a consistent response which we would otherwise have expected from an actor that has often been described as a frontrunner of promoting human rights and the rule of law (Rippoll-Servent 2018). The EPP group, time and again, embraced Fidesz, rather than sanctioning or excluding it by voting openly against any measures in light of rule of law backsliding in Hungary and preventing the EP from launching the Rule of Law Framework against Hungary (Kelemen 2017; Newsome and Stenberg, this volume). In the case of Poland's illiberal turn, however, the EP, particularly the EPP, as other EU actors, has had less difficulty in demanding decisive action as visible in the overwhelming support of the 2016 resolution on the developments in Poland (Gostyńska-Jakubowska 2016; Halmai 2018). Once more, partisan politics can also explain why Poland was the "easier case" to sanction as the governmental party PiS belongs to the small ECR group, thus making it an easier target for outspoken criticism (Kelemen 2017). It is noteworthy that the European Parliament eventually mustered the necessary supermajority to trigger Article 7(1) against Hungary faced with the country's worsening situation (European Parliament 2017), as normative democratic theory would have expected. Yet the lack of unity of the EPP's vote, the only partial expulsion of Fidesz from the group (Kelemen 2020)—even in light of Hungary's passage of the Enabling Act during the COVID-19 pandemic, enabling the Prime Minister to essentially rule by decree and suspend elections—as well as the overall delay in triggering Article 7 find resonance in post-functionalist theory. These theories would expect such problems, given the reduced and limited room for pro-integration maneuvres by traditional parties in times of Euroscepticism and European contestation.

These phenomena have been further intensified with the 2019 European elections, which saw the issue of the rule of law take center stage in the failure of the lead-candidate system. As De Wilde (2020) argues, both Weber's tacit support for Hungary's backsliding regime and Timmermans' vocal criticism thereof, made the two candidacies unacceptable to a politicized European Parliament, paving the way for Von der Leyen's presidency, which represents, to a certain extent, a victory for Hungary and Poland—and the preliminary end of the lead-candidate system (Raube 2020).

Expectations and Reality Aligned: The Responses of the Council and Court of Justice of the EU

When tracing back and analyzing the responses of two further EU actors, the Council and the Court of Justice of the EU (CJEU), to the rise of defective democracies theories of integration seem to provide quite an accurate picture with regard to expected actions.

Heavily informed by intergovernmental theories, expectations regarding the Council mirror the challenges faced by Member States when reaching agreements on common interests and instruments to deal with crises. Indeed, the role of governments and the Council, or rather its inaction, in relation to the protection of the rule of law and the EU's values and principles has been widely criticized (Hegedus 2019; Kochenov et al. 2016; Pech and Scheppele 2017). While governments can play a role beyond Article 7, namely by bringing another, noncompliant, Member State to the European Court of Justice for violating an obligation under the Treaties (Article 259 TFEU) this option has hardly ever been resorted to (Wilms 2017). Instead, faced with the consolidation of defective democracies and growing illiberal tendencies across the EU, the Council remained cautious in its approach, barely placing the issue on its agenda, and focusing mainly on rhetorical criticism through a dialogue mechanism recently developed to promote the rule of law (Kochenov et al. 2016). The lead up to the Council summit in February 2020 is a further clear indication of the divisiveness reigning in the Council in matters relating to the rule of law. As backed by the Commission and European Parliament, the linking of value compliance to the new EU budget, which has not yet been approved, was watered down even before the summit took place in order to make an agreement more plausible. According to reports, Council President Charles Michel presented a different proposal, which includes a qualified majority threshold in the Council in order to approve any decision by the Commission to cut funding in case of breach of values (Politico 2020).

In line with new intergovernmental theorizing, emphasizing the consensus reaching essence of the Council (Bickerton et al. 2015), the latter has additionally focused its efforts on developing a mechanism with no political or legal consequences, exhibiting a careful approach rather than a strong commitment from governments to solve the crisis. While dialogue can be merited for its engaging function, arguably important in keeping the deviating Member States close to the chest, critics would argue that these deliberation efforts did not generate any effect, no revision of problematic domestic measures or—in the best case—"upsliding" in some of the defect cases. Instead, the Council may even be seen as "falling forward," trying to find a solution, like the Commission, but trapped in a situation where only lowest common denominator options find support.

Despite the overall inactivity of the Council, a closer look into the Court of Justice of the EU reveals its potential role in upholding the integration project and order of the European Union, as anticipated by supranational theories. Given the genesis of the EU as a community of values, one whose integrity depends on its Member States' and institutions' respect for these, it comes as no surprise that the CJEU has been observing the rise of defective democracies with great concern (Scheppele 2018). In light of the developments in Poland and Hungary, both the Commission and national courts have made use of the possibility of referring cases to the Court of Justice of the EU. While the first infringement actions launched by the Commission against Hungary illustrated the limitations of EU treaties and the CJEU in protecting and enforcing the EU's fundamental values (Kovács and Scheppele 2018), recent developments have led to a potential breakthrough in the Court's capacity to enforce the rule of law, unlike post-functional and intergovernmental theories would suppose. In its landmark-ruling "*Commission v Poland*," the CJEU declared, for the first time, the incompatibility of national measures on the ground that they violated EU values, in particular Article 19 TEU on the judicial independence of national courts (see Case C-619/18 of June 2019). In doing so, the court, acting as an autonomous body beyond politics and Member State interests (Webber 2019), took yet another important step in operationalizing the rule of law through Article 19.[2] Given the problems with the highly political Article 7 procedure and the difficulties faced by other EU actors with regard to responding to the rise of defective democracies, the CJEU's role, as underlined by supranational integration theories, is likely to be quintessential in managing the ongoing crisis and protecting the European project. Its rulings, including subsequent judgments on further cases brought against Poland by the Commission (see Case C-192/18 of November 2019), have not only opened up strong avenues for enforcing and protecting values in Member States, they have also arguably emboldened the Commission in its quest to pursue solutions to the establishment of defective democracies, confirming the rationale and arguments it presents in the various launched infringement procedures. While such a supranational judicial power may put in question the Union's ability to respond to the democracy and rule of law crisis politically, the CJEU may at the same time as a federal constitutional court of the European Union and by means of its judicial review and decision-making—not the least because of its difference with other European institutions and decision-making processes (see Landfried 2019: 4)—increase "the overall rationality of democratic governance" in the European Union (ibid.).

Concluding Remarks: The Future of European Integration and Defective Democracies

Theories of European integration, as we argued above, have developed different arguments on how they would expect European Union actors to react in times of crisis (see above section "Conceptualizing the European Union's Crisis Response and Management"). At the same time, we argued that the different theories speak to the possible future scenarios developed by Riddervold et al. (2020) in multiple ways. Throughout the assessment of the European Union actors' responses to lingering crises, we showed that various theories can be used to explain their actions. This, we argue, has implications on what to expect in terms of the applicability of future scenarios.

Overall, we see that EU actors have great difficulties in responding to the democracy and rule of law crisis which currently affects several of its Member States. The crises in Poland and Hungary show that the EU is not a state-like order with vested powers in certain actors, which would imply the ability to intervene to safeguard its constitutional order against inconsistent practice. Undoubtedly, the EU's lack of response to increased executive powers in Hungary, most recently in response to the Corona crisis, as well as Poland's continuously problematic judicial reforms seems to suggest that the EU is *breaking down* in its defense of democratic values. And yet, while the EU's

---

[2] See Gremmelprez (2019) and Rosas (2019) for a more complete overview of the case law leading up to this decision.

capacity to act as a collective unit might be undermined by this crisis, we are not yet witnessing a complete Union-wide breakdown due to the rise of defective democracies. Rather, there are ongoing processes in the EU and by specific EU actors, which focus on these countries' breaches of the EU's core and treaty-based principles. These are indeed slow and not always efficient processes, over time suggesting the appropriateness of framing the EU's response in line with the *muddling through* scenario. In this sense, the EU and individual EU actors search for ways and instruments that allow it to keep relations with the Member States in crisis, while—at the same time—trying to establish red lines of what can normatively no longer be accepted. This approach implies, nonetheless, that the EU is losing precious time in the fight against defective democracies and that its effects are likely to have an impact on how the EU operates internally and is perceived externally. The EU can no longer that easily persuade third countries on the principles of rule of law and democracy, as long as it is not able to keep its own house in order (Raube et al. 2016; Pech 2016).

At the same time, there is still room to believe that some actors within the European Union are invested in *heading forward*, particularly as evident in the Court of Justice's decisive action. Yet, it may be questionable if affected Member States would accept and implement its rulings, as evidenced by the Polish government's open questioning of the authority of the Court of Justice of the EU. At the same time, the Court needs to be careful in its interpretative approach, e.g. in the Polish case, as it will possibly not want to claim that Member States judicial systems are no longer representing a rule of law system, as this would certainly undermine the implementation of European law overall.

As much as the *muddling through* scenario might lend itself to reflecting on the different EU actors' responses to the crisis in Poland and Hungary, returning to the *breaking down* scenario is important for some final reflections. As the latest developments as well as the EU's current handling of the rule of law challenges exacerbated by the COVID-19 pandemic clearly show, the democratic and rule of law crisis is the "other democratic deficit" of the Union and it rests with the Member States (Kelemen 2017). In other words, if the European Union is no longer able to treat the Member States equally, as their democratic and rule of law institutions differ fundamentally, then a more differentiated integration approach may become an option. This may be the case, if the Union decides not to cooperate and finance respective states in the long run, or to integrate further without them. This *break down* in scope of the old order would ultimately lead to a problem of nonengagement. While the European integration project has been about bringing together in diversity, such a scenario would clearly set the limits of what the European Union would be able to accept as diversity; it would also raise the question of how it will be possible to reintegrate defecting democracies again under the umbrella of the EU. In any case, so far, the functionalist logic seems to prevail: Despite the democracy and rule of law crisis the European Union keeps hanging on to its defective Member States, especially because of the deep economic interdependencies that have pushed integration and that have further grown because of it.

References

Bickerton, C., Hodson, D., & Pütter, U. (2015). The New Intergovernmentalism: European Integration in the Post-Maastricht Era. *Journal of Common Market Studies, 53*(4), 703–722.

Closa, C., & Kochenov, D. (2016). Introduction. In C. Closa & D. Kochenov (Eds.), *Reinforcing Rule of Law Oversight in the European Union* (pp. 1–12). Cambridge: Cambridge University Press.

Crum, B. (2020). Party-Groups and Ideological Cleavages in the European Parliament After the 2019 Elections. In S. Kritzinger, et al. (Eds.), *Assessing the 2019 European Elections* (pp. 54–66). Oxon: Routledge.

Committee on Civil Liberties, Justice and Home Affairs. (2013). Report on the Situation of Fundamental Rights: Standards and Practices in Hungary (Pursuant to the European Parliament Resolution of 16 February 2012). https://www.europarl.europa.eu/sides/getDoc.do?pubRef=-//EP//NONSGML+REPORT+A7-2013-0229+0+DOC+PDF+V0//EN. Accessed 24 June 2019.

Dahl, R. A. (1971). *Polyarchy: Participation and Opposition*. Yale University Press.

De Wilde, P. (2011). No Polity for Old Politics? A Famework for Analyzing the Politicization of European Integration. *Journal of European Integration, 33*(5), 559–575.

De Wilde, P. (2020). The Fall of the Spitzenkandidaten: Political Parties and Conflict in the 2019 European Elections. In S. Kritzinger et al. (Eds.), *Assessing the 2019 European Elections* (pp. 37–53). Oxon: Routledge.

Diamond, L., & Morlino, L. (2004). The Quality of Democracy: An Overview. *Journal of Democracy, 15*(4), 20–31.

Dinan, D., Nugent, N., & Paterson, W. E. (2017). *The European Union in Crisis*. Basingstoke: Palgrave Macmillan.

Eriksen, E. O. (2009a). *The Unfinished Democratization of the European Union*. Oxford: Oxford University Press.

Eriksen, E. O. (2009b). The EU: A Cosmopolitan Vanguard? *The Global Jurist, 9*(1), 1–23.

European Commission. (2019). *Rule of Law: European Commission Launches Infringement Procedure to Protect Judges in Poland from Political Control*. http://europa.eu/rapid/press-release_IP-19-1957_en.htm. Accessed 22 June 2019.

European Commission. (n.d.). *Rule of Law Framework*. https://ec.europa.eu/info/policies/justice-and-fundamental-rights/effective-justice/rule-law/rule-law-framework_en. Accessed 22 June 2019.

European Parliament. (2015). *Resolution of 10 June 2015 on the Situation in Hungary*. https://www.europarl.europa.eu/doceo/document/TA-8-2015-0227_EN.pdf. Accessed 18 June 2019.

European Parliament. (2017). *Resolution of 17 May 2017 on the Situation in Hungary*. https://www.europarl.europa.eu/doceo/document/TA-8-2017-0216_EN.pdf. Accessed 18 June 2019.

European Parliament. (2020). Resolution of 16 January 2020 on Ongoing Hearings Under Article 7(1) of the TEU Regarding Poland and Hungary. https://www.europarl.europa.eu/doceo/document/TA-9-2020-0014_EN.html. Accessed 28 May 2020.

Freedom House. (2018). *Nations in Transit 2018: Confronting Illiberalism.* https://freedomhouse.org/report/nations-transit/nations-transit-2018. Accessed 23 June 2019.

Freedom House. (2020). *Freedom in the World 2020: A Leaderless Struggle for Democracy.* https://freedomhouse.org/report/freedom-world/2020/leaderless-struggle-democracy. Accessed 26 May 2020.

Gostyńska-Jakubowska, A. (2016). *Why the Commission Is Treating Poland More Harshly Than Hungary in Its Rule of Law Review.* LSE Blogs. http://bit.ly/1o9D4Pj. Accessed 21 June 2019.

Gremmelprez, A. (2019). *The Legal vs. Political Route to Rule of Law Enforcement.* Verfassungsblog. https://verfassungsblog.de/the-legal-vs-political-route-to-rule-of-law-enforcement/. Accessed 22 June 2019.

Halmai, G. (2018). How the EU Can and Should Cope with Illiberal Member States. *Quaderni Costituzionali, 2,* 313–339.

Hegedus, D. (2019). *What Role for EU Institutions in Confronting Europe's Democracy and Rule of Law Crisis?* The German Marshall Fund of the United States. http://www.gmfus.org/sites/default/files/publications/pdf/Confronting%20Europe%E2%80%99s%20Democracy%20and%20Rule%20of%20Law%20Crisis.pdf. Accessed 21 June 2019.

Hooghe, L., & Marks, G. (2009). A Postfunctionalist Theory of European Integration: From Permissive Consensus to Constraining Dissensus. *British Journal of Political Science, 39*(1), 1–23.

Hooghe, L., & Marks, G. (2019). Grand Theories of European Integration in the Twenty-First Century. *Journal of European Public Policy, 26*(8), 1113–1133.

Ikenberry, J. (2008). Explaining Crisis and Change in Transatlantic Relations: An Introduction. In J. Anderson, G. J. Ikenberry & T. Risse (Eds.), *The End of the West? Crisis and Change in the Atlantic Order* (pp. 1–27). Cornell University Press.

Jones, E., Kelemen, D., & Meunier, S. (2017). Failing Forward? *The Euro Crisis and the Incomplete Nature of European Integration, Comparative Political Studies, 49*(7), 1010–1034.

Kelemen, D. (2017). Europe's Other Democratic Deficit: National Authoritarianism in Europe's Democratic Union. *Government and Opposition, 52*(2), 211–238.

Kelemen, R. D. (2020). The European Union's Authoritarian Equilibrium. *Journal of European Public Policy, 27*(3), 481–499.

Kelemen, R. D., & Orenstein, M. A. (2016). Europe's Autocracy Problem. *Foreign Affairs.* https://www.foreignaffairs.com/articles/poland/2016-01-07/europes-autocracy-problem.

Kochenov, D. (2017). The Acquis and Its Principles: The Enforcement of the 'Law' vs. the Enforcement of Values in the European Union. In A. Jakab & D. Kochenov (Eds.), *The Enforcement of EU Law and Values: Ensuring Member States' Compliance* (pp. 9–27). Oxford: Oxford University Press.

Kochenov, D., & Pech, L. (2016). Better Late Than Never? On the European Commission's Rule of Law Framework and Its First Activation. *JCMS: Journal of Common Market Studies, 54*(5), 1062–1074.

Kochenov, D., Magen, A., & Pech, L. (2016). Introduction: The Great Rule of Law Debate in the EU. *Journal of Common Market Studies, 54*(5), 1045–1049.

Kovács, K., & Scheppele, K. L. (2018). The Fragility of an Independent Judiciary: Lessons from Hungary and Poland—And the European Union. *Communist and Post-Communist Studies, 51*(3), 189–200.

Krastev, I. (2018). Eastern Europe's Illiberal Revolution: The Long Road to Democratic Decline. *Foreign Affairs, 97*(3), 49–56.

Landfried, C. (2019). Introduction. In C. Landfried (Ed.), *Judicial Power: How Constitutional Courts Affect Political Transformations* (pp. 1–17). Cambridge: Cambridge University Press.

Levitsky, S., & Ziblatt, D. (2018). *How Democracies Die*. New York: Viking.

Loewenstein, K. (1937). Militant Democracy and Fundamental Rights. *American Political Science Review, 31*(3), 417–432.

Magen, A. (2016). Cracks in the Foundations: Understanding the Great Rule of Law Debate in the EU. *Journal of Common Market Studies, 54*(5), 1050–1061.

Manners, I. (2002). Normative Power Europe—A Contradiction in Terms? *Journal of Common Market Studies, 40*(2), 235–258.

Mounk, Y. (2018). *The People vs Democracy*. Cambridge: Harvard University Press.

Müller, J. W. (2017). *What is populism?* London: Penguin Books.

Mycielski, M., & Pech, L. (2020). *When Will the Commission Act?* Verfassungsblog. https://verfassungsblog.de/when-will-the-eu-commission-act/. Accesses 25 May 202.

Norris, P., & Inglehart, R. (2019). *Cultural Backlash—Trump, Brexit and the Rise of Authoritarian Populism*. Cambridge: Cambridge University Press.

O'Donnell, G. (2004). The Quality of Democracy: Why the Rule of Law Matters. *Journal of Democracy, 15*(4), 32–46.

Offe, C. (1994). *Der Tunnel am Ende des Lichts – Erkundungen der politischen Transformation im Neuen Osten*, Frankfurt a.M.: Campus.

Pech, L. (2012). *The Rule of Law as a Guiding Principle of the EU's External Action* (Working Paper). Centre for the Law of EU External Relations. https://www.asser.nl/media/1632/cleer2012-3web.pdf. Accessed 21 June 2019.

Pech, L. (2016). The EU as a Global Rule of Law Promoter: The Consistency and Effectiveness Challenges. *Asia-Europe Journal, 14*(1), 7–24.

Pech, L., & Platon, S. (2017). *Systemic Threats to the Rule of Law in Poland: Between Action and Procrastination*. Foundation Robert Schuman. https://www.robert-schuman.eu/en/doc/questions-d-europe/qe-451-en.pdf. Accessed 18 June 2019.

Pech, L., & Scheppele, K. L. (2017). Illiberalism Within: Rule of Law Backsliding in the EU. *Cambridge Yearbook of European Legal Studies, 19*, 3–47.

Pech, L., Sadurski, W., & Scheppele, K. L. (2020). *Open Letter to the President of the European Commission Regarding Poland's "Muzzle Law"*. Verfassungsblog. https://verfassungsblog.de/open-letter-to-the-president-of-the-european-commission-regarding-polands-muzzle-law/. Accessed 25 May 2020.

Plattner, M. F. (2019). Illiberal Democracy and the Struggle on the Right. *Journal of Democracy, 30*(1), 5–19.

Politico. (2020). *4 Big Fights in Europe's Budget Battle*. https://www.politico.eu/article/eu-budget-battle-big-fights-cohesion-funding-agriculture/. Accessed 26 May 2020.

Polyakova, A. et al. (2019). *The Anatomy of Illiberal States: Assessing and Responding to Democratic Decline in Turkey and Central Europe*. Foreign Policy at Brookings. https://www.brookings.edu/wp-content/uploads/2019/02/illiberal-states-web.pdf. Accessed 23 June 2019.

Puddington. A. (2017). *Breaking Down Democracy: Goals, Strategies and Methods of Modern Authoritarians*. Freedom House. https://freedomhouse.org/sites/default/files/June2017_FH_Report_Breaking_Down_Democracy.pdf. Accessed 23 June 2019.

Raube, K. (2020). From Dawn to Doom: The Institutionalization of the Spitzenkandidaten-Process During European Elections and Its Final Negation. In S. Kritzinger, et al. (Eds.), *Assessing the 2019 European Elections* (pp. 19–36). Oxon: Routledge.

Raube, K., Burnay, M., & Wouters, J. (2016). By Way of Introduction: The Rule of Law as a Strategic Priority for EU External Action-Conceptualization and Implementation of EU Law and Policies. *Asia-Europe Journal, 14*(1), 1–6.

Riddervold, M., Trondal, J., & Newsome A. (2020). European Union Crisis: An Introduction. In M. Riddervold, A. Newsome, & J. Trondal (Eds.), *The Palgrave Handbook of EU Crises* (pp. 3–47). Palgrave MacMillan (forthcoming).

Rippoll-Servent, A. (2018). *The European Parliament*. Basingstoke: Palgrave.

Rosas, A. (2019). *The European Court of Justice: Do All Roads Lead to Luxembourg?* CEPS Policy Brief. https://www.ceps.eu/ceps-publications/european-court-justice-do-all-roads-lead-luxembourg/. Accessed 22 June 2019.

Sadurski, W., & Steinbeis, M. (2016). *What Is Going on in Poland Is an Attack Against Democracy*. Verfassungsblog. https://verfassungsblog.de/what-is-going-on-in-poland-is-an-attack-against-democracy/. Accessed 12 June 2019.

Sargentini, J., & Dimitrovs, A. (2016). The European Parliament's Role: Towards New Copenhagen Criteria for Existing Member States? *JCMS: Journal of Common Market Studies, 54*(5), 1085–1092.

Scheppele, K. L. (2011). *Hungary's Unconstitutional Constitution*. The Conscience of a Liberal Blog. http://krugman.blogs.nytimes.com/2011/12/31/hungarian-diplomatic-protest/. Accessed 23 June 2019.

Scheppele, K. L. (2018). *Distinguished Lecture*. https://www.youtube.com/watch?v=N8yxfHKPZ_Y. Accessed 24 June 2019.

Sedelmeier, U. (2014a). *Europe After the Eastern Enlargement of the European Union: 2004–2014*. Heinrich Böll Stiftung, 10. June 2014.

Sedelmeier, U. (2014b). Anchoring Democracy from Above? The European Union and Democratic Backsliding in Hungary and Romania after Accession. *Journal of Common Market Studies, 52*(1), 105–121.

Schimmelfennig, F., Leuffen, D., & Rittberger, B. (2015). The European Union as a System of Differentiated Integration: Interdependence, Politicization and Differentiation. *Journal of European Public Policy, 22*(6), 764–782.

Schimmelfennig, F. (2017), Theorising the European Union in Times of Crisis. In D. Dinan, N. Nugent, & W. E. Paterson (Eds.), *The European Union in Crisis* (pp. 316–336). Basingstoke: Palgrave Macmillan.

Szuleka, M. (2018). *First Victims or Last Guardians? The Consequences of Rule of Law Backsliding for NGOs: Case Studies of Hungary and Poland* (CEPS Paper in Liberty and Security in Europe). https://www.ceps.eu/ceps-publications/first-victims-or-last-guardians-consequences-rule-law-backsliding-ngos-case-studies/. Accessed 21 June 2019.

Treaty on European Union. (1992). https://europa.eu/european-union/sites/europaeu/files/docs/body/treaty_on_european_union_en.pdf. Accessed 29 September 2020.

Treaty of Amsterdam. (1997). https://europa.eu/european-union/sites/europaeu/files/docs/body/treaty_of_amsterdam_en.pdf. Accessed 29 September 2020.

Treaty of Lisbon. (2007). https://eur-lex.europa.eu/legal-content/en/TXT/?uri=CELEX%3A12007L%2FTXT. Accessed 29 September 2020.

Webber, D. (2019). *European Disintegration?: The Politics of Crisis in the European Union*. Basingstoke: Palgrave Macmillan.

Wilms, G. (2017). *Protecting Fundamental Values in the European Union Through the Rule of Law: Articles 2 and 7 TEU from a Legal, Historical and Comparative Angle*. European University Institute, Robert Schuman Centre for Advanced Studies. http://cadmus.eui.eu/bitstream/handle/1814/44987/RSCAS_Ebook_Wilms_EU_RuleOfLaw_2017.pdf?sequence=3&isAllowed=y. Accessed 23 June 2019.

Zakaria, F. (1997). The Rise of Illiberal Democracy. *Foreign Affairs, 76*(6), 22–34.

CHAPTER 38

Responding to Crises—Worries About Expertization

Cathrine Holst and Anders Molander

INTRODUCTION

Commentators do not agree on the true features of the recent crises of the European Union (EU). Where some analyze the Eurozone crisis, EU's troubles following the 2015 migration pressures, Brexit, etc., as largely separate incidents, spurred by relatively independent events, others see interrelated dysfunctionalities across social spheres and policy areas, and a more deep-seated crisis underlying what seems to be scattered problems and crises tendencies. Another controversy concerns the relationship between the EU's crises, however fundamental, and the role of experts and expert knowledge.

This chapter builds on three other co-authored articles by Holst and Molander (2018, 2019, 2020). Some sub-sections overlap across these pieces. The list and discussions of democratic worries over expertise are, however, unique to this chapter. The chapter is moreover framed specifically to address the role of experts in EU's recent crises, and includes a novel section that proposes reforms to address both democratic and epistemic worries, and with examples drawn from the EU context.

C. Holst (✉)
University of Oslo, Oslo, Norway
e-mail: cathrine.holst@sosgeo.uio.no

A. Molander
Oslo Metropolitan University, Oslo, Norway
e-mail: Anders.Molander@oslomet.no

© The Author(s) 2021
M. Riddervold et al. (eds.), *The Palgrave Handbook of EU Crises*,
Palgrave Studies in European Union Politics,
https://doi.org/10.1007/978-3-030-51791-5_38

Here one finds, roughly speaking, two main narratives, seemingly contradicting one another. According to the first narrative, expert bodies and communities are key to solving the Union's problems. The main claim, and hope, is that Europe's economic, social, political, and other crises can be overcome by more effective institutional coordination and through the formulation and implementation of knowledge-based policies. On the contrary, according to the second narrative, a larger role for experts and an expanded scope for expert judgment is one of the main sources of EU's legitimation problems. To address the different crises would thus require a rolling back of expert power and a shrinking of EU's expert institutions.

Clearly, both narratives are limited. On the one hand, the significant political power granted to expert communities and bodies in the EU, and experts' role in the decision-making leading up to the Union's recent crises, calls for critical scrutiny, and raises serious concerns. For one thing, there are democratic worries. If policy formulation is largely, and maybe increasingly, left in the hands of experts, will it not increase the EU's democratic deficit? In addition, come concerns from an epistemic perspective. Generally, the involvement of experts in policymaking is justified with reference to outcome improvements: expertise is supposed to be the "filter" that ensures "truth-sensitive" policies and legislation (Christiano 2012). Yet, critics take this to reflect a naive view of the reliability of expert knowledge and impartiality of experts, and experts are even accused of having made decisions and policies worse, the triggering of recent crises. Consequently, the narrative pointing to better guidance from EU's expert institutions and knowledge-based policymaking and implementation as a solution to crises underplays the democratic problems facing the EU currently, but also potentially severe epistemic challenges.

On the other hand, the alternative storyline that is almost dismissive of expertise is equally unhelpful. For one thing, both the democratic and the epistemic worries about the role of EU experts tend to be embedded in a rather sweeping critical discourse that does not distinguish between the different concerns involved. Secondly, it is often assumed—misleadingly—that the problems connected to the use of expertise in EU policymaking and approach to crisis cannot be addressed effectively through institutional measures. The implication seems to be that we have either to make public policies without expertise, or live with its supposed dysfunctional effects on policy and democracy, hoping that the benefits of our reliance on the decisions and advice of experts will outweigh the costs, and that crises when they occur, will pass, and institutions recover.

In what follows, we show that the substantive involvement of experts in policymaking does raise real concerns. Yet, we move beyond the general uneasiness that many critics articulate, and list ten discrete objections of each type: ten epistemic and ten democratic worries about expertization. These two ten-point lists make visible the considerable complexity of the challenge that arises from the use and reliance on expertise in policymaking. With examples from EU governance, we show that many of the problems that occur, unfortunately, are not marginal. Rather, they are accentuated in a time where the Union faces multiple crises. The fact that the listed worries are genuine, or at least not unreasonable, does not imply that the reliance on expertise in policymaking is ultimately misguided, or that it is impossible to institutionalize expert bodies in better ways. This chapter suggests both mechanisms tailored to tackle the epistemic uneasiness that the involvement of experts in policymaking has spurred, and ways to address the democratic challenge.

We proceed in the following two sections with a presentation of the different epistemic and democratic challenges with examples from EU governance. The section on the epistemic worries focuses its examples specifically on economic expertise, and the role of economists in EU's latter years economic and social crises; then, the following section relates the democratic worries to recent and ongoing debates on EU democracy. Next, we outline the proposed reform approach. Finally, the chapter discusses how the more detailed features of reform will depend on whether a *breaking down*, *muddling through*, or *heading forward* scenario of EU integration takes place.[1] At the same time, the shape and directions of reform will contribute to make one or more of these scenarios more likely than others.

TEN EPISTEMIC WORRIES

1. *We cannot know who the experts are*

Generally, experts are persons who have substantially more knowledge than other people within a specific domain.[2] Due to this epistemic asymmetry, nonexperts or lay people are often not in a position to know who among the putative experts are the "real" or the "best" experts, or to judge between competing claims when these experts disagree (for example, Hardwig 1985, 1991; Walton 1997; Goldman 2011). It is not hard to detect cases from the EU economic governance context where epistemic asymmetries are salient. Experts often provide knowledge that is technically complex. We see this, for example, in European Commission expert group reports in policy areas such as economic and monetary affairs, internal market, competition, external trade, and taxation,[3] or in the working paper series of the European Central Bank (ECB),[4] where recent published papers have titles such as "Sources of Borrowing and Fiscal Multipliers," "Trading ahead of Treasury Auctions," "Fiscal Equalization and the Tax Structure," and "The New Area-Wide Model II: An Extended Version of the ECB's Micro-founded Model for Forecasting

---

[1] See the introduction chapter to this handbook.
[2] See Alvin I. Goldman's (2011: 14) influential definition.
[3] The reports can be found in the Register of Commission Expert Groups, see http://ec.europa.eu/transparency/regexpert.
[4] https://www.ecb.europa.eu/pub/research/working-papers/html/index.en.html.

and Policy Analysis with a Financial Sector." It is no doubt hard for nonexperts to evaluate the quality and soundness of the discussions and analyses of several of these reports and papers, and to make direct judgments of whether the experts involved are truly knowledgeable in the relevant domains. Similarly, were putative economic experts to disagree on some of the conclusions made, it would require considerable expertise on the topics in question to formulate an informed and independent opinion on which of the competing claims to support.[5]

2. *There are no moral experts*

However, we should take into account how factual and technical considerations in policymaking are intertwined with norms and values. Experts may tell us something about is-questions, for example, about economic relationships and mechanisms, and the effects of different economic policies, and on the basis of this knowledge give recommendation about the choice of means to achieve certain predefined end. But what about questions of a noninstrumental kind concerning what we *ought* to will? A similar concern can be raised in the context of discussions of EU integration specifically. Here, there is scholarship concentrating on the features, mechanisms, effects, and the future scenarios of EU integration. However, there are also normative theories of how EU integration ought to develop, and what the proper role of economists and other experts ought to be. What is the status of this branch of theorizing? Can there be "experts" on normative diagnoses and prescriptions?

This raises the general question of whether there is at all such a thing as moral expertise. Arguably, all accounts of normative judgments that consider also noninstrumental ought-questions to be possible objects of rational discourse open up, in principle, to the existence of moral expertise: if some moral arguments are more qualified than others, then some persons may be more able to make qualified moral arguments than others. On this premise, one could think of moral expertise, for example, in the following way (see also, Gesang 2010):

> Someone familiar with moral concepts and with moral arguments, who has ample time to gather information and think about it, may reasonably be expected to reach a soundly based conclusion more often than someone who is unfamiliar with moral concepts and moral arguments and has little time. (Singer 1972: 117)

To talk about moral experts along these lines make it possible to identify some persons as more competent in answering moral questions than others. This

---

[5] On disagreement among economists, see Machlup (1965) and Fuchs et al. (1997).

makes the problem of epistemic asymmetry even more profound since it goes beyond the domain of factual and technical questions.

If we return to the expert bodies of EU economic governance, a key observation is how several of them have as a part of their mandate to address not only questions of facts and the technical efficiency of policies, but also questions about norms and values. We see this on several occasions in the European Central Bank and Eurosystem mission statements, and elaborating statements on "strategic intents" and "organisational principles."[6] For example, to ensure the "main objective" of the ECB and the Eurosystem— "the maintenance of price stability"—the ECB is mandated discretionary space to define "price stability for the common good," distinguished from price stability that is less "sound," and to interpret what it implies to show "due regard" to principles such as "independence," "decentralisation," "accountability," and "equal treatment." Similarly, we see in European Commission expert group mandates how economic and other experts are called upon to make judgments on distributive and other value-laden issues. The result is often discussions and recommendations that deal not only with issues which are technically complex, but which also include complicated normative considerations, relying, for example, on arguments from welfare, environmental or development economics. We can add to this the many papers and reports produced by EU economic experts responding to mandates that are seemingly purely technical, asking for "evidence", "mappings", "descriptions", "comparisons", "explanations," and/or "forecasts," but that will frequently involve deliberations on aims and goals, and on the interpretation and ranking of standards and parameters, since the latter, as they occur, for example, in the EU treaties and regulations, will typically be under-specified and under-determined. In all these cases, it can be hard for the untrained to grasp and assess the technical and noninstrumental normative claims involved, and even harder to review the relative merits of competing claims when putative experts disagree.

3. Proper expertise requires "normal science" and political "well orderedness"

One could argue that there are ways to identify relatively credible epistemic communities. Could we not soundly trust experts based on proxies such as academic credentials and past records, even if we cannot as nonexperts directly assess experts' explanations and judgments? If so, the additional worry arises that this only would apply under "normal" circumstances, and not in times of crisis. Generally, we often see how fields or disciplines are characterised by competing paradigms or research programs, and how, after periods of production of expert knowledge within the parameters of a certain cognitive framework, they undergo epistemic shifts that change the notions of what qualifies as expert knowledge. The sources of such shifts can be internal to

[6] https://www.ecb.europa.eu/ecb/orga/escb/html/index.en.html.

the epistemic community, spurred by theoretical or conceptual innovation, methodological breakthroughs or new technologies, but they can also be external and related to social and cultural changes, economic crisis, or political ruptures.

In the EU economic governance context, the 2008 crisis spurred opposed accounts within expert communities both of what caused the crisis, the role of the advice, models and predictions of economists, and of the viable ways ahead. On the one hand, some analyses connected the euro crisis to a shift in EU economic policy discourse "from pragmatism to dogmatism" rooted in "regulatory liberalism" and "monetary orthodoxy" (Mügge 2011: 201; see also, Jabko 1999; McKay 2005; Posner and Véron 2010; Broome 2013; Heipertz and Verdun 2004: 772), and to institutional asymmetries and dysfunctional fiscal, monetary and finance regulation policies resulting from this orthodoxy (Jabko 2010; Blankenburg et al. 2013; Mügge 2013), rooted in deep trends and flaws in economic thinking (for general arguments on the latter, see Reiss 2008; Quiggin 2008; Palley 2012; Schlefer 2012). In short, according to this approach, economists and economic expertise were hugely responsible for the economic, social, and political problems that Europe faced in the aftermath of the crisis.

On the other hand, competing accounts emphasized how EU economic expertise, institutions and governance adapted and readapted in a relatively functional way before, during, and in the aftermath of the euro crisis (for example, Salines et al. 2012; Rosen and Olsen, this volume). Others focused more generally, arguing that it was not economics and economic expertise as such that were to blame for the bad policy choices which preceded the 2008 crisis, but possibly certain flawed economic models (on the pluralism of perspectives and positions among contemporary economists, see, for example, Stiglitz et al. 2008; Blanchard et al. 2012), and particular epistemic communities of economists, powerful stakeholders and politicians dogmatically relying on these models, or on sound models that were, however, applied selectively or mechanically, without a proper understanding of the models' assumptions and conditions (see, for example, Schlefer 2012). Adding to the complexity, economic experts differed in their policy recommendation, where some spoke in favour of the austerity approach and "market conforming" measures, whereas others criticized austerity and emphasized the need for more "market shaping" measures (Jabko 2010). In such situations, which of the reputable experts and economists should the nonexpert trust? How can the novice assess directly and independently which camp to side with? In times of crises, when competing epistemic cultures and approaches typically occur, and expert standards and constellations shift, the question of who the "real" experts are, becomes, arguably, even harder.

4. *Experts make cognitive errors*

To the extent that proper experts can be identified, it is generally reasonable to assume that they, when they are using well-established scientific methods and follow the rules of scientific reasoning, are less prone to making errors than laypeople. Nonetheless, the fact that experts do make errors is well-known, and research in cognitive psychology has shown that expert judgments are more exposed to elementary fallacies than we would like to think (Tversky and Kahneman 1974; Tetlock 2005; Kahneman 2012). Experts have for example a dubious reputation as forecasters. In *Expert Political Judgment*, Philip Tetlock (2005) presents results from studies of the ability of experts to make economic and political predictions: Many turned out to be overconfident and scored badly on accuracy.

The problem of bad forecasting is generally a challenge for the many economic experts who develop and use models to produce predictions about economic trends and the effects of economic policy. Controversies surrounding the EU's economic forecasting endeavors, for example, the European Commission Economic Forecasts[7] or the ECB's Macroeconomic Projections[8] are illustrative. Forecasts and projections of the EU economic area and the Eurozone are criticized for being based upon uncertain, unlikely, or even random estimates, resulting in poorly founded scenarios and recommendations, and, in the end, failed policies. A standard accusation is how the Commission and the ECB made their estimates during the early 2000s clearly having "no clue" about the up-coming crisis and recession.[9] Later, they similarly failed to foresee the recovery. This criticism can be directed directly against economics and the economists who deliver "bad" advice, but it can also be more multilayered: The problem coming to the fore is maybe not so much that expert predictions are decisively false or flawed, but that economic experts tend to operate too confidently and exaggerate the certainty of estimates that are key to their problem framing and recommendations.

5. *Experts are one-eyed*

Experts are no doubt often too confident of their own competence (Angner 2006); they identify with their disciplines and are prone to frame problems so that they fall within their disciplinary matrices, paradigms, or epistemic cultures (Buchanan 2004). For example, studies of environmental policy show how engineers, lawyers, and economists tend to approach this policy area differently, focusing on technology, regulation, and taxes/dues, respectively (Tellmann 2016). In the aftermath of the 2008 euro crisis, this line of critique against disciplinary bias has been frequently raised against economists

---

[7] https://ec.europa.eu/info/business-economy-euro/economic-performance-and-forecasts/economic-forecasts_en.

[8] https://www.ecb.europa.eu/pub/projections/html/index.en.html.

[9] See for example https://www.opendemocracy.net/en/european-economic-forecasts-why-do-they-get-it-wrong/.

in particular. Critics argue that what they see as key features of "orthodox" economics—model building based upon idealized assumptions, over-simplified modeling of economic actors, etc.,—unduly colored the economic experts' advice before, during, and after the crisis. This, for example, is a central line of argument among the self-declared "anti-econocrats" (see, in particular, Earle et al. 2017), who list the narrow problem framing, along with the methodological rules and tool box of economics as one of several problems with this discipline's hold on policy advice. It was also one of the concerns for critics in the European Parliament and civil society when they in 2013 and 2014 accused the European Commission for composing its expert groups with biased and "unbalanced" expertise (Holst and Moodie 2015).

6. *Experts operate out of self-interest*

Another objection is that experts may be more or less biased by their self-interests. Researchers in a field may have particular interests, for example, increasing prestige of their research fields and possibilities of research funding. They may also have more private career-related interests. In a well-functioning political system, conflicting interests are normally taken care of by the procedures for the selection of experts. However, suspicions that the EU has not properly safeguarded against conflict of interests have fueled public demands for more transparency and better guidelines for expert selection.

7. *Experts are ideologically biased*

A related and frequent charge about bias is that economic and other experts have ideological commitments or other deeper normative orientations that influence their judgments. We see this when experts explicitly embed their decisions or advice in a particular ideological or moral outlook. In addition, there are not so easily detectable cases. Numerous examiners of economics from Gunnar Myrdal's classical examination of the value impregnation of classical and neoclassical economics ([1930] 1953) onward have noted how theoretical approaches may frame the problem at hand in such a way that some value options are tacitly favored. For example, neoclassical economics is said to frame problems in a way that favors market solutions. In the EU economic governance context, we see this when EU expert bodies and economic advisors are repeatedly accused of introducing market-conforming measures and "neoliberalism" with their recommendations and interventions.

8. *Experts fail to speak truth to power*

Yet another worry is that experts belong and identify with the societal or power élite, and that their elite position and frame of reference compromise their independence: Experts are supposed to "speak truth to power" (Wildavsky 1979), but their connections to the "establishment" tend to make them more affirmative than critical of the powers that be. This suspicion is a common ingredient in populist politics, but is also fueled by sober sociological scholarship on elite recruitment, formation, and networks.

Also, this worry is, no doubt, part of the criticism against EU "technocracy" and "expertocracy," for example, in the critique of the biased composition of the European Commission expert group system. Behind this criticism lies not only a democratic concern, but also a worry that economists and other experts will reproduce convenient élite conceptions and prejudices ultimately in line with "corporate interests" (Holst and Moodie 2015: 39). A related worry has come to the fore in the aftermath of the Brexit referendum where economists' forecasting of a severe "slow down" in the UK economy has been accused of being "politically motivated" and enmeshed in an establishment worldview.[10]

9. *Experts are bad at communicating their knowledge*

In addition, experts are often bad at stating arguments in a comprehensible way, or may be unwilling to communicate in ways that reach out more broadly to stakeholders and those affected, for example, due to elitist attitudes. Such translation problems add to the already troublesome situation of epistemic asymmetry between experts and nonexperts. Due to cognitive inequalities, it is hard for nonexperts to hold experts to account. The situation worsens if experts are also bad communicators. This is also an issue in the EU economic governance context where economic policy expert reports are accused of being unnecessarily technical, and framed in ways that exclude the average citizen from their readership.

10. *Experts lack political judgment*

Finally, it may be objected that experts lack an understanding of political processes and the ability to make political judgments, since they tend to view political questions as if they were questions of facts and logic. On the one hand, this may result in recommendations that are "right," in the sense that they are supported by solid evidence, but lack political feasibility, at least in the here and now (see Tranøy and Stensted, this volume). A variant of this is when experts give unfeasible recommendations because they ignore the institutional political conditions for their implementation (Swift and White 2008). On the other hand, experts may exaggerate the extent to which the space for political action is constrained by *Sachzwang*, by given circumstances and parameters.

---

[10] See for example https://eutoday.net/news/business-economy/2017/brexit-forecast-economists-admit-they-got-it-wrong.

The result in the first case is some kind of utopian intervention; in the other, the result is adaptive, technocratic engineering that considers revisable facts and questionable concerns as "necessities." In the contexts of economists and EU economic governance, technocracy, in the latter sense, represents a rather persuasive problem. In particular, we often see how considerations that necessarily involve normative interpretation and ranking, for example, when an expert group recommends one policy over others, are presented as if they were purely technical or scientific questions.

Ten Democratic Worries

To the epistemic worries, we can add different democratic concerns. We list first ten such concerns, before relating them to debates on EU democracy and legitimacy.

1. *Self-determination under fire*

The maybe most basic democratic objection to experts' political role originates from theories of democracy that consider democracy to be—not about "knowledge," "problem-solving," or "truth" at all—but about the self-governance of free and equal citizens (Urbinati 2014). From this perspective, democratic decision procedures are regarded as better irrespective of their epistemic credentials: There is a right to political self-determination even at the price that decisions may be wrong or bad in the sense of not being based on the best available reasons.

2. *Less collective wisdom*

The opposite camp in democratic theory, the so-called epistemic democrats, turns the previous objection upside down: Their contention is exactly that democracy's legitimacy as a form of rule depends on the truth-tracking qualities of its procedures. They argue also that democracy tends to deliver well from an epistemic point of view. The problem with expertization then is that it may lead to poorer decisions, since there is a "wisdom of the many" that make the many wiser than the most knowledgeable (Landemore 2012).

3. *A non-majoritarian source of political influence*

Beyond these fundamental democratic concerns, coming from the procedural (1) or epistemic (2) camp of democratic theory, there are democratic worries concerning the legitimate scope for expertise in democracies. The need for expert advice and some delegation to expert bodies is generally recognized. Yet, the fear is that expertization goes too far; that expert authority intrudes on and eventually replaces democratic political authority based on majoritarian procedures in certain area—that there is a shift from elected to unelected power (Vibert 2007).

4. *Expert versus public deliberation*

For democrats who emphasize the importance of public deliberation, there is furthermore a worry that deliberation over political issues becomes dominated by experts, and so less public, in the sense that expert knowledge narrows the space of viable reasons and devalues the contributions of ordinary citizens. Once more, this worry is compatible with recognizing the need to defer to expert authority in many questions. The concern is about what Jürgen Habermas (1968/1974) once called a "scientization of public opinion," not about the need for expertise in politics, and the hope is for a balanced interplay of expert knowledge and opinion formation in the public sphere (Christiano 2012).

5. *Unfair negotiation of social interests*

A range of other democratic concerns are also not necessarily *anti* expert, but take up problematic effects if expertization goes too far or takes the wrong track. Apart from voting and deliberation, bargaining is a central mechanism of political decision-making (Elster 1998), and for those who emphasize the importance of bargaining in the political process, there is the additional worry that the political role of experts interfere with a fair negotiation of social interests. The problem is in part that some interest groups in society are more capable of utilizing experts' cognitive resources than others, and that expertization will tend to come with increased and potentially undue influence for these groups. In addition, experts or particular expert communities will constitute powerful interest groups of their own. More fundamentally, the familiar grammar of politics comes under pressure: Expertization facilitates talk about political outcomes and policies as more or less "knowledge based," "rational," etc., and not as reflecting some groups' values and interests. Experts' extra influence in political processes is worrisome then, not only because it serves some social interests better than others, but also because interest promotion becomes harder to detect and challenge when it is disguised as "superior knowledge," "the best available expertise," "evidence," etc.

6. *Political alienation*

A democracy should express the will of the people, and an additional worry is that expertization may increase the feeling among large shares of the citizenry that they live under a rule rather expressing the will of experts and elites. This is what concerned Robert Dahl (1985), who argued that too much power to experts can come to produce "political alienation" among ordinary citizens: Many will not feel themselves responsible for, and thus see themselves as "alien" to, the collective decisions they are required to obey. Such feelings of alienation may have negative effects on public trust and democratic attitudes.

7. *Expert arrogance*

There is a tendency among experts to regard ordinary people as ill-informed, and to define "good policies" as those that are based on "knowledge" and "evidence," irrespective of public opinion. On this basis, some criticize self-proclaimed knowledge elites for underestimating the cognitive abilities, information levels and common sense of ordinary people, and fear that such expert arrogance can spur nondemocratic sentiments as well as reduce policy quality. Others concede that political ignorance may be widespread, but still worry over over-confident and arrogant experts. Such experts tend to overlook their own biases and cognitive limitations, but a minimal level of respect is also inherently valuable as part of a democratic ethos. Disrespectful attitudes can furthermore result in a popular disdain for experts and elites that pave the way for authoritarian populism and the erosion of democratic institutions over time.

8. *Free-floating experts*

Experts qua experts are moreover—or at least see themselves as—"freischwebende," to use Karl Mannheim's (1936) term, in the sense that their primary loyalties are often to epistemic communities or to their professions, and they tend to overlook the political context and the power relations in which their expert activities are embedded. This makes experts less capable of understanding the *modus operandi* of democratic politics and the motives of their fellow citizens: Most people who engage in politics have particular attachments and identities, and seek communities of like-minded (Mutz 2008).

9. *Depolitization of politics*

Expertization may also distort other features of democratic politics many will consider essential, such as the role of opinion in contrast to truth or evidence (Arendt 1968) or of contestation and conflict (Fawcett et al. 2017). Delegation to expert bodies implies to insulate policymaking from political debate and strife—to depoliticize it—and to convert political issues into questions that can be handled by "neutral" experts. An extensive role in governments for delegated expertise, critics worry, will take the "politics" out of politics, and distort our ideas of what democracy is, and of what experts can deliver (see Caporaso, this volume).

10. Damaged elite selection and circulation

Finally, even if one grants a role for elites in democracy (for a classical statement, see Schumpeter [1942] 1985), there is the worry that expertization may hamper processes of elite selection and circulation vital to good democratic governance. The problem can be that academic experts and professionals lack a social constituency and that the circulation in and out of governing epistemic communities is comparably low. Whereas leaders of political parties and interest groups in democracies will shift as a result of political mobilization or elections, expert groups and bodies will tend to be sheltered from political pressures. There can be good reasons for such sheltering, but an unfortunate side effect can be static and insensitive political leadership, to the extent that experts take on a political role.

With these ten democratic worries in mind, we can return to the EU context and the different controversies over the democratic qualities and deficits of the Union. Among these, we will limit our universe to three sets of debates, all central to the recent "crisis" discourse: those on the role and competences of the European Parliament relative to other EU institutions; those on the organization of EU's expert bodies (EU agencies, the European Central Bank, the European Commission expert group, etc.); and those surrounding national referendums on EU relations and policies, including the ongoing Brexit debate. A first observation is how fundamental democratic concerns are raised regularly in all of these debates, and fuel claims about a "political," "institutional," or even "constitutional" crisis in the Union, that needs to be urgently addressed. We find arguments about how a broader and more committed inclusion of "the people"—be it citizens' representatives in the European Parliament, lay or interest group representatives in agency boards or expert groups, or the voters of national referendums—can contribute to give the EU better and more anchored policies and a sounder and less crisis-ridden direction (2). We also see repeated appeals to the intrinsic value of democratic norms of inclusion and equal participation (1), and justifications on this basis for a vastly reformed EU, with a larger role for citizens, stakeholders and elected assemblies, and a more substantive curtailment of executives, courts and expert bodies (for general analyses, see Nikolaïdis 2013; Fossum 2015; Bellamy 2019).

As for the remaining worries, several of them come to fore in referendum debates, most recently in the quarrels over Brexit, where supporters of the Leave campaign express feelings of alienation (6) and distrust in arrogant EU experts (7) crowding in nonelected EU bodies (3), and without a proper understanding of ordinary people's identities and national sentiments (8) (see Oliver et al., this volume). However, we see some of the similar concerns raised in the other debates, for example, when the democratic credentials of the European Parliament as elected body is highlighted in contrast to the Central Bank, the Commission and other nonelected, bodies or when measures for a larger inclusion of lay perspectives are called for in EU agencies, to increase popular credibility (see Newsome and Stenberg, this volume). A potential conflict between a fair negotiation of social interests and EU's expert-driven problem-solving procedures tends to be assumed both in national referendum debates and by proponents of more stakeholder involvement in EU's executive branch (5), whereas an important argument both for a more pluralist composition of Commission expert groups and for increasing the European Central Bank's accountability commitments vis-à-vis the Parliament, is that this will ensure more public concerns to be included and so increase deliberative quality (4). Both the different measures taken to democratize EU agency boards and advisory fora, and to strengthen the European Parliament, can be interpreted as ways to counter an exaggerated depoliticization of politics (9), whereas the Brexit debate and similar national level debates are also debates about the relative power of national versus supranational elites and about who are best qualified for democratic leadership (10).

Reforming EU's Expert Arrangements

Overall then, the above listed worries about expertization, the epistemic as well as the democratic ones, are all worth our attention. Some concerns may be exaggerated, and concrete accusations can be more or less warranted. To be sure, not all that is said about "experts in Brussels" and "EU expert rule" hold water. Yet, none of the worries we have outlined seems generally unreasonable. Rather, scrutinizing EU governance and the discourse on European integration surrounding EU's recent crises, we find several of the listed concerns raised over and over again, and for quite sensible reasons. At the same time, it is hard to make rational policies in technologically advanced, complex societies like ours, and in a multilevel polity such as the EU, without expert knowledge, guidance, and decisions. Consequently, the proper answer is not to debunk expertise, but to organize and institutionalize expert arrangements more in accordance with democratic requirements, and in ways that ensure that experts operate like proper experts (Holst and Molander 2019).

To better address the epistemic worries, we believe at least three groups of mechanisms should be in place: those that target expert *behaviour*; those that target the *judgements* of experts, and a third group that addresses the *conditions* for expert inquiry and judgment. To the first category belong the "dos and don'ts" of scientific communities. Arguably, the adherence to such epistemic norms (Merton 1973; Tranøy 1976), is pre-supposed when political authorities and citizens appeal to expert opinion, and in the end, nonexperts have to rely on experts to behave in accordance with such norms—this is the predicament of epistemic asymmetry. Yet, governments can have an influence on the conditions for their own trust in the expertise used. Decisions taken about the external organization of science and research can have considerable effects on the internal functioning of scientific communities. This is central in an EU context. The Union is a large-scale funder of research, and whether funding policies emphasize academic independence and norm sets is key to the quality of knowledge production. The way expert bodies and expert groups are organized are also important for making the scientific ethos effective. In this connection, specific measures can be taken, such as checking scientific merit and past records, but also experts' vested interests and political affiliations, in order to exclude unsuitable persons from assignments. Once more, EU-level policies are decisive. Here the problem is sometimes a lack of regulations and guidelines. In other cases, expert arrangements are comparatively well-regulated on paper—European Commission expert groups can serve as an example (Holst and Moodie 2015), and the problem is rather that the high standards of EU regulatory discourse may be betrayed on the ground.

The second group of mechanisms aims at holding experts accountable by putting their judgments under review in different fora (Reiss 2008: 38 ff.). The primary forum for testing judgments and detecting fallacies and biases is the forum of peers; competent economic experts, for example, should review and control what other economic experts are doing. However, the testing of judgments and arguments can also be extended from this forum to experts in other relevant disciplines and to other relevant fora, such as administrative fora of regulators, elected assemblies, stakeholder fora, or publics of engaged citizens. Epistemic asymmetry will be an unavoidable challenge. Still, mechanisms that contribute to holding experts to account in different fora will influence to what extent experts are considered trustworthy, and in the best of cases they will also counteract expert failures, for example, when experts fall victim to overconfidence or are insensitive to the evaluative, nonscientific dimensions of a problem. Yet, overall, fora-based accountability mechanisms are underdeveloped both in the EU and other polities, despite what we know of their importance for ensuring the quality of expert judgments.

The third group of mechanisms targets the conditions for expert inquiry and judgment. It is for example vital to ensure that experts work in pluralist groups. Experts who reason alone are exposed to "confirmation bias" (the tendency to look only for arguments that confirm their own ideas), and to "reason-based choice" (the tendency to pick the option for which reasons can be most easily gathered), whereas deliberating groups are known to be less prone to such fallacies, typically work with a larger pool of ideas and information, and more often weed out bad arguments (Mercier 2011). However, the positive epistemic effects of deliberation are dependent on diversity. Without diversity deliberation may work in the opposite direction and create groupthink (Sunstein and Hastie 2015). Hence, organizing expert work along team and deliberative lines, and providing for the necessary diversity and exposure to criticism from the wider epistemic community is crucial. This insight should also guide EU institutional reform much more systematically. Even in EU contexts where pluralism in policy- and decision-making is high on the agenda, the reference is most often to member state or stakeholder pluralism, and less to cognitive diversity and disciplinary pluralism.

Finally, EU would need to respond to the recent crises with reforms that address the democratic worries about expertization. Here there are two main paths to follow. First, there are different ways to "democratize expertise" (Weingart 2005: 53–54): taking relevant lay knowledge more into account in knowledge production, giving laypeople better access to expert knowledge and experts, allowing laypeople to have more influence on the selection of experts, and taking political-representative concerns more into account in the selection of experts (through gender and national quotas, the balancing of ideological views, etc.). Reforms along these lines can sometimes go well together with reforms to better ensure the quality of expertise, but democratic and epistemic concerns can also draw in different directions (for examples, see Holst and Molander 2017). The second path is to democratize not only "expertise," but the relationship between institutions in the larger political system. Some of the democratic worries over experts' political power point toward more fundamental reform of EU's constitutional set-up, including a larger role and more and firmer competencies for European parliaments.

Conclusions

The relationship between reforms of EU expert arrangements of the kind suggested here and different scenarios of EU integration is at least two-fold. First, the more detailed reform paths will depend on whether a *breaking down*, *muddling through*, or *heading forward* scenario of EU integration takes place. The *breaking down* scenario predicts that the EU's multiple crises will contribute to an erosion of EU institutions and a strengthening of member states interests. Under this scenario, it is less likely to see a restructuring of EU level expert arrangements through sophisticated reform. Rather, national expert systems will regain importance, and their reform will depend on the capacity and will of national governments. The *muddling through* scenario suggests incremental changes based on pre-existing organizations and schemes. Under this scenario, familiar patterns will typically reoccur, to the advantage of reforms (of forum structures, to recompose expertise, to include lay perspectives, etc.) that resonate with EU institutions' *modus operandi* and established appropriate norms among EU regulators. Lastly, the *heading forward* scenario predicts a still deeper EU integration in the aftermath of recent crises and more unexpected and even radical institutional change. This may open for more *out of the box* reforms of EU expert arrangements. However, in the end, there is no guarantee that such reforms will concentrate on strengthening democratic and epistemic merits, even if the stability of a *heading forward* scenario would seem to depend on it.

At the same time, the shape and directions of reform will contribute to make one or more of these scenarios more likely than others. If reform energies in this area, are directed away from the EU level and EU institutions, the *breaking down* scenario moves closer. A *muddling through* approach to reform of EU expert arrangements, if pursued with a certain success over time, and even during crises, will tend to make the overall *muddling through* scenario more likely. Finally, advanced EU-level reforms of expert arrangements to ensure that experts operate as proper experts and to reduce democratic deficits are likely to be central to the manifestation of any successful *heading forward* scenario.

REFERENCES

Angner, E. (2006). Economists as Experts: Overconfidence in Theory and Practice. *Journal of Economic Methodology, 13*(1), 1–24.
Arendt, H. (1968). Truth and Politics. In H. Arendt (Ed.), *Between Past and Future: Eights Exercises in Political Thought*. New York: The Viking Press.
Bellamy, R. (2019). *A Republican Europe of States*. Cambridge: Cambridge University Press.
Blanchard, O., Romer, D., Spence, M., & Stiglitz, J. (2012). *In the Wake of the Crisis: Leading Economists Reassess Economic Policy*. Cambridge, MA: The MIT Press.
Blankenburg, S., King, L., Konselmann, S., & Wilkinson, F. (2013). Prospects for the Eurozone. *Cambridge Journal of Economics, 37*(3), 463–477.
Broome, A. (2013). The Politics of IMF-EU Co-operation: Institutional Change from the Maastricht Treaty to the Launch of the Euro. *Journal of European Public Policy, 20*(4), 589–605.
Buchanan, A. (2004). Political Liberalism and Social Epistemology. *Philosophy & Public Affairs, 32*(2), 95–130.
Christiano, T. (2012). Rational Deliberation Among Experts and Citizens. In J. Parkinson & J. Mansbridge (Eds.), *Deliberative Systems: Deliberative Democracy at the Large Scale* (pp. 27–51). Cambridge: Cambridge University Press.
Dahl, R. A. (1985). *Controlling Nuclear Weapons: Democracy versus Guardianship*. Syracuse NY: SUNY Press.
Earle, J., Moran, C., & Ward-Perkins, Z. (2017). *The Econocracy: The Perils of Leaving Economics to the Experts*. Manchester: Manchester University Press.
Elster, J. (1998). Introduction. In *Deliberative Democracy* (pp. 1–18). Cambridge: Cambridge University Press.
Fawcett, P., Flinders, M., Hay, C., & Wood, M. (2017). *Anti-politics, Depoliticization, and Governance*. Oxford: Oxford University Press.
Fossum, J. E. (2015). Democracya and Differentiation in Europe. *Journal of European Public Policy, 22*(6), 799–815.
Fuchs, V. R., Krueger, A. B., & Poterba, J. B. (1997). *Why Do Economist Disagree About Policy? The Roles of Beliefs About Parameters and Values* (NBER Working Paper 6151). Available at: www.nber.org/papers/w6151.pdf.
Gesang, B. (2010). Are Moral Philosophers Moral Experts? *Bioethics, 24*(4), 153–159.
Goldman, A. (2011). Experts: Which Ones Should You Trust? In A. Goldman & D. Whitcomb (Eds.), *Social Epistemology: Essential Readings* (pp. 109–133). Oxford: Oxford University Press.
Habermas. J. (1968/1974). The Scientization of Politics and Public Opinion. In *Toward a Rational Society*. Boston, MA: Beacon Press.
Hardwig, J. (1985). Epistemic Dependence. *Journal of Philosophy, 82*(7), 335–349.
Hardwig, J. (1991). The Role of Trust in Knowledge. *Journal of Philosophy, 88*(12), 693–708.

Heipertz, M., & Verdun, A. (2004). The Dog That Would Never Bite? What Can We Learn from the Origins of the Stability and Growth Pact. *Journal of European Public Policy*, 11(5), 765–780.

Holst, C., & Moodie, J. R. (2015). Cynical or Deliberative? An Analysis if the European Commission's Public Communication on Its Use of Expertise in Policy-Making. *Politics and Governance*, 3(1), 37–48.

Holst, C., & Molander, A. (2017). Public Deliberation and the Fact of Expertise: Making Experts Accountable. *Social Epistemology*, 31(3), 235–250.

Holst, C., & Molander, A. (2018). Asymmetry, Biases and Biases: Epistemic Worries About Expertise. *Social Epistemology*, 32(6), 358–371.

Holst, C., & Molander, A. (2019). Epistemic Democracy and the Role of Experts. *Contemporary Political Theory*. Available at: https://doi.org/10.1057/s41296-018-00299-4.

Holst, C., & Molander, A. (2020). Epistemic Worries About Economic Expertise. In J. Bátora and J. E. Fossum (Eds.), *Crises, EU Trajectories and the Question of Resilience*. London: Routledge.

Jabko, N. (1999). In the Name of the Market: How the European Commission Paved the Way for Monetary Union. *Journal of European Public Policy*, 6(3), 475–495.

Jabko, N. (2010). The Hidden Face of the Euro. *Journal of European Public Policy*, 17(3), 318–334.

Kahneman, D. (2012). *Thinking, Fast and Slow*. London: Penguin Books.

Landemore, H. (2012). *Democratic Reason: Politics. Collective Intelligence, and the Rule of the Many*. Princeton, NJ: Princeton University Press.

Machlup, F. (1965). Why Economist Disagree? *Proceedings of the American Philosophical Society*, 109(1), 1–7.

Mannheim, K. (1936). *Ideology and Utopia*. London: Routledge & Kegan Paul.

McKay, D. (2005). Economic Logic or Political Logic? Economic Theory, Federal Theory and EMU. *Journal of European Public Policy*, 12(3), 528–544.

Mercier, H. (2011). When Experts Argue: Explaining the Best and the Worst of Reasoning. *Argumentation*, 25(3), 313–327.

Merton, R. K. (1973). *The Sociology of Science: Theoretical and Empirical Investigations*. Chicago, IL and London: University of Chicago Press.

Mügge, D. (2011). From Pragmatism to Dogmatism: European Union Governance, Policy Paradigms and Financial Meltdown. *New Political Economy*, 16(2), 185–206.

Mügge, D. (2013). The Political Economy of Europeanized Financial Regulation. *Journal of European Public Policy*, 20(3), 458–470.

Mutz, D. (2008). Is Deliberative Democracy a Falsifiable Theory? *Annual Review of Political Science*, 11, 521–538.

Myrdal, G. ([1930] 1953). *The Political Element in the Development of Economic Theory*. London: Routledge.

Nikolaïdis, K. (2013). European Demoicracy and Its Crisis. *Journal of Common Market Studies*, 51(2), 351–369.

Palley, T. I. (2012). *From Financial Crisis to Stagnation: The Destruction of Shared Prosperity and the Role of Economics*. Cambridge: Cambridge University Press.

Peter Weingart. (2005). *Die Wissenschaft der Öffentlichkeit. Essays zum Verhältnis von Wissenschaft, Medien und Öffentlichkeit*. Weilerswist: Velbrück Wissenschaft.

Posner, E., & Véron, N. (2010). The EU and Financial Regulation: Power Without Purpose? *Journal of European Public Policy*, 17(3), 400–415.

Quiggin, J. (2008). Economists and Uncertainty. In G. Bammer & M. Smithson (Eds.), *Uncertainty and Risk: Multidisciplinary Perspectives*. London: Earthscan.

Reiss, J. (2008). *Error in Economics: Towards a More Evidence-Based Methodology*. London-New York: Routledge.

Salines, M., Glöckler, G., & Trchlewski, Z. (2012). Existential Crisis Incremental Response: The Eurozone's Dual Institutional Evolution. *Journal of European Public Policy, 19*(5), 665–681.

Schlefer, J. (2012). *The Assumptions Economists Make*. Cambridge MA: Harvard University Press.

Schumpeter, J. A. ([1942] 2005). *Capitalism, Socialism & Democracy*. Routledge: London.

Stiglitz, J. E., Edlin, A. S., & Bradford DeLong, J. (2008). *The Economists' Voice: Top Economists' Take on Today's Problems*. New York: Colombia University Press.

Singer, P. (1972). Moral Experts. *Analysis, 32*(4), 115–117.

Sunstein, C. R., & Hastie, R. (2015). *Wiser: Getting Beyond Groupthink to Make Groups Smarter*. Boston, MA: Harvard Business Review Press.

Swift, A., & White, S. (2008). Political Theory, Social Science, and Real Politics. In D. Leopold & M. Stears (Eds.), *Political Theory: Methods and Approaches* (pp. 49–69). Oxford: Oxford University Press.

Tellmann, S. M. (2016). *Experts in Public Policymaking: Influential, yet Constrained*. Doctoral Thesis. Oslo and Akershus University College of Applied Sciences.

Tetlock, P. E. (2005). *Expert Political Judgment: How Good Is It? How Can We Know?*. Princeton, NJ: Princeton University Press.

Tranøy, K. E. (1976). Norms of Inquiry: Methodologies as Normative Systems. In G. Ryle (Ed.), *Contemporary Aspects of Philosophy*. London: Oriel Press.

Tversky, A., & Kahneman, D. (1974). Judgment Under Uncertainty: Heuristics and Biases. *Science, 185*(4157), 1124–1131.

Urbinati, N. (2014). *Democracy Disfigured: Opinion, Truth, and the People*. Cambridge MA: Harvard University Press.

Vibert, F. (2007). *The Rise of the Unelected: Democracy and the New Separation of Powers*. Cambridge: Cambridge University Press.

Walton, D. (1997). *Appeal to Expert Opinion: Arguments from Authority*. University Park, PA: Pennsylvania State University Press.

Wildavsky, A. (1979). *Speaking Truth to Power: The Art and Craft of Policy Analysis*. London: Transaction.

CHAPTER 39

Rebound? The Short- and Long-Term Effects of Crises on Public Support and Trust in European Governance

Pieter de Wilde

INTRODUCTION

European crises such as the Euro crisis and refugee crisis contribute to rising Euroscepticism. This has been widely documented in recent studies documenting more skeptical public opinion and reduced citizen trust in European Union institutions (Clements et al. 2014; Serricchio et al. 2013; Usherwood and Startin 2013). Specifically, several studies document how the Euro crisis has resulted in reduced trust in the European Central Bank (Ehrmann et al. 2013; Gros and Roth 2010; see Caporaso; Rosen and Olsen; Tranoy and Stenstad, this volume). This kind of reduced trust may detrimentally affect the extent to which the EU can function and thus influence the course of European integration in the future. What is not clear, however, is how long such effects last. Both the Euro crisis and the refugee crisis have dissipated. Even if the underlying problems are far from solved, the risk of imminent collapse of the system and according media frenzy has faded from the political agenda. To investigate whether the crises have lasting effects on public opinion and citizens' trust in EU institutions, this chapter proceeds to analyze developments in the crises years and aftermath.

The great recession started in 2008 with the fall of Lehman Brothers. It spilled over into a government debt crisis as the Greek government revealed the true nature of its sovereign debt in 2010. In the period 2010–2012, the

---

P. de Wilde (✉)
Norwegian University of Science and Technology, Trondheim, Norway
e-mail: pieter.dewilde@ntnu.no

© The Author(s) 2021
M. Riddervold et al. (eds.), *The Palgrave Handbook of EU Crises*,
Palgrave Studies in European Union Politics,
https://doi.org/10.1007/978-3-030-51791-5_39

crisis held Europe in its grip as the EU came with late and half-baked solutions at the very last moment, barely averting collapse of the Eurozone. This period has been aptly described as "failing forward" (Jones et al. 2016; see also Tranoy and Stenstad, this volume). Ultimately, interventions by the European Central Bank in 2012 reduced pressure on the government debt of Greece and other EU member states in trouble. Slowly, bond spreads became lower. At the onset of 2014, the Euro crisis is over, even if it saw a short revival when the new SYRIZA government in Greece launched a referendum in early 2015. The refugee crisis started in 2013, peaked in 2015 and started dissipating in 2016. The number of refugees entering the EU in 2018 more or less equaled the number entering in 2014, about half as much as in the peak years of 2015 and 2016. Thus, at the time of writing, we are about five years out of the worst of the Euro crisis and about three years out of the worst of the refugee crisis. It is time for a first stocktaking about the long-term effects of both crises (see Schilde and Wallace Goodman, this volume).

This recent volatility of the Euro and refugee crises and its current dissipation provides a unique opportunity to study the long- and short-term effects of crises on public opinion. Is public opinion as volatile as market interest rates? Do people change their minds about the EU as quickly as markets do? In that case, we should see a pro-European rebound the past few years, just like we have seen a sharp decrease in government bond interest rates since 2012. Alternatively, the effects of crises could be more enduring, installing deeply engrained skepticism among European citizens that remains long after the crisis itself has left the front pages of newspapers. In other words, do crises have short- and long-term effects on public opinion about European integration and citizens' trust in EU institutions? That is the main question of this chapter. If so, what do these short- and long-term effects look like?

Finding out the extent to which crises have long-term effects on public opinion and citizens' trust could tell us a great deal about the viability of the three future scenarios of European integration laid out in the introduction of this volume. Lasting negative effects of crises on public opinion and citizen trust could lead to the EU *breaking down*. It would mean there is strong potential for Eurosceptics and populists to campaign on leaving the Union. If and when they see a chance to organize a referendum on leaving—like the Brexit referendum—lasting negativity due to past crises in public opinion would greatly increase the chances of Leave campaigns succeeding. Moreover, low levels of trust in government institutions are linked to low-quality governance. If governance institutions aren't trusted, their policies lose effectiveness, which in turn can reduce trust. In other words, there is a potential of a negative spiral where crises reduce citizen trust in EU institutions, which reduces the effectiveness of EU policies, which in turn reduces citizen trust, etc. This could lead to a gradual deterioration of the EU polity up until the point of full break down.

Alternatively, if there is at least a mild rebound of public opinion and citizens' trust after the immediacy of the crises has gone, the EU could return to status quo ante and resume a process of *muddling through*, much like it has done throughout the 1990s and early 2000s. In this scenario, public opinion and citizen trust would not support major leaps forward in integration that require Treaty changes. Nor would there be support for major enlargement rounds or new flagship projects of integration. But there would be support for gradual integration steps to improve and safeguard the achieved level of integration. Notably, the chances that crises provide a stepping stone to major leaps forward in integration are remote through public opinion and citizen trust. This is because it is clear that crises initially lead to more skeptical public opinion and lower citizen trust. It could be that the wider public can be sidelined or bypassed to enable future integration, but this chance seems remote since major leaps forward require Treaty changes and Treaty changes almost inevitably lead to referendum campaigns. Ireland is constitutionally obliged to hold referenda on Treaty change and once Ireland holds a referendum, there will be powerful calls in other member states to do the same. In short, through investigating long term the effects of crises on public opinion and citizen trust, this chapter investigates the comparative likelihood of scenario 1 (break down) and scenario 2 (*muddling through*) as outlined in the introduction.

The chapter proceeds as follows. First, we discuss the state of public opinion research on European integration. It shows the predominant focus in the literature to explain individual citizens' opinion rather than to document and discuss long-term aggregate trends. It also discusses the relevance of the public mood concept and postfunctionalist theory that would focus our attention on indifference among the EU population (Hooghe et al., this volume). I report short-term volatility in public support and trust in European governance and long-term effects on indifference. The implications of these findings as well as critical notes on the used data and dominant trends in academic research are discussed in the conclusion.

Public Support and Indifference

In the wake of the Euro crisis, many studies document its effect on public opinion (e.g. Clements et al. 2014; Hobolt and De Vries 2016; Serricchio et al. 2013; Usherwood and Startin 2013). These studies primarily analyze causal effects of exposure to the crisis and other individual characteristics, in the classic study to explain individual citizens' opinion about European integration (Hooghe and Marks 2005; Kritzinger 2003; McLaren 2007; Van Elsas and Van der Brug 2015; Weßels 2007). Aggregate studies of public opinion and its development over time are much rarer. Yet, as Anderson and Hecht (2018: 618) stress, it is not these individual characteristics that influence policymaking. "Politicians care about the views of states, districts, areas, cities, what-have-you. Individual opinion is useful only as an indicator of the aggregate. For a politician to pay attention to individual views is to miss the main game" (Stimson 1991: 12).

Albeit much fewer in number, there are also a range of studies analyzing the aggregate nature and developments in public opinion about Europe (Anderson and Hecht 2018; Bølstad 2015; Eichenberg and Dalton 1993, 2007). They often use the Eurobarometer question about membership as a key indicator. It has the advantage of asking citizens for a fairly clear appreciation of the European polity which is often foremost in people's minds when thinking about the EU and the integration process (Inglehart and Reif 1991). The question asks: "Generally speaking, do you think that (your country's) membership of the EU is …?", with as answer options "A Good Thing," "A Bad Thing," "Neither," and "Don't Know." Most of these studies subsequently construct a "net support" indicator, which is the percentage answering that membership is a good thing, minus the percentage answering membership is a bad thing. The answers Neither and Don't Know are ignored as missing values. The latter is common practice in public opinion research. Many scholars consider "don't know" answers useless and even try to design surveys in ways to reduce the amount of "don't know" answers to a bare minimum (Shoemaker et al. 2002).

Yet, the treatment of "don't know" answers as missing values is theoretically unwarranted in the context of European integration and other political issues that combine both recently salient political issues and abstract and distant political objects to relate to. While the EU in itself is not a policy issue like health care or taxation, the questions of membership and policy options that would increase or decrease the powers of supranational institutions vis-à-vis the member states or the amount of policy areas in which they have some sort of say do constitute European integration as a political issue. The rising salience of European integration as political issue has been well-documented in the literature. Since it is a comparatively new issue—and revolves around a set of distant, abstract political institutions in Brussels and elsewhere—it is no surprise to find a strong presence of a "permissive consensus" in public opinion. That is, for most of the history of post-WWII European integration, citizens did not care much about this process or were mildly in favor of it when asked (Lindberg and Scheingold 1970). Since the early 1990s, however, this permissive consensus has been replaced by a "constraining dissensus," where citizens increasingly do care about who rules over them from Brussels and become more critical about the powers and competencies of the EU (Hooghe and Marks 2009). Schmitter's (1969: 166) long awaited "widening of the audiences and clientele," in which citizens become increasingly aware of the impact the EU has in their daily lives and engaged in EU politics appears to finally happen.

In the politicization literature on European integration, many have argued that an increasing number of citizens becomes aware and engaged in EU politics as the Union has become more politicized over time (De Wilde and Zürn 2012; Hooghe and Marks 2009; Hutter and Grande 2014; Statham and Trenz 2013), even if this is not a uniform linear trend (De Wilde et al. 2016; Hutter and Grande 2014). That is, as political parties increase contestation over the EU and the integration project and as media provide more coverage of EU affairs, more citizens become aware of the EU's existence, impact on their lives and its functioning. As a result of the recognition that Brussels is increasingly an important political arena exercising political authority over EU citizens, citizens gain awareness and start mobilizing (De Wilde and Zürn 2012). If the theory of the politicization of European integration holds, we should see a reduction in indifference in public opinion over time, as the EU gains and exercises its authority.

To empirically measure this alleged *politicization* of European integration, Stoeckel (2013) argues we should study "don't know" answers to questions pertaining to European integration in surveys more in depth, rather than ignore them as missing values. He argues "don't know" answers can be considered a key indicator of indifference, and shows that indifference is a relevant and specific category in public opinion about European integration, with its own causes and implications for European governance (Stoeckel 2013). Even if European integration has become politicized as documented in electoral studies or media content analyses (De Vries 2011; Hutter and Grande 2014; Rauh 2016), indifference proves to be a persistent phenomenon in public opinion about the EU. Using focus groups, Van Ingelgom (2014) shows how large numbers of citizens across Europe remain indifferent to the unification project. Even in crisis-stricken Ireland, when the EU was having a major impact on citizens' lives through the Euro and bailout package, many citizens remained indifferent to European integration (Gora 2018).

Yet, "don't know" answers should be analyzed with caution. Because of the social desirability not to answer survey questions with "I don't know" (Converse 1970) and because pollsters have spent years trying to fine-tune questions in order to reduce "don't know" answers (Shoemaker et al. 2002), the number of indifferent citizens is likely to be vastly underestimated using traditional opinion polls like Eurobarometer. Focus groups reveal much higher levels of indifference. In analyzing survey data on indifference, we should also be cautious of spurious correlation. "Don't Know" answers have been shown to be negatively correlated with education. Higher educated people tend to answer "don't know" in survey questions less frequently than lower educated people (Converse 1976). Therefore, a drop in the percentage of "Don't Know" answers drop over time could indicate that people become aware of the EU and opinionated about integration, but it could also be that people become more educated over time. Nevertheless, relative and comparative "don't know" answers can still provide valuable insights into public indifference on certain issues compared to others and changes in indifference over time.

The question about the lasting effects of crises on public opinion about European integration thus includes both the effects of net support for integration and the effects on indifference. Unfortunately, the Eurobarometer discontinued a question for EU citizens about membership in 2011. This classic item to measure public support is thus no longer available to us. In order to gain traction on public opinion, I therefore rely on a series of other items in the Eurobarometer survey. To analyze public opinion about integration directly, this study relies on two items: Optimism about the EU and Image of the EU. The first item indirectly captures citizens' support: "Would you say that you are very optimistic, fairly optimistic, fairly pessimistic or very pessimistic about the future of the EU?" Beyond the four answer options contained in the question itself, it also allows "Don't Know" answers. The second item measures public opinion about the EU more directly: "In general, does the European Union conjure up for you a very positive, fairly positive, neutral, fairly negative or very negative image?" Again, it includes a non-named "Don't Know" option. The Image question has been asked biannually since 2002, while the optimism question has been asked biannually since 2007. McLaren (2007) shows that the Image question features similar patterns in causality as the membership question. Similar individual characteristics like economic situation, identity, and evaluation of other institutions influence citizens' feelings about the EU as their evaluation of membership of the EU. Gomez (2015) documents very similar trends in the Image indicator as in the classic membership question during the first years of the Great Recession, 2007–2011.

To further analyze the effects of the crisis on public opinion and to isolate possible generic effects of education on indifference, this chapter investigates developments in trust in various institutions. This includes general EU institutions, particularly the European Commission and the European Parliament, but also the key institution involved in the Euro crisis: the European Central Bank. If the crisis and politicization of European integration more generally have had an effect on indifference beyond the generic effects of education, we should see a different trend in people answering "Don't Know" to questions about trust in these EU institutions than in people answering "Don't Know" to trust questions on other, national institutions.

Public Support

Figure 39.1 shows public support in the EU from 2007, the start of the Great Recession, until 2018. First, this clearly shows that optimism and affective feelings correlate strongly. As EU citizens become less optimistic about the EU's future, their image of the EU also becomes more negative, or vice versa. It thus makes sense to consider both of them as indicators of a single public mood (Stimson 1991) on European integration. Second, we see that—with the exception of the period 2012–2014—public support remains on balance positive about the EU throughout the period of study. Thirdly and most importantly, we see a clear correlation between Europe's crises and support.

As the financial crisis starts in 2007, support decreases. When the crisis escalated from the financial crisis to the full government debt crisis in early 2010, public support decreases further. It reaches its lowest levels in 2012, at the heights of the Euro crisis and public support remains low until 2014, after which it starts recovering. This recovery does not last. Once the refugee

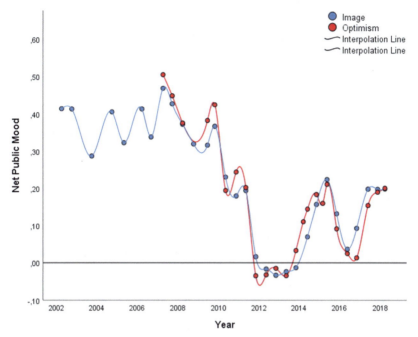

Fig. 39.1 Public Mood about the EU, 2007–2018 (Net Image and Net Optimism have been calculated where "very positive" and "very optimistic" are recoded as 2; fairly optimistic and fairly positive as 1; neutral as 0; fairly pessimistic and fairly negative as −1; and very pessimistic and very negative as −2. Both indicators thus run from a maximum of +2 to a minimum of −2.)

crisis hits in earnest in 2015, public support declines again. Finally, once the refugee crisis becomes less pronounced and less salient, public support starts recovering again. Both the negative effects of crises on public support and the recovery of support once these crises disappear are remarkable. The trend this figure shows clearly strengthens the notion that crises affect public opinion about European integration and the notion that these effects are short term, rather than lasting. In other words, unless crises lead to immediate break down of the system, it is likely that public opinion rebounds after the crisis dissipates, allowing the EU to return to a process of *muddling through*.

When it comes to indifference, we see a different trend. The percentage of EU citizens answering they don't know whether they are optimistic about the EU's future drops from around 8% in 2008 to 6% in 2018. The number of citizens for whom the EU conjures up neither a positive nor a negative image also drops. More precisely, the percentage of respondents to the survey which says they don't know what kind of image the EU creates for them drops from about 7% in 2002 to about 1.5% in 2018, with the largest decrease in the early years (Fig. 39.2).

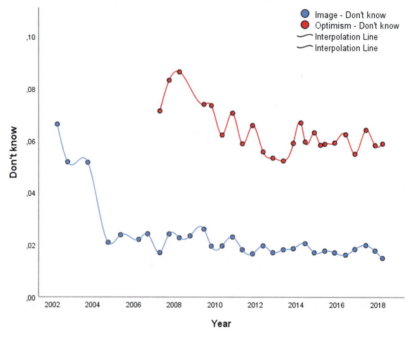

Fig. 39.2 Indifference about the EU (Y-axis reports fraction of the population answering «Don't Know»)

Even if there is fluctuation, this downward trend is in line with expectations from postfunctionalist theory that politicization causes an increasing number of EU citizens to become aware and opinionated about the EU over time, because of increases in its authority. While crises do not seem to impact this trend much, we see no return to indifference once crises have dissipated either.

Trust in European Governance

Citizens' trust in key national and European institutions sheds additional light on long- and short-term effects of crises. Trust in political institutions, often considered a measure of diffuse support for the political system, has been shown to be vital for the functioning of political systems. The more citizens trust political institutions, the more these institutions are able to effectively implement policies, delivering goods citizens want (Zmerli and Van der Meer 2017). Good governance and citizen trust can thus be part of a virtuous cycle and a decline in trust can conversely spell trouble for the effective functioning of the polity. While it is therefore highly relevant to study citizens' trust in political institutions, measures of *particular* trust (Hardin 2002) in political institutions can mean a variety of things. It inevitably combines a degree of trustworthiness of the institution with the inclination of citizens to trust strangers in general. Lack of trust does not necessarily mean that the stability of the system is at risk, it may also "... reflect a higher level of political sophistication and realism among the general public" (Citrin 1974: 975). In general, surveys consistently report that trust in EU institutions is higher than trust in national political institutions, which does not mean the former enjoy more legitimacy or stability than the latter. We should thus be careful not to overinterpret absolute levels of trust. Comparing developments in trust in institutions over time, however, does allow us to see whether public support shifts reported above might "trickle down" to more fundamental sentiments about the EU. Moreover, the Eurobarometer surveys contain a range of similar questions about citizens' trust in institutions, which measure trust in various EU institutions, national state institutions and non-state institutions. This allows us to analyze both the temporal effects of crisis and to isolate the changes in trust in EU institutions from changes in trust in general, which might be the product of higher levels of education and (political) sophistication, rather than crises.

Figures 39.3, 39.4, and 39.5 show striking similarities with the developments in the public mood indicators. For a long time, the number of citizens who responded that they trust EU institutions was higher than the number who said they tended not to trust them. The gap started to narrow as the Great Recession began in 2008 and the balance flipped around 2011. It closed again

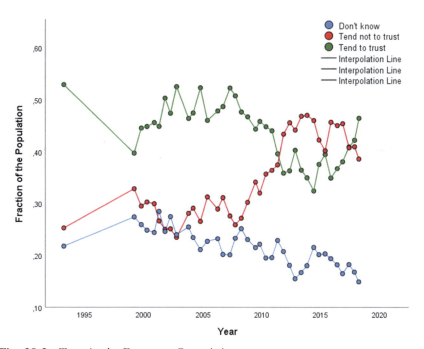

Fig. 39.3 Trust in the European Commission

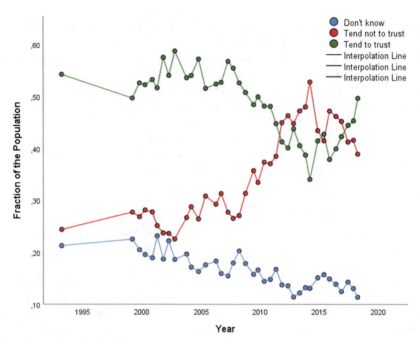

Fig. 39.4 Trust in the European Parliament

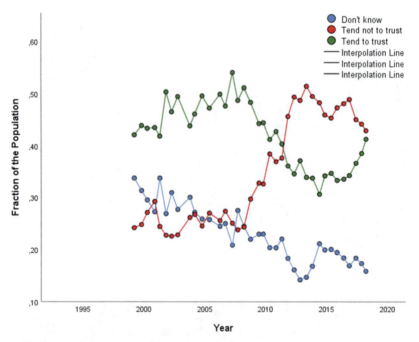

Fig. 39.5 Trust in the European Central Bank

briefly in late 2014–early 2015, in between the Euro and refugee crises, only to widen again in 2015–2016. Since 2017, citizens' trust in the EU institutions is on the rise again. Meanwhile, the percentage of people answering they don't know whether they trust EU institutions steadily declines. This is further support for postfunctionalist theory that citizens show a growing awareness and engagement with EU affairs as part of a more general politicization of European integration.

Yet, we still do not know whether such findings might be spurious effects of a general increase in the level of education of the EU population. To investigate this, I compare trends in "don't know" answers to various trust questions asked. The Eurobarometer regularly asks: "I would like to ask you a question about how much trust you have in certain media and institutions. For each of the following media and institutions, please tell me if you tend to trust it or tend not to trust it." Table 39.1 lists several of the institution's citizens have been regularly asked about, indicating the first year the question was included in the Eurobarometer, the percentage of "don't know" answers during that first survey, the most recent survey in which the question was asked and the percentage of "don't know" answers during that most recent survey, and finally the average annual change in the "don't know" category. Institutions have been ranked from those with the strongest change in "don't know" answers to those with the lowest change from top to bottom. First, this shows that the percentages of "don't know" answers are higher for EU institutions than they are for state and non-state institutions at national level. This fits with the politicization theory that EU institutions have long been

Table 39.1 Comparative trends in trust in institutions

Institution	First year of measurement	% 'Don't know' first year	Last year of measurement	% 'Don't know' last year	Average annual change in 'don't know' (%)
European Central Bank	1999	33.7	2018	15.8	−0.94
European Parliament	1993	21.3	2018	11.4	−0.40
European Commission	1993	21.8	2018	14.9	−0.27
Political Parties	2001	8.4	2018	5.5	−0.17
National Parliaments	2001	9.6	2018	6.7	−0.17
Radio	2000	9.3	2018	7.3	−0.11
Army	2001	7.8	2018	6.4	−0.08
Television	2001	4.6	2018	4.4	−0.01

Source Eurobarometer

less known and more remote to most citizens. We also see that EU institutions feature the strongest decline in "don't know" answers. Since the 1990s, the percentage of EU citizens who do not know whether they trust key EU institutions has dropped from 33.7 to 15.8% for the European Central Bank, 21.8 to 14.9% for the European Commission and from 21.3 to 11.4% for the European Parliament.

The percentage of citizens not knowing whether to trust national institutions also tends to decline, albeit only very marginally so in the case of trust in television. This implies that there could be a kind of inoculation effect of crises. If crises have the long-term effect of reducing the indifference among the population, then future crises will likely have less effects on public opinion and citizen trust. This is because events such as crises are more likely to sway citizens who do not have a clear opinion about the EU than the opinion of citizens who have a clear disposition before the crisis starts. For now, it is too early to tell whether this inoculation effect occurs. Only possible future crises in the context of a more "developed"—meaning less indifferent—public opinion would allow us to empirically assess the validity of such an inoculation hypothesis. Should it hold, however, this effect of crisis would strengthen the *muddling through* scenario rather than either the breakdown or leap forward scenarios. It would mean public opinion hardens in the proximity of a 50–50 distribution of positive and negative opinions which would hold each other in balance, allowing neither major changes in the direction of less integration nor major changes in the direction of more integration.

Conclusions

This chapter has investigated the long- and short-term effects of crises on public opinion about European integration. Drawing on public opinion theory and postfunctionalist integration theory, this chapter discussed the shifts in the public mood, trust in EU institutions and indifference toward the EU and the integration process. The effects of both the Euro crisis and the refugee crisis are clearly discernible in the public mood about the EU and in trust in EU institutions. We see a deterioration of the mood and trust starting with the onset of the Great Recession around 2007/2008. At the height of the Euro crisis around 2012, both the mood and trust had flipped from a plurality of EU citizens tending to be optimistic about the EU, having a positive image of the EU and tending to trust EU institutions, to a plurality of pessimistic, negative, and distrusting views. As the Euro crisis faded around 2014, these indicators become more positive again, only to turn negative again around the peak of the refugee crisis in 2015 and 2016. After 2016, both the public mood and trust in EU institutions improved again. This is evidence supporting the conclusion that crises have more or less immediate but short-term effects on the public mood about the EU and on trust in EU institutions.

The fact that the same trend is observable just after the Euro crisis and just after the refugee crisis, in multiple indicators ranging from citizens' optimism about the EU, image of the EU, and trust in key EU institutions means we are witnessing a rebound in public opinion. Soon after the crises dissipate, public opinion rebounds to more positive views about the EU and its institutions. At the same time, the long-term trend of decreasing indifference implies that shifts in public opinion may become smaller over time. If crises and general politicization affect public opinion, it is often not pro-Europeans becoming Eurosceptic or vice versa. Rather, shifts in public opinion are often caused by the undecideds, the indifferent people, becoming convinced of either side of the argument. The net deterioration in public opinion about European integration is primarily the result of indifferent people becoming Eurosceptic, rather than pro-Europeans changing sides. If this holds, then decreasing amounts of indifferent people means that fewer people will change their minds based on future events. We may see the emergence of a consolidated public opinion about European integration, which is fairly balanced: with approximately equal amounts of pro-European and Eurosceptic EU citizens. This implies crises may have an inoculation effect on public opinion, where each subsequent crisis has less effect on public opinion and citizens' trust, because the previous ones have already reduced the amount of indifferent citizens who could be easily swayed either way. Future research into crises should investigate this inoculation hypothesis further.

Drawing on postfunctionalist theory, this chapter identifies a long-term trend showing disappearing indifference about European integration. The percentage of people responding that they do not know whether they are optimistic about the EU, whether they have a positive image of the EU or whether they tend to trust EU institutions steadily declines. Crises may have a catalyzing effect on this trend, but it fits a longer trend of politicization of European integration that unfolds over decades, rather than years. EU citizens are increasingly aware of the EU and its influence in their daily lives. As Europe fills the news in positive and negative ways, citizens develop opinions, views, and feelings about the EU. This decreasing indifference is not merely the result of more general political sophistication or education of the EU population. When we compare trends in trust in EU institutions with trends in trust in national and non-state institutions, it shows clearly that the level of indifference concerning the EU drops considerably faster than the indifference about other institutions. This decreasing indifference in itself has implications for future developments in public opinion. It stands to reason that indifferent people can be more easily swayed one way or the other depending on events and media coverage. Once citizens have made up their minds about whether they see the EU in positive or negative light, it is likely that they are not swayed that easily anymore. If this is true, then decreasing indifference should go together with decreasing changes in net support for European integration. The more citizens develop an opinion about the EU, the less specific events will affect public opinion. Most longitudinal studies of public opinion to date have focused on net support for European integration, which is the percentage of EU supporters minus the percentage of EU opponents. They report a general drop in EU support or rising Euroscepticism, ignoring the "don't know" answers, as is often done in public opinion research. Analyzing the "don't knows," however, shows that changes in net support for European integration is to a large extent the result of a reduction of the percentage of indifferent people making place for more Eurosceptics than it is of pro-Europeans switching sides.

What does this imply for the EU itself and the various scenarios for future integration outlined in the introduction to this Handbook? The rebound in public opinion implies that the EU is unlikely to break up completely, as long as it manages to survive the worst of a crisis. Knowing that public opinion becomes more positive again when the EU manages to get itself out of the headlines of crisis-focused newspapers, provides an additional incentive for EU institutions to do "whatever it takes" to make it through the storm. At the same time, should future studies confirm the consolidation of public opinion thesis developed here, then the most likely scenario for future integration is a continuation of *muddling through*. As pro-Europeans and Eurosceptics hold each other in balance, neither major leaps forward in the integration process nor reversals of major accomplishments will be able to make it through the many checks and balances and veto points in EU decision-making. No one can predict the future, but based on the analysis of public opinion presented in this chapter, that is the most credible scenario.

A number of caveats need to be made, however. First, this chapter takes note that long-term trends are hard to assess, given that Eurobarometer stopped asking people whether they support membership of the EU and whether they think their country has benefitted from EU membership. The fact that the survey stopped asking these questions in the middle of the crisis should raise eyebrows and question the independence of Eurostat. Could it be that EU officials instructed Eurobarometer to stop asking these questions out of fear for negative results? Some critical investigation into the drafting process of Eurobarometer questions and the impact of crises on the survey design is warranted. Yet, insightful questions are still contained in Eurobarometer and their results have at least face validity. While a healthy dose of skepticism toward Eurobarometer seems warranted, it remains a very valuable tool for those of us interested in EU public opinion.

As a second caveat, I need to point out that this chapter has solely focused on aggregate descriptive trends. Careful checks on the impact of crises on individual citizens' opinion are warranted. Without multivariate analysis, this chapter is not able to rule out spurious correlation. It is especially daunting to corroborate the long-term effects of crises on citizens' indifference, given that it unlikely shows accurately in short-term panel surveys. While such words of caution are necessary, the choice made in this chapter also contains the critical note that too much focus on multivariate explanation in the discipline risks overlooking the general descriptive trends. In critically appraising such general trends often lies the potential to generate new, or fine-tune existing, theory. Finally, of course, we need to critically investigate how much time needs to pass by before we can say anything about long-term effects of crises. Is a span of three to five years after the height of a crisis enough to say something about lasting effects? Future research will have to answer that question.

References

Anderson, C. J., & Hecht, J. D. (2018). The Preference for Europe: Public Opinion about European Integration Since 1952. *European Union Politics, 19*(4), 617–638.

Bølstad, J. (2015). Dynamics of European Integration: Public Opinion in the Core and Periphery. *European Union Politics, 16*(1), 23–44.

Citrin, J. (1974). The Political Relevance of Trust in Government. *American Political Science Review, 68*(3), 973–988.

Clements, B., Nanou, K., & Verney, S. (2014). 'We No Longer Love You, But We Don't Want to Leave You': The Eurozone Crisis and Popular Euroscepticism in Greece. *Journal of European Integration, 36*(3), 247–265.

Converse, J. M. (1976). Predicting No Opinion in the Polls. *Public Opinion Quarterly, 40*(4), 515–530.

Converse, P. E. (1970). Attitudes and Non-attitudes: Continuation of a Dialogue. In E. R. Tufte (Ed.), *The Quantitative Analysis of Social Problems* (pp. 168–169). Reading, MA: Addison Wesley.

De Vries, C. E. (2011). EU Issue Voting: Asset or Liability? How European Integration Affects Parties' Electoral Fortunes. *European Union Politics, 11*(1), 89–117.

De Wilde, P., Leupold, A., & Schmidtke, H. (2016). Introduction: The Differentiated Politicisation of European Governance. *West European Politics, 39*(1), 3–22.

De Wilde, P., & Zürn, M. (2012). Can the Politicization of European Integration Be Reversed? *Journal of Common Market Studies, 50*(S1), 137–153.

Ehrmann, M., Soudan, M., & Stracca, L. (2013). Explaining European Citizens' Trust in the European Central Bank in Normal and Crisis Times. *The Scandinavian Journal of Economics, 115*(3), 781–807.

Eichenberg, R. C., & Dalton, R. J. (1993). Europeans and the European Community: The Dynamics of Public Support for European Integration. *International Organization, 47*(4), 507–534.

Eichenberg, R. C., & Dalton, R. J. (2007). Post-Maastricht Blues: The Transformation of Citizen Support for European Integration, 1973–2004. *Acta Politica, 42*(2/3), 128–152.

Gomez, R. (2015). The Economy Strikes Back: Support for the EU During the Great Recession. *Journal of Common Market Studies, 53*(3), 577–592.

Gora, A. (2018). *Irish Citizens and the Media During the Euro Crisis: An Inter-Arena Approach to Studying the Politicization of the EU*. Ph.D. thesis, Carleton University Ottawa, Ontario.

Gros, D., & Roth, F. (2010). *The Financial Crisis and Citizen Trust in the European Central Bank* (CEPS Working Document No. 334). Available at: https://papers.ssrn.com/sol3/papers.cfm?abstract_id=1650091.

Hardin, R. (2002). *Trust and Trustworthiness*. New York: Russell Sage Foundation.

Hobolt, S. B., & De Vries, C. E. (2016). Turning Against the Union? The Impact of the Crisis on the Eurosceptic Vote in the 2014 European Parliament Elections. *Electoral Studies, 44*: 504–514.

Hooghe, L., & Marks, G. (2005). Calculation, Community and Cues: Public Opinion on European Integration. *European Union Politics, 6*(4), 419–443.

Hooghe, L., & Marks, G. (2009). A Postfunctionalist Theory of European Integration: From Permissive Consensus to Constraining Dissensus. *British Journal of Political Science, 39*(1), 1–23.

Hutter, S., & Grande, E. (2014). Politicizing Europe in the National Electoral Arena: A Comparative Analysis of Five West European Countries, 1970-2010. *Journal of Common Market Studies, 52*(5), 1002–1018.

Inglehart, R., & Reif, K. (1991). Analyzing Trends in West European Opinion: The Role of the Eurobarometer Surveys. In K. Reif & R. Inglehart (Eds.), *Eurobarometer: The Dynamics of European Public Opinion* (pp. 1–26). London: MacMillan.

Jones, E., Kelemen, R. D., & Meunier, S. (2016). Failing Forward? The Euro Crisis and the Incomplete Nature of European Integration. *Comparative Political Studies, 49*(7), 1010–1034.

Kritzinger, S. (2003). The Influence of the Nation-State on Individual Support for the European Union. *European Union Politics, 4*(2), 219–242.

Lindberg, L. N., & Scheingold, S. A. (1970). *Europe's Would-Be Polity: Patterns of Change in the European Community.* Englewood Cliffs, NJ: Prentice-Hall.

McLaren, L. (2007). Explaining Mass-Level Euroscepticism: Identity, Interests, and Institutional Distrust. *Acta Politica, 42*(2/3), 233–251.

Rauh, C. (2016). *A Responsive Technocracy? EU Politicisation and Consumer Policies of the European Commission.* Colchester: ECPR Press.

Schmitter, P. C. (1969). Three Neo-Functional Hypotheses About International Integration. *International Organization, 23*(1), 161–166.

Serricchio, F., Tsakatika, M., & Quaglia, L. (2013). Euroscepticism and the Global Financial Crisis. *Journal of Common Market Studies, 51*(1), 51–64.

Shoemaker, P. J., Eichholz, M., & Skewes, E. A. (2002). Item Nonresponse: Distinguishing Between Don't Know and Refuse. *International Journal of Public Opinion Research, 14*(2), 193–201.

Statham, P., & Trenz, H.-J. (2013). *The Politicization of Europe: Contesting the Constitution in the Mass Media.* Abingdon: Routledge.

Stimson, J. A. (1991). *Public Opinion in America: Moods, Cycles and Swings.* Boulder, CO: Westview Press.

Stoeckel, F. (2013). Ambivalent or Indifferent? Reconsidering the Structure of EU Public Opinion. *European Union Politics, 14*(1), 23–45.

Usherwood, S., & Startin, N. (2013). Euroscepticism as a Persistent Phenomenon. *Journal of Common Market Studies, 51*(1), 1–16.

Van Elsas, E., & Van der Brug, W. (2015). The Changing Relationship Between Left-Right Ideology and Euroscepticism, 1973–2010. *European Union Politics, 16*(2), 194–215.

Van Ingelgom, V. (2014). *Integrating Indifference: A Comparative, Qualitative and Quantitative Approach to the Legitimacy of the European Union.* Colchester: ECPR Press.

Weßels, B. (2007). Discontent and European Identity: Three Types of Euroscepticism. *Acta Politica, 42*(2/3), 287–306.

Zmerli, S., & Van der Meer, T. (2017). *Handbook on Political Trust*. Cheltenham: Edward Elgar.

PART V

Commentaries

CHAPTER 40

A Differentiated European Union

Stefan Gänzle, Benjamin Leruth, and Jarle Trondal

INTRODUCTION

Jean Monnet, the first President of the High Authority, predecessor of the European Commission, famously maintained that "Europe will be forged in crises and will be the sum of the solutions adopted for those crises" (Monnet 1978: 417). Extrapolating on this almost proverbial, but certainly popular and often quoted statement by one of the founding fathers of European integration after Europe's so far largest crisis—World War II—one could intuitively assume that most of the solutions, which have hitherto been propelled in response to crises, would include some form of differentiation by which one or several member states deviate in terms of functionality of integration temporarily or even permanently. As this chapter suggests, differentiation can

---

S. Gänzle (✉) · J. Trondal
Department of Political Science and Management, University of Agder, Kristiansand, Norway
e-mail: stefan.ganzle@uia.no

J. Trondal
e-mail: jarle.trondal@uia.no

B. Leruth
University of Groningen, Groningen, The Netherlands
e-mail: b.j.j.leruth@rug.nl

J. Trondal
ARENA - Centre for European Studies, University of Oslo, Oslo, Norway

© The Author(s) 2021
M. Riddervold et al. (eds.), *The Palgrave Handbook of EU Crises*,
Palgrave Studies in European Union Politics,
https://doi.org/10.1007/978-3-030-51791-5_40

often be causally traced back to crises, albeit not exclusively, yet it should not be equated with 'crisis'.

The migration crisis of 2015 provides just for one example of the most recent large-scale EU crises, when member states could ultimately not agree on a common and long-term response *vis-à-vis* the challenge of migrants arriving from war-torn or economically deserted regions in the Middle East and Sub-Saharan Africa—and thus compromised the existing Dublin arrangements in terms of free movement. Another and perhaps more historical example would be the United Kingdom (UK)'s unwillingness to join a common currency in light of the country experiencing a 'Black Wednesday' in 1992, when the Conservative government lead by John Major was forced, following a speculative attack by the investor George Soros, to withdraw the pound sterling from the European Exchange Rate Mechanism (ERM) after it was unable to keep the pound above the ERM-agreed limits. This only sharpened and accentuated the British resistance, already informed by the UK awkward relationship to the European Community at the time (George 1990), to the projected Economic and Monetary Union (EMU) in Europe, one of the prime examples of differentiation in European integration today. As a consequence, the EU has gradually moved from a system of *relatively* uniform system of integration into a *relatively* differentiated system of integration (Leuffen et al. 2013; Schimmelfennig et al. 2015). Furthermore, Schimmelfennig and Winzen (2019) have pondered the idea whether the EU is not likely to be 'growing ever looser'—mirroring the famous postulate of the preamble of the EU Treaty on the creation of an ever-closer union of states and citizens—as a result of the tremendous growth of differentiation in light of crises.

Crises often, but not always, contribute to evolving forms of differentiation. Europe is abounding in crises today, which are increasingly intertwined and 'wicked' in character. Crisis appears to be here to stay, "to be the new normal for the European Union" (Haughton 2016: 5). The President of the European Commission, Jean-Claude Juncker aptly spoke of a "poly-crisis" (Juncker 2016 quoted in Börzel 2018: 478) in his state of the union address referring to the Eurozone, migration and Ukraine crises among others. Dinan et al. rightly emphasize the "multi-dimensional nature" (2017: 1–15) of crises in the contemporary EU. According to Boin et al. (2005: 3–4), the key properties of crisis include the notions of threat, urgency, and uncertainty—perhaps with the ultimate potential of presenting a tipping point of a historical juncture from the perspective of institutionalist thinking. Not only Jean Monnet, but also scholars of European integration perceive of crises just as "the natural ways of development for the EU" (Ágh 2014: 5). Ultimately, crises emerge toward the backdrop of a continuum composed between the extreme positions of nonexistential and existential threats. One of the editors of this volume has also contributed to thinking about additional concepts, such as turbulence, which complements, but is not identical with the concept of crisis (Ansell et al. 2016). Speaking about governance of organizations facing turbulence, such as the ensemble of the EU, is about how these organizations face governance challenges in situations where events, demands, and support interact in a highly variable, inconsistent, unexpected, and unpredictable manner. As a result, they must act to address situations of dynamic complexity where well-tested solutions may be inadequate and where failure is typically answered with critique. Governance in such circumstances entails balancing adaptability and experimentation—which has also been grasped by scholars of experimentalist governance (Sabel and Zeitlin 2010, 2012)—on the one hand with continuity and resilience on the other. This balancing act implies confronting the ambiguities associated with unruly problems while maintaining existing organizational capacities and functions (Ansell et al. 2016). It is perhaps fair to say that the institutional ensemble of the EU has been well-tested in the past in this regard and accounts among those compound organizations that are well-versed in accommodating both turbulence and crises.

The focus of this chapter is on differentiation: Differentiation and differentiated integration have become the trademark of European integration since the early 1990s. Differentiated integration can be distinguished in terms of internal—solely inside the scope of EU membership (e.g. the eurozone)—and external differentiated integration (e.g. membership in 'Schengen' which also comprises non-EU members such as Norway and Switzerland). In the wake of the cumbersome Brexit process, however, these concepts are now being complemented by differentiated *dis*integration. Thus, we understand differentiation as a holistic term encompassing both (differentiated) integration and disintegration. By this term, we conceive of processes under which a member state withdraws from participation in the process of European integration or under which EU policies are transferred back to member states (Schimmelfennig 2018, 2019). This cannot simply be captured by putting existing theories of European integration into "reverse gear" (see Radaelli and Salter 2019).

Differentiation can take various forms which are often intertwined, such as functional institutional and spatial/territorial as well as temporal differentiation (see Dyson and Sepos 2010). Turning to the EU, differentiated integration can almost be categorized as the 'natural' state of affairs because of the Union's very character as a 'composite polity' and as a 'compound of states'—as famously put in the Maastricht judgment of the German Constitutional Court. European integration is to be perceived as a process and polity borrowing federal(izing) as much as confederal(izing) aspects in terms of its governance. Only few of the EU's competences are exclusive, most being shared with member states or even completely left in the realm of the nation or member state completely. While EU states have morphed from 'nation-states' into 'member states' (Bickerton 2012), they also exhibit traits of hybrid statehood which also implies that they can easily revert to more classical notions of atavistic and autonomy-seeking 'nation statehood'. Turning from the EU's shape of polity to its policies, we find that many of the Community policies—such as the Common Agricultural Policy (CAP) or, more obviously, regional and cohesion policy—often benefitting from windows of opportunity or taking the form of side-payments to member states in order to ferment significant changes. With European integration advancing in a nonlinear way, one may understand differentiation in terms of both a cause and effect of regional integration.

Differentiation in the EU is not a new phenomenon to politics or to political science, neither in the history of other systems of regional integration nor in European integration itself. With regard to the latter, there has been a burgeoning literature devoted to the study of differentiation ever since the phenomenon became more pressing in the aftermath of the Treaty of Maastricht, one of the EU's major leaps in terms of integration. There are also several examples of disintegration—tentatively conceived as withdrawal from membership—that have occurred over time: Algeria (1962), Greenland (1985), and Saint Barthélémy (2012) have departed from the European Community/Union albeit for very different reasons (see Gänzle 2019).

Our chapter will first provide a short sketch of the development of differentiation in European integration; second it will turn to explore the scholarly debate *vis-à-vis* 'differentiated Europe'. How has differentiation been embraced as important aspect of European integration? Third, we charter the confines of differentiated (dis)integration as a new study field in European studies, and we argue that the Brexit as a crisis process provides a key instance of—and cause of—(differentiated) disintegration.

Differentiation—A Genuine and Persistent Feature of European Integration

As succinctly shown by Leuffen et al. (2013: 26), differentiation has increased in the course of European integration. In the early 1950s, integration was limited both functionally and territorially, but highly unified. It was only when the Community started to conclude association agreements with third countries in the wake of the Treaty of Rome of 1957 that a process of horizontal differentiation took off. Vertical differentiation increased at a time when new policies such as monetary and foreign policy cooperation in the framework of the European Political Cooperation (EPC) started life outside the Community framework at the intergovernmental level. In particular, with the advent of the European Council as the meeting of heads of state and government, and alternate and increasingly competitive center merged—outside the supranational scope. A major leap in differentiation occurred in the 1980s when a group of front-runner member states gathered and spear-headed cooperation in the realm of 'Schengen'. The agreement was the first of its kind signed by a limited group of pioneering members—at least according to the self-understanding of the heads of state and government involved. The Schengen agreement established an opt-in mechanism allowing for other countries to join in a later point of time. Monetary integration, which would start again at the end of the 1980s, established a reverse mechanism allowing member states for opt-outs.

The Treaty of Maastricht eventually contractually endorsed this new format of vertical differentiation by way of its pillar structure, where each of the pillars—Community, external and internal security—would go hand in hand with different integrationist logics and hence forms of vertical differentiation.

These developments have been proven remarkably stable, resembling the scenario of *muddling through* from Chapter 1 of this volume. Both opt-ins and opt-outs have been constant features in use by the EU since the early 1990s. The Treaty of Amsterdam adopted in 1997 eventually established the instrument of enhanced cooperation allowing a small group of member states to move ahead with integration in specific areas. Subsequent treaties, such as the Treaty of Nice, have also expanded the use of tailor-made protocols and legal clauses applying to individual member states and securing specific prerogative and exceptions. The Treaty of Lisbon eventually dismantled the pillar structure of the treaty, but continued to 'differentiate between policy-specific decision-making procedures' (Leuffen et al. 2013: 27). In terms of horizontal differentiation, the 1990s and 2002 have been characterized by a tremendous growth of differentiation in terms of membership: First in terms of several rounds of enlargements (1995, 2004, 2007, and 2013) pushing the numbers of members from 12 to 28. Second, it not only diversified the relationship with non-EU partners in the so-called developing world (e.g. Economic Partnership agreements, but created a wealth of different horizontal–vertical arrangements often blurring the line between EU members and non-members. In 1994, the European Economic Area (EEA) concluded with Iceland, Liechtenstein and Norway effectively turned these countries in quasi-members of the EU. Other bilateral agreements (e.g. Switzerland), Stabilization and Association Agreements with countries of the Western Balkan, as well as deep free trade and association agreements signed with countries of the European Neighborhood Policy and enhanced partnership agreements followed suit.

It seems fair to assume that none of these developments will go away easily and cede its place to a resuming unifying force in European integration. Thus, European integration is likely to be characterized by both increasing integration on the one hand and differentiation on the other. This leads us to the question how we need to theorize these developments in particular in light of sustained crises as well as turbulence. We will turn to this question in the following section and start with a reflection of how differentiation has been dealt with by the scholarly world and what the implications of expanding the scope of integration to effective disintegration ultimately holds for Europe's future political order.

REFLECTIONS ON DIFFERENTIATION IN EUROPEAN INTEGRATION

Most importantly, differentiation should not be, as already shown, just understood as yet another form of or response to crisis in general. The process of European integration is abundant of examples of fundamental crises, such as the ones triggered by the failure of the European Defense Community in 1954, the empty chair crisis of 1965/66 or the 'euro-sclerosis' of the 1970 in the past—or the Eurozone since 2009/10, Ukraine since 2013/14, and the Brexit crisis since 2016. Differentiation is not a crisis per se; it rather might be understood as a *variant* of integration and could partly be a response to crisis (Ansell et al. 2016). The following section outlines how differentiation has been explored in various fields of literature and research over the past two decades.

The First Stage (1990s and Early 2000s): Discovering Differentiated Integration

While certain limited elements of (legal) differentiation are present in the Treaty of Rome (see e.g. Hanf 2001), the idea of differentiation as a genuine strategy of integration finds its roots in the Tindemans (1975) report, which laid the foundations of a 'multi-speed Europe' without explicitly mentioning this notion (Stubb 1996). The broad concept of differentiation appeared for the first time in the primary Community law in 1986, as stated in Article 8c of the Single European Act (now Article 27 of the Treaty on the Functioning of the European Union [TFEU]):

> When drawing up its proposals with a view to achieving the objectives set out in Article 7a [now Article 26 TFEU, author's note], the Commission shall take into account the extent of the effort that certain economies showing differences in development will have to sustain for the establishment of the internal market and it may propose appropriate provisions. If these provisions take the form of derogations, they must be of a temporary nature and must cause the least possible disturbance to the functioning of the internal market.

Despite a few publications based on the Tindemans Report and the Single European Act written in the 1980s (Wallace et al. 1983; Ehlermann 1984; Grabitz 1984; Wallace and Ridley 1985), academic discussions on differentiated integration arose in the early 1990s for three main reasons. First, several opt-outs from the Maastricht Treaty were granted to the UK and Denmark in 1993, leading toward more institutionalized differentiation and raising questions on the future of European integration. Second, the end of the Cold War opened the door to the future 'big bang enlargement', creating new challenges for the future of European integration with the potential diversification of national interests (Centre for Economic Policy Research 1995). Finally, shortly after the ratification of the Maastricht Treaty, outlined the fact that "the next Intergovernmental Conference will (and should) open the door for more possibilities of non-traditional differentiation". Accordingly, discussions on the constitutionalization of differentiated integration in the Treaty of Amsterdam arose, and led to the introduction of the enhanced cooperation mechanism which, to date, has only been used in three cases (divorce law in

2010; unitary patent in 2013; and property regimes of international couples in 2016; see Philippart and Edwards 1999; Fabbrini 2012).

It is in this context that the first influent academic publications on differentiated integration emerged. Often used interchangeably with the notion of 'flexible integration' (see e.g. Kölliker 2001, 2006; Warleigh 2002; Holzinger and Schimmelfennig 2012), diverging views on the nature of this 'phenomenon' has led to the emergence of various definitions. Not surprisingly, a lack of conceptual consensus characterizes the first generation of academic literature; some leading observers even avoid offering an explicit definition on the term (see for instance Warleigh 2002; Andersen and Sitter 2006; de Neve 2007). One of the first attempts to grasp this 'moving target' was made by Alexander Stubb (1996: 283), who defined differentiated integration as "the general mode of integration strategies which try to reconcile heterogeneity within the European Union". Stubb's study is also the first attempt to conceptualize differentiated integration, by listing about 30 models of differentiation and classifying the mechanism into three categories linked to general concepts of European integration: 'time' (or 'temporal differentiation'), with 'multi-speed Europe' as main concept; 'space' (or 'territorial differentiation'), with 'variable geometry Europe' as the main concept; and 'matter' (or 'sectoral differentiation'), with '*à la carte* Europe' as the main concept. Based on his categorization, Stubb (1997) later summarized the member states' positions on differentiated integration at the 1996 intergovernmental conference: *à la carte* Europe is only favored by the UK; multispeed Europe is perceived as a viable options for all member states besides Greece; and variable geometry dividing the Union into two groups, as France, Germany, Belgium, the Netherlands, Luxembourg, Italy, Finland, Austria, and (to a lesser extent) Sweden favored more territorial flexibility.

In a study of the political dynamics of differentiated integration published in the *European Law Journal*, Walker (1998: 374) was particularly critical and defined it as a 'non-project', which could lead to irreconcilable divergences in terms of managing boundaries between legal orders, political efficacy, democratic credentials, and self-legitimation: "[c]ontingency, ambiguity and disagreement, rather than design, certainty and consensus, are key motifs in the composition of the new differentiated structure". In another influent discussion of the Economic and Monetary Union, Schengen and tax harmonization, Kölliker (2001: 147) found out that temporary differentiated mechanisms can trigger centripetal effects on 'reluctant' member states, but that only applies where policy design can "change the fundamental character of a common pool resource or a public good". One year later, Warleigh (2002: 2) argued that "flexibility offers the most useful means of balancing different (national) interests and thereby allowing progress to be made for (and in) the EU as a whole". The three aforementioned studies demonstrate that this first generation of studies of differentiation was trying to understand its effects on the process of European integration.

During this period, a series of influent case study analyses were also published. These studies were also influenced by the first generation of studies of Europeanization of the nation-state (see Mèny et al. 1996; Olsen 1996; Hanf and Soetendorp 1998; Knill 2001; Zeff and Pirro 2006; Featherstone and Radaelli 2003). Early case studies of differentiation mostly focused on the relations between the Nordic countries and the EU. Mouritzen (1993) was one of the first scholars to work on the Nordic countries as an instance of differentiation. Following the Norwegians' decision not to join the EU in 1994, Egeberg and Trondal (1999: 134) studied the relationship between Norway (as an EEA member state) and the EU; they established that Norway may be "even more sectorally penetrated or harmonized" than other EU members as far as policy harmonization is concerned, meaning that non-membership may still involve a great deal of integration—if not even greater than in the case of some member states. Advancing an organizational approach (see Trondal, this volume), they suggested that differentiated integration could be captured as two 'forms' of affiliation: a territorial form of affiliation between domestic ministries of foreign affairs and the Council, and a sectoral form of affiliation between domestic sectoral ministries and agencies and the EU's executive branch of government. Subsequently, Trondal (2002) conceptually questioned the membership/non-membership dichotomy by suggesting that different parts of member state administration might be connected differently to different parts of the EU institutional fabric (see below). The argument implies that the structure of the European Commission, to which the Norwegian government is coupled, works according to a sectoral logic that can be derived from its main principles of organizational specialization; i.e. purpose and function. The Commission structure may thus underpin tendencies of national executive fragmentation. The Council structure, on the other hand, from which the Norwegian government is decoupled, fosters a geographical or territorial logic that encourages horizontal coordination efforts in the member states, and the formulation of coordinated national interests. Thus, those who argued that sectorization and a weakening of the center of the nation-state follows from enhanced Europeanization (e.g. Siedentopf and Ziller 1988; Kassim and Wright 1991; Burnham and Maor 1995; Wessels and Rometsch 1996; Dehousse 1997) as well as those who observed a reassertion of the center of the nation-state (e.g. Moravcsik 1993; Milward 1996) were both partly right. Yet, in an EEA country, the integrative force of the Council structure is structurally absent, and thus the first observation is mostly observed (Egeberg and Trondal 1999).

Petersen (1998) studied Denmark's integration policy in what he called a 'dilemma' between influence capability and stress sensitivity. Gstöhl (2002a, b) also published studies on the so-called 'reluctant Europeans', i.e. European countries that did not join the EU (i.e. Norway and Switzerland) or did not join the Economic and Monetary Union (i.e. Sweden). Much like Kölliker, she also argued for the need to theorize differentiated integration following the ratification of the Treaty of Amsterdam (Gstöhl 2000).

Ingebritsen (1998) sparked a debate on the reasons why some Nordic states resisted EU membership and others do not. She argued that international security policy considerations and the political influence of leading economic sectors—in the case of Norway the oil industry—are the prime causes for dividing the Nordic states in their relations with the EU. Neumann (2003) as well as Tiilikainen (2003) have challenged this point of departure and emphasized the role of cultural identity and the different historical and political orientations of the five Nordic countries as explanatory variables for differential patterns of Nordic accession and association. Interestingly, and unlike this particular interest on the Nordic countries, there were few country-specific studies focusing on the UK as a case for differentiated integration, one exception being the UK-based Centre for Economic Policy Research's (1995) extensive, 191-pages long report advocating flexibility to shape the future of European integration.

The Second Stage: The Eurozone and 'Big Bang Enlargement' Studies

The introduction of the third stage of the EMU and the 2004 'big bang enlargement' effectively led to an increase in temporal differentiation, and to the emergence of what many will dub a 'two-speed Europe' (see e.g. Piris 2012). By 2010, more than half of EU policies were implemented in different ways. Majone (2009: 205) acknowledged that the EU was evolving into a "number of, often overlapping, state groupings established for cooperation in a variety of fields" (see also Jensen and Slapin 2012). During this period, academic studies extended the work conducted by the first generation of scholars by improving the theoretical and empirical depth of what started to become a subfield of European studies.

Conceptually, many studies focused on the scope and limits of differentiated integration in the EU. Andersen and Sitter (2006) asked 'how much differentiation can the EU accommodate?' and proposed a typology of European integration with four models: homogeneous integration; aligned integration; deviant integration; and autonomous integration. They argued that differentiation is now "a common and normal phenomenon" and that its study should also include formal and informal arrangements (ibid.: 327). De Neve (2007: 516) asked whether differentiated integration is reshaping "the European polity into what increasingly resembles a multi-layered European Onion" and questioned whether there could be 'too much' differentiated integration (an issue that is still being debated in a post-Brexit context). Following the first Irish vote on the Lisbon Treaty, Jensen and Slapin (2012) focused on the efficiency of what they call the 'multi-speed approach' and created a model under which opt-outs could lead to cascades (i.e. a 'domino effect' under which member states opt out because of other member states' decisions to opt out; with the authors using Sweden's informal EMU opt-out as a case study) or no cascades (with the authors using Schengen and the Social Charter as case studies). The latter study, however, reflects some of the semantic confusion in the existing literature, as it contradicts Stubb's original categorization of differentiated integration by using 'multi-speed integration' as a synonym of differentiation (see also Leruth and Lord 2015). The varied ideas on differentiation led Johan P. Olsen (2007) to generalize the question on what kind of political order Europe was in search of. The EU was depicted as "a conceptual battleground and an institutional building site" (Olsen 2010: 81). The EU was also viewed as a compound and unsettled system consisting of a varied mix of organizational forms, governance patterns, and ideas about legitimate forms and speeds of integration. Institutional differentiation was understood as "new institutional spheres have split off from older ones and developed their own identities" (ibid.: 142) and where political order consists of relatively autonomous institutional sub-systems with separate actors, structures, sources of legitimacy and resources. The overall institutional ecology was seen as consisting of nested and coevolving institutions that yet enjoy relative mutual independence.

During this period, Dyson and Sepos (2010: 4) edited one of the first books which focused on differentiated integration as a whole. The editors defined it as "... the process whereby European States, or sub-units, opt to move at different speeds and/or towards different objectives with regard to common policies, by adopting different formal and informal arrangements, whether inside or outside the EU treaty framework, and by assuming different rights and obligations". This extends Kölliker's definition by including "formal and informal arrangements" in the framework of differentiation, which were first introduced by Andersen and Sitter (2006). Nevertheless, both definitions only emphasize the 'demand' side of differentiated integration by member states, and not its 'supply' side (i.e. the power of supranational institutions to shape European integration). Dyson and Sepos' book contains a series of useful empirical studies which demonstrate the complexity of differentiated integration. Other influent empirical analyses published during this period focused on differentiated integration within specific policies and/or policy areas. These include a special issue of the *Journal of European Integration* on Euro-outsiders (Miles 2005); the impact of non-Eurozone membership (e.g. Marcussen 2009); opt-outs in Justice and Home Affairs (Adler-Nissen 2009, 2011, 2014; Balzacq and Hadfield 2012); the Single Market (e.g. Howarth and Sadeh 2010); and the Common Foreign and Security Policy (e.g. Lavenex 2011). During this period, two influential research networks (CONNEX and EUROGOV) concluded that the EU was characterized by multiple—and thus differentiated—'modes' of governance (e.g. Héritier and Rhodes 2011). This period also saw different subfields of social sciences and law entering the study field of European integration which led to several 'turns' in the literature— such as the constructivist (e.g. Risse 2000; Checkel 2007), the governance (e.g. Kohler-Koch and Rittberger 2006), or the public administration turns (e.g. Egeberg 2006; Trondal 2007).

The Third Phase: Post-Lisbon Studies and New Concepts

With the Great Recession of 2007–2008, the EU entered a new multifaceted crisis (Leruth 2017). The future of European integration became an increasingly debated issue, and so did the issue of differentiated integration. The possibility of scenarios such as Grexit (i.e. Greece leaving either the EU or the eurozone) and Brexit (re)emerged during the Euro crisis, and Eurosceptic political parties became increasingly prominent across Europe. And so did the potential for European disintegration (Vollaard 2014; Leruth et al. 2018).

The third generation of studies on differentiated integration has been dominated by what one could refer to as a 'Swiss-German' school, with scholars attempting to 'tidy up' existing literature. In a research agenda section of the *Journal of European Public Policy*, Holzinger and Schimmelfennig (2012: 293) outlined some of the existing shortcomings in this field of study: "empirical analysis has been limited to a few important cases of treaty law (such as EMU and Schengen), but there are no comprehensive data sets". They highlighted that differentiation always has territorial and sectoral impacts (see Egeberg and Trondal 1999), and that purely functional conceptions are not included in this categorization. They suggest, in turn, a categorization into six dimensions: (1) permanent vs. temporary differentiation; (2) territorial vs. purely functional differentiation; (3) differentiation across nation-states vs. multilevel differentiation; (4) differentiation takes place within the EU treaties vs. outside the EU treaties; (5) decision-making at EU level vs. at regime level (i.e. intergovernmental decisions); and (6) only for member states vs. also for non-member states/areas outside the EU territory.

The authors also underline that empirical examples can be found for almost all models, suggesting that "differentiated integration comes in an astonishing variety of forms and … the concepts of differentiated integration can and should be used systematically to describe these forms and their frequency" (ibid.: 297). The categorization offered by the authors provides a meticulous way of analyzing differentiated integration, which reflects the complex reality of European integration.

Another attempt at categorizing differentiated integration was made by Leuffen et al. (2013), describing the EU is a system of differentiated integration, i.e. "one Europe with a single organizational and member state core and a territorial extension that varies by function" (Schimmelfennig et al. 2015: 767). Basing their study on primary law, they start from the assumption that "the EU potentially covers the entire range of policies, but that each policy varies with regard to the level of centralization and the territorial extension" (Leuffen et al. 2013: 12). They determine that differentiated integration varies primarily along two dimensions: the variation in the level of centralization across policies (*vertical differentiation*), and the variation in territorial extension across policies (*horizontal differentiation*). Furthermore, they classify horizontal differentiation into four sub-categories: (1) no horizontal differentiation, where all EU rules apply uniformly to all EU member states (e.g. pre-Maastricht Europe); (2) external differentiation, where EU rules apply uniformly to all EU member states, but non-member states can also adopt these rules (e.g. the European Economic Area); (3) internal differentiation, where EU rules do not apply uniformly to all EU member states (e.g. Denmark through the Edinburgh Agreement or the enhanced cooperation procedure); and (4) internal and external differentiation, where EU rules from which some EU member states opted out, while non-member states opted in (e.g. Schengen).

Between 2012 and 2017, Frank Schimmelfennig and his team at ETH Zurich published a series of in-depth studies of differentiated integration, such as constitutional differentiation (Schimmelfennig and Winzen 2014), the impact of EU enlargement on differentiated integration (Schimmelfennig 2014; Schimmelfennig and Winzen 2017), and the impact of differentiation on EU governance (Schimmelfennig 2016a, b). Further studies also focused on differentiated integration within EU legislation, which demonstrate the increasing complexity of EU law and law-making (e.g. Kroll and Leuffen 2015; Duttle et al. 2017). Two special issues on differentiated integration were also published in this period. In 2015, a *Journal of European Public Policy* special issue edited by Leruth and Lord (2015) reflected on the evolution of the literature on differentiated integration, and included further theoretical and empirical papers reflecting on the future of the EU (see e.g. Fossum 2015; Lord 2015; Warleigh-Lack 2015). One year later, another special issue of *West European Politics* argued that a differentiated EU leads to differentiated politicization across times, countries, and settings (de Wilde et al. 2016).

In sum, this third 'generation' of studies extended the scope of differentiated integration, giving further theoretical and empirical depth to the debate and suggested conceptual ways of studying differentiation. By that time, it appeared clear that differentiation should be considered as a persistent and 'normal' feature of European integration (Leruth and Lord 2015). Yet, the study of differentiation still harbored a myriad of concepts and definitions of the subject as well as established theories to explain.

Toward a Fourth Stage: A Post-Brexit EU

The EU is at a turn in course of integration. As so is the scholarly literature. The UK's vote to leave the EU and the British government's subsequent decision to trigger Article 50 means that the Union is now facing a series of unprecedented challenges in uncharted territories. As a result, scholars have attempted to explain how and why 'Brexit' happened, as well as its most likely consequences for the future of the EU. For the first time in the history of the EU, one country chose to leave the Union, thus leading not only to differentiated European integration but toward a form of European *dis*integration. Yet, the existing literature on European disintegration is relatively scarce, mostly because of the lack of empirical evidence pre-Brexit (Zielonka 2014). In commentaries published shortly after the referendum, Jones (2016) and

Rosamond (2016), among others, emphasize the need to fill this new gap in the literature by developing ideas of European disintegration.

To date, one of the only articles that attempted to 'explain' European disintegration is the one written by Vollaard (2014) in the context of the Euro crisis. The author suggests that existing studies of differentiated integration (such as Leuffen et al. 2013) "only explain why some Member States do not join all integrative steps, and not whether the EU could become *less* integrated" (Vollaard 2014: 1143). Yet, by combining these insights on European disintegration with differentiated integration studies, it is possible to categorize Brexit as a ground-breaking case of *differentiated disintegration*. Conceptually, differentiated integration and disintegration involves merely variation on those dimensions that are thought to capture the phenomenon.

Drawing on the aforementioned work of Leuffen et al. (2013) on differentiation, differentiated disintegration can be defined as the general mode of processes and strategies under which a member state withdraws from participation in the process of European integration or under which EU policies are transferred back to member states (see also Leruth et al. 2019a, b). This concept of differentiated disintegration might take shape within the next couple of years, depending on the outcome of negotiations between the EU and the UK. Interestingly though, this discussion applies states as unit of analysis and does thus not disaggregate them into their constituent parts. The public administration turn in EU studies has done so, yet, the differentiated (dis)integration literature has not attended much to this public administration literature when conceptualizing and mapping differentiated European integration. One could imagine, for example, that administrative units such as agencies withdraw from cooperation within a member state, or that a member state withdraws from formal membership in the EU while some domestic agencies keep their membership in EU administrative networks (see Chapter 10 in this volume). This idea is captured by the public administration approach to European integration that sees the Union as consisting of interconnected sets of agencies, ministries, and regulatory networks (e.g. Egeberg 2006; Bauer and Trondal 2015; Heidbreder 2015; Knill and Bauer 2016).

Conclusions

EU studies have mirrored its unit of analysis through history (Rosamond 2000). With the advent of crisis in Europe EU scholars have become increasingly occupied with understanding causes and effects of crisis. Differentiation is one such effect of crisis. With prospects for ever more differentiated disintegration, new questions and scenarios arise for the Union and for the field of enquiry, and old ones have reappeared. The three scenarios outlined in Chapter 1 of this volume have become central in thinking about the consequences of crisis: *Breaking down, muddling through*, or *heading forward*. This chapter has demonstrated that much like the use of differentiated integration, academic studies of the phenomenon have evolved considerably over the past twenty years. From the Maastricht Treaty to the European Commission's White Paper on the Future of Europe of 2017 (EurActiv 2017), scholars have attempted to theorize and conceptualize a 'moving target'. Given the wide range of publications related to differentiation and following the Brexit vote, it is fair to consider differentiated disintegration as a next major theme in EU studies. While at least three sets of ideas as developed in Chapter 1 envisage, future EU studies should treat the dependent variable as a full continuum—from the possibility of *breaking down* to *heading forward* (Börzel 2018). Moreover, we should expect the study of European disintegration to largely follow existing theoretical threads within EU studies. The interesting avenue for future theorizing thus lies in determining the conditions under which each of the three scenarios outlined in Chapter 1 plays out in the case of differentiated (dis)integration. Even more, theorizing differentiated (dis)integration is likely to go beyond EU studies. First, studies of differentiated disintegration might learn from ideas about how organizations emerge, rise, and die, building on organizational theories on 'meta-governance' (Egeberg and Trondal 2018). Differentiated disintegration is thus seen as *muddling through* and contingent on existing organizational formats (Scenario 2). Scenario 1 might be explained by rational choice-based perspectives suggesting that the EU as we know it will *break up* due to member states' unwillingness to deal collectively with crises (Introduction this volume; Hodson and Puetter 2018). Moreover, both Scenarios 1 and 3 might be informed by historical institutionalism where crises may be seen as unlocking path-dependencies and institutional equilibria that trigger the potential for profound change. For example, crises may be viewed as situations of punctuation where more (1) or less (3) integration are perceived as effective solutions to address new challenges, leading to the delegation of more or less powers to EU institutions (Jones and Baumgartner 2005). Acknowledging that the theoretical menu is larger than this section can cover, the research challenge is mid-range theorizing in which scope conditions for each idea are specified and probed.

Following Scenario 1 from Chapter 1, neorealist perspectives might expect Brexit to *undermine and fragment* the EU project. To the extent that member states' willingness to agree on common action in the face of Brexit fades, EU policies might be increasingly oriented toward bolstering the member states' common *interests*. Also liberal integovernmentalist approaches might expect crisis such as Brexit to challenge a common EU project, unless member states expect that economic gains of common policies outweigh expected costs of working together. In general, scenario 1 would see member states as likely to share sovereignty or contribute to redistribution when faced with an EU skeptic population, and would strive to remain in power to veto future attempt to pool sovereignty.

As outlined in Chapter 1, the second scenario suggests how the EU will *muddle through* crisis through path-dependent and incremental responses that draw on preexisting institutional architectures: Preexisting institutions may thus serve as an important source of stability in the face of Brexit, enabling the EU to ride out short-term stressful times. Brexit would by this line of scholarship be profoundly path-dependent, structurally conditioned by preexisting organizations and institutions. As such, differentiated and disintegration would be assumed to be profoundly influenced by the present organizational-institutional architecture.

Scenario 3, as outlined in Chapter 1 to this volume, suggests that crises such as Brexit may unlock and trigger the potential for profound change. For example, Brixt may be viewed as situations where more integration is perceived as effective solutions to address new challenges, leading to the delegation of new powers to EU institutions in a variety of policy fields. Brexit may entail a questioning of preexisting governance arrangements in the EU and thus generate windows of opportunity for more integration in which it creates opportunity structures for *heading forward*. Contemporary examples include the rise of new European Union financial surveillance agencies, the structuring of the new EU banking union, and the emergent European energy union (Bauer and Trondal 2015). Although Scenario 1 suggests that crisis may lead to more integration, it does not specify what this might imply in terms of concrete institutional designs. That is an empirical question to be analyzed, but also a theoretical puzzle that might be informed by Scenario 2.

References

Adler-Nissen, R. (2009). Behind the Scenes of Differentiated Integration: Circumventing National Opt-Outs in Justice and Home Affairs. *Journal of European Public Policy*, 16(1), 62–80.

Adler-Nissen, R. (2011). Opting Out of an Ever Closer Union: The Integration Doxa and the Management of Sovereignty. *West European Politics*, 34(5), 1092–1113.

Adler-Nissen, R. (2014). *Opting Out of the European Union: Diplomacy, Sovereignty and European Integration*. Cambridge: Cambridge University Press.

Ágh, A. (2014). Decline of Democracy in East-Central Europe: The Last Decade as the Lost Decade in Democratization. *Journal of Comparative Politics*, 7(2), 4–33.

Andersen, S. S., & Sitter, N. (2006). Differentiated Integration: What Is It and How Much Can the EU Accommodate? *Journal of European Integration*, 28(4), 313–330.

Ansell, C., Trondal, J., & Ogard, M. (2016). *Governance in Turbulent Times*. Oxford: Oxford University Press.

Balzacq, T., & Hadfield, A. (2012). Differentiation and Trust: Prüm and the Institutional Design of EU Internal Security. *Cooperation and Conflict*, 47(4), 539–561.

Bauer, M. W., & Trondal, J. (2015). *The Palgrave Handbook of the European Administrative System*. Houndmills: Palgrave Macmillan.

Bickerton, C. (2012). *European Integration: From Nation-States to Member States*. Oxford: Oxford University Press.

Boin, A., Hart, P. T., Stern, E., & Sundelius, B. (2005). *The Politics of Crisis Management*. Cambridge: Cambridge University Press.

Börzel, T. A. (2018). Researching the EU (Studies) into Demise. *Journal of European Public Policy*, 25(3), 475–485.

Burnham, J., & Maor, M. (1995). Converging Administrative Systems: Recruitment and Training in EC Member-States. *Journal of European Public Policy,* 2(2), 185–204.

Centre for Economic Policy Research. (1995). Flexible Integration: Towards a More Effective and Democratic Europe. In *Monitoring European Integration 6.* London: Centre for Economic Policy Research.

Checkel, J. T. (2007). *International Institutions and Socialization in Europe.* Cambridge: Cambridge University Press.

de Neve, J.-E. (2007). The European Onion? How Differentiated Integration Is Reshaping the EU. *Journal of European Integration,* 29(4), 503–551.

de Wilde, P., Leupold, A., & Schmidtke, H. (2016). Introduction: The Differentiated Politicisation of European Governance. *West European Politics,* 39(1), 3–22.

Dehousse, R. (1997). European Integration and the Nation-State. In M. Rhodes, P. Heywood, & V. Wright (Eds.), *Developments in West European Politics.* Houndmills: Macmillan Press.

Dinan, D., Nugent, N., & Paterson, W. E. (2017). A Multi-Dimensional Crisis. In D. Dinan, N. Nugent, & W. E. Paterson (Eds.), *The European Union in Crisis* (pp. 1–15). Basingstoke: Palgrave Macmillan.

Duttle, T., Holzinger, K., Malang, T., Schläubli, T., Schimmelfennig, F., & Winzen, T. (2017). Opting Out from European Union Legislation: The Differentiation of Secondary Law. *Journal of European Public Policy,* 24(3), 406–428.

Dyson, K., & Sepos, A. (2010). Differentiation as Design Principle and as Tool in the Political Management of European Integration. In K. Dyson & A. Sepos (Eds.), *Which Europe? The Politics of Differentiated Integration* (pp. 3–23). Basingstoke: Palgrave Macmillan.

Ehlermann, C. D. (1984). 'How Flexible is Community Law? An Unusual Approach to the Concept of "Two Speeds". *Michigan Law Journal,* 4(30), 246–270.

Egeberg, M. (2006). *Multilevel Union Administration.* Houndmills: Palgrave Macmillan.

Egeberg, M., & Trondal, J. (1999). Differentiated Integration in Europe: The Case of EEA Country, Norway. *Journal of Common Market Studies,* 37(1), 133–142.

Egeberg, M., & Trondal, J. (2018). *An Organizational Approach to Public Governance.* Oxford: Oxford University Press.

EurActiv. (2017). *Juncker's Real Scenario' Is Multi-Speed Europe* [online]. Available at: http://www.euractiv.com/section/future-eu/news/junckers-re; http://www.euractiv.com/section/future-eu/news/junckers-real-scenario-is-multi-speed-eur ope/; http://www.euractiv.com/section/future-eu/news/junckers-real-scenario-is-multi-speed-europe/"l-scenario-is-multi-speed-europe/. Accessed 17 Mar 2017.

Fabbrini, F. (2012). The Enhanced Cooperation Procedure: A Study in Multispeed Integration. *Centro Studi sul Federalismo Research Paper October 2012.* Torino: Centro Studi sul Federalismo.

Featherstone, K., & Radaelli, C. M. (2003). *The Politics of Europeanization.* Oxford: Oxford University Press.

Fossum, J. E. (2015). Democracy and Differentiation in Europe. *Journal of European Public Policy,* 22(6), 799–815.

Gänzle, S. (2019). Differentiated (Dis)Integration in Europe and Beyond: A Historical and Comparative Perspective. In S. Gänzle, B. Leruth, & J. Trondal (Eds.), *Differentiated (Dis)integration in Light of Brexit: What Future for European Integration?* (pp. 202–218). London: Routledge.

Gänzle, S., Leruth, B., & Trondal, J. (2019). *Differentiated (Dis)integration in Light of Brexit: What Future for European Integration?* London: Routledge.

George, S. (1990). *An Awkward Partner: Britain and the European Community*. Oxford: Oxford University Press.

Grabitz, E. (1984). *Abgestufte Integration: Eine Alternative zum herkömmlichen Integrationskonzept?* Strasbourg: N.P. Engel Verlag.

Gstöhl, S. (2000). The European Union After Amsterdam: Towards a Theoretical Approach to (Differentiated) Integration. In M. Green Cowles & M. Smith (Eds.), *The State of the European Union 5: Risks, Reform, Resistance, and Revival* (pp. 42–63). Oxford: Oxford University Press.

Gstöhl, S. (2002a). *Reluctant Europeans: Norway, Sweden, and Switzerland in the Process of Integration*. London: Lynne Rienner.

Gstöhl, S. (2002b). Scandinavia and Switzerland: Small, Successful and Stubborn Towards the EU. *Journal of European Public Policy, 9*(4), 529–549.

Hanf, D. (2001). Flexibility Clauses in the Founding Treaties, from Rome to Nice. In B. De Witte, D. Hanf, & E. Vos (Eds.), *The Many Faces of Differentiation in EU Law*. Oxford: Hart Publishing.

Hanf, K., & Soetendorp, B. (1998). *Adapting to European Integration*. London: Longman.

Haughton, T. (2016). Is Crisis the New Normal? The European Union in 2015. *Journal of Common Market Studies, Annual Review, 54*, 5–7.

Heidbreder, E. G. (2015). Horizontal Capacity Pooling: Direct, Decentralized, Joint Policy Execution. In M. W. Bauer & J. Trondal (Eds.), *The Palgrave Handbook of the European Administrative System*. Houndmills: Palgrave Macmillan.

Héritier, A., & Rhodes, M. (2011). *New Modes of Governance in the EU*. Houndmills: Palgrave Macmillan.

Hodson, D., & Puetter, U. (2018). 'Studying EU after the Fall: Four Thoughts on Post-EU Studies'. *Journal of European Public Policy, 25*(30), 465–474.

Holzinger, K., & Schimmelfennig, F. (2012). Differentiated Integration in the European Union: Many Concepts, Sparse Theory, Few Data. *Journal of European Public Policy, 19*(2), 292–305.

Howarth, D., & Sadeh, T. (2010). The Ever Incomplete Single Market: Differentiation and the Evolving Frontier of Integration. *Journal of European Public Policy, 17*(7), 922–935.

Ingebritsen, C. (1998). *The Nordic States and European Unity*. Ithaca: Cornell University Press.

Jensen, C. B., & Slapin, J. B. (2012). Institutional Hokey-Pokey: The Politics of Multispeed Integration in the European Union. *Journal of European Public Policy, 19*(6), 779–795.

Jones, E. (2016). *Why We Need a Theory of Disintegration* [online]. Available at: https://erikjones.net/2016/11/12/why-we-need-a-theory-of-disintegration/. Accessed 12 Dec 2016.

Jones, B. D., & Baumgartner, F. R. (2005). *The Politics of Attention*. Chicago, IL: The University of Chicago Press.

Juncker, J.-C. (2016, June 21). *Speech at the Annual General Meeting of the Hellenic Federation of Enterprises (SEV)*. Athens: European Commission.

Kassim, H., & Wright, V. (1991). The Role of National Administrations in the Decision-Making Processes of the European Community. *Rivista Trimestrale de Diritto Pubblico, 3*, 832–850.

Knill, C. (2001). *The Europeanization of National Administrations*. Cambridge: Cambridge University Press.

Knill, C., & Bauer, M. W. (2016). Policy-Making by International Public Administrations: Concepts, Causes and Consequences. *Journal of European Public Policy, 23*(7), 949–959.

Kohler-Koch, B., & Rittberger, B. (2006). The "Governance Turn" in EU Studies. *Journal of Common Market Studies, 44,* 27–49.

Kölliker, A. (2001). Bringing Together or Driving Apart the Union? Towards a Theory of Differentiated Integration. *West European Politics, 24*(4), 125–151.

Kölliker, A. (2006). *Flexibility and European Unification: The Logic of Differentiated Integration*. Oxford: Rowman & Littlefield.

Kroll, D. A., & Leuffen, D. (2015). Enhanced Cooperation in Practice: An Analysis of Differentiated Integration in EU Secondary Law. *Journal of European Public Policy, 22*(3), 353–373.

Lavenex, S. (2011). Concentric Circles of Flexible 'EUropean' Integration: A Typology of EU External Governance Relations. *Comparative European Politics, 9*(4–5), 372–393.

Leruth, B. (2017). The Europeanization of the Welfare State: The Case for a 'Differentiated European Social Model'. In P. Taylor-Gooby, B. Leruth, & H. Chung (Eds.), *After Austerity: Welfare State Transformation in Europe After the Great Recession* (pp. 180–201). Oxford: Oxford University Press.

Leruth, B., Gänzle, S., & Trondal, J. (2019a). Exploring Differentiated Disintegration in a Post-Brexit European Union. *Journal of Common Market Studies*. Available from https://doi.org/10.1111/jcms.12869.

Leruth, B., Gänzle, S., & Trondal, J. (2019b). Differentiated Integration and Disintegration in the European Union After Brexit: Risks Versus Opportunities. *Journal of Common Market Studies, 57*(6), 1383–1394. https://doi.org/10.1111/jcms.12957.

Leruth, B., & Lord, C. (2015). Differentiated Integration in the European Union: A Concept, a Process, a System or a Theory? *Journal of European Public Policy, 22*(6), 754–763.

Leruth, B., Startin, N., & Usherwood, S. (2018). *The Routledge Handbook of Euroscepticism*. London: Routledge.

Leuffen, D., Rittberger, B., & Schimmelfennig, F. (2013). *Differentiated Integration: Explaining Variation in the European Union*. Basingstoke: Palgrave Macmillan.

Lord, C. (2015). Utopia or Dystopia? Towards a Normative Analysis of Differentiated Integration. *Journal of European Public Policy, 22*(6), 783–798.

Majone, G. (2009). *Europe as the Would-Be World Power: The EU at Fifty*. Cambridge: Cambridge University Press.

Marcussen, M. (2009). Out of the Box: Coping Successfully with Euro-Outsiderness. *Cooperation and Conflict, 44*(2), 167–187.

Mény, Y., Muller, P., & Quermonne, J.-L. (1996). *Adjusting to Europe*. London: Routledge.

Miles, L. (2005). Introduction: Euro-Outsiders and the Politics of Asymmetry. *Journal of European Integration, 27*(1), 3–23.

Milward, A. S. (1996). The Frontiers of National Sovereignty. In S. Gustavsson & L. Lewin (Eds.), *The Future of the Nation-State*. London: Routledge.

Monnet, J. (1978). *Memoirs*. London: Collins.

Moravcsik, A. (1993). Preferences and Power in the European Community: A Liberal Intergovernmentalist Approach. *Journal of Common Market Studies, 31*(4), 473–524.

Mouritzen, H. (1993). The Two *Musterknaben* and the Naughty Boy: Sweden, Finland and Denmark in the Process of European Integration. *Cooperation and Conflict, 28*(4), 373–402.

Neumann, I. B. (2003). The Nordic States and European Unity. Symposium on Christine Ingebrigtsen's Christine, The Nordic States and European Unity. *Cooperation and Conflict, 36*(1), 87–94.

Olsen, J. P. (1996). Europeanization and Nation-State Dynamics. In S. Gustavsson & L. Lewin (Eds.), *The Future of the Nation-State*. London: Routledge.

Olsen, J. P. (2007). *Europe in Search of Political Order*. Oxford: Oxford University Press.

Olsen, J. P. (2010). *Governing Through Institution Building*. Oxford: Oxford University Press.

Petersen, N. (1998). National Strategies in the Integration Dilemma: An Adaptation Approach. *Journal of Common Market Studies, 36*(1), 33–54.

Philippart, E., & Edwards, G. (1999). The Provisions on Closer Co-operation in the Treaty of Amsterdam: The Politics of Flexibility in the European Union. *Journal of Common Market Studies, 37*(1), 87–108.

Piris, J.-C. (2012). *The Future of Europe: Towards a Two-Speed EU?* Cambridge: Cambridge University Press.

Radaelli, C. M., & Salter, J.-P. (2019). Europeanization in Reverse Gear. In S. Gänzle, B. Leruthand, & J. Trondal (Eds.), *Differentiated (Dis)integration in Light of Brexit: What Future for European Integration?* (pp. 36–53). Routledge.

Risse, T. (2000). "Let's Argue!": Communicative Action in World Politics. *International Organization, 54*(1), 1–39.

Rosamond, B. (2000). *Theories of European Integration*. Houndmills: Macmillan.

Rosamond, B. (2016). Brexit and the Problem of European Disintegration. *Journal of Contemporary European Research, 12*(4), 865–871.

Sabel, C. F., & Zeitlin, J. (2010). Learning from Difference: The New Architecture of Experimentalist Governance in the European Union. In C. F. Sabel & J. Zeitlin (Eds.), *Experimentalist Governance in the European Union: Towards a New Architecture* (pp. 1–28). Oxford: Oxford University Press.

Sabel, C. F., & Zeitlin, J. (2012). Experimentalism in the EU: Common Ground and Persistent Difference. *Regulation and Governance, 6*(3), 410–426.

Schimmelfennig, F. (2014). EU Enlargement and Differentiated Integration: Discrimination or Equal Treatment? *Journal of European Public Policy, 21*(5), 681–698.

Schimmelfennig, F. (2016a). Good Governance and Differentiated Integration: Graded Membership in the European Union. *European Journal of Political Research, 55*, 789–810.

Schimmelfennig, F. (2016b). A Differentiated Leap Forward: Spillover, Path-Dependency, and Graded Members in European Banking Regulation. *West European Politics, 39*(3), 483–502.

Schimmelfennig, F. (2018). Brexit: Differentiated Disintegration in the European Union. *Journal of European Public Policy, 25*(8), 1154–1173.

Schimmelfennig, F. (2019). Negotiating Differentiated Integration and Disintegration in a Post-Brexit Era. In S. Gänzle, B. Leruth, & J. Trondal (Eds.), *Differentiated*

(Dis)integration in Light of Brexit: What Future for European Integration? (pp. 36-53). Routledge.

Schimmelfennig, F., Leuffen, D., & Rittberger, B. (2015). The European Union as a System of Differentiated Integration: Interdependence, Politicization and Differentiation. *Journal of European Public Policy, 22*(6), 764–782.

Schimmelfennig, F., & Winzen, T. (2014). Instrumental and Constitutional Differentiation in the European Union. *Journal of Common Market Studies, 52*(2), 354–370.

Schimmelfennig, F., & Winzen, T. (2017). Eastern Enlargement and Differentiated Integration: Towards Normalization. *Journal of European Public Policy, 24*(2), 239–258.

Schimmelfennig, F., & Winzen, T. (2019). *Differentiated European Integration: Towards Ever lLser Union?* Book Manuscript.

Siedentopf, H., & Ziller, J. (1988). *Making European Policies Work*. Bruylant: Sage.

Stubb, A. (1996). A Categorisation of Differentiated Integration. *Journal of Common Market Studies, 34*(2), 283–295.

Stubb, A. (1997). The 1996 Intergovernmental Conference and the Management of Flexible Integration. *Journal of European Public Policy, 4*(1), 37–55.

Tiilikainen, T. (2003). Nordic Integration Policy Seen from Abroad. Symposium on Christine Ingebrigtsen's Christine, The Nordic States and European Unity. *Cooperation and Conflict, 36*(1), 95–98.

Tindemans, L. (1975). European Union: Report by Mr. Leo Tindemans, Prime Minister of Belgium, to the European Council. *Bulletin of the European Communities* (Suppl. 1/76).

Trondal, J. (2002). Beyond the EU Membership—Non-membership Dichotomy? Explaining Supranational Identities among EU Decision-Makers. *Journal of European Public Policy, 9*(3), 468–487.

Trondal, J. (2007). The Public Administration Turn in Integration Research. *Journal of European Public Policy, 14*(6), 960–972.

Vollaard, H. (2014). Explaining European Disintegration. *Journal of Common Market Studies, 52*(5), 1142–1159.

Walker, N. (1998). Sovereignty and Differentiated Integration in the European Union. *European Law Journal, 4*(4), 355–388.

Wallace, H., & Ridley, A. (1985). *Europe the Challenge of Diversity (Chatham House Papers)*. London: Routledge.

Wallace, H., Wallace, W., & Webb, C. (1983). *Policy Making in European Community*. London: Wiley.

Warleigh, A. (2002). *Flexible Integration: Which Model for the European Union?* London: Sheffield Academic Press.

Warleigh-Lack, A. (2015). Differentiated Integration in the European Union: Towards a Comparative Regionalism Perspective. *Journal of European Public Policy, 22*(6), 871–887.

Wessels, W., & Rometsch, D. (1996). Conclusion: European Union and National Institutions. In D. Rometsch & W. Wessels (Eds.), *The European Union and Member States*. Manchester: Manchester University Press.

Zeff, E. E., & Pirro, E. B. (2006). *The European Union and Member States*. London: Boulder.

Zielonka, J. (2014). *Is the EU Doomed?* Cambridge: Polity Press.

CHAPTER 41

The European Union, Crisis Management, and International Order

Michael Smith

INTRODUCTION

This chapter is designed to draw upon a number of the areas explored in preceding chapters of the Handbook, and in particular to explore the implications of crisis within and outside the EU for the Union's broader commitment to and pursuit of world order. As noted by the Editors in their Introduction to the volume (Chapter 1), the incidence of crisis within the EU over the past decade has also been accompanied by turbulence, conflict, and crisis outside the Union, both in its neighborhood (eastern and southern) and in the broader global arena. A key argument in this chapter is that these crises are intimately linked, and that the intertwined externalities of the EU's efforts to cope with and manage the crises—as defined in Brussels and the capitals of EU member states—will be a continuing features of the Union's external action.

In taking this approach, the chapter works from the following initial positions. First, the global arena is currently characterized by a number of intersecting crises; these vary in geographical scope (global/regional/national); in duration and impact (long-term structural or chronic, short-term acute or contingent); and in the ways in which they intersect (in multilateral, plurilateral, bilateral, or bi-multilateral contexts). Second, these intersecting crises have important if not fundamental implications for ideas of world order

---

M. Smith (✉)
Department of Politics and International Studies, University of Warwick, Coventry, UK
e-mail: M.H.Smith@warwick.ac.uk

© The Author(s) 2021
M. Riddervold et al. (eds.), *The Palgrave Handbook of EU Crises*,
Palgrave Studies in European Union Politics,
https://doi.org/10.1007/978-3-030-51791-5_41

(defined in terms of power, institutions, ideas, and practices), since they potentially or actually corrode the foundations established in the Post-World War II period and the practices of the Liberal, rules-based world order of which the EU was and is an important component. Third, and as a consequence, the EU has a strong commitment to a particular form of world order based on multilateralism and liberal institutions, and this has been expressed in a number of formal strategy documents as well as in the 'reigning ideas' of EU external action and the practices of EU diplomacy. It is to be expected, therefore, that the EU will be profoundly challenged by the multiple crises outlined above, and that its self-perception as a defender of the liberal world order will be thrown into question. This challenge to the EU's role will be felt in the external realm, but also in the EU's internal workings and in the ideas on which the EU's global role is founded. As a result, the EU's role as a manager of world order and of international crisis will be challenged, and the task of (re)establishing a stable set of management practices and assumptions will potentially outrun the EU's capacities, at least in the short term. This argument relates strongly to the three scenarios set out by the Editors in their Introduction ('breakup', *muddling through*, and *heading forward*), and the conclusions to this chapter will focus on those as a way of evaluating the EU's prospects as an international crisis manager.

In order to explore the issues arising from these tensions and elements of crisis, the chapter proceeds as follows. First, it focuses on the EU and its commitment and contribution to world order in a number of linked domains, with the aim of identifying key areas of tension and potential difficulty. Second, it considers the changing nature of crises in the world arena and explores the growth of practices of EU crisis management in the global political economy and global security. Third, it identifies three key logics of EU external action and the ways in which they connect with practices of crisis management, with the aim of understanding their implications and impact. Fourth, it investigates the levels at which EU crisis management can be practiced, and the linkages and tensions between these levels. Finally, it assesses the linkages and externalities that imply that actions taken to manage crisis in specific areas of EU policy or external action can and do compromise the EU's capacity to manage in other areas by affecting resources, perceptions, and impacts. The chapter concludes by relating these arguments to the three scenarios set out in the Introduction to the volume: 'breakup', *muddling through*, and *heading forward*, and argues that *muddling through* is the most likely medium-term outcome.

The theoretical center of gravity of the chapter lies essentially in institutionalist accounts of EU policymaking, global governance, and world order (also see Ansell, this volume). This is not to say that rationalist and constructivist accounts are irrelevant to the argument here—rather, it is to contend that these accounts are best understood as being mediated, both historically and currently, by the role of institutions broadly defined (for more on these perspectives, see in this volume: Cross on Constructivism; Schimmelfennig on

Liberal Intergovernmentalism; Zimmermann on Neo-realism, and Reichvein on Realism). Thus, rational choice institutionalism and sociological institutionalism draw upon and enrich rationalist and constructivist understandings, while historical institutionalism provides the framework for understanding how successive institutional bargains and processes of path dependency contribute to the EU's external action in general, and in particular to its European and world order aspirations and actions. This focus in turn will enable the chapter to construct and evaluate a number of propositions relating to the EU's resilience and to the future engagement of the Union with questions of world order.

The EU and World Order

The EU has presented itself as a significant contributor to world order in (particularly) institutional and normative terms. Institutionally, the EU has presented itself (via the Commission especially) as a committed multilateralist in the broad sense and as a supporter of 'effective multilateralism' in a number of specific areas encompassing both political economy and the politics of security (Duke 2017; Orbie et al. 2015; Smith 2016). Normatively, one argument has been that the EU contributes to world order simply by existing—that is, to paraphrase Ian Manners, that the EU is an important buttress to world order not only because of what it does but also because of what it is (Manners 2002, 2006; see also Whitman 2010). In another sense, the EU's contribution to the framing of international rules and conventions constitutes a significant element in the maintenance and the consolidation of international norms and to practices of global governance in the general context of the Liberal world order (Wunderlich and Bailey 2011; Jørgensen and Laatikainen 2013).

The most recent systematic statement of the EU's approach to the global arena, the Global Strategy of 2016 (European Union 2016; see also European External Action Service 2015; Smith 2017; Tocci 2017) is in many ways an extended statement of the claims outlined above. It restates the Union's commitment to multilateral engagement, while setting out in detail the ways in which such engagement will be pursued within the EU's neighborhood, in key regional arenas and in global institutions. It also sets out the ways in which the EU's core values will continue to inform its involvement in processes of international conflict, competition, and cooperation. While developing the idea of 'principled pragmatism' as the centerpiece of Union activity, and emphasizing the need for 'strategic autonomy' as the foundation for EU influence, the Global Strategy in many ways underlines the continuity of the Union's engagement with world order issues. In particular, the Global Strategy draws upon the ideas of resilience, especially in specific regions, and the EU's capacity to support resilient societies and political systems—and also upon the notion of a 'comprehensive approach', mobilizing all of the Union's resources to prevent or to manage crises in key areas of European concern. Thus, the EU's approach to world order issues is reflected in the ambitions of the Global

Strategy and in the implied search for stability-centered on a rules-based multilateral system; but the Strategy also points to the 'complex, connected and contested' nature of the global arena in which this vision of order is to be pursued. As Simon Duke has pointed out, such a context raises major questions about EU capabilities, institutions, and capacity for strategic thinking (Duke 2017).

The EU's contributions to world order are also strongly linked to its hybrid nature as an international actor, and to the different levels of its engagement with world order issues (Manners 2002; Smith 2012, 2018). In the first case, it is clear that the EU's role is strongly affected by considerations of coherence and potential fragmentation, arising from its embodiment of supranational and intergovernmental elements and their institutionalization in the shape of the Commission and the Council. In this context, the achievement of coordinated and effective international engagement, either with key partners or in key regions or on key issues, is likely to be challenging (Gebhard 2017). In the second case, it seems clear that the EU's engagement with world order embodies three interconnected levels: the EU order itself (as the basis for external action and as a form of international order at the regional level), the European order (encompassing the EU's eastern and southern neighborhoods) and order at the global level (Smith 2007). Currently, all three of these areas of engagement are subject to challenge and to either acute short-term crisis or chronic long-term or structural crisis (see below). This has put intense pressure on the practices of crisis management in the EU, and created linkages between areas of crisis management that generate suboptimal processes and outcomes.

Crises, Crisis Management, and the EU

The nature of international crisis is often seen as reflecting three key challenges: first, a threat to actors' key values or interests, second a lack of anticipation and planning on the part of those involved, and third, time constraints lending urgency to any response (see for example the introduction and Anderson, this volume). In these circumstances, decision-making on the part of those involved can be both risky and stressful, with the accompanying dangers of under-reaction and overreaction. But this archetype only really defines one sort of international crisis; the acute crisis where there is the possibility of the use of military force. In reality, crises can be seen as falling across a wide spectrum, defined by the types of context in which they occur, the precipitating factors they reflect, and the scope of their actual or potential impacts. Thus, some crises can be described not as acute but as chronic, eroding over an extended period the certainties and structures surrounding interactions in the global arena. Additionally, except in rare cases, crises do not occur in isolation: very often, they intersect and impose multiple demands upon policymakers. The policymakers themselves are not inert: they can and do construct narratives of crisis, or can and do fail to recognize the potential scope and effects of their actions. A set of key distinctions can be made, on the one hand between crises *of* an order, crises *within* an order, and crises *for the participants*, and on the other hand between crises that are *contained, catalytic, cathartic*, or *catastrophic*. As noted in the introduction to this chapter, the current conjuncture in the global arena is characterized by intersecting and overlapping crises, and by the potential for crises to spread and have unexpected resonances across the global order.

The idea of international crisis management itself can be seen as a product of the Cold War period, and as a form of great-power doctrine, but it is also clear that the practice in general demands a number of key qualities in policymaking and implementation (Bell 1971; Brecher and Wilkenfeld 2000; Williams 1976; Winham 1988). In the first place, if effective crisis management is to occur, it demands a shared definition of the crisis that is confronting an actor or actors. This definition of the situation is an essential element in the construction of coordinated strategies and actions; it should simultaneously be clear and capable of adaptation in the light of novel developments or the acquisition of new information. Secondly, crisis management requires resources (attention, information, finance, policy instruments of a civilian, and a military nature) that can be mobilized for the management of crisis—and potentially for the management of more than one crisis at once. Thirdly, it requires processes of deliberation and internal coordination that generate a consensus on what should be done to address a recognized crisis, and finally, it requires the capacity to manage processes of communication and negotiation with those engaged in the crisis. Alongside these essentially 'positive' elements of a framework, there are other factors and forces that play important roles in the potential for and the practice of crisis management. One such factor is institutional: the extent to which crisis management takes place within a settled institutional context and according to established procedures, or the extent to which is creative (or perhaps chaotic) and conducted 'by the seat of the pants'. Another factor is ideational: while the 'definition of the situation' can encompass a wide range of elements, there are important issues relating to fundamental values and norms that will affect the propensity and the capacity for crisis management on the part of a given set of individuals or institutions. Each of these elements is redolent with implications for the roles that can be played by the EU in the contemporary global arena.

The EU has invested significantly during the past two decades in its capacity for crisis management, both civilian and military, political and economic, but this is part of a much more extended set of developments (Howorth 2014; Houber 2004; Jørgensen 1997). Indeed, there has been at least since the 1970s, and the crisis surrounding the 1973 October War in the Middle East, a consistent attempt to set up mechanisms that can enable the Union to cope with the challenges of international conflict and crises, either through systematic coordination between the member states or through more explicit action at the level of the Union. Most notably, the Maastricht Treaty of 1991 established the Common Foreign and Security Policy (CFSP), which gave the

Union a potentially significant role in areas of 'hard security' and diplomatic coordination. Such mechanisms are not confined to the 'hard security' end of the spectrum—they encompass measures in the global political economy, such as those relating to the internal and international financial crises after 2008 (see Trangy and Stenstad, this volume; Olsen and Rosén, this volume), or dealing with diplomatic and economic sanctions, and others dealing with the impact of regional and other crises surrounding migration (see Crawford, this volume; Bosilca, this volume; Schilde, this volume), political instability, and institutional decay (see Hooghe et al., this volume; de Wilde, this volume; Raube, this volume). In the security domain more specifically, the establishment of the Common Security and Defence Policy (CSDP) in the early years of the new millennium spawned a new range of devices for identifying, managing, and resolving international crises, and enabled the EU to present itself as a new kind of international conflict manager (Gross and Juncos 2011; Howorth 2014; Whitman and Wolff 2012).

The EU's capacity for crisis management has also been enhanced by the development since the 2009 Lisbon Treaty of the European External Action Service (EEAS) as the diplomatic arm of the Union, and the attendant role of the High Representative for Foreign Affairs and Security Policy, who is simultaneously a Vice-President of the European Commission (the HRVP for short), and who has oversight of the Common Foreign and Security Policy (CFSP). The implications of these developments, and of the Global Strategy, are that the EU is committed to the search for 'joined up policymaking'; in terms of crisis management, this implies the mobilization of all relevant resources across the Union and its institutions, and their use in a coordinated fashion via the 'comprehensive approach' outlined earlier. In principle, therefore, the evolution of the EU's system of diplomacy provides it with the potential to operate as a strategic actor and crisis manager, both within the European 'neighbourhood' and more broadly (Smith et al. 2016; see also Rieker, this volume on out of area crisis management operations).

Despite this, it can be argued that the EU, despite its best efforts via the CSDP and other channels in CFSP and external economic action, lacks the capacity consistently to fulfill the requirements of effective crisis management. First, there are persistent problems among institutions and member states in defining crisis situations, reflecting the limitations of institutional commitment, and the hybridity of decision-making as well as asymmetries of information and of evaluative capacity. Second, resources with which crisis management can be attempted are held at different levels in the EU system, and are subject to different criteria for their mobilization, either because of treaty commitments or because of national variations. Third, processes of deliberation and internal negotiation are intensely politicized when it comes to the management of crises, and this means that potential outcomes are subject to major variations in perceived legitimacy or operational effectiveness. As a result, the capacity at EU level to coordinate processes of communication and negotiation in crisis situations is limited and constrained. It should be noted that these are precisely some of the features identified in the EU's 2016 Global Strategy Paper, and are the subject of large parts of its call for 'joined up policy-making' in external action. Not only this, but they relate closely to the scenarios set out in the Introduction to this volume, and particularly to the 'breakup' and *muddling through* scenarios.

One further feature of the crisis management process should be underlined here, because it relates closely to the EU's status and role as identified earlier. There are two major external faces to crisis management: first, Crisis management as a tool for foreign policy and therefore as the basis for relative gains vis-à-vis competitors; and second, crisis management as an approach to the generation of global public goods, which can be loosely summarized as 'world order'. These two versions arise directly from the different 'faces' of crisis identified earlier: Crisis *of* a system, crisis *in* a system, and crisis *for* the participants. In this context, the incidence of crisis within the broader global or regional orders is likely to be mediated strongly by the capacities or inclinations of those involved to manage, and the purposes for which they define management as taking place. In the EU's case (and for that matter many national cases), it might be argued that there is a third 'face' to crisis management: its use as an internal device to protect domestic order and to maintain regime stability, or to project a specific type of image or identity for an actor. If we are to investigate the EU's practices of crisis management, one of the key questions that occur at a very early stage is thus 'who (or what) is this for?' and beyond the most general of tendencies to search for stability and support the rules-based global order, the answer is not self-evident. Such a question can be at least partly answered through an exploration of the logics of crisis management as practiced by the Union.

THE EU'S ROLE AS CRISIS MANAGER: THREE LOGICS

Following on from the points made above, it seems appropriate to identify (as I have elsewhere) three logics of EU crisis management, and of external action more generally (Smith 2009, 2013). The first logic is the internal logic: that crisis management is a means of protecting or promoting the European project, and that its effectiveness is therefore to be judged by the extent to which it protects, sustains, or enhances the EU order; at the same time, it is critically subject to the internal condition of the European project itself, and the degree of consensus or coordination that is possible in crisis situations. The second logic is the external logic: here, crisis management is to be evaluated in terms of its contribution on the one hand to promotion of the EU's roles in generating or sustaining European or world order, and on the other hand to the provision of regional or global public goods such as stability, prosperity, or dignity, but it is critically subject to international opportunity structures and the perceptions of key 'targets' or partners. The third logic is that of European identity: in other words, crisis management is to be seen as a projection of European values and as the realization of the internal normative foundations of the Union, but is subject to variations in the strength of those foundations and in the extent to which normative consensus exists within the Union.

It is possible to conceive of conditions in which the signs attached to all of these logics are positive, and therefore propitious for the expansion of the EU's roles in crisis management and world order. Equally, it is possible to conceive of conditions in which all three are negative, and thus there is no prospect of effective crisis management by the EU in pursuit of world order. Inevitably, the most likely situations are those in which the signs are mixed, and in which there is uncertainty about the EU's capacity to pursue or produce effective crisis management across related world order domains. In this context, a version of the question posed above becomes crucial for the EU's practices and for its prospects of success in any given crisis management process: 'what is crisis management for?'.

The current conjuncture for the EU is unpromising to say the least. Internally, the European project is subject to major (some would say, existential) challenges, which are linked to political tensions within member states and to the perceived ineffectiveness of institutions. These tensions include (but are not limited to) the long-lasting impact of financial and economic crisis, the associated rise of populism and 'new nationalism' in a number of EU member states, and the pressures exerted by the UK's decision to leave the Union after its referendum in June 2016.

Externally, there is a long-term shift in structural power within the global arena which challenges institutions and conventions, which closes down opportunities previously available to the EU and which also fragments some of the major building blocks on which the EU was founded and prospered. Thus, the rise of China and the responses to the challenge of China by the United States, the 'new geopolitics' reflected in Russian and other foreign policies, the rise of new security issues such as those linked to energy supply, to migration or to climate change, and the broader challenge to the idea of 'liberal world order' have all played roles in shaping the opportunities and risks attending the EU's pursuit of a congenial world order.

In relation to identity, there is uncertainty and instability of major images of the EU, both those shared within the Union and those held by major partners and competitors. The Union is faced by elements of structural crisis in the world economy and global security systems, by medium-term crisis in key regions, especially the eastern and southern neighborhoods, and by short-term conjunctural crises arising from these longer-term processes of adjustment, change, and challenge. It is not surprising in this context that responses at the EU level have been uncertain, fragmented, and often ineffective. Such an analysis again relates strongly to the arguments posed in the Introduction to the volume about the potential for 'breakup' (stressing the divergent preferences of member states and the fragmenting effects of external challenges) or *muddling through* (focusing on the inertia and path dependency generated through institutions and rules), but it adds an awareness of the ways in which identity can be challenged and disrupted by both internal and external forces in crisis conditions.

THE EU, CRISIS MANAGEMENT, AND WORLD ORDER: THREE LEVELS

As noted earlier, the EU's engagement with world order issues can be described in terms of different but interconnected levels of engagement and action: the EU order, the European order, and world order (Smith 2007). During the past decade, the EU has been faced with crises in each of these areas, and their interaction has been one of the key strands in EU crisis management.

Within the EU, and in line with the 'internal logic' outlined above, the financial and sovereign debt crises of the period 2007–2016 have corroded the institutional legitimacy and resources of the Union, and committed it to a seemingly never-ending process of fire-fighting and crisis management, often with the assistance of global institutions such as the IMF. One effect of this process, though, has been over time to erode the legitimacy and the impact of EU crisis management actions, and to bolster the positions of those in national contexts who wish to reign in the European project or to reverse it. The most obvious manifestation of this effect is to be found in the process of Brexit (see Oliver, this volume; Whitman, this volume), but several other member state governments, and many insurgent political parties or movements across the Union have contributed to a feeling that the internal EU order is contested in new and fundamental ways. This is not just a crisis in political economy; it extends to the stability and continued effectiveness of EU and national institutions, of political groupings and of social and cultural movements. If we reflect on the requirements of effective crisis management—shared definition of crisis, ability to mobilize resources, deliberation, capacity to communicate and negotiate—then the EU has not been in a strong position to fulfill these requirements internally, and this has generated externalities in terms of EU credibility and legitimacy in the wider world.

At the level of European order, the Union has been faced over the past decade with not only the spillover effects of its major achievement (the enlargements of 2004–2007) but also the declining effectiveness of the 'membership perspective'. The spillover effects have been felt in the form of a new security perimeter, which has had to be managed in a period when crises have erupted along with it and when there has also been a reinvigoration of geopolitics—an area in which the EU is not best placed to compete (Smith 2006, 2019). The declining effects of the 'membership perspective' arise from the potential end of enlargement—that process has gone from being a defining characteristic of EU external action to a busted flush, except in the Balkans. Rather than comfortable compliance with EU demands, the period since 2008 has seen a series of crises, such as those in Georgia, Moldova, and the Ukraine, in which the EU's search for a 'ring of friends' has been replaced by the need to respond to a 'ring of fire', and in which the EU does not have many tools for fire-fighting (in comparison with the area of political economy). The development of the European Neighbourhood Policy and then the Eastern and Southern Partnerships has proved to be a relatively fragile institutional structure when the issues at stake have led to the deployment of coercion and violence, as in the cases of Georgia and the Ukraine, and the uncertainty of EU and EU member state policies toward Russia has compounded the problems (Averre 2016; Haukkala 2015; Whitman and Wolff 2010a, b). As Lawrie Freedman has pointed out, the intersection of geopolitical and geo-economic forces in the Ukraine and other post-post-Cold War crises has posed challenges the EU has so far been unable to meet (Freedman 2014; on the impact of the Ukraine crisis as a driver of common EU policies see Juncos and Pomorska, and Riddervold, this volume). In the southern neighborhood, the initial hopes attached to the EU's engagement with the Arab Spring fostered a belief that the Union could capitalize on its long-term presence in the Maghreb and elsewhere to foster new institutions and patterns of cooperation, buttressed by the export of norms (Del Sarto 2016). But as the rebellions and insurgencies in Syria and then Libya have revealed, the transition from civilian political and social crisis to military force and coercion threatened to marginalize the Union and to reveal the limitations of its capabilities for collective action (Bicchi 2013; Duke 2017: Chapter 6; Peters 2012).

At the global level, and partly as a consequence of challenges at the levels of EU order and European order, the EU has found itself facing multiple tests of its crisis management potential. Economically, engagement with the G7-8 and the G20 has been not only a reflection of economic demands but also of perceptions of the EU's increasingly challenged political order. This is qualified by the EU's success in arriving at free trade agreements with important partners or regions, most notably Canada in 2016, Japan in 2018, and Mercosur in 2019—but these need to be placed into the context of an increasingly turbulent global political economy. In terms of security, although there have been diplomatic successes such as the 2015 agreement on Iranian nuclear programs (now challenged by the withdrawal of the United States and by the application of ever more severe sanctions on the Tehran regime), the Union has found itself powerless when the tools of crisis management move from the economic and the diplomatic to the military part of the spectrum, as in the aftermath of the 'Arab Spring' and potentially in the Persian Gulf. Regions in which the EU might once have claimed a certain predominance, such as Sub-Saharan Africa, have been less amenable and more penetrated by competitors such as China, who do not carry with them the baggage of colonialism (Carbone 2013). Global governance has experienced its own institutional and normative crises, and the EU along with others has been less able to exert its influence in the face of global power shifts and the widespread challenges to the multilateral rules-based system (Alcaro et al. 2016; Bouchard et al. 2014; Smith 2016). Global order (understood as liberal world order) is thus contested in new and challenging ways, closing off opportunities for effective EU action, and despite the good intentions expressed in the Global Strategy, the EU has found it impossible to respond decisively across the spectrum of its external action.

These arguments about the coexisting challenges posed by (internal) EU order, the European order, and the broader international order enable us to see more clearly the ways in which multiple and intersecting crises have come to be a dominating feature of the EU's international engagement. In the terms used earlier in this chapter, the Union is confronted with a series of crises at different levels and with different levels of acuteness. On the one hand, there is a long-term, chronic crisis affecting the liberal world order, of which the EU has been both a central part and a key beneficiary; this is a crisis not only of institutions and their effectiveness, but also of identities and of ideas, which have become routinely contested and challenged (Ikenberry 2018; Smith 2018; Youngs and Smith 2017). On the other hand, there are unpredictable and unanticipated acute crises that have sprung up both in the security and in the economic domain, and which also relate to the fragility of 'domestic' institutions. Tellingly, these crises of domestic order have occurred not only outside the Union but also within a number of its member states. They are related to many of the factors identified earlier—domestic and international power shifts, the demands of integration and the potential for disintegration, the impact of ideational convergence and divergence, the contestation of institutions. Taken together, these elements pose a compelling set of challenges to the EU's capacity to cope with crisis; they affect the key logics of the EU's international role(s), they affect the Union's capacity to generate resilience and adaptiveness, and thus they take further our understanding of the 'breakup' and *muddling through* scenarios. They also enable us to frame a number of propositions relating to the role of linkages and externalities in EU crisis management.

THE ROLE OF LINKAGES AND EXTERNALITIES

A key element of the argument in this chapter is that the different levels and arenas of EU crisis management link and intersect, and that externalities arising from each of the logics and levels of EU engagement make themselves felt in the EU's approaches to crisis management. What does this mean for the EU's capacity to identify and respond appropriately to the multiple crises outlined above?

First, it is clear that challenges linked to different logics and levels of EU engagement compromise the EU's capacity and inclination to contribute to world order broadly defined. Specifically, they lead to contestation (both within and outside the Union) of the EU's role as a manager of international crises, and thus to questions about its credibility and legitimacy both at home and abroad.

Second, it appears that the EU's efforts to manage crises in different logics and at different levels can generate negative externalities that then affect its capacity to manage crises as a whole. To put it in another form, crisis management in one domain can deflect attention and resources from others, and thus lead to overall failure even if the resolution is achieved at one level or in terms of one logic. To be specific, the efforts to manage the EU's internal financial and economic crises have put into question its capacity to pay attention to and to respond to crises in the broader European and world orders. Likewise, the impact of crisis in the EU's neighborhood, and the Union's inability to deal with questions of 'hard power' and 'hard security', can be felt both within the Union (in debates about the appropriate scale of EU external action) and in the wider global arena (for example in US questioning of the Union's capacity to act effectively in international conflicts). This judgment clearly has implications for the notion of resilience, since that notion encompasses not only material resources and the ability to deploy them, but also the reserves of legitimacy and credibility available to the Union.

Third, and as a consequence, the EU's capacity to achieve a shared definition of the challenges it and its member states confront, to mobilize resources for crisis management, to base decisions on deliberation and consensus, and to communicate and negotiate with targets and partners in the outside world has experienced a secular decline in the past decade, despite attempts in treaties and through institutional change to generate greater coherence and more effective external action. Thus its capacity for effective crisis management has declined even while its apparent institutional and treaty foundations have been elaborated, and this has potentially important implications for the resilience and adaptability of EU crisis management practices.

Finally, it is difficult at this stage to see a more favorable constellation of forces emerging in the near future, given the likely preoccupation with internal structure and the management of stability within the EU order that will characterize EU affairs for the next decade—especially when this is combined with a 'rogue' United States and the emergence of new challengers in regions that are of key interest for the EU.

Conclusions

In the Introduction to this handbook, the Editors identify not only the characteristics of the crises confronting the EU, but also the requirements for effective crisis response. Taking their cue from John Ikenberry, they define crisis (as distinct from turbulence) as 'an extraordinary moment when the existence and viability of the political order are called into question'. In this chapter, I have attempted to take this idea further, and to complement it with a sense of the multidimensional nature of international crises, so as to arrive at an evaluation of the future prospects for the EU in the broader international order.

One key contribution of this chapter is to extend the notion of international crisis. I have argued that international crises should be understood in several dimensions and at several levels. Equally, it is clear from the argument here that when it comes to the EU's presence in the global arena, the current period has thrown up a number of coexisting crises, both acute (in that they confront the EU with new threats that may be unanticipated and that demand an urgent response) and chronic (in that they are more extended, demand a sustained, multidimensional and deliberate approach to world or regional order and may challenge the basis of order itself). This set of multiple and differentiated (but linked) crises is the most challenging possible combination, and is inextricably linked to what some would identify as the 'internal' crisis of the EU order.

A second key contribution is to link this notion of multiple and differentiated crises to the potential for the EU as a crisis manager. I have argued that the management of crises demands a set of key attributes and resources, and that the EU possesses these attributes in varying and highly differentiated forms. This is a direct consequence of the EU's status as a hybrid and often contested international actor, and it has direct implications for the EU's ability to enact a role as an international crisis manager. Many of the resources are contested within the EU, between the EU institutions and member states or between the institutions themselves; they are available in qualified and often contingent ways that reflect the institutional complexity of the Union; when this is added to the complexity of the challenges faced by the Union, it is logical to expect a differentiated and contested set of crisis responses. As argued here, these responses reflect not only the availability of resources, but also the working out of key logics inherent to the European project as a whole, and the different directions in which those logics have worked at different times or in different policy domains.

This set of arguments then leads to a set of implications for the future capacity of the EU to manage and profit from the crises of international order with which it is confronted. The Editors in their Introduction focus on three scenarios: *breaking down*, *muddling through*, and *heading forward*. I argue that elements of all three of these scenarios are visible in the current conjuncture, and that this is likely to be the situation for the foreseeable future. There is clear evidence of *breaking down*, in the sense that the EU has proved incapable of creating a stable role for itself in key international crises such as those in the Middle East or eastern Europe and that its ability to manage events has actually moved backward rather than advancing. There is also evidence that the broader order around the EU—an order in which it has invested a great deal of political and economic capital—is changing in ways that limit the capacity of the Union to lead or to manage events. The liberal world order, or the multilateral system, is vital to the legitimacy and the credibility of the EU as an international crisis manager, but that order is in flux and its future is uncertain, in terms of power, institutions, and ideas.

At the same time, there is compelling evidence to support the *muddling through* scenario. The crises confronting the Union in the international arena have been met in many cases with a reinforcement of the Union's modes of action, and have led to incremental adjustment (often disjointed incremental adjustment) as new dimensions or expressions of the crises have become apparent. Although the Global Strategy of 2016 can be seen as a systematic attempt to address the nature of the 'complex, connected and contested world' and thus the multiple crises it generates, it fits very much within the framework of existing EU institutions and expresses the established consensus on the need for 'joined up policy-making' in response to multiple challenges and crises. It also expresses a reality that has emerged very clearly in this chapter: that multiple and differentiated crises, combined with the hybrid nature of the EU, have created highly differentiated responses, refracted through the institutional arrangements, the balance of material power, and the reigning ideas in specific policy domains. Thus, the differences between responses in commercial policy, security policy, environmental policy, and other areas are key indicators of the EU's varying presence and ability to create effects. The fact that these areas are often and increasingly linked is a key challenge to the EU.

This brings the argument logically to the third scenario: *heading forward*. According to the Editors, one crucial aspect of this scenario is that it requires 'windows of opportunity' for the Union, combined with the Union's capacity to exploit them. One possible way in which this might happen is through the 'purposeful opportunism' of policy entrepreneurs, who can muster the relevant resources and commitments at key moments. Another possible (and potentially linked) avenue for this kind of creative and innovative response is through the application of a 'grand strategy' that enables the Union to mobilize resources in accordance with agreed aims, depending upon the challenges that may emerge. In the first case—purposeful opportunism—there is a requirement for individuals or groups to recognize, respond to and learn from conditions as they change. In the second case—strategic leadership—there is a need for an underlying consensus on the strategic aims to be pursued, and recognition of the legitimacy and credibility of the leaders who have responsibility for implementing the strategy. Neither of these requirements is consistently fulfilled in the Union at present, given the conditions of flux within the European project, the lack of consensus among member states and within institutions and the perceived lack of legitimacy in crucial policy areas. But that does not mean that these requirements will never be met—indeed, there is evidence from the development of CSDP in the context of Brexit and from the development of new commercial policy instruments that they might well come to fruition in the longer term. The complicating factor in the case of external action and international order is that the EU is not alone—it cannot operate as a sealed universe of policymaking and institutional development, and there are strong links (both positive and negative) between internal EU policymaking and challenges within the European and the global orders.

As noted above, and emphasized throughout this chapter, the future of the EU as an international crisis manager will reflect both the hybrid nature of the Union and the complexity of the challenges it faces. Of the scenarios proposed by the Editors, the most likely to dominate is *muddling through*, reflecting a combination of institutional inertia, path dependency and member state divergence that will on the one hand prevent the collapse of the Union and on the other hand prevent the kind of creativity and strong leadership that could move the EU forward significantly as an international crisis manager. But EU responses will be highly differentiated, and influenced by the three logics presented in this chapter (internal, external, and identity) as well as by the several interconnected levels at which crises—and therefore crisis response and management—will occur (on differentiated integration, see Gänzle et al., this volume). Whatever the shape of the EU's future as a crisis manager in the world arena, it will also always be subject to the key question raised earlier in this chapter: who or what is crisis management for? Will it reflect the internal needs of the Union, the external opportunities available to it, or the Union's capacity to establish a stable identity and role for itself in relation to European and world order?

REFERENCES

Averre, D. (2016). The Ukraine Conflict: Russia's Challenge to European Security Governance. *Europe-Asia Studies, 68*(4), 699–725.

Alcaro, R., Peterson, J., & Greco, E. (Eds.), (2016). *The West and the Global Power Shift: Transatlantic Relations and Global Governance*. Basingstoke: Palgrave Macmillan.

Bell, C. (1971). *The Conventions of Crisis: A Study in Diplomatic Management*. Oxford: Oxford University Press.

Bicchi, F. (2013). Europe and the Arab Uprisings: The Irrelevant Power? In F. A. Gerges (Ed.), *The New Middle East: Protest and Revolution in the Arab World*. Cambridge: Cambridge University Press.

Bouchard, C., Peterson, J., & Tocci, N. (2014). *Multilateralism in the 21st Century: Europe's Quest for Effectiveness*. London: Routledge.

Brecher, M., & Wilkenfeld, J. (2000). *A Study of Crisis*. Ann Arbor, MI: University of Michigan Press.

Carbone, M. (2013). *The European Union in Africa: Incoherent Policies, Asymmetrical Partnership, Declining Relevance?* Manchester: Manchester University Press.

Del Sarto, R. (2016). Normative Empire Europe: The European Union, Its Borderlands and the "Arab Spring". *Journal of Common Market Studies, 54*(2), 215–232.

Duke, S. (2017). *Europe as a Stronger Global Actor: Challenges and Strategic Responses*. Basingstoke: Palgrave Macmillan.

European External Action Service. (2015). *The European Union in a Changing Global Environment: A More Connected, Contested and Complex World*. Brussels: EEAS.

European Union. (2016, June). *Shared Vision, Common Action: A Stronger Europe: A Global Strategy for the EU's Common Foreign and Security Policy*. Brussels.

Freedman, L. (2014). Ukraine and the Art of Crisis Management. *Survival, 56*(3), 7–42.

Gebhard, C. (2017). The Problem of Coherence in the European Union's International Relations. In C. Hill, M. Smith, & S. Vanhoonacker (Eds.), *International Relations and the European Union* (3rd ed., pp. 123–142). Oxford: Oxford University Press.

Gross, E., & Juncos, A. (2011). *EU Conflict Prevention and Crisis Management: Role, Institutions and Policies*. London: Routledge.

Haukkala, H. (2015). From Cooperative to Contested Europe? The Conflict in Ukraine as a Culmination of a Long-Term Crisis in EU–Russia Relations. *Journal of Contemporary European Studies*, 23(1), 25–40.

Houber, M. (2004). *International Crisis Management: The Approach of European States*. London: Routledge.

Howorth, J. (2014). *Security and Defence Policy in the European Union*. Basingstoke: Palgrave Macmillan.

Ikenberry, J. (2018). The End of Liberal International Order? *International Affairs*, 94(1), 7–23.

Jørgensen, K. E. (1997). *European Approaches to Crisis Management*. The Hague: Kluwer.

Jørgensen, K. E., & Laatikainen, K. (2013). *Routledge Handbook on the European Union and International Institutions: Performance, Policy, Power*. London: Routledge.

Manners, I. (2002). Normative Power Europe: A Contradiction in Terms? *Journal of Common Market Studies*, 40(2), 235–258.

Manners, I. (2006). Normative Power Europe Reconsidered: Beyond the Crossroads. *Journal of European Public Policy*, 13(2), 182–199.

Orbie, J., Saenen, B., Vershaeve, J., & De Ville, F. (2015). The EU's Relations with Multilateral Institutions. In K. E. Joergensen, A. Aarstad, E. Drieskens, K. Laatikainenand, & B. Tonra (Eds.), *The SAGE Handbook of European Foreign Policy* (pp. 721–35). London, UK: Sage.

Peters, J. (2012). *The European Union and the Arab Spring: Promoting Democracy and Human Rights in the Middle East*. Lanham, MD: Lexington Books.

Smith, K. (2017). European Union Global Strategy for a Changing World. *International Politics*, 54, 503–518.

Smith, M. (2006). The Shock of the Real: Trends in European Foreign and Security Policy Since September 2001. *Studia Diplomatica*, 59(1), 27–44.

Smith, M. (2007). The European Union and International Order: European and Global Dimensions. *European Foreign Affairs Review*, 12, 437–456.

Smith, M. (2009). Between Soft Power and a Hard Place: European Union Foreign and Security Policy Between the Islamic World and the United States. *International Politics*, 46(5), 596–615.

Smith, M. (2012). Still Rooted in Maastricht: European Union External Relations as a 'Third-Generation Hybrid'. *Journal of European Integration*, 34(7), 699–715.

Smith, M. (2013). Beyond the comfort zone: internal crisis and external challenges in the European Union's response to rising powers. *International Affairs*, 89(3), 653–671.

Smith, M. (2016, September). *Is the EU an Effective Multilateralist? Role Conceptions and Role Performance in the EU's Approach to Global Governance*. Paper presented at the UACES Annual Conference, Queen Mary University of London.

Smith, M. (2018). The European Union, the United States and the Crisis of Contemporary Multilateralism. *Journal of European Integration*, 40(5), 539–553. https://doi.org/10.1080/07036337.2018.1488836.

Smith, M. (2019, May). *Testing the Boundaries of Order? Europe, the European Union and a Changing World Arena*. Paper presented at the European Union Studies Association Biennial International Conference, Denver, CO.

Smith, M., Keukeleire, S., and Vanhoonacker, S. (Eds.), (2016). *The Diplomatic System of the European Union: Evolution, Change and Challenge*. London: Routledge.

Tocci, N. (2017). *Framing the EU Global Strategy: A Stronger Europe in a Fragile World*. Basingstoke: Palgrave Macmillan.

Whitman, R. (2010). *Normative Power Europe: Empirical and Theoretical Perspectives*. Basingstoke: Palgrave Macmillan.

Whitman, R., & Wolff, S. (2010a). *The European Neighbourhood Policy in Perspective: Context, Implementation and Impact*. Basingstoke: Palgrave Macmillan.

Whitman, R., & Wolff, S. (2010b). The EU as a Conflict Manager? The Case of Georgia and Its Implications. *International Affairs, 86*(1), 87–107.

Whitman, R., & Wolff, S. (2012). *The European Union as a Global Conflict Manager*. London: Routledge.

Williams, P. (1976). *Crisis Management: Confrontation and Diplomacy in the Nuclear Age*. London: Martin Robertson.

Winham, G. (1988). *New Issues in International Crisis Management*. Boulder, CO: Westview Press.

Wunderlich, U., & Bailey, D. (2011). *The European Union and Global Governance: A Handbook*. London: Routledge.

Youngs, R., & Smith, M. (2017). The EU and the Liberal Order: Contingent Liberalism. *The International Spectator*.

Crises and the EU's Response: Increasing the Democratic Deficit?

Anne Elizabeth Stie

Introduction

Founded on the ruins of two world wars, it is common to teach new students of European integration that not only was the European Union (EU) a result of crisis, crisis—or the narrative of crisis—is often highlighted as one of the important triggers of wider and deeper European integration.[1] As further integration often has involved a strengthening of institutions with a popular anchoring, notably the European Parliament (EP), the potential effect of crisis could, for defenders of European-level democracy, therefore also been seen as

---

[1] But see Martill and Oliver's chapter (this volume: 7–8) nuancing this assumption: "The idea of crisis as a driver of integration is deeply woven into the narrative of the EU, and there is some evidence that integration has indeed resulted from specific times of crisis (Börzel 2018: 475; Lefkofridi and Schmitter 2015: 4; Mény 2014: 1350). But as Dinan (2017) has shown, closer inspection raises questions about the link between crises and European integration. Integration has been the result of a variety of factors, with crises sometimes playing a part, but by no means being the key factor and sometimes playing little or no part at all. Giving credit to crises distract from longer-running developments and work that integration has depended on. Moreover, arguably only certain kinds of crises – those that highlight policy failures from incomplete contracts – facilitate further integration. Other crises, like Brexit, which call into question the basis on which the Union is constructed, are less likely to spur greater integration."

A. E. Stie (✉)
University of Agder, Kristiansand, Norway
e-mail: anne.e.stie@uia.no

a welcome opportunity to add new stepping-stones to the democratic organization of the Union. Today, however, the passing note is far less optimistic as crises pile up and common and acceptable solutions seem hard to find. Now, the European integration project is increasingly criticized, more loudly and uncompromisingly by populists and Eurosceptics, but more often also by mainstream and less tabloid commentators. Arguments and intensity obviously differ, but in some way or the other they all question the EU's ability to solve the crises in a manner that makes the everyday life better for ordinary citizens. In some cases, the critique has also resulted in recourse to differentiated responses as well as (disintegration) efforts to withdraw from the Union, as in the case of Brexit (see Gänzle et al., Martill and Oliver, this volume). Thus, apart from a few positive signs (e.g., increase in the EP voter turnout in 2019), this time most commentators seem to agree that the chances are bleak that crisis could bear the promise of a democratization of the EU institutions and decision-making processes. Rather, the most pessimistic voices contend that the EU's handling of the crises demonstrates that the Union has taken an "authoritarian turn" and that there has been a "shift towards decisionist authority structures at both the domestic and the European level" (Kreuder-Sonnen 2018: 452; Scicluna and Auer 2019), and "emergency rule" (White 2015). One of the main reasons for this, or so I argue, stems from the Union's inability to deal with the crises in a manner that properly addresses the underlying legitimacy problems of the Union, namely it is inclination to handle genuinely political challenges through technocratic procedures and solutions. As a result, solving the EU's crises by opting for the technocratic approach, does not only contribute to further undermine democracy in Europe (both at the national and European levels), disguising or treating political matters as neutral technical and pragmatic issues also contributes to hollow out the legitimate use of expertise and technocratic means in public policy-making as citizens lose trust in European decision-making institutions. Hence, even if the previous chapters demonstrate the Union's ability to cope and muddle through the crises quite successfully in individual policy areas and institutions, with its unresolved legitimacy question and looking from the vantage point of the overall polity level, the EU appears more vulnerable in the volatile, geopolitical environment of the world today.

Against this background, the aim of this chapter is to make two interrelated arguments. Firstly, to show that democratic decision-making requires both citizen participation (input legitimacy) and expertise (output legitimacy). This implies that output legitimacy can only to some extent compensate for the lack of input legitimacy. In the EU, the reliance on output legitimacy has been written into the structural architecture from the start but has now developed too far making populists and Eurosceptics the big winners. Secondly, not only is democracy hollowed out—at both the national and the European levels—the credibility of expertise is also at risk. In a polity where insulated and relatively independent technocratic institutions dominate and when decisions taken by these institutions are (no longer) neither perceived as desirable nor as contributing in solving, but rather exacerbating citizens' problems (as many found in the euro and migration crises), people start questioning the credibility of these institutions and consequently also the quality of the expertise they claim to hold.

THE PATH DEPENDENCY OF EXECUTIVE DOMINANCE IN THE EU

In 1994, after the adoption of the Maastricht Treaty, Featherstone (1994: 150–151) argued that "… Monnet established the European integration process with a particular character – which was marked by technocracy and elitism – and that the legacy of this early strategy has been to afford the Commission a weak and fragile democratic legitimacy. In that sense, the [popular] backlash against the Maastricht Treaty is a direct consequence of Monnet's original strategy. As Jacques Delors has commented: 'Europe began as an elitist project [in which it was believed] that all that was required was to convince the decision-makers. That phase of benign despotism is now over' (Independent, 26 July 1993)." In other words, there has from the start been a profound (and intended) discrepancy between the power of the technocratic elites and the citizenry in Europe. This discrepancy is, as Featherstone contends, inherent in the Monnet method which attempts to depoliticize issues by strengthening the powers of supranational institutions resulting in a widening and deepening of integration. However, as long as there was a "permissive consensus" in mass public opinion supporting and not questioning the EU integration process, elite-driven technocratic and executive cooperation was possible without much protest and interference from citizens (cf. Lindberg and Scheingold 1970).

With the negotiations and adoption of the Maastricht Treaty, this situation changed. The fall of the Soviet empire and the end of the cold war represented new possibilities for the reunification of Europe (and Germany), and the Maastricht Treaty thus, in many ways, signified a decisive turning point in the history of European integration and Weiler (1999) even talked about a "constitutional moment." The new treaty provisions represented a major leap forward in the integration process not only because of the establishment of the Economic and Monetary Union (EMU), but also because it created the European Union implying a more political dimension of the integration process. However, for the first time, the state and future of the Union was seriously questioned, epitomized by Denmark's "no" vote against the Maastricht Treaty. The legitimacy question moved forever beyond the pragmatic level and the era of the "permissive consensus" was undoubtedly over (Abromeit 1998: 6). As a result of this critical juncture in Europe, Hooghe and Marks (2008, 2018) also identify this period (the beginning of the 1990s) as the nascent start of a new, (and by now blooming) transnational cleavage in European politics between those who favor international and European cooperation and those who find themselves in a more disadvantaged position by the opening up of national borders and the upload of decision-making processes to supranational and intergovernmental bodies. In short, the transnational cleavage is "..a political reaction against European integration and immigration (...), [and] relate to the defense of national community against transnational shocks. The European Union is itself such a shock, because it introduces rule by those who are regarded as foreigners, diminishes the authority exercised by national states over their own populations, produces economic insecurity among those who lack mobile assets, and facilitates immigration" (Hooghe and Marks 2018: 109–110).[2] Since Maastricht, then, the Union has been in a state of "constraining dissensus" (Hooghe and Marks 2008) where the scope and direction of European integration has become politicized and can no longer develop unnoticed by the publics.

The politicization that followed in the wake of the adoption of the Maastricht Treaty also offset a vivid scholarly debate on the Union's many alleged democratic deficits, ranging from the lack of a European demos, the lack of a European public sphere, an unelected and not sufficiently democratically accountable executive (in general executive dominance), a second-order European Parliament, technocratic, depoliticized, informal, and publicly inaccessible decision-making processes, etc. Epitomized in the well-known and customized European version of the input–output legitimacy debate (cf. Easton 1965; Scharpf 1999), it revolved around the issue of whether the EU could rely on being legitimated by its ability to produce desirable and effective outcomes at the European level, i.e., output legitimacy, because it was backed indirectly by the democratic legitimacy (i.e., the input legitimacy) of its member states. The two major proponents of this position (although coming from different starting points), Andrew Moravcsik and Giandomenico Majone, claimed that output legitimacy could compensate for the weak or lack of input legitimacy at the European level. This was possible because the Union is not a self-standing polity, but dependent, controlled and legitimized by and through the democratic systems of the member states. Whereas Moravcsik (1998, 2002) primarily focused his perspective on the political side of how European integration and cooperation can be explained by how the member states negotiate "grand bargains" in order to achieve goals they otherwise would not reach alone, Majone (1996, 1998) concentrates on how the delegation of regulatory powers to the supranational level, to institutions like the European Commission, could be seen to be on a par with how such powers often are delegated to non-majoritarian bodies at the national level. Uploading limited, regulatory powers in this way could contribute to insulate and depoliticize such tasks and consequently ensure that they are not subjected to short-sighted and short-term electoral goals of politicians (primarily) aiming

---

[2]Hooghe and Marks (2008, 2018) refer to this cleavage as the GAL/TAN divide, i.e. between those defending green/alternative/libertarian (GAL) positions, on the one hand, and those defending tradition/authority/national (TAN) positions, on the other.

to be reelected. As long as the EU dealt with regulatory and not redistributive functions, and, as long as the powers of the European non-majoritarian bodies (mainly the Commission) were limited and narrowly defined, European integration only raised "…relatively minor legitimacy problems.." and could be seen as a positive-sum game, according to Majone (2014: 1216). Against (Moravcsik and) Majone, proponents of the other strand, argued that the depoliticized policymaking in the hands of non-majoritarian bodies and insulated from real or weak influence by directly elected majoritarian bodies, were too broad and exceeding their remit as they also included redistributive issues. Hence, the EU did indeed suffer from a democratic deficit primarily because the EU fails to meet the core democratic requirement, namely contestation for political leadership over policy (Føllesdal and Hix 2006; Schmidt 2006; Eriksen and Fossum 2000).

However, over the years and exacerbated by the crises, also Majone (2014: 1217) have concluded that the conditions for output legitimacy alone at the European level have expired as particularly the Commission has obtained more and different types of functions which "..expands the scope of the Commission's discretionary choice, greatly complicating the task of evaluating the overall quality of its performance." In short, it was doing more than just regulatory tasks. In addition to the growth in the Commission's portfolio, other non-majoritarian bodies, such as the ECB as well as multiple agencies, have been established and obtained (more) power. This contrasts strongly with the situation of the popularly elected bodies. Even if the EP has obtained new competencies particularly with the coming into force of the Lisbon Treaty and the increase in legislative powers, this is far from matching the powers gained by technocratic bodies. This mismatch in favor of the unelected aggravates the legitimacy problem as the Union's own source of (output) legitimacy—its ability for effective and efficient problem-solving—is increasingly perceived to be overstretched and outright authoritarian (Kreuder-Sonnen 2018; Scicluna and Auer 2019).

Prior to the eurozone crisis, as described above, the jury was still out as scholars disagreed on how far it was possible for the EU to let result-oriented output legitimacy compensate for lacking and not doing enough to cultivate the sources from where the Union could draw its own input legitimacy (Schmidt 2013). After the crises kicked in and the Union has increasingly been unsuccessful in "delivering" outcomes European citizens find desirable, however, there is now widespread agreement that the situation where the Union's mode of governance is captured in the slogan "policy without politics," i.e., depoliticized, binding decision-making with miniscule popular input and accountability at the European level, on the on hand, and, on the other hand, removing decision-making responsibilities at the member state level leaving national democracies with popular input and accountability through public debate, but with no possibility to influence actual policy outcomes, i.e., "politics without policy" (cf. Schmidt 2006, 2013).[3]

Concurrently with the Europeanisation of public policymaking, the disconnect between actual decision-makers at the European level and affected parties/citizens at the national level has been growing and has, as a result, made national party politics "…more divisive on the issue of European integration (…), while electoral politics have become more volatile, risking the twin problems of growing voter disaffection and political extremism in response to Europeanisation" (Schmidt 2006: 155–156; Hooghe and Marks 2018). Hence, this situation has slowly but steadily been developing in scope and scale leading up to the financial crisis hit Europe in 2008, setting the ground for the democratic quagmire the Union has now gotten itself into.

The negative reactions from citizens and affected parties to the EU's handling of the crises contribute to show that the lack of input legitimacy is only sustainable or tolerable up to a certain point before it peaks. In following its old technocratic paths, the Union now seems to have reached a tipping point and has "..undergone a profound transformation in terms of institutional structure and political process" (Kreuder-Sonnen 2018: 452; Eriksen and Fossum 2018: 843). Moreover, by today the "…rise of nationalist populism and the spread of EU-level "politics of emergency"[4] are linked and mutually reinforcing—building a "cycle of authoritarianism": the complex and opaque forms of transnational emergency politics feed domestic populism, which builds on the critique of intangible elites. The anti-European discourse which thus emerges exacerbates the "constraining dissensus" in European publics and renders constitutional reform for further integration less feasible" (Kreuder-Sonnen 2018: 453; Scicluna and Auer 2019). In other words, more technocracy arguably feeds more, not less populism and Euroscepticism and should therefore be seen as two sides of the same coin complementing rather than opposing each other (cf. Bickerton and Invernizzi-Accetti 2017; Caramani 2017). Moreover, commentators also point to the (underlying and

---

[3] "..this makes for *policy without politics* at the EU level, as policies are made without the kind of debate along a left-right divide normally found at the national level. By setting this system on top of those of its member-states, the EU has 'de-politicised' national politics by marginalising national partisan politics at the EU level while Europeanizing more and more policies, thereby removing them from the national political arena. This makes for *politics without policy* at the national level" (Schmidt 2006: 155–156).

[4] See White (2015). Wilkinson (2013: 528) labels it 'politics of necessity' in his analysis of the euro crisis and argues that "The specter of authoritarian liberalism is outlined here only with broad brushstrokes. These highlight the dominance of the economic over the political and legal constitution in the various formal and informal responses to the crisis. Integration through law and politics is replaced by integration through fear, and the 'whip of necessity' and a disarmingly cavalier attitude towards normative principles is displayed. Integration proceeds and legal and political norms are ignored or suspended for the sake of preserving financial stability, economic unity and market liberalism, rather than for the sake of preserving social cohesion, security or political unity. The practice of authoritarian liberalism is to conceal, rather than to confront, the conflict between democracy and capitalism, and it utilizes a powerful motto of depoliticization, 'there is no alternative'."

path dependent) assumption that seems to guide the European elites' in their efforts to solve Europe's problems, namely that what is needed is more integration and supranational competence. When the Union does not develop in this manner, they are treated as "…deviations; mistakes in need of correction. It is in this context that technocrats take on ever-expanding political roles. If national publics, and even national governments, are fickle and short-sighted, then it is for technocratic experts – dispassionate, objective, far-sighted – to keep the process of European integration on the right track. However, these attitudes are very much part of the problem. They are based on the fallacy of technocratic reason. (…) Excessive reliance on technocratic logic tends to impoverish democracy and fuel the turn to populism within member states" (Scicluna and Auer 2019: 1434).[5]

Citizen Participation and Expertise: Forming the European Common Interest

All democracies have non-majoritarian bodies[6] that are not subject to strict democratic authorization—without the polities themselves being criticized for being undemocratic. In fact, studies show that people seem to tolerate and accept "…large doses and place considerable trust in procedures and institutions that privilege experts and expert opinions. This acceptance and trust is intimately linked to contemporary societies' dependency on expertise (…): it is hard to make rational political decisions without relying extensively on expert advice and even expert decisions" (Holst and Molander 2017: 235). But despite this "fact of expertise" (ibid.), the input–output debate in the EU illustrates that exactly where the line should be drawn and when the balance tilts toward too much power to expert institutions is a contested issue (cf. Majone 1996, 2014; Holst and Molander 2017; Chambers 2017).

To Majone, the value of non-majoritarian bodies pertains to their aptitude in achieving societies' long-term interests and goals because they can operate in an environment shielded from the often short-sighted electoral cycle of majoritarian bodies where politicians are susceptible to take decisions that are not necessarily good for the polity, but rather for their own self-interest in reelection. In other words, it is the non-majoritarian bodies' independence or "separateness" from "politics and organised interests" that make it possible for

---

[5] Kreuder-Sonnen (2018) argues that also European studies to a great extent is subject to this type of theorising as many scholars have a tendency to still argue that more integration can—in the end—solve Europe's legitimacy and democratic deficit problems, without paying enough attention to the development of a 'cycle of authoritarianism' the crises have institutionalised and normalised.

[6] Maggetti (2010: 2) describes them as "..non-elective and non-representative bodies, which are separated from the politico-administrative state hierarchy, and exert a distinctive form of political power through the application of public authority – that is, regulatory power."

them to act in accordance with and make a credible commitment to the polity's long-term interests (Maggetti 2010; see also Landwehr and Wood 2019). In this sense, they function as a "fourth branch of government" or a checks-and-balances mechanism that buffer or protect "…some pre-established 'basic principles' from the 'populist' component of democracy and from the risk of an arbitrary use of political decision makers" (Maggetti 2010: 3). When we think about how dominating populist, partisan and strategically one-sided the pursuit of particular agendas often are in the political climate we have today, and how this distracts or hinders an informed public debate, recourse to "neutral" and knowledge-based expertise obviously appears appealing.

However, the pitfall is to make this inherent skepticism toward "politics" and democratically anchored institutions and processes end up as an either-or choice between citizen participation or expertise, or as the dilemma is formulated by Simone Chambers (2017: 270) as either prioritizing "…truth and epistemic quality in which case we need to limit and circumscribe equal participation as ordinary citizens have low epistemic competence; or we prioritize equality and autonomy in which case we value democracy not because it produces the most rational decisions or policies but because it treats citizens as free and equal." Instead of striving toward finding a balance between expertise and citizen participation, the EU's rigid, technocratic handling of the crises have, in many ways, pushed Europe toward making this exactly an either-or choice on which only populist and Eurosceptics are now scoring points. (cf. Holst and Molander, this volume). This is an unfortunate situation as a democratic polity needs both in order to function. Public policymaking is not only about finding solutions to pragmatic factual and technical matters, it is also about making decisions that will impact a society's values and norms, that is, ethical-political questions concerning collective identity and the common good, and moral questions concerning what is just and which are universal in nature, reaching beyond the borders of the community (cf. Habermas 1996; Landwehr and Wood 2019). Analytically, these questions are possible to distinguish from one another, but in actual decision-making processes this is (almost) impossible as political issues are (usually) a mix of "is"- and "ought"-questions. Whereas technocrats obviously have something to bring to the table also in "ought"-questions about "what we as a society should do" (such as in the euro or migration crises), they are, however, not the only ones possessing competence in such questions. They do not sit on the full answer to how burdens and goods should legitimately be (re-)distributed.

In forming public opinion or the common European interest or good, the viewpoints of citizens and other affected parties must also be included. In other words, experts cannot do this job alone. To be effective and contribute to problem-solving, as is the task of non-majoritarian bodies, require that "someone" has articulated, prioritized, and decided that "something" is a (common) goal. From the EU's institutions, there are numerous examples of formulations about the "common good" or the "European interest" coming from press conferences, speeches, and other formal documents every year. The question is whose European interest or common good is it the EU officials claim to protect and pursue? What kind of collective European opinion-formation process has preceded such statements? At some point, the question of "in whose interest" are decisions "desirable" and considered "efficient"? How can unelected actors in technocratic institutions claim to know what is the European interest a priori when they have not been in contact with those who are going to be affected by their decisions? The process of public opinion formation is not a one-way street where public authorities can simply postulate or "inform" citizens about the decisions they have reached in insulated and secretive settings (cf. Chambers 2017). Forming a common European interest is a dialogical and reflective process between (the often chaotic and unorganized) discussions in the public sphere and democratically anchored institutions at the decision-making level. The latter contribute to transmit the opinion-formation processes in the public sphere into the will-formation processes in formal decision-making bodies (ibid.; Habermas 1996; Stie 2013).

Hence, effectiveness and problem-solving is dependent upon there being a prior process of formulating and legitimately authorizing something as a common goal. Landwehr and Wood (2019: 69) remind us that it is neither the autonomy of non-majoritarian institutions per se, nor that they are populated by individuals with expertise[7] in various fields that make their decisions credible, but their quality. A decision that has been tested through some kind of accountability arrangement can be "…'externally' credible *if the validity claims it is based upon are made explicit and successfully defended*" (ibid.: 71). Moreover, "…credibility is the quality of a particular decision or piece of advice, which is based on *contestable* claims that do not carry prima facie authority over the public" (Landwehr and Wood 2019: 69, my emphasis). In short, the argument that credibility is more likely when non-majoritarian bodies operate insulated and independently of democratic institutions is thus insufficient because the validity claims their decisions are founded on are themselves in need of justification (cf. Landwehr and Wood 2019). The argument of credibility via independence should therefore be replaced by credibility via accountability mechanisms. In other words, "[c]redibility should be seen as obtained as a result of accountability mechanisms rather than as a Madisonian check on majoritarian will" (Landwehr and Wood 2019: 80), that is, non-majoritarian bodies (and other expert arrangements) should complement, *not take over*, public policymaking processes.

Majone too admits "that delegation to IRAs [independent regulatory agencies] implies a 'net loss' of legitimacy for the political system (…). In fact,

---

[7] It is a necessary, but not sufficient condition that non-majoritarian bodies are populated by individuals who are experts in different fields. Getting a position in such institutions must be decided according to meritocratic standards. For a definition of what can be deemed and 'expert', see Holst and Molander (2017, this volume).

(…), the political 'principal' can transfer his powers to the independent delegate, *but not his legitimacy*; hence IRAs must rely on other *external* sources of legitimacy" (see Maggetti 2010: 3, my emphases). To compensate for this legitimacy loss, non-majoritarian institutions must demonstrate that their *effectiveness* and *credibility* outshine the proficiency of democratic institutions by "…producing qualitatively better policy outputs…" (ibid.; see also Landwehr and Wood 2019; Holst and Molander 2017). As we have seen, instead of operating in splendid isolation, the chances for this to happen are higher when non-majoritarian bodies are subject to accountability mechanisms which ensure that the validity claims underpinning their decisions are somehow tested externally, i.e., outside the non-majoritarian institutions themselves. Exactly how this should be organized cannot be detailed here, but there are obviously institutional requirements involved as efficiency and problem-solving are only necessary, but not sufficient conditions for the authorization of democratically legitimate decisions (see Landwehr and Wood 2019; Holst and Molander 2017). In other words, it is not an option to hide political discussions and decision-making in technocratic bodies which are practically inaccessible to citizens and subsequently expect the latter to blindly defer to decisions they have not participated in making (cf. Lafont 2015, 2019; Landwehr, this volume). Whereas taking this "expertocratic shortcut" may be tolerated up to a point, it will turn out as a "…dead end, because citizens eventually cannot be bypassed as decision-takers (…). Moreover, the implementation and effectiveness of decisions is significantly reduced where citizens are unable to understand and share the reasons they are based on" (Landwehr, this volume).

Against this background, it is natural to assume that the EU's propensity to concentrate the bulk of decision-making processes in the hands of technocratic and executive bodies subject to minimal democratic accountability will (arguably) backfire. The populist and Eurosceptic parties and movements have already contributed to a more polarized and fragmented Europe where it is harder to reach compromises and decisions that are deemed legitimate in the eyes of the citizens. Moreover, they accuse and question—with considerable success—the publicly unjustified and untested policy advice coming out of EU institutions as disguised political and partisan positions advocating self-interested agendas rather than reflecting the best possible solution given the knowledge available at the time (see also Höegenauer 2019). To (the majority of) citizens and other affected parties, it is exactly the standards of effectiveness and credibility the European institutions have failed to meet in their efforts to handle and solve the crises. They have not been able to demonstrate their ability to provide effective and credible problem-solving. There are, of course, many reasons for this—including circumstances beyond European decision-makers' control—but in the heat of notably the euro and migration crises, it was striking how fast the decision-making elites withdrew into insulated and secretive settings, evading public debate and democratically anchored procedures. When proper accountability procedures are not available and outcomes fail to happen, trust in expertise may plummet. This, of course, is detrimental to the functioning of the Union. Hence it is in the EU's own self-interest to avoid this to happen.

Conclusions

Whereas the EU has always been dominated by technocratic bodies and suffered from a democratic deficit, the crises have exacerbated this situation as the Unions' way of dealing with the crises have mainly been to further strengthen existing technocratic and executive bodies as well as establishing new ones. Part of the problem is the EU's seeming inability to respond to crises in a manner that properly addresses the underlying legitimacy problems of the Union. What the majority of the previous chapters in this book directly or indirectly demonstrate, but hardly problematize, is that the EU seems to be stuck in a pattern where genuinely political questions and challenges—such as how to deal with the eurozone and migration crises—(more or less) as a rule are met with technocratic processes and solutions "everyone" knows is not the right or sufficient medicine to solve the crises in manner that both ensures (long-term) effectiveness and legitimacy. To the contrary, opting for these technocratic solutions only seems to deepen the problems because the measures and reforms are unable to address the political nature of the crises (cf. Scicluna and Auer 2019). This is so either the Union follows a *muddling through* (scenario 2) or *heading forward* (scenario 3) approach to crisis management. Whereas the former perpetuates the democratic deficits already inherent in the EU's institutional architecture, the latter deepens the democratic deficits as the majority of the substantial changes resulting from the Union's handling of the crises—particularly in economic governance—amounts to the strengthening of technocratically founded bodies such as the Commission and the ECB, as well as the establishment of new non-majoritarian agencies, without compensating popularly elected bodies.

This way of trying to settle the crises could be labelled the curse or rather the path dependency of the Monnet method described as the gradual, by stealth integration of Europe through the means of an elitist and technocratically driven process with no final blueprint and with little or no room for popularly or democratically based bodies that could function as channels between decision-makers and citizens. More powers and influence in the hands of executives and experts contribute to further insulate and depoliticize policymaking in the EU. This, in turn, has further disconnected the formal decision-making processes from public debate in Europe and given rise to more polarization, alienation and fragmentation among the citizenry (Mair 2013). Moreover, "[t]he paradoxical effect of the euro crisis is that it has led to both more politicisation *and* more technocracy. As a result, the EU is still a regulatory state, but not of the sort that Majone (1994) envisaged, i.e., one focusing on areas of high technical complexity and low political salience. The EU today is a *highly politicised regulatory state* in which democratic politics

– and publics – are not trusted. (…) There is a sense in which the euro and the integration project are too important to be left to the voters" (Scicluna and Auer 2019: 1435 emphasis in original; cf. also Börzel and Risse 2018). The result is poorer circumstances for ensuring political inclusion in European public policymaking, thus moving the EU even further away from meeting the core principle of democratic self-government, namely that those subject to law can also see themselves as its authors.

So, can the vicious circle be broken? Here I side with Lafont (2019) and Landwehr (this volume), that there are no possible shortcuts or quick fix to be made if the aim is democratic self-government. In the words of Lafont (2019: 356, emphasis in original): "Unfortunately, there are no shortcuts to making a political community better than its members, nor can a community achieve progress faster by leaving its citizens behind. The *only road* to better political outcomes is the long, participatory road that is taken when citizens forge a collective political will by changing one another's hearts and minds. Commitment to democracy simply *is* the realization that there are no shortcuts. However arduous, fragile, and risky the process of mutual justification of political decisions through public deliberation may be, simply skipping it cannot get us any closer to the democratic ideal. In fact, it will move us further away."

References

Abromeit, H. (1998). *Democracy in Europe: Legitimizing Politics in a Non-State Polity*. New York: Berghahn Books.

Bickerton, C., & Invernizzi Accetti, C. (2017). Populism and Technocracy: Opposites or Complements? *Critical Journal of International Social and Political Philosophy*, 20(2), 186–206.

Börzel, T. A., & Risse, T. (2018). From the Euro to the Schengen Crises: European Integration Theories, Politicisation, and Identity Politics. *Journal of European Public Policy*, 25(1), 83–108.

Caramani, D. (2017). Will vs. Reason: The Populist and Technocratic Forms of Political Representation and Their Critique to Party Government. *American Political Science Review*, 111(1), 54–67.

Chambers, S. (2017). Balancing Epistemic Quality and Equal Participation in a System Approach to Deliberative Democracy. *Social Epistemology*, 31(3), 266–276.

Easton, D. (1965). *A Systems Analysis of Political Life*. Chicago, IL: Chicago University Press.

Eriksen, E. O., & Fossum, J. E. (Eds.). (2000). *Democracy in the European Union: Integration Through Deliberation?* London and New York: Routledge.

Eriksen, E. O., & Fossum, J. E. (2018). Deliberation Constrained: An Increasingly Segmented European Union. In A. Bächtinger, J. Dryzek, J. Mansbridge, & M. Warren (Eds.), *The Oxford Handbook of Deliberative Democracy* (pp. 842–855). Oxford: Oxford University Press.

Featherstone, K. (1994). Jean Monnet and the 'Democratic Deficit' in the European Union. *Journal of Common Market Studies*, 32(2), 149–170.

Føllesdal, A., & Hix, S. (2006). Why There Is a Democratic Deficit in the EU: A Response to Majone and Moravcsik. *Journal of Common Market Studies, 44*(3), 533–562.
Gänzle, S., Leruth, B., & Trondal, J. (this volume).
Habermas, H. (1996). *Between Facts and Norms Contributions to a Discourse Theory of Law and Democracy*. Cambridge, MA: The MIT Press.
Höegenauer, A.-L. (2019). The Politicisiation of the European Central Bank and the Bundestag. *Politics and Governance, 7*(3), 291–302.
Holst, C., & Molander, A. (2017). Public Deliberation and the Fact of Expertise: Making Experts Accountable. *Social Epistemology, 31*(3), 235–250.
Holst, C., & Molander, A. (this volume).
Hooghe, L., & Marks, G. (2008). A Postfunctionalist Theory of European Integration: From Permissive Consensus to Constraining Dissensus. *British Journal of Political Science, 39*(1), 1–23.
Hooghe, L., & Marks, G. (2018). Cleavage Theory Meets Europe's Crises: Lipset, Rokkan, and the Transnational Cleavage. *Journal of European Public Policy, 25*(1), 109–135.
Kreuder-Sonnen, C. (2018). An Authoritarian Turn in Europe and European Studies? *Journal of European Public Policy, 25*(3), 452–464.
Lafont, C. (2015). Deliberation, Participation, and Democratic Legitimacy: Should Deliberative Mini-Publics Shape Public Policy? *The Journal of Political Philosophy, 23*(1), 40–63.
Lafont, C. (2019). Democracy Without Shortcuts. *Constellations, 26,* 355–360.
Landwehr, C. (this volume). Deliberative Theory.
Landwehr, C., & Wood, M. (2019). Reconciling Credibility and Accountability: How Expert Bodies Achieve Credibility Through Accountability Processes. *European Politics and Society, 20*(1), 66–82.
Lindberg, L. N., & Scheingold, S. A. (1970). *Europe's Would-Be Polity: Patterns of Change in the European Community*. Princeton, NJ: Prentice-Hall.
Maggetti, M. (2010). Legitimacy and Accountability of Independent Regulatory Agencies: A Critical Review. *Living Reviews in Democracy, 2,* 1–9.
Mair, P. (2013). *Ruling the Void: The Hollowing of Western Democracy*. London and New York: Verso.
Majone, G. (1996). *Regulating Europe*. London: Routledge.
Majone, G. (1998). Europe's 'Democratic Deficit': The Question of Standards. *European Law Journal, 4*(1), 5–28.
Majone, G. (2014). From Regulatory State to a Democratic Default. *Journal of Common Market Studies, 52*(6), 1216–1223.
Martill, B., & Oliver, T. (this volume).
Moravcsik, A. (1998). *The Choice for Europe: Social Purpose and State Power from Messina to Maastricht*. Ithaca, NY: Cornell University Press, European edition with London: Routledge/UCL Press.
Moravcsik, A. (2002). In Defence of the 'Democratic Deficit': Reassessing the Legitimacy of the European Union. *Journal of Common Market Studies, 40*(4), 603–634.
Scharpf, F. (1999). *Governing in Europe: Effective and Democratic?* Oxford: Oxford University Press.
Schmidt, V. (2006). *Democracy in Europe: The EU and National Polities*. Oxford: Oxford University Press.

Schmidt, V. (2013). Democracy and Legitimacy in the European Union Revisited: Input, Output and 'Throughput'. *Political Studies*, 61(1), 2–22.

Scicluna, N., & Auer, S. (2019). From the Rule of Law to the Rule of Rules: Technocracy and the Crisis of EU Governance. *West European Politics*, 42(7), 1420–1442.

Stie, A. E. (2013). *Democratic Decision-Making in the EU: Technocracy in Disguise?* London: Routledge.

Weiler, J. H. H. (1995). Does Europe Need a Constitution? Reflections on Demos, Telos and the German Maastricht Decision. *European Law Journal*, 1(3), 219–258.

Weiler, J. H. H. (1999). *The Constitution of Europe: 'Do the New Clothes Have an Emperor?' and Other Essays on European Integration*. Cambridge: Cambridge University Press.

White, J. (2015). Emergency Europe. *Political Studies*, 63(2), 300–318.

Wilkinson, M. A. (2013). The Specter of Authoritarian Liberalism: Reflections on the Constitutional Crisis of the European Union. *German Law Journal*, 14(5), 527–560.

CHAPTER 43

The Perfect Storm

Martin Shapiro

When this volume was first initiated, the EU was sailing in troubled waters. Subsequently it has encountered the perfect storm, a storm which hovers over both sides of the Atlantic.

The origins of this storm, paradoxically enough, was the great success of liberalism. With the fall of Soviet communism, the movement of European socialist parties away from true socialism (government ownership of the means of production) to welfare statism and the continuing New Deal consensus of the U.S., liberalism achieved trans-Atlantic dominance. In doing so, however, liberalism persuaded most people that government was responsible for achieving and then guaranteeing their economic success.

Free trade was part of the liberal agenda along with government regulation and individual rights. The EU was one of the achievements of liberalism. Rooted in a base of free trade, it must be remembered that any free trade community will also inevitably become a regulatory community. For once tariffs and the like have been eliminated, member states can and will resort to idiosyncratic health, safety, consumer protection, and other regulation to achieve the same results as tariffs. A German requirement that refrigerators must have two inches of insulation when the French require only one will keep French-built refrigerators out of Germany just as effectively as a German tariff on French refrigerators. To preserve free trade within a community of member

M. Shapiro (✉)
University of California, Berkeley, CA, USA
e-mail: mshapiro@law.berkeley.edu

© The Author(s) 2021
M. Riddervold et al. (eds.), *The Palgrave Handbook of EU Crises*,
Palgrave Studies in European Union Politics,
https://doi.org/10.1007/978-3-030-51791-5_43

states thus requires the supplanting of diverse member state regulations with transnational, and thus uniform, ones.

If liberalism succeeded in persuading nearly everyone in the trans-Atlantic domain that government was responsible not only for their initial and increasingly growing economic prosperity, then it followed that government was also responsible for any lapse in their prosperity and its continuing growth.

If and when large numbers and categories of persons feel themselves to be losing prosperity and their children threatened by the stagnation of prosperity, then the faith in liberalism is necessarily undermined. People begin to blame liberal governments for their and their children's prosperity problems. That storm is now upon us.

In some part, the cause of this malaise may be some long term, little understood evolution of Western culture. There are, however, more concrete probable causes. The liberal pursuit of the welfare state has proven to be so expensive that some of the champion welfare states of the EU, such as the Scandinavian countries and the Netherlands, have been cutting back benefits. Such cutbacks are very concrete generators of economic unease among large categories of citizens.

It was always understood that the Euro would work as long as all the member state economies were doing well or badly in unison. When Greece, Italy, and Spain suffered severe economic distress and Germany served as their taskmaster, citizens of the three delinquent states suffered real economic pain, pain that has continued or only slowly decreased.

In the U.S. a major recession almost escaped correction by government intervention showing that the promised liberal, welfare, regulatory state gravy train did not always run smoothly.

Everywhere in the West automation, the climate crisis, and advances in food growing technologies were more and more perceived as economic threats especially to the economic interests of major segments of the industrial and agricultural work forces. Late marriage and declining birth rates across the West were seen as both causes and effects of economic malaise.

As it became clearer and clearer that the liberal welfare state necessarily chose increased benefits for some and not or even at a cost to others through political processes, those groups and interests who saw themselves, rightly or wrongly, as perennial losers and others as turning political advantage into economic gain at a cost to others, distrust of electoral politics in the usual vein and of government more generally gained momentum.

Often this distrust takes the form of denunciation of government bureaucracies as arrogant, corrupt and captured by special interest, and generally as "far away" from the people they are supposed to serve. And indeed, in federal arrangements such as the U.S. and the EU, regulation that deeply effects vital local interests is largely the product of faraway bureaucratic experts often captured by the very interests they are supposed to regulate for the general welfare. The traditionally governing political parties are often seen the same way.

As liberal governments have become more and more involved in increasingly complex health, safety, consumer protection and other big science interests, what had been seen as liberal democracy, that is rule by the people, became more and more obviously technocratic government, that is rule by the experts. The demos became more and more suspicious, not without some justification, of people who say that they should tell you what to do because they know more than you do what is good for you. One response is increased suspicion of scientific expertise and even of the notion of true facts that underlies that expertise.

The Brussels bureaucracy has been, again not without justification, seen as the height of bureaucratic arrogance. That is likely when someone far away tells you that the way you have been making cheese for hundreds of years is wrong and must be changed.

At the heart of our perfect storm has been globalization along two dimensions. The first of these is economic or market globalization. There is little doubt, except among its extreme enemies, that this globalization has increased the overall gross production of the world. Although there is some doubt, it appears clear to most people that it has also caused considerable, although geographically concentrated, unemployment, enormous profits for segments of the wealthy, and stagnation or slow growth for the incomes of the not so wealthy. The huge wealth gap between the rich and the rest is now widely, negatively, celebrated and generally attributed, at least in part, to market globalization. Given that free trade has been an element in liberal ideology, those who perceive themselves, rightly or wrongly, as its economic victims, are prone to blame liberal governments for their economic plight. This blame is sharpened by the high unemployment rate, particularly for the young, in many Western nation states, many of them EU member states.

The second globalization dimension has been massive refugee problems too familiar to require explanation here and, to an extent, attributed to market globalization but largely the result of various failures of various political regimes and/or attributable to widespread wars, insurrections, illicit drug trades, and national or tribal irredentism. These phenomena in a number of differing combinations have caused tragic suffering and subsequent migrations into the Western world.

Entangled with the immigration problem has been the feeling of many persons, reacting to liberal governments' attempts to correct discrimination against and protect the rights of minority groups, that the government, the bureaucracy and the established political parties are paying attention to "them" but not to "us." The "government" the "bureaucracy" and "globalization" and even the "parties" are a bit too abstract to easily hate. And declaring hatred for any of them too easily appears to be a rejection of national or transnational patriotism. Massive flows of immigrants are very tangible and "foreign" and so, real or imagined, easier to hate. These are real people not institutions, and hating them appears patriotic rather than unpatriotic.

I do not mean to suggest that concerns about refugees are wholly irrational. If one's family has lived in and loved life in a Danish village for generations, some discomfort naturally arises when it turns into a Middle Eastern souk. That this is not merely the rich trying to protect themselves from the poor is shown by the anti "gentrification" movement in many working-class American neighborhoods seeking to protect their long term community from displacement by suburbanites rediscovering the charms of city life. "Multi-culturalism" may be the current trope of the chattering classes but cannot entirely disguise the pain that occurs by the displacement of one day to day culture by an entirely different one. The "free movement of persons" of the EU, and thus the EU itself, is naturally the object of such cultural fears and, of course, the fear of potential job displacement of old comers by newcomers.

The EU has encountered all these, often mutually contradictory, anxieties. From the very beginning, it has been the target of concerns about its "democratic deficit," concerns that have not been alleviated by the enhancement of the powers of its democratic branch, the European Parliament. The Commission has always been the most proactive branch of the EU, and it is the very model of the far away, technocratic bureaucracy that pays no attention to "us" in giving orders that subject everyone to the same, uniform orders disregarding differences in the member states political, economic, and cultural preferences.

The Union's very heart and soul, internal free trade, inevitably harmed some investors and work forces. That those harmed were often concentrated in particular member states or regions within them aggravates member state, nationalist opposition to the Union. That the Union is a "transnational" institution is a two edged sword. In the context of international trade with outside states, it projects a stronger collective national interest against nonmember states' national interests than could member states aching alone. Internally, particularly as a regulator, which it inevitably must be, it often appears to be an enemy of one or another of its member states' national interests. For "make America great again" or "America first" substitute "Italy" or the "UK" for America. Rightly or wrongly the EU becomes a target for the member states' nationalisms that World War II was supposed to have ended. The financial dominance of Germany in the Union, furthers nationalist appeals to those who feel that things are not getting better or are getting worse for them and for the prospects of their children. The world trade, capitalist economy imagined, probably correctly, to have aggravated the gaps between the rich and the poor, can neatly be concretized by reference to the contrast between the northern and southern member states' economies.

One declared purpose of the Union is to protect and expand individual rights and liberties a la the liberal democratic ideal. The expansion of the Union into Eastern Europe has now created an openly expressed admiration for non-liberal democracy in several member states that is bound to create hostility to the Union from within.

The free movement of persons, which has been central to the Union, at first caused trouble within the Union—the famous "Polish plumber" problem. Now, however, the enormous problems of Africa and the Middle East have caused an alarming refugee phenomenon for all of Europe. Union free movement of persons imports that phenomena to all of its members and makes the Union a plausible target for all of those who, rightly or wrongly see the refugee phenomena as an economic and cultural threat to the West. Indeed that perceived threat tends to push together liberals who seek to protect Western values and conservatives who seek to preserve Western economies. That the refugees may take your jobs, marry your children and substitute Islam for religious (often Catholic) freedom is a rallying cry that can bring some liberals and some conservatives together against a Union that is seen as a gateway for refugees.

So, what is the Union to do, and can it survive, all of this.

Most of the contributions to this volume concern the reactions of the various EU institutions to various past and present crises. The overall impression is that those institutions have a mixed record of success and failure in adjusting their organizations and ways of doing business to such situations. The repeated message is that for the most part the Parliament, Councils, Commission and Agencies have "muddled thru" and sometimes even muddled forward a bit (see Section III, this volume). Uncertainty about the future, even the possibility of major retreat or collapse, is frequently expressed. Both the internal relations of the EU with the member states and with the international actors are discussed. There is some confidence in offering at least probablistic, predictions about internal EU matters. For obvious reasons, given today's massive uncertainties, there is far less confidence in predicting EU international relations.

The chapters cover usual crises and EU responses: the Euro-zone and general financial crises, refugee and border control crises both real and imagined, and more generally EU entanglements in the ongoing middle eastern, seemingly endless, uproar, Russia-Ukraine, the authoritarian swings in several central European members and the trumpetings of international free trade versus protectionism. While some attention is paid to the causes of the various crises, central attention is paid to EU institutional responses.

Only a few of the chapters, most notably those on political parties and specifically on public opinion deal with the responses to crisis of the general EU population and of the member state political parties and their EU parliamentary coalitional parties.

Those pieces also suggest that internal popular disagreements and the fragmented state of EU parliamentary parties have resulted and probably will continue to result in EU *muddling through*. The public opinion study suggests some increase in in public trust of the EU following each crisis, but generally argues that very substantial trust and distrust segments of public opinion and a large "undecided" segment exist now and will persist. Again such finding support a *muddling through* EU future with the "the undecided" swinging back and forth from crisis to crisis.

The problems of the EU are so many, so complex and so constantly changing that no single volume should be expected to deal with every relevant issue. Most of the chapters in this one deal with organizational and decision-making process changes to meet various crisis situations. Only a few examine changes in substantive policy, most notably EU foreign policy, as modes of EU self-defense and development. The Middle Eastern, African, and Chinese–U.S. problems are so intractable and so largely beyond EU control, that foreign policy changes that have been or might be made to bolster the EU present a particularly gloomy picture. Future volumes might well take up internal policy changes, particularly in EU transnational regulatory policies in health, safety, and consumer protection areas.

Finally, the greatest problem of all are the causes and possible cures for the popular syndrome that lies behind many of the largest problems for national, transnational, and international governance on both sides of the Atlantic and indeed much of the world. I hope the reader will forgive a move from a meteorological to a medical metaphor, but syndrome seems an appropriate word for a massive but very complex condition with multiple, interactive, uncertain, overlapping symptoms, and causes that may vary from case to case.

The syndrome to which I refer is the current popular movement to distrust in and fear government or "the establishment" in general, government bureaucrats, technical experts, scientific findings, "far away" decision-makers, professional politicians and the "chattering classes." This syndrome is now prominent in the U.S., a number of EU states, most notably the UK, Hungary, Poland, and Italy, and manifested in increasing chaos in the political party system and processes of governmental decision-making.

The syndrome may well be a principal cause of the EU's "muddling thru" rather than taking dynamic action as traditional liberal forces and "the new right" divide voters, parties and governments over a host of issues. The causes of this syndrome obviously involve economic globalization, rapid technological change, large population displacements, the now evident income "gap" between the rich and everybody else, the widespread dimming of hope on the improvement in prosperity for this and future generations and the creation of local areas of economic despair amidst global economic growth.

The syndrome appears to spring from deep, psychological processes rather than simple economic self-interest, party identification or other such phenomena that are the familiar explanatory constructs of economic and political science. Some of the possible cures may have intolerable side effects. Attempts at vigorous cure may often do more harm than good. We do not know how to cure or raise sufficient resources to adequately respond to the syndrome as a whole or to such of its elements as racial hatred, political authoritarianism, anarchy, and the massive denial of objective facts.

To switch metaphors again, it would be foolish to deny this elephant in the room when studying the EU and its member states which are among its grazing grounds. Yet hunting this elephant moves us toward only partially understood, and deeply contested areas of psychological investigation.

As if economic analysis and the study of externally visible political phenomena were not difficult enough, adding deep psychological analysis is hard to contemplate. Perhaps it would be better to stick to globalization and income gaps. There are many volumes to come.

CHAPTER 44

The COVID-19 Pandemic: Failing Forward in Public Health

Scott L. Greer, Anniek de Ruijter, and Eleanor Brooks

INTRODUCTION: THE TRANSFORMATION OF EUROPEAN UNION PUBLIC HEALTH

Although most governments were heavily scrutinized and looked bad early in the COVID-19 pandemic, the EU was most noticeable for its absence. As spring 2020 turned to summer it has become clear that most European citizens, and most European governments, expected their local, regional, and especially member state governments to protect them, not the EU. They are not wrong; the role of the EU in responding to a ramifying crisis such as COVID-19, with components ranging from public health to liquidity to trade to demand crises, is far from obvious. The law and politics are clear: the EU can only help save Europeans from a human public health crisis if member states instruct it to (Anderson et al. 2020).

S. L. Greer (✉)
University of Michigan, Ann Arbor, MI, USA
e-mail: slgreer@umich.edu

A. de Ruijter
Universiteit van Amsterdam, Amsterdam, The Netherlands
e-mail: a.deruijter@uva.nl

E. Brooks
University of Edinburgh, Edinburgh, UK
e-mail: Eleanor.Brooks@ed.ac.uk

S. L. Greer
European Observatory on Health Systems and Policies, Brussels, Belgium

© The Author(s) 2021
M. Riddervold et al. (eds.), *The Palgrave Handbook of EU Crises*,
Palgrave Studies in European Union Politics,
https://doi.org/10.1007/978-3-030-51791-5_44

This chapter first presents the standard crisis narrative of EU public health policy. It then discusses the EU's COVID-19 response in terms of the three faces of European health policy—explicit health-focused policy such as public health protection, market-making and -regulating policies, and fiscal governance (Greer 2014). For decades, the second face of EU health policy, market regulation and integration, had dominated health policy, while explicit health policy was tightly constrained by member states and fiscal governance difficult to enforce on member states. With the crisis, however, European member states shifted the EU's emphasis considerably. They adopted a much more ambitious health policy agenda and a very different, if contradictory and contested, approach to fiscal governance that might lead it to look more like a federation. The conclusion returns to the European integration theories, arguing that the stylized debates of neofunctionalists and intergovernmentalists always obscured the extent to which member states have used the EU to rescue themselves before, and in the COVID-19 crisis are doing so again. The focus of the chapter is on the EU's own internal politics and policies. What is beyond the scope of this chapter is the course of its international engagement in COVID-19 response, including aid and vaccine politics, as it is politically and legally a different topic.

Initially, in March and April 2020, member states made minimal practical use of EU health law and policy, outside of sharing information and data through existing coordination mechanisms.[1] Instead, the first months of the crisis saw acute regulatory variation (Alemanno 2020). Member states showed little sense of solidarity in the face of a shared risk. Export bans on needed personal protective equipment (PPE), poorly coordinated border closures and widespread member state egotism all looked bad and fed into preexisting media narratives of EU crisis. Arguments about shared debt felt more like 2010 than 2020, with governments of self-styled "frugal" northern creditor states arguing for conditionality, and framing shared debt as bailouts for southern Europe.

This stage passed quickly as states reached an agreement about the goal of regulation, namely the reduction of transmission, and noted the need for some commonality in their pursuit of this goal (Alemanno 2020). Export bans were lifted, shared public procurements were organized and the funding for EU public procurement was increased. By late summer 2020, there was a huge new health budget, and a substantial enough program of shared debt to create an expert debate about whether there had been a transformation in the EU's basic political economy. European integration was once again being forged through crisis.

The constitutional place of public health, at least from the position of the EU institutions shifted almost overnight. European Union law had traditionally, and in line with world trade law, defined "public health" as a justification

---

[1] Decision No. 1082/2013/EU of the European Parliament and of the Council of 22 October 2013 on serious crossborder threats to health.

for member states to adopt measures in exception to the Art. 36 TFEU prohibition of infringement the freedom of movement of goods, services, or people. Although the determination as to the legality of the invocation of public health as an exception was made by European Union Judges, the substantive protection of public health was only ever intended to protect the health of national populations; never that of the population of the whole of the EU. It was a member state level concept that could justify member state level exceptions to EU policies (Weatherill and Beaumont 1999). The protection of public health of the whole of the EU was done through regulation of standards, for e.g. food, and pharmaceuticals, toys, medical devices, chemicals, blood, and blood products—never in opposition to other (EU) public policy objectives, but rather as its by-product.

European law accordingly looked on it with skepticism (the foundational *Cassis de Dijon* decision was actually about whether Germany was overusing the public health exception to discriminate against the French drink) (Greer and Jarman, forthcoming). Faced with member states' initial rush to close borders, including export bans, the Commission articulated a new logic: public health was a *European* concept and its invocation should be on behalf not of member states but EU citizens. Public health was an exception to EU law; now it is EU law (Purnhagen et al. 2020; de Ruijter et al. 2020).

A legal statement from the Commission is one thing, but money is something else. The European Union Health Programme had been losing its distinctive organizational identity for years while its small size (€446m 2014–2020) meant it had limited influence. The new "EU4Health" plan for 2021–2027, was €1.7 billion, reduced from an initial Commission proposal of €9.6 billion, and was accompanied by a huge increase in RescEU, the civil protection mechanism, and a separate vaccines strategy. EU4Health included crisis response, health systems strengthening (e.g. broader investment in the capacity and resilience of health systems so they can address unexpected consequences of COVID-19 as well as future problems), and continuing work on the preexisting priority areas of cancer, pharmaceuticals, and eHealth.[2]

It is worth noting that both crisis response and health systems strengthening open up space for direct and useful assistance to health systems, which has been a taboo topic for richer countries that are well aware of the scale of the Union's territorial inequalities. But it seems that member states have adopted an argument that neofunctionalists (see Niemann, this volume) and public health experts share: if the EU is to be an integrated area, that means every member state must have the public health capacity (surveillance, testing, tracing, and eventually vaccination) and health care capacity to keep the whole

---

[2] Brussels, 28.5.2020 COM(2020) 405 final. Proposal for a Regulation of the European Parliament and of the Council on the establishment of a Programme for the Union's action in the field of health—for the period 2021–2027 and repealing regulation (EU) No. 282/2014 ("EU4Health Programme").

Union safe from this highly infectious virus. There will undoubtedly be disappointments in store for both neofunctionalists and public health advocates, but it is a major alteration to the old equilibrium in which cohesion funds for capital projects, best understood as side payments, were the most health systems could really get from the EU.

Beyond the specific health budget, the EU responded relatively quickly to the unprecedentedly large and unusual economic crisis that the virus brought. Data on the scale of the catastrophe in Europe was staggering, with the EU economy contracting by 3.5% and the Eurozone economy shrinking by 3.8% in the first quarter of 2020, before the economic impact had really hit.[3] Most member states passed elaborate plans for income support and replacement in order to enable their firms and workers to survive the shutdowns and the contraction of overall trade that affected Europe's small and open economies. The initial, obvious, response from the EU level was to activate the "general escape clause" that suspended the operation of the fiscal compact and fiscal governance system in general.[4] This might take some pressure off, but it did nothing to address a Eurozone structure that been slowly asphyxiating economies such as Italy, Greece, and Spain for a decade. The innovation, possibly the one that will most impress historians, was the creation of an explicit and unconditional EU debt facility to support member states in managing the pandemic and its effects—a remarkably integrative step.

A Health Policy Forged in Crisis

More so than some other policy areas, the progress of EU public health policy has been written in terms of crisis and response. The eruption of a crisis opens a window of political opportunity (see also Ansell, this volume, Chapter 1 this volume). It increases the political will behind the search for a solution and makes it easier to achieve consensus on a common response, while the element of urgency reduces the time made available for debate and, potentially, obstruction. In health these factors are amplified by the presence of fear, which is readily present around issues such as communicable disease and is a powerful tool for shifting both public opinion and political commitment. Without a frightening crisis as a focusing event and problem, it has proven very difficult to get public health policy onto the EU agenda (Kingdon 2003). Member states guarded their autonomy, and many public health proposals encounter powerful resistance from big industries in areas such as tobacco, chemicals, and junk food (Greer and Kurzer 2013; Passarani 2019; Guigner 2018).

---

[3] https://ec.europa.eu/eurostat/documents/2995521/10294708/2-30042020-BP-EN.pdf/526405c5-289c-30f5-068a-d907b7d663e6.

[4] European Council (ECFIN): 23 March 2020 Statement of EU ministers of finance on the Stability and Growth Pact in light of the COVID-19 crisis 23 March 2020. https://www.consilium.europa.eu/en/press/press-releases/2020/03/23/statement-of-eu-ministers-of-finance-on-the-stability-and-growth-pact-in-light-of-the-covid-19-crisis/.

While there had long been speculative proposals for European public health integration (Davesne and Guigner 2013), the first inklings of an EU health policy were partly in response to perceptions of a crisis in abuse of illegal drugs, and the first treaty language explicitly focused on that as a target of EU public health action. AIDS was also seen as a crisis where member states could productively work together through the EU (Steffen 2012). In retellings of the history of EU public health policy, though, the variant Creuzfeld-Jakobsen (vCJD) episode occupies a central role in the crisis story (Ansell and Vogel 2006; Ansell and Gingrich 2007; Farrell 2005).

Nicknamed "mad cow disease," the story fit with broad neofunctionalist narratives as well as a Kingdonian multiple-streams approach. The problem was that integration of European food systems had radically outpaced the regulatory system, and an innovative agricultural sector had adopted practices few voters knew about or, it turns out, liked. Variant CJD was a relative of scrapie, a sheep disease, that spread into cattle through feed that included ground-up sheep and cattle. When this became public, it turned out that many Europeans were repelled by the idea of a food system that involved forcing herbivores to become not just carnivores but cannibals. Revulsion at the system that created the disease came with concern about the inability of any authorities to monitor what was happening in the food system, with the traffic in animals and animal products across borders essentially unregulated. As neofunctionalists would predict, increasing integration in one area (food production) led to problems that created a demand for European solutions to the new European problems (see Niemann, this volume).

The disease itself was a perfect focusing event and political problem, with garish images that everybody alive at the time is likely to remember—cows writhing in agony, a British agriculture minister trying to instill public confidence by feeding his young daughter a beef burger on television. While member states indeed resorted immediately to domestic actions—in 1996 France put an embargo on British beef—they also moved to creating a Europe-wide system of food safety and regulation including amendments to the Amsterdam treaty enabling broader EU powers. Their food systems were simply too integrated to do otherwise, and so the EU failed forward into a much broader set of standards and tightly integrated information systems. By now there is an entrenched EU regulatory framework laid out in the 2002 General Food Law Regulation. It is managed by DG SANTE (the Commission's health directorate), an EU agency (the European Food Safety Authority) and an established and integrated network of food safety and agriculture regulators operating across the EU to police production and handling of food as well as keep records on what is going where in the integrated European market (Grant 2012). The system is still far from perfect, as we saw with "Horsegate" in 2013 (Brooks et al. 2017), and the 2011 scandal of e.coli in German vegetables. But then, its ambition is immense and its successes impressive. Measured purely in terms of the magnitude of the policy output, it was a dramatic, expensive, and largely implemented commitment to Europeanize food production and safety.

Variant CJD might be a landmark in the broad relationship of the EU to public health, but it also was substantially limited to the food system. That is partly because vCJD was fundamentally a problem of food safety and veterinary health with only limited opportunities for human to human transmission (primarily via the blood supply). It is also because of the strong treaty bases, in agriculture and consumer protection, that exist in food policy. These were supplemented in the 1997 Amsterdam Treaty by new specific treaty powers for the EU to regulate blood and blood products, filling in that gap and also responding to issues about blood safety triggered by the scandal of HIV-infected blood supplies in France (Farrell 2005; Steffen 1992).

Reflecting the lowest-common denominator nature of EU policymaking and the sheer difficulty of Europeanizing a sector like food and agriculture, as well as health ministries' resistance to European action, the vCJD public health crisis produced an animal health response. It created a situation in which the EU has dramatic executive powers in animal health that vanish in questions of human health that do not involve blood. Had COVID-19 been a disease of pigs or sheep, the EU could have taken radical steps such as closing borders or ordering mass culls. But as it came in humans, there was little it could initially do; health ministers had done a good job of defending health systems and public health policies against EU imposition even as agriculture ministers, who were long comfortable in Brussels, had settled into a new, Europeanized, system.

The twenty-first century produced an increasing number and intensity of human health crises. They brought pressure on member state governments to act, and that sometimes meant acting through the EU. The 2001 terrorist attacks in the US and wars in Afghanistan and Iraq were the backdrop for a series of anthrax attacks that pushed public health up the global agenda while giving it a strong securitized tone (Greer 2017; also see Fidler and Gostin 2008). The 2003 SARS crisis had essentially no impact on European public health, but it changed the politics of public health in Europe as elsewhere (Fidler 2004). By showing the speed with which new communicable disease risks could emerge and travel the world, it inspired the first real efforts to build a European capacity in communicable disease control (Greer 2012).

The 2009 H1N1 influenza pandemic is widely remembered as a policy failure, in part because the pandemic strain of influenza was less harmful than seasonal influenza but also because it exposed a variety of dysfunctions in the European system, especially the hoarding and then wasting of vaccines and antiviral medication. Within the world of EU public health, though, there was considerable learning (de Ruijter 2019). H1N1 might turn out to have been the critical juncture at which the trajectory of EU health emergencies policy was set.

A 2013 decision set up a clearer framework and role for the EU in addressing health threats—a small role, but a bigger and more formal one than before.[5] In a sector-specific replay of the kinds of socialization mechanisms that Europeanize politics more broadly (Van Middelaar 2013; also see Ansell, this volume; Cross, this volume), the Health Security Committee of member state representatives became an increasingly clear coordinating body with shared understandings among its members. Its role extended beyond its legal mandate into areas where member states wanted coordination. For example, radiologic emergencies and threats to health are governed under the EURATOM treaty. There is no desire to revise that treaty, so member states just agree to coordinate through the standard health threats system with the Health Security Committee at its core. It contributed to a sense among public health policymakers and advisors that the EU was indeed a community of fate in public health matters (Pacces and Weimer 2020).

The concrete problems of procuring medicines and vaccines during the H1N1 pandemic also led to the elaboration of the Joint Procurement mechanism which is effectively an EU buyers' club for medicines. It allows EU member states, most of which are not especially big pharmaceutical markets, to negotiate for better prices and terms. The West African Ebola outbreak in 2014 had similarly little impact on European morbidity and mortality but efforts to coordinate responses further developed mechanisms that member states could use when they chose (even if they frequently chose not to coordinate).

The EU's civil protection system after Lisbon changed focus as well. EU civil protection evolved largely in response to natural disasters and the obvious fact that global heating would expose more and more of the continent to more and severe kinds of disasters, from floods to wildfires to heat waves. Initially EU disaster response action had been largely targeted abroad, operating under external relations DGs and coordinating member state resources (e.g. search and rescue teams) with EU foreign aid. Gradually, it began to work inwards, supported by TFEU Articles 196 (on mutual aid among states) and 214 (authorizing the EU to aid victims of disasters worldwide), which provide a solid legal base for the development of EU civil protection capacity. It was primarily a matchmaking service, smoothing the process by which member states with spare resources (e.g. firefighting equipment) could loan them to member states with unexpected needs (e.g. fires). The scheme, called RescEU from March 2019, did not really have its own resources (equipment, people, or money) or foresight capacities. It did preparatory coordinating work, such as identifying and classifying medical and health resources that member states could volunteer in order to speed requests and avoid mismatches while making some efforts to harmonize or at least familiarize teams with each other.

By 2020 the cumulation of these different disaster responses meant that the EU had an agency responsible for coordinating communicable disease

---

[5] Decision No. 1082/2013/EU of the European Parliament and of the Council of 22 October 2013 on serious crossborder threats to health.

response (ECDC), a thin but institutionalized public health and health emergencies capacity in the Commission, and a useful-looking bridge between its civil protection system and health. The informal dimensions of this structure were bigger than they looked on paper and rooted it more deeply in member state politics than an outside observer might have thought, with groups like the Health Security Committee coordinating formally and informally.

No simple linear relationship between crisis and response exists, of course. As this book shows, crises are socially constructed (see Chapter 1 this volume; Ansell, this volume; Cross, this volume), as with the illegal drug crisis of the 1980s and 1990s, not all crises lead to actions, not all are stimuli to political action are actual crises, and there is no reason to expect that a crisis leads to a logical solution.

COVID-19 AND EUROPEAN INTEGRATION

At the start of 2020 European Union public health policymakers and researchers, a small group, were cautiously optimistic about the future (Brooks and Guy 2020, forthcoming). The Juncker Commission had once considered abandoning health policy entirely (European Commission 2017) and had systematically sidelined the small Directorate-General for Health and Food Safety (SANTE). After that experience, the survival of the DG and a comparatively expansive mandate letter for the new Commissioner was cause for optimism (Greer et al. 2019). In the specific area of communicable disease control and health emergencies, the decade since the H1N1 influenza pandemic had been put to good use, developing and testing networks and legal forms to enable useful coordination in future health emergencies. But there was still no designated health emergencies budget line, the public health treaty base (Art. 168 TFEU) was very limiting, and the EU's civil protection mechanism was still being built.

By June, the situation looked quite different. Europe had been a global epicenter of the pandemic and the pandemic had reshaped EU health politics. The COVID-19 crisis hit Europe hard, starting with an outbreak in Italy in February, and the continent was clearly the global epicenter of the disease by late March and April. European governments, member state, and regional, acted, and Europeans turned to their governments to protect them. Much as it might frustrate us, it is hard to say how well any of them did. Despite citizens' desire to find heroes and villains among governments, and political scientists' desire to have mortality figures prove pet theories, the data is just not good enough and the causality too complex. Epidemiological factors such as transmission routes, social factors such as intergenerational living, and population health factors such as age profile and comorbidities (such as diabetes) all feed into the eventual outcome, and even that is hard to measure due to sampling problems with tests (Karanikolos and McKee 2020). But while it is not clear whether most governments did especially well or poorly, what is clear is that European member states initially moved on their own, revealing strengths that had been easy to forget earlier. Only as the crisis evolved and governments realized their shared fates did they begin to work together.

This section frames the EU's change of course in terms of the three faces of EU health policy. Conversations about EU health policy were long bedeviled by the fact that most of EU health policy was not named as such, making EU health policies a constant "treaty base game" (Rhodes 1995) and leading to legal-epistemological debates about whether things like the General Food Law Regulation, which promoted human health primarily on agricultural, internal market, and consumer protection treaty bases, was "health" (Hervey and McHale 2015; Hervey 2017).

The three faces framework identifies three major and quite different ways in which the EU shapes health. The first face, health policy, is the face that resembles health policy elsewhere: built on Article 168, run by DG SANTE or agencies such as the ECDC or the EMCDDA (European Monitoring Centre for Drugs and Drug Addiction), and with the stated intent of promoting health. This has been by far the least consequential dimension of EU health policy to date; member states worked, in treaties, legislation, and daily politics, to restrain EU powers over human health and health systems, and succeeded. The second face is where the EU has had its most significant impact on health to date. It is the law of the internal market and its regulation. This includes the other policy areas that have human health named as an explicit policy goal, including labor law (social policy), environmental protection, and consumer protection. It also includes ones that have no legal, political, or historical commitment to human health, including law on the regulation of services, state aids, competition, cross-border mobility, and insurance. The irruption of these policy logics into health care systems was perhaps the biggest story in EU health policy for two decades; while member states had barred the door against EU action in health systems regulation and development, they were vulnerable to a simple reclassification of health systems as "services" and regulation of them on that basis. Efforts to establish the "specificity" of health care in the eyes of courts, and turn back challenges to see it as a service, or as a case of public procurement, state aids, competition law, or one of the other kinds of EU law, led to a directive and shaped EU health politics.

The third face of EU health policy is fiscal governance. Fiscal governance refers to the set of rules that were instituted to preserve the Eurozone by requiring member state adherence to budgetary limits, notably a deficit ceiling of 3% and a debt ceiling of 60% of GDP. The logic is that since the EU does not have internal redistribution on a large scale, and the ECB's defense of the Euro creates a soft budget constraint, member states will be tempted to issue too much debt, avoid making necessary structural changes, and eventually create debt crises (see Hjertaker and Tranøy, this volume for further discussion). EU fiscal governance is largely a history of failure. No matter how elaborate and legalized the system, it was hard to compel member states to make the kinds of austere policies that the system demanded. Furthermore, it is not clear that EU fiscal governance could be expected to work. All stick and no carrot, it asked member states to pursue often brutal policies of internal devaluation right when the good policy would ask for countercyclical spending or social investment. Failing to address the alarming and growing scale of internal divergence between EU economies, it coded deficits and debt simply as failings of individual governments. Its crude moralism poisoned European political debate while blocking policies, such as the issuance of European debt, that might have addressed the internal divergence within the EU. A rigidly liberal framework in a rapidly diverging economy could point to a terminal crisis of some sort, but also pointed to a future in which much of southern and central Europe would become a permanent periphery—a giant *mezzogiorno* (Greer 2020).

Such a policy attracted not just principled and political opposition, but also led to numerous efforts to undermine it by those whom it would make suffer. Just as with previous efforts to impose fiscal governance rules in Europe, it began to decay quickly as opponents worked to undermine it (Zeitlin and Vanhercke 2018). The fiscal governance scheme set up in 2012 was, predictably, becoming rotten by 2020. Threats to act against member states with deficits were not credible while the vast and elaborate surveillance system that advocates of austerity had built was being undermined as opponents of austerity expanded goals, added and queried indicators, and increased the scope of conflict until the old, crude, rules were hard to apply at all (Greer and Brooks 2020).

By January of 2020, then, advocates of more ambitious EU health policies were relieved that DG SANTE had not been abolished and the new Commissioner actually had a more expansive mandate than under the Juncker Commission (see also Kassim and Tholoniat, this volume). They were nonetheless still struck in a structural trap: the only kinds of consequential policy affecting health that could plausibly be proposed could not be made in the name of health. There was only one open legislative file in health (on health technology assessment). Insinuating health objectives and engagement with health sector actors into the second and third faces seemed the rational strategy, whether it meant trying to promote health objectives in EU research policy or turn the European Semester from a crude tool of austerity into something less dangerous to health and social policy, or even a way to push up the salience of health objectives (Zeitlin and Vanhercke 2018). The fact that the UN Sustainable Development Goals were integrated into the Semester gave hope that the Semester would be more socially oriented, or at least less effective as a tool of austerity. Undermining the institutionalized austerity of EU fiscal governance, and the neoliberalism of internal markets policy under Juncker and Barroso, was hard, slow, and essentially defensive work.

Health Policy: From Exception to Policy

The EU's immediate health policy responses to COVID-19 used the two key resources that were already available at the start of 2020: the ECDC, the health emergencies system, and the RescEU civil protection mechanism. The ECDC fulfilled its function without visible hitches. It gathered and circulated data, its systems for transmitting information worked well, and its expertise was used. No member state government chose to rely on the EU (or WHO) directly for advice, and the ECDC, knowing its role, did not produce the kinds of detailed guidance that was being published by state-level institutions or WHO. Governments filtered EU and other information and advice through their own committees of experts, whose composition and transparency varied greatly. ECDC's role was always limited. It had fewer than 300 staff and was manifestly not designed to be the front line of European health emergency response (in the language of the field, its role is risk assessment). Rather, it was designed to be a hub for member state level experts and information, and it fulfilled that role (Greer 2012; Guigner 2004, 2006; Deruelle 2016). The Commission and member states in the Health Security Committee are in charge of risk management, where decisions are made, and actions are taken. Again, the system worked as one might have predicted; the Committee coordinated as intended. It was a vehicle through which EU member states coordinated more and more issues, as the first wave of panic and national egotism subsided, and they realized the benefits of coordination as well as safety in numbers (see Trondal, this volume).

The system worked, but it was a small and historically unambitious system made up of a committee whose informal role exceeded its formal powers, a supranational agency that was dwarfed by many of the national agencies it coordinated, and a small Luxembourg-based unit of a small DG that lacked its own budget line, supported by an administrative agency (CHAFEA) with no independent legal basis. Already tested by the crisis, it was then given a new challenge. The Commission rapidly prepared a new work plan and the EU budget was amended, increasing money for health work in the EU4Health program as well as RescEU's dramatic expansion. Whether this substantial increment will stay remains to be seen (historically, public health emergency response has a way of declining as memory of the last crisis diminishes). It is also unclear whether the funding and priority-setting mechanisms will be politically sustainable now that their policy role is central and the amounts of money far greater. However, the guidance and initiatives issued by the Commission may well raise the expectations of citizens, market actors, and member states (Alemanno 2020: 316) and, as neofunctional theory anticipates, underpin relocation of the political debate to the European level.

Civil protection (RescEU), like the EU, initially disappointed. A matchmaking service is of no great value in a moment of autarchy and egotism, and was not designed for a situation in which all states face the same needs. Member states were either in deep crisis or feared that they were about to descend into crisis. That made them reluctant to offer up any current surpluses to states in need, lest they should soon need these themselves. But as the unevenness of the pandemic became clear as well as the long-term nature of its threat, member states came to the view enlightened self-interest meant a policy that stockpiled EU resources, even ones that were immediately relevant to COVID-19 and scarce. Accordingly, by April RescEU was stockpiling equipment of immediate usefulness and by late summer its budget was much larger.

Markets: Preserving the Internal Market

Legal scholars often write that the "four freedoms" of movement of capital, goods, people, and services are constitutional principles of the EU. When member states initially started closing borders to each other's citizens and imposing export bans on important equipment such as personal protective equipment (PPE), it could be regarded as necessary emergency measures but also as a blow to the heart of the EU. As noted above, member states either were in crisis or feared crisis. They accordingly hoarded supplies and applied export bans, creating a new and unexpected landscape of inequality based on who happened to have a given kind of factory within their borders. There was a barely plausible public health case for closing borders to people in some states, especially if combined with domestic restrictions on movement. Export bans, on the other hand, were a direct assault on the internal market and solidarity. Member states turned a public health crisis into what could have been an EU constitutional crisis.

The Commission reacted forcefully to the export bans (de Ruijter et al. 2020). They fought back with infringement proceedings against illegal restraint of trade in goods. There would be little reason to expect courts applying EU law to support member state actions that reverse principles dating to 1956. But courts, of course, live in political worlds; so why did the EU so quickly manage to reestablish its market? The Commission's success might be partly due to revulsion at some cases of apparent national egotism (Italy receiving masks from China before Germany, Czechia seizing a shipment of masks Italy had bought) several of which later turned out to be less clearcut than they looked, but which looked very bad at the time. Furthermore, member states quickly started to recognize that the pandemic would hit them unevenly. A functioning European market would serve them all better than a weird landscape of plenty and want based on what kinds of factories were located where.

Restrictions on personal mobility took longer to undo and at the time of writing are still widespread. The EU, with energetic input from the Commission, began to try to coordinate and slowly reduce personal movement restrictions, even developing an app to make it easier to work out who could travel where and what would be permitted when they arrived. Schengen states developed common external border policies, setting standards that tightly restricted arrivals from countries which did not have their epidemics under control such as Brazil, Russia, and the United States. In this area, the Home Affairs Council formation led. Its increasingly tight coordination led, by July 2020, to integrated European decision-making on entrances. Given that its first decisions in 2020 were to effectively close Europe to some of the world's most powerful countries and Europe's biggest trading partners, the European decision to act together and formulate transparent rules was a test passed for integration. At the time of writing in autumn 2020, the key question was how the UK would be handled. Schengen might be European, but member states control border guards, and Southern European countries which had never really recovered from 2010 and faced bleak economic prospects opted to admit British tourists despite the manifest failure of the government to control the virus in England.

Fiscal Governance: A Hamiltonian Moment?

The first line of defense for the Euro and Eurozone economies is always the European Central Bank (Dyson 2001, also see Hjertaker and Tranøy, this volume). The ECB wobbled early in the crisis, with a wayward statement by its head Christine Lagarde that disrupted Italian bond markets. But it quickly reverted to its de facto role as guarantor of the Eurozone's financial stability, a role that sophisticated political observers had identified soon after its birth. Its clear and continued commitment to ensuring the smooth functioning of the Eurozone monetary system meant that potential liquidity crises in the early period were averted. However, the problem with relying on central banks to compensate for fiscal policy failure, as the EU, US, and other countries show, is that all of their tools increase inequality and finance-sector rentierism.

The elaborate structure of EU fiscal governance collapsed almost immediately. The Commission quickly invoked the "general escape clause," which lifted the Stability and Growth Pact's restrictions on member state spending. The Semester's surveillance continues, but it had become an increasingly diffuse process with health goals included, and it is unclear how much it will matter. In mid-2020, it was a sideshow and by late 2020 it was being integrated into a new Recovery and Resilience Facility. There will inevitably be a pro-austerity backlash from the right in European and world politics, but it is not at all clear that proponents of austerity will find the existing fiscal governance structures a promising tool when they renew their push. Others float the idea that the Semester might be used to strengthen the EU's resilience in the face of pandemics (Renda and Castro 2020), linking this to integration of the Sustainable Development Goals (SDGs) in a further dilution of the framework's original purpose. The integration of the Recovery and Resilience Facility, below, with the Semester might suggest just such an outcome.

The real excitement was the unprecedented issuance of common European debt as a response to the crisis. This might turn out to be the biggest single change that the crisis precipitates, and seems to constitute an early, significant evidence of *heading forward*. Students of political economy debated whether this was the EU's "Hamiltonian moment," referring to the critical juncture in American political economy when the federal government assumed states' war debts and created its own debt in 1790. In an object lesson in the difficulties of historical analogy, the discussion of whether the EU had a Hamiltonian moment in 2020 fell immediately into conceptual confusion. The question was not whether the EU had suddenly turned into the US. It was whether the EU would start to develop the fiscal capacity that every other viable federal government has and uses to stabilize its internal divergence (Greer 2020; Greer and Elliott 2019). The original Hamiltonian moment in eighteenth-century North America was a very limited federal decision (assuming debts plausibly related to the revolutionary war against the UK) that turned out to have enormous path-dependent consequences for the country's fiscal structure. It put the US on a road to convergence with most other federations with a big role for the central government and its debt. 2020 produced nothing like a Europeanization of the crushing debt burdens of Greece or Italy, but on the other hand it created a mechanism to issue very solid debt for member states without any conditionality.

The impact of this could be far-reaching. As is well known, the EU grew up as a regulatory polity, a law-state (Kelemen 2019; Majone 1994; Page 2001). Compared to other federations it has combined an unusually deep regulatory reach into the affairs of its member states with nugatory fiscal capacity and essentially no implementation capacity. But now, it will issue European debt to sustain its member states through at least one big crisis, without conditionality and with a role for the European institutions in allocating the money. The debt is for response to the specific and unprecedented crisis of COVID-19, but since the crisis will last a long time, the virtues of shared debt as a way to maintain the EU's internal economic and political coherence might start to appeal to policymakers. Even if it is wound down, which is clearly the preference of "creditor" member states, the experience of having issued and distributed shared debt is a precedent for European action that will be hard to forget.

Conclusion: Another European Rescue of the Nation-State?

European integration, and on bad days EU studies in general, has long been understood through a literature that focused on stylized duels of neofunctionalists and intergovernmentalists. While interesting and theoretically productive, the debate distracted us from the fact that the empirical stories of European advance were often very similar. Member states confront a problem that they share; they identify a shared approach, typically after initial attempts to address it individually or through intergovernmental mechanisms; they formalize a least-common-denominator response through the EU institutions, reining in ambitious EU actors (Kleine 2013); the result is integration, but rarely integration at the scale that advocates of European Union or comprehensive policy solutions would like to see. In other words, they fail forward (Jones et al. 2015, also see Stenstad and Trangy, this volume). Faced with what the introduction refers to as disintegration (scenario 1), member states will try *muddling through* and might find themselves taking major steps. To the extent that they muddle, they might create the conditions for another crisis that will require another European rescue of the nation-state (Milward 1999).

This chapter is being written early in the COVID-19 crisis. Epidemiologically, the virus is likely to stay endemic in our species for a long time to come; the opportunity to stamp it out worldwide was lost in January or February 2020 at the latest. Even suppressing it consistently in an age of interconnected economies and personal mobility is likely to be impossible. If some EU countries, formally or informally, adopt a "herd immunity" strategy of letting the disease circulate more or less unconstrained, they will eventually export the disease to the rest of the Union, just like a few major disease-exporting trading partners are a threat so long as there is no vaccine. At some point, either there will be a widely distributed vaccine that is safe and effective, or countries will, at enormous cost, start to overshoot and then stabilize around the "herd immunity" threshold of 60–70% infection. Until then, economic disruption is the best-case scenario, and many more deaths the worst. The vaccine itself will pose serious policy problems, from trials of a vaccine on a very short timescale, to distributional decisions about who gets what vaccine when. These problems will test EU solidarity and clout in the global marketplace. The upshot is that this chapter, written in September 2020, is at most a half-time discussion. More likely is that we are early in a reckoning with a pandemic that could easily last four or five years.

The likely long duration of the crisis matters in understanding the EU's behavior because European integration can be slow, or at least slower than politics in most member states. The vCJD crisis was in 1996, but the General Food Law Regulation passed in 2002. A financial crisis that started in 2008 and morphed into a debt crisis in Europe in 2010 led to frantic improvisation at first (the Troika). The fiscal governance system that was intended to prevent another such crisis was only really built in 2012. The EU is not a quick-moving machine, and the ordinary legislative process in particular was not designed to be fast or decisive. Treaty changes are still less so. The existing mechanisms which embody genuine solidarity—collective purchase of vaccines via the Joint Procurement Agreement and emergency response mechanisms like RescEU—are voluntary, intergovernmental and do not move quickly enough to accommodate urgent needs (de Ruijter et al. 2020: 18). But the length of the crisis and the disruptions it entails give more than enough time for member states to learn and conclude that they want still more, or different, Europe. A crisis that lingers for years—and whose economic and social consequences are visible for longer—creates plenty of time for evolution in areas such as the management of the expanded health budget or shared debt. There will be time and pressure to build capacity and harder law, and to develop bigger ambitions for EU health.

What we can say, from the perspective of June 2020, is that the EU has actually had a good crisis. The predictable, if demoralizing, phase of disorganization and national egotism lasted only about a month (March–April). In May and June 2020 it created a substantial new first-face health policy agenda, reasserted its second-face market-preserving powers, and shifted its fiscal stance in a much more supportive direction. "To the uninitiated, there is something quite logical in assuming that the EU is competent where its Member States are mutually dependent. Yet, public health is far from integrated" wrote Deruelle (Deruelle 2020), highlighting the tension that neofunctionalist theory would have us expect to produce integration. The COVID-19 crisis exposed European Union member states' interdependence. It has, so far, also led to integration.

REFERENCES

Alemanno, A. (2020). The European Response to COVID-19: From Regulatory Emulation to Regulatory Coordination? *European Journal of Risk Regulation, 11*(2), 307–316.

Anderson, M., Mckee, M., & Mossialos, E. (2020). Covid-19 Exposes Weaknesses in European Response to Outbreaks. *BMJ, 368,* 1075.

Ansell, C., & Vogel, D. (Eds.). (2006). *What's the Beef? The Contested Governance of European Food Safety.* Cambridge, MA: MIT Press.

Ansell, C. K., & Gingrich, J. (2007). *The United Kingdom's Response to the BSE Epidemic.* Charlotte: Information Age Publishing.

Brooks, E., & Guy, M. (2020, forthcoming). EU Health Law and Policy: Shaping a Future Research Agenda. *Health Economics, Policy and Law.* https://doi.org/10.1017/S1744133120000274.

Brooks, S., Elliott, C. T., Spence, M., Walsh, C., & Dean, M. (2017). Four Years Post-Horsegate: An Update of Measures and Actions Put in Place Following the Horsemeat Incident of 2013. *npj Science of Food, 1,* 5.

Davesne, A., & Guigner, S. (2013). La Communauté Européenne De La Santé (1952–1954). Une Redécouverte Intergouvernementaliste Du Projet Fonctionnaliste De «Pool Blanc». *Politique Européenne, 41,* 40–63.

de Ruijter, A. (2019). *EU Health Law & Policy: The Expansion of EU Power in Public Health and Health Care.* Oxford: Oxford University Press.

de Ruijter, A., Beetsma, R. M. W. J., Burgoon, B. Nicoli, F., & Vandenbroucke, F. (2020). EU Solidarity and Policy in Fighting Infectious Diseases: State of Play, Obstacles, Citizen Preferences and Ways Forward. *Amsterdam Centre for European Studies Research Paper.*

Deruelle, T. (2016). Bricolage or Entrepreneurship? Lessons from the Creation of the European Centre for Disease Prevention and Control. *European Policy Analysis, 2,* 43–67.

Deruelle, T. (2020). *Beyond Health: Looking for Europe's Strategy Vis-À-Vis the Covid-19 Crisis.* Doha: Al Jazeera Centre for Studies.

Dyson, K. (2001). *The Politics of the Euro-Zone: Stability or Breakdown?.* Oxford: Oxford University Press.

European Commission. (2017). *White Paper on the Future of Europe: Five Scenarios.* Brussels: European Commission.

Farrell, A.-M. (2005). The Emergence of EU Governance in Public Health: The Case of Blood Policy and Regulation. In M. Steffen (Ed.), *Health Governance in Europe: Issues, Challenges and Theories.* Abingdon: Routledge.

Fidler, D. P. (2004). *Sars, Governance and the Globalization of Disease.* Basingstoke: Palgrave Macmillan.

Fidler, D. P., & Gostin, L. O. (2008). *Biosecurity in the Global Age Biological Weapons, Public Health, and the Rule of Law.* Stanford: Stanford University Press.

Grant, W. (2012). Agricultural Policy, Food Policy and Communicable Diseases Policy. *Journal of Health Politics, Policy and Law, 37,* 1031–1048.

Greer, S. L. (2012). The European Centre for Disease Prevention and Control: Hub or Hollow Core? *Journal of Health Politics, Policy and Law, 37,* 1001–1030.

Greer, S. L. (2014). The Three Faces of European Union Health Policy: Policy, Markets and Austerity. *Policy and Society, 33,* 13–24.

Greer, S. L. (2017). Constituting Public Health Surveillance in Twenty-First Century Europe. In M. Weimer & A. de Ruijter (Eds.), *Regulating Risks in the European Union: The Co-Production of Expert and Executive Power.* London: Bloomsbury.

Greer, S. L. (2020). Health, Federalism and the European Union: Lessons from Comparative Federalism About the European Union. *Health Economics, Policy and Law,* 1–14.

Greer, S. L., & Brooks, E. (2020). Termites of Solidarity in the House of Austerity: Undermining Fiscal Governance in the European Union. *Journal of Health Politics, Policy and Law, xxx,* xxx.

Greer, S. L., & Elliott, H. (Eds.). (2019). *Federalism and Social Policy: Patterns of Redistriubtion in Eleven Democracies.* Ann Arbor: University of Michigan Press.

Greer, S. L., Fahy, N., Rozenblum, S., Jarman, H., Palm, W., Elliott, H. A., et al. (2019). *Everything You Always Wanted to Know About European Union Health Policy but Were Afraid to Ask* (2nd Rev. ed.). Brussels: European Observatory on Health Systems and Policies.

Greer, S. L., & Jarman, H. (Forthcoming). What Is EU Public Health and Why? Explaining the Scope and Organization of Public Health in the European Union. *Journal of Health Politics, Policy, and Law, xxx,* xxx–xxx.

Greer, S. L., & Kurzer, P. (Eds.). (2013). *European Union Public Health Policies: Regional and Global Perspectives.* Abingdon: Routledge.

Guigner, S. (2004). Institutionalizing Public Health in the European Commission: The Thrills and Spills of Politiciziation. In A. Smith (Ed.), *Politics and the European Commission: Actors, Interdependence, Legitimacy.* London: Routledge.

Guigner, S. (2006). The Eu's Role(s) in European Public Health: The Interdependence of Roles Within a Saturated Space of International Organizations. In O. Elgström & M. Smith (Eds.), *The European Union's Roles in International Politics.* London: Routledge.

Guigner, S. (2018). L'union Européenne Et La Santé: Des Lobbies Sous Pression. In G. Coron (Ed.), *L'europe De La Santé: Enjeux Et Pratiques Des Politiques Publiques.* Paris: Hygee.

Hervey, T. K. (2017). Telling Stories About European Union Health Law: The Emergence of a New Field of Law. *Comparative European Politics, 15,* 352–369.

Hervey, T. K., & McHale, J. V. (2015). *European Union Health Law: Themes and Implications.* Cambridge: Cambridge University Press.

Jones, E., Kelemen, R. D., & Meunier, S. (2015). Failing Forward? The Euro Crisis and the Incomplete Nature of European Integration. *Comparative Political Studies, 49,* 1010–1034.

Karanikolos, M., & McKee, M. (2020). How Comparable Is COVID-19 Mortality Across Countries? *COVID-19 Health System Response Monitor.*

Kelemen, R. Dl. (2019). Is Differentiation Possible in Rule of Law. *Comparative European Politics, 17,* 246–260.

Kingdon, J. W. (2003). *Agendas, Alternatives, and Public Policies*. New York: HarperCollins.

Kleine, M. (2013). *Informal Governance in the European Union: How Governments Make International Organizations Work*. Ithaca: Cornell University Press.

Majone, G. (1994). The Rise of the Regulatory State in Europe. *West European Politics, 17*, 77–102.

Milward, A. (1999). *The European Rescue of the Nation State*. London: Routledge.

Pacces, A. M., & Weimer, M. (2020). From Diversity to Coordination: A European Approach to COVID-19. *European Journal of Risk Regulation, 11*, 283–296.

Page, E. C. (2001). The European Union and the Bureaucratic Mode of Production. In A. Menon (Ed.), *From the Nation State to Europe: Essays in Honour of Jack Hayward*. Oxford: Oxford University Press.

Passarani, I. (2019). *Role of Evidence in the Formulation of European Public Health Policies: A Comparative Case Study Analysis*.

Purnhagen, K. P., De Ruijter, A., Flear, M. L., Hervey, T. K., & Herwig, A. (2020). More Competences Than You Knew? The Web of Health Competence for European Union Action in Response to the COVID-19 Outbreak. *European Journal of Risk Regulation, 11*(2), 297–306.

Renda, A., & Castro, R. (2020). Towards Stronger EU Governance of Health Threats After the COVID-19 Pandemic. *European Journal of Risk Regulation, 11*(2), 273–282.

Rhodes, M. (1995). A Regulatory Conundrum: Industrial Relations and the Social Dimension. In S. Leibfried & P. Pierson (Eds.), *European Social Policy: Between Fragmentation and Integration*. Washington, DC: Brookings.

Steffen, M. (1992). France: Social Solidarity and Scientific Expertise. In D. L. Kirp & R. Bayer (Eds.), *AIDS in the Industrialized Democracies: Passions, Politics and Policies*. New Brunswick: Rutgers University Press.

Steffen, M. (2012). The Europeanization of Public Health: How Does It Work? The Seminal Role of the AIDS Case. *Journal of Health Politics, Policy and Law, 37*, 1057–1089.

Van Middelaar, L. (2013). *The Passage to Europe: How a Continent Became a Union*. New Haven: Yale University Press.

Weatherill, S., & Beaumont, P. (1999). *EU Law*. London: Penguin.

Zeitlin, J., & Vanhercke, B. (2018). Socializing the European Semester: EU Social and Economic Policy Co-Ordination in Crisis and Beyond. *Journal of European Public Policy, 25*, 149–174.

CHAPTER 45

A Series of Unfortunate Events: Crisis Response and the European Union After 2008

Jeffrey J. Anderson

European integration has been driven by crisis since the 1950s. What distinguishes the most recent crisis context in Europe is its degree of complexity, duration, and interdependence. To understand the current chapter in European integration, one must first evaluate the unusual, combined effects of the five overlapping crises that have surfaced since 2008. I develop a general framework of analysis designed to help us understand Europe's novel crisis context, and then apply it to the Eurozone crisis, the Russia–Ukraine crisis, the crisis of migration, Brexit, and the crisis in the transatlantic relationship. What emerges from the comparative analysis is that the level of interactive complexity generated by this succession of crises has prompted the EU to respond in ways that has brought the Union incrementally closer to "stateness."

European integration has been driven by crisis. Since the 1950s, the seminal grand bargains that now define modern Europe have followed in response to exogenous shocks. What distinguishes the most recent crisis context in Europe is its degree of complexity, duration, and interdependence. Five overlapping and continuing shocks—the Eurozone crisis (2008+); the Russia/Ukraine crisis (2014+); the immigration crisis (2015+); Brexit (2016+); and Donald Trump (2017+)—have confronted the European Union with novel, intractable challenges, triggering responses that have led to new political dynamics and new European-level outcomes. To understand this

J. J. Anderson (✉)
Georgetown University, Washington, DC, USA
e-mail: jja5@georgetown.edu

unprecedented chapter in European integration, one must first evaluate the unusual combined effects of the intersecting crises that have given rise to it.

Following a review of how crisis has been analyzed in theories of European integration as well as the broader literature on crisis response, I will develop a general framework of analysis designed to help us understand Europe's crisis context since 2008. The remainder of the chapter will then focus on the five overlapping crises, which specific attention to five dimensions of each crisis: intensity, scope, duration, interactivity, and conflict. What emerges from the analysis is that the level of interactive complexity generated by the succession of crises has prompted the EU to respond in ways that, by taking into account the radically changed domestic circumstances in which integration now proceeds, has brought the Union incrementally closer to "stateness."

Crisis and European Integration Theory

To state that the European integration process has been shaped by intermittent crisis is to utter a truism. To state that the European integration process has been determined by crisis is to invite a theoretical debate. The goal of this paper is to navigate the fault line between these two statements. Tellingly, the role of crisis in triggering decisive steps toward enhanced cooperation in postwar Europe, while a recurring theme, has not featured consistently as a fully integrated component in any of the first generation theories of regional integration: federalism, functionalism, neofunctionalism, and intergovernmentalism.[1] To be sure, these various schools, while they disagree profoundly about the main agents, motors, and processes of integration, typically acknowledge the critical role played by the original historical crisis—fierce interstate rivalries culminating in two world wars—in launching the European project. Beyond serving as a catalyst, however, crisis features hardly at all in these theories.

The second generation of integration theory accords a more explicit and at times coherent role for crisis in the integration process. The reason behind this is straightforward: since the goal is to explain first the unexpected restarting of integration in 1987 with the ratification of the Single European Act, and then the even more ambitious revisions to the treaty framework outlined in the Treaty on European Union in 1993, the search for precipitating events or processes encompasses both internal and external causal sources. Although integration scholars disagree vehemently over which actors were driving the integration process, there is general agreement that the impetus for change came at least in part from exogenous shocks to the European project.

For the heirs of intergovernmentalism, the environment external to the European integration project plays a role insofar as it acts as a source (among many) of changes in the preference distributions of the member state national

---

[1] For an excellent overview of these traditional European integration theories, see Rosamond (2000).

executives.[2] This inherently realist perspective, according to which changes in the distribution and balance of power and influence at the international level affects the interests and actions of state actors in the system, represents a distinct improvement in the capacity of the intergovernmental approach to cope with the empirical reality of exogenous shocks to the European integration process, but it still falls well short of a fully articulated analytical framework.

A more promising approach can be found within the functionalist lineage. A particularly good example is Sandholtz and Zysman (1989), which identifies an explicit international trigger for the bargaining that eventually culminated in the Single European Act (SEA). Significant changes in the balance of power and potential in the international economy—specifically, the rise of Japan and the relative decline of the United States in the 1970s and early 1980s—exposed vulnerabilities within the European Community, which subsequently "triggered" sustained policy efforts to redress these weaknesses.[3]

Sandholtz and Zysman's "trigger" connects causally to the integration process via the grand bargain on which the European project rests. In this sense, their causal mechanism is tied to their conception of regional integration, which is predicated on a hierarchy of bargains dating back to the founding period in the 1950s. These bargains reflect the core features of the international system at the time the bargains were struck. As such, significant changes in the structure of the international system, which can follow from incremental change but are even more likely to result from the severe international crisis, can trigger a drive on the part of European elites to recast the bargains holding together the European project. "When the global context changed, the European bargains had to be adjusted for new realities… Changing international … structures altered the choices and constraints facing European elites" (Sandholtz and Zysman 1989: 103).

The most recent wave of theorizing about the European project—postfunctionalism and the new intergovernmentalism[4]—seeks to explain integration dynamics that have emerged since the Treaty on European Union went into effect in 1993. Postfunctionalism attaches central importance to the end of the permissive consensus during the 1990s, when European integration ceased to be an elite game and grew increasingly politicized at the domestic level. The impact has been to elevate the importance of domestic identity politics and interests in the European integration process, which has placed significant constraints on what is possible at the supranational level. European issues are

[2] See for example the discussion of "intergovernmental institutionalism" in Moravcsik (1991).

[3] Sandholtz, in a later piece, advances a similar argument, one that stresses the importance of the geopolitical security crisis resulting from the unification of Germany and the end of the Cold War in providing the main impetus for the Maastricht Treaty in the early 1990s (Sandholtz 1993).

[4] For an overview of postfunctionalism and the new intergovernmentalism, see Hooghe and Marks (2019).

now tightly woven into the fundamental political divides that drive domestic politics across the European space. The result is a "constraining dissensus" that curbs both the supranational aspirations of European politicians and the ambitions of supranational actors as well. "A brake on European integration has been imposed not because people have changed their minds, but because, on a range of vital issues, legitimate decision making has shifted from an insulated elite to mass politics" (Hooghe and Marks 2009: 13).

Crisis plays an important but nevertheless implicit role in the postfunctionalist perspective. The end of the Cold War—an exogenous shock—triggers an elite response at the European level—the Maastricht grand bargain—that in turn sparks a politicization of Europe at the domestic level from which there is no going back. In short, 1989/90 ushers in a disequilibrium in the politics of European integration, one in which the permissive consensus disintegrates and takes with it the freedom of maneuver on European matters previously enjoyed by both national executives and supranational actors alike. Integration is still possible, but far less likely and when on the agenda, in far smaller doses.

Enter the new intergovernmentalists, who accept the domestic paradigm identified by the postfunctionalists, but unlike them posit a fundamental clash between pro-integration elites at both the national and supranational levels and their increasingly Euro-skeptical publics. Rather than a stable, constraining dissensus, the new intergovernmentalists see "a destructive dissensus that casts doubt on the future sustainability of the EU. "In short, Europe currently finds itself" in a persistent state of disequilibrium," with potentially dire implications for the future of the European project (Hodson and Puetter 2019: 2).

Many of the seminal contributions to the new intergovernmentalism have appeared since 2008, so it is not surprising that crisis features, sometimes prominently, in the discussions. Little new ground is broken, however. In Jones et al. (2016), for example, the Euro crisis functions as an external trigger that tips the European Union into a veritable preprogrammed internal crisis, one foreordained by the incomplete intergovernmental bargains—the result of the lowest common denominator dynamic inherent to intergovernmentalism—forged in response to earlier exogenous shocks. The analytical focus is squarely on the ensuing internal crisis, which leads to bargaining and outcomes that, like their predecessors, are incomplete owing to the intergovernmentalist logic of lowest common denominator bargaining, thereby guaranteeing a repeat of the sequence and process: "failing forward." The content and precise impact of the exogenous crisis are of secondary importance in the analysis.

Exogenous crisis is given an equally perfunctory place in the theoretical framework advanced by Bickerton, Hodson, and Puetter; the authors identify a changing dynamic of integration since Maastricht, in which the member states "pursue more integration but stubbornly resist further supranationalism" (Bickerton et al. 2015: 705). Their brand of new intergovernmentalism consists of intensified policy coordination among member states, marked by deliberation and consensus-building at all levels. Delegation of national policy responsibilities, or what might have been described in a previous scholarly era as the pooling of sovereignty, has occurred, but the beneficiaries are not supranational actors like the Commission, but rather de novo bodies like the European Central Bank, the European External Action Service, and other regulatory and executive agencies.

The sources of "integration without supranationalism" are "Europe's changing political economy and transformations in domestic politics within European states" in the years after the ratification of the Maastricht Treaty (Bickerton et al. 2015: 707). The authors acknowledge that the post-Maastricht period has been a time of considerable exogenous change, even transformation, but they argue that the effects of such exogenous shifts are always indeterminate. They move quickly past potential exogenous triggers, arguing "[w]e seek to go beyond this indeterminacy by focusing on mid-range causal mechanisms that mediate between these exogenous forces and EU-level institutional change" (Bickerton et al. 2015: 707).

Undeniably, external and internal crises have featured prominently in the empirical record of integration since the early 1950s. Despite consistent acknowledgment of a clear causal connection between crisis and integration, European studies scholars generally have not accorded crisis a fully articulated role in the theoretical pantheon. Only Sandholtz and Zysman's focus on triggers and the recasting of grand bargains, and to a much lesser extent Bickerton, Hodson, and Puetter, who acknowledge the importance of international structural change in the post-Maastricht era as a distant factor in the rise of the new intergovernmentalism, provide anything like starting points for thinking about how better to conceptualize crisis in the broader sequence and process of integration. To assist in the construction of an analytical framework that will help shed light on the impact and import of the cascade of overlapping crises that has washed over Europe since 2008, we will need to go beyond the corpus of theory in European integration studies.

Crisis Response[5] and European Integration: A Framework of Analysis

What are the distinguishing characteristics of a crisis? A crisis—defined as "a situation of large-scale public dissatisfaction or even fear stemming from wide-ranging economic problems and/or an unusual degree of social unrest and/or threats to national security" (Keeler 1993: 184)—takes on causal significance

---

[5] Crisis response emerged as a systematic approach in the 1980s in the field of comparative political economy. The early literature, although critically important in framing the general puzzle—if an exogenous shock hits a set of actors simultaneously, how can one account for variations in the ways these actors respond?—nevertheless suffers from some of the same analytical weaknesses as the European studies literature. Early contributions include Katzenstein (1978), Lange et al. (1982), Gourevitch et al. (1984), Goldthorpe (1984), Katzenstein (1984, 1985), Hall (1986), and Gourevitch (1986).

insofar as it generates an opportunity for structural change by discrediting institutions or raising concerns about the adequacy of current policymaking processes (Cortell and Petersen 1999: 185). According to the literature, a crisis opens a "window of opportunity"[6] or creates a "critical juncture" (Capoccia and Kelemen 2007), heralding the possibility of significant change in the political status quo. Increased demands for institutional and policy changes flow from the domestic costs generated by the crisis. At the same time, state officials may find themselves less constrained to act as a result of the crisis. In other words, citizens may be more willing to allow policymakers greater latitude in crafting a response if the pressures for a prompt and effective response to crisis are great enough. Similarly, institutional and political veto points may weaken in a context of acute crisis, opening up a wider field of maneuver for state officials. Following this logic, complex crises like war and economic depression create the possibility for change across a number of policy fronts whereas narrowly framed crises—e.g., a spike in the cost of energy or the collapse of a key economic sector like steel or coal—will elicit responses that are confined to the area in question, with little or no opportunity for state actors to widen the scope of institutional change or reform.[7]

A frequently overlooked aspect of a crisis or critical juncture is time, or more specifically duration and sequencing. All of the causal implications of crisis outlined above—increased societal demands, diminished constraints, etc.—are shaped by temporality. For example, slow-building crises, because they are more open to alternative framings and interpretations, may present state actors with a very different political context in terms of societal demands and autonomy than crises that explode on the scene in full, disruptive glory.

Paul Pierson, in *Politics in Time*, seeks to illuminate the variability of the time horizons attached to cause and effect. He offers up a metaphor-based typology consisting of four very different kinds of natural events: a tornado, an earthquake, a large-scale meteor strike, and global warming (Pierson 2004: 79–82). Each of these represents a unique combination of short-term and long-term cause and effect. A tornado represents a situation in which the causal time horizon is short, coming together on short notice and imparting its effects over the short term. An earthquake, by contrast, is the product of an accumulation of stresses and strains that build over long periods of time, yet its impact is experienced in a very compact time frame. A meteor strike represents an example of a "quick/slow" event, in which the impact is experienced over a short duration, whereas the effects—up to and including changes to the global climate and mass extinctions—unfold over a much longer period of time. Finally, global warming is an example of a "slow/slow" event—both the

---

[6]Here, Cortell and Petersen (1999) build on the work of Kingdon (1984) and Keeler (1993).

[7]The connection between crisis and citizen demands, state autonomy, veto points, and scope of response are highlighted in much of the literature on crisis response, including Cortell and Petersen (1999) and Capoccia and Kelemen (2007).

Table 45.1 The time horizons of different causal accounts

		Time horizon of outcome	
		Short	Long
Time horizon of cause	Short	I (tornado)	II (meteorite)
	Long	III (earthquake)	IV (global warming)

cause and the ensuing effects are experienced over significantly long and drawn out time horizons. Pierson captures these differences in Table 45.1 (Pierson 2004: 81).

Pierson presents this typology as a heuristic for reminding researchers that not all cause-and-effect sequences take place in the short term (Quadrant I), and that one should always be on the lookout both for transformative causal impacts with long time horizons, as well as effect-chains (i.e., path-dependent dynamics) that are unleashed over long periods of time. The typology provides useful insights into how best to approach the analysis of specific crises or critical junctures, by helping to categorize the likely cause-effect sequence presented to the researcher.

Pierson's typology is intended for the classification of single events and their aftermaths. Of relevance to the question addressed in this article, it also provides insight into situations in which more than one crisis occurs in a given time frame. To take but one example, imagine a situation in which a territory increasingly experiencing the impact of global warming is suddenly hit by a massive earthquake. The observer is not only faced with the challenge of disentangling the short- and long-term effects of the two overlapping crises, but also looking for evidence of interaction effects. This is a major part of the research challenge confronting researchers in the recent European context.

Stepping back from these observations drawn from the literature on crises, we can identify several key dimensions along which crises can be categorized. Crises differ in their level of *intensity, scope, duration, interactivity, and conflict*.[8] Although none of these characteristics are causally determinative—a consistent refrain in the theoretical literature—they can point the researcher in potentially fruitful directions when it comes to identifying and evaluating the ensuing political responses (or non-responses) to the crisis. As we prepare to explore the characteristics of crises that have washed over Europe since 2008, the following dimensions will be at the forefront of the analysis. Several can be ascertained in advance—that is, gleaned from the very nature of the crisis as it presents itself in real time. Other characteristics, however, can be determined only after the fact, drawn from the political assessments and reactions to

---

[8] For a discussion of crisis that focuses on two dimensions—time and intensity—see Seabrooke and Tsingou (2019).

the changed circumstances. Much will depend, of course, on the perceptions of those embroiled in the crisis. In this sense, a crisis is very much what one (collectively) makes of it.

- *Intensity*: To qualify as a crisis, an unanticipated challenge to the status quo must already carry a certain level of intensity. Be that as it may, not all crises are alike. The key difference is to be found in the relative urgency of the ensuing response, which will be a function of the political, economic, and/or social costs generated by the change in circumstances as well as the volume and nature of the resulting demands for change and action. If a political reaction is demanded or called forth in the short term, then the crisis can be said to carry a level of intensity that is greater than a crisis that permits a longer-term evaluation and response.
- *Scope*: Crises can differ in terms of their reach. The starkest contrast is between an all-encompassing, manifold crisis like a full-scale war or national economic emergency and a much narrower one that is confined to a particular sector or even to a limited geographical region, such as a city. A crisis that lacks scope can nevertheless be very intense for those affected. There are multiple dimensions to the scope of a crisis: the range of issue areas or sectors—and by implication policies—affected; the number of actors impacted; and the geographical range of the crisis's effects.
- *Duration*: Per Pierson, crises can materialize over long or short time horizons, and similarly their effects can be transmitted in a concentrated burst or linger over a much longer period of time. In terms of responses to and the eventual resolution of the crisis, duration matters not only for each individual crisis, but also in cases when two or more crises occur within a finite period of time, as this creates the potential for overlapping effects, which brings us to our fourth dimension of comparison.
- *Interactivity*: This is less an innate characteristic than one that emerges in a specific context of overlapping or simultaneous crises. The issue is whether a crisis interacts with a prior, ongoing crisis, or produces synergistic impulses that are activated by a subsequent crisis. As such, interactivity emerges as a phenomenon not in isolation, but only when two or more crises are present and active. The effects produced by interactivity span a range of possibilities—amplification (or cancellation) of costs imposed on actors; the creation (or narrowing) of options and opportunities for political actors; and so on. The potential for interactivity is certainly influenced, but in no way determined, by the other dimensions of crisis elaborated on above. As a case in point, a crisis of long duration and broad scope very likely creates high probability of interactivity with a subsequent crisis.
- *Conflict*: It is rare that a crisis of the scale we are considering here does not generate political conflict. The key question is—what types of conflict? At the EU level, are there conflict lines that separate large from

small states? The wealthy from the indigent? Core from periphery? At the level of domestic politics, do the conflicts produced by the crisis fall neatly along the lines generated by the political party system, or do they cut across the traditional choices offered up to voters (typically, along the left–right dimension)? Is there a potential for intergovernmental conflicts, say between national and subnational governments? Naturally, the greater the intensity and scope of the crisis, and the longer it persists, the more we should expect conflict lines to multiply. And as multiple crises carry the potential to interact, the researcher should be on the lookout for resonance or amplification effects, as the conflicts generated by a previous crisis are exacerbated by subsequent ones.

THE CASCADE OF CRISES IN EUROPE AFTER 2008

Between 2008 and 2019, Europe sustained five successive shocks: the Eurozone crisis (2008+), the Russia/Ukraine crisis (2014+), the immigration-refugee crisis (2015+), the crisis of Brexit (2016+), and last but not least the Trump challenge (2017+). Not one of these crises has passed, which is another way of saying they are now in a state of cumulative overlap—a "polycrisis." In this penultimate section of the chapter, I will evaluate each of the crises in succession, describing their essential characteristics and how they have interacted with each other. Although the aim is to analyze the crises and not the EU responses—that task is left to the other chapters in this volume—the discussion will at times reference the political responses to crisis as a way of highlighting the importance of particular features of the individual crises and their interactions.

The Eurozone Crisis: The 2008 collapse of the international financial system and the ensuing pressures on European stock exchanges, the banking system, and eventually public finances across the EU rank at the very top in terms of crisis intensity, scope, and duration. The numbers posted at the height of the crisis—loss in stock market value, increase in private and public indebtedness, government budget deficits, unemployment—rival those of the Great Depression (Cameron 2012).

Although it is accurate to say that the perception of the crisis was, for all intents and purposes, EU-wide, the actual intensity of the crisis varied greatly across national space. Member states like Poland and Slovakia escaped the brunt of the crisis, at least in terms of the contraction of their national economies. Even for those countries that endured the painful effects of the Eurozone crisis at a high level of intensity, there was nothing like a "typical" condition; indeed, imagine a spectrum of affliction, with the Federal Republic of Germany anchoring one end and Greece holding down the other. Any analysis of EU-level responses to the Eurozone crisis must take into account these differentiated impacts and resulting political-economic contexts and tensions.

In those countries affected by the Eurozone crisis, as well as in Brussels, the pressure for political responses was ubiquitous, and touched on all levels of governance, from local and regional authorities to national governments to the European Union. The policy scope of the crisis was immense; public actors were confronted with demands for action across a broad range of policy areas: private sector banking; EU-level banking and fiscal policy; key sectors of the national welfare states, such as labor market policy, unemployment insurance, and industrial/sectoral policy.[9] Cataloguing and explaining the broad range of responses, as well as those initiatives that either failed or were not even considered, represents an enormous research challenge.

The considerable scope of the Eurozone crisis also extended to state-society relations and the number of actors impacted. Not only elites (investors, bankers, politicians, bureaucrats) but also and perhaps even especially ordinary citizens and social groups took the brunt of the crisis, in the form of massive economic dislocation and unemployment.[10] The end political effect was to lead to widespread upheaval in the domestic politics of member states throughout the EU, and specifically to the rise of populist movements and political parties in key countries like Greece, Spain, France, Italy, and Germany. Thus, the post-Maastricht sea change in the relationship between EU politics and domestic politics in Europe, acknowledged by postfunctionalists and new intergovernmentalists alike, received further reinforcement from the far-reaching effects of the Eurozone crisis. Reflecting back on the insights of the crisis response literature, one could expect a flood of demands for action as a result of the Eurozone crisis; would there be a parallel loosening of political constraints on state action, especially at the EU level?

Perhaps the thorniest aspect of the Eurozone crisis to evaluate is its duration. The antecedents of the crisis originate in the United States in 2007, and once its effects appeared on European soil the following year in Ireland, the crisis took hold quickly, peaking in terms of economic effects in 2012–2013. By the time its impact had spread from private equity markets and the banking system to public budgets and sovereign debt levels, the Eurozone crisis was threatening to engulf the entire politico-economic institutional edifice of the EU constructed after Maastricht. The EU's responses, which involved both short-term assistance for chronically indebted member states like Greece and longer-term institutional fixes for the EU's banking and fiscal regimes, were largely in place by 2015, which could conceivably serve as a convenient end point for the crisis. As such, recalling Pierson's typology, the Eurozone crisis resembles a long, drawn out, continental earthquake, followed by recurring aftershocks.

However, it would be premature to describe the Eurozone crisis as over. At the insistence of key member states like Germany and the Netherlands, the EU's short-term strategy for crisis-prone member states (e.g., Greece) has

---

[9] For an overview and analysis of the Eurozone crisis, see Bermeo and Pontusson (2012).

[10] Contrast this with the two signature crises of the pre-Maastricht period (the changing international economy in the 1980s and the end of the Cold War in 1989/90), which were primarily if not exclusively experienced at the elite level.

avoided permanent solutions like debt forgiveness or sustained fiscal transfers, and instead relied on long-term austerity programs and rigid adherence to preordained schedules for debt retirement, which have left the member states in question highly exposed to political vagaries at home and unfavorable economic developments abroad. The EU's approach to longer-term institutional reform, although impressive, still falls well short of a fully articulated fiscal, monetary, and banking union, leaving it vulnerable to the "failing forward" syndrome identified by Jones et al. (2016). In short, the potential for a recurrence of intense economic crisis, beginning in a place like Greece and quickly escalating to a Eurozone-wide shock, remains very much alive, and the resulting level of uncertainty[11] means that although the intensity of the crisis has diminished considerably and the scope of the crisis has been admirably contained, the crisis nevertheless persists.

There is no interactivity to evaluate in the Eurozone crisis, at least until 2014, when the second crisis breaks in Europe. As we shall see, Europe's first and arguably most complex crisis offers up numerous elements for amplification as subsequent crises came online; a full accounting takes place in the sections below.

The last dimension of the Eurozone crisis to be outlined is conflict, and we find ourselves confronted with numerous lines of division. At the European level, the most salient conflict was between those member states advocating an approach emphasizing austerity, balanced budgets, and building down of sovereign debt levels on the one hand, and those member states pushing coordinated stimulus-based solutions at both the European and national levels to spur growth and employment on the other. This difference in policy approach tended to coincide with core versus peripheral states in the EU economic space, with repeated clashes between Greek and German political elites personifying this divide.[12] Domestically, the Eurozone crisis opened up confrontations between different levels of government, particularly in those countries where national governments pursued austerity policies that entailed significant budget cuts from regional and local authorities. By far the most significant conflict line was the one that emerged in the party systems of most member states, reflecting deep societal divides over who bore responsibility for the crisis and what measures should be taken in response. The populist backlash in Central and Eastern Europe (the rise of illiberal democracy) as well as populist challenges in places like Germany, France, Italy, and the Netherlands were fueled by the impact of the Eurozone crisis.

---

[11] As we shall see below, a marked drop-off in intensity accompanied by lingering uncertainty is a feature of subsequent crises in Europe, most notably the Russia/Ukraine crisis and the Trump crisis.

[12] A second line of conflict was between members and non-members of the Eurozone, although this ultimately proved to be less salient over the course of the Eurozone crisis.

The Russia/Ukraine Crisis: The second of five significant crises in Europe since 2008 began to take shape in late 2013, when the Ukrainian pro-democracy movement began holding continuous mass demonstrations on the main square of the nation's capital, the Maidan in Kiev, calling for new leadership and an openly pro-Western, pro-European Union foreign policy. In early 2014, escalating violence on the streets of Kiev and elsewhere in the western regions of the country eventually forced the pro-Russian Ukrainian President, Viktor Yanukovych, to flee the country, inflaming separatist sentiments in eastern Ukraine that culminated in a bold move by Russian-backed security forces and paramilitaries to occupy the breakaway region, with Russian President Vladimir Putin eventually annexing Crimea in March (Allison 2014). The focus of tensions quickly shifted to the Donbass, a region in eastern Ukraine with long historical ties to Russia. Pro-Russian political authorities there, backed by indigenous paramilitary forces, engaged in armed clashes with Ukrainian troops, and evidence soon accumulated that the separatist forces were drawing clandestine military support, both material and personnel, from Russia.

The Russia/Ukraine crisis represents not only the first incidence of armed conflict on the EU's borders since the Balkan Wars of the 1990s, but the first time the European Union has confronted an overt, militarized security challenge in the post-Cold War era. Russian authorities voiced support for "self-determination" in Crimea and issued resolute denials of direct involvement in eastern Ukraine, at the same time condemning EU and NATO policies toward Ukraine and other former Soviet republics. In short, Russia blamed EU foreign policy for provoking the crisis in Ukraine, and has placed the EU on notice about incursions into its sphere of interest.

The intensity of the Russia/Ukraine crisis has tracked closely Russian escalation and de-escalation of the military conflict. The crisis peaked in July 2014 and ensuing months, in the direct aftermath of the shooting down of Malaysian Airlines flight MH17, which killed 298 passengers, many of them European (Dutch). All evidence pointed to the culpability of the Russian military in the shootdown, and the European Union and the United States issued the first round of coordinated sanctions on Russia soon after the tragedy (Speck 2016). When the fighting in eastern Ukraine subsided in the aftermath of the signing of the Minsk Protocol by Russia and Ukraine in September 2014, the level of intensity of the crisis fell as well, only to resume again as ceasefire violations picked up in January 2015. For the most part, the crisis has been on a low but still salient boil since February 2015, when the Minsk II Protocol came into effect. The most recent flare-up in tensions occurred in November 2018, when Russian ships attacked and boarded three Ukrainian vessels in Crimean port of Azov near the Black Sea, claiming that Ukraine had violated Russian waters.

If we think about how the intensity of the crisis has been distributed across Europe spatially, a more differentiated picture emerges. For many member states on or near the fault line of the crisis—specifically Poland and the Baltic

States—the Russian presence has awakened old fears and elicited persistent calls for solidarity and resolute action from EU partners and especially from NATO allies. For those member states further away from the conflict, perceptions in many instances have been leavened by concerns about the economic and security implications of a worsening relationship with Russia (e.g., Greece, Italy).

Unlike the Eurozone crisis, the Russia/Ukraine conflict has been quite limited in scope; perhaps a better way of describing it would be institutional compartmentalization. The military-security dimension has not featured prominently on the EU's agenda; rather, this has been NATO's purview. For its part, the EU has focused on geo-economic responses to the crisis (sanctions), as well as the troubling implications and challenges for EU foreign policy in the region, specifically the Eastern Partnership program (Cadier 2014). Unlike other crises, the crisis has not extended to subnational actors or to societal groups and citizens; it remains very much an elite preoccupation.

As for duration, the crisis, despite the clear drop-off in intensity since the peak of hostilities in 2014/15, must still be characterized as ongoing, given the continuing absence of international recognition of the annexation of Crimea, the presence of Russian forces in eastern Ukraine, and the consistent renewal of U.S.–European economic sanctions against Russia. As the flare-up of the crisis in November 2018 demonstrates, the Russians and their proxies in eastern Ukraine retain the initiative, which translates into a constant and significant level of uncertainty in the region and, from the standpoint of Brussels and 27 European capitals, the ever-present possibility of escalation. In this regard, the crisis resembles a serious, regionally confined earthquake, again with the very real possibility of aftershocks.

In terms of interactivity, the Russia/Ukraine crisis has generated at least two points of contact across existing and future crises. First, the dominant response by EU members—the levying of economic sanctions against Russian individuals and economic enterprises, which requires unanimous consent—raises potential conflicts among the EU member states, which were still coping with the effects of the economic downturn caused by the Eurozone crisis and very sensitive to any disruptions in trade and business relations with third party countries.[13] Second, the crisis introduced an active agent into the complex of crises that was building in Europe—the Russian government. Although Russia had been seeking to foment and exploit divisions within the European Union long before the opportunity in Ukraine presented itself, the 2014 crisis provides both pretext and potential for intensifying these activities on EU soil. Playing on resentments in Greece and Italy directed at the EU and key member states like Germany arising out of the Eurozone crisis,

---

[13] "… Austrian banks have extensive business relations with Russia, the Czech Republic fears for its engineering exports, Poland is concerned about the food export, Finland and the Baltic countries are dependent on Russian gas supplies…" (Veebel and Markus 2016: 137).

the Russians made overtures to potential allies in these countries, hoping to undermine support for the sanctions regime and generally sew division within the ranks of an already fractious European Union.[14] The interactivity of the Russia/Ukraine crisis with other European crises is potentially significant, insofar as the crisis generates additional opportunities for Russia as an active agent to put pressure on the EU.

Finally, the conflict lines generated by the Russia/Ukraine crisis within the EU have been generally quite modest in import and impact. EU solidarity over sanctions has been maintained since 2015, although occasional disagreements have arisen between countries like Germany, which have stood on principle in their stand-off with Russia, and those like Greece and Italy, where governments are more concerned about the economic opportunity costs of the sanctions policy. Conflicts have not materialized at the societal level to any appreciable extent, although there are both parties and substrata of the electorates across the EU that are more open to rapprochement with Russia.

The Immigration-Refugee Crisis: The European Union has been a destination point for economic and political refugees from nearby regions in southern and eastern Europe, Eurasia, Africa, and the Middle East for decades. The situation in Europe began to grow critical in 2014, as the crisis in Libya led to an upsurge in refugees and asylum seekers attempting to cross the Mediterranean and enter Italy. That 2015 became the year of an all-encompassing continental immigration crisis has much to do with the Russia-inspired escalation of the civil war in Syria, as well as the deterioration of living conditions in many parts of Central and Northern Africa, all of which contributed to a major increase in the flow of refugees bound for Europe. The number of first-time asylum seekers entering Europe doubled from the previous year to 1.2 million. Most of these refugees made their way across frontier states like Greece, Italy, and Hungary in order to register for asylum in northern countries like Germany and Sweden, and the resulting pressures at the local, national, and supranational levels threatened to overwhelm the European Union and many of its member states.

The intensity of the crisis closely tracked the refugee flows and the attendant media coverage of the refugees' plight. The peculiarities of asylum protocols in the European Union shaped not only the severity of the crisis, but its territorial distribution as well—entry and transit states like Greece and Hungary confronted challenges of humanitarian assistance and security, but also strong incentives to move refugees along to destination states like Germany and Sweden, where both the short- and long-term problems of assistance and social integration exploded. Thus, the level and types of challenges manifested themselves very differently across the EU space.

The scope of the immigration crisis was similarly very large. The precise contours of the refugee crisis also depended on the level of government

---

[14] Russian efforts enjoy a mixed record of success. See for example Hope (2018) and Konstandaris (2018).

involved. For cities and towns, the short-term challenge was to house and feed the newcomers, and to begin the arduous task of developing longer-term programs to integrate those permitted to stay, which involved everything ranging from housing policy to education to vocational training and labor market policy. For member states and the European Union, the agenda was enormous: external border security; whether and how to control and regulate the flow of people across internal borders, which raised the thorny issue of modifications to the Schengen Accords; and lastly policing and counterintelligence, as the influx of refugees carried with it the potential for importing terrorism from hotspots on Europe's periphery (e.g., ISIS/Syria).[15] The one common element facing policymakers at all levels was the need to cope with the rapid politicization of the issue, in particular the growing populist backlash against the presence of foreigners.

The duration of the immigration-refugee crisis should be characterized, much like the Eurozone crisis, as ongoing, despite the fact that the actual number of border crossings dropped dramatically after March 2016, when the European Union and Turkey reached an agreement to house refugees bound for the European Union on Turkish soil in exchange for financial assistance and modifications to the EU's visa policies toward Turkish citizens. Even though the number of immigrants seeking to enter the EU space has declined to pre-2014 levels, media attention on the plight of refugees making the dangerous sea crossings to Greece, Italy, and Spain has continued unabated, keeping the issue alive and salient in the minds of citizens and policymakers alike. In terms of Pierson's typology, one is tempted to reach for the earthquake category again, but in light of the long antecedents and the increasingly real possibility that mass migration flows represent the new normal in Europe, the immigration-refugee crisis seems more like a tipping point in a longer-term instance of climate change.

One of the characteristics of the immigration-refugee crisis is the extent to which political reactions and responses to the evolving situation have generated additional fuel for the crisis. For example, German Chancellor Angela Merkel's attempt to take the lead in the EU's response to the crisis in August 2015, by welcoming to Germany any and all Syrian refugees regardless of their point of entry into the EU (Hall 2015), while laudable from a moral standpoint, inflamed tensions among EU members, particularly those "frontier states" like Greece and Hungary, and created a powerful political backlash at home, propelling the populist Alternative for Germany (AfD) to new heights (Art 2018). Similarly, EU efforts beginning in 2016 to distribute Syrian refugees who had been granted political asylum equitably around the EU space ran into fierce opposition from newer member states in Central and Eastern Europe, which not only made for fireworks in Brussels but also stoked populist

[15] For an overview of these and other issues relating to the EU's refugee crisis, see the JCMS Special issue edited by Niemann and Zaun (2018).

resentments and political backlash throughout the European Union (Niemann and Zaun 2018).

The immigration-refugee crisis has generated a significant level of interactivity. It has aggravated and reinforced two fault lines exposed by the Eurozone crisis. One of these resides at the level of domestic politics—populist movements and parties that drew strength from the economic upheavals beginning in 2008 found fresh political sustenance in the panic accompanying the refugee crisis; indeed, in the case of Germany the AfD essentially reinvented itself around the issue of immigration, pushing its Euroskepticism into the background (Art 2018). The second fault line cut through the European Union; it was no coincidence that precisely those member states that suffered most as a result of the Eurozone crisis, clustered on the EU's economic periphery, also struggled to cope with the significant influx of asylum seekers and economic migrants across Europe's geographical periphery. In particular, Greece and Italy bore the brunt of costs of coping with the in-migration. The lines of political division exacerbated by the immigration crisis mirrored almost perfectly the ones opened up during the Eurozone crisis, with the leading "core" member state, the Federal Republic of Germany, clashing frequently with vulnerable peripheral member states like Greece.

Interaction effects extending beyond the Eurozone abound. The immigration crisis, which in many ways was sparked by Russia's intervention in the Syrian conflict, also created additional opportunities for Russian meddling in EU affairs. Just as Russia attempted to use the fallout from the Eurozone crisis to peel off Greece with speculative offers of financial assistance, Russia has sought to exploit the nationalist-populist backlash to immigration in countries like Hungary and Italy to its advantage, and to the EU's disadvantage. Finally, as subsequent sections attest, the immigration-refugee crisis soon set up resonance with the two crises soon to come, Brexit and Trump.

The conflict lines generated by the immigration-refugee crisis are similar in breadth and number to those generated by the Eurozone crisis. At the EU level, the main conflicts involve transit countries like Greece, Hungary, and Italy, which sit astride the principal migratory routes from the Middle East and Northern Africa, and countries further away from the action, which either rest generally outside the fray of the crisis (e.g., Ireland, UK) or are considered destination states by refugees and thus confront a different set of challenges (Germany, Netherlands). These conflicts entail external border security and the issue of temporary suspension of Schengen protocols. As the EU has grappled with collective responses, a second line of conflict has emerged, pitting those countries who are unwilling to accept quotas of refugees who have been granted asylum (Poland, Hungary) and most of the rest of the EU membership. At the level of domestic politics, the immigration-refugee crisis has generated tensions between levels of government, which face very different challenges in this context. Most salient are the party political ramifications, since the conflict lines tend to reinforce the ones exacerbated by the

Eurozone crisis, further fueling the rise of populist nationalism that is opposed to immigration and opposed to Europe.

The Brexit Crisis: Of the five crises examined here, Brexit is the odd one out, for several reasons. In the first place, it is not an external shock, but rather a political crisis internal to the EU. Second, Brexit, precipitated as it was by the outcome of the UK referendum in June 2016 to leave the EU, was a crisis of and within the European integration process itself. In other words, this was not a crisis that originated in the security realm or the economy or social relations, which then impinged on the EU. Instead, Brexit represented an internal schism in the fabric of the European Union itself, a breakdown in trust and solidarity that was resolved by the UK's decision to remove itself from the community of member states.

Brexit's intensity was sudden. When the results of the referendum were announced late on June 23, 2016—51.9% in favor of Leave, 48.1% in support of Remain—the news came as a complete shock, and pitched the EU overnight into its fourth overlapping crisis since 2008. Since that date, and in particular since the UK government invoked Article 50 on March 29, 2017, thereby commencing the two-year countdown on negotiations with the EU over the terms of exit, the crisis has certainly persisted, but has been contained by the structure and procedures of the EU treaty framework. After multiple extensions and bitterly contested negotiations, the UK exited the European Union on January 31, 2020. This has not, however, ended the affair; indeed, the lingering effects of the crisis remain very real, especially since a probable outcome remains a failure to agree on a future terms of the trade relationship which experts agree would leave both parties, the EU and the UK, in very difficult positions.

The scope of the Brexit crisis is not easy to pin down. Viewed from one perspective, it is fairly narrow, consisting of a set of procedures culminating in a pre-determined outcome (exit) that was initiated voluntarily by a member state, acting in accordance with the treaty framework. Viewed from another, it is potentially limitless in scope, affecting any and all relations and connections between the United Kingdom and the European Union (and by extension its 27 other members). Again pointing up the unique nature of the Brexit crisis in comparison with the other four confronting the EU, the scope of the crisis— or at least a good portion of it—was something at least in theory capable of being managed actively by the EU, particularly once Article 50 was invoked. In other words, one can look for evidence of the widening or narrowing of the scope of the crisis in the way the EU responded to the challenges associated with Brexit. At the outset of the Brexit process, particularly in the months immediately following the referendum before the invocation of Article 50, the greatest concerns within the European Commission and among stalwart proEU member states like Germany and France were that the UK's decision to leave would provide destabilizing momentum to Euroskeptic movements and governments across the European Union. Fears of a Brexit contagion have not materialized; in this sense, the crisis has been contained, in large part because of expert negotiating tactics employed by the Commission as well as the member states (McTague 2019).

One would think that Brexit's duration is the most straightforward of its characteristics to define. Commencing with the outcome of the referendum in June 2016, the official endpoint of the process was supposed to fall on March 29, 2019—the end of the two-year disengagement period stipulated under the terms of Article 50. However, this was not the case, and all signs are that the Brexit issue will drag on well beyond the formal date of the UK's exit. If one were to contrast the current political situations in the UK and the EU, one is tempted to conclude that the crisis has already been largely processed and in many ways ended at the European level, but is just beginning for the UK. In terms of Pierson's typology, Brexit most closely resembles a meteor strike on UK soil.

As for interactivity, the Brexit crisis retains a measure of uniqueness in comparison to the other four crises covered here. One can in fact interpret Brexit as a collective British decision to leave that was shaped not only by doubts about the idea and aims of the European project that long predate the accession of the United Kingdom in 1973, but also shorter-term judgments by elites and the mass public about the ineffectiveness of the EU in dealing with the host of challenges that had confronted Europe since 2008, in particular the Eurozone and immigration crises. In addition, there is evidence of a significant part played by Russian disinformation, particularly through social media platforms like Facebook and Twitter but also through direct, covert financing of the Leave campaign, in shaping the eventual referendum outcome (Martin 2019). In short, the Brexit crisis was in some ways the spawn of earlier, adjacent crises. Once in full swing, the Brexit crisis also offered up potential interactions with the other crises, particularly with the looming crisis of the Trump Presidency, which was just about to wash over an already battered and beleaguered Europe.

The conflict lines generated by the Brexit crisis have been far less varied and consequential (for the EU) than original anticipated or feared. As mentioned above, Brexit contagion has not materialized, at least not yet. The EU has in fact remained remarkably unified in its bargaining position vis-à-vis the United Kingdom, despite the plethora of issues that could have seen divisions within the EU camp proliferate (the Ireland–Northern Ireland border, Gibraltar, fisheries policy, etc.). Indeed, the main division follows the line established by the Brexit exercise: the UK versus the EU. To the extent that internal domestic divisions have materialized around the Brexit issue within the EU, they are concentrated exclusively within the United Kingdom.

The Transatlantic Crisis: The fifth and final European crisis since 2008 dates from the election of Donald J. Trump as 45th President of the United States on November 9, 2016. Like three of the four earlier crises, this one was exogenous to the European Union. Unlike the other four, it has been more of an ambient crisis, residing in the realm of political relations and perceptions. And like one of the other crises—Russia/Ukraine—it has been driven by actors, led by the U.S. president, who appear to be committed to a radical change in the ties that have bound Europe and the United States since the end of the Second World War.

The Trump challenge to Europe should be seen in the broader historical context of the relationship, which has rested on fundamental bargains between the United States and Europe involving mutual security and defense, access to markets and a commitment to a liberal international order, and partnership under the aegis of U.S. leadership (Ikenberry 2008: 9–10). Over the 60+ years of the relationship, occasional crises have buffeted the relationship; these have involved differences over interests and objectives as well as over the institutional arrangements (e.g., NATO) that have underpinned these overarching bargains. Setting the Trump challenge apart from previous crises in the transatlantic relationship is the fact that the rupture engineered by the U.S. administration directly calls into question the essential bargains underpinning the relationship.

Europeans saw early indications that a Trump presidency would be deeply problematic. Trump's 2016 campaign rhetoric repeatedly questioned the pillars of the transatlantic relationship: free trade within recognized international regimes like the WTO; the mutual defense pact organized around NATO; and European integration. Once in power after January 2017, President Trump has gone out of his way repeatedly to disparage core elements of the Atlantic alliance. He has trained his fire principally on Germany, criticizing this key ally's perennial export surplus with the United States and its defense expenditures in relation to NATO commitments. Trump also signaled an unusually conciliatory approach to Putin, raising legitimate questions about the future of the Russia sanctions policy. Although Trump's consistently derogatory rhetoric about Europe has been matched far less frequently by action,[16] and his more inflammatory statements usually have been softened by subsequent reassurances from members of his administration, there is no denying that current U.S.–European relations rest on a knife's edge, with few prospects for improvement in sight.

In terms of intensity, the Trump crisis has yet to match the urgency of the early years of the Eurozone crisis or the first 18 months of the immigration-refugee crisis. Although there can be no denying that Europe is held in poor regard by the Trump Administration and may well be in the crosshairs, this has not (yet) precipitated anything like a formal response by the EU. The intensity of the crisis seems to spike with the formal occasions that bring the partners together (e.g., G-7 and NATO summits, the annual Munich Security Conference, etc.).

The scope of the crisis is as broad as the bargains that define the relationship. To date, the principal conflicts have involved security, in particular the

---

[16]The list includes the U.S. abandonment of the Paris Climate Accords in 2017 and of the Iran nuclear treaty in 2018, as well as the levying of tariffs on aluminum and steel in 2018.

integrity and future of NATO, as well as trade. Given the sweep of the transatlantic agenda, however, the reverberations of the Trump-induced chill extend much more broadly. International human rights, the Iran nuclear agreement, climate change and the Paris Accords, the Syrian conflict, the Middle East Peace Process, relations with China: these and other issues have been impacted by transatlantic rift and drift.

The transatlantic crisis is ongoing, with no change in the offing, at least until the 2020 presidential election in the United States. Although not an especially intense crisis to date, the Trump challenge has been pervasive and durable, testament to the single-minded consistency of the U.S. president when it comes to Europe. Should Trump lose in 2020, there is every reason to expect a marked improvement in relations between the United States and Europe starting in 2021. Few are predicting a return to the good old days of the Obama Administration—warts and all[17]—but fewer still expect the crisis to continue. Should Trump win reelection, however, one can anticipate the crisis to worsen as European countries and the EU take concrete steps, individually and collectively, to protect themselves from what is already seen as a corrosive relationship with a fundamentally changed United States (Stelzenmuller 2019). The crisis resembles a change in climate (Pierson's metaphor of global warming comes to mind)—a generally deteriorating forecast, occasionally punctuated by partly cloudy skies and more often by especially bad storms.

This fifth and (so far) most recent European crisis offers up many possibilities for interactivity. Again, because so much of the Trump crisis has been in the realms of rhetoric and perception, its impact on other crises has been more symbolic than real, and laced with uncertainty. For example, President Trump has played repeatedly on tensions within Europe arising from the immigration-refugee crisis, stoking fears of Islamization and terrorism, as well as from Brexit, calling it a good move for the United Kingdom and a model for others to emulate. And although Trump was constrained by the congressional and executive investigations into Russian interference in the 2016 presidential election, the publication of the Mueller Report in March 2019 ushers in the very real possibility of dramatic change in U.S. policy toward the Putin regime after the 2020 presidential election. Were this to occur, Europe's calculations vis-à-vis the Russia/Ukraine crisis would have to be reset on short notice. One area where concrete actions have been undertaken by the Trump Administration is trade, where tariffs on European exports of steel and aluminum were imposed in 2017, with the threat of even more damaging duties on automobiles held over Europe's head. The possibility of a costly trade war hangs over the transatlantic relationship as never before, and with it the very real prospect of recessionary impulses at a time when the European economy is still struggling to overcome the persistent effects of the

---

[17] For a review and analysis of transatlantic relations between 2008 and 2016, see Anderson (2018).

Eurozone crisis. All of which is to say that the interactivity of the Trump crisis is at least potentially wide-ranging and negative.

Finally, the conflict lines created by the Trump-induced crisis in the transatlantic relationship resemble those of Brexit. Many initially feared that Trump would play successfully on internal European divisions, but unlike previous crisis in U.S.–European relations such as the U.S. invasion of Iraq in 2003 (Anderson 2018), Europe has remained unified in the face of U.S. criticism and actions directed at their transatlantic partners. The crisis has not penetrated to the level of public opinion in Europe; here too, there is precious little evidence of pro-Trump constituencies anywhere within the EU, and even nationalist and populist parties, which have frequently been singled out for praise by the U.S. president, have steered clear of open endorsements of Trump.

Analysis and Conclusions

This chapter is an attempt to improve the analytical toolkit available to help us understand the causal connection between crisis and European integration. In particular, the level of empirical complexity posed by the past decade of polycrisis in Europe calls for a more nuanced framework of analysis. Drawing on the literature in European studies as well as the more general findings of the scholarship on crisis response on critical junctures, I have constructed a simple but usable schema for evaluating the specific characteristics of individual crises as well as their interconnections under conditions of overlap, and then applied this schema to the five overlapping crises that have affected Europe since 2008.

There are two principal take-aways that deserve attention here at the end of the analysis. First, recall Sandholtz and Zysman's argument that European integration is constructed on a hierarchy of bargains that take account of the prevailing core features of the international system (Sandholtz and Zysman 1989). Any significant changes in the structure of the international system, such as those following from the impact of severe international crisis, can trigger a drive on the part of European elites to recast the bargains holding together the European project to reflect the new prevailing circumstances.

There is no question that these five crises have already ushered in significant changes to the international system in which the EU is embedded. Indeed, just about any one of them, with the possible exception of Brexit, would have been sufficient to introduce significant changes. In combination, the imprint on the EU's environment is indelible, spanning economic vulnerabilities (Eurozone), security threats (Russia/Ukraine; Trump), and social pressures (immigration-refugee). Even a quick examination of the sheer number of actors affected and the profusion of political cleavages aggravated by these crises—both related to the scope properties of each crisis, and many of them reinforcing—indicates just how much more impactful this period has been as compared to the pre-Maastricht crises that occasionally shook the European project into a recasting mode. In those cases, the actors affected were confined to supranational and national elites in Europe, and the cleavages similarly resided at the European and intermember state levels, and did not extend to European civil society or beyond EU borders at all. Today's "polycrisis" is much more far-reaching. To mix Pierson's metaphors, the confluence of earthquake and climate change-like shocks will permanently alter the context within which the EU is operating, putting great pressure on the EU to recast the foundational bargains on which it rests.

In what way then can we say the hierarchy of European bargains is being recast? Although a complete answer lies beyond the purview of this paper, it is possible to sketch the outlines of the evolving grand bargain. Although the responses have been halting and even half-hearted in some sectors, particularly on Eurozone reforms (e.g., fiscal union), the overall pattern suggests a number of deliberate, incremental steps in the general direction of greater "stateness" for the European Union. The two crises relating to security concerns—Russia/Ukraine and Trump—have provided motive and impetus for greater coordination on economic diplomacy (sanctions; tariffs) as well as the first inklings of a change in the European vision of security, while the Eurozone and immigration-refugee crises have led directly to significant if rather understated reforms on financial and banking union, external border security, and internal policing and intelligence sharing. In light of the changing environment in which the EU operates—shaped by these overlapping crises—the new hierarchy of bargains is taking a coherent and logical shape.

This point brings us to the second take-away of this analysis, one that addresses an apparent paradox between the third generation European integration theory literature and the more general works on critical junctures. We know that crises or critical junctures can, under the right circumstances, generate for state officials a usable degree of autonomy from short-term political constraints (Cortell and Petersen 1999). However, from both post-functionalism and new intergovernmentalism we also know that the domestic political constraints on both pro-EU national elites and supranational actors have never been tighter. This suggests that crises will be less likely than in the past to generate significant "windows of opportunity" for policymakers to propose and to implement ambitious, European-level solutions to the problems generated by crisis.

Clearly, EU and state officials pushing European solutions have been fully aware of the constraints imposed by the ubiquitous politicization of Europe on the continent, as other chapters in this volume attest. In some instances, this has led to explicit decisions *not* to pursue institutional reforms that would likely provoke sharp political backlash or opposition, as the case of Germany and the Eurozone exemplifies. Yet if we look carefully at the impressive list of significant reforms put in place by the EU during this period in response to the crisis context, a clear pattern emerges—all have been justified with public appeals to security and efficacy. These values resonate with a generally warier European public, and the end result has been to bring the EU closer to "stateness."

REFERENCES

Allison, R. (2014). Russian 'Deniable' Intervention in Ukraine: How and Why Russia Broke the Rules. *International Affairs, 90*(6), 1255–1297.

Anderson, J. (2018). Rancor and Resilience in the Atlantic Political Order: The Obama Years. *Journal of European Integration, 40*(5), 621–636. https://doi.org/10.1080/07036337.2018.1488841.

Art, A. (2018). The AfD and the End of Containment in Germany? *German Politics and Society.* https://doi.org/10.3167/gps.2018.360205.

Bermeo, N., & Pontusson, J. (Eds.). (2012). *Coping with Crisis: Government Reactions to the Great Recession.* New York: Russel Sage Foundation.

Bickerton, C., Hodson, D., & Puetter, U. (2015). The New Intergovernmentalism: European Integration in the Post-Maastricht Era. *Journal of Common Market Studies, 53*(4), 703–722.

Cadier, D. (2014). Eastern Partnership vs. Eurasian Union: The EU–Russia Competition in the Shared Neighborhood and the Ukraine Crisis. *Global Policy, 5*(1), 76–85.

Cameron, D. (2012). European Fiscal Responses to the Great Recession. In N. Bermeo & J. Pontusson (Eds.), *Coping with Crisis: Government Reactions to the Great Recession* (pp. 91–129). New York: Russel Sage Foundation.

Capoccia, G., & Kelemen, D. (2007). The Study of Critical Junctures: Theory, Narrative, and Counterfactuals in Historical Institutionalism. *World Politics, 59*(3), 341–369.

Cortell, A., & Petersen, S. (1999). Altered States: Explaining Domestic Institutional Change. *British Journal of Political Science, 29*(1), 177–203.

Goldthorpe, J. (Ed.). (1984). *Order and Conflict in Contemporary Capitalism.* Oxford: Clarendon Press.

Gourevitch, P. (1986). *Politics in Hard Times.* Ithaca, NY: Cornell University Press.

Gourevitch, P., et al. (1984). *Unions and Economic Crisis: Britain, West Germany, and Sweden.* London: George Allen & Unwin.

Hall, P. (1986). *Governing the Economy.* Oxford: Oxford University Press.

Hall, A. (2015, August 24). Germany Opens Its Gates. *The Independent.* https://www.independent.co.uk/news/world/europe/germany-opens-its-gates-berlin-says-all-syrian-asylum-seekers-are-welcome-to-remain-as-britain-is-10470062.html.

Hodson, D., & Puetter, U. (2019). The European Union in Disequilibrium: New Intergovernmentalism, Postfunctionalism, and Integration Theory in the Post-Maastricht Period. *Journal of European Public Policy.* https://doi.org/10.1080/13501763.2019.1569712.

Hooghe, L., & Marks, G. (2009). A Postfunctionalist Theory of European Integration: From Permissive Consensus to Constraining Dissensus. *British Journal of Political Science.* https://doi.org/10.1017/S0007123408000409.

Hooghe, L., & Marks, G. (2019). Grand Theories of European Integration in the Twenty-First Century. *Journal of European Public Policy.* https://doi.org/10.1080/13501763.2019.1569711.

Hope, K. (2018, July 13). Russia Meddles in Greek Town to Push Back the West. *Financial Times.* https://www.ft.com/content/b5728090-86b0-11e8-96dd-fa565ec55929.

Ikenberry, G. J. (2008). Explaining Crisis and Change in Atlantic Relations: An Introduction. In J. Anderson, G. J. Ikenberry, & T. Risse (Eds.), *End of the West? Crisis and Change in the Atlantic Order* (pp. 1–27). Ithaca: Cornell University Press.

Jones, E., Kelemen, R. D., & Meunier, S. (2016). Failing Forward? The Euro Crisis and the Incomplete Nature of European Integration. *Comparative Political Studies*, 49(7), 1010–1034.

Katzenstein, P. (Ed.). (1978). *Between Power and Plenty*. Madison, WI: University of Wisconsin Press.

Katzenstein, P. (1984). *Corporatism and Change*. Ithaca: Cornell University Press.

Katzenstein, P. (1985). *Small States and World Markets*. Ithaca, NY: Cornell University Press.

Keeler, J. T. S. (1993). Opening the Window for Reform: Mandates, Crises, and Extraordinary Policymaking. *Comparative Political Studies*, 25(4), 433–486.

Kingdon, J. (1984). *Agendas, Alternatives, and Public Policies*. New York: HarperCollins.

Konstandaris, N. (2018, July 23). Athens and Moscow's Stunning Falling Out. *New York Times*. https://www.nytimes.com/2018/07/23/opinion/athens-moscow-greece-russia-tensions.html.

Lange, P., Ross, G., & Vannicelli, M. (1982). *Unions, Change, and Crisis: French and Italian Union Strategy and the Political Economy, 1945–1980*. London: George Allen & Unwin.

Martin, A. (2019, February 18). MPs Call for Government to Examine Russian Influence on Brexit. *Sky News*. https://news.sky.com/story/mps-call-for-government-to-examine-russian-influence-on-brexit-11640694.

McTague, T. (2019, March 27). How the UK Lost the Brexit Battle. *Politico*. https://www.politico.eu/article/how-uk-lost-brexit-eu-negotiation/?utm_source=POLITICO.EU&utm_campaign=6ce3f2f806-EMAIL_CAMPAIGN_2019_03_28_05_45&utm_medium=email&utm_term=0_10959edeb5-6ce3f2f806-189581421.

Moravcsik, A. (1991). Negotiating the Single European Act: National Interests and Conventional Statecraft in the European Community. *International Organization*, 45(1), 19–56.

Niemann, A., & Zaun, N. (Eds.). (2018). EU Refugee Policies and Politics in Times of Crisis: Theoretical and Empirical Perspectives [Special Issue]. *Journal of Common Market Studies*, 56(1), 3–22. https://doi.org/10.1111/jcms.12650.

Pierson, P. (2004). *Politics in Time: Historical Institutions and Social Analysis*. Princeton: Princeton University Press.

Rosamond, B. (2000). *Theories of European Integration*. New York: St. Martin's Press.

Sandholtz, W. (1993). Choosing Union: Monetary Politics and Maastricht. *World Politics*, 47(1), 1–39.

Sandholtz, W., & Zysman, J. (1989). 1992: Recasting the European Bargain. *World Politics*, 42(1), 95–128.

Seabrooke, L., & Tsingou, E. (2019). Europe's Fast- and Slow-Burning Crises. *Journal of European Public Policy*. https://doi.org/10.1080/13501763.2018.1446456.

Speck, U. (2016). The West's Response to the Ukraine Conflict: A Transatlantic Success Story. *Transatlantic Academy 2015–16 Paper Series No. 4*. Washington, DC: German Marshall Fund of the United States.

Stelzenmuller, C. (2019, March 12). Order from Chaos: A New Franco-German Narrative for Europe. *Foreign Affairs*. https://www.brookings.edu/blog/order-from-chaos/2019/03/12/a-new-franco-german-narrative-for-europe/.

Veebel, V., & Markus, R. (2016). At the Dawn of a New Era of Sanctions: Russian-Ukrainian Crisis and Sanctions. *Orbis, 60*(1), 128–139.

Correction to: The Palgrave Handbook of EU Crises

Marianne Riddervold, Jarle Trondal, and Akasemi Newsome

Correction to:
M. Riddervold et al. (eds.),
The Palgrave Handbook of EU Crises, **Palgrave Studies in European Union Politics, https://doi.org/10.1007/978-3-030-51791-5**

In the original version of this book, in the list of contributors, the affiliation for "Hubert Zimmermann" which was incorrectly included as "Gutenberg University in Mainz" instead of "Philipps University of Marburg (Germany)" has now been corrected. Also, in Chapter 16, the author name H. Kassim which was mistakenly added twice has been removed and the disclaimer for Luc Tholoniat has been added. The corrections to the book have been updated with the changes.

The updated version of the book can be found at https://doi.org/10.1007/978-3-030-51791-5

INDEX

A
Agencies
  constitutional *lacunae*, 320
  delegation, 326
  European Union (EU), 18, 24, 35, 38, 72, 155, 160, 164, 234, 235, 237, 308, 315–324, 328, 329, 333, 476, 659
  political abdication, 328
Arab spring, 236, 358, 361–363, 366–369, 424, 716
Arguing, 13, 14, 20, 22, 30, 126, 143, 147, 213, 341, 343, 387, 509, 514, 526, 532, 547, 574–576, 610, 652, 748, 769
Article 50, 74, 75, 517–520, 781
Asylum, 25, 29, 70–72, 233, 242, 244, 247, 249, 265, 271, 279, 285, 289, 307, 330, 333, 444–446, 448–460, 462–464, 469–473, 475–477, 482, 492, 495–498, 500–503, 778–780
Axis, 81, 82, 90

B
Balance of power, 80, 82, 85, 86, 93, 94, 140, 267, 767
Balancing, 16, 81, 82, 89, 102, 104, 109, 155, 529, 548, 575, 578, 581, 662, 689, 693

Bargaining, 10, 12, 13, 52, 63, 65–67, 69, 71–74, 76, 119, 121, 147, 148, 213, 239, 243, 247, 286, 387, 406, 412–414, 438, 451, 470–472, 474, 475, 480, 483, 517–520, 557, 558, 609, 634, 657, 767, 768, 782
Brexit
  Article 50, 280, 508, 509, 513, 515, 519, 698, 781, 782
  crisis, 17, 52, 62, 73, 223, 281, 607, 692, 781, 782
  differentiated integration, 17, 31, 242, 514, 689, 695, 697, 699
  disintegration, 13, 17, 20, 26, 31, 107, 507, 526, 527, 690, 698
  withdrawal agreement, 73–75, 280, 509, 513
Britain, 25, 26, 107–109, 246, 376, 379, 411, 412, 509, 511, 513–518, 611

C
Cameron, David, 108, 221, 263, 289, 427, 511, 773
Classical realism, 12, 23, 52, 53, 80, 83, 87, 90, 93
Cleavage theory, 23, 52, 56, 175, 179, 189
Common European Asylum System (CEAS), 265, 449, 451, 457

© The Editor(s) (if applicable) and The Author(s), under exclusive license to Springer Nature Switzerland AG 2021
M. Riddervold et al. (eds.), *The Palgrave Handbook of EU Crises*, Palgrave Studies in European Union Politics,
https://doi.org/10.1007/978-3-030-51791-5

Consensus, 119, 215–217, 222–225, 233, 243–245, 247, 249, 260, 268, 282, 299, 319, 345, 472, 475, 480, 491, 495, 499, 530, 554, 557, 559, 563, 565, 582, 590, 593, 594, 632, 635, 639, 670, 693, 711, 713, 714, 718, 720, 739, 750, 767
Constitutional treaty crisis, 205
Constructivism, 15, 54, 121, 122, 195, 439
Cooperative hegemony, 92
Council of the European Union, 236, 239, 261, 300, 359, 461, 586, 587, 597
  consensus, 260
  Coreper, 19
Court of Justice of the European Union (CJEU), 24, 28, 29, 233, 234, 277–279, 289, 316, 324–326, 435, 436, 518, 571, 621, 622, 635, 638–641
Crisis
  Brexit, 17, 52, 62, 73, 75, 223, 281, 437, 607, 692, 781, 782
  Corona, 4, 6, 22, 28–30, 33, 34, 37, 38, 640
  Covid-19, 748, 754, 761, 762
  institutional, 55, 381, 387
  legitimacy, 24, 27–29, 34, 242, 261, 268, 389, 546, 607, 620–622, 624
  migration, 9, 13, 14, 18–20, 22, 24–26, 29, 32, 34, 36–38, 55, 56, 58, 89, 101, 108, 160, 190, 233, 242, 247, 260, 261, 264, 265, 271, 279, 310, 358, 362, 365, 368, 379, 444–447, 450, 451, 460, 546, 582, 628, 688, 727, 732, 734, 735, 782
  refugee, 34, 129, 203, 233, 299, 302, 306, 308, 309, 379, 421, 422, 424–427, 429, 432, 434, 437–439, 443, 445, 447–450, 455, 456, 470–474, 476, 479, 481–483, 490–492, 495, 498, 503, 613, 614, 667, 668, 673, 677–679, 778–780
  Ukraine, 19, 20, 27, 53, 94, 104, 105, 109, 141, 145, 163, 261, 270, 358, 362, 367, 369, 492, 547, 548, 554, 556, 559, 562, 565, 569, 570, 573–576, 580, 581, 605, 614, 688, 716

D
de Laroisiére Report, 378
Deliberation
  -meta, 38, 58, 215, 223–225
Deliberative
  processes, 213, 215, 221
  theory, 23, 52, 57, 213, 214, 221, 224
Democratic legitimacy, 27, 28, 30, 32, 35, 37, 221, 261, 269, 282, 283, 396, 608, 620, 622, 727, 728
Disjuncture, 449
Dissensus, 101
Dual leadership, 84, 89, 91–93
Dublin Convention, 265, 445, 448, 455, 458, 476

E
Economic
  crisis, 18, 33, 206, 223, 298, 304, 363, 512, 555, 652, 714, 718, 750, 775
  governance, 303, 394, 395, 423, 649, 651, 652, 654–656, 735
  politics, 70, 88, 386
Economists, 17, 138, 159, 346, 386, 389, 411, 415, 422, 649, 650, 652, 653, 655, 656
EFTA Court, 280
EU citizenship, 278, 281–289
EU Foreign and Security Policy
  Arctic, 574, 614
  CFSP, 27, 547, 551
  Crimea, 547
  EU-Turkey Statement, 19, 233, 266, 271, 448, 503
  EU-US relations, 550
  external relations, 163, 242, 270, 360
  special relationship, 610
  transatlantic relations, 550
  Ukraine, 547, 569, 575, 581, 614
EUNAVOR Sophia, 444

European
  differentiation, 17, 328
  disintegration, 16, 17, 526, 697, 699, 700
  integration, 4, 6, 9, 13–15, 17, 19–21, 23, 25, 26, 30, 33, 35, 37, 39, 52, 53, 58, 61, 62, 64, 65, 71, 76, 80, 81, 87, 89, 92, 93, 99–102, 109, 115, 117, 120, 176, 177, 185, 203, 213, 216, 218, 219, 221, 222, 241, 243, 248, 259, 260, 282, 283, 333, 390, 392–394, 396, 403, 448, 450–453, 460, 470, 492, 508, 512, 515–517, 527, 607, 623, 629, 633, 634, 640, 641, 660, 667–673, 677–680, 687–693, 695–699, 725–731, 748, 760, 761, 765–768, 781, 783, 785, 786
  solidarity, 4, 491–493, 497, 499, 503
European Central Bank (ECB), 18, 21, 24, 25, 29, 30, 33, 38, 124, 127–129, 148, 234, 235, 237, 267, 268, 278, 298, 304, 305, 316, 327–329, 339–352, 377–379, 384, 388, 391, 394, 395, 408–413, 415, 493, 494, 649, 651, 653, 659, 660, 667, 668, 672, 678, 729, 735, 755, 759, 769
European Commission, 5, 11, 18, 19, 21, 24, 29, 38, 74, 119, 148, 207, 222, 233, 237, 263, 269, 277, 298, 346, 357, 384, 385, 392, 395, 408, 410, 414, 455, 460, 463, 464, 469, 473–475, 478, 480, 481, 497, 498, 500–502, 509, 513, 548, 558, 560, 588, 596, 621, 632, 634–636, 649, 651, 654, 655, 659, 661, 672, 678, 687, 688, 694, 712, 728, 754, 781
European Council, 24, 74, 125, 233, 234, 236, 239–242, 248, 265, 267, 269–271, 286, 297–303, 305–307, 309, 390, 394, 395, 427, 434, 435, 444, 447, 455, 459, 460, 462, 463, 480, 483, 498, 526, 534, 564, 571, 585, 589, 594, 634, 690
European External Action Service (EEAS), 19, 24, 235, 236, 242, 262, 304, 357–370, 548, 558, 563, 570–572, 574, 577, 580, 581, 588–595, 597, 709, 712, 769
European foreign policy (CFSP), 19, 20, 27, 270, 357, 359, 365, 545–548, 550, 551, 556–558, 562, 570–572, 574, 575, 578, 586, 590, 593, 616, 630, 711, 712
European Parliament (EP), 18, 19, 21, 24, 29, 38, 71, 75, 127, 164, 232, 233, 236, 237, 244, 259–271, 278, 286, 301, 304, 305, 307, 317, 330, 360, 362, 363, 392, 395, 396, 427, 435, 464, 476, 483, 514, 518, 532, 538, 546, 571–573, 575, 590, 596, 621, 622, 632, 635–639, 654, 659, 660, 672, 678, 725, 728, 729, 742
European Stability Mechanism (ESM), 70, 106, 125, 127, 304–306, 379, 384, 386–388, 394, 413, 428, 430
European Union agencies
  Frontex, 72, 160, 368, 455, 464
Eurozone crisis
  Euro, 242, 384
  Euroscepticism, 516
  institutions, 149
Expertise
  democratic worry, 648, 649, 662
  epistemic worry, 648, 649

F

Failing forward, 9, 10, 17, 52, 76, 147, 377, 401, 402, 416, 452, 502, 634, 637, 668, 768, 775
Financial crisis, 7, 11, 16–18, 22, 24, 25, 30, 34, 38, 54, 69, 105, 147, 148, 235, 264, 267, 271, 302, 315, 318, 341, 343, 350, 358, 362–364, 366, 369, 376, 377, 379, 382, 383, 385–390, 393, 394, 396, 397, 403, 405, 407, 409–412, 415, 421, 422, 425–428, 432, 438, 446–448, 494, 556, 580, 624, 672, 730, 761
Foreign policy, 19, 20, 63, 83, 87, 234, 236, 242, 249, 271, 280, 298, 299, 357–362, 364, 365, 367–370, 491, 493, 546–551, 556, 560, 565, 570, 572, 576–578, 580–582, 586, 587,

603–605, 607–616, 690, 713, 744, 776, 777
France, 12, 53, 72, 74, 80, 81, 84–87, 89–92, 94, 102, 106, 107, 204–206, 208, 221, 266, 287, 303, 308, 363, 367, 411, 413, 414, 423, 438, 460, 476, 495, 498, 500, 558–564, 693, 751, 752, 774, 775, 781
Free movement of workers/persons, 284

G
GAL-TAN, 56, 174, 185
General Court, 277, 279, 281
Germany, 12, 20, 26, 30, 56, 69, 71, 72, 74, 80–94, 100, 102–109, 190, 251, 278, 282, 287, 288, 303, 342, 346, 362, 367, 378, 391, 392, 411, 413, 414, 422, 423, 425, 426, 430–434, 438, 445, 447–449, 451, 454, 462, 474–476, 490–503, 554, 558–564, 573, 575, 604, 693, 727, 739, 740, 742, 749, 758, 773–775, 777–781, 783, 786
Governance
  -meta, 55, 153–155, 157–162, 165–167, 700
  public, 39, 154, 156, 167

H
High Representative, 242, 303, 357, 564, 571, 572, 575, 589, 590, 593
Hoffmann, Stanley, 62, 80, 81, 83, 86, 88–90, 120, 124

I
Improvised practices, 250
Indifference, 669, 671–674, 678–680
Institutionalism
  discursive, 55, 136, 137, 142, 145, 146, 299
  historic, 135, 136, 138–140, 144–148, 281, 445, 470, 554, 700, 709
  pragmatist, 137, 148
  rational choice, 135, 136, 141, 142, 709
  sociological, 135–138, 141, 142, 145, 709

Interaction of crises, 782

J
Johnson, Boris, 281, 289, 516, 611

L
Legislative override, 286, 289
legitimacy, 18, 20, 22, 27, 31, 32, 37, 38, 146, 197, 214, 216, 218, 220–222, 233, 242, 250, 278, 319, 332, 350, 364, 365, 388, 389, 396, 428, 490, 509, 513, 620, 629, 656, 675, 696, 712, 715, 717–720, 726–730, 733–735
Legitimacy crisis
  Article 7 TEU, 278, 279, 285, 621, 632, 634, 636
  Eurobarometer, 28
  euroscepticism, 620
  illiberal democracy, 620
  populism, 606
  technocracy, 28
Liberal intergovernmentalism (LI), 10, 13, 14, 52, 61, 62, 64–67, 70, 73–76, 147, 281, 299, 406, 446, 470, 471, 474, 476, 482, 483
Logic of appropriateness, 137, 247
Logic of diversity, 90
Loose coupling, 155, 163, 165, 244

M
May, Theresa, 73, 75, 101, 281, 289, 511, 516, 519, 534, 611
Media, 14, 15, 57, 107, 190, 195, 197–209, 269, 346, 392, 425, 444, 620, 623, 631, 667, 670, 671, 677, 679, 748, 778, 779, 782
Migration, 5, 18, 19, 25, 26, 29, 36, 65, 70–72, 76, 79, 82, 87–90, 92, 93, 164, 173, 176, 222, 233, 234, 241, 265, 278, 288, 289, 298, 302, 306, 307, 425, 427, 433, 435, 437, 438, 443, 445, 446, 449–457, 461–465, 469–471, 474, 475, 477, 478, 480, 492, 495, 500, 502, 503, 517, 615, 647, 688, 712, 714, 741, 765, 779

Migration crisis, 9, 13, 14, 18–20, 22, 24–26, 29, 34, 36, 38, 55, 56, 58, 89, 101, 107, 108, 160, 190, 233, 242, 247, 260, 261, 264, 265, 271, 279, 310, 358, 362, 365, 368, 376, 379, 444–447, 450, 451, 460, 546, 582, 628, 688
Moral, 90, 93, 196, 199–202, 408, 434, 493, 604, 622, 650, 654, 732, 779
  hazard, 414, 423, 424, 430, 499, 514
  leadership, 489
Morgenthau, Hans J., 84–88

N
NATO, 82, 86, 89, 428, 529, 537, 538, 575, 577, 579, 587, 591, 592, 594, 604, 605, 608, 610–612, 631, 776, 777, 783, 784
Neo-functionalism, 10, 14, 406
Neo-realism, 52–54, 80, 82, 709
Norway model, 280

O
Organizational
  culture, 232, 239, 241–245, 247, 252, 253
  demography, 157
  design, 8, 154, 162
  engineering, 163
  reform, 161, 163
  structure, 29, 55, 153, 157, 158, 163, 165, 166, 613
  theory, 23, 52, 55, 155, 163, 166, 196

P
Panic
  integrational, 57, 196, 199, 200, 203–206, 208
Participation, 11, 17, 25, 32, 38, 73, 165, 201, 214, 219–221, 223, 267, 305, 323, 332, 396, 412, 473, 494, 509, 514, 527, 529, 530, 532, 534, 537, 538, 623, 624, 632, 659, 689, 699, 726, 732
Political
  conflict, 56, 102, 174, 175, 326, 331, 772
  ideology, 185
  order, 7, 40, 157, 220, 244, 279, 392, 394, 450, 632, 691, 696, 716, 718
  party, 179, 185, 270, 494, 744, 773
  process, 109, 136, 138, 213, 330, 377, 432, 452, 526, 535, 655, 657, 740
  structure, 422
  system, 83, 153, 154, 216, 332, 362, 389, 470, 654, 662, 674, 709, 733
Politicization, 13, 14, 128, 240, 282, 284, 377, 527–529, 532, 535, 538, 624, 633, 637, 670–672, 674, 677, 679, 698, 768, 779, 786
Polycrisis, 8, 16, 20, 31–34, 37, 38, 231–234, 236, 237, 302, 376, 377, 546, 620, 622–624, 628, 773, 785, 786
Populism, 32, 37, 220, 222, 235, 241, 447, 605, 607, 611, 612, 615, 630, 631, 658, 714, 730, 731
Post-functionalism, 9, 13, 14, 17, 101, 637
Public
  administration, 154, 156, 157, 164, 363, 508, 696, 699
  mood, 289, 669, 672, 675, 678
  opinion, 14, 35, 117, 176, 190, 199, 202, 221, 241, 379, 563, 623, 658, 667–673, 678–680, 727, 732, 733, 743, 750, 785
  policy, 23, 51, 70, 200, 454, 470, 749
  support, 26, 28, 37, 222, 396, 613, 669, 671–673, 675

R
Re-constitutionalization, 38, 215, 223–225
Reform
  constitutional, 730
  democratic, 37, 369
  institutional, 67, 70, 173, 251, 317, 379, 387, 389, 477, 622, 661, 775, 786

organizational, 161, 163
process, 157, 158, 161, 164, 357, 367
Refugees, 70–72, 90, 190, 234, 264, 279, 307, 368, 421, 424–427, 432–435, 437–439, 444, 446, 447, 451, 452, 455, 456, 461–463, 469, 470, 474–478, 482, 492, 495–503, 585, 613, 668, 741–743, 778–780
Relative gains, 102, 103, 106
Resilience, 5, 37, 39, 221, 222, 241, 309, 369, 472, 689, 709, 717, 718, 749, 759
  dynamic, 155, 156, 166, 248
  static, 155, 156

S
Schengen, 29, 52, 61, 62, 70–72, 75, 76, 129, 203, 306, 308, 330, 379, 425, 435, 445–447, 454, 456, 461, 462, 469, 471, 475–477, 480–482, 500, 513, 689, 690, 693, 695, 697, 698, 758, 759, 779, 780
Securitization, 358, 378, 410, 478, 479
Social
  construction, 57, 145, 196, 198, 199, 201
  constructivism, 14, 23, 52, 401
Spillover
  functional, 9–11, 54, 121, 123, 378, 406
  political, 13, 58

System attitude, 232, 236, 241, 243, 244, 252, 253

T
Technocracy, 4, 220, 395, 608, 622, 623, 655, 656, 727, 730, 735
Temporal sorting, 155, 163
Transatlantic relations, 21, 547, 550, 603, 604, 606, 609, 611, 612, 614
Trump, Donald, 34, 104, 105, 489, 546, 547, 550, 604–607, 609, 611, 612, 614, 616, 765, 780, 782–785
Trust
  in institutions, 675
  relationships, 623
Turbulence
  environmental, 7
  of scale, 35, 36, 241, 244
  organizational, 689

U
Ukraine, 19, 21, 27, 29, 79, 93, 101, 102, 104, 105, 214, 233, 234, 270, 271, 278, 279, 298, 302, 303, 309, 358, 365, 367, 370, 494, 547–551, 554, 558–562, 565, 573–579, 585, 586, 608, 609, 615, 715, 716, 776, 777
Unintended consequences, 11, 30, 35, 36, 39, 118, 122, 241, 444, 621

Printed in the United States
By Bookmasters